# THE
# BOOK
## OF THE
# STATES

---

## 2012 EDITION
## VOLUME 44

The Council of State Governments
Lexington, Kentucky

Headquarters: (859) 244-8000
Fax: (859) 244-8001
Internet: www.csg.org

## Sharing capitol ideas.

*Headquarters:*
David Adkins, Executive Director/CEO
2760 Research Park Drive, P.O. Box 11910
Lexington, KY 40578-1910
Phone: (859) 244-8000
Internet: www.csg.org

*Southern:*
Colleen Cousineau, Director
P.O. Box 98129
Atlanta, GA 30359
Phone: (404) 633-1866
Internet: www.slcatlanta.org

*Eastern:*
Wendell M. Hannaford, Director
100 Wall Street, 20th Floor
New York, NY 10005
Phone: (212) 482-2320
Internet: www.csgeast.org

*Western:*
Edgar Ruiz, Director
1107 9th Street, Suite 730
Sacramento, CA 95814
Phone: (916) 553-4423
Internet: www.csgwest.org

*Midwestern:*
Michael H. McCabe, Director
701 E. 22nd Street, Suite 110
Lombard, IL 60148
Phone: (630) 925-1922
Internet: www.csgmidwest.org

*Washington, D.C.:*
Christopher Whatley, Director
444 N. Capitol Street, NW, Suite 401
Washington, D.C. 20001
Phone: (202) 624-5460
Internet: www.csgdc.org

# Foreword

Dear Friends,

The Council of State Governments was founded by the states and territories to provide a civil and productive forum in which the best ideas and information could be shared. In our federal system of government, the states matter. State government impacts the lives of every American. On economic development, education, energy, environment, health care, human services and social issues, public safety and transportation, the decisions made in state capitols shape our lives and the future of our nation. The taxation and spending policies of each state determine priorities and outcomes for the public. We all live with the opportunities and consequences created by the laws, regulations and actions of state government.

At CSG, we believe the complexity of these issues is growing, that solutions in an increasingly polarized political world are more elusive, and that state leaders need and want reliable information upon which to base their actions and opinions. CSG was created to empower state leaders to craft the common sense solutions necessary to move America forward. This issue of *The Book of the States* is designed to do just that.

With more than 225 employees in 18 states and a total annual operating budget of $36 million, CSG is a partner that state leaders can rely on to help them better understand and address the significant challenges facing the states today.

I want to thank the authors whose work appears in the pages of this edition. Their insights and information make this book the resource that it is. Their commitment to CSG and its members is appreciated.

I also want to acknowledge the work of our dedicated CSG staff members whose commitment to this publication makes it possible. Audrey Wall leads this effort and somehow makes a very difficult task look easy. She is assisted by Heather Perkins and Chris Pryor who, in addition to many other duties, work tirelessly to make sure every number, chart and table is correct. This team is assisted by many of CSG's policy experts under the leadership of our director of Policy, John Mountjoy. The design and publication of the book is overseen by our director of Membership, Marketing and Media, Kelley Arnold. I appreciate the work all of these dedicated professionals do every day to serve our members.

We also rely on the states and territories to provide us with the data to populate the tables that appear in this book. Over the years we have developed a vast array of friends in the states who respond to our requests for information. They make this resource possible.

*The Book of the States* has become an iconic CSG product. No other organization or association can or does publish such a resource. This book reflects our intense commitment to serve the states and their leaders and our desire to place in the hands of state leaders and their staff a relevant and timely resource. In addition to the print version of *The Book of the States*, we also have developed a singular online resource to help state leaders access policy information: CSG's Knowledge Center (*http://knowledgecenter.csg.org*). In the Knowledge Center, users will find not only online versions of past volumes of *The Book of the States*, but also powerful tools that enable customization of data—allowing users to sift and sort detailed information to suit their needs.

We hope you value this book as much as we enjoy compiling the information shared within its pages. I remain confident that the creativity, passion, commitment and dedication of state leaders is sufficient to address any challenge, solve any problem and achieve excellence in governing. At CSG, we are proud of the role we play in helping state leaders achieve great things for the people they serve.

Very truly yours,

David Adkins
Executive Director / CEO
The Council of State Governments

The Council of State Governments is our nation's only organization serving all three branches of state government. CSG is a region-based forum that fosters the exchange of insights and ideas to help state officials shape public policy. This offers unparalleled regional, national and international opportunities to network, develop leaders, collaborate and create problem-solving partnerships.

# Staff Acknowledgements

The staff wishes to thank the authors who shared their expertise and insights, the hundreds of individuals in the states who responded to surveys conducted by The Council of State Governments, national organizations of state officials, federal agencies and think tank organizations who made their most recent data and information available for this volume.

# The Book of the States 2012

*Managing Editor* ....... Audrey S. Wall

*Associate Editor* ........ Heather M. Perkins

*Graphic Designers*..... Chris Pryor
Jessica Hughes

*Copy Editors*.............. Mary Branham
Jennifer Ginn

*Other CSG Staff
Contributors*............... Jennifer Horne
Paige Anderson
Jennifer Burnett
Ericka Harney
Kasey D. Cooke

# Table of Contents

# CONTENTS

# CONTENTS

**Chapter Five**
## STATE JUDICIAL BRANCH ...............................................................................291

# CONTENTS

## TABLES

*State Finance*

## ARTICLES

*Post-Recession State Tax Revenues and Taxation of Digitized Transactions*

*Amazon and the States: New Momentum for States to Recoup Sales Taxes on e-Commerce Transactions*

## TABLES

*Taxes*

*Revenue and Expenditure*

# CONTENTS

# CONTENTS

TABLES

*Criminal Justice/Corrections*

ARTICLE

*Hydraulic Fracturing—An Introduction and Policy Considerations for States*

**Chapter Ten**

## STATE PAGES ...................................................................................... 551

TABLES

## INDEX ................................................................................................. 589

# Chapter One

# STATE
# CONSTITUTIONS

# State Constitutional Developments in 2011
## By John Dinan

*Several of the 26 amendments on the 2011 ballot attracted significant attention, including an unsuccessful Mississippi personhood amendment and a successful Ohio amendment exempting residents from health insurance mandates. Voters also considered high-profile amendments regarding voter identification, eminent domain and sports betting. Additionally, the Alabama and Ohio legislatures established constitutional revision commissions charged with reviewing and recommending changes to these state constitutions.*

Relatively few state constitutional amendments appeared on the ballot in 2011, as is typical of odd-year elections. The two highest profile amendments were initiated measures—an unsuccessful Mississippi amendment stipulating that personhood begins at the moment of fertilization and a successful Ohio amendment exempting residents from health insurance mandates. A good deal of attention focused on qualifying amendments for the 2012 ballot on topics including abortion, health insurance, same-sex marriage and religious liberty. Meanwhile, the Alabama and Ohio legislatures established constitutional revision commissions, at the same time the Utah legislature reduced the power of its long-standing revision commission.

## Constitutional Amendment and Revision Methods

Constitutional amendments were formally proposed in 2011 in nine states. This is well below the 37 states that considered amendments in 2010, but slightly above the comparable rates for recent odd-year elections; five states considered amendments in 2009 and eight states considered amendments in 2007.

Twenty-six amendments were proposed and 20 were enacted in 2011. Again, this is far below the level of amendment activity in 2010, when 165 amendments were proposed and 116 enacted. It is, however, comparable to recent odd-year elections, when 21 amendments were proposed and 17 enacted in 2009 and 34 amendments were proposed and 33 enacted in 2007. As is typical of odd-year elections, Texas accounted for a good portion of the 2011 amendment activity, contributing 10 of the 26 proposed amendments and seven of the 20 enacted amendments. Alabama also has, in recent years, accounted for a significant amount of constitutional amendment activity. In 2011,

Alabama approved just one amendment, a local amendment that applies to Hale County and was voted on only by residents of that county.

### Legislative Proposals and Constitutional Initiatives

All the amendments on the ballot in 2011 were proposed by legislatures or through the initiative process. Voters approved 16 of the 22 amendments proposed by legislatures, for a passage rate of 73 percent. This is comparable to the passage rate for legislature-referred amendments in prior years.

Three of the four amendments proposed via the constitutional initiative process were approved, for a passage rate of 75 percent, which is much higher than the usual passage rate for citizen-initiated amendments. Mississippi accounted for two of the three successful initiated amendments, marking the first time the constitutional initiative process was used successfully in the state since the process was reintroduced there in 1992.[1]

One amendment was adopted in Delaware, which is unique among the 50 states in that constitutional amendments there are not submitted for popular ratification. Rather, the legislature enacts amendments by approving them by a two-thirds vote in consecutive sessions.

### Constitutional Commissions and Conventions

Three constitutional commissions were operating or set to begin operating in 2011—a longstanding Utah commission and new commissions in Alabama and Ohio. The Utah Constitutional Revision Commission, created by legislative statute in 1977, has long been the only commission in the country with an ongoing charge to review the state constitution and recommend constitutional changes for consideration by the legislature and possible submission to voters. Utah commissioners also have long had the power to give advice on pro-

## Table A: State Constitutional Changes by Method of Initiation: 2006–07, 2008–09 and 2010–11

| Method of initiation | Number of states involved | | | Total proposals (a) | | | Total adopted (b) | | | Percentage adopted (c) | | |
|---|---|---|---|---|---|---|---|---|---|---|---|---|
| | 2006– 2007 | 2008– 2009 | 2010– 2011 | 2006– 2007 | 2008– 2009 | 2010– 2011 | 2006– 2007 | 2008– 2009 | 2010– 2011 | 2006– 2007 | 2008– 2009 | 2010– 2011 |
| All methods................. | 37 | 32 | 40 | 200 (d) | 161 (e) | 191 | 158 (d) | 104 (e) | 136 (f) | 78.0 | 64.6 | 70.2 |
| Legislative proposal... | 36 | 31 | 37 | 167 (d) | 127 (e) | 170 | 147 (d) | 88 (e) | 124 (f) | 86.8 | 69.3 | 71.8 |
| Constitutional initiative..................... | 12 | 10 | 9 | 33 | 30 | 21 | 11 | 13 | 12 | 33.3 | 43.3 | 57.1 |
| convention .............. | ... | ... | ... | ... | ... | ... | ... | ... | ... | ... | ... | ... |
| commission.............. | ... | 1 | ... | ... | 4 | ... | ... | 3 | ... | ... | 75.0 | ... |

*Source:* John Dinan and The Council of State Governments.
*Key:*
(a) Excludes Delaware, where proposals are not submitted to voters.
(b) Includes Delaware.
(c) In calculating the percentages, the amendments adopted in Delaware (where proposals are not submitted to voters) are excluded (two amendments were adopted in 2007, one in 2010 and one in 2011).
(d) Excludes one Alabama amendment that was proposed by the legislature and appeared on the ballot but was determined by the governor's office prior to the vote not to have received enough votes in the legislature to properly appear on the ballot, and thus even though the amendment was approved by voters in November 2006 and the vote totals were certified by the state canvassing board, the governor did not proclaim the results for the amendment and so it has not received an official amendment number.
(e) Excludes one New Mexico amendment approved by voters in November 2008 but declared invalid by the state supreme court on single-subject grounds in December 2008.
(f) Excludes one Alabama local amendment approved by voters in November 2010 but not certified pursuant to a court order.

posed amendments upon the request of the governor, the chief officer or minority leader of the house or senate, or the legislative sponsor of the amendment. In 2011, however, the Utah legislature enacted a statute reducing the commission's power in each of these respects. The commission will no longer have the power to recommend constitutional changes to the legislature. In addition, the commission will only be able to offer advice on proposed amendments when requested to do so by the governor, the legislature as a whole acting through a joint resolution or the legislative management committee.

The Alabama legislature in its 2011 session created a Constitutional Revision Commission charged with recommending changes to selected constitutional articles and removing unconstitutional language throughout the document. The group Alabama Citizens for Constitutional Reform has for the past decade urged the legislature to call a constitutional convention to reduce the length of the state's 376,000-word constitution and eliminate outdated or inoperative provisions.

The 2011 Alabama legislature, controlled by Republicans for the first time since Reconstruction, was no more prepared than its recent predecessors to call a convention. At the urging of Senate President Pro Tem Del Marsh, however, the legislature approved and Gov. Robert Bentley signed a law creating a 16-member commission made up of the governor, senate president pro tem, house speaker and three people appointed by each of these officials, as well as the chairs of the judiciary committees and the constitution and elections committees in the house and senate. These commission members chose former Gov. Albert Brewer to chair the body.

The enabling statute sets out a specific schedule for the Alabama Constitutional Revision Commission to follow in recommending changes to 11 of the state constitution's 18 articles between 2011 and 2014. The statute directs the commission to recommend changes to the banking and corporations articles and identify unconstitutional language throughout the document in 2011, and then to recommend changes to nine other constitutional articles in piecemeal fashion in the following three years. Certain articles are explicitly excluded from the commission's consideration, including, most importantly, the taxation article.

The Ohio legislature in its 2011 session also established a constitutional revision commission, partly in anticipation of a popular referendum to take place in 2012 on calling a constitutional convention. Ohio is one of 14 states whose constitution requires that a convention referendum be placed before voters at periodic intervals, and it is one of three states—along with Alaska and New Hampshire—with a convention referendum scheduled for 2012. Partly out of a desire to prepare for this referendum but also with an eye toward conducting an extensive assessment of the suitability of the current state constitution, the Ohio legislature approved a bill spearheaded by House Speaker William Batchelder establishing the Ohio Constitutional Modernization Commission.

The 32-member Ohio commission includes 12 members appointed by the Democratic and Republican leaders of the House and Senate—three appointees for each legislative leader—and 20 public members to be selected by a majority of the legislative appointees. In the event that a convention is called, the commission is directed by the enabling statute to make recommendations to the legislature regarding how it should be organized. The commission also is charged by the statute with reviewing the state constitution and making recommendations, by a two-thirds vote of commissioners, to the legislature, which may then by a three-fifths vote, propose amendments to the electorate. The commission is required to make its first report to the legislature by January 2013 and is expected to make biennial reports until its charge expires in 2021.

The creation of the Alabama and Ohio constitutional commissions, in part out of a desire to blunt calls for constitutional conventions, is illustrative of legislators' determined opposition to conventions and their reliance on commissions as an alternative mechanism for achieving constitutional reform. This is a longstanding feature of state constitutional politics that has intensified since the 1970s. In fact, outside of an unusual situation in 1992 when legislators in Louisiana temporarily convened as a convention, no state constitutional conventions have been held in the quarter century since Rhode Island's 1986 convention was called through a mandatory convention referendum. The 2012 election will provide another test of popular support for constitutional conventions. Voters will face mandatory convention referendums in Ohio, where such votes are held every 20 years, and in Iowa and New Hampshire, where such referendums are held every 10 years.

## Constitutional Changes

Voters in 2011 considered rights-related amendments on topics such as abortion, health insurance and the eminent domain power. Amendments also were proposed regarding electoral and governing institutions on topics including redistricting, voter identification and the judicial retirement age. Policy amendments dealt with taxation, rainy day funds and gambling, among other topics. At the same time voters were considering these amendments on the 2011 ballot, attention also focused on qualifying amendments for the 2012 ballot.

### Individual Rights

None of the amendments on the 2011 ballot attracted more attention than an unsuccessful initiated amendment in Mississippi defining personhood as beginning at the moment of fertilization, cloning or the functional equivalent. Personhood amendments have been proposed in several states in recent years, with supporters viewing them as a means of creating a conflict between state and federal law and thereby helping to generate a legal challenge to the U.S. Supreme Court's abortion jurisprudence, in the hopes that a majority of justices might be open to modifying prior precedents.[2] Two prior personhood amendments that qualified for a state ballot, in Colorado in 2008 and 2010, were soundly defeated.

Polling conducted several weeks before Mississippi's November 2011 vote, as well as support from both the Republican and Democratic gubernatorial candidates, indicated that the Mississippi measure stood a good chance of passing. As a result, in the campaign's final weeks, the measure attracted significant national attention and a good deal of criticism, not only from abortion rights supporters who decried its sweeping nature, but also from some pro-life groups who viewed it as unlikely to bring about a modification of the Supreme Court's previous rulings on abortion. In the end, Mississippi voters rejected the amendment by a 58-42 percent margin.

Other abortion-related amendments could appear on the 2012 ballot. Supporters of personhood amendments are seeking to qualify them via the initiative process in Colorado, for a third time, and Nevada, although they have encountered difficulties in crafting ballot language capable of satisfying a Nevada district judge. Meanwhile, the Florida legislature approved an amendment for placement on the 2012 ballot that would prohibit public funds from being spent on abortions or for health insurance coverage that provides for abortions. Additionally, employing wording included in several prior Florida amendments designed to prevent state courts from interpreting state criminal procedure guarantees more broadly than corresponding federal bill of rights clauses, the proposed amendment stipulates that the Florida Constitution "may not be interpreted to create broader rights to an abortion than those contained in the United States Constitution."

## Table B: Substantive Changes in State Constitutions: Proposed and Adopted: 2006–07, 2008–09 and 2010–11

| Subject matter | Total proposed (a) | | | Total adopted (b) | | | Percentage adopted (c) | | |
|---|---|---|---|---|---|---|---|---|---|
| | 2006–2007 | 2008–2009 | 2010–2011 | 2006–2007 | 2008–2009 | 2010–2011 | 2006–2007 | 2008–2009 | 2010–2011 |
| Proposals of statewide applicability | 172 | 123 (d) | 147 | 134 (b) | 77 (d) | 108 (b) | 76.7 (c) | 62.6 | 72.1 (c) |
| Bill of Rights | 30 (e) | 16 | 22 | 26 (e) | 12 | 17 | 86.7 | 75.0 | 77.3 |
| Suffrage & elections | 7 | 11 | 18 | 4 | 6 | 15 | 57.1 | 54.5 | 83.3 |
| Legislative branch | 12 | 13 | 6 | 7 | 8 | 5 | 58.3 | 61.5 | 83.3 |
| Executive branch | 1 | 5 | 6 | 1 | 4 | 5 (b) | 100.0 | 80.0 | 66.7 (c) |
| Judicial branch | 8 | 1 | 7 | 6 (b) | 0 | 5 (b) | 50.0 (c) | 0.0 | 57.1 (c) |
| Local government | 1 | 3 | 7 | 0 | 0 | 4 | 0.0 | 0.0 | 57.1 |
| Finance & taxation | 65 | 37 | 42 | 51 | 18 | 32 | 78.5 | 48.6 | 76.2 |
| State & local debt | 10 | 6 | 16 | 9 | 6 | 13 | 90.0 | 100.0 | 81.3 |
| State functions | 5 | 4 | 9 | 4 | 3 | 3 | 80.0 | 75.0 | 33.3 |
| Amendment & revision | 1 | 0 | 0 | 1 | 0 | 0 | 100.0 | 0.0 | 0.0 |
| General revision proposals | 0 | 0 | 0 | 0 | 0 | 0 | 0.0 | 0.0 | 0.0 |
| Miscellaneous proposals | 32 | 27 | 14 | 25 | 20 | 9 | 78.1 | 74.1 | 64.3 |
| Local amendments | 28 (f) | 38 | 44 | 24 (f) | 27 | 28 (g) | 85.7 | 71.1 | 63.6 |

*Source:* John Dinan and The Council of State Governments.

*Key:*

(a) Excludes Delaware, where amendments do not require popular approval.

(b) Includes Delaware.

(c) In calculating the percentages, the amendments adopted in Delaware (where proposals are not submitted to voters) are excluded (two amendments were adopted in 2007, one in 2010 and one in 2011).

(d) Excludes one New Mexico amendment approved in November 2008 but declared invalid by the state supreme court in December 2008.

(e) Includes amendments restricting the use of eminent domain, regardless of whether these protections were actually inserted in the bill of rights or in other articles.

(f) Excludes one Alabama amendment that was proposed by the legislature and appeared on the ballot but was determined by the governor's office prior to the vote not to have received enough votes in the legislature to properly appear on the ballot, and thus even though the amendment was approved by voters in November 2006 and the vote totals were certified by the state canvassing board, the governor did not proclaim the results for the amendment and so it has not received an official amendment number.

(g) Excludes one Alabama local amendment approved by voters in November 2010 but not certified pursuant to a court order.

Next to Mississippi's failed personhood amendment, a successful Ohio amendment exempting residents from health insurance mandates attracted the most attention in 2011. Arizona and Oklahoma approved constitutional amendments along these lines in 2010, at the same time that six state legislatures were passing such measures on a statutory basis. With voters' approval of a citizen-initiated amendment in 2011, Ohio became the third state to enact such a measure as a constitutional amendment, and votes on similar amendments are scheduled to take place in 2012 in Alabama, Florida and Wyoming.

Supporters are presumably seeking to create a conflict between these state measures and the individual mandate provision of the federal Patient Protection and Affordable Care Act of 2010, in hopes of generating a justiciable lawsuit presenting the U.S. Supreme Court with an opportunity to strike down the individual mandate. Framing these measures as constitutional amendments rather than statutes, however, does not have any advantages in this regard. In any event, the Supreme Court agreed to hear a challenge in March 2012 to the legitimacy of the federal individual mandate and is expected to resolve the question of whether Congress has the power to enact such a provision.

If personhood and health insurance amendments are directed to the judiciary in the sense of presenting the U.S. Supreme Court with an opportunity to reconsider its prior decisions or invalidate federal statutes, a successful Mississippi eminent domain amendment is directed to the judiciary in the sense of securing greater protection for rights than the U.S. Supreme Court has guaranteed. In its 2005 ruling in *Kelo v. City of New London*, the Supreme Court declined to interpret the takings clause of the federal Bill of Rights to prohibit the use of eminent domain to condemn land for economic development purposes. But in the ruling's aftermath, a number of states took the opportunity to provide greater restrictions on the eminent domain power than the Supreme Court was willing to require. Some states enacted increased protection for property rights by passing statutes to this effect, while other states enacted constitutional amendments along these lines. By approving a citizen-initiated amendment prohibiting use of eminent domain to transfer property to other persons or businesses, Mississippi became the 10th state to adopt a major eminent domain amendment in response to the *Kelo* decision. Similar amendments are scheduled to appear on the ballot in future years in other states, including Virginia, where the legislature gave the required second approval for an eminent domain amendment to be voted on in the November 2012 election.

Although no same-sex marriage ban amendments appeared on the 2011 ballot, the North Carolina and Minnesota legislatures approved amendments for placement on the 2012 ballot and the Indiana legislature gave the first of two required approvals for placing an amendment on a future ballot. The North Carolina amendment will appear on the May 2012 primary ballot. The Minnesota amendment will be voted on at the 2012 general election.

To date, 30 states have adopted constitutional amendments regarding same-sex marriage, largely out of a desire to prevent state courts from legalizing same-sex marriage, or, in the case of California's Proposition 8, to overturn a state court decision legalizing same-sex marriage. Hawaii's amendment, one of the first enacted in 1998, is unique in that it reserves to the legislature the power to legalize same-sex marriage and thereby prohibits state courts from assuming this power. The other 29 amendments enacted from 1998 through 2008 go further in prohibiting state courts, as well as state legislatures, from legalizing same-sex marriage and, in many cases, civil unions.

Two religious liberty amendments scheduled to appear on the 2012 ballot in North Dakota and Florida respond to judicial decisions in quite different ways. A citizen-initiated amendment on the June 2012 North Dakota primary election ballot would prohibit government from burdening the free exercise of religion absent a compelling government interest. The U.S. Supreme Court in *Oregon v. Smith* in 1990 held that the free exercise clause of the federal Bill of Rights does not require state governments to meet such a high standard before enacting generally applicable laws that incidentally burden the exercise of religion. In the ensuing two decades, however, some states have nevertheless sought to require governments to satisfy the compelling governmental-interest test. The proposed North Dakota amendment is the latest effort to enact a state constitutional amendment to provide greater protection for religious liberty than the U.S. Supreme Court has provided based on the federal Bill of Rights.

Meanwhile, the Florida legislature approved a measure for the 2012 ballot eliminating a provision in the state constitution's religious liberty clause prohibiting public funds from supporting sectarian institutions. Blaine amendments of this sort originally were added to state constitutions in the 19th century, largely out of a desire to limit state financial support of Catholic schools, and the Florida Supreme Court and other state courts have relied on these provisions in recent years to impose greater restrictions on school voucher programs than the U.S. Supreme Court has imposed. A Florida district judge in December 2011 initially ordered the removal of the amendment because of what he deemed misleading ballot language. By virtue of an important statutory change in state elections law adopted earlier in the year making it more difficult for judges to disqualify amendments, however, the attorney general was able to rewrite the language and place the amendment back on the ballot.

Various other rights-related amendments will appear on the 2012 ballot. Amendments in Kentucky and Wyoming would secure hunting and fishing rights. Similar amendments have passed in other states in recent years. An Alabama amendment would secure the right to a secret ballot in union-organizing elections, following four states that enacted such amendments in 2010. An Oklahoma amendment would eliminate any preference based on race or gender in public hiring, contracting or education, following four states that have enacted amendments restricting affirmative action since the mid-1990s.

### Governing Institutions

Several amendments were approved in 2011 or qualified for the 2012 ballot regarding voting and elections, especially voter identification requirements. Mississippi voters initiated and approved an amendment requiring voters to submit photo identification after the legislature declined to adopt a statute along these lines. Because all election-related changes in Mississippi must be pre-cleared by the U.S. Justice Department pursuant to Section 5 of the Voting Rights Act, this amendment has not yet taken effect.

In Missouri, the legislature placed a similar amendment on the 2012 ballot as a way of overcoming a 2011 gubernatorial veto of a photo ID law and as a response to a 2006 state supreme court ruling invalidating a prior legislative effort along these lines. Legislative supporters of a photo ID requirement in Minnesota are also scheduled in their 2012 session to consider such a measure as a constitutional amendment for submission to the voters. This is a way for the Republican-controlled legislature to bypass the Democratic governor's veto of a statutory photo ID measure in the previous year's session.

In other election-related amendments in 2011, Washington state voters approved an amendment removing an unenforceable 60-day residency requirement to vote for president; the amendment makes clear that a 30-day residency requirement in another clause of the constitution applies to all elections, including presidential elections. Meanwhile, Maine voters approved an amendment making several changes to the state's redistricting process. The amendment stipulates that beginning after the next census, the legislature shall redraw legislative districts not three years after the census is taken, as is currently done, but one year after the census, as is the norm in other states. The amendment also constitutionalizes a current statutory requirement that congressional district maps be approved by a two-thirds legislative supermajority.

One amendment considered in 2011 dealt with the judicial branch. Ohio voters defeated an amendment increasing the judicial retirement age and making several other changes to the judicial article. Currently, Ohio judges may not begin a term on the bench if they are older than 70. The defeated amendment would have raised the age limit to 75.

Several amendments approved by voters in 2011 affect the executive branch. Texas voters approved an amendment authorizing the governor to issue pardons not only to people convicted of an offense, but also to people who have completed deferred adjudication programs. The Delaware legislature provided the requisite second approval—no popular referendum is required in Delaware—for an amendment increasing the annual amount of compensation an officer must receive before senate confirmation is required for filling that position.

Although no amendments affecting the legislative branch were voted on in 2011, several have qualified for the 2012 ballot. Among them, opponents of California's legislative term limits provision have qualified an amendment via the initiative process that would adjust the current rules. As a result of a 1990 California amendment, individuals may serve no more than six years in the state assembly and no more than eight years in the state senate, for a lifetime limit of 14 years of legislative service. The amendment on the 2012 ballot would establish a lifetime limit of 12 years of legislative service, but would allow legislators to serve up to 12 years in the assembly or the senate or some combination of the two offices. California voters defeated a similar effort to relax existing legislative term limits in 2008, but a key difference between that amendment and the pending 2012 one is the proposed new limits on legislative service would not apply to current officeholders.

*Policy*

Voters in 2011 approved several amendments regarding taxation, including a complex Louisiana amendment. The main purpose of the amendment is to dedicate additional money from the state's tobacco settlement fund to the Taylor Opportunity Program for Students—known as TOPS—that provides financial aid for students enrolled in the state's public and private colleges. After Gov. Bobby Jindal vetoed a legislative effort to renew a 4-cent cigarette tax increase and legislators could not override his veto, they added a renewal of this tax to the proposed constitutional amendment and dedicated the tax revenue to the TOPS scholarship fund. Voters approved this multi-faceted amendment in an October 2011 election.

Louisiana voters also approved, in a late-November election, an amendment prohibiting imposition of new real estate transfer taxes. By enacting the amendment, Louisiana joins Missouri and Montana, both of which added bans to their constitution in 2010, in order to prevent imposition of such taxes that are collected in all but 13 states. Meanwhile, Texas voters approved an amendment exempting surviving spouses of totally disabled veterans from property taxes.

Voters in two states considered amendments regarding state rainy day funds. Louisiana voters rejected a technical change that would have given the legislature more time to replenish the state rainy day fund after making a withdrawal. Washington state voters approved an amendment requiring the legislature to set aside additional money for the state rainy day fund in any year when tax revenues increase by a specified amount.

Voters approved several amendments dealing with other fiscal policy matters. Texas voters approved a pair of amendments authorizing the Texas Water Development Board to issue additional general obligation bonds to pay for wastewater treatment plants and permitting the Texas Higher Education Coordinating Board to issue more bonds to support student financial aid. Texas voters rejected an amendment though that would have given to counties the same power currently possessed by cities to issue bonds for the redevelopment of blighted property.

Louisiana voters approved an amendment dedicating a portion of any nonrecurring revenue in the next several years to addressing unfunded liabilities in two of the state's retirement systems. Louisiana voters also approved an amendment elevating to constitutional status a medical malpractice fund and preventing any possibility that a future legislature might dip into the fund to make up a budget shortfall.

New Jersey voters approved one gambling-related amendment. The amendment authorizes the legislature to enact a statute allowing Atlantic City casinos and racetracks to permit betting on sporting events. Currently, federal law does not permit sports betting in New Jersey. The New Jersey amendment, as well as a state law allowing for sports betting that was enacted several months after the amendment's passage, are meant to anticipate a possible change in the federal law.

## Conclusion

Several trends emerge from a review of state constitutional developments in 2011. First, the constitutional amendment process continues to serve as a vehicle for achieving goals unattainable through the legislative process. This was evident in Mississippi, where supporters of stricter voter identification requirements were unable to secure legislative passage of a statutory measure and turned instead to the constitutional initiative process and were successful in approving this measure as a constitutional amendment. In Missouri, legislators supported stricter voter identification requirements, but they were blocked by a gubernatorial veto. Legislators turned instead to the constitutional amendment process, where the governor does not play a role, and have placed the issue before voters in 2012. Louisiana legislators also relied successfully on the constitutional amendment process to bypass a gubernatorial veto, in this case for the purpose of renewing a cigarette tax increase by attaching it to a broader amendment approved by voters.

Second, many constitutional amendments in recent years have been responsive to federal or state court decisions. At times, state constitutional amendments are passed to secure protection for more rights than the U.S. Supreme Court is willing to guarantee through its interpretation of the U.S. Constitution. A Mississippi amendment restricting use of the eminent domain power is the latest example of relying on state constitutional amendments to respond to the U.S. Supreme Court's 2005 *Kelo* decision by providing greater protection for property rights. Also of note is a North Dakota amendment on the 2012 ballot that would respond to the U.S. Supreme Court's 1990 *Oregon v. Smith* decision by requiring the government to satisfy a compelling interest test before burdening the exercise of religion.

At other times, state constitutional amendments are enacted for a quite different purpose—to prevent state courts from expanding rights beyond the federal Bill of Rights guarantees. This is

### Table C: State Constitutional Changes by Legislative and Initiative Proposal: 2011

| State | Legislative proposal | | | Constitutional initiative | | |
|---|---|---|---|---|---|---|
| | Number proposed | Number adopted | Percentage adopted | Number proposed | Number adopted | Percentage adopted |
| Alabama | 1 | 1 | 100.0% | | | |
| Delaware | (a) | 1 | (a) | | | |
| Louisiana | 6 | 4 | 66.7 | | | |
| Maine | 1 | 1 | 100.0 | | | |
| Mississippi | | | | 3 | 2 | 66.7% |
| New Jersey | 1 | 1 | 100.0 | | | |
| Ohio | 1 | 0 | 0.0 | 1 | 1 | 100.0 |
| Texas | 10 | 7 | 70.0 | | | |
| Washington | 2 | 2 | 100.0 | | | |
| Totals | 22 | 17 | 72.7(b) | 4 | 3 | 75.0 |

*Source:* John Dinan and The Council of State Governments.
*Key:*
(a) Delaware does not provide for submission of amendments to the people.
(b) Excludes Delaware's legislature-approved amendment.

most evident in the 30 state constitutional amendments enacted from 1998 to 2008 to prevent state courts from legalizing same-sex marriage, as well as in the same-sex marriage amendments placed on the North Carolina and Minnesota ballot in 2012. This is also evident in a pair of Florida amendments on the 2012 ballot. One proposed Florida amendment would prevent state courts from interpreting the state constitution to provide greater protection for abortion rights than the U.S. Supreme Court has guaranteed. Another proposed Florida amendment would eliminate state constitutional language that has been relied on by state courts to provide greater restrictions on public aid of religious schools than the U.S. Supreme Court has required.

A third development is the continuing reliance on commissions instead of conventions to achieve constitutional reform. For much of American history, state constitutional conventions were held regularly, though somewhat more frequently in some states than others. In fact, 233 constitutional conventions have been held since 1776. With the exception of an unusual and short-lived 1992 Louisiana convention, however, no state constitutional conventions have been held in the last quarter century. All seven mandatory convention referendums in recent years—three in 2008 and four in 2010—were defeated.[3] And there is little expectation that any of the three mandatory convention referendums on the ballot in 2012 in Alaska, Ohio and New Hampshire will meet with success. Legislatures, however, have generally looked more favorably on constitutional commissions, viewing them as an alternative to constitutional conventions and occasionally as a way of blunting support for conventions. The creation in 2011 of the Alabama Constitutional Revision Commission and Ohio Constitutional Modernization Commission are the most recent examples.

## Notes

[1] Mississippi originally adopted the constitutional initiative process in 1914, but the state supreme court in 1922 invalidated the amendment providing for the initiative process. It was not until 1992 that voters approved an amendment reinstating the constitutional initiative. Amendments had been proposed in Mississippi via the initiative process in 1995 and then again in 1999, but were defeated by voters on both occasions.

[2] This phenomenon of relying on state constitutional amendments to assist in generating challenges to U.S. Supreme Court precedents is discussed in John Dinan, "State Constitutional Amendment Processes and the Safeguards of American Federalism," *Penn State Law Review* 115 (Spring 2011): 1007–1034.

[3] The results of recent mandatory convention referendums are detailed in John Dinan, "The Political Dynamics of Mandatory State Constitutional Convention Referendums: Lessons from the 2000s Regarding Obstacles and Pathways to their Passage," *Montana Law Review* 71 (Summer 2010): 395–432.

## Acknowledgements

The Council of State Governments and the author would like to thank the following individuals for their contribution.

| | |
|---|---|
| Alabama | Nancy Ekberg |
| Alaska | Jerry McBeath |
| Arizona | Toni McClory |
| Arkansas | Art English |
| Colorado | Richard B. Collins |
| Florida | Rebecca Mae Salokar |
| Georgia | Robert M. Schaefer |
| Hawaii | Anne Feder Lee |
| Indiana | Andrew Downs |
| Kentucky | Michael W. Hail |
| Louisiana | Warren M. Billings |
| Michigan | Robert A. Sedler |
| Minnesota | Mary Jane Morrison |
| Mississippi | John W. Winkle III |
| Nebraska | Anthony B. Schutz |
| New Jersey | Robert F. Williams |
| New Mexico | K. Seckler |
| New York | Robert N. Wells |
| North Carolina | John Dinan |
| North Dakota | Dana Michael Harsell |
| Ohio | Steven H. Steinglass |
| Pennsylvania | Joel Fishman |
| Rhode Island | Mel A. Topf |
| South Dakota | Michael Card |
| Utah | Robert H. Rees |
| Virginia | John Dinan |
| Washington | Hugh D. Spitzer |
| Wisconsin | Michael Richter Fine |

## About the Author

**John Dinan** is professor of political science at Wake Forest University in North Carolina. He is the author of *The American State Constitutional Tradition* and numerous articles on state constitutionalism.

## Table 1.1
## GENERAL INFORMATION ON STATE CONSTITUTIONS
## (As of January 1, 2012)

| State or other jurisdiction | Number of constitutions* | Dates of adoption | Effective date of present constitution | Estimated length (number of words)** | Number of amendments Submitted to voters | Adopted |
|---|---|---|---|---|---|---|
| Alabama | 6 | 1819, 1861, 1865, 1868, 1875, 1901 | Nov. 28, 1901 | 376,006 (a)(b) | 1,180 | 855 (c) |
| Alaska | 1 | 1956 | Jan. 3, 1959 | 13,479 | 42 | 29 |
| Arizona | 1 | 1911 | Feb. 14, 1912 | 47,306 | 266 | 147 |
| Arkansas | 5 | 1836, 1861, 1864, 1868, 1874 | Oct. 30, 1874 | 59,120 | 196 | 98 (d) |
| California | 2 | 1849, 1879 | July 4, 1879 | 67,048 | 891 | 525 |
| Colorado | 1 | 1876 | Aug. 1, 1876 | 66,140 | 336 | 155 |
| Connecticut | 4 | 1818 (f), 1965 | Dec. 30, 1965 | 16,401 | 31 | 30 |
| Delaware | 4 | 1776, 1792, 1831, 1897 | June 10, 1897 | 25,445 | (e) | 142 |
| Florida | 6 | 1839, 1861, 1865, 1868, 1886, 1968 | Jan. 7, 1969 | 56,705 | 154 | 118 |
| Georgia | 10 | 1777, 1789, 1798, 1861, 1865, 1868, 1877, 1945, 1976, 1982 | July 1, 1983 | 41,684 | 94 (g) | 71 (g) |
| Hawaii | 1 (h) | 1950 | Aug. 21, 1959 | 21,498 | 131 | 110 |
| Idaho | 1 | 1889 | July 3, 1890 | 24,626 | 210 | 123 |
| Illinois | 4 | 1818, 1848, 1870, 1970 | July 1, 1971 | 16,401 | 18 | 12 |
| Indiana | 2 | 1816, 1851 | Nov. 1, 1851 | 11,476 | 79 | 47 |
| Iowa | 2 | 1846, 1857 | Sept. 3, 1857 | 11,089 | 59 | 54 (i) |
| Kansas | 1 | 1859 | Jan. 29, 1861 | 14,097 | 125 | 95 (i) |
| Kentucky | 4 | 1792, 1799, 1850, 1891 | Sept. 28, 1891 | 27,234 | 75 | 41 |
| Louisiana | 11 | 1812, 1845, 1852, 1861, 1864, 1868, 1879, 1898, 1913, 1921, 1974 | Jan. 1, 1975 | 69,876 | 239 | 168 |
| Maine | 1 | 1819 | March 15, 1820 | 16,313 | 205 | 172 (j) |
| Maryland | 4 | 1776, 1851, 1864, 1867 | Oct. 5, 1867 | 43,198 | 261 | 225 (k) |
| Massachusetts | 1 | 1780 | Oct. 25, 1780 | 45,283 (l) | 148 | 120 |
| Michigan | 4 | 1835, 1850, 1908, 1963 | Jan. 1, 1964 | 31,164 | 68 | 30 |
| Minnesota | 1 | 1857 | May 11, 1858 | 11,734 | 215 | 120 |
| Mississippi | 4 | 1817, 1832, 1869, 1890 | Nov. 1, 1890 | 26,229 | 161 | 125 |
| Missouri | 4 | 1820, 1865, 1875, 1945 | March 30, 1945 | 69,394 | 175 | 114 |
| Montana | 2 | 1889, 1972 | July 1, 1973 | 12,790 | 56 | 31 |
| Nebraska | 2 | 1866, 1875 | Oct. 12, 1875 | 34,934 | 350 (m) | 228 (m) |
| Nevada | 1 | 1864 | Oct. 31, 1864 | 37,418 | 232 | 136 (i) |
| New Hampshire | 2 | 1776, 1784 | June 2, 1784 | 13,060 | 287 (n) | 145 |
| New Jersey | 3 | 1776, 1844, 1947 | Jan. 1, 1948 | 26,360 | 80 | 45 |
| New Mexico | 1 | 1911 | Jan. 6, 1912 | 33,198 | 293 (y) | 160 (y) |
| New York | 4 | 1777, 1822, 1846, 1894 | Jan. 1, 1895 | 44,397 | 295 | 220 |
| North Carolina | 3 | 1776, 1868, 1970 | July 1, 1971 | 17,177 | 37 | 30 |
| North Dakota | 1 | 1889 | Nov. 2, 1889 | 18,746 | 265 | 150 (o) |
| Ohio | 2 | 1802, 1851 | Sept. 1, 1851 | 53,239 | 286 | 172 |
| Oklahoma | 1 | 1907 | Nov. 16, 1907 | 81,666 | 354 (p) | 187 (p) |
| Oregon | 1 | 1857 | Feb. 14, 1859 | 49,016 | 490 (q) | 249 (q) |
| Pennsylvania | 5 | 1776, 1790, 1838, 1873, 1968 (r) | 1968 (r) | 26,078 | 36 (r) | 30 (r) |
| Rhode Island | 3 | 1842 (f), 1986 (s) | Dec. 4, 1986 | 11,407 | 12 (s) | 10 (s) |
| South Carolina | 7 | 1776, 1778, 1790, 1861, 1865, 1868, 1895 | Jan. 1, 1896 | 27,421 | 686 (t) | 497 (t) |
| South Dakota | 1 | 1889 | Nov. 2, 1889 | 27,774 | 229 | 215 |
| Tennessee | 3 | 1796, 1835, 1870 | Feb. 23, 1870 | 13,960 | 62 | 39 |
| Texas | 5 (u) | 1845, 1861, 1866, 1869, 1876 | Feb. 15, 1876 | 86,936 | 652 (v) | 474 |
| Utah | 1 | 1895 | Jan. 4, 1896 | 17,849 | 167 | 115 |
| Vermont | 3 | 1777, 1786, 1793 | July 9, 1793 | 8,565 | 212 | 54 |
| Virginia | 6 | 1776, 1830, 1851, 1869, 1902, 1970 | July 1, 1971 | 21,899 | 54 | 46 |
| Washington | 1 | 1889 | Nov. 11, 1889 | 32,578 | 178 | 105 |
| West Virginia | 2 | 1863, 1872 | April 9, 1872 | 33,324 | 121 | 71 |
| Wisconsin | 1 | 1848 | May 29, 1848 | 15,102 | 194 | 145 (i) |
| Wyoming | 1 | 1889 | July 10, 1890 | 26,349 | 125 | 98 |
| American Samoa | 2 | 1960, 1967 | July 1, 1967 | 6,000 | 15 | 7 |
| No. Mariana Islands | 1 | 1977 | Jan. 9, 1978 | 11,000 | 60 | 56 (w)(x) |
| Puerto Rico | 1 | 1952 | July 25, 1952 | 9,281 | 6 | 6 |

See footnotes at end of table.

## GENERAL INFORMATION ON STATE CONSTITUTIONS — Continued
### (As of January 1, 2012)

*Source:* John Dinan and The Council of State Governments, with research assistance from Wake Forest students Bradley Harper and Alec Papovich.

*The constitutions referred to in this table include those Civil War documents customarily listed by the individual states.

**In calculating word counts, supplemental information regarding dates of adoption and other material not formally a part of the constitution are generally excluded. In some cases, word counts are taken from the total as of January 2012.

(a) The Alabama constitution includes numerous local amendments that apply to only one county. An estimated 70 percent of all amendments are local. A 1982 amendment provides that after proposal by the legislature to which special procedures apply, only a local vote (with exceptions) is necessary to add them to the constitution.

(b) Computer word count.

(c) The total number of Alabama amendments includes one that is commonly overlooked.

(d) Eight of the approved amendments have been superseded and are not printed in the current edition of the constitution. The total adopted does not include five amendments proposed and adopted since statehood.

(e) Proposed amendments are not submitted to the voters in Delaware.

(f) Colonial charters with some alterations served as the first constitutions in Connecticut (1638, 1662) and in Rhode Island (1663).

(g) The Georgia constitution requires amendments to be of "general and uniform application throughout the state," thus eliminating local amendments that accounted for most of the amendments before 1982.

(h) As a kingdom and republic, Hawaii had five constitutions.

(i) The figure includes amendments approved by the voters and later nullified by the state supreme court in Iowa (three), Kansas (one), Nevada (six) and Wisconsin (two).

(j) The figure does not include one amendment approved by the voters in 1967 that is inoperative until implemented by legislation.

(k) Two sets of identical amendments were on the ballot and adopted in the 1992 Maryland election. The four amendments are counted as two in the table.

(l) The printed constitution includes many provisions that have been annulled.

(m) The 1998 and 2000 Nebraska ballots allowed the voters to vote separately on "parts" of propositions. In 1998, 10 of 18 separate propositions were adopted; in 2000, 6 of 9.

(n) The constitution of 1784 was extensively revised in 1792. Figure shows proposals and adoptions since the constitution was adopted in 1784.

(o) The figures do not include submission and approval of the constitution of 1889 itself and of Article XX; these are constitutional questions included in some counts of constitutional amendments and would add two to the figure in each column.

(p) The figures include five amendments submitted to and approved by the voters which were, by decisions of the Oklahoma or U.S. Supreme Courts, rendered inoperative or ruled invalid, unconstitutional, or illegally submitted.

(q) One Oregon amendment on the 2000 ballot was not counted as approved because canvassing was enjoined by the courts.

(r) Certain sections of the constitution were revised by the limited convention of 1967–68. Amendments proposed and adopted are since 1968.

(s) Following approval of the eight amendments and a "rewrite" of the Rhode Island Constitution in 1986, the constitution has been called the 1986 Constitution. Amendments since 1986 total 12 proposed and 10 adopted. Otherwise, the total is 106 proposals and 60 adopted.

(t) In 1981 approximately two-thirds of 626 proposed and four-fifths of the adopted amendments were local. Since then the amendments have been statewide propositions.

(u) The Constitution of the Republic of Texas preceded five state constitutions.

(v) The number of proposed amendments to the Texas Constitution excludes three proposed by the legislature but not placed on the ballot.

(w) By 1992, 49 amendments had been proposed and 47 adopted. Since then, one was proposed but rejected in 1994, all three proposals were ratified in 1996 and in 1998, of two proposals one was adopted.

(x) The total excludes one amendment ruled void by a federal district court.

(y) The total excludes one amendment approved by voters in November 2008 but later declared invalid on single subject grounds by the state supreme court.

## Table 1.2
## CONSTITUTIONAL AMENDMENT PROCEDURE: BY THE LEGISLATURE
### Constitutional Provisions

| State or other jurisdiction | Legislative vote required for proposal (a) | Consideration by two sessions required | Vote required for ratification | Limitation on the number of amendments submitted at one election |
|---|---|---|---|---|
| Alabama | 3/5 | No | Majority vote on amendment | None |
| Alaska | 2/3 | No | Majority vote on amendment | None |
| Arizona | Majority | No | Majority vote on amendment | None |
| Arkansas | Majority | No | Majority vote on amendment | 3 |
| California | 2/3 | No | Majority vote on amendment | None |
| Colorado | 2/3 | No | Majority vote on amendment | None (b) |
| Connecticut | (c) | (c) | Majority vote on amendment | None |
| Delaware | 2/3 | Yes | Not required | No referendum |
| Florida | 3/5 | No | 3/5 vote on amendment (d) | None |
| Georgia | 2/3 | No | Majority vote on amendment | None |
| Hawaii | (e) | (e) | Majority vote on amendment (f) | None |
| Idaho | 2/3 | No | Majority vote on amendment | None |
| Illinois | 3/5 | No | (g) | 3 articles |
| Indiana | Majority | Yes | Majority vote on amendment | None |
| Iowa | Majority | Yes | Majority vote on amendment | None |
| Kansas | 2/3 | No | Majority vote on amendment | 5 |
| Kentucky | 3/5 | No | Majority vote on amendment | 4 |
| Louisiana | 2/3 | No | Majority vote on amendment (h) | None |
| Maine | 2/3 (i) | No | Majority vote on amendment | None |
| Maryland | 3/5 | No | Majority vote on amendment | None |
| Massachusetts | Majority (j) | Yes | Majority vote on amendment | None |
| Michigan | 2/3 | No | Majority vote on amendment | None |
| Minnesota | Majority | No | Majority vote in election | None |
| Mississippi | 2/3 (k) | No | Majority vote on amendment | None |
| Missouri | Majority | No | Majority vote on amendment | None |
| Montana | 2/3 (i) | No | Majority vote on amendment | None |
| Nebraska | 3/5 | No | Majority vote on amendment (f) | None |
| Nevada | Majority | Yes | Majority vote on amendment | None |
| New Hampshire | 3/5 | No | 2/3 vote on amendment | None |
| New Jersey | (l) | (l) | Majority vote on amendment | None (m) |
| New Mexico | Majority (n) | No | Majority vote on amendment (n) | None |
| New York | Majority | Yes | Majority vote on amendment | None |
| North Carolina | 3/5 | No | Majority vote on amendment | None |
| North Dakota | Majority | No | Majority vote on amendment | None |
| Ohio | 3/5 | No | Majority vote on amendment | None |
| Oklahoma | Majority | No | Majority vote on amendment | None |
| Oregon | (o) | No | Majority vote on amendment (p) | None |
| Pennsylvania | Majority (p) | Yes (p) | Majority vote on amendment | None |
| Rhode Island | Majority | No | Majority vote on amendment | None |
| South Carolina | 2/3 (q) | Yes (q) | Majority vote on amendment | None |
| South Dakota | Majority | No | Majority vote on amendment | None |
| Tennessee | (r) | Yes (r) | Majority vote in election (s) | None |
| Texas | 2/3 | No | Majority vote on amendment | None |
| Utah | 2/3 | No | Majority vote on amendment | None |
| Vermont | (t) | Yes | Majority vote on amendment | None |
| Virginia | Majority | Yes | Majority vote on amendment | None |
| Washington | 2/3 | No | Majority vote on amendment | None |
| West Virginia | 2/3 | No | Majority vote on amendment | None |
| Wisconsin | Majority | Yes | Majority vote on amendment | None |
| Wyoming | 2/3 | No | Majority vote in election | None |
| American Samoa | 2/3 | No | Majority vote on amendment (u) | None |
| No. Mariana Islands | 3/4 | No | Majority vote on amendment | None |
| Puerto Rico | 2/3 (v) | No | Majority vote on amendment | 3 |

See footnotes at end of table.

## CONSTITUTIONAL AMENDMENT PROCEDURE: BY THE LEGISLATURE — Continued
## Constitutional Provisions

*Source:* John Dinan and The Council of State Governments, February 2012.

*Key:*

(a) In all states not otherwise noted, the figure shown in the column refers to the proportion of elected members in each house required for approval of proposed constitutional amendments.

(b) Legislature may not propose amendments to more than six articles of the constitution in the same legislative session.

(c) Three-fourths vote in each house at one session, or majority vote in each house in two sessions between which an election has intervened.

(d) Three-fifths vote on amendment, except amendment for "new state tax or fee" not in effect on Nov. 7, 1994 requires two-thirds of voters in the election.

(e) Two-thirds vote in each house at one session, or majority vote in each house in two sessions.

(f) Majority vote on amendment must be at least 50 percent of the total votes cast at the election (at least 35 percent in Nebraska); or, at a special election, a majority of the votes tallied which must be at least 30 percent of the total number of registered voters.

(g) Majority voting in election or three-fifths voting on amendment.

(h) If five or fewer political subdivisions of the state are affected, majority in state as a whole (and also in affected subdivisions) is required.

(i) Two-thirds of both houses.

(j) Majority of members elected sitting in joint session.

(k) The two-thirds must include not less than a majority elected to each house.

(l) Three-fifths of all members of each house at one session, or majority of all members of each house for two successive sessions.

(m) If a proposed amendment is not approved at the election when submitted, neither the same amendment nor one which would make substantially the same change for the constitution may be again submitted to the people before the third general election thereafter.

(n) Amendments concerning certain elective franchise and education matters require three-fourths vote of members elected and approval by three-fourths of electors voting in state and two-thirds of those voting in each county.

(o) Majority vote to amend constitution, two-thirds to revise ("revise" includes all or a part of the constitution).

(p) Emergency amendments may be passed by two-thirds vote of each house, followed by ratification by majority vote of electors in election held at least one month after legislative approval. There is an exception for an amendment containing a supermajority voting requirement, which must be ratified by an equal supermajority.

(q) Two-thirds of members of each house, first passage; majority of members of each house after popular ratification.

(r) Majority of members elected to both houses, first passage; two-thirds of members elected to both houses, second passage.

(s) Majority of all citizens voting for governor.

(t) Two-thirds vote senate, majority vote house, first passage; majority both houses, second passage. As of 1974, amendments may be submitted only every four years.

(u) Within 30 days after voter approval, governor must submit amendment(s) to U.S. Secretary of the Interior for approval.

(v) If approved by two-thirds of members of each house, amendment(s) submitted to voters at special referendum; if approved by not less than three-fourths of total members of each house, referendum may be held at next general election.

## Table 1.3
## CONSTITUTIONAL AMENDMENT PROCEDURE: BY INITIATIVE
### Constitutional Provisions

| State or other jurisdiction | Number of signatures required on initiative petition | Distribution of signatures | Referendum vote |
|---|---|---|---|
| Arizona | 15% of total votes cast for all candidates for governor at last election. | None specified. | Majority vote on amendment. |
| Arkansas | 10% of voters for governor at last election. | Must include 5% of voters for governor in each of 15 counties. | Majority vote on amendment. |
| California | 8% of total voters for all candidates for governor at last election. | None specified. | Majority vote on amendment. |
| Colorado | 5% of total legal votes for all candidates for secretary of state at last general election. | None specified. | Majority vote on amendment. |
| Florida | 8% of total votes cast in the state in the last election for presidential electors. | 8% of total votes cast in each of 1/2 of the congressional districts. | Three-fifths vote on amendment except amendment for "new state tax or fee" not in effect Nov. 7, 1994 requires 2/3 of voters voting in election. |
| Illinois (a) | 8% of total votes cast for candidates for governor at last election. | None specified. | Majority voting in election or 3/5 voting on amendment. |
| Massachusetts (b) | 3% of total votes cast for governor at preceding biennial state election (not less than 25,000 qualified voters). | No more than 1/4 from any one county. | Majority vote on amendment which must be 30% of total ballots cast at election. |
| Michigan | 10% of total voters for all candidates at last gubernatorial election. | None specified. | Majority vote on amendment. |
| Mississippi (c) | 12% of total votes for all candidates for governor in last election. | No more than 20% from any one congressional district. | Majority vote on amendment and not less than 40% of total vote cast at election. |
| Missouri | 8% of legal voters for all candidates for governor at last election. | The 8% must be in each of 2/3 of the congressional districts in the state. | Majority vote on amendment. |
| Montana | 10% of qualified electors, the number of qualified voters to be determined by number of votes cast for governor in preceding election in each county and in the state. | The 10% to include at least 10% of qualified voters in 1/2 of the counties. | Majority vote on amendment. |
| Nebraska | 10% of registered voters. | The 10% must include 5% in each of 2/5 of the counties. | Majority vote on amendment which must be at least 35% of total vote at the election. |
| Nevada | 10% of voters who voted in entire state in last general election. | None in effect after a U.S. District Court ruling in 2004 invalidated the requirement. | Majority vote on amendment in two consecutive general elections. |
| North Dakota | 4% of population of the state. | None specified. | Majority vote on amendment. |
| Ohio | 10% of total number of electors who voted for governor in last election. | At least 5% of qualified electors in each of 1/2 of counties in the state. | Majority vote on amendment. |
| Oklahoma | 15% of legal voters for state office receiving highest number of voters at last general state election. | None specified. | Majority vote on amendment. |
| Oregon | 8% of total votes for all candidates for governor at last election at which governor was elected for four-year term. | None specified. | Majority vote on amendment except for supermajority equal to supermajority voting requirement contained in proposed amendment. |
| South Dakota | 10% of total votes for governor in last election. | None specified. | Majority vote on amendment. |
| No. Mariana Islands | 50% of qualified voters of commonwealth. | In addition, 25% of qualified voters in each senatorial district. | Majority vote on amendment if legislature approved it by majority vote; if not, at least 2/3 vote in each of two senatorial districts in addition to a majority vote. |

Source: John Dinan and The Council of State Governments, February 2012.

Key:
(a) Only Article IV, the Legislature Article, may be amended by initiative petition.
(b) Before being submitted to the electorate for ratification, initiative measures must be approved at two sessions of a successively elected legislature by not less than one-fourth of all members elected, sitting in joint session.
(c) Before being submitted to the electorate, initiated measures are sent to the legislature, which has the option of submitting an amended or alternative measure alongside the original measure.

## Table 1.4
## PROCEDURES FOR CALLING CONSTITUTIONAL CONVENTIONS
### Constitutional Provisions

| State or other jurisdiction | Provision for convention | Provision for calling a convention by initiative | Legislative vote for submission of convention question (a) | Popular vote to authorize convention | Periodic submission of convention question required (b) | Popular vote required for ratification of convention proposals |
|---|---|---|---|---|---|---|
| Alabama | Yes | No | Majority | ME | No | Not specified |
| Alaska | Yes | No | No provision (c)(d) | (c) | 10 years; 2002 (c) | Not specified (c) |
| Arizona | Yes | No | Majority | (e) | No | MP |
| Arkansas | No | No | No | | | |
| California | Yes | No | 2/3 | MP | No | MP |
| Colorado | Yes | No | 2/3 | MP | No | ME |
| Connecticut | Yes | No | 2/3 | MP | 20 years; 2008 (f) | MP |
| Delaware | Yes | No | 2/3 | MP | No | No provision |
| Florida | Yes (m) | Yes (m) | (g) | MP | No | 3/5 voting on proposal |
| Georgia | Yes | No | (d) | No | No | MP |
| Hawaii | Yes | No | Not specified | MP | 9 years; 2008 | MP (h) |
| Idaho | Yes | No | 2/3 | MP | No | Not specified |
| Illinois | Yes | No | 3/5 | (i) | 20 years; 2008 | MP |
| Indiana | No | No | No | | | |
| Iowa | Yes | No | Majority | MP | 10 years; 2010 | MP |
| Kansas | Yes | No | 2/3 | MP | No | MP |
| Kentucky | Yes | No | Majority (j) | MP (k) | No | No provision |
| Louisiana | Yes | No | (d) | No | No | MP |
| Maine | Yes | No | (d) | No | No | No provision |
| Maryland | Yes | No | Majority | ME | 20 years; 2010 | MP |
| Massachusetts | No | No | | No | | |
| Michigan | Yes | No | Majority | MP | 16 years; 2010 | MP |
| Minnesota | Yes | No | 2/3 | ME | No | 3/5 voting on proposal |
| Mississippi | No | No | No | | | |
| Missouri | Yes | No | Majority | MP | 20 years; 2002 | Not specified (l) |
| Montana | Yes (m) | Yes (m) | 2/3 | MP | 20 years; 2010 | MP |
| Nebraska | Yes | No | 3/5 | MP (o) | No | MP |
| Nevada | Yes | No | 2/3 | ME | No | No provision |
| New Hampshire | Yes | No | Majority | MP | 10 years; 2002 | 2/3 voting on proposal |
| New Jersey | No | No | No | | | |
| New Mexico | Yes | No | 2/3 | MP | No | Not specified |
| New York | Yes | No | Majority | MP | 20 years; 1997 | MP |
| North Carolina | Yes | No | 2/3 | MP | No | MP |
| North Dakota | No | No | No | | | |
| Ohio | Yes | No | 2/3 | MP | 20 years; 1992 | MP |
| Oklahoma | Yes | No | Majority | (e) | 20 years; 1970 | MP |
| Oregon | Yes | No | Majority | (e) | No | No provision |
| Pennsylvania | No | No | No | | | |
| Rhode Island | Yes | No | Majority | MP | 10 years; 2004 | MP |
| South Carolina | Yes | No | (d) | ME | No | No provision |
| South Dakota | Yes (m) | Yes (m) | (d) | No | No | (p) |
| Tennessee | Yes (q) | No | Majority | MP | No | MP |
| Texas | No | No | No | | | |
| Utah | Yes | No | 2/3 | ME | No | ME |
| Vermont | No | No | No | | | |
| Virginia | Yes | No | (d) | No | No | MP |
| Washington | Yes | No | 2/3 | ME | No | Not specified |
| West Virginia | Yes | No | Majority | MP | No | Not specified |
| Wisconsin | Yes | No | Majority | MP | No | No provision |
| Wyoming | Yes | No | 2/3 | ME | No | Not specified |
| American Samoa | Yes | No | (r) | No | No | ME (s) |
| No. Mariana Islands | Yes | No | Majority (t) | 2/3 | 10 years | MP and at least 2/3 in each of 2 senatorial districts |
| Puerto Rico | Yes | No | 2/3 | MP | No | MP |

See footnotes at end of table.

## PROCEDURES FOR CALLING CONSTITUTIONAL CONVENTIONS — Continued
## Constitutional Provisions

*Source:* John Dinan and The Council of State Governments, February 2012.

*Key:*

MP — Majority voting on the proposal.

ME — Majority voting in the election.

(a) In all states not otherwise noted, the entries in this column refer to the proportion of members elected to each house required to submit to the electorate the question of calling a constitutional convention.

(b) The number listed is the interval between required submissions on the question of calling a constitutional convention; where given, the date is that of the most recent submission of the mandatory convention referendum.

(c) Unless provided otherwise by law, convention calls are to conform as nearly as possible to the act calling the 1955 convention, which provided for a legislative vote of a majority of members elected to each house and ratification by a majority vote on the proposals. The legislature may call a constitutional convention at any time.

(d) In these states, the legislature may call a convention without submitting the question to the people. The legislative vote required is two-thirds of the members elected to each house in Georgia, Louisiana, South Carolina and Virginia; two-thirds concurrent vote of both branches in Maine; three-fourths of all members of each house in South Dakota; and not specified in Alaska, but bills require majority vote of membership in each house.

(e) The law calling a convention must be approved by the people.

(f) The legislature shall submit the question 20 years after the last convention, or 20 years after the last vote on the question of calling a convention, whichever date is last.

(g) The power to call a convention is reserved to the people by petition.

(h) The majority must be 50 percent of the total votes cast at a general election or at a special election, a majority of the votes tallied which must be at least 30 percent of the total number of registered voters.

(i) Majority voting in the election, or three-fifths voting on the question.

(j) Must be approved during two legislative sessions.

(k) Majority must equal one-fourth of qualified voters at last general election.

(l) Majority of those voting on the proposal is assumed.

(m) The question of calling a constitutional convention may be submitted either by the legislature or by initiative petition. In Montana and South Dakota, conventions can be called by initiative petition in the same manner as provided for initiated amendments (see Table 1.3), and with approval by a majority of voters. In Florida, conventions can be called by filing an initiative petition with signatures equal to 15 percent of the votes cast in the preceding presidential election and also equal to 15 percent of signatures in half of the congressional districts in the state and then obtaining a majority of the voters at the ensuing election.

(n) Two-thirds of all members of the legislature.

(o) Majority must be 35 percent of total votes cast at the election.

(p) Convention proposals are submitted to the electorate at a special election in a manner to be determined by the convention. Ratification by a majority of votes cast.

(q) Conventions may not be held more often than once in six years.

(r) Five years after effective date of constitutions, governor shall call a constitutional convention to consider changes proposed by a constitutional committee appointed by the governor. Delegates to the convention are to be elected by their county councils. A convention was held in 1972.

(s) If proposed amendments are approved by the voters, they must be submitted to the U.S. Secretary of the Interior for approval.

(t) The initiative may also be used to place a referendum convention call on the ballot. The petition must be signed by 25 percent of the qualified voters or at least 75 percent in a senatorial district.

# A Statistical Approach to Ohio's Constitutional History ... And a Calculation of Its Future

### By Robert Hern

*Ohio began its statehood with a constitution of slightly more than 6,000 words. Today, its constitution is almost 54,000 words, more than 9,000 of which are in sections that are "collecting dust", and is growing at an exponential rate. If Ohio stays true to its current course, by 2050 it will have a constitution around 71,500 words long.*

## Introduction

In 1802, Ohio began with a constitution that contained just over 6,000 words, and in its nearly five decades of existence, was never amended. In 1851, Ohio adopted its second constitution, which was 50 percent longer than its predecessor at more than 9,000 words. Ohioans touted that this constitution was "of reasonable length, full and plain in its provisions, and well considered and well arranged by its authors, who embraced many of the wisest and soundest men of the state."[1]

Then in 1874, after the 1873–74 Constitutional Convention, Ohio voted on whether to adopt its third constitution, which totaled around 15,000 words. The proposed 1874 Constitution was overwhelmingly rejected by a vote of 250,169 to 102,885,[2] in part, because it was overly "complex"[3] and it had "too much legislation in it."[4]

Today, the 1851 Constitution now contains over 50,000 words, making it the tenth longest state constitution in the United States[5] and in a condition that does not produce the same praising words as it did in 1851. Most notably, Ohio Supreme Court Justice Paul E. Pfeifer dubbed the current Ohio Constitution "a mess"[6] when he pointed to the 2009 casino amendment and livestock standards as provisions clogging the Constitution.[7]

This paper creates a detailed and complete statistical analysis of Ohio's constitutional history.[8] Furthermore, potential causes of Ohio's constitutional growth

will be explored and, using statistical analysis, Ohio's constitutional future will be calculated.

## Ohio's Constitutional History

In 1802, Ohio's constitution had only eight articles, 106 sections and 6,265 words. It remained unaltered until its replacement in 1851 with a constitution containing 16 articles, 168 sections and 9,447 words. Today, the Buckeye State's constitution is made up

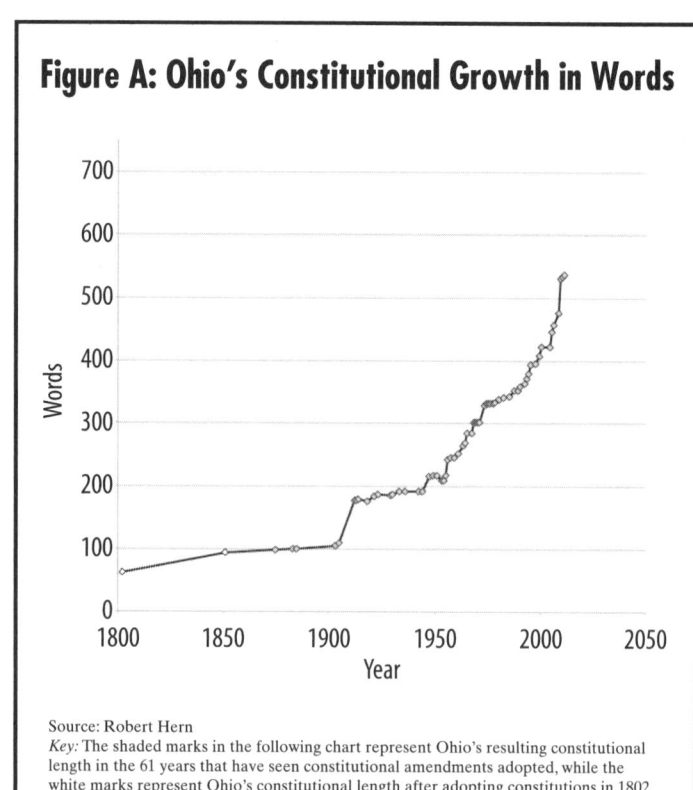

# Figure A: Ohio's Constitutional Growth in Words

Words

Year

Source: Robert Hern
*Key:* The shaded marks in the following chart represent Ohio's resulting constitutional length in the 61 years that have seen constitutional amendments adopted, while the white marks represent Ohio's constitutional length after adopting constitutions in 1802 and 1851.[10]

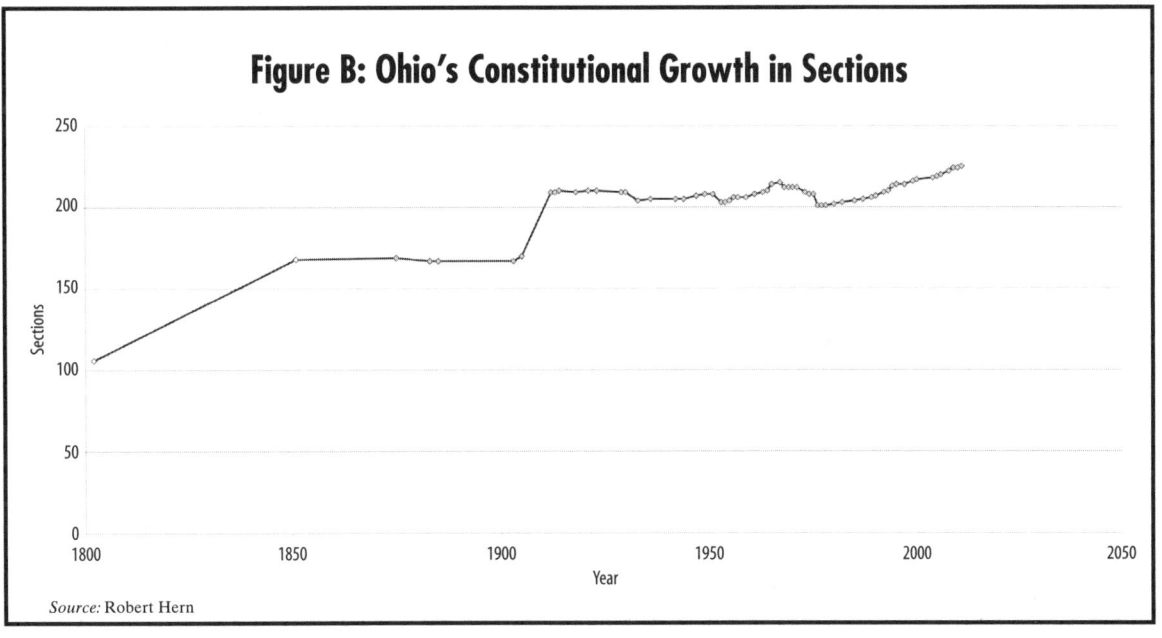

Figure B: Ohio's Constitutional Growth in Sections

*Source:* Robert Hern

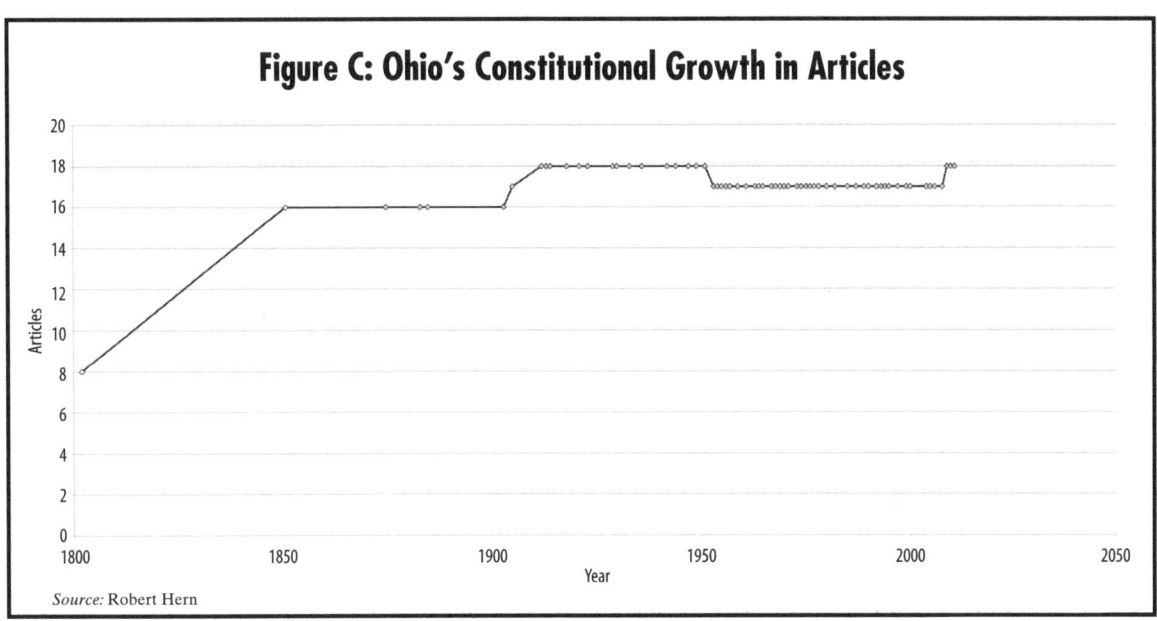

Figure C: Ohio's Constitutional Growth in Articles

*Source:* Robert Hern

of 18 articles, 224 sections and 53,421 words. This equates to a current constitutional length 8.5 times longer than the 1802 constitution and more than 5.5 times longer than the 1851 constitution as adopted.

While these numbers show considerable constitutional growth, they may be discounted as a natural consequence to more than 200 years of history.

To determine the validity of such a claim, the rate of growth should be evaluated.

Linear growth may indicate Ohio has maintained consistent principles concerning how to determine whether subject is worthy of constitutional inscription and the style in which provisions ought to be written. If this is true, Ohio should have experienced a growth rate of about 227 words

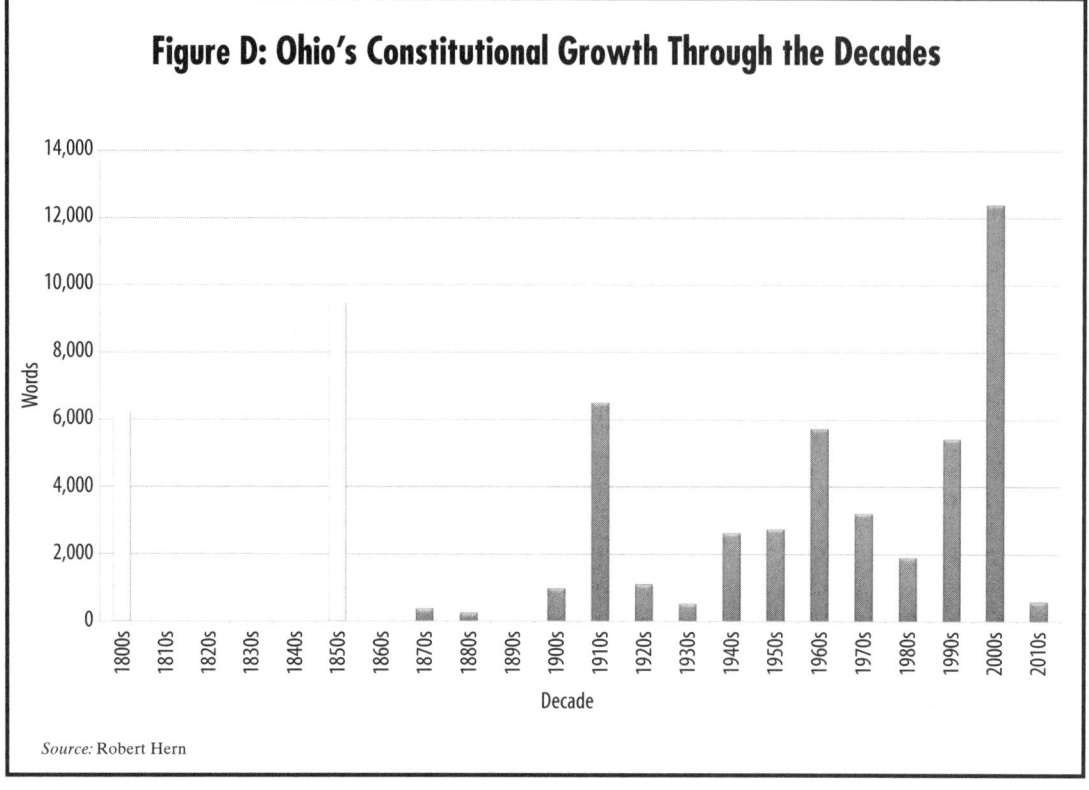

Figure D: Ohio's Constitutional Growth Through the Decades

*Source:* Robert Hern

per year since the 1802 constitution. Applying this same thought process to the 1851 constitution, it should have grown at 276 words per year.

Figure A depicts Ohio's actual constitutional growth, in words, throughout its history. That growth is the result of 164 amendments—76 percent of which have increased the document by more than 47,000 words, while 38 amendments (23 percent) have removed 3,376 words, and two amendments[9] (one percent) have had no net effect. Those expecting linear growth may be disappointed to see that the constitution has been growing at an exponential rate.

This chart cannot answer questions about the causes of Ohio's constitutional growth, but it does indicate the residents are either expanding what they believe is constitutional subject matter or how they write constitutional provisions, or a combination of the two.

Also noteworthy are the two following charts that illustrate Ohio's constitutional growth since 1802 in terms of the number of sections, as well as the number of articles.

### Growth Through the Decades

Figure D depicts Ohio's constitutional growth throughout the decades and helps to emphasize the seriousness of the rate in which the Constitution is increasing.

Before the turn of the 21st century, the decade in which the most words were added to the Ohio Constitution by amendment was the 1910s, when 6,502 words were added in 40 amendments. That decade's growth was primarily due to the 1912 Constitutional Convention, which resulted in 34 adopted amendments that added almost 7,000 words to the constitution.

The 2000s, a decade in which only 10 amendments were adopted, increased the Ohio Constitution by 12,394 words—nearly twice as many as the 1910s and accomplished in one-fourth the amendments. This is even more shocking in that the 2000s added 31 percent more words than the entire 1851 constitution as adopted.

The volume of words added in so few amendments during the 2000s suggests that Ohio has made a dramatic shift in how it *writes* constitutional amendments.

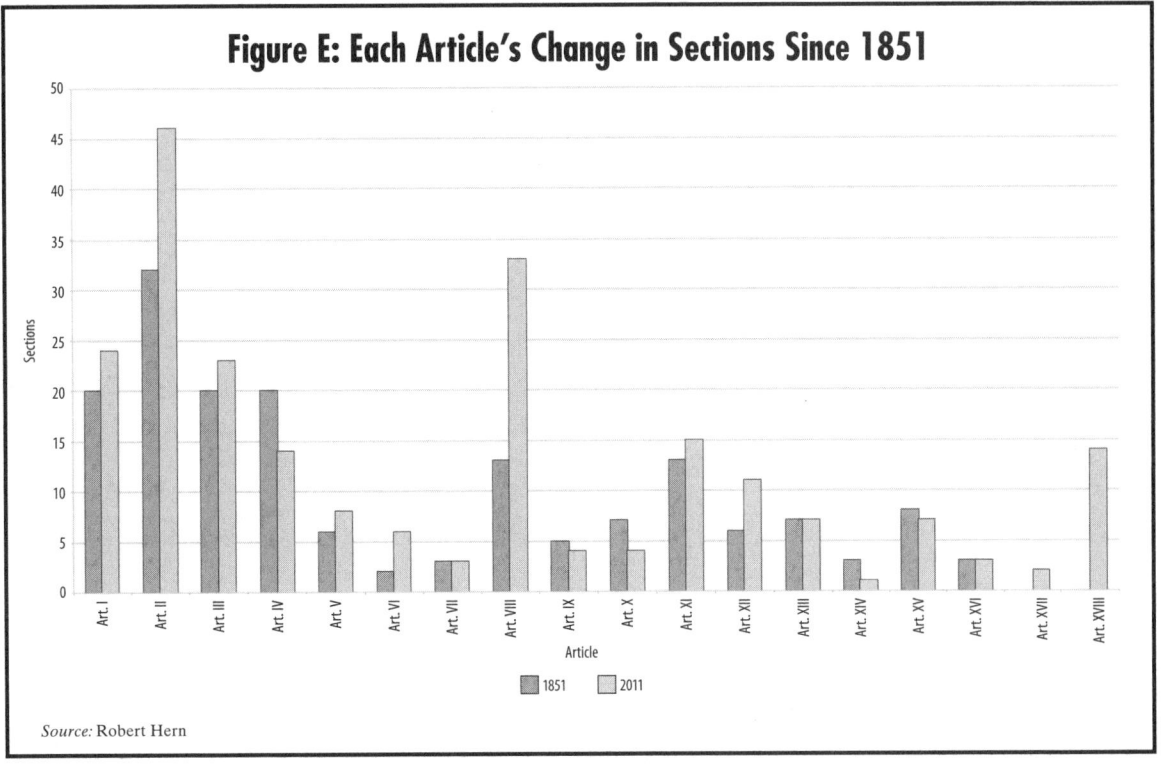

## Figure E: Each Article's Change in Sections Since 1851

*Source:* Robert Hern

### The Location of Ohio's Constitutional Growth

To obtain an even more comprehensive understanding of Ohio's constitutional growth, it is beneficial to look at how each article has changed since 1851. Such an evaluation can be done by comparing either the amount of sections or total words that made up each article in 1851 versus today. The following chart illustrates how each article has changed, in terms of sections, since 1851.

As seen in Figure E, article II, establishing the legislative branch, contained the most sections in 1851 with 32 and continues to do so today, containing 46. The article experiencing the most growth since 1851, however, is article VIII, providing for public debt and public works, experiencing an increase of 20 sections.

Although article II of the Ohio Constitution contains 13 more sections than the next closest article, article VIII; in terms of length, article II does not even compare to article VIII, the Constitution's longest article.

In 1851, article VIII contained only 873 words, 701 less words than article II. Today, article VIII totals an astonishing 26,279 words, 2.8 times larger than the entire Ohio Constitution as adopted in

1851. Article II is now the second longest article, containing 7,410 words. Figures E and F together show just how concentrated Ohio's constitutional growth has been in article VIII. While article II has 39 percent more sections than article VIII, article VIII contains more than 3.5 times as many words.

### Is Ohio Forgetting How to Effectively Write Constitutional Amendments?

Ohio's constitutional history illustrates that, at some level, its residents have forgotten how to effectively write constitutional amendments.

In 1851, Ohio's constitution had 168 sections averaging 56 words per section. Today, the constitution has 225 sections. If it took roughly the same number of words today to express each subject matter as it did in 1851, a constitution consisting of 225 sections should contain approximately 12,600 words today. The state's constitution, however, is 53,684 words long, averaging 239 words per section.

This disparity is even more striking considering that 70 of the 168 original sections in the 1851 Constitution have never been altered. Those unaltered sections constitute 31 percent of the total sections in Ohio's current constitution, but

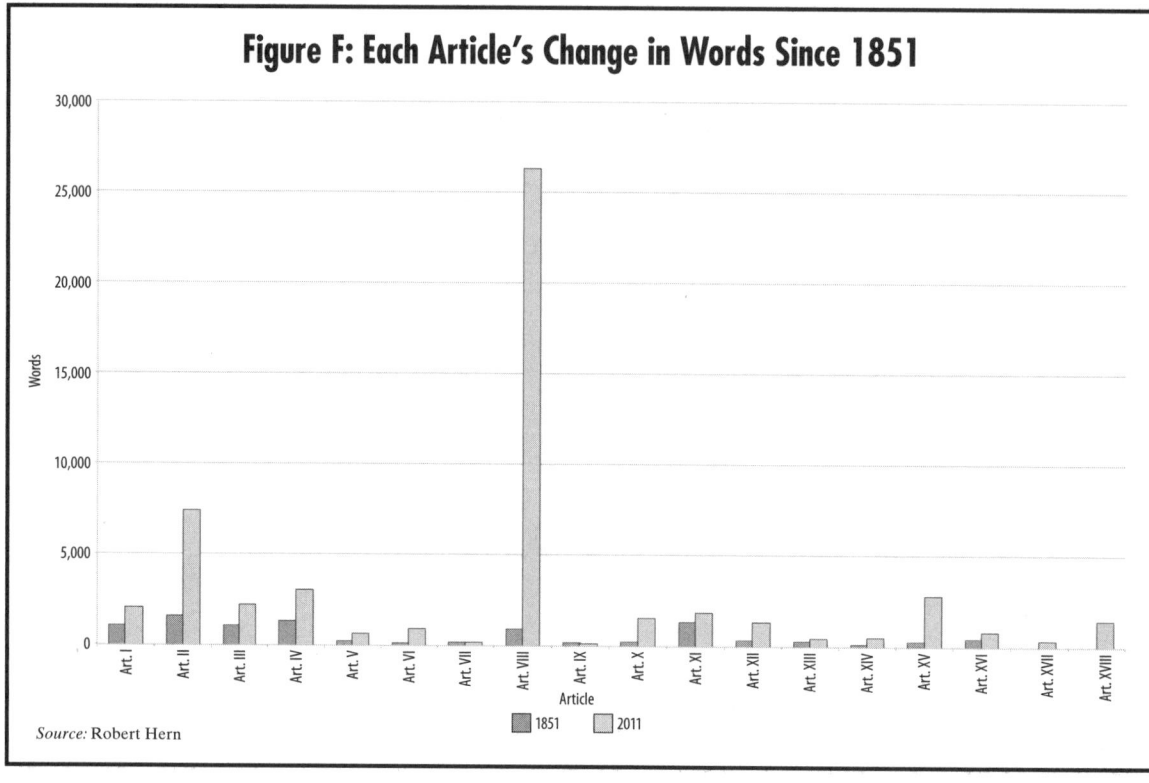

Figure F: Each Article's Change in Words Since 1851

Source: Robert Hern

■ 1851    □ 2011

only account for 6 percent—3,352 words—of its length.[11] Thus, the remaining 155 sections represent 50,332 words and average 325 words per section. This growth in the average number of words per section supports the conclusion that Ohio is increasingly writing lower and lower quality constitutional amendments.

The following chart, in addition to Figure F above, illustrates that this lapse has been a relatively recent phenomenon.

Until the 1910s the average number of words per section remained virtually constant. Thereafter, until the 2000s, the constitution experienced gradual and consistent growth in the average number of words per section. In the 2000s, however, 10 amendments increased the average number of words per section of the entire constitution by 48 words. Again, this is more data supporting the conclusion that the writing quality of constitutional amendments has diminished drastically in Ohio over recent years.

### Examples of Ineffective Writing

A prime example of ineffective writing is the 2009 constitutional amendment that allowed four casi-

nos in Ohio, which took article XV, section 6 from 125 words to 2,533 words. As a result, section 6 became flooded with a nearly 1,000-word definition section, which in less than a year became a straightjacket for the state.[12]

Article XV, section 6, defines "casino facility," "casino gaming," "casino operator," "gross casino revenue," "majority interest," "slot machines" and "table game"—seemingly all well understood terms. "Casino facility" is defined in such detail that it lists the parcels on which the four permitted casinos in Ohio may be built.[13] Unsurprisingly, when disagreement resulted in the location of one of the casinos, to change the location, a constitutional amendment had to be proposed and adopted. Was this level of micromanagement necessary, or, could the amendment have been better written and therefore avoided an additional but necessary 2010 amendment?

A critic could say the quality of the casino amendment was not as high because it was proposed by initiative petition, not the General Assembly. Unfortunately, it is just as easy to locate a great example of micromanagement in an amendment proposed by the General Assembly.

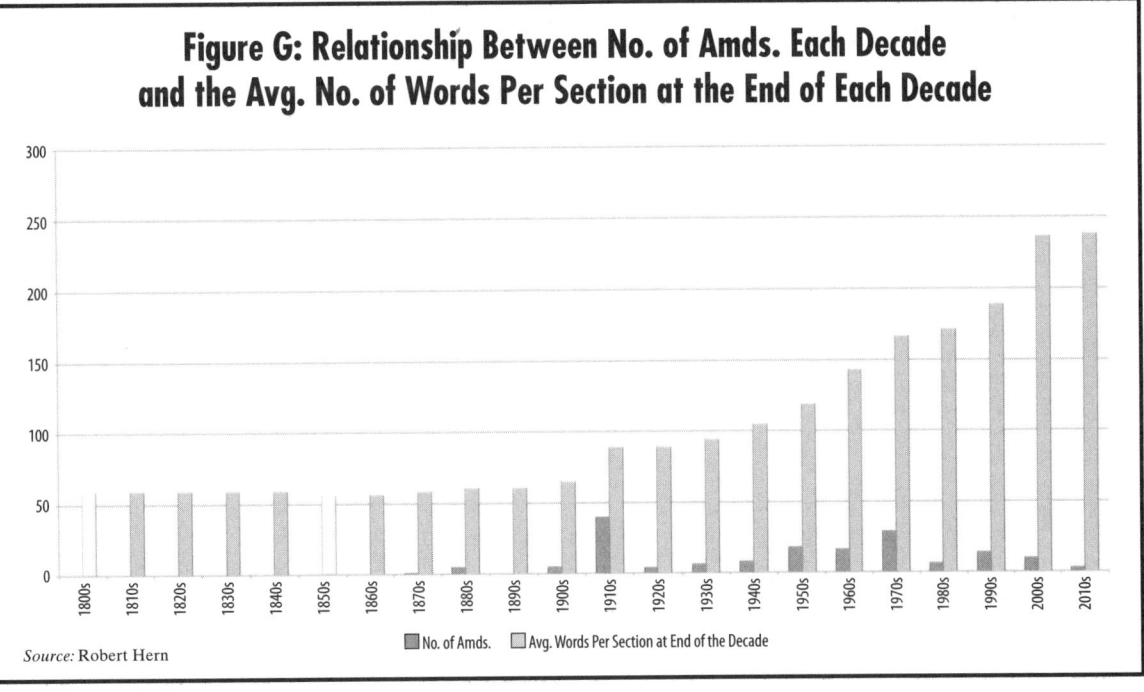

**Figure G: Relationship Between No. of Amds. Each Decade and the Avg. No. of Words Per Section at the End of Each Decade**

■ No. of Amds.　　□ Avg. Words Per Section at End of the Decade

*Source:* Robert Hern

## Table A: Eight "Expired" Article VIII Sections

| Sec. | Purpose | Last Year in Which a Debt Obligation Pursuant to the Section Could Expire | Words |
|---|---|---|---|
| 2b | WWII Veterans | 1966 | 2,301 |
| 2c | Highways | 1972 | 434 |
| 2d | Korean War Veterans | 1976 | 1,945 |
| 2e | State Bldgs | 1984 | 831 |
| 2f | State Bldgs | 2002 | 1,190 |
| 2g | State Highways | 1989 | 469 |
| 2h | State Capital Improvements | 2000 | 724 |
| 2j | Vietnam War Veterans | 1992 | 1,453 |
| Total | | | 9,347 |

*Source:* Robert Hern

In 2009, the General Assembly proposed, and the voters adopted, the single largest constitutional amendment in Ohio constitutional history—article VIII, section 2r, grants the authority to issue bonds to provide compensation to veterans of the Persian Gulf, Afghanistan, and Iraq conflicts, which added 2,681 words to the Ohio Constitution.

Colossal constitutional amendments such as the casino amendment and article VIII, section 2r do not need to be dissected. Regardless of the purpose for the provision, it should not take 2,500 words to enunciate. If it's not possible to write the provision in a more succinct way, then the subject matter of the provision may not be the kind that should be within a constitution.

### *Ohio Does Not Do Any "House Cleaning"*

In 1953, six separate amendments were adopted for "deleting or repealing obsolete, unused or unusable sections or parts of sections" of Ohio's constitution.[14] As a result of that joint resolution, 1,334 words were removed from the document—40 percent of words ever removed from the constitution through adopted amendments.

Then, in 1976, six amendments were proposed through six separate joint resolutions to remove or clarify unnecessary or obsolete constitutional language.[15] As a result, 459 words were removed—14

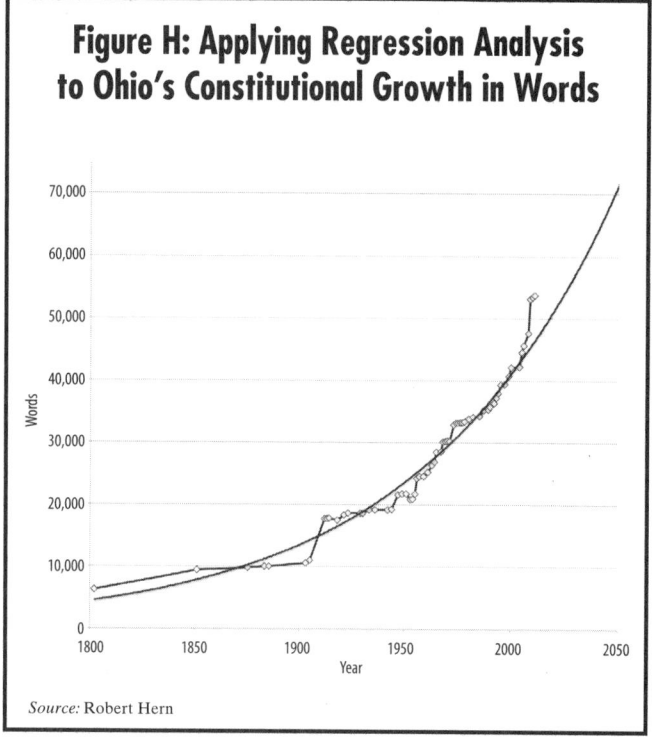

## Figure H: Applying Regression Analysis to Ohio's Constitutional Growth in Words

*Source:* Robert Hern

'divested' States of any power to add qualifications.[16]

As a result of the case, Ohio has since knowingly kept an unconstitutional provision in its state constitution for 16 years.

Article VIII is the area with the most serious problem of articles collecting dust—an article that places restrictions on state and local governments concerning state debt.[17] The article's debt limitation, however, may be overcome by specific amendments[18] to the constitution and has been bypassed by 22 amendments.[19] Of these amendments, 18 were adopted to raise money for a specified purpose through the sale of bonds.[20] Nine of those 18 amendments have expired, meaning the bonds have been sold and the debt has been satisfied by the state.[21]

So how many of the expired constitutional amendments have been repealed now that they no longer serve any function? One. Article VIII, section 2a was repealed in 1953, as part of Amended House Joint Resolution No. 94, the purpose of which was "[t]o amend the constitution of the state of Ohio by deleting or repealing obsolete, unused or unusable sections or parts of sections thereof ..."[22]

By simply removing an unconstitutional provision and the eight provisions that are collecting dust, Ohio could reduce its constitution by 18 percent and absolutely nothing would change.

percent of the total words ever removed from the constitution through amendments. Thus, the 100th and 111th Ohio General Assembly, or two of 129 Ohio General Assemblies, were responsible for more than half of all words ever removed from the constitution.

## Actual Provisions "Collecting Dust"

So what "house cleaning" should be done now? A prime example of a provision of the Ohio Constitution that needs to be removed is section 8, article V, which was adopted in 1992 and limits the terms of Ohio's U.S. senators and representatives. Three years after adoption, a similar state constitutional provision from Arkansas was held unconstitutional by the United States Supreme Court.

In *United States Term Limits v. Thornton*, the Supreme Court ruled:

"First, ... the power to add qualifications is not within the 'original powers' of the States, and thus is not reserved to the States by the Tenth Amendment. Second, even if States possessed some original power in this area, we conclude that the Framers intended the Constitution to be the exclusive source of qualifications for Members of Congress, and that the Framers thereby

## Calculating Ohio's Constitutional Future: Applying Regression Analysis

### *In Terms of Overall Length*

So what will happen to the Ohio Constitution if Ohio does not change how constitutional amendments are written? Using regression analysis, one is not only able to determine the relationship between two variables, but also may be able to forecast the variables' future relationships.[23] Regression analysis is the process of finding the equation of a line that best fits a set of data.[24] Speaking generally, one may determine the accuracy by which the line represents the relationship between two variables by looking to the line's

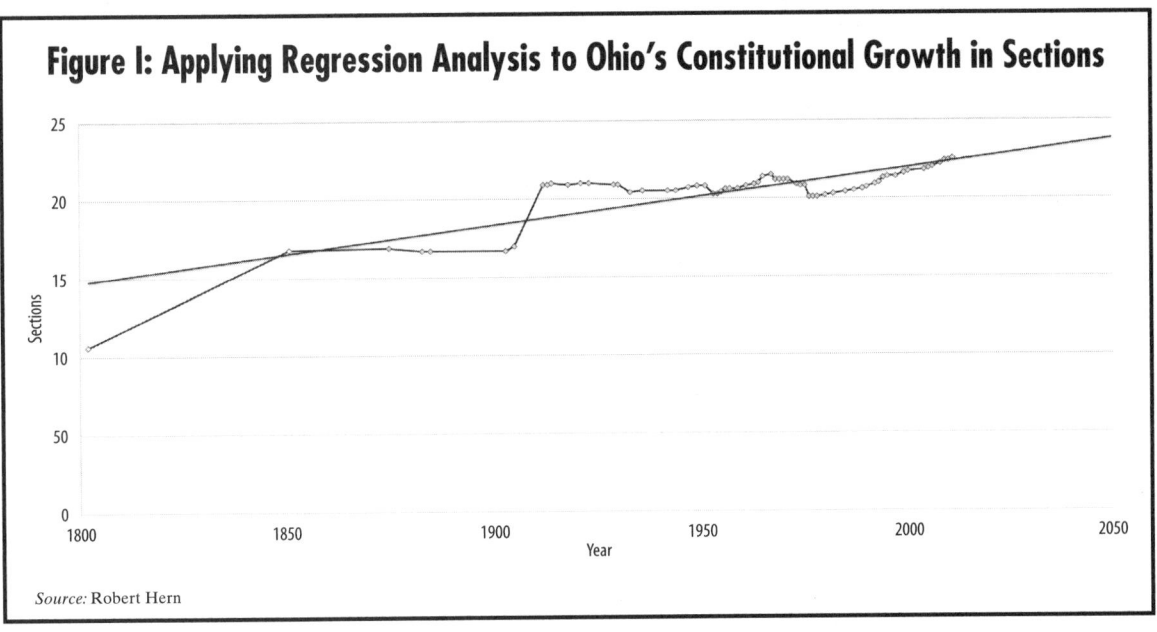

Figure I: Applying Regression Analysis to Ohio's Constitutional Growth in Sections

*Source:* Robert Hern

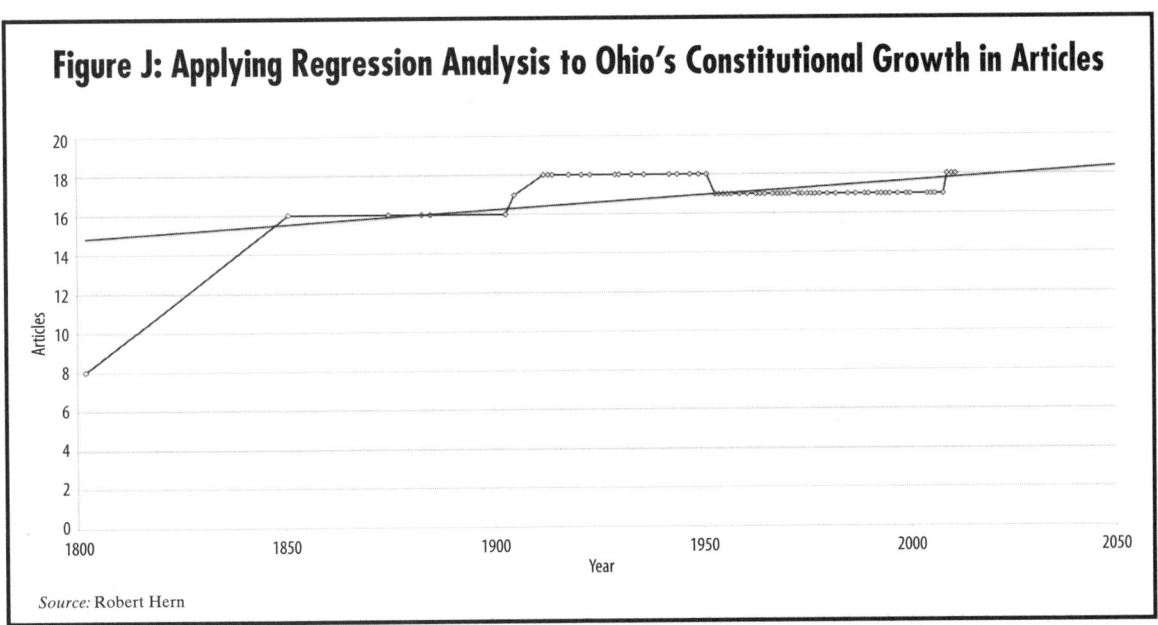

Figure J: Applying Regression Analysis to Ohio's Constitutional Growth in Articles

*Source:* Robert Hern

squared correlation coefficient value, or R2.[25] This number will be between zero and one, with a value of one indicating the strongest relationship possible.[26] In other words, the higher the R2 value for a regression line, the more accurately it represents the relationship between the two variables. The following applies regression analysis to the data of Ohio's constitutional history.

As discussed above, Ohio's constitutional growth over time has not been linear, but rather exponential. Figure H applies an exponential regression line to the data of the constitutional growth through the years.

The above exponential regression line has a R2 value of 0.96—indicating this regression line illustrates Ohio's constitutional growth through time quite accurately. With this strength of the regression line, and using the exponential regression line equation of, where *y* represents the year and *x* the amount of words in the Ohio Constitution, we can confidently forecast what the Ohio Constitution may look like in the future if the way in which Ohio drafts constitutional amendments continues on its current path. Therefore, in 2050 Ohio may expect to see a constitution that will contain 71,533 words—33% larger than Ohio's constitution currently.

### In Terms of Sections

Concerning constitutional growth of the amount of sections in the Ohio Constitution, the growth has been almost continually increasing. However, using regression analysis here is only moderately helpful. The linear regression line drawn below has a R2 value of 0.67.

Therefore, using the linear regression line's equation of , where *y* represents the year and *x* the amount of sections in the Ohio Constitution, in 2050, Ohio may expect to see a constitution that contains around 238 sections—only around 6% larger than Ohio's constitution currently.

### In Terms of Articles

Finally, the amount of articles in Ohio's constitution has not drastically changed over the past 160 years. While a lack of change does mean regression analysis is not useful, here, the change of articles in Ohio's constitutional history does not produce a reliable regression line, as its R2 value is 0.22. Thus, any forecasts of the amount of Articles in Ohio's constitutional future would be more along the lines of speculation.

## Conclusion

States must aim to create a constitution that is flexible and adaptable to potential changes. To do so, the drafters must first determine whether the subject matter is one that should be provided for at the highest level of state legal authority and is so important as to justify the invalidation of all legislative and other governmental action in conflict with it. If the subject matter is of constitutional importance, the provision must be written in a way that does not micromanage the state government and be kept simple. If it is not possible to do so, the subject matter may be more appropriate as a statutory matter.

After a complete analysis of every adopted amendment's effect on the Ohio Constitution, it is apparent that the constitution is growing in an exponential manner. Additionally, it is clear that Ohio is radically deviating from quality constitutional writing.

As a practical matter, however, correcting Ohio's constitutional writing style is a long-term goal. In the short-term, Ohio could reduce the length of its constitution by 18 percent if it eliminated all the provisions that are collecting dust. If Ohio chooses not to make any changes in the way constitutional amendments are written and doesn't remove the obsolete and unconstitutional provisions, the state could have a constitution that is almost 71,000 words long, or 33 percent longer than the current constitution, in less than 40 years.

In the end, Ohio state Supreme Court Justice Paul E. Pfeifer's claim that the Ohio Constitution is "a mess" appears to be more than just an opinion. Rather, it is more closely aligned as a fact supported by an abundance of data.

## Note on Methodology

The final word count of the Ohio Constitution used in this paper is 53,684 words. It was calculated using the word count feature in Microsoft Word. Therefore, for example, "Article I" or "§ 1" would each be considered as two words.

The word count includes the titles of the constitution itself and the 18 articles. The titles of the sections, however, are not included, as those are not approved by the voters and are instead supplied by the various publishing companies. Additionally, the word count includes the preamble, but excludes the various schedules.

## Notes

[1] Editorial, Clev. Evening Herald, Mar. 13, 1851.

[2] Steven H. Steinglass and Gino J. Scarselli, The Ohio State Constitution: A Reference Guide, 30 (2004).

[3] Editorial, *New Constitution–Yes or No?*, Clev. Plain Dealer, Aug. 17, 1874 ("Indeed the proposed new constitution has to do with so much that is complex and beyond the scope of the popular information that the work of the convention, as a whole, will hardly be voted on intelligently.").

[4] Editorial, *The Election on Tuesday*, Clev. Plain Dealer, Aug. 19, 1874 ("It was very generally believed that the proposed constitution had too much legislation in it; and that it was too much 'a lawyers' constitution.'").

[5] John Dinan, State Constitutional Developments in 2009, *in* 2010 The Book of the States 1, 11 (2010) (using an Ohio Constitution word count of 53,421).

[6] Alan Johnson, *Pfeifer: Revise Constitution, End Death Penalty*, The Columbus Dispatch, Jan. 20, 2011, *http://www.dispatchpolitics.com/live/content/local_news/stories/2011/01/20/copy/pfeifer-revise-constitution-end-death-penalty.html?sid=101.*

[7] *Id.*

[8] *See infra* Appendix, Note on Methodology.

[9] The first amendment was in 1912, adopting the schedule of the amendments, which as stated in the Note on Methodology, do not become a part of the constitution. The second amendment was in 1918, that conflicted with another adopted amendment. Ultimately, one was held unconstitutional in *State ex rel. Greenlund v. Fulton*, 99 Ohio St. 168, 124 N.E. 172 (1919).

[10] This shaded and white theme will be used consistently in the charts throughout.

[11] The seventy unchanged sections average 48 words per section.

[12] Today, after article XV, section 6 now has a total length of 2531 words—of which 984 are "definitions" of the terms listed in the following paragraph. OH Const. art. XV, § 6(C)(9).

[13] Oh Const. art. XV, § 6.

[14] H.J.R. 94, 100th Gen. Assem., Reg. Sess. (Ohio 1953).

[15] *See* H.J.R. 14, 111th Gen. Assem., Reg. Sess. (Ohio 1976); H.J.R. 15, 111th Gen. Assem., Reg. Sess. (Ohio 1976); H.J.R. 36, 111th Gen. Assem., Reg. Sess. (Ohio 1976); H.J.R. 37, 111th Gen. Assem., Reg. Sess. (Ohio 1976); S.J.R. 16, 111th Gen. Assem., Reg. Sess. (Ohio 1976); S.J.R. 17, 111th Gen. Assem., Reg. Sess. (Ohio 1976).

[16] *Id* at 800–01.

[17] *Supra* note 2 at p 219.

[18] *State ex rel. Ohio Funds Management Bd. v. Walker*, 55 Ohio St. 3d 1, 9, 561 N.E.2d 927 (1990).

[19] Ohio Const. Art. VIII, §§ 2a-2r, 13–16.

[20] Ohio Const. Art. VIII, §§ 2a-2r.

[21] Ohio Const. Art. VIII, §§ 2a-2h, 2j.

[22] *Supra* note 16.

[23] For a well written article on the basics of regression analysis, see Alan O. Sykes, *Introduction to Regression Analysis, in* Law and Economics Working Papers (1993) *available at* http://www.law.uchicago.edu/Lawecon/ wp1-50.html.

[24] *Id.*

[25] *Id.*

[26] *Id.*

## About the Author

**Robert Hern** is an attorney in Cincinnati. He is a 2011 graduate of the Cleveland-Marshall College of Law.

# Table B: Analysis of Each Adopted Amendment in Ohio's Constitutional History
## From 1801–2011

| No. | Year | Amendment | Total Length (In Words) | Words Before Amd. | Words After Amd. | Net Change | Articles / Sections Affected | Net Article Change | Total Articles | Net Section Change | Total Sections |
|---|---|---|---|---|---|---|---|---|---|---|---|
| | | | | | **1800** | | | | | | |
| | 1802 | Ohio Constitution of 1802 | 6,265 | | | | | | 8 | | 106 |
| | | *Title* | 0 | | | | | | | | |
| | | *Preamble* | 164 | | | | | | | | |
| | | *Body* | 6,101 | | | | | | | | |
| | | | | | **1810, 1820, 1830, 1840** | | | | | | |
| | | | | | None | | | | | | |
| | | | | | **1850** | | | | | | |
| | 1851 | 1851 Constitution, *as adopted* | 9,447 | | | | | | 16 | | 168 |
| | | *Title* | 6 | | | | | | | | |
| | | *Preamble* | 28 | | | | | | | | |
| | | *Body* | 9,413 | | | | | | | | |
| | | | | | **1860** | | | | | | |
| | | | | | None | | | | | | |
| | | | | | **1870** | | | | | | |
| 1 | 1875 | Supreme Court Commission | 9,817 | 0 | 370 | 370 | ADDED § 21 to Art. IV | 0 | 16 | 1 | 169 |
| | | | | | **1880** | | | | | | |
| 2 | 1883 | Judicial Constitutional | 10,046 | 359 | 588 | 229 | §§ 1, 2 and 6 of Art. IV / REPEALED §§ 5 and 11 of Art. IV | 0 | 16 | -2 | 167 |
| 3 | 1885 | Changing Fall Election to Nov. (First Prop.) | 10,050 | 42 | 46 | 4 | § 2 of Art. II | 0 | 16 | 0 | 167 |
| 4 | | Changing Fall Election to Nov. (Second Prop.) | 10,055 | 49 | 54 | 5 | § 1 of Art. III | 0 | 16 | 0 | 167 |
| 5 | | Changing Fall Election to Nov. (Third Prop.) | 10,053 | 42 | 40 | -2 | § 2 of Art. X | 0 | 16 | 0 | 167 |
| 6 | | Township Officers | 10,056 | 43 | 46 | 3 | § 4 of Art. X | 0 | 16 | 0 | 167 |
| | | | | | **1890** | | | | | | |
| | | | | | None | | | | | | |
| | | | | | **1900** | | | | | | |
| 7 | 1903 | Single Liability of Stockholders | 10,035 | 60 | 39 | -21 | § 3 of Art. XIII | 0 | 16 | 0 | 167 |
| 8 | | Governor's Veto | 10,556 | 85 | 606 | 521 | § 16 of Art. II | 0 | 16 | 0 | 167 |
| 9 | | Giving Each County At Least One Representative | 10,565 | 61 | 70 | 9 | § 2 of Art. XI | 0 | 16 | 0 | 167 |
| 10 | 1905 | State & County Elections in Even Years | 10,994 | 0 | 429 | 429 | ADDED Art. XVII / ADDED §§ 1, 2 and 3 to Art. XVII | 1 | 17 | 3 | 170 |
| 11 | | Non-tax of Public Bonds | 11,026 | 120 | 152 | 32 | § 2 of Art. XII | 0 | 17 | 0 | 170 |
| | | | | | **1910** | | | | | | |
| 12 | 1912 | Double Liability of Stockholders and Inspection of Private Banks | 11,158 | 39 | 171 | 132 | § 3 of Art. XIII | 0 | 17 | 0 | 170 |
| 13 | | Registering & Warranting Land Titles | 11,257 | 0 | 99 | 99 | ADDED § 40 to Art. II | 0 | 17 | 1 | 171 |
| 14 | | Investigations by Each House of General Assembly | 11,307 | 65 | 115 | 50 | § 8 of Art. II | 0 | 17 | 0 | 171 |

| No. | Year | Amendment | Total Length (In Words) | Words Before Amd. | Words After Amd. | Net Change | Articles / Sections Affected | Net Article Change | Total Articles | Net Section Change | Total Sections |
|---|---|---|---|---|---|---|---|---|---|---|---|
| 15 | 1912 | Primary Elections | 11,455 | 0 | 148 | 148 | ADDED § 7 to Art. V | 0 | 17 | 1 | 172 |
| 16 | | Welfare of Employes | 11,498 | 0 | 43 | 43 | ADDED § 34 to Art. II | 0 | 17 | 1 | 173 |
| 17 | | Removal of Officials | 11,561 | 0 | 63 | 63 | ADDED § 38 to Art. II | 0 | 17 | 1 | 174 |
| 18 | | Damage for Wrongful Death | 11,592 | 0 | 31 | 31 | ADDED § 19a to Art. I | 0 | 17 | 1 | 175 |
| 19 | | Regulating Expert Testimony in Criminal Trials | 11,615 | 0 | 23 | 23 | ADDED § 39 to Art. II | 0 | 17 | 1 | 176 |
| 20 | | Reform in Civil Jury System | 11,642 | 11 | 38 | 27 | § 5 of Art. I | 0 | 17 | 0 | 176 |
| 21 | | Regulating State Printing | 11,656 | 56 | 70 | 14 | § 2 of Art. XV | 0 | 17 | 0 | 176 |
| 22 | | Limiting Power of General Assembly in Extra Sessions | 11,710 | 29 | 83 | 54 | § 8 of Art. III | 0 | 17 | 0 | 176 |
| 23 | | Conservation of Natural Resources | 11,834 | 0 | 124 | 124 | ADDED § 36 to Art. II | 0 | 17 | 1 | 177 |
| 24 | | Regulating Insurance | 11,896 | 54 | 116 | 62 | § 6 of Art. VIII | 0 | 17 | 0 | 177 |
| 25 | | Abolishing Prison Contract Labor | 12,098 | 0 | 202 | 202 | ADDED § 41 to Art. II | 0 | 17 | 1 | 178 |
| 26 | | Workmen's Compensation | 12,264 | 0 | 166 | 166 | ADDED § 35 to Art. II | 0 | 17 | 1 | 179 |
| 27 | | Civil Service | 12,310 | 0 | 46 | 46 | ADDED § 10 to Art. XV | 0 | 17 | 1 | 180 |
| 28 | | Eight Hour Day on Public Work | 12,362 | 0 | 52 | 52 | ADDED § 37 to Art. II | 0 | 17 | 1 | 181 |
| 29 | | Suits Against the State | 12,384 | 37 | 59 | 22 | § 16 of Art. I | 0 | 17 | 0 | 181 |
| 30 | | Regulation of Corporations & Sale of Personal Property | 12,466 | 22 | 104 | 82 | § 2 of Art. XIII | 0 | 17 | 0 | 181 |
| 31 | | Municipal Home Rule | 13,829 | 0 | 1,363 | 1,363 | ADDED Art. XVIII and 14 Sections | 1 | 18 | 14 | 195 |
| 32 | | Organization of Boards of Education | 13,909 | 0 | 80 | 80 | ADDED § 3 to Art. VI | 0 | 18 | 1 | 196 |
| 33 | | License to Traffic in Intoxicating Liquors | 14,469 | 0 | 560 | 560 | ADDED § 9 to Art. XV | 0 | 18 | 1 | 197 |
| 34 | | Abolishing Board of Public Works | 14,412 | 117 | 60 | -57 | § 12 of Art. VIII / REPEALED § 13 of Art. VIII | 0 | 18 | -1 | 196 |
| 35 | | Initiative and Referendum | 16,640 | 25 | 2,253 | 2,228 | § 1 of Art. II / ADDED §§ 1a, 1b, 1c, 1d, 1e, 1f and 1g to Art. II | 0 | 18 | 7 | 203 |
| 36 | | Judge of Court of Common Pleas for Each County | 16,801 | 307 | 468 | 161 | §§ 3, 7, 12 and 15 of Art. IV | 0 | 18 | 0 | 203 |
| 37 | | Depositions by State and Comment on Failure of Accused to Testify in Criminal Cases | 16,937 | 172 | 308 | 136 | § 10 of Art. I | 0 | 18 | 0 | 203 |
| 38 | | Mechanics' and Builders' Liens | 16,987 | 0 | 50 | 50 | ADDED § 33 to Art. II | 0 | 18 | 1 | 204 |
| 39 | | Limiting Veto Power of Governor | 16,783 | 606 | 402 | -204 | § 16 of Art. II | 0 | 18 | 0 | 204 |
| 40 | | Methods of Submitting Amendments to the Constitution | 16,854 | 402 | 473 | 71 | §§ 1, 2 and 3, of Art. XVI | 0 | 18 | 0 | 204 |
| 41 | | Change in Judicial System | 17,383 | 588 | 1,117 | 529 | §§ 1, 2 and 6 of Art. IV | 0 | 18 | 0 | 204 |

| No. | Year | Amendment | Total Length (In Words) | Words Before Amd. | Words After Amd. | Net Change | Articles / Sections Affected | Net Article Change | Total Articles | Net Section Change | Total Sections |
|---|---|---|---|---|---|---|---|---|---|---|---|
| 42 | | Taxation of State & Municipal Bonds, Inheritances, Incomes, Franchises & Production of Minerals | 17,680 | 194 | 491 | 297 | §§ 1, 2 and 6 of Art. XII / ADDED §§ 7, 8, 9, 10 and 11 to Art. XII | 0 | 18 | 5 | 209 |
| 43 | | Abolition of Justices of the Peace in Certain Cities | 17,639 | 41 | 0 | -41 | REPEALED § 9 of Art. IV | 0 | 18 | -1 | 208 |
| 44 | | Creating the Office of Superintendent of Public Instruction to Replace State Commissioner of Common Schools | 17,708 | 0 | 69 | 69 | ADDED § 4 of Art. VI | 0 | 18 | 1 | 209 |
| 45 | | Schedule of Amendments (Excluded) | 17,708 | | | | ADDED 1912 Schedule | | | | |
| 46 | 1913 | Women Eligible to Serve on Boards or Commissions Affecting Women & Children | 17,751 | 23 | 66 | 43 | § 4 of Art. XV | 0 | 18 | 0 | 209 |
| 47 | 1914 | Home Rule on Subjects of Intoxicating Liquor | 17,842 | 0 | 91 | 91 | ADDED § 9a to Art. XV | 0 | 18 | 1 | 210 |
| 48 | 1918 | Referendum; Voters May Approve or Reject Action of Legislature Ratifying Any Proposed Amd. to U.S. Constitution | 18,086 | 142 | 386 | 244 | § 1 of Art. II | 0 | 18 | 0 | 210 |
| 49 | | Prohibition of Sale & Manufacture of Intoxicating Liquors | 17,484 | 651 | 49 | -602 | § 9 of Art. XV / REPEALED § 9a of Art. 15 | 0 | 18 | -1 | 209 |
| 50 | | General Assembly To Provide Against Double Taxation Resulting from Real Estate & Mortgage or Secured Debt on Real Estate Taxation | 17,528 | 176 | 220 | 44 | § 2 of Art. XII | 0 | 18 | 0 | 209 |
| 51 | | General Assembly to Classify Property for Taxation * | 17,528 | 0 | 0 | 0 | § 2 of Art. XII | 0 | 18 | 0 | 209 |
| | | | | | 1920 | | | | | | |
| 52 | 1921 | To Provide for a Soldier Bonus | 18,365 | 0 | 837 | 837 | ADDED § 2a to Art. VIII | 0 | 18 | 1 | 210 |
| 53 | 1923 | Expand Indus. Commission's Power in Workmen's Compensation | 18,647 | 166 | 448 | 282 | § 35 of Art. II | 0 | 18 | 0 | 210 |
| 54 | | Delete "White Male" from Voter Qualifications | 18,644 | 66 | 63 | -3 | § 1 of Art. V | 0 | 18 | 0 | 210 |
| 55 | 1929 | $15M on Unvoted Real Estate Taxes | 18,615 | 287 | 258 | -29 | § 2 of Art. XII / REPEALED § 3 of Art. XII | 0 | 18 | -1 | 209 |
| | | | | | 1930 | | | | | | |
| 56 | 1930 | Distribution of Income & Inheritance Taxes | 18,630 | 38 | 53 | 15 | § 9 of Art. XII | 0 | 18 | 0 | 209 |
| 57 | 1933 | Repeal of Statewide Prohibition | 18,581 | 49 | 0 | -49 | REPEALED § 9 of Art. XV | 0 | 18 | -1 | 208 |
| 58 | | $10m Limit on Unvoted Real Estate Taxes | 18,579 | 258 | 256 | -2 | § 2 of Art. XII | 0 | 18 | 0 | 208 |
| 59 | | Home Rule for Counties & Townships | 19,156 | 341 | 918 | 577 | §§ 1-4 of Art. X / REPEALED § 16 of Art. 4 and §§ 5-7 of Art. X | 0 | 18 | -4 | 204 |
| 60 | 1936 | Eliminate Additional Liability of Stockholders of Banking & Other Depository Corps. | 19,100 | 171 | 115 | -56 | § 3 of Art. XIII | 0 | 18 | 0 | 204 |

| No. | Year | Amendment | Total Length (In Words) | Words Before Amd. | Words After Amd. | Net Change | Articles / Sections Affected | Net Article Change | Total Articles | Net Section Change | Total Sections |
|---|---|---|---|---|---|---|---|---|---|---|---|
| 61 | | Prohibit Sales Tax on Food for Consumption off Premises | 19,131 | 0 | 31 | 31 | ADDED § 12 to Art. XII | 0 | 18 | 1 | 205 |
| | | | | | **1940** | | | | | | |
| 62 | 1942 | Vacancies in Judicial Office | 19,177 | 68 | 114 | 46 | § 13 of Art. IV | 0 | 18 | 0 | 205 |
| 63 | 1944 | Permit Temporary or Substitute Judges in the S.Ct | 19,282 | 426 | 531 | 105 | § 2 of Art. IV | 0 | 18 | 0 | 205 |
| 64 | | Jurisdiction of Cts of App. | 19,229 | 647 | 594 | -53 | § 6 of Art. IV | 0 | 18 | 0 | 205 |
| 65 | 1947 | Provide a Bonus to Veterans | 21,530 | 0 | 2,301 | 2,301 | ADDED § 2b to Art. VIII | 0 | 18 | 1 | 206 |
| 66 | | 6-yr Term for Probate Judges; Delete Req't That Compensation Be Paid From Cty Treasury | 21,501 | 555 | 526 | -29 | § 7 of Art. IV and § 2 of Art. XVII | 0 | 18 | 0 | 206 |
| 67 | | Expand Sinking Fund Commission to Include Governor and Treasurer of State | 21,505 | 28 | 32 | 4 | § 8 of Art. VIII | 0 | 18 | 0 | 206 |
| 68 | | Limit Use of Motor Vehicle License and Fuel Taxes for Road and Related Purposes | 21,597 | 0 | 92 | 92 | ADDED § 5a to Art. XII | 0 | 18 | 1 | 207 |
| 69 | 1949 | Adopt Office-Type Ballot | 21,756 | 0 | 159 | 159 | ADDED § 2a to Art. V | 0 | 18 | 1 | 208 |
| | | | | | **1950** | | | | | | |
| 70 | 1951 | Permit More Than One Probate Judge Per Cty | 21,765 | 215 | 224 | 9 | § 7 of Art. IV | 0 | 18 | 0 | 208 |
| 71 | 1953 | Authorize Bond Issue for Highway System | 22,199 | 0 | 434 | 434 | ADDED § 2c to Art. VIII | 0 | 18 | 1 | 209 |
| 72 | | Create State Bd. of Educ. w/ Power to Appoint Superintendent of Public Instruction | 22,192 | 69 | 62 | -7 | § 4 of Art VI | 0 | 18 | 0 | 209 |
| 73 | | Delete "white" Re: Males Eligible or Req'd to Serve in State Militia | 22,190 | 53 | 51 | -2 | § 1 of Art. IX | 0 | 18 | 0 | 209 |
| 74 | | Eliminate Conflicts w/ US Const. | 21,940 | 463 | 213 | -250 | §§ 1 and 27 of Art. II | 0 | 18 | 0 | 209 |
| 75 | | Eliminate Obsolete Provisions Re: Eligibility of Women for Office | 21,897 | 66 | 23 | -43 | § 4 of Art. XV | 0 | 18 | 0 | 209 |
| 76 | | Adjusted Compensation for WWI Vets. | 21,060 | 837 | 0 | -837 | REPEALED § 2a of Art. VIII | 0 | 18 | -1 | 208 |
| 77 | | Repeal Provision for Electing Militia Officers | 21,033 | 27 | 0 | -27 | REPEALED § 2 of Art. IX | 0 | 18 | -1 | 207 |
| 78 | | Repeal Obsolete Provisions Re: 1851 Commission to Modernize Ct Procedure | 20,896 | 137 | 0 | -137 | REPEALED Art. XIV and §§ 1-3 of Art. XIV | -1 | 17 | -3 | 204 |
| 79 | | Repeal Obsolete Provision Re: Incumbents in Office in 1905 | 20,856 | 40 | 0 | -40 | REPEALED § 3 of Art. XVII | 0 | 17 | -1 | 203 |
| 80 | 1954 | 4-yr Terms for Governor, etc.; Limit Governor to 2 Successive Terms | 20,939 | 413 | 496 | 83 | § 2 of Art. III and §§ 1 and 2 of Art. XVII | 0 | 17 | 0 | 203 |
| 81 | 1955 | Authorize Bond Issue for Construction Program for Public Bldgs. | 21,770 | 0 | 831 | 831 | ADDED § 2e to Art. VIII | 0 | 17 | 1 | 204 |
| 82 | 1956 | Korean Veterans' Bonuses | 23,715 | 0 | 1,945 | 1,945 | ADDED § 2d to Art. VIII | 0 | 17 | 1 | 205 |
| 83 | | 4-yr Terms for State Senators | 24,215 | 130 | 630 | 500 | § 2 of Art. II and § 1 of Art. XI / ADDED § 6a to Art. XI | 0 | 17 | 1 | 206 |

| No. | Year | Amendment | Total Length (In Words) | Words Before Amd. | Words After Amd. | Net Change | Articles / Sections Affected | Net Article Change | Total Articles | Net Section Change | Total Sections |
|---|---|---|---|---|---|---|---|---|---|---|---|
| 84 | 1957 | Allow New OH Residents to Vote for President & VP | 24,308 | 63 | 156 | 93 | § 1 of Art. V | 0 | 17 | 0 | 206 |
| 85 | | Permit Adoption of Cty Charters | 24,502 | 252 | 446 | 194 | § 3 of Art. X | 0 | 17 | 0 | 206 |
| 86 | 1959 | Remove Limitation on Extra-Territorial Sale of Water and Sewer Services by Municipalities | 24,520 | 71 | 89 | 18 | § 6 of Art. XVIII | 0 | 17 | 0 | 206 |
| 87 | | Permit GA to Increase # of Ct of App Judges in Districts Where Needed | 24,499 | 594 | 573 | -21 | § 6 of Art. IV | 0 | 17 | 0 | 206 |
| | | | | | 1960 | | | | | | |
| 88 | 1961 | Change Method of Filing Vacancies in GA | 24,849 | 25 | 375 | 350 | § 11 of Art. II | 0 | 17 | 0 | 206 |
| 89 | | Continuity of State Gov't in Case of Attack | 24,937 | 0 | 88 | 88 | ADDED § 42 to Art. II | 0 | 17 | 1 | 207 |
| 90 | | Increase Militia Age Limits; Calling Militia In Disaster; Conform to Fed. Law | 24,913 | 138 | 114 | -24 | §§ 1, 3 and 4 of Art. IX | 0 | 17 | 0 | 207 |
| 91 | | Provide for Advice and Consent of Senate Re: Appointments to Office | 25,194 | 0 | 281 | 281 | ADDED § 21 to Art. III | 0 | 17 | 1 | 208 |
| 92 | 1963 | Authorize Bond Issue for Public Improvements | 26,384 | 0 | 1,190 | 1,190 | ADDED § 2f to Art. VIII | 0 | 17 | 1 | 209 |
| 93 | 1964 | Authorize Bond Issue for Highways | 26,853 | 0 | 469 | 469 | ADDED § 2g to Art. VIII | 0 | 17 | 1 | 210 |
| 94 | 1965 | Guarantee College Loans for OH Residents | 27,069 | 0 | 216 | 216 | ADDED § 5 to Art. VI | 0 | 17 | 1 | 211 |
| 95 | | Authorize Bond Issue for State Development | 27,793 | 0 | 724 | 724 | ADDED § 2h to Art. VIII | 0 | 17 | 1 | 212 |
| 96 | | Guarantee Loans for Indus. Dev. | 28,233 | 0 | 440 | 440 | ADDED § 13 to Art. VIII | 0 | 17 | 1 | 213 |
| 97 | | Authorize Same Judge to Serve More Than One Court in Counties Under 40,000 | 28,436 | 0 | 203 | 203 | ADDED § 23 to Art. IV | 0 | 17 | 1 | 214 |
| 98 | 1967 | Apportion OH House and Senate into Single-Member Districts | 28,539 | 1,885 | 1,988 | 103 | § 2 and 3 of Art. II and §§ 1-6 and 7-13 of Art. XI / ADDED §§ 14 and 15 to Art. XI / REPEALED § 6a of Art. XI | 0 | 17 | 1 | 215 |
| 99 | 1968 | Disposition of School and Ministerial Lands Trust Funds | 28,530 | 56 | 47 | -9 | § 1 of Art. VI | 0 | 17 | 0 | 215 |
| 100 | | Filling Vacancies in OH House | 28,600 | 375 | 445 | 70 | § 11 of Art. II | 0 | 17 | 0 | 215 |
| 101 | | Revise Administration and Org. of OH Court System ("Modern Courts Amd't") | 28,690 | 1,761 | 1,851 | 90 | §§ 1-4 and 6 of Art. IV and §§ 12 and 13 of Art. XI / ADDED § 5 of Art. V / REPEALED §§ 7, 8, 10, 12 and 14 of Art. IV | 0 | 17 | -4 | 211 |
| 102 | | Authorize Bond Issue for Highways and Other Capital Improvements | 30,143 | 0 | 1,453 | 1,453 | ADDED § 2i to Art. VIII | 0 | 17 | 1 | 212 |

| No. | Year | Amendment | Total Length (In Words) | Words Before Amd. | Words After Amd. | Net Change | Articles / Sections Affected | Net Article Change | Total Articles | Net Section Change | Total Sections |
|---|---|---|---|---|---|---|---|---|---|---|---|
| 103 | 1969 | Dispense w/ Short-Term Elections to Fill Vacancies | 30,212 | 432 | 501 | 69 | § 18 of Art. III and § 2 of Art. XVII | 0 | 17 | 0 | 212 |
| | | | | | | **1970** | | | | | |
| 104 | 1970 | Real Estate Tax Homestead Reduction for Residents 65 and Older | 30,250 | 256 | 294 | 38 | § 2 of Art. XII | 0 | 17 | 0 | 212 |
| 105 | | Reduce Voter Residence Req't From 1 yr to 6 mos. | 30,250 | 156 | 156 | 0 | § 1 of Art. V | 0 | 17 | 0 | 212 |
| 106 | | Permit Notice by Publication Instead of Mail of Proposed Municipal Charter Amd'ts | 30,269 | 157 | 176 | 19 | § 9 of Art. XVIII | 0 | 17 | 0 | 212 |
| 107 | 1971 | Require Notice by Publication Instead of Mail of Const'l Amd'ts or Laws Proposed or Referred by Initiative and Referendum | 30,235 | 888 | 854 | -34 | § 1g of Art. II | 0 | 17 | 0 | 212 |
| 108 | 1973 | Authorize State Lottery | 30,283 | 20 | 68 | 48 | § 6 of Art. XV | 0 | 17 | 0 | 212 |
| 109 | | Revise Org., Admin. and Procedures of GA | 30,524 | 1,391 | 1,632 | 241 | §§ 4, 6-9, 11 and 14-16 of Art. II / REPEALED §§ 17-19 and 25 of Art. II | 0 | 17 | -4 | 208 |
| 110 | | Tax Valuation of Farmland According to Agricultural Use | 30,636 | 124 | 236 | 112 | § 36 of Art. II | 0 | 17 | 0 | 208 |
| 111 | | Authorize GA to Provide for Amt of Income Exempt from Taxation | 30,635 | 52 | 51 | -1 | § 8 of Art. XII | 0 | 17 | 0 | 208 |
| 112 | | Re: Ct Org. and Admin. | 30,797 | 1,108 | 1,270 | 162 | §§ 1 and 4-6 of Art. IV | 0 | 17 | 0 | 208 |
| 113 | | Vietnam Vets' Bonuses | 32,879 | 0 | 2,082 | 2,082 | ADDED § 2j to Art. VIII | 0 | 17 | 1 | 209 |
| 114 | 1974 | Preparing Ballot Language and Informing Voters Re: Proposed Const'l Amd'ts | 33,217 | 164 | 502 | 338 | § 1 of Art. XVI | 0 | 17 | 0 | 209 |
| 115 | | Real Estate Tax Homestead Reduction for Disabled | 33,223 | 294 | 300 | 6 | § 2 of Art. XII | 0 | 17 | 0 | 209 |
| 116 | | Repeal Req't that Gov. Appoint Public Works Superintendent for 1-Yr Term | 33,163 | 60 | 0 | -60 | REPEALED § 12 of Art. VIII | 0 | 17 | -1 | 208 |
| 117 | | Indus. Dev. Revenue Bonds & Loan Guarantee Programs | 33,169 | 440 | 446 | 6 | § 13 of Art. VIII | 0 | 17 | 0 | 208 |
| 118 | 1975 | Give Candidates Reasonably Equal Treatment on Ballot, by Name Rotation or Otherwise | 33,162 | 159 | 152 | -7 | § 2a of Art. V | 0 | 17 | 0 | 208 |
| 119 | | Voters to Elect Delegates to Nat'l Party Conventions | 33,153 | 148 | 139 | -9 | § 7 of Art. V | 0 | 17 | 0 | 208 |
| 120 | | Permit Charitable Bingo | 33,174 | 68 | 89 | 21 | § 6 of Art. XV | 0 | 17 | 0 | 208 |
| 121 | 1976 | Require Joint Election of Gov. and Lt. Gov; Revise Lt. Gov's Duties | 33,209 | 198 | 233 | 35 | § 2a of Art. V / ADDED §§ 1a and 1b to Art. III / REPEALED § 16 of Art. III | 0 | 17 | 1 | 209 |

| No. | Year | Amendment | Total Length (In Words) | Words Before Amd. | Words After Amd. | Net Change | Articles / Sections Affected | Net Article Change | Total Articles | Net Section Change | Total Sections |
|---|---|---|---|---|---|---|---|---|---|---|---|
| 122 | | Qualifications of Electors; Remove Unconst'l & Unnecessary Language | 33,029 | 255 | 75 | -180 | §§ 1 and 4 of Art. V / REPEALED §§ 3 and 5 of Art. V | 0 | 17 | -2 | 207 |
| 123 | | Elections, Terms of Office, & Vacancies; Remove Unnecessary Language | 32,916 | 429 | 316 | -113 | §§ 1 and 2 of Art. XVII | 0 | 17 | 0 | 207 |
| 124 | | Require at least 50% of Estate Taxes to Be Returned to Political Subdivisions (Clarify Language) | 32,923 | 87 | 94 | 7 | §§ 4 and 9 of Art. XII | 0 | 17 | 0 | 207 |
| 125 | | Consolidate Provisions for Imposing Taxes; Clarify Language | 32,883 | 198 | 158 | -40 | ADDED § 3 of Art XII / REPEALED §§ 7, 8, 10 and 12 of Art. XII | 0 | 17 | -3 | 204 |
| 126 | | Succession in Case of Disability or Vacancy in Office of Gov or Lt. Gov | 33,350 | 131 | 598 | 467 | §§ 15 and 17 of Art. III / ADDED § 22 to Art. III | 0 | 17 | 1 | 205 |
| 127 | | Repeal Obsolete Provisions on Public Printing, Dueling, & Bureau of Statistics | 33,224 | 126 | 0 | -126 | REPEALED §§ 2, 5 & 8 of Art. XV | 0 | 17 | -3 | 202 |
| 128 | | Declaration of Election Results for State Officers at Next Regular GA Session | 33,208 | 167 | 151 | -16 | § 3 of Art. III / REPEALED § 4 of Art. III | 0 | 17 | -1 | 201 |
| 129 | 1977 | Person Entitled to Vote if Registered for 30 Days; Elector Failing to Vote at Least once in 4 Years must Re-register | 33,247 | 48 | 87 | 39 | § 1 of Art. V | 0 | 17 | 0 | 201 |
| 130 | 1978 | Ballot Bd. to Write Language for State Issues; Advertising Proposals; Initiative and Referendum Petitions | 33,201 | 854 | 808 | -46 | § 1g to Art. II | 0 | 17 | 0 | 201 |
| 131 | | Modify Procedures to Adopt, Amend or Repeal Cty Charter | 33,583 | 476 | 858 | 382 | § 4 of Art. X | 0 | 17 | 0 | 201 |
| 132 | | GA to Regulate Prison Labor; Remove Const'l Restrictions on Sale of Prison-Made Goods | 33,408 | 202 | 27 | -175 | § 41 of Art. II | 0 | 17 | 0 | 201 |
| | | | | | **1980** | | | | | | |
| 133 | 1980 | Authorize GA to Classify Real Property for Taxation | 33,809 | 0 | 401 | 401 | ADDED § 2a to Art. XII | 0 | 17 | 1 | 202 |
| 134 | 1982 | Authorize Bonds to Subscribe Low Cost Housing | 34,113 | 0 | 304 | 304 | ADDED § 14 to Art. VIII | 0 | 17 | 1 | 203 |
| 135 | 1985 | Authorize Bond Issue to Finance Coal Research | 34,298 | 0 | 185 | 185 | ADDED § 15 to Art. VIII | 0 | 17 | 1 | 204 |
| 136 | 1987 | Entire Net Proceeds of State Lottery to Be Used for Support of Education | 34,334 | 89 | 125 | 36 | § 6 of Art. XV | 0 | 17 | 0 | 204 |
| 137 | | Permit State to Finance or Assist Local Gov'ts to Improve Roads, Water, Sewer & Waste Collection & Treatment Facilities | 35,258 | 0 | 924 | 924 | ADDED § 2k to Art. VIII | 0 | 17 | 1 | 205 |
| 138 | 1989 | Method for Filling Vacancy in Office of Lt. Gov. | 35,301 | 0 | 43 | 43 | ADDED § 17a to Art. III | 0 | 17 | 1 | 206 |

| No. | Year | Amendment | Total Length (In Words) | Words Before Amd. | Words After Amd. | Net Change | Articles / Sections Affected | Net Article Change | Total Articles | Net Section Change | Total Sections |
|---|---|---|---|---|---|---|---|---|---|---|---|
| | | | | | 1990 | | | | | | |
| 139 | 1990 | Authorize Public Financial Support for Low-Cost Housing | 35,848 | 0 | 547 | 547 | ADDED § 16 to Art. VIII | 0 | 17 | 1 | 207 |
| 140 | | Extend Homestead Exemption to Surviving Spouses | 35,826 | 300 | 278 | -22 | § 2 of Art. XII | 0 | 17 | 0 | 207 |
| 141 | 1992 | Term Limits for State Senators & Reps. | 36,020 | 119 | 313 | 194 | § 2 of Art. II | 0 | 17 | 0 | 207 |
| 142 | | Term Limits for State Exec. Branch Officers other than Gov. | 36,225 | 101 | 306 | 205 | § 2 of Art. III | 0 | 17 | 0 | 207 |
| 143 | | Term Limits for US Senators & Reps. | 36,429 | 0 | 204 | 204 | ADDED §§ 8 and 9 to Art. V | 0 | 17 | 2 | 209 |
| 144 | 1993 | Authorize Bond Issue for Capital Improvements for Parks, Conservation & Natural Resources | 37,198 | 0 | 769 | 769 | ADDED § 21 to Art. VIII | 0 | 17 | 1 | 210 |
| 145 | 1994 | Protect Rights of Crime Victims | 37,321 | 0 | 123 | 123 | ADDED § 10a to Art. I | 0 | 17 | 1 | 211 |
| 146 | | Eliminate Intermediate Appeal & Provide for Direct Appeal to S.Ct in Death Penalty Cases | 37,371 | 743 | 793 | 50 | §§ 2 and 3 of Art. IV | 0 | 17 | 0 | 211 |
| 147 | | Protect Viability of Prepaid Tuition Program & Prevent Fed Taxation of Program Income | 37,807 | 0 | 436 | 436 | ADDED § 6 to Art. VI | 0 | 17 | 1 | 212 |
| 148 | | Repeal Soft Drink Excise Tax | 37,950 | 0 | 143 | 143 | ADDED § 13 to Art. XII | 0 | 17 | 1 | 213 |
| 149 | 1995 | Limit Unrestricted Power of Gov. to Commute Sentences | 37,957 | 138 | 145 | 7 | § 11 of Art. III | 0 | 17 | 0 | 213 |
| 150 | | Public Works & Highways; Issuance of Obligations | 39,311 | 0 | 1,354 | 1,354 | ADDED § 2m to Art. VIII | 0 | 17 | 1 | 214 |
| 151 | 1997 | Denial of Bail to Persons Charged w/ Certain Felonies | 39,455 | 39 | 183 | 144 | § 9 of Art. I | 0 | 17 | 0 | 214 |
| 152 | 1999 | Authorize the State to Issue Bonds for School Facilities | 40,718 | 0 | 1,263 | 1,263 | ADDED §§ 2n and 17 to Art. VIII | 0 | 17 | 2 | 216 |
| | | | | | 2000 | | | | | | |
| 153 | 2000 | Issuance of Bonds for Environmental Conservation | 42,147 | 0 | 1,429 | 1,429 | ADDED § 2o to Art. VIII | 0 | 17 | 1 | 217 |
| 154 | 2004 | Defining Marriage | 42,204 | 0 | 57 | 57 | ADDED § 11 to Art. XV | 0 | 17 | 1 | 218 |
| 155 | 2005 | Create Jobs & Stimulate Economic Growth in Ohio | 44,589 | 0 | 2,385 | 2,385 | ADDED § 2p to Art. VIII | 0 | 17 | 1 | 219 |
| 156 | 2006 | Raise the State Min. Wage | 45,615 | 0 | 1,026 | 1,026 | ADDED § 34a to Art. II | 0 | 17 | 1 | 220 |
| 157 | 2008 | To Provide for Earlier Filing Deadlines for Statewide Ballot Issues (Issue One) | 45,857 | 1,796 | 2,038 | 242 | §§ 1a, 1b, 1c and 1g of Art. II | 0 | 17 | 0 | 220 |
| 158 | | To Authorize the State to Issue Bonds to Continue the Clear Ohio program for Environmental Revitalization & Conservation (Issue Two) | 47,287 | 0 | 1,430 | 1,430 | ADDED § 2q to Art. VIII | 0 | 17 | 1 | 221 |
| 159 | | To Protect Private Property Rights in Ground Water, Lakes & Other Watercourses | 47,569 | 0 | 282 | 282 | ADDED § 19b to Art. I | 0 | 17 | 1 | 222 |

| No. | Year | Amendment | Total Length (In Words) | Words Before Amd. | Words After Amd. | Net Change | Articles / Sections Affected | Net Article Change | Total Articles | Net Section Change | Total Sections |
|---|---|---|---|---|---|---|---|---|---|---|---|
| 160 | 2009 | To Authorize State to Issue Bonds to Provide Compensation to the Vets of the Persian Gulf, Afghan & Iraq | 50,250 | 0 | 2,681 | 2,681 | ADDED § 2r to Art. VIII | 0 | 17 | 1 | 223 |
| 161 | | To Create the Ohio Livestock Care Standards Bd (Issue Two) | 50,704 | 0 | 454 | 454 | ADDED Art. XIV and § 1 to Art. XIV | 1 | 18 | 1 | 224 |
| 162 | | Allowance & Tax on Casinos | 53,112 | 125 | 2,533 | 2,408 | § 6 of Art. XV | 0 | 18 | 0 | 224 |
| | | | | **2010** | | | | | | | |
| 163 | 2010 | Extend the Ohio 3rd Frontier Program | 53,423 | 2,385 | 2,696 | 311 | § 2p of Art. VIII | 0 | 18 | 0 | 224 |
| 164 | | Change the Location of Casinos | 53,421 | 2,533 | 2,531 | -2 | § 6 to Art. XV | 0 | 18 | 0 | 224 |
| 165 | 2011 | Freedom to Choose Healthcare | 53,684 | 0 | 263 | 263 | ADDED § 21 to Art. I | 0 | 18 | 1 | 225 |

*Sources:* Robert Hern, 2011–2012.

# Chapter Two

# FEDERALISM AND INTERGOVERNMENTAL RELATIONS

# State-Federal Relations:
# Revolt Against Coercive Federalism?

### By John Kincaid

*Partisan polarization characterizes the current period of coercive federalism, shaping state-federal relations in often conflictual ways. Major clashes have occurred over health care, immigration, education, environmental protection, voting rights and numerous cultural issues such as abortion. State-federal disputes over health care and immigration have, moreover, generated two U.S. Supreme Court contests that could mark a pivotal advance or rollback of federal power over the states. At the same time, austerity and scrambles for tax revenue continue to characterize intergovernmental fiscal relations, while social welfare spending drives state budgets and squeezes funding for nonwelfare functions and for local governments.*

Although 2012 is a presidential election year, the election will have little impact on federalism because coercive federalism[1] has been a bipartisan enterprise since the late 1960s. The parties differ on what they want to nationalize, but each nationalizes its policy preferences whenever possible.

The year, however, may be pivotal for federalism, if the U.S. Supreme Court uses several cases to restrain federal power. Potentially most potent is the court's case on President Barack Obama's Patient Protection and Affordable Care Act of 2010,[2] for which the justices held six hours of oral argument over three days.

At the same time, partisan polarization has revived a kind of dual, competitive federalism in which the party not in power in Washington, D.C., uses its dominance in a majority or sizable number of states to challenge policies of the party in power in Washington. Hence, state-based Republicans will continue challenging federal policies promulgated under President Obama, as they also did during Clinton's presidency, thereby generating intergovernmental conflict, just like state-based Democrats opposed some federal policies promulgated under President Ronald Reagan and the two Bush presidencies.

## Partisan Polarization and Federalism

In recent years, elected officials, media pundits and many voters have polarized into boisterous ideological monologues. Maine Republican Olympia Snowe's announced retirement from the U.S. Senate in 2012 marked, perhaps, the death knell for bipartisanship.

In 2011, for the second year in a row and only the third time in 30 years, "no Senate Democrat compiled a voting record to the right of any Senate Republican, and no Republican came down on the left of any Senate Democrat."[3] Another indication of polarization is the rise of the Senate filibuster, which reached historic highs during the 110th and 111th Congresses, from 2007 to 2011.

Polarization has had two notable impacts on the federal system. It contributed significantly to centralization and coercive federalism because control of Congress, the White House, and a majority of the state legislatures and governorships by one party smooths the way for expansive federal policymaking. State partisan allies of the party in power in Washington, D.C., usually embrace policies emanating from their federal counterparts. Polarization also escalates state-federal conflict when the party in power in Washington, D.C., faces many states controlled by the other party.

The parties also differ rhetorically on federalism. According to Karl Rove, for example, Republican House members believe "that the federal government is doing too much dictating to states and localities and that state and local governments ought to be freed from constraints."[4] Democrats rarely express these concerns.

The much publicized photo of Arizona Republican Gov. Jan Brewer pointing her finger at President Obama during a heated exchange at the Phoenix-Mesa Gateway Airport in January 2012 dramatically symbolized federal-state clashes arising from polarization. She had given the president a letter stating, "We both love this country, but we fundamentally disagree on how to best make America grow and prosper once again."[5]

In his 2012 state-of-the-state address, Republican Gov. Gary Herbert of Utah inveighed against "the regulatory colossus created by an overarching, out-of-control and out-of-touch federal government."[6] Texas Gov. Rick Perry has stood out for his frequent flaying of the Environmental Protection Agency,[7] criticism of the Obama administration over federal disaster assistance during the state's summer wildfires and clashes with federal officials over Planned Parenthood. One can see the heightened stridency of today's anti-Washington rhetoric by comparing the Republican Perry's 2010 book *Fed Up!*[8] with former Utah Republican Gov. Scott M. Matheson's 1986 book *Out of Balance*.[9]

Not all state challenges have a partisan hue, though. Vermont, with a Democratic governor, Peter Shumlin, and legislature, has challenged in court the federal Nuclear Regulatory Commission's decision to allow the Vermont Yankee nuclear power plant to operate for 20 years beyond its 40-year design. The Democratic attorney general of Massachusetts has appealed the commission's decision to relicense the Pilgrim Nuclear Station in Plymouth, and New York's Democratic governor, Andrew Cuomo, wants to close the Indian Point Energy Center. The Vermont case might decide who can pull the plug on nuclear plants, the federal government or the plant's host state.

A number of states, both Democratic and Republican, oppose massive new regulations issued by the Federal Energy Regulatory Commission that require all electric utilities to join regional planning organizations, which, among other things, have substantial authority to decide who should pay for long-distance power line construction. States fear the new regional groups will curtail their regulatory authority, especially over local power lines.

## Federal Clashes with States and Localities

The federal government has not been quiescent in the face of state innovations and pushbacks. The Obama administration is, for example, challenging states' voter ID laws. A spate of new laws, mostly in Republican-controlled states, require a photo ID to register or vote, demand proof of citizenship, reduce early voting and regulate registration drives by third-party groups such as the NAACP and the League of Women Voters. An ID is required to vote in about 32 states, 16 of which have enacted photo ID laws.

The U.S. Department of Justice found voter ID laws in South Carolina and Texas in violation of the U.S. Voting Rights Act. Polls indicate that about 70 percent of Americans support a photo ID for voting. The U.S. Supreme Court upheld Indiana's photo ID law in 2008, but left open a door to challenge such laws if they are applied discriminatorily.[10]

In May 2011, the administration objected to an Indiana law banning the use of Medicaid funds at Planned Parenthood clinics; a federal court later enjoined enforcement of the law. The Centers for Medicare and Medicaid Services warned all state officials that states cannot exclude physicians, clinics, or other providers from Medicaid "because they separately provide abortion services." In March 2012, the Centers for Medicare and Medicaid Services also announced it would phase out its 90 percent share of the Texas Women's Health Program because Texas lawmakers banned Planned Parenthood from the program.

Federal courts have blocked all or parts of many state laws involving such Republican-supported policies as abortion restrictions, immigration enforcement and funding cutoffs for Planned Parenthood. These federal interventions have brought relief to Democrats, who hope some of the cases will overturn laws they couldn't stop.[11]

The proposed Child Interstate Abortion Notification Act, however, has picked up steam in Congress. This bill would criminalize the act of knowingly taking a minor across state lines to obtain an abortion so as to evade her home state's parental involvement law. It also would prohibit performance of an abortion on an out-of-state minor without notification of one of her parents.

In June 2011, after the Texas House of Representatives passed a bill banning intrusive airport screening, the federal government threatened to halt all flights to Texas.

The administration is pressing suburban communities to provide more low-income housing and welcome more minority residents. Commenting on litigation involving Westchester County, N.Y., the deputy secretary of the U.S. Department of Housing and Urban Development said: "We're clearly messaging other jurisdictions across the country that ... we're going to ask them to pursue similar goals."[12]

Under pressure from the Obama administration, St. Paul, Minn., withdrew its appeal in *Magner v. Gallagher*, which would have given the U.S. Supreme Court an occasion to decide whether the disparate-impact method of proving discrimination under the Fair Housing Act is constitutional. Even though the case was scheduled for oral argument, city officials announced, "The City of Saint Paul, national civil rights organizations, and legal scholars believe that, if Saint Paul prevails in the U.S. Supreme Court, such a result could completely eliminate 'disparate impact' civil rights enforcement, including under the Fair Housing Act and the Equal Credit Opportunity Act."[13]

Illinois, Massachusetts, New York and various communities have sought to opt out of Secure Communities because they object to having every arrested person's fingerprints run through immigration databases. The program, they argue, ensnares too many innocent people and instills fear among Latino victims and witnesses of crime. The Obama administration declared their participation to be mandatory, however, and began terminating agreements with localities, arguing that the federal government needs no intergovernmental agreements to allow Homeland Security to search local arrest records for illegal immigrants.

Another facet of coercive federalism has been the nationalization of criminal law. Federal criminal cases have increased by 70 percent over the past decade alone.[14] The federal courts are backlogged with criminal and civil cases. Many observers have raised civil liberties concerns about this nationalization, concerns that were heightened in early 2012 when U.S. District Court Judge Emmet G. Sullivan reported "systematic concealment of significant exculpatory evidence" in the U.S. Justice Department's prosecution of former Alaska Sen. Ted Stevens, who was convicted of corruption in October 2008. Six months later, Sullivan dismissed the charges against Stevens after first learning of prosecutorial misconduct. Sen. Lisa Murkowski of Alaska contended that Stevens would have been re-elected in November 2008 had this misconduct not led to his conviction.[15]

## Affordable Care Act at the U.S. Supreme Court

The blockbuster state-federal constitutional clash for 2012 is the court battle over the Affordable Care Act. At a U.S. Capitol press briefing in October 2009, then House Speaker Nancy Pelosi was asked, "Where specifically does the Constitution grant Congress the authority to enact an individual health insurance mandate?" She replied: "Are you serious? Are you serious?" Now this issue has come to a head.

The attorneys general and governors of 27 states, virtually all Republicans, petitioned the U.S. Supreme Court to overturn the Affordable Care Act's individual mandate to buy health insurance

and its mandatory expansion of state Medicaid programs. In early 2012, the Democratic governor of Washington, Chris Gregoire, 12 Democratic state attorneys general and 500 liberal state legislators filed amicus briefs defending the Medicaid expansion. Before reaching the high court, the Fourth, Sixth and District of Columbia federal appeals courts had upheld the Affordable Care Act, while the 11th Court of Appeals had struck it down.

The individual mandate requires uninsured citizens and legal residents to purchase federally approved health insurance by 2014 unless they are exempt (e.g., for religious reasons). Those who do not buy insurance will have to pay to the U.S. Treasury a penalty of up to 2.5 percent of their annual income. When Congress debated this mandate, the president said the penalty was "absolutely not" a tax, but when states challenged the mandate in court, the U.S. Department of Justice defended the mandate as a proper exercise of Congress's "power to lay and collect taxes."[16] The key constitutional points of contention are the suing states' arguments that the mandate exceeds Congress's commerce and tax powers and violates the 10th Amendment.

The Supreme Court also agreed unexpectedly to review the act's mandatory Medicaid expansion. The suing states argued that the penalty of losing all Medicaid funding for not complying with the expansion is coercive and an illegal commandeering of states' autonomy. States, they contend, have no real choice to leave Medicaid. Starting in 2014, individuals who earn up to 138 percent of the federal poverty line, effectively, will qualify for Medicaid. The federal government will pay all additional costs—other than administrative costs—until 2016. By 2020, states will pay 10 percent of the expanded program.

In 1936, the Supreme Court opined that unrestrained conditional grants "could become the instrument for the total subversion of the government power reserved to the individual states."[17] In 1987, the court seemed to suggest that, "in some circumstances, the financial inducement offered by Congress might be so coercive as to pass the point at which 'pressure turns into compulsion.'"[18]

If the Supreme Court voids the individual mandate or the entire Affordable Care Act, the suing states will have blocked a significant expansion of federal power and reinforced the court's occasional willingness since *United States v. Lopez* (1995) to limit Congress's interstate commerce reach. The justices, however, likely would frame such a rejection as an exception rather than a precedent readily applicable to other cases.

If the court strikes down the Medicaid expansion as unconstitutionally coercive, it will set an entirely new precedent. Again, though, the Supreme Court likely would cast such a ruling as an exception because Medicaid is such a gargantuan federal aid program. If the Affordable Care Act falls, health reform could shift to the states.

## Health Reform in the States

The states have received federal funds to set up the exchanges and implement other facets of the law. As of January 2012, 14 states had made substantial progress toward establishing health insurance exchanges as set forth in the Affordable Care Act, 21 had made moderate progress, and another 15 had made little progress.[19] Florida and Louisiana have refused to implement much of the law, and many states are holding back because of the litigation.

The 14 states that have elected to operate their own exchange—a website allowing people to compare and purchase health insurance policies—will need to meet a Jan. 1, 2013, deadline to receive more federal funds. States also need to establish health information exchanges containing electronic health records accessible to health care providers so as to minimize treatment errors and duplications. Exchanges are supposed to open in January 2014.

In a November 2011 letter to U.S. Department of Health and Human Services Secretary Kathleen Sebelius, the National Governors Association expressed concern about curtailments of state autonomy. "Under the proposed federal-state partnership models, states would be required to cede many operations that have been traditionally handled at the state level, such as Medicaid eligibility, regardless of whether they implement a state-based exchange, implement a state-federal partnership model or turn over responsibility for the exchange entirely to the federal government."

In a surprise move toward flexibility, HHS in December 2011 authorized states to define the "essential health benefits" insurance packages to be offered citizens by 2014; however, the packages must be comparable to benchmark private plans.[20] The Affordable Care Act requires a standard set of covered benefits involving 10 general areas, but states will have some flexibility.

A few states, such as Oregon and Vermont, want waivers to implement programs that go beyond the health care reform law. The act already includes State Innovation Waivers, but those waivers do not become available until 2017, after states will have set up programs. Vermont wants to establish a single-payer plan. Some Republican governors want a block grant.

## State Budget Stress and Tax Quests

Although tax collections have improved for state and local governments, most are still experiencing the depressing effects of the recession. About 280,000 state and local employee jobs were eliminated in 2011. As of January 2012, states owed the federal government some $38.5 billion for unemployment benefit loans.

In November 2011, the National Governors Association and National Association of State Budget Officers predicted dire fiscal straits for states for the foreseeable future. Additionally, the U.S. Government Accountability Office paints a bleak picture of the long-term fiscal health of the federal, state and local governments.[21] The principal drivers of fiscal stress are rising debt-service and entitlement spending, especially for health care.

President Obama's $3.8 trillion 2013 fiscal year budget, up from $3 trillion in 2008, maintains entitlement spending, proposes to increase taxes on high-income people by $1.5 trillion and spends more on popular programs, such as infrastructure. The president's 2013 budget calls for a 3.5 percent increase in education spending, for example, but reductions of 2.7 percent in agriculture, 7.6 percent in housing and urban development, 8.4 percent in health and human services, and 9.1 percent in labor—all areas important to state and local governments. The president projects a $1.33 trillion federal budget deficit for FY 2012.

States and localities are concerned about Obama's proposals to reduce the tax exemption for municipal bond interest and to limit a provider-fee technique states use to reduce their share of Medicaid costs. Many state officials also express concern about maintenance-of-effort rules under the Affordable Care Act and the absence of triggers for federal aid if the economy plunges again.

States, therefore, are also scrambling to find new revenue sources. For example, since the U.S. Department of Justice reversed its position in 2011 that the Federal Wire Act of 1961 banned Internet gambling, many states are moving to allow intrastate Internet gambling. It is not clear whether states can legalize interstate Internet gambling.

To the amazement of many observers, bipartisan movement in Congress could authorize state taxation of Internet sales. Amazon, Best Buy, Home

Depot, JCPenney, Target, Wal-Mart, and some other large retailers now support state Internet sales taxes. Although eBay and some other Internet retailers oppose this movement, big brick-and-click retailers—such as Wal-Mart—have aligned with brick-and-mortar retailers on Main streets to enlist support from some otherwise tax-shy Republicans. The National Conference of State Legislatures estimates that states will lose $23.3 billion from not collecting sales taxes from online and catalog purchases in 2012. Online retailers say this estimate is too high.

Meanwhile, a number of states have passed nexus laws requiring out-of-state sellers to collect and remit the state's sales tax when they advertise through affiliates located in the state. This policy, however, presents a dilemma for states because the big retailers usually then cut off these affiliates, harming many in-state small businesses and families that sell online.

More states also are becoming aggressive about collecting their use tax from residents for online purchases. Pennsylvania, for example, added a use tax line to its income tax form and included a table showing presumed use tax amounts due for filers in various income categories.

## Federal Aid Diversions and Dilemmas

In June 2011, the U.S. Conference of Mayors urged an end to the wars in Afghanistan and Iraq so the peace dividend can be spent on urban programs.[22] The Iraq war has ended, and the Afghan war is expected to end soon, but no peace dividend will flow to cities. Money saved from the wars will be used to soften some federal budget cuts, counteract some tax cuts, and, above all, pay for increased social welfare and debt service spending.

For example, the Community Development Block Grant was cut by nearly 12 percent for 2012.[23] Some localities lost even more than that due to data from Census's American Community Survey being used for the first time in the allocation formula. President Obama's 2013 budget proposal preserves almost $3 billion for Community Development Block Grants and $1 billion for HOME, which was cut by 38 percent in 2011, but these are at the same levels as in 2012. Community Oriented Policing Services was cut by 60 percent to $199 million for FY 2012. Other state and local law enforcement and first responder grants also were cut. The Partnership for Sustainable Communities and Choice Neighborhoods programs were slashed to $100 million each for 2012. Workforce training was cut by nearly $1

billion. Grants for Public Health Emergency Preparedness have been reduced by about $72 million since 2010. The federal highway program was cut by $900 million for 2012.

One major feature of coercive federalism has been a huge shift in federal aid from places to persons since 1978.[24] That year was an historic high point in federal aid to state and local governments; only 31.8 percent of aid was dedicated to Medicaid and other social welfare payments to individuals. In 1988, that figure increased to 54.7 percent of aid, and by 2008, it was 65.2 percent of aid. In 2017, three-quarters of all aid will go to Medicaid and other social welfare for individuals (see Figure 1). Thus, even though total aid is projected to increase by 18.6 percent from 2011 to 2017, aid for persons is expected to increase by 39.9 percent, while aid to places will drop by 19.2 percent.

This change in the composition of federal aid is the main reason local governments have seen a precipitous decline in federal aid since the late 1970s. Local governments have principal responsibility for most nonwelfare functions such as infrastructure, education, libraries, criminal justice, housing, parks and recreation, economic development and similar public services. The portions of state budgets devoted to nonwelfare services have likewise experienced sharp declines in federal aid. In turn, most states have reduced aid to their local governments.

Additionally, the federal government plans to shut some military bases and close various regional facilities. The U.S. Department of Agriculture plans to close 249 offices in 2012, though members of Congress likely will resist some of those closures. Congress has approved closing 12 Agricultural Research Service laboratories. The federal government also plans to close about 1,200 of its 3,100 data centers by the end of 2015. Many communities will lose post offices over the next several years.

The current ban on congressional earmarks also will reduce federal funding for local projects. Adding to federal aid woes is Congress' failure to pass federal budgets and to reauthorize major multi-year programs such as education and surface transportation. These failures are rooted in partisan polarization. Even surface transportation, an historically bipartisan favorite, has been rent by party conflict.

The parties also differ on how to deliver federal aid. Republicans propose issuing block grants for Medicaid and other entitlement programs and returning some programs, such as surface transpor-

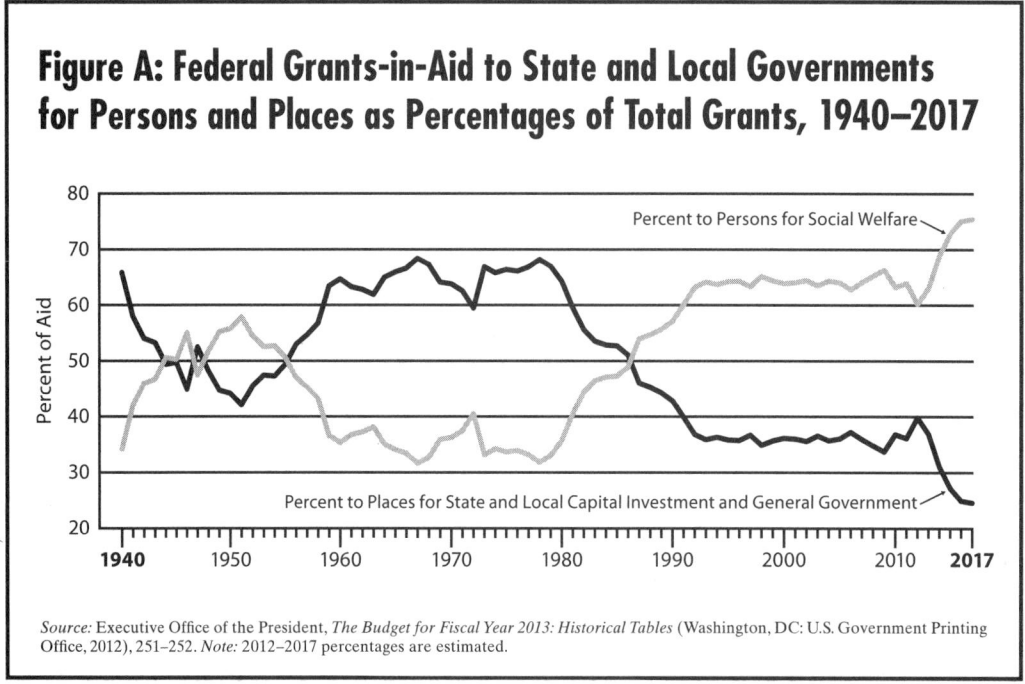

# Figure A: Federal Grants-in-Aid to State and Local Governments for Persons and Places as Percentages of Total Grants, 1940–2017

Source: Executive Office of the President, *The Budget for Fiscal Year 2013: Historical Tables* (Washington, DC: U.S. Government Printing Office, 2012), 251–252. *Note:* 2012–2017 percentages are estimated.

tation, to the states entirely. Such policies would give states more flexibility and perhaps foster innovation and efficiencies. Many Democrats contend that such policies would degrade program quality by fostering interstate races to the bottom and greater differences in recipient treatments across states.

The Office of Management and Budget established a Council on Financial Assistance Reform in the wake of a July 2011 GAO report highlighting problems in the grants-in-aid system,[25] especially weak federal oversight and recipient accountability that resulted in, among other things, about $125.4 billion in improper payments in 2010. In November 2011, the Big Seven state and local associations and other state groups complained that the council consisted only of federal officials and requested representation.

Policy conditions attached to federal aid are another feature of coercive federalism. States sometimes resist these rules. About 34 states, for example, have not complied with the Adam Walsh Child Protection and Safety Act of 2006, which requires states to upload sex offender data into a three-tiered national public registry. Consequently, these states could lose 10 percent of their Byrne Justice Assistance Grant funds in 2012. This block grant totaled about $250 million in 2011. Many state officials regard the requirement as an unfunded

mandate entailing costs to install technology to upload digital DNA data and fingerprints and palm prints and to pay for additional processing time by police personnel.

For some states, compliance costs will exceed federal grant funds. Texas estimated that compliance would cost $38.8 million, while the federal funding loss would be $1.4 million.[26] New York reached a similar conclusion. As of July 2011, only eight states were deemed to be in substantial compliance with the law.

Nearly one-third of the states could lose 5 percent of their federal highway funds for not meeting a probable January 2014 deadline for their licensing bureaus to upload into a national database medical certifications that their licensed interstate truck drivers are healthy enough to drive.

## Medicaid's Upward Budget March

Medicaid is, by far, the largest federal aid program. It benefits more than 63 million people. State spending on Medicaid is expected to increase by 28.7 percent in 2012. The additional federal money states received for Medicaid under the American Recovery and Reinvestment Act of 2009 ended in June 2011, although states remained bound by the act's maintenance-of-effort requirement not to reduce Medicaid eligibility.

In 2011, Medicaid was the single largest category of state spending, accounting for 23.6 percent of state spending, compared to 21.9 percent in 2009. By contrast, state spending on elementary and secondary education dropped from 21.5 percent in 2009 to 20.1 percent in 2011. Recently, both red and blue states united to combat a proposed $41 billion federal cutback in Medicaid funding.

A growing concern for state officials is that the Affordable Care Act will add about 17 million people to Medicaid by 2014. Although the federal government will provide 100 percent of the funding for newly eligible individuals from 2014 to 2016, phasing down to 90 percent by 2020, the expansion gradually will increase costs for states. State and local Medicaid spending is expected to increase from $130 billion in 2009 to $357 billion in 2020. Two Republican senators introduced a bill in September 2011 to allow states to opt out of the Medicaid expansion required by health care reform, but the bill is unlikely to succeed.

Many Republicans support converting Medicaid to a block grant.[27] Democrats oppose that, although Rhode Island has experimented with a block grant since January 2009. After a *Wall Street Journal* editorialist characterized Washington's Democratic Gov. Christine Gregoire as having signed a bill authorizing the state to apply for a Medicaid block grant waiver,[28] Gregoire penned a heated reply saying that she opposes "any congressional effort to impose Medicaid as a block grant."[29]

States, therefore, will continue to seek cost containments by trying to limit eligibility, which will be prohibited by the Affordable Care Act, cut benefits, and reduce provider payments. In light of program constraints, pressure is likely to build from governors for federal waivers to experiment with structural changes in Medicaid. In March 2012, the Bipartisan Policy Center's Governors' Council proposed to streamline and speed up the waiver process and allow successful waivers to become permanent or semi-permanent rather than requiring states to reapply regularly.

## Whither Education?

Another titanic partisan battle is being fought over reauthorization of the 1965 Elementary and Secondary Education Act, now called the No Child Left Behind Act of 2001. The education act's renewal is five years overdue. The Elementary and Secondary Education Act covered a mere five titles in 32 pages; the No Child Left Behind Act has 600 pages, 10 titles and more than 50 programs. States want a new law, but they have been seeking waivers under No Child Left Behind. While Democrats and Republicans want to jettison the act's overly prescriptive features, they agree on little else.

In September 2011, President Obama warned that if Congress failed to reauthorize the Elementary and Secondary Education Act, he would exercise executive authority to waive portions of No Child Left Behind for states. If states do not fulfill waiver promises, the waivers will be taken away. In February 2012, Obama issued waivers freeing 10 states from some of the act's toughest requirements, especially the 2014 deadline for 100 percent student proficiency in math and reading. Another 26 states applied for waivers in early 2012.

Some members of Congress as well as constitutional scholars have challenged conditional waivers. It is not clear that the executive branch can unilaterally depart so far from the law and also make waivers contingent upon states making policy changes that fall outside current law. Waivers allow the president to pressure states to pursue his preferred education agenda regardless of Congress's intent behind No Child Left Behind and proposed reforms. Waivers also will create separate accountability systems for waiver states and No Child Left Behind states. More generally, the proliferation of waivers in a number of policy fields over the past two decades raises questions about the politicization of law and diminution of the rule of law.[30]

In further federal effort to improve education, 11 states and Washington, D.C., received $4 billion in aid in 2011 from the Race to the Top competition, which was funded at $700 million for 2012. This is a competitive program that awards federal funds to states willing to implement federally approved reforms. Most of these states have had major problems implementing their intended innovations, especially new teacher evaluation systems.[31]

Obama has proposed a competitive $5 billion grant—Recognizing Education Success, Professional Excellence and Collaborative Teaching—for states to reform teaching by awarding tenure only with proof of good teaching, raising salaries in response to student achievement and improving teacher education. However, NCSL and the National Association of State Boards of Education expressed concern that states needing the most help might be among the least able to compete for grants effectively.

The president also has focused on higher education, proposing in early 2012 to reduce Supplemental Education Opportunity grants, Perkins loans and Work Study funds for colleges and universities that increase tuition too heftily or fail to provide good value for tuition dollars. Such extensions of federal accountability rules into higher education are likely to continue, although the ability of state universities to restrain tuition increases is substantially defeated by state budget constraints arising from Medicaid costs, which ordinarily win out over higher education in appropriations battles.

## Whither Transportation?

Reauthorization of surface transportation is another partisan bone of contention; hence, Congress enacted only a short-term extension in March 2012. A key structural problem is the decline in motor fuel tax revenue, which has necessitated appropriations of general revenues for highways and mass transit. Congress spent $35 billion of general revenues bailing out the Highway Trust Fund in 2008, 2009 and 2010. This stalemate has led to a revival of calls for Congress to turn back transportation to the states.[32]

The governors of Florida, Ohio and Wisconsin rejected federal funds for high-speed rail, arguing that such rail service is not cost effective. In turn, Congress rejected Obama's funding proposals for high-speed rail and a national infrastructure bank.

## Environmental Protection Regulation

The Obama administration has given environmental protection high priority. This policy area produced more bipartisan action and state-federal alliances than many other areas, although many state-federal conflicts still exist.

After six years of controversial development, the U.S. Environmental Protection Agency issued its Cross-State Air Pollution Rule in 2011, which aims to slash emissions from power plants in 27 states in the eastern half of the country. Efforts to block the regulation failed in Congress. The EPA, however, also proposed to give 10 of the 27 states more enforcement flexibility, including permission to emit more pollution than before the new rule was issued. Texas sued the EPA over the rule and a federal appeals court stayed implementation of the rule in December 2011.

In November 2011, New York led 10 states in filing suit in federal court to compel the EPA to issue new, stricter air quality standards for fine particles. The states contend that the EPA has not complied with a 2009 court order.

The Supreme Court held 8-0 in June 2011, however, that eight states, New York City and three private land trusts could not proceed under the federal common law of nuisance to sue utility companies to cap global warming emissions because the Clean Air Act authorizes the EPA to manage greenhouse gas emissions. There is no basis for parallel judicial action so long as the EPA enforces emissions limits.[33]

## Culture Wars

The so-called culture wars are an integral part of today's polarization. One area of cultural controversy has been medical marijuana, which is legal in 18 states. After saying at the outset of his administration that he would not pursue medical marijuana prosecutions, the Obama administration has become aggressive.[34] The Internal Revenue Service has sought to extract extra taxes from dispensaries, the Treasury Department has pressured banks to close the accounts of marijuana businesses that are legal under state law, and the Bureau of Alcohol, Tobacco, Firearms and Explosives has ruled that patients using medical marijuana cannot buy firearms. U.S. Attorneys have threatened to target media outlets that run ads for dispensaries and to seize properties rented to dispensaries and possibly jail the landlords.[35] In June 2011, a federal judge ordered Michigan to turn over to federal officials the medical marijuana records of six people.

In November 2011, the governors of Rhode Island and Washington petitioned the U.S. Drug Enforcement Administration to reclassify marijuana as suitable for medical use. Meanwhile, Arizona, Florida, Indiana and Missouri have passed laws requiring drug tests for people applying for benefits such as food stamps, job training, public housing, unemployment and welfare. Thirty-six other states are considering such a policy.

The U.S. Court of Appeals for the Ninth Circuit invalidated California's 2008 voter-approved ban on gay marriage, perhaps setting the stage for a Supreme Court review of the issue. Same-sex marriage has been legalized in eight states and Washington, D.C., while 30 states have a constitutional ban on gay marriage. North Carolinians will vote on a constitutional ban in May 2012.

A federal appeals court held that Oklahoma's "Save Our State" constitutional amendment, approved by 70 percent of voters in November 2010, "is likely unconstitutional." The amendment prohibits Oklahoma courts from enforcing Sharia. Arizona, Louisiana and Tennessee have passed similar statutes. Another 21 states are considering such laws. Opponents of the "American laws for

American courts" movement charge that such laws "are unnecessary, unconstitutional and motivated by anti-Muslim bigotry."[36]

## Federal Pre-emption and Court Orders

Federal pre-emptions of state law and federal court orders are other leading characteristics of coercive federalism. In January 2012, for example, the Supreme Court held that the Federal Meat Inspection Act pre-empts a California animal rights slaughterhouse law that prohibited the slaughter or sale of animals unable to walk.[37] The court also ruled, by a 5-4 vote, that the Federal Arbitration Act of 1925 pre-empts state laws that bar contracts from forbidding class action lawsuits, thus making it harder for consumers to file such suits.[38]

A potentially forthcoming pre-emption is the National Right-to-Carry Reciprocity Act, which passed the House in 2011 and was introduced in the Senate in 2012 by two Democrats. The bill would allow anyone with a state-issued concealed firearms permit to carry a concealed handgun in any other state that issues such permits or does not forbid the carrying of concealed firearms for lawful purposes. Forty-eight states issue concealed-carry permits; Vermont requires no permit. More than half the states do not recognize other states' permits, or do so only under certain conditions. Only about 12 states unconditionally recognize other states' permits.

The bill's opponents argue that it would override states' rights and create "a locked-and-loaded race to the bottom in which states with strict requirements, like New York, would be forced to allow people with permits from states with lax screening to carry hidden loaded guns."[39] For instance, about 38 states deny carry permits to people convicted of violent or sex crimes; 36 require individuals to be at least 21 years old to obtain a permit; and 35 states require gun-safety training.

Federal court orders continue to be significant factors in state and local governance. For example, by a 5-4 vote, the Supreme Court upheld, on Eighth Amendment grounds, a lower federal court order requiring California to relieve overcrowding in its prisons by releasing about 40,000 inmates.[40]

## Supreme Court Litigation

For a presidential election year, the Supreme Court has granted *certiorari* to some politically charged cases, especially the Affordable Care Act and Arizona's immigration law,[41] which have substantial federalism implications. Here are some of the issues pending before the Supreme Court:

*Immigration.* Although illegal immigration has declined since 2008, states have pursued immigration legislation. According to NCSL, all 50 state legislatures and Puerto Rico considered 1,607 immigration bills in 2011. Forty-two states and Puerto Rico enacted 197 laws and 109 resolutions. The Obama administration has challenged immigration laws recently enacted by Alabama, Arizona, South Carolina and Utah.

The contested Arizona law contains four parts rejected by the Obama administration as conflicting with federal laws. These include:

- State law enforcement officials must determine the immigration status of anyone they stop or arrest when they believe the individual might be an illegal immigrant.

- The immigration status of arrestees must be determined before their release.

- Police may arrest individuals without a warrant if they have probable cause to believe they have committed acts subject to deportation under federal law.

- It is a crime under state law for an immigrant to fail to register under a federal law and for an illegal immigrant to work or seek work.

The U.S. Court of Appeals for the Ninth Circuit blocked all four provisions.

A major sore point is whether the federal government has exclusive authority to enforce immigration law. In enacting its law, Arizona relied, in part, on an April 2, 2002, memorandum to the U.S. attorney general from the U.S. Justice Department's Office of Legal Counsel, which opined that states "have inherent power, subject to federal pre-emption, to make arrests for violation of federal law" and that federal law does not prohibit state police from arresting "aliens on the basis of civil deportability."

*Voting Rights Act.* In early 2012, the Supreme Court rejected redistricting maps drawn by a federal district court in Texas that favored Democratic candidates after Democrats and minority groups had challenged the maps. The redistricting plan had not yet received preclearance from the federal court in Washington, D.C., under the federal Voting Rights Act. The justices opined that redistricting is primarily the responsibility of elected state officials and the court had not given due deference to the maps drawn by the Republican-controlled legislature.[42] The justices remanded the case, thereby prolonging uncertainty about the future of the Voting Rights Act. The Texas plan had preserved 10 majority-minority districts and added a Latino "opportunity district." The U.S. Department of Justice wants more minority districts.

The Voting Rights Act, especially Section 5— which covers only nine states, mostly in the South, and parts of seven other states, and requires federal preclearance of voting rule changes by those states —could return to the court through cases involving Alabama, Arizona or Texas because decennial redistricting has heightened Voting Rights Act matters. A key point of challenge is that Section 5 was intended to be temporary. For example, Arizona contends that discrimination against Spanish-speaking voters ended long ago and that the formula for determining which states are covered by Section 5 relies on conditions deemed prevalent in 1972. Arizona came under Section 5 when the Voting Rights Act was amended in 1975 to include any state having language minorities accounting for 5 percent or more of the population if it did not have bilingual ballots in 1972 and minority voter turnout fell below certain levels. Arizona came under the act even though it already had bilingual ballots and had elected the country's second Hispanic governor in 1974. Objecting states, therefore, argue that Congress failed in 2006 to justify the extension of Section 5 for another 25 years.

In 2009, the Supreme Court hinted that Section 5 may have outlived its rationale by opining that the act "imposes current burdens that must be justified by current needs."[43]

Challengers also contest the disparate treatment of states whereby Wisconsin, but not South Carolina, can enact a voter ID law without federal interference. This might violate the constitutional principle of equal state sovereignty. In October 2011, however, the federal government ordered Milwaukee, Wis., to provide ballots and other voter information in Spanish. This was the first time a Wisconsin jurisdiction had come under the Voting Rights Act. The act's language requirement now applies to about 248 jurisdictions in 30 states.

*Court Rulings.* In a potentially important federalism case, the Supreme Court unanimously ruled that a citizen had standing to argue that a federal statute enforcing the Chemical Weapons Convention violated state sovereignty because the convention had no link to interstate commerce and encroached upon Tenth Amendment police powers reserved to the states. Justice Anthony Kennedy contended that "an action that exceeds the National Government's enumerated powers undermines the sovereign interests of states" and

that a litigant in a justiciable case can argue that her injury stems from disregard of our federal structure of government. "Fidelity to principles of federalism," he added, "is not for the states alone to vindicate."[44]

By contrast, the court held 6-2 that *Ex Parte Young* (1908) prohibits Virginia from invoking its sovereign immunity to prevent a state agency established to comply with a federal law, which funds states to care for people with disabilities, from suing for a federal court order to require state officials to comply with the federal law.[45]

Otherwise, the court issued an unusual number of First Amendment rulings affecting states during its 2010–11 term. In a very controversial 5-4 decision, the court struck down an Arizona matching funds law that provided additional campaign money to a publicly funded candidate when spending by a privately financed candidate and independent groups exceeded the funding allotted to the publicly financed candidate.[46]

The court struck down Vermont's Prescription Confidentiality Law, which required that files containing a physician's prescription records not be sold or used for marketing purposes without the doctor's consent.[47] The Supreme Court also held that federal regulations of prescription drug labels pre-empt state law's failure-to-warn claims against generic drug manufacturers. Hence, individuals harmed by mislabeled generics cannot recover damages under state law.[48]

The court struck down a 2005 California law that barred the sale of certain violent video games to children without parental supervision.[49] The court unanimously held, however, that the First Amendment does not protect an elected official from a state ethics charge for voting for a development project for which a friend and campaign manager was a paid consultant.[50]

The court also upheld the Legal Arizona Workers Act of 2007, which requires employers to check the immigration status of new employees through the federal E-Verify program. The state law, opined the five-justice majority, "falls well within the confines of the authority Congress chose to leave to the states."[51]

## U.S. Constitutional Change Proposals

In developments reminiscent of the 1995 States' Federalism Summit cosponsored by The Council of State Governments, proposals for constitutional change and even a constitutional convention[52] have garnered attention.

Some Tea Party supporters advocate a "Repeal Amendment" stating: "Any provision of law or regulation of the United States may be repealed by the several states, and such repeal shall be effective when the legislatures of two-thirds of the several states approve resolutions for this purpose that particularly describe the same provision or provisions of law or regulation to be repealed."

Texas Gov. Rick Perry and some other conservatives want to repeal the 17th Amendment. Another proposal would allow two-thirds of the states to propose an amendment that would be ratified by conventions or referendums in states representing three-quarters of the Electoral College.[53]

Some Democrats support an amendment to overturn the Supreme Court's 2010 *Citizens United* ruling,[54] which held that the First Amendment prohibits the government from restricting corporations or unions from spending their general treasury funds on independent political communications supporting or opposing candidates in elections.

Ironically, both the left and the right assailed the States' Federalism Summit for plotting to trigger a constitutional convention, even though the summit's leaders expressly disavowed that intention.[55]

The probability of constitutional change remains as small, but the flurry of amendment proposals illustrates the continuing salience of the issues addressed by the summit and the extent to which polarization has pushed activists on the left and the right toward constitutional change.

## Conclusion

Although the Supreme Court might roll back federal power in 2012, the rollback is likely to be modest and the political process, no matter who wins the presidential and congressional elections, will not likely alter the current balance of state-federal power significantly. Partisan polarization will continue to infect state-federal relations, although gridlock in Washington, D.C., could unlock if one party wins the presidency and sizable majorities in Congress.

## Notes

[1] For background, see John Kincaid, "The Rise of Social Welfare and Onward March of Coercive Federalism," *Networked Governance: The Future of Intergovernmental Management*, eds., Jack W. Meek and Kurt Thurmaier. Los Angeles: Sage/CQ Press, 2011, pp. 8–38; John Kincaid, "State-Federal Relations: Civil War Redux?" *The Book of the States* (Lexington, KY: The Council of State Governments, 2011), 21–28; John Kincaid, "State-Federal Relations: Cooperative Coercion," *The Book of the States*. Lexington, KY: The Council of State Governments, 2010, pp. 21–30; and chapters in previous volumes of *The Book of the States*.

[2] *Florida v. United States Department of Health and Human Services* (2012).

[3] John Aloysius Farrell, "Divided We Stand," *National Journal* 44 (February 25, 2012): 10.

[4] Interview, "State and local governments ought to be freed from constraints," *State Legislatures* 38 (February 2012): 31.

[5] Available at *http://www.azgovernor.gov/Newsroom/Gov_PR.asp*.

[6] Quoted in Robert Gehrke, "Utah governor defiant of feds in election-year State of The State," *The Salt Lake Tribune*, January 26, 2012, 1.

[7] Anon, "Rick Perry's Air War," *National Journal* (September 10, 2011): 45–46.

[8] New York: Little, Brown, 2010.

[9] With James Edwin Kee (Salt Lake City: Peregrine Smith Books, 1986).

[10] *Crawford v. Marion County Election Board*, 553 U.S. 181 (2008).

[11] A.G. Sulzberger, "Courts Put The Brakes On Agenda Of G.O.P.," *New York Times*, September 6, 2011, A14.

[12] Quoted in Editorial, "Social Engineering in Suburbia," *Wall Street Journal*, September 19, 2011, A16.

[13] St. Paul website: *http://www.stpaul.gov/index.aspx?NID=4874*.

[14] Gary Fields and John R. Emshwiller, "Criminal Case Glut Impedes Civil Suits," *Wall Street Journal*, November 10, 2011, A21.

[15] Charlie Savage and Michael S. Schmidt, "An Alaska Senator Calls for Firing of Prosecutors in Botched Stevens Trial," *New York Times*, March 17, 2012, A11.

[16] J. Kenneth Blackwell and Kenneth A. Klukowski, "Why the ObamaCare Tax Penalty Is Unconstitutional," *Wall Street Journal*, July 22, 2010, A19.

[17] *United States v. Butler*, 297 U.S. 1 (1936).

[18] *South Dakota v. Dole*, 483 U.S. 203 (1987) and *Steward Machine Company v. Davis*, 301 U.S. 548 (1937).

[19] Frederic Blavin, Matthew Buettgens, and Jeremy Roth, *State Progress Toward Health Reform Implementation* (Washington, DC: Urban Institute, January 2012), 1–2.

[20] Robert Pear, "Health Care Law Will Let States Tailor Benefits," *New York Times*, December 17, 2011, A1, A4, and Louise Radnofsky, "States Told They Can Decide on Coverage by Health Plans," *Wall Street Journal*, December 17–18, 2011, A4.

[21] U.S. Government Accountability Office, *The Federal Government's Long-Term Fiscal Outlook: Fall 2011 Update*. (Washington, DC: GAO-12-28SP, Fall 2011).

[22] Michael Cooper, "Mayors See End to Wars as Fix for Struggling Cities," *New York Times*, June 18, 2011, A10.

[23] Michael Cooper, "Tough Choices for Cities as Federal Aid Shrinks," *New York Times*, December 22, 2011, A16.

[24] John Kincaid, "The State of U.S. Federalism, 2000–2001: Continuity in Crisis," *Publius: The Journal of Federalism* 31 (Summer 2001): 1–69.

[25] U.S. Government Accountability Office, *Federal Grants: Improvements Needed in Oversight and Accountability Processes* (Washington, DC: GAO-11-773T, June 23, 2011).

[26] Criminal Justice Committee, Senate of the State of Texas, Interim Report (Austin: Senate, December 15, 2010), 14.

[27] Joanne Kenen, "Fifty Ways to Run Your Program," *CQ Weekly* 69 (June 27, 2011): 1362–1364.

[28] Nansen Malin, "Liberal Washington State Tries to Kiss Medicaid Goodbye," *Wall Street Journal*, June 4–5, 2012, A13.

[29] "We Say No to Medicaid Block Grants," *Wall Street Journal*, June 11, 2011, A12.

[30] Kincaid, "The State of U.S. Federalism, 2000–2001," 21–22.

[31] Lauren Smith, "'Race' Hits Obstacles," *CQ Weekly* 70 (January 20, 2012): 84.

[32] Ronald D. Utt, "'Turn Back' Transportation to the States," *Backgrounder* No. 2651 (Washington, DC: Heritage Foundation, February 6, 2012). See also U.S. Advisory Commission on Intergovernmental Relations, *Devolving Selected Federal-Aid Highway Programs and Revenue Bases: A Critical Appraisal* (Washington, DC: ACIR, September 1987).

[33] *American Electric Power Co., Inc. v. Connecticut*, 564 U.S. ___ (2011).

[34] William Yardley, "New Federal Crackdown Confounds States That Allow Medical Marijuana," *New York Times*, May 8, 2011, 13.

[35] Ethan Nadelmann, "Reefer Madness," *New York Times*, November 7, 2011, A25.

[36] Ashby Jones and Joe Palazzolo, "States Target Foreign Law," *Wall Street Journal*, February 7, 2012, A3.

[37] *National Meat Association v. Harris*, 565 U.S. ___ (2012).

[38] *AT&T Mobility LLC v. Concepcion*, 131 S. Ct. 1740 (2011).

[39] Editorial, "Packing Heat Everywhere," *New York Times*, September 9, 2011, A26.

[40] *Brown v. Plata*, 131 S. Ct. 1910 (2011).

[41] *Arizona v. United States*, No. 11-182 (2012).

[42] *Perry v. Perez*, 565 U. S. ___ (2012).

[43] *Northwest Austin Municipal Utility District No. 1 v. Holder*, 557 U.S. 193 (2009).

[44] *Bond v. United States*, 564 U.S. ___ (2011).

[45] *Virginia Office for Protection and Advocacy v. Stewart*, 563 U.S. ___ (2011).

[46] *Arizona Free Enterprise Club's Freedom Club PAC v. Bennett*, 564 U.S. ___ (2011).

[47] *Sorrell v. IMS Health Inc.*, 564 U.S. ___ (2011).

[48] *PLIVA v. Mensing*, 131 S. Ct. 2567 (2011).

[49] *Brown v. Entertainment Merchants Association*, 564 U.S. ___ (2011).

[50] *Nevada Commission on Ethics v. Carrigan*, 564 U.S. ___ (2011).

[51] *Chamber of Commerce of the United States v. Whiting* 131 S. Ct. 1968 (2011).

[52] Christopher Shea, "Unconventional Meeting of Minds: Scholars and Tea Partyers gather to consider changing the Constitution," *The Chronicle of Higher Education*, September 23, 2011, A1, A4, A6.

[53] Michael B. Rappaport, "Renewing Federalism by Reforming Article V Defects in the Constitutional Amendment Process and a Reform Proposal," *Policy Analysis* No. 691 (Washington, DC: Cato Institute, January 18, 2012).

[54] *Citizens United v. Federal Election Commission*, 558 U.S. ___ (2010).

[55] The Council of State Governments, *Restoring Balance to the American Federal System* (Lexington, KY: CSG, 1996), 75.

## About the Author

**John Kincaid** is the Robert B. and Helen S. Meyner Professor of Government and Public Service and Director of the Meyner Center for the Study of State and Local Government, Lafayette College, Easton, Pennsylvania. He is former editor of *Publius: The Journal of Federalism*; former executive director of the U.S. Advisory Commission on Intergovernmental Relations; co-editor of *Constitutional Origins, Structure, and Change in Federal Countries* (2005) and editor of *Federalism* (4 vols., 2011).

# Congressional Pre-emption Trends

### By Joseph F. Zimmerman

*Congress slowly exercised its power of pre-emption to remove regulatory powers from state and local governments commencing from 1790 through the mid-1960s, when the pace accelerated. A significant number of acts contain mandates requiring state and/or local governments to initiate a compliance action(s) or impose prohibitions. No pre-emption mandate relief act has been enacted since 1996. This article focuses on the pre-emption acts signed by President Barack Obama since January 2009.*

The U.S. Constitution delegates to Congress a number of broad pre-emption powers which remove regulatory powers from states completely, partially or contingently without guidelines or restrictions other than the presidential veto or court invalidation of pre-emption acts. The number of such statutes totaled 678 on Nov.1, 2011, and produced a silent revolution that restructured in a fundamental manner national and state-local governmental regulation.

## Pre-emption Types

There are 10 types of pre-emption: (1) complete pre-emption removes all regulatory power in a field from states (*Copyright Act of 1790*); (2) partial pre-emption removes some, but not all, regulatory powers in a field from states and may assume the form of a savings clause (*Commodity Futures Act of 2000*); (3) national minimum regulatory standards permit a state to continue to regulate in a given field provided the state standards meet or exceed the national standards and the state has qualified personnel and necessary equipment (*Air Quality Act of 1967*); (4) maximum standards place caps on the stringency of state regulations (*Gramm-Leach-Bliley Financial Modernization Act of 1999*); (5) procedural pre-emption specifies the appeals procedure (*Gramm-Leach-Bliley Financial Modernization Act of 1999*); (6) contingent pre-emption applies to a state or a local government only if a specified condition(s) exists (*Voting Rights Act of 1965*); (7) complete pre-emption may provide for a limited regulatory authority turn-back to states (*United States Grain Standards Act of 1968*); (8) complete pre-emption may authorize cooperative state enforcement (*Consumer Credit Reporting Reform Act of 1996*); (9) complete pre-emption may exempt from pre-emption a state whose legislature enacted a specified uniform state law (*Electronic Signatures in Global and National Commerce Act of 2000*); and (10) complete pre-emption may allow states to enact only a regulatory standard identical to the federal standard (*Health and Safety Act of 1968*).

## The Obama Pre-emption Record

President Obama has not held a state or a local government executive office, and his views on pre-emption were not known when he assumed the presidency. He signed 49 pre-emption acts between Jan. 20, 2009, and Nov. 1, 2011.

### Antiterrorism

The four antiterrorism acts removed little power from state and local governments as most had been removed by earlier antiterrorism acts and two acts simply extended earlier acts.

### Banking, Commerce, Energy and Finance

President Obama signed 11 bills relating to banking, commerce, energy and finance. The most important one is the complex 847-page *Dodd-Frank Wall Street Reform and Consumer Protection Act of 2010.* The *Credit Card Accountability Responsibility and Disclosure Act* was enacted in 2009 and was amended later in the year to extend its effective date to Jan. 31, 2013. The act provides greater protection for credit and prepaid gift cardholders; places limits on increases in interest rates, fees and finance charges; enhances consumer information disclosures; and provides special protection for young consumers. The other acts removed relatively little power from states.

### Environment, Health and Safety

President Obama signed 19 pre-emption bills pertaining to environment, health and safety, and a health bill that may or may not be pre-emptive depending upon a forthcoming U.S. Supreme Court decision. The 905-page *Patient Protection and Affordable Care Act of 2010* is the most controversial pre-emption act because of its requirement that everyone not covered by another person's insurance policy—with specified exceptions—must purchase health insurance or pay a penalty. The other acts removed small amounts of powers from subnational governments.

### Foreign Affairs

President Obama signed 10 foreign affairs pre-emption bills, including free trade agreements with Columbia, Panama and South Korea. Three acts extend the Burmese import restrictions and three acts extend the *Andean Trade Preference Act*. The *Securing the Protection of Our Enduring and Established Constitutional Heritage Act of 2010* seeks to protect freedom of speech and the press against individuals who obstruct the free expression of U.S. authors and publishers by filing lawsuits in foreign jurisdictions offering less protection to authors and publishers than they have in the United States.

### Intellectual Property

President Obama signed one intellectual property act. The 57-page *Leahy-Smith America Invents Act of 2011* is a major revision of patent law that includes provisions relating to the first inventor to file a patent application, derived patents, appeal to the patent and trial and appeal board, inter partes review, among others. The act also stipulates "no patent may issue on a claim directed to or encompassing a human organism."

### Political Privileges

The *Military and Overseas Voter Empowerment Act of 2009* seeks to facilitate voting in federal elections by military personnel and civilians residing in other nations. The *Military Spouses Residency Relief Act of 2009* applies to voting for federal offices, and provides that a spouse accompanying a member of the U.S. armed forces does not lose residency in a state regardless of whether the person intends to return to the state, and the spouse is deemed not to have become a resident of another state.

### Telecommunications

President Obama signed five telecommunications bills. The most important one is the *Twenty-First Century Communications and Video Accessibility Act of 2010* that seeks, among other goals, to ensure that hearing aids are compatible with telephones and relay services utilized by deaf-blind individuals. Shortly thereafter, the act was amended to make technical corrections. Two acts extended three existing acts, and the other two acts removed little state regulatory authority.

## Pre-emption Impact

The number of complete pre-emption acts and other acts containing a pre-emption provision(s) during any time period is not an accurate indicator of the amount and importance of discretionary regulatory authority removed from state and local governments. Ten bills signed by President Obama simply extend the sunset provisions of acts. An 11th act redefined a switchblade knife. A 12th act made technical corrections to a 2010 act. The *Formaldehyde Standards for Composite Wood Products Act of 2010* applies only to composite wood. Many of the other acts made relatively minor changes to existing laws. Republican control of the U.S. House of Representatives following the 2010 general elections will lead to the enactment of fewer pre-emption acts in 2011 and 2012 because of the differing views of the House and the Democrat-controlled Senate on important issues.

Two major 2010 pre-emption acts have, or will have, a major impact on the federal system.

### Dodd-Frank Wall Street Reform and Consumer Protection Act of 2010

The Dodd-Frank act affects nearly every aspect of financial markets, does not seek the reform of regulatory agencies and cannot be explained adequately in a short article.

The act amends a relatively large number of existing acts containing pre-emption provisions, generally strengthening them, and directs 11 federal financial departments and agencies to promulgate 385 new administrative regulations.

The act focuses primarily on financial services companies and neglects the "parallel (shadow) banking sector" consisting of "money market funds collecting uninsured short-term deposits and funding financial firms ..." The act establishes a Financial Stability Oversight Council, composed of federal regulators and chaired by the secretary of the Treasury. All 26 bank holding companies with consolidated assets equal to or exceeding $50 billion as of Jan. 1, 2010, that "received financial assistance under the Capital Purchase Program established under the Troubled Asset Relief Program" are subject to more stringent regulations than smaller bank holding companies. The council determines the financial market utilities that are systemically important.

The act seeks to "mitigate systemic risk in the financial system and promote financial stability" by granting the Board of Governors "an enhanced role in the supervision of risk management standards for systemically important payment, clearing, and settlement activities by financial institutions." The terms "systemically important" and "systemic importance" are defined as "a situation where the failure of or a disruption to the functioning of a financial market utility or the conduct of a payment, clearing, or settlement activity could create, or increase, the risk of significant liquidity or credit problems spreading among financial institutions or markets and thereby threaten the stability of the financial system of the United States." Section 1044 clarifies state law applicable to national banks and subsidiaries by stipulating, "State consumer financial laws are pre-empted, only if (A) application of a State consumer financial law would have a discriminatory effect on national banks, in comparison with the effect of the law on a bank chartered by that State; (B) ...the State consumer financial law prevents or significantly interferes with the exercise by the national bank of its powers; (C) the State consumer financial law is pre-empted by a provision of Federal law other than this title."

The act created a federal Bureau of Consumer Financial Protection, an independent agency within the Federal Reserve System, with authority to regulate "the offering and provision of consumer financial products or services under the Federal consumer financial laws." It also mandated the agency director to establish an Office of Fair Lending and Equal Opportunity to oversee and to enforce federal laws "to ensure the fair, equitable, and nondiscriminatory access to credit for both individuals and communities. ..." The act delegated broad rulemaking authority subject to exceptions and exceptions to exceptions to the director.

Subtitle D, preservation of state law, stipulates Title X of the act with the exceptions of five sections "may not be construed as annulling, altering or affecting, or exempting any persons subject to the provisions of this title from complying with the statutes, regulations, orders or interpretations in effect in any State, except to the extent that any such provision of law is inconsistent with the provisions of this title, and then only to the extent of the inconsistency." In addition, the act stipulates a state statute, regulation or order is not inconsistent with the title if the protection offered is greater than the protection provided under the title. The provision in effect is a national minimum standards one. The act also specifically preserves the enforcement powers of the states by allowing state attorneys general to bring a civil action in any U.S. District Court located in their state.

The section also contains a savings clause providing this title of the act and section of 24 of the *Federal Reserve Act* do not pre-empt state banking laws applicable to a subsidiary or affiliate of a national bank with the exceptions of a subsidiary or an affiliate chartered as a national bank. Furthermore, the comptroller of the currency is directed to review every five years a determination that a provision of federal law pre-empts a state consumer financial law, and to publish a notice in the *Federal Register* to continue or rescind the determination or advance a proposal to amend the determination. In addition, a section stipulates the act, relative to federal savings associations, "does not occupy the field in any area of State law."

The act's proponents contend it will prevent another financial crisis as severe as the most recent one. Opponents disagree, with some contending the act is unworkable.

### Patient Protection and Affordable Care Act of 2010

The *Affordable Care Act* and its companion, *Health Care and Education Reconciliation Act of 2010*, are primarily conditional grant-in-aid programs in terms of their impact on state and local governments, with the exception of the mandate that individuals with specified exceptions must purchase health insurance, effective Jan. 1, 2014. The mandate pre-empts current state law in Idaho, Utah and Virginia.

McKinsey & Co. in 2011 released a report, based on a survey of business owners, concluding "that nearly a third of employers would definitely or probably drop coverage for employees" when the act's provisions take effect. Other reports, including one by the Urban Institute, reached conflicting conclusions.

The act's most controversial provision is the individual mandate to purchase health insurance, which was included because of the fear numerous healthy young individuals would delay purchasing insurance for many years until they become ill, thereby threatening to bankrupt the national health care system. Shortly after the act's enactment, Congress enacted the *Health Care and Education Reconciliation Act of 2010*, which amended several provisions of the act and lowered the penalty for not purchasing insurance from $750 to $695.

The act contains two religious exemptions from the individual mandate for people of a denomination, such as the Amish and the Christian Scientists, whose religious conscience bars the acceptance of the benefits of private or public insurance, and members of a health-sharing ministry "that share a common set of ethical and religious beliefs and share medical expenses among members in accordance with those beliefs …" Individuals who cannot afford the cost of the insurance coverage are also exempted from the mandate.

President Obama on April 14, 2011, signed the *Comprehensive 1099 Taxpayer Protection and Repayment of Exchange Subsidy Overpayments Act of 2011*. This act, among other provisions, repealed the requirement in the *Patient Protection and Affordable Care Act* that all businesses must file a 1099 form with the Internal Revenue Service for each vendor with whom they have annual cumulative transactions of $600 or more, and a second 1099 reporting requirement imposed on owners of rental real estate. Small businesses in particular strongly opposed them. A second provision repealed the expansion of information reporting requirements for rental property expense payments.

Twenty-nine challenges to the law were filed by May 31, 2011, with nine pending in U.S. District Courts, seven awaiting action by circuits of the Court of Appeals, and 13 suits dismissed. States presented two types of challenges: They contend (1) the individual mandate is an unconstitutional regulation and (2) provisions of the act regulating the states violate the structural principles of federalism. The federal government, in its defense of the act, has relied primarily on the interstate commerce clause and, alternatively, on the necessary and proper clause and the taxation power.

Judge Henry Hudson of the United States District Court for the Eastern District of Virginia in 2010 invalidated the mandate, thereby continuing the validity of the Virginia law that stipulates: "No resident of this Commonwealth … shall be required to obtain or maintain a policy of individual insurance coverage." The law otherwise would have been invalidated under the supremacy of the law provision of article VI of the U.S. Constitution.

Judge Roger Vinson of the United States District Court for the Northern District of Florida in 2011 also struck down the mandate as unconstitutional and opined, "Because the individual mandate is unconstitutional and not severable, the entire Act must be declared void."

The U.S. District Court for the Eastern District of Michigan, the Western District of Virginia and the District of Columbia rejected challenges to the law. Judge Norman K. Moon of the District Court for the Western District of Virginia upheld the individual mandate on the ground the decision not to purchase insurance was an economic decision within the scope of Congress' powers under the interstate commerce clause.

Judge Gladys Kessler of the U.S. District Court for the District of Columbia on Feb. 22, 2011, rejected challenges that the penalty provided by the act is a tax, and the individual mandate exceeds the scope of the interstate commerce clause and is a burden placed on religious freedom.

The Court of Appeals for the Sixth Circuit in Cincinnati on June 1, 2011, commenced oral hearings on a district court's affirmation of the constitutionality of the act. Judge James L. Graham asked Acting U.S. Solicitor General Neal K. Katyal a most pertinent question: "Where, ultimately, is the limit on Congress' power?" He replied the government did not suggest there are no limits. Graham responded by asking, "Where are they? I want to find them." Katyal did not respond to the question directly, but contended the mandate "regulates the way they pay for health care they will inevitably consume." He also argued the lawsuit should be dismissed because Jann DeMars, a plaintiff, purchased an insurance policy in October 2010. Her lawsuit filed in March 2010 maintained she had standing to sue because she did not have health insurance.

The Sixth Circuit of the Court of Appeals, by a 2-to-1 vote June 30, upheld the constitutionality of the act, opining the mandate regulates economic activity and the decision to forego insurance "is no less economic than the activity of purchasing an insurance plan." The 11th Circuit of the Court, by a 2-to-1 vote Aug. 12, opined the individual mandate exceeded Congress's power under the interstate commerce clause, and was a civil penalty, not a tax, authorized by the constitution's taxing and spending clause. The court held the mandate could be severed from the act.

Should the individual mandate survive constitutional scrutiny by the U.S. Supreme Court, collecting the penalties from defaulting individuals will be difficult since the act waived criminal penalties and prohibited the imposition of levies or liens on taxpayer property for failure to pay.

## Conclusions

With the exception of the *Dodd-Frank Wall Street Reform and Consumer Protection Act of 2010*, the pre-emption acts signed by President Obama did not remove important regulatory powers from state and local governments. Experience with the Dodd-Frank law is too limited to permit drawing firm conclusions relative to whether it will achieve its ambitious stated goals. Several television, radio and blog commentators do not anticipate the act will be successful in preventing another major recession. Nevertheless, it is reasonable to conclude various interest groups will continue to seek amendments to the act and will lobby energetically the federal agencies drafting implementing rules and regulations.

A strong possibility exists that the United States Supreme Court will invalidate the provision in the *Patient Protection and Affordable Care Act of 2010* imposing a mandate on individuals, with a few exceptions, to purchase health insurance or to pay a penalty. Proponents maintain the mandate is within the scope of the power to regulate interstate commerce delegated by the U.S. Constitution to Congress or the necessary and proper clause, or the taxation clause. Contending a decision not to purchase health insurance is interstate commerce stretches the interstate commerce clause to unimaginable limits. Such an interpretation of the mandate bears only an extremely tenuous relationship with the interstate commerce clause. Proponents of the law rely upon what is labeled an aggregation theory, positing individual decisions not to purchase health insurance collectively impact interstate commerce.

Predicting the success of the act is impossible at this time as various provisions, including the key individual mandate, will be phased in over a period of several years.

Evidence suggests Congress will continue to enact new pre-emption statutes in response to inventions, technological developments, and lobbying by private and public sector groups. Such statutes primarily will involve banking, environmental protection, financial services, foreign trade, health and telecommunications. Although no transportation act, other than the transportation-related *Pedestrian Safety Enhancement Act of 2010*, has been enacted to date during the Obama administration, such a pre-emption act probably will be enacted in the future.

Congress generally continues to ignore the controversies over apportionment of the waters of major rivers and state taxation of interstate commerce, subjects Congress has plenary authority to address. Congress deliberately left the settlement of these controversies to the courts and, in particular, to the U.S. Supreme Court, which has opined on numerous occasions the political branch, not the judiciary, is best qualified to address these controversies.

## About the Author

**Joseph F. Zimmerman** is a professor of political science at Rockefeller College of the State University of New York in Albany. He is the author of more than 40 books and numerous articles.

# Supreme Court Hears
# A Number of Significant Federalism Cases

## Lisa Soronen

*In its October Term 2011, the U.S. Supreme Court will decide four significant and prominent federalism cases involving states. These cases include the Affordable Care Act cases, the Arizona immigration case, the Texas redistricting case and the California Medicaid case. The State and Local Legal Center (SLLC)* filed amicus curiae *briefs in four cases to be decided this term affecting state and local government, including the California Medicaid case.*

Arguably the two most prominent cases of the United States Supreme Court's October Term 2011 are the Affordable Care Act cases and the Arizona immigration case. States are a party in both cases and states' rights are a central issue in both cases. Two other cases from this term where states are a party, the Texas redistricting case and the California Medicaid case, also involve important federalism questions. What makes these four cases different from many of the prominent federalism cases of the past few decades is that they involve politically charged topics—health insurance and immigration in particular—and concern issues that directly impact the lives of your average American. And as usual, the implications of the court's decisions in these cases may extend well beyond the specific facts litigated.

## Affordable Care Act

The court is considering four questions in the Affordable Care Act cases—two of which address federalism head on. First, the court will decide whether the individual mandate, which requires almost all Americans by 2014 to obtain health insurance or pay a fine, violates the Commerce Clause. One of the reasons the 11th Circuit concluded the individual mandate is unconstitutional is that insurance and health care are traditional areas of state concern. Second, the Affordable Care Act requires states to expand Medicaid coverage or lose *all* federal Medicaid funding, not just additional federal funding that will cover the cost of the expansion. The court will decide whether the Medicaid expansion is permissible under the Spending Clause or fails the coercion test because states are essentially compelled to participate in Medicaid.

Whether the court considers the requirement to buy health insurance interstate commerce or the Medicaid expansion coercive will impact both legal

doctrines in contexts well beyond the individual mandate and Medicaid. The argument that Congress can regulate inactivity (not buying health insurance) is novel. Likewise, the court has only twice ruled on the coercion doctrine in the Spending Clause context, making any ruling—much less a ruling regarding a program as big as Medicaid—significant.

## Arizona Immigration

In *Arizona v. United States*, the Supreme Court will decide whether four provisions of Arizona's immigration statute are pre-empted by federal law. Arizona argued in its *certiorari* petition that Senate Bill 1070 "authorizes cooperative law enforcement and imposes sanctions that consciously parallel federal law." But the Ninth Circuit disagreed, concluding that federal immigration law pre-empts all four provisions of Senate Bill 1070.

Regarding police being required to determine if a person is in the United States legally, the Ninth Circuit concluded that the federal Immigration and Naturalization Act allows state and local police to aid in immigration enforcement *only* under the supervision of the U.S. attorney general. Regarding state criminalization of failing to carry immigration papers, the Ninth Circuit concluded this requirement is pre-empted because Congress did not provide for state participation in this section of the immigration act, though it did in other sections of the law. Regarding Arizona criminalizing employment for undocumented immigrants, the Ninth Circuit noted that the Immigration and Naturalization Act only sanctions employers. Regarding police officers being allowed to arrest a person, without a warrant, who is likely subject to deportation, because of a crime committed, the Ninth Circuit concluded this section is pre-empted because "states do not have the inherent authority to enforce the civil provisions of federal immigration law."

Other states have adopted immigration laws similar to Arizona's. These laws also may be pre-empted by federal law, depending on how the court rules in this case.

## Texas Redistricting

The issue in *Perry v. Perez* was whether and how much a federal district court must defer to a state legislature's drawing of electoral maps when the federal district court creates *interim* electoral maps. Texas gained four U.S. House of Representative seats due to population growth, requiring the Texas state legislature to redraw its electoral maps. The state legislature's redistricting plan likely would allow Republicans to gain three of the four additional seats.

Per the Voting Rights Act, Texas' redistricting plan had to be precleared to ensure it wasn't discriminatory on the basis of race or color. While preclearance of Texas' plan was being litigated in a federal district court for the District of Columbia, the candidate filing period for the 2012 election was closing. So a federal district court in San Antonio drew an interim redistricting map. The court's interim map would likely give Democrats two of the new Congressional seats and, according to Texas, substantially changed all but nine of the 36 districts. Texas sued, claiming the federal district court should have deferred to the state legislature's electoral map when drawing up an interim map.

The Supreme Court's opinion in this case was favorable to the Texas legislature. The court vacated the federal district court's interim maps. It instructed the district court to "take guidance from the State's recently enacted plan in drafting an interim plan. That plan reflects the State's policy judgments on where to place new districts and how to shift existing ones in response to massive population growth."

## California Medicaid

In a 5-4 decision in *Douglas v. Independent Living Center of Southern California*, the Supreme Court left it to the Ninth Circuit to decide whether a Supremacy Clause claim can be brought against a state to enforce Medicaid.

The California legislature passed three statutes reducing state Medicaid payments to various providers and placing a limit on state contributions for certain services. Medicaid providers and beneficiaries sued California, arguing that the rate reductions were pre-empted by § (30)(A) of the federal Medicaid statute that involves state payments. The Ninth Circuit held that plaintiffs could sue California under the Supremacy Clause and that § (30)(A) of Medicaid

pre-empted the state laws. After the Supreme Court heard oral argument in this case, the Centers for Medicare and Medicaid Services approved several of California's statutory amendments to its Medicaid plan, indicating that it did not believe Medicaid pre-empted California's statutes.

The Supreme Court remanded this case to the Ninth Circuit to determine whether the Supremacy Clause claim against California may proceed in light of the Centers for Medicare and Medicaid Service's action. The majority of the court seemed skeptical that the Supremacy Clause provides a cause of action in this case, noting that the Medicaid providers and beneficiaries may now be required to seek review of the Centers for Medicare and Medicaid Services' decision under the Administrative Procedure Act instead of suing California under the Supremacy Clause. The dissent concluded that the Supremacy Clause provides no private right of action to enforce § (30)(A) of the Medicaid statute, as the Supremacy Clause is "not a source of any federal rights."

At least one significant concern for states following this case, particularly if the Ninth Circuit allows the Supremacy Clause claim to proceed, is that lower courts and the Supreme Court will allow Supremacy Clause causes of action to be read into other federal statutes.

## Conclusion

The Supreme Court already has issued an opinion in the Texas redistricting case and the California Medicaid case. It will issue an opinion in the Affordable Care Act and Arizona immigration cases no later than the end of its term in June 2012.

Not all the cases from this term affecting state and local government have been as prominent, controversial or partisan as the cases described. The State and Local Legal Center filed an *amicus curiae* brief supporting California in *Douglas v. Independent Living Center of Southern California*. The SLLC also filed *amicus* briefs in the three cases below. All these cases will likely have a greater impact on local government than state government. Visit the SLLC's website at *http://www.statelocallc.org/* for more information about these cases and to read the SLLC's briefs. To read opinions in these cases decided after this article is published, visit the Supreme Court's website.

### Filarsky v. Delia

In a unanimous decision in *Filarsky v. Delia,* the court held that contract attorneys and other individuals working for the government on a part-time basis are eligible for qualified immunity from lawsuits, like their full-time government employee counterparts.

### *Reichle v. Howards*

The issue in *Reichle v. Howards* is whether a person arrested based on probable cause can bring a First Amendment retaliatory arrest claim.

### *Armour v. Indianapolis*

The issue in *Armour v. Indianapolis* is whether a city violated the Equal Protection Clause when it forgave the assessments of homeowners who paid for sewer improvements in multi-year installments, but issued no refunds to homeowners who paid for the same improvements in a lump sum.

---

## About the Author

**Lisa Soronen** is the executive director of the State and Local Legal Center. She files *amicus curiae* briefs to the U.S. Supreme Court on behalf of members of the Big Seven in cases involving federalism, organizes moot courts for attorneys representing state and local government at the Supreme Court, and is a resource to Big Seven members on legal issues affecting state and local government, particularly at the Supreme Court level. Members of the Big Seven are The Council of State Governments, National Governors Association, National Conference of State Legislatures, National League of Cities, U.S. Conference of Mayors, National Association of Counties and the International City/County Management Association.

# State-Federal Relations in the Age of Austerity

## By Chris Whatley

*With the flow of federal funding slowing dramatically, states will need to look to Washington for flexibility rather than dollars to meet their own budget challenges.*

## Introduction

In the words of author David Osborne, the business of state government is to "educate, medicate, and incarcerate." In the new age of austerity, however, the state-federal funding mechanisms that have underpinned these priorities for nearly half a century are beginning to fray.

## Domestic Policymaking

The wave election of 2010 brought to a close one of the most intense periods of domestic policymaking in U.S. history. Over the span of a little more than a year, the Obama administration and its allies in Congress enacted both the $800 billion American Recovery and Reinvestment Act and the most extensive restructuring of health care in America since the creation of Medicare and Medicaid. But in the face of mounting deficits and divided partisan control, the 112th Congress has ushered in a new era underpinned by partisan gridlock and fiscal austerity.

The legislative achievements of the 111th Congress were a mixed bag for states. The Recovery Act played a decisive role in stemming the historic state budget crisis of 2008–10 by moving more than $140 billion in short-term deficits off of state balance sheets and onto the national debt. The Affordable Care Act, however, has created troubling new long-term costs for states as millions of patients will be added to a Medicaid system that already is crowding out virtually every other category of state expenditure.

The public's reaction to the very costs of these programs propelled the GOP into the majority in the U.S. House. Given the mandate of the new majority, it is no surprise that standoffs between the president, House and Senate over budget resolutions and debt ceiling votes have defined the 112th Congress and led directly to the only significant piece of legislation to emerge in the session, the Budget Control Act of 2011.

## Budget Control Act or Sequestration

The Budget Control Act was designed to reduce projected federal deficits by at least $2.1 trillion through a two-part process. The first part included a $917 billion commitment to reduce the projected deficit by shaving more than 10 percent from discretionary spending over the next 10 years. These cuts will fall equally on defense and non-defense spending in the first two years, with Congress retaining the authority to redistribute the cuts across all discretionary categories in future years.

The second part of the act mandated the creation of the ill-fated supercommittee to attempt to identify an additional $1.2 trillion to $1.5 trillion in cuts and/or revenue measures. Knowing it would be difficult to reach a deal, Congress included an automatic trigger in the act that mandates a further $1.2 trillion in cuts through a process known as "sequestration" if the supercommittee failed.

Barring an unlikely effort to defang the automatic trigger in the Budget Control Act, Congress will be required to sequester, or remove from consideration, set amounts of discretionary spending below the $1.05 trillion 2011 fiscal year baseline spending level to achieve $1.2 trillion in savings by the end of 2020. Beginning in 2013, federal discretionary spending will dive nearly $100 billion to a total discretionary level of $967 billion and will then slowly increase each year thereafter. Total federal discretionary spending will not crest above the 2011 fiscal year level until 2019.

Sequestration cuts will be shared equally between security and non-security spending. The security spending includes not only defense, but also the State Department budget, foreign aid, intelligence agencies and many other aspects of America's national security posture. Because the Department of Defense dwarfs these other budget components, however, the military will inevitably bear the brunt of the security cuts. Anticipating the impact of these cuts, some observers are already speculating that DOD will need to conduct another round of Base Realignment and Closure—or BRAC—as early as 2015.

One provision of the Budget Control Act could help ease the sting of these defense cuts. Defense Secretary Leon Panetta frequently mentions that his department is already grappling with plans to cut $450 billion over 10 years as a result of this summer's $917 billon debt ceiling compromise. That $450 billion assumes that the cuts included in the $917 billion agreement, which are already taking effect, will be shared equally among security and non-security accounts.

Unlike the sequester cuts, however, the Budget Control Act only requires that the cuts used to generate $917 billion in savings be shared equally for the first two years. If sequestration kicks in as expected in 2013, triggering another $500 billion in security cuts, expect Congress to use this flexibility to dial back some of the $450 billion in scheduled cuts under the $917 billion compromise by forcing non-security accounts to cut even more. Given that grants-in-aid to state and local government constitute nearly 40 percent of federal non-defense discretionary spending, any effort to raid these funds will have an immediate impact on states.

The push to shift more cuts from the $917 billion compromise to domestic spending will be reinforced by the fact that domestic spending will fare much better than defense under sequestration. While at first glance it would appear that domestic discretionary spending is headed to a similar $500 billion dive, dramatically reducing intergovernmental transfers for everything from education to public transit, the blow will be lessened by the fact that domestic discretionary spending includes some areas of mandatory spending that also will be cut.

Although cuts to Medicare are capped at 2 percent per year, the cap still allows for $123 billion in Medicare spending to be trimmed over nine years. In addition, while Medicaid, welfare (Temporary Assistance to Needy Families), and food stamps (Supplemental Nutrition Assistance Program) are exempt, some other categories of mandatory domestic spending including farm subsidies and the new health exchange insurance subsidies under the Affordable Care Act are not exempt and can be expected to experience cuts of almost $50 billion. As a result, the total amount of domestic discretionary spending subject to sequestration comes in at roughly $300 billion.

## Grants-In-Aid

The combined impact of sequestration and the initial Budget Control Act cuts will reduce grants-in-aid to state and local governments across 150 separate grant programs by a total of $12 billion.[1] Final cuts could go even deeper, as even small cuts to federal agencies of 2 to 5 percent often translate into magnified cuts to state grant accounts of 20 percent or higher.

As the cuts will be spread out across a broad range of programs, covering everything from the Low Income Heating Assistance Program—known as LIHEAP—to emergency management grants, states will be able to pass on many of these cuts to local governments or community service providers. Some of the education funds set to meet the chopping block, particularly Title I disadvantaged schools funding and IDEA special education money, however, will need to be back-filled with state general fund dollars on a near one-to-one basis or risk court actions that could force states to spend even more money than they would otherwise.

While the Budget Control Act may be the most visible sign of the new age of austerity, it is not the only one. Recent debates in Congress over transportation reauthorization and the House budget resolution have witnessed proposals to cap federal expenditures on two of the most fundamental elements of the state-federal partnership, surface transportation and Medicaid, and to shift the programs into block grants to states. With Congress locked in partisan gridlock, it will become ever more tempting to devolve large components of public works and the social safety net to the states. In essence, these efforts are an attempt to shift political risk to a level of government that has proved more capable of making the hard choices over revenue increases or spending cuts that Congress is increasingly unable to make.

## Conclusion

With Congress looking to reduce its share of the bill for the "educate, medicate, and incarcerate" programs that define state budgets, calls to reduce maintenance of effort requirements and other federal funding restrictions are sure to be at the top of the list in the state-federal dialogue for years to come. History will tell if the push to devolve will lead to a damaging reduction of programs and services or if it sparks a wave of state-led innovation in managing costs and speeding service delivery. Without clear and convincing advocacy from states, however, there is a real danger that Congress will shift the risk of devolution to the states without giving them the authority to reform and manage the programs that have underpinned the state-federal partnership for more than 50 years.

## Notes

[1] Federal Funds Information for States, Special Analysis 12-01, February 7, 2012.

## About the Author

**Chris Whatley** serves as Washington director and deputy executive director of The Council of State Governments, leading CSG's federal advocacy and international outreach efforts.

# The Evolution of Interstate Compacts
## By Crady deGolian

*First referenced in Article I, Section 10, Clause 3 of the United States Constitution, interstate compacts are the most formal mechanism available to policymakers seeking state-driven solutions to a wide range of policy challenges. Of all the tools available to state policymakers trying to work cooperatively across borders, interstate compacts are the most formal and perhaps the least understood.[1] Compacts hold a unique place in American history for several different reasons. First, while the use of interstate compacts dates back to the founding of the country, the frequency with which they are used has expanded considerably over the last half century. Second, compacts provide state policymakers with a sustainable tool capable of promoting interstate cooperation without federal intervention. Third, interstate compacts can be used to address a wide range of policy challenges, ranging from insurance reform to environmental regulation and virtually everything in between.*

Interstate compacts hold a unique place in American history. They were first referenced in Article I, Section 10, Clause 3 of the United States Constitution and still are the most structured and perhaps the least understood mechanism available to policymakers seeking state-driven solutions to a wide range of policy challenges. While the use of interstate compacts dates back to the founding of the country, the frequency with which they are used has expanded considerably over the past half century. Compacts provide state policymakers with a sustainable tool capable of promoting interstate cooperation without federal intervention. They also can be used to address a wide range of policy challenges, ranging from insurance reform to environmental regulation and virtually everything in between.[2]

## About Interstate Compacts

Compacts initially were used to resolve disputes between colonies. Since 1789, they have grown beyond bi-state agreements into national and regional creations with both advisory and regulatory responsibilities.[3]

Interstate compacts are contracts between two or more states creating an agreement on a variety of issues, including specific policy challenges, regulatory matters and boundary settlements. As such,

## Table A:
## Interstate Compacts: Advantages and Disadvantages

| *Advantages* | *Disadvantages* |
|---|---|
| Flexible and enforceable | Lengthy and challenging process |
| Interstate uniformity without federal intervention | Lack of familiarity with the mechanism among state government officials and the public |
| States maintaining collective sovereignty | Perceived loss of individual state sovereignty |
| Alternative to federal pre-emption | Delegation of state regulatory authority to an interstate agency |

compacts are governed by the tenants of contract law, meaning an offer to enter the agreement is expressed by the first state to join the compact and accepted by each subsequent jurisdiction that also joins.[4]

States have used interstate compacts to address a variety of challenges, including:

- Resolving boundary disputes;
- Managing the interstate allocation of natural resources; and
- Creating interstate administrative agencies in a wide range of policy areas, including tax reform, education, criminal justice, licensing, and energy and environment.

This diversity is one of the primary benefits interstate compacts provide. They can be used to address a variety of challenges, from the very simple to the extremely complex.

Compacts also provide other advantages, such as allowing states to maintain their sovereignty by providing a means to act collectively outside the confines of federal legislation or regulation. Compacts let states develop a dynamic, self-regulatory system that remains flexible enough to address changing needs.

## The History of Interstate Compacts

The use of interstate compacts has evolved considerably throughout the course of American history. As of 2011, approximately 215 interstate compacts were active, with each state belonging to an average of 25. Virginia is the member of the most compacts, adopting approximately 40 different agreements, while Hawaii is the member of the fewest agreements, with approximately 15 active compacts.[5]

Most of the earliest compacts were bi-state agreements intended to resolve border disputes. Border compacts represent the simplest form of the mechanism, with no oversight authority or governing structure required for enforcement.[6] As the use of compacts became more common, compacts grew in sophistication. In the early part of the 20th century, states began entering into what would eventually become known as advisory compacts. These agreements between two or more states often were used to create study commissions to examine a problem and report their findings to the respective member states.[7] While advisory compacts represented an evolution in the use of interstate compacts, they still lacked any kind of formal governance structure or enforcement procedures.

The creation of the Port Authority of New York and New Jersey in 1922 through an interstate compact signaled a significant shift in the use and application of interstate compacts.[8] For the first time, states began using them to establish regulatory agencies with the authority to act on the state's behalf. While the formation of the port authority ushered in a new era, states really began using compacts as a means to resolve challenging policy questions beginning in approximately 1955

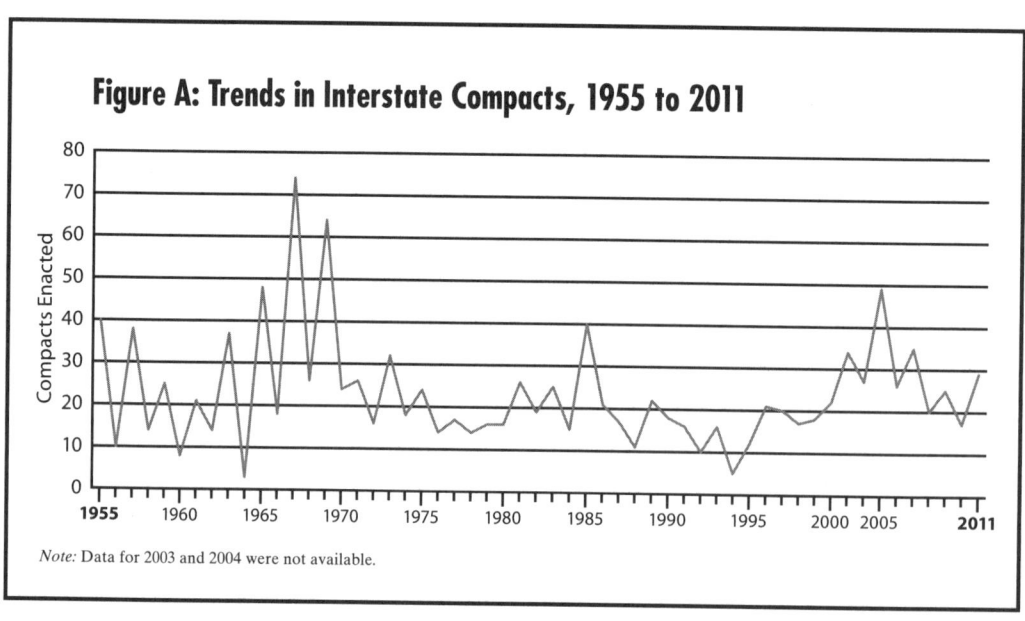

## Figure A: Trends in Interstate Compacts, 1955 to 2011

*Note:* Data for 2003 and 2004 were not available.

through the creation of administrative compacts. Since then, the use of interstate compacts has grown dramatically, including:

- The adoption of nearly 1,300 compact bills by states;
- An average of 23 state adoptions per year, with a high of 74 adoptions in 1974 and a low of five in 1994;
- The formation of numerous regional and national compacts; and
- The creation of interstate administrative agencies intended to address a wide range of policy challenges.[9]

The past four decades have seen some fairly dramatic ebbs and flows in the use of compacts. In a 26-year period from 1974 to 2000, state adoptions were above the annual average of 23 only four times. Compact adoptions were above average in none of the eight years of the Clinton administration. Conversely, from 2001 to 2011, the number of state adoptions was above average in seven legislative cycles.[10]

While the reasons for the increased use of compacts over the course of the past decade is impossible to determine, one possible explanation may be attributed to recent Republican electoral successes. Both the Bush administration and the recent shift to a Republican-controlled House of Representatives have resulted in calls for a less centralized federal government and more emphasis on state-driven solutions.

## Current Trends

This argument seems to carry more water when analyzing compact adoptions during the past two state legislative sessions. In 2010, there were 17 pieces of compact legislation adopted by state legislatures across the country. While this number is not extremely low when looking across the past 66 years, it is well below the annual average number of state adoptions. Conversely, state legislatures in the first half of 2011 took action on 29 compacts adoptions, which is well above the annual average. These include compacts concerning juvenile justice, surplus lines insurance, Thoroughbred and harness horse racing, education, health insurance and insurance product regulation.

Once again, such a dramatic jump in the use of compacts from 2010 to 2011 is difficult to explain. It seems reasonable to conclude that the November 2010 elections, which resulted in Republicans gaining control of the U.S. House of Representatives and

making significant gains in the number of gubernatorial seats held, and the number of state houses and senates controlled, played a significant role. With Republicans advocating a reduced reliance on the federal government, states have become more active in addressing policy challenges by working on an interstate basis.

## Modern Administrative Compacts

Administrative compacts are often the most intricate of the compacts and therefore have the most extensive administrative apparatus. Administrative compacts typically require the creation of an interstate agency to oversee an ongoing area of interstate policy. These agencies, typically known as commissions, often serve as quasi-governmental agencies and have the authority to pass rules, form committees, establish organizational policy, seek grants and ensure compliance with the compact. Additionally, many modern administrative compacts create a national office and hire staff to carry out the day-to-day operations of the compact.

While opponents of interstate compacts would argue that these functions simply result in another level of bureaucratic red tape, administrative compacts have the unique ability to create economies of scale, in turn saving states valuable resources during challenging fiscal times. For example, the Interstate Compact for Adult Offender Supervision, which was redrafted in 1999 by The Council of State Governments and the Department of Justice, is tasked with tracking the movement of adult criminal offenders and parolees across state lines. In order to streamline this process, the commission and national office worked to develop an online tracking system to create a more efficient monitoring process. The online monitoring system reduced what used to be a multiweek process down to a matter of minutes. With all 50 states and four of the U.S. territories as members, the compact and the work of its commission have saved dollars and reduced staff time, in turn saving states valuable resources.

Modern administrative compacts also provide states a number of additional advantages. Frequently, administrative compacts have a clearly defined governance structure, ensuring that mechanisms are in place to resolve disputes between member states. The compacts also typically call for the creation of standing committees, which have the ability to make decisions and allow the compact to evolve over time.

Equally important, administrative compacts allow for flexibility and necessary adjustments through the promulgation of rules. Given the changing nature of today's world, it is nearly impossible to predict what the future holds. While each member state of an interstate compact adopts nearly identical language, the rule-making authority that is frequently granted to commissions in administrative compacts ensures that the compact can evolve in a changing world.

By their very nature, interstate compacts ensure that states can act jointly to solve an immediate problem, while continuing to work cooperatively well into the future as the scope and nature of the problem change. While interstate compacts are not new, their evolution has provided state policymakers a sustainable and long-term solution to address complex cross-border challenges.

For more information about which compacts your state is a member of, visit the National Center for Interstate Compacts Database at *www.csg.org/ncic.*

## Notes

[1] *The Evolving Use and the Changing Roll of Interstate Compacts: A Practitioners Guide.* Broun, Buenger, McCabe, and Masters. Published by the ABA. p. 4.

[2] Ibid, p. 12.

[3] *Interstate Compacts: Background History.* Published March 18, 2011. Accessed on 3/27/12 at *http://knowledge center.csg.org/drupal/content/interstate-compacts-back ground-and-history.*

[4] *Compacts as a Tool of the Game.* Accessed on 3/27/12 at *http://www.csg.org/knowledgecenter/docs/ncic/ToolGame.pdf.*

[5] *Trends in Interstate Compacts.* Published August 25, 2011. Accessed on 3/27/12 at *http://knowledgecenter.csg.org/dru pal/content/capitol-research-trends-interstate-compacts.*

[6] *Best Practices for Compact Development.* Published June 2, 2011. Accessed on 3/27/12 at *http://knowledgecenter.csg. org/drupal/content/best-practices-compact-development.*

[7] Ibid.

[8] *Trends in Interstate Compacts.* Published August 25, 2011. Accessed on 3/27/12 at *http://knowledgecenter.csg.org/dru pal/content/capitol-research-trends-interstate-compacts.*

[9] Ibid.

[10] Ibid.

## About the Author

**Crady deGolian** is the director of CSG's National Center for Interstate Compacts. In his current role, deGolian manages each of the National Center's compact projects from development to implementation. He worked extensively on The Interstate Compact on Educational Opportunity for Military Children and The Interstate Compact for Juveniles. He has also helped lead the development of several compact efforts, including the Prescription Monitoring Program Compact, the Interstate Reciprocity Compact, and the Electric Transmission Line Siting Compact. In addition to managing CSG's compact activities, deGolian has written extensively, delivered national presentations, and provided oral testimony before Congress about interstate compacts. Originally from Louisville, Ky., deGolian holds a BA in history and political science from Furman University in Greenville, S.C. and a MA in diplomacy and international relations from the University of Kentucky.

# The Uniform Law Commission:
# Preserving the Roles of Federal and State Law

## By Eric M. Fish

*The Uniform Law Commission is actively engaging with the federal government on behalf of the states to create and preserve an effective balance of federalism. It is also serving to increase the dialogue about the benefits of cooperative federalism and developing guiding principles on how responsibilities can be best allocated to preserve the balance of state and federal roles.*

The Constitution of the United States is a delicate instrument that divides governing power between two sovereigns whose purpose is to provide for the betterment of the whole. The Founding Fathers acknowledged that "federal and state governments are in fact but different agents and trustees of the people, constituted with different powers and designed for different purposes."[1] The federal government is responsible for integrating citizens of states with different histories, resources, and needs together into one unified nation. At the same time, the Constitution circumscribes the powers of the federal government. States remain sovereign, free to a separate and independent existence, so far as the exercise of power does not conflict with powers specifically enumerated as within the purview of the federal government. Maintaining this constitutional division of power between state and federal authority is ultimately dependant on the political process. A robust Federalism has been, and will continue to be, a dynamic arrangement of governance with its sustainability dependent on the spirited exploration of its limits by the people.

Although the structure of the Constitution has not changed, the authority of the federal government with respect to the powers reserved to the states has changed over the years. From the ever expanding and contracting conception of the commerce clause, to the tendency for a legislator to draft legislation attuned more to popular opinion than the structural benefits of federalism, the choices made during the political process often create unforeseen implications on the balance of federal and state powers. As such, the powers of the state are in need of constant protection from federal encroachment.

The inherent tendency in protecting state law is to wait until an intrusion into state law is perceived to violate the 10th Amendment and seek judicial intervention. Advocates rely on the courts to fulfill their role as ultimate arbiter of the bounds of federalism, swayed by claims that the action in controversy will, for example, be a "death-knell for the Constitution's finely calibrated system of federalism."[2]

Without question, the judiciary plays a significant role maintaining the design contemplated by the Constitution's framers. But the role is passive and unpredictable, and should be one of last resort. By design, the judiciary is not to be an active participant in the political process. The balance of federalism is best maintained through the political process, with the representatives of the people engaged in debate and competition to establish the proper bounds of federal and state authority.[3]

Unique state-based institutions, such as the Uniform Law Commission, offer an alternative to the reliance on litigation to advance the cause of state law. The active participation of the Commission in the political process is providing considerable protection from federal encroachment on state power and helping to shape future discussions on the issue of federalism.

## The Uniform Law Commission

For well over a century, the more than 250 uniform acts drafted by the Uniform Law Commission have brought consistency, clarity and stability to state statutory law. While one of the original intentions of state governments when founding the Commission was to have a forum where state leaders could consider state law, determine in which areas of the law uniformity is important, and then draft uniform and model acts for consideration by the states, the Uniform Law Commission plays an important role in preserving the balance of federalism. Although uniform legislation was initially characterized by some as tending toward the same sort of centralization imposed by federal mandate, voluntary state action through uniform laws "takes from the general government any excuse for absorbing powers now confined to the states, and therefore directly tends to preserve intact the independence of the states."[4]

As the debate over federalism intensifies, the Uniform Law Commission is continuing to preserve the role of state law within a federal system. Recently, the Commission has served as a bulwark against federal legislation that would federalize areas of family law, while at the same time offering a state solution. It also has worked with the federal government to integrate international obligations into state law without damaging existing laws. And, much in the same way, it has played an important role in addressing the feasibility of federal initiatives and provides commentary that can help guide federal policy. Expounding on these examples, the importance of the Uniform Law Commission as a political institution of state government able to engage in the political pursuit of federalism becomes clear.

## Defending State Law from Federal Encroachment

The Uniform Law Commission, which has drafted ubiquitous laws such as the Uniform Child Custody Jurisdiction and Enforcement Act (UCCJEA) and the Uniform Interstate Family Support Act (UIFSA), has defended against departures from the longstanding deference to state laws in matters involving child custody and domestic relations. Complex family matters are best reserved to the state courts, which, over the course of time, have developed appropriate expertise and mechanisms to make fact-driven determinations needed in such cases.

Recently introduced federal legislation addressing the child custody arrangements of deployed military service members threatens the harmonious balance of state and federal law as it relates to family matters. More than 30 states have laws affording protections for service men and women involved in child custody arrangements.[5] But with relentless determination, U.S. Rep. Michael Turner of Ohio has made the issue a core item of his agenda. His proposed legislation would prohibit state courts from using past deployments or the possibility of deployment against service members when making child custody determinations. The language also would prohibit courts from permanently altering custody orders during a parent's deployment, and requires pre-deployment custody to be reinstated unless that is not in the best interests of the child. Variations of the bill have been introduced on multiple occasions.[6] On each occasion, the Uniform Law Commission, joined by other groups

such as the American Bar Association and the National Center for State Courts, has been vocal in opposing the legislation on grounds that the changes to federal law hinders the powers of the states to legislate in the area of family law.[7] Even after its most recent defeat, the bill was reintroduced.[8]

Under the threat of federal pre-emption, this important issue remains ripe for a national solution that is rooted in state law. The Uniform Law Commission is spearheading a project to draft a uniform statute that states may adopt to govern child custody and visitation rights when a service member is deployed for military service. Based in part on existing statutes, the uniform law will go well beyond the proposed federal legislation and will establish a comprehensive set of state law procedures and protections for the custody issues that military families face. The Uniform Law Commission is expected to give the uniform act final approval in July 2012.

This example illustrates how the Uniform Law Commission can work within the political process to concurrently defend traditional areas of state law while offering solutions to national problems without departing from the balance of state and federal law. Providing a forum for each state to have a voice in crafting a uniform act respectful of existing law, the commission is able to reform law in a way that achieves the objectives sought by Congress without eradicating the deference to the states in matters of traditional state authority.

## Cooperative Federalism

In addition to its involvement with domestic law, the Uniform Law Commission has recently embarked on an effort to aid the federal government in implementing international treaties through indigenous state law, thereby preserving the existing balance of domestic law. This method of implementation is termed "conditional pre-emption" or "cooperative federalism." While the states and federal government have used cooperative federalism in the past to achieve specific domestic policy objectives,[9] its use to implement international obligations is a fairly new idea.

The involvement of the Uniform Law Commission in the process ensures that any resulting changes in domestic law are brought about in a way that is respectful of state interests, and ensures certainty in the application of the treaty terms. Just as important, the Commission provides a method that is transparent and allows states to have a voice in the process.

The fundamental approach revolves around a set of principles and procedures designed to maintain the balance of state and federal power without disrupting larger policy objectives. First, federal law would implement the international agreement at the federal level. The U.S. Senate would provide advice and consent on the treaty or convention, and legislation would be introduced that would execute the agreement. State law would implement the convention at the state level if a state adopted the uniform act. If a state did not adopt the act, federal law would govern in that particular state. This process creates a mechanism for the instantaneous implementation of the act and an opportunity for the states to preserve an important balance in existing state and federal law.

## Effective Implementation of International Obligations Through State Law

In 2007, the U.S. participated in the drafting of the Hague Convention on the International Recovery of Child Support and Other Forms of Family Maintenance. The Convention aims to increase cooperation among nations for the international recovery of child support and other forms of family assistance through administrative cooperation premised on clear rules of jurisdiction. The Convention also applies to the establishment and modification of spousal support in cases where no related request for child support is present. State child support agencies will administer the convention provisions at the state level. The U.S. Department of Health and Human Services will serve as central authority under this convention, but many of the responsibilities of the central authority will be delegated to the individual state child support agencies.

Working in conjunction with the Departments of State and Health and Human Services, the Uniform Law Commission established a drafting committee to determine how the parts of the Convention affecting state law could be best integrated with the Uniform Interstate Family Support Act, a framework that is law in all states. The drafting committee determined that it should refrain from any temptation to amend provisions of the Uniform Interstate Family Support Act (UIFSA) except to the extent necessary to accommodate the procedures of enforcement and recognition contained in the Convention. The uniform act was completed in July 2008.

Despite what appears to be an agreed upon and formulaic approach to implementing the Convention, the process has not been without its share of disruptions. When the Uniform Law Commission completed the necessary changes to UIFSA, all parties involved, both state and federal, envisioned quick passage of the federal implementing legislation. However, concern over language in the preamble of the Convention caused the Senate to delay its advice and consent; specifically the reference to principles espoused in the United Nations Convention on the Rights of the Child.

While the United States was a signatory to the Convention, it has never been ratified because of concerns that the Convention changes the relationship of the child, the parent and the state. Core principles of the U.N. Convention on the Rights of the Child—the "best interests of the child" and the child's "evolving capacities"—have been seen as potentially contrary to American principles. The Hague Convention on Family Maintenance does not change the relationship of the family to the state. It is strictly a procedural Convention, focusing on procedures for the collection of child support across borders and ensuring reciprocal enforcement of orders between the U.S. and other signatory countries.

Nonetheless, when the Senate acted to provide advice and consent, Sen. Jim DeMint offered an amendment reinforcing that "The United States is not a party to the Convention on the Rights of the Child and understands that a mention of the convention in the preamble of this treaty does not create any obligations and does not affect or enhance the status of the convention as a matter of United States or international law." With the amendment, the treaty was approved.[10]

Pursuant to the idea of cooperative federalism, legislation had to be introduced to fully implement the treaty. Both the Senate and the House of Representatives are considering the use of conditional spending to ensure national adoption of the changes to UIFSA.[11] This approach is not new to the area of child support. The 1996 Welfare Reform Act[12] made major changes to welfare programs requiring modification of state law. With the Welfare Reform Act, Congress made the enactment of UIFSA a condition of state eligibility for federal support of child support enforcement.[13] In conformity with this requirement, all states adopted UIFSA within the two-year window provided in the legislation. Just as was the case with the Welfare Reform Act, states will be given a similar timeframe when the legislation to implement the Convention is passed.

Throughout the process of implementing the Convention, the Uniform Law Commission work illustrates that state law can be used as the vehicle to reach substantial national conformity with the language of treaties that are federal priority. But the Uniform Law Commission can play another role when international obligations may affect state law: that of a protector of state interests.

## Protecting State Law
## Impacted by International Agreements

More than 12 years of discussion on international judgment recognition concluded with the completion of the Hague Convention on Choice of Court Agreements in the summer of 2005. The Convention provides rules for the enforcement of exclusive choice of forum clauses and for recognition and conventions with other countries. The Convention and this act contain three key rules. These rules govern when a court must hear a case; when a court must decline to hear a case; and when a court must recognize and enforce a judgment from another court.

Recognizing the Convention's potential impact on state law, especially the terms governing the exclusive choice of forum clauses and recognition and enforcement of foreign judgments, the Department of State asked the Uniform Law Commission to study how these terms could be implemented without detrimentally affecting the internal administration of state courts. Equally as important was the recognition that ordering state courts to administer their courts in a particular manner through federal legislation has both constitutional and practical political implications.

The Uniform Law Commission established a study committee on this matter in July 2007. The study committee found that ratifying the Convention would facilitate the participation of the United States commercial entities in cross-border commercial transactions and would provide an excellent judicial alternative to international arbitration. The conclusions that the Convention could be implemented through cooperative federalism further encouraged the Department of State to sign the convention, which it did in January 2009.

Since then, a drafting committee has been working on comprehensive uniform state legislation that would implement the Convention in a manner that is consistent with the Convention and in harmony with state law. The committee continues its work to resolve certain policy differences regarding the scope of the federal act and its impact on existing state law. First among the issues is the scope of federal court jurisdiction in actions for recognition

and enforcement of a judgment of a court chosen under the convention. Although some voiced support for federal question jurisdiction along the lines of provisions in the Federal Arbitration Act, a possible compromise would involve the minimal diversity jurisdiction based on the approach in the Class Action Fairness Act. The second issue concerned the applicable law in federal court in a state that has adopted the uniform act.

All parties are hopeful that compromise can be reached and the final version of the uniform act will be approved in 2012. But until compromise is reached, the Uniform Law Commission continues to ensure that federal initiatives do not unduly burden areas of traditional state interest.

## Forging a Principled Approach

In light of its experience as a defender of state law in overreaching federal legislation, a partner with federal authorities in finding workable solutions to issues of national importance, and the growing need to further explore the responsible coordination of state and federal law to address emerging policy issues, the Uniform Law Commission formed the Committee on Federalism and State Law in July 2009. The task of the committee is to study and make recommendations on how to advance the public understanding of the importance of areas of traditional state law within the federal system.

The committee is working to issue "Principles of Federalism" that would promote a healthy balance of federal and state responsibilities, re-evaluate the current balance between federal and state law, and identify specific criteria to guide future decisions about the relative roles of the federal and state governments. In particular, standards will provide guidance on the appropriate circumstances in which federal law should substantially pre-empt state law and areas where federal law should establish minimum standards for the states, which would thereby encourage states to engage in the healthy experimentation that would further refine the approach to reach policy objectives. The principles also illustrate how pre-emption can be avoided and intergovernmental cooperation encouraged.

One of the committee's other goals is to foster the conversation between state and federal leaders on important federalism issues. In October 2010, the Uniform Law Commission hosted a symposium on federalism in Washington, D.C., that brought together state lawmakers, federal stakeholders and policy experts to discuss the role of state law in the federal system. Participants debated banking regulation, pharmaceutical regulation and unfunded mandates levied on the states by federal legislation. The Uniform Law Commission will continue to sponsor these forums, with the next program anticipated in the winter of 2013.

By working cooperatively with federal agencies in the implementation of international agreements, defending encroachments on areas of traditional state law and actively working to foster an understanding of the importance of state law during times of comprehensive discussions over the expanding role of federal power, the Uniform Law Commission will continue to be an important asset of state government in the political debates involving federalism. Engaging state and federal leaders through symposia on federalism, joint projects with state judicial and legislative organizations, and vigorous assertion of the rights and benefits of state law, especially when federal legislation or regulations threaten pre-emption, will help maintain federal and state interests and the continued vitality of state law. The continued involvement of the Uniform Law Commission in engaging political actors in debate over the proper role of state law in the federal system will help shape how federalism is understood and protected for decades to come.

## Notes

[1] The Federalist Papers No. 46 (James Madison).

[2] Brief of the Independence Institute as Amicus Curiae Supporting Petition in State of Florida, et al., v. Dept. of Health and Human Services, 565 U.S. ___, (2012) (No. 11-400).

[3] South Carolina v. Baker, 485 U.S. 505, 512 (1988).

[4] Walter P. Armstrong, Jr. *A Century of Service: A Centennial History of the National Conference of Commissioners on Uniform State Laws* 21 (1991).

[5] For example, in 2009, South Carolina enacted the Military Parent Equal Protection Act (S.C. Acts 63-5-900), which makes custody orders issued upon deployment of a service member temporary, provides for expedited hearings and contains several other provisions designed to protect service members and the best interests of the child.

[6] H.R. 6048, (2008), H.R. 4469, 111th Cong. (2011), Senate Amdt 1119, 112th Cong. (2012).

[7] Hearing on H.R. 4469, Hearing Before Subcomm. on Economic Opportunity of H. Comm. On Veterans Affairs, 111th Cong. (February 25, 2010).

[8] H.R. 4201, 112th Cong. (2012).

[9] *E.g.*, Federal Water Pollution Control Act ("Clean Water Act"), 33 U.S.C. §§ 1251–1387 (2006); Occupational Safety and Health Act of 1970, 29 U.S.C. §§ 651–678 (2006). Senate Amdt 4683, 111th Cong. (2010).

[10] Senate Amdt 4683, 111th Cong. (2010).

[11] S. 3848, 111th Cong. (2010), S. 1318, 112th Cong. (2012).

[12] Personal Responsibility and Work Opportunity Reconciliation Act of 1996, Pub. L. No.104-193, 110 Stat. 2105.

[13] 28 U.S.C. 666(f).

## About the Author

Eric M. Fish serves as interim legal counsel to the Uniform Law Commission. In this capacity, he works with state and federal legislators, as well as the executive branches of state government on public policy issues, including federalism, commercial law, criminal law, and family and elder law. He is a graduate of the Loyola University of Chicago School of Law, where he was the editor-in-chief of the Loyola University Chicago *International Law Review*. He received an undergraduate degree with honors from the University of Chicago. The statements contained within are attributable to the author and do not necessarily represent the official position of the Uniform Law Commission.

## Table 2.1
## SUMMARY OF STATE INTERGOVERNMENTAL EXPENDITURES: 1944–2010
(In thousands of dollars)

| Fiscal year | Total | To Federal government (a) | To local governments Total | For general local government support | Education | Public welfare | Highways | Health | Miscellaneous and combined |
|---|---|---|---|---|---|---|---|---|---|
| 1944 | $1,842,000 | … | $1,842,000 | $274,000 | $861,000 | $368,000 | $298,000 | … | $41,000 |
| 1946 | 2,092,000 | … | 2,092,000 | 357,000 | 953,000 | 376,000 | 339,000 | … | 67,000 |
| 1948 | 3,283,000 | … | 3,283,000 | 428,000 | 1,554,000 | 648,000 | 507,000 | … | 146,000 |
| 1950 | 4,217,000 | … | 4,217,000 | 482,000 | 2,054,000 | 792,000 | 610,000 | … | 279,000 |
| 1952 | 5,044,000 | … | 5,044,000 | 549,000 | 2,523,000 | 976,000 | 728,000 | … | 268,000 |
| 1953 | 5,384,000 | … | 5,384,000 | 592,000 | 2,737,000 | 981,000 | 803,000 | … | 271,000 |
| 1954 | 5,679,000 | … | 5,679,000 | 600,000 | 2,930,000 | 1,004,000 | 871,000 | … | 274,000 |
| 1955 | 5,986,000 | … | 5,986,000 | 591,000 | 3,150,000 | 1,046,000 | 911,000 | … | 288,000 |
| 1956 | 6,538,000 | … | 6,538,000 | 631,000 | 3,541,000 | 1,069,000 | 984,000 | … | 313,000 |
| 1957 | 7,440,000 | … | 7,440,000 | 668,000 | 4,212,000 | 1,136,000 | 1,082,000 | … | 342,000 |
| 1958 | 8,089,000 | … | 8,089,000 | 687,000 | 4,598,000 | 1,247,000 | 1,167,000 | … | 390,000 |
| 1959 | 8,689,000 | … | 8,689,000 | 725,000 | 4,957,000 | 1,409,000 | 1,207,000 | … | 391,000 |
| 1960 | 9,443,000 | … | 9,443,000 | 806,000 | 5,461,000 | 1,483,000 | 1,247,000 | … | 446,000 |
| 1962 | 10,906,000 | … | 10,906,000 | 839,000 | 6,474,000 | 1,777,000 | 1,327,000 | … | 489,000 |
| 1963 | 11,885,000 | … | 11,885,000 | 1,012,000 | 6,993,000 | 1,919,000 | 1,416,000 | … | 545,000 |
| 1964 | 12,968,000 | … | 12,968,000 | 1,053,000 | 7,664,000 | 2,108,000 | 1,524,000 | … | 619,000 |
| 1965 | 14,174,000 | … | 14,174,000 | 1,102,000 | 8,351,000 | 2,436,000 | 1,630,000 | … | 655,000 |
| 1966 | 16,928,000 | … | 16,928,000 | 1,361,000 | 10,177,000 | 2,882,000 | 1,725,000 | … | 783,000 |
| 1967 | 19,056,000 | … | 19,056,000 | 1,585,000 | 11,845,000 | 2,897,000 | 1,861,000 | … | 868,000 |
| 1968 | 21,950,000 | … | 21,950,000 | 1,993,000 | 13,321,000 | 3,527,000 | 2,029,000 | … | 1,080,000 |
| 1969 | 24,779,000 | … | 24,779,000 | 2,135,000 | 14,858,000 | 4,402,000 | 2,109,000 | … | 1,275,000 |
| 1970 | 28,892,000 | … | 28,892,000 | 2,958,000 | 17,085,000 | 5,003,000 | 2,439,000 | … | 1,407,000 |
| 1971 | 32,640,000 | … | 32,640,000 | 3,258,000 | 19,292,000 | 5,760,000 | 2,507,000 | … | 1,823,000 |
| 1972 | 36,759,246 | … | 36,759,246 | 3,752,327 | 21,195,345 | 6,943,634 | 2,633,417 | … | 2,234,523 |
| 1973 | 40,822,135 | … | 40,822,135 | 4,279,646 | 23,315,651 | 7,531,738 | 2,953,424 | … | 2,741,676 |
| 1974 | 45,941,111 | 341,194 | 45,599,917 | 4,803,875 | 27,106,812 | 7,028,750 | 3,211,455 | … | 3,449,025 |
| 1975 | 51,978,324 | 974,780 | 51,003,544 | 5,129,333 | 31,110,237 | 7,136,104 | 3,224,861 | … | 4,403,009 |
| 1976 | 57,858,242 | 1,179,580 | 56,678,662 | 5,673,843 | 34,083,711 | 8,307,411 | 3,240,806 | … | 5,372,891 |
| 1977 | 62,459,903 | 1,386,237 | 61,073,666 | 6,372,543 | 36,964,306 | 8,756,717 | 3,631,108 | … | 5,348,992 |
| 1978 | 67,287,260 | 1,472,378 | 65,814,882 | 6,819,438 | 40,125,488 | 8,585,558 | 3,821,135 | … | 6,463,263 |
| 1979 | 75,962,980 | 1,493,215 | 74,469,765 | 8,224,338 | 46,195,698 | 8,675,473 | 4,148,573 | … | 7,225,683 |
| 1980 | 84,504,451 | 1,746,301 | 82,758,150 | 8,643,789 | 52,688,101 | 9,241,551 | 4,382,716 | … | 7,801,993 |
| 1981 | 93,179,549 | 1,872,980 | 91,306,569 | 9,570,248 | 57,257,373 | 11,025,445 | 4,751,449 | … | 8,702,054 |
| 1982 | 98,742,976 | 1,793,284 | 96,949,692 | 10,044,372 | 60,683,583 | 11,965,123 | 5,028,072 | … | 9,228,542 |
| 1983 | 100,886,902 | 1,764,821 | 99,122,081 | 10,364,144 | 63,118,351 | 10,919,847 | 5,277,447 | … | 9,442,292 |
| 1984 | 108,373,188 | 1,722,115 | 106,651,073 | 10,744,740 | 67,484,926 | 11,923,430 | 5,686,834 | … | 10,811,143 |
| 1985 | 121,571,151 | 1,963,468 | 119,607,683 | 12,319,623 | 74,936,970 | 12,673,123 | 6,019,069 | … | 13,658,898 |
| 1986 | 131,966,258 | 2,105,831 | 129,860,427 | 13,383,912 | 81,929,467 | 14,214,613 | 6,470,049 | … | 13,862,386 |
| 1987 | 141,278,672 | 2,455,362 | 138,823,310 | 14,245,089 | 88,253,298 | 14,753,727 | 6,784,699 | … | 14,786,497 |
| 1988 | 151,661,866 | 2,652,981 | 149,008,885 | 14,896,991 | 95,390,536 | 15,032,315 | 6,949,190 | … | 16,739,853 |
| 1989 | 165,415,415 | 2,929,622 | 162,485,793 | 15,749,681 | 104,601,291 | 16,697,915 | 7,376,173 | … | 18,060,733 |

See footnotes at end of table.

# SUMMARY OF STATE INTERGOVERNMENTAL EXPENDITURES: 1944–2010—Continued
## (In thousands of dollars)

| Fiscal year | Total | To Federal government (a) | To local governments Total | For general local government support | Education | Public welfare | Highways | Health | Miscellaneous and combined |
|---|---|---|---|---|---|---|---|---|---|
| 1990 | 175,027,632 | 3,243,634 | 171,783,998 | 16,565,106 | 109,438,131 | 18,403,149 | 7,784,316 | … | 19,593,296 |
| 1991 | 186,398,234 | 3,464,364 | 182,933,870 | 16,977,032 | 116,179,860 | 20,903,400 | 8,126,477 | … | 20,747,101 |
| 1992 | 201,313,434 | 3,608,911 | 197,704,523 | 16,368,139 | 124,919,686 | 25,942,234 | 8,480,871 | … | 21,993,593 |
| 1993 | 214,094,882 | 3,625,051 | 210,469,831 | 17,690,986 | 131,179,517 | 31,339,777 | 9,298,624 | … | 20,960,927 |
| 1994 | 225,635,410 | 3,603,447 | 222,031,963 | 18,044,015 | 135,861,024 | 30,624,514 | 9,622,849 | … | 27,879,561 |
| 1995 | 240,978,128 | 3,616,831 | 237,361,297 | 18,996,435 | 148,160,436 | 30,772,525 | 10,481,616 | … | 28,926,886 |
| 1996 | 252,079,335 | 3,896,667 | 248,182,668 | 20,019,771 | 156,954,115 | 31,180,345 | 10,707,338 | 10,790,396 | 18,530,703 |
| 1997 | 264,207,209 | 3,839,942 | 260,367,267 | 21,808,828 | 164,147,715 | 35,754,024 | 11,431,270 | 11,772,189 | 15,453,241 |
| 1998 | 278,853,409 | 3,515,734 | 275,337,675 | 22,693,158 | 176,250,998 | 32,327,325 | 11,648,853 | 12,379,498 | 20,037,843 |
| 1999 | 308,734,917 | 3,801,667 | 304,933,250 | 25,495,396 | 192,416,987 | 35,161,151 | 12,075,195 | 13,611,228 | 26,173,293 |
| 2000 | 327,069,829 | 4,021,471 | 323,048,358 | 27,475,363 | 208,135,537 | 40,206,513 | 12,473,052 | 15,067,156 | 19,690,737 |
| 2001 | 350,326,546 | 4,290,764 | 346,035,782 | 31,693,016 | 222,092,587 | 41,926,990 | 12,350,136 | 16,518,461 | 21,454,592 |
| 2002 | 364,789,480 | 4,370,330 | 360,419,150 | 28,927,053 | 227,336,087 | 47,112,496 | 12,949,850 | 20,816,777 | 23,276,887 |
| 2003 | 382,781,397 | 4,391,095 | 378,390,302 | 30,766,480 | 240,788,692 | 49,302,737 | 13,337,114 | 20,241,742 | 23,953,537 |
| 2004 | 388,559,152 | 4,627,356 | 383,931,796 | 29,718,225 | 249,256,844 | 42,636,305 | 14,008,581 | 19,959,396 | 28,352,445 |
| 2005 | 405,925,287 | 4,620,167 | 401,305,120 | 28,320,648 | 263,625,820 | 48,370,718 | 14,500,232 | 17,515,138 | 28,972,564 |
| 2006 | 432,265,206 | 6,502,059 | 425,763,147 | 30,486,739 | 280,090,982 | 48,409,237 | 15,495,306 | 18,144,795 | 33,136,088 |
| 2007 | 460,184,110 | 4,670,648 | 455,513,462 | 31,207,955 | 301,091,116 | 57,343,557 | 14,868,267 | 20,067,198 | 30,935,369 |
| 2008 | 479,009,669 | 4,761,135 | 474,248,534 | 32,035,268 | 315,461,936 | 58,263,287 | 16,535,299 | 20,342,928 | 31,609,816 |
| 2009 | 491,321,871 | 4,819,716 | 486,502,155 | 30,334,682 | 324,495,673 | 59,183,863 | 16,453,767 | 21,019,353 | 35,014,817 |
| 2010 | 485,545,580 | 4,339,166 | 481,206,414 | 27,821,356 | 316,843,198 | 59,519,344 | 17,914,186 | 18,777,149 | 40,331,181 |

*Source:* U.S. Census Bureau, 1944–2010 Census of Governments. For information on sampling and nonsampling errors and definitions, see *http://www.census.gov/govs/state/how_data_collected.html.* Data users who create their own estimates from this table should cite the U.S. Census Bureau as the source of the original data only.

*Note:* Detail may not add to total due to rounding.

*Key:*
… — Not available.
(a) Represents primarily state reimbursements for the supplemental security income program.

**Table 2.2**
## STATE INTERGOVERNMENTAL EXPENDITURES, BY STATE: 2000–2010
(In thousands of dollars)

| State | 2010 | 2009 | 2008 | 2007 | 2006 | 2005 | 2004 | 2003 | 2002 | 2001 | 2000 |
|---|---|---|---|---|---|---|---|---|---|---|---|
| United States | 485,545,580 | 491,321,871 | 479,009,669 | 460,184,110 | 432,265,206 | 405,925,287 | 388,559,152 | 382,781,397 | 364,789,480 | 350,326,546 | 327,069,829 |
| Alabama | 6,604,013 | 6,535,634 | 6,720,814 | 6,088,940 | 5,759,949 | 5,281,804 | 4,164,719 | 4,074,005 | 4,095,562 | 3,892,653 | 3,908,350 |
| Alaska | 1,655,467 | 1,616,689 | 1,487,649 | 1,365,793 | 1,217,110 | 1,145,032 | 1,049,706 | 1,091,391 | 1,055,596 | 986,921 | 1,026,962 |
| Arizona | 9,179,514 | 9,618,970 | 10,320,506 | 10,341,643 | 9,063,746 | 8,028,519 | 7,556,518 | 6,936,753 | 6,968,635 | 6,439,144 | 5,940,651 |
| Arkansas | 4,791,989 | 4,698,889 | 4,392,340 | 4,300,048 | 4,039,533 | 3,886,756 | 3,212,815 | 3,210,582 | 3,071,214 | 2,941,918 | 2,725,242 |
| California | 90,517,531 | 94,909,240 | 94,872,980 | 93,537,044 | 88,317,088 | 80,948,431 | 80,132,150 | 84,468,847 | 74,687,370 | 69,747,365 | 65,389,054 |
| Colorado | 7,177,794 | 6,845,674 | 6,233,384 | 6,000,582 | 5,621,254 | 5,187,797 | 4,860,577 | 4,666,350 | 4,295,239 | 3,909,362 | 3,702,849 |
| Connecticut | 4,877,144 | 4,351,337 | 4,231,032 | 3,831,974 | 3,727,280 | 3,534,857 | 3,313,737 | 3,030,485 | 3,734,962 | 3,252,917 | 3,362,551 |
| Delaware | 1,235,608 | 1,205,247 | 1,172,083 | 1,157,652 | 1,129,736 | 983,773 | 922,710 | 903,476 | 822,544 | 788,160 | 856,008 |
| Florida | 18,478,449 | 17,677,928 | 19,703,095 | 19,680,891 | 19,402,818 | 17,475,959 | 15,285,893 | 14,460,722 | 14,053,858 | 15,010,631 | 14,073,445 |
| Georgia | 10,747,620 | 10,816,572 | 10,415,395 | 10,515,856 | 9,991,603 | 9,548,675 | 9,331,174 | 9,016,458 | 8,644,827 | 8,383,261 | 7,179,698 |
| Hawaii | 156,881 | 159,452 | 137,771 | 138,054 | 157,863 | 147,201 | 134,452 | 125,434 | 130,387 | 124,448 | 157,902 |
| Idaho | 2,022,896 | 2,077,028 | 2,037,507 | 1,931,829 | 1,606,232 | 1,519,654 | 1,496,785 | 1,449,076 | 1,407,058 | 1,363,345 | 1,277,688 |
| Illinois | 15,383,259 | 15,235,221 | 14,749,988 | 14,259,666 | 13,946,155 | 14,212,820 | 13,303,609 | 13,369,662 | 13,090,976 | 12,770,065 | 12,050,100 |
| Indiana | 9,705,254 | 8,204,196 | 7,969,434 | 8,178,674 | 7,817,176 | 7,876,764 | 7,963,397 | 6,760,945 | 6,556,774 | 7,052,415 | 6,735,704 |
| Iowa | 4,528,319 | 4,660,802 | 4,142,960 | 3,892,136 | 3,881,967 | 3,642,335 | 3,529,971 | 3,442,552 | 3,326,499 | 3,284,057 | 3,211,878 |
| Kansas | 4,176,958 | 4,314,940 | 4,214,475 | 3,869,984 | 3,594,505 | 3,281,217 | 3,123,152 | 2,925,220 | 2,971,413 | 2,953,527 | 2,853,333 |
| Kentucky | 5,078,845 | 4,769,871 | 4,700,971 | 4,526,996 | 4,384,427 | 3,915,278 | 3,963,425 | 3,693,634 | 3,559,669 | 3,620,278 | 3,280,144 |
| Louisiana | 6,658,397 | 6,505,389 | 6,022,791 | 6,175,010 | 5,654,409 | 4,588,748 | 4,410,251 | 4,329,053 | 4,168,290 | 3,800,785 | 3,721,576 |
| Maine | 1,338,300 | 1,325,723 | 1,335,469 | 1,272,764 | 1,217,377 | 1,093,027 | 1,049,160 | 1,051,164 | 1,009,582 | 976,233 | 912,376 |
| Maryland | 8,592,779 | 8,654,935 | 8,509,003 | 7,568,283 | 6,916,136 | 5,679,626 | 5,632,520 | 5,358,342 | 5,235,506 | 5,003,670 | 4,355,724 |
| Massachusetts | 9,107,584 | 8,890,500 | 8,840,769 | 8,909,899 | 7,231,774 | 7,271,036 | 5,393,684 | 6,435,841 | 6,283,972 | 6,886,054 | 6,240,692 |
| Michigan | 19,410,018 | 19,629,569 | 19,514,672 | 19,395,333 | 19,409,591 | 19,307,932 | 19,035,055 | 19,851,778 | 19,067,058 | 18,145,167 | 17,201,031 |
| Minnesota | 10,427,657 | 11,199,230 | 11,188,797 | 10,686,237 | 10,867,738 | 10,108,813 | 9,638,153 | 9,618,471 | 8,271,462 | 8,196,532 | 7,610,072 |
| Mississippi | 5,272,442 | 5,156,650 | 5,111,703 | 5,086,220 | 4,826,721 | 4,005,786 | 3,880,446 | 3,665,580 | 3,456,588 | 3,354,226 | 3,248,019 |
| Missouri | 6,227,630 | 5,888,392 | 5,743,498 | 5,559,734 | 5,386,306 | 5,489,120 | 5,260,101 | 5,159,094 | 5,073,185 | 4,802,371 | 4,528,746 |
| Montana | 1,334,478 | 1,276,112 | 1,318,649 | 1,175,674 | 1,088,009 | 1,005,091 | 955,378 | 938,000 | 910,845 | 863,553 | 760,511 |
| Nebraska | 2,192,338 | 2,064,173 | 1,981,940 | 1,793,817 | 1,721,265 | 1,659,130 | 1,695,613 | 1,784,749 | 1,820,137 | 1,684,159 | 1,585,847 |
| Nevada | 3,703,574 | 3,864,223 | 3,860,236 | 3,826,539 | 3,667,299 | 3,272,860 | 2,948,274 | 2,648,660 | 2,432,909 | 2,271,654 | 2,250,330 |
| New Hampshire | 1,261,454 | 1,278,589 | 1,451,976 | 1,408,445 | 1,385,014 | 1,224,831 | 1,278,988 | 1,283,091 | 1,178,642 | 1,040,566 | 1,053,267 |
| New Jersey | 11,940,861 | 11,135,809 | 10,927,571 | 10,671,445 | 11,060,423 | 10,642,426 | 10,565,755 | 8,997,417 | 9,320,357 | 9,081,634 | 8,639,491 |
| New Mexico | 4,308,854 | 4,740,669 | 4,342,730 | 4,144,807 | 3,745,089 | 3,617,407 | 3,234,697 | 2,951,328 | 2,768,420 | 2,561,979 | 2,447,354 |
| New York | 54,318,363 | 55,107,082 | 52,820,634 | 50,527,547 | 45,615,561 | 43,731,212 | 44,112,115 | 40,874,514 | 38,982,253 | 34,712,602 | 31,273,000 |
| North Carolina | 13,429,946 | 13,562,079 | 13,152,908 | 12,499,778 | 11,721,637 | 11,637,674 | 10,226,422 | 10,356,152 | 9,450,766 | 9,309,537 | 9,301,095 |
| North Dakota | 1,245,686 | 933,974 | 805,351 | 741,535 | 735,705 | 701,125 | 613,513 | 1,190,923 | 585,521 | 569,034 | 589,807 |
| Ohio | 18,373,625 | 18,988,114 | 18,105,626 | 18,042,563 | 17,347,300 | 16,368,355 | 15,730,201 | 15,249,395 | 15,052,074 | 14,594,220 | 12,932,081 |
| Oklahoma | 4,546,446 | 4,506,456 | 4,391,706 | 4,014,883 | 3,871,758 | 3,711,117 | 3,669,052 | 3,395,494 | 3,377,045 | 3,486,043 | 3,089,257 |
| Oregon | 5,864,882 | 5,703,775 | 5,640,993 | 5,047,346 | 4,947,578 | 4,764,615 | 4,637,052 | 4,071,501 | 4,212,673 | 4,027,505 | 3,919,771 |
| Pennsylvania | 18,615,065 | 19,110,552 | 17,801,247 | 17,009,062 | 13,650,400 | 13,307,866 | 12,061,035 | 11,943,470 | 12,787,590 | 13,120,752 | 11,369,795 |
| Rhode Island | 1,124,458 | 963,902 | 1,053,782 | 1,063,067 | 998,505 | 908,479 | 865,956 | 828,198 | 749,034 | 711,439 | 677,552 |
| South Carolina | 5,369,519 | 5,520,979 | 5,719,235 | 4,870,680 | 4,699,299 | 4,245,394 | 4,159,942 | 4,155,920 | 4,241,010 | 4,168,449 | 3,806,116 |

See footnotes at end of table.

# STATE INTERGOVERNMENTAL EXPENDITURES, BY STATE: 2000–2010—Continued

| State | 2010 | 2009 | 2008 | 2007 | 2006 | 2005 | 2004 | 2003 | 2002 | 2001 | 2000 |
|---|---|---|---|---|---|---|---|---|---|---|---|
| South Dakota.......... | 737,190 | 707,862 | 679,868 | 652,117 | 633,891 | 608,209 | 566,853 | 514,949 | 506,347 | 480,960 | 448,131 |
| Tennessee ............. | 6,664,828 | 6,797,935 | 6,516,598 | 6,034,661 | 5,910,319 | 5,705,768 | 5,301,665 | 4,952,923 | 4,477,936 | 4,582,883 | 4,364,404 |
| Texas...................... | 27,461,315 | 29,252,364 | 26,089,474 | 21,919,511 | 19,785,626 | 17,489,900 | 17,032,016 | 17,332,957 | 16,680,780 | 17,204,468 | 16,231,378 |
| Utah........................ | 3,027,680 | 3,120,527 | 3,050,173 | 2,601,367 | 2,384,402 | 2,189,527 | 2,112,921 | 2,165,151 | 2,170,884 | 2,100,657 | 1,977,703 |
| Vermont.................. | 1,518,129 | 1,532,766 | 1,340,755 | 1,415,922 | 1,357,660 | 1,266,715 | 981,307 | 938,085 | 918,858 | 919,865 | 931,604 |
| Virginia.................. | 10,959,394 | 11,810,753 | 11,052,058 | 10,458,913 | 10,019,166 | 9,720,411 | 8,820,012 | 8,352,635 | 8,369,313 | 7,869,121 | 7,132,350 |
| Washington............ | 9,798,444 | 10,043,789 | 9,143,766 | 8,602,204 | 7,820,778 | 7,443,361 | 6,911,826 | 6,785,341 | 6,806,350 | 6,576,757 | 6,370,710 |
| West Virginia......... | 2,382,633 | 2,232,558 | 2,131,100 | 2,074,429 | 2,067,829 | 2,004,862 | 1,942,069 | 1,544,758 | 1,453,707 | 988,322 | 1,359,668 |
| Wisconsin .............. | 10,253,124 | 10,199,520 | 10,093,198 | 9,747,672 | 9,560,976 | 9,200,766 | 9,285,137 | 9,478,166 | 9,523,191 | 8,895,941 | 8,170,504 |
| Wyoming ................ | 1,760,946 | 1,919,231 | 1,769,009 | 1,568,884 | 1,301,223 | 1,337,226 | 1,207,193 | 952,705 | 974,608 | 818,841 | 838,308 |

*Source:* U.S. Census Bureau, 1999–2010 Census of Governments. For information on sampling and nonsampling errors and definitions, see *http://www.census.gov/govs/state/how_data_collected.html.* Data users who create their own estimates from this table should cite the U.S. Census Bureau as the source of the original data only.

*Note:* Includes payments to the federal government, primarily state reimbursements for the supplemental security income program.
*Note:* Detail may not add to total due to rounding.

## Table 2.3
## STATE INTERGOVERNMENTAL EXPENDITURES, BY FUNCTION AND BY STATE: 2010
### (In thousands of dollars)

| State | Total | General local government support | Education | Public welfare | Highways | Health | Miscellaneous and combined |
|---|---|---|---|---|---|---|---|
| United States ............... | $485,545,580 | $27,821,356 | $316,843,198 | $59,519,344 | $17,914,186 | $18,777,149 | $44,670,347 |
| Alabama....................... | 6,604,013 | 194,354 | 5,034,522 | 75,467 | 208,391 | 34,864 | 1,056,415 |
| Alaska.......................... | 1,655,467 | 44,278 | 1,003,548 | 36,015 | 3,761 | 173,560 | 394,305 |
| Arizona........................ | 9,179,514 | 2,057,983 | 5,067,052 | 1,012,710 | 673,600 | 82,356 | 285,813 |
| Arkansas...................... | 4,791,989 | 285,306 | 4,006,074 | 750 | 160,520 | 836 | 338,503 |
| California ..................... | 90,517,531 | 788,978 | 42,707,787 | 27,892,047 | 4,714,447 | 6,070,483 | 8,343,789 |
| Colorado...................... | 7,177,794 | 65,132 | 4,420,650 | 1,611,501 | 368,351 | 92,410 | 619,750 |
| Connecticut................. | 4,877,144 | 119,650 | 3,632,957 | 541,287 | 9,143 | 289,228 | 284,879 |
| Delaware ..................... | 1,235,608 | 0 | 1,109,108 | 8,236 | 9,175 | 15,034 | 94,055 |
| Florida......................... | 18,478,449 | 1,600,436 | 14,259,205 | 86,329 | 597,883 | 11,523 | 1,923,073 |
| Georgia........................ | 10,747,620 | 0 | 9,560,202 | 412,395 | 133,974 | 223,376 | 417,673 |
| Hawaii.......................... | 156,881 | 101,101 | 0 | 335 | 0 | 5,631 | 49,814 |
| Idaho........................... | 2,022,896 | 179,009 | 1,674,706 | 0 | 121,809 | 3,036 | 44,336 |
| Illinois......................... | 15,383,259 | 1,620,368 | 9,681,433 | 1,705,295 | 674,938 | 141,480 | 1,559,745 |
| Indiana........................ | 9,705,254 | 731,836 | 7,778,727 | 19,499 | 784,557 | 75,095 | 315,540 |
| Iowa ............................ | 4,528,319 | 129,478 | 3,110,347 | 173,012 | 441,538 | 128,476 | 545,468 |
| Kansas ......................... | 4,176,958 | 77,208 | 3,674,612 | 343 | 162,864 | 38,968 | 222,963 |
| Kentucky ..................... | 5,078,845 | 828 | 4,105,845 | 139,927 | 189,292 | 166,915 | 476,038 |
| Louisiana..................... | 6,658,397 | 186,530 | 4,644,651 | 117,234 | 68,531 | 0 | 1,641,451 |
| Maine .......................... | 1,338,300 | 125,776 | 1,116,975 | 16,743 | 23,248 | 0 | 55,558 |
| Maryland ..................... | 8,592,779 | 122,065 | 6,873,914 | 552 | 145,418 | 713,832 | 736,998 |
| Massachusetts ............. | 9,107,584 | 988,746 | 6,707,854 | 296,274 | 197,478 | 22,125 | 895,107 |
| Michigan...................... | 19,410,018 | 1,035,263 | 13,286,444 | 2,709,835 | 1,124,806 | 134,828 | 1,118,842 |
| Minnesota.................... | 10,427,657 | 1,522,506 | 6,333,547 | 525,989 | 907,709 | 190,293 | 947,613 |
| Mississippi .................. | 5,272,442 | 534,972 | 3,210,588 | 286,148 | 347,634 | 53,623 | 839,477 |
| Missouri....................... | 6,227,630 | 2,341 | 5,328,920 | 78,848 | 311,285 | 7,709 | 498,527 |
| Montana....................... | 1,334,478 | 216,916 | 890,926 | 39,047 | 17,962 | 13,885 | 155,742 |
| Nebraska ..................... | 2,192,338 | 431,662 | 1,482,109 | 39,342 | 10,847 | 81,448 | 146,930 |
| Nevada......................... | 3,703,574 | 937,870 | 2,478,887 | 117,580 | 97,902 | 17,377 | 53,958 |
| New Hampshire .......... | 1,261,454 | 58,805 | 1,048,582 | 61,356 | 41,171 | 2,247 | 49,293 |
| New Jersey .................. | 11,940,861 | 1,857,507 | 8,145,885 | 961,371 | 212,769 | 45,445 | 717,884 |
| New Mexico ................. | 4,308,854 | 1,150,712 | 3,082,232 | 0 | 44,831 | 0 | 31,079 |
| New York...................... | 54,318,363 | 1,690,955 | 27,224,713 | 11,640,746 | 13,349 | 5,871,795 | 7,876,805 |
| North Carolina............. | 13,429,946 | 183,020 | 10,436,308 | 1,745,619 | 216,342 | 193,522 | 655,135 |
| North Dakota............... | 1,245,686 | 190,325 | 797,280 | 14,078 | 87,814 | 17,999 | 138,190 |
| Ohio............................. | 18,373,625 | 1,967,210 | 11,698,386 | 1,587,999 | 789,927 | 1,008,711 | 1,321,392 |
| Oklahoma..................... | 4,546,446 | 98,661 | 3,514,239 | 48,795 | 362,362 | 218,572 | 303,817 |
| Oregon......................... | 5,864,882 | 142,765 | 4,041,864 | 596,022 | 425,135 | 129,541 | 529,555 |
| Pennsylvania ............... | 18,615,065 | 201,053 | 11,868,611 | 2,103,402 | 696,021 | 1,047,423 | 2,698,555 |
| Rhode Island............... | 1,124,458 | 157,306 | 873,523 | 79,946 | 0 | 467 | 13,216 |
| South Carolina............. | 5,369,519 | 1,744,583 | 3,182,149 | 61,247 | 83,446 | 28,436 | 269,658 |
| South Dakota............... | 737,190 | 25,967 | 595,399 | 6,558 | 39,363 | 5,872 | 64,031 |
| Tennessee ................... | 6,664,828 | 285,408 | 4,828,377 | 815,336 | 99,664 | 68,454 | 567,589 |
| Texas........................... | 27,461,315 | 172,216 | 24,811,637 | 724,208 | 289,948 | 305,584 | 1,157,722 |
| Utah............................. | 3,027,680 | 0 | 2,740,809 | 26,403 | 100,705 | 49,711 | 110,052 |
| Vermont....................... | 1,518,129 | 19,158 | 1,427,546 | 26 | 49,399 | 313 | 21,687 |
| Virginia........................ | 10,959,394 | 1,000,303 | 6,370,932 | 725,288 | 419,527 | 343,374 | 2,099,970 |
| Washington.................. | 9,798,444 | 71,099 | 7,827,512 | 25,248 | 797,298 | 355,387 | 721,900 |
| West Virginia............... | 2,382,633 | 89,839 | 1,882,350 | 42,539 | 12,667 | 59,804 | 295,434 |
| Wisconsin .................... | 10,253,124 | 2,207,443 | 6,195,738 | 310,282 | 599,731 | 236,089 | 703,841 |
| Wyoming ..................... | 1,760,946 | 406,429 | 1,067,536 | 135 | 25,654 | 12 | 261,180 |

*Source:* U.S. Census Bureau, 2010 Annual Survey of State Government Finances. For information on sampling and nonsampling errors and definitions, see *http://www.census.gov/govs/state/how_data_collected.html.*

Data users who create their own estimates from this table should cite the U.S. Census Bureau as the source of the original data only.
  *Note:* Detail may not add to total due to rounding.

## Table 2.4
## STATE INTERGOVERNMENTAL EXPENDITURES, BY TYPE OF RECEIVING GOVERNMENT AND BY STATE: 2010
### (In thousands of dollars)

| State | Total intergovernmental expenditure | Federal | School districts | Other local governments |
|---|---|---|---|---|
| United States ...................... | $485,545,580 | $4,339,166 | $254,495,467 | $226,710,947 |
| Alabama............................. | 6,604,013 | 0 | 5,017,677 | 1,586,336 |
| Alaska................................ | 1,655,467 | 0 | 0 | 1,655,467 |
| Arizona.............................. | 9,179,514 | 0 | 5,047,444 | 4,132,070 |
| Arkansas............................ | 4,791,989 | 30 | 4,006,074 | 785,885 |
| California........................... | 90,517,531 | 2,878,157 | 39,842,641 | 47,796,733 |
| Colorado............................ | 7,177,794 | 3,037 | 4,405,112 | 2,769,645 |
| Connecticut........................ | 4,877,144 | 61,780 | 30,187 | 4,785,177 |
| Delaware ........................... | 1,235,608 | 1,093 | 1,105,372 | 129,143 |
| Florida............................... | 18,478,449 | 0 | 13,904,925 | 4,573,524 |
| Georgia.............................. | 10,747,620 | 0 | 9,560,202 | 1,187,418 |
| Hawaii................................ | 156,881 | 335 | 0 | 156,546 |
| Idaho................................. | 2,022,896 | 312 | 1,674,706 | 347,878 |
| Illinois............................... | 15,383,259 | 17 | 9,636,113 | 5,747,129 |
| Indiana.............................. | 9,705,254 | 31,707 | 7,778,327 | 1,895,220 |
| Iowa .................................. | 4,528,319 | 0 | 3,107,356 | 1,420,963 |
| Kansas .............................. | 4,176,958 | 921 | 3,670,871 | 505,166 |
| Kentucky ........................... | 5,078,845 | 209 | 4,105,845 | 972,791 |
| Louisiana........................... | 6,658,397 | 0 | 4,637,238 | 2,021,159 |
| Maine................................ | 1,338,300 | 5,902 | 0 | 1,332,398 |
| Maryland ........................... | 8,592,779 | 0 | 0 | 8,592,779 |
| Massachusetts ..................... | 9,107,584 | 208,719 | 934,232 | 7,964,633 |
| Michigan............................ | 19,410,018 | 29,999 | 13,261,370 | 6,118,649 |
| Minnesota.......................... | 10,427,657 | 0 | 6,320,216 | 4,107,441 |
| Mississippi......................... | 5,272,442 | 0 | 3,190,305 | 2,082,137 |
| Missouri............................. | 6,227,630 | 89,617 | 5,328,920 | 809,093 |
| Montana ............................ | 1,334,478 | 193 | 890,068 | 444,217 |
| Nebraska ........................... | 2,192,338 | 39,342 | 1,482,109 | 670,887 |
| Nevada.............................. | 3,703,574 | 1,535 | 2,478,887 | 1,223,152 |
| New Hampshire .................. | 1,261,454 | 0 | 185,349 | 1,076,105 |
| New Jersey ......................... | 11,940,861 | 0 | 6,003,332 | 5,937,529 |
| New Mexico ....................... | 4,308,854 | 0 | 3,082,232 | 1,226,622 |
| New York............................ | 54,318,363 | 702,171 | 13,505,829 | 40,110,363 |
| North Carolina.................... | 13,429,946 | 0 | 0 | 13,429,946 |
| North Dakota...................... | 1,245,686 | 0 | 797,270 | 448,416 |
| Ohio .................................. | 18,373,625 | 9,987 | 11,698,386 | 6,665,252 |
| Oklahoma........................... | 4,546,446 | 61,162 | 3,514,175 | 971,109 |
| Oregon............................... | 5,864,882 | 0 | 4,039,978 | 1,824,904 |
| Pennsylvania ...................... | 18,615,065 | 148,571 | 10,438,075 | 8,028,419 |
| Rhode Island...................... | 1,124,458 | 22,249 | 52,532 | 1,049,677 |
| South Carolina.................... | 5,369,519 | 0 | 3,164,293 | 2,205,226 |
| South Dakota...................... | 737,190 | 0 | 595,399 | 141,791 |
| Tennessee .......................... | 6,664,828 | 9,330 | 288,489 | 6,367,009 |
| Texas................................. | 27,461,315 | 0 | 24,566,262 | 2,895,053 |
| Utah.................................. | 3,027,680 | 0 | 2,739,051 | 288,629 |
| Vermont............................. | 1,518,129 | 26 | 1,427,546 | 90,557 |
| Virginia.............................. | 10,959,394 | 2,410 | 16,262 | 10,940,722 |
| Washington......................... | 9,798,444 | 4,853 | 7,823,845 | 1,969,746 |
| West Virginia...................... | 2,382,633 | 0 | 1,877,691 | 504,942 |
| Wisconsin........................... | 10,253,124 | 0 | 6,195,738 | 4,057,386 |
| Wyoming ........................... | 1,760,946 | 25,502 | 1,067,536 | 667,908 |

*Source:* U.S. Census Bureau, 2010 Annual Survey of State Government Finances. For information on sampling and nonsampling errors and definitions, see *http://www.census.gov/govs/state/how_data_collected.html.*

Data users who create their own estimates from this table should cite the U.S. Census Bureau as the source of the original data only.
   *Note:* Detail may not add to total due to rounding.

## Table 2.5
## STATE INTERGOVERNMENTAL REVENUE FROM FEDERAL AND LOCAL GOVERNMENTS: 2010
(In thousands of dollars)

| State | Total intergovernmental revenue | From federal government | | | | | From local governments | | | | |
|---|---|---|---|---|---|---|---|---|---|---|---|
| | | Total (a) | Education | Public welfare | Health & hospitals | Highways | Total (a) | Education | Public welfare | Health & hospitals | Highways |
| United States | $575,561,683 | $555,296,681 | $105,404,764 | $315,517,460 | $26,186,596 | $42,969,373 | $20,265,002 | $3,256,778 | $8,115,056 | $1,247,061 | $2,755,234 |
| Alabama | 9,369,725 | 8,840,961 | 2,103,803 | 4,386,117 | 324,065 | 905,200 | 528,764 | 12,928 | 434,250 | 45,511 | 21,804 |
| Alaska | 2,961,501 | 2,955,497 | 357,617 | 1,116,201 | 114,176 | 483,539 | 6,004 | 4,924 | 0 | 0 | 0 |
| Arizona | 12,577,215 | 12,337,706 | 2,005,908 | 8,018,977 | 315,051 | 610,521 | 239,509 | 15,402 | 83,068 | 58,835 | 19,570 |
| Arkansas | 5,978,147 | 5,961,108 | 854,312 | 3,350,763 | 130,344 | 500,880 | 17,039 | 16,181 | 0 | 703 | 0 |
| California | 67,805,353 | 62,958,004 | 12,662,571 | 36,391,508 | 2,046,788 | 4,237,867 | 4,847,349 | 195,956 | 857,576 | 6,761 | 1,524,214 |
| Colorado | 6,371,099 | 6,294,236 | 1,400,596 | 2,717,142 | 1,107,724 | 631,746 | 76,863 | 16,821 | 386 | 656 | 20,344 |
| Connecticut | 6,229,831 | 6,217,632 | 866,828 | 3,939,146 | 231,395 | 594,868 | 12,199 | 912 | 0 | 0 | 0 |
| Delaware | 2,035,019 | 1,976,903 | 349,022 | 1,005,671 | 107,661 | 249,331 | 58,116 | 58,116 | 0 | 0 | 0 |
| Florida | 25,447,682 | 24,996,716 | 5,381,394 | 14,092,539 | 1,777,297 | 1,844,897 | 450,966 | 8,354 | 0 | 331,521 | 0 |
| Georgia | 16,193,428 | 15,938,771 | 4,164,539 | 6,577,586 | 1,964,982 | 1,625,290 | 254,657 | 198,299 | 0 | 0 | 19,087 |
| Hawaii | 2,592,047 | 2,586,608 | 543,066 | 1,056,860 | 123,863 | 177,935 | 5,439 | 0 | 0 | 0 | 0 |
| Idaho | 2,672,926 | 2,659,457 | 548,618 | 1,165,627 | 223,184 | 368,692 | 13,469 | 494 | 7,616 | 0 | 5,326 |
| Illinois | 19,345,760 | 18,956,139 | 4,394,535 | 10,486,980 | 628,731 | 1,786,699 | 389,621 | 37,667 | 260,879 | 0 | 74,907 |
| Indiana | 10,400,713 | 10,276,593 | 1,817,152 | 5,743,884 | 367,755 | 1,104,955 | 124,120 | 14,906 | 24,511 | 4,176 | 66,732 |
| Iowa | 6,743,091 | 6,535,811 | 1,430,557 | 3,423,102 | 179,421 | 581,492 | 207,280 | 477 | 164,820 | 21,291 | 11,344 |
| Kansas | 4,624,104 | 4,580,934 | 1,082,915 | 2,181,309 | 138,662 | 453,302 | 43,170 | 10,050 | 0 | 0 | 33,120 |
| Kentucky | 9,149,028 | 9,117,626 | 1,691,169 | 5,341,768 | 244,383 | 724,995 | 31,402 | 17,818 | 0 | 0 | 0 |
| Louisiana | 13,255,001 | 13,174,285 | 1,726,902 | 6,284,801 | 385,506 | 866,415 | 80,716 | 20,476 | 0 | 2,923 | 0 |
| Maine | 3,212,892 | 3,201,555 | 364,058 | 2,144,000 | 90,950 | 242,722 | 11,337 | 2,808 | 0 | 87 | 7,452 |
| Maryland | 10,534,111 | 10,162,959 | 2,070,782 | 5,328,335 | 910,203 | 613,804 | 371,152 | 47,416 | 26,758 | 206,452 | 23,423 |
| Massachusetts | 13,326,217 | 13,126,642 | 2,234,682 | 8,295,687 | 537,113 | 777,168 | 199,575 | 9,347 | 0 | 0 | 264 |
| Michigan | 19,527,609 | 19,320,406 | 3,811,469 | 10,881,001 | 1,030,315 | 1,020,293 | 207,203 | 18,603 | 74,190 | 53,869 | 25,652 |
| Minnesota | 10,024,802 | 9,930,013 | 1,874,212 | 5,997,105 | 349,358 | 813,538 | 94,789 | 2,080 | 53,851 | 0 | 23,645 |
| Mississippi | 8,807,805 | 8,645,642 | 1,179,978 | 4,667,116 | 229,061 | 648,775 | 162,163 | 5,503 | 320 | 5 | 108,221 |
| Missouri | 11,798,319 | 11,444,588 | 2,053,102 | 6,177,319 | 1,126,210 | 1,133,781 | 353,731 | 4,363 | 245,872 | 20,365 | 67,609 |
| Montana | 2,504,673 | 2,498,169 | 386,468 | 997,963 | 121,484 | 526,449 | 6,504 | 18 | 2,494 | 0 | 3,022 |
| Nebraska | 3,202,752 | 3,146,417 | 209,043 | 2,314,143 | 49,962 | 297,410 | 56,335 | 35,301 | 970 | 3 | 16,423 |
| Nevada | 2,917,112 | 2,758,834 | 521,718 | 1,264,804 | 104,937 | 357,736 | 158,278 | 40,080 | 97,094 | 1,729 | 12,762 |
| New Hampshire | 2,360,687 | 2,138,110 | 383,988 | 993,559 | 49,983 | 218,896 | 222,577 | 4,456 | 196,862 | 364 | 4,287 |
| New Jersey | 15,476,911 | 14,753,302 | 3,305,313 | 7,522,766 | 459,102 | 1,071,737 | 723,609 | 252,810 | 2,166 | 77,899 | 156,008 |
| New Mexico | 6,247,462 | 6,065,367 | 756,279 | 4,035,161 | 163,106 | 493,674 | 182,095 | 48,860 | 0 | 133,235 | 0 |
| New York | 55,725,570 | 49,619,082 | 6,070,297 | 35,499,876 | 1,278,034 | 1,943,715 | 6,106,488 | 234,697 | 4,977,219 | 1,593 | 31,819 |
| North Carolina | 15,698,831 | 15,350,128 | 2,886,677 | 8,940,484 | 1,678,454 | 788,960 | 348,703 | 131,019 | 134,928 | 3,231 | 31,963 |
| North Dakota | 1,741,931 | 1,687,395 | 380,255 | 604,624 | 56,442 | 311,055 | 54,536 | 1 | 6,490 | 43,028 | 0 |
| Ohio | 22,461,873 | 21,953,202 | 3,621,021 | 14,364,653 | 764,389 | 1,191,868 | 508,671 | 8,092 | 196,181 | 0 | 72,462 |
| Oklahoma | 8,007,066 | 7,892,192 | 1,020,393 | 3,663,506 | 1,280,074 | 990,473 | 114,874 | 784 | 3,162 | 2,549 | 32,024 |
| Oregon | 6,857,718 | 6,843,589 | 1,569,661 | 3,485,298 | 281,957 | 526,095 | 14,129 | 9,504 | 0 | 0 | 0 |
| Pennsylvania | 21,338,641 | 21,116,037 | 3,834,449 | 13,036,167 | 645,285 | 1,929,718 | 222,604 | 199,854 | 0 | 682 | 14,404 |
| Rhode Island | 2,966,972 | 2,851,196 | 323,195 | 1,350,025 | 283,925 | 248,571 | 115,776 | 4,452 | 0 | 0 | 0 |
| South Carolina | 7,933,502 | 7,499,023 | 1,543,905 | 4,335,883 | 215,624 | 638,919 | 434,479 | 78,459 | 212,335 | 3,426 | 79,494 |

See footnotes at end of table.

# STATE INTERGOVERNMENTAL REVENUE FROM FEDERAL AND LOCAL GOVERNMENTS: 2010 — Continued
## (In thousands of dollars)

| State | Total intergovernmental revenue | From federal government | | | | | From local governments | | | | |
|---|---|---|---|---|---|---|---|---|---|---|---|
| | | Total (a) | Education | Public welfare | Health & hospitals | Highways | Total (a) | Education | Public welfare | Health & hospitals | Highways |
| South Dakota.......... | 1,794,047 | 1,766,695 | 322,807 | 708,131 | 110,736 | 328,921 | 27,352 | 11,141 | 0 | 6,420 | 9,222 |
| Tennessee ............ | 11,371,391 | 11,321,262 | 1,840,460 | 7,225,852 | 291,055 | 846,798 | 50,129 | 22,320 | 1,903 | 3,391 | 7,084 |
| Texas..................... | 41,450,202 | 40,779,780 | 10,286,616 | 22,409,302 | 1,352,670 | 2,867,784 | 670,422 | 555,888 | 4,446 | 108,491 | 0 |
| Utah...................... | 4,373,886 | 4,369,605 | 954,367 | 2,226,512 | 169,211 | 503,997 | 4,281 | 4,184 | 0 | 0 | 0 |
| Vermont................ | 1,904,907 | 1,902,523 | 269,463 | 1,085,437 | 61,955 | 211,941 | 2,384 | 0 | 0 | 0 | 2,384 |
| Virginia................. | 9,779,654 | 9,221,138 | 2,449,479 | 4,828,325 | 403,680 | 877,929 | 558,516 | 395,211 | 0 | 62,031 | 82,268 |
| Washington............ | 11,176,371 | 10,890,811 | 2,632,803 | 4,901,465 | 1,208,895 | 898,805 | 285,560 | 132,744 | 0 | 21,989 | 69,096 |
| West Virginia.......... | 4,426,116 | 4,353,106 | 588,792 | 2,531,241 | 143,916 | 507,115 | 73,010 | 2,562 | 0 | 0 | 0 |
| Wisconsin ............. | 10,403,378 | 10,229,562 | 1,819,595 | 5,975,640 | 231,872 | 961,586 | 173,816 | 13,797 | 44,709 | 21,434 | 70,002 |
| Wyoming .............. | 2,456,605 | 2,093,364 | 457,933 | 446,099 | 95,650 | 430,516 | 363,241 | 350,643 | 0 | 2,411 | 7,796 |

*Source:* U.S. Census Bureau, 2010 Annual Survey of State Government Finances. For information on sampling and nonsampling errors and definitions, see *http://www.census.gov/govs/state/how_data_collected.html.* Data users who create their own estimates from this table should cite the U.S. Census Bureau as the source of the original data only.

*Note:* Detail may not add to total due to rounding.
*Key:*
(a) Total includes other types of intergovernmental revenue not shown separately in this table.

## Table 2.6
## SUMMARY OF FEDERAL GOVERNMENT EXPENDITURE, BY STATE AND OUTLYING AREA: FISCAL YEAR 2010
### (In millions of dollars)

| State and outlying area | Total | Retirement and disability | Other direct payments | Grants | Procurement | Salaries and wages |
|---|---|---|---|---|---|---|
| United States ...................... | $3,276,422 | $914,844 | $818,570 | $683,361 | $516,714 | $342,933 |
| Alabama............................. | 56,496 | 17,977 | 13,151 | 9,273 | 10,482 | 5,613 |
| Alaska................................ | 12,615 | 1,591 | 1,040 | 3,465 | 2,464 | 4,055 |
| Arizona.............................. | 64,427 | 18,535 | 13,738 | 14,361 | 12,813 | 4,980 |
| Arkansas............................ | 28,904 | 10,364 | 7,529 | 6,843 | 1,751 | 2,418 |
| California .......................... | 333,809 | 84,843 | 87,976 | 78,869 | 57,537 | 24,585 |
| Colorado............................ | 49,687 | 12,839 | 9,169 | 8,793 | 10,367 | 8,519 |
| Connecticut....................... | 55,978 | 10,148 | 23,672 | 8,299 | 11,957 | 1,903 |
| Delaware ........................... | 8,076 | 3,056 | 1,895 | 2,055 | 363 | 708 |
| Florida .............................. | 186,704 | 64,375 | 63,317 | 28,066 | 17,981 | 12,964 |
| Georgia.............................. | 92,387 | 26,060 | 19,744 | 16,751 | 12,461 | 17,372 |
| Hawaii................................ | 20,855 | 4,368 | 2,819 | 3,026 | 2,745 | 7,898 |
| Idaho................................. | 14,252 | 4,558 | 2,835 | 2,980 | 2,633 | 1,245 |
| Illinois............................... | 109,967 | 33,844 | 32,513 | 24,060 | 11,601 | 7,949 |
| Indiana.............................. | 58,603 | 19,682 | 17,098 | 11,965 | 5,498 | 4,360 |
| Iowa .................................. | 28,379 | 9,464 | 8,246 | 6,394 | 2,373 | 1,902 |
| Kansas ............................... | 29,046 | 8,586 | 6,845 | 4,736 | 3,060 | 5,818 |
| Kentucky ........................... | 57,271 | 14,836 | 16,241 | 9,502 | 7,486 | 9,205 |
| Louisiana........................... | 53,214 | 13,033 | 13,101 | 15,088 | 7,291 | 4,703 |
| Maine................................. | 14,644 | 4,893 | 3,094 | 3,787 | 1,736 | 1,134 |
| Maryland ........................... | 96,261 | 19,119 | 21,137 | 14,441 | 26,522 | 15,041 |
| Massachusetts ................... | 82,454 | 18,412 | 21,196 | 22,352 | 15,987 | 4,506 |
| Michigan............................ | 90,921 | 32,404 | 26,675 | 20,577 | 6,467 | 4,798 |
| Minnesota.......................... | 44,376 | 14,273 | 13,256 | 10,528 | 2,950 | 3,368 |
| Mississippi......................... | 31,419 | 9,784 | 8,081 | 7,871 | 2,666 | 3,017 |
| Missouri............................. | 70,348 | 19,221 | 16,801 | 14,003 | 13,002 | 7,321 |
| Montana ............................ | 10,758 | 3,404 | 2,401 | 2,939 | 819 | 1,195 |
| Nebraska ........................... | 16,532 | 5,457 | 4,478 | 3,507 | 1,307 | 1,783 |
| Nevada............................... | 19,771 | 7,245 | 4,475 | 3,702 | 2,407 | 1,942 |
| New Hampshire ................. | 11,335 | 4,304 | 2,405 | 2,311 | 1,435 | 880 |
| New Jersey......................... | 80,990 | 24,824 | 24,895 | 15,457 | 10,236 | 5,578 |
| New Mexico ....................... | 27,959 | 6,629 | 4,343 | 6,720 | 7,499 | 2,768 |
| New York............................ | 202,266 | 53,810 | 57,533 | 63,104 | 13,883 | 13,936 |
| North Carolina................... | 90,737 | 29,611 | 19,587 | 20,099 | 6,091 | 15,349 |
| North Dakota...................... | 8,696 | 2,205 | 2,485 | 2,237 | 685 | 1,083 |
| Ohio................................... | 106,449 | 35,139 | 31,106 | 24,399 | 8,829 | 6,975 |
| Oklahoma........................... | 38,475 | 12,571 | 9,098 | 7,855 | 3,375 | 5,575 |
| Oregon............................... | 33,974 | 12,078 | 8,586 | 8,694 | 2,047 | 2,569 |
| Pennsylvania ..................... | 145,934 | 43,458 | 44,909 | 29,411 | 19,352 | 8,803 |
| Rhode Island...................... | 11,759 | 3,333 | 3,276 | 3,152 | 1,001 | 997 |
| South Carolina................... | 46,578 | 15,926 | 9,653 | 8,210 | 8,171 | 4,618 |
| South Dakota..................... | 9,507 | 2,625 | 2,688 | 2,250 | 913 | 1,031 |
| Tennessee .......................... | 68,866 | 21,116 | 19,677 | 14,094 | 10,141 | 3,837 |
| Texas................................. | 225,725 | 60,423 | 50,157 | 44,624 | 40,594 | 29,926 |
| Utah................................... | 23,545 | 6,026 | 5,580 | 4,987 | 3,758 | 3,195 |
| Vermont............................. | 7,405 | 2,007 | 1,362 | 2,380 | 932 | 724 |
| Virginia.............................. | 136,083 | 28,304 | 16,101 | 12,228 | 58,338 | 21,112 |
| Washington........................ | 70,437 | 20,483 | 13,650 | 14,725 | 10,041 | 11,539 |
| West Virginia..................... | 21,511 | 7,741 | 5,081 | 4,970 | 1,783 | 1,936 |
| Wisconsin .......................... | 54,866 | 16,833 | 13,310 | 11,992 | 9,805 | 2,926 |
| Wyoming ........................... | 6,211 | 1,644 | 1,034 | 2,254 | 569 | 709 |
| Dist. of Columbia .............. | 61,920 | 2,787 | 3,982 | 10,872 | 21,250 | 23,030 |
| American Samoa ............... | 515 | 61 | 15 | 408 | 25 | 6 |
| Fed. States of Micronesia ... | 239 | 1 | 0 | 234 | 4 | 0 |
| Guam ................................. | 2,012 | 294 | 140 | 450 | 752 | 377 |
| Marshall Islands................. | 128 | 0 | 1 | 126 | 1 | 0 |
| No. Mariana Islands .......... | 250 | 33 | 6 | 190 | 12 | 9 |
| Palau ................................. | 29 | 0 | 3 | 24 | 1 | 0 |
| Puerto Rico........................ | 21,118 | 7,951 | 4,960 | 6,313 | 1,043 | 851 |
| U.S. Virgin Islands............. | 821 | 239 | 135 | 334 | 51 | 63 |
| Undistributed..................... | 21,927 | 20 | 285 | 23 | 19,370 | 2,230 |

*Source:* U.S. Census Bureau, *Consolidated Federal Funds Report for Fiscal Year 2010.* Released September 2011.
*Note:* All amounts are aggregates from data included in Tables 2.7–2.11. Data are rounded to millions of dollars. Total expenditure does not include data on contingent liabilities (loans and insurance), which are separately listed in Tables 2.12–2.14. For additional information, see the complete report at *http://www.census.gov/govs/cffr/.*

## Table 2.7
## FEDERAL GOVERNMENT EXPENDITURE FOR DIRECT PAYMENTS FOR INDIVIDUALS FOR RETIREMENT AND DISABILITY, FOR SELECTED PROGRAMS, BY STATE AND OUTLYING AREA: FISCAL YEAR 2010
### (In thousands of dollars)

| State and outlying area | Total | Social Security payments | | | Supplemental security income payments | Federal retirement and disability benefits | | Veterans benefits | | Other |
|---|---|---|---|---|---|---|---|---|---|---|
| | | Retirement insurance payments | Survivors insurance payments | Disability insurance payments | | Civilian | Military | Payments for service connected disability | Other benefit payments | |
| United States | $914,844,281 | $439,520,354 | $134,385,878 | $121,915,341 | $47,309,384 | $71,298,307 | $38,938,539 | $33,504,791 | $5,787,890 | $22,183,796 |
| Alabama | 17,976,710 | 7,022,609 | 2,639,225 | 3,150,665 | 1,040,164 | 1,738,920 | 1,072,132 | 758,641 | 211,165 | 343,189 |
| Alaska | 1,590,715 | 585,920 | 189,305 | 180,155 | 59,414 | 241,705 | 177,176 | 130,570 | 6,763 | 19,706 |
| Arizona | 18,534,733 | 9,401,560 | 2,419,237 | 2,235,109 | 692,633 | 1,468,698 | 1,074,974 | 799,620 | 102,644 | 340,259 |
| Arkansas | 10,363,578 | 4,355,491 | 1,479,403 | 1,900,132 | 641,336 | 670,462 | 437,072 | 537,508 | 87,405 | 254,769 |
| California | 84,843,120 | 42,083,369 | 11,996,531 | 10,220,047 | 6,775,261 | 5,834,653 | 3,416,228 | 2,669,987 | 452,831 | 1,394,212 |
| Colorado | 12,838,967 | 5,816,455 | 1,664,485 | 1,384,768 | 388,572 | 1,333,685 | 1,108,827 | 665,770 | 76,630 | 399,775 |
| Connecticut | 10,148,333 | 6,100,611 | 1,519,851 | 1,207,376 | 365,288 | 414,567 | 189,530 | 197,182 | 31,569 | 122,359 |
| Delaware | 3,055,821 | 1,556,717 | 411,318 | 409,412 | 98,445 | 262,539 | 149,964 | 93,311 | 12,266 | 61,849 |
| Florida | 64,374,873 | 33,155,556 | 8,372,392 | 7,240,671 | 2,927,188 | 4,630,728 | 3,873,088 | 2,557,197 | 453,864 | 1,164,189 |
| Georgia | 26,059,533 | 11,351,876 | 3,655,220 | 3,669,575 | 1,340,554 | 2,290,881 | 1,704,434 | 1,185,604 | 229,046 | 632,343 |
| Hawaii | 4,368,434 | 2,086,678 | 465,732 | 350,655 | 150,417 | 688,205 | 347,016 | 181,502 | 18,543 | 79,685 |
| Idaho | 4,558,243 | 2,190,139 | 626,376 | 561,264 | 167,433 | 397,739 | 234,980 | 202,921 | 23,376 | 154,014 |
| Illinois | 33,844,226 | 17,653,892 | 5,674,343 | 4,196,490 | 1,831,430 | 1,861,351 | 655,689 | 719,759 | 133,480 | 1,117,793 |
| Indiana | 19,682,084 | 10,187,459 | 3,272,126 | 2,789,577 | 745,131 | 970,752 | 385,113 | 537,425 | 100,988 | 693,513 |
| Iowa | 9,463,840 | 5,070,620 | 1,564,521 | 1,023,933 | 289,093 | 562,149 | 187,212 | 259,704 | 50,980 | 455,627 |
| Kansas | 8,585,999 | 4,204,897 | 1,285,329 | 998,676 | 280,350 | 668,296 | 405,329 | 276,304 | 46,820 | 419,998 |
| Kentucky | 14,836,487 | 5,809,404 | 2,359,723 | 2,914,969 | 1,187,419 | 934,676 | 451,554 | 627,309 | 100,986 | 450,448 |
| Louisiana | 13,032,975 | 5,089,099 | 2,667,275 | 2,117,223 | 1,073,288 | 758,907 | 452,391 | 504,724 | 125,607 | 244,463 |
| Maine | 4,892,633 | 2,221,116 | 651,736 | 792,288 | 213,283 | 389,965 | 206,223 | 303,791 | 32,509 | 81,722 |
| Maryland | 19,118,589 | 7,417,117 | 2,187,063 | 1,747,722 | 674,467 | 4,878,422 | 1,145,329 | 543,275 | 76,372 | 448,822 |
| Massachusetts | 18,412,164 | 9,506,531 | 2,622,752 | 2,819,179 | 1,098,669 | 1,153,894 | 320,372 | 546,649 | 90,031 | 254,086 |
| Michigan | 32,453,554 | 17,025,380 | 5,394,952 | 4,865,536 | 1,634,664 | 1,189,195 | 429,306 | 766,462 | 165,862 | 932,197 |
| Minnesota | 14,272,953 | 7,784,787 | 2,100,895 | 1,691,211 | 546,047 | 758,512 | 273,409 | 601,862 | 70,246 | 445,984 |
| Mississippi | 9,784,007 | 3,935,597 | 1,524,916 | 1,814,931 | 742,052 | 706,115 | 458,799 | 329,288 | 82,829 | 189,479 |
| Missouri | 19,221,076 | 9,117,644 | 2,896,729 | 2,899,708 | 813,322 | 1,477,880 | 632,104 | 682,038 | 143,491 | 558,161 |
| Montana | 3,403,858 | 1,549,239 | 468,643 | 366,170 | 102,861 | 365,009 | 154,892 | 188,261 | 21,231 | 187,551 |
| Nebraska | 5,457,220 | 2,615,780 | 796,594 | 562,607 | 149,685 | 359,111 | 273,788 | 316,256 | 39,357 | 344,041 |
| Nevada | 7,245,056 | 3,565,926 | 867,062 | 864,300 | 252,015 | 611,071 | 526,384 | 322,527 | 44,632 | 191,138 |
| New Hampshire | 4,304,020 | 2,227,109 | 543,449 | 662,433 | 105,177 | 343,070 | 187,581 | 153,664 | 20,835 | 60,702 |
| New Jersey | 24,823,721 | 14,275,546 | 3,732,822 | 3,049,774 | 983,094 | 1,478,229 | 331,080 | 524,247 | 77,244 | 371,686 |
| New Mexico | 6,628,644 | 2,673,069 | 848,916 | 840,297 | 367,926 | 791,427 | 426,379 | 424,922 | 46,944 | 208,763 |
| New York | 53,810,003 | 28,886,409 | 7,907,557 | 7,660,882 | 4,025,241 | 2,521,136 | 563,429 | 1,104,218 | 208,532 | 932,599 |
| North Carolina | 29,611,049 | 14,098,082 | 3,805,301 | 4,584,024 | 1,297,027 | 2,074,033 | 1,648,746 | 1,438,434 | 204,027 | 461,374 |
| North Dakota | 2,205,046 | 929,576 | 352,772 | 181,825 | 45,655 | 172,123 | 79,631 | 89,033 | 11,226 | 343,206 |
| Ohio | 35,139,148 | 17,243,645 | 6,419,579 | 4,443,158 | 1,849,691 | 2,003,442 | 773,921 | 905,011 | 233,348 | 1,267,353 |

See footnotes at end of table.

# FEDERAL GOVERNMENT EXPENDITURE FOR DIRECT PAYMENTS FOR INDIVIDUALS FOR RETIREMENT AND DISABILITY, FOR SELECTED PROGRAMS, BY STATE AND OUTLYING AREA: FISCAL YEAR 2010—Continued

(In thousands of dollars)

| State and outlying area | Total | Social Security payments | | | Supplemental security income payments | Federal retirement and disability benefits | | Veterans benefits | | Other |
|---|---|---|---|---|---|---|---|---|---|---|
| | | Retirement insurance payments | Survivors insurance payments | Disability insurance payments | | Civilian | Military | Payments for service connected disability | Other benefit payments | |
| Oklahoma | 12,571,476 | 5,298,983 | 1,848,786 | 1,722,201 | 577,756 | 1,301,374 | 595,148 | 881,412 | 128,918 | 216,899 |
| Oregon | 12,078,061 | 6,221,514 | 1,660,695 | 1,438,250 | 457,848 | 966,161 | 377,022 | 612,127 | 81,066 | 263,379 |
| Pennsylvania | 43,458,124 | 22,116,709 | 7,079,628 | 5,559,914 | 2,314,513 | 2,911,617 | 853,213 | 998,742 | 253,109 | 1,370,679 |
| Rhode Island | 3,333,043 | 1,721,654 | 422,269 | 501,581 | 193,146 | 223,865 | 114,863 | 107,485 | 19,789 | 28,391 |
| South Carolina | 15,925,573 | 7,286,724 | 2,108,537 | 2,467,244 | 640,488 | 1,197,855 | 1,047,958 | 755,691 | 135,808 | 285,269 |
| South Dakota | 2,624,575 | 1,232,513 | 387,168 | 241,659 | 79,863 | 273,322 | 127,231 | 127,385 | 19,810 | 135,624 |
| Tennessee | 21,115,983 | 9,525,674 | 3,103,122 | 3,336,661 | 1,054,423 | 1,638,362 | 923,786 | 805,196 | 190,181 | 538,579 |
| Texas | 60,422,731 | 26,035,911 | 9,638,015 | 7,738,427 | 3,608,643 | 4,511,248 | 3,804,435 | 3,177,566 | 484,710 | 1,423,777 |
| Utah | 6,025,588 | 2,736,644 | 819,846 | 616,792 | 170,534 | 1,008,201 | 289,627 | 189,001 | 26,337 | 168,605 |
| Vermont | 2,006,915 | 1,062,188 | 283,074 | 291,817 | 77,786 | 123,443 | 60,887 | 70,353 | 8,518 | 28,850 |
| Virginia | 28,304,390 | 10,473,953 | 3,116,684 | 2,995,057 | 891,291 | 4,871,388 | 3,913,394 | 1,225,974 | 154,553 | 662,097 |
| Washington | 20,483,118 | 9,616,430 | 2,563,689 | 2,373,326 | 918,740 | 1,889,329 | 1,398,303 | 1,023,124 | 118,556 | 581,620 |
| West Virginia | 7,740,791 | 2,986,962 | 1,362,703 | 1,461,319 | 513,036 | 497,866 | 170,074 | 360,410 | 55,391 | 333,030 |
| Wisconsin | 16,832,509 | 9,356,610 | 2,603,462 | 2,154,683 | 652,669 | 728,828 | 306,563 | 561,075 | 102,496 | 366,124 |
| Wyoming | 1,643,992 | 781,778 | 228,513 | 172,968 | 36,134 | 162,677 | 90,500 | 75,146 | 8,923 | 87,354 |
| Dist. of Columbia | 2,786,717 | 545,756 | 161,469 | 168,092 | 162,917 | 1,605,221 | 60,259 | 42,639 | 10,366 | 29,998 |
| American Samoa | 60,732 | 16,732 | 17,319 | 15,258 | 0 | 1,882 | 1,603 | 6,909 | 838 | 142 |
| Fed. States of Micronesia | 577 | 0 | 0 | 0 | 0 | 301 | 0 | 268 | 8 | 0 |
| Guam | 294,106 | 110,217 | 51,479 | 26,132 | 0 | 57,295 | 23,861 | 21,393 | 2,591 | 1,138 |
| Marshall Islands | 104 | 0 | 0 | 0 | 0 | 33 | 0 | 62 | 8 | 2 |
| No. Mariana Islands | 32,971 | 8,840 | 6,469 | 2,208 | 5,305 | 7,841 | 853 | 1,066 | 65 | 324 |
| Palau | 296 | 0 | 10 | 1 | 0 | 189 | 0 | 57 | 39 | 0 |
| Puerto Rico | 7,951,300 | 3,439,821 | 1,501,662 | 2,208,140 | 0 | 299,200 | 22,873 | 314,132 | 131,627 | 33,846 |
| Virgin Islands | 239,101 | 149,834 | 37,149 | 26,871 | 0 | 19,140 | 2,004 | 2,604 | 504 | 995 |
| Undistributed | 20,141 | 0 | 0 | 0 | 0 | 125 | 0 | | 20,000 | 16 |

*Source:* U.S. Census Bureau, *Consolidated Federal Funds Report for Fiscal Year 2010.* Released September 2011.

*Note:* Reported amounts represent obligations of federal funds during the fiscal year. Detail may not add to total because of rounding. For additional information see the complete report at *http://www.census.gov/govs/cffr/.*

Table 2.8
## FEDERAL GOVERNMENT EXPENDITURE FOR DIRECT PAYMENTS OTHER THAN FOR RETIREMENT AND DISABILITY, FOR SELECTED PROGRAMS, BY STATE AND OUTLYING AREA: FISCAL YEAR 2010
(In thousands of dollars)

| State and outlying area | Total | Medicare benefits | | | Excess earned income tax credits | Unemployment compensation |
|---|---|---|---|---|---|---|
| | | Hospital insurance | Supplementary medical insurance | Medical prescription drug coverage | | |
| United States ................. | $818,569,598 | $246,104,816 | $205,150,069 | $60,374,211 | $51,987,860 | $67,805,206 |
| Alabama ............................ | 13,150,613 | 4,610,035 | 3,336,335 | 339,634 | 1,251,833 | 532,526 |
| Alaska ................................ | 1,040,048 | 205,670 | 142,990 | 0 | 85,428 | 227,725 |
| Arizona .............................. | 13,737,523 | 3,552,474 | 3,334,796 | 153,377 | 1,110,735 | 860,353 |
| Arkansas............................ | 7,528,636 | 2,459,005 | 1,878,416 | 79,275 | 669,992 | 451,347 |
| California .......................... | 87,975,802 | 26,936,049 | 25,312,585 | 4,012,440 | 5,579,213 | 10,191,136 |
| Colorado ........................... | 9,169,422 | 2,457,480 | 2,101,044 | 96,805 | 612,650 | 1,083,620 |
| Connecticut ...................... | 23,671,786 | 3,569,357 | 2,927,307 | 14,104,997 | 349,697 | 1,335,289 |
| Delaware ........................... | 1,895,122 | 626,214 | 523,584 | 0 | 133,898 | 168,447 |
| Florida ............................... | 63,317,425 | 18,589,503 | 18,987,624 | 9,016,761 | 3,866,796 | 2,687,146 |
| Georgia .............................. | 19,744,248 | 5,734,981 | 4,492,684 | 12,772 | 2,362,954 | 1,364,786 |
| Hawaii................................ | 2,818,818 | 728,692 | 712,979 | 47,212 | 192,101 | 328,139 |
| Idaho.................................. | 2,835,379 | 709,077 | 590,114 | 20,918 | 259,802 | 306,064 |
| Illinois............................... | 32,513,201 | 11,190,731 | 8,536,869 | 77,891 | 1,970,092 | 3,605,000 |
| Indiana............................... | 17,098,384 | 5,020,907 | 3,819,751 | 146,915 | 1,055,909 | 1,217,206 |
| Iowa ................................... | 8,245,693 | 2,163,114 | 2,056,568 | 389,205 | 381,386 | 586,857 |
| Kansas ............................... | 6,845,131 | 2,157,921 | 1,921,866 | 45,689 | 412,734 | 568,252 |
| Kentucky ........................... | 16,240,943 | 3,563,967 | 2,666,541 | 5,462,945 | 793,317 | 784,440 |
| Louisiana ........................... | 13,100,565 | 5,229,186 | 3,398,906 | 74,847 | 1,235,788 | 463,765 |
| Maine.................................. | 3,094,131 | 1,025,888 | 807,840 | 3,251 | 166,073 | 233,323 |
| Maryland ........................... | 21,136,992 | 4,454,325 | 3,875,244 | 6,201,324 | 726,911 | 900,650 |
| Massachusetts ................... | 21,196,285 | 7,982,779 | 5,394,565 | 313,196 | 633,653 | 2,308,801 |
| Michigan............................ | 26,675,409 | 8,807,550 | 7,989,918 | 310,135 | 1,558,842 | 2,570,944 |
| Minnesota.......................... | 13,256,139 | 3,226,311 | 2,596,482 | 1,751,952 | 579,073 | 1,435,381 |
| Mississippi ........................ | 8,081,114 | 2,720,910 | 1,885,083 | 0 | 972,651 | 258,604 |
| Missouri............................. | 16,801,445 | 5,375,938 | 4,255,941 | 214,424 | 1,024,431 | 912,212 |
| Montana ............................ | 2,401,167 | 620,824 | 528,467 | 3,941 | 149,597 | 178,168 |
| Nebraska ............................ | 4,478,144 | 1,128,858 | 1,008,005 | 5,203 | 251,788 | 197,811 |
| Nevada ............................... | 4,475,356 | 1,159,055 | 1,070,022 | 52,227 | 422,423 | 900,876 |
| New Hampshire ................. | 2,404,840 | 844,213 | 633,360 | 0 | 121,951 | 196,081 |
| New Jersey ......................... | 24,895,378 | 8,184,437 | 7,199,537 | 1,449,730 | 1,025,619 | 3,639,044 |
| New Mexico ....................... | 4,343,264 | 1,024,214 | 937,987 | 48,804 | 448,767 | 456,650 |
| New York ........................... | 57,532,891 | 19,626,810 | 16,549,087 | 1,626,915 | 3,047,551 | 4,729,790 |
| North Carolina................... | 19,586,868 | 5,804,776 | 4,445,335 | 120,727 | 1,871,955 | 2,289,141 |
| North Dakota..................... | 2,485,932 | 493,785 | 427,040 | 286 | 77,602 | 74,250 |
| Ohio.................................... | 31,106,418 | 10,301,948 | 8,437,371 | 1,720,276 | 1,851,942 | 2,516,781 |
| Oklahoma........................... | 9,098,454 | 3,291,923 | 2,239,069 | 52,636 | 717,909 | 400,246 |
| Oregon................................ | 8,585,949 | 2,243,861 | 2,047,767 | 323,596 | 484,135 | 1,239,530 |
| Pennsylvania ..................... | 44,909,415 | 15,423,832 | 12,229,119 | 4,092,196 | 1,659,351 | 4,168,690 |
| Rhode Island...................... | 3,276,159 | 1,117,464 | 828,458 | 42,852 | 146,882 | 380,654 |
| South Carolina................... | 9,652,828 | 2,837,121 | 2,306,502 | 60,081 | 1,051,273 | 666,028 |
| South Dakota..................... | 2,688,397 | 542,563 | 452,563 | -182 | 121,008 | 47,057 |
| Tennessee .......................... | 19,677,186 | 5,683,446 | 3,607,646 | 3,993,012 | 1,331,437 | 852,777 |
| Texas.................................. | 50,157,177 | 15,485,358 | 11,289,018 | 937,555 | 5,717,800 | 3,555,053 |
| Utah.................................... | 5,579,665 | 968,250 | 743,464 | 1,827,366 | 374,770 | 377,550 |
| Vermont.............................. | 1,362,318 | 439,297 | 316,875 | 566 | 67,992 | 151,003 |
| Virginia.............................. | 16,101,200 | 4,525,252 | 3,819,546 | 63,642 | 1,121,187 | 815,085 |
| Washington........................ | 13,649,579 | 3,620,546 | 3,255,752 | 99,600 | 776,043 | 2,085,924 |
| West Virginia..................... | 5,080,665 | 1,921,685 | 1,495,298 | 0 | 306,071 | 265,777 |
| Wisconsin .......................... | 13,310,062 | 3,773,697 | 3,207,952 | 554,390 | 692,116 | 1,530,428 |
| Wyoming ............................ | 1,033,868 | 320,355 | 247,083 | 0 | 65,994 | 127,654 |
| Dist. of Columbia .............. | 3,981,710 | 683,975 | 585,375 | 10,899 | 94,822 | 196,873 |
| American Samoa ............... | 14,817 | 0 | 0 | 0 | 0 | 0 |
| Fed. States of Micronesia ... | 98 | 0 | 0 | 0 | 0 | 0 |
| Guam .................................. | 140,497 | 1,304 | 1,026 | 0 | 0 | 0 |
| Marshall Islands................. | 583 | 0 | 0 | 0 | 0 | 0 |
| No. Mariana Islands .......... | 6,352 | 0 | 0 | 0 | 0 | 0 |
| Palau .................................. | 3,386 | 0 | 0 | 0 | 0 | 0 |
| Puerto Rico ........................ | 4,959,551 | 914,968 | 1,676,897 | 411,926 | 3,916 | 371,510 |
| U.S. Virgin Islands ............. | 135,150 | 22,937 | 18,422 | 0 | 0 | 12,762 |
| Undistributed..................... | 284,557 | 0 | 0 | 0 | 0 | 0 |

See footnotes at end of table.

## FEDERAL GOVERNMENT EXPENDITURE FOR DIRECT PAYMENTS OTHER THAN FOR RETIREMENT AND DISABILITY, FOR SELECTED PROGRAMS, BY STATE AND OUTLYING AREA: FISCAL YEAR 2010 — Continued
### (In thousands of dollars)

| State and outlying area | Supplemental Nutrition Assistance Program (SNAP) | Housing assistance | Agricultural assistance | Federal employees life and health insurance | Student financial assistance | Other |
|---|---|---|---|---|---|---|
| United States .................... | $64,739,425 | $14,174,051 | $17,319,993 | $26,931,571 | $50,036,521 | $13,945,876 |
| Alabama............................ | 1,226,019 | 331,280 | 241,399 | 426,626 | 678,879 | 176,046 |
| Alaska................................ | 159,414 | 20,984 | 19,219 | 2,178 | 34,905 | 141,536 |
| Arizona.............................. | 1,587,702 | 82,403 | 132,847 | 377,517 | 1,990,198 | 555,121 |
| Arkansas............................ | 686,401 | 90,856 | 525,985 | 147,096 | 439,865 | 100,399 |
| California.......................... | 5,694,137 | 1,114,049 | 795,332 | 1,999,631 | 4,932,653 | 1,408,577 |
| Colorado............................ | 687,709 | 155,333 | 290,763 | 414,982 | 974,248 | 294,788 |
| Connecticut ...................... | 569,684 | 230,155 | 33,190 | 164,436 | 262,392 | 125,282 |
| Delaware ........................... | 171,155 | 50,181 | 66,904 | 64,979 | 58,139 | 31,620 |
| Florida............................... | 4,416,943 | 483,155 | 335,312 | 1,286,527 | 2,767,856 | 879,804 |
| Georgia.............................. | 2,565,170 | 416,925 | 395,265 | 735,379 | 1,114,066 | 549,266 |
| Hawaii................................ | 358,145 | 44,558 | 14,515 | 218,175 | 73,906 | 100,396 |
| Idaho.................................. | 299,552 | 27,587 | 266,938 | 101,867 | 177,841 | 75,620 |
| Illinois............................... | 2,784,474 | 739,582 | 855,342 | 693,174 | 1,693,692 | 366,355 |
| Indiana............................... | 1,291,225 | 288,301 | 457,789 | 351,305 | 3,313,203 | 135,872 |
| Iowa ................................... | 526,119 | 55,742 | 878,982 | 208,928 | 909,022 | 89,771 |
| Kansas................................ | 402,630 | 86,370 | 741,704 | 153,009 | 264,592 | 90,362 |
| Kentucky ........................... | 1,186,291 | 195,728 | 460,302 | 273,969 | 690,429 | 163,013 |
| Louisiana........................... | 1,286,199 | 151,975 | 350,015 | 228,134 | 528,197 | 153,554 |
| Maine................................. | 356,097 | 73,843 | 102,027 | 116,953 | 141,840 | 66,996 |
| Maryland............................ | 877,976 | 341,960 | 92,782 | 3,012,564 | 402,861 | 250,395 |
| Massachusetts ................... | 1,172,300 | 851,806 | 40,290 | 475,556 | 1,800,574 | 222,766 |
| Michigan............................ | 2,808,763 | 333,461 | 301,881 | 394,404 | 1,344,002 | 255,508 |
| Minnesota.......................... | 631,789 | 192,803 | 693,427 | 355,578 | 1,575,769 | 217,573 |
| Mississippi ........................ | 846,543 | 105,759 | 516,732 | 192,352 | 465,940 | 116,541 |
| Missouri ............................ | 1,361,301 | 199,927 | 546,618 | 1,725,397 | 996,726 | 188,529 |
| Montana ............................ | 176,546 | 27,160 | 378,117 | 112,844 | 125,618 | 99,885 |
| Nebraska............................ | 237,577 | 42,874 | 685,470 | 140,594 | 703,265 | 76,699 |
| Nevada............................... | 414,596 | 43,067 | 25,113 | 112,428 | 183,163 | 92,385 |
| New Hampshire ................. | 151,814 | 73,141 | 44,821 | 164,559 | 120,385 | 54,515 |
| New Jersey ........................ | 1,030,293 | 654,440 | 59,635 | 537,841 | 796,765 | 318,038 |
| New Mexico ....................... | 541,806 | 36,474 | 74,383 | 209,611 | 279,135 | 285,432 |
| New York........................... | 4,984,900 | 2,334,802 | 157,086 | 911,977 | 3,023,651 | 540,322 |
| North Carolina.................. | 2,072,127 | 304,085 | 753,755 | 530,399 | 1,033,597 | 360,970 |
| North Dakota..................... | 95,015 | 19,867 | 1,051,791 | 61,336 | 81,816 | 102,605 |
| Ohio................................... | 2,737,409 | 736,346 | 357,065 | 613,735 | 1,494,978 | 338,567 |
| Oklahoma.......................... | 899,656 | 87,784 | 282,184 | 411,132 | 513,207 | 202,709 |
| Oregon............................... | 1,073,261 | 85,209 | 211,314 | 310,082 | 415,582 | 151,612 |
| Pennsylvania ..................... | 2,332,575 | 649,207 | 138,960 | 1,088,192 | 2,755,643 | 371,649 |
| Rhode Island..................... | 237,618 | 190,742 | 10,020 | 65,842 | 187,579 | 68,050 |
| South Carolina.................. | 1,256,298 | 205,605 | 236,073 | 267,489 | 565,536 | 200,821 |
| South Dakota..................... | 153,075 | 19,781 | 705,608 | 36,330 | 472,566 | 138,030 |
| Tennessee .......................... | 1,966,108 | 320,836 | 260,688 | 384,643 | 825,968 | 450,625 |
| Texas................................. | 5,447,397 | 502,699 | 1,368,387 | 1,536,417 | 3,278,298 | 1,039,195 |
| Utah................................... | 367,516 | 18,902 | 40,943 | 314,676 | 458,104 | 88,124 |
| Vermont............................. | 128,139 | 30,355 | 39,872 | 43,966 | 111,335 | 32,919 |
| Virginia............................. | 1,213,496 | 263,751 | 215,822 | 1,872,150 | 1,463,899 | 727,368 |
| Washington........................ | 1,386,586 | 166,170 | 538,774 | 683,407 | 606,475 | 430,302 |
| West Virginia..................... | 486,940 | 69,189 | 21,782 | 184,110 | 232,558 | 97,256 |
| Wisconsin .......................... | 1,000,496 | 118,168 | 347,951 | 316,214 | 1,566,248 | 202,402 |
| Wyoming ........................... | 51,675 | 13,901 | 71,936 | 60,267 | 50,843 | 24,160 |
| Dist. of Columbia ............. | 195,893 | 115,235 | 54,059 | 1,723,418 | 64,457 | 256,704 |
| American Samoa .............. | 6,624 | 0 | 116 | 0 | 6,570 | 1,507 |
| Fed. States of Micronesia ... | 0 | 0 | 0 | 0 | 0 | 98 |
| Guam ................................ | 96,695 | 6,180 | 414 | 20,698 | 8,829 | 5,351 |
| Marshall Islands................ | 575 | 0 | 0 | 0 | 0 | 8 |
| No. Mariana Islands .......... | 35 | 1,339 | 0 | 0 | 2,866 | 2,112 |
| Palau................................. | 0 | 0 | 0 | 0 | 3,386 | 0 |
| Puerto Rico........................ | 0 | 343,891 | 31,729 | 95,051 | 966,682 | 142,981 |
| U.S. Virgin Islands ............. | 42,942 | 28,126 | 563 | 1,448 | 5,722 | 2,228 |
| Undistributed..................... | 0 | 0 | 0 | 0 | 0 | 284,557 |

*Source:* U.S. Census Bureau, *Consolidated Federal Funds Report for Fiscal Year 2010.* Released September 2011.

*Note:* Reported amounts represent obligations of federal funds dur-ing the fiscal year. Detail may not add to total because of rounding. For additional information see the complete report at *http://www.census. gov/govs/cffr/*.

## Table 2.9
## FEDERAL GOVERNMENT EXPENDITURE FOR GRANTS, BY AGENCY, BY STATE AND OUTLYING AREA: FISCAL YEAR 2010 (In thousands of dollars)

| State and outlying area | Total | Agency for International Development | Dept. of Agriculture | Appalachian Regional Commission | Dept. of Commerce | Corporation for Nat'l & Community Service | Corporation for Public Broadcasting | Dept. of Defense | Delta Regional Authority |
|---|---|---|---|---|---|---|---|---|---|
| United States ............... | $683,361,474 | $6,914,881 | $36,138,937 | $74,778 | $6,276,841 | $729,643 | $164,629 | $4,854,393 | $137,564 |
| Alabama ...................... | 9,273,415 | 13,078 | 535,177 | 5,154 | 197,991 | 8,182 | 1,275 | 42,272 | 2,743 |
| Alaska.......................... | 3,465,207 | 0 | 274,298 | 0 | 73,422 | 3,786 | 2,095 | 36,558 | 0 |
| Arizona........................ | 14,360,990 | 23,114 | 696,173 | 0 | 86,169 | 10,027 | 5,362 | 126,677 | 0 |
| Arkansas...................... | 6,843,035 | 38,242 | 623,757 | 0 | 120,426 | 6,943 | 645 | 41,434 | 2,311 |
| California .................... | 78,868,861 | 383,251 | 4,054,728 | 0 | 493,176 | 53,169 | 8,929 | 379,558 | 0 |
| Colorado...................... | 8,792,919 | 4,106 | 398,873 | 0 | 277,731 | 10,460 | 440 | 57,518 | 0 |
| Connecticut................. | 8,298,863 | 118,405 | 226,696 | 500 | 110,780 | 6,111 | 105 | 54,724 | 0 |
| Delaware ..................... | 2,055,157 | 1,400 | 117,109 | 0 | 24,885 | 2,143 | 0 | 22,456 | 0 |
| Florida ........................ | 28,066,276 | 16,041 | 1,609,695 | 0 | 165,144 | 22,444 | 10,252 | 146,578 | 0 |
| Georgia........................ | 16,750,617 | 65,970 | 1,238,634 | 4,752 | 95,050 | 14,504 | 10,184 | 104,670 | 0 |
| Hawaii.......................... | 3,025,551 | 0 | 137,170 | 0 | 92,419 | 4,767 | 0 | 97,606 | 0 |
| Idaho........................... | 2,979,516 | 0 | 182,414 | 0 | 12,520 | 4,210 | 1,836 | 35,235 | 0 |
| Illinois......................... | 24,060,063 | 11,778 | 1,078,143 | 0 | 265,352 | 18,214 | 2,989 | 137,782 | 1,408 |
| Indiana......................... | 11,964,781 | 18,052 | 604,189 | 0 | 48,211 | 9,790 | 3,863 | 128,092 | 0 |
| Iowa ............................ | 6,394,423 | 0 | 413,157 | 0 | 98,344 | 9,563 | 4,113 | 60,877 | 0 |
| Kansas ......................... | 4,736,253 | 444 | 379,270 | 0 | 21,391 | 6,435 | 1,641 | 43,534 | 0 |
| Kentucky ..................... | 9,502,246 | 2,400 | 686,290 | 12,187 | 68,256 | 13,292 | 5,209 | 61,942 | 4,039 |
| Louisiana..................... | 15,087,553 | 0 | 648,865 | 0 | 177,969 | 11,152 | 786 | 43,667 | 3,615 |
| Maine........................... | 3,787,423 | 2,667 | 136,855 | 0 | 97,912 | 4,394 | 86 | 59,106 | 0 |
| Maryland ..................... | 14,441,372 | 762,983 | 514,329 | 2,440 | 218,869 | 28,340 | 4,421 | 350,500 | 0 |
| Massachusetts ............. | 22,351,806 | 332,191 | 493,016 | 8 | 166,041 | 56,716 | 606 | 275,968 | 0 |
| Michigan...................... | 20,577,316 | 11,987 | 951,205 | 0 | 175,488 | 18,636 | 8,128 | 120,529 | 0 |
| Minnesota.................... | 10,527,842 | 27,303 | 569,048 | 0 | 54,333 | 23,826 | 2,505 | 102,551 | 0 |
| Mississippi................... | 7,871,132 | 687 | 521,818 | 5,516 | 168,519 | 15,388 | 2,682 | 14,365 | 3,151 |
| Missouri....................... | 14,002,545 | 200 | 697,760 | 0 | 122,421 | 11,293 | 6,002 | 58,976 | 32,228 |
| Montana ...................... | 2,939,432 | 0 | 224,513 | 0 | 27,443 | 7,915 | 1,750 | 34,878 | 0 |
| Nebraska...................... | 3,506,958 | 4,083 | 216,413 | 0 | 27,870 | 5,288 | 3,623 | 72,415 | 0 |
| Nevada......................... | 3,701,764 | 0 | 203,002 | 0 | 47,128 | 4,487 | 1,734 | 47,042 | 0 |
| New Hampshire ........... | 2,311,054 | 0 | 94,369 | 0 | 74,551 | 5,820 | 1,871 | 43,392 | 0 |
| New Jersey ................... | 15,456,752 | 2,700 | 644,183 | 0 | 72,841 | 13,200 | 3,439 | 98,274 | 0 |
| New Mexico ................. | 6,720,212 | 2,075 | 382,783 | 0 | 91,474 | 7,168 | 4,093 | 27,923 | 0 |
| New York...................... | 63,103,569 | 510,274 | 1,959,327 | 2,768 | 211,003 | 69,164 | 4,686 | 205,647 | 0 |
| North Carolina............. | 20,098,865 | 260,952 | 1,063,377 | 5,471 | 172,336 | 10,452 | 5,435 | 143,318 | 0 |
| North Dakota............... | 2,237,318 | 0 | 146,327 | 0 | 22,480 | 1,993 | 0 | 32,399 | 0 |
| Ohio............................. | 24,398,975 | 0 | 983,976 | 5,330 | 199,305 | 19,517 | 5,262 | 110,971 | 0 |
| Oklahoma.................... | 7,854,822 | 2,568 | 617,501 | 0 | 103,850 | 6,572 | 3,306 | 46,472 | 0 |
| Oregon......................... | 8,694,475 | 142,174 | 440,488 | 0 | 110,909 | 14,254 | 1,491 | 84,166 | 0 |
| Pennsylvania ............... | 29,411,180 | 11,748 | 987,072 | 6,708 | 211,885 | 25,111 | 4,429 | 239,540 | 0 |
| Rhode Island............... | 3,152,040 | 12,544 | 87,008 | 0 | 37,686 | 4,109 | 0 | 25,538 | 0 |
| South Carolina............. | 8,210,467 | 2,950 | 530,667 | 2,679 | 53,412 | 6,338 | 3,692 | 85,393 | 0 |
| South Dakota............... | 2,250,151 | 0 | 141,165 | 0 | 29,415 | 1,992 | 1,714 | 22,771 | 0 |
| Tennessee .................... | 14,094,421 | 3,178 | 732,109 | 8,481 | 36,686 | 10,579 | 1,525 | 69,516 | 88,070 |
| Texas............................ | 44,624,108 | 18,539 | 3,087,506 | 0 | 139,270 | 25,833 | 7,299 | 239,785 | 0 |
| Utah............................. | 4,986,698 | 450 | 291,468 | 0 | 41,384 | 7,517 | 5,959 | 36,743 | 0 |
| Vermont....................... | 2,379,905 | 44,631 | 169,068 | 0 | 53,568 | 3,322 | 0 | 16,770 | 0 |
| Virginia........................ | 12,227,540 | 282,829 | 606,172 | 3,561 | 179,613 | 8,170 | 1,836 | 192,788 | 0 |
| Washington.................. | 14,725,393 | 184,149 | 669,907 | 0 | 305,030 | 26,475 | 5,103 | 69,837 | 0 |
| West Virginia............... | 4,970,193 | 300 | 287,168 | 9,036 | 159,771 | 7,674 | 1,713 | 52,489 | 0 |
| Wisconsin.................... | 11,992,040 | 3,468 | 629,943 | 0 | 123,376 | 23,408 | 5,077 | 76,533 | 0 |
| Wyoming ..................... | 2,254,133 | 0 | 54,879 | 0 | 12,322 | 2,920 | 1,241 | 15,315 | 0 |
| Dist. of Columbia ........ | 10,871,983 | 3,593,671 | 127,847 | 186 | 148,181 | 29,049 | 0 | 134,819 | 0 |
| American Samoa ......... | 407,747 | 0 | 114,186 | 0 | 10,063 | 926 | 719 | 0 | 0 |
| Fed. States of Micronesia............ | 234,260 | 0 | 2,131 | 0 | 0 | 0 | 0 | 0 | 0 |
| Guam ........................... | 449,636 | 0 | 25,143 | 0 | 10,980 | 291 | 0 | 4,463 | 0 |
| Marshall Islands........... | 126,383 | 0 | 614 | 0 | 0 | 0 | 0 | 0 | 0 |
| No. Mariana Islands .... | 189,560 | 0 | 27,927 | 0 | 3,475 | 0 | 0 | 0 | 0 |
| Palau............................ | 24,350 | 0 | 263 | 0 | 0 | 0 | 0 | 0 | 0 |
| Puerto Rico.................. | 6,313,385 | 0 | 2,771,856 | 0 | 56,793 | 5,560 | 3,478 | 18,609 | 0 |
| U.S. Virgin Islands ....... | 333,716 | 0 | 29,912 | 0 | 69,918 | 754 | 0 | 3,416 | 0 |
| Undistributed............... | 22,825 | 0 | 0 | 0 | 0 | 0 | 0 | 0 | 0 |

*Source:* U.S. Census Bureau, *Consolidated Federal Funds Report for Fiscal Year 2010.* Released September 2011.

*Note:* Grants data in the CFFR generally cover obligations, which may or may not result in actual expenditures. Obligations that do not result in expenditures may become deobligated.

## FEDERAL GOVERNMENT EXPENDITURE FOR GRANTS, BY AGENCY, BY STATE AND OUTLYING AREA: FISCAL YEAR 2010 (In thousands of dollars) — Continued

| State and outlying area | Dept. of Education (a) | Election Assistance Commission | Dept. of Energy | Environmental Protection Agency | Dept. of Health & Human Services | Dept. of Homeland Security | Dept. of Housing & Urban Development | Institute of Museum & Library Services |
|---|---|---|---|---|---|---|---|---|
| United States ............... | $58,435,480 | $91,411 | $17,213,880 | $5,039,275 | $407,400,747 | $6,715,966 | $36,444,479 | $267,910 |
| Alabama...................... | 816,732 | 0 | 259,080 | 72,267 | 5,456,000 | 46,609 | 382,004 | 4,470 |
| Alaska......................... | 354,919 | 1,425 | 56,174 | 93,276 | 1,260,343 | 15,824 | 174,410 | 2,051 |
| Arizona....................... | 1,186,137 | 1,211 | 220,161 | 81,059 | 9,386,327 | 12,737 | 710,896 | 4,118 |
| Arkansas..................... | 539,715 | 647 | 44,258 | 37,423 | 4,100,153 | 76,899 | 265,117 | 2,276 |
| California .................... | 6,113,724 | 0 | 1,832,381 | 437,157 | 49,943,908 | 148,663 | 4,890,767 | 27,287 |
| Colorado...................... | 778,909 | 19 | 392,569 | 75,498 | 4,343,686 | 7,671 | 399,628 | 4,025 |
| Connecticut................. | 497,262 | 0 | 143,767 | 37,325 | 5,420,795 | 20,386 | 522,237 | 4,038 |
| Delaware ..................... | 285,844 | 0 | 72,951 | 25,064 | 1,103,347 | 8,283 | 78,158 | 1,612 |
| Florida ........................ | 3,471,678 | 1 | 622,648 | 127,959 | 16,341,958 | 110,247 | 1,635,945 | 11,322 |
| Georgia........................ | 1,976,991 | 0 | 225,425 | 119,165 | 9,172,807 | 99,227 | 936,769 | 6,162 |
| Hawaii......................... | 350,842 | 1,075 | 72,399 | 27,348 | 1,465,159 | 5,983 | 170,262 | 3,313 |
| Idaho........................... | 244,390 | 850 | 84,658 | 57,606 | 1,642,179 | 8,562 | 71,033 | 1,509 |
| Illinois........................ | 2,151,486 | 11,951 | 504,210 | 217,454 | 14,084,379 | 259,938 | 1,735,324 | 13,740 |
| Indiana........................ | 977,661 | 58,985 | 472,619 | 109,841 | 7,023,977 | 24,767 | 633,733 | 4,271 |
| Iowa ........................... | 469,729 | 736 | 50,766 | 29,182 | 3,407,244 | 245,420 | 698,135 | 4,392 |
| Kansas ........................ | 508,550 | 2,612 | 103,316 | 28,273 | 2,608,122 | 122,998 | 133,497 | 1,957 |
| Kentucky ..................... | 784,187 | 983 | 52,383 | 35,438 | 6,107,278 | 78,325 | 357,776 | 3,591 |
| Louisiana..................... | 943,295 | 0 | 82,242 | 52,103 | 6,937,961 | 2,909,663 | 1,731,715 | 3,129 |
| Maine.......................... | 229,614 | 0 | 183,580 | 52,819 | 2,436,400 | 6,334 | 151,823 | 3,095 |
| Maryland..................... | 1,112,755 | 3,896 | 485,408 | 118,595 | 8,458,757 | 53,144 | 710,244 | 5,103 |
| Massachusetts .............. | 1,343,654 | 0 | 691,495 | 147,290 | 15,222,188 | 87,255 | 1,328,902 | 5,692 |
| Michigan...................... | 1,689,622 | 1 | 819,572 | 166,255 | 13,132,716 | 7,056 | 937,605 | 9,286 |
| Minnesota.................... | 755,198 | 2,924 | 72,479 | 107,572 | 6,856,108 | 26,374 | 437,235 | 3,827 |
| Mississippi................... | 632,854 | 694 | 149,086 | 54,267 | 4,924,541 | 185,699 | 233,352 | 4,030 |
| Missouri...................... | 936,184 | 34 | 866,236 | 68,420 | 8,645,222 | 87,345 | 519,590 | 4,505 |
| Montana ...................... | 263,460 | 372 | 22,003 | 63,178 | 1,265,305 | 6,608 | 95,468 | 1,420 |
| Nebraska ..................... | 308,745 | 1,271 | 39,333 | 51,191 | 1,965,746 | 37,606 | 119,913 | 2,399 |
| Nevada........................ | 338,977 | 1,194 | 271,427 | 53,158 | 1,572,771 | 4,336 | 225,116 | 2,030 |
| New Hampshire ........... | 195,684 | 0 | 47,220 | 28,872 | 1,287,951 | 14,252 | 120,850 | 1,281 |
| New Jersey ................... | 1,236,620 | 0 | 402,604 | 157,992 | 9,386,960 | 130,453 | 1,041,943 | 5,430 |
| New Mexico ................. | 619,256 | 1,320 | 117,480 | 43,326 | 4,060,150 | 3,898 | 159,898 | 2,100 |
| New York..................... | 4,360,822 | 4,622 | 755,902 | 404,385 | 44,871,269 | 142,982 | 3,570,223 | 18,691 |
| North Carolina............. | 1,865,552 | 7,980 | 825,237 | 118,072 | 12,816,624 | 25,193 | 644,469 | 8,125 |
| North Dakota............... | 201,997 | 350 | 68,828 | 18,458 | 779,242 | 141,098 | 75,372 | 1,108 |
| Ohio............................ | 2,193,617 | 275 | 762,797 | 67,838 | 15,831,507 | 15,763 | 1,215,539 | 7,607 |
| Oklahoma.................... | 703,853 | 1,182 | 175,668 | 96,250 | 4,563,995 | 117,824 | 352,726 | 4,809 |
| Oregon........................ | 608,024 | 11 | 180,302 | 84,775 | 4,965,170 | 49,359 | 345,864 | 2,990 |
| Pennsylvania ............... | 3,813,410 | 7,568 | 979,062 | 265,877 | 18,241,843 | 31,953 | 1,242,090 | 10,330 |
| Rhode Island................ | 269,474 | 850 | 16,161 | 40,863 | 1,972,920 | 53,325 | 144,434 | 1,808 |
| South Carolina............. | 667,410 | 1,011 | 119,898 | 22,247 | 5,287,002 | 7,830 | 250,187 | 4,535 |
| South Dakota............... | 251,002 | 367 | 39,620 | 40,827 | 907,796 | 56,151 | 88,977 | 1,068 |
| Tennessee .................... | 1,441,113 | 0 | 185,651 | 71,855 | 8,865,614 | 199,524 | 545,274 | 5,107 |
| Texas .......................... | 3,710,850 | 19,492 | 691,962 | 315,503 | 26,352,699 | 533,666 | 3,383,050 | 17,268 |
| Utah............................ | 447,493 | 0 | 427,267 | 45,985 | 2,380,279 | 11,118 | 122,504 | 2,407 |
| Vermont....................... | 140,070 | 0 | 111,465 | 38,149 | 1,231,473 | 402 | 72,421 | 1,175 |
| Virginia....................... | 1,214,548 | 65 | 198,315 | 124,876 | 6,206,563 | 276,838 | 592,716 | 5,135 |
| Washington.................. | 1,188,119 | 1,408 | 838,778 | 179,560 | 8,256,187 | 45,701 | 656,344 | 6,103 |
| West Virginia................ | 338,197 | 1,413 | 49,736 | 71,540 | 2,815,304 | 31,960 | 131,573 | 1,891 |
| Wisconsin.................... | 860,129 | 5,673 | 541,198 | 72,715 | 7,512,866 | 56,274 | 460,550 | 4,586 |
| Wyoming ..................... | 134,423 | 0 | 31,054 | 32,608 | 521,623 | 453 | 27,710 | 1,001 |
| Dist. of Columbia ........ | 730,240 | 0 | 667,679 | 95,265 | 2,593,072 | 16,786 | 342,565 | 5,050 |
| American Samoa ......... | 42,765 | 0 | 10,221 | 20,759 | 30,358 | 41,693 | 1,510 | 130 |
| Fed. States of Micronesia............ | 0 | 0 | 0 | 0 | 0 | -252 | 0 | 103 |
| Guam.......................... | 153,834 | 0 | 26,776 | 5,605 | 54,181 | -1,079 | 40,806 | 141 |
| Marshall Islands........... | 0 | 0 | 0 | 0 | 0 | -2 | 0 | 103 |
| No. Mariana Islands .... | 62,636 | 0 | 9,886 | 14,356 | 0 | 218 | 5,856 | 187 |
| Palau........................... | 3,277 | 0 | 0 | 0 | 0 | 0 | 0 | 320 |
| Puerto Rico.................. | 808,957 | 33 | 39,698 | 11,631 | 1,292,139 | 7,894 | 499,156 | 2,559 |
| U.S. Virgin Islands ....... | 109,177 | 0 | 787 | 2,899 | 30,583 | 733 | 23,215 | 110 |
| Undistributed............... | 0 | 0 | 0 | 0 | 0 | 0 | 0 | 0 |

Deobligations are shown as negative amounts in the data. *http://www.census.gov/govs/cffr/.*
Detail may not add to total because of rounding.

Key:
(a) Data for certain programs come from *Federal Aid to States for Fiscal Year 2010.*

## FEDERAL GOVERNMENT EXPENDITURE FOR GRANTS, BY AGENCY, BY STATE AND OUTLYING AREA: FISCAL YEAR 2010 (In thousands of dollars) — Continued

| State and outlying area | Dept. of the Interior | Dept. of Justice | Dept. of Labor | NASA | National Archives and Records Admin. | National Endowment for the Arts | National Endowment for the Humanities | National Science Foundation |
|---|---|---|---|---|---|---|---|---|
| United States ............. | $6,528,169 | $3,766,198 | $10,124,288 | $926,694 | $9,711 | $139,414 | $140,318 | $6,932,870 |
| Alabama...................... | 52,041 | 64,408 | 137,544 | 25,165 | 106 | 1,417 | 855 | 43,766 |
| Alaska......................... | 151,421 | 17,285 | 56,014 | 6,076 | 0 | 985 | 871 | 64,151 |
| Arizona....................... | 147,958 | 95,354 | 146,416 | 28,649 | 80 | 1,465 | 1,775 | 121,162 |
| Arkansas..................... | 30,764 | 28,960 | 100,754 | 1,307 | 0 | 1,005 | 1,204 | 28,808 |
| California .................... | 524,904 | 554,187 | 1,299,569 | 123,321 | 990 | 12,388 | 10,634 | 954,606 |
| Colorado...................... | 235,309 | 60,550 | 129,952 | 51,332 | 130 | 3,461 | 1,534 | 388,631 |
| Connecticut ................ | 8,083 | 37,969 | 140,561 | 2,929 | 310 | 1,954 | 2,087 | 63,638 |
| Delaware ..................... | 6,977 | 17,708 | 27,688 | 3,494 | 133 | 932 | 1,043 | 35,794 |
| Florida ........................ | 56,990 | 244,083 | 393,618 | 31,152 | 0 | 2,272 | 2,031 | 197,639 |
| Georgia........................ | 23,873 | 137,415 | 217,305 | 10,494 | 59 | 3,694 | 2,352 | 137,267 |
| Hawaii......................... | 54,677 | 9,884 | 50,181 | 18,370 | 73 | 1,086 | 1,696 | 70,359 |
| Idaho.......................... | 60,985 | 19,516 | 68,516 | 6,216 | 55 | 1,013 | 6,932 | 21,213 |
| Illinois........................ | 48,482 | 140,752 | 405,038 | 10,195 | 243 | 4,536 | 5,938 | 350,259 |
| Indiana........................ | 28,781 | 43,486 | 226,316 | 6,512 | 139 | 1,559 | 2,174 | 166,046 |
| Iowa ........................... | 20,103 | 31,707 | 92,096 | 5,063 | 244 | 942 | 1,230 | 57,883 |
| Kansas ........................ | 26,544 | 25,744 | 62,645 | 2,508 | 105 | 996 | 1,089 | 48,521 |
| Kentucky ..................... | 73,274 | 52,390 | 137,319 | 4,885 | 0 | 1,421 | 1,098 | 25,542 |
| Louisiana..................... | 105,678 | 31,325 | 116,995 | 5,355 | 74 | 2,213 | 1,302 | 50,122 |
| Maine.......................... | 14,247 | 14,459 | 58,326 | 4,478 | 70 | 1,344 | 1,059 | 33,843 |
| Maryland ..................... | 27,335 | 108,607 | 256,309 | 124,083 | 435 | 4,307 | 3,279 | 150,760 |
| Massachusetts ............. | 28,404 | 72,358 | 215,281 | 55,680 | 637 | 5,419 | 10,095 | 481,923 |
| Michigan...................... | 46,512 | 83,206 | 542,064 | 16,472 | 357 | 2,169 | 3,478 | 194,998 |
| Minnesota.................... | 43,620 | 48,437 | 186,987 | 7,060 | 193 | 7,579 | 32,558 | 103,438 |
| Mississippi................... | 57,489 | 30,618 | 95,560 | 12,695 | 64 | 984 | 1,143 | 33,731 |
| Missouri...................... | 37,413 | 62,449 | 199,314 | 9,505 | 216 | 3,044 | 2,281 | 54,530 |
| Montana ...................... | 212,876 | 23,849 | 54,025 | 6,464 | 17 | 1,172 | 954 | 28,134 |
| Nebraska ..................... | 41,289 | 21,691 | 51,028 | 4,731 | 86 | 1,083 | 1,358 | 41,181 |
| Nevada........................ | 138,692 | 55,612 | 91,973 | 3,760 | 39 | 924 | 704 | 16,674 |
| New Hampshire ........... | 26,096 | 16,843 | 43,316 | 14,053 | 0 | 997 | 1,128 | 27,702 |
| New Jersey .................. | 11,672 | 85,333 | 272,689 | 10,676 | 636 | 1,880 | 4,109 | 163,843 |
| New Mexico ................. | 470,928 | 32,442 | 60,068 | 6,439 | 0 | 1,542 | 1,643 | 58,226 |
| New York ..................... | 182,063 | 210,514 | 553,152 | 42,649 | 655 | 22,422 | 15,917 | 500,988 |
| North Carolina............. | 32,848 | 77,608 | 302,849 | 11,517 | 85 | 2,422 | 3,757 | 176,024 |
| North Dakota............... | 230,326 | 14,160 | 23,783 | 7,550 | 0 | 910 | 790 | 19,202 |
| Ohio........................... | 17,566 | 85,713 | 404,604 | 15,967 | 225 | 2,183 | 4,326 | 130,034 |
| Oklahoma.................... | 32,706 | 53,586 | 90,655 | 8,300 | 10 | 949 | 866 | 34,037 |
| Oregon........................ | 192,068 | 48,552 | 206,833 | 7,262 | 347 | 1,605 | 2,176 | 84,219 |
| Pennsylvania ................ | 91,973 | 130,153 | 427,445 | 19,798 | 335 | 4,442 | 6,468 | 284,941 |
| Rhode Island................ | 860 | 17,831 | 55,008 | 4,380 | 141 | 1,148 | 1,610 | 51,691 |
| South Carolina............. | 15,015 | 42,722 | 143,997 | 4,031 | 0 | 1,255 | 1,120 | 53,081 |
| South Dakota............... | 153,692 | 15,155 | 34,181 | 4,136 | 5 | 988 | 811 | 17,171 |
| Tennessee ................... | 28,196 | 66,093 | 149,874 | 6,068 | 259 | 1,658 | 2,274 | 65,058 |
| Texas.......................... | 109,868 | 253,043 | 492,153 | 55,837 | 286 | 4,041 | 2,857 | 245,575 |
| Utah........................... | 323,304 | 25,632 | 75,633 | 4,286 | 81 | 1,844 | 1,223 | 42,496 |
| Vermont...................... | 11,500 | 12,663 | 34,850 | 3,002 | 0 | 1,348 | 1,562 | 10,521 |
| Virginia....................... | 105,134 | 153,137 | 273,709 | 46,974 | 806 | 1,879 | 6,505 | 117,731 |
| Washington.................. | 111,645 | 86,132 | 259,128 | 15,115 | 0 | 2,993 | 2,264 | 149,028 |
| West Virginia................ | 301,353 | 35,995 | 53,358 | 14,171 | 0 | 888 | 732 | 14,985 |
| Wisconsin.................... | 41,162 | 62,192 | 210,050 | 13,348 | 292 | 1,367 | 2,066 | 117,531 |
| Wyoming ..................... | 1,065,326 | 8,796 | 25,254 | 3,401 | 197 | 867 | 666 | 12,806 |
| Dist. of Columbia ........ | 107,337 | 67,130 | 226,017 | 16,480 | 476 | 6,539 | 5,574 | 562,325 |
| American Samoa ......... | 67,604 | 1,981 | 27,438 | 0 | 0 | 307 | 344 | 26 |
| Fed. States of Micronesia............. | 207,627 | 0 | 0 | 0 | 0 | 0 | 0 | 0 |
| Guam.......................... | 81,214 | 3,341 | 4,816 | 0 | 0 | 308 | 404 | 170 |
| Marshall Islands........... | 117,668 | 0 | 0 | 0 | 0 | 0 | 0 | 0 |
| No. Mariana Islands .... | 47,464 | 1,539 | 1,459 | 0 | 0 | 0 | 391 | 95 |
| Palau.......................... | 13,305 | 0 | 186 | 0 | 0 | 0 | 0 | 0 |
| Puerto Rico.................. | 6,577 | 20,967 | 105,292 | 3,305 | 19 | 925 | 824 | 25,575 |
| U.S. Virgin Islands........ | 11,349 | 2,935 | 7,505 | 0 | 0 | 342 | 399 | 3,167 |
| Undistributed............... | 8,005 | 0 | 0 | 0 | 0 | 0 | 0 | 0 |

See additional footnotes on next page.

## FEDERAL GOVERNMENT EXPENDITURE FOR GRANTS, BY AGENCY, BY STATE AND OUTLYING AREA: FISCAL YEAR 2010 (In thousands of dollars) — Continued

| State and outlying area | Small Business Admin. | Social Security Admin. | Dept. of State | State Justice Institute | Tennessee Valley Authority (b) | Dept. of Transportation | Dept. of the Treasury (c) | Dept. of Veterans Affairs | Other |
|---|---|---|---|---|---|---|---|---|---|
| United States ............ | $299,811 | $44,343 | $505,734 | $3,256 | $550,309 | $64,330,217 | $1,043,059 | $848,385 | $267,883 |
| Alabama ...................... | 4,468 | 703 | 3,921 | 67 | 125,443 | 956,778 | 2,034 | 10,578 | 1,088 |
| Alaska......................... | 1,780 | 16 | 895 | 12 | 0 | 815,195 | 197 | 649 | 1,079 |
| Arizona....................... | 3,689 | 427 | 7,283 | 73 | 0 | 1,243,352 | 640 | 8,223 | 4,274 |
| Arkansas..................... | 2,922 | 402 | 3,629 | 0 | 0 | 723,488 | 707 | 18,174 | 665 |
| California .................... | 22,574 | 6,351 | 42,212 | 309 | 0 | 6,452,313 | 11,098 | 58,963 | 27,741 |
| Colorado...................... | 4,021 | 291 | 90,321 | 245 | 0 | 1,140,295 | 627 | 12,470 | 3,910 |
| Connecticut ................ | 5,513 | 283 | 4,882 | 1 | 0 | 854,327 | 255 | 10,455 | 2,483 |
| Delaware ..................... | 1,785 | 175 | 997 | 0 | 0 | 208,045 | 328 | 5,573 | 1,233 |
| Florida ........................ | 12,112 | 1,449 | 13,327 | 46 | 0 | 2,772,309 | 12,860 | 27,002 | 7,475 |
| Georgia........................ | 5,923 | 795 | 8,931 | 77 | 8,777 | 2,075,275 | 18,131 | 15,299 | 14,641 |
| Hawaii......................... | 1,091 | 130 | 23,783 | 2 | 0 | 356,144 | 943 | 7,370 | 1,422 |
| Idaho........................... | 1,691 | 175 | 844 | 3 | 0 | 444,050 | 334 | 6,175 | 1,442 |
| Illinois......................... | 12,881 | 1,004 | 18,151 | 4 | 495 | 2,508,207 | 7,856 | 46,434 | 5,437 |
| Indiana........................ | 4,509 | 537 | 8,560 | 81 | 0 | 1,396,448 | 1,015 | 10,735 | 2,922 |
| Iowa............................ | 3,665 | 255 | 6,866 | 7 | 0 | 660,978 | 212 | 19,669 | 1,845 |
| Kansas ........................ | 6,738 | 230 | 3,302 | 27 | 0 | 590,227 | 501 | 4,690 | 345 |
| Kentucky ..................... | 9,269 | 696 | 4,662 | 0 | 49,473 | 849,397 | 755 | 15,303 | 3,187 |
| Louisiana..................... | 6,787 | 572 | 4,681 | 2 | 0 | 1,179,138 | 854 | 32,864 | 3,431 |
| Maine.......................... | 6,181 | 203 | 1,966 | 0 | 0 | 273,169 | 1,766 | 10,778 | 848 |
| Maryland ..................... | 4,564 | 396 | 9,366 | 127 | 0 | 891,843 | 2,197 | 9,964 | 18,015 |
| Massachusetts ............. | 5,049 | 7,783 | 26,831 | 30 | 0 | 1,248,019 | 3,362 | 22,217 | 17,696 |
| Michigan...................... | 7,278 | 3,440 | 10,855 | 84 | 0 | 1,596,603 | 2,056 | 15,023 | 4,634 |
| Minnesota.................... | 4,988 | 365 | 12,607 | 195 | 0 | 1,040,780 | 497 | 13,409 | 12,845 |
| Mississippi .................. | 7,895 | 427 | 1,666 | 4 | 34,587 | 661,447 | 223 | 15,019 | 931 |
| Missouri ...................... | 6,970 | 595 | 8,123 | 15 | 0 | 1,508,001 | 1,911 | 48,487 | 3,275 |
| Montana ...................... | 2,661 | 302 | 3,316 | 0 | 0 | 584,369 | 175 | 4,732 | 2,075 |
| Nebraska ..................... | 3,479 | 177 | 2,811 | 36 | 0 | 468,745 | 86 | 12,242 | 1,040 |
| Nevada........................ | 2,224 | 190 | 2,007 | 39 | 0 | 605,638 | 984 | 8,498 | 1,403 |
| New Hampshire ........... | 1,277 | 175 | 2,616 | 14 | 0 | 253,692 | 592 | 4,770 | 1,669 |
| New Jersey .................. | 9,361 | 602 | 6,091 | 0 | 0 | 1,665,657 | 8,255 | 18,747 | 3,264 |
| New Mexico ................. | 3,788 | 242 | 3,052 | 92 | 0 | 552,775 | 135 | 4,196 | 1,699 |
| New York..................... | 24,555 | 1,823 | 47,291 | 32 | 0 | 4,342,886 | 17,857 | 31,753 | 17,247 |
| North Carolina............. | 6,809 | 905 | 7,716 | 0 | 2,889 | 1,480,419 | 3,725 | 11,716 | 4,981 |
| North Dakota............... | 2,157 | 175 | 1,238 | 0 | 0 | 444,650 | 48 | 2,083 | 594 |
| Ohio............................ | 9,913 | 967 | 13,199 | 4 | 0 | 2,257,211 | 1,516 | 23,717 | 12,526 |
| Oklahoma.................... | 2,799 | 371 | 3,753 | 5 | 0 | 786,746 | 374 | 41,764 | 1,326 |
| Oregon......................... | 2,951 | 290 | 7,477 | 30 | 0 | 1,099,067 | 1,210 | 6,718 | 3,693 |
| Pennsylvania ............... | 8,102 | 1,177 | 17,208 | 11 | 0 | 2,293,719 | 4,455 | 33,876 | 8,449 |
| Rhode Island............... | 2,600 | 175 | 1,361 | 4 | 0 | 305,536 | 287 | 40,603 | 2,084 |
| South Carolina............. | 3,587 | 387 | 3,168 | 4 | 0 | 873,948 | 2,235 | 14,731 | 5,936 |
| South Dakota............... | 2,121 | 177 | 947 | 38 | 0 | 433,848 | 55 | 2,462 | 1,497 |
| Tennessee .................... | 5,349 | 654 | 4,190 | 3 | 327,324 | 1,151,873 | 789 | 18,319 | 2,157 |
| Texas........................... | 14,966 | 1,554 | 16,062 | 65 | 0 | 4,809,460 | 24,249 | 37,053 | 14,318 |
| Utah ............................ | 892 | 175 | 4,719 | 23 | 0 | 667,217 | 212 | 17,227 | 1,160 |
| Vermont....................... | 2,466 | 175 | 2,970 | 78 | 0 | 402,827 | 326 | 8,713 | 4,389 |
| Virginia........................ | 11,117 | 738 | 11,561 | 938 | 1,321 | 1,588,913 | 1,688 | 5,675 | 5,690 |
| Washington.................. | 2,703 | 507 | 13,009 | 55 | 0 | 1,632,799 | 1,825 | 12,854 | 2,633 |
| West Virginia............... | 7,614 | 365 | 1,902 | 2 | 0 | 560,669 | 149 | 17,512 | 734 |
| Wisconsin .................... | 5,029 | 3,617 | 7,735 | 4 | 0 | 1,129,848 | 571 | 17,874 | 3,559 |
| Wyoming ..................... | 1,136 | 175 | 1,363 | 0 | 0 | 297,137 | 341 | 980 | 320 |
| Dist. of Columbia ........ | 1,843 | 50 | 78,872 | 46 | 0 | 786,815 | 519,196 | 1,152 | 7,721 |
| American Samoa ........ | 556 | 25 | 0 | 0 | 0 | 36,139 | 0 | 0 | 0 |
| Fed. States of Micronesia........... | 0 | 0 | 0 | 0 | 0 | 24,650 | 0 | 0 | 0 |
| Guam .......................... | 840 | 25 | 25 | 58 | 0 | 37,204 | 0 | 91 | 0 |
| Marshall Islands........... | 0 | 0 | 0 | 0 | 0 | 8,000 | 0 | 0 | 0 |
| No. Mariana Islands .... | 0 | 25 | 0 | 0 | 0 | 14,046 | 0 | 0 | 0 |
| Palau ........................... | 0 | 0 | 0 | 0 | 0 | 7,000 | 0 | 0 | 0 |
| Puerto Rico.................. | 1,965 | 398 | 248 | 0 | 0 | 245,029 | 380,362 | 2,802 | 733 |
| U.S. Virgin Islands....... | 611 | 25 | 0 | 11 | 0 | 35,859 | 0 | 0 | 10 |
| Undistributed............... | 0 | 0 | 2,456 | 253 | 0 | 0 | 0 | 0 | 12,111 |

(b) Payments in lieu of taxes have been categorized as "grants."

(c) Includes Treasury payments to recipients that are separate from the government of the District of Columbia and Washington Metropolitan Area Transit Authority (WMATA), as well as distributions to state and local governments of seized cash assets and proceeds from the sale of other seized assets.

Table 2.10
# FEDERAL GOVERNMENT EXPENDITURE FOR PROCUREMENT CONTRACTS, BY AGENCY, BY STATE AND OUTLYING AREA: FISCAL YEAR 2010
(In thousands of dollars)

| State and outlying area | Dept. of Defense and nondefense Total | Department of Defense | | | | |
|---|---|---|---|---|---|---|
| | | Total | Army | Navy | Air Force | Other defense |
| United States ............ | $516,713,547 | $331,221,413 | $115,479,251 | $85,135,094 | $61,735,351 | $68,871,718 |
| Alabama .................... | 10,481,742 | 8,140,104 | 4,850,039 | 594,567 | 768,719 | 1,926,779 |
| Alaska...................... | 2,464,278 | 1,776,348 | 875,959 | 155,244 | 516,949 | 228,196 |
| Arizona..................... | 12,813,125 | 10,831,380 | 3,825,695 | 2,438,531 | 1,810,190 | 2,756,964 |
| Arkansas................... | 1,750,994 | 1,137,523 | 585,577 | 15,015 | 70,978 | 465,954 |
| California ................. | 57,536,893 | 41,323,271 | 5,843,352 | 11,941,630 | 13,690,120 | 9,848,169 |
| Colorado.................... | 10,367,046 | 5,631,588 | 969,700 | 152,707 | 3,683,125 | 826,055 |
| Connecticut.............. | 11,956,601 | 11,113,554 | 3,102,705 | 5,086,372 | 1,866,130 | 1,058,346 |
| Delaware .................. | 362,660 | 218,117 | 103,467 | 18,355 | 71,630 | 24,665 |
| Florida ..................... | 17,980,742 | 12,814,205 | 5,174,407 | 2,547,419 | 3,511,777 | 1,580,603 |
| Georgia..................... | 12,460,681 | 8,377,523 | 2,969,595 | 505,632 | 4,306,077 | 596,218 |
| Hawaii...................... | 2,744,816 | 2,350,783 | 881,078 | 1,054,472 | 216,910 | 198,323 |
| Idaho........................ | 2,633,326 | 264,896 | 116,158 | 14,401 | 60,491 | 73,847 |
| Illinois...................... | 11,600,509 | 7,118,663 | 2,433,229 | 1,913,483 | 1,029,622 | 1,742,329 |
| Indiana..................... | 5,498,401 | 4,369,925 | 1,936,952 | 1,219,429 | 281,106 | 932,438 |
| Iowa ........................ | 2,372,595 | 1,556,732 | 564,337 | 358,065 | 522,757 | 111,573 |
| Kansas ..................... | 3,059,665 | 1,940,809 | 878,426 | 43,342 | 930,533 | 88,508 |
| Kentucky .................. | 7,486,132 | 5,180,542 | 1,492,656 | 160,079 | 88,233 | 3,439,574 |
| Louisiana.................. | 7,290,637 | 5,841,727 | 4,743,993 | 564,513 | 139,590 | 393,631 |
| Maine....................... | 1,735,708 | 1,336,189 | 231,405 | 804,606 | 2,362 | 297,816 |
| Maryland .................. | 26,522,496 | 12,017,561 | 4,608,712 | 4,942,339 | 1,170,542 | 1,295,968 |
| Massachusetts ........... | 15,987,355 | 12,673,540 | 5,130,986 | 3,387,735 | 2,484,247 | 1,670,572 |
| Michigan................... | 6,466,608 | 4,080,256 | 2,785,433 | 569,923 | 166,413 | 387,383 |
| Minnesota................. | 2,950,444 | 1,520,342 | 433,093 | 467,834 | 63,110 | 556,305 |
| Mississippi................ | 2,665,904 | 1,634,043 | 796,109 | 318,617 | 240,727 | 278,591 |
| Missouri.................... | 13,002,391 | 10,334,525 | 3,644,967 | 3,777,522 | 1,695,429 | 1,216,607 |
| Montana ................... | 819,401 | 312,740 | 184,962 | 2,602 | 93,970 | 31,205 |
| Nebraska .................. | 1,306,732 | 793,150 | 152,089 | 20,652 | 480,913 | 139,495 |
| Nevada ..................... | 2,407,149 | 1,315,017 | 221,200 | 133,329 | 913,515 | 46,973 |
| New Hampshire ....... | 1,435,344 | 1,091,883 | 427,049 | 336,335 | 168,889 | 159,610 |
| New Jersey ................ | 10,236,358 | 7,857,550 | 4,207,869 | 1,378,826 | 347,356 | 1,923,499 |
| New Mexico .............. | 7,498,864 | 1,519,707 | 740,965 | 72,134 | 597,413 | 109,195 |
| New York................... | 13,883,205 | 8,809,787 | 2,653,402 | 3,741,519 | 835,111 | 1,579,755 |
| North Carolina.......... | 6,090,513 | 3,626,519 | 1,454,713 | 1,207,003 | 190,651 | 774,153 |
| North Dakota............ | 685,259 | 288,154 | 151,987 | 4,228 | 106,904 | 25,044 |
| Ohio........................ | 8,829,337 | 6,064,282 | 1,433,857 | 721,880 | 1,763,982 | 2,144,562 |
| Oklahoma................. | 3,374,782 | 2,409,881 | 1,004,807 | 127,131 | 927,687 | 350,255 |
| Oregon...................... | 2,047,066 | 891,456 | 643,930 | 116,355 | 18,012 | 113,159 |
| Pennsylvania ............. | 19,352,447 | 11,900,948 | 4,216,121 | 3,571,331 | 846,771 | 3,266,725 |
| Rhode Island............. | 1,001,400 | 776,927 | 60,252 | 613,443 | 14,755 | 88,478 |
| South Carolina.......... | 8,171,374 | 4,496,729 | 819,946 | 2,429,595 | 166,467 | 1,080,721 |
| South Dakota............ | 912,913 | 560,697 | 143,093 | 65,417 | 38,853 | 313,334 |
| Tennessee ................. | 10,140,621 | 3,100,865 | 801,300 | 160,557 | 500,290 | 1,638,718 |
| Texas ....................... | 40,594,474 | 30,331,486 | 10,296,066 | 8,627,935 | 7,851,337 | 3,556,148 |
| Utah........................ | 3,758,424 | 2,521,626 | 1,177,681 | 133,965 | 1,033,511 | 176,470 |
| Vermont.................... | 931,642 | 711,273 | 588,789 | 69,538 | 12,712 | 40,234 |
| Virginia..................... | 58,337,629 | 40,377,677 | 15,160,542 | 12,171,205 | 3,510,098 | 519,778 |
| Washington............... | 10,040,842 | 5,150,536 | 926,514 | 2,512,047 | 1,192,197 | 519,778 |
| West Virginia............. | 1,782,542 | 344,646 | 211,011 | 80,647 | 30,534 | 22,454 |
| Wisconsin ................. | 9,805,065 | 8,468,971 | 7,212,107 | 545,057 | 26,636 | 685,171 |
| Wyoming .................. | 569,384 | 155,353 | 45,576 | 2,212 | 77,360 | 30,205 |
| Dist. of Columbia ..... | 21,249,887 | 4,650,999 | 1,182,057 | 2,499,790 | 542,584 | 426,568 |
| American Samoa ...... | 25,432 | 7,952 | 7,821 | 44 | 0 | 88 |
| Fed. States of Micronesia......... | 4,346 | 974 | 0 | 974 | 0 | 0 |
| Guam ....................... | 751,623 | 734,142 | 3,766 | 656,121 | 48,548 | 25,707 |
| Marshall Islands........ | 772 | -24 | -24 | 0 | 0 | 0 |
| No. Mariana Islands... | 12,000 | 2,183 | 52 | 1,592 | 22 | 517 |
| Palau ....................... | 1,246 | 135 | 3 | 131 | 0 | 0 |
| Puerto Rico............... | 1,043,306 | 580,768 | 347,298 | 63,415 | 9,895 | 160,160 |
| U.S. Virgin Islands .... | 50,547 | 22,402 | 22,397 | 0 | 0 | 4 |
| Undistributed (a)...... | 19,369,876 | 7,759,880 | 2,028 | 16,253 | 615 | 7,740,984 |

See footnotes at end of table.

## FEDERAL GOVERNMENT EXPENDITURE FOR PROCUREMENT CONTRACTS, BY AGENCY, BY STATE AND OUTLYING AREA: FISCAL YEAR 2010 — Continued
### (In thousands of dollars)

| State and outlying area | Total | Dept. of Agriculture | Dept. of Commerce | Dept. of Education | Dept. of Energy | Environmental Protection Agency | General Services Admin. | Dept. of Health and Human Services |
|---|---|---|---|---|---|---|---|---|
| United States ............. | $185,492,134 | $6,341,976 | $3,982,344 | $1,618,094 | $25,735,029 | $1,685,923 | $17,107,540 | $18,283,674 |
| Alabama..................... | 2,341,638 | 77,904 | 4,077 | 229 | 1,677 | 1,231 | 238,803 | 134,176 |
| Alaska....................... | 687,931 | 70,339 | 42,840 | 817 | 2,994 | 1,805 | 72,786 | 21,155 |
| Arizona...................... | 1,981,745 | 72,136 | 2,538 | 14,375 | 9,480 | 2,330 | 253,429 | 152,457 |
| Arkansas.................... | 613,471 | 92,947 | 214 | 189 | 3,441 | 121 | 43,130 | 66,363 |
| California ................... | 16,213,622 | 732,228 | 127,282 | 77,970 | 2,708,655 | 74,055 | 1,336,290 | 602,788 |
| Colorado..................... | 4,735,458 | 241,281 | 201,553 | 6,122 | 678,994 | 59,759 | 594,134 | 89,960 |
| Connecticut .............. | 843,048 | 6,168 | 5,475 | 466 | 3,258 | 2,190 | 38,900 | 40,284 |
| Delaware ................... | 144,543 | 3,681 | 1,345 | 273 | 167 | 1,118 | 14,657 | 11,001 |
| Florida ...................... | 5,166,537 | 58,491 | 131,152 | 1,067 | 2,971 | 24,322 | 555,590 | 192,038 |
| Georgia...................... | 4,083,159 | 84,895 | 4,766 | 35,942 | 2,717 | 39,213 | 435,336 | 1,803,89 |
| Hawaii....................... | 394,033 | 9,503 | 18,732 | 4,536 | 0 | 100 | 148,370 | 4,465 |
| Idaho......................... | 2,368,430 | 167,580 | 368 | 201 | 1,344,342 | 1,165 | 27,407 | 1,699 |
| Illinois....................... | 4,481,846 | 222,214 | 7,062 | 66,259 | 1,135,623 | 33,937 | 458,002 | 130,303 |
| Indiana...................... | 1,128,476 | 20,844 | 28,888 | 14,565 | 222 | 5,065 | 116,368 | 162,566 |
| Iowa ......................... | 815,863 | 94,761 | 508 | 22,950 | 32,333 | 173 | 173,452 | 38,568 |
| Kansas ...................... | 1,118,856 | 184,621 | 959 | 1,447 | 11 | 25,630 | 61,884 | 10,691 |
| Kentucky ................... | 2,305,590 | 38,808 | 9,183 | 210 | 264,134 | 4,422 | 171,696 | 15,430 |
| Louisiana .................. | 1,448,910 | 186,963 | 47,587 | 277 | 149,809 | 6,855 | 126,640 | 14,146 |
| Maine........................ | 399,519 | 8,461 | 3,678 | 69 | 0 | 1,082 | 102,129 | 11,110 |
| Maryland................... | 14,504,935 | 148,900 | 1,903,034 | 98,909 | 349,649 | 60,384 | 973,071 | 5,007,655 |
| Massachusetts .......... | 3,313,816 | 41,045 | 65,715 | 39,585 | 2,149 | 93,969 | 215,795 | 327,393 |
| Michigan.................... | 2,386,351 | 132,431 | 7,927 | 2,052 | 4,775 | 53,461 | 788,228 | 270,834 |
| Minnesota.................. | 1,430,102 | 271,528 | 8,431 | 6,881 | 1,352 | 5,816 | 234,869 | 84,371 |
| Mississippi ................ | 1,031,860 | 96,430 | 48,425 | 171 | 339 | 636 | 100,676 | 10,316 |
| Missouri..................... | 2,667,866 | 290,370 | 7,602 | 1,419 | 621,837 | 49,568 | 528,807 | 151,891 |
| Montana .................... | 506,661 | 114,960 | 1,112 | 179 | 1,908 | 255 | 103,201 | 32,298 |
| Nebraska ................... | 513,582 | 91,390 | 8,171 | 176 | 1,396 | 12,874 | 52,304 | 26,709 |
| Nevada...................... | 1,092,133 | 23,401 | 1,773 | 202 | 601,903 | 10,451 | 42,315 | 6,022 |
| New Hampshire ........ | 343,461 | 5,976 | 25,540 | 5,111 | 487 | 10,830 | 18,294 | 19,780 |
| New Jersey ................ | 2,378,808 | 21,255 | 36,391 | 42,322 | 91,595 | 42,574 | 385,546 | 150,752 |
| New Mexico .............. | 5,979,156 | 61,218 | 679 | 208 | 4,810,369 | 3,335 | 84,227 | 177,146 |
| New York ................... | 5,073,418 | 96,010 | 164,115 | 53,693 | 769,403 | 36,696 | 640,333 | 213,998 |
| North Carolina.......... | 2,463,994 | 70,079 | 28,268 | 38,515 | 1,437 | 192,785 | 117,189 | 503,766 |
| North Dakota............. | 397,105 | 74,035 | 335 | 168 | 3,639 | 0 | 38,277 | 115,307 |
| Ohio.......................... | 2,765,055 | 59,630 | 8,574 | 16,120 | 262,253 | 77,006 | 494,402 | 156,862 |
| Oklahoma................... | 964,902 | 42,313 | 2,007 | 5,210 | 23,166 | 5,905 | 92,598 | 134,620 |
| Oregon....................... | 1,155,609 | 255,960 | 20,657 | 4,969 | 5,578 | 4,629 | 221,114 | 25,690 |
| Pennsylvania ............. | 7,451,496 | 143,209 | 70,670 | 35,195 | 919,351 | 72,086 | 302,742 | 3,462,122 |
| Rhode Island............. | 224,473 | 1,612 | 4,256 | 247 | 635 | 7,379 | 25,390 | 15,537 |
| South Carolina.......... | 3,674,645 | 18,827 | 19,368 | 181 | 2,312,193 | 1,068 | 112,112 | 223,111 |
| South Dakota............. | 352,216 | 14,972 | 172 | 154 | 3,969 | 731 | 17,532 | 41,185 |
| Tennessee ................. | 7,039,756 | 162,155 | 9,241 | 238 | 3,459,562 | 2,708 | 81,899 | 126,280 |
| Texas......................... | 10,262,989 | 167,694 | 21,125 | 85,027 | 594,971 | 43,329 | 767,171 | 320,833 |
| Utah.......................... | 1,236,798 | 52,258 | 4,354 | 190 | 39,744 | 4,852 | 123,714 | 25,064 |
| Vermont..................... | 220,368 | 7,756 | 650 | 186 | 12 | 2,422 | 28,490 | 2,089 |
| Virginia...................... | 17,959,952 | 226,786 | 391,088 | 378,081 | 459,183 | 298,039 | 1,885,442 | 1,612,188 |
| Washington................ | 4,890,306 | 118,743 | 52,935 | 3,342 | 3,123,491 | 40,197 | 374,719 | 72,495 |
| West Virginia............. | 1,437,896 | 29,462 | 42,774 | 325 | 285,045 | 2,603 | 124,376 | 20,110 |
| Wisconsin .................. | 1,336,094 | 189,630 | 85,024 | 1,116 | 965 | 22,167 | 71,349 | 92,449 |
| Wyoming ................... | 414,032 | 16,833 | 327 | 202 | 12,668 | 32 | 9,394 | 1,844 |
| Dist. of Columbia ..... | 16,598,888 | 397,708 | 121,764 | 546,429 | 530,257 | 203,121 | 2,842,158 | 753,887 |
| American Samoa ...... | 17,479 | 8,139 | 2,359 | 0 | 0 | 0 | 542 | 85 |
| Fed. States of Micronesia......... | 3,372 | 6 | 1,292 | 0 | 0 | 0 | 0 | 0 |
| Guam......................... | 17,481 | 161 | 2,900 | 0 | 0 | 0 | 8,546 | 0 |
| Marshall Islands........ | 796 | 0 | 453 | 0 | 0 | 0 | 0 | 0 |
| No. Mariana Islands... | 9,818 | 10 | 2,877 | 0 | 0 | 0 | 2,005 | 0 |
| Palau......................... | 1,111 | 9 | 259 | 0 | 0 | 0 | 0 | 765 |
| Puerto Rico................ | 462,538 | 8,407 | 752 | 165 | 53 | 243 | 152,948 | 3,057 |
| U.S. Virgin Islands .... | 28,145 | 186 | 2,967 | 0 | 0 | 7 | 5,756 | 0 |
| Undistributed (a)....... | 11,609,966 | 506,657 | 167,777 | 3,162 | 98,866 | 39,299 | 71,011 | 592,068 |

See footnotes at end of table.

# FEDERAL GOVERNMENT EXPENDITURE FOR PROCUREMENT CONTRACTS, BY AGENCY, BY STATE AND OUTLYING AREA: FISCAL YEAR 2010—Continued
## (In thousands of dollars)

| State and outlying area | Dept. of Homeland Security | Dept. of Housing and Urban Development | Dept. of the Interior | Dept. of Justice | Dept. of Labor | NASA | National Archives and Records Admin. | National Science Foundation |
|---|---|---|---|---|---|---|---|---|
| | | | | Nondefense agencies—continued | | | | |
| United States ............ | $13,754,011 | $1,120,879 | $5,946,225 | $6,780,794 | $2,778,774 | $16,076,522 | $249,764 | $301,582 |
| Alabama...................... | 129,421 | 627 | 18,067 | 59,523 | 15,989 | 935,430 | 0 | 367 |
| Alaska........................ | 102,612 | 84 | 122,948 | 1,880 | 11,046 | 25,494 | 0 | 4 |
| Arizona....................... | 294,162 | 5,409 | 343,388 | 63,280 | 36,353 | 114,401 | 0 | 0 |
| Arkansas..................... | 7,529 | 485 | 11,923 | 23,702 | 8,004 | 1,540 | 562 | 0 |
| California ................... | 731,347 | 46,364 | 953,649 | 307,123 | 148,567 | 3,613,764 | 16,987 | 6,320 |
| Colorado..................... | 102,732 | 14,088 | 392,528 | 38,219 | 10,244 | 1,547,196 | 79 | 35,397 |
| Connecticut ................ | 61,913 | 101 | 5,897 | 17,160 | 11,852 | 123,004 | 39 | 189 |
| Delaware .................... | 5,115 | 108 | 3,596 | 1,341 | 4,165 | 6,223 | 196 | 5 |
| Florida ....................... | 543,058 | 44,150 | 68,887 | 199,429 | 48,649 | 888,812 | 43 | 490 |
| Georgia....................... | 311,324 | 39,112 | 39,824 | 299,798 | 61,287 | 16,837 | 8,751 | 82 |
| Hawaii........................ | 28,276 | 15,949 | 42,508 | 3,044 | 17,020 | 20,212 | 0 | 9 |
| Idaho.......................... | 10,078 | 97 | 64,354 | 3,496 | 10 | 7,077 | 0 | 0 |
| Illinois........................ | 70,228 | 20,272 | 20,804 | 95,182 | 26,444 | 19,897 | 3,097 | 6,087 |
| Indiana........................ | 19,843 | 14,292 | 8,620 | 65,140 | 18,674 | 110,916 | 65 | 53 |
| Iowa ........................... | 51,460 | 0 | 8,273 | 6,359 | 9,793 | 5,990 | 1,111 | 0 |
| Kansas ....................... | 4,391 | 18,519 | 28,567 | 12,218 | 7,642 | 2,699 | 1,632 | 1 |
| Kentucky .................... | 63,669 | 386 | 37,083 | 75,339 | 69,537 | 4,961 | 15 | 19 |
| Louisiana ................... | 118,359 | 13,107 | 73,661 | 50,378 | 21,882 | 305,725 | 44 | 12 |
| Maine......................... | 52,320 | 221 | 20,883 | 2,896 | 18,937 | 4,226 | 0 | 0 |
| Maryland .................... | 500,298 | 69,645 | 266,105 | 366,734 | 132,531 | 1,568,518 | 123,725 | 22,271 |
| Massachusetts ........... | 296,557 | 4,580 | 74,079 | 63,627 | 63,568 | 175,765 | 21,995 | 251 |
| Michigan..................... | 69,625 | 40,481 | 42,175 | 37,020 | 44,031 | 23,040 | 3,861 | 88 |
| Minnesota................... | 28,178 | 4,611 | 25,708 | 24,290 | 11,215 | 15,308 | 132 | 168 |
| Mississippi ................. | 125,975 | 3 | 31,911 | 17,542 | 33,016 | 320,272 | 0 | 0 |
| Missouri...................... | 144,811 | 2,320 | 47,943 | 98,359 | 30,842 | 18,375 | 9,214 | 411 |
| Montana ..................... | 8,966 | 3,634 | 61,124 | 4,576 | 6,570 | 7,590 | 0 | 0 |
| Nebraska .................... | 36,370 | 9,845 | 14,520 | 3,570 | 847 | 5,630 | 37 | 0 |
| Nevada....................... | 12,931 | 1,192 | 116,235 | 7,136 | 40,830 | 4,204 | 0 | 0 |
| New Hampshire ........ | 9,363 | 31,870 | 9,056 | 8,427 | 104 | 20,157 | 13 | 236 |
| New Jersey ................. | 232,289 | 784 | 37,523 | 70,017 | 28,426 | 19,394 | 328 | 495 |
| New Mexico .............. | 50,210 | 1,241 | 247,273 | 126,263 | 23,322 | 114,960 | 0 | 61 |
| New York.................... | 236,519 | 12,161 | 82,885 | 117,269 | 93,783 | 66,265 | 13,629 | 3,502 |
| North Carolina.......... | 153,500 | 22,794 | 52,194 | 109,539 | 14,572 | 14,793 | 2,284 | 3,315 |
| North Dakota............. | 8,174 | 42 | 27,596 | 4,084 | 7,510 | 7,436 | 0 | 0 |
| Ohio........................... | 76,476 | 68,291 | 35,983 | 43,432 | 40,385 | 331,272 | 160 | 90 |
| Oklahoma................... | 43,555 | 28,156 | 33,754 | 61,584 | 33,930 | 10,885 | 278 | -42 |
| Oregon....................... | 34,400 | 5,614 | 126,349 | 11,904 | 27,623 | 9,183 | 0 | 35 |
| Pennsylvania ............. | 97,739 | 28,078 | 114,827 | 159,567 | 96,287 | 39,241 | 338 | 974 |
| Rhode Island.............. | 24,328 | 518 | 2,067 | 2,804 | 4,637 | 5,865 | 0 | 21 |
| South Carolina.......... | 63,144 | 1,355 | 10,381 | 32,328 | 8,835 | 4,965 | 153 | 0 |
| South Dakota............. | 8,320 | 56 | 144,866 | 3,674 | 748 | 4,163 | 0 | 0 |
| Tennessee .................. | 105,160 | 680 | 69,529 | 57,608 | 22,251 | 36,232 | 555 | 29 |
| Texas.......................... | 644,942 | 31,974 | 195,166 | 240,496 | 140,423 | 3,943,696 | 10,812 | 946 |
| Utah........................... | 5,294 | 6,810 | 101,154 | 18,051 | 34,698 | 581,391 | 0 | 6 |
| Vermont...................... | 68,258 | 12 | 2,281 | 1,657 | 7,582 | 3,234 | 0 | 0 |
| Virginia...................... | 3,972,722 | 82,384 | 817,166 | 1,270,123 | 47,006 | 647,337 | 9,421 | 133,028 |
| Washington................. | 230,994 | 1,462 | 143,303 | 14,968 | 29,984 | 30,973 | 12 | 176 |
| West Virginia............. | 129,746 | -5 | 32,182 | 291,477 | 21,418 | 53,009 | 3,255 | 117 |
| Wisconsin .................. | 125,469 | 352 | 70,971 | 62,495 | 6,631 | 17,277 | 32 | 0 |
| Wyoming .................... | 706 | 0 | 114,809 | 1,843 | 7 | 3,579 | 0 | 0 |
| Dist. of Columbia ..... | 2,955,696 | 411,282 | 518,787 | 1,353,375 | 1,133,399 | 132,661 | 8,624 | 80,238 |
| American Samoa ...... | 4,821 | 0 | 300 | 732 | 0 | 4 | 0 | 0 |
| Fed. States of Micronesia......... | 1,652 | 0 | 0 | 0 | 0 | 0 | 0 | 0 |
| Guam ......................... | 500 | 0 | 230 | 382 | 44 | 0 | 0 | 0 |
| Marshall Islands........ | 0 | 0 | 0 | 0 | 0 | 0 | 0 | 0 |
| No. Mariana Islands... | 81 | 0 | 1,855 | 0 | 15 | 0 | 0 | 0 |
| Palau ......................... | 0 | 0 | 0 | 0 | 0 | 0 | 0 | 0 |
| Puerto Rico................ | 22,596 | 81 | 4,166 | 15,196 | 23,590 | 3,040 | 0 | 0 |
| U.S. Virgin Islands .... | 2,307 | 1,574 | 3,861 | 355 | 0 | 0 | 0 | 0 |
| Undistributed (a)...... | 513,501 | 13,630 | 0 | 753,442 | 22,021 | 82,406 | 8,285 | 6,133 |

See footnotes at end of table.

## FEDERAL GOVERNMENT EXPENDITURE FOR PROCUREMENT CONTRACTS, BY AGENCY, BY STATE AND OUTLYING AREA: FISCAL YEAR 2010—Continued
### (In thousands of dollars)

| State and outlying area | U.S. Postal Service (b) | Small Business Admin. | Social Security Admin. | Dept. of State | Dept. of Transportation | Dept. of the Treasury | Dept. of Veterans Affairs | Other nondefense (c) |
|---|---|---|---|---|---|---|---|---|
| | | | | Nondefense agencies—continued | | | | |
| United States ............ | $15,315,806 | $130,740 | $1,072,619 | $3,862,040 | $5,660,601 | $5,933,343 | $23,398,187 | $8,355,666 |
| Alabama.................... | 204,402 | 957 | 3,755 | 21,811 | 7,359 | 4,167 | 167,952 | 313,714 |
| Alaska....................... | 36,670 | 0 | 42,917 | 35,205 | 71,377 | 884 | 23,155 | 920 |
| Arizona..................... | 225,343 | 0 | 1,002 | 4,866 | 88,436 | 4,330 | 288,954 | 5,075 |
| Arkansas................... | 132,169 | 2,766 | 682 | 23,564 | 7,114 | 583 | 182,142 | 4,410 |
| California .................. | 1,577,359 | 5,503 | 27,359 | 72,131 | 293,313 | 1,480,533 | 1,243,736 | 30,298 |
| Colorado.................... | 254,002 | 139 | 9,115 | 4,466 | 84,708 | 18,796 | 276,716 | 75,232 |
| Connecticut .............. | 205,440 | 616 | 4,678 | 223,421 | 9,900 | 3,608 | 74,790 | 3,698 |
| Delaware................... | 44,500 | 0 | 74 | 276 | 146 | 589 | 45,464 | 503 |
| Florida ..................... | 821,265 | 97 | 2,950 | 62,360 | 198,979 | 8,837 | 1,266,999 | 45,902 |
| Georgia..................... | 417,763 | 851 | 10,381 | 5,498 | 98,705 | 20,254 | 290,320 | 55,607 |
| Hawaii....................... | 555,512 | 0 | 1,410 | 986 | -5,956 | 461 | 27,452 | 1,445 |
| Idaho........................ | 59,867 | 0 | 315 | 2,496 | 31,714 | 600,976 | 44,621 | 566 |
| Illinois...................... | 734,047 | 1,273 | 43,010 | 89,587 | 28,869 | 94,536 | 1,096,187 | 78,925 |
| Indiana...................... | 292,906 | 31 | 2,248 | 4,804 | 17,079 | 44,223 | 157,728 | 23,339 |
| Iowa ......................... | 182,829 | 35 | 1,145 | 1,257 | 17,370 | 78,445 | 87,495 | 1,555 |
| Kansas ...................... | 181,746 | 4 | 1,660 | 584 | 29,997 | 485 | 539,452 | 4,017 |
| Kentucky ................... | 194,067 | 8 | 9,559 | 1,876 | 2,983 | 13,242 | 136,248 | 1,192,735 |
| Louisiana .................. | 191,043 | 313 | 1,034 | 6,234 | 20,179 | 1,890 | 102,658 | 10,112 |
| Maine........................ | 82,524 | 10 | 25,259 | 234 | 6,488 | 78 | 58,645 | 269 |
| Maryland ................... | 313,215 | 6,958 | 360,243 | 98,005 | 517,872 | 899,768 | 370,606 | 346,839 |
| Massachusetts ........... | 402,035 | 1,781 | 15,597 | 28,987 | 309,679 | 334,092 | 399,955 | 335,618 |
| Michigan.................... | 517,279 | 600 | 17,812 | 40,852 | 10,881 | 31,286 | 241,314 | 6,298 |
| Minnesota.................. | 305,881 | 646 | 974 | 11,741 | 8,335 | 14,848 | 325,684 | 39,134 |
| Mississippi ................ | 114,454 | 600 | 1,766 | -109 | 11,942 | 7,059 | 102,327 | 8,110 |
| Missouri.................... | 364,011 | 7 | 18,223 | 1,856 | 10,817 | 12,772 | 253,746 | 2,664 |
| Montana .................... | 52,714 | 8 | 624 | 140 | 72,671 | 249 | 33,468 | 414 |
| Nebraska ................... | 109,197 | 3,559 | 527 | 1,543 | 4,149 | 487 | 119,987 | 10,296 |
| Nevada...................... | 100,847 | 25 | 370 | 742 | 24,753 | 734 | 95,302 | 764 |
| New Hampshire ........ | 79,252 | 102 | 787 | 56,394 | 9,516 | 4,348 | 26,624 | 1,193 |
| New Jersey ................ | 554,896 | 729 | 6,471 | 10,806 | 439,034 | 21,335 | 157,931 | 27,915 |
| New Mexico .............. | 78,597 | 11 | 1,397 | 68,615 | 19,043 | 816 | 108,946 | 859 |
| New York................... | 1,085,737 | 2,094 | 14,978 | 42,948 | 95,779 | 397,326 | 789,128 | 45,168 |
| North Carolina.......... | 429,813 | 0 | 7,409 | 86,035 | 53,836 | 3,195 | 243,127 | 315,548 |
| North Dakota............. | 42,627 | 0 | 269 | 4 | 3,186 | 4,455 | 59,537 | 426 |
| Ohio.......................... | 585,044 | 589 | 4,973 | 15,708 | 34,591 | 35,958 | 398,073 | 19,183 |
| Oklahoma.................. | 167,349 | 0 | 257 | 26,235 | 134,433 | 5,282 | 108,023 | 5,403 |
| Oregon...................... | 160,940 | 174 | 448 | 12,191 | 69,921 | 2,179 | 154,928 | 1,124 |
| Pennsylvania ............. | 732,084 | 177 | 8,759 | 18,111 | 225,143 | 38,360 | 617,600 | 268,836 |
| Rhode Island............. | 63,839 | 0 | 85 | 64 | 3,461 | 4,015 | 57,366 | 347 |
| South Carolina.......... | 171,185 | 599 | 1,238 | 106,183 | 34,084 | 943 | 531,685 | 20,259 |
| South Dakota............. | 49,352 | 0 | 310 | 72 | 3,687 | 20 | 58,023 | 209 |
| Tennessee ................. | 290,762 | 425 | 4,949 | 13,216 | 82,295 | 74,719 | 720,842 | 1,718,420 |
| Texas........................ | 973,472 | 748 | 47,808 | 337,850 | 88,138 | 177,154 | 1,373,963 | 55,249 |
| Utah.......................... | 121,788 | 125 | 575 | 2,939 | 12,631 | 8,841 | 107,645 | -15,325 |
| Vermont.................... | 41,431 | 0 | 196 | 175 | 1,588 | 1 | 47,713 | 4,637 |
| Virginia..................... | 393,031 | 17,215 | 216,686 | 1,268,328 | 1,318,718 | 545,282 | 583,544 | 1,387,153 |
| Washington................ | 284,286 | -41 | 16,487 | 1,687 | 35,227 | 2,723 | 286,353 | 25,791 |
| West Virginia............. | 93,739 | 0 | 705 | 10,283 | 1,202 | 71,531 | 215,306 | 9,236 |
| Wisconsin ................. | 286,384 | 0 | 3,105 | 3,011 | 19,645 | 3,783 | 265,983 | 8,257 |
| Wyoming ................... | 26,199 | 0 | 205 | 71 | 27,790 | 2,373 | 54,305 | 140,844 |
| Dist. of Columbia ..... | 121,021 | 75,395 | 43,411 | 930,750 | 755,728 | 748,068 | 729,455 | 1,205,675 |
| American Samoa ...... | 316 | 0 | 0 | 104 | 82 | 0 | 655 | 0 |
| Fed. States of Micronesia......... | 0 | 0 | 0 | 422 | 0 | 0 | 0 | 0 |
| Guam........................ | 2,437 | 0 | 0 | 0 | 2,107 | 9 | 156 | 11 |
| Marshall Islands........ | 0 | 0 | 0 | 271 | 0 | 0 | 0 | 72 |
| No. Mariana Islands... | 248 | 0 | 0 | 26 | 0 | 0 | 0 | 2,702 |
| Palau ........................ | 0 | 0 | 0 | 78 | 0 | 0 | 0 | 0 |
| Puerto Rico............... | 64,900 | 125 | 359 | 344 | 769 | 300 | 160,721 | 726 |
| U.S. Virgin Islands .... | 4,355 | 0 | 0 | 0 | 4,923 | 237 | 310 | 1,308 |
| Undistributed (a)...... | 237,633 | 5,483 | 86,082 | 103,712 | 203,823 | 101,877 | 7,487,144 | 505,984 |

See footnotes at end of table.

# FEDERAL GOVERNMENT EXPENDITURE FOR PROCUREMENT CONTRACTS, BY AGENCY, BY STATE AND OUTLYING AREA: FISCAL YEAR 2010—Continued

*Source:* U.S. Census Bureau, *Consolidated Federal Funds Report for Fiscal Year 2010.* Released September 2011.

*Note:* Detail may not add to total because of rounding. Data shown for U.S. Postal Service represent actual outlays for contractual commitments, while all other amounts shown represent the value of contract actions, and do not reflect federal government expenditures. Nonpostal data generally involve only current-year contract actions; however, multiple-year obligations may be reflected for contract actions of less than three years duration. Negative amounts represent the deobligation of prior-year contracts. For additional information, see the complete report at *http://www.census.gov/govs/www/cffr.html.*

*Key:*

(a) For all agencies, this line includes procurement purchases made using government-issued purchase cards.

(b) Data shown for U.S. Postal Service represent actual outlays for contractual commitments.

(c) Includes Fiscal Year 2000 procurement data for the Tennessee Valley Authority, which did not provide Fiscal Year 2010 procurement data.

## Table 2.11
## FEDERAL GOVERNMENT EXPENDITURE FOR SALARIES AND WAGES, BY AGENCY, BY STATE AND OUTLYING AREA: FISCAL YEAR 2010
(In thousands of dollars)

| | | | | | Department of Defense | | | | | |
| | | | | | | Military services | | | Army | |
| State and outlying area | Total | Nondefense civilian (a) | Total | Other defense civilian | Total | Active military | Inactive military | Civilian | Total | Active military |
|---|---|---|---|---|---|---|---|---|---|---|
| United States ............ | $342,932,897 | $160,986,795 | $181,946,102 | $4,639,006 | $177,307,096 | $117,123,493 | $33,992,042 | $26,191,561 | $132,972,125 | $90,972,416 |
| Alabama ..................... | 5,613,172 | 1,838,220 | 3,774,952 | 163,807 | 3,611,145 | 1,792,554 | 959,608 | 858,983 | 3,213,328 | 1,534,648 |
| Alaska........................ | 4,055,081 | 833,775 | 3,221,306 | 11,259 | 3,210,047 | 2,918,191 | 111,568 | 180,288 | 2,537,499 | 2,348,736 |
| Arizona...................... | 4,980,419 | 2,750,909 | 2,229,510 | 52,871 | 2,176,639 | 1,603,575 | 260,606 | 312,458 | 1,299,525 | 919,144 |
| Arkansas.................... | 2,417,754 | 1,066,248 | 1,351,506 | 3,412 | 1,348,094 | 532,801 | 695,713 | 119,580 | 1,005,934 | 244,001 |
| California .................. | 24,584,616 | 13,953,654 | 10,630,962 | 301,261 | 10,329,701 | 5,734,898 | 1,947,557 | 2,647,246 | 4,310,569 | 2,150,600 |
| Colorado.................... | 8,518,503 | 3,105,486 | 5,413,017 | 74,118 | 5,338,899 | 4,480,378 | 440,515 | 418,006 | 4,374,434 | 3,836,987 |
| Connecticut............... | 1,902,732 | 1,280,597 | 622,135 | 37,211 | 584,924 | 248,145 | 259,571 | 77,208 | 410,762 | 145,443 |
| Delaware.................... | 707,577 | 281,075 | 426,502 | 2,207 | 424,295 | 250,336 | 112,364 | 61,595 | 169,022 | 56,262 |
| Florida....................... | 12,964,458 | 7,150,991 | 5,813,467 | 93,924 | 5,719,543 | 3,231,117 | 1,277,050 | 1,211,376 | 2,578,648 | 1,221,522 |
| Georgia...................... | 17,372,039 | 4,764,869 | 12,607,170 | 105,793 | 12,501,377 | 9,841,524 | 1,346,060 | 1,313,793 | 10,843,422 | 9,097,251 |
| Hawaii........................ | 7,897,604 | 689,616 | 7,207,988 | 37,312 | 7,170,676 | 6,066,537 | 416,927 | 687,212 | 5,609,317 | 5,043,963 |
| Idaho......................... | 1,245,268 | 701,387 | 543,881 | 1,789 | 542,092 | 299,271 | 190,273 | 52,548 | 304,926 | 96,735 |
| Illinois....................... | 7,949,473 | 5,419,135 | 2,530,338 | 58,611 | 2,471,727 | 925,078 | 979,567 | 567,082 | 1,738,322 | 486,284 |
| Indiana....................... | 4,359,723 | 2,095,528 | 2,264,195 | 208,946 | 2,055,249 | 519,947 | 1,282,602 | 252,700 | 1,818,634 | 492,851 |
| Iowa........................... | 1,902,300 | 1,125,751 | 776,549 | 2,352 | 774,197 | 208,450 | 516,348 | 49,399 | 721,584 | 190,964 |
| Kansas ....................... | 5,818,464 | 1,287,109 | 4,531,355 | 12,078 | 4,519,277 | 3,788,378 | 491,264 | 239,635 | 4,280,536 | 3,601,893 |
| Kentucky ................... | 9,204,720 | 1,646,671 | 7,558,049 | 32,393 | 7,525,656 | 6,696,409 | 579,397 | 249,850 | 7,473,297 | 6,669,454 |
| Louisiana................... | 4,702,517 | 1,742,949 | 2,959,568 | 11,389 | 2,948,179 | 2,028,830 | 702,234 | 217,115 | 2,457,265 | 1,658,614 |
| Maine......................... | 1,134,025 | 583,793 | 550,232 | 21,349 | 528,883 | 131,927 | 134,991 | 261,965 | 209,711 | 70,045 |
| Maryland ................... | 15,041,483 | 9,877,623 | 5,163,860 | 137,103 | 5,026,757 | 2,672,245 | 627,029 | 1,727,483 | 2,939,369 | 1,693,258 |
| Massachusetts........... | 4,505,976 | 3,213,810 | 1,292,166 | 57,724 | 1,234,442 | 425,744 | 525,430 | 283,268 | 881,870 | 288,159 |
| Michigan.................... | 4,798,229 | 3,371,766 | 1,426,463 | 77,578 | 1,348,885 | 385,084 | 648,846 | 314,955 | 1,238,475 | 335,805 |
| Minnesota.................. | 3,368,345 | 2,150,242 | 1,218,103 | 10,956 | 1,207,147 | 297,292 | 830,763 | 79,182 | 1,130,770 | 269,161 |
| Mississippi................ | 3,016,702 | 1,054,121 | 1,962,581 | 9,240 | 1,953,341 | 751,844 | 875,489 | 326,008 | 1,259,953 | 286,201 |
| Missouri..................... | 7,320,606 | 3,212,726 | 4,107,880 | 32,307 | 4,075,573 | 1,916,028 | 1,879,076 | 280,469 | 3,735,244 | 1,700,125 |
| Montana ..................... | 1,194,568 | 750,775 | 443,793 | 1,026 | 442,767 | 225,902 | 166,774 | 50,091 | 253,497 | 76,271 |
| Nebraska ................... | 1,782,751 | 809,950 | 972,801 | 2,866 | 969,935 | 495,561 | 320,005 | 154,369 | 502,544 | 140,725 |
| Nevada...................... | 1,941,696 | 934,382 | 1,007,314 | 4,407 | 1,002,907 | 684,563 | 232,752 | 85,592 | 338,448 | 109,863 |
| New Hampshire ........ | 880,039 | 600,058 | 279,981 | 8,697 | 271,284 | 99,154 | 140,647 | 31,483 | 218,411 | 66,482 |
| New Jersey ............... | 5,577,865 | 3,513,392 | 2,064,473 | 37,231 | 2,027,242 | 687,135 | 691,807 | 648,300 | 1,491,905 | 378,163 |
| New Mexico .............. | 2,768,001 | 1,505,941 | 1,262,060 | 20,236 | 1,241,824 | 744,123 | 207,712 | 289,989 | 486,687 | 182,116 |
| New York................... | 13,936,494 | 8,270,409 | 5,666,085 | 85,996 | 5,580,089 | 4,108,369 | 1,114,394 | 357,326 | 5,253,456 | 3,949,961 |
| North Carolina.......... | 15,349,417 | 3,161,081 | 12,188,336 | 76,929 | 12,111,407 | 10,414,617 | 1,073,523 | 623,267 | 10,285,323 | 8,960,987 |
| North Dakota............. | 1,083,469 | 444,560 | 638,909 | 1,778 | 637,131 | 390,444 | 184,160 | 62,527 | 273,039 | 78,307 |
| Ohio........................... | 6,974,864 | 3,969,933 | 3,004,931 | 464,147 | 2,540,784 | 786,217 | 898,921 | 855,646 | 1,274,216 | 372,368 |
| Oklahoma.................. | 5,575,449 | 1,618,451 | 3,956,998 | 55,810 | 3,901,188 | 2,370,682 | 671,632 | 858,874 | 2,678,192 | 1,866,537 |
| Oregon....................... | 2,568,512 | 1,760,746 | 807,766 | 1,361 | 806,405 | 201,441 | 492,020 | 112,944 | 718,311 | 157,409 |
| Pennsylvania............. | 8,802,627 | 5,542,788 | 3,259,839 | 405,238 | 2,854,601 | 829,671 | 1,365,715 | 659,215 | 2,354,930 | 739,205 |
| Rhode Island............. | 996,769 | 425,718 | 571,051 | 4,205 | 566,846 | 156,177 | 169,678 | 240,991 | 276,170 | 107,966 |
| South Carolina.......... | 4,617,901 | 1,395,419 | 3,222,482 | 23,097 | 3,199,385 | 2,055,362 | 785,588 | 358,435 | 2,304,929 | 1,432,936 |
| South Dakota............ | 1,030,554 | 561,642 | 468,912 | 1,114 | 467,798 | 238,742 | 183,598 | 45,458 | 272,959 | 77,687 |
| Tennessee ................. | 3,837,329 | 2,284,969 | 1,552,360 | 31,230 | 1,521,130 | 390,483 | 918,065 | 212,582 | 1,322,460 | 310,030 |
| Texas......................... | 29,926,435 | 10,053,334 | 19,873,101 | 167,238 | 19,705,863 | 15,788,502 | 2,334,585 | 1,582,776 | 16,904,285 | 13,799,771 |
| Utah........................... | 3,194,814 | 1,261,216 | 1,933,598 | 49,699 | 1,883,899 | 554,765 | 723,470 | 605,664 | 1,099,286 | 312,535 |
| Vermont..................... | 724,043 | 411,725 | 312,318 | 1,810 | 310,508 | 92,197 | 199,527 | 18,784 | 282,209 | 77,807 |
| Virginia..................... | 21,112,167 | 7,480,928 | 13,631,239 | 1,514,851 | 12,116,388 | 7,921,948 | 891,299 | 3,303,141 | 6,726,891 | 4,872,090 |
| Washington............... | 11,538,560 | 3,193,500 | 8,345,060 | 40,926 | 8,304,134 | 6,444,790 | 784,381 | 1,074,963 | 6,622,084 | 5,572,010 |
| West Virginia............ | 1,936,395 | 1,374,647 | 561,748 | 584 | 561,164 | 157,122 | 335,783 | 68,259 | 503,365 | 133,242 |
| Wisconsin ................. | 2,926,401 | 1,798,124 | 1,128,277 | 5,307 | 1,122,970 | 331,447 | 714,317 | 77,206 | 1,057,800 | 298,693 |
| Wyoming ................... | 709,271 | 349,473 | 359,798 | 952 | 358,846 | 203,902 | 115,390 | 39,554 | 165,051 | 44,437 |
| Dist. of Columbia ..... | 23,029,513 | 19,176,708 | 3,852,805 | 62,302 | 3,790,503 | 2,746,632 | 162,365 | 881,506 | 2,742,568 | 2,416,551 |
| American Samoa ...... | 6,373 | 6,266 | 107 | 0 | 107 | 0 | 0 | 107 | 107 | 0 |
| Fed. States of Micronesia......... | 0 | 0 | 0 | 0 | 0 | 0 | 0 | 0 | 0 | 0 |
| Guam ......................... | 376,595 | 46,425 | 330,170 | 6,357 | 323,813 | 241,496 | 15,751 | 66,566 | 341 | 43 |
| Marshall Islands........ | 0 | 0 | 0 | 0 | 0 | 0 | 0 | 0 | 0 | 0 |
| No. Mariana Islands... | 9,098 | 9,034 | 64 | 0 | 64 | 39 | 0 | 25 | 25 | 0 |
| Palau ......................... | 0 | 0 | 0 | 0 | 0 | 0 | 0 | 0 | 0 | 0 |
| Puerto Rico............... | 850,584 | 789,163 | 61,421 | 6,622 | 54,799 | 13,481 | 6,991 | 34,327 | 18,120 | 118 |
| U.S. Virgin Islands .... | 62,756 | 58,186 | 4,570 | 0 | 4,570 | 1,946 | 434 | 2,190 | 2,190 | 0 |
| Undistributed............ | 2,229,800 | 2,229,800 | 0 | 0 | 0 | 0 | 0 | 0 | 0 | 0 |

See footnotes at end of table.

## FEDERAL GOVERNMENT EXPENDITURE FOR SALARIES AND WAGES, BY AGENCY, BY STATE AND OUTLYING AREA: FISCAL YEAR 2010—Continued
### (In thousands of dollars)

| State and outlying area | Army—continued Inactive military | Civilian | Navy Total | Active military | Inactive military | Civilian | Air Force Total | Active military | Inactive military | Civilian |
|---|---|---|---|---|---|---|---|---|---|---|
| United States ............ | $32,971,473 | $9,028,236 | $18,878,241 | $9,159,977 | $494,770 | $9,223,494 | $25,456,730 | $16,991,100 | $525,799 | $7,939,831 |
| Alabama ................... | 946,986 | 731,604 | 19,791 | 9,988 | 4,735 | 5,068 | 378,116 | 247,918 | 7,887 | 122,311 |
| Alaska ...................... | 99,395 | 89,368 | 4,518 | 2,511 | 678 | 1,329 | 668,030 | 566,944 | 11,495 | 89,591 |
| Arizona .................... | 234,780 | 145,601 | 99,038 | 67,035 | 6,815 | 25,188 | 778,076 | 617,396 | 19,011 | 141,669 |
| Arkansas .................. | 679,740 | 82,193 | 3,516 | 1,680 | 1,562 | 274 | 338,644 | 287,120 | 14,411 | 37,113 |
| California ................. | 1,855,453 | 304,516 | 4,311,831 | 2,471,933 | 62,941 | 1,776,957 | 1,707,301 | 1,112,365 | 29,163 | 565,773 |
| Colorado .................. | 415,317 | 122,130 | 30,930 | 20,589 | 7,137 | 3,204 | 933,535 | 622,802 | 18,061 | 292,672 |
| Connecticut .............. | 251,973 | 13,346 | 147,022 | 92,205 | 3,738 | 51,079 | 27,140 | 10,497 | 3,860 | 12,783 |
| Delaware ................. | 105,858 | 6,902 | 2,096 | 470 | 1,441 | 185 | 253,177 | 193,604 | 5,065 | 54,508 |
| Florida ..................... | 1,219,118 | 138,008 | 1,160,846 | 603,234 | 37,933 | 519,679 | 1,980,049 | 1,406,361 | 19,999 | 553,698 |
| Georgia .................... | 1,315,526 | 430,645 | 367,044 | 171,147 | 15,380 | 180,517 | 1,290,911 | 573,126 | 15,154 | 702,631 |
| Hawaii ..................... | 394,814 | 170,540 | 1,020,095 | 604,718 | 4,405 | 410,972 | 541,264 | 417,856 | 17,708 | 105,700 |
| Idaho ....................... | 187,114 | 21,077 | 5,445 | 1,029 | 1,317 | 3,099 | 231,721 | 201,507 | 1,842 | 28,372 |
| Illinois ..................... | 948,271 | 303,767 | 174,815 | 83,126 | 16,999 | 74,690 | 558,590 | 355,668 | 14,297 | 188,625 |
| Indiana .................... | 1,271,886 | 53,897 | 171,789 | 6,422 | 4,814 | 160,553 | 64,826 | 20,674 | 5,902 | 38,250 |
| Iowa ........................ | 503,697 | 26,923 | 4,618 | 2,990 | 1,393 | 235 | 47,995 | 14,496 | 11,258 | 22,241 |
| Kansas ..................... | 485,753 | 192,890 | 4,593 | 3,106 | 1,355 | 132 | 234,148 | 183,379 | 4,156 | 46,613 |
| Kentucky ................. | 574,392 | 229,451 | 16,997 | 4,882 | 2,634 | 9,481 | 35,362 | 22,073 | 2,371 | 10,918 |
| Louisiana ................. | 679,986 | 118,665 | 88,511 | 37,509 | 16,687 | 34,315 | 402,403 | 332,707 | 5,561 | 64,135 |
| Maine ...................... | 131,049 | 8,617 | 294,500 | 51,543 | 1,279 | 241,678 | 24,672 | 10,339 | 2,663 | 11,670 |
| Maryland ................. | 614,957 | 631,154 | 1,355,636 | 390,281 | 4,902 | 960,453 | 731,752 | 588,706 | 7,170 | 135,876 |
| Massachusetts .......... | 502,778 | 90,933 | 33,063 | 18,000 | 5,981 | 9,082 | 319,509 | 119,585 | 16,671 | 183,253 |
| Michigan .................. | 630,256 | 272,414 | 29,300 | 17,340 | 10,464 | 1,496 | 81,110 | 31,939 | 8,126 | 41,045 |
| Minnesota ................ | 818,363 | 43,246 | 16,951 | 9,951 | 6,063 | 937 | 59,426 | 18,180 | 6,247 | 34,999 |
| Mississippi ............... | 113,033 | 239,379 | 124,145 | 3,883 | 111,351 | 106,515 | 424,009 | 341,498 | 10,887 | 101,624 |
| Missouri ................... | 1,834,542 | 200,577 | 86,773 | 29,428 | 29,428 | 34,327 | 253,556 | 186,475 | 10,207 | 56,874 |
| Montana ................... | 161,709 | 15,517 | 1,126 | 167 | 932 | 27 | 188,144 | 149,464 | 4,133 | 34,547 |
| Nebraska ................. | 314,643 | 47,176 | 20,942 | 17,634 | 2,488 | 820 | 446,449 | 337,202 | 2,874 | 106,373 |
| Nevada .................... | 214,688 | 13,897 | 35,177 | 20,574 | 3,232 | 11,371 | 629,282 | 554,126 | 14,832 | 60,324 |
| New Hampshire ........ | 135,268 | 16,661 | 21,724 | 17,660 | 3,002 | 1,062 | 31,149 | 15,012 | 2,377 | 13,760 |
| New Jersey ............... | 672,087 | 441,665 | 129,530 | 9,060 | 10,366 | 110,104 | 405,807 | 299,912 | 9,354 | 96,541 |
| New Mexico ............. | 201,798 | 102,773 | 8,768 | 4,129 | 1,959 | 2,680 | 746,369 | 557,878 | 3,955 | 184,536 |
| New York .................. | 1,072,949 | 230,546 | 81,193 | 52,916 | 21,037 | 7,240 | 245,440 | 105,492 | 20,408 | 119,540 |
| North Carolina .......... | 1,056,876 | 267,460 | 1,340,797 | 1,036,362 | 10,188 | 294,247 | 485,287 | 417,268 | 6,459 | 61,560 |
| North Dakota ............ | 181,411 | 13,321 | 1,224 | 370 | 721 | 133 | 362,868 | 311,767 | 2,028 | 49,073 |
| Ohio ........................ | 855,023 | 46,825 | 35,101 | 18,741 | 12,527 | 3,833 | 1,231,467 | 395,108 | 31,371 | 804,988 |
| Oklahoma ................ | 650,146 | 161,509 | 53,065 | 44,522 | 4,490 | 4,053 | 1,169,931 | 459,623 | 16,996 | 693,312 |
| Oregon ..................... | 474,313 | 86,589 | 13,988 | 8,835 | 4,174 | 979 | 74,106 | 35,197 | 13,533 | 25,376 |
| Pennsylvania ............ | 1,331,654 | 284,071 | 387,360 | 47,918 | 14,920 | 324,522 | 112,311 | 42,548 | 19,141 | 50,622 |
| Rhode Island ............ | 161,396 | 6,808 | 264,495 | 31,955 | 5,467 | 227,073 | 26,181 | 16,256 | 2,815 | 7,110 |
| South Carolina .......... | 771,287 | 100,706 | 359,566 | 173,150 | 6,145 | 180,271 | 534,890 | 449,276 | 8,156 | 77,458 |
| South Dakota ............ | 181,467 | 13,805 | 698 | 25 | 561 | 112 | 194,141 | 161,030 | 1,570 | 31,541 |
| Tennessee ................ | 904,093 | 108,337 | 102,004 | 43,959 | 8,661 | 49,384 | 96,666 | 36,494 | 5,311 | 54,861 |
| Texas ....................... | 2,280,052 | 824,462 | 233,099 | 138,581 | 40,363 | 54,155 | 2,568,479 | 1,850,150 | 14,170 | 704,159 |
| Utah ........................ | 716,759 | 69,992 | 9,185 | 4,361 | 2,638 | 2,186 | 775,428 | 237,869 | 4,073 | 533,486 |
| Vermont ................... | 89,992 | 8,884 | 1,726 | 1,043 | 598 | 85 | 26,568 | 13,323 | 2,211 | 11,034 |
| Virginia .................... | 841,080 | 1,013,721 | 3,894,064 | 1,919,078 | 31,350 | 1,943,636 | 1,495,433 | 1,130,780 | 18,869 | 345,784 |
| Washington ............... | 751,923 | 298,151 | 1,204,462 | 497,998 | 13,338 | 693,126 | 477,588 | 374,782 | 19,120 | 83,686 |
| West Virginia ............ | 330,669 | 39,454 | 13,080 | 8,127 | 1,608 | 3,345 | 44,719 | 15,573 | 3,506 | 25,460 |
| Wisconsin ................. | 704,657 | 54,450 | 11,403 | 5,021 | 4,801 | 1,581 | 53,767 | 27,733 | 4,859 | 21,175 |
| Wyoming .................. | 112,912 | 7,702 | 353 | 24 | 304 | 25 | 193,442 | 159,441 | 2,174 | 31,827 |
| Dist. of Columbia ..... | 133,152 | 192,865 | 778,901 | 112,784 | 28,216 | 637,901 | 269,034 | 217,297 | 997 | 50,740 |
| American Samoa ....... | 0 | 107 | 0 | 0 | 0 | 0 | 0 | 0 | 0 | 0 |
| Micronesia ................ | 0 | 0 | 0 | 0 | 0 | 0 | 0 | 0 | 0 | 0 |
| Guam ....................... | 0 | 298 | 176,429 | 114,351 | 0 | 62,078 | 147,043 | 127,102 | 15,571 | 4,190 |
| Marshall Islands ........ | 0 | 0 | 0 | 0 | 0 | 0 | 0 | 0 | 0 | 0 |
| No. Mariana Islands... | 0 | 25 | 39 | 39 | 0 | 0 | 0 | 0 | 0 | 0 |
| Palau ....................... | 0 | 0 | 0 | 0 | 0 | 0 | 0 | 0 | 0 | 0 |
| Puerto Rico .............. | 0 | 18,002 | 9,628 | 5,295 | 1,841 | 2,492 | 27,051 | 8,068 | 5,150 | 13,833 |
| U.S. Virgin Islands .... | 0 | 2,190 | 12 | 12 | 0 | 0 | 2,368 | 1,934 | 434 | 0 |
| Undistributed ............ | 0 | 0 | 0 | 0 | 0 | 0 | 2,229,800 | 0 | 0 | 0 |

See footnotes at end of table.

## FEDERAL GOVERNMENT EXPENDITURE FOR SALARIES AND WAGES, BY AGENCY, BY STATE AND OUTLYING AREA: FISCAL YEAR 2010—Continued
### (In thousands of dollars)

| State and outlying area | Total (a) | Dept. of Agriculture | Dept. of Commerce | Dept. of Education | Dept. of Energy | Environmental Protection Agency | Federal Deposit Insurance Corporation | General Services Admin. | Dept. of Health and Human Services |
|---|---|---|---|---|---|---|---|---|---|
| | | | | Nondefense agencies | | | | | |
| United States ........... | $160,986,795 | $6,738,707 | $6,447,961 | $428,877 | $1,556,456 | $1,916,191 | $838,269 | $1,080,395 | $6,238,750 |
| Alabama.................... | 1,838,220 | 76,585 | 18,056 | 209 | 138 | 4,278 | 5,157 | 3,173 | 7,358 |
| Alaska...................... | 833,775 | 61,930 | 72,831 | 0 | 131 | 3,416 | 0 | 2,899 | 21,351 |
| Arizona.................... | 2,750,909 | 121,411 | 32,081 | 0 | 20,401 | 501 | 4,784 | 4,324 | 289,868 |
| Arkansas.................. | 1,066,248 | 122,227 | 7,748 | 0 | 4,293 | 0 | 2,943 | 1,380 | 32,502 |
| California ................. | 13,953,654 | 571,009 | 209,680 | 15,237 | 41,540 | 103,161 | 93,789 | 79,276 | 129,979 |
| Colorado.................. | 3,105,486 | 260,661 | 197,396 | 5,422 | 72,149 | 75,027 | 5,535 | 31,455 | 46,965 |
| Connecticut.............. | 1,280,597 | 12,521 | 13,562 | 12 | 0 | 660 | 3,767 | 1,260 | 5,008 |
| Delaware ................. | 281,075 | 16,514 | 2,027 | 0 | 0 | 0 | 1,876 | 381 | 975 |
| Florida .................... | 7,150,991 | 122,202 | 138,584 | 512 | 193 | 8,616 | 43,252 | 8,645 | 46,394 |
| Georgia ................... | 4,764,869 | 179,956 | 58,248 | 16,148 | 5,250 | 113,705 | 30,581 | 58,833 | 743,569 |
| Hawaii..................... | 689,616 | 38,032 | 50,589 | 0 | 128 | 617 | 0 | 3,664 | 4,042 |
| Idaho....................... | 701,387 | 168,682 | 15,136 | 0 | 31,391 | 2,900 | 0 | 886 | 3,808 |
| Illinois..................... | 5,419,135 | 119,332 | 60,713 | 13,585 | 28,624 | 129,527 | 36,725 | 65,419 | 60,978 |
| Indiana.................... | 2,095,528 | 61,182 | 252,286 | 126 | 253 | 403 | 4,142 | 3,195 | 3,771 |
| Iowa........................ | 1,125,751 | 145,129 | 12,174 | 103 | 982 | 237 | 9,290 | 1,357 | 3,513 |
| Kansas .................... | 1,287,109 | 69,468 | 20,667 | 0 | 0 | 53,648 | 3,899 | 1,004 | 14,255 |
| Kentucky ................. | 1,646,671 | 78,277 | 17,499 | 0 | 4,143 | 338 | 7,552 | 1,341 | 2,953 |
| Louisiana................. | 1,742,949 | 175,872 | 26,626 | 0 | 7,516 | 615 | 6,211 | 3,008 | 10,649 |
| Maine...................... | 583,793 | 19,476 | 12,627 | 0 | 0 | 26 | 0 | 475 | 2,748 |
| Maryland ................. | 9,877,623 | 322,697 | 1,706,691 | 0 | 129,613 | 10,980 | 4,492 | 12,334 | 3,355,790 |
| Massachusetts .......... | 3,213,810 | 31,028 | 112,142 | 5,775 | 26 | 71,906 | 25,576 | 24,902 | 57,231 |
| Michigan.................. | 3,371,766 | 84,271 | 58,663 | 0 | 0 | 34,987 | 5,777 | 6,200 | 14,412 |
| Minnesota................ | 2,150,492 | 137,361 | 21,015 | 104 | 72 | 8,372 | 8,323 | 3,066 | 33,125 |
| Mississippi............... | 1,054,121 | 123,026 | 36,026 | 0 | 0 | 2,718 | 3,382 | 1,281 | 1,808 |
| Missouri................... | 3,212,726 | 306,682 | 75,440 | 7,136 | 8,228 | 669 | 29,913 | 65,614 | 34,509 |
| Montana................... | 750,775 | 187,398 | 15,893 | 0 | 11,930 | 3,357 | 1,145 | 1,067 | 61,162 |
| Nebraska ................. | 809,950 | 98,039 | 12,558 | 0 | 1,387 | 91 | 5,189 | 1,453 | 8,457 |
| Nevada .................... | 934,382 | 29,514 | 15,407 | 0 | 29,363 | 15,869 | 0 | 1,621 | 7,134 |
| New Hampshire ........ | 600,058 | 25,825 | 5,766 | 0 | 155 | 26 | 3,694 | 1,699 | 1,726 |
| New Jersey ............... | 3,513,392 | 37,600 | 43,176 | 12 | 1,341 | 23,172 | 7,010 | 14,790 | 15,367 |
| New Mexico ............. | 1,505,941 | 173,962 | 11,968 | 10 | 107,719 | 51 | 1,954 | 2,493 | 181,058 |
| New York.................. | 8,270,409 | 82,388 | 91,258 | 9,207 | 14,475 | 77,482 | 32,291 | 53,928 | 81,633 |
| North Carolina.......... | 3,161,081 | 151,696 | 79,422 | 169 | 92 | 137,783 | 9,452 | 3,766 | 83,925 |
| North Dakota............ | 444,560 | 61,395 | 9,083 | 0 | 4,882 | 0 | 3,881 | 1,022 | 24,048 |
| Ohio........................ | 3,969,933 | 69,935 | 32,561 | 2,716 | 16,019 | 61,754 | 4,117 | 5,258 | 63,948 |
| Oklahoma................ | 1,618,451 | 68,072 | 45,277 | 0 | 7,069 | 5,378 | 6,002 | 3,224 | 83,392 |
| Oregon.................... | 1,760,746 | 272,543 | 46,551 | 0 | 132,686 | 10,240 | 2,100 | 3,329 | 16,201 |
| Pennsylvania ............ | 5,542,788 | 114,126 | 54,653 | 8,427 | 36,666 | 89,542 | 8,942 | 52,197 | 80,349 |
| Rhode Island............ | 425,718 | 4,291 | 8,599 | 11 | 0 | 7,287 | 0 | 783 | 3,635 |
| South Carolina.......... | 1,395,419 | 63,778 | 45,354 | 98 | 43,172 | 0 | 2,533 | 1,870 | 5,271 |
| South Dakota............ | 561,642 | 64,707 | 12,138 | 10 | 14,350 | 106 | 3,493 | 909 | 71,032 |
| Tennessee................ | 2,284,969 | 81,765 | 22,875 | 119 | 61,040 | 644 | 15,655 | 2,324 | 11,840 |
| Texas ...................... | 10,053,334 | 267,092 | 123,107 | 11,128 | 20,279 | 91,258 | 116,211 | 82,834 | 69,839 |
| Utah........................ | 1,261,216 | 118,969 | 17,456 | 0 | 1,715 | 173 | 6,197 | 1,888 | 6,181 |
| Vermont................... | 411,725 | 21,029 | 5,123 | 0 | 0 | 26 | 0 | 514 | 1,012 |
| Virginia.................... | 7,480,928 | 163,894 | 1,706,422 | 116 | 1,983 | 144,904 | 1,772 | 126,279 | 14,267 |
| Washington............... | 3,193,500 | 152,532 | 218,219 | 5,057 | 181,680 | 55,497 | 6,938 | 35,879 | 58,650 |
| West Virginia............ | 1,374,647 | 54,674 | 7,227 | 0 | 26,865 | 2,642 | 1,875 | 1,908 | 30,044 |
| Wisconsin ................ | 1,798,124 | 113,269 | 19,338 | 0 | 0 | 317 | 9,233 | 1,431 | 4,855 |
| Wyoming ................. | 349,473 | 56,139 | 7,578 | 0 | 4,943 | 0 | 0 | 482 | 7,185 |
| Dist. of Columbia ..... | 19,176,708 | 736,069 | 550,982 | 326,990 | 489,201 | 554,697 | 248,729 | 289,355 | 309,189 |
| American Samoa ...... | 6,266 | 496 | 1,039 | 0 | 0 | 0 | 0 | 0 | 0 |
| Micronesia................ | 0 | 0 | 0 | 0 | 0 | 0 | 0 | 0 | 0 |
| Guam....................... | 46,425 | 4,537 | 2,093 | 0 | 0 | 0 | 0 | 120 | 67 |
| Marshall Islands........ | 0 | 0 | 0 | 0 | 0 | 0 | 0 | 0 | 0 |
| No. Mariana Islands... | 9,034 | 311 | 0 | 0 | 0 | 9,034 | 311 | 0 | 0 |
| Palau....................... | 0 | 0 | 0 | 0 | 0 | 0 | 0 | 0 | 0 |
| Puerto Rico .............. | 789,163 | 36,354 | 8,208 | 449 | 0 | 5,178 | 2,136 | 2,202 | 9,277 |
| U.S. Virgin Islands .... | 58,186 | 777 | 0 | 0 | 0 | 165 | 0 | 127 | 195 |
| Undistributed............ | 0 | 0 | 0 | 0 | 0 | 0 | 0 | 0 | 0 |

See footnotes at end of table.

# FEDERAL GOVERNMENT EXPENDITURE FOR SALARIES AND WAGES, BY AGENCY, BY STATE AND OUTLYING AREA: FISCAL YEAR 2010—Continued
## (In thousands of dollars)

| State and outlying area | Dept. of Homeland Security | Dept. of Housing and Urban Development | Dept. of the Interior | Dept. of Justice | Dept. of Labor | NASA | National Archives and Records | National Science Foundation |
|---|---|---|---|---|---|---|---|---|
| United States ............ | $15,822,760 | $1,005,898 | $4,280,273 | $10,102,168 | $1,699,528 | $1,951,032 | $199,470 | $172,816 |
| Alabama...................... | 115,782 | 6,939 | 8,802 | 91,939 | 13,091 | 257,066 | 0 | 0 |
| Alaska........................ | 211,045 | 3,663 | 150,223 | 17,192 | 1,674 | 0 | 379 | 124 |
| Arizona...................... | 544,054 | 9,946 | 232,710 | 190,379 | 5,342 | 110 | 92 | 0 |
| Arkansas.................... | 26,107 | 4,842 | 17,554 | 67,056 | 3,482 | 0 | 2,373 | 0 |
| California .................. | 1,888,043 | 66,383 | 428,404 | 836,050 | 91,618 | 215,757 | 9,109 | 0 |
| Colorado.................... | 147,887 | 33,056 | 490,739 | 169,935 | 39,901 | 1,271 | 2,025 | 603 |
| Connecticut............... | 132,493 | 6,375 | 3,522 | 64,736 | 6,580 | 106 | 107 | 0 |
| Delaware ................... | 8,545 | 369 | 2,109 | 11,815 | 1,255 | 0 | 0 | 0 |
| Florida ...................... | 1,129,873 | 23,032 | 78,245 | 505,111 | 49,445 | 213,548 | 97 | 0 |
| Georgia...................... | 397,900 | 43,850 | 63,753 | 215,289 | 59,638 | 0 | 5,155 | 0 |
| Hawaii........................ | 197,152 | 2,956 | 34,785 | 39,346 | 2,436 | 108 | 0 | 0 |
| Idaho......................... | 24,575 | 897 | 120,298 | 21,994 | 3,205 | 0 | 0 | 0 |
| Illinois...................... | 302,357 | 43,763 | 14,555 | 285,267 | 85,678 | 0 | 4,298 | 0 |
| Indiana...................... | 79,915 | 6,545 | 13,621 | 98,854 | 8,939 | 120 | 0 | 0 |
| Iowa .......................... | 25,072 | 2,728 | 8,013 | 22,964 | 2,719 | 0 | 1,097 | 0 |
| Kansas ....................... | 38,539 | 14,758 | 21,814 | 56,507 | 5,338 | 0 | 4,295 | 0 |
| Kentucky ................... | 64,592 | 5,596 | 18,739 | 170,631 | 42,510 | 0 | 0 | 0 |
| Louisiana................... | 229,587 | 9,089 | 66,442 | 153,486 | 8,192 | 2,556 | 0 | 0 |
| Maine......................... | 102,915 | 371 | 10,712 | 11,930 | 2,224 | 0 | 205 | 0 |
| Maryland ................... | 323,734 | 12,183 | 49,743 | 134,197 | 9,252 | 321,159 | 81,689 | 0 |
| Massachusetts ........... | 315,001 | 20,841 | 66,669 | 137,753 | 48,516 | 72 | 5,704 | 31 |
| Michigan.................... | 325,266 | 15,613 | 23,717 | 144,441 | 10,572 | 130 | 1,830 | 0 |
| Minnesota.................. | 117,728 | 8,120 | 48,583 | 117,154 | 5,826 | 138 | 0 | 0 |
| Mississippi ................ | 80,438 | 5,914 | 22,902 | 70,747 | 4,246 | 36,314 | 0 | 0 |
| Missouri..................... | 140,091 | 10,092 | 41,434 | 145,990 | 33,301 | 206 | 33,696 | 0 |
| Montana .................... | 60,432 | 673 | 113,301 | 17,403 | 2,275 | 0 | 0 | 0 |
| Nebraska ................... | 74,442 | 3,545 | 26,043 | 24,110 | 3,238 | 0 | 0 | 0 |
| Nevada ...................... | 87,632 | 2,575 | 116,713 | 43,194 | 3,664 | 0 | 0 | 0 |
| New Hampshire ......... | 35,351 | 3,505 | 5,484 | 14,552 | 3,991 | 0 | 0 | 0 |
| New Jersey ................ | 377,720 | 13,250 | 19,946 | 201,170 | 19,067 | 183 | 0 | 0 |
| New Mexico ............... | 180,668 | 3,243 | 249,424 | 49,247 | 2,708 | 6,299 | 100 | 0 |
| New York.................... | 875,327 | 48,334 | 57,350 | 561,631 | 63,444 | 3,432 | 2,792 | 31 |
| North Carolina........... | 244,393 | 9,211 | 34,089 | 164,041 | 7,518 | 175 | 0 | 0 |
| North Dakota.............. | 52,417 | 674 | 48,038 | 9,386 | 1,495 | 0 | 0 | 0 |
| Ohio........................... | 140,727 | 21,938 | 16,236 | 138,293 | 43,045 | 167,577 | 3,203 | 0 |
| Oklahoma................... | 40,786 | 11,423 | 58,432 | 95,497 | 5,178 | 0 | 0 | 0 |
| Oregon....................... | 117,813 | 5,227 | 181,549 | 67,586 | 4,293 | 120 | 0 | 31 |
| Pennsylvania ............. | 243,888 | 42,281 | 64,717 | 389,375 | 93,391 | 106 | 3,277 | 0 |
| Rhode Island.............. | 43,838 | 2,193 | 3,044 | 13,122 | 2,572 | 0 | 0 | 0 |
| South Carolina........... | 109,385 | 6,713 | 12,836 | 128,765 | 3,297 | 108 | 121 | 0 |
| South Dakota............. | 9,234 | 530 | 79,754 | 21,322 | 1,221 | 0 | 0 | 0 |
| Tennessee .................. | 80,191 | 11,902 | 37,103 | 100,183 | 10,648 | 0 | 0 | 0 |
| Texas......................... | 1,839,054 | 53,416 | 69,335 | 762,580 | 83,439 | 362,608 | 9,420 | 0 |
| Utah........................... | 40,940 | 2,029 | 105,202 | 39,416 | 10,249 | 1,346 | 0 | 0 |
| Vermont..................... | 156,167 | 466 | 4,607 | 8,716 | 443 | 0 | 0 | 0 |
| Virginia...................... | 1,273,515 | 8,397 | 297,843 | 852,961 | 50,104 | 213,370 | 0 | 171,996 |
| Washington................ | 403,940 | 17,148 | 135,738 | 98,676 | 28,621 | 0 | 1,780 | 0 |
| West Virginia............. | 45,112 | 2,023 | 44,009 | 333,190 | 47,141 | 3,717 | 363 | 0 |
| Wisconsin .................. | 58,994 | 6,209 | 39,213 | 61,223 | 9,516 | 74 | 0 | 0 |
| Wyoming ................... | 6,825 | 165 | 95,892 | 9,939 | 1,986 | 0 | 0 | 0 |
| Dist. of Columbia ..... | 2,043,037 | 363,219 | 311,469 | 2,034,891 | 648,878 | 143,256 | 26,263 | 0 |
| American Samoa ...... | 1,042 | 0 | 1,006 | 305 | 0 | 0 | 0 | 0 |
| Micronesia................. | 0 | 0 | 0 | 0 | 0 | 0 | 0 | 0 |
| Guam......................... | 17,191 | 82 | 1,258 | 5,465 | 210 | 0 | 0 | 0 |
| Marshall Islands........ | 0 | 0 | 0 | 0 | 0 | 0 | 0 | 0 |
| No. Mariana Islands... | 4,976 | 0 | 610 | 1,328 | 199 | 0 | 0 | 0 |
| Palau......................... | 0 | 0 | 0 | 0 | 0 | 0 | 0 | 0 |
| Puerto Rico............... | 163,774 | 7,606 | 7,577 | 66,907 | 2,717 | 0 | 0 | 0 |
| U.S. Virgin Islands .... | 25,257 | 0 | 4,477 | 6,961 | 0 | 0 | 0 | 0 |
| Undistributed............ | 0 | 0 | 0 | 0 | 0 | 0 | 0 | 0 |

See footnotes at end of table.

## FEDERAL GOVERNMENT EXPENDITURE FOR SALARIES AND WAGES, BY AGENCY, BY STATE AND OUTLYING AREA: FISCAL YEAR 2010—Continued
### (In thousands of dollars)

| State and outlying area | U.S. Postal Service | Small Business Admin. | Social Security Admin. | Dept. of State | Dept. of Transportation | Dept. of the Treasury | Dept. of Veterans Affairs | All other nondefense (a) |
|---|---|---|---|---|---|---|---|---|
| | | | | | *Nondefense agencies—continued* | | | |
| United States ........... | $60,348,026 | $327,960 | $4,950,908 | $1,507,294 | $5,676,593 | $6,840,341 | $10,621,641 | $10,234,481 |
| Alabama................... | 818,088 | 4,631 | 165,979 | 0 | 23,751 | 34,619 | 172,240 | 10,339 |
| Alaska..................... | 146,764 | 1,014 | 4,587 | 108 | 105,587 | 5,414 | 21,913 | 1,529 |
| Arizona.................... | 901,902 | 1,615 | 42,416 | 4,110 | 52,621 | 46,293 | 223,587 | 22,362 |
| Arkansas.................. | 528,984 | 4,498 | 34,689 | 784 | 17,755 | 15,510 | 167,185 | 4,335 |
| California ................ | 6,313,131 | 37,159 | 485,428 | 13,554 | 454,885 | 749,824 | 971,445 | 149,192 |
| Colorado.................. | 1,016,604 | 11,790 | 55,237 | 2,640 | 144,708 | 99,566 | 153,347 | 41,568 |
| Connecticut............. | 822,242 | 1,008 | 29,606 | 2,783 | 18,827 | 44,495 | 105,232 | 5,694 |
| Delaware ................. | 178,104 | 761 | 7,296 | 0 | 3,724 | 9,507 | 34,328 | 1,488 |
| Florida .................... | 3,286,983 | 6,986 | 170,329 | 24,066 | 267,763 | 206,318 | 778,743 | 42,054 |
| Georgia.................... | 1,672,031 | 11,442 | 131,699 | 190 | 284,630 | 327,726 | 266,281 | 78,995 |
| Hawaii..................... | 222,179 | 1,284 | 7,648 | 1,565 | 35,397 | 10,457 | 31,134 | 6,097 |
| Idaho...................... | 239,610 | 962 | 8,699 | 0 | 10,124 | 7,059 | 40,170 | 991 |
| Illinois.................... | 2,937,909 | 5,332 | 244,574 | 7,956 | 227,334 | 167,136 | 401,847 | 176,226 |
| Indiana.................... | 1,172,310 | 1,574 | 56,413 | 0 | 109,046 | 53,417 | 156,866 | 12,550 |
| Iowa....................... | 731,745 | 1,563 | 23,413 | 0 | 16,727 | 14,798 | 99,022 | 3,105 |
| Kansas .................... | 727,410 | 1,110 | 20,448 | 0 | 87,672 | 20,086 | 119,557 | 6,634 |
| Kentucky ................. | 776,723 | 2,358 | 54,700 | 587 | 38,185 | 215,382 | 141,105 | 3,460 |
| Louisiana................. | 764,620 | 3,154 | 53,454 | 9,710 | 30,486 | 30,462 | 141,731 | 9,503 |
| Maine...................... | 330,288 | 1,043 | 13,899 | 92 | 12,973 | 7,326 | 53,396 | 1,067 |
| Maryland ................. | 1,253,595 | 1,784 | 1,076,003 | 2,522 | 54,120 | 409,056 | 145,565 | 460,415 |
| Massachusetts ........... | 1,609,081 | 2,862 | 90,613 | 4,668 | 117,193 | 169,167 | 251,562 | 45,492 |
| Michigan.................. | 2,070,328 | 2,558 | 99,787 | 1,806 | 70,497 | 130,781 | 252,019 | 18,112 |
| Minnesota................ | 1,224,242 | 1,533 | 34,360 | 1,213 | 112,446 | 55,299 | 199,270 | 12,892 |
| Mississippi .............. | 458,086 | 1,365 | 43,177 | 0 | 13,991 | 13,298 | 127,543 | 7,736 |
| Missouri.................. | 1,456,897 | 4,564 | 173,682 | 237 | 87,255 | 283,013 | 256,577 | 17,500 |
| Montana .................. | 210,980 | 854 | 8,598 | 0 | 13,717 | 6,019 | 32,641 | 1,931 |
| Nebraska ................. | 437,042 | 1,127 | 12,318 | 0 | 13,785 | 15,782 | 68,446 | 2,898 |
| Nevada .................... | 403,625 | 1,352 | 14,901 | 0 | 34,042 | 23,796 | 99,612 | 4,368 |
| New Hampshire ........ | 317,192 | 1,004 | 10,916 | 38,595 | 87,680 | 13,594 | 27,823 | 1,510 |
| New Jersey .............. | 2,220,886 | 2,281 | 67,312 | 1,032 | 182,243 | 111,761 | 139,911 | 14,163 |
| New Mexico ............. | 314,573 | 1,307 | 54,555 | 380 | 61,467 | 10,577 | 85,569 | 6,609 |
| New York................. | 4,345,494 | 14,298 | 301,228 | 23,128 | 271,485 | 486,020 | 640,886 | 132,867 |
| North Carolina.......... | 1,720,261 | 2,787 | 85,937 | 2,218 | 50,747 | 64,650 | 292,593 | 16,157 |
| North Dakota............ | 170,608 | 939 | 5,812 | 0 | 11,732 | 5,872 | 32,435 | 841 |
| Ohio....................... | 2,341,549 | 3,396 | 112,084 | 64 | 137,481 | 159,983 | 402,875 | 25,174 |
| Oklahoma................ | 669,788 | 1,592 | 36,731 | 0 | 296,056 | 35,018 | 145,215 | 4,301 |
| Oregon.................... | 644,138 | 1,645 | 30,833 | 0 | 27,931 | 38,402 | 159,154 | 3,601 |
| Pennsylvania ............ | 2,930,052 | 4,597 | 287,967 | 5,122 | 82,396 | 356,060 | 453,134 | 141,523 |
| Rhode Island............ | 255,506 | 835 | 11,832 | 0 | 8,512 | 10,252 | 47,989 | 1,428 |
| South Carolina.......... | 685,142 | 1,362 | 45,059 | 48,964 | 23,784 | 17,279 | 145,554 | 4,974 |
| South Dakota............ | 197,522 | 867 | 6,516 | 0 | 6,919 | 5,529 | 64,870 | 613 |
| Tennessee ................. | 1,163,730 | 1,492 | 72,274 | 33 | 107,139 | 187,678 | 298,229 | 18,106 |
| Texas...................... | 3,896,168 | 49,788 | 239,267 | 26,210 | 447,223 | 602,612 | 740,350 | 90,116 |
| Utah....................... | 487,439 | 1,774 | 12,314 | 0 | 67,901 | 249,239 | 85,536 | 5,252 |
| Vermont................... | 165,821 | 836 | 3,992 | 0 | 4,996 | 4,292 | 33,063 | 622 |
| Virginia................... | 1,573,044 | 18,339 | 165,888 | 1,449 | 227,295 | 100,117 | 222,914 | 144,059 |
| Washington.............. | 1,137,809 | 3,911 | 107,976 | 7,130 | 222,264 | 81,862 | 212,527 | 19,666 |
| West Virginia............ | 375,175 | 1,093 | 30,547 | 0 | 13,362 | 187,601 | 161,624 | 4,455 |
| Wisconsin................ | 1,146,208 | 1,670 | 46,067 | 0 | 23,625 | 34,691 | 214,192 | 7,999 |
| Wyoming ................. | 104,858 | 988 | 3,098 | 0 | 5,453 | 3,144 | 40,272 | 526 |
| Dist. of Columbia ..... | 484,368 | 91,463 | 22,266 | 1,274,164 | 830,287 | 872,090 | 339,240 | 6,186,605 |
| American Samoa ...... | 1,264 | 0 | 250 | 0 | 369 | 0 | 483 | 11 |
| Micronesia................ | 0 | 0 | 0 | 0 | 0 | 0 | 0 | 0 |
| Guam...................... | 9,754 | 267 | 699 | 0 | 3,943 | 0 | 722 | 17 |
| Marshall Islands........ | 0 | 0 | 0 | 0 | 0 | 0 | 0 | 0 |
| No. Mariana Islands... | 993 | 0 | 246 | 214 | 92 | 0 | 49 | 15 |
| Palau...................... | 0 | 0 | 0 | 0 | 0 | 0 | 0 | 0 |
| Puerto Rico.............. | 259,751 | 2,038 | 24,368 | 0 | 14,084 | 30,031 | 121,592 | 24,914 |
| U.S. Virgin Islands .... | 17,431 | 108 | 921 | 0 | 886 | 381 | 476 | 24 |
| Undistributed............ | 0 | 0 | 0 | 0 | 0 | 0 | 0 | 2,229,800 |

*Source:* U.S. Census Bureau, *Consolidated Federal Funds Report for Fiscal Year 2010.* Released September 2011.

*Note:* Department of Defense data represent salaries, wages and compensation, such as housing allowances; distributions by state are based on duty station. State details for all other federal government agencies are estimates, based on place of employment. Detail may not add to total because of rounding. For additional information, see the complete repoprt at *http://www.census.gov/govs/www/cffr.html.*

*Key:*
(a) The "undistributed" amount includes the salaries and wages for the Federal Judiciary that could not be geographically allocated.

Table 2.12
## FEDERAL GOVERNMENT DIRECT LOAN PROGRAMS — VOLUME OF ASSISTANCE PROVIDED BY STATE AND OUTLYING AREA: FISCAL YEAR 2010
(In thousands of dollars)

| State and outlying area | Total | Department of Agriculture | | Federal direct student loans | Other direct loans |
|---|---|---|---|---|---|
| | | Commodity loans— price supports | Other loans | | |
| United States ..................... | $88,482,586 | $85,379 | $8,803,522 | $73,035,436 | $1,558,249 |
| Alabama............................. | 1,255,728 | 110,825 | 89,096 | 1,049,265 | 6,542 |
| Alaska................................ | 207,050 | 12 | 142,652 | 62,171 | 2,215 |
| Arizona.............................. | 5,035,397 | 2,552 | 90,421 | 4,941,037 | 1,387 |
| Arkansas............................ | 1,000,425 | 419,983 | 155,156 | 419,599 | 5,686 |
| California........................... | 6,994,239 | 402,486 | 371,764 | 6,137,804 | 82,185 |
| Colorado............................ | 1,794,488 | 137,316 | 88,396 | 1,567,583 | 1,193 |
| Connecticut........................ | 795,026 | 0 | 86,454 | 703,150 | 5,421 |
| Delaware ........................... | 303,977 | 1,473 | 73,002 | 228,992 | 510 |
| Florida ............................... | 4,236,250 | 126,846 | 172,103 | 3,780,251 | 157,050 |
| Georgia.............................. | 2,250,051 | 141,905 | 159,172 | 1,879,851 | 69,123 |
| Hawaii................................ | 200,495 | 8 | 83,793 | 113,109 | 3,585 |
| Idaho................................. | 625,170 | 104,046 | 120,141 | 400,983 | 0 |
| Illinois............................... | 3,459,721 | 120,253 | 139,604 | 3,161,793 | 38,071 |
| Indiana.............................. | 2,692,385 | 109,010 | 309,169 | 2,268,156 | 6,051 |
| Iowa .................................. | 2,573,008 | 236,493 | 252,716 | 2,072,654 | 11,145 |
| Kansas ............................... | 983,600 | 29,569 | 189,790 | 763,661 | 580 |
| Kentucky ........................... | 1,571,107 | 29,778 | 381,607 | 1,134,909 | 24,813 |
| Louisiana........................... | 1,180,080 | 215,902 | 341,505 | 596,864 | 25,709 |
| Maine................................. | 367,193 | 219 | 91,128 | 273,716 | 2,130 |
| Maryland ........................... | 1,495,757 | 5,506 | 81,076 | 1,080,053 | 329,122 |
| Massachusetts .................... | 2,828,403 | 755 | 100,966 | 2,647,178 | 70,504 |
| Michigan............................ | 4,246,468 | 185,825 | 257,382 | 3,797,975 | 5,285 |
| Minnesota.......................... | 2,892,947 | 361,982 | 294,368 | 2,231,182 | 5,415 |
| Mississippi ........................ | 1,122,465 | 497,256 | 158,882 | 456,274 | 10,053 |
| Missouri ............................ | 1,845,572 | 58,343 | 331,088 | 1,453,956 | 2,185 |
| Montana ............................ | 284,173 | 45,834 | 112,819 | 125,284 | 235 |
| Nebraska ........................... | 638,856 | 93,685 | 95,277 | 448,382 | 1,512 |
| Nevada.............................. | 347,472 | 8 | 33,233 | 314,056 | 175 |
| New Hampshire .................. | 384,242 | 21 | 71,094 | 312,857 | 270 |
| New Jersey ......................... | 1,484,220 | 12,459 | 52,629 | 1,401,932 | 17,200 |
| New Mexico ........................ | 274,568 | 3,061 | 72,148 | 198,519 | 840 |
| New York............................ | 5,353,098 | 21,444 | 170,249 | 4,701,861 | 459,545 |
| North Carolina.................... | 2,069,488 | 223,068 | 588,913 | 1,253,465 | 4,042 |
| North Dakota...................... | 384,404 | 109,954 | 124,483 | 146,335 | 3,633 |
| Ohio .................................. | 3,290,578 | 64,083 | 141,388 | 3,081,215 | 3,892 |
| Oklahoma........................... | 890,957 | 7,466 | 186,932 | 688,685 | 7,874 |
| Oregon............................... | 1,094,408 | 4,324 | 96,506 | 992,436 | 1,141 |
| Pennsylvania ...................... | 3,872,137 | 11,319 | 327,684 | 3,527,286 | 5,847 |
| Rhode Island...................... | 423,438 | 0 | 21,612 | 374,031 | 27,795 |
| South Carolina.................... | 1,039,680 | 18,461 | 224,739 | 795,402 | 1,079 |
| South Dakota...................... | 383,387 | 78,232 | 136,742 | 167,593 | 820 |
| Tennessee .......................... | 1,606,630 | 218,769 | 231,521 | 1,225,875 | -69,535 |
| Texas................................. | 4,753,856 | 778,947 | 376,388 | 3,501,426 | 97,095 |
| Utah.................................. | 662,293 | 1,766 | 144,162 | 511,851 | 4,514 |
| Vermont............................. | 251,647 | 0 | 79,820 | 171,384 | 442 |
| Virginia.............................. | 2,282,180 | 34,995 | 265,407 | 1,973,512 | 8,266 |
| Washington........................ | 1,349,574 | 12,582 | 277,075 | 1,049,406 | 10,511 |
| West Virginia...................... | 814,415 | 1,903 | 90,447 | 718,911 | 3,153 |
| Wisconsin .......................... | 1,270,655 | 43,946 | 192,457 | 1,029,539 | 4,713 |
| Wyoming............................ | 93,670 | 708 | 26,982 | 65,922 | 59 |
| Dist. of Columbia ............... | 750,111 | 1 | 0 | 678,232 | 71,878 |
| American Samoa ................. | 23,903 | 0 | 10,088 | 0 | 13,815 |
| Fed. States of Micronesia................... | 83 | 0 | 83 | 0 | 0 |
| Guam ................................ | 48,048 | 0 | 42,684 | 5,364 | 0 |
| Marshall Islands................. | 452 | 0 | 452 | 0 | 0 |
| No. Mariana Islands .......... | 7 | 0 | 7 | 0 | 0 |
| Palau................................. | 55 | 0 | 55 | 0 | 0 |
| Puerto Rico......................... | 399,932 | 0 | 47,102 | 350,621 | 2,209 |
| U.S. Virgin Islands ............. | 2,964 | 0 | 908 | 1,787 | 270 |
| Undistributed...................... | 0 | 0 | 0 | 0 | 0 |

See footnotes at end of table.

# FEDERAL GOVERNMENT DIRECT LOAN PROGRAMS — VOLUME OF ASSISTANCE PROVIDED BY STATE AND OUTLYING AREA: FISCAL YEAR 2010 — Continued

*Source:* U.S. Census Bureau, *Consolidated Federal Funds Report for Fiscal Year 2010.* Released September 2011.

*Note:* Amounts represent dollar volume of direct loans made during the fiscal year. For additional information see the complete report at *http://www.census.gov/govs/www/cffr.html.* Detail may not add to total because of rounding.

The CFDA defines "Direct Loans" as "Financial assistance provided through the lending of federal monies for a specific period of time, with a reasonable expectation of repayment. Such loans may or may not require the payment of interest." The CFDA defines "Guaranteed/ Insured Loans" as "Programs in which the federal government makes an arrangement to indemnify a lender against part or all of any defaults by those responsible for the repayment of loans." Loan program amounts reflect the volume of loan activities. These amounts represent either direct loans made to certain categories of borrowers, or the federal government contingent liability for loans guaranteed. Loan data does not represent actual expenditures associated with the loan programs.

Any actual outlays under these programs, appear in the direct payments categories in the CFFR. Federal government contingent liability can vary by program, and caution should be used in comparing one federal loan program to another, or in interpreting the data presented to reflect actual federal outlays over time.

The following also should be noted:

1. Amounts guaranteed do not necessarily represent future outlays.

2. All amounts reflect the dollar value of loans provided during the fiscal year, and not the cumulative totals of such activity over the life of the program.

3. Direct loans are not reported on a net basis, as in the federal budget, but rather are shown in terms of total amounts loaned.

4. Programs otherwise similar can vary in the share of the total liability that the federal government guarantees or insures. Certain veterans guaranteed loan programs are guaranteed only up to a stated maximum dollar value, for example. In these cases, the federal government contingent liability is less than the total value of the loan or insured policy agreement.

## Table 2.13
## FEDERAL GOVERNMENT GUARANTEED LOAN PROGRAMS—VOLUME OF COVERAGE PROVIDED BY STATE AND OUTLYING AREA: FISCAL YEAR 2010
### (In thousands of dollars)

| State and outlying area | Total | Mortgage insurance for homes | Federal Family Education Loan program | Veterans housing guaranteed and insured loans— VA home loans | Mortgage insurance— condominiums | U.S.D.A. guaranteed loans | Small business loans | Other guaranteed loans |
|---|---|---|---|---|---|---|---|---|
| United States ............ | $426,580,579 | $279,240,004 | $23,285,635 | $63,140,000 | $17,467,015 | $28,011,183 | $14,241,718 | $1,195,023 |
| Alabama ................ | 5,894,898 | 3,779,780 | 264,354 | 1,079,299 | 29,464 | 582,583 | 159,249 | 169 |
| Alaska.................... | 1,640,993 | 832,967 | 20,323 | 526,698 | 104,708 | 112,252 | 44,045 | 0 |
| Arizona.................. | 14,968,820 | 7,347,504 | 3,588,742 | 2,936,636 | 223,248 | 606,228 | 264,999 | 1,462 |
| Arkansas................. | 4,015,091 | 1,910,349 | 145,806 | 496,627 | 6,001 | 1,369,953 | 86,289 | 66 |
| California ................ | 53,237,387 | 39,653,126 | 2,090,086 | 3,515,851 | 4,541,713 | 849,481 | 2,449,498 | 137,631 |
| Colorado.................. | 13,232,570 | 8,590,442 | 563,397 | 2,436,201 | 610,223 | 659,792 | 371,787 | 728 |
| Connecticut.............. | 4,863,846 | 3,796,705 | 155,170 | 216,738 | 422,360 | 132,148 | 135,596 | 5,129 |
| Delaware ................ | 1,816,185 | 1,316,382 | 23,584 | 279,412 | 34,108 | 77,430 | 13,270 | 72,000 |
| Florida .................. | 20,745,993 | 12,136,176 | 1,566,829 | 4,903,960 | 401,097 | 1,062,497 | 659,775 | 15,659 |
| Georgia.................. | 13,981,000 | 8,791,568 | 523,061 | 2,585,948 | 342,276 | 1,222,021 | 515,786 | 341 |
| Hawaii.................... | 1,370,455 | 615,764 | 39,268 | 179,905 | 238,941 | 263,523 | 32,794 | 261 |
| Idaho..................... | 2,679,718 | 1,705,901 | 70,147 | 482,208 | 9,296 | 306,261 | 105,667 | 239 |
| Illinois................... | 14,738,484 | 9,427,237 | 1,252,592 | 1,597,863 | 1,268,521 | 574,285 | 608,207 | 9,781 |
| Indiana................... | 7,863,447 | 5,380,797 | 551,449 | 1,043,670 | 60,190 | 571,040 | 255,576 | 724 |
| Iowa ..................... | 4,120,546 | 2,178,132 | 969,685 | 330,501 | 61,361 | 389,725 | 189,821 | 1,322 |
| Kansas ................... | 3,572,804 | 2,385,397 | 153,233 | 608,633 | 10,319 | 290,491 | 124,494 | 237 |
| Kentucky ................. | 4,753,305 | 2,976,384 | 288,124 | 669,216 | 106,278 | 600,865 | 112,267 | 171 |
| Louisiana................. | 4,783,313 | 3,036,576 | 234,719 | 570,842 | 36,524 | 786,732 | 117,649 | 272 |
| Maine.................... | 1,352,266 | 795,897 | 42,989 | 161,079 | 20,282 | 257,028 | 74,666 | 325 |
| Maryland................. | 14,406,373 | 9,906,936 | 136,557 | 2,918,603 | 897,833 | 286,674 | 159,744 | 100,027 |
| Massachusetts .......... | 8,076,811 | 6,286,445 | 286,537 | 274,919 | 602,028 | 129,671 | 300,479 | 196,732 |
| Michigan................. | 8,411,895 | 4,998,790 | 625,829 | 1,052,268 | 471,637 | 896,733 | 366,300 | 337 |
| Minnesota................ | 8,610,684 | 5,884,579 | 410,179 | 666,135 | 374,731 | 756,928 | 455,782 | 62,351 |
| Mississippi .............. | 3,006,211 | 1,475,609 | 189,887 | 519,401 | 2,143 | 672,504 | 144,290 | 2,377 |
| Missouri.................. | 9,253,650 | 5,667,438 | 597,662 | 1,216,129 | 156,047 | 1,332,168 | 283,467 | 740 |
| Montana ................. | 1,502,302 | 861,341 | 55,137 | 185,698 | 22,706 | 307,632 | 688,761 | 917 |
| Nebraska ................ | 3,063,462 | 1,833,239 | 127,639 | 685,346 | 8,349 | 299,675 | 108,980 | 234 |
| Nevada .................. | 5,755,223 | 3,939,428 | 53,939 | 1,538,039 | 46,515 | 93,252 | 83,881 | 169 |
| New Hampshire ........ | 1,926,028 | 1,317,206 | 76,155 | 166,526 | 130,038 | 151,382 | 84,432 | 291 |
| New Jersey .............. | 13,200,261 | 10,482,890 | 313,950 | 688,578 | 1,215,012 | 149,576 | 349,983 | 272 |
| New Mexico .............. | 3,136,621 | 1,925,304 | 94,274 | 750,681 | 23,308 | 254,329 | 88,476 | 250 |
| New York................. | 15,480,682 | 11,806,299 | 1,028,598 | 550,073 | 445,398 | 373,373 | 899,472 | 377,469 |
| North Carolina........... | 12,054,310 | 6,711,449 | 307,053 | 3,205,760 | 118,296 | 1,287,096 | 424,289 | 367 |
| North Dakota............ | 1,619,492 | 583,581 | 54,734 | 144,657 | 12,019 | 776,808 | 47,473 | 220 |
| Ohio..................... | 12,543,044 | 8,538,269 | 708,157 | 1,891,981 | 308,251 | 708,657 | 380,787 | 6,941 |
| Oklahoma................ | 4,773,282 | 3,124,642 | 223,373 | 782,894 | 16,891 | 492,009 | 133,126 | 347 |
| Oregon................... | 6,175,093 | 4,121,839 | 325,203 | 973,074 | 121,563 | 496,556 | 136,302 | 582 |
| Pennsylvania ............ | 14,608,719 | 10,802,857 | 1,115,368 | 1,358,448 | 374,857 | 538,960 | 417,984 | 245 |
| Rhode Island............ | 1,462,741 | 1,154,901 | 98,554 | 67,775 | 51,115 | 24,298 | 66,028 | 70 |
| South Carolina.......... | 5,142,739 | 3,337,936 | 208,501 | 903,226 | 36,302 | 567,912 | 88,803 | 59 |
| South Dakota............ | 1,183,399 | 623,413 | 88,119 | 177,636 | 9,000 | 233,216 | 51,613 | 312 |
| Tennessee ................ | 8,630,482 | 5,926,135 | 377,964 | 1,481,258 | 149,918 | 559,265 | 135,730 | 211 |
| Texas .................... | 27,813,957 | 17,799,490 | 956,818 | 5,974,814 | 286,631 | 1,578,901 | 1,203,312 | 13,993 |
| Utah ..................... | 7,759,918 | 5,753,527 | 328,249 | 785,135 | 339,508 | 338,200 | 213,849 | 1,450 |
| Vermont.................. | 563,717 | 256,537 | 68,219 | 57,964 | 26,494 | 104,667 | 49,436 | 400 |
| Virginia.................. | 19,602,236 | 10,974,532 | 486,202 | 5,113,527 | 1,219,739 | 1,603,534 | 199,464 | 5,239 |
| Washington............... | 14,467,246 | 9,260,181 | 290,799 | 3,175,672 | 738,392 | 597,580 | 402,191 | 2,431 |
| West Virginia............. | 1,220,590 | 717,409 | 86,623 | 165,341 | 2,088 | 218,410 | 30,523 | 196 |
| Wisconsin................ | 6,242,345 | 3,809,144 | 319,327 | 803,235 | 111,636 | 779,120 | 418,453 | 1,430 |
| Wyoming ................. | 1,225,036 | 672,123 | 60,776 | 147,827 | 2,021 | 307,305 | 34,833 | 151 |
| Dist. of Columbia ..... | 1,921,774 | 798,099 | 499,692 | 23,618 | 404,084 | 0 | 24,580 | 171,701 |
| American Samoa ...... | 16,747 | 0 | 0 | 0 | 0 | 16,672 | 75 | 0 |
| Fed. States of Micronesia......... | 26 | 0 | 0 | 0 | 0 | 13,120 | 26 | 0 |
| Guam .................... | 62,593 | 0 | 8,245 | 5,073 | 0 | 42,436 | 6,840 | 0 |
| Marshall Islands........ | 0 | 0 | 0 | 0 | 0 | 0 | 0 | 0 |
| No. Mariana Islands... | 900 | 0 | 0 | 0 | 0 | 0 | 900 | 0 |
| Palau .................... | 0 | 0 | 0 | 0 | 0 | 0 | 0 | 0 |
| Puerto Rico.............. | 1,997,164 | 1,215,886 | 133,761 | 665,721 | 214,107 | 308,540 | 58,299 | 0 |
| U.S. Virgin Islands .... | 31,705 | 15,469 | 0 | 857 | 1,356 | 12,809 | 1,214 | 0 |
| Undistributed............ | 0 | 0 | 0 | 0 | 0 | 0 | 0 | 0 |

See footnotes at end of table.

## FEDERAL GOVERNMENT GUARANTEED LOAN PROGRAMS — VOLUME OF COVERAGE PROVIDED BY STATE AND OUTLYING AREA: FISCAL YEAR 2010 — Continued

*Source:* U.S. Census Bureau, *Consolidated Federal Funds Report for Fiscal Year 2010.* Released September 2011.

*Note:* Amounts represent dollar volume of loans guaranteed during the fiscal year. For additional information see the complete report at *http://www.census.gov/govs/www/cffr.html.* Detail may not add to total because of rounding.

The CFDA defines "Guaranteed/Insured Loans" as "Programs in which the federal government makes an arrangement to indemnify a lender against part or all of any defaults by those responsible for the repayment of loans." Loan and program amounts reflect the volume of loan activities. These amounts represent the federal government contingent liability for loans guaranteed. Loans and insurance data do not represent actual expenditures associated with the loan or insurance programs. Any actual outlays under these programs, such as insurance claims paid by the federal government, appear in the direct payments categories in the CFFR. Federal government contingent liability can vary by program, and caution

should be used in comparing one federal loan or insurance program to another, or in interpreting the data presented to reflect actual federal outlays over time.

The following also should be noted:

1. Amounts guaranteed or insured do not necessarily represent future outlays.

2. All amounts reflect the dollar value of loans or insurance coverage provided during the fiscal year, and not the cumulative totals of such activity over the life of the program.

3. Direct loans are not reported on a net basis, as in the federal budget, but rather are shown in terms of total amounts loaned.

4. Programs otherwise similar can vary in the share of the total liability that the federal government guarantees or insures. Certain veterans guaranteed loan programs are guaranteed only up to a stated maximum dollar value, for example. In these cases, the federal government contingent liability is less than the total value of the loan or insured policy agreement.

## Table 2.14
## FEDERAL GOVERNMENT INSURANCE PROGRAMS — VOLUME OF COVERAGE PROVIDED BY STATE
## AND OUTLYING AREA: FISCAL YEAR 2010
### (In thousands of dollars)

| State and outlying area | Total | Flood insurance | Crop insurance | Foreign investment insurance | Life insurance for veterans | Other insurance |
|---|---|---|---|---|---|---|
| | | | | *Insurance programs by volume of coverage provided* | | |
| United States .............. | $1,324,168,480 | $1,233,560,464 | $763,680,134 | $134,309 | $13,597,220 | $508,474 |
| Alabama....................... | 11,996,351 | 11,441,711 | 357,195 | 0 | 196,506 | 939 |
| Alaska.......................... | 680,455 | 653,664 | 376 | 0 | 19,568 | 6,846 |
| Arizona........................ | 8,150,539 | 7,639,032 | 208,346 | 0 | 301,175 | 1,986 |
| Arkansas...................... | 3,789,974 | 2,582,595 | 1,085,422 | 0 | 120,213 | 1,745 |
| California..................... | 73,929,226 | 68,009,958 | 4,490,152 | 1,373 | 1,347,151 | 80,592 |
| Colorado...................... | 5,325,471 | 4,166,201 | 871,897 | 7,000 | 249,975 | 55,398 |
| Connecticut................. | 8,800,221 | 8,518,978 | 63,939 | 7,290 | 208,864 | 1,149 |
| Delaware ..................... | 6,090,115 | 5,948,314 | 93,543 | 0 | 43,700 | 4,558 |
| Florida ........................ | 472,732,970 | 468,567,622 | 2,855,011 | 0 | 1,291,834 | 18,504 |
| Georgia........................ | 24,243,680 | 22,937,655 | 968,545 | 0 | 330,489 | 6,992 |
| Hawaii.......................... | 11,873,888 | 11,642,548 | 106,906 | 0 | 124,434 | 0 |
| Idaho........................... | 2,348,301 | 1,501,455 | 776,802 | 0 | 61,403 | 8,641 |
| Illinois......................... | 16,458,448 | 8,091,016 | 7,799,770 | 4,500 | 553,076 | 10,087 |
| Indiana........................ | 8,907,091 | 5,029,944 | 3,663,565 | 0 | 207,174 | 6,408 |
| Iowa............................. | 12,182,519 | 2,684,210 | 9,321,308 | 0 | 168,747 | 8,255 |
| Kansas ........................ | 5,609,149 | 1,955,092 | 3,518,177 | 0 | 129,384 | 6,496 |
| Kentucky ..................... | 4,333,071 | 3,243,258 | 939,624 | 0 | 144,459 | 5,730 |
| Louisiana..................... | 107,505,758 | 106,619,368 | 716,368 | 0 | 157,158 | 12,865 |
| Maine........................... | 1,995,324 | 1,843,480 | 74,695 | 0 | 77,149 | 0 |
| Maryland ..................... | 15,016,697 | 14,425,036 | 261,748 | 31,437 | 277,885 | 20,590 |
| Massachusetts ............. | 12,231,285 | 11,801,652 | 60,699 | 14,580 | 348,766 | 5,588 |
| Michigan...................... | 5,893,265 | 4,093,951 | 1,415,474 | 0 | 373,104 | 10,753 |
| Minnesota.................... | 8,975,492 | 2,542,674 | 6,137,646 | 0 | 292,644 | 2,528 |
| Mississippi .................. | 16,639,287 | 15,606,212 | 937,371 | 384 | 94,555 | 765 |
| Missouri....................... | 6,354,556 | 3,982,783 | 2,092,583 | 0 | 260,036 | 19,154 |
| Montana ...................... | 1,675,394 | 819,076 | 793,133 | 0 | 55,849 | 7,336 |
| Nebraska ..................... | 7,459,826 | 1,909,199 | 5,445,878 | 0 | 103,706 | 1,042 |
| Nevada......................... | 3,725,244 | 3,598,174 | 27,592 | 0 | 92,012 | 7,466 |
| New Hampshire ........... | 1,832,537 | 1,753,112 | 5,652 | 0 | 73,293 | 481 |
| New Jersey .................. | 51,696,174 | 51,143,521 | 87,786 | 0 | 452,952 | 11,915 |
| New Mexico ................. | 3,011,548 | 2,777,736 | 120,161 | 0 | 108,607 | 5,044 |
| New York...................... | 39,837,829 | 38,563,788 | 360,588 | 64,374 | 847,143 | 1,936 |
| North Carolina............. | 33,397,868 | 31,607,337 | 1,395,281 | 0 | 393,989 | 1,261 |
| North Dakota............... | 6,813,235 | 2,823,964 | 3,953,999 | 0 | 34,593 | 679 |
| Ohio ............................ | 9,169,388 | 6,169,246 | 2,481,784 | 0 | 484,961 | 33,398 |
| Oklahoma.................... | 3,536,232 | 2,707,111 | 658,123 | 0 | 166,608 | 4,390 |
| Oregon......................... | 7,907,793 | 7,136,628 | 588,444 | 0 | 178,595 | 4,126 |
| Pennsylvania ............... | 12,960,341 | 11,846,702 | 380,313 | 0 | 692,054 | 41,272 |
| Rhode Island............... | 3,788,494 | 3,733,325 | 925 | 0 | 54,245 | 0 |
| South Carolina............. | 48,142,415 | 47,564,968 | 360,830 | 0 | 216,591 | 26 |
| South Dakota............... | 4,308,322 | 1,075,153 | 3,186,949 | 0 | 45,979 | 241 |
| Tennessee ................... | 7,058,268 | 6,162,643 | 671,055 | 1,800 | 217,775 | 4,996 |
| Texas........................... | 162,994,364 | 158,989,049 | 3,147,649 | 0 | 828,638 | 29,028 |
| Utah............................. | 1,060,701 | 923,193 | 24,557 | 0 | 86,934 | 26,017 |
| Vermont....................... | 698,911 | 642,680 | 25,254 | 0 | 30,977 | 0 |
| Virginia........................ | 26,938,440 | 26,109,706 | 418,014 | 0 | 395,736 | 14,984 |
| Washington.................. | 14,903,235 | 12,880,865 | 1,719,993 | 0 | 296,784 | 5,594 |
| West Virginia............... | 2,679,943 | 2,580,631 | 16,663 | 0 | 82,238 | 411 |
| Wisconsin .................... | 4,799,267 | 2,660,735 | 1,835,040 | 0 | 300,514 | 2,978 |
| Wyoming ...................... | 643,995 | 509,809 | 105,755 | 0 | 24,993 | 3,437 |
| Dist. of Columbia ........ | 317,783 | 285,234 | 0 | 1,571 | 22,946 | 8,031 |
| American Samoa ......... | 13,695 | 13,695 | 0 | 0 | 0 | 0 |
| Fed. States of Micronesia............ | 0 | 0 | 0 | 0 | 0 | 0 |
| Guam........................... | 49,924 | 49,924 | 0 | 0 | 0 | 0 |
| Marshall Islands........... | 0 | 0 | 0 | 0 | 0 | 0 |
| No. Mariana Islands .... | 0 | 0 | 0 | 0 | 0 | 0 |
| Palau............................ | 0 | 0 | 0 | 0 | 0 | 0 |
| Puerto Rico................. | 5,605,626 | 5,570,292 | 0 | 0 | 35,334 | 0 |
| U.S. Virgin Islands ....... | 363,058 | 358,472 | 0 | 0 | 4,586 | 0 |
| Undistributed............... | 600 | 600 | 0 | 0 | 0 | 0 |

See footnotes at end of table.

## FEDERAL GOVERNMENT INSURANCE PROGRAMS — VOLUME OF COVERAGE PROVIDED BY STATE AND OUTLYING AREA: FISCAL YEAR 2010 — Continued

*Source:* U.S. Census Bureau, *Consolidated Federal Funds Report for Fiscal Year 2010.* Released September 2011.

*Note:* Amounts represent dollar volume of the face value of insurance coverage provided during the fiscal year. Detail may not add to total because of rounding. For additional information see the complete report at *http://www.census.gov/govs/www/cffr.html.*

The CFDA defines "Insurance" as "financial assistance provided to assure reimbursement for losses sustained under specified conditions. Coverage may be provided directly by the federal government or through private carriers and may or may not involve the payment of premiums."

All data on insurance programs of the federal government, with the exception of data on flood insurance, come from the FAADS. Flood Insurance data, reflecting insurance in force on September 30, 2010, are from FEMA, Department of Homeland Security.

Insurance program amounts reflect the volume of insurance activities. Insurance data do not represent actual expenditures associated with the loan or insurance programs. Any actual outlays under these programs, such as insurance claims paid by the federal government, appear in the direct payments categories in the CFFR. Federal government contingent liability can vary by program, and caution should be used in comparing one federal loan or insurance program to another, or in interpreting the data presented to reflect actual federal outlays over time.

The following also should be noted:

1. Amounts insured do not necessarily represent future outlays.

2. All amounts reflect the dollar value of insurance coverage provided during the fiscal year, and not the cumulative totals of such activity over the life of the program.

3. Programs otherwise similar can vary in the share of the total liability that the federal government guarantees or insures.

## Table 2.15
## PER CAPITA AMOUNTS OF FEDERAL GOVERNMENT EXPENDITURE, BY MAJOR OBJECT CATEGORY, BY STATE AND OUTLYING AREA: FISCAL YEAR 2010
### (In dollars)

| State and outlying area | United States resident population— April 1, 2010 (a) | Total | Retirement and disability | Other direct payments | Grants | Procurement | Salaries and wages |
|---|---|---|---|---|---|---|---|
| United States totals ........... | $308,745,538 | $10,459.69 | $2,935.25 | $2,633.32 | $2,187.11 | $1,604.73 | $1,099.28 |
| Alabama .............................. | 4,779,736 | 11,819.83 | 3,761.03 | 2,751.33 | 2,751.33 | 1,940.15 | 1,174.37 |
| Alaska.................................. | 710,231 | 17,762.29 | 2,239.71 | 1,464.38 | 4,878.99 | 3,469.68 | 5,709.52 |
| Arizona................................ | 6,392,017 | 10,079.26 | 2,899.67 | 2,149.17 | 2,246.71 | 2,004.55 | 779.16 |
| Arkansas.............................. | 2,915,918 | 9,912.49 | 3,554.14 | 2,581.91 | 2,346.79 | 600.49 | 829.16 |
| California ............................ | 37,253,956 | 8,960.37 | 2,277.43 | 2,361.52 | 2,117.06 | 1,544.45 | 659.92 |
| Colorado.............................. | 5,029,196 | 9,879.68 | 2,552.89 | 1,823.24 | 1,748.37 | 2,061.37 | 1,693.81 |
| Connecticut ........................ | 3,574,097 | 15,662.23 | 2,839.41 | 6,623.15 | 2,321.95 | 3,345.35 | 532.37 |
| Delaware ............................. | 897,934 | 8,994.35 | 3,403.17 | 2,110.54 | 2,288.76 | 403.88 | 788.01 |
| Florida................................. | 18,801,310 | 9,930.36 | 3,423.96 | 3,367.71 | 1,492.78 | 956.36 | 689.55 |
| Georgia................................ | 9,687,653 | 9,536.58 | 2,689.97 | 2,038.08 | 1,729.07 | 1,286.24 | 1,793.21 |
| Hawaii.................................. | 1,360,301 | 15,331.33 | 3,211.37 | 2,072.20 | 2,224.18 | 2,017.80 | 5,805.78 |
| Idaho................................... | 1,567,582 | 9,091.54 | 2,907.82 | 1,808.76 | 1,900.71 | 1,679.87 | 794.39 |
| Illinois................................. | 12,830,632 | 8,570.70 | 2,637.77 | 2,534.03 | 1,875.20 | 904.13 | 619.57 |
| Indiana................................ | 6,483,802 | 9,038.43 | 3,035.58 | 2,637.09 | 1,845.33 | 848.02 | 672.40 |
| Iowa .................................... | 3,046,355 | 9,315.67 | 3,106.61 | 2,706.74 | 2,099.04 | 778.83 | 624.45 |
| Kansas................................. | 2,853,118 | 10,180.27 | 3,009.34 | 2,399.18 | 1,660.03 | 1,072.39 | 2,039.34 |
| Kentucky ............................. | 4,339,367 | 13,197.90 | 3,419.04 | 3,742.70 | 2,189.78 | 1,725.17 | 2,121.21 |
| Louisiana............................. | 4,533,372 | 11,738.34 | 2,874.90 | 2,889.81 | 3,328.11 | 1,608.22 | 1,037.31 |
| Maine................................... | 1,328,361 | 11,024.05 | 3,683.21 | 2,329.28 | 2,851.20 | 1,306.65 | 853.70 |
| Maryland ............................. | 5,773,552 | 16,672.74 | 3,311.41 | 3,661.00 | 2,501.30 | 4,593.79 | 2,605.24 |
| Massachusetts .................... | 6,547,629 | 12,592.89 | 2,812.04 | 3,237.25 | 3,413.73 | 2,441.70 | 688.18 |
| Michigan.............................. | 9,883,640 | 9,199.15 | 3,278.50 | 2,698.95 | 2,081.96 | 654.27 | 485.47 |
| Minnesota............................ | 5,303,925 | 8,366.58 | 2,691.02 | 2,499.31 | 1,984.92 | 556.28 | 635.07 |
| Mississippi .......................... | 2,967,297 | 10,588.38 | 3,297.28 | 2,723.39 | 2,652.63 | 898.43 | 1,016.65 |
| Missouri............................... | 5,988,927 | 11,746.36 | 3,209.44 | 2,805.42 | 2,338.07 | 2,171.07 | 1,222.36 |
| Montana .............................. | 989,415 | 10,873.52 | 3,440.27 | 2,426.86 | 2,970.88 | 828.17 | 1,207.35 |
| Nebraska.............................. | 1,826,341 | 9,051.87 | 2,988.06 | 2,451.98 | 1,920.21 | 715.49 | 976.13 |
| Nevada................................. | 2,700,551 | 7,321.11 | 2,682.81 | 1,657.20 | 1,370.74 | 891.35 | 719.00 |
| New Hampshire ................... | 1,316,470 | 8,610.37 | 3,269.36 | 1,826.73 | 1,755.49 | 1,090.30 | 668.48 |
| New Jersey........................... | 8,791,894 | 9,211.90 | 2,823.48 | 2,831.63 | 1,758.07 | 1,164.29 | 634.43 |
| New Mexico ......................... | 2,059,179 | 13,577.73 | 3,219.07 | 2,109.22 | 3,263.54 | 3,641.68 | 1,344.23 |
| New York.............................. | 19,378,102 | 10,437.87 | 2,776.85 | 2,968.96 | 3,256.44 | 716.44 | 719.19 |
| North Carolina..................... | 9,535,483 | 9,515.69 | 3,105.35 | 2,054.10 | 2,107.80 | 638.72 | 1,609.72 |
| North Dakota........................ | 672,591 | 12,929.83 | 3,278.44 | 3,695.25 | 3,326.42 | 1,018.83 | 1,610.89 |
| Ohio .................................... | 11,536,504 | 9,227.12 | 3,045.91 | 2,696.35 | 2,114.94 | 765.34 | 604.59 |
| Oklahoma............................ | 3,751,351 | 10,256.30 | 3,351.19 | 2,425.38 | 2,093.86 | 899.62 | 1,486.25 |
| Oregon................................. | 3,831,074 | 8,868.03 | 3,152.66 | 2,241.13 | 2,269.46 | 534.33 | 670.44 |
| Pennsylvania ....................... | 12,702,379 | 11,488.70 | 3,421.26 | 3,535.51 | 2,315.41 | 1,523.53 | 692.99 |
| Rhode Island........................ | 1,052,567 | 11,172.13 | 3,166.59 | 3,112.54 | 2,994.62 | 951.39 | 946.99 |
| South Carolina..................... | 4,625,364 | 10,070.16 | 3,443.10 | 2,086.93 | 1,775.10 | 1,766.64 | 998.39 |
| South Dakota....................... | 814,180 | 11,676.28 | 3,223.58 | 3,301.97 | 2,763.70 | 1,121.27 | 1,265.76 |
| Tennessee ........................... | 6,346,105 | 10,851.62 | 3,327.67 | 3,100.67 | 2,220.96 | 1,597.93 | 604.67 |
| Texas................................... | 25,145,561 | 8,976.73 | 2,402.92 | 1,994.67 | 1,774.63 | 1,614.38 | 1,190.13 |
| Utah.................................... | 2,763,885 | 8,518.87 | 2,180.12 | 2,018.78 | 1,804.24 | 1,359.83 | 1,155.91 |
| Vermont............................... | 625,741 | 11,833.69 | 3,207.26 | 2,177.13 | 3,803.34 | 1,488.86 | 1,157.10 |
| Virginia................................ | 8,001,024 | 17,008.19 | 3,537.60 | 2,012.39 | 1,528.25 | 7,291.27 | 2,638.68 |
| Washington.......................... | 6,724,540 | 10,474.69 | 3,046.03 | 2,029.82 | 2,189.80 | 1,493.16 | 1,715.89 |
| West Virginia........................ | 1,852,994 | 11,608.56 | 4,177.45 | 2,741.87 | 2,682.25 | 961.98 | 1,045.01 |
| Wisconsin ........................... | 5,686,986 | 9,647.65 | 2,959.83 | 2,340.44 | 2,108.68 | 1,724.12 | 514.58 |
| Wyoming.............................. | 563,626 | 11,019.09 | 2,916.81 | 1,834.32 | 3,999.34 | 1,010.22 | 1,258.41 |
| Dist. of Columbia ............... | 601,723 | 102,904.18 | 4,631.23 | 6,617.18 | 18,068.00 | 35,315.07 | 38,272.62 |
| American Samoa ................. | 66,000 | 7,803.81 | 919.45 | 224.49 | 6,177.99 | 385.33 | 96.55 |
| Fed. States of Micronesia... | 107,000 | 2,236.27 | 5.40 | 0.92 | 2,189.34 | 40.61 | 0 |
| Guam................................... | 181,000 | 11,118.55 | 1,624.89 | 776.23 | 2,484.18 | 4,152.61 | 2,080.64 |
| Marshall Islands.................. | 66,000 | 1,937.02 | 1.58 | 8.83 | 1,914.90 | 11.7 | 0 |
| No. Mariana Islands .......... | 48,000 | 5,207.94 | 686.90 | 132.34 | 3,949.16 | 250.01 | 189.53 |
| Palau................................... | 21,000 | 1,394.20 | 14.08 | 161.23 | 1,159.55 | 59.34 | 0 |
| Puerto Rico ......................... | 3,725,789 | 5,668.09 | 2,134.13 | 1,331.14 | 1,694.51 | 280.02 | 228.30 |
| U.S. Virgin Islands ............. | 110,000 | 7,466.10 | 2,173.64 | 1,228.64 | 3,033.78 | 459.52 | 570.51 |
| Undistributed...................... | 0 | 0 | 0 | 0 | 0 | 0 | 0 |

Source: U.S. Census Bureau, *Consolidated Federal Funds Report for Fiscal Year 2010.* Released September 2011.

Note: Data are not subject to sampling error. Data users who create their own estimates from these tables should cite the U.S. Census Bureau as the source of the original data only. U.S. total population and per capita figures in the top line include only the 50 states and the District of Columbia; the U.S. Outlying Areas displayed at the bottom of the table are excluded.

Key:
(a) All population figures represent resident population as of April 1, 2010.

## Table 2.16
## PERCENT DISTRIBUTION OF FEDERAL GOVERNMENT EXPENDITURE, BY MAJOR OBJECT CATEGORY, BY STATE AND OUTLYING AREA: FISCAL YEAR 2010
(In dollars)

| State and outlying area | Percent distribution of United States resident population— July 1, 2010 (a) | Total | Retirement and disability | Other direct payments | Grants | Procurement | Salaries and wages |
|---|---|---|---|---|---|---|---|
| United States ..................... | 100% | 100% | 100% | 100% | 100% | 100% | 100% |
| Alabama ............................. | 1.5 | 1.7 | 2.0 | 1.6 | 1.4 | 2.0 | 1.6 |
| Alaska................................. | 0.2 | 0.4 | 0.2 | 0.1 | 0.5 | 0.5 | 1.2 |
| Arizona............................... | 2.0 | 2.0 | 2.0 | 1.7 | 2.1 | 2.5 | 1.5 |
| Arkansas............................. | 0.9 | 0.9 | 1.1 | 0.9 | 1.0 | 0.3 | 0.7 |
| California ........................... | 11.9 | 10.2 | 9.3 | 10.7 | 11.5 | 11.1 | 7.2 |
| Colorado............................. | 1.6 | 1.5 | 1.4 | 1.1 | 1.3 | 2.0 | 2.5 |
| Connecticut........................ | 1.1 | 1.7 | 1.1 | 2.9 | 1.2 | 2.3 | 0.6 |
| Delaware............................. | 0.3 | 0.2 | 0.3 | 0.2 | 0.3 | 0.1 | 0.2 |
| Florida ............................... | 6.0 | 5.7 | 7.0 | 7.7 | 4.1 | 3.5 | 3.8 |
| Georgia............................... | 3.1 | 2.8 | 2.8 | 2.4 | 2.5 | 2.4 | 5.1 |
| Hawaii................................ | 0.4 | 0.6 | 0.5 | 0.3 | 0.4 | 0.5 | 2.3 |
| Idaho.................................. | 0.5 | 0.4 | 0.5 | 0.3 | 0.4 | 0.5 | 0.4 |
| Illinois................................ | 4.1 | 3.4 | 3.7 | 4.0 | 3.5 | 2.2 | 2.3 |
| Indiana................................ | 2.1 | 1.8 | 2.2 | 2.1 | 1.8 | 1.1 | 1.3 |
| Iowa ................................... | 1.0 | 0.9 | 1.0 | 1.0 | 0.9 | 0.5 | 0.6 |
| Kansas ................................ | 0.9 | 0.9 | 0.9 | 0.8 | 0.7 | 0.6 | 1.7 |
| Kentucky ............................ | 1.4 | 1.7 | 1.6 | 2.0 | 1.4 | 1.4 | 2.7 |
| Louisiana............................ | 1.4 | 1.6 | 1.4 | 1.6 | 2.2 | 1.4 | 1.4 |
| Maine.................................. | 0.4 | 0.4 | 0.5 | 0.4 | 0.6 | 0.3 | 0.3 |
| Maryland ............................ | 1.8 | 2.9 | 2.1 | 2.6 | 2.1 | 5.1 | 4.4 |
| Massachusetts .................... | 2.1 | 2.5 | 2.0 | 2.6 | 3.3 | 3.1 | 1.3 |
| Michigan............................. | 3.2 | 2.8 | 3.5 | 3.3 | 3.0 | 1.3 | 1.4 |
| Minnesota........................... | 1.7 | 1.4 | 1.6 | 1.6 | 1.5 | 0.6 | 1.0 |
| Mississippi ......................... | 0.9 | 1.0 | 1.1 | 1.0 | 1.2 | 0.5 | 0.9 |
| Missouri.............................. | 1.9 | 2.1 | 2.1 | 2.1 | 2.0 | 2.5 | 2.1 |
| Montana ............................. | 0.3 | 0.3 | 0.4 | 0.4 | 0.4 | 0.1 | 0.4 |
| Nebraska............................. | 0.6 | 0.5 | 0.6 | 0.5 | 0.5 | 0.3 | 0.5 |
| Nevada................................ | 0.9 | 0.6 | 0.8 | 0.5 | 0.5 | 0.5 | 0.6 |
| New Hampshire .................. | 0.4 | 0.3 | 0.5 | 0.3 | 0.3 | 0.3 | 0.3 |
| New Jersey ......................... | 2.8 | 2.5 | 2.7 | 3.0 | 2.3 | 2.0 | 1.6 |
| New Mexico ....................... | 0.7 | 0.9 | 0.7 | 0.5 | 1.0 | 1.5 | 0.8 |
| New York............................ | 6.2 | 6.2 | 5.9 | 7.0 | 9.2 | 2.7 | 4.1 |
| North Carolina.................... | 3.0 | 2.8 | 3.2 | 2.4 | 2.9 | 1.2 | 4.5 |
| North Dakota....................... | 0.2 | 0.3 | 0.2 | 0.3 | 0.3 | 0.1 | 0.3 |
| Ohio ................................... | 3.7 | 3.2 | 3.8 | 3.8 | 3.6 | 1.7 | 2.0 |
| Oklahoma............................ | 1.2 | 1.2 | 1.4 | 1.1 | 1.1 | 0.7 | 1.6 |
| Oregon................................ | 1.2 | 1.0 | 1.3 | 1.0 | 1.3 | 0.4 | 0.7 |
| Pennsylvania ...................... | 4.1 | 4.5 | 4.8 | 5.5 | 4.3 | 3.7 | 2.6 |
| Rhode Island....................... | 0.3 | 0.4 | 0.4 | 0.4 | 0.5 | 0.2 | 0.3 |
| South Carolina.................... | 1.5 | 1.4 | 1.7 | 1.2 | 1.2 | 1.6 | 1.3 |
| South Dakota....................... | 0.3 | 0.3 | 0.3 | 0.3 | 0.3 | 0.2 | 0.3 |
| Tennessee ........................... | 2.0 | 2.1 | 2.3 | 2.4 | 2.1 | 2.0 | 1.1 |
| Texas.................................. | 8.0 | 6.9 | 6.6 | 6.1 | 6.5 | 7.9 | 8.7 |
| Utah ................................... | 0.9 | 0.7 | 0.7 | 0.7 | 0.7 | 0.7 | 0.9 |
| Vermont.............................. | 0.2 | 0.2 | 0.2 | 0.2 | 0.3 | 0.2 | 0.2 |
| Virginia............................... | 2.6 | 4.2 | 3.1 | 2.0 | 1.8 | 11.3 | 6.2 |
| Washington......................... | 2.1 | 2.1 | 2.2 | 1.7 | 2.2 | 1.9 | 3.4 |
| West Virginia...................... | 0.6 | 0.7 | 0.8 | 0.6 | 0.7 | 0.3 | 0.6 |
| Wisconsin .......................... | 1.8 | 1.7 | 1.8 | 1.6 | 1.8 | 1.9 | 0.9 |
| Wyoming ............................ | 0.2 | 0.2 | 0.2 | 0.1 | 0.3 | 0.1 | 0.2 |
| Dist. of Columbia ............... | 0.2 | 1.9 | 0.3 | 0.5 | 1.6 | 4.1 | 6.7 |
| American Samoa ................. | 0.0 | 0.0 | 0.0 | 0.0 | 0.1 | 0.0 | 0.0 |
| Fed. States of Micronesia ... | 0.0 | 0.0 | 0.0 | 0.0 | 0.0 | 0.0 | 0.0 |
| Guam .................................. | 0.1 | 0.1 | 0.0 | 0.0 | 0.1 | 0.1 | 0.1 |
| Marshall Islands................. | 0.0 | 0.0 | 0.0 | 0.0 | 0.0 | 0.0 | 0.0 |
| No. Mariana Islands .......... | 0.0 | 0.0 | 0.0 | 0.0 | 0.0 | 0.0 | 0.0 |
| Palau .................................. | 0.0 | 0.0 | 0.0 | 0.0 | 0.0 | 0.0 | 0.0 |
| Puerto Rico........................ | 1.2 | 0.6 | 0.9 | 0.6 | 0.9 | 0.2 | 0.2 |
| U.S. Virgin Islands............. | 0.0 | 0.0 | 0.0 | 0.0 | 0.1 | 0.0 | 0.0 |
| Undistributed...................... | 0.0 | 0.7 | 0.0 | 0.0 | 0.0 | 3.7 | 0.7 |

*Source:* U.S. Census Bureau, *Consolidated Federal Funds Report for Fiscal Year 2010.* Data are not subject to sampling error, but for information on processing and response error, see the Reliability of the Data section in the Introduction. Data users who create their own estimates from these tables should cite the U.S. Census Bureau as the source of the original data only.

*Note:* Values for the 50 states, the District of Columbia, and the U.S. Outlying Areas were used in calculating these distributions.

*Key:* (a) All population figures represent resident population as of April 1, 2010.

## Table 2.17
## FEDERAL GOVERNMENT EXPENDITURE FOR DEFENSE DEPARTMENT AND ALL OTHER AGENCIES, BY STATE AND OUTLYING AREA: FISCAL YEAR 2010

| State and outlying area | Federal expenditure (millions of dollars) | | Per capita federal expenditure (dollars) (a) | | Percent distribution of federal expenditure | | Exhibit: Dept. of Energy, defense-related activities (millions of dollars) (b) |
|---|---|---|---|---|---|---|---|
| | Dept. of Defense | All other federal agencies | Dept. of Defense | All other federal agencies | Dept. of Defense | All other federal agencies | |
| United States ............ | $556,959 | $2,719,463 | $1,772.90 | $8,686.78 | 100% | 100% | $16,108 |
| Alabama..................... | 13,029 | 43,466 | 2,725.98 | 9,093.85 | 2.3 | 1.6 | 0 |
| Alaska...................... | 5,211 | 7,404 | 7,337.59 | 10,424.71 | 0.9 | 0.3 | 0 |
| Arizona...................... | 14,263 | 50,164 | 2,231.31 | 7,847.95 | 2.6 | 1.8 | 0 |
| Arkansas.................... | 2,968 | 25,936 | 1,017.70 | 8,894.78 | 0.5 | 1.1 | 0 |
| California ................ | 55,750 | 278,059 | 1,496.49 | 7,463.89 | 10.0 | 10.2 | 1,124 |
| Colorado.................... | 12,211 | 37,476 | 2,428.01 | 7,451.67 | 2.2 | 1.4 | 128 |
| Connecticut.............. | 11,980 | 43,998 | 3,351.88 | 12,310.35 | 2.2 | 1.6 | 0 |
| Delaware .................. | 817 | 7,259 | 909.91 | 8,084.45 | 0.1 | 0.3 | 0 |
| Florida...................... | 22,647 | 164,056 | 1,204.56 | 8,725.80 | 4.1 | 6.0 | 8 |
| Georgia...................... | 22,794 | 69,594 | 2,352.85 | 7,183.74 | 4.1 | 2.6 | 0 |
| Hawaii....................... | 10,003 | 10,852 | 7,353.81 | 7,977.52 | 1.8 | 0.4 | 0 |
| Idaho........................ | 1,079 | 13,173 | 688.32 | 8,403.22 | 0.2 | 0.5 | 751 |
| Illinois...................... | 10,442 | 99,525 | 813.87 | 7,756.83 | 1.9 | 3.7 | 74 |
| Indiana...................... | 7,147 | 51,456 | 1,102.34 | 7,936.09 | 1.3 | 1.9 | 0 |
| Iowa ........................ | 2,581 | 25,797 | 847.36 | 8,468.31 | 0.5 | 0.9 | 0 |
| Kansas ..................... | 6,921 | 22,124 | 2,425.78 | 7,754.49 | 1.2 | 0.8 | 0 |
| Kentucky ................. | 13,252 | 44,018 | 3,053.92 | 10,143.98 | 2.4 | 1.6 | 23 |
| Louisiana.................. | 9,297 | 43,917 | 2,050.87 | 9,687.47 | 1.7 | 1.6 | 0 |
| Maine....................... | 2,152 | 12,492 | 1,619.85 | 9,404.20 | 0.4 | 0.5 | 0 |
| Maryland .................. | 18,677 | 77,584 | 3,234.97 | 13,437.77 | 3.4 | 2.9 | 0 |
| Massachusetts ........... | 14,562 | 67,892 | 2,224.02 | 10,368.87 | 2.6 | 2.5 | 0 |
| Michigan................... | 6,057 | 84,865 | 612.79 | 8,586.37 | 1.1 | 3.1 | 0 |
| Minnesota................. | 3,114 | 41,261 | 587.19 | 7,779.39 | 0.6 | 1.5 | 0 |
| Mississippi................ | 4,070 | 27,349 | 1,371.55 | 9,216.83 | 0.7 | 1.0 | 4 |
| Missouri.................... | 15,133 | 55,215 | 2,526.91 | 9,219.44 | 2.7 | 2.0 | 433 |
| Montana ................... | 946 | 9,812 | 956.43 | 9,917.10 | 0.2 | 0.4 | 0 |
| Nebraska .................. | 2,112 | 14,420 | 1,156.49 | 7,895.38 | 0.4 | 0.5 | 0 |
| Nevada ..................... | 2,896 | 16,875 | 1,072.28 | 624,882.00 | 0.5 | 0.6 | 492 |
| New Hampshire ........ | 1,603 | 9,732 | 1,217.53 | 7,392.85 | 0.3 | 0.4 | 0 |
| New Jersey ................ | 10,351 | 70,639 | 1,177.38 | 8,034.53 | 1.9 | 2.6 | 0 |
| New Mexico .............. | 3,236 | 24,723 | 1,571.53 | 12,006.20 | 0.6 | 0.9 | 3,718 |
| New York .................. | 15,244 | 187,023 | 786.64 | 9,651.23 | 2.7 | 6.9 | 500 |
| North Carolina.......... | 17,607 | 73,130 | 1,846.46 | 7,669.23 | 3.2 | 2.7 | 0 |
| North Dakota............. | 1,039 | 7,657 | 1,544.91 | 11,384.92 | 0.2 | 0.3 | 0 |
| Ohio......................... | 9,954 | 96,495 | 862.84 | 8,364.29 | 1.8 | 3.5 | 135 |
| Oklahoma.................. | 7,008 | 31,466 | 1,868.26 | 8,388.04 | 1.3 | 1.2 | 0 |
| Oregon...................... | 2,160 | 31,814 | 563.92 | 8,304.11 | 0.4 | 1.2 | 0 |
| Pennsylvania ............. | 16,254 | 129,680 | 1,279.57 | 10,209.13 | 2.9 | 4.8 | 434 |
| Rhode Island............. | 1,488 | 10,271 | 1,414.05 | 9,758.08 | 0.3 | 0.4 | 0 |
| South Carolina.......... | 8,853 | 37,726 | 1,913.92 | 8,156.24 | 1.6 | 1.4 | 2,359 |
| South Dakota............. | 1,180 | 8,327 | 1,448.83 | 10,227.44 | 0.2 | 0.3 | 0 |
| Tennessee ................. | 5,647 | 63,219 | 889.76 | 9,961.86 | 1.0 | 2.3 | 1,381 |
| Texas........................ | 54,249 | 171,476 | 2,157.39 | 6,819.34 | 9.7 | 6.3 | 556 |
| Utah......................... | 4,782 | 18,764 | 1,730.03 | 6,788.85 | 0.9 | 0.7 | 0 |
| Vermont.................... | 1,101 | 6,304 | 1,759.91 | 10,073.78 | 0.2 | 0.2 | 0 |
| Virginia..................... | 58,115 | 77,968 | 7,263.42 | 9,744.77 | 10.4 | 2.9 | 0 |
| Washington............... | 14,964 | 55,474 | 2,225.24 | 8,249.45 | 2.7 | 2.0 | 2,580 |
| West Virginia............. | 1,129 | 20,382 | 609.26 | 10,999.30 | 0.2 | 0.7 | 19 |
| Wisconsin ................. | 9,980 | 44,886 | 1,754.94 | 7,892.71 | 1.8 | 1.7 | 0 |
| Wyoming................... | 621 | 5,590 | 1,101.73 | 9,917.36 | 0.1 | 0.2 | 16 |
| Dist. of Columbia ..... | 8,699 | 53,221 | 14,456.62 | 88,447.56 | 1.6 | 2.0 | 1,372 |
| American Samoa ...... | 10 | 505 | 146.40 | 7,657.41 | 0.0 | 0.0 | 0 |
| Fed. States of Micronesia........ | 1 | 238 | 9.10 | 2,227.17 | 0.0 | 0.0 | 0 |
| Guam ....................... | 1,093 | 920 | 6,036.66 | 5,081.89 | 0.2 | 0.0 | 0 |
| Marshall Islands........ | 0 | 128 | -0.36 | 1,937.38 | 0.0 | 0.0 | 0 |
| No. Mariana Islands... | 3 | 247 | 64.57 | 5,143.36 | 0.0 | 0.0 | 0 |
| Palau........................ | 0 | 29 | 6.42 | 1,387.79 | 0.0 | 0.0 | 0 |
| Puerto Rico .............. | 684 | 20,434 | 183.50 | 5,484.60 | 0.1 | 0.8 | 0 |
| U.S. Virgin Islands .... | 322 | 789 | 294.47 | 7,171.62 | 0.0 | 0.0 | 0 |
| Undistributed............ | 7,760 | 14,167 | 0.00 | 0.00 | 1.4 | 0.5 | 0 |

Source: U.S. Census Bureau, *Consolidated Federal Funds Report for Fiscal Year 2010*. Released September 2011.
Note: Detail may not add to total because of rounding. For additional information see the complete report at *http://www.census.gov/govs/www/cffr.html.*

Key:
(a) All population figures represent resident population as of April 1, 2010.
(b) These data are presented for illustrative purposes only. They were compiled from preliminary FY 2010 state budget allocation tables that were prepared for submission to Congress and that were found on the Department of Energy website.

## Table 2.18
## STATE RANKINGS FOR PER CAPITA AMOUNTS
## OF FEDERAL GOVERNMENT EXPENDITURE: FISCAL YEAR 2010

| State | Total | Retirement and disability | Other direct payments | Grants | Procurement | Salaries and wages |
|---|---|---|---|---|---|---|
| Alabama | 11 | 2 | 15 | 35 | 7 | 19 |
| Alaska | 1 | 49 | 50 | 1 | 4 | 2 |
| Arizona | 27 | 36 | 34 | 22 | 11 | 32 |
| Arkansas | 30 | 4 | 22 | 16 | 47 | 29 |
| California | 44 | 48 | 29 | 27 | 19 | 41 |
| Colorado | 31 | 46 | 47 | 45 | 9 | 9 |
| Connecticut | 4 | 38 | 1 | 18 | 5 | 48 |
| Delaware | 42 | 11 | 35 | 20 | 50 | 31 |
| Florida | 29 | 8 | 6 | 49 | 33 | 36 |
| Georgia | 33 | 43 | 40 | 46 | 25 | 7 |
| Hawaii | 5 | 21 | 38 | 23 | 10 | 1 |
| Idaho | 39 | 35 | 48 | 37 | 15 | 30 |
| Illinois | 47 | 45 | 23 | 38 | 35 | 45 |
| Indiana | 41 | 30 | 21 | 39 | 39 | 38 |
| Iowa | 35 | 26 | 18 | 31 | 41 | 44 |
| Kansas | 26 | 31 | 28 | 47 | 29 | 6 |
| Kentucky | 7 | 10 | 2 | 26 | 13 | 5 |
| Louisiana | 13 | 37 | 12 | 5 | 17 | 23 |
| Maine | 18 | 3 | 31 | 11 | 24 | 28 |
| Maryland | 3 | 14 | 4 | 15 | 2 | 4 |
| Massachusetts | 9 | 40 | 8 | 4 | 6 | 37 |
| Michigan | 38 | 16 | 19 | 33 | 45 | 50 |
| Minnesota | 49 | 42 | 24 | 34 | 48 | 42 |
| Mississippi | 22 | 15 | 17 | 14 | 37 | 24 |
| Missouri | 12 | 22 | 14 | 17 | 8 | 16 |
| Montana | 20 | 7 | 26 | 10 | 40 | 17 |
| Nebraska | 40 | 32 | 25 | 36 | 44 | 26 |
| Nevada | 50 | 44 | 49 | 50 | 38 | 34 |
| New Hampshire | 46 | 18 | 46 | 44 | 28 | 40 |
| New Jersey | 37 | 39 | 13 | 43 | 26 | 43 |
| New Mexico | 6 | 20 | 36 | 7 | 3 | 13 |
| New York | 24 | 41 | 11 | 8 | 43 | 33 |
| North Carolina | 34 | 27 | 39 | 30 | 46 | 11 |
| North Dakota | 8 | 17 | 3 | 6 | 30 | 10 |
| Ohio | 36 | 29 | 20 | 28 | 42 | 47 |
| Oklahoma | 25 | 12 | 27 | 32 | 36 | 12 |
| Oregon | 45 | 25 | 32 | 21 | 49 | 39 |
| Pennsylvania | 16 | 9 | 5 | 19 | 20 | 35 |
| Rhode Island | 17 | 24 | 9 | 9 | 34 | 27 |
| South Carolina | 28 | 6 | 37 | 41 | 12 | 25 |
| South Dakota | 14 | 19 | 7 | 12 | 27 | 14 |
| Tennessee | 21 | 13 | 10 | 24 | 18 | 46 |
| Texas | 43 | 47 | 44 | 42 | 16 | 18 |
| Utah | 48 | 50 | 42 | 40 | 23 | 21 |
| Vermont | 10 | 23 | 33 | 3 | 22 | 20 |
| Virginia | 2 | 5 | 43 | 48 | 1 | 3 |
| Washington | 23 | 28 | 41 | 25 | 21 | 8 |
| West Virginia | 15 | 1 | 16 | 13 | 32 | 22 |
| Wisconsin | 32 | 33 | 30 | 29 | 14 | 49 |
| Wyoming | 19 | 34 | 45 | 2 | 31 | 15 |

*Source:* U.S. Census Bureau, *Consolidated Federal Funds Report for Fiscal Year 2010.* Released September 2011.

*Note:* For additional information see the complete report at *http://www. census.gov/govs/www/cffr.html.* States are ranked from largest per capita amount of federal funds (1) to smallest per capita amount of federal funds (50). Rankings are based upon per capita amounts shown in Table 2.10. Federal funds for loans and insurance coverage are excluded from consideration in this table. Also excluded are per capita amounts for the District of Columbia and the U.S. Outlying Areas.

# Chapter Three

# STATE LEGISLATIVE BRANCH

# 2011 Legislative Elections

## By Tim Storey

*In the relatively few state legislative and gubernatorial elections in 2011, Republicans continued their winning streak in Southern states, coming closer to complete control of states in the region by taking over the Mississippi House for the first time since Reconstruction and by taking back functional control of the Virginia Senate. The four odd-year election states of Louisiana, Mississippi, New Jersey and Virginia staged regular elections for 578 legislative seats in 2011. In the end, Republicans picked up 25 seats in the off-year elections, adding to their dramatic gains from the year before and putting the party in its strongest position in state legislatures since 1928.*

## Republicans Extend Winning Streak in Legislative Races

Louisiana, Mississippi, New Jersey and Virginia held regular elections in 2011 for all of the seats in the state legislature. Some 578 seats were up for grabs in those four states, representing 7.8 percent of the 7,382 legislative seats in the 50 states. The outcome of the elections was good for the GOP, continuing a trend of Republican success in legislative elections going back to 2009. That's when the pendulum began to swing back in the direction of Republicans after several consecutive election cycles favoring Democrats. Republicans added 25 legislative seats in November 2011, bringing their tally to just shy of 4,000 Republican legislators in the 50 states as 2012 legislative sessions convened. With the 2011 gains, Republicans earned control of 54.4 percent of all legislative seats.

In addition to padding their overall seats total, Republicans notched key wins by taking control of the Mississippi House outright and by picking up two seats in the Virginia Senate to tie the chamber at 20 Democrats to 20 Republicans. That left the GOP with functional control of the Old Dominion's Senate. The battle for control of the Virginia Senate was hard fought before, during and after the election. On election night, control came down to the race between incumbent Democratic Sen. Edd Houck and his Republican challenger, Bryce Reeves. Reeves eked out a victory of only 226 votes out of more than 44,000 votes cast. Reeves win meant that Republicans picked up the two Senate seats they needed to tie the chamber which triggered a lawsuit, ultimately dismissed, by Democratic loyalists about which party would organize the Senate. When the Senate convened in January 2012, Republican Lt. Gov. Bill Bolling acted as the tiebreaking vote under the state's constitution, allowing Republicans to organize as the "majority" party even though the chamber was technically tied.

The victory for Republicans in the Mississippi House was easier. Including a few post-election party switchers, Republicans gained 10 seats to take control of the chamber by a relatively comfortable six-seat margin—64 Republicans and 58 Democrats. It was the first Republican majority in the chamber since the elections of 1875. That led to the eventual election of Rep. Philip Gunn as the Magnolia State's first Republican house speaker in nearly 140 years. In Mississippi Senate elections, Republicans gained three seats to gain a 10-seat edge in the chamber, 31 Republicans to 21 Democrats. Republican Phil Bryant won the race to succeed Haley Barbour as Mississippi's governor to give Republicans complete control in Jackson.

Louisiana voters also handed small gains to the GOP in both the House and Senate, helping the party pad a majority that was gained through party changes and special elections since the last general elections in the Bayou State. Republicans picked up two seats in the Louisiana Senate, giving them a 24-15 majority. The Republican-controlled Senate selected former Democrat and former House Speaker John Alario as the Senate president. Alario joined a short list of only a half dozen people to serve in the top spot in both the House and Senate. He is the only person to accomplish that feat as a member of two different parties. In Louisiana's House, Republicans netted one seat to gain a majority of 58 to 45 with two Independents.

Legislative elections in New Jersey were a bright spot for Democrats in the off-year. They added one seat in the Garden State's Assembly and maintained their 24-16 advantage in the Senate.

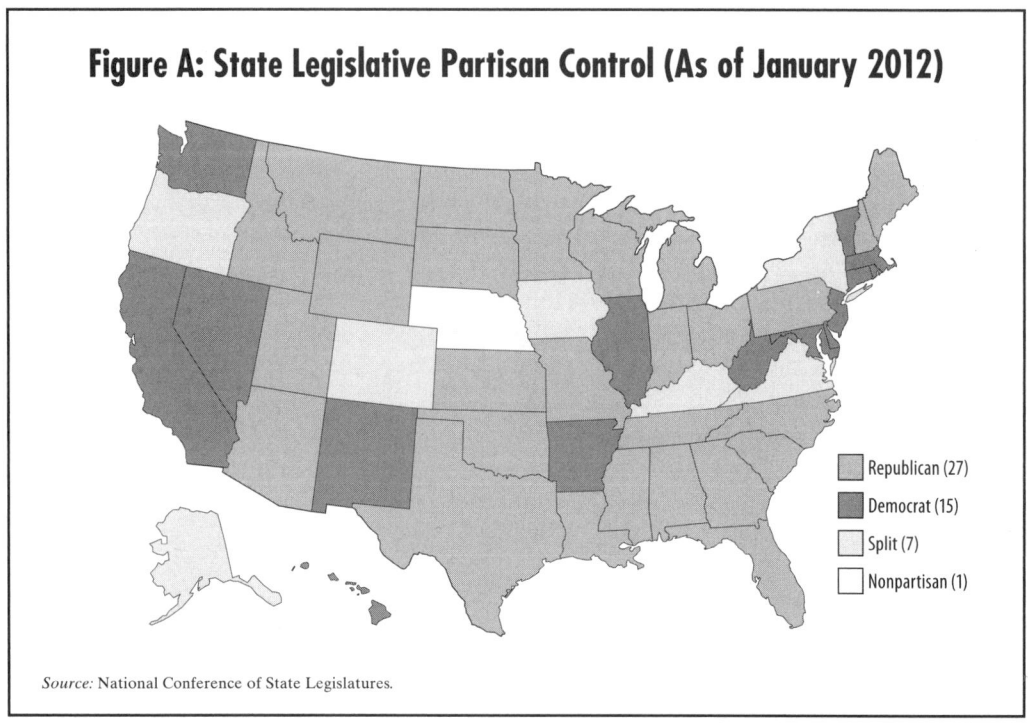

# Figure A: State Legislative Partisan Control (As of January 2012)

Republican (27)
Democrat (15)
Split (7)
Nonpartisan (1)

*Source:* National Conference of State Legislatures.

## Overall Partisan Breakdown

Factoring in the shift of the Mississippi House to the GOP column, Republicans entered 2012 controlling both chambers of the legislature in 27 states. The last time they controlled that many states was before the elections of 1930. Democrats, on the other hand, saw the states where they held both bodies fall to 15, a fairly dramatic reversal from just two years before when they controlled the entire legislature in 27 states. In seven states, the legislative branch is divided. That reflects the fewest number of states with split control since 1982. That tallies up to 49 states because in addition to being unicameral, Nebraska's legislature is also nonpartisan, so it is not included in those totals.

At the beginning of legislative sessions in 2012, Republicans held the majority in 59 legislative chambers. Democrats had the majority in 36 chambers. Three chambers were tied. The Alaskan Senate remained tied at 10 Democrats and 10 Republicans; Republican Sen. Gary Stevens, who was elected by a bipartisan coalition, leads the Alaska Senate. In Oregon, the House was tied at 30 Democrats and 30 Republicans after the 2010 election and remained tied headed into 2012. The House has a power-sharing arrangement that includes co-speakers and co-chairs for all of the committees.

## Solidified GOP Control in the South

With Republicans winning the Mississippi House and functional control of the Virginia Senate—even though the chamber is still considered tied—in 2011, Southern state legislatures are now almost entirely run by Republicans. It marks an incredible shift of party dominance in the region during the past two decades. In 1992, Republicans did not hold the majority in a single legislative chamber in the South. They now control 22 of the region's 28 chambers outright; 23 if the tally includes the Virginia Senate. The map in Figure A shows the extent of Republican control in the South. With the switch in the Mississippi House combined with legislative wins in 2010 by the GOP in Alabama and North Carolina, Arkansas is now the only state where one party has had uninterrupted party control for more than a century. Democrats have been in command of both chambers of the Arkansas legislature since the elections of 1874.

The party breakdown for governors did not change in 2011 elections, with Democrats holding on to the top job in Kentucky and Republicans in Louisiana and Mississippi. That left the overall partisan control of state government only slightly different from before the election. In 22 states, Republicans held the governor's mansion and both chambers of the legislature, while Democrats have the trifecta of political control in 11 states. Power remained divided in the other 17 states.

## Running in New Districts and Turnover

With the delivery of new 2010 census data to states in early 2011, states were required to draw new legislative districts for use in the 2011 fall elections. Louisiana, New Jersey and Virginia accomplished the task. Mississippi legislators, however, were unable to agree on new district plans, so a court ruled that 2011 legislative elections would be run under the maps from the previous decade.

Somewhat surprisingly, in the three states where incumbents and challengers were running in new districts, turnover did not increase substantially, which often happens in the first election following redistricting. The overall turnover in the 2002 elections in states with legislative elections following the 2002 redistricting cycle was slightly more than 26 percent, compared to an average election turnover in legislatures of about 18 percent. In the four states holding 2011 elections, overall turnover was 21.7 percent.

For several reasons, Louisiana experienced the highest turnover of the four states holding elections in 2011. Both Louisiana representatives and senators serve four-year terms, so the last general elections there were in 2007. Fifteen states have term limits for state legislators, but Louisiana was the only state holding elections in 2011 where legislators were subject to term limits. Nine Louisiana House incumbents and six senators were prohibited from running for re-election in 2011 because of term limits. In addition to term limits and the four-year lag since the most recent election, redistricting undoubtedly contributed to high turnover in the Pelican State. Louisiana's redistricting was heavily influenced by the considerable population displacement in the wake of Hurricane Katrina in 2005, which led to considerable changes to districts throughout the state. After the election, 31 percent of Louisiana House members and 26 percent of Louisiana Senate members were new.

As in Louisiana, Mississippi House and Senate members serve four-year terms. The terms are not staggered, so the last legislative elections there were also in 2007. Although they were not subject to redistricting, a number of incumbents in the Magnolia State still opted to retire. Retirements combined with a handful of primary and general election losses led to 27 percent turnover in the Mississippi Senate and 25 percent turnover in the House.

The other two odd-year election states experienced notably lower turnover, in part due to redistricting plans that were friendlier to incumbents. In New Jersey, turnover in the Senate was only 5 percent, while turnover in the Assembly was 19 percent. A bipartisan commission that was chaired in 2011 by Rutgers professor and pre-eminent legislative scholar Alan Rosenthal completed legislative redistricting in New Jersey. Virginia's new legislative maps were drawn by the legislature and led to 13 percent turnover in the Senate and 16 percent in the House.

## High Profile Special Elections

In addition to the regularly scheduled general election in the odd-year election states, a couple of notable special elections were held in November 2011. In Iowa, a senate seat vacated when Republican Gov. Terry Branstad appointed a Democratic senator to the state utilities board set up a special election that could have shifted control of the chamber from 25 Democrats to 24 Republicans, with one vacancy, to tied. Democrat Liz Mathis won the special election to fill the vacant seat by defeating Republican Cindy Golding, 56 percent to 44 percent, after outspending her 2-to-1 in what the *Des Moines Register* dubbed the most expensive legislative race in Iowa history. With independent spending added in, the race easily topped $1 million.

In Arizona, Senate President Russell Pierce lost a recall election to fellow Republican Jerry Lewis. Lewis got 53 percent of the vote to defeat Pierce, who had been the primary sponsor of controversial immigration legislation passed by the Arizona legislature in the previous session. While it was highly unusual for a leader to be recalled, the election did not change the party composition in the Arizona Senate, which stayed at 21 Republicans and nine Democrats. Pierce was only the 16th state legislator to be successfully recalled in U.S. history.

## 2012 Elections

The 2011 legislative elections were good for Republicans and built on their massive wave of success in 2010, when they picked up 720 seats and Democrats lost control of a stunning 23 legislative chambers. In November 2012, almost 6,000 of the nation's legislative seats will be up for grabs. It also will be the first major election following redistricting using 2010 census data, which will add a high degree of uncertainty to many races as well as lead to higher than normal turnover of legislative seats. The biggest political factor is likely to be what happens at the top

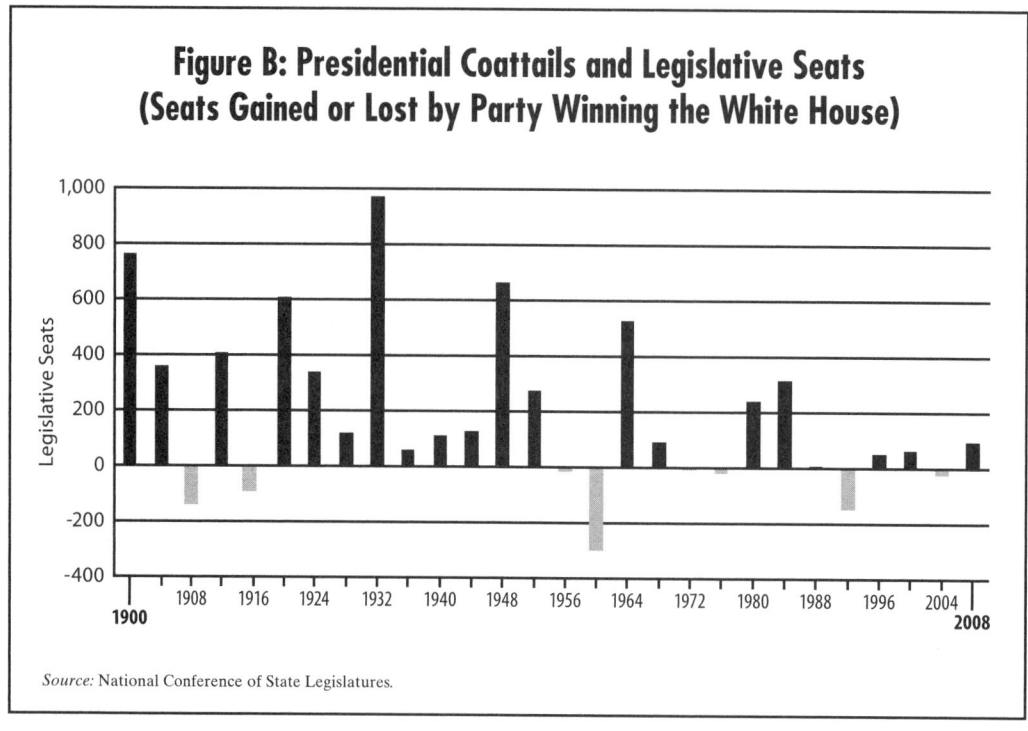

**Figure B: Presidential Coattails and Legislative Seats
(Seats Gained or Lost by Party Winning the White House)**

*Source:* National Conference of State Legislatures.

of the ticket. In presidential election years, the party winning the White House has a good track record in legislative elections. The party winning the White House has netted legislative seats in 20 of the 28 elections since 1900. See Figure B.

With a close race for the White House expected, 2012 may be less of a wave election than the past three major election cycles, all of which led to huge shifts in legislative seats. A switch of only three seats in 13 state senates, would be sufficient to change the majority, and a shift of five or fewer seats would alter control in nine state houses. In every two-year election cycle, the average number of chambers that switch party control is 13. Two, the Mississippi House and Virginia Senate, already have changed hands in this cycle.

## About the Author

**Tim Storey** is a senior fellow in the Legislative Management Program of the Denver, Colo.-based National Conference of State Legislatures. He specializes in elections and redistricting, as well as legislative organization and management. He has staffed NCSL's Redistricting and Elections Committee since 1990 and authored numerous articles on the topics of elections and redistricting. Every two years, he leads NCSL's StateVote project to track and analyze legislative election results. He graduated from Mars Hill College in North Carolina and received his master's degree from the University of Colorado's Graduate School of Public Affairs.

## Table 3.1
## NAMES OF STATE LEGISLATIVE BODIES AND CONVENING PLACES

| State or other jurisdiction | Both bodies | Upper house | Lower house | Convening place |
|---|---|---|---|---|
| Alabama | Legislature | Senate | House of Representatives | State House |
| Alaska | Legislature | Senate | House of Representatives | State Capitol |
| Arizona | Legislature | Senate | House of Representatives | State Capitol |
| Arkansas | General Assembly | Senate | House of Representatives | State Capitol |
| California | Legislature | Senate | Assembly | State Capitol |
| Colorado | General Assembly | Senate | House of Representatives | State Capitol |
| Connecticut | General Assembly | Senate | House of Representatives | State Capitol |
| Delaware | General Assembly | Senate | House of Representatives | Legislative Hall |
| Florida | Legislature | Senate | House of Representatives | The Capitol |
| Georgia | General Assembly | Senate | House of Representatives | State Capitol |
| Hawaii | Legislature | Senate | House of Representatives | State Capitol |
| Idaho | Legislature | Senate | House of Representatives | State Capitol |
| Illinois | General Assembly | Senate | House of Representatives | State House |
| Indiana | General Assembly | Senate | House of Representatives | State House |
| Iowa | General Assembly | Senate | House of Representatives | State Capitol |
| Kansas | Legislature | Senate | House of Representatives | State Capitol |
| Kentucky | General Assembly | Senate | House of Representatives | State Capitol |
| Louisiana | Legislature | Senate | House of Representatives | State Capitol |
| Maine | Legislature | Senate | House of Representatives | State House |
| Maryland | General Assembly | Senate | House of Delegates | State House |
| Massachusetts | General Court | Senate | House of Representatives | State House |
| Michigan | Legislature | Senate | House of Representatives | State Capitol |
| Minnesota | Legislature | Senate | House of Representatives | State Capitol |
| Mississippi | Legislature | Senate | House of Representatives | State Capitol |
| Missouri | General Assembly | Senate | House of Representatives | State Capitol |
| Montana | Legislature | Senate | House of Representatives | State Capitol |
| Nebraska | Legislature | (a) | | State Capitol |
| Nevada | Legislature | Senate | Assembly | Legislative Building |
| New Hampshire | General Court | Senate | House of Representatives | State House |
| New Jersey | Legislature | Senate | General Assembly | State House |
| New Mexico | Legislature | Senate | House of Representatives | State Capitol |
| New York | Legislature | Senate | Assembly | State Capitol |
| North Carolina | General Assembly | Senate | House of Representatives | State Legislative Building |
| North Dakota | Legislative Assembly | Senate | House of Representatives | State Capitol |
| Ohio | General Assembly | Senate | House of Representatives | State House |
| Oklahoma | Legislature | Senate | House of Representatives | State Capitol |
| Oregon | Legislative Assembly | Senate | House of Representatives | State Capitol |
| Pennsylvania | General Assembly | Senate | House of Representatives | Main Capitol Building |
| Rhode Island | General Assembly | Senate | House of Representatives | State House |
| South Carolina | General Assembly | Senate | House of Representatives | State House |
| South Dakota | Legislature | Senate | House of Representatives | State Capitol |
| Tennessee | General Assembly | Senate | House of Representatives | State Capitol |
| Texas | Legislature | Senate | House of Representatives | State Capitol |
| Utah | Legislature | Senate | House of Representatives | State Capitol |
| Vermont | General Assembly | Senate | House of Representatives | State House |
| Virginia | General Assembly | Senate | House of Delegates | State Capitol |
| Washington | Legislature | Senate | House of Representatives | State Capitol |
| West Virginia | Legislature | Senate | House of Delegates | State Capitol |
| Wisconsin | Legislature | Senate | Assembly (b) | State Capitol |
| Wyoming | Legislature | Senate | House of Representatives | State Capitol |
| Dist. of Columbia | Council of the District of Columbia | (a) | | Council Chamber |
| American Samoa | Legislature | Senate | House of Representatives | Maota Fono |
| Guam | Legislature | (a) | | Congress Building |
| No. Mariana Islands | Legislature | Senate | House of Representatives | Civic Center Building |
| Puerto Rico | Legislative Assembly | Senate | House of Representatives | The Capitol |
| U.S. Virgin Islands | Legislature | (a) | | Capitol Building |

*Source:* The Council of State Governments, *Directory I— Elective Officials 2010.*

*Key:*

(a) Unicameral legislature. Except in the District of Columbia, members go by the title Senator.

(b) Members of the lower house go by the title Representative.

## Table 3.2
## LEGISLATIVE SESSIONS: LEGAL PROVISIONS

| State or other jurisdiction | Regular sessions | | | | Special sessions | | |
|---|---|---|---|---|---|---|---|
| | Year | Month | Day | Limitation on length of session (a) | Legislature may call | Legislature may determine subject | Limitation on length of session |
| Alabama ............ | Annual | Jan. Mar. Feb. | 2nd Tues. (b) 1st Tues. (c)(d) 1st Tues. (e) | 30 L in 105 C | No | Yes (f) | 12 L in 30 C |
| Alaska .............. | Annual | Jan. | 3rd Tues. (g) | 121 C; 90 Statutory (g) | By petition, 2/3 members, each house | Yes | 30 C |
| Arizona ............ | Annual | Jan. | 2nd Mon. | (h) | By petition, 2/3 members, each house | Yes | None |
| Arkansas .......... | Annual | Jan. Feb. | 2nd Mon. 2nd Mon. | 60 C (i) 30 C | No | No (j) | None |
| California .......... | Biennium (k) | Jan. | 1st Mon. (d) | None | No | No | None |
| Colorado .......... | Annual | Jan. | No later than 2nd Wed. | 120 C | By petition, 2/3 members, each house | Yes (l) | None |
| Connecticut ...... | Annual | Jan. Jan. | Wed. after 1st Mon. (odd years) Wed. after 1st Mon. (even years) | (m) | By petition, 2/3 members, each house (n) | Yes | None |
| Delaware .......... | Annual | Jan. | 2nd Tues. | June 30 | Joint call, presiding officers, both houses | No | None |
| Florida ............. | Annual | Mar. | 1st Tues. after 1st Mon. (o) | 60 C (i) | Joint call, presiding officers, both houses or by petition | Yes | 20 C (i) |
| Georgia............. | Annual | Jan. | 2nd Mon. | 40 L | By petition, 3/5 members, each house | No (p) | 40 L |
| Hawaii .............. | Annual | Jan. | 3rd Wed. | 60 L (i) | By petition, 2/3 members, each house | Yes | 30 L (i) |
| Idaho ............... | Annual | Jan. | Mon. on or nearest 9th day | None | No | No | 20 C |
| Illinois ............. | Annual | Jan. | 2nd Wed. | None (q) | Joint call, presiding officers, both houses | Yes (l) | None |
| Indiana ............ | Annual | Jan. | 2nd Mon. (r) | odd–61 C or Apr. 29; even–30 C or Mar. 14 | No | Yes | 30 L or 40 C |
| Iowa ................ | Annual | Jan. | 2nd Mon. | None | By petition, 2/3 members, each house | Yes | None |
| Kansas ............. | Annual | Jan. | 2nd Mon. | odd–None; even–90 C (i) | Petition to governor of 2/3 members, each house | Yes | None |
| Kentucky .......... | Annual | Jan. | 1st Tues after 1st Mon. | even–60 L; odd–30 L (s) | No | No | None |
| Louisiana ......... | Annual | Mar. (even years) Apr. (odd years) | last Mon. (even years) last Mon. (odd years) | even–60 L in 85 C; odd–45 L in 60 C | By petition, majority, each house | Yes | 30 C |
| Maine............... | (t) | Dec. (even years) Jan. (subsequent even year) | 1st Wed. (quadrennial election year) Wed. after 1st Tues. | Calendar days set by statute (u) | Joint call, presiding officers of both houses with the consent of a majority of the members of each political party | Yes | None |
| Maryland........... | Annual | Jan. | 2nd Wed. | 90 C | By petition, 2/3 members, each house | Yes | 30 C |
| Massachusetts ... | Biennium | Jan. | 1st Wed. | (v) | By petition, majority, each house | Yes | None |
| Michigan........... | Annual | Jan. | 2nd Wed. | None | By petition (w) | No | None |
| Minnesota.......... | Biennium | Feb. | Feb. 12, 2008 | 120 L | No (x) | Yes | None |
| Mississippi......... | Annual | Jan. | Tues. after 1st Mon. | 125 C (y); 90 C (y) | No | No | None |

See footnotes at end of table.

# LEGISLATIVE SESSIONS: LEGAL PROVISIONS — Continued

| State or other jurisdiction | Regular sessions Legislature convenes Year | Month | Day | Limitation on length of session (a) | Special sessions Legislature may call | Legislature may determine subject | Limitation on length of session |
|---|---|---|---|---|---|---|---|
| Missouri | Annual | Jan. | Wed. after 1st Mon. | May 30 | By petition, 3/4 members, each house | Yes (l) | 30 C (z) |
| Montana | Biennial–odd year | Jan. | 1st Mon. | 90 L | By petition, majority, each house | Yes | None |
| Nebraska | Annual | Jan. | Wed. after 1st Mon. | odd–90 L; even–60 L | By petition, 2/3 members, each house | Yes | None |
| Nevada | Biennial–odd year | Feb. | 1st Mon. | 120 C | No | No | None (aa) |
| New Hampshire | Annual | Jan. | Wed. after 1st Tues. | 45 L | By petition, 2/3 members, each house | Yes | 15 L (bb) |
| New Jersey | Biennium | Jan. | 2nd Tues. of even year | None | By petition, majority, each house (cc) | Yes | None |
| New Mexico | Annual | Jan. | 3rd Tues. | odd–60 C; even–30 C | By petition, 3/5 members, each house (l) | Yes (l) | 30 C |
| New York | Annual | Jan. (dd) | Wed. after 1st Mon. | None | By petition, 2/3 members, each house | Yes (l) | None |
| North Carolina | (ee) | Jan. | 3rd Wed. after 2nd Mon. (odd years) | None | By petition, 3/5 members, each house | Yes | None |
| North Dakota | Biennial–odd year | Jan. | Tues. after Jan. 3, but not later than Jan. 11 | 80 L in the biennium | Yes (ff) | Yes | None (ff) |
| Ohio | Biennium | Jan. | 1st Mon. (gg) | None | Joint call, presiding officers, both houses | Yes | None |
| Oklahoma | Annual | Feb. | 1st Mon. | last Fri. in May | By petition, 2/3 members, each house | Yes | None |
| Oregon | Biennial–odd year | Jan. | 2nd Mon. | None | By petition, majority, each house | Yes | None |
| Pennsylvania | Biennium (hh) | Jan. | 1st Tues. | None | Governor may call | No | None |
| Rhode Island | Annual | Jan. | 1st Tues. | None | Joint call, presiding officers, both houses | Yes | None |
| South Carolina | Biennium | Jan. | 2nd Tues. | (ii) | By vote, 2/3 members, each house | Yes | None |
| South Dakota | Annual | Jan. | 2nd Tues. | odd–40 L; even–40 L | By petition, 2/3 members, each house | Yes (jj) | None |
| Tennessee | Biennium (kk) | Jan. | 2nd Tues. | 90 L (ll) | By petition, 2/3 members, each house | Yes | 30 L (ll) |
| Texas | Biennial–odd year | Jan. | 2nd Tues. | 140 C | No | No | 30 C |
| Utah | Annual | Jan. | 4th Mon. | 45 C | No | No | 30 C |
| Vermont | Annual | Jan. | Wed. after 1st Mon. | None | No | Yes | None |
| Virginia | Annual | Jan. | 2nd Wed. | odd–30 C (i); even–60 C (i) | (tt) | Yes | None (mm) |
| Washington | Annual | Jan. | 2nd Mon. | odd–105 C; even–60 C | By vote, 2/3 members, each house | Yes | 30 C |
| West Virginia | Annual | Jan | 2nd Wed. | 60 C (i) | By petition, 3/5 members, each house | Yes (l) | None |
| Wisconsin | Biennium | Jan. | 1st Mon. | None | (nn) | No | None |
| Wyoming | Biennium | Jan. (odd years) Feb. (even years) | 2nd Tues. (odd years) 2nd Mon. (even years) | odd–40 L; even–20 L; biennium–60 L | By petition, majority members, each house | Yes | 20 L |
| Dist. of Columbia | (oo) | Jan. | 2nd day | None | ... | ... | ... |
| American Samoa | Annual | Jan. July | 2nd Mon. 2nd Mon. | 45 L 45 L | No | No | None |
| Guam | (pp) | Jan. | 2nd Mon. | None (pp) | Only the governor may call | No | None (pp) |

See footnotes at end of table.

# LEGISLATIVE SESSIONS: LEGAL PROVISIONS—Continued

| State or other jurisdiction | Regular sessions | | | | Special sessions | | |
|---|---|---|---|---|---|---|---|
| | Legislature convenes | | | Limitation on length of session (a) | Legislature may call | Legislature may determine subject | Limitation on length of session |
| | Year | Month | Day | | | | |
| No. Mariana Islands | Annual | (rr) | (d)(rr) | 90 L (qq) | Upon request of presiding officers, both houses | Yes (j) | 10 C |
| Puerto Rico | Annual (rr) | Jan. Aug. | 2nd Mon. 3rd Mon. | 5 mo. 4 mo. | No | No | 20 C |
| U.S. Virgin Islands | Annual | Jan. (ss) | 2nd Mon. (ss) | None | No, governor calls | No | None |

*Source:* The Council of State Governments' survey, March 2012.

*Key:*

Annual — holds legislative sessions every year.

Biennial–odd year — holds legislative sessions every other year.

Biennium — holds legislative sessions in a two-year term of activity.

C — Calendar day

L — Legislative day (in some states called a session day or workday; definition may vary slightly, however, generally refers to any day on which either house of legislature is in session).

(a) Applies to each year unless otherwise indicated.

(b) General election year (quadrennial election year).

(c) Year after quadrennial election.

(d) Legal provision for organizational session prior to stated convening date. Alabama—in the year after quadrennial election, second Tuesday in January for 10 C. California—in the even-numbered general election year, first Monday in December for an organizational session, recess until the first Monday in January of the odd-numbered year. No. Mariana Islands—in year after general election, second Monday in January.

(e) Other years.

(f) By 2/3 vote each house.

(g) Convening date is statutory. Length of session is 121 calendar days, 90 by statute.

(h) No constitutional or statutory provision; however, by legislative rule regular sessions shall be adjourned sine die no later than Saturday of the week during which the 100th day from the beginning of each regular session falls. The Speaker/President may by declaration authorize the extension of the session for a period not to exceed seven additional days. Thereafter the session can be extended only by a majority vote of the House/Senate.

(i) Session may be extended by vote of members in both houses. Arkansas—2/3 vote. Florida—3/5 vote, session may be extended by vote of members in each house. Hawaii—petition of 2/3 membership for maximum 15-day extension. Kansas—2/3 vote. Virginia—2/3 vote for 30 C extension. West Virginia—may be extended by the governor.

(j) After governor's business has been disposed of, members may remain in session up to 15 C days by a 2/3 vote of both houses.

(k) Regular sessions begin after general election, in December of even-numbered year. In California, in the even-numbered general election year, first Monday in December for an organizational session, recess until the first Monday in January of the odd-numbered year.

(l) Only if legislature convenes itself. In Illinois, governor may call a special session and determine its subject. The Constitution does not mention limiting the subject(s) of a special session called by legislative leaders. In New York, special sessions may also be called by the governor. Legislature may determine subject only if it has convened itself. In New Mexico, special sessions may only be called by the governor and subjects are limited to issues included in governor's proclamation; extraordinary session may only be called by the legislature and have no limitations on subject.

(m) Odd-numbered years—not later than Wednesday after first Monday in June; even-numbered years—not later than Wednesday after first Monday in May.

(n) Notice sent to secretary of state.

(o) A regular session of the legislature shall convene on the first Tuesday after the first Monday of each odd-numbered year, and on the first Tuesday after the first Monday in March, or such other date as may be fixed by law, of each even-numbered year.

(p) If three-fifths of the General Assembly certifies to governor that an emergency exists, governor must convene a special session for all purposes.

(q) Constitution encourages adjournment by May 31.

(r) Legislators may reconvene at any time after organizational meeting; however, second Monday in January is the final date by which regular session must be in process.

(s) During the odd-year session, the members convene for four days, then break until February.

(t) Regular session begins after general election in even-numbered years. Session which begins in December of general election year runs into the following year (odd-numbered); second session begins in next even-numbered year. The second session is limited to budgetary matters; legislation in the governor's call; emergency legislation; legislation referred to committee for study.

(u) Statutory adjournment for the First Regular Session (beginning in December of even-numbered years and continuing into the following odd-numbered year) is the third Wednesday of June; statutory adjournment for the Second Regular Session (beginning in January of the subsequent even-numbered year) is the third Wednesday in April. The statutes provide for up to two extensions of up to five legislative days each for each session.

(v) Legislative rules say formal business must be concluded by Nov. 15th of the 1st session in the biennium, or by July 31st of the 2nd session for the biennium.

(w) Joint rules provide for the submission of a written statement requesting special session by a specified number of members of each chamber.

(x) Special session is called by the governor.

(y) 90 C sessions every year, except the first year of a gubernatorial administration during which the legislative session runs for 125 C.

(z) 30 C if called by legislature; 60 C if called by governor.

(aa) No limit, however legislators are only paid up to 20 calendar days during a special session.

(bb) Limitation is on legislative pay and mileage.

(cc) Or by joint call, presiding officers, both houses.

(dd) Session officially begins on the first Wednesday following the first Monday of the new legislative term (commencing the first of the year), and lasts until the legislature completes its business and adjourns sine die. However, over the past several years, both houses have adopted the tactic of declaring a recess at the call of the leaders, in order to facilitate easy recall of the legislature to override vetoes, etc. Over time the custom has become to formally adjourn both houses just before the new session opens. This leads to the rather interesting convention that when the governor calls the legislature into session, it is considered "special" or "executive," even though the regular session is ongoing.

# LEGISLATIVE SESSIONS: LEGAL PROVISIONS—Continued

(ee) Legal provision for session in odd-numbered year; however, legislature may divide, and in practice has divided, to meet in even-numbered years as well.

(ff) Legislative Council may reconvene the Legislature assembly. However, a reconvened session may not exceed the number of days available (80) but not used by the last regular session.

(gg) Unless Monday is a legal holiday; in second year, the General Assembly convenes on the same date.

(hh) Sessions are two years and begin on the 1st Tuesday of January of the odd-numbered year. Session ends on November 30 of the even-numbered year. Each calendar year receives its own legislative number.

(ii) The regular session ends the first Thursday in June; it can be extended with a two-thirds majority vote.

(jj) Legislators must address topic for which the special session was called.

(kk) Each General Assembly convenes for a First and Second Regular Session over a two-year period.

(ll) 90 legislative days over a two-year period. During special sessions members will be paid up to 30 legislative days; further days will be without pay or per diem.

(mm) No limitation, but the convening of the new General Assembly following an election would by operation end the special session.

(nn) The Legislature may call itself into Extraordinary Session on any subject by a majority vote of the organizing committees of each house, by joint resolution, or by a petition of a majority of each house.

(oo) Each Council period begins on January 2 of each odd-numbered year and ends on January 1 of the following odd-numbered year.

(pp) Legislature meets on the first Monday of each month following its initial session in January. One legislative day or one special session day may become several calendar days. Special sessions may address only one subject.

(qq) 60 L before April 1 and 30 L after July 31.

(rr) Legislature meets twice a year. During general election years, the legislature only convenes on the January session.

(ss) The legislature convenes in January on the second Monday; March, June and September, the third Wednesday.

(tt) The Constitution provides that the governor must call a special session upon "application" of 2/3 of the members of each house.

## Table 3.3
## THE LEGISLATORS: NUMBERS, TERMS, AND PARTY AFFILIATIONS: 2012

| State or other jurisdiction | Senate | | | | | | House/Assembly | | | | | | Senate and House/Assembly totals |
|---|---|---|---|---|---|---|---|---|---|---|---|---|---|
| | Democrats | Republicans | Other | Vacancies | Total | Term | Democrats | Republicans | Other | Vacancies | Total | Term | |
| **State and territory totals** | 915 | 1,069 | 16 | 5 | 2,072* | ... | 2,447 | 2,985 | 29 | 24 | 5,505 | ... | 7,577* |
| State totals...................... | 875 | 1,039 | 5 | 3 | 1,971* | ... | 2,430 | 2,939 | 18 | 24 | 5,411 | ... | 7,382* |
| **Alabama**........................ | 12 | 22 | 1 (b) | ... | 35 | 4 | 40 | 65 | ... | ... | 105 | 4 | 140 |
| Alaska............................. | 10 | 10 | ... | ... | 20 | 4 | 16 | 24 | ... | ... | 40 | 2 | 60 |
| Arizona............................ | 9 | 21 | ... | ... | 30 | 2 | 20 | 40 | ... | ... | 60 | 2 | 90 |
| Arkansas.......................... | 20 | 15 | ... | ... | 35 | 4 | 54 | 46 | ... | ... | 100 | 2 | 135 |
| California ........................ | 25 | 15 | ... | ... | 40 | 4 | 52 | 28 | ... | ... | 80 | 2 | 120 |
| Colorado.......................... | 20 | 15 | ... | ... | 35 | 4 | 32 | 33 | ... | ... | 65 | 2 | 100 |
| Connecticut...................... | 22 | 14 | ... | ... | 36 | 2 | 99 | 52 | ... | ... | 151 | 2 | 187 |
| Delaware ......................... | 14 | 7 | ... | ... | 21 | 4 | 26 | 15 | ... | ... | 41 | 2 | 62 |
| Florida............................. | 12 | 28 | ... | ... | 40 | 4 | 39 | 81 | ... | ... | 120 | 2 | 160 |
| Georgia............................ | 20 | 36 | ... | ... | 56 | 2 | 63 | 115 | 1 (b) | 1 | 180 | 2 | 236 |
| Hawaii.............................. | 24 | 1 | ... | ... | 25 | 4 | 42 | 8 | ... | 1 | 51 | 2 | 76 |
| Idaho............................... | 7 | 28 | ... | ... | 35 | 2 | 13 | 57 | ... | ... | 70 | 2 | 105 |
| Illinois............................. | 35 | 24 | ... | ... | 59 | (a) | 64 | 54 | ... | ... | 118 | 2 | 177 |
| Indiana............................ | 13 | 37 | ... | ... | 50 | 4 | 40 | 60 | ... | ... | 100 | 2 | 150 |
| Iowa ................................ | 26 | 24 | ... | ... | 50 | 4 | 40 | 60 | ... | ... | 100 | 2 | 150 |
| Kansas ............................. | 8 | 32 | ... | ... | 40 | 4 | 33 | 92 | ... | ... | 125 | 2 | 165 |
| Kentucky ......................... | 15 | 22 | 1 (b) | ... | 38 | 4 | 59 | 40 | ... | 1 | 100 | 2 | 138 |
| Louisiana......................... | 15 | 24 | ... | ... | 39 | 4 | 45 | 58 | 2 (b) | ... | 105 | 4 | 144 |
| Maine............................... | 14 | 20 | 1 (c) | ... | 35 | 2 | 72 | 77 | 1 (c) | 1 | 151 | 2 | 186 |
| Maryland.......................... | 35 | 12 | ... | ... | 47 | 4 | 98 | 43 | ... | ... | 141 | 4 | 188 |
| Massachusetts ................. | 36 | 4 | ... | ... | 40 | 2 | 125 | 33 | ... | 2 | 160 | 2 | 200 |
| Michigan.......................... | 12 | 26 | ... | ... | 38 | 4 | 46 | 62 | ... | 2 | 110 | 2 | 148 |
| Minnesota........................ | 30 (d) | 37 | ... | ... | 67 | 4 | 62 (d) | 72 | ... | ... | 134 | 2 | 201 |
| Mississippi....................... | 21 | 31 | ... | ... | 52 | 4 | 58 | 64 | ... | ... | 122 | 4 | 174 |
| Missouri........................... | 8 | 26 | ... | ... | 34 | 4 | 56 | 106 | ... | 1 | 163 | 2 | 197 |
| Montana .......................... | 22 | 28 | ... | ... | 50 | 4 | 32 | 68 | ... | ... | 100 | 2 | 150 |
| Nebraska ......................... | ..Nonpartisan election.. | | | | 49 | 4 | .........................Unicameral......................... | | | | | | 49 |
| Nevada............................. | 11 | 10 | ... | ... | 21 | 4 | 26 | 16 | ... | ... | 42 | 2 | 63 |
| New Hampshire .............. | 5 | 19 | ... | ... | 24 | 2 | 104 | 292 | ... | 4 | 400 | 2 | 424 |
| New Jersey ...................... | 24 | 16 | ... | ... | 40 | 4 (f) | 47 | 32 | ... | 1 | 80 | 2 | 120 |
| New Mexico ..................... | 28 | 14 | ... | ... | 42 | 4 | 36 | 33 | 1 (b) | ... | 70 | 2 | 112 |
| New York.......................... | 29 | 32 | ... | 1 | 62 | 2 | 96 | 49 | 1 (e) | 4 | 150 | 2 | 212 |
| North Carolina................. | 19 | 31 | ... | ... | 50 | 2 | 52 | 68 | ... | ... | 120 | 2 | 170 |
| North Dakota.................... | 12 | 35 | ... | ... | 47 | 4 | 25 | 69 | ... | ... | 94 | 4 | 141 |
| Ohio ................................ | 10 | 23 | ... | ... | 33 | 4 | 40 | 59 | ... | ... | 99 | 2 | 132 |
| Oklahoma......................... | 15 | 31 | ... | 2 | 48 | 4 | 33 | 68 | ... | ... | 101 | 2 | 149 |
| Oregon............................. | 16 | 14 | ... | ... | 30 | 4 | 30 | 30 | ... | ... | 60 | 2 | 90 |
| Pennsylvania ................... | 20 | 30 | ... | ... | 50 | 4 | 87 | 110 | ... | 6 | 203 | 2 | 253 |
| Rhode Island.................... | 29 | 8 | 1 (b) | ... | 38 | 2 | 65 | 10 | ... | ... | 75 | 2 | 113 |
| South Carolina................. | 19 | 27 | ... | ... | 46 | 4 | 48 | 76 | ... | ... | 124 | 2 | 170 |
| South Dakota ................... | 5 | 30 | ... | ... | 35 | 2 | 19 | 50 | 1 (b) | ... | 70 | 2 | 105 |
| Tennessee ........................ | 13 | 20 | ... | ... | 33 | 4 | 34 | 64 | 1 (q) | ... | 99 | 2 | 132 |
| Texas ............................... | 12 | 19 | ... | ... | 31 | 4 | 49 | 101 | ... | ... | 150 | 2 | 181 |
| Utah ................................ | 7 | 22 | ... | ... | 29 | 4 | 17 | 58 | ... | ... | 75 | 2 | 104 |
| Vermont........................... | 21 | 8 | 1 (r) | ... | 30 | 2 | 94 | 48 | 8 (g) | ... | 150 | 2 | 180 |
| Virginia............................ | 20 | 20 | ... | ... | 40 | 4 | 32 | 67 | 1 (b) | ... | 100 | 2 | 140 |
| Washington...................... | 27 | 22 | ... | ... | 49 | 4 | 56 | 42 | ... | ... | 98 | 2 | 147 |
| West Virginia................... | 28 | 6 | ... | ... | 34 | 4 | 65 | 35 | ... | ... | 100 | 2 | 134 |
| Wisconsin ........................ | 16 | 17 | ... | ... | 33 (h) | 4 | 39 | 59 | 1 (b) | ... | 99 (h) | 2 | 132 |
| Wyoming .......................... | 4 | 26 | ... | ... | 30 | 4 | 10 | 50 | ... | ... | 60 | 2 | 90 |
| Dist. of Columbia (i) ..... | 11 | 0 | 2 (b) | ... | 13 | 4 | ............................Unicameral............................ | | | | | | 13 |
| American Samoa ........... | ..........Nonpartisan election.......... | | | | 18 (j) | 4 | ..........Nonpartisan election ........ | | | | 20 (j) | 2 | 38 |
| Guam............................... | 9 | 6 | ... | ... | 15 | 2 | ............................Unicameral............................ | | | | | | 15 |
| No. Mariana Islands ...... | 1 | 4 | 4 (k) | ... | 9 | 4 | ... | 9 | 11 (l) | ... | 20 | 2 | 29 |
| Puerto Rico...................... | 9 (m) | 20 (n) | ... | 2 | 31 (p) | 4 | 17 (m) | 37 (n) | ... | ... | 54 (p) | 4 | 85 |
| U.S. Virgin Islands ......... | 10 | ... | 5 (o) | ... | 15 | 2 | ............................Unicameral............................ | | | | | | 15 |

See footnotes at end of table.

## THE LEGISLATORS: NUMBERS, TERMS, AND PARTY AFFILIATIONS: 2012—Continued

*Source:* The Council of State Governments, February 2012.

*\*Note:* Senate and combined body (Senate and House/Assembly) totals include Unicameral legislatures.

*Key:*

... — Does not apply

(a) The entire Senate comes up for election in every year ending in "2" with districts based on the latest decennial Census. Senate districts are divided into three groups. One group elects senators for terms of four years, four years and two years; the second group for terms of four years, two years and four years; the third group for terms of two years, four years, and four years.

(b) Independent.

(c) Unenrolled.

(d) Democratic-Farmer-Labor.

(e) Independence Party.

(f) All 40 Senate terms are on a ten-year cycle which is made up of a two-year term, followed by twp consecutive four-year terms, beginning after the decennial census.

(g) Independent (3); Progressive (5).

(h) All House seats contested in even-numbered years; In the Senate, 17 seats contested in gubernatorial years; 16 seats contested in presidential years.

(i) Council of the District of Columbia.

(j) Senate: senators are not elected by popular vote, but by county council chiefs. House: 21 seats; 20 are elected by popular vote and one appointed, non-voting delegate from Swains Island.

(k) Independent (3); Covenant (1).

(l) Covenant (7); Independent (4).

(m) Popular Democratic Party.

(n) New Progressive Party.

(o) Independent (3); Independent Citizens Movement (2).

(p) Constitutionally, the Senate consists of 27 seats and the House consists of 51 seats. However, extra at-large seats can be granted to the opposition to limit any party's control to 2/3. After the 2008 election, extra seats for the minority party were added in both the Senate and House.

(q) Carter County Republican.

(r) Progressive Party.

## Table 3.4
## MEMBERSHIP TURNOVER IN THE LEGISLATURES: 2011

| State or other jurisdiction | Senate | | | House/Assembly | | |
|---|---|---|---|---|---|---|
| | Total number of members | Number of membership changes | Percentage change of total | Total number of members | Number of membership changes | Percentage change of total |
| Alabama | 35 | 0 | 0 | 105 | 2 | 2 |
| Alaska | 20 | 0 | 0 | 40 | 0 | 0 |
| Arizona | 30 | 2 | 7 | 60 | 0 | 0 |
| Arkansas | 35 | 0 | 0 | 100 | 1 | 1 |
| California | 40 | 0 | 0 | 80 | 0 | 0 |
| Colorado | 35 | 1 | 3 | 65 | 0 | 0 |
| Connecticut | 36 | 0 | 0 | 151 | 1 | 1 |
| Delaware | 21 | 0 | 0 | 41 | 0 | 0 |
| Florida | 40 | 0 | 0 | 120 | 0 | 0 |
| Georgia | 56 | 2 | 4 | 180 | 4 | 2 |
| Hawaii | 25 | 0 | 0 | 51 | 0 | 0 |
| Idaho | 35 | 1 | 3 | 70 | 1 | 1 |
| Illinois | 59 | 0 | 0 | 118 | 3 | 3 |
| Indiana | 50 | 0 | 0 | 100 | 0 | 0 |
| Iowa | 50 | 1 | 0 | 100 | 0 | 0 |
| Kansas | 40 | 0 | 0 | 125 | 1 | 1 |
| Kentucky | 38 | 0 | 0 | 100 | 1 | 1 |
| Louisiana | 39 | 9 | 23 | 105 | 24 | 23 |
| Maine | 35 | 0 | 0 | 151 | 2 | 1 |
| Maryland | 47 | 0 | 0 | 141 | 0 | 0 |
| Massachusetts | 40 | 1 | 3 | 160 | 2 | 1 |
| Michigan | 38 | 0 | 0 | 110 | 0 | 0 |
| Minnesota | 67 | 2 | 3 | 134 | 1 | 1 |
| Mississippi | 52 | 15 | 29 | 122 | 32 | 26 |
| Missouri | 34 | 1 | 3 | 163 | 4 | 16 |
| Montana | 50 | 1 | 2 | 100 | 0 | 0 |
| Nebraska | 49 | 1 | 2 | ...................... Unicameral .................. | | |
| Nevada | 21 | 0 | 0 | 42 | 0 | 0 |
| New Hampshire | 24 | 0 | 0 | 400 | 1 | 0 |
| New Jersey | 40 | 2 | 5 | 80 | 13 | 16 |
| New Mexico | 42 | 1 | 2 | 70 | 0 | 0 |
| New York | 62 | 0 | 0 | 150 | 7 | 5 |
| North Carolina | 50 | 2 | 4 | 120 | 2 | 2 |
| North Dakota | 47 | 1 | 2 | 94 | 0 | 0 |
| Ohio | 33 | 5 | 15 | 99 | 4 | 4 |
| Oklahoma | 48 | 1 | 0 | 101 | 0 | 0 |
| Oregon | 30 | 0 | 0 | 60 | 0 | 0 |
| Pennsylvania | 50 | 0 | 0 | 203 | 0 | 0 |
| Rhode Island | 38 | 0 | 0 | 75 | 0 | 0 |
| South Carolina | 46 | 0 | 0 | 124 | 2 | 2 |
| South Dakota | 35 | 0 | 0 | 70 | 1 | 1 |
| Tennessee | 33 | 1 | 3 | 99 | 0 | 0 |
| Texas | 31 | 0 | 0 | 150 | 1 | 1 |
| Utah | 29 | 3 | 10 | 75 | 4 | 5 |
| Vermont | 30 | 0 | 0 | 150 | 2 | 1 |
| Virginia | 40 | 6 | 15 | 100 | 16 | 16 |
| Washington | 49 | 2 | 4 | 98 | 1 | 1 |
| West Virginia | 34 | 1 | 3 | 100 | 2 | 2 |
| Wisconsin | 33 | 1 | 3 | 99 | 1 | 1 |
| Wyoming | 30 | 0 | 0 | 60 | 0 | 0 |
| Dist. of Columbia | 13 | 0 | 0 | ...................... Unicameral .................. | | |
| American Samoa | 18 | 0 | 0 | 20 | 0 | 0 |
| Guam | 15 | 0 | 0 | ...................... Unicameral .................. | | |
| No. Mariana Islands | 9 | 0 | 0 | 18 | 1 | 6 |
| Puerto Rico | 31 | 1 | 3 | 54 | 2 | 4 |
| U.S. Virgin Islands | 15 | 0 | 0 | ...................... Unicameral .................. | | |

*Source:* The Council of State Governments, April 2012.

**Table 3.5**
**THE LEGISLATORS: QUALIFICATIONS FOR ELECTION**

| State or other jurisdiction | House/Assembly | | | | | Senate | | | | |
|---|---|---|---|---|---|---|---|---|---|---|
| | Minimum age | U.S. citizen (years) (a) | State resident (years) (b) | District resident (years) | Qualified voter (years) | Minimum age | U.S. citizen (years) (a) | State resident (years) (b) | District resident (years) | Qualified voter (years) |
| Alabama | 21 | ... | 3 (c) | 1 | ... | 25 | ... | 3 (c) | 1 | ... |
| Alaska | 21 | ★ | 3 | 1 | ★ | 25 | ... | 3 | 1 | ★ |
| Arizona | 25 | ★ | 3 | 1 | ★ | 25 | ★ | 3 | 1 | ★ |
| Arkansas | 21 | ★ | 2 | 1 | ★ | 25 | ★ | 2 | 1 | ★ |
| California | 18 | 3 | 3 | 1 | ★ | 18 | 3 | 3 | 1 | ★ |
| Colorado | 25 | ★ | 1 | 1 | ★ | 25 | ★ | 1 | 1 | ★ |
| Connecticut | 18 | ★ | ★ | ★ | ★ | 18 | ★ | ★ | ★ | ★ |
| Delaware | 24 | ★ | 3 | 1 | ★ | 27 | ★ | 3 (c) | 1 | ★ |
| Florida | 21 | ... | 2 | 2 | ★ | 21 | ... | 2 | 2 | ★ |
| Georgia | 21 | ★ | 2 (c) | 1 | ★ | 25 | ★ | 2 (c) | 1 | ★ |
| Hawaii | 18 | ★ | 3 | ★ | ★ | 18 | ★ | 3 | ★ | ★ |
| Idaho | 21 | ★ | 30 days | 1 | ★ | 21 | ★ | 30 days | 1 | ★ |
| Illinois | 21 | ★ | 2 | 2 (d) | ★ | 21 | ★ | 2 | 2 (d) | ★ |
| Indiana | 21 | ★ | 2 | 1 | ★ | 25 | ★ | 2 | 1 | ★ |
| Iowa | 21 | ★ | 1 | 60 days | ... | 25 | ★ | 1 | ... | ... |
| Kansas | 18 | ★ | ★ (c) | ★ | ★ | 18 | ★ | ★ (c) | ★ | ★ |
| Kentucky | 24 | ★ | 2 (c) | 1 | ★ | 30 | ★ | 6 (c) | 1 | ★ |
| Louisiana | 18 | ★ | 2 | 1 | ★ | 18 | 5 | 2 | 1 | ★ |
| Maine | 21 | 5 | ... | 3 mo. | ... | 25 | ... | 1 | 3 mo. | ★ |
| Maryland | 21 | ★ | 1 (c) | 6 mo. (e) | ... | 25 | ★ | 1 (c) | 6 mo. (e) | 3 |
| Massachusetts | 18 | ... | 5 | 1 | ★ | 18 | ... | 5 | 5 | ★ |
| Michigan | 21 | ★ | ★ | (f) | ★ | 21 | ★ | 1 | (f) | ★ |
| Minnesota | 18 | ... | 1 | 6 mo. | ★ | 21 | ... | 1 | 6 mo. | ★ |
| Mississippi | 21 | ... | 4 (c) | 2 | ★ | 25 | ... | 4 (c) | 2 | ★ |
| Missouri | 24 | ★ | ★ | 1 | 2 | 30 | ★ | ★ | 1 | 3 |
| Montana | 18 | U | 1 | 6 mo. (g) | U | 18 | U | 1 | 6 mo. (g) | U |
| Nebraska | U | ... | U | U | ... | 21 | ★ | 1 (c) | 1 | ★ |
| Nevada | 21 | ★ | 1 (c) | 30 days (h) | ★ | 21 | ★ | 1 (c) | 30 days (h) | ★ |
| New Hampshire | 18 | ... | 2 (c) | ★ | ★ | 30 | ... | 7 (c) | 1 | ★ |
| New Jersey | 21 | ★ | 2 (c) | 1 | ★ | 30 | ★ | 2 (c) | 1 | ★ |
| New Mexico | 21 | ★ | ★ (c) | ★ | ★ | 25 | ★ | 5 | 1 (i) | ★ |
| New York | 18 | ★ | 5 | 1 (i) | ★ | 18 | ★ | 5 | 1 | ★ |
| North Carolina | 21 | ... | ... | 1 | ★ | 25 | ... | 2 | 1 | ★ |
| North Dakota | 18 | ... | 1 | 1 | ★ | 18 | ... | 1 | 1 | ★ |
| Ohio | 18 | ★ | 30 days | 1 | ★ | 18 | ★ | 30 days | 30 days | ★ |
| Oklahoma | 21 | ★ | ★ (c) | ★ | ★ | 25 | ★ | ★ (c) | 1 | ★ |
| Oregon | 21 | ★ | ... | 1 | ... | 21 | ★ | ... | 1 | ... |
| Pennsylvania | 21 | ... | 4 (c) | 4 | ★ | 25 | ★ | 4 (c) | 4 | ★ |
| Rhode Island | 18 | ★ | 30 days | 30 days | ★ | 18 | ★ | 30 days | 30 days | ★ |
| South Carolina | 21 | ... | ... | ★ (j) | ... | 25 | ... | ... | ★ (j) | ... |

See footnotes at end of table.

# THE LEGISLATORS: QUALIFICATIONS FOR ELECTION—Continued

| State or other jurisdiction | House/Assembly | | | | | Senate | | | | |
|---|---|---|---|---|---|---|---|---|---|---|
| | Minimum age | U.S. citizen (years) (a) | State resident (years) (b) | District resident (years) | Qualified voter (years) | Minimum age | U.S. citizen (years) (a) | State resident (years) (b) | District resident (years) | Qualified voter (years) |
| South Dakota | 21 | ★ | 2 | ★ | ★ | 21 | ★ | 2 | ★ | ★ |
| Tennessee | 21 | ★ | (c) | 1 | ★ | 30 | ★ | 3 | 1 | ★ |
| Texas | 21 | ★ | 2 | 1 | ★ | 26 | ★ | 5 | 1 | ★ |
| Utah | 25 | ★ | 3 (c) | 6 mo. | ... | 25 | ★ | 3 (c) | 6 mo. | ... |
| Vermont | 18 | ★ | 2 | 1 | ... | 18 | ★ | 2 | 1 | ... |
| Virginia | 21 | ★ | ★ | ★ | ★ | 21 | ★ | ★ | ★ | ★ |
| Washington | 18 | ★ | 1 (c) | ... | ★ | 18 | ★ | 5 (c) | ... | ★ |
| West Virginia | 18 | ★ | 1 | 1 | ★ | 25 | 5 | 1 | 1 | ★ |
| Wisconsin | 18 | ★ | 1 | ★(k) | ★(k) | 18 | ★ | 1 | ★(k) | ★(k) |
| Wyoming | 21 | ★ | ★(c) | 1 | ★ | 25 | ★ | ★(c) | 1 | ★(k) |
| Dist. of Columbia | U | U | U | U | U | 18 | ... | 1 | 1 | U |
| American Samoa | 25 | ★(l) | 5 | 1 | U | 30 (m) | ★(l) | 1 | 1 | ★ |
| Guam | U | U | U | U | U | 25 | ★(l) | 5 | 1 | ... |
| No. Mariana Islands | 21 | ... | 3 | (f) | ★ | 25 | ... | 5 | (f) | ★ |
| Puerto Rico | 25 | ... | 2 | 1 (n) | ... | 30 | ★ | 2 | 1 (n) | ... |
| U.S. Virgin Islands | U | U | U | U | U | 21 | ... | 3 (c) | 3 | ★ |

Source: The Council of State Governments survey, April 2012.

Note: Many state constitutions have additional provisions disqualifying persons from holding office if they are convicted of a felony, bribery, perjury or other infamous crimes.

Key:
U — Unicameral legislature; members are called senators, except in District of Columbia.
★ — Formal provision; number of years not specified.
... — No formal provision.

(a) In some states candidate must be a U.S. citizen to be an elector, and must be an elector to run.
(b) In some states candidate must be a state resident to be an elector, and must be an elector to run.
(c) State citizenship requirement. In Tennessee—must be a citizen for three years.
(d) In the first election after a redistricting, a candidate may be elected from any district that contains a part of the district in which (s)he resided at the time of redistricting, and may be re-elected if a resident of the district (s)he represents for 18 months before re-election.

(e) If the district was established for less than six months, residency is length of establishment of district.
(f) Must be a qualified voter of the district; number of years not specified.
(g) Shall be a resident of the county if it contains one or more districts or if the district contains all or parts of more than one county.
(h) 30 days prior to close of filing for declaration of candidacy.
(i) After redistricting, candidate must have been a resident of the county in which the district is contained for one year immediately preceding election.
(j) At the time of filing.
(k) Ten days prior to election.
(l) Or U.S. national.
(m) Must be registered matai.
(n) The district legislator must live in the municipality he/she represents.

# Table 3.6
## SENATE LEADERSHIP POSITIONS: METHODS OF SELECTION

| State or other jurisdiction | President | President pro tem | Majority leader | Assistant majority leader | Majority floor leader | Assistant majority floor leader | Majority whip | Majority caucus chair | Minority leader | Assistant minority leader | Minority floor leader | Assistant minority floor leader | Minority whip | Minority caucus chair |
|---|---|---|---|---|---|---|---|---|---|---|---|---|---|---|
| Alabama (b) | (a) | ES | (b) | | (b) | | | | (b) | | (b) | | | |
| Alaska | ES | AP | EC | EC | | | EC | EC | EC | | EC | | EC | EC |
| Arizona | ES | ES | EC | EC | | | EC | EC | EC | EC | EC | | EC | EC |
| Arkansas | (a) | ES | EC | EC | | | EC | EC | EC | | EC | | EC | EC |
| California | (a) | ES | EC | EC | | | EC | EC | EC | | EC | | EC | EC |
| Colorado | ES | ES | EC | EC | | | AP | EC | EC | EC | EC | AL | AL | EC |
| Connecticut (c) | (a) | ES | AP | AP | AP | AP | AP | AP | EC | AL | AL | AL | AL | AL |
| Delaware | ES | AP | EC | AL | AP or AL | AP or AL | AP or AL | AP or AL | EC | AL | AL | AL | AL | AL |
| Florida | EC/ES | AP | EC | | AP or AL | | EC | AP or AL | EC | AL | EC | | EC | EC |
| Georgia | (a) | ES | EC | | | | EC | EC (f) | EC | | EC | | | |
| Hawaii (d) | ES | ES (e) | EC | EC | EC | | EC | EC (f) | EC | | EC | | EC | EC |
| Idaho | (a) | ES | EC | EC | EC | | AP/3 | AP | EC | EC/5 | EC | | AL | AL |
| Illinois (g) | ES | | AP (g) | AP/5 | AT | AT | AT | EC | EC | EC | EC | (h) | (h) | EC |
| Indiana | (a) | ES | EC | EC | | | EC | EC | EC | | EC | | EC | EC |
| Iowa | ES | ES | EC | EC | | | EC | EC | EC | EC | EC | | EC | EC |
| Kansas | ES | ES (e) | EC | EC | EC | | EC | EC | EC | EC | EC | | EC | EC |
| Kentucky (i) | ES | ES | EC | EC | EC | | EC | EC | EC | EC | EC | | EC | EC |
| Louisiana | ES | ES | | | | | | | EC (o) | | | | | |
| Maine | ES | AP | EC | AP (n) | (j) | (j) | (k) | (j) | EC (o) | EC | (l) | (l) | (m) | (p) |
| Maryland | ES | ES | AP (n) | AP (n) | (n) | (n) | AP | EC | EC | EC | (o) | | EC | EC |
| Massachusetts | EC | | AP | AP | EC | | EC | (p) | EC | EC | EC | EC | EC | (p) |
| Michigan (q) | (a) | ES | EC | EC | EC | EC | EC | EC | EC | EC | EC | EC | EC | EC |
| Minnesota | (a) | ES | EC | EC | EC | | AL/7 | AP | EC | EC | EC | | EC/5 | EC |
| Mississippi | (a) | ES | | | | | | | EC | | | | | EC |
| Missouri | ES | ES | AP (n) | | (n) | (n) | AP | EC | EC | EC | | | EC | EC |
| Montana | (a) | ES | AP | AP | EC | EC | ES | MA | EC | ES | ES | | ES | |
| Nebraska (U) | (a) | ES (r) | | | | | ES | MA | EC | EC | EC | | EC | EC |
| Nevada (s) | (a) | AP | AP | AP | EC | EC | AP | AP | EC | AL | MI | EC | AL | AL |
| New Hampshire | ES | AP | MA | MA | MA | MA | MA | MA | MI | MI | MI | MI | MI | MI |
| New Jersey | ES | ES | | | | | ES | | ES (x) | ES | ES | ES | ES | |
| New Mexico | (a) | ES | EC (t) | AT (v) | EC (t) AT (v) | | EC | EC AT (v) | EC (t) AT (v) | AT (v) | EC (t) AT (v) | | EC | AL (v) |
| New York (u) | (a) | ES | EC | EC | AT (v) | | AT | | EC | EC | | | EC | EC |
| North Carolina (u) | (a) | ES | EC | EC | EC | | EC | EC | EC | EC | EC | | EC | EC |
| North Dakota | (a) | ES | EC | EC | | | ES | EC | EC | ES | ES | | ES | EC |
| Ohio (w)(x) | ES (x) | ES | | | ES | ES | ES | MA | ES (x) | ES | ES | ES | ES | ES |
| Oklahoma | (a) | ES | EC | EC | EC | | EC | EC | EC | EC | EC | EC | EC | EC |
| Oregon | ES | ES | EC | EC | EC | | EC | EC | EC | EC | EC | | EC | EC |
| Pennsylvania | ES | ES | EC | EC | EC | | EC | EC | EC | EC | EC | EC | EC | EC |
| Rhode Island (y) | ES | ES | EC | AL | EC | | AL | EC | EC | EC | EC | AL | AL | EC |
| South Carolina | (a) | ES | EC | AL | | | | | EC | | | | | |
| South Dakota | (a) | ES | EC | EC | EC | | EC | EC | EC | EC | EC | | EC | EC |
| Tennessee | (a) | AP | EC | EC | | | EC | EC | EC | EC | EC | | EC | EC |
| Texas | (a) | ES | EC | EC | EC (z) | EC (z) | EC | EC | EC | EC | EC (z) | EC (z) | EC | EC (z) |
| Utah | ES | ES | EC | EC | EC (aa) | EC (aa) | EC (aa) | EC (aa) | EC | EC | EC (aa) | EC (aa) | EC (aa) | EC (aa) |
| Vermont | (a) | ES | EC | EC | | | | | EC | | EC | | EC | EC |

See footnotes at end of table.

## SENATE LEADERSHIP POSITIONS: METHODS OF SELECTION—Continued

| State or other jurisdiction | President | President pro tem | Majority leader | Assistant majority leader | Majority floor leader | Assistant majority floor leader | Majority whip | Majority caucus chair | Minority leader | Assistant minority leader | Minority floor leader | Assistant minority floor leader | Minority whip | Minority caucus chair |
|---|---|---|---|---|---|---|---|---|---|---|---|---|---|---|
| Virginia.......... | (a) | ES | EC (bb) | ... | EC (bb) | ... | ... | EC | EC | EC | EC | ... | ... | EC |
| Washington (cc)...... | (a) | ES | EC | EC (bb) | EC | ... | EC | EC | EC | EC | EC | EC | EC | EC |
| West Virginia...... | ES | AP | AP | EC | ... | ... | AP | ... | EC | EC | ... | ... | AL | EC |
| Wisconsin.......... | ES (dd) | EC | EC | ... | EC | ... | EC | EC | EC | EC | EC | ... | EC | EC |
| Wyoming........... | ES (e) | EC | ... | ... | ... | ... | ... | ... | ... | ... | ... | ... | ... | ... |
| Dist. of Columbia (U)...... | (ee) | (ff) | ... | ... | ... | ... | ... | ... | ... | ... | ... | ... | ... | ... |
| American Samoa...... | ES | ES | ... | ... | ... | ... | ... | ... | EC | ... | ... | ... | ... | ... |
| Guam (U)(gg)...... | ES (r) | ES (e) | EC | ... | EC | ... | ... | EC | EC | EC | EC | ... | EC | ... |
| No. Mariana Islands...... | ES (hh) | ... | (hh) | ... | ... | ... | ... | (kk) | EC (p) | ... | ... | ... | ... | ... |
| Puerto Rico...... | ES (p) | EC | EC | ... | EC | ... | ... | ... | ES | EC | EC (jj) | ... | ... | (p) |
| U.S. Virgin Islands (U)...... | ES | EC | ES | ... | EC (jj) | ... | ... | ES | ES | ... | ... | ... | ... | ES |

Source: The Council of State Governments' survey, January 2012.

Note: In some states, the leadership positions in the Senate are not empowered by the law or by the rules of the chamber, but rather by the party members themselves. Entry following slash indicates number of individuals holding specified position.

Key:
ES — Elected or confirmed by all members of the Senate.
EC — Elected by party caucus.
AP — Appointed by president.
AT — Appointed by president pro tempore.
... — Position does not exist or is not selected on a regular basis.
AL — Appointed by party leader.
MA — Elected by majority party.
MI — Elected by minority party.
(U) — Unicameral legislative body.

(a) Lieutenant governor is president of the Senate by virtue of the office.

(b) Majority leader and majority floor leader appointed by president pro tempore and the Senate Democratic Caucus. Minority leader and minority floor leader elected by active members of the minority party. Additional leadership positions: deputy president pro tempore—appointed by Committee on Assignments and Dean of Senate—appointed by Committee on Assignments.

(c) Position titles are as follows: chief deputy president pro tem, two deputy presidents pro tem, a chief assistant president pro tem, three assistant presidents pro tem, three deputy majority leaders (AP); a minority leader pro tem, two chief deputy minority leaders, a deputy minority leader-at-large, and three deputy minority leaders (AL).

(d) An additional position of President Emeritus exists.

(e) Official title is vice president. In Guam, vice speaker.

(f) Official title is majority caucus leader.

(g) The president can appoint a majority leader, and has done so in the current General Assembly. Additional leadership positions: the minority leader appoints a deputy minority leader and four assistant minority leaders.

(h) Appointed by minority leader.

(i) In each chamber, the membership elects Chief Clerk; Assistant Clerk; Enrolling Clerk; Sergeant-at-Arms; Doorkeeper; Janitor; Cloakroom Keeper; and Pages.

(j) Same position as assistant majority leader.

(k) Same position as assistant majority leader.

(l) Same position as minority leader.

(m) Same position as assistant minority leader.

(n) Majority leader also serves as majority floor leader; deputy majority leader is official title and serves as assistant majority floor leader. There is also an assistant deputy majority leader, a majority whip, deputy majority whip, and two assistant majority whips.

(o) Minority leader also serves as the minority floor leader.

(p) President and minority floor leader also serves as caucus chairs. In Puerto Rico, president and minority leader. In Oregon, majority leader and minority leader.

(q) Senate Rule 1.104 provides that the president pro tempore (ES), assistant president pro tempore (ES), and the associate president pro tempore (ES) are elected by a majority of the Senate. The rules also provide

for the selection of additional positions: assistant majority caucus whip (EC), assistant minority caucus whip (EC), assistant majority caucus chairperson (EC), and assistant minority caucus chairperson (EC).

(r) Official title is speaker. In Guam the Speaker is elected on the Floor by majority and minority members on Inauguration Day.

(s) Additional leadership positions: Assistant Majority and Minority Whips, elected by caucus.

(t) Majority leader also serves as majority floor leader. Minority leader also serves as minority floor leader.

(u) Additional positions appointed by the majority leader, Senate Finance Comm. Chair, Vice President pro tem, Majority Program Development Comm. Chair, Majority Steering Comm. Chair, two assistant majority leaders, various deputies and assistants. Additional positions appointed by the minority leader, Senate Finance Comm. ranking member, Minority Policy Comm. chair, Minority Program Development chair, three (additional assistant minority leaders, various deputies and assistants.

(v) The assistant majority leader bears the title of senior assistant majority leader; majority floor leader bears the title of deputy majority leader for legislative operations; Majority caucus chair bears the title of majority conference chair; assistant minority leader bears the title deputy minority leader; minority floor leader bears the title assistant minority leader for floor operations; minority caucus chair bears the title minority conference chair.

(w) While the entire membership actually votes on the election of leaders, selections generally have been made by the members of each party prior to the date of this formal election.

(x) In Ohio president acts as majority leader and caucus chair; minority leader also acts as minority caucus chair; the fourth ranking minority leadership position is assistant minority whip (ES).

(y) Additional positions include deputy president pro tempore.

(z) Official title for majority floor leader is known as the assistant majority whip; the assistant minority floor leader is known as the assistant minority whip and the minority caucus chair is known as minority caucus manager.

(aa) Majority leader serves as majority floor leader and majority caucus chair. Assistant majority leader serves as assistant majority floor leader and majority whip. Minority leader serves as minority floor leader and minority caucus chair. Assistant minority leader serves as assistant minority floor leader and minority whip.

(bb) Majority party and Minority party in Senate elects caucus officers.

(cc) Washington Senate also has the leadership position of vice-president pro tem.

(dd) Caucus nominee elected by whole membership.

(ee) Chair of the Council, which is an elected position.

(ff) Appointed by the chair; official title is chair pro tem.

(gg) Additional positions include: Parliamentarian, elected by majority caucus and Senior Senator, elected by majority caucus.

(hh) Speaker also serves as majority leader.

(ii) Official title is floor leader.

(jj) Official title is alternate floor leader.

(kk) Official title is caucus chair.

# Table 3.7
# HOUSE/ASSEMBLY LEADERSHIP POSITIONS: METHODS OF SELECTION

| State or other jurisdiction | Speaker | Speaker pro tem | Majority leader | Assistant majority leader | Majority floor leader | Assistant majority floor leader | Majority whip | Majority caucus chair | Minority leader | Assistant minority leader | Minority floor leader | Assistant minority floor leader | Minority whip | Minority caucus chair |
|---|---|---|---|---|---|---|---|---|---|---|---|---|---|---|
| Alabama | EH | EH | EC | | | | | | EC | | | | EC | |
| Alaska | EH | | EC | | | | EC | EC | EC | | | | EC | EC |
| Arizona | EH | AS | EC | | | | EC | EC | EC | EC | EC | EC | EC | EC |
| Arkansas | EH | AS | AS | AS | AS | AS | AS | AS | AS | AL | AS | AL | AS | AL |
| California | EH | AS | EC | AS | AS | AS | AS | AS | EC | | | | EC | EC |
| Colorado (a) | EH | AS | EC | EC | | | EC | EC | EC | EC | | | EC | EC |
| Connecticut | EH | AS/4 (b) | EC | EC/4 (b) | | | AS | AS | EC | AL | AL | AL | AL | AL |
| Delaware | EH | EH | AS | AS | AS | | AS | AS | AS | AL | AL | | AL | AL |
| Florida | EH | EH | AS | AS | AS | | EC | EC | AL | EC | AL | EC | EC | EC |
| Georgia | EH | EH | EC | | EC | EC | EC | EC | EC | EC | EC | EC | EC | EC |
| Hawaii (c) | EH | EH (d) | EC | EC | | | EC | EC (e) | EC | EC (e) | | | EC | EC (e) |
| Idaho | EH | | AS (e) | AS (e) | | | AL | AL | AL (e) | AL | AL | AL | AL | AL |
| Illinois | EH | AL | EC | AL | AL | | AS | AL | EC | EC | EC | EC | EC | EC |
| Indiana | EH | EH | EC | EC | EC | | EC | EC | EC | EC | EC | EC | EC | EC |
| Iowa | EH | EH | EC | EC | EC | | EC | EC | EC | EC | | | EC | EC |
| Kansas (f) | EH | EH | EC | EC | | | EC | EC | EC | EC | EC | EC | EC | EC |
| Kentucky (g) | EH | EH | EC (h) | EC (h) | | | EC (h) | EC | EC (h) | EC (h) | EC (h) | EC (h) | EC (h) | EC |
| Louisiana | EH | AS (h) | AS (j) | AS (j) | | | AS | | EC | AL | EC (l) | EC (l) | EH | (k) |
| Maine | EH (i) | EH (i) | AS | AS | | | AS | AS | EC | AL | EC | EC | EC | EC |
| Maryland (bb) | EH (k) | | | | | | | (k) | EC (l) | EC | EC (l) | EC (l) | EH | EC (k) |
| Massachusetts | EC | EH | AS | AS | AS | AS | AS | EC | AS | AL | EC | EC | EC | EC |
| Michigan (n) | EH | EH | EC | EC | EC | EC | EC | EC | EC | EC | EC | EC | EC | EC |
| Minnesota | EH | AS | | | | | | | EC | AL | EC | EC | EC | EC |
| Mississippi | EH | EH | EC | | | | EC | EC | AL | AL | EC | EC | EC | EC |
| Missouri | EH | EH | EC | EC | EC | EC | EC | EC | EC | EC | EC | EC | EC | EC |
| Montana | EH | EH | | | | | EH | | EH | EH | EH | EH | EH | |
| Nebraska | | | | | | | | | | | | | | |
| Nevada | EH | EH | AS | EC | EC | EC | EC | EC | AL | AL | EC | EC | AL | |
| New Hampshire | EH | AS (d) | MA | MA | MA | MA | MA | MA | MI | MI | MI | MI | MI | MI |
| New Jersey | EH | EH | EC | EC | EC (m) | | EC | EC | EC | EC | EC (l) | EC (l) | EC | EC |
| New Mexico | EH | EH | EC | | EC (m) | | EC | EC | EC | EC | EC | EC | EC | EC |
| New York (p) | EH | | AS | AS | AS | AS | AS | AS (q) | AL | EC | MI | AL | AL | AL (q) |
| North Carolina | EH | AS | AS | EC | EC | EC | MA | AS | AL | AL | MI | MI | MI | AL |
| North Dakota | EH | | EC | | | | EC | EC | EC | EC | EC | EC | EC | EC |
| Ohio (r) | EH (k) | EH | EC | EC | EC | EH | EH | AS (q) | EH | EH | EH | EH | EH | EC |
| Oklahoma | EH | EH | AS | AS | AS | AS | AS | AS | EC | EC | EC | EC | EC | EC |
| Oregon | EH | EH | EC | EC | EC | EC | EC | EC | EC | EC | EC | EC | EC | EC |
| Pennsylvania | EH | EH | EC | EC | EC | EC | EC | EC | EC | EC | EC | EC | EC | EC |
| Rhode Island | EH | EH | EC | AL | | | AL | AL | AL | AL | | | AL | AL |
| South Carolina | EH | EH | AL | EC | | | EC | EC | EC | EC | | | EC | EC |
| South Dakota | EH | EH | EC | EC | EC | EC | EC | EC | EC | EC | EC | | EC | EC |
| Tennessee | EH | EH | EC | EC | EC | EC | EC | EC | EC | EC | EC | AL | EC | EC |
| Texas | EH | AS | EC (s) | EC (s) | | | | | EC (s) | EC | EC (s) | EC (s) | EC | EC (s) |
| Utah | EH | AS | EC | EC | | | EC | | EC | EC | | | EC | EC |
| Vermont | EH | | EC | | (t) | | (t) | (t) | EC | EC | (t) | (t) | (t) | (t) |

See footnotes at end of table.

# HOUSE/ASSEMBLY LEADERSHIP POSITIONS: METHODS OF SELECTION — Continued

| State or other jurisdiction | Speaker | Speaker pro tem | Majority leader | Assistant majority leader | Majority floor leader | Assistant majority floor leader | Majority whip | Majority caucus chair | Minority leader | Assistant minority leader | Minority floor leader | Assistant minority floor leader | Minority whip | Minority caucus chair |
|---|---|---|---|---|---|---|---|---|---|---|---|---|---|---|
| Virginia (u) | EH | ... | EC(v) | EC(v) | EC(v) | ... | EC | EC | EC(w) | ... | EC(w) | ... | AL | EC |
| Washington | EH | EH | EC | EC | EC | EC | EC | EC | EC | EC | EC | EC | EC | EC |
| West Virginia | EH | AS | AS | AS | ... | ... | AS | AS | EC | EC | EC | ... | ... | ... |
| Wisconsin | EH(x) | EH(x) | EC | EC | EC | EC | EC | EC | EC | EC | EC | EC | EC | EC |
| Wyoming | EH | EH | EC | EC | EC | ... | EC | EC | EC | EC | EC | ... | EC | EC |
| Dist. of Columbia | ... | ... | ... | ... | ... | ... | ... | ... | ... | ... | ... | ... | ... | ... |
| American Samoa | EH | EH(d) | ... | ... | ... | ... | (o) | ... | ... | ... | ... | ... | ... | ... |
| Guam | ... | ... | ... | ... | ... | ... | (o) | ... | ... | ... | ... | ... | ... | ... |
| No. Mariana Islands | EH(y) | ... | (y) | ... | EH(z) | ... | (o) | ... | EC | ... | EC | ... | ... | ... |
| Puerto Rico | EH(k) | EH(d) | EC | ... | EC(aa) | ... | ... | ... | EC(k) | ... | EC | ... | ... | ... |
| U.S. Virgin Islands | ... | ... | ... | ... | ... | ... | ... | ... | ... | ... | ... | ... | ... | (k) |

*Source:* The Council of State Governments' survey, January 2009 and March 2011.

*Note:* In some states, the leadership positions in the House are not empowered by the law or by the rules of the chamber, but rather by the party members themselves. Entry following slash indicates number of individuals holding specified position.

*Key:*

EH — Elected or confirmed by all members of the House.
EC — Elected by party caucus.
AS — Appointed by speaker.
AL — Appointed by party leader.
MA — Elected by majority party.
MI — Elected by minority party.
... — Position does not exist or is not selected on a regular basis.

(a) Additional positions include deputy majority whip (EC) and assistant majority caucus chair (EC).
(b) Official titles: speaker pro tem—deputy speaker; assistant majority leader—deputy majority leader.
(c) Other positions in Hawaii include speaker emeritus.
(d) Official title is deputy speaker. In Hawaii, American Samoa and Puerto Rico, vice speaker.
(e) The two deputy majority leaders appointed by the speaker are among eight assistant majority leaders; and the two deputy Republican (minority) leaders appointed by the Republican (minority) leader are among the eight assistant leaders. (The term "Minority" is in the state constitution, but has not been recently used by the leadership of the Republican (Minority) party.)
(f) Additional positions include minority agenda chair (EC) and minority policy chair (EC).
(g) In each chamber, the membership elects chief clerk; assistant chief clerk; enrolling clerk; sergeant-at-arms; doorkeeper; janitor; cloakroom keeper; and pages.
(h) Speaker pro tem each occurrence. Majority leader also serves as majority floor leader; assistant majority leader also serves as assistant majority floor leader and majority whip; minority leader also serves as minority floor leader; assistant minority floor leader also serves as assistant minority floor leader and minority whip.
(i) There is also a deputy speaker pro tem.
(j) Majority leader also serves as majority floor leader. Official title of assistant majority leader is deputy majority leader. There are also an assistant majority floor leader, majority whip, chief deputy majority whips, and deputy majority whips.
(k) Speaker and minority leader are also caucus chairs.
(l) Minority leader also serves as the minority floor leader. There are also a minority whip, assistant minority leader, a chief deputy minority whip, an assistant minority whip, and several deputy minority whips.

(m) Majority leader also serves as majority floor leader; minority leader also serves as minority floor leader.
(n) Other positions include: two associate speakers pro tempore (EH); majority caucus chair (EC); assistant majority whip (EC); assistant associate minority floor leader (EC); minority assistant caucus chair (EC); assistant minority whip (EC).
(o) Unicameral legislature; see entries in Table 3.6, "Senate Leadership Positions—Methods of Selection."
(p) Additional majority positions appointed by the speaker: deputy speaker (AS), deputy majority leader, Ways and Means Committee chair, Democratic Program Committee chair, Democratic Steering Committee chair, various deputies and assistants. Additional minority positions appointed by the minority leader: deputy minority leader, Ways and Means Committee ranking member, Republican Steering Committee chair, Republican Program Committee chair, various deputies and assistants.
(q) Official titles: the majority caucus chair is majority conference chair; minority caucus chair is minority conference chair.
(r) While the entire membership actually votes on the election of leaders, selections generally have been made by the members of each party prior to the date of this formal election. Additional positions include assistant majority whip, the 6th ranking majority leadership position (EH) and assistant minority whip, the 4th ranking minority leadership position (EH).
(s) Assistant majority leader is known as majority assistant whip; assistant minority floor leader known as majority assistant whip; minority caucus chair known as minority caucus manager.
(t) Majority leader also serves as majority floor leader; assistant majority leader also serves as assistant majority floor leader and majority whip; minority leader also serves as minority floor leader; assistant minority floor leader also serves as assistant minority floor leader and minority whip.
(u) The majority caucus also has a secretary, who is appointed by the speaker; the minority caucus has 2 vice-chairs, 1 vice-chair/treasurer and an interim sergeant-at-arms.
(v) The title of majority leader is not used in Virginia; the title is majority floor leader.
(w) The title of minority leader is not used in Virginia; the title is minority floor leader.
(x) Caucus nominee elected by whole membership.
(y) Speaker also serves as majority leader.
(z) Official title is floor leader.
(aa) Official title is alternate floor leader.
(bb) There is a parliamentarian for the majority appointed by the Speaker and a minority parliamentarian elected by the minority party caucus.

## Table 3.8
# METHOD OF SETTING LEGISLATIVE COMPENSATION

| State | Method |
|---|---|
| Alabama | Constitutional Amendment 57 |
| Alaska | Compensation Commission; Alaska Stat. §24.10.100, §24.10.101; §39.23.200 thru 39.23.260 |
| Arizona | Compensation Commission Send to a Public Vote; Arizona Revised Statutes 41-1103 and 41-1904 |
| Arkansas | Amendment 70, Ark. Stat. Ann. §10-2-212 et seq. |
| California | State Constitution—Art. III, §8, which establishes a Compensation Commission. |
| Colorado | Colorado Stat. 2-2-307 (1) |
| Connecticut | Conn. Gen. Stat. Ann. §2-9a; The General Assembly takes independent action pursuant to recommendations of a Compensation Commission. |
| Delaware | Del. Code Ann. Title 29, §710 et seq.; §§3301–3304; Are implemented automatically if not rejected by resolution. |
| Florida | §11.13(1), Florida Statutes; Statute provides members same percentage increase as state employees. |
| Georgia | Ga. Code Ann. §45-7-4 and §28-1-8 |
| Hawaii | Art. III, §9; Commission recommendations take effect unless rejected by concurrent resolution or the governor. Any change in salary that becomes effective does not apply to the legislature for which the recommendation was submitted. |
| Idaho | A Citizen's Committee on Legislative Compensation makes recommendations that the Legislature can reduce or reject, but not increase. Idaho Code 67-406a and 406b |
| Illinois | 25 ILCS 120-Compensation Review Act and 25 ILCS 115-General Assembly Compensation Act |
| Indiana | IC 2-3-1-1: An amount equal to 18% of the annual salary of a judge under IC 33-38-5-6, as adjusted under IC 33-38-5-8.1. |
| Iowa | Iowa Code Ann. §2.10; Iowa Code Ann. §2A.1 thru 2A.5 |
| Kansas | Kan. Stat. Ann. §46-137a et seq.; §75-3212 |
| Kentucky | Ky. Rev. Stat. Ann. §6.226-229; The Kentucky committee has not met since 1995. The most recent pay raise was initiated and passed by the General Assembly. |
| Louisiana | La. Rev. Stat. 24:31 & 31.1 |
| Maine | Maine Constitution Article IV, Part Third, §7 and 3 MRSA, §2 and 2-A; Increase in compensation is presented to the legislature as legislation; the legislature must enact and the governor must sign into law. Takes effect only for subsequent legislatures. |
| Maryland | Art. III, §15; Commission meets before each four-year term of office and presents recommendations to the General Assembly for action. Recommendations may be reduced or rejected. |
| Massachusetts | Mass. Gen. Laws Ann. ch. 3, §§9, 10; In 1998, the voters passed a legislative referendum that starting with the 2001 session, members will receive an automatic increase or decrease according to the median household income for the commonwealth for the following 2-year period. |
| Michigan | Art. IV §12; Compensation Commission recommends, legislature by majority vote must approve or reduce for change to be effective for the session immediately following the next general election. |
| Minnesota | Minn. Stat. Ann §3.099 et seq.; §15A.082; The Council submits salary recommendations to the presiding officers by May 1 in odd-numbered years. |
| Mississippi | Miss. Code Ann. 5-1-41 |
| Missouri | Art. III, §§16, 34; Mo. Ann. Stat. §21.140; Recommendations are adjusted by legislature or governor if necessary. |
| Montana | Mont. Laws 5-2-301; Tied to executive broadband pay plan. |
| Nebraska | Neb. Const. Art. III, §7; Neb. Rev. Stat. 50-123.01 |
| Nevada | §218.210–§218.225 |
| New Hampshire | Art. XV, part second |
| New Jersey | Art. IV, Sec IV 7 & 8; NJSA 52:10A-1; NJSA 52:14-15.111 to 52:14-15.114 |
| New Mexico | Art. IV. §10; 2-1-8 NMSA |
| New York | Constitution—Art. 3, §6; Consolidated Laws of NY—Legislative Law, Section 5 |
| North Carolina | N.C.G.S. 120-3 |
| North Dakota | NDCC 54-03-10 and 54-03-20 |
| Ohio | Art. II, §31; Ohio Rev. Code Ann. title 1 ch. 101.27 thru 101.272 |
| Oklahoma | Okla. Stat. Ann. title 74, §291 et seq.; Art V, §21; Title 74, §291.2 et seq.; Legislative Compensation Board |
| Oregon | Or. Rev. Stat. §171.072 |
| Pennsylvania | Pa. Cons. Stat. Ann. 46 PS §5; 65 PS §366.1 et seq.; Legislators receive annual cost of living increase that is tied to the Consumer Price Index. |
| Rhode Island | Art. VI, §3 |

## METHOD OF SETTING LEGISLATIVE COMPENSATION — Continued

| State | Method |
|---|---|
| South Carolina | S.C. Code Ann. 2-3-20 and the annual General Appropriations Act |
| South Dakota | Art. III, §6 and Art. XXI, §2; S.D. Codified Laws Ann. §20402 et seq. |
| Tennessee | Art. II, §23; Tenn. Code Ann. §3-1-106 et seq. |
| Texas | Art. III, §24; In 1991, a constitutional amendment was approved by voters to allow Ethics Commission to recommend the salaries of members. Any recommendations must be approved by voters to be effective. The provision has yet to be used. |
| Utah | Art. VI, §9; Utah Code Ann. §36-2-2, et seq. |
| Vermont | Vt. Stat. Ann. title 32, §1051 and §1052 |
| Virginia | Art. IV, §5; Va. Code Ann. §30-19.11 thru §30-19.14 |
| Washington | Art. II, §23; §43.03.060; Wash. Rev. Code Ann. §43.03.028; Salary Commission sets salaries of legislature and other state officials based on market study and input from citizens. |
| West Virginia | Art. 6, §33; W. Va. Code §4-2A-1 et seq.; Submits by resolution and must be concurred by at least four members of the commission. The Legislature must enact the resolution into law and may reduce, but shall not increase, any item established in such resolution. |
| Wisconsin | Sections 20.923 and 230.12, Wis. Statutes, created by Chapter 90, Laws of 1973, and amended by 1983 Wis. Act 27 and Wis. Act 33, provide the current procedure for setting salaries of elected state officials. Generally, compensation is determined as part of the state compensation plan for non-represented employees and is approved by vote of the joint committee on employment relations. |
| Wyoming | Wyo. Stat. §28-5-101 thru §28-5-105 |

*Source:* National Conference of State Legislatures, 2012.

# Table 3.9
## LEGISLATIVE COMPENSATION AND LIVING EXPENSE ALLOWANCES DURING SESSIONS

| State | Salaries — Regular sessions — Per-diem salary | Salaries — Regular sessions — Limit on days | Annual salary | Mileage cents per mile | Session per diem rate |
|---|---|---|---|---|---|
| Alabama | $10 C | ... | ... | 10/mile for a single roundtrip per session. 48.5/mile interim cmte. attendance. | $4,308/month plus $50/day for three days during each week that the legislature actually meets during any session (U). Effective April 1, 2012. |
| Alaska | ... | ... | $50,400 | 40.5/mile for approved travel. | $238 or $253/day (depending on the time of year) tied to federal rate. Legislators who reside in the Capitol area receive 75% of the federal rate. |
| Arizona | ... | ... | $24,000 | 44.5/mile on actual miles. | $35/day for the 1st 120 days of regular session and for special session and $10/day thereafter. Members residing outside Maricopa County receive an additional $25/day for the 1st 120 days of reg. session and for special session and an additional $10/day thereafter (V). Set by statute. |
| Arkansas | ... | ... | $15,869 | 51/mile. | $136/d (V) plus mileage tied to federal rate. |
| California | ... | ... | $95,291 | 53/mile. | $141.86/day for each day they are in session. |
| Colorado | ... | ... | $30,000 | 50/mile. State reimbursement rate is 90% of federal rate. | $45/day for members living in the Denver metro area. $150/day for members living outside Denver. Effective 7/1/12 non-metro per diem will be 85% of federal per diem for Denver. |
| Connecticut | ... | ... | $28,000 | 51/mile. | No per diem is paid. |
| Delaware | ... | ... | $42,750 | 40/mile. | $7,334 expense allowance annually. |
| Florida | ... | ... | $29,687 | 44.5/mile for business travel. | $131/day earned based on the number of days in session. Travel vouchers are filed to substantiate. |
| Georgia | ... | ... | $17,342 | 50/mile. Ga. Code Ann. §50-19-7 sets rate of reimbursement at the same mileage rate established by the U.S. General Services Administration. | $173/d (U) set by the Legislative Services Committee. |
| Hawaii | ... | ... | $46,273 | ... | $150/day for members living outside Oahu during session; $10/day for members living on Oahu during the interim while conducting official legislative business. |
| Idaho | ... | ... | $16,116 | One roundtrip per wk. at state rate. | $122/day for members establishing second residence in Boise; $49/day if no second residence is established and up to $25/day travel (V) set by Compensation Commission. |
| Illinois | ... | ... | $67,836—Members are mandatorily required to forfeit one day of compensation per month. | Mileage rate is 39/mile. | $111/per session day. |
| Indiana | ... | ... | $22,616 | 55/mile. | $152/day (U) tied to federal rate. |
| Iowa | ... | ... | $25,000 | 39/mile. | $135/day (U). $101.25/day for Polk County legislators (U) set by the legislature to coincide with federal rate. State mileage rates apply. |

See footnotes at end of table.

# LEGISLATIVE COMPENSATION AND LIVING EXPENSE ALLOWANCES DURING SESSIONS — Continued

| State | Salaries Regular sessions Per-diem salary | Limit on days | Annual salary | Mileage cents per mile | Session per diem rate |
|---|---|---|---|---|---|
| Kansas | $88.66 C | ... | ... | 51/mile, set by Dept. of Admin. | $123/day (U) tied to federal rate. |
| Kentucky | $188.22 C | ... | ... | 55.5/mile. | $135.30/day (U) tied to federal rate. (110% Federal per diem rate). |
| Louisiana | ... | ... | $16,800 plus additional $6,000/yr. (U) expense allowance. | 55.5/mile based on federal mileage rate. | $149/day (U) tied to federal rate (26 U.S.C. Section 162(h)(1)(B)(ii)). |
| Maine | ... | ... | $13,852 for first regular session; $9,661 for second regular session. | 44/mile. | $38/day housing, or mileage and tolls in lieu of housing (at rate of $0.44/mile up to $38/day) plus $32/day for meals. Per diem limits are set by statute. |
| Maryland | ... | ... | $43,500 | 55.5/mile. $500 annual allowance for in-district travel as taxable income; members may decline the allowance. | Lodging $101/day; meals $42/day tied to federal rate and compensation commission. Out-of-state travel per diem is $225/day for meals and lodging. |
| Massachusetts | ... | ... | $61,300 | Between $10–$100, determined by distance from State House. | From $10/day–$100/day, depending on distance from State House (V) set by the legislature. |
| Michigan | ... | ... | $71,865 | 55.5/mile. | $10,800 yearly expense allowance for session and interim (V) set by compensation commission. |
| Minnesota | ... | ... | $31,140.90 | House: range of $100–$1,650 per month for mileage reimbursement for travel in the legislative district during interim. During session, House members can request up to one roundtrip per week if they live more than 50 miles from the Capitol. Senate: a reasonable allowance. | Senators receive $96/day and Representatives receive $66/legislative day set by the legislature. |
| Mississippi | ... | ... | $10,000 | Determined by Federal Register and Legislature. | $109/day (U) tied to federal rate. |
| Missouri | ... | ... | $35,915 | 37/mile. | $104.00/day tied to federal rate. Verification of per diem is by roll call. |
| Montana | $82.64 L | ... | ... | 55/mile; Rate is based on IRS rate. Reimbursement for actual mileage traveled in connection with legislative business | $105.31/day (U). |
| Nebraska | ... | ... | $12,000 | 55.5/mile; tied to federal rate. | $123/day outside 50-mile radius from Capitol; $46/day if member resides within 50 miles of Capitol (V) tied to federal rate. |
| Nevada | $146.29/day | Max of 60 days of session. | ... | Federal rate, currently 40.5/mile. | Federal rate for Capitol area (U). Legislators who live more than 50 miles from the capitol, if require lodging, will be paid HUD single-room rate for Carson City area for each month of session. |

See footnotes at end of table.

# LEGISLATIVE COMPENSATION AND LIVING EXPENSE ALLOWANCES DURING SESSIONS—Continued

| State | Salaries | | | Mileage cents per mile | Session per diem rate |
|---|---|---|---|---|---|
| | Regular sessions | | | | |
| | Per-diem salary | Limit on days | Annual salary | | |
| New Hampshire | … | 2-yr. term. | $200 | Roundtrip home to State House at 38/mile for first 45 miles and 19/mile thereafter; or members will be reimbursed for actual expenses and mileage will be paid at the maximum IRS mileage rate. | No per diem is paid. |
| New Jersey | … | … | $49,000 | None. | No per diem is paid. |
| New Mexico | … | … | … | 55.5/mile, tied to federal rate. | $154/d (V) tied to federal rate and the constitution. |
| New York | … | … | $79,500 | Varies (V) tied to Federal GSA rate—currently 55.5/mile. | $171/full day and $61/half day. |
| North Carolina | … | … | $13,951 | 29/mile, 1 roundtrip/week during session; 1 roundtrip for attendance at interim cmte. mtgs. | $104/day (U) set by statute. $559/month expense allowance. |
| North Dakota | $152/day during legislative sessions (C) | … | … | 51/mile; one roundtrip/week during session. | Lodging reimbursement up to 30 times 65 percent of the daily lodging rate ($1,351 per month as of 8/1/2011 (V)). |
| Ohio | … | … | $60,583 | 45/mile; one roundtrip/week from home to Statehouse for legislators outside Franklin County only. | No per diem is paid. |
| Oklahoma | … | … | $38,400 | 55.5/mile, tied to federal rate. | $147/day (U) tied to federal rate. |
| Oregon | … | … | $21,936 | 51/mile. | $123/day (U) tied to federal rate. |
| Pennsylvania | … | … | $82,026 | 55.5/mile; rate tied to federal rate. | $159/day (V) tied to federal rate. Can receive actual expenses or per diem. |
| Rhode Island | … | … | $14,186 | 44.5/mile. | No per diem is paid. |
| South Carolina | … | … | $10,400 | 44.5/mile. | $131/day for meals and housing for each statewide session day and committee meeting; tied to federal rate. |
| South Dakota | … | 2-yr. term. | $12,000 | 37/mile for one roundtrip from Pierre to home each weekend. One trip is also paid at 5/mile. During the interim, 37/mile for scheduled committee meetings. | $110/L (U) set by the legislature. |
| Tennessee | … | … | $19,009 | 46/mile. | $173/L (U) tied to federal rate. |
| Texas | … | … | $7,200 | 50/mile set by General Appropriations bill; an allowance for single, twin and turbo engines from $1.24/mile is also given. | $150/d (U) set by Ethics Commission. |
| Utah | $117/day C | … | … | 51/mile, roundtrip from home to capitol. | $95/day (U) lodging allotment for each calendar day, tied to federal rate, $61/day meals (U). |

See footnotes at end of table.

# LEGISLATIVE COMPENSATION AND LIVING EXPENSE ALLOWANCES DURING SESSIONS—Continued

| State | Salaries | | | Mileage cents per mile | Session per diem rate |
|-------|----------|--|--|------------------------|------------------------|
| | Regular sessions | | | | |
| | Per-diem salary | Limit on days | Annual salary | | |
| Vermont | ... | ... | $604.79/week during session; $112 per day for special sessions or interim cmte. meetings. | Federal mileage rate, now about 51/mile, state employee reimbursement rate. | Federal per diem rate for Montpelier is $101/day for lodging and $61/day for meals for non-commuters; commuters receive $61/day for meals plus mileage. |
| Virginia | ... | ... | $18,000/year Senate, $17,640/year House, | 55.5/mile. | House—$135/day (U) tied to federal rate. Senate—$169/day(U) tied to federal rate. |
| Washington | ... | ... | $42,106 | 51/mile. | $90/day. |
| West Virginia | ... | ... | $20,000 | 48.5/mile based on Dept. of Admin. travel regs. | $131/day during session (U) set by compensation commission. |
| Wisconsin | ... | ... | $49,943 | 48.5/mile; one roundtrip/week to Capitol. | $88/day maximum (U) set by compensation commission (90% of federal rate). Per diem authorized under 13.123 (1), Wis. Statutes, and Leg. Joint Rule 85. 20.916(8) State Statutes and Joint Committee on Employment Relations (JCOER) establishes the max. amount according to the recommendations of the Director of the Office of State Employment Relations. The leadership of each house then determines, within that maximum, what amount to authorize for the session. |
| Wyoming | $150/day during session. Members other than leadership receive $300/mo. when not in session. | ... | ... | 55/mile. | $109/day (V) set by the legislature, includes travel days for those outside of Cheyenne. |

*Source:* National Conference of State Legislatures, 2012.
*Key:*
C — Calendar day
L — Legislative day
(U) — Unvouchered
(V) — Vouchered
d — day
w — week
m — month
y — year
... — Not applicable
N.R. — Not reported

# Table 3.10
# LEGISLATIVE COMPENSATION: OTHER PAYMENTS AND BENEFITS

| State | Legislator's compensation for office supplies, district offices and staffing | Phone allowance | Transportation offered to legislators | Insurance benefits | | | | |
|---|---|---|---|---|---|---|---|---|
| | | | | Health | Dental | Optical | Disability insurance | Life insurance benefits |
| Alabama.......... | None, although annual appropriation to certain positions may be so allocated. | Yes (a) | None | S.A., O.P. | S.A., O.P. | N.A. | N.A. | N.A. |
| Alaska.......... | Senators receive $20,000/year or $10,00/year and Representatives receive $16,000/year or $8,000/year for postage per their choice for postage, stationery and other legislative expenses. Staffing allowance determined by rules and presiding officers, depending on time of year. | Yes (a) | None | S.P.P. | S.P.P. | O.P.; unless included in Health Ins. | Optional; if selected is included in health insurance | Small policy available; additional is optional at legislator's expense. |
| Arizona.......... | None. | No | (b) | S.A. | S.A. | S.A. | S.P.P. | State pays 15K policy; additional amount is paid by legislator. |
| Arkansas.......... | Legislators are entitled to receive a maximum reimbursement of up to $14,400/year for legislative expenses. Committee chairs, vice chairs, and standing subcommittee chairs may claim additional reimbursement up to $3,600/year. | No | None | O.P. | O.P. | O.P. | O.P. | State provides $30,000 coverage with option to purchase greater amount. |
| California.......... | Assembly members have an annual base allowance of $263,000 to cover these expenses. Senate member expenses are paid directly and maintained by the Senate Rules Committee. | No | (c) | S.P.P. | S.P.P. | S.P. | S.P. | S.P. |
| Colorado.......... | None. | Yes (a) | None | S.P.P. | S.P.P. | N.A. | N.A. | State pays full amount for $50,000 policy; additional is optional at legislator's expense. |
| Connecticut.......... | Senators receive $5,500 and Representatives receive $4,500 in unvouchered expense allowance. | Yes. (d) | None | S.P.P. | S.P.P. | Some health insurance plans include discounts on eyewear. | O.P. | O.P. |
| Delaware.......... | Reimbursement provided for office expenses. | Yes (a) | None | S.P.P. – After three months the state pays entire amount for basic plan. | O.P. | O.P. | N.A. | O.P. |

See footnotes at end of table.

# LEGISLATIVE COMPENSATION: OTHER PAYMENTS AND BENEFITS — Continued

| State | Legislator's compensation for office supplies, district offices and staffing | Phone allowance | Transportation offered to legislators | Insurance benefits Health | Dental | Optical | Disability insurance | Life insurance benefits |
|---|---|---|---|---|---|---|---|---|
| Florida | Senate $2,921/month for district office expenses; House $2,482/month for district office expenses. | No | (e) | Legislators pay $8.34 for individual coverage and $30.00 for family coverage. | S.P. | O.P. | S.P. | S.P. |
| Georgia | Legislators have $7,000/year reimbursable expense account. If the member requests and provides receipts, the member is reimbursed for personal services, office equipment, rent, supplies, transportation, telecommunications, etc. | No | None | S.A., S.P.P. | O.P. | O.P. | S.P.P. | S.P.P. |
| Hawaii | There is no set dollar amount for office supplies. All supplies are provided by the House Supply room. Any item not carried in the Supply Room may be purchased with statutory legislative allowance funds which is currently $10,200/year. House members do not have district offices. With the exception of the Speaker's Office and Majority and Minority Leadership offices, the House Finance, Judiciary and Consumer Protection offices, each House Majority and Minority member is allowed 1 permanent full-time Office Manager. During the session each committee chair receives $5,100/month for temporary staff salaries, and all other members receive $4,800 month. | Yes (a) | (f) | S.P.P. | S.P.P. | S.P.P. | S.P.P. | S.P.P. |
| Idaho | $1,875/year for unvouchered constituent expense. No staffing allowance. | Yes (g) | None | S.P.P. | S.P.P. | S.P.P. | S.P.P. | S.P.P. |
| Illinois | Senators receive $83,063/y and Representatives $69,409/y for office expenses, including district offices and staffing. | No | None | S.P.P. | S.P.P. | S.P.P. | S.P. | S.P.P. |
| Indiana | All of these come out of one main Senate budget. We do not have district offices. | No | None | S.A. | S.A. | S.A. | N.A. | S.A. |
| Iowa | $300/m to cover district constituency postage, travel, telephone and other expenses. No staffing allowance. | No | None | S.P.P. | S.P.P. | N.A. | S.P. | State pays first $20,000, additional at legislator expense. |
| Kansas | Allowed $7,083/year which is taxable income to the legislators. Staffing allowances vary for leadership who have their own budget. Legislators provided with secretaries during session only. | Yes | None | S.P.P. | S.P., legislator pays dep. portion | O.P. | S.P. | 150% of annual salary if part of KPERS. Additional insurance is optional at legislator's expense. |

See footnotes at end of table.

# LEGISLATIVE COMPENSATION: OTHER PAYMENTS AND BENEFITS—Continued

| State | Legislator's compensation for office supplies, district offices and staffing | Phone allowance | Transportation offered to legislators | Insurance benefits | | | | |
|---|---|---|---|---|---|---|---|---|
| | | | | Health | Dental | Optical | Disability insurance | Life insurance benefits |
| Kentucky .............. | $1,788.51 for district expenses during interim. | No | Yes (h) | S.A. | O.P. | O.P. | O.P. | State pays $20,000; extra available at legislator's expense. |
| Louisiana.............. | Allowed $500/month. Senators and Representatives receive an additional $1,500 supplemental allowance for vouchered office expenses, rent, travel mileage in district. Senators and Representatives staff allowance $2,000/month starting salary up to $3,000 with annual increases. | Yes (i) | None | S.P.P. | S.P.P.—Senators pay 100%. | O.P. | O.P. | State pays half; legislator pays half. |
| Maine.............. | None. However, supplies for staff offices are provided and paid for out of general legislative account. | No | None | S.A. | S.A. | O.P. | N.A. | O.P. |
| Maryland.............. | Members, $18,265/year for normal expenses of an office with limits on postage, telephone and publications. Members must document expenses. Legislators must use $5,800 for clerical services. Senators receive one administrative assistant and session secretary. | No | None | S.A. | S.A., O.P. | Covered under medical plan. | N.A. | Term insurance; optional at legislator's expense. |
| Massachusetts ....... | Allowed $7,200/yearly for office expenses. | No | None | S.P.P. | S.P.P. | S.P.P. | O.P. | $5,000 policy provided; Additional up to 8 times salary at legislator's expense. |
| Michigan.............. | Allowed $46,800 per majority Senator for office budget, $46,800 for minority Senator for office budget. | Yes (a) | None | Health, vision, life, cancer, prescription, offered via cafeteria plan. | | | N.A. | Offered at different levels as part of cafeteria plan. |
| Minnesota............. | No district offices. Supples provided in State Capitol. In the House, Staffing provided centrally. For Senators, one legislative assistant plus $75/week for interns. | Yes (j) | (k) | S.A. | State pays 81% single, 60% family. | S.A. | O.P. | State pays premium for benefit of $35,000. |
| Mississippi............ | A total of $1,500/m out of session. | Yes | None | S.P.—legislator only premiums. | O.P. | N.A. | None | S.P.P. |
| Missouri.............. | $700/month to cover all reasonable and necessary business expenses. | Yes (l) | None | S.P.P. | O.P. | O.P. | S.P. | S.P.—Additional amounts are optional at legislator's expense. |
| Montana.............. | None. | Yes (m) | Limited | S.P. | S.P. | O.P. | N.A. | State pays $14,000 term policy. Additional at legislator's expense. |

See footnotes at end of table.

# LEGISLATIVE COMPENSATION: OTHER PAYMENTS AND BENEFITS—Continued

| State | Legislator's compensation for office supplies, district offices and staffing | Phone allowance | Transportation offered to legislators | Insurance benefits | | | | |
|---|---|---|---|---|---|---|---|---|
| | | | | Health | Dental | Optical | Disability insurance | Life insurance benefits |
| Nebraska | No allowance; however, each member is provided with two full-time capitol staff year-round. | Yes (a) | None | O.P. | O.P. | O.P. | O.P. | O.P. |
| Nevada | None. | $2,800 allowance | (n) | O.P. | O.P. | O.P. | O.P. | O.P. |
| New Hampshire | None. | No | None | O.P. | O.P. | N.A. | N.A. | N.A. |
| New Jersey | Allowed $1,250 for office supplies; equipment and furnishings supplied through a district office program and $110,000/year for district office personnel. State provides stationery for each legislator and $10,000 for postage stamps. | No | (o) | S.A. | S.A. | S.A. | It depends on the retirement plan they are enrolled in. | Depends on retirement plan enrollment. If State Pension Plan same as all state employees. |
| New Mexico | None. | No | None | N.A. | N.A. | N.A. | N.A. | N.A. |
| New York | Staff allowance set by majority leader for majority members and by minority leader for minority members. Staff allowance covers both district and capitol; geographic location; seniority and leadership responsibilities will cause variations. | Yes (a) | (p) | S.P.P. | S.P.P. | No cost if participating provider used. | S.P. | O.P. |
| North Carolina | Non-leaders receive $6,708/y for any legislative expenses not otherwise provided. Full-time secretarial assistance is provided during session. | Yes (q) | None | S.P.; O.P. family coverage | O.P. | O.P. | O.P. | O.P. |
| North Dakota | None. | Yes (r) | None | S.P. | O.P. | O.P. | O.P. | State pays for $1,300 term life policy. |
| Ohio | None. | Yes (a) | None | S.P.P. | S.P. | S.P. | N.A. | Amount equal to salary; premium paid by state. Member may purchase a supplemental policy, which is also offered to state employees. |
| Oklahoma | $350/y for unvouchered office supplies plus $500 per month credit for postage. | Yes (s) | None | Allowance ranging from $608.57 for legislator only to $1,596.95 per month for family. | S.A. | S.A. | S.A. | S.A. |

See footnotes at end of table.

# LEGISLATIVE COMPENSATION: OTHER PAYMENTS AND BENEFITS — Continued

| State | Legislator's compensation for office supplies, district offices and staffing | Phone allowance | Transportation offered to legislators | Insurance benefits | | | | |
|---|---|---|---|---|---|---|---|---|
| | | | | Health | Dental | Optical | Disability insurance | Life insurance benefits |
| Oregon.............. | For interim periods, legislators receive $16,476 per biennium. They can spend as they choose. For session, they receive $24,290 for session staffing and $2,325 for services and supplies. They also receive an additional $450–$750/month as a district allowance, depending on geographic size of district. | Yes (t) | None | S.A. | S.A. | S.A. | O.P. | O.P. |
| Pennsylvania ........ | Staffing is determined by leadership. | No | (u) | Medical/hospital, dental, vision, Rx. Senate members and employees pay 1% of salary for health benefits. | | | | Group life up to salary. |
| Rhode Island.......... | None. | No | None | S.A. | Legislators pay 1% of salary toward benefits. | Legislators pay 1% of salary toward benefits. | O.P. | O.P. |
| South Carolina........ | Senate $3,400/year for postage, stationery and telephone. House $1,800/year for telephone and $600/year for postage. Legislators also receive $1,000/m for in district expenses that is treated as income. | Yes (a) | None | S.P.P. | S.P.P. | N.A. | S.P.P. | S.P.P. |
| South Dakota......... | None. | Yes (v) | None | N.A. | N.A. | N.A. | S.P. for accidental death/dismemberment ins. only. | N.A. |
| Tennessee............... | Allowed $1,000/m for expenses in district (U). | Yes (w) | (x) | State pays 80%, legislator pays 20%. | O.P. | N.A. | N.A. | State pays $15,000; Legislator pays $7,000. |
| Texas................... | Approved allowance for staff salaries, supplies, stationery, postage, district office rental, telephone expense, etc. Senate and House allocations are not the same. | No | None | S.P. | O.P. | Included in health coverage | O.P. | O.P. |
| Utah.................. | None. | No | None | S.P.P. | S.P.P. | S.P.P. | S.P. | S.P. |
| Vermont.............. | None. | Yes | None | O.P. | N.A. | N.A. | N.A. | N.A. |
| Virginia.............. | Legislators receive $1,250/month; leadership receives $1,750/month office expense allowance. Legislators receive a staffing allowance of $39,765/year; leadership staffing receives $59,644/year. | Yes | None | S.P.P. | S.P.P. | S.P.P. | S.P.—only permanent disability retirement through retirement system. | S.P.P. |

See footnotes at end of table.

# LEGISLATIVE COMPENSATION: OTHER PAYMENTS AND BENEFITS — Continued

| State | Legislator's compensation for office supplies, district offices and staffing | Phone allowance | Transportation offered to legislators | Insurance benefits | | | | |
|---|---|---|---|---|---|---|---|---|
| | | | | Health | Dental | Optical | Disability insurance | Life insurance benefits |
| **Washington** | Senate—$7,800/year for legislative expenses, for which the legislator has not been otherwise entitled to reimbursement. No staffing allowance. | Yes (a) | None | S.P.P. | S.P. | Included in medical. | S.P.P. | S.P.P. |
| **West Virginia** | None. | Yes | None | O.P. | O.P. | O.P. | N.A. | O.P. |
| **Wisconsin** | Allowed $12,000 for two-year session in the Assembly. N/A staffing. DO. $45,000 for two-year period for office expenses. Allowed $191,700 for two-year period for staffing allowance. | (y) | None | S.P.P. | Some HMOs cover. | O.P. | O.P. | O.P. |
| **Wyoming** | Up to $750 quarter through the constituent service allowance. | (z) | No | N.A. | N.A. | N.A. | N.A. | N.A. |

*Source:* National Conference of State Legislatures, 2012.

*Key:*
(U) — Unvouchered.
(V) — Vouchered.
d — day.
m — month.
w — week.
y — year.
N.A. — Not available.
S.P. — State pays full amount.
S.P.P. — State pays portion and legislator pays portion.
S.A. — Same as state employees.
O.P. — Optional at legislator's expense.
(a) Official state business only.
(b) Access to motor pool for legislative trips only.
(c) One round trip flight for each week of Session; Use of a pool car for those members who fly to Sacramento.
(d) Official business only; charges for personal calls are reimbursed by legislator.
(e) Rental cars for official business.
(f) Neighbor Island members are allowed 1 round trip from their home island every week — during session and during the interim. Additional trips are allowed when authorized by the Speaker.
(g) During session only.

(h) State cars are available but not assigned to members.
(i) District office line with one extension.
(j) House members are allowed $75 per month for a communications allowance.
(k) Car rental is available with prior approval.
(l) Phone cards issued but expenditures deducted from monthly expense allowance.
(m) Leadership positions only.
(n) Motor pool or private; legislative police shuttle to/from Reno airport.
(o) Automobiles for some top leadership positions.
(p) Top leadership has access to vehicles.
(q) Allowance of $2,275 for postage, stationery and telephone.
(r) Only Legislative Council members or chairs of interim cmtes.
(s) Senate members receive phone credit card for state-related business use away from capitol.
(t) State-provided office and district office phone for legislative business only.
(u) Mileage basis or vehicle from Department of General Services fleet.
(v) Telephone allowance: $600/6 m for legislators and $900/6 m for leadership.
(w) Phone cards for in-state long distance (only).
(x) In lieu of mileage, members residing greater than 100 miles from the seat of government may be reimbursed for coach class airline fare for attendance at session or committee meetings. Limited to one round trip per week during session.
(y) Members' office expenses, including phone expense, are limited to the amount of each legislator's office budget, as established by the committees, on Senate and Assembly organization.
(z) Telephone credit card for official business only with a $2,000 limit during 2 yrs.

# Table 3.11
## ADDITIONAL COMPENSATION FOR SENATE LEADERS

| State | Presiding officer | Majority leader | Minority leader | Other leaders and committee chairs |
|---|---|---|---|---|
| Alabama | $2/day plus $1,500/mo. expense allowance | None | None | None |
| Alaska | $500/year | None | None | None |
| Arizona | Generally approved for additional interim per diem. | Generally approved for additional interim per diem. | Generally approved for additional interim per diem. | None |
| Arkansas | None | None | None | None |
| California | $109,584/year for the Senate President pro Tem. | $102,437/year for the Majority Floor Leader. | $109,584/year for the Minority Leader. | $102,437/year for the Second Ranking Minority Leader. |
| Colorado | All leaders receive $99/day salary during interim when in attendance at committee or leadership meetings. | | | None |
| Connecticut | $10,689 | $8,835 | $8,835 | Leaders: Dep. min. and maj. ldrs. $6,446/year; asst. maj. and min. ldrs. and maj. and min. whips $4,241/yr. Committee chairs: All cmte. chairs, $4,241. |
| Delaware | $19,983 | $12,376 | $12,376 | Leaders: Maj. and min. whips $7,794. |
| Florida | $11,484 | None | None | None |
| Georgia | None | $200/mo. | $200/mo. | President pro tem, $400/mo; admin. flr. ldr., $200/mo; asst. admin. flr. ldr., $100/mo. |
| Hawaii | Salary differential for presiding officer is $7,500. | None | None | None |
| Idaho | None | None | None | None |
| Illinois | $27,477 | $20,649 | $27,477 | Dpty.min. leader $20,649; Asst. maj. and min. ldr., $20,649; maj and min caucus chair, $20,649 |
| Indiana | $7,000 | Maj. floor ldr. $5,500; asst. maj. floor ldr. $3,500 | Min. floor ldr. $6,000; min. asst. floor ldr. $5,000; min. ldr. pro tem. emeritus $1,500 | Asst. Pres. Pro Tem. $3,000; Maj. Cauc. Chairman $5,500; Asst. Maj. Cauc. Chair $1,500; Appropriations Comm. Ranking Maj. Mem. $2,000; Tax & Fiscal Policy Ranking Maj. Mem. $2,000; Maj. Whip $4,000; Asst. Maj. Whip $2,000; Min. Cauc. Chair $5,000; Asst. Min. Cauc. Chair $1,000; Appropriations Comm. Ranking Min. Mem. $2,000; Tax & Fiscal Policy Ranking Min. Mem.$2,000; Min. Whip $3,000; Asst. Min. Whip $1,000. Committee Chairs: $1,000 |
| Iowa | $11,593 | $11,593 | $11,593 | Pres. Pro Tem $1,243. |
| Kansas | $14,039.22/yr | $12,665.64/yr | $12,665.64/yr | Asst. maj., min. ldrs., vice pres., $7,165.34/yr. |
| Kentucky | $47.35/day | $37.40/day | $37.40/day | Leaders: Maj., min. caucus chairs and whips, $28.66/day. |
| Louisiana | $32,000 | None | None | Pres. Pro Tem $24,500. |
| Maine | 150% of base salary | 125% of base salary | 112.5% of base salary | None |
| Maryland | $13,000/yr. | None | None | None |
| Massachusetts | $35,000 | $22,500 | $22,500 | Leaders: asst. maj. and min. ldr., (and 2nd and 3rd assistant), Pres. Pro Tem., each $15,000. |
| Michigan | $4,962 | $23,400 | $19,800 | Leaders: Maj. flr. ldr., $10,800; min. flr. ldr., $9,000. |

## ADDITIONAL COMPENSATION FOR SENATE LEADERS — Continued

| State | Presiding officer | Majority leader | Minority leader | Other leaders and committee chairs |
|---|---|---|---|---|
| Minnesota | None | Additional compensation is 40% of base salary | Additional compensation is 40% of base salary | Assistant Majority Leader: $4,152/year. Tax Committee chair: $4,152/year. Finance Committee chair: $4,152/year. Senate Tax Cmte. and Cmte. on Finance Chair: $35,292 |
| Mississippi | Lt. Gov., $60,000 total salary; Pres. Pro Tem, $15,000 | None | None | None |
| Missouri | None | None | None | None |
| Montana | $5/day during session | None | None | None |
| Nebraska | None | None | None | None |
| Nevada | $900 | $900 | $900 | None |
| New Hampshire | $50/two-yr term | None | None | Leaders: Pres. Pro Tem, $900. Committee Chairs: Standing cmte. chairs $900. |
| New Jersey | 1/3 above annual salary | None | None | None |
| New Mexico | None | None | None | None |
| New York | $41,500 | None | $34,500 | None |
| North Carolina | $38,151 and $16,956 expense allowance. | $17,048 and $7,992 expense allowance | $17,048 and $7,992 expense allowance | Leaders: 24 other leaders with compensation ranging from $13,000 to $34,000. Committee Chairs: between $9,000 and $34,000. |
| North Dakota | None | $15/day during legislative sessions, $284 ($298 effective 7/1/10) per month during term of office. | $15/day during legislative sessions, $307 per month during term of office. | Leaders: Asst. ldrs., $10/day during session. |
| Ohio | President $94,437.36 | President Pro Tem $86,165; Maj Flr Leader $81,163; Asst Maj Flr Leader $76,169; Maj Whip $71,173; Asst Maj Whip $66,175 | Minority Leader $86,165 | Compensation for committee leadership (See Committee Chair Table). |
| Oklahoma | $17,932 | $12,364 | $12,364 | None |
| Oregon | President receives additional $21,612/year in salary. | None | None | None |
| Pennsylvania | $46,022/year | $36,819/year | $36,819/year | Maj. and min. whips, $27,942 maj. and min. caucus chairs, $17,422; maj. and min. caucus secretaries $11,506; maj. and min. policy chairs, $11,506. |
| Rhode Island | Senate President receives double the annual rate for Senators | None | None | None |
| South Carolina | Lt. gov. holds this position | None | None | Leaders: President pro tem, $11,000. |
| South Dakota | None | None | None | None |
| Tennessee | None | None | None | None |
| Texas | $57,027 | None | None | None |

# ADDITIONAL COMPENSATION FOR SENATE LEADERS — Continued

| State | Presiding officer | Majority leader | Minority leader | Other leaders and committee chairs |
|---|---|---|---|---|
| Utah | $3,000 | $2,000 | $2,000 | Leaders: Maj. whip, asst. maj. whip, min. whip and asst. min. whip, $2,000. Committee Chairs: $2,000 for Executive Appropriations Chair (Co-chair) |
| Vermont | Presiding officer is Lt. Governor who is paid an annual salary $60,507. For Senate Leader, Pres. Pro Tem, see above. | None | None | None |
| Virginia | None | $200/day only for days that official meetings are attended | $200/day only for days that official meetings are attended | President pro tem $200/day only for days that official meetings are attended |
| Washington | Lt. gov. holds this position | $50,106 ($8,000 addition to base salary) | $46,106 ($4,000 addition to base salary) | None |
| West Virginia | $150/day during session. | $50/day during session. | $50/day during session. | The Chairman of Finance & Judiciary may receive $150.00/day up to 30 days when the Legislature is not in session or meeting for interims. Up to six add'l people named by presiding officer receive $150 for a maximum of 30 days when the Legislature is not in session or meeting for interims. |
| Wisconsin | None | None | None | None |
| Wyoming | $3/day during session; $978/mo when not in session | $600/mo when not in session | $600/Mo when not in session | None |

*Source:* National Conference of State Legislatures, 2012.

## Table 3.12
## ADDITIONAL COMPENSATION FOR HOUSE/ASSEMBLY LEADERS

| State | Presiding officer | Majority leader | Minority leader | Other leaders and committee chairs |
|---|---|---|---|---|
| Alabama............... | $2/day plus $1,500/mo. expense allowance | None | None | None |
| Alaska................. | $500/year | None | None | None |
| Arizona............... | Generally approved for additional interim per diem. | Generally approved for additional interim per diem. | Generally approved for additional interim per diem. | None |
| Arkansas............. | None | None | None | None |
| California ........... | The speaker of the Assembly and Pro Tem of the Senate each get paid $109,584 per year. | They get $102,437 per year. | They get $109,584 per year. | 2nd ranking min. ldrs. receive $102,437/yr. |
| Colorado.............. | ------- All leaders receive $99/day salary during interim when in attendance at committee or leadership matters.------- | | | |
| Connecticut.......... | $10,689 | $8,835 | $8,835 | Leaders: Dep. spkr., dep. maj. and min. ldrs. $6,446/yr; asst. maj. and min.ldrs.:maj. and min whips. $4,241/yr. Cmte Chairs: $4,241. |
| Delaware ............. | $19,893 | $12,376 | $12,376 | Leaders: maj. and min. whips. $7,794. |
| Florida............... | $11,484/yearly | None | None | None |
| Georgia............... | $6,812/mo. | $200/mo. | $200/mo. | Governor's flr. ldr., $200/mo; asst. flr. ldr., $100/mo.; spkr. pro tem. $400/mo. |
| Hawaii................ | Salary differential for presiding officer is $7,500/year | None | None | None |
| Idaho.................. | $4,000 | None | None | None |
| Illinois............... | $27,477 | $23,300 | $27,477 | Leaders: dpty. maj. and min., $19,791; asst. maj. and asst. min., maj. and min. conference chr. $18,066. |
| Indiana............... | $6,500 | $5,000 | $5,500 | Leaders: Speaker pro tem, $5,000; maj. caucus chair, $5,000; min. caucus chair, $4,500; asst. min. flr. leader, $3,500; asst. maj. flr. ldr., $1,000; maj. whip, $3,500; min. whip, $1,500. |
| Iowa .................. | $11,593 | $11,593 | $11,593 | Speaker pro tem. $1,243 |
| Kansas ............... | $14,039.22/yr. | $12,665.64/yr. | $12,665.64/yr. | Leaders: asst. maj. and min. ldrs., spkr. pro tem, $7,165.34/yr. |
| Kentucky ............. | $47.35/day | $37.40/day | $7.40/day | Leaders: maj. and min. caucus chairs & whips, $28.66/day. |
| Louisiana ............ | $32,000 (a) | None | None | Leaders: Speaker pro tem, $24,500 (a). |
| Maine ................ | 150% of base salary | 125% of base salary | 112.5% of base salary | None |
| Maryland ............. | $13,000/year | None | None | None |

See footnotes at end of table.

# ADDITIONAL COMPENSATION FOR HOUSE/ASSEMBLY LEADERS — Continued

| State | Presiding officer | Majority leader | Minority leader | Other leaders and committee chairs |
|---|---|---|---|---|
| Massachusetts | $35,000 | $22,500 | $22,500 | Leaders: asst. maj. and min. ldr. (and 2nd and 3rd asst.), and spkr. pro tem, $15,000 each. |
| Michigan | $27,000 | No position | $22,000 | Committee Chairs: $7,000 for Appropriation Committee chairs. |
| Minnesota | 40% of base salary | 40% of base salary | 40% of base salary | $35,292 for Committee on Finance. |
| Mississippi | $60,000 (a) | None | None | None |
| Missouri | $208.34/mo. | $125/mo. | $125/mo. | None |
| Montana | $5/day during session | None | None | None |
| Nebraska | None | None | None | None |
| Nevada | $900 | $900 | $900 | Leaders: Speaker pro tem, $900. |
| New Hampshire | $50/two-year term | None | None | None |
| New Jersey | 1/3 above annual base salary | None | None | None |
| New Mexico | None | None | None | None |
| New York | $41,500 | $34,500 | $34,500 | Leaders: 31 leaders with compensation ranging from $9,000 to $25,000. |
| North Carolina | $38,151 (a) and $16,956 expense allowance | $17,048 (a) and $7,992 expense allowance | $17,048 (a) and $7,992 expense allowance | Speaker pro tem, $21,739 and $10,032 expense allowance. |
| North Dakota | $15/day during legislative session. | $15/day during legislative session, $270/m during term of office. | $15/day during legislative session, $270/m during term of office. | Leaders: Asst. ldrs., $10/day during legislative sessions. |
| Ohio | $94,437.36 (a) | Speaker pro tem $86,165; maj ftr. leader $81,163; asst. maj. ftr. leader $76,169; maj. whip $71,173; asst. maj. whip $66,175 | Minority leader $86,165; asst. min. ldr. $78,668; min. whip $71,173; asst. min. whip $63,381 | Compensation for committee leadership |
| Oklahoma | $17,932 | $12,364 | $12,364 | Leaders: Speaker pro tem, $12,364. |
| Oregon | Speaker receives additional $21,936/year in salary | None | None | None |
| Pennsylvania | $46,022/year | $36,819/year | $36,819/year | Maj. and min. whips, $27,942; maj. and min. caucus chairs, $17,422; maj. and min. caucus secretaries, $11,506; maj. and min. policy chairs, $11,506; maj. and min. caucus admin., $11,506. |

See footnotes at end of table.

## ADDITIONAL COMPENSATION FOR HOUSE/ASSEMBLY LEADERS — Continued

| State | Presiding officer | Majority leader | Minority leader | Other leaders and committee chairs |
|---|---|---|---|---|
| Rhode Island | Speaker of the House receives double annual rate for Representatives. | None | None | None |
| South Carolina | $11,000/yr | None | None | Leaders: Speaker pro tem, $3,600/yr. |
| South Dakota | None | None | None | None |
| Tennessee | $57,027 | None | None | None |
| Texas | None | None | None | None |
| Utah | $3,000 | $2,000 | $2,000 | Leaders: whips and asst. whips, $2,000. |
| Vermont | $669/week during session plus an additional $10,080 in salary. | None | None | None |
| Virginia | $8,000 addition to base salary | $4,000 addition to base salary | $4,000 addition to base salary | None |
| Washington | $50,106, $8,000 additional to base salary (a) | None | $46,106, $4,000 additional to base salary (a) | None |
| West Virginia | The Speaker may receive $150.00/day when not in session or interim committees not meeting for attending to legislative business. | $50/day during session | $50/day during session | Leaders: The Chairman of Finance & Judiciary may receive $150.00/day up to 30 days when the Legislature is not in session or meeting for interims. Up to six add'l people named by presiding officer receive $150 for a maximum of 30 days when the Legislature is not in session or meeting for interims. |
| Wisconsin | $25/month | None | None | None |
| Wyoming | $3/day during session; $978/mo when not in session. | $600/mo when not in session. | $600/mo when not in session. | None |

*Source:* National Conference of State Legislatures, 2011.
(a) Total annual salary for this position.

# Table 3.13
## STATE LEGISLATIVE RETIREMENT BENEFITS

| State or other jurisdiction | Participation | Plan name | Requirements for regular retirement | Employee contribution rate | Benefit formula |
|---|---|---|---|---|---|
| **Alabama** | None available. | | | | |
| **Alaska** | Optional | Public Employees Retirement System | Age 60 with 10 yrs. | Employee 6.75% | 2% (first 10 yrs.); or 2.25% (second 10 yrs.); or 2.5% over 20 yrs. x average salary over 5 highest consecutive yrs. x yrs. of service. |
| **Arizona** | Mandatory—except that officials subject to term limits may opt out for a term of office. | Elected Officials Retirement System | Age 65, 5+ yrs. service: age 62, 10+ yrs. service; or 20 yrs. service; earlier retirement with an actuarial reduction of benefits. Vesting at 5 yrs. | Employee 7% | 4% x years of credited service x highest 3 yr. average in the past 10 yrs. The benefit is capped at 80% of FAS. An elected official may purchase service credit in the plan for service earned in a non-elected position by buying it at an actuarially-determined amount. |
| **Arkansas** | Optional. Those elected before 7/1/99 may have service covered as a regular state employee but must have 5 years of regular service to do so. | Arkansas Public Employees Retirement System | Age 65, 10 yrs. service; or age 55, 12 yrs. service; or any age, 28 yrs. service; any age if serving in the General Assembly on 7/1/79; any age if in elected office on 7/1/79 with 17 and 1/2 yrs. of service. As a regular employee, age 65, 5 yrs. service, or any age and 28 yrs. Members of the contributory plan established in 2005 must have a minimum of 10 yrs. legislative service if they have only legislative state employment. | Non-contributory plan in effect for those elected before 2006. For those elected then and thereafter, a contributory plan that requires 5% of salary. | For service that began after 7/1/99: 2.07% x FAS x years of service. FAS based on three highest consecutive years of service. For service that began after July 1, 1991, $35 x years of service equals monthly benefit. For contributory plan, 2% x FAS x years of service. |
| **California** | Legislators elected after 1990 are not eligible for retirement benefits for legislative service. | | | | |
| **Colorado** | Mandatory | Either Public Employees' Retirement Association or State Defined Contribution Plan. A choice is not irrevocable. | PERA: age 65, 5 yrs. service; age 50, 30 yrs. service; when age + service equals 80 or more (min. age of 55). DCP: no age requirement & vested immediately. | Employee: 8% | PERA: 2.5% x FAS x yrs. of service, capped at 100% of FAS. DCP benefit depends upon contributions and investment returns. |
| **Connecticut** | Mandatory | State Employees Retirement System Tier IIA | Age 60, 25 yrs. credited service; age 62, 10–25 yrs. credited service; age 62, 5 yrs. actual state service. Reduced benefit available with earlier retirement ages. | 2% | (.0133 x avg. annual salary) + (.005 x avg. annual salary in excess of "breakpoint" x credited service up to 35 years.<br>2003 — $36,400    2007 — $46,000<br>2004 — $38,600    2008 — $48,800<br>2005 — $40,900    2009 — $51,700<br>2006 — $43,400<br>After 2009 · increase breakpoint by 6% per year rounded to nearest $100. |

See footnotes at end of table.

## STATE LEGISLATIVE RETIREMENT BENEFITS—Continued

| State or other jurisdiction | Participation | Plan name | Requirements for regular retirement | Employee contribution rate | Benefit formula |
|---|---|---|---|---|---|
| Delaware | Mandatory | State Employees Pension Plan | Age 60, 5 yrs. credited service | 3% of total monthly compensation in excess of $6,000 | 2% times FAS times years of service before 1997 + 1.85% times FAS times years of service from 1997 on. FAS = average of highest 3 years. |
| Florida | Optional. Elected officials may opt out and may choose between DB and DC plans. | Florida Retirement System | Vesting in DB plan, 6 years; in DC plan, 1 year. DB plan: Age 62 with 6 years; 30 years at any age. DC plan: any age | No employee contribution. Employer contribution for 2004–2005 for legislators is 12.49% of salary. | DB plan: 3% x years of creditable service x average final compensation (average of highest 5 yrs). DC plan: Dependent upon investment experience. |
| Georgia | Optional: Choice when first elected. | Georgia Legislative Retirement System | Vested after 8 yrs.; age 62, with 8 yrs. of service; age 60 with reduction for early retirement. | Employee rate 3.75% + $7 month | $36 month for each year of service. |
| Hawaii | Mandatory | Public Employees Retirement System; elected officials' plan | Age 55 with 5 years of service, any age with 10 years service. Vesting at 5 years. | Main plan is non-contributory; 7.8% for elected officials' plan for annuity. | 3.5 x yrs. of service as elected official x highest average salary plus annuity based on contributions as an elected official. Highest average salary = average of 3 highest 12-month periods as elected official. |
| Idaho | Mandatory | | Age 65 with 5 yrs. service; reduced benefit at age 55 with 5 yrs. of service. | 6.97% | Avg. monthly salary for highest 42 consecutive months x 2% x months of credited service. |
| Illinois | Optional | General Assembly Retirement System | Age 55, 8 yrs. service; or age 62, 4 yrs. service | 8.5% for retirement; 2% for survivors; 1% for automatic increases; 11.5% total | 3% of each of 1st 4 yrs.; 3.5% for each of next 2 yrs.; 4% for each of next 2 yrs.; 4.5% for each of the next 4 yrs.; 5% for each yr. above 12. |
| Indiana | DB plan is optional for those serving on April 30, 1989. Defined contribution plan is optional for those serving on April 30, 1989 and mandatory for those elected or appointed since April 30, 1989. | Legislator's Retirement System and Defined Benefit (DB) Plan and Defined Contribution Plan (DC). | DB plan: Vesting at 10 yrs. Age 65 with 10 yrs. of legislative service; or if no longer in the legislature, these options apply: at least 10 yrs. service; no state salary; at age 55+ Rule of 85 applies; or age 60 with 15 yrs. of service. Early retirement with reduced benefit. Immediate vesting in the DC plan, | DC plan: 5% employee, 20% state (of taxable income). DB plan and employer contributions funded by appropriation. | DB benefit plan monthly benefit: Lesser of (a) $40 x years of General Assembly service completed before November 8, 1989 or (b) 1/12 of the average of the three highest consecutive years of General Assembly service salary. DC plan: numerous options for withdrawing accumulations in accord with IRS regulations. Loans are available. A participant in both plans may receive a benefit from both plans. |
| Iowa | Optional | Public Employees Retirement System | Age 65; age 62 with 20 yrs. service Rule of 88; reduced benefit at 55 with at least 4 years of service. | 3.7% individual | 2% times FAS x years of service for first 30 years, + 1% times FAS times years in excess of 30 but no more than 5 in excess of 30. FAS is average of 3 highest years. |
| Kansas | Optional | Public Employees Retirement System | Age 65, age 62 with 10 yrs. of service or age plus yrs. of service equals 85 pts. | 4% of salary, (4% annualized salary for Legislators). | 3 highest yrs. x 1.75% x yrs. service divided by 12. |

See footnotes at end of table.

# STATE LEGISLATIVE RETIREMENT BENEFITS — Continued

| State or other jurisdiction | Participation | Plan name | Requirements for regular retirement | Employee contribution rate | Benefit formula |
|---|---|---|---|---|---|
| Kentucky ........... | Optional. Those who opt out are covered by the state employees' plan. | Kentucky Legislator's Retirement Plan | Age 65 with five years of service; any age with 30 years of service, and intermediate provisions. Early retirement with reduced benefits. | 5% of creditable compensation, set by law at $27,500: not the same as actual salary. Revised to be payable on compensation reported on W-2 forms beginning in 2005. | 2.75% of FAS (based on creditable compensation) x years of service. FAS is the average monthly earnings for the 60 months preceding retirement. |
| Louisiana ........... | None available | | | | |
| Maine ........... | Mandatory | Maine State Retirement Plan | Age 60 (if 10 yrs. of service on 7/1/93) and age 62 (if less than 10 yrs. of service on 7/1/93). Reduced benefit available for earlier retirement. | 7.65% legislators; employer contribution is actuarially determined. | 2% of average final compensation (the average of the 3 high salary years) times years of service. |
| Maryland ........... | Optional | State Legislator's Pension Plan | Age 60, with 8 yrs.; age 50, 8+yrs creditable service (early reduced retirement) | 5% of annual salary | 3% of legislative salary for each yr of service up to a max. of 22 yrs. 3 months. Benefits are recalculated when legislative salaries are changed. |
| Massachusetts ........... | Optional after each election or re-election to the General Court. | State Retirement System legislator's plan | Age 55 with 6 years service; unreduced benefit at 65. Vesting at 6 years. Reduced benefits for retirement before age 65. | 9%. Some legislators are grandfathered at lower rates. | 2.5 times years of service times FAS. FAS = average of highest 36 months. Service credit is allowed for membership in other Massachusetts retirement plans. |
| Michigan ........... | Optional | Legislative Retirement System (DB) for legislators elected before 3/31/97. Others may join the state defined contribution plan. | Age 55, 5 yrs. or age plus service equals 70 | 7%–13% for DB plan. For the DC plan, the state contributes 4% of salary. Members may contribute up to 3% of salary. The state will match the member's contribution in addition to the state 4% contribution. | For DB plans, various provisions, depending on when service started. For the DC plan, benefits depend upon contributions and earnings. |
| Minnesota ........... | Mandatory | Legislators Retirement Plan before 7/1/97; Defined Contribution Plan (DCP) since then. | LRP: Age 62, 6 yrs. service and fully vested. DCP: age 55 and vested immediately. LRP members do not have Social Security coverage. DCP members have Social Security coverage. | LRP: 9% DCP: 4% from member, 6% from state. | 2.7% x high 5 yr. avg. salary x length of service (yrs.). DCP benefit depends upon contributions and investment return. |
| Mississippi ........... | Mandatory | Legislators' plan within the Public Employees' Retirement System | Age 60 with 4 or more years of service, or 25 years of service. | Regular: 7.25% state 9.75% to 10.75% effective July 1, 2005; Supplement for legislative service: 3%/6.33% | Legislators who qualify for regular state retirement benefits also automatically qualify for the legislators' supplemental benefits. Regular: 2% times FAS times years of service up to and including 25 years of service + 2.5% times FAS times service in excess of 25 years FAS is based on the high 4 years. Supplement: 1% times FAS times years of legislative service through 25 years, + 1.25% times FAS times years of service in excess of 25. |

See footnotes at end of table.

## STATE LEGISLATIVE RETIREMENT BENEFITS — Continued

| State or other jurisdiction | Participation | Plan name | Requirements for regular retirement | Employee contribution rate | Benefit formula |
|---|---|---|---|---|---|
| Missouri | Mandatory | Missouri State Employee Retirement System | Age 55; three full biennial assemblies (6 years) or Rule of 80. Vesting at 6 years of service. | Non-contributory | Monthly pay divided by 24 x years of creditable service, capped at 100% of salary. Benefit is adjusted by the percentage increase in pay for an active legislator. |
| Montana | Optional | Public Employees Retirement System. Either a DB or a DC plan is available. | Vesting at 5 years. Age 60 with at least 5 years service; age 65 regardless of years of service; or 30 years of service regardless of age | 6.9% for DB plan. Employer contribution of 4.19% plus employee contribution of 6.9 % for DC plan. | DB plan: 1/56 times years of service times FAS. Early retirement with reduced benefits is available. DC plan: Employee contributions and earnings are immediately vested. Employer contributions and earnings are vested after 5 years. |
| Nebraska | None available | | | | |
| Nevada | Mandatory; but Chapter 380, Laws of 2005, allows legislators to withdraw from the system at will. The decision is final. | Legislator's Retirement System | Age 60, 10 yrs. service | 15% of session salary | Number of years x $25 = monthly allowance |
| New Hampshire | None available | | | | |
| New Jersey | Mandatory | Public Employees' Retirement System | Age 60; no minimum service requirement. Early retirement with no benefit reduction with 25 years of service. Vesting at 8 years. | 5% of salary | 3% x Final Average Salary x years of service. FAS = higher of three highest years or three final years. Benefit is capped at 2/3 of FAS. Other formulas apply if a legislator also has other service covered by the Public Employee Retirement System. |
| New Mexico | Optional | Legislative Retirement Plan | Plans 1A and 1B: Age 65 with 5 years of service; 64/8; 63/11; 60/12; or any age with 14 years of service. Plan 2: 65 with five years of service or at any age with 10 years of service. | Plan 1A: $100 per year for service after 1959 Plan 1B: $200 per year (now closed to new enrollments). Plan 2: $500/year | Plan 1A: $250 per year of service. Plan 1B: $500 per year of service after 1959. Plan 2: 11 percent of the IRS per diem rate in effect on December 31st of the year a legislator retires x 60 x the years of credited service. For a legislator who retired in 2003 the benefit would be $957 per year of credited service. Annual 3% COLA. |
| New York | Mandatory | New York State and Local Retirement System | Age 62 with 5 years of service; 55 with 30 years; reduced benefit available at 55/5. Vesting at 5 years. | 3% for first 10 years of membership (Tier 4 provisions). | Tier 4: For less than 20 yrs. of service, pension = 1/60th for (1.66%) of final average salary (FAS) x years of service: for 20 years service, pension = 1/50th (2%) of FAS x years of service; each year of service beyond 39, pension = 3/200th (1.5%) of FAS. |
| North Carolina | Mandatory | Legislative Retirement System | Age 65 with 5 years of service; reduced benefit available at earlier ages. | 7% | Highest annual compensation x 4.02% x years of service. |
| North Dakota | None available. | | | | |
| Ohio | Optional | Public Employees Retirement System | Age 60 with 5 years service or 55 with 25 years service or at any age with 30 years service | 8.5% of gross salary. A 10% contribution rate for legislators will be phased in over three years starting in 2006. | 2.2% of final average salary times years of service up to and through 30 years of service. 2.5% starting with the 31st year of service and every year thereafter. |

See footnotes at end of table.

# STATE LEGISLATIVE RETIREMENT BENEFITS—Continued

| State or other jurisdiction | Participation | Plan name | Requirements for regular retirement | Employee contribution rate | Benefit formula |
|---|---|---|---|---|---|
| Oklahoma | Legislators may retain membership as regular public employees if they have that status when elected; one time option to join Elected Officials' Plan. | Public Employee Retirement System, as regular member or elected official member. [Information here is for the Elected Officials' Plan]. | Elected Officials' Plan: Age 60 with 6 years service, vesting at 6 years. | Optional contribution of 4.5%, 6%, 7.5%, 8.5%, 9%, or 10% of total compensation. | Avg. participating salary x length of service x computation factor depending on optional contributions ranging from 1.9% for a 4.5% contribution to 4% for a 10% contribution. |
| Oregon | Optional | Public Employee Retirement System legislator plan | Age 55, 30+ yrs. Service, 5 years vesting. | 16.317% of subject wages | 1.67% x yrs. service and final avg. monthly salary. |
| Pennsylvania | Optional | State Employees' Retirement System | Age 50, 3 yrs. service, any age with 35 years of service; early retirement with reduced benefit. | 7.5% | 3% x final avg. salary x credited yrs. of service (x withdrawal factor if under regular retirement age—50 for legislators). |
| Rhode Island | Legislators elected after January 1995 are ineligible for retirement benefits based on legislative service. (a) | | | | |
| South Carolina | Mandatory, but members may opt out six months after being sworn into office. | South Carolina Retirement System | Age 60, 8 yrs. service; 30 yrs. of service regardless of age | 10% | 4.82% of annual compensation x yrs. service. |
| South Dakota | None available. | | | | |
| Tennessee | Optional | | Age 55, 4 yrs. service | 5.43% | $70 per month x yrs. service with a $1,375 monthly cap. |
| Texas | Optional | Employee Retirement System: Elected Class Members | Age 60, 8 yrs. service; age 50, 12 yrs. service. Vesting at 8 years. | 8% | 2.3% x district judge's salary x length of service, with the monthly benefit capped at the level of a district judge's salary, and adjusted when such salaries are increased. Various annuity options are available. Military service credit may be purchased to add to elective class service membership. In July 2005, a district judge's salary was set at $125,000, a year. |
| Utah | Mandatory | Governors' and Legislators' Retirement Plan | Age 62 with 10 years and an actuarial reduction; age 65 with 4 years of service for full benefits. | Non-contributory | $24.80/month (as of July 2004) x years of service; adjusted semi-annually according to consumer price index up to a maximum increase of 2%. |
| Vermont | None available. Deferred compensation plan available. | | | | |
| Virginia | Mandatory | | Age 50, 30 yrs. service (unreduced); age 55, 5 yrs. service; age 50, 10 yrs. service (reduced). | 8.91% of creditable compensation | 1.7% of average final compensation x yrs. of service. |

See footnotes at end of table.

## STATE LEGISLATIVE RETIREMENT BENEFITS—Continued

| State or other jurisdiction | Participation | Plan name | Requirements for regular retirement | Employee contribution rate | Benefit formula |
|---|---|---|---|---|---|
| Washington | Optional. If before an election the legislator belonged to a state public retirement plan, he or she may continue in that by making contributions. Otherwise the new legislator may join PERS Plan 2 or Plan 3. | See column to left. PERS plan 2 is a DB plan. PERS plan 3 is a hybrid DB/DC plan. | PERS plan 2: Age 65 with 5 years of service credit. Plan 3: Age 65 with 10 years of service credit for the DB side of the plan; immediate benefits (subject to federal restrictions) on the DC side of the plan. The member may choose various options for investment of contributions to the DC plan. | PERS plan 2: Employee contribution of 2.43% for 2002. Estimated at 3.33% for 2005–2007. Plan 3: No required member contribution for the DB component. The member may contribute from 5% to 15% of salary to the DC component. | PERS plan 2: 2% x years of service credit x average final compensation. Plan 3: DB is 1% x service credit years x average final compensation. DC benefit depends upon the value of accumulations. |
| West Virginia | Optional | | Age 55, if yrs. of service + age equal 80. | 4.5% gross income | 2% of final avg. salary x yrs. service. Final avg. salary is based on 3 highest yrs. out of last 10 yrs. |
| Wisconsin | Mandatory | | Age 62 normal; age 57 with 30 years of service. | 2.6% of salary in 2003, adjusted annually | Higher benefit of formula (2.165% x years of service x salary for service before 2000; 2% x years of service x salary for service 2000 and after) or money-purchase calculation. |
| Wyoming | None available | | | | |
| Dist. of Columbia | Mandatory | | Age 62, 5 yrs. service; age 55, 30 yrs. service; age 60, 20 yrs. service. | Before 10/1/87, 7%; after 10/1/87, 5% | Multiply high 3 yrs. average pay by indicator under applicable yrs. or months of service. |
| Puerto Rico | Optional | Retirement System of the Employees of the Government of Puerto Rico | After 1990, age 65 with 30 years of service. | 8.28% | 1.5% of average earnings multiplied by the number of years of accredited service. |
| Guam | Optional | | Age 60, 30 yrs. service; age 55, 15 yrs. service | 5% or 8.5% | An amount equal to 2% of avg. annual salary for each of the first 10 yrs. of credited service and 2.5% of avg. annual salary for each yr. or part thereof of credited service over 10 yrs. |
| U.S. Virgin Islands | Optional | | Age 60, 10 yrs. service | 8% | At age 60 with at least 10 yrs. of service, at 2.5% for each yr. of service or at any time with at least 30 yrs. service |

*Source:* National Conference of State Legislatures, January 2006 and updated January 2009.

*Notes:* This table shows the retirement plans effective for state legislators elected in 2003, 2004 and thereafter. In general the table does not include information on closed plans, plans that continue in force for some legislators who entered the plans in previous years, but which have been closed to additional members. The information in this table was updated for all states and Puerto Rico in 2004 and updated for 2005 state legislation. Information for the District of Columbia, Guam and the Virgin Islands dates from 2002.

*Key:*

N.A. — Information not available.

None available. — No retirement benefit provided.

(a) Constitution has been amended effective 1/95. Any legislator elected after this date is not eligible to join the State Retirement System, but will be compensated for $10,000/yr. with cost of living increases to be adjusted annually.

## Table 3.14
## BILL PRE-FILING, REFERENCE AND CARRYOVER

| State or other jurisdiction | Pre-filing of bills allowed (b) | Bills referred to committee by: Senate | Bills referred to committee by: House/Assembly | Bill referral restricted by rule (a) Senate | Bill referral restricted by rule (a) House/Assembly | Bill carryover allowed (c) |
|---|---|---|---|---|---|---|
| Alabama | ★(d) | (e) (f) | Speaker (f) | L, M | L, M | ... |
| Alaska | ★ | President | Speaker | L, M | L, M | ★ |
| Arizona | ★ | President | Speaker | L | L | ... |
| Arkansas | ★ | President (g) | Speaker | L | L | ... |
| California | ★(h) | Rules Cmte. | Rules Cmte. | L | L | ★(h) |
| Colorado | ★ | President | Speaker | L, M (i) | L (i) | ... |
| Connecticut | ★ | Pres. Pro Tempore | Speaker | M | M | ... |
| Delaware | ★ | Pres. Pro Tempore | Speaker | L | L | ★ |
| Florida | ★ | President | Speaker | L, M | M | ... |
| Georgia | ★ | President (f) | Speaker | ... | ... | ★ |
| Hawaii | (j) | (j) | Speaker | ... | ... | ★ |
| Idaho | ... | President (e) | Speaker | L | L | ... |
| Illinois | ★ | Rules Cmte. | Rules Cmte. | (k) | (k) | ★ |
| Indiana | ★(l) | Pres. Pro Tempore | Speaker | (m) | ... | ... |
| Iowa | ★ | President | Speaker | M | M | ★ |
| Kansas | ★ | President | Speaker | L (n) | L (n) | ★ |
| Kentucky | ★ | Cmte. on Cmtes. | Cmte. on Cmtes. | L, M | L, M | ... |
| Louisiana | ★ | President (o) | Speaker (o) | L | L | ... |
| Maine | ★ | Secy. of Senate | Clerk of House | (p) | (p) | ★ |
| Maryland | ★ | President (q) | Speaker (q) | L | L | ... |
| Massachusetts | ★ | Clerk | Clerk | M | M | ★ |
| Michigan | ... | Majority Ldr. | Speaker | ... | ... | ★ |
| Minnesota | ★(r) | President | Speaker | L, M | L, M | ★(r) |
| Mississippi | ★ | President (e) | Speaker | L | L | ... |
| Missouri | ★ | Pres. Pro Tempore | Speaker | L | L | ... |
| Montana | ★ | President | Speaker | ... | ... | ... |
| Nebraska | ★ | Reference Cmte. (s) | U | L | U | ★(t) |
| Nevada | ★ | President (u) | Speaker (u) | L (v) | ... | ... |
| New Hampshire | ★ | President | Speaker | L | M | ★ |
| New Jersey | ★ | President | Speaker | L, M | L, M | ★ |
| New Mexico | ★ | (w) | Speaker | L, M | M (x) | ... |
| New York | ★ | Pres. Pro Tempore | Speaker | M | M | ★ |
| North Carolina | ... | Rules Chair | Speaker | M | M | ★ |
| North Dakota | ★ | President | Speaker | L | L | ... |
| Ohio | ★(y) | Reference Cmte. | Rules & Reference Cmte. | L (z) | L, M (aa) | ★(bb) |
| Oklahoma | ★ | Majority Leader | Speaker | L | L | ★(cc) |
| Oregon | ★ | President | Speaker | (dd) | (ee) | ... |
| Pennsylvania | ★ | President Pro Tempore | Chief Clerk | M | M | ★ |
| Rhode Island | ★ | President | Speaker | M | M | ★ |
| South Carolina | ★ | President | Speaker | M | M | ★(ff) |
| South Dakota | ★ | President Pro Tempore | Speaker | L | L | ... |
| Tennessee | ★ | Speaker | Speaker | L, M | L, M | ★(gg) |
| Texas | ★ | President | Speaker | L | L | ... |
| Utah | ★ | President | Speaker | L | L | ... |
| Vermont | (hh) | President | Speaker | M | M | ★ |
| Virginia | ★ | Clerk | Clerk (ii) | L, M (jj) | (kk) | ★(ll) |
| Washington | ★ | (mm) | Speaker | L | L | ★ |
| West Virginia (nn) | ★ | President | Speaker | L, M | L, M | ... |
| Wisconsin | ... | President | Speaker | ... | ... | ★(oo) |
| Wyoming | ★ | President | Speaker | M | M | ... |
| American Samoa | ... | ... | ... | ... | ... | ... |
| Guam | ★ | Cmte. on Calendar Chairs | U | L, M (pp) | U | ★ |
| Puerto Rico | ... | President | Secretary | M | M | ... |
| U.S. Virgin Islands | ... | Senate President in Pro-Forma meeting | U | L | U | ★ |

See footnotes at end of table.

# BILL PRE-FILING, REFERENCE AND CARRYOVER — Continued

*Source*: The Council of State Governments' survey, January 2009 with March 2010 update.

*Key*:

★ — Yes

. . . — No

L — Rules generally require all bills be referred to the appropriate committee of jurisdiction.

M — Rules require specific types of bills be referred to specific committees (e.g., appropriations, local bills).

U — Unicameral legislature.

(a) Legislative rules specify all or certain bills go to committees of jurisdiction.

(b) Unless otherwise indicated by footnote, bills may be introduced prior to convening each session of the legislature. In this column only: ★ — pre- filing is allowed in both chambers (or in the case of Nebraska, in the unicameral legislature); . . . — pre-filing is not allowed in either chamber.

(c) Bills carry over from the first year of the legislature to the second (does not apply in Alabama, Arkansas, Montana, Nevada, North Dakota, Oregon and Texas, where legislatures meet biennially). Bills generally do not carry over after an intervening legislative election.

(d) Except between the end of the last regular session of the legislature in any quadrennium and the organizational session following the general election and special sessions.

(e) Lieutenant governor is the president of the Senate.

(f) Senate bills by president with concurrence of president pro tem. House bills by president pro tem with concurrence of president, if no concurrence, referred to Majority Leader for assignment.

(g) Senate Chief Counsel makes recommendations to the Presiding officer.

(h) Bills drafted prior to session. Introduction on the first day. Bills introduced in the first year of the regular session and passed by the house of origin on or before the January 31st constitutional deadline are carryover bills.

(i) In either house, state law requires any bill which affects the sentencing of criminal offenders and which would result in a net increase of imprisonment in state correctional facilities must be assigned to the appropriations committee of the house in which it was introduced. In the Senate, a bill must be referred to the Appropriations Committee if it contains an appropriation from the state treasury or the increase of any salary. Each bill which provides that any state revenue be devoted to any purpose other than that to which it is devoted under existing law must be referred to the Finance Committee.

(j) Prefiling allowed only in the House, seven calendar days before the commencement of the regular session, in even-numbered years. Senate bills are referred to committee by the members of the majority leadership appointed by the President.

(k) In even-numbered years, the Rules Committee is to refer to substantive committees only appropriation bills implementing the budget, and bills deemed by the Rules Committee to be of an emergency nature or of substantial importance to the operation of government.

(l) Only in the Senate

(m) At the discretion of President Pro Tempore.

(n) Appropriation bills are the only "specific type" mentioned in the rules to be referred to either House Appropriation Cmte. or Senate Ways and Means.

(o) Subject to approval or disapproval. Louisiana–majority members present.

(p) Maine Joint Rule 308 sections 1,2,3, "All bills and resolves must be referred to committee, except that this provision may be suspended by a majority vote in each chamber."

(q) The President and Speaker may refer bills to any of the standing committees or the Rules Committees, but usually bills are referred according to subject matter.

(r) Pre-filing of bills allowed prior to the convening of the 2nd year of the biennium. Bill carryover allowed if in second year of a two-year session.

(s) The Nebraska Legislature's Executive Board serves as the Reference Committee.

(t) Bills are carried over from the 90-day session beginning in the odd-numbered year to the 60-day session, which begins in even-numbered year. Bills that have not passed by the last day of the 60-day session are all indefinitely postponed by motion on the last day of the session. The odd-numbered year shall be carried forward to the even-numbered year.

(u) In the Senate any member may make a motion for referral, but committee referrals are under the control of the Majority Floor Leader. In the House any member may make a motion for referral, and a chart is used to guide bill referrals based on statutory authority of committee, but committee referrals are under the control of the Majority Floor Leader.

(v) Rules do not require specific types of bills be referred to specific committees.

(w) Sponsor and members.

(x) Speaker has discretion.

(y) Senate Rule 33: Between the general election and the time for the next convening session, a holdover member or member-elect may file bills for introduction in the next session with the Clerk's office. Those bills shall be treated as if they were bills introduced on the first day of the session. House Rule 61: Bills introduced prior to the convening of the session shall be treated as if they were bills introduced on the first day of the session. Between the general election and the time for the next convening session, a member-elect may file bills for introduction in the next session with the Clerk's office. The Clerk shall number such bills consecutively, in the order in which they are filed, beginning with the number "1."

(z) Senate Rule 35: Unless a motion or order to the contrary, bills are referred to the proper standing committee. All Senate bills and resolutions referred by the Committee on Reference on or before the first day of April in an even-numbered year shall be scheduled for a minimum of one public hearing.

(aa) House Rule 37: All House bills and resolutions introduced, in compliance with House Rules, on or before the fifteenth day of May in an even-numbered year shall be referred to a standing select, or special committee, and shall be scheduled for a minimum of one public hearing. House Rule 65: All bills carrying an appropriation shall be referred to the Finance and Appropriations Committee for consideration and report before being considered the third time.

(bb) Bills carry over between the first and second year of each regular annual session, but not to the next biennial 2-year General Assembly.

(cc) A legislature consists of two years. Bills from the first session can carry over to the second session only. 2007 will begin a new Legislature, the 51st, and no bills will carry over to 2007.

(dd) The President can refer bills to any standing or special committee and may also attach subsequent referrals to other committees following action by the first committee.

(ee) Rules specify bills shall be referred by the Speaker to any standing or special committee and may also attach subsequent referrals to other committees following action by the first committee.

(ff) Allowed during the first year of the two year session.

(gg) Bills and resolutions introduced in the First Regular Session may carry over to the Second Regular Session (odd-numbered year to even-numbered year) only.

(hh) Bills are drafted prior to session but released starting first day of session.

(ii) Under the direction of the speaker.

(jj) Jurisdiction of the committees by subject matter is listed in the Rules.

(kk) The House Rules establish jurisdictional committees. The Speaker refers legislation to those committees as he deems appropriate.

(ll) Even-numbered year session to odd-numbered year session.

(mm) By the floor leader.

(nn) Prefiling allowed only in the house in even-numbered years.

(oo) From odd-year to even-year, but not between biennial sessions.

(pp) Substantive resolutions referred to sponsor for public hearing.

# Table 3.15
# TIME LIMITS ON BILL INTRODUCTION

| State or other jurisdiction | Time limit on introduction of bills | Procedures for granting exception to time limits |
|---|---|---|
| Alabama...................... | House: no limit. Senate: 24th legislative day of regular session (a). | Unanimous vote to suspend rules. |
| Alaska ...................... | 35th C day of 2nd regular session. | Introduction by committee or by suspension of operation of limiting rule. |
| Arizona ...................... | House: 29th day of regular session; 10th day of special session. Senate: 22nd day of regular session; 10th day of special session. | House: Permission of rules committee. Senate: Permission of rules committee. |
| Arkansas .................... | 55th day of regular session (50th day for appropriations bills). Retirement and health care legislation affecting licensures shall be introduced during the first 15 days. | 2/3 vote of membership of each house. |
| California ................... | Deadlines established by the Joint Rules Committee. | House: Rules Committee grants exception with 3/4 vote of House. Senate: Approval of Rules Committee and 3/4 vote of membership. |
| Colorado .................... | House: 22nd C day of regular session. Senate: 17th C day of regular session. | Committees on delayed bills may extend deadline. |
| Connecticut ................. | 10 days into session in odd-numbered years, 3 days into session in even-numbered years (b). | 2/3 vote of members present. |
| Delaware.................... | House: no limit. Senate: no limit. | |
| Florida...................... | House: noon of the first day of regular session. Senate: noon first day of regular session (c)(d). | Existence of an emergency reasonably compelling consideration notwithstanding the deadline. |
| Georgia ..................... | Only for specific types of bills. | |
| Hawaii ...................... | Actual dates established during session. | Majority vote of membership. |
| Idaho ....................... | House: 20th day of session for personal bills; 36th day of session for all committees; beyond that only privileged cmtes. Senate: 12th day of session for personal bills; 36th day of session for all committees; beyond that only privileged cmtes. | House and Senate: speaker/president pro tempore may designate any standing committee to serve as a privileged committee temporarily. |
| Illinois...................... | House: determined by speaker. Senate: determined by senate president. | House: the speaker may set deadlines for any action on any category of legislative measure, including deadlines for introduction of bills. Senate: At any time, the president may set alternative deadlines for any legislative action with written notice filed with the secretary. |
| Indiana ..................... | House: Mid-January. Senate: Date specific—set in Rules, different for long and short session. Mid-January. | House: 2/3 vote. Senate: If date falls on weekend/Holiday—extended to next day. Sine die deadline set by statute, does not change. |
| Iowa........................ | House: Friday of 6th week of 1st regular session; Friday of 2nd week of 2nd regular session. Senate: Friday of 7th week of 1st regular session; Friday of 2nd week of 2nd regular session. | Constitutional majority. |
| Kansas ...................... | Actual dates established in the Joint Rules of the House and Senate every two years when the joint rules are adopted. | Resolution adopted by majority of members of either house may make specific exceptions to deadlines. |
| Kentucky.................... | House: No introductions during the last 14 L days of odd-year session, during last 22 L days of even-year session. Senate: No introductions during the last 14 L days of odd-year session, during last 20 L days of even-year session. | None. |
| Louisiana ................... | House: 10th C day of odd-year sessions and 23rd C day of even-year sessions. Senate: 10th C day of odd-year sessions and 23rd C day of even-year sessions. | None. |
| Maine ...................... | House: Cloture dates established by the Legislative Council. Cloture for 1st session of 124th legislature was January 16, 2009. Senate: Cloture dates established by the Legislative Council. Cloture for 1st session of 124th legislature was January 16, 2009. | House: Bills filed after cloture date must be approved by a majority of the Legislative Council. Senate: Appeals heard by Legislative Council. Six votes required to allow introduction of legislation. |

See footnotes at end of table.

# TIME LIMITS ON BILL INTRODUCTION — Continued

| State or other jurisdiction | Time limit on introduction of bills | Procedures for granting exception to time limits |
|---|---|---|
| Maryland............................ | House and Senate: No introductions during the last 35 days of regular session, unless 2/3 of the elected members of a chamber vote yes. Additional limitations involve committee action. Senate bills introduced after the 24th calendar day must be referred to the Senate Rules Committee and also Senate bills introduced after the 10th calendar day on behalf of the administration, i.e. the governor, must be referred to the Senate Rules Committee. House bills introduced during the last 59 calendar days (after the 31st day) are referred to the House Rules Committee. The Senate Rules and House Rules contain further provisions concerning the requirements for forcing legislation out of these committees. | House: 2/3 vote of elected members of each house. |
| Massachusetts................. | 1st Wednesday in December even-numbered years, 1st Wednesday in November odd-numbered years. | 2/3 vote of members present and voting. |
| Michigan .......................... | No limit. | |
| Minnesota ........................ | No limit. | |
| Mississippi........................ | 14th C day in 90 day session; 49th C day in 125 day session (e). | 2/3 vote of members present and voting. |
| Missouri ........................... | House: 60th L day of regular session. Senate: March 1. | Majority vote of elected members each house; governor's request for consideration of bill by special message. |
| Montana............................ | General bills & resolutions: 10th L day; revenue bills: 17th L day; committee bills and resolutions: 36th L day; committee bills implementing provisions of a general appropriation act: 75th L day; committee revenue bills: 62nd L day; interim study resolutions: 75th L day (c). | 2/3 vote of members. |
| Nebraska........................... | 10th L day of any session (f). | 3/5 vote of elected membership. |
| Nevada ............................. | Actual dates established at start of session. | Waiver granted by majority leader of the Senate and speaker of the Assembly acting jointly. |
| New Hampshire ............. | Determined by rules. | 2/3 vote of members present. |
| New Jersey....................... | No limit. | |
| New Mexico.................... | House: 15 days in short session/even years, 30 days in long session/odd years. Senate: 15 days in short session/even years, 30 days in long session/odd years. | None. Statutory limit for legislators; governor not limited and can send bill with message. |
| New York ......................... | Assembly: for unlimited introduction of bills, the final day is the last Tuesday in May of the 2nd year of the legislative term; for introduction of 10 or fewer bills, last Tuesday in May. Senate: 1st Tuesday in March. | Assembly: By unanimous consent or by introduction by Rules Cmte. or by message from the Senate. Senate: Exceptions are granted by the president pro tem or by introduction by Rules Cmte. or by message from Assembly. |
| North Carolina .............. | Actual dates established during session. | Senate: 2/3 vote of membership present and voting shall be required. |
| North Dakota ................. | Proposed limits for 2009 session; House: January 19. Senate: January 26. | 2/3 vote of the floor or by approval of Delayed Bills Committee. |
| Ohio.................................. | No limit. | |
| Oklahoma ........................ | Time limit set in rules. | 2/3 vote of membership. |
| Oregon ............................. | House: 50th C day of session. Senate: 50th C day of session. Rules adopted every 2 years. | House: Bills approved by the speaker: appropriation or fiscal measures sponsored by the Cmte. on Ways and Means; measures drafted by the Legislative Counsel and introduced as members' priority drafting requests. Senate: Measures approved by the senate president: appropriation or fiscal measures sponsored by the Committee on Ways and Means; measures drafted by the Legislative Counsel and introduced as members' priority drafting requests. |
| Pennsylvania................... | No limit. | |

See footnotes at end of table.

# TIME LIMITS ON BILL INTRODUCTION — Continued

| State or other jurisdiction | Time limit on introduction of bills | Procedures for granting exception to time limits |
|---|---|---|
| **Rhode Island** | Second week of February for Public Bills. | Sponsor must give one legislative day's notice. |
| **South Carolina** | House: Prior to April 15 of the 2nd yr. of a two-yr. legislative session; May 1 for bills first introduced in Senate. Rule 5.12. Senate: May 1 of regular session for bills originating in House. Rule 47. | House: 2/3 vote of members present and voting. Senate: 2/3 vote of membership. |
| **South Dakota** | Individual bills: 40-day session: 15th L day; 35-day session: 10th L day. Committee bills: 40-day session: 16th L day; 35-day session: 11th L day. | 2/3 approval of members-elect. |
| **Tennessee** | General bills, 10th L day of regular session (g). | Unanimous approval by Delayed Bills Committee. |
| **Texas** | 60th C day of regular session. | 4/5 vote of members present and voting. |
| **Utah** | 12 p.m. on 11th day of session. | Motion for request must be approved by a constitutional majority vote. |
| **Vermont** | House: 1st session—last day of February; 2nd session—last day of January. Senate: 1st session—53 C day; 2nd session—25 C days before start of session. | Approval by Rules Committee. |
| **Virginia** | Set by joint procedural resolution adopted at the beginning of the session (usually the second Friday of the session is the last day to introduce legislation that does not have any earlier deadline). | As provided in the joint procedural resolution (usually unanimous consent or at written request of the governor). |
| **Washington** | Until 10 days before the end of session unless 2/3 vote of elected members of each house. | 2/3 vote of elected members of each house. |
| **West Virginia** | House: 45th C day. Senate: 41st C day. | 2/3 vote of members present. |
| **Wisconsin** | No limit. | |
| **Wyoming** | House: 15th L day of session. Senate: 12th L day of session. | 2/3 vote of elected members. |
| **American Samoa** | House: After the 25th L day of the fourth Regular Session Senate: After the 15th L day. | |
| **Guam** | Public hearing on bill must be held no more than 120 days after date of bill introduction. | |
| **Puerto Rico** | 1st session—within first 125 days; 2nd session—within first 60 days. | None. |
| **U.S. Virgin Islands** | No limit. | |

*Source*: The Council of State Governments' survey, January 2009.
*Key*:
C — Calendar
L — Legislative
(a) Not applicable to local bills, advertised or otherwise.
(b) Specific dates set in Joint Rules.
(c) Not applicable to appropriations bills.
(d) Not applicable to local bills and joint resolutions. Florida: Not applicable to local bills (which have no deadline) or claim bills (deadline is August 1 of the year preceding consideration or within 60 days of a senator's election).
(e) Except Appropriation and Revenue bills (51st/86th C day) and Local & Private bills (83rd/118th C day).
(f) Except appropriations bills and bills introduced at the request of the governor, bills can be introduced during the first 10 legislative days of the session. Appropriation bills and bills introduced at the request of the governor can be introduced at any time during the session.
(g) Local bills have no cutoff.

# Table 3.16
# ENACTING LEGISLATION: VETO, VETO OVERRIDE AND EFFECTIVE DATE

| State or other jurisdiction | Governor may item veto appropriation bills | | Days allowed governor to consider bill (a) | | | Votes required in each house to pass bills or items over veto (c) | Effective date of enacted legislation (d) |
|---|---|---|---|---|---|---|---|
| | Amount | Other (b) | During session — Bill becomes law unless vetoed | After session — Bill becomes law unless vetoed | After session — Bill dies unless signed | | |
| Alabama | ★(e) | ... | 6 (f) | | 10A | Majority of elected body | Date signed by governor, unless otherwise specified. |
| Alaska | ★ | ... | 15 | | | 2/3 elected (g) | 90 days after enactment |
| Arizona | ★ | ... | 5 | 10A | | 2/3 elected (h) | 90 days after adjournment |
| Arkansas | ★ | ... | 5 | 20A | | Majority elected | 91st day after adjournment |
| California | ★(i) | ... | 12 (j) | 30A | | 2/3 elected | (k) |
| Colorado | ★(l) | ... | 10 (m) | 30A (m) | | 2/3 elected | 90 days after adjournment (n) |
| Connecticut | ★ | ... | 5 | 15P | (o) | 2/3 elected | Oct. 1, unless otherwise specified. |
| Delaware | ★ | ... | 10 | 10P | | 3/5 elected | Immediately |
| Florida | ★ | ★ | 7 (m)(p) | 15P (m) | 30A | 2/3 present | 60 days after adjournment |
| Georgia | ★ | ★ | 6 | 40A | | 2/3 elected | Unless other date specified, July 1 for generals, date signed by governor for locals. |
| Hawaii (q) | ★(r) | ... | 10 (s) | 45A (s)(p) | (p) | 2/3 elected | Immediately |
| Idaho | ★(r) | ... | 7 | 10P | | 2/3 present | July 1 |
| Illinois | ★(r) | ... | 60 (m) | 60 (m) | | 3/5 elected (g) | Usually Jan. 1 of next year (t) |
| Indiana | ... | ★ | 7 | 7P | | Majority elected | (u) |
| Iowa | ... | ★ | 3 | | 30A | 2/3 elected | July 1 (t) |
| Kansas | ★ | ... | 10 (m) | 90A | | 2/3 membership | Upon publication or specified date after publication |
| Kentucky | ★ | ... | 10 | | 10P | Majority elected | 90 days after adjournment sine die. Unless the bill contains an emergency clause or special effective date. |
| Louisiana (q) | ★ | ... | 10 (m) | 20P (m) | | 2/3 elected | Aug. 15 |
| Maine | ★ | ... | 10 | | (v) | 2/3 elected | 90 days after adjournment unless enacted as an emergency. |
| Maryland | ★(w) | ★ | 6 (x) | 30P (y) | (z) | 3/5 elected (aa) | June 1 (bb) |
| Massachusetts | ★ | ... | 10 | 10P | 10A | 2/3 present | 90 days after enactment |
| Michigan | ★ | ... | 14 | | 14P | 2/3 elected and serving | 90 days after adjournment |
| Minnesota | ★ | (i) | 3P | 14A, 3P | 3A, 14P | 2/3 elected—90 House; 45 Senate | Aug. 1 (cc) |
| Mississippi | ★ | ... | 5 | 15P (dd) | | 2/3 elected | July 1 unless specified otherwise. |
| Missouri | ★ | ... | 15 | 45A | | 2/3 elected | Aug. 28 (ee) |
| Montana (q) | ★ | ... | 10 (m) | 25A (m) | | 2/3 present | Oct. 1 (cc) |
| Nebraska | ★ | ★ | 5 | 5A, 5P | (ff) | 3/5 elected | 90 days following adjournment sine die. Unless bill contains an emergency clause. |
| Nevada | ... | ... | 5 (gg) | 10A (gg) | | 2/3 elected | Oct. 1, unless measure stipulates a different date. |
| New Hampshire | ... | ... | 5 | 5P | | 2/3 present | 60 days after enactment, unless otherwise noted. |
| New Jersey | ... | ... | 45 | | | 2/3 elected | Dates usually specified |
| New Mexico | ★ | ★ | 3 (hh) | | 20A | 2/3 present | 90 days after adjournment unless other date specified. |
| New York | ★ | ... | 10 (ii) | | 30A | 2/3 votes in each house | 20 days after enactment |
| North Carolina | ... | ... | 10 | (ii) | | 3/5 elected | 60 days after enactment |
| North Dakota | ... | ... | 3 | 30A | | 2/3 elected | 60 days after adjournment |
| Ohio | ★ | ★ | 10 | 10P | 10A | 3/5 elected (kk) | (jj) 91st day after filing with secretary of state. (ll) |

See footnotes at end of table.

# ENACTING LEGISLATION: VETO, VETO OVERRIDE AND EFFECTIVE DATE—Continued

| State or other jurisdiction | Governor may item veto appropriation bills | | Days allowed governor to consider bill (a) | | | Votes required in each house to pass bills or items over veto (c) | Effective date of enacted legislation (d) |
| --- | --- | --- | --- | --- | --- | --- | --- |
| | Amount | Other (b) | During session: Bill becomes law unless vetoed | After session: Bill becomes law unless vetoed | After session: Bill dies unless signed | | |
| Oklahoma | ★ | ... | 5 (mm) | | 15A (mm) | 2/3 elected | 90 days after adjournment unless specified in the bill. |
| Oregon | ★ | ... | 5 | 30A (s) | | 2/3 present | Jan. 1st of following year. (nn) |
| Pennsylvania | ★ | ★ | 10 | 10P | | Majority | 60 days after signed by governor |
| Rhode Island | ... | ... | 6 | 10P (oo) | (oo) | 3/5 present | Immediately (pp) |
| South Carolina | ★ | ... | 5 | (qq) | | 2/3 elected | Date of signature |
| South Dakota | ★ | ... | 5 (rr) | 15P (rr) | | 2/3 elected | July 1 |
| Tennessee | ★ | ... | 10 | (ss) | | Constitutional majority | 40 days after enactment unless otherwise specified |
| Texas | ★ | ... | 10 | 20A | | 2/3 elected | 90 days after adjournment |
| Utah | ★ | ... | 10P | 20A | | 2/3 elected | 60 days after adjournment of the session at which it passed. |
| Vermont | ... | ... | 5 | | 3A | 2/3 present | July 1 |
| Virginia | ★(tt) | ★ | 7 (m) | 30A (uu) | | 2/3 present (vv) | July 1 (ww) |
| Washington | ★ | ★ | 5 | 20A | | 2/3 present | 90 days after adjournment |
| West Virginia | ... | (i) | 5 | 15A (xx) | | Majority elected | 90 days after enactment |
| Wisconsin | ★ | ... | 6 | 6P | | 2/3 present | Day after publication date unless otherwise specified |
| Wyoming | ★ | ★ | 3 | 15A | | 2/3 elected | Specified in act |
| American Samoa | ★ | ... | 10 | | 30A | 2/3 elected | 60 days after adjournment (yy) |
| Guam | ★ | ★ | 10 | 10P | 30P (zz) | 10 votes to override | Immediately (bbb) |
| No. Mariana Islands | ★ | ... | 40 (m)(aaa) | | | 2/3 elected | Immediately |
| Puerto Rico | ★ | ... | 10 | | 30P | 2/3 elected | Specified in act |
| U.S. Virgin Islands | ★(ccc) | ★(ccc) | 10 | 10P | 30A | 2/3 elected | Immediately |

*Source:* The Council of State Governments' survey, April 2012.

Key:
★ – Yes
... – No
A – Days after adjournment of legislature.
P – Days after presentation to governor.
(a) Sundays excluded, unless otherwise indicated.
(b) Includes language in appropriations bill.
(c) Bill returned to house of origin with governor's objections.
(d) Effective date may be established by the law itself or may be otherwise changed by vote of the legislature. Special or emergency acts are usually effective immediately.
(e) The governor may line item distinct items or item veto amounts in appropriation bills, if returned prior to final adjournment.
(f) Except bills presented within five days of final adjournment, Sundays are included.
(g) Different number of votes required for revenue and appropriations bills. Alaska–3/4 elected. Illinois–3/5ths members elected to override any gubernatorial change except a reduction in an item, which a majority of the members elected to each house can restore to its original amount.
(h) Several specific requirements of 3/4 majority.
(i) Line item veto.
(j) For a bill to become law during session, if 12th day falls on a Saturday, Sunday, or holiday, the period is extended to the next day that is not a Saturday, Sunday, or holiday.

(k) For legislation enacted in regular sessions: January 1 of the following year. Urgency legislation: immediately upon chaptering by Secretary of State. Legislation enacted in Special Session: 91st day after adjournment of the special session at which the bill was passed.
(l) Must veto entire amount of any item; an item is an indivisible sum of money dedicated to a stated purpose.
(m) Sundays included.
(n) An act takes effect on the date stated in the act, or if no date is stated in the act, then upon signature of the governor. If no safety clause on a bill, the bill takes effect 90 days after sine die if no referendum petition has been filed. The state constitution allows for a 90 day period following adjournment when petitions may be filed for bills that do not contain a safety clause.
(o) Bill enacted if not signed/vetoed within time frames.
(p) The governor must notify the legislature 10 days before the 45th day of his intent to veto a measure on that day. The legislature may convene on the 45th day after adjournment to consider the vetoed measures. If the legislature fails to reconvene, the bill does not become law. If the legislature reconvenes, it may pass the measure over the governor's veto or it may amend the law to meet the governor's objections. If the law is amended, the governor must sign the bill within 10 days after it is presented to him in order for it to become law.
(q) Constitution withholds right to veto constitutional amendments.
(r) Governor can also reduce amounts in appropriations bills. In Hawaii, governor can reduce items in executive appropriations measures, but cannot reduce or item veto amounts appropriated for the judicial or legislative branches.

# ENACTING LEGISLATION: VETO, VETO OVERRIDE AND EFFECTIVE DATE—Continued

(s) Except Sundays and legal holidays. In Hawaii, except Saturdays, Sundays, holidays and any days in which the legislature is in recess prior to its adjournment. In Oregon, if the governor does not sign the bill within 30 days after adjournment, it becomes law without the governor's signature, Saturdays and Sundays are excluded.

(t) Effective date for bills which become law on or after July 1. Illinois–Unless specified in the act. Exception: An act enacted by a bill passed after May 31 cannot take effect before June 1 of the following year unless it was passed by 3/5ths of the members elected to each house.

(u) Varies with date of the veto.

(v) "If the bill or resolution shall not be returned by the governor within 10 days (Sundays excepted) after it shall have been presented to the Governor, it shall have the same force and effect as if the Governor had signed it unless the Legislature by their adjournment prevent its return, in which case it shall have such force and effect, unless returned within 3 days after the next meeting of the same Legislature which enacted the bill or resolution; if there is no such next meeting of the Legislature which enacted the bill or resolution, the bill or resolution shall not be a law." (excerpted from Article IV, Part Third, Section 2 of the Constitution of Maine).

(w) The governor cannot veto the budget bill but may exercise a total veto or item veto on a supplementary appropriations bill. In practice this means the governor may strike items in the annual general capital loan bill. Occasionally the governor will also veto a bond bill or a portion of a bond bill.

(x) If a bill is presented to the governor in the first 83 days of session, the governor has only six days (not including Sunday) to act before the bill automatically becomes law.

(y) All bills passed at regular or special sessions must be presented to the governor no later than 20 days after adjournment. The governor has a limited time to sign or veto a bill after it is presented. If the governor does not act within that time, the bill becomes law automatically; there is no pocket veto. The time limit depends on when the presentment is made. Any bill presented in the last 7 days of the 90-day session or after adjournment must be acted on within 30 days after presentment. Bills vetoed after adjournment are returned to the legislature for reconsideration at the next meeting of the same General Assembly.

(z) The governor has a limited time to sign or veto a bill after it is presented. If the governor does not act within that time, the bill becomes law automatically; there is no pocket veto. The time limit depends on when the presentment is made.

(aa) Vetoed bills are returned to the house of origin immediately after that house has organized at the next regular or special session. When a new General Assembly is elected and sworn in, bills vetoed from the previous session are not returned. These vetoed bills are not subject to any further legislative action.

(bb) Unless otherwise provided, June 1 is the effective date for bond bills, July 1 for budget, tax and revenue bills. By custom October 1 is the usual effective date for other legislation. If the bill is an emergency measure, it may take effect immediately upon approval by the governor or at a specified date prior to June 1. For vetoed legislation, 30 days after the veto is overridden or on the date specified in the bill, whichever is later. An emergency bill passed over the governor's veto takes effect immediately.

(cc) Different date for fiscal legislation. Minnesota, Montana–July 1.

(dd) Bills vetoed after adjournment are returned to the legislature for reconsideration. Mississippi–returned within three days after the beginning of the next session.

(ee) If bill has an emergency clause, it becomes effective upon governor's signature.

(ff) Bills are carried over from the 90-day session beginning in the odd-numbered year to the 60-day session, which begins in even-numbered years. Bills that have not passed by the last day of the 60-day session are all indefinitely postponed by motion on the last day of the session.

(gg) The day of delivery and Sundays are not counted for purposes of calculating these periods.

(hh) Except bills going up in the last three days of session, for which the governor has 20 days.

(ii) If the legislature adjourns during the governor's consideration of a 10-day bill, the bill shall not become law without the governor's approval.

(jj) August 1 after filing with the secretary of state. Appropriations and tax bills July 1 after filing with secretary of state, or date set in legislation by Legislative Assembly, or by date established by emergency clause.

(kk) The exception covers such matters as emergency measures and court bills that originally required a 2/3 majority for passage. In those cases, the same extraordinary majority vote is required to override a veto.

(ll) Emergency, current appropriation, and tax legislation effective immediately. The General Assembly may also enact an uncodified section of law specifying a desired effective date that is after the constitutionally established effective date.

(mm) During session the governor has 5 days (except Sunday) to sign or veto a bill or it becomes law automatically. After Session a bill becomes a pocket veto if not signed 15 days after sine die.

(nn) Unless emergency declared or date specific in text of measure.

(oo) Bills become effective without signature if not signed or vetoed.

(pp) Date signed, date received by Secretary of State if effective without signature, date that veto is overridden, or other specified date.

(qq) Two days after the next meeting.

(rr) During a session, a bill becomes law if a governor signs it or does not act on it within five days. If the legislature has adjourned or recessed or is within 5 days of a recess or an adjournment, the governor has 15 days to act on the bill. If he does not act the bill becomes law.

(ss) Adjournment of the legislature is irrelevant; the governor has 10 days to act on a bill after it is presented to him or it becomes law without his signature.

(tt) If part of the item.

(uu) The governor has thirty days after adjournment of the legislature to act on any bills. The Constitution of Virginia provides that: "If the governor does not act on any bill, it shall become law without his signature."

(vv) Must include majority of elected members.

(ww) Unless a different date is stated in the bill. Special sessions–first day of fourth month after adjournment.

(xx) Five days for supplemental appropriation bills.

(yy) Laws required to be approved only by the governor. An act required to be approved by the U.S. Secretary of the Interior only after it is vetoed by the governor and so approved takes effect 40 days after it is returned to the governor by the secretary.

(zz) After Legislature adjourns sine die at end of two-year term.

(aaa) Twenty days for appropriations bills.

(bbb) U.S. Congress may annul.

(ccc) May item veto language or amounts in a bill that contains two or more appropriations.

## Table 3.17
## LEGISLATIVE APPROPRIATIONS PROCESS: BUDGET DOCUMENTS AND BILLS

| State or other jurisdiction | Legal source of deadline | | Budget document submission — Submission date relative to convening | | | | | Budget bill introduction | | |
|---|---|---|---|---|---|---|---|---|---|---|
| | Constitutional | Statutory | Prior to session | Within one week | Within two weeks | Within one month | Over one month | Same time as budget document | Another time | Not until committee review of budget document |
| Alabama | ★ | ★ | (a) | ... | ... | ... | ... | ★ | ... | ... |
| Alaska | ★ | ★ | ... | (a) | ... | ... | ... | ★ | ... | ... |
| Arizona | ... | ★ | ★ | ... | ... | ... | ... | ... | ... | ★ |
| Arkansas | ... | ★ | ★ | ... | ... | ... | ... | ... | ... | ★ |
| California | ★ | ... | ... | ... | ... | ... | ... | ★(b) | ... | ... |
| Colorado | ... | ★ | ★(a) | ... | ... | ... | ... | ... | 76th day by rule | ... |
| Connecticut | ... | ★ | ... | ... | ... | (a) | ... | ★ | ... | ... |
| Delaware | ... | ... | ... | ... | ... | ... | ... | ... | ... | ... |
| Florida | ★ | ★ | ★ | ... | ... | ... | ... | ... | ... | ★ |
| Georgia | ★ | ... | ... | (a) | ... | ... | ... | ★ | ... | ... |
| Hawaii | ... | ★ | 30 days | ... | ... | ... | ... | ... | ★ | ... |
| Idaho | ... | ★ | ... | ★ | ... | ... | ... | ... | ... | ★ |
| Illinois | ... | ★ | ... | ... | ... | ... | ★(a) | ... | ★(c) | ... |
| Indiana | ... | ★ | ... | ... | ... | ... | ... | ... | ★ | ... |
| Iowa | ... | ★ | ... | ... | ... | (a) | ... | ... | ... | ★(d) |
| Kansas | ... | ★ | ... | ... | ★(e) | ... | ... | ... | ★ | ... |
| Kentucky | ★ | ... | ... | ... | (a) | ... | ... | ★ | ... | ... |
| Louisiana | ... | ★ | (f) | (f) | ... | ... | ... | (g) | ... | ... |
| Maine | ... | ★ | ... | (a) | ... | ... | ... | ★ | ... | ... |
| Maryland | ★ | ... | ... | ★(e) | ... | ... | ... | ★(h) | ... | ... |
| Massachusetts | ... | ★ | ... | ... | ... | ★ | ... | ★ | ... | ... |
| Michigan | ... | ★ | ... | ... | ... | ★ | ... | ★ | ... | ... |
| Minnesota | ... | ★ | ... | ... | ... | (a) | ... | ... | ... | ★ |
| Mississippi | ... | ★ | ★ | ... | ... | ... | ... | ... | ★ | ... |
| Missouri | ★ | ... | ... | ... | ... | ★ | ... | ... | ... | ★ |
| Montana | ... | ★ | ★ | ... | ... | ... | ... | ... | ★ | ... |
| Nebraska | ... | ★ | ... | ... | ... | ★ | ... | ★(i) | ... | ... |
| Nevada | ★ | ... | (a) | ... | ... | ... | ... | ... | ... | ★ |
| New Hampshire | ... | ★ | ... | ... | ... | ... | (a) | ★ | ... | ... |
| New Jersey | ... | ★ | ... | ... | ... | ... | ... | ... | ... | ★ |
| New Mexico | ... | ★ | ... | ... | ... | (a) | ... | ... | ★ | ... |
| New York | ★ | ... | ... | ... | ★(a) | ... | ... | ... | ★(j) | ... |
| North Carolina | ... | ... | ... | ... | ... | ... | ... | ★ | ... | ... |
| North Dakota | ... | ★ | (k) | ... | ... | ... | ... | ... | ... | ★ |
| Ohio | ... | ★ | ... | ... | ... | ★(d)(e) | ... | ★ | ... | ... |
| Oklahoma | ... | ★ | ★ | ★ | ... | ... | ... | ★ | ... | ... |
| Oregon | ... | ★ | ... | ... | ... | ... | ★(l) | ★(m) | ... | ... |
| Pennsylvania | ★ | ... | ... | ... | ... | ... | ★ | ... | ... | ★ |
| Rhode Island | ... | ★ | ... | ... | ... | ... | ★ | ... | ★ | ... |
| South Carolina | ... | ★ | ... | ★ | ... | ... | ... | ... | ... | ★(n) |
| South Dakota | ... | ★ | ... | ... | ... | ... | ★(o) | ... | ★(p) | ... |
| Tennessee | ... | ★ | ... | ... | ★(a)(e) | ★(a)(e) | ... | ★ | ... | ... |
| Texas | ... | ★ | ... | 6th day | ... | ... | ... | ... | ★(q) | ... |
| Utah | ... | ★ | (a) | ... | ... | ... | ... | ... | ... | ★ |
| Vermont | ... | ... | ... | (s) | ... | ... | ... | ... | ... | ★ |
| Virginia | ... | ★ | Dec. 20 | ... | ... | ... | ... | ★ | ... | ... |
| Washington | ★(t) | ... | Dec. 20 (u) | ... | ... | ... | ... | ★ | ... | ... |
| West Virginia | ★ | ... | ... | ★ | ... | ... | ... | ★ | ... | ... |
| Wisconsin | ... | ★ | ... | ... | ... | ★(v) | ... | ★ | ... | ... |
| Wyoming | ... | ★ | Dec. 1 | ... | ... | ... | ... | ★ | ... | ... |
| American Samoa | ... | ★ | ★ | ... | ... | ... | ... | ★ | ... | ... |
| Guam | ... | ★ | ... | ... | ... | ★(w) | ... | ★ | ... | ... |
| No. Mariana Islands | ... | ★ | (a) | ... | ... | ... | ... | ... | (v) | ★ |
| Puerto Rico | ... | ★ | ... | ... | ... | ★ | ... | ... | ... | ★ |
| U.S. Virgin Islands | ... | ★ | May 30 | ... | ... | ... | ... | ... | ★ | ... |

See footnotes at end of table.

## LEGISLATIVE APPROPRIATIONS PROCESS: BUDGET DOCUMENTS AND BILLS — Continued

*Source*: The Council of State Governments' survey, January 2010.
*Key*:
★ — Yes
... — No

(a) Specific time limitations: Alabama—five days; Alaska—December 15, 4th legislative day; Connecticut— not later than the first session day following the third day in February, in each odd numbered year; Colorado—presented by November 1 to the Joint Budget Committee; Georgia—first five days of session; Illinois— Third Wednesday in February; Iowa—no later than February 1; Kentucky—10th legislative day; Maine—The Governor shall transmit the budget document to the Legislature not later than the Friday following the first Monday in January of the first regular legislative session ... A Governor-elect elected to a first term of office shall transmit the budget document to the Legislature not later than the Friday following the first Monday in February of the first regular legislative session (Maine Revised Statutes, Title 5, Chapter 149, Section 1666; Minnesota—by the 4th Tuesday in January each odd-numbered year; Nevada—no later than 14 days before commencement of regular session; New Hampshire—by February 15; New Mexico—by January 1 each year; New York—The executive budget must be submitted by the governor to the legislature by the 2nd Tuesday following the opening of session (or February 1 for the first session following a gubernatorial election); Tennessee—on or before February 1 for sitting governor; Utah— Must submit to the legislature by the calendared floor time on the first day of the annual session; No. Mariana Islands—no later than 6 months before the beginning of the fiscal year.

(b) Budget and Budget Bill are annual—to be submitted within the first 10 days of each calendar year.

(c) Deadlines for introducing bills in general are set by Senate president and House speaker.

(d) Executive budget bill is introduced and used as a working tool for committee.

(e) Later for first session of a new governor; Kansas—21 days; Maryland—10 days after; New Jersey—February 15; Ohio—by March 15; Tennessee—March 1.

(f) The governor shall submit his executive budget to the Joint Legislative Committee on the budget no later than 45 days prior to each regular session; except that in the first year of each term, the executive budget shall be submitted no later than 30 days prior to the regular session. Copies shall be made

available to the entire legislature on the first day of each regular session.

(g) Bills appropriating monies for the general operating budget and ancillary appropriations, bills appropriating funds for the expenses of the legislature and the judiciary must be submitted to the legislature for introduction no later than 45 days prior to each regular session, except that in the first year of each term, such appropriation bills shall be submitted no later than 30 days prior to the regular session.

(h) Appropriations bill other than the budget bill (supplementary) may be introduced at any time. They must provide their own tax source and may not be enacted until the budget bill is enacted.

(i) Governor's budget bill is introduced and serves as a working document for the Appropriations Committee. The governor must submit the budget proposal by January 15 of each odd-numbered year. (Neb. Rev. Stat. sec. 81–125). The statute extends this deadline to February 1 for a governor who is in his first year of office.

(j) Submission of the governor's budget bills to the legislature occurs with submission of the executive budget.

(k) Legislative Council's Budget Section hears the executive budget recommendations during legislature's December organizational session.

(l) By December 1st of even-numbered year unless new governor is elected; if new governor is elected, then February 1st of odd-numbered year.

(m) Legislature often introduces other budget bills during legislative session that are not part of the governor's recommended budget.

(n) The Ways and Means Committee introduces the Budget Bill within five days after the beginning of the session (S.C. Code 11-11-70).

(o) It is usually over a month. The budget must be delivered to the Legislature not later than the first Tuesday after the first Monday in December.

(p) It must be introduced no later than the 16th legislative day.

(q) Within first 30 days of session.

(r) Legislative rules require budget bills to be introduced by the 43rd day of the session.

(s) No official submission dates. Occurs by custom early in the session.

(t) And Rules.

(u) For fiscal period other than biennium, 20 days prior to first day of session.

(v) Last Tuesday in January. A later submission date may be requested by the governor.

(w) Usually January before end of current fiscal year.

## Table 3.18
## FISCAL NOTES: CONTENT AND DISTRIBUTION

| State or other jurisdiction | Content | | | | | | Distribution — Legislators | | | Appropriations Committee | | | |
| --- | --- | --- | --- | --- | --- | --- | --- | --- | --- | --- | --- | --- | --- |
| | Intent or purpose of bill | Cost involved | Projected future cost | Proposed source of revenue | Fiscal impact on local government | Other | All | Available on request | Bill sponsor | Members | Chair only | Fiscal staff | Executive budget staff |
| Alabama | ★ | ★ | ... | ★ | ★ | ★(a) | ... | ★ | ★ | ... | ... | ... | ... |
| Alaska | ... | ★ | ★ | ★ | ... | ... | ★ | ★ | ★ | ... | ... | ★ | ★ |
| Arizona | ★ | ★ | ★ | ★ | ★ | ★ | ★ | ★ | ★ | ★ | ... | ★ | ★ |
| Arkansas (b) | ... | ★ | ★ | ... | ★ | ★ | ★ | ... | ... | ... | ... | ... | ... |
| California | ★ | ★ | ★ | ★ | ★ | ... | ★ | ★ | ★ | ... | ... | ★ | ★ |
| Colorado | ★ | ★ | ★ | ★ | ★ | ... | ★ | ... | ... | ... | ... | ... | ... |
| Connecticut | ★ | ★ | ★ | ★ | ★ | ... | (c) | ... | ... | ... | ... | ... | ... |
| Delaware | ... | ★ | ... | ... | ... | ... | ★ | ... | ... | ... | ... | ... | ... |
| Florida | ★ | ★ | ★ | ★ | ★ | ★ | ★ | ... | ... | ... | ... | ★ | ... |
| Georgia | ... | ★ | ★ | ... | ★ | ... | ★ | ★ | ... | ... | ... | ... | ... |
| Hawaii | ... | ... | ... | ... | ... | ★ | ... | ... | ... | ... | ★ | ★ | ★ |
| Idaho | ★ | ★ | ★ | ★ | ★ | ★(d) | ★ | ... | ... | ... | ... | (e) | (e) |
| Illinois | ... | ★ | ★ | ★ | ★ | ... | (f) | ★ | ★ | ... | ... | ... | ... |
| Indiana | ★ | ★ | ★ | ★ | ★ | ... | ★ | ... | ... | ... | ... | ★ | ★ |
| Iowa | ★ | ★ | ★ | ★ | ★ | ... | ..................(g).................. | | | | | | |
| Kansas | ★ | ★ | ★ | ★ | ★ | ... | ★ | ★ | ★ | ... | ★ | ★ | ★ |
| Kentucky | ★ | ★ | ★ | ★ | ★ | ★ | ... | ★ | ★ | ★ | (h) | ★ | ... |
| Louisiana | ... | ★ | ★ | ... | ★ | ... | ★ | ★ | ... | ... | ★(h) | ★ | ★ |
| Maine | ... | ★ | ★ | ★ | ★ | ... | ... | ★(i) | ★ | ... | ... | ★ | ★ |
| Maryland | ★ | ★ | ★ | ★ | ★ | ★(j) | ... | ... | ★(k) | ... | ... | ... | ... |
| Massachusetts | ... | ★(l) | ★ | ... | ... | ★ | ★ | ... | ... | ... | ★ | ... | ... |
| Michigan | ★ | ★ | ★ | ★ | ★ | ★(m) | ★(n) | ... | ... | ... | ★ | ★ | ★ |
| Minnesota | ★ | ★ | ★ | ★ | ★ | ... | ... | ... | ★ | ... | ★ | ★ | ★ |
| Mississippi | ... | ★ | ★ | ★ | ... | ... | ... | ... | ★(o) | ... | ... | ... | ... |
| Missouri | ★ | ★ | ★ | ★ | ★ | ... | ... | ★ | ★ | ... | ... | ... | ★ |
| Montana | ... | ★ | ★ | ... | ★ | ★(p) | ★ | ... | ... | ... | ... | ★ | ★ |
| Nebraska | ... | ★ | ★ | ★ | ★ | ... | ★ | ★ | ... | ... | ... | ★ | ★ |
| Nevada | ... | ★ | ★ | ★ | ★ | ★ | ★ | ... | ... | ... | ... | ... | ... |
| New Hampshire | ★ | ★ | ... | ★ | ★ | ... | ... | ★ | ... | ... | ★ | ★ | ★ |
| New Jersey | ... | ★ | ... | ★ | ★ | ... | ★ | ... | ... | ... | ... | ★ | ★ |
| New Mexico | ★ | ★ | ★ | ★ | ★ | ... | ... | ★ | ★ | ★ | ... | (q) | (q) |
| New York | ... | ★ | ★ | ... | ★ | ★(r) | ... | ★ | ★ | ★ | ... | ★ | ... |
| North Carolina | ... | ★ | ★ | ... | ★ | ★ | (s) | ... | ... | ... | ... | ... | ... |
| North Dakota | ... | ... | ★ | ★ | ★ | ★(t) | (u) | ★ | ... | ... | ... | ★ | ★ |
| Ohio | ★ | ★ | ★ | ★ | ★ | ... | (v) | ... | ... | ... | ... | ... | ... |
| Oklahoma | ★ | ★ | ★ | ★ | ... | ... | ... | ★ | ★ | ... | ★ | ★ | ... |
| Oregon | ★ | ★ | ★ | ★ | ★ | ... | ★ | ... | ... | ... | ... | ★ | ★ |
| Pennsylvania | ... | ★ | ★ | ★ | ★ | ... | ... | ... | ... | ★ | ★ | ★ | ★ |
| Rhode Island | ★ | ★ | ★ | ★ | ★ | ... | ... | ★ | ... | ... | ★ | ★ | ★ |
| South Carolina | ★ | ★ | ★ | ★ | ★ | ... | ... | ★ | ... | (w) | ... | ★ | ★ |
| South Dakota | ... | ★ | ★ | ★ | ★ | ... | ... | ★ | ... | ... | ... | ... | ... |
| Tennessee | ★ | ★ | ★ | ... | ★ | ... | ★ | ★ | ★ | ... | ... | ... | ★ |
| Texas | ... | ★ | ★ | ★ | ★ | ★(x) | ★ | ★ | ★ | ★ | ... | ... | ★ |
| Utah | ... | ★ | ★ | ★ | ★ | ★(y) | ★ | ★ | ★ | ... | ... | ★ | ★ |
| Vermont | ..............(z).............. | | | | | | ... | ★ | ... | ★ | ... | ... | ... |
| Virginia | ★ | ★ | ★ | ★ | ★ | ★(aa) | (bb) | ... | ★ | ★ | ... | ★ | ★(cc) |
| Washington | ... | ★ | ★ | ★ | ★ | ★(dd) | ★ | ★ | ★ | ★ | ★ | ★ | ... |
| West Virginia | ... | ★ | ★ | ★ | ★ | ... | ... | ... | ... | ★ | ... | ... | ... |
| Wisconsin | ... | ★ | ★ | ★ | ★ | ... | (ee) | ... | ... | ... | ... | (ee) | ... |
| Wyoming | ... | ★ | ★ | ★ | ... | ... | ★ | ... | ... | ... | ... | ... | ... |
| Guam | ... | ★ | ... | ... | ★ | ★(ff) | ★ | ... | ... | ... | ★ | ★ | ... |
| No. Mariana Islands | ★ | ★ | ★ | ★ | ★ | ★ | ... | ... | ... | ... | ★ | ★ | ★ |
| Puerto Rico | ..............(gg).............. | | | | | | | | | | | | |
| U.S. Virgin Islands | ★ | ★ | ... | ★ | ... | ... | ★ | ... | ... | ... | ... | ... | ... |

See footnotes at end of table.

# FISCAL NOTES: CONTENT AND DISTRIBUTION — Continued

*Source:* The Council of State Governments' survey, March 2011.

*Note:* A fiscal note is a summary of the fiscal effects of a bill on government revenues, expenditures and liabilities.

*Key:*

★ — Yes

... — No

(a) Fiscal notes included on final passage calendar.

(b) Only retirement, corrections, revenue, tax and local government bills require fiscal notes. During the past session, fiscal notes were provided for education.

(c) The fiscal notes are printed with the bills favorably reported by the committees.

(d) Statement of purpose.

(e) Attached to bill, so available to both fiscal and executive budget staff.

(f) A summary of each fiscal note is attached to the summary of its bill in the printed Legislative Synopsis and Digest, and on the General Assembly's Web site. Fiscal notes are prepared for the sponsor and attached to the bill on file with the House Clerk or Senate Secretary.

(g) Fiscal notes are available to everyone.

(h) Prepared by the Legislative Fiscal Office when a state agency is involved and prepared by Legislative Auditor's office when a local board or commission is involved; copies sent to House and Senate staff offices respectively.

(i) Distributed to members of the committee of reference; also available on the Legislature's Web site.

(j) A fiscal note is now known as a fiscal and policy note to better reflect the contents. Fiscal and policy notes also identify any mandate on local government and include analyses of the economic impact on small businesses.

(k) In practice fiscal and policy notes are prepared on all bills and resolutions prior to a public hearing on the bills/resolutions. After initial hard copy distribution to sponsor and committee, the note is released to member computer system and thereafter to the legislative Web site.

(l) Fiscal notes are prepared only if cost exceeds $100,000 or matter has not been acted upon by the Joint Committee on Ways and Means.

(m) Other relevant data.

(n) At present, fiscal information is part of the bill analysis on the legislative Web site.

(o) And committee to which bill referred.

(p) Mechanical defects in bill.

(q) Fiscal impact statements prepared by Legislative Finance Committee staff are available to anyone on request and on the legislature's Web site.

(r) Bills impacting workers compensation benefits must have an actuarial impact statement; bills proposing changes in state or local government retirement systems must have an actuarial note.

(s) Fiscal notes are posted on the Internet and available to all members.

(t) Notes required only if impact is $5,000 or more. Bills impacting workforce safety and insurance benefits or premiums have actuarial statements as do bills proposing changes in state and local retirement systems.

(u) Fiscal notes are available online to anyone from the legislative branch Web site.

(v) Fiscal notes are prepared for bills before being voted on in any standing committee or floor session. Upon distribution to the legislators preparing to vote, the fiscal notes are made public.

(w) Fiscal impact statements on proposed legislation are prepared by the Office of State Budget and sent to the House or Senate standing committee that requested the impact. All fiscal impacts are posted on the OSB Web page.

(x) Equalized education funding impact statement and criminal justice policy impact statement.

(y) Fiscal notes are to include cost estimates on all proposed bills that anticipate direct expenditures by any Utah resident and the cost to the overall Utah resident population.

(z) Fiscal notes are not mandatory and their content will vary.

(aa) Technical amendments, if needed. Fiscal notes do not provide statements or interpretations of legislative intent for legal purposes. A summary of the stated objective, effect, and impact may be included.

(bb) Fiscal impact statements are widely available because they are also posted on the Internet shortly after they are distributed. The Joint Legislative Audit Review Commission (JLARC) also prepares a review of the fiscal impact statement if requested by a standing committee chair. The review statement is also available on the Internet.

(cc) Legislative budget directors.

(dd) Impact on private sector

(ee) The fiscal estimate is printed as an appendix to the bill; anyone that has a copy of the bill has a copy of the fiscal estimate.

(ff) Fiscal impact on local economy.

(gg) The Legislature of Puerto Rico does not prepare fiscal notes, but upon request the economics unit could prepare one. The Department of Treasury has the duty to analyze and prepare fiscal notes.

## Table 3.19
## BILL AND RESOLUTION INTRODUCTIONS AND ENACTMENTS:
## 2011 REGULAR SESSIONS

| State | Duration of session** | Introductions | | Enactments/Adoptions | | Measures vetoed by governor | Length of session |
|---|---|---|---|---|---|---|---|
| | | Bills | Resolutions* | Bills | Resolutions* | | |
| Alabama | Mar. 1–Jun. 9, 2011 | 1,205 | 1,135 | 296 | 413 | 0 | 105L |
| Alaska | Jan. 18–Apr. 17, 2011 | 375 | 82 | 32 | 40 | 1 | 90C |
| Arizona | Jan. 10–Apr. 20, 2011 | 1,350 | 146 | 357 | 36 | 29 | 109C |
| Arkansas | Jan. 10–Apr. 27, 2011 | 2,235 | 132 | 1,242 | 87 | 0 | 108C |
| California | Dec. 6, 2010–Sept. 10, 2011 | 2,417 | 219 | 814 | 125 | 125 | 130L (c) |
| Colorado | Jan. 12–May 11, 2011 | 712 | 107 | 404 | 92 | 1 | 120L |
| Connecticut | Jan. 5–Jun. 8, 2011 | 3,132 | 299 | 273 | 299 | 0 | 25L |
| Delaware | Jan. 11–Jun. 30, 2011 | 381 | 63 | 161 | 54 | 4 | 138L |
| Florida | Mar. 8–May 6, 2011 | 1,953 | 200 | 277 | 117 | 5 | 60C |
| Georgia | Jan. 10–Apr. 20, 2011 | 958 | 1,734 | 257 | 1,542 | 9 | 211C |
| Hawaii | Jan. 19–May 5, 2011 | 1,665 | 918 | 235 | 187 | 17 | 60L |
| Idaho | Jan. 10–Apr. 7, 2011 | 565 | 47 | 336 | 35 | 1 | 88L |
| Illinois | Jan. 12–Dec. 13, 2011 (d) | 6,491 | 1,316 | 650 | 1,101 | 8 | 72L (e) |
| Indiana | Nov. 16, 2010–Apr. 29, 2011 | 600 | 15 | 116 | 1 | 1 | 115C |
| Iowa | Jan. 10–Jun. 30, 2011 | 1,377 | N.A. | 138 | N.A. | 1 | 172C |
| Kansas | Jan. 11–May 13, 2011 | 659 | 36 | 118 | 10 | 0 | 90C |
| Kentucky | Jan. 4–Mar. 9, 2011 | 653 | 587 | 102 | 379 | 2 | 30L |
| Louisiana | Apr. 25–Jun. 23, 2011 | 905 | 649 | 425 | 600 | 18 | 60C |
| Maine | Dec. 1, 2010–Jun. 29, 2011 | 1,588 | 38 | 595 | 38 | 12 | 65L |
| Maryland | Jan. 12–Apr. 11, 2011 | 2,353 | 17 | 625 | 1 | 82 | 90C |
| Massachusetts | Jan. 5–Dec. 31, 2011 | 6,304 | N.A. | 226 | N.A. | N.A. | 136L (f) |
| Michigan | Jan. 12–Dec. 28, 2011 | 2,123 | 402 | 323 | 239 | 2 | 351C |
| Minnesota | Jan. 4–May 23, 2011 | 3,238 | 100 | 117 | N.A. | 23 | 64L |
| Mississippi | Jan. 4–Apr. 7, 2011 | 2,721 | 719 | 417 | 613 | 3 | 94C |
| Missouri | Jan. 5–May 30, 2011 | 1,461 | 60 | 133 | 2 | 14 | 73L |
| Montana | Jan. 3–Apr. 28, 2011 | 1,075 | 104 | 419 | 65 | 78 | 88L |
| Nebraska (U) | Jan. 5–May 26, 2011 | 704 | 355 | 272 | 207 | 4 | 87L |
| Nevada | Feb. 7–Jun. 7, 2011 | 1,089 | 50 | 560 | 32 | 28 | 120C |
| New Hampshire | Jan. 5, 2011–Jan. 4, 2012 | 621 | 52 | 265 | 25 | 13 | 24L |
| New Jersey | Jan. 11, 2011–Jan. 9, 2012 | 559 (g) | 127 (h) | 232 | 6 | 76 | 41L (i) |
| New Mexico | Jan. 18–Mar. 19, 2011 | 1,203 | 53 | 284 | 7 | 98 | 60C |
| New York | Jan. 5, 2011–Jan. 4, 2012 | 15,746 | | 602 | 3,407 | 89 | 365C |
| North Carolina | Jan. 26–Jun. 18, 2011 | 1,691 | 30 | 396 | 9 | 16 | 144C |
| North Dakota | Jan. 4–Apr. 28, 2011 | 841 | 79 | 514 | 60 | 0 | 115C |
| Ohio | Jan. 3–Dec. 29, 2011 (j) | 678 | 59 | 70 | 13 | 1 | 129L (k) |
| Oklahoma | Feb. 7–May 20, 2011 | 985 | 92 | 192 | 40 | 4 | 58L |
| Oregon | Feb. 1–Jun. 30, 2011 | 2,806 | 212 | 732 | 74 | 1 | 150C |
| Pennsylvania | Jan. 4–Dec. 21, 2011 | 3,468 | 962 | 134 | N.A. | 1 | 143L |
| Rhode Island | Jan. 4–Nov. 17, 2011 | 2,443 | N.A. | 550 | 461 | 3 | 67C (l) |
| South Carolina | Jan. 11–Jul. 26, 2011 | 1,337 | 1,076 | 101 | 827 | 5 | 62L |
| South Dakota | Jan. 11–Mar. 28, 2011 | 458 | 27 | 226 | 15 | 434 | 38L |
| Tennessee | Jan. 11–May 21, 2011 | 4,282 | 1,202 | 542 | N.A. | 0 | 39L |
| Texas | Jan. 11–May 30, 2011 | 5,796 | 439 | 1,379 | 153 | 24 | 140C |
| Utah | Jan. 24–Mar. 10, 2011 | 685 | 97 | 444 | 60 | 4 | 103C |
| Vermont | Jan. 5–May 6, 2011 | 571 | 301 | 74 | 5 | 1 | 69L |
| Virginia (m) | Jan. 12–Feb. 27, 2011 | 1,882 | 744 | 888 | 645 | 6 (n) | 47C |
| Washington | Jan. 10–Apr. 22, 2011 | 2,061 | 70 | 378 | 12 | 1 | 103C |
| West Virginia | Jan. 12–Mar. 18, 2011 | 1,894 | N.A. | 191 | N.A. | 3 | 66C |
| Wisconsin | Jan. 3–Mar. 15, 2011 | 1,325 | 259 | 164 | 138 | 0 | 65L |
| Wyoming | Jan. 11–Mar. 3, 2011 | 338 | 10 | 199 | 5 | 0 | 38L |

See footnotes at end of table.

# BILL AND RESOLUTION INTRODUCTIONS AND ENACTMENTS:
## 2011 REGULAR SESSIONS — Continued

*Sources:* The Council of State Governments' survey of legislative agencies and state websites, April 2012.

\* Includes Joint and Concurrent resolutions.

\*\*Actual adjournment dates are listed regardless of constitutional or statutory limitations. For more information on provisions, see Table 3.2, "Legislative Sessions: Legal Provisions."

*Key:*

C — Calendar day.

L — Legislative day (in some states, called a session or workday; definition may vary slightly; however, it generally refers to any day on which either chamber of the legislature is in session).

U — Unicameral legislature.

N.A. — Not available.

(a) Line item or partial vetoes: Alaska—2; Arkansas—1; California—4; Colorado—1; Florida—1; Illinois—19; Iowa—11; Kansas—7; Louisiana—16; Missouri—1; Montana—4; New Jersey—2; New Mexico—2; New York—22; North Dakota—2; South Carolina—35; Texas—33; Washington—25; Wisconsin—3; Wyoming—2.

(b) Number of vetoes overridden: Colorado—1; Illinois—3; Missouri—1; Nebraska—2; New Hampshire—7; New York—67; North Carolina—7; Rhode Island—2; South Carolina—6; South Dakota—2; Utah—2; Virginia—2; Wyoming—2.

(c) Senate only; 129 Assembly days in session.

(d) Dates given are Senate only. House dates: Jan. 12–Dec. 12, 2011.

(e) Senate only; 88 House days in session.

(f) 103 days were informal session days; 33 days were formal session days.

(g) Senate only; 697 Assembly.

(h) Senate only; 109 Assembly.

(i) Senate only; 30 Assembly days in session; 2 joint days.

(j) Dates given are Senate only. House dates: Jan. 3–Dec. 28, 2011.

(k) Senate only; 113 House days in session.

(l) Senate only; 69 House days in session.

(m) The General Assembly reconvened 04/06/2011 for a one day session to act on Governor's vetoes and executive amendments.

(n) The Governor proposed 86 amendments to the Appropriations Bill, of which the General Assembly accepted 66 and rejected 20. The Governor proposed executive amendments to an additional 131 bills. The General Assembly accepted the amendments to 115 bills, rejected amendments to 11 bills, and accepted in part and rejected in part the amendments to five bills.

## Table 3.20
## BILL AND RESOLUTION INTRODUCTIONS AND ENACTMENTS:
## 2011 SPECIAL SESSIONS

| State or other jurisdiction | Duration of session** | Introductions | | Enactments/adoptions | | Measures vetoed by governor (a)(b) | Length of session |
|---|---|---|---|---|---|---|---|
| | | Bills | Resolutions* | Bills | Resolutions* | | |
| Alabama | No special session in 2011 | | | | | | |
| Alaska | Apr. 18 – May 14, 2011 | 0 | 0 | 7 | 0 | 0 | 27C |
| | Jun. 27 – Jun. 28, 2011 | 0 | 0 | 0 | 0 | 0 | 2C |
| Arizona | Jan. 19 – Jan. 20, 2011 (c) | 6 | 2 | 1 | 0 | 0 | 2C |
| | Feb. 14 – Feb. 16, 2011 (d) | 1 | 0 | 1 | 0 | 0 | 3C |
| | Jun. 10 – Jun. 13, 2011 (e) | 1 | 0 | 0 | 0 | 0 | 3C |
| | Nov. 1, 2011 (f) | 0 | 0 | 0 | 0 | 0 | 1C |
| Arkansas | No special session in 2011 | | | | | | |
| California (g) | Dec. 6, 2010 – Sep. 10, 2011 | 77 | 4 | 16 | 1 | 3 | 63L (h) |
| Colorado | No special session in 2011 | | | | | | |
| Connecticut | Jun. 30 – Sep. 1, 2011 (i) | 2 | 3 | 2 | 3 | 0 | 2L |
| | Oct. 26 – Nov. 1, 2011 (j) | 2 | 3 | 2 | 3 | 0 | 1L |
| Delaware | No special session in 2011 | | | | | | |
| Florida | No special session in 2011 | | | | | | |
| Georgia | No special session in 2011 | | | | | | |
| Hawaii | No special session in 2011 | | | | | | |
| Idaho | No special session in 2011 | | | | | | |
| Illinois | No special session in 2011 | | | | | | |
| Indiana | No special session in 2011 | | | | | | |
| Iowa | No special session in 2011 | | | | | | |
| Kansas | No special session in 2011 | | | | | | |
| Kentucky | Mar. 14 – Apr. 6, 2011 | 6 | 63 | 1 | N.A. | 0 | 24C |
| Louisiana | Mar. 20 – Apr. 13, 2011 | 82 | 97 | 43 | 91 | 0 | 24C |
| Maine | Sep. 27, 2011 | 3 | 1 | 2 | 1 | 0 | 1L |
| Maryland | Oct. 17 – Oct. 20, 2011 | 55 | 0 | 3 | 0 | 0 | 4C |
| Massachusetts | No special session in 2011 | | | | | | |
| Michigan | No special session in 2011 | | | | | | |
| Minnesota | Jul. 19, 2011 | 38 | 3 (k) | 12 | N.A. | 0 | 1L |
| Mississippi | Sep. 2, 2011 (l) | 3 | 39 | 1 | 28 | 0 | 1L |
| Missouri | Sep. 15 – Oct. 25, 2011 | 21 | 1 | 2 | 0 | 0 | 22L |
| Montana | No special session in 2011 | | | | | | |
| Nebraska (U) | Nov. 11 – Nov. 22, 2011 | 6 | 35 | 4 | 33 | 0 | 11C |
| Nevada | No special session in 2011 | | | | | | |
| New Hampshire | No special session in 2011 | | | | | | |
| New Jersey | No special session in 2011 | | | | | | |
| New Mexico | Sep. 6 – Sep. 24, 2011 | 91 | 1 | 9 | 0 | 4 | 19C |
| New York | Dec. 7, 2011 | 4 | 4 | 4 | 4 | 0 | 1L |
| North Carolina | No special session in 2011 | | | | | | |
| North Dakota | Nov. 7 – Nov. 11, 2011 | 7 | 3 | 6 | 3 | 0 | 4C |
| Ohio | No special session in 2011 | | | | | | |
| Oklahoma | No special session in 2011 | | | | | | |
| Oregon | No special session in 2011 | | | | | | |
| Pennsylvania | No special session in 2011 | | | | | | |
| Rhode Island | No special session in 2011 | | | | | | |
| South Carolina | No special session in 2011 | | | | | | |
| South Dakota | Oct. 24, 2011 | 2 | 0 | 2 | 0 | 0 | 1L |
| Tennessee | No special session in 2011 | | | | | | |
| Texas | May 31 – Jun. 29, 2011 | 114 | 31 | 8 | 14 | 0 | 30C |
| Utah | Mar. 18, 2011 (m) | 0 | 0 | 0 | 0 | 0 | 1L |
| | May 6 – May 7, 2011 (n) | 0 | 0 | 0 | 0 | 0 | 2L |
| Vermont | No special session in 2011 | | | | | | |
| Virginia | Feb. 26, 2011 – Jan. 10, 2012 | 9 | 148 | 2 | 121 | 1 | 14L (o) |
| Washington | Apr. 26 – May 25, 2011 | 1,713 (p) | 62 (q) | 50 | 4 | 0 | |
| | Nov. 28 – Dec. 14, 2011 | 1,749 (r) | 62 (s) | 50 | 4 | 0 | 17C |
| West Virginia | Aug. 1 – Aug. 5, 2011 | 15 | 5 | 9 | 5 | 1 | 5C |
| | Aug. 18 – Aug. 21, 2011 | 3 | 5 | 3 | 4 | 0 | 4C |
| | Nov. 13 – Nov. 15, 2011 | 0 | 4 | 0 | 4 | 0 | 3C |
| | Dec. 11 – Dec. 14, 2011 | 2 | 4 | 1 | 4 | 0 | 4C |
| Wisconsin | Jan. 4 – Sep. 27, 2011 | 27 | 4 | 12 | 2 | 0 | 87L |
| | Sep. 29 – Dec. 8, 2011 | 48 | 0 | 7 | 0 | 0 | 23L |
| Wyoming | No special session in 2011 | | | | | | |

See footnotes at end of table.

# BILL AND RESOLUTION INTRODUCTIONS AND ENACTMENTS:
## 2011 SPECIAL SESSIONS — Continued

*Source:* The Council of State Governments' survey of state legislative agencies, April 2012.

\* Includes Joint and Concurrrent resolutions.

\*\* Actual adjournment dates are listed regardless of constitutional or statutory limitations. For more information on provisions, see Table 3.2, "Legislative Sessions: Legal Provisions."

*Key:*

N.A. — Not available.

C — Calendar day.

L — Legislative day (in some states, called a session or workday; definition may vary slightly.

U — Unicameral legislature.

(a) Line item or partial vetoes: Washington — 11; Wisconsin — 1.

(b) Number of vetoes overridden: Utah — 2.

(c) Topic of focus was proposed amendments to state-sponsored health care.

(d) Topics included the creation of the Arizona Commerce Authority and amendments to business and individual property tax laws.

(e) Topic of focus was employment security.

(f) This special session had only one introduced and passed memorial. Focused on the Independent Redistricting Commission and the removal of one member.

(g) Statistics are for the first half of the 2011–2012 First Extraordinary Session.

(h) Session days shown are for Assembly only. Senate session days: 74L.

(i) Adjournment date records calendar day adjournment.

(j) Senate dates only; House session was convened and adjourned on Oct. 26, 2011.

(k) House only.

(l) Session and all bill introductions were for bonds.

(m) Repealed H.B. 477 from the 2011 General Session.

(n) 2011 Veto Override Special Session.

(o) The 2011 Special Session 1 covered a period of 318 calendar days; the General Assembly actually met on 14 days throughout that period.

(p) Thirty bills were introduced the first time during this session, 1,683 bills were reintroduced during this session, which equals 1,713 bills in total introduced.

(q) Four resolutions were introduced the first time during this session, 58 were reintroduced during this session, which equals 62 resolutions in total introduced.

(r) Eighty-six bills were introduced the first time during this session, 1,663 bills were reintroduced during this session, which equals 1,749 bills in total introduced.

(s) Three resolutions were introduced the first time during this session, 58 were reintroduced during this session, which equals 61 resolutions in total introduced.

## Table 3.21
## STAFF FOR INDIVIDUAL LEGISLATORS

| State or other jurisdiction | Senate Capitol Personal | Senate Capitol Shared | Senate District | House/Assembly Capitol Personal | House/Assembly Capitol Shared | House/Assembly District |
|---|---|---|---|---|---|---|
| Alabama | ... | YR/2 | (a) | ... | YR/10 | (a) |
| Alaska (b) | YR/SO | ... | YR | YR/SO | ... | YR |
| Arizona | YR (c) | ... | ... | ... | YR (c) | ... |
| Arkansas | ... | YR | ... | ... | YR (d) | ... |
| California | YR | ... | YR | YR | ... | YR |
| Colorado | (e) | (e) | ... | (e) | (e) | ... |
| Connecticut (f) | YR/36 | ... | ... | ... | YR/38 | ... |
| Delaware | ....................................................................(g)........................................ | | | | | |
| Florida | YR (h) | ... | YR (h) | YR (h) | ... | YR (h) |
| Georgia | ... | YR/3, SO/68 | ... | ... | YR/25, SO/113 | ... |
| Hawaii | YR | ... | ... | YR | ... | ... |
| Idaho | ... | SO, YR (i) | ... | ... | SO, YR (i) | ... |
| Illinois | ... | YR/1 (j) | YR (j) | YR | YR/2 (j) | YR (j) |
| Indiana | ... | YR/2 (k) | ... | ... | YR | ... |
| Iowa | SO | ... | ... | SO | ... | ... |
| Kansas | SO/1 | ... | ... | (l) | SO/3 | ... |
| Kentucky | ... | YR (m) | ... | ... | YR (m) | ... |
| Louisiana | (n) | YR (o) | YR (n) | (n) | YR (o) | YR (n) |
| Maine | YR, SO (p) | YR/27, SO/7 | YR | ... | YR (q) | ... |
| Maryland | YR, SO (r) | ... | YR (r) | YR (r) | SO (r) | YR (r) |
| Massachusetts | YR | ... | ... | YR | ... | ... |
| Michigan | YR (s) | ... | ... | YR/2 (s) | ... | ... |
| Minnesota | YR (t) | Varies | ... | YR/3 | Varies | ... |
| Mississippi | ... | YR | ... | ... | YR | ... |
| Missouri | YR | YR | ... | YR | YR | ... |
| Montana | ... | SO | ... | ... | SO | ... |
| Nebraska | YR (u) | ... | ... | .........................Unicameral......................... | | |
| Nevada | SO (v) | YR | ... | SO (s)(v) | YR | ... |
| New Hampshire | ... | YR | ... | ... | YR | ... |
| New Jersey | YR (h) | ... | YR (h) | YR (h) | ... | YR (h) |
| New Mexico | SO (w) | ... | ... | ... | SO/2 | ... |
| New York | YR (x) | ... | YR (x) | YR (x) | ... | YR (x) |
| North Carolina | YR (y) | YR | ... | YR (y) | YR | ... |
| North Dakota | ... | SO (v) | ... | ... | SO (v) | ... |
| Ohio | YR/2 (z) | ... | (aa) | YR/1 (bb) | ... | (aa) |
| Oklahoma | YR/1 (cc) | YR (cc) | ... | YR (cc) | YR/1 (cc) | ... |
| Oregon | YR (dd) | YR | YR (ee) | YR (dd) | YR | YR (ee) |
| Pennsylvania | YR | ... | YR | YR | ... | YR |
| Rhode Island | ... | YR (ff) | ... | ... | YR (ff) | ... |
| South Carolina | ... | YR/2 | ... | YR/4 | ... | ... |
| South Dakota | (gg) | (gg) | ... | (gg) | (gg) | ... |
| Tennessee | YR/1 | ... | ... | (hh) | YR/1 | ... |
| Texas | YR/6 (ii) | ... | ... | YR/3 (ii) | ... | ... |
| Utah | (jj) | ... | ... | (jj) | ... | ... |
| Vermont | YR/1 (kk) | ... | ... | YR/1 (kk) | ... | ... |
| Virginia | SO/1 (ll) | ... | (ll) | SO (ll) | SO/2 | (ll) |
| Washington | YR/1 | ... | YR/1 | YR/1 | ... | YR/1 |
| West Virginia | SO | ... | ... | ... | SO/17 | ... |
| Wisconsin | YR (mm) | YR | YR (mm) | YR (mm) | YR | YR (mm) |
| Wyoming | ... | ... | ... | ... | ... | ... |
| American Samoa | ... | ... | ... | ... | ... | ... |
| Guam | ... | ... | ... | .........................Unicameral......................... | | |
| No. Mariana Islands | YR (nn) | (nn) | ... | YR (nn) | (nn) | (mm) |
| Puerto Rico | YR (nn) | ... | ... | YR (nn) | ... | ... |
| U.S. Virgin Islands | YR (nn) | ... | ... | .........................Unicameral......................... | | |

See footnotes at end of table.

## STAFF FOR INDIVIDUAL LEGISLATORS — Continued

*Source:* The Council of State Governments' survey, January 2011.

*Note:* For entries under column heading "Shared," figures after slash indicate approximate number of legislators per staff person, where available.

*Key:*

... — Staff not provided for individual legislators.

YR — Year-round.

SO — Session only.

IO — Interim only.

(a) Six counties have local delegation offices with shared staff.

(b) The number of staff per legislator varies depending on their position.

(c) Representatives share a secretary with another legislator; however, House leadership and committee chairs usually have their own secretarial staff. All legislators share professional research staff.

(d) The legislators share 21 staff people; 4.76 legislators per staff person.

(e) Senate: has 17 session only staff and 18 year-round staff. There are no district staffers, and since the entire staff works for multiple senators, they are not listed as shared. There are five session only staff in the bill room who are jointly managed by the Colorado Senate and House. House: year-round staff consists of five majority caucus staff; four minority caucus staff; 6 chief clerk non-partisan staff. The Colorado session only staff consists of three majority caucus staff; two minority caucus staff; 23 chief clerk non-partisan staff. The Colorado House of Representatives may have up to 65 legislative aides who serve as the legislator's personal staff. The legislative aides are employed for a total of 330 hours per legislator during the session only and they can work only in the capitol, and not in the district office. All of the legislators may hire an aide.

(f) The numbers are for staff assigned to specific legislators. There is additional staff working in the leadership offices that also support the rank and file members.

(g) Staffers are a combination of full time, part time, shared, personal, etc. and their assignments change throughout the year.

(h) Personal and district staff are the same. In Florida, two out of the three district employees may travel to the capitol for sessions.

(i) Idaho has 2 year-round full-time, 3 part-time year-round employees and 32 session only employees in the Senate. The House has 2 full-time and 1 part-time person year-round and 37 additional people during session.

(j) The only staff working for individual rank-and-file legislators are (1) one secretary in the Capitol complex for each two members and (1–2) district staff, whom legislators select and pay from a separate allowance for that purpose. Partisan staffers help individual legislators with many issues in addition to staffing committees.

(k) Leadership has one legislative assistant. During session, college interns are hired to provide additional staff — one for every two members. Leadership has one intern.

(l) One clerical staff person for three individual House members is the norm. Chairpersons are provided their own individual clerical staff person.

(m) The General Assembly is provided professional and clerical staff services by a centralized, non-partisan staff, with the exception of House and Senate leadership which employs partisan staff. No district staff provided.

(n) Each legislator may hire as many assistants as desired, but pay from public funds ranges from $2,000 to $3,000 per month per legislator.

Assistant(s) generally work in the district office but may also work at the capitol during the session.

(o) The six caucuses are assigned one full-time position each (potentially 24 legislators per one staff person).

(p) President's office: six year-round; Majority office: 7 year-round, 1 session only; Secretary's office: nine year-round, five session only.

(q) The 151 House members do not have individual staff. There are 21 people who work year-round in the two partisan offices, 12 of whom are legislative aides who primarily work directly with legislators.

(r) Senators have one year-round administrative aide and one session only secretary. Delegates have one part-time year-round administrative aide and a shared session only secretary. Legislators may increase staff and also hire student interns if their district office funds are used.

(s) Senate — majority, 5 staff per legislator; minority, 3 staff per legislator. House — 2 staff per legislator.

(t) One to two staff persons per legislator.

(u) Two to five staff persons per legislator.

(v) Secretarial staff; in North Dakota, leadership only.

(w) One plus; clerical plus attendant or analyst.

(x) House/party leaders determine allowances/funds for members once allocations are made. Members have considerable independence in hiring personal and committee staffs.

(y) Part time during interim.

(z) Some leadership offices have more.

(aa) Some legislators maintain district offices at their own expense.

(bb) Some offices have more.

(cc) Senate; Pro Tem — 5 staff persons; House: year-round one to five, majority party only; minority party one staff person per legislator. Committee, fiscal and legal staffs are available to legislators year-round.

(dd) Two staff persons per legislator during session.

(ee) Senate — Equivalent of one full-time staff. House — 1 during interim.

(ff) The General Assembly has a total of 280 full-time positions, 267 full-time shared staff and additional 13 full-time positions for the House.

(gg) The non-partisan Legislative Research Council serves all members of both houses year-round. Committee secretaries and legislative interns and pages provide support during the sessions.

(hh) Several House members have year-round personal staff. It depends on seniority, duties (such as committee chairs), and committee assignments.

(ii) Average staff numbers are from staff member totals from each chamber.

(jj) Most legislators are assigned student interns during session who are temporarily employed by OLRGC. Some legislators provide their own personal interns (volunteer/financial arrangements made between them).

(kk) No personal staff except one administrative assistant for the Speaker and one for the Senate Pro Tempore.

(ll) Senate — One administrative assistant (secretary) provided to the members during the session by the Clerk's offices. Members also receive a set dollar allowance to hire additional legislative assistants who may serve year-round at the capitol and in the district. House — Members also receive a set dollar allowance to hire additional legislative assistants who may serve year-round at the capitol and in the district.

(mm) Staffing levels vary according to majority/minority status and leadership or committee responsibilities. Members may assign staff to work in the district office.

(nn) Individual staffing and staff pool arrangements are at the discretion of the individual legislator.

## Table 3.22
## STAFF FOR LEGISLATIVE STANDING COMMITTEES

| State or other jurisdiction | Committee staff assistance | | | | Source of staff services ** | | | | | | | |
| | Senate | | House/Assembly | | Joint central agency (a) | | Chamber agency (b) | | Caucus or leadership | | Committee or committee chair | |
| | Prof. | Cler. | Prof. | Cler. | Prof. | Cler. | Prof. | Cler. | Prof. | Cler. | Prof. | Cler. |
|---|---|---|---|---|---|---|---|---|---|---|---|---|
| Alabama | • | ★ | • | ★ | B | B | B | B | ... | ... | ... | ... |
| Alaska | ★ | ★ | ★ | ★ | B | B | ... | ... | ... | ... | B | B |
| Arizona | ★ | ★ | ★ | ★ | B | B | B | B | B | B | B | B |
| Arkansas | ★ | ★ | ★ | ★ | B | B | B | B | ... | ... | ... | ... |
| California | ★ | ★ | ★ | ★ | B | B | B | B | B | B | B | B |
| Colorado | ★ | ... | ★ | ... | B | ... | B | B | B | B (c) | ... | ... |
| Connecticut | ... | ★ | ... | ★ | B | ... | ... | ... | B | B | ... | B |
| Delaware | • | ★ | • | ★ | B | ... | B | ... | B | ... | ... | B |
| Florida | ★ | ★ | ★ | ★ | B | B | B | B | B | B | B | B |
| Georgia | • | ★ | • | ★ | B | B | B | B | B | B | B | ... |
| Hawaii | • | ★ | ★ | ★ | B | B | B | B | B | B | B | B |
| Idaho | ... | ★ | ... | ★ | B (d) | B (d) | ... | ... | ... | B (e) | ... | ... |
| Illinois | ★ | ★ | ★ | ★ | ... | ... | B | B | B | B | ... | ... |
| Indiana | ★ | ... | • | ... | ... | ... | S | ... | S | ... | ... | ... |
| Iowa | ★ | ... | ★ | ... | B | ... | (f) | B | B | ... | ... | ... |
| Kansas | ★ | ★ | ★ | ★ | B | B (g) | B | B | B | B | B | B |
| Kentucky | ★ | ★ | ★ | ★ | B | B | ... | ... | B (h) | B (h) | ... | ... |
| Louisiana | ★(i) | ★ | ★(i) | ★ | B | B | B | B | B | B | B (j) | B (j) |
| Maine | ★(k) | ★(k) | ★(k) | ★(k) | B | B | B | B | B | B | ... | B |
| Maryland | ★(l) | ★(l) | ★(l) | ★(l) | B | B | ... | ... | ... | ... | ... | .. |
| Massachusetts | ★ | ★ | ★ | ★ | ... | ... | ... | ... | ... | ... | ... | ... |
| Michigan | ★ | ★ | ★ | ★ | B | ... | ... | H | B | ... | ... | S |
| Minnesota | ★ | ★ | ★ | ★ | ... | ... | B | S | B | S | B | B |
| Mississippi | • | ★ | • | ★ | ... | ... | B | B | ... | ... | B | B |
| Missouri | ★ | ... | ★ | ... | B | ... | B | ... | S | S | B | ... |
| Montana | ★ | ★ | ★ | ★ | B | ... | ... | B | ... | ... | ... | ... |
| Nebraska | ★ | ★ | U | U | (m) | ... | (m) | ... | (m) | ... | (m) | ... |
| Nevada | ★ | ★ | ★ | ★ | B | ... | ... | B | ... | ... | ... | ... |
| New Hampshire | • | ★ | ★ | ★ | B | B | B | B | ... | H | ... | H |
| New Jersey | ★ | ★ | ★ | ★ | B | B | B | B | ... | ... | ... | ... |
| New Mexico | ★ | ★ | ★ | ★ | ... | ... | B | B | ... | ... | ... | ... |
| New York | ★ | ★ | ★ | ★ | B | B | B | B | B | B | B | B |
| North Carolina | ★ | ★(n) | ★ | ★(n) | B | ... | ... | ... | ... | ... | ... | B (n) |
| North Dakota | • | ★ | • | ★ | B | B | ... | ... | ... | ... | ... | ... |
| Ohio | ★ | ★ | ★ | ★ | B | ... | ... | ... | ... | B | B | B |
| Oklahoma | ★ | ★ | ★ | ★ | ... | ... | B | B | ... | ... | B | B |
| Oregon | ★ | ★ | ★ | ★ | B | B | B | B | B | B | B | B |
| Pennsylvania | ★ | ★ | ★ | ★ | B | B | B | B | B | B | B | B |
| Rhode Island | • | ★ | • | ★ | B | B | ... | B | ... | ... | B | ... |
| South Carolina | ★ | ★ | ★ | ★ | B | B | B | B | B | B | B | B |
| South Dakota | ★ | ★ | ★ | ★ | B | ... | ... | (l) | ... | (l) | ... | (l) |
| Tennessee | ★ | ★ | ★ | ★ | B | ... | B | B | ... | ... | ... | B |
| Texas | ★ | ★ | ★ | ★ | B | B | ... | B | ... | ... | B | B |
| Utah | ★ | ★(r) | ★ | ★(r) | B | B | ... | B | B (s) | B | ... | ... |
| Vermont | ★ | • | ★ | • | B | ... | ... | ... | ... | ... | ... | ... |
| Virginia | ★ | ★ | ★ | ★ | B | ... | B | B | ... | ... | (o) | (o) |
| Washington | ★ | ★ | ★ | ★ | ... | ... | B | B | B | B | B | B |
| West Virginia | ★ | ★ | ★ | ★ | B | B | B | B | B | B | B | B |
| Wisconsin | ★ | ★ | ★ | ★ | B | ... | ... | ... | ... | ... | (p) | B |
| Wyoming | ... | ★ | ... | ★ | ... | ... | ... | B | ... | ... | ... | ... |
| American Samoa | • | ★ | • | ★ | B | B | B | B | ... | ... | B | ... |
| Guam | ★ | ★ | U | U | ... | ... | S | S | ... | ... | ... | ... |
| No. Mariana Islands | ★ | ★ | ★ | ★ | B (q) | B (q) | B (q) | B (q) | B (q) | B (q) | B (q) | B (q) |
| Puerto Rico | ★ | ★ | ★ | ★ | B (q) | B (q) | B (q) | B (q) | B (q) | B (q) | B (q) | B (q) |
| U.S. Virgin Islands | ★ | ★ | U | U | S (q) | S (q) | S (q) | S (q) | S (q) | S (q) | S (q) | S (q) |

See footnotes at end of table.

# STAFF FOR LEGISLATIVE STANDING COMMITTEES — Continued

*Source:* The Council of State Governments' survey, February 2011.

** — Multiple entries reflect a combination of organizations and location of services.

*Key:*

★ — All committees

● — Some committees

... — Services not provided

B — Both chambers

H — House

S — Senate

U — Unicameral

(a) Includes legislative council or service agency or central management agency.

(b) Includes chamber management agency, office of clerk or secretary and House or Senate research office.

(c) Senate—there is secretarial staff for both majority and minority offices for the Senate in the Capitol. Most of the clerical work is done by caucus staff.

House—the clerical and secretarial staff for the House is more centralized and is supervised by the Clerk of the House.

(d) Professional staff and clerical support is provided via the Legislative Services Office, a non-partisan office serving all members on a year round basis.

(e) Leadership in each party hire their respective support staff.

(f) The Senate secretary and House clerk maintain supervision of committee clerks.

(g) Senators and House chairpersons select their secretaries and notify the central administrative services agency; all administrative employee matters handled by the agency.

(h) Leadership employs partisan staff to provide professional and clerical services. However, all members, including leadership are also served by the centralized, non-partisan staff.

(i) House Appropriations and Senate Finance Committees have Legislative Fiscal Office staff at their hearings.

(j) Staff are assigned to each committee but work under the direction of the chair.

(k) Standing committees are joint House and Senate committees.

(l) The clerical support comes from employees who are hired to work only during the legislative sessions. They are employees of either the House or the Senate, and are not part of the central agency.

(m) Professional services are not provided, except that the staff of the Legislative Fiscal Office serves the Appropriations Committee. Individual senators are responsible for the process of hiring their own staff.

(n) Member's personal secretary serves as a clerk to the committee or subcommittee that the member chairs.

(o) The House Appropriations Committee and the Senate Finance Committees have their own staff. The staff members work under the direction of the chair.

(p) Standing committees are staffed by subject specialist from the Joint Legislative Council.

(q) In general, the legislative service agency provides legal and staff assistance for legislative meetings and provides associated materials. Individual legislators hire personal or committee staff as their budgets provide and at their own discretion.

(r) Clerical staff not assigned to Rules Cmtes.

(s) Refers only to Chief Deputy of the Senate and Chief of Staff in the House.

**Table 3.23**
**STANDING COMMITTEES: APPOINTMENT AND NUMBER**

| State or other jurisdiction | Committee members appointed by: | | Committee chairpersons appointed by: | | Number of standing committees during regular 2011–12 session | | |
|---|---|---|---|---|---|---|---|
| | Senate | House/Assembly | Senate | House/Assembly | Senate | House/Assembly | Joint |
| Alabama | CC | S | CC | S | 24 | 31 | 5 |
| Alaska | CC | CC | CC | CC | 10 | 10 | 7 |
| Arizona | P | S | P | S | 15 | 17 | 16 |
| Arkansas | (a) | (b) | (a) | S | 9 | 10 | 24 |
| California | CR | S | CR | S | 24 | 30 | 7 |
| Colorado | MjL | S | MjL | S | 10 | 10 | 6 |
| Connecticut | CC | CC | CC | CC | (c) | (c) | 21(c) |
| Delaware | PT | S | PT | S | 25 | 25 | 3 |
| Florida | P | S | P | S | 19 | 10 | 5 |
| Georgia | CC | S | CC | S | 28 | 38 | 1 |
| Hawaii | P | (e) | P | (d) | 14 | 20 | ... |
| Idaho | PT (f) | S | PT | S | 10 | 14 | 3 |
| Illinois | P, MnL | S, MnL | P | S | 27 | 47 | 4 |
| Indiana | PT | S | PT | S | 20 | 24 | ... |
| Iowa | MjL, MnL | S | MjL | S | 17 | 19 | 1 |
| Kansas | (g) | S | (g) | S | 18 | 30 | 19 |
| Kentucky | P | S | P | S | 15 | 19 | 15 |
| Louisiana | P | S (h) | P | S | 17 | 16 | 2 |
| Maine | P | S | P | S | 5 | 6 | 17 (i) |
| Maryland | P | S | P | S | 6 | 7 | 19 |
| Massachusetts | P | S | P | S | 7 | 9 | 27 |
| Michigan | MjL | S | MjL | S | 20 | 19 | ... |
| Minnesota | CR | S | MjL | S | 16 | 21 | ... |
| Mississippi | P | S | P | S | 433 | 46 | 2 |
| Missouri | PT (j) | S | PT | S | 18 | 43 | 20 |
| Montana | CC | S | CC | S | 17 | 16 | 6 |
| Nebraska | CC | U | E | U | 14 | U | U |
| Nevada | MjL | S | MjL | S | 11 | 10 | ... |
| New Hampshire | P (k) | S (k) | P (k) | S (k) | 12 | 16 | ... |
| New Jersey | CC | CC | CC | CC | 16 | 23 | 5 |
| New Mexico | CC | S | CC | S | 9 (l) | 16 (l) | ... |
| New York | PT | S | PT | S | 33 | 37 | ... |
| North Carolina | CC | CC | CC | CC | 18 | 19 | ... |
| North Dakota | CC | CC | MjL | MjL | 11 | 12 (n) | ... |
| Ohio | P (m) | S (m) | P (m) | S (m) | 14 | 17 | 5 |
| Oklahoma | PT | S | PT | S | 15 | 19 | 0 |
| Oregon | P | S | P | S | 10 | 13 | 7 |
| Pennsylvania | PT | S | PT | S | 22 | 27 | ... |
| Rhode Island | P | S | P | S | 10 | 11 | 3 |
| South Carolina | (o) | S | (p) | E | 15 | 11 | ... |
| South Dakota | PT | S | PT | S | 13 | 13 | 1 |
| Tennessee | S | S | S | S | 9 | 14 | 15 |
| Texas | P | S (q) | P | S | 18 | 36 | 1 |
| Utah | P | S | P | S | 12 | 15 | 0 |
| Vermont | CC | S | CC | S | 12 | 15 | 13 |
| Virginia | E | S | (r) | S | 11 | 14 | ... |
| Washington | P(s) | S | E (t) | S | 15 | 21 | 7 |
| West Virginia | P | S | P | S | 18 | 18 | 5 |
| Wisconsin | MjL | S | MjL | S | 17 | 32 | 10 |
| Wyoming | P | S | P | S | 12 | 12 | 12 |
| Dist. of Columbia | (u) | U | (u) | U | 14 | U | U |
| American Samoa | P | S | E | S | 16 | 20 | ... |
| Guam | (v) | U | (v) | U | 12 | U | ... |
| No. Mariana Islands | P | S | P | S | 9 | 7 | ... |
| Puerto Rico | P | S | P | S | 23 | 30 | ... |
| U.S. Virgin Islands | E | U | E | U | 10 | U | U |

See footnotes at end of table.

# STANDING COMMITTEES: APPOINTMENT AND NUMBER — Continued

*Source:* The Council of State Governments' survey January 2010 and The Council of State Governments' survey April 2012.

*Key:*
CC — Committee on Committees
CR — Committee on Rules
E — Election
MjL — Majority Leader
MnL — Minority Leader
P — President
PT — President pro tempore
S — Speaker
U — Unicameral Legislature
. . . — None reported.

(a) Selection process based on seniority.

(b) Members of the standing committees shall be selected by House District Caucuses with each caucus selecting five members for each "A" standing committee and five members for each "B" standing committee.

(c) Substantive standing committees are joint committees. Connecticut, 21 (there are also three statutory and four select committees for the House and the Senate).

(d) By resolution with members of majority party designating the chair, vice-chairs and majority party members of committees, and members of minority party designating minority party members.

(e) By resolution, with members of majority party designating the chair, vice-chairs and majority party members of committees, and members of minority party designating minority party members.

(f) Committee members appointed by the Senate leadership under the direction of the president pro tempore, by and with the Senate's consent.

(g) Committee on Organization, Calendar and Rules.

(h) Speaker appoints only 12 of the 19 members of the Committee on Appropriations.

(i) There are currently 17 Joint Standing Committees, two Joint Select Committees, and a joint Government Oversight Committee.

(j) Senate minority committee members chosen by minority caucus, but appointed by president pro tempore.

(k) Senate president and House speaker consult with minority leaders.

(l) Senate: includes eight substantive committees and one procedural committee. House: includes 12 substantive committees and three procedural committees.

(m) The minority leader may recommend for consideration minority party members for each committee.

(n) The House had a Constitutional Revision Committee.

(o) Appointment based on seniority (Senate Rule 19D).

(p) Appointed by seniority which is determined by tenure within the committee rather than tenure within the Senate. Also, chair is based on the majority party within the committee (Senate Rule 19E).

(q) For each standing substantive committee of the House, except for the appropriations committee, a maximum of one-half of the membership, exclusive of chair and vice-chair, is determined by seniority; the remaining membership of the committee is determined by the speaker.

(r) Senior member of the majority party on the committee is the chair.

(s) Lieutenant governor is president of the Senate.

(t) Recommended by the Committee on Committees, approved by the president, then confirmed by the Senate.

(u) Chair of the Council.

(v) Members are appointed by the Chairperson; Chairperson is elected during majority caucus prior to inauguration.

# Table 3.24
## RULES ADOPTION AND STANDING COMMITTEES: PROCEDURE

| State or other jurisdiction | Constitution permits each legislative body to determine its own rules | Committee meetings open to public* | | Specific, advance notice provisions for committee meetings or hearings | Voting/roll call provisions to report a bill to floor |
|---|---|---|---|---|---|
| | | Senate | House/ Assembly | | |
| Alabama................ | ★ | ★ | ★ | Senate: 4 hours, if possible<br>House: 24 hours, except Rules & Local Legislations Committee. Exceptions after 27th legislative day and special sessions. | Senate: final vote on a bill is recorded.<br>House: recorded vote if requested by member of committee and sustained by one additional committee member. |
| Alaska................... | ... | ★ | ★ | For meetings, by 4 p.m. on the preceding Thurs.; for first hearings on bills, 5 days | Roll call vote on any measure taken upon request by any member of either house. |
| Arizona................. | ★ | ★ | ★ | Senate: Written agenda for each regular and special meeting containing all bills, memorials and resolutions to be considered shall be distributed to each member of the committee and to the Secretary of the Senate at least five days prior to the committee meeting<br>House: The committee chair shall prepare an agenda and distribute copies to committee members, the Information Desk and the Chief Clerk's Office by 4 p.m. each Wednesday for all standing committees meeting on Monday of the following week and 4 p.m. each Thursday for all standing committees meeting on any day except Monday of the following week. | Senate: roll call vote.<br>House: roll call vote. |
| Arkansas............ | ★ | ★ | ★ | Senate: 2 days<br>House: 18 hours (2 hours with 2/3's vote of the committee) | Senate: roll call votes are recorded.<br>House: report of committee recommendation signed by committee chair. |
| California ........... | ★ | ★ | ★ | Senate: advance notice provisions exist.<br>House: advance notice provisions exist. | Senate: roll call.<br>House: roll call. |
| Colorado.............. | ★ | ★ | ★ | Senate: final action on a measure is prohibited unless notice is posted one calendar day prior to its consideration. The prohibition does not apply if the action receives a majority vote of the committee.<br>House: Meeting publicly announced while the House is in actual session as much in advance as possible. | Senate: final action by recorded roll call vote.<br>House: final action by recorded roll call vote. |
| Connecticut.......... | ★ | ★ | ★ | Senate: one day notice for meetings, five days notice for hearings.<br>House: one day notice for meetings, five days notice for hearings. | Senate: roll call required.<br>House: roll call required. |
| Delaware ............. | ★ | ★ | ★ | Senate: agenda released one day before meetings<br>House: agenda for meetings released four days before meetings | Senate: results of all committee reports are recorded.<br>House: results of all committee reports are recorded. |
| Florida ................ | ★ | ★ | ★ | Senate: during session — 3 hours notice for first 50 days, 4 hours thereafter<br>House: two days. | Senate: vote on final passage is recorded.<br>House: vote on final passage is recorded. |
| Georgia................ | ★ | ★ | ★ | Senate: a list of committee meetings shall be posted by 10 a.m. the preceding Friday<br>House: none | Senate: bills can be voted out by voice vote or roll call.<br>House: bills can be voted out by voice vote or roll call. |

See footnotes at end of table.

# RULES ADOPTION AND STANDING COMMITTEES: PROCEDURE — Continued

| State or other jurisdiction | Constitution permits each legislative body to determine its own rules | Committee meetings open to public* | | Specific, advance notice provisions for committee meetings or hearings | Voting/roll call provisions to report a bill to floor |
|---|---|---|---|---|---|
| | | Senate | House/ Assembly | | |
| Hawaii | ★ | ★(a) | ★(a) | Senate: 72 hours before 1st referral committee meetings, 48 hours before subsequent referral committee<br>House: 48 hours | Senate: A quorum of committee members must be present before voting.<br>House: A quorum of committee members must be present before voting. |
| Idaho | ★ | ★(a) | ★(a) | Senate: none<br>House: per rule; chair provides notice of next meeting dates and times to clerk to be read prior to adjournment each day of session. | Senate: bills can be voted out by voice vote or roll call.<br>House: bills can be voted out by voice vote or roll call. |
| Illinois | ★ | ★(b) | ★(b) | Senate: 6 days<br>House: 6 days | Senate: votes on all legislative measures acted upon are recorded.<br>House: votes on all legislative matters acted upon are recorded. |
| Indiana | ★ | ★ | ★ | Senate: 48 hours<br>House: prior to adjournment of the meeting day next preceding the meeting or announced during session | Senate: committee reports—do pass; do pass amended, reported out without recommendation.<br>House: majority of quorum; vote can be by roll call or consent. |
| Iowa | ★ | ★ | ★ | Senate: none<br>House: none | Senate: final action by roll call.<br>House: committee reports include roll call on final disposition. |
| Kansas | ★ | ★ | ★ | Senate: none<br>House: none | Senate: vote recorded upon request of member.<br>House: total for and against actions recorded. |
| Kentucky | ★ | ★ | ★ | Senate: none<br>House: none | Senate: each member's vote recorded on each bill.<br>House: each member's vote recorded on each bill. |
| Louisiana | ★ | ★(a) | ★(a) | Senate: no later than 1 p.m. the preceding day<br>House: no later than 4 p.m. the preceding day | Senate: any motion to report an instrument is decided by a roll call vote.<br>House: any motion to report an instrument is decided by a roll call vote. |
| Maine | ★ | ★ | ★ | Senate: must be advertised two weekends in advance.<br>House: must be advertised two weekends in advance. | Senate: recorded vote is required to report a bill out of committee.<br>House: recorded vote is required to report a bill out of committee. |
| Maryland | ★ | ★ | ★ | Senate: none (c)<br>House: none (c) | Senate: the final vote on any bill is recorded.<br>House: the final vote on any bill is recorded. |
| Massachusetts | ★ | ★ | ★ | Senate: 48 hours for public hearings<br>House: 48 hours for public hearings | Senate: voice vote or recorded roll call vote at the request of 2 committee members.<br>House: recorded vote upon request by a member. |
| Michigan | ★ | ★ | ★ | Senate and House: Notice shall be published in the journal in advance of a hearing. Notice of a special meeting shall be posted at least 18 hours before a meeting. Special provisions for conference committees. | Senate: committee reports include the vote of each member on any bill.<br>House: the daily journal reports the roll call on all motions to report bills. |
| Minnesota | ★ | ★ | ★ | Senate: 3 days<br>House: 3 days | Senate: not needed.<br>House: not needed. |

See footnotes at end of table.

# RULES ADOPTION AND STANDING COMMITTEES: PROCEDURE—Continued

| State or other jurisdiction | Constitution permits each legislative body to determine its own rules* | Committee meetings open to public* | | Specific, advance notice provisions for committee meetings or hearings | Voting/roll call provisions to report a bill to floor |
|---|---|---|---|---|---|
| | | Senate | House/ Assembly | | |
| Mississippi | ★ | ★ | ★ | Senate: none<br>House: none | House: recorded roll call vote upon request by a member.<br>Senate: bills are reported out by voice vote or recorded roll call vote. |
| Missouri | ★ | ★ | ★ | Senate: 24 hours<br>House: 24 hours | House: bills are reported out by voice vote or recorded roll call vote.<br>Senate: yeas and nays are reported in journal. |
| Montana | ★ | ★ | ★ | Senate: 3 legislative days<br>House: none | House: bills are reported out by a recorded roll call vote.<br>Senate: every vote of each member is recorded and made public. |
| Nebraska | ★ | ★ | U | Seven calendar days notice before hearing a bill. | House: every vote of each member is recorded and made public. In executive session, majority of the committee must vote in favor of the motion made. |
| Nevada | ★ | ★ | ★ | Senate: by rule—"adequate notice" shall be provided. (d)<br>House: by rule—"adequate notice" shall be provided. (d) | Senate: recorded vote is taken upon final committee action on bills.<br>House: recorded vote is taken upon final committee action on bills. |
| New Hampshire | ★ | ★ | ★ | Senate: 4 days<br>House: no less than 4 days | Senate: committees may report a bill out by voice or recorded roll call vote.<br>House: committees may report a bill out by voice or recorded roll call vote. |
| New Jersey | ★ | ★ | ★ | Senate: 5 days<br>House: 5 days | Senate: the chair reports the vote of each member present on a motion to report a bill.<br>House: the chair reports the vote of each member present on motions with respect to bills. |
| New Mexico | ★ | ★ | ★ | Senate: none<br>House: none | Senate: vote on the final report of the committee taken by yeas and nays. Roll call vote upon request.<br>House: vote on the final report of the committee taken by yeas and nays. Roll call vote upon request. |
| New York | ★ | ★(a) | ★(a) | Senate: Rules require that notice be given for public hearings, but the Rules are silent as to how long.<br>House: 1 week for hearings, Thursday of prior week for meetings. | Senate: majority vote required<br>House: majority vote required |
| North Carolina | (f) | ★ | ★ | Senate: none (e)<br>House: none (e) | Senate: no roll call vote may be taken in any committee.<br>House: roll call vote taken on any question when requested by member & sustained by one-fifth of members present. |
| North Dakota | ★ | ★ | ★ | Senate: hearing schedule printed Friday mornings.<br>House: hearing schedule printed Friday mornings. | Senate: included with minutes from standing committee.<br>House: included with minutes from standing committee. |

See footnotes at end of table.

# RULES ADOPTION AND STANDING COMMITTEES: PROCEDURE — Continued

| State or other jurisdiction | Constitution permits each legislative body to determine its own rules | Committee meetings open to public* | | Specific, advance notice provisions for committee meetings or hearings | Voting/roll call provisions to report a bill to floor |
|---|---|---|---|---|---|
| | | Senate | House/Assembly | | |
| Ohio | ★ | ★ | ★ | Senate: 2 days. In a case of necessity, the notice of hearing may be given in a shorter period by such reasonable method as prescribed by the Committee on Rules. House: 5 days. If an emergency requires consideration of a matter at a meeting not announced on notice, the chair may revise or supplement the notice at any time before or during the meeting to include the matter. | Senate: the affirmative votes of a majority of all members of a committee shall be necessary to report or to postpone further consideration of bills or resolutions. Every member present shall vote, unless excused by the chair. At discretion of chair the roll call may be continued for a vote by any member who was present at the prior meeting, but no later than 10 a.m. of next calendar day. House: the affirmative votes of a majority of all members of a committee shall be necessary to report or to postpone further consideration of bills or resolutions. Every member present shall vote, unless excused by the chair. At discretion of chair the roll call may be continued for a vote by any member who was present at the prior meeting, but no later than 12 noon one day following the meeting. Members must be present in order to vote on amendment. |
| Oklahoma | ★ | ★ | ★ | Senate: 3 day notice. House: 3 day notice. | Senate: roll call vote. House: roll call vote. |
| Oregon | ★ | ★ | ★ | Senate: At least 48 hrs. notice except at the end of session when President invokes 1 hr. notice when adjournment sine die is imminent. House: First public hearing on a measure must have at least 72 hours notice, all other meetings at least 48 hours notice except in case of emergency. | Senate: affirmative roll call vote of majority of members of committee and recorded in committee minutes. House: affirmative roll call vote of majority of members of committee and recorded in committee minutes. |
| Pennsylvania | ★ | ★ | ★ | Senate: written notice to members containing date, time, place and agenda. House: written notice to members containing date, time, place and agenda | Senate: a majority vote of committee members. House: a majority vote of committee members. |
| Rhode Island | ★ | ★ | ★ | Senate: notice required. House: notice required. | Senate: majority vote of the members present. House: majority vote of the members present. |
| South Carolina | ★ | ★ | ★ | Senate: 24 hours House: 24 hours | Senate: before the expiration of five days from the date of reference, any bill, may be recalled from committee by the vote of three-fourths of the Senators present and voting. House: favorable report out of committee (majority of committee members voting in favor). |
| South Dakota | ★ | ★ | ★ | Senate and House: at least one legislative day must intervene between the date of posting and the date of consideration in both houses. | Senate and House: a majority vote of the members-elect taken by roll call is needed for final disposition on a bill. This applies to both houses. |
| Tennessee | ★ | ★ | ★ | Senate: 6 days House: 72 hours | Senate: majority referral to Calendar and Rules Committee, majority of Calendar and Rules Committee referral to floor. House: majority referral to Calendar and Rules Committee, majority of Calendar and Rules Committee referral to floor. |

See footnotes at end of table.

# RULES ADOPTION AND STANDING COMMITTEES: PROCEDURE — Continued

| State or other jurisdiction | Constitution permits each legislative body to determine its own rules | Committee meetings open to public* — Senate | Committee meetings open to public* — House/ Assembly | Specific, advance notice provisions for committee meetings or hearings | Voting/roll call provisions to report a bill to floor |
|---|---|---|---|---|---|
| Texas | ★ | ★ | ★ | Senate: 24 hours<br>House: The House requires five calendar days notice before a public hearing at which testimony will be taken, and two hours notice or an announcement from the floor before a formal meeting (testimony cannot be taken at a formal meeting). 24 hour advance notice is required during special session | Senate: bills are reported by recorded roll call vote.<br>House: committee reports include the record vote by which the report was adopted, including the vote of each member. |
| Utah | ★ | ★ | ★ | Senate: Not less than 24 hours public notice.<br>House: Not less than 24 hours public notice. | Senate: Voice vote accepting the recommendation of the committee.<br>House: Voice vote accepting the recommendation of the committee. |
| Vermont | ★ | ★ | ★ | Senate: none<br>House: none | Senate: vote is recorded for each committee member for every bill considered.<br>House: vote is recorded for each committee member for every bill considered. |
| Virginia | ★ | ★(a) | ★(a) | Senate: none<br>House: none | Senate: recorded vote, except resolutions that do not have a specific vote requirement under the Rules. In these cases, a voice vote is sufficient.<br>House: vote of each member is taken and recorded for each measure. |
| Washington | ★ | ★ | ★ | Senate: 5 days<br>House: 5 days | Senate: bills reported from a committee carry a majority report which must be signed by a majority of the committee.<br>House: every vote to report a bill out of committee is by yeas and nays; the names of the members voting are recorded in the report. |
| West Virginia | ★ | ★ | ★ | Senate: none<br>House: none | Senate: majority of committee members voting.<br>House: majority of committee members voting. |
| Wisconsin | ★ | ★ | ★ | Senate: Monday noon of the preceding week.<br>House: Monday noon of the preceding week. | Senate: number of ayes and noes, and members absent or not voting are reported.<br>House: number of ayes and noes are recorded. |
| Wyoming | ★ | ★ | ★ | Senate: by 3 p.m. of previous day<br>House: by 3 p.m. of previous day | Senate: bills are reported out by recorded roll call vote.<br>House: bills are reported out by recorded roll call vote. |
| American Samoa | ★ | ★(g) | ★(g) | Senate: At least 3 calendar days in advance.<br>House: At least 3 calendar days in advance. | Senate/House: There are four methods of ascertaining the decision upon any matter: by raising of hands; by secret ballot, when authorized by law; by rising; and by call of the members and recorded by the Clerk of the vote of each. |
| Guam | ★ | ★ | U | Five days prior to public hearings. | Majority vote of committee members. |
| Puerto Rico | ★ | ★ | ★ | Senate: Must be notified every Thurs., one week in advance.<br>House: 24 hours advanced notice, no later than 4 p.m. previous day | Senate: bills reported from a committee carry a majority vote<br>House: bills reported from a committee carry a majority vote by referendum or in an ordinary meeting. |
| U.S. Virgin Islands | ★ | ★ | U | Seven calendar days. | Bills must be reported to floor by Rules Committee. |

See footnotes at end of table.

## RULES ADOPTION AND STANDING COMMITTEES: PROCEDURE — Continued

*Source:* The Council of State Governments' survey, January 2009 with update August 2010.

*Key:*

★ – Yes

* – Notice of committee meetings may also be subject to state open meetings laws; in some cases, listed times may be subject to suspension or enforceable only to the extent "feasible" or "whenever possible."

U – Unicameral.

(a) Certain matters may be discussed in executive session. (Other states permit meetings to be closed for various reasons, but their rules do not specifically mention "executive session.")

(b) A session of a house or one of its committees can be closed to the public if two-thirds of the members elected to that house determine that the public interest so requires. A meeting of a joint committee or commission can be closed if two-thirds of the members of both houses so vote.

(c) General directive in the Senate and House rules to the Department of Legislative Services to compile a list of the meetings and to arrange for distribution which in practice is done on a regular basis.

(d) Senate: This rule may be suspended for emergencies by a two thirds vote of appointed committee members. House: This rule may be suspended for emergencies by a two thirds vote of appointed committee members. In the Assembly this rule does not apply to committee meetings held on the floor during recess or conference committee meetings.

(e) If public hearing, five calendar days.

(f) Not referenced specifically, but each body publishes rules.

(g) Unless privileged information is being discussed with counsel or the security of the territory is involved.

# Table 3.25
# LEGISLATIVE REVIEW OF ADMINISTRATIVE REGULATIONS: STRUCTURES AND PROCEDURES

| State or other jurisdiction | Type of reviewing committee | Rules reviewed | Time limits in review process |
|---|---|---|---|
| Alabama | Joint bipartisan, standing committee | P | If not approved or disapproved within 35 days of filing, rule is approved. If disapproved by committee, rule suspended until adjournment, next regular session or until legislature by resolution revokes suspension. Rule takes effect upon final adjournment unless committee's disapproval is sustained by legislature. The committee may approve a rule. |
| Alaska | Joint bipartisan, standing committee and Legislative Affairs Agency review of proposed regulations. | P,E | ... |
| Arizona | Joint bipartisan | P,E | ... |
| Arkansas | Joint bipartisan | P,E | ... |
| California | ... | P,E | Regulation review conducted by independent executive branch agency. The only existing rules that are reviewed are emergency regulations—all others are reviewed prior to implementation. |
| Colorado | Joint bipartisan | E | Rules continue unless the annual legislative Rule Reviews Bill discontinues a rule. The Rule Reviews Bill is effective upon the governor's signature. |
| Connecticut | Joint bipartisan, standing committee | P | Submittal of proposed regulation shall be on the first Tuesday of month; after first submittal committee has 65 days after date of submission. Second submittal: 35 days for committee to review/take action on revised regulation. |
| Delaware | Attorney General review | P | The attorney general shall review any rule or regulation promulgated by any state agency and inform the issuing agency in writing as to the potential of the rule or regulation to result in a taking of private property before the rule or regulation may become effective. |
| Florida | Joint bipartisan | P,E | ... |
| Georgia | Standing committee | P | The agency notifies the Legislative Counsel 30 days prior to the effective dates of proposed rules. |
| Hawaii | Legislative agency | P,E | In Hawaii, the legislative reference bureau assists agencies to comply with a uniform format of style. This does not affect the status of rules. |
| Idaho | Germane joint subcommittees | P | Germane joint subcommittees vote to object or not object to a rule. They cannot reject a proposed rule directly, only advise an agency which may choose to adopt a rule subject to review by the full legislature. The legislature as a whole reviews rules during the first three weeks of session to determine if they comport with state law. The Senate and House may reject rules via resolution adopted by both. Rules imposing fees must be approved or are deemed approved unless rejected. Temporary rules expire at the end of session unless extended by concurrent resolution. |
| Illinois | Joint bipartisan | P,E | An agency proposing non-emergency regulations must allow 45 days for public comment. At least five days after any public hearing on the proposal, the agency must give notice of the proposal to the Joint Committee on Administrative Rules, and allow it 45 days to approve or object to the proposed regulations. |
| Indiana | Joint bipartisan | P | ... |
| Iowa | Joint bipartisan | P,E | ... |
| Kansas | Joint bipartisan | P | Agencies must give a 60-day notice to the public and the Joint Committee of their intent to adopt or amend specific rules and regulations, a copy of which must be provided to the committee. Within the 60-day comment period, the Joint Committee must review and comment, if it feels necessary, on the proposals. Final rules and regulations are resubmitted to the committee to determine whether further expression of concern is necessary. |
| Kentucky | Joint bipartisan statutory committee | P,E | 45 days. |

See footnotes at end of table.

## LEGISLATIVE REVIEW OF ADMINISTRATIVE REGULATIONS: STRUCTURES AND PROCEDURES — Continued

| State or other jurisdiction | Type of reviewing committee | Rules reviewed | Time limits in review process |
|---|---|---|---|
| Louisiana (b) | Standing committee | P | All proposed rules and fees are submitted to designated standing committees of the legislature. If a rule or fee is unacceptable, the committee sends a written report to the governor. The governor has 10 days to disapprove the committee report. If both Senate and House committees fail to find the rule unacceptable, or if the governor disapproves the action of a committee within 10 days, the agency may adopt the rule change. (d) |
| Maine | Joint bipartisan, standing committee | P | One legislative session. |
| Maryland | Joint bipartisan | P,E | Proposed regulations are submitted for review at least 15 days before publication. Publication triggers 45 day review period which may be extended by the committee, but if agreement cannot be reached, the governor may instruct the agency to modify or withdraw the regulation, or may approve its adoption. |
| Massachusetts (b) | Public hearing by agency | P | In Massachusetts, the General Court (Legislature) may by statute authorize an administrative agency to promulgate regulations. The promulgation of such regulations are then governed by Chapter 30A of the Massachusetts General Laws. Chapter 30A requires 21 day notice to the public of a public hearing on a proposed regulation. After public hearing the proposed regulation is filed with the state secretary who approves it if it is in conformity with Chapter 30A. The state secretary maintains a register entitled "Massachusetts Register" and the regulation does not become effective until published in the register. The agency may promulgate amendments to the regulations following the same process. |
| Michigan | Joint bipartisan | P | Joint Committee on Administrative Rules (JCAR) has 15 session days in which to consider the rule and to object to the rule by filing a notice of objection. If no objection is made, the rules may be filed and go into effect. If JCAR does formally object, bills to block the rules are introduced in both houses of the legislature simultaneously by the committee chair and placed directly on the Senate and House calendars for action. If the bills are not enacted by the legislature and presented to the governor within 15 session days, the rules may go into effect. Between legislative sessions the committee can meet and suspend rules promulgated during the interim between sessions. |
| Minnesota | Joint bipartisan, standing committee | P,E | Minnesota Statute Sec. 3.842, subd. 4a |
| Mississippi | | | .................................(a)................................. |
| Missouri | Joint bipartisan, standing committee | P,E | The committee must disapprove a final order of rulemaking within 30 days upon receipt or the order of rulemaking is deemed approved. |
| Montana | Germane joint bipartisan committees | P | Prior to adoption. |
| Nebraska | Standing committee | P | If an agency proposes to repeal, adopt or amend a rule or regulation, it is required to provide the Executive Board Chair with the proposal at least 30 days prior to the public hearing, as required by law. The Executive Board Chair shall provide to the appropriate standing committee of the legislature, the agency proposal for comment. |
| Nevada | Ongoing statutory committee (Legislative Commission) | P | Proposed regulations are either reviewed at the Legislative Commission's next regularly scheduled meeting (if the regulation is received more than three working days before the meeting), or they are referred to the Commission's Subcommittee to Review Regulations. If there is no objection to the regulation, then the Commission will "promptly" file the approved regulation with the secretary of state. If the Commission or its subcommittee objects to a regulation, then the Commission will "promptly" return the regulation to the agency for revision. Within 60 days of receiving the written notice of objection to the regulation, the agency must revise the regulation and return it to the Legislative Counsel. If the Commission or its subcommittee objects to the revised regulation, the agency shall continue to revise and resubmit it to the Commission or subcommittee within 30 days after receiving the written notice of objection to the revised regulation. |

See footnotes at end of table.

# LEGISLATIVE REVIEW OF ADMINISTRATIVE REGULATIONS: STRUCTURES AND PROCEDURES — Continued

| State or other jurisdiction | Type of reviewing committee | Rules reviewed | Time limits in review process |
|---|---|---|---|
| **New Hampshire** | Joint bipartisan | P | Under APA, for regular rulemaking, the joint committee of administrative rules has 45 days to review a final proposed rule from an agency, Otherwise the rule is automatically approved. If JLCAR makes a preliminary or revised objection, the agency has 45 days to respond, and JLCAR has another 50 days to decide to vote to sponsor a joint resolution, which suspends the adoption process. JLCAR may also, or instead, make a final objection, which shifts the burden of proof in court to the agency. There is no time limit on making a final objection. If no JLCAR action in the 50 days to vote to sponsor a joint resolution, the agency may adopt the rule. |
| **New Jersey** | Joint bipartisan | ... | ... |
| **New Mexico** | ...................................................... (g) ...................................................... | | |
| **New York** | Joint bipartisan commission | P,E | ... |
| **North Carolina** | Rules Review Commission; Public membership appointed by legislature | P,E | The Rules Review Commission must review a permanent rule submitted to it on or before the 20th of the month by the last day of the next month. The commission must review a permanent rule submitted to it after the 20th of the month by the last day of the second subsequent month. |
| **North Dakota** | Interim committee | E | The Administrative Rules Committee meets in each calendar quarter to consider rules filed in previous 90 days. |
| **Ohio** | Joint bipartisan | P,E (h) | The committee's jurisdiction is 65 days from date of original filing plus an additional 30 days from date of re-filing. Rules filed with no changes, pursuant to the five-year review, are under a 90 day jurisdiction. |
| **Oklahoma** | Standing committee (c) | P,E | The legislature has 30 legislative days to review proposed rules. |
| **Oregon** | Office of Legislative Counsel | E | Agencies must copy Legislative Counsel within 10 days of rule adoption. |
| **Pennsylvania** | Joint bipartisan, standing committee | E | Time limits decided by the president pro tempore and speaker of the House. |
| **Rhode Island** | ...................................................... (a) ...................................................... | | |
| **South Carolina** | Standing committee (e) | P | General Assembly has 120 days to approve or disapprove. If not disapproved by joint resolution before 120 days, regulation is automatically approved. It can be approved during 120 day review period by joint resolution. |
| **South Dakota** | Joint bipartisan | P | Rules must be adopted within 75 days of the commencement of the public hearing; emergency rules must be adopted within 30 days of the date of the publication of the notice of intent. Many other deadlines exist; see SDCL 1-26-4 for further details. |
| **Tennessee** | Joint bipartisan | P | All permanent rules take effect 165 days after filing with the secretary of state. Emergency rules take effect upon filing with the secretary of state. |
| **Texas** | Standing committee | P | No time limit. |
| **Utah** | (f) | P,E | Except as provided in Subsection (2)(b), every agency rule that is in effect on February 28 of any calendar year expires May 1 of that year unless it has been reauthorized by the legislature. (UCA 63G-3-502) |
| **Vermont** | Joint bipartisan | P | The Joint Legislative Committee on Rules must review a proposed rule within 30 days of submission to the committee. |
| **Virginia** | Joint bipartisan, standing committee | P | Standing committees and the Joint Commission on Administrative Rules may object to a proposed or final adopted rule before it becomes effective. This delays the process for 21 days and the agency must respond to the objection. In addition or as an alternative, standing committees and the Commission may suspend the effective date of all or a part of a final regulation until the end of the next regular session, with the concurrence of the Governor. |
| **Washington** | Joint bipartisan | P,E | If the committee determines that a proposed rule does not comply with legislative intent, it notifies the agency, which must schedule a public hearing within 30 days of notification. The agency notifies the committee of its action within seven days after the hearing. If a hearing is not held or the agency does not amend the rule, the objection may be filed in the state register and referenced in the state code. The committee's powers, other than publication of its objections, are advisory. |

See footnotes at end of table.

## LEGISLATIVE REVIEW OF ADMINISTRATIVE REGULATIONS: STRUCTURES AND PROCEDURES — Continued

| State or other jurisdiction | Type of reviewing committee | Rules reviewed | Time limits in review process |
|---|---|---|---|
| **West Virginia**............. | Joint bipartisan | P,E | ... |
| **Wisconsin** .................. | Joint bipartisan, standing committee | P,E | The standing committee in each house has 30 days to conduct its review for a proposed rule. If either objects the Joint Committee for the Review of Administrative Rules has 30 days to introduce legislation in each house overturning the rules. After 40 days the bills are placed on the calendar. If either bill passes, the rules are overturned. If they fail to pass, the rules go into effect. |
| **Wyoming** ................... | Joint bipartisan | E | An agency shall submit copies of adopted, amended or repealed rules to the legislative service office for review within five days after the date of the agency's final action adopting, amending or repealing those rules. The legislature makes its recommendations to the governor who within 15 days after receiving any recommendation, shall either order that the rule be amended or rescinded in accordance with the recommendation or file in writing his objections to the recommendation. |
| **American Samoa** ...... | Standing committee | P | ... |
| **Guam** ........................ | Standing committee | | 45 Calendar days |
| **Puerto Rico**.............. | ............................................................................ (a)............................................................................ | | |
| **U.S. Virgin Islands** .... | ............................................................................ (a)............................................................................ | | |

*Source*: The Council of State Governments' survey, February 2009 with update August 2010.

*Key*:
P — Proposed rules
E — Existing rules
... — No formal time limits
(a) No formal rule review is performed by both legislative and executive branches.
(b) Review of rules is performed by both legislative and executive branches.
(c) House has a standing committee to which all rules are generally sent for review. In the Senate rules are sent to standing committee which deals with that specific agency.
(d) If the committees of both houses fail to find a fee unacceptable, it can be adopted. Committee action on proposed rules must be taken within 5 to 30 days after the agency reports to the committee on its public hearing (if any) and whether it is making changes on proposed rules.
(e) Submitted by General Assembly for approval.
(f) Created by statute (63G-3-501).
(g) No formal review is performed by legislature. Periodic review and report to legislative finance committee is required of certain agencies.
(h) The Committee reviews proposed new, amended, and rescinded rules. The Committee participates in a five-year review of every existing rule.

## Table 3.26
## LEGISLATIVE REVIEW OF ADMINISTRATIVE RULES/REGULATIONS: POWERS

| State or other jurisdiction | Reviewing committee's powers | | | Legislative powers |
| | Advisory powers only (a) | No objection constitutes approval of proposed rule | Committee may suspend rule | Method of legislative veto of rules |
| --- | --- | --- | --- | --- |
| Alabama .................. | ... | ★ | ★ | If not approved or disapproved within 35 days of filing, rule is approved. If disapproved by committee, rule suspended until adjournment, next regular session or until legislature by resolution revokes suspension. Rule takes effect upon final adjournment unless committee's disapproval is sustained by legislature. The committee may approve a rule. |
| Alaska ......................... | ★ | ... | (b) | Statute |
| Arizona ...................... | ★ | N.A. | N.A. | N.A. |
| Arkansas.................... | ★ | ... | ... | ... |
| California ................... | ... | ★ | ★ | ... |
| Colorado..................... | ... | ★ | ... | Rules that the General Assembly has determined should not be continued are listed as exceptions to the continuation. |
| Connecticut .............. | ... | ★ | ... | Statute CGS 4-170 (d) and 4-171; see footnote (c) |
| Delaware ................... | N.A. | N.A. | N.A. | N.A. |
| Florida ........................ | ★ | ... | ... | Statute |
| Georgia...................... | ... | ★ | ... | Resolution (d) |
| Hawaii........................ | ★ | ... | ... | ... |
| Idaho............................ | ... | ★ | ... | Concurrent resolution. All rules are terminated one year after adoption unless the legislature reauthorizes the rule. |
| Illinois.......................... | ... | (e) | ★(f) | (f) |
| Indiana....................... | ★ | ... | ... | (g) |
| Iowa ............................ | ... | ... | (h) | E-mail legislation |
| Kansas ....................... | ★ | ... | ... | Statute |
| Kentucky ................... | ... | ★ | ★ | Enacting legislation to void. |
| Louisiana.................... | ... | ★ | (i) | Concurrent resolution to suspend, amend or repeal adopted rules or fees. For proposed rules and emergency rules, see footnote (i). |
| Maine........................... | ... | ★ | ... | (j) |
| Maryland .................... | ★(k) | ... | ... | ... |
| Massachusetts ........... | ... | ... | ... | The legislature may pass a bill which would supersede a regulation if signed into law by the governor. |
| Michigan...................... | ... | ... | (l) | Joint Committee on Rules has 15 session days to approve the filing of a notice of objection. The filing of the notice of objection starts another 15 day session period that stays the rules and causes committee members to introduce legislation in both houses of the legislature for enactment and presentment to the governor. Any member of the legislature, pursuant to statute, can introduce a bill at a session, which in effect amends or rescinds a rule. |
| Minnesota................... | ★ | ... | ... | (m) |
| Mississippi .................. | ...........................................................................(n).......................................................................... | | | |
| Missouri...................... | ... | ★ | ★ | Concurrent resolution passed by both houses of the General Assembly. |
| Montana ..................... | ... | ... | ★(o) | Statute |
| Nebraska ................... | ★ | ★ | ... | ... |
| Nevada........................ | N.A. | ★ | ★ | Proposed regulations are either reviewed at the Legislative Commission's next regularly scheduled meeting (if the regulation is received more than three working days before the meeting), or they are referred to the Commission's Subcommittee to Review Regulations. If there is no objection to the regulation, then the Commission will "promptly" file the approved regulation with the Secretary of State. If the Commission or its subcommittee objects to a regulation, then the Commission will "promptly" return the regulation to the agency for revision. Within 60 days of receiving the written notice of objection to the regulation, the agency must revise the regulation and return it to the Legislative Counsel. If the Commission or its subcommittee objects to the revised regulation, the agency shall continue to revise and resubmit it to the Commission or subcommittee within 30 days after receiving the written notice of objection to the revised regulation. |
| New Hampshire ........ | ★ | (q) | ... | (r) |

See footnotes at end of table.

## LEGISLATIVE REVIEW OF ADMINISTRATIVE RULES/REGULATIONS: POWERS — Continued

| | Reviewing committee's powers | | | Legislative powers |
|---|---|---|---|---|
| State or other jurisdiction | Advisory powers only (a) | No objection constitutes approval of proposed rule | Committee may suspend rule | Method of legislative veto of rules |
| New Jersey | ★ | ★ | ★ | (s) |
| New Mexico | N.A. | N.A. | N.A. | No formal mechanism exists for legislative review of administrative rules. |
| New York | ★ | ... | ... | Reviewing commission's powers are advisory; it may, via its chair, introduce legislation with regard to agency rulemaking. |
| North Carolina | ★ | ★ | ★ | ... |
| North Dakota | ... | ★(t) | ... | The Administrative Rules Committee can void a rule. |
| Ohio | ★ | ... | ... | Concurrent resolution. Committee recommends to the General Assembly that a rule be invalidated. The General Assembly invalidates a rule through adoption of concurrent resolution. |
| Oklahoma | ★ | ★(p) | ★(p) | The legislature may disapprove (veto) proposed rules by concurrent or joint resolution. A concurrent resolution does not require the governor's signature. Existing rules may be disapproved by joint resolution. A committee may not disapprove; only the full legislature may do so. Failure of the legislature to disapprove constitutes approval. |
| Oregon | ★ | ★ | ★ | ... |
| Pennsylvania | ... | ★ | ★ | Written or oral. |
| Rhode Island | | | | ...(n)... |
| South Carolina | ... | ★ | ... | ... |
| South Dakota | ... | ★ | ★ | The Interim Rules Review Committee may, by statute, suspend rules that have not become effective yet by an affirmative vote of the majority of the committee. |
| Tennessee | ... | ... | ★ | Bill approved by Constitutional majority of both hoses declaring rule invalid. |
| Texas | ★ | ... | ... | N.A. |
| Utah | ★ | ... | ... | All rules must be reauthorized by the legislature annually. This is done by omnibus legislation, which also provides for the sunsetting of specific rules listed in the bill. |
| Vermont | | ...(u)... | | Statute |
| Virginia | ... | ... | (v) | The General Assembly must pass a bill enacted into law to directly negate the administrative rule. |
| Washington | ★ | ★ | ★ | N.A. |
| West Virginia | ★ | ... | ... | (w) |
| Wisconsin | ... | ★ | ★ | The standing committee in each house has 30 days to conduct its review for a proposed rule. If either objects the Joint Committee for the Review of Administrative Rules has 30 days to introduce legislation in each house overturning the rules. After 40 days the bills are placed on the calendar. If either bill passes, the rules are overturned. If they fail to pass, the rules go into effect. |
| Wyoming | ★ | ★ | ... | Action must be taken by legislative order adopted by both houses before the end of the next succeeding legislative session to nullify a rule. |
| American Samoa | | | | The enacting clause of all bills shall be: Be it by the Legislature of American Samoa, and no law shall be except by bill. Bills may originate in either house, and may be amended or rejected by the other. The Governor may submit proposed legislation to the Legislature for consideration by it. He may designate any such proposed legislation as urgent, if he so considers it. |
| Guam | N.A. | N.A. | N.A. | Legislation to disapprove rules and regulations. |
| U.S. Virgin Islands | | | | ...(n)... |

See footnotes at end of table.

# LEGISLATIVE REVIEW OF ADMINISTRATIVE RULES/REGULATIONS: POWERS — Continued

*Source:* The Council of State Governments' survey, January 2009 with update August 2010.

*Key:*

★ — Yes

... — No

N.A. — Not applicable

(a) This column is defined by those legislatures or legislative committees that can only recommend changes to rules but have no power to enforce a change.

(b) Authorized, although constitutionally questionable.

(c) Disapproval of proposed regulations may be sustained, or reversed by action of the General Assembly in the ensuing session. The General Assembly may by resolution sustain or reverse a vote of disapproval.

(d) The reviewing committee must introduce a resolution to override a rule within the first 30 days of the next regular session of the General Assembly.

If the resolution passes by less than a two-thirds majority of either house, the governor has final authority to affirm or veto the resolution.

(e) The Administrative Procedure Act is not clear on this point, but implies that the Joint Committee should either object or issue a statement of no objections.

(f) Joint Committee on Administrative Rules can send objections to issuing agency. If it does, the agency has 90 days from then to withdraw, change, or refuse to change the proposed regulations. If the Joint Committee determines that proposed regulations would seriously threaten the public good, it can block their adoption. Within 180 days the Joint Cmte., or both houses of the General Assembly, can "unblock" those regulations; if that does not happen, the regulations are dead.

(g) None — except by passing statute.

(h) Committee may delay rules.

(i) If the committee determines that a proposed rule is unacceptable, it submits a report to the governor who then has 10 days to accept or reject the report. If the governor rejects the report, the rule change may be adopted by the agency. If the governor accepts the report, the agency may not adopt the rule. Emergency rules become effective upon adoption or up to 60 days after adoption as provided in the rule, but a standing committee or governor may void the rule by finding it unacceptable within 2 to 61 days after adoption and reporting such finding to agency within four days.

(j) No veto allowed. Legislation must be enacted to prohibit agency from adopting objectionable rules.

(k) Except for emergency regulations which require committee approval for adoption.

(l) Committee can suspend rules during interim.

(m) The Legislative Commission to Review Administrative Rules (LCRAR) ceased operating, effective July 1, 1996. The Legislative Coordinating Commission (LCC) may review a proposed or adopted rule. Contact the LCC for more information. See Minn. Stat. 3.842, subd. 4a.

(n) No formal mechanism for legislative review of administrative rules. In Virginia, legislative review is optional.

(o) A rule disapproved by the reviewing committee is reinstated at the end of the next session if a joint resolution in the legislature fails to sustain committee action.

(p) Full legislature may suspend rules.

(q) Failure to object or approve within 45 days of agency filing of final proposal constitutes approval.

(r) The legislature may permanently block rules through legislation. The vote to sponsor a joint resolution suspends the adoption of a proposed rule for a limited time so that the full legislature may act on the resolution, which would then be subject to governor's veto and override.

(s) Article V, Section IV of the Constitution, as amended in 1992, says the legislature may review any rule or regulation to determine whether the rule or regulation is consistent with legislative intent. The legislature transmits its objections to existing or proposed rules or regulations to the governor and relevant agency via concurrent resolutions. The legislature may invalidate or prohibit an existing or proposed rule from taking effect by a majority vote of the authorized membership of each house.

(t) Unless formal objections are made or the rule is declared void, rules are considered approved.

(u) JLCAR may recommend that an agency amend or withdraw a proposal. A vote opposing rule does not prohibit its adoption but assigns the burden of proof in any legal challenge to the agency.

(v) Standing committees and The Joint Commission on Administrative Rules may suspend the effective date of all or a part of a final regulation until the end of the next regular legislative session with the concurrence of the governor.

(w) State agencies have no power to promulgate rules without first submitting proposed rules to the legislature which must enact a statute authorizing the agency to promulgate the rule. If the legislature during a regular session disapproves all or part of any legislative rule, the agency may not issue the rule nor take action to implement all or part of the rule unless authorized to do so. However, the agency may resubmit the same or a similar proposed rule to the committee.

**Table 3.27**
## SUMMARY OF SUNSET LEGISLATION

| State | Scope | Preliminary evaluation conducted by | Other legislative review | Other oversight mechanisms in law | Phase-out period | Life of each agency (in years) | Other provisions |
|---|---|---|---|---|---|---|---|
| Alabama | C | Dept. of Examiners of Public Accounts | Standing Cmte. | Perf. audit | No later than Oct. 1 of the year following the regular session or a time as may be specified in the Sunset bill. | (Usually 4) | Schedules of licensing boards and other enumerated agencies are repealed according to specified time tables. |
| Alaska | C | Budget & Audit Cmte. | ... | ... | 1/y | ... | ... |
| Arizona | C | Legislative staff | Joint Cmte. | ... | 6/m | 10 | ... |
| Arkansas | D | ... | ... | ... | ... | ... | ... |
| California | S | St. Legis. Sunset Review Cmte. (a) | ... | Perf. eval. | ... | Varies up to 15 | ... |
| Colorado | R | Dept. of Regulatory Agencies | Legis. Cmtes. of Reference | Bills need adoption by the legislature. | 1/y | 5 years | State law provides certain criteria that are used to determine whether a public need exists for an entity or function to continue and that its regulation is the least restrictive regulation consistent with the public interest. |
| Connecticut | S | Legis. Program Review & Investigations Cmte. | ... | Programs or entities must be affirmatively re-established by legislature. | 1/y (b) | 4 | (c) |
| Delaware | C | Agencies under review submit reports to Del. Sunset Comm. based on criteria for review and set forth in statute. Comm. staff conducts separate review. | ... | Perf. audit | Dec. 31 of next succeeding calendar year | 10 | Yearly sunset review schedules must include at least nine agencies. If the number automatically scheduled for review or added by the General Assembly is less than a full schedule, additional agencies shall be added in order of their appearance in the Del. Code to complete the review schedule. |
| Florida | C | Cmte. charged with oversight of the subject area. | Jt. cmte. charged with oversight of the subject area. | ... | 4–6/y | ... | ... |
| Georgia | R | Dept. of Audits | Standing Cmtes. | Perf. audit | ... | Established by the legislature | A performance audit of each regulatory agency must be conducted upon the request of the Senate or House standing committee to which an agency has been assigned for oversight and review. (d) |

See footnotes at end of table.

# SUMMARY OF SUNSET LEGISLATION—Continued

| State | Scope | Preliminary evaluation conducted by | Other legislative review | Other oversight mechanisms in law | Phase-out period | Life of each agency (in years) | Other provisions |
|---|---|---|---|---|---|---|---|
| Hawaii | R | Legis. Auditor | Standing Cmtes. | Perf. eval. | None | ... | Schedules various professional and vocational licensing programs for repeal. Proposed new regulatory measures must be referred to the Auditor for sunrise analysis. |
| Idaho | (e) | ... | ... | ... | ... | Usually 10 | ... |
| Illinois | R,S (f) | Governor's Office of Mgmt. and Budget | Cmte. charged with re-enacting law | (g) | ... | ... | ... |
| Indiana | S | Non-partisan staff units | Interim cmte. formed to review | ... | ... | ... | Smaller program review process now in place after about a dozen years of formal sunset program. |
| Iowa | | | | ------------No Program------------ | | | |
| Kansas | (h) | ... | ... | ... | ... | ... | ... |
| Kentucky | R | Administrative Regulation Review Subcommittee | Joint committee with subject matter jurisdiction | ... | ... | ... | ... |
| Louisiana | C | Standing cmtes. of the two houses with subject matter jurisdiction. | ... | Perf. eval. | 1/y | Up to 6 | Act provides for termination of a department and all offices in a department. Also permits committees to select particular agencies or offices for more extensive evaluation. Provides for review by Jt. Legis. Cmte. on Budget of programs that were not funded during the prior fiscal year for possible repeal. |
| Maine | S | Joint standing cmte. of jurisdiction. | Office of Program Evaluation & Government Accountability | None | ... | Generally 10 | ... |
| Maryland | R | Dept. of Legislative Services | Standing Cmtes. | Perf. eval. | ... | Varies (usually 10) | ... |
| Massachusetts | | | | ------------No Program------------ | | | |
| Michigan | (e) | ... | ... | ... | ... | ... | ... |
| Minnesota | S(e) | ... | ... | ... | ... | ... | ... |

See footnotes at end of table.

# SUMMARY OF SUNSET LEGISLATION — Continued

| State | Scope | Preliminary evaluation conducted by | Other legislative review | Other oversight mechanisms in law | Phase-out period | Life of each agency (in years) | Other provisions |
|---|---|---|---|---|---|---|---|
| Mississippi.............. | (i) | ... | ... | ... | ... | ... | ... |
| Missouri.................. | R | Oversight Division of Cmte. on Legislative Research | ... | ... | ... | 6, not to exceed total of 12 | ... |
| Montana.................. | (e) | ... | ... | ... | ... | ... | ... |
| Nebraska ............... | D(e)(j) | ... | ... | ... | ... | ... | ... |
| Nevada.................... | (e) | ... | ... | ... | ... | ... | ... |
| New Hampshire ..... | (k) | ... | ... | ... | ... | ... | ... |
| New Jersey ............. | (e) | ... | ... | ... | ... | ... | ... |
| New Mexico ........... | S | Legis. Finance Cmte. | ... | Public hearing before termination | 1/y | 6 | ... |
| New York................ | (e) | ... | ... | ... | ... | ... | ... |
| North Carolina........ | (l) | ... | ... | ... | ... | ... | ... |
| North Dakota.......... | | | | -----No Program----- | | | |
| Ohio....................... | C(m) | Sunset Review Cmte. | ... | Perf. eval. | (n) | 4 | ... |
| Oklahoma............... | S, D | Jt. Cmtes. with jurisdiction over sunset bills | Appropriations and Budget Cmte. | ... | 1/y | 6 | ... |
| Oregon.................... | D(o) | ... | (o) | Perf. eval. | 1/y | ... | ... |
| Pennsylvania .......... | R | Leadership Cmte. | ... | ... | ... | Varies | ... |
| Rhode Island........... | (p) | ... | No | ... | ... | ... | ... |

See footnotes at end of table.

# SUMMARY OF SUNSET LEGISLATION—Continued

| State | Scope | Preliminary evaluation conducted by | Other legislative review | Other oversight mechanisms in law | Phase-out period | Life of each agency (in years) | Other provisions |
|---|---|---|---|---|---|---|---|
| South Carolina | (q) | ... | ... | ... | ... | ... | |
| South Dakota | (r) | ... | ... | ... | ... | ... | |
| Tennessee | C | Office of the Comptroller | Government Operations Committees | ... | 1/y | Up to 6 years | ... |
| Texas | S | Sunset Advisory Commission staff | ... | ... | 1/y | 12 | ... |
| Utah | S | Interim cmtes. | Standing cmtes. as amendments may be made to bill | ... | (v) | (v) | ... |
| Vermont | (s) | Legis. Council staff | Legis. Council staff | Senate and House Government Operations Cmtes. | ... | ... | ... |
| Virginia | S(e) | ... | ... | ... | ... | ... | Sunset provisions vary in length. The only standard sunset required by law is on bills that create a new advisory board or commission in the executive branch of government. The legislation introduced for these boards and commissions must contain a sunset provision to expire the entity after three years. |
| Washington | D | ... | ... | Perf. Eval. | 1/y | ... | ... |
| West Virginia | S | Jt. Cmte. on Govt. Operations | Performance Evaluation and Research Division | Perf. audit | 1/y | 6 | Jt. Cmte. on Govt. Operations composed of five House members, five Senate members and five citizens appointed by governor. Agencies may be reviewed more frequently. |
| Wisconsin | (e) | ... | ... | ... | ... | ... | ... |
| Wyoming | D(t) | Program evaluation staff who work for Management Audit Cmte. | ... | Perf. eval. (u) | ... | ... | ... |

See footnotes at end of table.

# SUMMARY OF SUNSET LEGISLATION — Continued

*Source:* The Council of State Governments' survey, January 2009 with updates August 2010.

Key:

C — Comprehensive
R — Regulatory
S — Selective
D — Discretionary
d — day
m — month
y — year
. . . — Not applicable

(a) Review by the Jt. Legislative Sunset Review Cmte. of professional and vocational licensing boards terminated on January 1, 2004. Sunset clauses are included in other selected programs and legislation.

(b) Upon termination a program shall continue for one year to conclude its affairs.

(c) Since the sunset law was enacted in 1977, only one five-year cycle has been carried out. P.A. 01-160 enacted the last sunset postponement. Per that legislation, 28 entities or programs are scheduled for termination on July 1, 2008, the first year of a five-year cycle, unless affirmatively reestablished by the legislature. This termination date means that 28 entities or programs will be the subjects of PRI performance audits during calendar 2007 in order for the committee to meet its obligation under the Connecticut sunset law. H.B. 6997 (P.A. 07-33) was enacted to postpone the sunset cycle until 2010 to allow for this study.

(d) The automatic sunsetting of an agency every six years was eliminated in 1992. The legislature must pass a bill in order to sunset a specific agency.

(e) While they have not enacted sunset legislation in the same sense as the other states with detailed information in this table, the legislatures in Idaho, Michigan, Minnesota, Montana, Nebraska, Nevada, New Jersey, New York, Virginia and Wisconsin have included sunset clauses in selected programs or legislation.

(f) Many tax laws provide that tax breaks enacted since 1994 will last only five years after taking effect unless the laws creating those breaks establish other sunset periods.

(g) Governor is to read GOMB report and make recommendations to the General Assembly every even-numbered year.

(h) Sunset legislation terminated July 1992. Legislative oversight of designated state agencies, consisting of audit, review and evaluation, continues.

(i) Sunset Act terminated December 31, 1984.

(j) Sunset legislation is discretionary, meaning that senators are free to offer sunset legislation or attach termination dates to legislative proposals. There is no formal sunset commission. Nebraska. Revised Statutes section 50-1303 directs the Legislature's Government, Military and Veteran's Committee to conduct an evaluation of any board, commission, or similar state entity. The review must include, among other things, a recommendation as to whether the board, commission, or entity should be terminated, continued or modified.

(k) New Hampshire's Sunset Committee was repealed July 1, 1986.

(l) North Carolina's sunset law terminated on July 30, 1981. Successor vehicle, the Legislative Committee on Agency Review, operated until June 30, 1983.

(m) There are statutory exceptions.

(n) Authority for latest review (HB 548 of the 123rd General Assembly) expired December 31, 2004. H.B. 516 of the 125 General Assembly re-established the Sunset Review Cmte, but postpones its operation until the 128th General Assembly. The bill terminates the Sunset Review Law on December 31, 2010.

(o) Sunset legislation was repealed in 1993. No general law sunsetting rules or agencies.

(p) No standing sunset statutes or procedures at this time.

(q) Law repealed by 1998 Act 419, Part II, Sect. 35E.

(r) South Dakota suspended sunset legislation in 1979. Under current law, the Executive Board of the Legislative Research Council is directed to establish one or more interim committees each year to review state agencies so that each state agency is reviewed once every ten years.

(s) Sunsets are at the legislature's discretion. Their structure will vary on an individual basis.

(t) Wyoming repealed sunset legislation in 1988.

(u) The program evaluation process evolved out of the sunset process, but Wyoming currently does not have a scheduled sunset of programs.

(v) Default is ten years, although years may be decreased by legislative decisions.

# Chapter Four

# STATE EXECUTIVE BRANCH

# The State of State Addresses:
# The New Normal Fosters Gubernatorial Funnel Vision[1]

### By Katherine Willoughby

*The National Bureau of Economic Research determined the end of the Great Recession in June 2009 because, "the trough marks the end of the recession that began in December 2007 and the beginning of an expansion."[2] Now three years into an expansion, governors are beating the bushes for ways to stretch a dollar. This year, governors presented many ideas for keeping government going, though primarily in the areas of education and economic development. Chief executives did not shy away from talking about revenues, though most of this talk addressed the creation of tax credits, exemptions or incentives to promote job creation. Continued fiscal stress in the states is evidenced by the fact that for the second straight year, the number of issues addressed by at least two-thirds of governors declined. Governors exhibit "funnel vision" as fiscal malaise continues; they have honed down their budget and policy agendas and focus on just the most primary of state functions.*

## The Situation

Politically, red remains the overriding color of states in 2012. According to the Council of State Governments, 29 states have Republican governors, 27 states have predominantly Republican legislatures, and 22 states are Republican controlled (up one from last year)—with the GOP in control of both branches of government. On the other hand, 20 states have Democratic governors, 15 have predominantly Democratic legislatures and 11 are Democratic controlled. Seventeen states are split, with the governor and legislature of different parties, or the legislature is split, with one house of the legislature of a different party.[3] Republican governors working with a split or Democratic legislature include Sean Parnell of Alaska, Terry Branstad of Iowa, Chris Christie of New Jersey, Susana Martinez of New Mexico, Bryan Sandoval of Nevada and Bob McDonnell of Virginia. Democratic governors working with split or Republican legislatures include John Hickenlooper of Colorado, Steven Beshear of Kentucky, Mark Dayton of Minnesota, Brian Schweitzer of Montana, Jay Nixon of Missouri, Beverly Purdue of North Carolina, John Lynch of New Hampshire, Andrew Cuomo of New York and John Kitzhaber of Oregon. Gov. Lincoln Chafee of Rhode Island is an Independent working with a Democratic legislature, and Nebraska Gov. Dave Heineman is a Republican with a nonpartisan legislature.

Fiscally, in the red remains a threat to states in 2012 and beyond. Scott Pattison, executive director of the National Association of State Budget Officers, reviewed data from NASBO's most recent fiscal survey and explained that states are far from out of the woods. While revenues— particularly personal income tax receipts—are stronger than last year and budgets are improving, state spending has not returned to pre-recession levels. In fact, total 2012 state revenues fall below those in the 2008 fiscal year by almost $21 billion.[4] In a study by McNichol, Oliff and Johnson, the authors conclude that "even though the revenue outlook is trending upward, states are still addressing large budget shortfalls by historical standards as they consider budgets for the upcoming year."[5] Scott Pattison concurs that "state budget growth for at least a couple more fiscal years will be tepid."[6] Since the onset of the Great Recession, states have slashed budgets to close gaps and accommodate first plunging, but now sluggish, revenues. Also this past year, states grappled with the end of federal stimulus money; funds from the American Recovery and Reinvestment Act of 2009 have been used or expired. Pattison laments, "I hope I'm wrong, but slow growth for state finances appears at this point to be how things are going."[7]

## Checking the List

Education and jobs remain at the top of the list of gubernatorial agendas. More than 90 percent of governors discussed their plans in these two areas this year. While jobs have been second to education since 2009, this is the first year jobs and economic development have found their way into the speeches of at least 90 percent of state chief executives. Issues considered by more governors this year than last include surplus/deficits/rainy days and reserves, transparency, natural resources and energy, safety and corrections, and tax and revenue initiatives. Issues mentioned by fewer governors this year than last include performance and accountability (down by 27.2 percent) and health care (down by 16.5 percent). Transportation is a consistent agenda item over the years, with almost half of governors again having outlined their plans for state transportation systems, roads and bridges. Compared with last year, however, when five issues were considered by at least two-thirds of governors (education, jobs, performance, health care and taxes), just three issues—education, jobs

and taxes—make the cut this year. Ethics reform and debt reduction continue to be addressed by the fewest number of governors.

### Getting Schooled

Popular reforms in education this year include rebalancing the relationship between state and local governments, innovation of curricula and schools, greater program rigor, and better evaluation of student achievement and teacher performance. Many governors discussed "bold steps" to change community colleges, technical schools and universities to prepare students to be work-ready. Just as almost every state is asking for a waiver from the federal No Child Left Behind prescriptive, many state chief executives emphasized that a one-size-fits-all mantra for education does not work, especially because as some claimed, "college

## Table A:
## Issues Expressed by Governors in
## State of the State Addresses, 2007–2012

| Issue expressed by governors | 2007 percentage of governors mentioning the issue (N=43) | 2008 percentage of governors mentioning the issue (N=43) | 2009 percentage of governors mentioning the issue (N=43) | 2010 percentage of governors mentioning the issue (N=43) | 2011 percentage of governors mentioning the issue (N=43) | 2012 percentage of governors mentioning the issue (N=43) |
|---|---|---|---|---|---|---|
| | N=43 | N=42 | N=44 | N=42 | N=47 | N=43 |
| Education | 100% | 90.5% | 86.4% | 90.5% | 93.6% | 95.3% |
| Economic development/jobs | 79.5 | 81.0 | 79.5 | 88.1 | 87.2 | 90.7 |
| Tax/revenue initiative | 84.1 | 59.5 | 65.9 | 83.3 | 70.2 | 81.4 |
| Natural resources/energy | 84.1 | 71.4 | 79.5 | 73.8 | 44.7 | 65.1 |
| Surplus/deficit/rainy day funds/reserves | 70.5 | 54.8 | 45.5 | 78.6 | 34.0 | 60.5 |
| Health care | 86.4 | 83.3 | 79.5 | 57.1 | 72.3 | 55.8 |
| Safety/corrections | 75.0 | 59.5 | 50.0 | 54.8 | 38.3 | 55.8 |
| Performance/accountability | 72.7 | 42.9 | 52.3 | 73.8 | 83.0 | 55.8 |
| Transportation/roads/bridges | 52.3 | 59.5 | 65.9 | 50.0 | 46.8 | 48.8 |
| Pensions/OPEBs | 36.4 | 21.4 | 18.2 | 19.0 | 36.2 | 32.6 |
| Local government | 52.3 | 35.7 | 20.5 | 11.9 | 17.0 | 25.6 |
| Transparency | 20.5 | 14.3 | 31.8 | 14.3 | 2.1 | 25.6 |
| Borders/illegal immigrants | 11.4 | 16.7 | 6.8 | 4.8 | 8.5 | 11.6 |
| Ethics reform | 13.6 | 11.9 | 15.9 | 26.2 | 8.5 | 7.0 |
| Debt reduction | 13.6 | 9.5 | 4.5 | 0.0 | 8.5 | 7.0 |

*Source:* Content analysis of 2007-2009 State of the State Addresses from Table C of Katherine G. Willoughby, 2008, "The State of the States: Governors Keep Agendas Short," The Book of the States, Vol. 40 (Lexington, KY: The Council of State Governments): 157-64; Content analysis of 2009 State of State Addresses conducted by Tanya Smilley, MPA candidate and Soyoung Park, Ph.D. candidate, Public Policy; Content analysis of 2010 State of State Addresses conducted by Soyoung Park, Ph.D. candidate, Public Policy and Scott Allen, MPA candidate; Content analysis of 2011 State of State Addresses conducted by Byungwoo Cho, MPA candidate; Content analysis of 2012 State of State Addresses conducted by Megan Phillips, MPA candidate and Sarah Beth Gehl, Ph.D. candidate, Public Policy, all students of Andrew Young School of Policy Studies, Georgia State University, Atlanta, Georgia.

is not for everyone" or "individuals learn in different ways."

Alabama Gov. Robert Bentley promoted greater school flexibility as an avenue to let local systems innovate free from state or federal bureaucracy. Pennsylvania's Tom Corbett concurs, "local districts know better how to spend and allocate resources than do bureaucrats in Harrisburg." Virginia's McDonnell explained releasing school districts from a mandated calendar, while Gov. Nikki Haley spoke of giving districts more control over school buses, identifying South Carolina as the only state in the nation to still run a bus fleet. Under her proposal, individual districts would decide whether to operate bus fleets, choose a private operation or to develop a hybrid solution. South Dakota Gov. Dennis Daugaard pressed for local school flexibility to decide on which factors to use when evaluating teachers and classrooms. Gov. Earl Ray Tomblin of West Virginia wants legislation for a pilot program "in which local administrators and educators will be granted flexibility to attract qualified teachers to obtain better results for our students."

Some governors pushed specific funding as an avenue to greater flexibility. Kansas Gov. Sam Brownback asked for $45 million for the state's poorest school districts. Utah Gov. Gary Herbert pushed $111 million in new funding for public schools, including a modest pay increase for teachers. Maryland Gov. Martin O'Malley discussed education reform as a shared responsibility between the state and counties, calling for rebalancing teacher retirement system costs with the state providing $244.5 million to the counties to cover the additional costs in the first year. Similarly, McDonnell proposed an increase in funding for K-12 education of $438 million among other things, to strengthen the Virginia Retirement System for teachers and school employees. Oklahoma Gov. Mary Fallin explained that her state "must keep its commitment to fund teachers' health benefits" through supplemental funding. Alaska's Parnell wants $400 million set aside to build a "strong fence of moral obligation" toward student scholarships. Rhode Island's Chafee combines education funding with taxpayer relief emphasizing a commitment "to education ($40 million to cities and towns), while also reducing the financial burden on property taxpayers." Lynch of New Hampshire pushed a constitutional amendment to restructure state-local responsibilities for education funding, as well as legislation "that will establish a build-ing aid budget, prioritize projects, and increase the match available to school districts with the greatest needs."

Governors comments about education hit on natural transition points—pre-K, K-12, technical schools and universities. Kitzhaber pointed out a frightening possibility for his state: "that this generation of Oregon children could be the first to be less educated than their parents and their peers around the United States." His agenda includes an early learning bill "to streamline disparate programs." Delaware Gov. Jack Markell spoke of proper training for childcare professionals, an upgrade of facilities and teaching tools, and raising "the percentage of high-need children in quality-rated programs from 20 percent to nearly 80 percent." Hawaii Gov. Neil Abercrombie believes early childhood education to be "a fundamental necessity" and mapped out a plan to improve the quality of early care and learning programs. Kentucky's Beshear explained his Early Childhood Advisory Council to advance kindergarten readiness while Gov. Phil Bryant wants to improve early education in Mississippi "by monitoring the learning opportunities in licensed child care centers to include more than just the room size and number of bathrooms."

New Mexico's Martinez bemoaned the consequences of lackluster reading ability in young children, concluding, "children who can't read by the third grade are four times more likely to dropout. And 80 percent of our fourth-graders cannot read proficiently." In describing reading readiness as "everyone's responsibility," she said her favorite job as governor is reading to children. "I've gotten really good at sitting 'crisscross applesauce' on the floor." Her plan calls for $17 million for reading reforms in schools. She was unique in announcing that the $500,000 it cost to operate that state's luxury jet, now sold, should be used to buy every New Mexico first-grader a reading book of their own. In addition, "every school will receive an official letter grade—A, B, C, D, or F, to support a school rating system that is uniquely our own. Not a one-size-fits-all federal system." Other governors, like Virginia's McDonnell singled out reading by third grade as an important goal, because in his words, "social promotions are not acceptable." West Virginia's Tomblin announced his Save the Children program will match $1 million in state funds with a $500,000 investment in McDowell County and partner with three elementary schools and their administrators to focus on literacy.

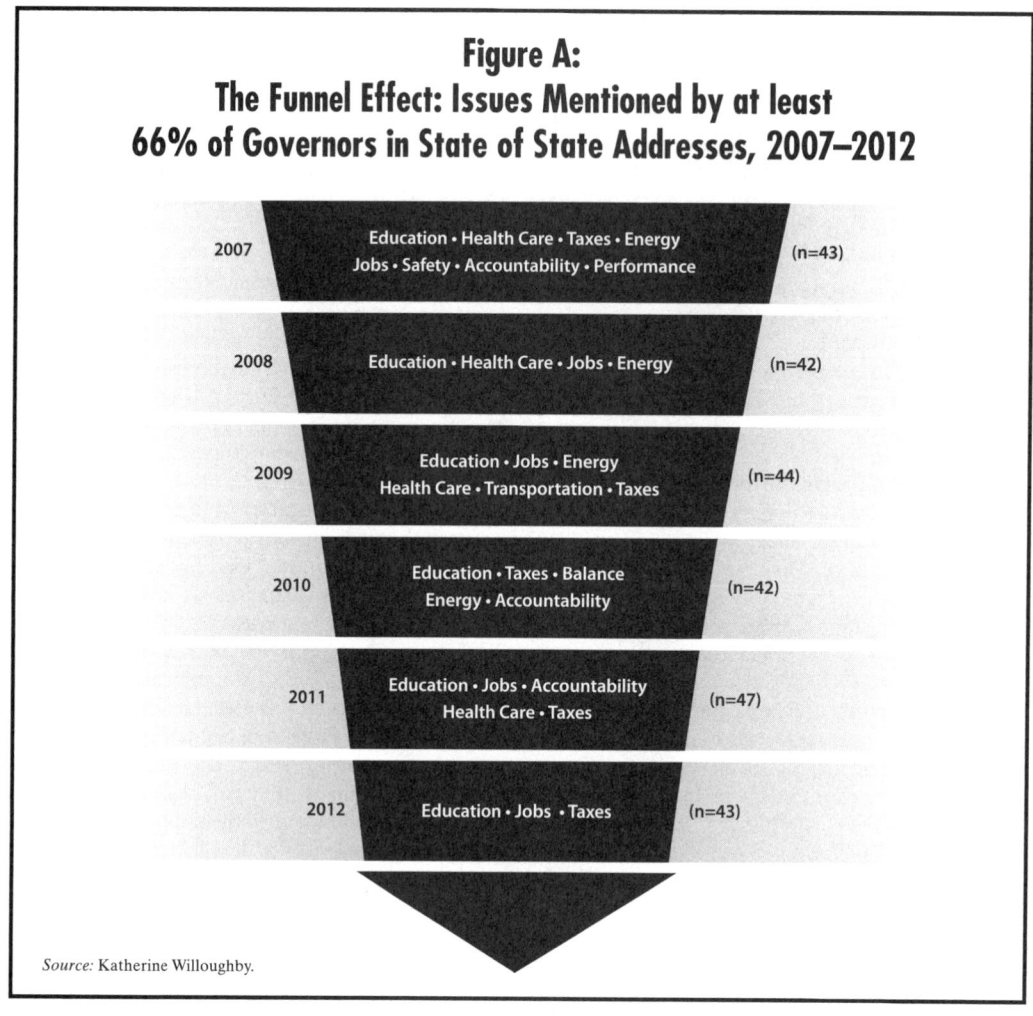

## Figure A:
## The Funnel Effect: Issues Mentioned by at least
## 66% of Governors in State of State Addresses, 2007–2012

**2007** — Education · Health Care · Taxes · Energy / Jobs · Safety · Accountability · Performance — (n=43)

**2008** — Education · Health Care · Jobs · Energy — (n=42)

**2009** — Education · Jobs · Energy / Health Care · Transportation · Taxes — (n=44)

**2010** — Education · Taxes · Balance / Energy · Accountability — (n=42)

**2011** — Education · Jobs · Accountability / Health Care · Taxes — (n=47)

**2012** — Education · Jobs · Taxes — (n=43)

*Source:* Katherine Willoughby.

Christie of New Jersey admitted, "more money does not necessarily lead to a better education." His reforms concentrate on public-private partnerships to "build and operate renaissance schools." He also wants to reform the process for authorizing charter schools "to attract the best operators." Nixon made a similar call, while Haley and McDonnell discussed charter schools as innovators. Christie also called for tenure reform by giving it to teachers "with strong evaluations, and taking it away from those whose ratings are unacceptably weak." Daugaard talked of ending teacher tenure altogether in South Dakota. Rounding out Christie's education agenda is enhanced pay for teachers assigned to a failing school or for those who teach a difficult subject, an end to forced teacher placements and establishing tax credits to provide scholarships for low-income students in the worst performing schools.

Governors were not shy about discussing novel ideas to improve education. Maine Gov. Paul LePage recognized that "some students learn best working with their hands. Woodworking requires a strong working knowledge of geometry. Some kids aren't going to pick up geometry in a textbook, but will in the context of trades such as woodworking, welding, or machining." Cuomo of New York presented his vision for entrée into public service through a student intern program that "will bring students into state government to allow them to experience the work of governing and the complex policy challenges facing New York state."

Delaware's Markell envisions partial immersion programs where students spend half the school day learning in another language. McDonnell promoted dual enrollment of students in high school and community colleges to speed their journey through these institutions.

Many governors this year consider technical and trade schools and community colleges to be vital to creating economically thriving states. Massachusetts Gov. Deval Patrick explained that "middle-skills jobs (such as lab technicians or solar installers) require more than a high school diploma but not necessarily a four-year degree." He discussed strengthening and unifying the state's community college system to give students a combination of classroom learning and on-the-job training. Gov. Nathan Deal of Georgia promoted workforce development through Go Build Georgia, a public-private initiative to upgrade skilled trades. Pennsylvania Gov. Tom Corbett promoted trade schools as the means to prepare students for high-demand occupations. Dayton in Minnesota discussed better coordination of state and federal workforce development funds for higher education, "so that all of our students come out of our educational systems, skilled and ready to succeed." His plans called for educational infrastructure repairs and upgrades, as well as expansion of the state's GI Bill for veterans. Haley also mentioned a restructuring of workforce training in her state.

Ohio Gov. John Kasich issued a long, rather rambling discourse on educational improvements that concentrate on community colleges and universities. "They've got to do a much better job of focusing kids on realistic job propositions." Kasich also asked The Ohio State University President Gordon Gee to bring university presidents together to develop a capital bill that benefits all the universities. Gordon also was tasked with increasing graduation rates for the state's universities.

Gov. Mitch Daniels of Indiana wants greater accountability and performance enhancement in higher education by limiting "credit creep that increases time to graduation and student expense." Likewise, Corbett said "higher education can't be a luxury." He is creating a panel to study Pennsylvania's system and come up with recommendations. Virginia's McDonnell proposed greater accountability measures for higher education as well, including a new funding model, rewards for increasing the number of degrees (especially in STEM), improving graduation rates and expanding practical research, and greater leveraging of facilities and technology. Nixon made a similar call for higher education in Missouri to "look for more ways to cut overhead and administrative costs and run smarter, more efficient operations."

Governors in Iowa and South Dakota presented a list of reforms to advance education. Branstad talked of the need for greater expertise—being more selective about who can become an educator, requiring mastery of subject matter for a state teaching license and improving management knowledge of instructional leaders. He presented a list of reforms including: a new kindergarten assessment; a requirement for reading by third grade; improved standards in the hard and soft sciences and fine arts; character as well as physical education programs; entrepreneurship; applied arts and foreign languages; end-of-course tests for core subjects; state funding of SATs for high school juniors; student internships; and increased online learning opportunities. Daugaard proposed a similar focus on math and science, enhancing teaching careers by expanding the health career camps already held in South Dakota to include engineering, technical and math careers. His call for the expansion of technical training in the state was novel. "Our state does not have enough welders. ... We need to expand the welding program in our corrections facility at Springfield," he said. Daugaard's suggested investment in teachers is certainly noteworthy:

"Under the Investing in Teachers, every teacher in the top 20 percent would receive a bonus of $5,000; this could be earned every year by a teacher who remains in the top 20 percent. Beginning in the 2013-14 school year, the state will pay every middle school and high school math or science teacher a bonus of $3,500; a teacher who stays in these fields will qualify for the $3,500 bonus every year. And a teacher can qualify for both bonuses. That means that a math or science teacher who is in the top 20 percent of teachers in his or her district would receive a bonus of $8,500. For a teacher earning a salary of about $35,000, that is a bonus of nearly 25 percent. These bonuses will be paid entirely with state dollars and they will be in addition to the annual funding formula increases."

### Priming the Pump

For the fourth year in a row, jobs were second to education on governors' minds. More than 90 percent of governors discussed ideas for jumpstarting their state economies. Those in Alabama, Massachusetts, Missouri, New Hampshire and

West Virginia discussed workforce development, career training and business-community college partnerships to secure knowledgeable workers. In Alabama, Arizona, Utah and Wisconsin, governors talked about cutting red tape and/or regulations to streamline business activities. Chief executives in Maine and New Jersey asked for lower taxes, while those in Georgia, Illinois, Iowa, Kentucky, New Mexico, Pennsylvania and New York discussed increased or new tax credits, exemptions and/or incentives. Public-private partnerships were advanced in New York, Pennsylvania, South Dakota and Wyoming, while employing veterans and veteran-preference programs were promoted in Colorado, Missouri, New Mexico, Oklahoma and West Virginia. Governors in Connecticut, South Dakota and West Virginia spoke about recruiting workers into their states and/or reaching out to those who left to return, to reduce the number of jobs shipped out of state or "sent overseas." Daugaard said his goal is to "identify and place 1,000 professional and skilled workers from outside of our state into jobs in South Dakota."

Chief executives presented lofty economic development goals. Alaska's Parnell set a goal of increasing oil production to 1 million barrels a day over the next decade. Gov. Pat Quinn wants to double Illinois' exports by 2014, because "a quarter of our soybean crop is sold in just one country—China." Similarly, Nixon pushed exports to "take the Made in Missouri label global." Virginia's McDonnell also pushed increasing state exports. New York's Cuomo envisions making his state "the number 1 convention site in the nation" by building the country's largest convention center and legalizing gambling. Hawaii's Abercrombie also spoke of aggressively putting projects into action, because bonding and refinancing "will spur an immediate rise in job growth." Pennsylvania's Corbett called for deepening the Delaware River channel and building supertankers—both the projects and subsequent, increased exports will advance jobs in the state. Governors in Maryland and Minnesota expressed similar goals. Governors in South Carolina and Utah claimed no rest until "every state citizen that wants a job, has a job" or "can find a job." Likewise, Bryant claimed, "my first job is to make sure every Mississippian has a job." Utah's Herbert followed up with his goal "to accelerate private sector job creation of 100,000 jobs in 1,000 days." Haley took a different tact to fulfill this goal, emphasizing South Carolina as one of the least unionized states in the country. She

proposed allowing every employee in both the public and private sectors the right to refuse to join a union. She plans to issue an executive order to "make it clear that our state will not subsidize striking workers by paying them unemployment benefits."

Some governors' ideas about job growth were a bit more complex, if no less earnest. For example, Colorado's Hickenlooper pointed to the expected economic dividends of hosting the USA Pro Cycling Challenge and the Pedal the Plains, bike tour that will "be great for the sport of cycling and give folks an opportunity to see where our food comes from." He also is exploring the feasibility of hosting the Olympic Winter Games in 2022. Cuomo discussed expanding food access to underserved communities throughout New York to "lower costs related to obesity and diet-related disease, while fostering community and economic development."

## Making Promises

Pattison points out that states "actually decreased their enacted taxes—in the aggregate—this past year."[8] State chief executives held firm to this credo in their 2012 addresses, with more governors asking for tax cuts than for tax hikes, in spite of continued fiscal malaise. Alabama Gov. Robert Bentley was emphatic that he "will oppose any effort to raise taxes on Alabama families, and I will veto any tax increase," just as Corbett in Pennsylvania claimed, "We will not raise taxes." Arizona Gov. Jan Brewer stated, "I'm here today to say: (the 1-cent sales tax) will end on my watch!" Gov. Peter Shumlin said he would not increase "broad-based taxes on Vermonters." He took pride in his state's "progressive income tax structure—the most progressive in the country, where unlike the federal government, we require our wealthiest citizens to pay their fair share of income tax." Cuomo noted closing New York's $2 billion budget deficit with no new taxes and no new fees. He also asked a Tax Reform and Fairness Commission "to propose additional, long-term changes to our corporate, sales and personal income tax systems" to "close tax loopholes, promote efficiency in administration, enhance collection and enforcement, and simplify the tax code to improve New York's business climate."

Many governors pushed business related tax cuts to pump state economies. Florida Gov. Rick Scott pressed the "need to lower burdensome taxes on small businesses." Deal's tax cuts were more specific—eliminate sales tax on energy used in manufacturing, sales and use tax exemptions for construction materials, and a restructuring of Georgia's job tax credits programs. Hawaii's Abercrombie requested legislation to make an existing TV and film tax credit permanent. Branstad lobbied the Iowa General Assembly to reduce commercial and industrial property taxes by 40 percent over the next eight years, while Hickenlooper focused on property tax relief for seniors in Colorado, "until we can restore the full senior homestead exemption." Dayton pushed his Jobs Now tax credit to "encourage businesses to hire unemployed Minnesotans, veterans and recent college graduates." Similarly, Bryant called for enhancing medically underserved areas in Mississippi by capping the state income tax for new physicians who choose to practice in underserved communities. Martinez pushed exempting half of New Mexico's small businesses from gross receipts tax. She also proposed a tax credit for high-tech research and development and a $1,000 tax credit for employers who hire returning veterans. She rounded out her tax cut package with a proposal for retiring veterans to exempt 25 percent of their pension income from state taxes. Haley presented a budget that includes nearly$140 million in tax cuts. She discussed phasing out South Carolina's corporate income tax and flattening the state's individual income tax.

Personal income tax cuts are especially pleasing to the public and several governors delivered. Fallin drew a "bold tax reform plan that represents the most significant tax cut in state history,…to cut income taxes in all brackets, simplify the code and chart a course towards the gradual elimination of the tax" in Oklahoma. Fallin believes lost revenues can be recouped by eliminating tax loopholes and government waste, by increasing government efficiencies and through economic growth. Brownback proposed overhauling Kansas' tax code "to make it fairer, flatter and simpler," including lowering individual income tax rates and eliminating individual state income tax on most small business income. LePage vowed to reduce Maine's tax burden—the ninth highest in the country—after comparing it with the lower burdens in surrounding states. "We must break the cycle where retired Mainers live in Florida for six months and one day to avoid our high taxes. It's one thing to go south for some beach weather in January and February; it's entirely different when you have to escape the tax man." Heineman spoke similarly of changing Nebraska's income tax structure to allow "hard-

working, middle class families to keep more of their income"; he also proposed eliminating inheritance tax and reducing corporate income taxes. Gov. Bill Haslam proposed raising the exemption level on the estate tax in Tennessee, to reach the federal exemption level of $5 million, given that "our current estate tax is chasing people and capital out of our state and discourages people who don't live here from investing here." He is pushing to decrease the state sales tax on groceries, too.

Herbert reported, "due to wise trust fund management and a nation-leading record of helping people move from unemployment back into the workforce, Utah is in a position to reduce unemployment insurance tax rates." McDonnell proposed a pro-business investor tax credit along with an extension of time to take advantage of the business facility job tax credit and a tax credit for companies that contribute to an educational scholarship fund in Virginia. He also called for the elimination of accelerated sales tax policy for 96 percent of Virginia's merchants. Lynch was proud that New Hampshire has among the lowest state taxes per capita in the nation and noted commitment to veto an income or a sales tax and double the research-and-development tax credit. Alternatively, he explained the need to roll back a previous cut to tobacco taxes and "use the revenue to invest in our economic future."

New Hampshire's Lynch joined a very small percentage of governors asking for tax hikes, restorations or exemption repeals. California Gov. Jerry Brown admitted determination "to press ahead both with substantial budget cuts and my tax initiative," that he characterizes as fair, temporary and earmarked for public safety and education programs. O'Malley quoted The Baltimore Sun to sell his tax hike: "If Maryland continues to embrace a 1992 tax rate, it will have to settle for crumbling 1992-era infrastructure." He wants to repeal the state's sales tax exemption on gasoline, phasing it out by 2 percent a year, with a braking mechanism to protect consumers if the price of gas spikes. Chafee of Rhode Island framed his request for a 2-percentage point increase in the food and beverage tax in terms of an honest, fiscally responsible budget. He proposed a modest expansion of the sales tax to a handful of nonessential goods and services. In addition, he proposed increasing vehicle registration and driver's license fees to "responsibly address our state's transportation deficit and provide much-needed revenue for urgent maintenance and repair projects for our roads and bridges." Finally, Washington Gov. Christine Gregoire expressed the need to close tax loopholes and pass a temporary, three-year, half-cent sales tax increase to pay for human welfare and education services. "Remember, the last time we raised the state sales tax was in 1983, under a Republican governor during the worst recession until this one," she said. She also asked for a $1.50 fee on every barrel of oil produced in the state.

### Doing Better, Being Good

While 27 percent fewer governors mentioned performance and accountability concerns in their speeches this year, their consideration of government transparency increased by 23 percent. Still, governors offered many ideas to streamline government services and more effectively allocate resources. Improved budget scrutiny, expansive program evaluation and reorganizations were all mentioned. Georgia's Deal promoted zero-based budgeting to "bring a new level of accountability to state government and verify that taxpayer dollars are being spent to meet the priorities of Georgians." Similarly, Tennessee's Haslam discussed his recommendations for savings, process improvements and restructurings based on top-to-bottom reviews of state agencies, boards and commissions. Minnesota's Dayton highlighted efforts to consolidate state information technology functions as well as implement "lean practices of continuous improvement" to save money and improve services." Mississippi's Bryant asked his legislature to pass the Smart Budget Act to budget "on performance, not politics," Nebraska's Heineman specified improvements to his state's child welfare system for measurable results, while New Hampshire's Lynch emphasized consolidations, streamlined processes and cuts to red tape to better provide "direct services to our citizens, rather than writing reports that no one reads." Fallin, together with the Oklahoma Office of State Finance, will use new software to measure agency and program performance and efficiency to better "align expenditures with outcomes...to right-size government" and ensure effective operations. In Florida, Scott wants to improve accountability by requiring "job training for those who are receiving unemployment checks."

Reorganization is on the executive brain as well. Haley pressed for restructuring legislation to create a Department of Administration, replacing South Carolina's unique Budget and Control Board, a joint executive-legislative body that oversees man-agement of state operations. Heineman spoke of merging Nebraska's labor department with one for economic development to provide business, labor and state government "coordinated and an even greater focus on job creation, worker training and worker retraining." Pennsylvania's Corbett discussed restructuring an authority, to "merge several programs under a single umbrella...to more flexibly direct loans to expanding businesses." Chafee discussed his efforts to improve state operations and the employment landscape through his newly developed "Jobs Cabinet" to grow businesses and develop a skilled workforce. His secretary of state is developing a "one-stop system to make it easier to start and conduct business in Rhode Island."

Daugaard brought fruits of labor from his Red Tape Review to South Dakota residents—22 bills, 168 pages, repealing "unnecessary regulations and statutes,...eliminating nearly 1,100 rules and 200,000 words from state administrative rules, repealing over 400 sections of codified law."Hickenlooper claimed, "We are scrubbing every Colorado state agency to eliminate red tape." In Maine, LePage wants a Certified Business Friendly Community Program to reduce red tape and promote job creation. Haslam introduced the Tennessee Excellence, Accountability and Management Act, claiming, "We are like a college football team that can't recruit. We can only take players that come to us, and then we decide who plays based on who has been on the team the longest, not necessarily who the best players are." He specifically addressed bumping, in which longevity, not performance, influences who remains on the job. Virginia's McDonnell was alone in proposing a one-time bonus for state employees, contingent on employee achievement of savings and meeting performance goals.

Electronic government and IT advancements also were mentioned. Cuomo highlighted his one-stop-shop that will allow "citizens young and old to easily access information about an array of New York state agencies." Lynch mentioned a similar online Business One Stop to provide business owners with streamlined access to information about operating effectively in New Hampshire. Delaware's Markell pointed to his "I found it cheaper" website, where state employees report "when contracts fail to offer the best value to taxpayers." Daugaard talked about improvements to South Dakota's homepage, while Gov. Matthew Mead called for restructuring Wyoming's IT services and expanding teleconferencing.

While few mentioned ethics reform, those who did framed reform in terms of greater transparency and improved democracy. Nixon called for a new law in Missouri to restrict campaign contributions. "When one person with an ax to grind can make an unlimited contribution to advance a narrow agenda...when lobbyists for powerful interests can tip the balance of an election...the very foundations of our democracy are at risk." Cuomo listed a number of ideas around ethics: (1) a system of public funding of elections; (2) lowering contribution limits; (3) enacting pay-to-play restrictions "because companies and individuals who do business with the state should have no undue influence over elected officials"; (4) creating an enforcement unit with independence and authority to investigate alleged violations of campaign finance laws; and (5) independent redistricting "to restore public trust." Michigan's Snyder also mentioned campaign finance reform.

Addressing fraud, Martinez in New Mexico signed an executive order prohibiting state government from doing business with companies involved in corruption and requiring her appointees to disclose their financial interests online and barring them from lobbying state government for two years after serving in her administration. Rhode Island's Chafee recommended new funding for the state's Office of Health and Human Services to crack down on waste and fraud. Beshear proposes to improve transparency in Kentucky with his Child Protection Act that includes creation of an independent review panel " to examine child fatalities and near-fatalities where abuse and/or neglect are alleged. Wisconsin Gov. Scott Walker pointed to his Commission on Waste, Fraud and Abuse—which identified more than $400 million in savings—as reason enough to create a Waste, Fraud and Abuse *Elimination*

Task Force charged with the responsibility to follow through with the first commission's recommendations. Finally, Daugaard discussed his efforts at greater transparency—releasing the names of guests to various gubernatorial events, event sponsors, information from the Department of Corrections, as well the names of state loan recipients and public tours of the Governor's Mansion.

## Conclusions

During and following the Great Recession, governors have been honing in on the primary tasks of states—education and economic development. Years of examining these speeches indicates that throughout the slow recovery period, governors exhibit "funnel vision" by focusing their talks each year on fewer and fewer functions generally viewed as traditional state services. For example, in 2007, at least two-thirds of governors discussed education, health care, natural resources, taxes, jobs, public safety, performance and budget balance issues in their addresses. By 2012, just three issues were discussed by at least 66 percent of chief executives—education, jobs and taxes. Governors consistently present new ideas, conceive of new programs, outline lofty goals or make commitments—rethinking how states provide educational services, to whom and for what purposes; decreasing taxes or increasing incentives; and continuing to lay out plans to downsize, resize or "right size" government itself. The economic recovery period likely will remain extremely slow for states, certainly in the near term. In light of this, expect governors to continue to focus on education and jobs to the exclusion of other state functions. The issue of how to fund—and in the case of jobs, promote—these activities will undoubtedly necessitate keeping taxes and revenues on their list as well.

## Notes

[1]Governors report annually or biennially to their legislatures regarding the fiscal condition of their state, commonwealth or territory. They often use their address to lay out their policy and budget agendas for their upcoming or continuing administration. The 2012 state of the state addresses were accessed from January 1 through March 10, 2012, via *www.nga.org* or *www.stateline.org* or the state government's homepage. This research considers those 43 states with transcripts available at these sites as of March 10, 2012. Speeches not available by this date included Arkansas, Louisiana, Montana, North Carolina, North Dakota, Nevada, and Texas. All quotes and data presented here are from the addresses accessed on these websites, unless otherwise noted.

To conduct a content analysis of governors' state of state addresses, as in the past, topics were considered addressed if the chief executive specifically discussed them as relevant to state operations and the budget *going forward*. The governor needed to relay that the function, activity or issue is an important item in next year's—fiscal 2013—budget and policy direction. Just mentioning a state function or policy area like health care in a speech did not classify the issue as an agenda item addressed by a governor. Further, a review by a governor of his or her past accomplishments in any particular issue area did not count in this content analysis.

[2]National Bureau of Economic Research 2010. *Business Cycle Dating Committee Report*. September 20. (Cambridge, Massachusetts) Accessed on February 2, 2012 at: *http://www.nber.org/cycles/sept2010.pdf*.

[3]National Conference of State Legislatures 2012. StateVote: 2012 State and Legislative Partisan Composition (January 12). Accessed on February 2, 2012 at: *http://www. ncsl.org/documents/statevote/2012_Legis_and_State.pdf*.

[4]National Association of State Budget Officers 2011. *Fiscal Survey of the States*. (Washington, D.C.) Fall, p. vii.

[5]McNichol, Elizabeth, Oliff, Phil and Johnson, Nicholas. 2012. "States Continue to Feel Recession's Impact." February 27 (Washington, D.C.: Center on Budget and Policy Priorities). Accessed on February 29, 2012 at: *http://www. cbpp.org/files/9-8-08sfp.pdf*.

[6]Pattison, Scott D. 2011. Blogged on November 29th, 2011. Accessed on February 2, 2012 at: *http://www.nasbo. org/budget-blog/states-not-yet-back-pre-recession-levels*.

[7]Ibid.

[8]Ibid.

## About the Author

**Katherine Willoughby** is professor of public management and policy in the Andrew Young School of Policy Studies at Georgia State University in Atlanta. Her research concentrates on state and local government budgeting and financial management, public policy development and public organization theory. She has conducted extensive research in the area of state budgeting practices, with a concentration on performance measurement applicability at this level of government in the United States.

# Gubernatorial Elections, Campaign Costs and Winning Governors

## By Thad Beyle

*Governors remain in the forefront of activity in the 21st century. While the governorship was not the stepping stone to the White House for President Barack Obama—as it was for the country's two previous presidents, Democratic Gov. Bill Clinton from Arkansas (1993–2001) and Republican Gov. George W. Bush from Texas (2001–09)—governors continue to be in the middle of addressing the problems facing the country's weak economy. The demands on governors to propose state budgets and then keep them in balance have increased greatly during the current recession as severe revenue shortfalls have hit the states. This has placed severe limits on states' abilities to address the many growing needs of people trying to live through tough times. Politically, this has led to fallout from unhappy voters as they vent their anger and frustration toward leaders on election days.*

## 2011 Gubernatorial Politics

The three Southern states—Kentucky, Louisiana and Mississippi—which traditionally hold gubernatorial elections in the year before a presidential election, had a fourth state—West Virginia—join them in 2011. West Virginia held a special election to decide who would succeed Gov. Joe Manchin, who nominated himself to fill the U.S. Senate seat vacated after the death of Robert Bird in late 2010. State Senate President Earl Ray Tomblin, who had been serving as interim governor, defeated Republican Bill Maloney by a 2.3 point margin.

This margin compares poorly with the margins in the three Southern races. In Louisiana, incumbent Gov. Bobby Jindal won a second term by a 47.9 point margin, while in Kentucky, incumbent Gov. Steven Beshear won his second term by a 20 point margin. The new Mississippi governor, Phil Bryant, won his first term by 22 points. The political makeup following the 2011 elections was no different than the makeup following the 2010 elections, with 29 Republicans, 20 Democrats and one Independent serving as governors.

## Gubernatorial Elections

As seen in Table A, incumbents were eligible to seek another term in 437 of the 576 gubernatorial contests held between 1970 and 2011 (75.9 percent). In those contests, 341 incumbents sought re-election (78 percent), and 259 of them succeeded (75.9 percent). Those who were defeated were more likely to lose in the general election than in their own party primary by a 3-to-1 ratio. In 2010, Nevada Gov. Jim Gibbons was defeated in the Republican

primary, the third such loss since the 2000 election, and the 21st since 1970.

Democratic candidates held a winning edge in 308 of the 576 elections (53.5 percent) held between 1970 and 2011. In 222 of these races (38.5 percent), the results led to a party shift. But these party shifts have evened out over the years so that neither of the two major parties has an edge in the past four decades of gubernatorial elections.

Between 1970 and 1992, Democrats won 200 of the 324 races for governor (62 percent). Then, from 1993 to 2003, Republicans leveled the playing field by winning 85 of the 145 races for governor (59 percent). From 2004 to 2011, there has been a virtual tie in which party has won the 106 governor's races, with Republicans winning 54 (51 percent), Democrats winning 51 (48 percent), and an Independent winning a single race (1 percent).

Another factor in determining how many governors have served in the states is the number of newly elected governors who are new to the office as compared to those who are returning after complying with constitutional term limits or after holding other positions. Of new governors taking office over a decade, states dropped from a rate of 2.3 new governors per state in the 1950s to 1.9 in the 1970s and to 1.1 in the 1980s. In the 1990s, the rate began to move up a bit to 1.4 new governors per state. In the first decade of the 21st century, many new faces filled governor's mansions. From 2000–2009 alone, new governors were elected in 61 of the 118 elections (51.7 percent). Nine new governors succeeded to office upon the incumbent vacating the office from

## Table A: Gubernatorial Elections: 1970–2011

| | | Democratic winner | | Number of incumbent governors | | | | | | | | | |
| | | | | Eligible to run | | Actually ran | | Won | | Lost | | | |
| Year | Number of races | Number | Percent | Number | Percent | Number | Percent | Number | Percent | Number | Percent | In primary | In general election |
|---|---|---|---|---|---|---|---|---|---|---|---|---|---|
| 1970 | 35 | 22 | 63 | 29 | 83 | 24 | 83 | 16 | 64 | 8 | 36 | 1 (a) | 7 (b) |
| 1971 | 3 | 3 | 100 | 0 | ... | ... | ... | ... | ... | ... | ... | ... | ... |
| 1972 | 18 | 11 | 61 | 15 | 83 | 11 | 73 | 7 | 64 | 4 | 36 | 2 (c) | 2 (d) |
| 1973 | 2 | 1 | 50 | 1 | 50 | 1 | 100 | ... | ... | 1 | 100 | 1 (e) | ... |
| 1974 | 35 | 27 (f) | 77 | 29 | 83 | 22 | 76 | 17 | 77 | 5 | 24 | 1 (g) | 4 (h) |
| 1975 | 3 | 3 | 100 | 2 | 66 | 2 | 100 | 2 | 100 | ... | ... | ... | ... |
| 1976 | 14 | 9 | 64 | 12 | 86 | 8 | 67 | 5 | 63 | 3 | 33 | 1 (i) | 2(j) |
| 1977 | 2 | 1 | 50 | 1 | 50 | 1 | 100 | 1 | 100 | ... | ... | ... | ... |
| 1978 | 36 | 21 | 58 | 29 | 81 | 23 | 79 | 16 | 73 | 7 | 30 | 2 (k) | 5 (l) |
| 1979 | 3 | 2 | 67 | 0 | ... | ... | ... | ... | ... | ... | ... | ... | ... |
| 1980 | 13 | 6 | 46 | 12 | 92 | 12 | 100 | 7 | 58 | 5 | 42 | 2 (m) | 3 (n) |
| 1981 | 2 | 1 | 50 | 0 | ... | ... | ... | ... | ... | ... | ... | ... | ... |
| 1982 | 36 | 27 | 75 | 33 | 92 | 25 | 76 | 19 | 76 | 6 | 24 | 1 (o) | 5 (p) |
| 1983 | 3 | 3 | 100 | 1 | 33 | 1 | 100 | ... | ... | 1 | 100 | 1 (q) | ... |
| 1984 | 13 | 5 | 38 | 9 | 69 | 6 | 67 | 4 | 67 | 2 | 33 | ... | 2 (r) |
| 1985 | 2 | 1 | 50 | 1 | 50 | 1 | 100 | 1 | 100 | ... | ... | ... | ... |
| 1986 | 36 | 19 | 53 | 24 | 67 | 18 | 75 | 15 | 83 | 3 | 18 | 1 (s) | 2 (t) |
| 1987 | 3 | 3 | 100 | 2 | 67 | 1 | 50 | ... | ... | 1 | 100 | 1 (u) | ... |
| 1988 | 12 | 5 | 42 | 9 | 75 | 9 | 100 | 8 | 89 | 1 | 11 | ... | 1 (v) |
| 1989 | 2 | 2 | 100 | 0 | ... | ... | ... | ... | ... | ... | ... | ... | ... |
| 1990 | 36 | 19 (w) | 53 | 33 | 92 | 23 | 70 | 17 | 74 | 6 | 26 | ... | 6 (x) |
| 1991 | 3 | 2 | 67 | 2 | 67 | 2 | 100 | ... | ... | 2 | 100 | 1 (y) | 1 (z) |
| 1992 | 12 | 8 | 67 | 9 | 75 | 4 | 44 | 4 | 100 | ... | ... | ... | ... |
| 1993 | 2 | 0 | 0 | 1 | 50 | 1 | 100 | ... | ... | 1 | 100 | ... | 1 (aa) |
| 1994 | 36 | 11 (bb) | 31 | 30 | 83 | 23 | 77 | 17 | 74 | 6 | 26 | 2 (cc) | 4 (dd) |
| 1995 | 3 | 1 | 33 | 2 | 67 | 1 | 50 | 1 | 100 | ... | ... | ... | ... |
| 1996 | 11 | 7 | 64 | 9 | 82 | 7 | 78 | 7 | 100 | ... | ... | ... | ... |
| 1997 | 2 | 0 | 0 | 1 | 50 | 1 | 100 | 1 | 100 | ... | ... | ... | ... |
| 1998 | 36 | 11 (ee) | 31 | 27 | 75 | 25 | 93 | 23 | 92 | 2 | 8 | ... | 2 (ff) |
| 1999 | 3 | 2 | 67 | 2 | 67 | 2 | 100 | 2 | 100 | ... | ... | ... | ... |
| 2000 | 11 | 8 | 73 | 7 | 88 | 6 | 86 | 5 | 83 | 1 | 17 | ... | 1 (gg) |
| 2001 | 2 | 2 | 100 | 0 | ... | ... | ... | ... | ... | ... | ... | ... | ... |
| 2002 | 36 | 14 | 39 | 22 | 61 | 16 | 73 | 12 | 75 | 4 | 25 | ... | 4 (hh) |
| 2003 | 4 (ii) | 1 | 25 | 2 | 50 | 2 | 100 | ... | ... | 2 | 100 | ... | 2 (jj) |
| 2004 | 11 | 6 | 55 | 11 | 100 | 8 | 73 | 4 | 50 | 4 | 50 | 2 (kk) | 2 (ll) |
| 2005 | 2 | 2 | 100 | 1 | 50 | ... | ... | ... | ... | ... | ... | ... | ... |
| 2006 | 36 | 20 | 56 | 31 | 86 | 27 | 87 | 25 | 93 | 2 | 7 | 1 (mm) | 1 (nn) |
| 2007 | 3 | 1 | 33 | 3 | 100 | 2 | 67 | 1 | 50 | 1 | 50 | ... | 1 (oo) |
| 2008 | 11 | 7 | 64 | 9 | 82 | 8 | 89 | 8 | 100 | ... | ... | ... | ... |
| 2009 | 2 | 0 | 0 | 1 | 50 | 1 | 100 | ... | ... | 1 | 100 | ... | 1 (pp) |
| 2010 | 37 | 13 | 35 | 22 | 60 | 14 | 64 | 11 | 79 | 3 | 21 | 1 (qq) | 2 (rr) |
| 2011 | 4 | 2 | 50 | 3 | 75 | 3 | 100 | 3 | 100 | 0 | 0 | 0 | 0 |
| **Totals:** | | | | | | | | | | | | | |
| Number | 576 | 308 | | 437 | | 341 | | 259 | | 82 | | 21 | 61 |
| Percent | 100 | 53.5 | | 75.9 | | 78.0 | | 75.9 | | 24.0 | | 25.6 | 74.4 |

See footnotes on the next page.

2000 to 2009.[1] So, during the first few years of the previous decade, 70 new governors were sworn into office, continuing the 1.4 rate per state.

In the 2010 and 2011 elections, considerable turnover among governors continued. In 2010, 26 new governors were elected in 37 races, and two other new governors succeeded to the office upon the resignation of the incumbent to take over as one of the state's new U.S. senators.[2] In 2011, one new governor was elected in one of the four races

—Mississippi's Phil Bryant. As noted earlier, in a 2011 special election, West Virginia's successor Gov. Earl Ray Tomlin was required to win the voters' approval to fill out former Gov. Joe Manchin's remaining term, which he did by a narrow margin. And in the two other elections in 2011, both incumbents won their second terms.[3] In sum, in the 41 governor's elections in 2010–11, 27 new governors were elected (65.9 percent), while 14 incumbent governors won another term (34 percent).

## Table A: Gubernatorial Elections: 1970–2011, Footnotes

*Source:* The Council of State Governments, *The Book of the States,* *2011,* (Lexington, KY: The Council of State Governments, 2011), 128, updated.

*Key:*

(a) Albert Brewer, D-Ala.

(b) Keith Miller, R-Alaska; Winthrop Rockefeller, R-Ark.; Claude Kirk, R-Fla.; Don Samuelson, R-Idaho; Norbert Tieman, R-Neb.; Dewey Bartlett, R-Okla.; Frank Farrar, R-S.D.

(c) Walter Peterson, R-N.H.; Preston Smith, D-Texas.

(d) Russell Peterson, R-Del.; Richard Ogilvie, R-Ill.

(e) William Cahill, R-N.J.

(f) One independent candidate won: James Longley of Maine.

(g) David Hall, D-Okla.

(h) John Vanderhoof, R-Colo.; Francis Sargent, R-Mass.; Malcolm Wilson, R-N.Y.; John Gilligan, D-Ohio.

(i) Dan Walker, D-Ill.

(j) Sherman Tribbitt, D-Del.; Christopher 'Kit' Bond, R-Mo.

(k) Michael Dukakis, D-Mass.; Dolph Briscoe, D-Texas.

(l) Robert F. Bennett, R-Kan.; Rudolph G. Perpich, D-Minn.; Meldrim Thompson, R-N.H.; Robert Straub, D-Ore.; Martin J. Schreiber, D-Wis.

(m) Thomas L. Judge, D-Mont.; Dixy Lee Ray, D-Wash.

(n) Bill Clinton, D-Ark.; Joseph P. Teasdale, D-Mo.; Arthur A. Link, D-N.D.

(o) Edward J. King, D-Mass.

(p) Frank D. White, R-Ark.; Charles Thone, R-Neb.; Robert F. List, R-Nev.; Hugh J. Gallen, D-N.H.; William P. Clements, R-Texas.

(q) David Treen, R-La.

(r) Allen I. Olson, R-N.D.; John D. Spellman, R-Wash.

(s) Bill Sheffield, D-Alaska.

(t) Mark White, D-Texas; Anthony S. Earl, D-Wis.

(u) Edwin Edwards, D-La.

(v) Arch A. Moore, R-W.Va.

(w) Two Independent candidates won: Walter Hickel (Alaska) and Lowell Weiker (Conn.). Both were former statewide Republican office holders.

(x) Bob Martinez, R-Fla.; Mike Hayden, R-Kan.; James Blanchard, D-Mich.; Rudy Perpich, DFL-Minn.; Kay Orr, R-Neb.; Edward DiPrete, R-R.I.

(y) Buddy Roemer, R-La.

(z) Ray Mabus, D-Miss.

(aa) James Florio, D-N.J.

(bb) One Independent candidate won: Angus King of Maine.

(cc) Bruce Sundlun, D-R.I.; Walter Dean Miller, R-S.D.

(dd) James E. Folsom, Jr., D-Ala.; Bruce King, D-N.M.; Mario Cuomo, D-N.Y.; Ann Richards, D-Texas.

(ee) Two Independent candidates won: Angus King of Maine and Jesse Ventura of Minnesota.

(ff) Fob James, R-Ala.; David Beasley, R-S.C.

(gg) Cecil Underwood, R-W.Va.

(hh) Don Siegelman, D-Ala.; Roy Barnes, D-Ga., Jim Hodges, D-S.C.; and Scott McCallum, R-Wis.

(ii) The California recall election and replacement vote of 2003 is included in the 2003 election totals and as a general election for the last column.

(jj) Gray Davis, D-Calif., Ronnie Musgrove, D-Miss.

(kk) Bob Holden, D-Mo.; Olene Walker, R-Utah, lost in the pre-primary convention.

(ll) Joe Kernan, D-Ind.; Craig Benson, R-N.H.

(mm) Frank Murkowski, R-Alaska.

(nn) Robert Ehrlich, R-Md.

(oo) Ernie Fletcher, R-Ky.

(pp) Jon Corzine, D-N.J.

(qq) Jim Gibbons, R-Nev.

(rr) Chet Culver, D-Iowa; Ted Strickland, D-Ohio.

## The New Governors

During the 2008–11 gubernatorial elections and resignations, new governors took several routes to office. Twenty-one had previously held an elective office. These include:

- Eight lieutenant governors: Alaska Gov. Sean Parnell, North Dakota Gov. Jack Dalrymple, South Dakota Gov. Dennis Daugaard and Utah Gov. Gary Herbert, all Republicans; and Illinois Gov. Pat Quinn, Kentucky Gov. Steve Beshear (who served as lieutenant governor from 1983 to 87), New York Gov. David Paterson and North Carolina Gov. Beverly Perdue, all Democrats;

- Five attorneys general: California Gov. Jerry Brown (who also served as governor from 1975 to 83), Missouri Gov. Jay Nixon and New York Gov. Andrew Cuomo—all Democrats; and Pennsylvania Gov. Tom Corbett and Virginia Gov. Robert McDonald—both Republicans;

- Two former governors in addition to Jerry Brown: Oregon Gov. John Kitzhaber, a Democrat, elected in 1994 and 1998, and Iowa Gov. Terry Branstad, a Republican, elected in 1982, 1986, 1990 and 1994;

- One secretary of state: Arizona Gov. Jan Brewer, a Republican, who succeeded to office upon the resignation of Gov. Janet Napolitano in 2009;

- Three U.S. senators: Kansas Gov. Sam Brownback, a Republican; Minnesota Gov. Mark Dayton, a Democrat; and Rhode Island Gov. Lincoln Chafee, an Independent;

- One state treasurer: Delaware Gov. Jack Markell, Democrat.

Fourteen new governors had previously held elected or appointed sub-state offices. These include:

- Five former members of Congress: Hawaii Gov. Neil Abercrombie, a Democrat; and Georgia Gov. Nathan Deal, Louisiana Gov. Bobby Jindal, Ohio Gov. John Kasich and Oklahoma Gov. Mary Fallin, all Republicans;

- Four mayors or former mayors: Colorado Gov. John Hickenlooper, Denver, and Connecticut Gov. Dannel Malloy, Stamford—both Democrats; and Maine Gov. Paul LePage, Waterville, and Tennessee Gov. Bill Haslam, Knoxville—both Republicans;

- Three state legislators: South Carolina Gov. Nikki Haley, a Republican state representative; and Vermont Gov. Peter Shumlin and West Virginia Gov. Earl Ray Tomlin, both Democratic state senate presidents;
- Two county officials: New Mexico Gov. Susana Martinez, district attorney, and Wisconsin Gov. Scott Walker, county CEO—both Republicans.

Six new governors followed a unique path to the governorship:

- Three former federal attorneys or judges: New Jersey Gov. Christopher Christie, a former U.S. attorney; Nevada Gov. Brian Sandoval, a former federal district court judge; and Wyoming Gov. Matt Mead, a former U.S. attorney, all Republicans;
- Two businessmen: Florida Gov. Rick Scott, a health care company executive, and Michigan Gov. Rick Snyder, a venture capitalist in computers, both Republicans;
- One doctor: Alabama Gov. Robert Bentley, a dermatologist, Republican.

Two of these new governors have a family heritage tied to the office, as their fathers also had served as the state's top executive. New York Gov. Andrew Cuomo is the son of former Gov. Mario Cuomo, elected in 1982, 1986 and 1990. Rhode Island Gov. Lincoln Chafee is the son of former Gov. John Chafee, who was elected in 1962, 1964 and 1966.

In the 466 gubernatorial races between 1977 and 2011—the last political step taken prior to this election—among the candidates were 117 lieutenant governors (33 won), 102 attorneys general (29 won), 35 secretaries of state (eight won), 29 state treasurers (eight won), and 18 state auditors or comptrollers (three won). Looking at these numbers from a bettor's point of view, the odds of a lieutenant governor becoming governor stand at 3.55-to-1, an attorney general at 3.5-to-1; a secretary of state at 4.38-to-1; a state treasurer at 4.1-to-1; and a state auditor or comptroller stands at 6-to-1.

One other unique aspect about the current governors is that six women will be serving in 2012—the same number as were serving in 2010 and 2011. Three of these women were elected in 2010 to their first term,[4] while three others will continue terms they won or succeeded to earlier.[5] Six other women were major party candidates in the 2010 races, but they were not able to win.[6]

Women are becoming more of a part of the gubernatorial scene from 2004 to 2011. Twenty-nine women ran for governor either as incumbents seeking another term or as a major party candidate, with 14 of them winning (48 percent).

## Cost of Gubernatorial Elections

Table B presents data on the total cost of gubernatorial elections from 1977 to 2011 and reveals two very clear patterns. First is the rhythm of gubernatorial elections in each four-year cycle. In the odd year following a presidential election year, only two states hold their elections. In the mid-year between presidential elections, 36 states hold their elections. In the year before a presidential election, only three states hold their elections. And during a presidential election year, 13—now 11 states—hold their elections, as Arkansas and Rhode Island both switched to a four-year term for the governor in 1986 and 1994 respectively.

The second pattern is the consistent growth in the amounts of money spent in gubernatorial elections over the four-decade period, with only a few drops between comparable years in the cycles. These drops usually were tied to relatively uncontested races when an incumbent was successful in his or her re-election bid.

- The recent drop in the amount of money spent between the 2005 and 2009 races could have signaled the impact of the Great Recession on how much money was available for these elections. Other reasons could account for this slight drop. In 2005, both elections were open seat races in which Democrats won. In 2009, one election was an open seat race and the other saw an incumbent lose in a bid for a second term; Republicans won both races.
- The changes in the amount of money spent in the most recent mid-presidential term races is also interesting. In 2002, the total amount spent was slightly more than $841 million. In 2006, the total amount spent was down to $727.7 million,. Then in 2010, it rose up to more than $920 million!

A major part of these ups and downs is tied to the number of incumbents running and the number of open seat races. In 2002, 16 incumbents ran and 12 won; the other 20 elections were open seat races. In 2006, 31 incumbents ran and 25 won; the other five were open seat races. And in 2010, 14 incumbents ran for another term and 11 won; 23 were open seat races. Other reasons may be tied to some of the specific races.

## Table B: Total Cost of Gubernatorial Elections: 1977–2011 (in thousands of dollars)

| Year | Number of races | Total campaign costs Actual $ | Total campaign costs 2010$ (a) | Average cost per state (2010$) | Democrats Amount | Democrats Percent | Republicans Amount | Republicans Percent | Others Amount | Others Percent |
|---|---|---|---|---|---|---|---|---|---|---|
| 1977 | 2 | 12,312 | 43,505 | 21,753 | 7,051 | 57.3 | 5,261 | 42.7 | 0 | 0.0 |
| 1978 | 36 | 102,392 | 336,651 | 9,351 | 51,495 | 48.3 | 46,985 | 44.1 | 8,063 | 7.6 |
| 1979 | 3 | 32,744 | 96,876 | 32,292 | 24,546 | 75.0 | 8,197 | 25.0 | 0 | 0.0 |
| 1980 | 13 | 35,634 | 92,797 | 7,138 | 25,159 | 70.6 | 10,451 | 29.3 | 23 | 0.1 |
| 1981 | 2 | 24,648 | 58,132 | 29,066 | 12,725 | 51.6 | 11,923 | 48.4 | 0 | 0.0 |
| 1982 | 36 | 181,832 | 404,071 | 11,224 | 88,850 | 48.9 | 92,114 | 50.7 | 867 | 0.5 |
| 1983 | 3 | 39,966 | 86,134 | 28,711 | 23,804 | 72.3 | 9,076 | 27.6 | 41 | 0.1 |
| 1984 | 13 | 47,156 | 97,430 | 7,495 | 24,374 | 51.7 | 19,796 | 42.0 | 2,985 | 6.3 |
| 1985 | 2 | 18,859 | 37,568 | 18,784 | 11,532 | 61.2 | 7,326 | 38.9 | 0 | 0.0 |
| 1986 | 36 | 270,605 | 529,560 | 14,710 | 149,863 | 55.4 | 116,271 | 43.0 | 4,471 | 1.6 |
| 1987 | 3 | 40,212 | 75,872 | 25,291 | 35,786 | 89.0 | 4,426 | 11.0 | 0 | 0.0 |
| 1988 | 12 (b) | 52,208 | 94,580 | 7,882 | 25,229 | 48.3 | 26,479 | 50.7 | 501 | 1.0 |
| 1989 | 2 | 47,902 | 82,875 | 41,438 | 16,468 | 34.4 | 31,435 | 65.6 | 0 | 0.0 |
| 1990 | 36 | 345,493 | 567,312 | 15,759 | 186,060 | 53.9 | 154,681 | 44.8 | 4,751 | 1.4 |
| 1991 | 3 | 34,564 | 64,432 | 18,144 | 24,737 | 71.6 | 9,821 | 28.4 | 6 | 0.0 |
| 1992 | 12 | 60,278 | 92,168 | 7,681 | 31,106 | 51.6 | 28,311 | 47.0 | 861 | 1.4 |
| 1993 | 2 | 36,195 | 53,702 | 26,851 | 15,663 | 43.3 | 20,282 | 56.0 | 251 | 0.7 |
| 1994 | 36 | 417,873 | 604,737 | 16,798 | 194,209 | 46.5 | 210,044 | 50.3 | 13,620 | 3.3 |
| 1995 | 3 | 35,693 | 50,272 | 16,757 | 20,268 | 56.8 | 15,406 | 43.2 | 18 | 0.0 |
| 1996 | 11 (c) | 68,610 | 93,858 | 8,533 | 32,048 | 46.7 | 36,416 | 53.1 | 142 | 0.2 |
| 1997 | 2 | 44,823 | 59,924 | 29,962 | 22,530 | 50.3 | 21,432 | 47.8 | 861 | 1.9 |
| 1998 | 36 | 470,326 | 618,850 | 17,190 | 218,136 | 46.7 | 231,983 | 49.7 | 17,089 | 3.7 |
| 1999 | 3 | 16,276 | 20,947 | 6,982 | 8,226 | 50.5 | 7,987 | 49.1 | 64 | 0.4 |
| 2000 | 11 | 97,098 | 120,919 | 10,993 | 51,403 | 52.9 | 45,173 | 46.5 | 522 | 0.5 |
| 2001 | 2 | 70,400 | 85,230 | 42,615 | 35,202 | 50.0 | 34,977 | 49.7 | 221 | 0.3 |
| 2002 | 36 | 841,427 | 1,002,893 | 27,858 | 412,831 | 49.1 | 342,835 | 40.8 | 85,750 | 10.2 |
| 2003 | 4 (d) | 69,939 | 81,514 | 27,171 | 45,969 | 51.6 | 42,609 | 47.9 | 400 | 0.5 |
| 2004 | 11 | 112,625 | 127,838 | 11,622 | 58,766 | 52.0 | 54,253 | 48.0 | 74 | 0.0 |
| 2005 | 2 | 131,996 | 145,051 | 72,525 | 65,284 | 49.5 | 66,556 | 50.4 | 156 | 0.1 |
| 2006 | 36 | 727,552 | 773,991 | 21,500 | 384,196 | 52.8 | 328,250 | 45.1 | 15,035 | 2.1 |
| 2007 | 3 | 93,803 | 97,104 | 32,368 | 33,353 | 35.6 | 60,418 | 64.4 | 31 | 0.0 |
| 2008 | 11 | 118,912 | 118,438 | 10,767 | 62,083 | 52.2 | 56,584 | 47.6 | 306 | 0.3 |
| 2009 | 2 | 92,911 | 92,911 | 46,455 | 61,111 | 57.3 | 43,877 | 41.2 | 1,632 | 1.5 |
| 2010 | 37 | 920,735 | 920,735 | 24,885 | 334,814 | 36.4 | 563,688 | 61.2 | 22,233 | 2.4 |
| 2011 | 4 | 40,934 | (e) | 10,234 | 19,692,029 | 48.1 | 21,045,580 | 51.4 | 194,637 | 0.5 |

*Source:* Thad Beyle.
*Key:*
(a) Developed from the Table, "Historical Consumer Price Index for All Urban Consumers (CPI-U)," Bureau of Labor Statistics, U.S. Department of Labor. Each year's actual expenditures are converted to the 2010 value of the dollar to control for the effect of inflation over the period.
(b) As of the 1986 election, Arkansas switched to a four-year term for the governor, hence the drop from 13 to 12 for this off-year.

(c) As of the 1994 election, Rhode Island switched to a four-year term for the governor, hence the drop from 12 to 11 for this off-year.
(d) California held a special recall and replacement election in which the voters agreed to recall Gov. Gray Davis (D) from the office he was reelected to in 2002, and replace him with Arnold Schwarzenegger (R).
(e) The 2011$ were not converted into equivalent 2010$. In the next edition of *The Book of the States*, dollars spent will be converted into equivalent 2012$.

Table C shows the costs of elections from 2007 through 2010. The range in cost of these races is considerable: From the high-cost 2010 race in California ($219,802,866 in 2010 dollars), to the low-cost 2008 race in Missouri ($1,192,038). Both races were for an open seat and the winner posed a shift from a Republican to a Democratic governor.

The most money spent by the winning candidates in these elections were in Texas (just over $41 million in 2010 dollars) by Gov. Rick Perry in 2010; in California ($36.03 million) by newly elected Gov. Jerry Brown in 2010; in Michigan ($36.3 million) by newly elected Gov. Rick Snyder in 2010; in Indiana ($28 million) by Gov. Mitch Daniels win-

## Table C: Cost of Gubernatorial Campaigns, Most Recent Elections, 2007–2011

| | | | | Total campaign expenditures | | Winner | | |
| State | Year | Winner | Point margin | All candidates (2010$) | Cost per vote (2010$) | Spent (2010$) | Percent of all expenditures | Vote percent |
|---|---|---|---|---|---|---|---|---|
| Alabama | 2010 | R# | +15.7 | $28,924,325 | $19.36 | $8,306,741 | 28.7% | 57.6% |
| Alaska | 2010 | R★ | +21.4 | 2,781,674 | 10.86 | 513,698 | 18.5 | 59.1 |
| Arizona | 2010 | R★ | +11.86 | 7,828,002 | 4.53 | 1,820,004 | 23.3 | 54.3 |
| Arkansas | 2010 | D★ | +30.79 | 6,044,112 | 7.74 | 5,425,861 | 89.8 | 64.4 |
| California | 2010 | D# | +12.9 | 219,802,866 | 21.77 | 36,305,490 | 16.5 | 53.8 |
| Colorado | 2010 | D# | +14.67 | 9,483,214 | 5.30 | 3,921,135 | 41.4 | 51.1 |
| Connecticut | 2010 | D# | +0.56 | 34,056,201 | 29.72 | 8,763,028 | 25.7 | 49.5 |
| Delaware | 2008 | D# | +35.5 | 10,410,137 | 26.34 | 8,080,186 | 77.6 | 67.5 |
| Florida | 2010 | R# | +1.15 | 22,199,829 | 4.14 | 2,310,269 | 10.4 | 48.9 |
| Georgia | 2010 | R# | +10 | 27,831,419 | 10.80 | 8,340,566 | 30.0 | 53.0 |
| Hawaii | 2010 | D# | +17.1 | 11,887,573 | 31.07 | 4,601,607 | 38.7 | 58.2 |
| Idaho | 2010 | R★ | +26.2 | 3,208,692 | 7.09 | 1,797,892 | 56.0 | 59.1 |
| Illinois | 2010 | D★ | +0.85 | 32,813,221 | 8.80 | 2,007,401 | 6.1 | 46.8 |
| Indiana | 2008 | R★ | +17.8 | 36,632,483 | 13.55 | 28,062,109 | 76.6 | 57.8 |
| Iowa | 2010 | R★★★ | +9.6 | 17,658,265 | 15.77 | 8,505,180 | 48.2 | 52.9 |
| Kansas | 2010 | R# | +31.1 | 3,376,623 | 4.03 | 2,684,620 | 79.5 | 63.3 |
| Kentucky | 2011 | D★★★ | +20.4 | 15,060,810 | 18.08 | 12,013,516 | 79.8 | 55.7 |
| Louisiana | 2011 | R★ | +47.9 | 6,615,023 | 6.46 | 6,559,054 | 99.2 | 65.8 |
| Maine | 2010 | R# | +1.7 | 12,903,339 | 22.53 | 1,205,924 | 9.4 | 38.1 |
| Maryland | 2010 | D★ | +12.45 | 18,503,072 | 9.96 | 10,904,491 | 58.9 | 56.2 |
| Massachusetts | 2010 | D★ | +6.4 | 17,647,433 | 7.68 | 4,601,357 | 26.1 | 48.4 |
| Michigan | 2010 | R# | +18.2 | 47,346,738 | 14.68 | 36,292,790 | 76.7 | 58.1 |
| Minnesota | 2010 | D# | +0.42 | 16,536,147 | 7.85 | 4,743,437 | 28.7 | 46.6 |
| Mississippi | 2011 | R# | +21.9 | 8,801,588 | 9.85 | 6,317,982 | 71.8 | 61.0 |
| Missouri | 2008 | D# | +18.9 | 1,192,038 | 0.41 | 856,117 | 71.8 | 58.4 |
| Montana | 2008 | D★ | +33.0 | 1,542,312 | 3.17 | 794,052 | 51.5 | 65.5 |
| Nebraska | 2010 | R★ | +47.8 | 1,389,992 | 2.85 | 1,085,847 | 78.2 | 73.9 |
| Nevada | 2010 | R★★ | +11.75 | 9,869,684 | 13.77 | 4,333,271 | 43.9 | 53.4 |
| New Hampshire | 2010 | D★ | +7.6 | 1,979,841 | 4.34 | 1,027,383 | 51.9 | 52.6 |
| New Jersey | 2009 | R★★★ | +3.6 | 54,159,909 | 22.35 | 16,879,130 | 31.2 | 48.5 |
| New Mexico | 2010 | R# | +6.8 | 16,848,747 | 28.00 | 6,746,981 | 40.0 | 53.3 |
| New York | 2010 | D# | +25.85 | 38,253,647 | 7.33 | 23,259,271 | 60.8 | 61.6 |
| North Carolina | 2008 | D# | +3.3 | 36,617,448 | 8.58 | 15,991,217 | 43.7 | 50.3 |
| North Dakota | 2008 | R★ | +50.9 | 2,199,415 | 6.97 | 1,855,161 | 84.4 | 74.4 |
| Ohio | 2010 | R★★★ | +2 | 31,873,437 | 8.27 | 16,217,299 | 50.9 | 49.0 |
| Oklahoma | 2010 | R# | +20.9 | 10,607,876 | 10.25 | 4,055,657 | 38.2 | 60.5 |
| Oregon | 2010 | D# | +1.53 | 19,220,048 | 13.22 | 7,400,541 | 38.5 | 49.3 |
| Pennsylvania | 2010 | R# | +9 | 67,880,692 | 17.02 | 24,240,005 | 35.7 | 54.5 |
| Rhode Island | 2010 | IN# | +2.5 | 6,165,600 | 18.01 | 2,484,238 | 40.3 | 36.1 |
| South Carolina | 2010 | R# | +4.46 | 12,420,771 | 9.24 | 3,943,130 | 31.8 | 51.4 |
| South Dakota | 2010 | R# | +23.02 | 4,710,454 | 14.86 | 1,915,733 | 40.7 | 61.5 |
| Tennessee | 2010 | R# | +31.9 | 23,841,630 | 14.89 | 16,651,661 | 69.8 | 65.0 |
| Texas | 2010 | R# | +12.68 | 97,399,214 | 19.56 | 41,022,276 | 42.1 | 55.0 |
| Utah | 2010 | R★ | +32.43 | 4,695,884 | 7.90 | 2,578,015 | 54.9 | 64.2 |
| Vermont | 2010 | D★ | +1.8 | 4,359,884 | 18.00 | 1,433,984 | 32.9 | 49.5 |
| Virginia | 2009 | R# | +17.35 | 54,193,343 | 27.30 | 24,173,238 | 44.6 | 58.6 |
| Washington | 2008 | D★ | +5.5 | 25,607,830 | 8.53 | 13,833,235 | 54.0 | 53.2 |
| West Virginia | 2011 (a) | D★ | +2.33 | 10,458,277 | 34.74 | 4,156,910 | 39.7 | 49.5 |
| Wisconsin | 2010 | R# | +5.77 | 24,484,825 | 11.33 | 9,769,516 | 39.9 | 52.3 |
| Wyoming | 2010 | R# | +42.8 | 3,911,115 | 20.75 | 1,923,177 | 49.2 | 65.7 |

*Source:* Thad Beyle, *www.unc.edu/~beyle.*
*Note:* All dollar figures are in equivalent 2010$. Using the 2010 CPI-U Index which was 2.18 of the 1982–84 Index = 1.00, the actual 2007 expenditures were based on a 207.3 CPI-U index value or .9509 of the 2010$ index, the 2008 expenditures were based on a 215.3 CPI-U index value or .9876 of the 2010$ index, the 2009 expenditures were based on a 214.5 CPI-U index value or 0.984 of the 2010$ index, and the 2010 expenditures were the exact dollars spent in that election year. Then the actual expenditures of each state's governor's race were divided by the .9 value for that year to get the equivalent 2010$ value of those expenditures.

*Key:*
D — Democrat     I — Independent     R — Republican
# — Open seat     ★ — Incumbent ran and won.
★★ — Incumbent ran and lost in party primary.
★★★ — Incumbent ran and lost in general election.
(a) The 2011 election was a special election called for under West Virginia law. The law requires a governor who succeeds to office upon the resignation of a previously elected governor to get the vote of the people in order for the successor to continue to fill out the term. In Nov. 2010, Gov. Joe Manchin was elected to U.S. Congress and then-Senate President/Lt. Gov. Earl Ray Tomblin succeeded to the office of governor.

## Figure A: Gubernatorial Elections Expenditures (by millions)

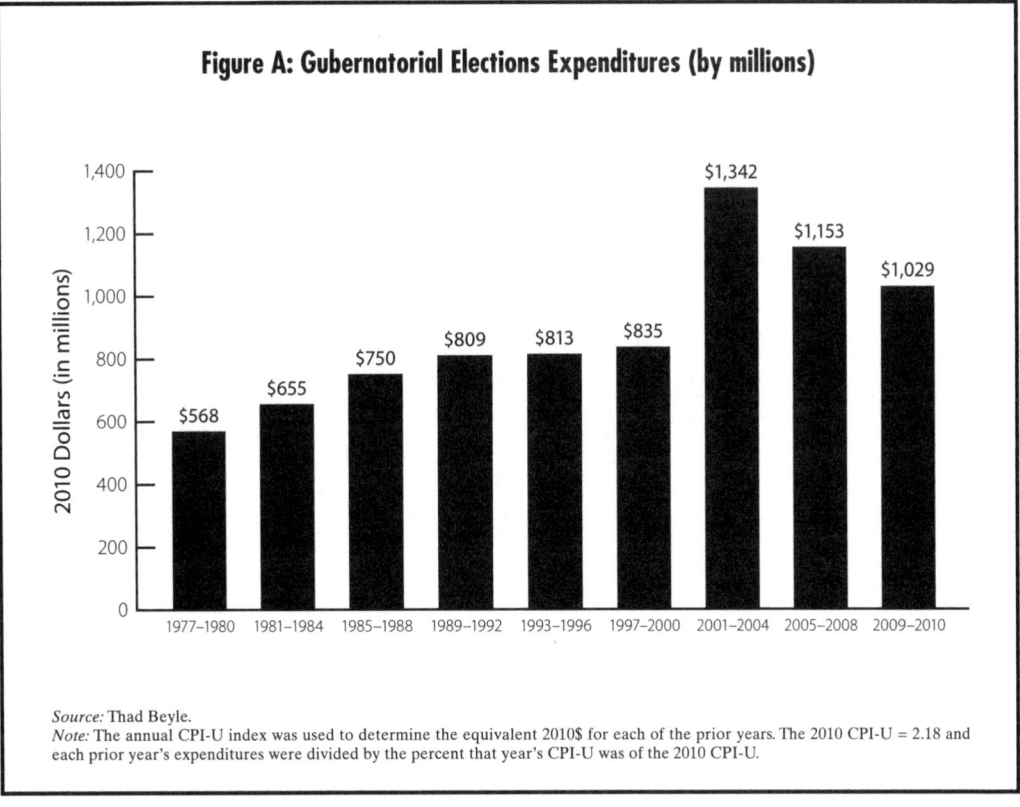

Source: Thad Beyle.
Note: The annual CPI-U index was used to determine the equivalent 2010$ for each of the prior years. The 2010 CPI-U = 2.18 and each prior year's expenditures were divided by the percent that year's CPI-U was of the 2010 CPI-U.

ning a second term in 2008; in Pennsylvania ($24.24 million) by newly elected Tom Corbett in 2010; in Virginia ($24.17 million) by newly elected Gov. Robert McDonnell in 2009; and in New York ($23.6 million) by newly elected Gov. Andrew Cuomo in 2010. The most money spent by a losing candidate was in California ($154 million) by the Republican candidate, former ebay CEO Meg Whitman, in 2010.

The least money spent by winning candidates in these elections was in Alaska ($513,698) by Gov. Sean Parnell who won a full term in 2010 after succeeding former Gov. Sarah Palin; in Montana ($794,052) by Gov. Brian Schweitzer winning his second term in 2008; in Missouri ($856,117) by newly elected Gov. Jay Nixon in 2008; in New Hampshire ($1.03 million) by Gov. John Lynch winning a fourth term in 2010; in Nebraska ($1.08 million) by Gov. Dave Heineman winning his second full term in 2010; and in Maine ($1.2 million) by newly elected Gov. Paul LePage in 2010.

But looking at the amount of money spent per general election vote shows a slightly different picture. In 2007, the most expensive races per general election vote occurred in Louisiana at $33.60 per

vote, and in Kentucky at $33.02 per vote. The Louisiana race was for an open seat, while the Kentucky race saw an incumbent defeated in the general election. The least expensive races per vote in 2008 were held in Missouri at 41 cents per vote, and in Utah at 97 cents per vote. The Missouri race was for an open seat, while in the Utah race, an incumbent won his second term.

In Figure A, by converting the actual dollars spent each year into equivalent 2010 dollars, the cost of these elections has generally increased over time. The actual dollars spent between 1977 and 2010 totaled $5.744 billion. When converted into equivalent 2010 dollars, the total was $7.954 billion. The starkness of the changes over this 34-year period can be demonstrated by comparing the amounts spent in the first four years involved (1977–80) with the amount spent in the last four years (2007–10). In the earlier 1977–80 cycle, those in the 54 races spent $567,758,192. In the latest 2007–10 cycle, those in the 53 races spent $1,248,141,978—an increase of $680,391,786, or 1.198 percent. Clearly, money really counts for a lot in gubernatorial politics.

## Table D: Women Governors in the States

| Governor | State | Year elected or succeeded to office | How woman became governor | Tenure of service | Previous offices held | Last elected position held before governorship |
|---|---|---|---|---|---|---|
| **Phase I—From initial statehood to adoption of the 19th Amendment to U.S. Constitution (1920)** | | | | | | |
| No women elected or served as governor | | | | | | |
| **Phase II—Wives of former governors elected governor, 1924–1966** | | | | | | |
| Nellie Tayloe Ross (D) | Wyoming | 1924 | E | 1/1925–1/1927 | F | ... |
| Miriam "Ma" Ferguson (D) | Texas | 1924 | E | 1/1925–1/1927 1/1933–1/1935 | F | ... |
| Lurleen Wallace (D) | Alabama | 1966 | E | 1/1967–5/1968 | F | ... |
| **Phase III—Women who became governor on their own merit, 1970 to date** | | | | | | |
| Ella Grasso (D) | Connecticut | 1974 | E | 1/1975–12/1980 | SH, SOS, (a) | (a) |
| Dixy Lee Ray (D) | Washington | 1976 | E | 1/1977–1/1981 | (b) | ... |
| Vesta M. Roy (R) | New Hampshire | 1982 | S (c) | 12/1982–1/1983 | (d) | (d) |
| Martha Layne Collins (D) | Kentucky | 1983 | E | 12/1983–12/1987 | (e), LG | LG |
| Madeleine M. Kunin (D) | Vermont | 1984 | E | 1/1985–1/1991 | SH, LG | LG |
| Kay A. Orr (R) | Nebraska | 1986 | E | 1/1987–1/1991 | T | T |
| Rose Mofford (D) | Arizona | 1988 | S (f) | 4/1988–1/1991 | SOS | SOS |
| Joan Finney (D) | Kansas | 1990 | E | 1/1991–1/1995 | T | T |
| Barbara Roberts (D) | Oregon | 1990 | E | 1/1991–1/1995 | (g), C, SH, SOS | SOS |
| Ann Richards (D) | Texas | 1990 | E | 1/1991–1/1995 | C, T | T |
| Christy Whitman (R) | New Jersey | 1993 | E | 1/1994–1/2001 | (h) | (h) |
| Jeanne Shaheen (D) | New Hampshire | 1996 | E | 1/1997–1/2003 | (d) | (d) |
| Jane Dee Hull (R) | Arizona | 1997 | S (i) | 9/1997–1/2003 | (j), SOS | SOS |
| Nancy P. Hollister (R) | Ohio | 1998 | S (k) | 12/1998–1/1999 | LG | LG |
| Ruth Ann Minner (D) | Delaware | 2000 | E | 1/2001–1/2009 | SH, SS, LG | LG |
| Judy Martz (R) | Montana | 2000 | E | 1/2001–1/2005 | LG | LG |
| Sila Calderón (Pop D) | Puerto Rico | 2000 | E | 1/2001–1/2005 | M | M |
| Jane Swift (R) | Massachusetts | 2001 | S (l) | 4/2001–1/2003 | SS, LG | LG |
| Janet Napolitano (D) | Arizona | 2002 | E | 1/2003–1/2009 | (m), AG | AG |
| Linda Lingle (R) | Hawaii | 2002 | E | 12/2002–12/2010 | C, M (n) | M |
| Kathleen Sebelius (D) | Kansas | 2002 | E | 1/2003–4/2009 | SH, (o) | (o) |
| Jennifer Granholm (D) | Michigan | 2002 | E | 1/2003–1/2011 | (p), AG | AG |
| Olene Walker (R) | Utah | 2003 | S (q) | 11/2003–1/2005 | SH, LG | LG |
| Kathleen Blanco (D) | Louisiana | 2003 | E | 1/2004–1/2008 | SH, LG | LG |
| M. Jodi Rell (R) | Connecticut | 2004 | S (r) | 7/2004–1/2011 | SH, LG | LG |
| Christine Gregoire (D) | Washington | 2004 | E | 1/2005– | AG | AG |
| Sarah Palin (R) | Alaska | 2006 | E | 1/2007–7/2009 | M (s) | M |
| Beverly Perdue (D) | North Carolina | 2008 | E | 1/2009– | SH, SS, LG | LG |
| Jan Brewer (R) | Arizona | 2009 | S (t) | 1/2009– | C, SH, SS, SOS | SOS |
| Susana Martinez (R) | New Mexico | 2010 | E | 1/2011– | (u) | (u) |
| Mary Fallin (R) | Oklahoma | 2010 | E | 1/2011– | (a) | (a) |
| Nikki Haley (R) | South Carolina | 2010 | E | 1/2011– | SH | SH |

*Sources:* National Governors Association website, *www.nga.org*, and individual state government websites.

*Key:*

S — Succeeded to office upon death, resignation or removal of the incumbent governor.

AG — Attorney general
C — City council or county commission
E — Elected governor
F — Former first lady
LG — Lieutenant governor

M — Mayor
SH — State House member
SOS — Secretary of state
SS — State Senate member
T — State treasurer

(a) Congresswoman.

(b) Ray served on the U.S. Atomic Energy Commission from 1972 to 1975 and was chair of the AEC from 1973 to 1975.

(c) Roy as state Senate president succeeded to office upon the death of Gov. Hugh Gallen.

(d) State Senate president.

(e) State Supreme Court clerk.

(f) Mofford as secretary of state became acting governor in February 1988 and governor in April 1988 upon the impeachment and removal of Gov. Evan Mecham.

(g) Local school board member.

(h) Whitman was a former state utilities official.

(i) Hull as secretary of state became acting governor when Gov. Fife Symington resigned. Elected to full term in 1998.

(j) Speaker of the state House.

(k) Hollister as lieutenant governor became governor when Gov. George Voinovich stepped down to serve in the U.S. Senate.

(l) Swift as lieutenant governor succeeded Gov. Paul Celluci who resigned after being appointed ambassador to Canada. Was the first governor to give birth while serving in office.

(m) U.S. attorney.

(n) Lingle was mayor of Maui for two terms, elected in 1990 and 1996.

(o) Insurance commissioner.

(p) Federal prosecutor.

(q) Walker as lieutenant governor succeeded to the governorship upon the resignation of Gov. Mike Leavitt in 2003.

(r) Rell as lieutenant governor succeeded to the governorship upon the resignation of Gov. John Rowland in 2004.

(s) Palin was a two-term Mayor of Wasilla, Alaska, and had unsuccessfully sought the lieutenant governor's office in 2002. In 2008, Palin was nominated to be the vice presidential candidate on the Republican ticket with U.S. Sen. John McCain.

(t) Brewer as secretary of state succeeded to the governorship upon the resignation of Gov. Janet Napolitano in January 2009 after her confirmation as head of the U.S. Department of Homeland Security. Brewer then won a full term in the 2010 election.

(u) District Attorney—Dona Ana County, N.M.

## Table E: 2008–2011 Governors' Race Winners by Party and Margin

| | Democratic winners | | | | Republican winners | | | | Independent winners | | |
|---|---|---|---|---|---|---|---|---|---|---|---|
| State | Election Year | Percent of win | Point margin | State | Election Year | Percent of win | Point margin | State | Election Year | Percent of win | Point margin |
| New Hampshire .. | 2008 | 70.2% | +42.6 | Utah..................... | 2008 | 77.7% | +58.0 | Rhode Island ....... | 2010 | 36.1% | +2.5 |
| West Virginia ....... | 2008 | 69.8 | +44.1 | Nebraska.............. | 2010 | 74.9 | +47.8 | | | | |
| Delaware.............. | 2008 | 67.5 | +35.5 | North Dakota ...... | 2008 | 74.4 | +50.9 | | | | |
| Montana............... | 2008 | 65.5 | +33.0 | Louisiana.............. | 2011 | 65.8 | +47.9 | | | | |
| Arkansas ............. | 2010 | 64.4 | +30.8 | Wyoming.............. | 2010 | 65.7 | +42.8 | | | | |
| New York ............ | 2010 | 61.6 | +27.0 | Utah..................... | 2010 | 64.2 | +32.4 | | | | |
| Missouri .............. | 2008 | 58.4 | +18.9 | Kansas ................. | 2010 | 63.3 | +31.1 | | | | |
| Hawaii ................. | 2010 | 58.2 | +17.1 | South Dakota ...... | 2010 | 61.5 | +23.0 | | | | |
| Maryland............. | 2010 | 56.2 | +14.4 | Mississippi............ | 2011 | 61.1 | +22.1 | | | | |
| California ............ | 2010 | 53.8 | +12.9 | Oklahoma ............ | 2010 | 60.4 | +20.9 | | | | |
| Washington ......... | 2008 | 53.2 | +6.5 | Idaho .................. | 2010 | 59.1 | +26.2 | | | | |
| New Hampshire .. | 2010 | 52.6 | +7.6 | Alaska ................. | 2010 | 59.1 | +20.9 | | | | |
| North Carolina .... | 2008 | 50.3 | +1.8 | Virginia................ | 2009 | 58.6 | +17.4 | | | | |
| Colorado ............. | 2010 | 50.0 | +14.6 | Michigan ............ | 2010 | 58.1 | +18.2 | | | | |
| Vermont .............. | 2010 | 49.5 | +1.8 | Indiana................ | 2008 | 57.8 | +17.8 | | | | |
| Connecticut ........ | 2010 | 49.5 | +0.56 | Alabama.............. | 2010 | 57.6 | +15.7 | | | | |
| West Virginia ....... | 2011 | 49.5 | +2.3 | Kentucky.............. | 2011 | 55.1 | +19.8 | | | | |
| Oregon ................ | 2010 | 49.3 | +1.5 | Texas.................... | 2010 | 55.0 | +12.7 | | | | |
| Massachusetts...... | 2010 | 48.4 | +0.85 | Pennsylvania........ | 2010 | 54.5 | +9.0 | | | | |
| Illinois.................. | 2010 | 46.8 | +0.8 | Arizona .............. | 2010 | 54.3 | +14.5 | | | | |
| Minnesota ........... | 2010 | 43.6 | +0.42 | Vermont .............. | 2008 | 53.4 | +31.6 | | | | |
| | | | | Nevada ............... | 2010 | 53.4 | +11.8 | | | | |
| | | | | New Mexico......... | 2010 | 53.3 | +6.8 | | | | |
| | | | | Georgia ............... | 2010 | 53.0 | +10 | | | | |
| | | | | Iowa.................... | 2010 | 52.9 | +9.6 | | | | |
| | | | | Wisconsin............. | 2010 | 52.3 | +5.8 | | | | |
| | | | | South Carolina .... | 2010 | 51.4 | +4.4 | | | | |
| | | | | Ohio..................... | 2010 | 49.0 | +2.0 | | | | |
| | | | | Florida ................. | 2010 | 48.9 | +1.15 | | | | |
| | | | | New Jersey........... | 2009 | 48.5 | +3.6 | | | | |
| | | | | Maine................... | 2010 | 38.1 | +1.7 | | | | |

*Source:* Thad Beyle.

*Overall results by victory point margin: party and region*

| Point margin | Number of states | Number of Republicans | Number of Democrats | Number of Independents | East | South | Midwest | West |
|---|---|---|---|---|---|---|---|---|
| 10+ points | 33 | 22 | 11 | 0 | 5 | 11 | 6 | 11 |
| 5/-10 points | 6 | 4 | 2 | 0 | 2 | 0 | 2 | 2 |
| 0/-5 points | 14 | 5 | 8 | 1 | 6 | 4 | 3 | 1 |
| **Totals:** | 53 | 31 | 21 | 1 | 13 | 15 | 11 | 14 |

*Source:* Thad Beyle.

## Table F: New Governors Elected Each 4-Year Period, 1970–2011 (a)

| Year | Number of gubernatorial elections | New Governors | | Incumbents Running | | | |
|------|------|------|------|------|------|------|------|
| | | Won | Percent | Number | Won | Lost | Percent Lost |
| 1970 | 35 | 19 | 54 | 24 | 16 | 8 | 36 |
| 1971 | 3 | 3 | 100 | ... | ... | ... | ... |
| 1972 | 18 | 11 | 61 | 11 | 7 | 4 | 36 |
| 1973 | 2 | 2 | 100 | 1 | ... | 1 | 100 |
| 1974 | 35 | 18 | 51 | 22 | 17 | 5 | 24 |
| 1975 | 3 | 1 | 33 | 2 | 2 | ... | ... |
| 1976 | 14 | 9 | 64 | 8 | 5 | 3 | 33 |
| 1977 | 2 | 1 | 50 | 1 | 1 | ... | ... |
| 1978 | 36 | 20 | 56 | 23 | 16 | 7 | 30 |
| 1979 | 3 | 3 | 100 | ... | ... | ... | ... |
| 1980 | 13 | 6 | 46 | 12 | 7 | 5 | 42 |
| 1981 | 2 | 2 | 100 | ... | ... | ... | ... |
| 1982 | 36 | 17 | 47 | 25 | 19 | 6 | 24 |
| 1983 | 3 | 3 | 100 | 1 | ... | 1 | 100 |
| 1984 | 13 | 9 | 69 | 6 | 4 | 2 | 33 |
| 1985 | 2 | 1 | 50 | 1 | 1 | ... | ... |
| 1986 | 36 | 21 | 58 | 18 | 15 | 3 | 18 |
| 1987 | 3 | 3 | 100 | 1 | ... | 1 | 100 |
| 1988 | 12 | 4 | 33 | 9 | 8 | 1 | 11 |
| 1989 | 2 | 2 | 100 | ... | ... | ... | ... |
| 1990 | 36 | 19 | 53 | 23 | 17 | 6 | 26 |
| 1991 | 3 | 3 | 100 | 2 | ... | 2 | 100 |
| 1992 | 12 | 8 | 67 | 4 | 4 | ... | ... |
| 1993 | 2 | 1 | 50 | 1 | ... | 1 | 100 |
| 1994 | 36 | 19 | 53 | 23 | 17 | 6 | 26 |
| 1995 | 3 | 2 | 67 | 1 | 1 | ... | ... |
| 1996 | 11 | 4 | 36 | 7 | 7 | ... | ... |
| 1997 | 2 | 1 | 50 | 1 | 1 | ... | ... |
| 1998 | 36 | 13 | 36 | 25 | 23 | 2 | 8 |
| 1999 | 3 | 1 | 33 | 2 | 2 | ... | ... |
| 2000 | 11 | 6 | 55 | 6 | 5 | 1 | 17 |
| 2001 | 2 | 2 | 100 | ... | ... | ... | ... |
| 2002 | 36 | 24 | 67 | 16 | 12 | 4 | 25 |
| 2003 (b) | 4 | 4 | 100 | 2 | ... | 2 | 100 |
| 2004 | 11 | 7 | 64 | 8 | 4 | 4 | 50 |
| 2005 | 2 | 2 | 100 | ... | ... | ... | ... |
| 2006 | 36 | 9 | 25 | 27 | 25 | 2 | 7 |
| 2007 | 3 | 2 | 67 | 2 | 1 | 1 | 50 |
| 2008 | 11 | 3 | 24 | 8 | 8 | ... | ... |
| 2009 | 2 | 2 | 100 | 1 | ... | 1 | 100 |
| 2010 | 37 | 26 | 70 | 14 | 11 | 3 | 21 |
| 2011 | 4 | 1 | 25 | 3 | 3 | 0 | 0 |
| **Totals:** | 576 | 316 | 55 | 341 | 259 | 82 | 24 |

Key:
(a) Table A: Gubernatorial Elections: 1970–2010, *The Book of the States, 2011* (Lexington, KY: The Council of State Governments, 2011): 128.

(b) In 2003, there was a recall and replacement election vote in California in which the incumbent Gov. Gray Davis-D was recalled and Republican Arnold Schwarzenegger was elected as his replacement.

## The 2009–12 Cycle in Process

We are now three years through the current four-year cycle. In the 43 races held from 2009 to 2011, we saw 29 states elect new governors and five other states gain successor governors (North Dakota Gov. John Hoeven and West Virginia Gov. Joe Manchin were elected to U.S. Senate seats; Kansas Gov. Kathleen Sebelius and Arizona Gov. Janet Napolitano were appointed by President Obama to cabinet positions; and Illinois Gov. Rod Blagojevich was impeached).

In 2012, 11 states will hold gubernatorial elections.[7] These seats are now held by eight Democrats and three Republicans, but four incumbents—in Indiana, Montana, New Hampshire and Washington —face term limits. So, there will be at least four new governors elected in 2012.

## Notes

[1] Five of these new governors succeeded governors who resigned upon moving on to a new responsibility before the end of their elected terms: Alaska (2009), Arizona (2009), Kansas (2009), Nebraska (2005), Texas (2000); four others succeeded due to problems the incumbents had and were removed from office in California (2003) and Illinois (2009), or the incumbent governor resigned to avoid efforts to remove them due to certain activities they had performed while governors in New Jersey (2010) and New York (2008).

[2] In North Dakota, Lt. Gov. Jack Dalrymple-R, succeeded outgoing Gov. John Hoeven-R, who was elected to the U.S. Senate in the 2010 election. In West Virginia, state Senate President Earl Ray Tomlin-D, succeeded outgoing Gov. Joe Manchin-D, who appointed himself to fill the remaining years of deceased Democratic U.S. Senator Robert Byrd's term.

[3] Steve Beshear-D, in Kentucky and Bobby Jindal-R, in Louisiana.

[4] New Mexico Gov. Susana Martinez, Oklahoma Gov. Mary Fallin and South Carolina Gov. Nikki Haley—all Republicans.

[5] Arizona Gov. Jan Brewer-R, succeeded to office in January 2009, North Carolina Gov. Beverly Perdue-D, won in 2008 and Washington Gov. Christine Gregoire-D, won in 2004 and 2008.

[6] In California, Meg Whitman-R; in Florida, Alex Sink-D; in Maine, Libby Mitchell-D; in New Mexico, Diane Denish-D; in Oklahoma, Jari Adkins-D; and in Wyoming, Leslie Petersen-D.

[7] Eleven gubernatorial elections will be held in 2012: Delaware, Indiana, Missouri, Montana, New Hampshire, North Carolina, North Dakota, Utah, Vermont, Washington and West Virginia.

## About the Author

**Thad Beyle** is a professor-emeritus of political science at the University of North Carolina at Chapel Hill. A Syracuse University A.B. and A.M., he received his Ph.D. at the University of Illinois. He spent a year in the North Carolina governor's office in the mid-1960s followed by two years with Terry Sanford's "A Study of American States" project at Duke University, and has worked with the National Governors Association in several capacities on gubernatorial transitions.

**Table 4.1**
**THE GOVERNORS, 2012**

| State or other jurisdiction | Name and party | Length of regular term in years | Date of first service | Present term ends | Number of previous terms | Term limits | Joint election of governor and lieutenant governor (a) | Official who succeeds governor | Birthdate | Birthplace |
|---|---|---|---|---|---|---|---|---|---|---|
| Alabama | Robert Bentley (R) | 4 | 1/2011 | 1/2015 | ... | 2-4 | No | LG | 2/3/1943 | AL |
| Alaska | Sean Parnell (R) | 4 | 7/2009 (b) | 12/2014 | 1(b) | 2-4 | Yes | LG | 11/19/1962 | CA |
| Arizona | Jan Brewer (R) | 4 | 1/2009 (c) | 1/2015 | 1 (c) | 2-4 | (d) | SS | 9/26/1944 | CA |
| Arkansas | Mike Beebe (D) | 4 | 1/2007 | 1/2015 | 1 | 2A | No | LG | 12/28/1946 | AR |
| California | Edmund Gerald "Jerry" Brown (D) | 4 | 1/1975 (e) | 1/2015 | 2 (e) | 2A (e) | No | LG | 4/7/1938 | CA |
| Colorado | John Hickenlooper (D) | 4 | 1/2011 | 1/2015 | ... | 2-4 | Yes | LG | 2/7/1952 | NY |
| Connecticut | Dan Malloy (D) | 4 | 1/2011 | 1/2015 | ... | ... | Yes | LG | 7/21/1955 | CT |
| Delaware | Jack Markell (D) | 4 | 1/2009 | 1/2013 | ... | 2A | No | LG | 11/26/1960 | DE |
| Florida | Rick Scott (R) | 4 | 1/2011 | 1/2015 | ... | 2-4 | Yes | LG | 12/2/1952 | IL |
| Georgia | Nathan Deal (R) | 4 | 1/2011 | 1/2015 | ... | 2-4 | No | LG | 8/25/1942 | GA |
| Hawaii | Neil Abercrombie (D) | 4 | 12/2010 | 12/2014 | ... | 2-4 | Yes | LG | 6/26/1938 | NY |
| Idaho | C.L. "Butch" Otter (R) | 4 | 1/2007 | 1/2015 | 1 | ... | No | LG | 5/3/1942 | ID |
| Illinois | Patrick Quinn (D) | 4 | 1/2009 (f) | 1/2015 | 1(f) | ... | Yes | LG | 12/16/1948 | IL |
| Indiana | Mitch Daniels (R) | 4 | 1/2005 | 1/2013 | 1 | 2-12 | Yes | LG | 4/7/1949 | PA |
| Iowa | Terry Branstad (R) | 4 | 1/1983 (g) | 1/2015 | 4 (g) | ... | Yes | LG | 11/17/1946 | IA |
| Kansas | Sam Brownback (R) | 4 | 1/2011 | 1/2015 | ... | 2-4 | Yes | LG | 9/12/1956 | KS |
| Kentucky | Steven L. Beshear (D) | 4 | 12/2007 | 12/2015 | 1 | 2-4 | Yes | LG | 9/21/1944 | KY |
| Louisiana | Bobby Jindal (R) | 4 | 1/2008 | 1/2016 | 1 | 2-4 | No | LG | 6/10/1971 | LA |
| Maine | Paul LePage (R) | 4 | 1/2011 | 1/2015 | ... | 2-4 | (d) | PS | 10/9/1948 | ME |
| Maryland | Martin O'Malley (D) | 4 | 1/2007 | 1/2015 | 1 | 2-4 | Yes | LG | 1/18/1963 | MD |
| Massachusetts | Deval L. Patrick (D) | 4 | 1/2007 | 1/2015 | 1 | ... | Yes | LG | 7/31/1956 | IL |
| Michigan | Rick Snyder (R) | 4 | 1/2011 | 1/2015 | ... | 2A | Yes | LG | 8/19/1958 | MI |
| Minnesota | Mark Dayton (D) | 4 | 1/2011 | 1/2015 | ... | ... | Yes | LG | 1/26/1947 | MN |
| Mississippi | Phil Bryant (R) | 4 | 1/2012 | 1/2016 | ... | 2A | Yes | LG | 12/9/1954 | MS |
| Missouri | Jay Nixon (D) | 4 | 1/2009 | 1/2013 | ... | 2A | No | LG | 2/13/1956 | MO |
| Montana | Brian Schweitzer (D) | 4 | 1/2005 | 1/2013 | 1 | 2-16 | Yes | LG | 9/4/1955 | MT |
| Nebraska | Dave Heineman (R) | 4 | 1/2005 (h) | 1/2015 | 1 (h) | 2-4 | Yes | LG | 5/12/1948 | NE |
| Nevada | Brian Sandoval (R) | 4 | 1/2011 | 1/2015 | ... | 2A | No | LG | 8/5/1963 | CA |
| New Hampshire | John Lynch (D) | 2 | 1/2005 | 1/2013 | 3 | ... | (d) | PS | 11/25/1952 | MA |
| New Jersey | Christopher J. Christie (R) | 4 | 1/2010 | 1/2014 | ... | 2-4 | Yes | LG | 9/6/1962 | NJ |
| New Mexico | Susana Martinez (R) | 4 | 1/2011 | 1/2015 | ... | 2-4 | Yes | LG | 7/14/1959 | TX |
| New York | Andrew Cuomo(D) | 4 | 1/2011 | 1/2015 | ... | ... | Yes | LG | 12/6/1957 | NY |
| North Carolina | Beverly Perdue (D) | 4 | 1/2009 | 1/2013 | 1 | 2-4 | No | LG | 1/14/1947 | VA |
| North Dakota | Jack Dalrymple (R) | 4 | 12/2010 (i) | 12/2012 | ... | ... | Yes | LG | 10/16/1948 | MN |
| Ohio | John Kasich (R) | 4 | 1/2011 | 1/2015 | ... | 2-4 | Yes | LG | 5/13/1952 | PA |
| Oklahoma | Mary Fallin (R) | 4 | 1/2011 | 1/2015 | ... | 2-A | No | LG | 12/9/1954 | MO |
| Oregon | John Kitzhaber (D) | 4 | 1/1995 (j) | 1/2015 | 2 | 2-12 | (d) | SS | 3/5/1947 | WA |
| Pennsylvania | Tom Corbett (R) | 4 | 1/2011 | 1/2015 | ... | 2-4 | Yes | LG | 6/17/1949 | PA |
| Rhode Island | Lincoln Chafee (I) | 4 | 1/2011 | 1/2015 | ... | 2-4 | No | LG | 3/26/1953 | RI |
| South Carolina | Nikki Haley (R) | 4 | 1/2011 | 1/2015 | ... | 2-4 | No | LG | 1/20/1972 | SC |

See footnotes at end of table.

# THE GOVERNORS, 2012—Continued

| State or other jurisdiction | Name and party | Length of regular term in years | Date of first service | Number of previous terms | Present term ends | Term limits | Joint election of governor and lieutenant governor (a) | Official who succeeds governor | Birthdate | Birthplace |
|---|---|---|---|---|---|---|---|---|---|---|
| South Dakota | Dennis Daugaard (R) | 4 | 1/2011 | ... | 1/2015 | 2-4 | Yes | LG | 6/11/1953 | SD |
| Tennessee | Bill Haslam (R) | 4 | 1/2011 | ... | 1/2015 | 2-4 | No | SpS (k) | 8/23/1952 | TN |
| Texas | Rick Perry (R) | 4 | 12/2000 (l) | 3 (l) | 1/2015 | ... | No | LG | 3/4/1950 | TX |
| Utah | Gary Herbert (R) | 4 | 8/2009 (m) | 1 | 1/2013 (m) | ... | Yes | LG | 5/7/1947 | UT |
| Vermont | Peter Shumlin (D) | 2 | 1/2011 | ... | 1/2013 | ... | No | LG | 3/24/1956 | VT |
| Virginia | Robert McDonnell (R) | 4 | 1/2010 | ... | 1/2014 | 1-4 | No | LG | 6/15/1954 | PA |
| Washington | Christine Gregoire (D) | 4 | 1/2005 | 1 | 1/2013 | ... | No | LG | 3/24/1957 | WA |
| West Virginia | Earl Ray Tomblin (D) | 4 | 11/2010 (n) | ... | 1/2013 | 2-4 | (d) | PS (k) | 3/15/1952 | WV |
| Wisconsin | Scott Walker (R) | 4 | 1/2011 | ... | 1/2015 | ... | Yes | LG | 11/2/1967 | CO |
| Wyoming | Matt Mead (R) | 4 | 1/2011 | ... | 1/2015 | 2-16 | (d) | SS | 3/11/1962 | WY |
| American Samoa | Togiola Tulafono (D) | 4 | 4/2003 (o) | 2 (o) | 1/2013 | 2-4 | Yes | LG | 2/28/1947 | AS |
| Guam | Eddie Calvo (R) | 4 | 1/2011 | ... | 1/2015 | 2-4 | Yes | LG | 8/29/1961 | Guam |
| No. Mariana Islands | Benigno Fitial (C) | 4 (p) | 1/2006 | 1 | 1/2015 (p) | 2A | Yes | LG | 11/27/1945 | CNMI |
| Puerto Rico | Luis G. Fortuño (R) (NPP) | 4 | 1/2009 | ... | 1/2013 | ... | (d) | SS | 10/31/1960 | PR |
| U.S. Virgin Islands | John deJongh Jr. (D) | 4 | 1/2007 | 1 | 1/2015 | 2-4 | Yes | LG | 11/13/1957 | USVI |

*Source:* The Council of State Governments, January 2012.

*Key:*
C — Covenant
D — Democrat
I — Independent
NPP — New Progressive Party
R — Republican
LG — Lieutenant Governor
SS — Secretary of State
PS — President of the Senate
SpS — Speaker of the Senate
... — Not applicable
2A — Two terms, absolute.
2-4 — Two terms, re-eligible after four yrs.
2-12 — Two terms, eligible for eight out of 12 yrs.
2-16 — Two terms, eligible for eight out of 16 yrs.
1-4 — One term, re-eligible after four years.

(a) The following also choose candidates for governor and lieutenant governor through a joint nomination process: Florida, Kansas, Maryland, Minnesota, Montana, North Dakota, Ohio, Utah, American Samoa, Guam, No. Mariana Islands and U.S. Virgin Islands.

(b) Lieutenant Governor Sean Parnell was sworn in as governor on July 26, 2009 after Governor Palin resigned. He was elected to a full term in the November 2010 general election.

(c) Secretary of State Jan Brewer succeeded to the office of governor on January 21, 2009, upon Governor Napolitano's appointment as U.S. Secretary of Homeland Security. Her partial term will serve as the first of two terms allowed by Arizona law.

(d) No lieutenant governor.

(e) Governor Brown previously served two terms as governor of California from 1975–1983. He was elected again in November 2010 and was inaugurated on January 3, 2011 to begin serving his third

term. California instituted absolute term-limits of two four-year terms for the office of governor in 1990. Those who served as governor prior to that date are eligible for re-election. Gov. Brown will now be limited to serving two more terms.

(f) Lieutenant Governor Patrick Quinn became governor on January 29, 2009 after Governor Blagojevich was removed from office. He was elected to a full term in November 2010.

(g) Governor Branstad was first elected in 1983 and served for four terms until 1999. He was elected to a fifth term in November of 2010.

(h) Governor Heineman, as lieutenant governor, was sworn-in as Nebraska's governor on Friday, January 21, 2005 after Governor Johanns resigned on January 20, 2005 upon being confirmed as the United States Secretary of Agriculture. He was then elected to full terms in the 2006 and 2010 general elections.

(i) Lt. Gov. Dalrymple was sworn in on December 21, 2010 to complete Governor Hoeven's term as governor of North Dakota after Hoeven was elected to the Senate.

(j) John Kitzhaber previously served two terms as governor of Oregon from 1995–2003 and was elected again in November 2010 and was inaugurated on January 10, 2011 to begin serving his third term.

(k) Official bears the additional title of "lieutenant governor."

(l) Lt. Gov. Perry was sworn in on December 21, 2000 to complete President George W. Bush's term as governor of Texas. He was elected to serve four-year terms in 2002, 2006 and 2010.

(m) Lieutenant Governor Gary Herbert was sworn in as governor on August 10, 2009 after Governor Huntsman resigned to accept President Obama's appointment as Ambassador to China. Utah law states that a replacement governor elevated in a term's first year will face a special election at the next regularly scheduled general election, November 2010, instead of serving the remainder of the term. Utah's next regular scheduled gubernatorial election will be held in Nov. 2012.

(n) Senate President Earl Ray Tomblin was sworn in as governor on November 15, 2010 after Gov. Manchin was elected in the November election to fill Sen. Robert Byrd's seat.

(o) Governor Tulafono, as lieutenant governor, became governor in April 2003 after Governor Sunia's death. He was elected to four-year terms in November 2004 and 2008.

(p) The current governor will serve a five-year term to change future CNMI elections to even-numbered years. The next election will occur in November 2014.

## Table 4.2
## THE GOVERNORS: QUALIFICATIONS FOR OFFICE

| State or other jurisdiction | Minimum age | State citizen (years) | U.S. citizen (years) (a) | State resident (years) (b) | Qualified voter (years) |
|---|---|---|---|---|---|
| Alabama | 30 | ... | 10 | 7 | ★ |
| Alaska | 30 | ★ | 7 | 7 | ★ |
| Arizona | 25 | 5 | 10 | ... | ... |
| Arkansas | 30 | ★ | ★ | 7 | ★ |
| California | 18 | ... | 5 | 5 | ★ |
| Colorado | 30 | ... | ★ | 2 | ... |
| Connecticut | 30 | (c) | ★ | ★ | (c) |
| Delaware | 30 | ... | 12 | 6 | ... |
| Florida | 30 | ★ | ... | 7 | 7 |
| Georgia | 30 | ... | 15 | 6 | ... |
| Hawaii | 30 | ... | 5 | 5 | ★ |
| Idaho | 30 | 2 | ★ | 2 | ... |
| Illinois | 25 | 3 | ★ | 3 | ★ |
| Indiana | 30 | ... | 5 | 5 | ★ |
| Iowa | 30 | 2 | 2 | 2 | ★ |
| Kansas | ... | ... | ... | ... | ... |
| Kentucky | 30 | 6 | ... | 6 | ... |
| Louisiana | 25 | 5 | 5 | 5 | ★ |
| Maine | 30 | ... | 15 | 5 | ... |
| Maryland | 30 | ... | (d) | 5 | 5 |
| Massachusetts | ... | ... | ... | 7 | ... |
| Michigan | 30 | ... | ★ | ★ | 4 |
| Minnesota | 25 | ... | ★ | 1 | ★ |
| Mississippi | 30 | ★ | 20 | 5 | ★ |
| Missouri | 30 | ... | 15 | 10 | ... |
| Montana | 25 | ★ | ★ | 2 | ★ |
| Nebraska | 30 | 5 | 5 | 5 | ... |
| Nevada | 25 | 2 | 2 | 2 | ★ |
| New Hampshire | 30 | ... | ... | 7 | ... |
| New Jersey | 30 | ... | 20 | 7 | ... |
| New Mexico | 30 | ... | ★ | 5 | ★ |
| New York | 30 | ... | ★ | 5 | ... |
| North Carolina | 30 | ... | 5 | 2 | ★ |
| North Dakota | 30 | ... | ★ | 5 | ★ |
| Ohio | 18 | ... | ★ | ★ | ★ |
| Oklahoma | 31 | ... | 10 | 10 | 10 |
| Oregon | 30 | ... | ★ | 3 | ... |
| Pennsylvania | 30 | ★ | ★ | 7 | ★ |
| Rhode Island | 18 | 30 days | 30 days | 30 days | 30 days |
| South Carolina | 30 | 5 | 5 | 5 | ... |
| South Dakota | 18 | ★ | ★ | ★ | ★ |
| Tennessee | 30 | 7 | ★ | ... | ... |
| Texas | 30 | ... | ★ | 5 | ... |
| Utah | 30 | 5 | 3 | 5 | ★ |
| Vermont | 18 | 1 | ... | 4 | ★ |
| Virginia | 30 | ★ | ★ | ★ | 5 |
| Washington | 18 | ... | ★ | ★ | ★ |
| West Virginia | 30 | 5 | ★ | 1 | ★ |
| Wisconsin | 18 | ★ | ★ | ★ | ★ |
| Wyoming | 30 | ★ | ★ | 5 | ★ |
| American Samoa | 35 | ... | ★ | 5 | ... |
| Guam | 30 | ... | 5 | 5 | ★ |
| No. Mariana Islands | 35 | ... | ★ | 10 | ★ |
| Puerto Rico | 35 | 5 | 5 | 5 | ... |
| U.S. Virgin Islands | 30 | ... | 5 | 5 | ★ |

*Source:* The Council of State Governments' survey of governor's offices, December 2009 and state websites February 2012.

*Key:*

★ — Formal provision; number of years not specified.

... — No formal provision.

(a) In some states you must be a U.S. citizen to be an elector, and must be an elector to run.

(b) In some states you must be a state resident to be an elector, and must be an elector to run.

(c) Must be an elector of the state, not a state citizen.

(d) *Crosse v. Board of Supervisors of Elections* 243 Md. 555, 221 A.2d 431 (1966) — opinion rendered indicated that U.S. citizenship was, by necessity, a requirement for office.

## Table 4.3
## THE GOVERNORS: COMPENSATION, STAFF, TRAVEL AND RESIDENCE

| State or other jurisdiction | Salary | Governor's office staff (a) | Access to state transportation | | | Receives travel allowance | Reimbursed for travel expenses | Official residence |
|---|---|---|---|---|---|---|---|---|
| | | | Automobile | Airplane | Helicopter | | | |
| Alabama | (c) | 60 | ★ | ★ | ★ | ... | ... | ★ |
| Alaska | 145,000 | 71 | ★ | ★ | ... | ... | ★(b) | ★ |
| Arizona | 95,000 | 34 | ★ | ★ | ... | ... | ★(b) | ... |
| Arkansas | 86,890 | 67 | ★ | ★ | ... | ... | ★ | ★ |
| California | 173,987 | 185 | ★ | ... | ... | (b) | (d) | (e) |
| Colorado | 90,000 | 50 | ★ | ★ | ... | ★ | ★ | (e) |
| Connecticut | 150,000 | 37 | ★ | ... | ... | ... | ... | (e) |
| Delaware | 171,000 | 32 | ★ | ... | ... | ... | ... | ★ |
| Florida | 130,273 (c) | 325 (f) | ★ | ★ | ★ | ... | ★(b) | ★ |
| Georgia | 139,339 | 56 (f) | ★ | ★ | ★ | ... | ... | ★ |
| Hawaii | 117,312 | 67 | ★ | ★ | ★ | ★ | ★ | ★ |
| Idaho | 115,348 | 22 | ★ | ★ | ... | ★(b) | ★(b) | (e) |
| Illinois | 177,412 | 130 | ★ | ★ | ★ | ★ | (d) | ★ |
| Indiana | 107,881 | 34 | ★ | ★ | ★ | ★(b) | ★(b) | ★ |
| Iowa | 130,000 | 32 | ★ | ... | ... | ... | ★ | ★ |
| Kansas | 99,636 | 24 | ★ | ★ | ★ | ... | ★ | ★ |
| Kentucky | 151,643 (c) | 65 | ★ | ★ | ★ | ★ | ... | ★ |
| Louisiana | 130,000 | 93 (f) | ★ | ★ | ★ | ... | ★ | ★ |
| Maine | 70,000 | 19 | ★ | ... | ... | ★ | ★ | ★ |
| Maryland | 150,000 | 85 (f) | ★ | ★ | ★ | (b) | (b) | ★ |
| Massachusetts | 139,832 | 70 | ★ | ... | ★ | ★(b) | ★(b) | ... |
| Michigan | 159,300 (c) | 92 | ★(h) | ★(i) | ... | (b) | (b) | (e) |
| Minnesota | 120,303 | 43 | ★ | ★ | ★ | ... | ★ | ★ |
| Mississippi | 122,160 | 46 | ★ | ★ | ... | ... | ★ | ★ |
| Missouri | 133,821 | 38 | ★ | ★ | ... | (b) | (d) | ★ |
| Montana | 108,167 | 65 (f) | ★ | ★ | ★ | ... | ★(b) | ★ |
| Nebraska | 105,000 | 9 | ★ | ★ | ... | ★ | ★ | ★ |
| Nevada | 141,000 | 21 | ★ | ★ | ... | (b) | ... | ★ |
| New Hampshire | 113,834 | 23 | ★ | ... | ... | (b) | (d) | (e) |
| New Jersey | 175,000 | 125 | ★ | ... | ★ | ... | ★(b) | (e) |
| New Mexico | 110,000 | 39.3 | ★ | ★ | ★ | ... | ... | ★ |
| New York | 179,000 (c) | 180 | ★ | ★ | ★ | ... | ★ | ★ |
| North Carolina | 139,590 | 68 | ★ | ★ | ★ | ★(b) | ★(b) | ★ |
| North Dakota | 110,283 | 17 | ★ | ★ | ... | ... | ★ | ★ |
| Ohio | 148,886 | 60 | ★ | ★ | ★ | (b) | (d) | (e) |
| Oklahoma | 147,000 | 30 | ★ | ★ | ... | ★(b) | ★(b) | ★ |
| Oregon | 93,600 | 65 (f) | ★ | ... | ... | ★(b) | ★(b) | ★ |
| Pennsylvania | 183,255 (c) | 68 | ★ | ★ | ... | ... | ★(b) | ★ |
| Rhode Island | 129,210 | 46 | ★ | ... | ★ | ... | ★ | ... |
| South Carolina | 106,078 | 29 | ★ | ★ | ... | ... | ★ | ★ |
| South Dakota | 98,031 | 21.5 | ★ | ★ | ... | ... | ★ | ★ |
| Tennessee | 170,340 (c) | 32 | ★ | ★ | ★ | ★(b) | ★(b) | ★ |
| Texas | 150,000 | 266 | ★ | ★ | ★ | ... | ★ | ★ |
| Utah | 109,470 | 16 | ★ | ★ | ★ | ... | ★ | ★ |
| Vermont | 142,542 (c) | 12 | ★ | ... | ... | ★ | ... | ... |
| Virginia | 175,000 | 44 | ★ | ★ | ★ | ... | ★ | ★ |
| Washington | 166,891 | 36 | ★ | ★ | ... | (b) | (d) | ★ |
| West Virginia | 150,000 | 49 | ★ | ★ | ★ | (b) | (d) | ★ |
| Wisconsin | 144,423 | 25 | ★ | ★ | ... | ... | (d) | ★ |
| Wyoming | 105,000 | 22 | ★ | ★ | ... | ... | ★(b) | ★ |
| American Samoa | 50,000 | 23 | ★ | ... | ... | (b) | ... | ★ |
| Guam | 90,000 | 42 | ★ | ... | ... | $218/day | ... | ★ |
| No. Mariana Islands | 70,000 | 16 | ★ | ... | ... | (b) | ... | ★ |
| Puerto Rico | 70,000 | 28 | ★ | (g) | (g) | ... | ★ | ★ |
| U.S. Virgin Islands | 80,000 | 86 | ★ | ... | ... | ... | ★ | ★ |

See footnotes at end of table.

## THE GOVERNORS: COMPENSATION, STAFF, TRAVEL AND RESIDENCE — Continued

*Source:* The Council of State Governments, March 2012.
*Key:*
★ — Yes
. . . — No
N.A. — Not available.

(a) Definitions of "governor's office staff" vary across the states—from general office support to staffing for various operations within the executive office.

(b) Travel expenses.

Alaska—$60/day per diem plus actual lodging expenses.

American Samoa—$105,000. Amount includes travel allowance for entire staff.

Arizona—The rate depends on the location and the date. The default $34/day for meals and $60/day lodging.

California—$145,000 in state; $36,000 out of state.

Florida—State can reimburse. Reimbursed at same rate as other state officials: in-state, choice between $80 per diem ($20/per quarter of a day) or actual hotel expenses, meals, transportation; out-of-state, same as in-state. Foreign travel: actual transportation, per diem and meals based on Federal reimbursement rates.

Idaho—Travel allowance included in office budget. The Governor is reimbursed for actual travel expenses, but he must turn in travel vouchers with appropriate receipts.

Indiana—Statute allows $12,000 but due to budget cuts the amount has been reduced to $9,800 and reimbursed for actual expenses for travel/lodging.

Maryland—Travel allowance included in office budget.

Massachusetts—As necessary.

Michigan—The Governor is provided a $60,000 annual expense allowance, as determined by the State Officers Compensation Commission in 2000. "Expense allowance" is for normal, reimbursable personal expenses such as food, lodging, and travel costs incurred by an individual in carrying out the responsibilities of state office.

Montana—Statutory rate applicable to all state employees.

Missouri—Amount includes travel allowance for entire staff. Amount not available.

Nevada—Amount includes travel allowance for entire staff. The following figures include travel expenses for governor and staff, $45,750 in state; $32,800 out of state.

New Hampshire—Travel allowance included in office budget.

New Jersey—Reimbursement may be provided for necessary expenses.

North Carolina—Travel allowance—receives $11,500, expense allowance, not just travel. Reimbursed for actual out-of-state travel expenses.

Northern Mariana Islands—Travel allowance included in office budget. Governor has a "contingency account" that can be used for travel expenses and expenses in other departments or other projects.

Ohio—Set administratively.

Oklahoma—Reimbursed for actual and necessary expenses.

Oregon—$1,000 a month for expenses, not specific to travel. Reimbursed for actual travel expenses.

Pennsylvania—Reimbursed for reasonable expenses.

Tennessee—Travel allowance included in office budget.

Washington—Travel allowance included in office budget.

West Virginia—Included in general expense account.

Wyoming—$99/day or actual.

(c) Governor's salary:

Alabama—Gov. Robert Bentley is not accepting his salary, $119,950, until the unemployment rate in Alabama drops.

Florida—Gov. Rick Scott does not collect his salary.

Kentucky—Reflects a voluntary 10 percent salary reduction.

Michigan—Gov. Rick Snyder returns all but $1.00 of his salary.

New York—Gov. Andrew Cuomo has reduced his salary by 5 percent:

Pennsylvania—1.7 percent of Gov. Corbett's salary is being repaid as part of the management pay freeze.

Tennessee—Gov. Haslam returns his salary to the state. Tennessee statute mandates the governor and the chief justice of the Supreme Court receive the same salary, currently, $170,340.

Vermont—Governor has taken a voluntary five percent reduction in the annual salary set in statue.

(d) Information not provided.

(e) Governor's residence: Many governors are choosing to live in their own residences even when an official residence is provided.

California—provided by Governor's Residence Foundation, a non-profit organization which provides a residence for the governor of California. No rent is charged; maintenance and operational costs are provided by California Department of General Services. The original residence was sold in a cost-savings attempt.

Colorado—The governor chooses to live in his private home and allow cabinet members who live farther away to occupy the governor's mansion.

Connecticut—maintained by the Department of Public Works.

Idaho—J.R. and Esther Simplot donated their home to the state of Idaho in December 2004 for use as the future Governor's residence. The governor has never occupied the mansion even though the state allocates funds for maintenance every year.

Michigan—Constitution mandates official residence in Lansing.

New Hampshire—The current governor does not occupy the official residence.

New Jersey—The governor chooses not to live in the state-provided housing.

Ohio—The governor chooses not to live in the state-provided housing.

(f) Governor's staff:

Florida—The Governor's office budget includes the following staff for the Executive Office: 116 Drug Control, 7 Office of Tourism, 21 Trade and Economic Dev., 48 System Design, 105 Office of Policy and Budget, 14 Energy Office and 14 the Agency for Enterprise Information Technology (a Cabinet Agency administratively housed in the EOG).

Georgia—Full-time employees—56 and 2 part-time employees.

Louisiana—Full-time employees—93, part-time (non-student)—21, students—25.

Maryland—Full-time employees—85 and 1 part-time employee.

Montana—Including 20 employees in the Office of Budget and Program Planning.

Oregon—Of this total, 45 are true Governor's staff and 20 are on loan for agency staff.

Vermont—Voluntary 5 percent salary reduction.

(g) The Governor's office pays for access to an airplane or helicopter with a corporate credit card and requests a refund of those expenses with the corresponding documentation to the Dept. of Treasury.

(h) Provided for security reasons as determined by the state police.

(i) When not in use by other state agencies.

## Table 4.4
## THE GOVERNORS: POWERS

| State or other jurisdiction | Budget making power | | Item veto power | | | | | Authorization for reorganization through executive order (a) |
|---|---|---|---|---|---|---|---|---|
| | Full responsibility | Shares responsibility | Governor has item veto power on all bills | Governor has item veto power on appropriations only | Governor has no item veto power | Item veto— 2/3 legislators present or 3/5 elected to override | Item veto— majority legislators elected to override | |
| Alabama | ★(b) | | ★ | | | ★ | | ★ |
| Alaska | ★ | | | ★ | | ★ | | |
| Arizona | ★(b) | ★ | | ★ | | ★ | | ★ |
| Arkansas | | ★ | | ★ | | | (c) | ★(d) |
| California | ★(b) | ★ | | ★ | | ★ | | ★ |
| Colorado | | ★ | | ★ | | ★ | | ★ |
| Connecticut | ★(b) | ★ | | ★ | | ★ | | ★ |
| Delaware | | ★ | ★ | | | ★ | | ★ |
| Florida | ★ | ★ | | ★ | | ★ | | ★ |
| Georgia | | ★ | | ★ | | (c) | | ★ |
| Hawaii | | ★ | ★ | | | ★ | | ★ |
| Idaho | (e) | (e) | | ★ | | ★ | | ★ |
| Illinois | ★ | ★ | ★ | | | ★ | | ★ |
| Indiana | ★ | ★ | | | ★ | | | ★ |
| Iowa | ★ | ★ | | ★ | | ★ | | ★ |
| Kansas | ★(b) | ★ | | ★(f) | | ★ | ★(g) | ★ |
| Kentucky | | ★ | | ★ | | ★ | ★ | ★(h) |
| Louisiana | ★ | ★ | | ★ | | ★ | | ★ |
| Maine | | ★ | | | ★ | | | ★ |
| Maryland | ★ | | ★ | | | | | |
| Massachusetts | ★(i) | ★ | ★ | ★(f) | | | ★(g) | ★(d) |
| Michigan | ★(i) | ★ | | ★ | | ★ | ★(g) | ★ |
| Minnesota | | ★(k) | | ★ | | ★ | ★(g) | ★(i) |
| Mississippi | ★(b) | | | ★ | | ★ | | ★ |
| Missouri | ★(b) | ★ | | ★ | | ★ | | ★(m) |
| Montana | ★ | ★ | | ★ | | ★(l) | | |
| Nebraska | ★ | ★ | | ★ | | ★(n) | | |
| Nevada | ★(b) | ★ | | | ★ | | | |
| New Hampshire | ★(b) | ★ | | | ★ | | ★(g) | ★(o) |
| New Jersey | ★(b) | ★ | | ★ | | ★ | | |
| New Mexico | ★ | ★ | | ★ | | ★ | | ★ |
| New York | | ★ | ★ | | | ★ | | |
| North Carolina | ★ | ★ | | | ★ | | | ★(p) |
| North Dakota | ★ | ★ | | ★ | | ★ | | ★ |
| Ohio | | ★ | | ★ | | ★ | | ★ |
| Oklahoma | | ★ | | ★ | | ★ | ★(g) | ★ |
| Oregon | ★ | ★ | | ★ | | ★ | | |
| Pennsylvania | ★ | ★ | | ★ | | ★ | | |
| Rhode Island | | ★ | | | ★ | | | |
| South Carolina | | ★ | | ★ | | ★ | | |

See footnotes at end of table.

# THE GOVERNORS: POWERS — Continued

| State or other jurisdiction | Budget making power | | Item veto power | | | | | Authorization for reorganization through executive order (a) |
|---|---|---|---|---|---|---|---|---|
| | Full responsibility | Shares responsibility | Governor has item veto power on all bills | Governor has item veto power on appropriations only | Governor has no item veto power | Item veto — 2/3 legislators present or 3/5 elected to override | Item veto — majority legislators elected to override | |
| South Dakota | ★ | . . . | . . . | ★ | . . . | ★(q) | . . . | ★ |
| Tennessee | . . . | ★ | . . . | ★ | . . . | . . . | ★ | ★ |
| Texas | . . . | ★ | . . . | ★ | . . . | ★ | . . . | ★ |
| Utah | . . . | ★ | . . . | ★ | . . . | ★ | . . . | ★ |
| Vermont | ★ | . . . | . . . | . . . | ★ | . . . | . . . | ★ |
| Virginia | ★ | . . . | . . . | ★ | . . . | ★(q) | . . . | ★ |
| Washington | ★ | . . . | ★(r) | . . . | . . . | ★ | . . . | . . . |
| West Virginia | ★(b) | . . . | . . . | ★ | . . . | ★ | . . . | . . . |
| Wisconsin | ★ | . . . | . . . | ★(s) | . . . | ★ | . . . | . . . |
| Wyoming | . . . | ★ | ★ | . . . | . . . | . . . | . . . | . . . |
| American Samoa | ★ | . . . | . . . | . . . | . . . | . . . | . . . | . . . |
| Guam | . . . | ★ | ★ | . . . | . . . | ★ | . . . | ★ |
| No. Mariana Islands | . . . | ★ | . . . | ★ | . . . | ★ | . . . | ★ |
| Puerto Rico | . . . | ★ | . . . | ★ | . . . | ★ | . . . | . . . |
| U.S. Virgin Islands | ★ | . . . | . . . | ★ | . . . | ★ | . . . | ★(t) |

*Source:* The Council of State Governments' survey of governor's offices, August 2011.

Key:
★ — Yes; provision for.
. . . — No; not applicable.
(a) For additional information on executive orders, see Table 4.5.
(b) Full responsibility to propose; legislature adopts or revises and governor signs or vetoes.
(c) 2/3 of members to which each house is entitled required to override veto.
(d) Authorization for reorganization provided for in state constitution.
(e) The Legislature has full responsibility with regard to setting the State's budget.
(f) Governor may veto any distinct item or items appropriating money in any appropriations bill.
(g) 2/3 of elected legislators of each house to override.
(h) Only for agencies and offices within the Governor's Office.
(i) Governor has sole authority to propose annual budget. No money may be paid out of state treasury except in pursuance of appropriations made by law.
(j) Statute provides for reorganization by the Commissioner of Administration with the approval of the governor.
(k) Governor has the responsibility of presenting a balanced budget. The budget is based on revenue estimated by the Governor's office and the Legislative Budget Committee.

(l) If the Legislature is not in session when the Governor vetoes a bill, the Secretary of State must poll the Legislature as to the question of an override but only if the bill had passed by a vote of 2/3 of the members present.
(m) The office of the governor shall continuously study and evaluate the organizational structure, management practices, and functions of the executive branch and each agency. The governor shall, by executive order or other means within his authority, take action to improve the manageability of the executive branch. The Governor may not, however, create an agency of state government by administrative action, except that the Governor may establish advisory councils and must approve the internal organizational structures of departments.
(n) 3/5 majority required to override line item veto.
(o) Executive reorganization plans can be disapproved by majority vote in both houses of the legislature.
(p) Executive Order must be approved by the legislature if changes affect existing law.
(q) Requires 2/3 of legislators present to override.
(r) Governor has veto power of selections for nonappropriations and item veto in appropriations.
(s) In Wisconsin, governor has "partial" veto over appropriation bills. The partial veto is broader than item veto.
(t) Only if it is not prohibited by law.

## Table 4.5
## GUBERNATORIAL EXECUTIVE ORDERS: AUTHORIZATION, PROVISIONS, PROCEDURES

| State or other jurisdiction | Authorization for executive orders | Provisions | | | | | | | | Procedures | | |
|---|---|---|---|---|---|---|---|---|---|---|---|---|
| | | Civil defense disasters, public emergencies | Energy emergencies and conservation | Other emergencies | Executive branch reorganization plans and agency creation | Create advisory, coordinating, study or investigative committees/commissions | Respond to federal programs and requirements | State personnel administration | Other administration | Filing and publication procedures | Subject to administrative procedure act | Subject to legislative review |
| Alabama | S, I, Case Law | ★ | ★ | … | … | ★ | … | … | … | ★ | … | … |
| Alaska | C | … (a) | … (a) | ★ (a) | ★ | ★ | ★ | ★ | … | ★ (b) | … | (b) |
| Arizona | I | ★ (a) | ★ (a) | ★ | ★ | ★ | ★ | ★ | ★ | (b) | … | … |
| Arkansas | S, I, Common Law | ★ | ★ | ★ | ★ | ★ | ★ | ★ | … | … | … | … |
| California | I | ★ | ★ | ★ | ★ | ★ | ★ | ★ | ★ | ★ | ★ | … |
| Colorado | C | ★ | ★ | ★ | ★ | ★ | ★ | ★ | … | ★ | ★ | … |
| Connecticut | C,S | ★ | ★ | ★ | ★ | ★ | ★ | ★ | … | ★ | ★ | … |
| Delaware | C | ★ | ★ | ★ | ★ | ★ | ★ | ★ | … | … | ★ (c) | … |
| Florida | C,S | ★ | ★ | ★ | ★ | ★ | ★ | ★ | … | … | ★ | … |
| Georgia | S,I (d) | ★ | ★ | ★ | ★ | ★ | ★ | ★ | … | … | … | ★ |
| Hawaii | C | ★ | I | … | … | ★ | I | ★ | (g) | (b)(e) | … | … |
| Idaho | S | ★ | I | I | … | ★ | I | ★ | … | ★ | … | ★ |
| Illinois | C,S | … | ★ | ★ | ★ | ★ | ★ | ★ | (g) | ★ | … | ★ |
| Indiana | C,S, Case Law | ★ | I | ★ | ★ (limited) | I | I | ★ | I | ★ (b) | … | (h) |
| Iowa | (f) | ★ | ★ | ★ | ★ | ★ | ★ | ★ | ★ (j)(k)(l) | ★ | … | … |
| Kansas | C,S | ★ | ★ | ★ (i) | ★ | ★ | ★ | ★ | ★ (j)(k)(l) | ★ | ★ | ★ (o) |
| Kentucky | C,S | ★ | ★ | ★ | ★ | ★ | ★ | ★ | … | ★ (b) | … | ★ (o) |
| Louisiana | C,S (m) | ★ | ★ | ★ | ★ | ★ | ★ | ★ | … | ★ | ★ | … |
| Maine | I | ★ | I | … | ★ | ★ | I | ★ | ★ (n) | ★ | … | … |
| Maryland | C,S | ★ | ★ | ★ | ★ | ★ | ★ | ★ | … | ★ | … | … |
| Massachusetts | C,S | ★ | ★ | ★ | ★ | ★ | ★ | ★ | … | ★ (p) | … | … |
| Michigan | C,S,I | ★ | ★ (q) | ★ | ★ (p) | ★ | ★ | ★ | (r) | ★ (b) | … | ★ (o) |
| Minnesota | S | ★ | I | I | … | ★ | ★ | ★ | … | (s) | (s) | … |
| Mississippi | C, S,Common Law | ★ | ★ | … | ★ | ★ | ★ | ★ | (n) | ★ (o) | … | ★ (o)(t) |
| Missouri | C,S | ★ | ★ | ★ | ★ | ★ | ★ | ★ | … | ★ | … | … |
| Montana | C, S,Common Law | ★ | ★ | ★ | ★ | ★ | ★ | ★ | I | ★ | ★ | … |
| Nebraska | S, I, Common Law | ★ | ★ | I | ★ | ★ | ★ | ★ | … | … | … | … |
| Nevada | S,I | ★ | ★ | ★ | ★ | ★ | ★ | ★ | ★ (k) | ★ | … | … |
| New Hampshire | S | ★ | ★ (a) | … | ★ | ★ | ★ | ★ | ★ (u) | ★ | … | … |
| New Jersey | C,S,I | ★ | ★ | ★ | ★ | ★ | ★ | ★ | … | ★ | … | … |
| New Mexico | C,S | ★ | ★ | ★ | ★ | ★ | ★ | ★ | … | ★ | … | … |
| New York | C,S | ★ | ★ | ★ | ★ | ★ | ★ | ★ | (l)(r)(u)(w)(x)(y) | ★ | … | ★ (v) |
| North Carolina | C,S | ★ | ★ | ★ | ★ | ★ | ★ | ★ | … | ★ | … | … |
| North Dakota | S,I | ★ | ★ | ★ | ★ | ★ | ★ | ★ | … | ★ | … | … |
| Ohio | S,I (z) | ★ | ★ | ★ | ★ (aa) | ★ | ★ | ★ | … | ★ | … | … |
| Oklahoma | C,S | ★ | ★ | ★ | ★ | ★ | ★ | ★ | … | ★ | … | … |
| Oregon | I | ★ | I | I | ★ | ★ | ★ | ★ | … | … | … | … |
| Pennsylvania | C,S | ★ (n)(bb)(cc)(dd) | ★ | ★ | ★ | ★ | ★ | ★ | (dd) | ★ (b)(bb) | ★ (s) | … |
| Rhode Island | I, Case Law | ★ | ★ | ★ | ★ | ★ | ★ | ★ | ★ | ★ (b)(bb) | … | … |
| South Carolina | S | ★ | ★ | ★ | ★ | ★ | ★ | ★ | ★ | ★ | … | … |

See footnotes at end of table.

## GUBERNATORIAL EXECUTIVE ORDERS: AUTHORIZATION, PROVISIONS, PROCEDURES — Continued

| State or other jurisdiction | Authorization for executive orders | Provisions | | | | | | | | Procedures | | |
|---|---|---|---|---|---|---|---|---|---|---|---|---|
| | | Civil defense, disasters, public emergencies | Energy emergencies and conservation | Other emergencies | Executive branch reorganization plans and agency creation | Create advisory, coordinating, study committees/commissions or investigative | Respond to federal programs and requirements | State personnel administration | Other administration | Filing and publication procedures | Subject to administrative procedure act | Subject to legislative review |
| South Dakota | C | ★ | ★ | ★ | ★ | ★ | ★ | ★ | ★ | ★ (b) | ... | ... |
| Tennessee | S | ★ | ★ | ★ | ★ | ★ | ★ | ★ | ★ | ... | ... | ... |
| Utah | I | ★ | ★ | ★ | ★ | ★ | ★ | ★ | ★ | ... | ... | ... |
| Vermont | S,I | ★ | ★ | ★ | (ee) | ★ | ★ | ★ | ★ | ... | ★ | ★ (ff) |
| Virginia | S | ★ | ★ | ... | ... | ★ | ★ | ★ | ... | ... | ... | ... |
| Washington | S | ★ | ... | ... | ... | ★ | ★ | ★ | ... | ... | ... | ... |
| West Virginia | C,S | ★ | ★ | ★ | ... | ★ | ★ | ★ | ★ | ... | ... | ... |
| Wisconsin | S | ... | ... | ★ | ... | ★ | ★ | ★ | ... | ★ | ★ | ... |
| Wyoming | (gg) | ★ | ★ | ★ | ... | ... | ... | ... | ... | ★ | ... | ★ |
| American Samoa | C,S | ★ | ★ | ★ | (ii) | ★ | ★ | ★ | ★ | ★ (hh) | ★ (hh) | ... |
| Guam | C | ★ | ★ | ... | C | ★ | S | ★ | ★ | S | S | I |
| No. Mariana Islands | C | ★ | I | ★ | ... | S,I | S | ... | ... | ... | I | ★ |
| Puerto Rico | C, S, I, Case Law | ★ | ★ | ★ | C | ★ | ★ | ★ | ★ | (jj) | ... | ★ |
| U.S. Virgin Islands | C | ★ | ★ | ★ | ★ | ★ | ★ | ★ | ★ | | | |

*Source:* The Council of State Governments' survey, December 2011.

*Key:*
C — Constitutional
S — Statutory
I — Implied
★ — Formal provision.
... — No formal provision.
(a) Broad interpretation of gubernatorial authority.
(b) Executive orders must be filed with secretary of state or other designated officer. In Idaho, must also be published in state general circulation newspaper.
(c) Under some circumstances the Cabinet must approve before an order becomes law. The Joint Administrative Procedure Committee must make sure agency rules have legislative authority to do so.
(d) Implied from Constitution.
(e) Some implied.
(f) Constitution, statute, implied, case law, common law.
(g) Executive clemency.
(h) Only for EROs. When an ERO is submitted the legislature has 30 days to veto the ERO or it becomes law.
(i) To give immediate effect to state regulation in emergencies.
(j) To control administration of state contracts and procedures.
(k) To impound or freeze certain state matching funds.
(l) To reduce state expenditures in revenue shortfall.
(m) Inherent.
(n) To control procedures for dealing with public.
(o) Reorganization plans and agency creation.

(p) Executive reorganizations not effective if rejected by both houses of legislature within 60 calendar days. Executive orders reducing appropriations not effective unless approved by appropriations committees of both houses of legislature.
(q) If an energy emergency is declared by the state's Executive Council or legislature.
(r) To assign duties to lieutenant governor, issue writ of special election.
(s) Governor is exempt from the Administrative Procedures Act and filing and administrative procedures Miss. Code Ann. § 25-43-102 (1972).
(t) Reorganization plans and agency creation and for meeting federal program requirements.
(u) To administer and govern the armed forces of the state.
(v) Must submit to the Secretary of State who must compile, index and publish Executive Orders. Copies must also be sent to President of the Senate, Speaker of House and Principal Clerk of each chamber
(w) To suspend certain officials and/or other civil actions.
(x) To designate game and wildlife areas or other public areas.
(y) Appointive powers.
(z) Executive authority implied except for emergencies which are established by statute.
(aa) Limited authority in executive branch reorganization/agency creation.
(bb) Filing.
(cc) For fire emergencies.
(dd) To transfer funds in an emergency.
(ee) Subject to legislative approval.
(ff) Only if reorganization order filed with the legislature.
(gg) No specific authorization granted, general authority only.
(hh) If executive order fits definition of rule.
(ii) Can reorganize, but not create.
(jj) Executive Orders are filed in the Department of State.

**Table 4.6**
## STATE CABINET SYSTEMS

| State or other jurisdiction | Authorization for cabinet system | | | | Criteria for membership | | | Number of members in cabinet (including governor) | Frequency of cabinet meetings | Open cabinet meetings |
|---|---|---|---|---|---|---|---|---|---|---|
| | State statute | State constitution | Governor created | Tradition in state | Appointed to specific office (a) | Elected to specified office (a) | Gubernatorial appointment regardless of office | | | |
| Alabama | ★ | ... | ★ | ★ | ★ | ... | ... | 25 | Quarterly | ... |
| Alaska | ... | ... | ★ | ... | ★ | ... | ... | 19 | Gov.'s discretion | ★(b) |
| Arizona | ... | ... | ★ | ... | ★ | ... | ★ | 38 | Monthly | ... |
| Arkansas | ... | ... | ★ | ... | ★ | ... | ... | 47 | Monthly | ... |
| California | ★ | ... | ★ | ... | ★ | ... | ★ | 11 | Every two weeks | ... |
| Colorado | ★ | ... | ★ | ... | ... | ... | ★ | 21 | Monthly | ... |
| Connecticut | ★ | ... | ... | ... | ... | ... | ★ | 27 | Gov.'s discretion | ... |
| Delaware | ★ | ... | ... | ... | ★ | ... | ★ | 16 | Gov.'s discretion | ... |
| Florida | ... | ★ | ... | ... | ... | ★ | ... | 4 | Semi-weekly | ★ |
| Georgia | | | | | | | (d) | | | |
| Hawaii | ... | ★ | ... | ... | ★ | ... | ★ | 22 | Monthly | ... |
| Idaho | | | | (d) | | | | 43 | Gov.'s discretion | ... |
| Illinois | ★ | ... | ... | ... | ... | ... | ★ | 18 | N.A. | ... |
| Indiana | ... | ... | ★ | ... | ... | ... | ★ | 16 | Bi-monthly | ... |
| Iowa | ★ | ... | ★ | ★ | ★ | ... | ... | 30 | (c) | ... |
| Kansas | ★ | ... | ... | ... | ... | ... | ★ | 14 | Bi-weekly | ... |
| Kentucky | ★ | ★ | ★ | ... | ★ | ... | ★ | 15 | Weekly | ... |
| Louisiana | ★ | ... | ★ | ★ | ★ | ... | ... | 16 | Monthly | ... |
| Maine | ... | ... | ... | ★ | ... | ... | ★ | 16 | Weekly | ... |
| Maryland | ★ | ... | ... | ... | ★ | ... | ... | 25 | Every other week | ... |
| Massachusetts | ★ | ... | ... | ... | ★ | ... | ... | 10 | Bi-weekly | ... |
| Michigan | ... | ... | ★ | ★ | ... | ... | (e) | 18 | Bi-weekly and Gov.'s discretion | ... |
| Minnesota | ... | ... | ★ | ... | ★ | ... | ... | 24 | Regularly | ... |
| Mississippi | | | | | | | (d) | | | |
| Missouri | ... | ★ | ... | ★ | ★ | ... | ... | 17 | Gov.'s discretion | ... |
| Montana | ★ | ★ | ... | ... | ★ | ... | ... | 21 | Weekly | ★ |
| Nebraska | ... | ... | ★ | ★ | ★ | ... | ★ | 30 | Monthly | ... |
| Nevada | | | | (d) | | | | 23 | At call of the governor | ... |
| New Hampshire | | | | | | | (d) | | | |
| New Jersey | ★ | ★ | ... | ... | ★ | ... | ... | 24 | Gov.'s discretion | ... |
| New Mexico | ★ | ... | ... | ★ | ★ | ... | ... | 25 | Gov.'s discretion | ... |
| New York | ... | ... | ★ | ... | ... | ... | ★ | 75 | Gov.'s discretion | ... |
| North Carolina (f) | ... | ★ | ★ | ... | ... | ... | ★ | 10 | Weekly (g) | ... |
| North Dakota | ... | ... | ★ | ... | ... | ... | ★ | 18 | Monthly | ★ |
| Ohio | ★ | ... | ... | ... | ★ | ... | ... | 24 | Gov.'s discretion | ★ |
| Oklahoma | ★ | ... | ... | ... | ... | ... | ★ | 16 (h) | Monthly | ... |
| Oregon | | | | | | | (d) | | | |
| Pennsylvania | ★ | ★ | ★ | ... | ★(i) | ... | ★ | 28 | Gov.'s discretion | ★ |
| Rhode Island | ... | ... | ... | ★ | ... | ... | ★ | 20 | Bi-monthly | ... |
| South Carolina | ★ | ... | ... | ... | ★(i) | ... | ... | 16 | Monthly | ★ |
| South Dakota | ★ | ★ | ... | ... | ★ | ... | ... | 19 | Monthly | ... |
| Tennessee | ★ | ... | ... | ... | ★ | ... | ... | 28 | Monthly | ... |
| Texas | | | | | | | (d) | | | |
| Utah | ★ | ... | ★ | ... | ★ | ... | ... | 21 | Monthly, weekly during legislative session | ... |
| Vermont | ★ | ... | ... | ... | ★ | ... | ... | 7 | Gov.'s discretion | ... |
| Virginia | ★ | ... | ... | ... | ... | ... | ★(j) | 14 | Weekly | ... |
| Washington | ... | ... | ★ | ... | ★ | ... | ... | 28 | Bi-weekly, weekly during legislative session | ... |
| West Virginia | ... | ... | ★ | ★ | ★ | ... | ... | 9 | Weekly | ... |
| Wisconsin | ★ | ... | ... | ... | ★ | ... | ... | 16 | Gov.'s discretion | ★ |
| Wyoming | ... | ... | ★ | ... | ... | ... | ★ | 20 | Monthly | ... |
| American Samoa | ★ | ★ | ... | ... | ★ | ... | ★ | 16 | Gov.'s discretion | ★ |
| Guam | ... | ... | ★ | ... | ★ | ... | ... | 55 | Bi-monthly | ... |
| No. Mariana Islands | ... | ★ | ... | ... | ★ | ... | ... | 16 | Gov.'s discretion | ★ |
| Puerto Rico | ★ | ★ | ... | ... | ... | ... | ★ | 10 (k) | Every 6 weeks | ... |
| U.S. Virgin Islands | ... | ★ | ... | ... | ★ | ... | ... | 21 | Monthly | ★ |

See footnotes at end of table.

## STATE CABINET SYSTEMS — Continued

*Source*: The Council of State Governments, January 2011.

*Key*:

★ — Yes

... — No

N.A. — Not available

(a) Individual is a member by virtue of election or appointment to a cabinet-level position.

(b) Except when in executive session.

(c) Every other month, and every month during session.

(d) No formal cabinet system. In Idaho, however, sub-cabinets have been formed by executive order; the chairs report to the governor.

(e) Membership determined by governor. Some officers formally designated as cabinet member by executive order.

(f) There is a Council of State Elected Officials created by the state Constitution: Lieutenant Governor; Treasurer; Secretary of State; Labor; Auditor; Attorney General; Agriculture; Public Instruction; and Insurance. A few statutes mention Cabinet secretaries or agencies, but the Cabinet is not specifically authorized by statute. Cabinet members are appointed by the Governor. Cabinet agencies are as follows: Transportation; Environment And Natural Resources; Commerce; Correction; Health and Human Services; Revenue; Administration; Crime Control and Public Safety; Juvenile Justice and Delinquency Prevention; and Cultural Resources.

(g) Frequency of meetings may fluctuate with Governor's schedule.

(h) Maximum of 16.

(i) With the consent of the Senate.

(j) Appointed by the governor and confirmed by each house.

(k) The Constitutional Cabinet has 10 members including the governor. There are other members of the Cabinet provided by statute.

## Table 4.7
## THE GOVERNORS: PROVISIONS AND PROCEDURES FOR TRANSITION

| State or other jurisdiction | Legislation pertaining to gubernatorial transition | Appropriation available to gov-elect ($) | Provision for: Gov-elect's participation in state budget for coming fiscal year | Gov-elect to hire staff to assist during transition | State personnel to be made available to assist gov-elect | Office space in buildings to be made available to gov-elect | Acquainting gov-elect staff with office procedures and routine office functions | Transfer of information (files, records, etc.) |
|---|---|---|---|---|---|---|---|---|
| Alabama | ... | ... | ★ | ● | ● | ● | ● | ● |
| Alaska | ● | ★(a) | ... | ● | ● | ● | ● | ★ |
| Arizona | ... | ... | ★ | ... | ● | ● | ● | ● |
| Arkansas | ● | 10,000 | ... | ... | ... | ... | ... | ... |
| California | ★ | 450,000 | ★ | ★ | ★ | ★ | ● | ● |
| Colorado | ★ | 10,000 | ★ | ★ | ★ | ★ | ● | ★ |
| Connecticut | ★ | ★ | ★ | ★ | ★ | ★ | ★ | ★ |
| Delaware | ★ | 15,000 | ● | ★ | ● | ● | ● | ● |
| Florida | ★ | 2,500,000 (b) | ● | ★ | ● | ★(b) | ● | ● |
| Georgia | ★ | 50,000 | ★ | ★ | ★ | ● | ● | ★ |
| Hawaii | ★ | 50,000 | ★ | ● | ★ | ★ | ★ | ● |
| Idaho | ★ | 15,000 | ★ | ★ | ★ | ★ | ★ | ★ |
| Illinois | ... | ... | ... | ★ | ... | ★ | ★ | ★ |
| Indiana | ★ | 40,000 | ... | ... | ... | ★ | ★ | ★ |
| Iowa | ● | 100,000 | ★ | ● | ● | ● | ● | ★ |
| Kansas | ★ | 150,000 (c) | ★ | ★ | ★ | ★ | ★ | ★ |
| Kentucky | ★ | ★(d) | ★ | ★ | ★ | ★ | ★ | ★ |
| Louisiana | ★ | ● 65,000 | ★ | ★ | ... | ★ | ... | ● |
| Maine | ● | 5,000 | ★ | ● | ● | ● | ● | ★ |
| Maryland | ★ | ● | ... | ★ | ★ | ★ | ★ | ★ |
| Massachusetts | ● | ● | ● | ... | ● | ● | ● | ★ |
| Michigan | ● | ● | ● | ● | ● | ● | ● | ● |
| Minnesota | ★ | (e) | ★ | ★ | ★ | ★ | ● | ★ |
| Mississippi | ● | ★(f) | ★ | ★ | ★ | ★ | ★ | ★ |
| Missouri | ★ | 100,000 | ★ | ★ | ● | ★ | ● | ●(g) |
| Montana | ★ | ★ | ★ | ★ | ★ | ★ | ● | ●(h) |
| Nebraska | ★ | ... | ★ | ... | ★ | ★ | ★ | ★ |
| Nevada | ★ | Reasonable amount | ★ | ... | ... | ... | ... | ★(i) |
| New Hampshire | ★ | 75,000 | ★ | ★ | ★ | ★ | ★ | ... |
| New Jersey | ★ | ★(j) | ● | ★ | ★ | ● | ● | ★ |
| New Mexico | ★ | (k) | ★ | ★ | ● | ★ | ★ | ★ |
| New York | ... | ... | ... | ... | ★ | ★ | ★ | ★ |
| North Carolina | ★ | ★(l) | ... | ★ | ● | ★ | ● | ★ |
| North Dakota | ● | 10,000 | (m) | (n) | ● | ... | ● | ★ |
| Ohio | ★ | Unspecified (o) | ● | ★ | ● | ... | ● | ● |
| Oklahoma | ● | ● | ★ | ● | ● | ★ | ● | ● |
| Oregon | ★ | ★ | ★ | ★ | ★ | ★ | ★ | ★ |
| Pennsylvania | ★ | ... | ... | ★ | ● | ● | ● | ... |
| Rhode Island | ★ | 500,000 | ... | ★ | ★ | ★ | ● | ● |
| South Carolina | ... | ● | ● | ● | ● | ● | ● | ● |
| South Dakota | ★ | ... | ... | ... | ... | ... | ... | ... |
| Tennessee | ★ | ★ | ● | ★ | ★ | ★ | ● | ● |
| Texas | ● | ● | ● | ● | ● | ● | ● | ● |
| Utah | ★ | ★(p) | ★ | ★ | ★ | ★ | ★ | ★ |
| Vermont | ... | ★(q) | ... | ... | ... | ... | ... | ... |
| Virginia | ★ | ★(r) | ★ | ★ | ★ | ★ | ★ | ★ |
| Washington | ★ | ★ | ● | ★ | ● | ★ | ● | ● |
| West Virginia | ... | ● | ... | ● | ... | ● | ● | ● |
| Wisconsin | ★ | Unspecified | ★ | ★ | ★ | ★ | ★ | ★ |
| Wyoming | ● | ... | ● | ● | ● | ● | ● | ● |
| American Samoa | ... | Unspecified | ★(s) | ★ | ● | ● | ★ | ● |
| Guam | ★ | (t) | ... | ... | ★ | ★ | ★ | ... |
| No. Mariana Islands | ★ | Unspecified | ... | ★ | ★ | ★ | ★ | ★ |
| Puerto Rico | ★ | ... | ★ | ★ | ★ | ★ | ★ | ★ |
| U.S. Virgin Islands | ★ | 100,000 | ... | ★ | ★ | ★ | ★ | ★ |

See footnotes at end of table.

# THE GOVERNORS: PROVISIONS AND PROCEDURES FOR TRANSITION — Continued

*Source*: The Council of State Governments' survey, January 2011.
*Key*:
. . . — No provisions or procedures.
★ — Formal provisions or procedures.
● — No formal provisions, occurs informally.
N.A. — Not applicable.
(a) Varies.
(b) There is a budget for the governor-elect to use during transition. Very specific procedures including legislative review to access the funds. Some of these funds may be shared with Cabinet transitions: CFO and Commissioner of Agriculture. Transition information is available with no formal provisions. Budget allows for space, etc., but actual office space determined by availability at the time.
(c) Transition funds are used by both the incoming and outgoing administrations.
(d) Amount to be determined.
(e) 1.5% of amount appropriated for the fiscal year to the Governor's office.
(f) Miss. Code Ann.§ 7-1-101 provides as follows: the governor's office of general services shall provide a governor-elect with office space and office equipment for the period between the election and inauguration. A special appropriation to the governor's office of general services is hereby authorized to defray the expenses of providing necessary staff employees and for the operation of the office of governor-elect during the period

between the election and inauguration. The state fiscal management board shall make available to a governor-elect and his designated representatives information on the following: (a) all information and reports used in the preparation of the budget report; and (b) all information and reports on projected income and revenue estimates for the state.
(g) Activity is traditional and routine, although there is no specific statutory provision.
(h) In addition to the informal transfer of information, by statute, a successor department head has full access to all agency records prior to assuming office.
(i) As determined in budget.
(j) No specific amount - necessary services and facilities.
(k) Legislature required to make appropriation; no dollar amount stated in legislation.
(l) Governor receives $80,000 and lieutenant governor receives $10,000.
(m) Responsible for submitting budget for coming biennium.
(n) Governor usually hires several incoming key staff during transition.
(o) Determined in budget.
(p) Appropriated by legislature at the time of transition.
(q) Governor-elect entitled to 70% of Governor's salary.
(r) Determined every 4 years.
(s) Can submit reprogramming or supplemental appropriation measure for current fiscal year.
(t) Appropriations given upon the request of governor-elect.

# Table 4.8
# IMPEACHMENT PROVISIONS IN THE STATES

| State or other jurisdiction | Governor and other state executive and judicial officers subject to impeachment | Legislative body which holds power of impeachment | Vote required for impeachment | Legislative body which conducts impeachment trial | Chief justice presides at impeachment trial (a) | Vote required for conviction | Official who serves as acting governor if governor impeached (b) | Legislature may call special session for impeachment |
|---|---|---|---|---|---|---|---|---|
| Alabama | ★ | H | maj. mbrs. | S | ... | majority of elected mbrs. | LG | ★ |
| Alaska | ★ | S | 2/3 mbrs. | H | (c) | 2/3 mbrs. | LG | ★ |
| Arizona | ★(d) | H | maj. mbrs. | S | (e) | 2/3 mbrs. | SS | ★ |
| Arkansas | ★ | H | maj. mbrs. | S | ★(e) | 2/3 mbrs. | LG | ... |
| California | ★ | H | ... | S | ★ | 2/3 mbrs. | LG | ... |
| Colorado | ★ | H | maj. mbrs. | S | ... | 2/3 mbrs. | LG | ★ |
| Connecticut | ★ | H | maj. mbrs. | S | ★(f) | 2/3 mbrs. must be present | LG | ★ |
| Delaware | ★ | H | 2/3 mbrs. | S | (g) | 2/3 mbrs. | LG | ★ |
| Florida | ★ | H | 2/3 mbrs. | S | ★(g) | 2/3 mbrs. present (h) | LG (i) | ★(j) |
| Georgia | ★ | H | ... | S | ★(e) | 2/3 mbrs. | ... | ★ |
| Hawaii | ★ | H | 2/3 mbrs. | S | ★ | 2/3 mbrs. | LG | ... |
| Idaho | ★ | H | 2/3 mbrs.(k) | S | ★ | 2/3 mbrs. | LG | ★ |
| Illinois | ★(l) | H | 2/3 mbrs. | S | ★ | 2/3 mbrs. | LG | ★ |
| Indiana | ★ | H | 2/3 mbrs. | S | ... | 2/3 mbrs. | LG | ★ |
| Iowa | ★ | H | maj. mbrs. | S | ... | majority of elected mbrs. | LG | ★ |
| Kansas | ★ | H | (m) | S | ★ | 2/3 mbrs. present | LG | ... |
| Kentucky | ★ | H | (n) | S | ... | (n) | LG | ★ |
| Louisiana | ★ | H | 2/3 mbrs. | S | ... | 2/3 mbrs. present | PS | ... |
| Maine | ★ | H | ... | S | ... | 2/3 mbrs. | LG | ★ |
| Maryland | ★ | H | maj. mbrs. | S | ★ | 2/3 mbrs. | LG | ... |
| Massachusetts | ★ | H | maj. mbrs. | S | ★(p) | 2/3 mbrs.(q) | LG | ★ |
| Michigan | ★ | H | maj. mbrs.(o) | S | ... | 2/3 mbrs. present | LG | ★ |
| Minnesota | ★ | H | maj. mbrs. | S | ★(r) | 2/3 mbrs. present (s) | LG | (u) |
| Mississippi | ★ | H | 2/3 mbrs. present | S | ★(t) | (t) | LG | ... |
| Missouri | ★ | H | ... | (t) | (t) | (t) | LG | ★ |
| Montana | ★ | H | 2/3 mbrs. | S | ★(w) | 2/3 mbrs. | LG | ★ |
| Nebraska | ★ | S (v) | maj. mbrs. | (w) | (w) | (w) | LG | ★ |
| Nevada | ★(d) | H | maj. mbrs. | S | ★ | 2/3 mbrs. | PS | ★ |
| New Hampshire | ★ | H | ... | S | ★ | ... | LG | ★ |
| New Jersey | ★ | H | maj. mbrs. | S | ★ | 2/3 mbrs. | LG | ★ |
| New Mexico | ★ | H | maj. mbrs. | S | ★(p) | 2/3 mbrs. | LG | ★ |
| New York | ★ | H | maj. mbrs. | S | ★ | 2/3 mbrs. present | LG | ★ |
| North Carolina | ★ | H | 2/3 mbrs. | S | ★(x) | 2/3 mbrs. present | LG | ★ |
| North Dakota | ★(d) | H | maj. mbrs. | S | ... | 2/3 mbrs. present | LG | ... |
| Ohio | ★ | H | maj. mbrs. | S | ... | 2/3 mbrs. present | LG | ... |
| Oklahoma | ★ | H | maj. mbrs. | S | ★ | 2/3 mbrs. present | LG | ★ |
| Oregon | ... | ... | ... | (y) | ... | ... | LG | ★ |
| Pennsylvania | ★ | H | 2/3 maj. mbrs. | S | ... | 2/3 maj. mbrs. | LG | ★ |
| Rhode Island | ★ | H | 2/3 mbrs. | S | ★ | 2/3 maj. mbrs. | LG | ★ |
| South Carolina | ★ | H | 2/3 mbrs. | S | ★ | 2/3 mbrs. | LG | ... |

See footnotes at end of table.

# IMPEACHMENT PROVISIONS IN THE STATES — Continued

| State or other jurisdiction | Governor and other state executive and judicial officers subject to impeachment | Legislative body which holds power of impeachment | Vote required for impeachment | Legislative body which conducts impeachment trial | Chief justice presides at impeachment trial (a) | Vote required for conviction | Official who serves as acting governor if governor impeached (b) | Legislature may call special session for impeachment |
|---|---|---|---|---|---|---|---|---|
| South Dakota | ★ | H | maj. mbrs. | S | ★ | 2/3 mbrs. | LG | ★ |
| Tennessee | ★ | H | maj. mbrs. | S | ★ | 2/3 mbrs. (z) | PS | ★ |
| Texas | ★ | H | maj. mbrs. | S | ... | 2/3 mbrs. present | LG | ★ |
| Utah | ★ | H | 2/3 mbrs. | S | ★ | 2/3 mbrs. | LG | ★ |
| Vermont | ★ | H | 2/3 mbrs. | S | ... | 2/3 mbrs. | LG | ... |
| Virginia | ★(d) | H | maj. mbrs. | S | ... | 2/3 mbrs. present | LG | ★ |
| Washington | ★ | H | maj. mbrs. | S | ★ | 2/3 mbrs. | LG | ★ |
| West Virginia | ★ | H | ... | S | ★ | 2/3 mbrs. | PS | ★ |
| Wisconsin | ★ | H | maj. mbrs. | S | ... | 2/3 mbrs. | LG | ... |
| Wyoming | ★ | H | maj. mbrs. | S | ★ | 2/3 mbrs. | SS | ★ |
| Dist. of Columbia | (bb) | | | ...... (aa) | | | | |
| American Samoa | | H | 2/3 mbrs. | S | ★ | 2/3 mbrs. | ... | ... |
| Guam | | | | ...... (aa) | | | | |
| No. Mariana Islands | ★ | H | 2/3 mbrs. | S | ... | 2/3 mbrs. | LG | ... |
| Puerto Rico | ★ | H | 2/3 mbrs. | S | ★ | 3/4 mbrs. | SS | ★ |
| U.S. Virgin Islands | | | | ...... (aa) | | | | |

*Source:* The Council of State Governments, January 2011.

*Key:*

★ — Yes; provision for.

... — Not specified, or no provision for.

H — House or Assembly (lower chamber).

S — Senate.

LG — Lieutenant Governor

PS — President or Speaker of the Senate

SS — Secretary of state.

(a) Presiding justice of state court of last resort. In many states, provision indicates that chief justice presides only on occasion of impeachment of governor.

(b) For provisions on official next in line of succession if governor is convicted and removed from office, refer to Chapter 4, "The Governors."

(c) An appointed Supreme Court justice presides.

(d) With exception of certain judicial officers. In Arizona and Washington—justices of courts not of record. In Nevada—justices of the peace. In North Dakota—county judges, justices of the peace, and police magistrates.

(e) Should the Chief Justice be on trial, or otherwise disqualified, the Senate shall elect a judge of the Supreme Court to preside.

(f) Only if Governor is on trial.

(g) Except in a trial of the chief justice, in which case the governor shall preside.

(h) An officer impeached by the house of representatives shall be disqualified from performing any official duties until acquitted by the senate, and, unless impeached, the governor may by appointment fill the office until completion of the trial.

(i) Governor may appoint someone to serve until the impeachment procedures are final.

(j) Special sessions of the General Assembly shall be limited to a period of 40 days unless extended by 3/5 vote of each house and approved by the Governor or unless at the expiration of such period an impeachment trial of some officer of state government is pending, in which event the House shall adjourn and the

Senate shall remain in session until such trial is completed.

(k) No person shall be convicted without the concurrence of two-thirds of there senators elected. When the governor is impeached, the chief justice shall preside.

(l) Judges not included.

(m) No statute, simple majority is the assumption.

(n) Concurrence of 2/3 of the elected senators.

(o) A majority of the members of the House elected and serving is necessary to direct an impeachment.

(p) Only if governor or lieutenant governor is on trial.

(q) Must have concurrence of two-thirds members of Senate elected and serving.

(r) When the governor is tried; if Chief Justice is unable to preside, the next longest serving justice shall preside.

(s) No person shall be convicted without concurrence of 2/3 of all senators present. Miss Const. 1890 Art. IV § 52.

(t) All impeachments are tried before the state Supreme Court, except that the governor or a member of the Supreme Court is tried by a special commission of seven eminent jurists to be elected by the Senate. A vote of 5/7 of the court of special commission is necessary to convict.

(u) It is implied but not addressed directly in Miss Const. 1890 Art. IV §§ 49-53.

(v) Unicameral legislature; members use the title "senator".

(w) Court of impeachment is composed of chief justice and supreme court. A vote of 2/3 present of the court is necessary to convict.

(x) Chief Justice presides if it is the Governor or Lieutenant Governor; otherwise , the President of the Senate presides.

(y) No provision for impeachment. Public officers may be tried for incompetence, corruption, malfeasance, or delinquency in office in same manner as criminal offenses.

(z) Vote of 2/3 of members sworn to try the officer impeached.

(aa) Removal of elected officials by recall procedure only.

(bb) Governor, lieutenant governor.

## Table 4.9
## CONSTITUTIONAL AND STATUTORY PROVISIONS FOR
## NUMBER OF CONSECUTIVE TERMS OF ELECTED STATE OFFICIALS
### (All terms are four years unless otherwise noted)

| State or other jurisdiction | Governor | Lt. Governor | Secretary of state | Attorney general | Treasurer | Auditor | Comptroller | Education | Agriculture | Labor | Insurance |
|---|---|---|---|---|---|---|---|---|---|---|---|
| Alabama | 2 | 2 | 2 | 2 | 2 | ... | ... | ... | 2 | ... | ... |
| Alaska | 2 | 2 | (a) | ... | (b) | ... | ... | ... | ... | ... | ... |
| Arizona | 2 (c) | (d) | 2 | 2 | 2 | ... | ... | 2 | ... | ... | ... |
| Arkansas | 2 (c) | 2 | 2 | 2 | 2 | ... | ... | ... | ... | ... | ... |
| California | 2 | 2 | 2 | 2 | 2 | ... | 2 | 2 | ... | ... | ... |
| Colorado | 2 | 2 | 2 | 2 | 2 | ... | ... | ... | ... | ... | ... |
| Connecticut | N | N | N | N | N | ... | N | ... | ... | ... | ... |
| Delaware | 2 (f)(c) | 2 | ... | N | N | N | ... | ... | ... | ... | N |
| Florida | 2 | 2 | ... | 2 | 2 (g)(e) | ... | 2 | N | N | ... | (g)(e) |
| Georgia | 2 | N | N | N | ... | ... | ... | N | N | N | N |
| Hawaii | 2 | 2 | (a) | ... | ... | ... | ... | ... | ... | ... | ... |
| Idaho | N | N | N | N | N | ... | 2 | N | ... | ... | ... |
| Illinois | N | N | N | N | N | ... | N | ... | ... | ... | ... |
| Indiana | 2 (h) | 2 | 2 | ... | (f) | ... | 2 (g) | ... | ... | ... | ... |
| Iowa | N | N | N | N | N | N | ... | ... | ... | ... | ... |
| Kansas | 2 | 2 | N | N | ... | ... | ... | ... | ... | ... | ... |
| Kentucky | 2 | 2 | 2 | 2 | 2 | 2 | ... | ... | 2 | 2 | ... |
| Louisiana | 2 (h) | N | N | N | N | ... | ... | N | N | ... | N |
| Maine | 2 | (i) | (j) | (j) | (j) | ... | ... | ... | ... | ... | ... |
| Maryland | 2 (h) | 2 | ... | N | ... | ... | N | ... | ... | ... | ... |
| Massachusetts | N | N | N | 2 | N | N | ... | ... | ... | ... | ... |
| Michigan | 2 | 2 | 2 | 2 | ... | ... | ... | ... | ... | ... | ... |
| Minnesota | N | N | N | N | (k) | N | ... | ... | ... | ... | (l) |
| Mississippi | 2 | 2 (h) | N | N | N | N | ... | ... | ... | ... | ... |
| Missouri | 2 | N | N | N | 2 (c) | N | ... | ... | ... | ... | ... |
| Montana | 2 (m) | 2 (m) | 2 (m) | 2 (m) | ... | N | ... | 2 (m) | ... | ... | ... |
| Nebraska | 2 (h) | 2 (h) | N | N | 2 (h) | N | ... | ... | ... | ... | ... |
| Nevada | 2 | 2 | 2 | 2 | 2 | ... | 2 | ... | ... | ... | ... |
| New Hampshire | (t) | (i) | ... | ... | ... | ... | ... | ... | ... | ... | ... |
| New Jersey | 2 | 2 | ... | ... | ... | ... | ... | ... | ... | ... | ... |
| New Mexico | 2 | 2 (h) | 2 (h) | 2 (h) | 2 (h) | 2 (h) | ... | ... | ... | ... | ... |
| New York | N | N | ... | N | ... | N (p) | N | ... | ... | ... | ... |
| North Carolina | 2 | 2 | N | N | N | N | ... | N | N | N | N |
| North Dakota | N | N | N (n) | N (n) | N | N | ... | N | N (n)(o) | N (n) | N |
| Ohio | 2 (h) | 2 | 2 | 2 | 2 | 2 | ... | ... | ... | ... | ... |
| Oklahoma | 2 (h) | N | ... | N | N | N | ... | 2 (h) | ... | 2 (h) | N |
| Oregon | 2 (f) | (q) | 2 (f) | N | 2 (f) | ... | ... | ... | ... | ... | ... |
| Pennsylvania | 2 | 2 | ... | 2 | 2 (r) | 2 (h) | ... | ... | ... | ... | ... |
| Rhode Island | 2 | 2(h) | 2 (h) | 2 (h) | 2 (h) | ... | ... | ... | ... | ... | ... |
| South Carolina | 2 (h) | 2 | N | N | N | ... | N | N | N | ... | ... |
| South Dakota | 2 | 2 (h) | 2 (h) | 2 (h) | 2 (h) | ... | 2 | ... | ... | ... | ... |
| Tennessee | 2 (h) | (i) | ... | (s) | ... | ... | ... | ... | ... | ... | ... |
| Texas | N | N | ... | N | (p) | ... | N | ... | ... | ... | ... |
| Utah | N | N | (a) | N | N | N | ... | ... | ... | ... | ... |
| Vermont | (t) | (t) | (t) | (t) | (t) | (t) | ... | ... | ... | ... | ... |
| Virginia | (v) | (u) | ... | (u) | ... | ... | ... | ... | ... | ... | ... |
| Washington | N | N | N | N | N | N | ... | N | ... | ... | ... |
| West Virginia | 2 | N (i) | N | N | N | ... | N | ... | N | ... | ... |
| Wisconsin | N | N | N | N | N | ... | ... | N | N | ... | ... |
| Wyoming | 2 (m) | (q) | N | ... | 2 | ... | 2 | N | ... | ... | ... |
| Dist. of Columbia | N (w) | 2 | ... | ... | ... | ... | ... | ... | ... | ... | ... |
| American Samoa | 2 | 2 | (a) | ... | ... | ... | (x) | ... | ... | ... | ... |
| Guam | 2 | 2 | (a) | ... | ... | ... | (y) | ... | ... | ... | ... |
| No. Mariana Islands | 2 (f) | 2 | ... | ... | ... | 2 | (x) | ... | ... | ... | (l) |
| Puerto Rico | (h) | (d) | ... | ... | ... | 1 | ... | ... | ... | ... | ... |
| U.S. Virgin Islands | 2 (h) | 2 | (p) | ... | (d) | ... | (d) | ... | ... | ... | (a) |

See footnotes at end of table.

## CONSTITUTIONAL AND STATUTORY PROVISIONS FOR
## NUMBER OF CONSECUTIVE TERMS OF ELECTED STATE OFFICIALS—Continued
### (All terms are four years unless otherwise noted)

*Source:* The Council of State Governments, March 2012.

*Note:* All terms last four years unless otherwise noted. Footnotes specify if a position's functions are performed by an appointed official under a different title.

*Key:*

N — No provision specifying number of terms allowed.

. . . — Position is appointed or elected by governmental entity (not chosen by the electorate).

(a) Lieutenant Governor performs this function.

(b) Deputy Commissioner of Department of Revenue performs function.

(c) Absolute two-term limitation, but not necessarily consecutive.

(d) Finance Administrator performs function.

(e) Chief Financial Officer performs this function as of January 2003.

(f) Eligible for eight out of any period of twelve years.

(g) State auditor performs this function.

(h) After two consecutive terms, must wait four years and/or one full term before being eligible again.

(i) President or Speaker of the Senate is next in line of succession to the governorship. In Tennessee and West Virginia, Speaker of the Senate has the statutory title "Lieutenant Governor."

(j) Serves 2-year term and is eligible to serve 4 terms.

(k) Office of the State Treasurer was abolished on the first Monday in January 2003.

(l) Commerce administrator performs this function.

(m) Eligible for eight out of sixteen years. Due to a recent Wyoming Supreme Court ruling, term limits may be unconstitutional.

(n) The terms of the office of the elected officials are four years, except that in 2004 the agricultural commissioner, attorney general, secretary of state and the tax commissioner were elected to a term of two years.

(o) Constitution provides for a secretary of agriculture and labor. However, the legislature was given constitutional authority to provide for (and has provided for) a department of labor distinct from agriculture, and a commissioner of labor distinct from the commissioner of agriculture.

(p) Comptroller performs this function.

(q) Secretary of State is next in line to the governorship.

(r) Treasurer must wait four years before being eligible for the office of auditor general.

(s) Term is for eight years and official is appointed by judges of the State Supreme Court.

(t) Serves two-year term, no provision specifying the number of terms allowed.

(u) Provision specifying individual may hold office for an unlimited number of terms.

(v) Cannot serve consecutive terms, but after 4-year respite can seek re-election.

(w) Mayor.

(x) State treasurer performs this function.

(y) General services administrator performs function.

## Table 4.10
## SELECTED STATE ADMINISTRATIVE OFFICIALS: METHODS OF SELECTION

| State or other jurisdiction | Governor | Lieutenant governor | Secretary of state | Attorney general | Treasurer | Adjutant general | Administration | Agriculture | Auditor | Banking |
|---|---|---|---|---|---|---|---|---|---|---|
| Alabama | CE | CE | CE | CE | CE | GS | G | SE | CE | GS |
| Alaska | CE | CE | (a-1) | GB | AG | GB | GB | AG | L | AG |
| Arizona | CE | (a-2) | CE | CE | CE | GS | GS | GS | L | GS |
| Arkansas | CE | CE | CE | CE | CE | AG | AG | AG | CE | GS |
| California | CE | CE | CE | CE | CE | GS | N.O. | G | GB | GS |
| Colorado | CE | CE | CE | CE | CE | GS | GS | GS | L | A |
| Connecticut | CE | CE | CE | CE | CE | GE | GE | GE | L | GE |
| Delaware | CE | CE | GS | CE | CE | GS | (c) | GS | CE | GS |
| Florida | CE | CE | GS | CE | CE (b) | G | GS | CE | L | (b) |
| Georgia | CE | CE | CE | CE | B | G | G | CE | (d) | G |
| Hawaii | CE | CE | ... | GS | GS | GS | N.O. | GS | CL | AG |
| Idaho | CE | CE | CE | CE | CE | GS | GS | GS | ... | (a-24) |
| Illinois | CE | CE | CE | CE | CE | GS | GS | GS | CL | GS |
| Indiana | CE | CE | CE | SE | CE | G | G | LG | CE | G |
| Iowa | CE | CE | CE | CE | CE | GS | GS | CE | CE | GS |
| Kansas | CE | CE | CE | CE | CE | GS | GS | GS | N.A. | GS |
| Kentucky | CE | CE | CE | CE | CE | G | ... | CE | CE | G |
| Louisiana | CE | CE | CE | CE | CE | GS | GS | CE | G | GLS |
| Maine | CE | (e) | CL | CL | CL | GLS | GLS | GLS | L | GLS |
| Maryland | CE | CE | GS | CE | CL | G | GS | GS | N.A. | AG |
| Massachusetts | CE | CE | CE | CE | CE | G | G | CG | CE | G |
| Michigan | CE | CE | CE | CE | GS | GS | GS | GS | CL | GS |
| Minnesota | CE | CE | CE | CE | (a-24) | GS | GS | GS | CE | A |
| Mississippi | CE | CE | CE | CE | CE | GE | GS | SE | CE | GS |
| Missouri | CE | CE | CE | CE | CE | G | GS | GS | CE | N.O. |
| Montana | CE | CE | CE | CE | GS | GS | GS | GS | CE | A |
| Nebraska | CE | CE | CE | CE | CE | GS | GS | GS | CE | GS |
| Nevada | CE | CE | CE | CE | CE | G | G | BG | ... | A |
| New Hampshire | CE | (e) | CL | GC | CL | GC | GC | GC | ... | GC |
| New Jersey | CE | CE | GS (f) | GS | GS | GS | ... | BG | (g) | GS |
| New Mexico | CE | CE | CE | CE | CE | G | (a-26) | A | CE | N.A. |
| New York | CE | CE | GS | CE | GS | G | G | GS | (a-14) | GS |
| North Carolina | CE | CE | CE | CE | CE | A | G | CE | CE | G |
| North Dakota | CE | CE | CE | CE | CE | G | ... | CE | CE | GS |
| Ohio | CE | CE | CE | CE | CE | G | GS | GS | CE | A |
| Oklahoma | CE | CE | GS | CE | CE | GS | GS | GS | CE | GS |
| Oregon | CE | (a-2) | CE | SE | CE | G | GS | GS | SS | ... |
| Pennsylvania | CE | CE | GS | CE | CE | GS | G | GS | CE | GS |
| Rhode Island | CE | CE | CE | SE | SE | GS | GS | GS | LS | GS |
| South Carolina | CE | CE | CE | CE | CE | CE | B | CE | B | A |
| South Dakota | CE | CE | CE | CE | CE | GS | GS | GS | L | A |
| Tennessee | CE | CL (e) | CL | CT | CL | G | G | G | (a-14) | G |
| Texas | CE | CE | G | CE | (a-14) | G | A | SE | L | B |
| Utah | CE | CE | (a-1) | CE | CE | GS | GS | GS | CE | GS |
| Vermont | CE | CE | (a-1) | CE | CE | GS | GS | GS | CE | GS |
| Virginia | CE | CE | GB | CE | GB | GB | GB | GB | SL | B |
| Washington | CE | CE | CE | CE | CE | G | G | G | CE | G |
| West Virginia | CE | (e) | CE | CE | CE | GS | GS | CE | CE | GS |
| Wisconsin | CE | CE | CE | CE | CE | G | GS | GS | LS | A |
| Wyoming | CE | (a-2) | CE | G | CE | G | GS | GS | CE | A |
| American Samoa | CE | CE | (a-1) | GB | GB | N.A. | GB | GB | N.A. | N.A. |
| Guam | CE | CE | ... | CE | CS | GS | GS | GS | CE | GS |
| No. Mariana Islands | CE | CE | GS | CS | ... | G | G | ... | GB | C |
| U.S. Virgin Islands | SE | SE | (a-1) | GS | GS | GS | GS | GS | GS | LG |

*Sources:* The Council of State Governments' survey of state personnel agencies and state websites, April 2012.

*Key:*
N.A.– Not available.
. . . — No specific chief administrative official or agency in charge of function.
CE — Constitutional, elected by public.
CL — Constitutional, elected by legislature.
SE — Statutory, elected by public.
SL — Statutory, elected by legislature.
L — Selected by legislature or one of its organs.
CT — Constitutional, elected by state court of last resort.
CP — Competitve process.

*Appointed by:*
G — Governor
GS — Governor
GB — Governor
GE — Governor
GC — Governor
GD — Governor
GLS — Governor

GOC — Governor &
        Council or cabinet
LG — Lieut. Governor
LGS — Lieut. Governor
AT — Attorney General
ATS — Attorney General
SS — Secretary of State

*Approved by:*

Senate (in Neb., unicameral legislature)
Both houses
Either house
Council
Departmental board
Appropriate legislative committee
        & Senate

Senate
Senate

## SELECTED STATE ADMINISTRATIVE OFFICIALS: METHODS OF SELECTION — Continued

| State or other jurisdiction | Budget | Civil rights | Commerce | Community affairs | Comptroller | Consumer affairs | Corrections | Economic development | Education | Election admin. |
|---|---|---|---|---|---|---|---|---|---|---|
| Alabama | CS | N.O. | G | G | CS | CS | G | (a-12) | B | CS |
| Alaska | G | GB | GB | (a-12) | AG | (a-13) | GB | (a-13) | GD | AG |
| Arizona | L | AT | GS | AT | A | AT | GS | GS | CE | (a-2) |
| Arkansas | A | N.A. | (a-17) | N.A. | A | AT | B | GS | BG | B |
| California | (a-24) | N.O. | N.O. | GS | CE | G | GS | N.O. | CE | G |
| Colorado | G | A | ... | A | A | AT | GS | G | AB | CS |
| Connecticut | CS | GE | GE | GE | CE | GE | GE | GE | BG | CS |
| Delaware | GS | CG | (a-2) | N.O. | CG | AT | GS | GS | GS | GS |
| Florida | G | AB | G | A | CE (b) | A | GS | G | GS | A |
| Georgia | G | G | B | B | CE | G | GD | B | CE | A |
| Hawaii | GS | B | GS | N.O. | GS | A | GS | GS | B | B |
| Idaho | GS | B | GS | ... | CE | (a-3) | B | (a-12) | CE | (a-2) |
| Illinois | G | GS | GS | (a-12) | CE | (a-3) | GS | (a-12) | B | B |
| Indiana | G | G | G | G | (a-8) | AT | G | G | CE | (h) |
| Iowa | GS | GS | GS | A | N.O. | ATS | GS | GS | GS | SS |
| Kansas | G | B | GS | C | C | AT | GS | C | B | (a-2) |
| Kentucky | G | B | G | G | CG | AT | G | GC | B | B |
| Louisiana | CS | B | GS | G | GS | A | GS | GS | BG | A |
| Maine | A | B | (a-17) | (a-17) | A | GLS | GLS | GLS | GLS | SS |
| Maryland | GS | G | GS | ... | CE | A | GS | GS | B | B |
| Massachusetts | CG | G | G | G | G | G | CG | G | B | CE |
| Michigan | GS | B | GS | ... | CS | ... | GS | ... | B | (i) |
| Minnesota | (a-24) | GS | GS | (a-17) | (a-24) | A | GS | GS | GS | (a-2) |
| Mississippi | GS | ... | SE | A | (a-6) | A | GS | GS | BS | A |
| Missouri | AGS | AGS | GS | A | A | CE | GS | GS | BG | SS |
| Montana | G | CP | GS | CP | CP | CP | GS | G | CE | SS |
| Nebraska | A | B | GS | A | A | (a-3) | GS | GS | B | A |
| Nevada | (a-5) | G | G | ... | CE | A | G | GD | B | (j) |
| New Hampshire | GC | CS | GC | G | AGC | AGC | GC | AGC | B | CL |
| New Jersey | GS | A | (a-17) | GS | GS | A | GS | G | GS | A |
| New Mexico | G | N.A. | (a-17) | N.A. | N.A. | AT | GS | GS | GS | CE |
| New York | G | GS | GS | GS | CE | GS | GS | GS | B | B |
| North Carolina | (a-24) | A | G | A | G | (k) | G | A | CE | G |
| North Dakota | A | G | G | ... | A | AT | G | N.A. | CE | SS |
| Ohio | GS | B | GS | A | GS | A | GS | GS | B | (a-2) |
| Oklahoma | A | B | GS | (k) | A | B | B | GS | CE | L |
| Oregon | A | A | GS | G | A | GS | GS | GS | SE | A |
| Pennsylvania | G | B | GS | AG | G | AT | GS | GS | GS | G |
| Rhode Island | A | B | GS | ... | A | SE | GS | GS (l) | B | B |
| South Carolina | A | B | GS | N.A. | CE | B | GS | (a-12) | CE | B |
| South Dakota | (a-24) | N.A. | (a-44) | (a-48) | (a-40) | N.A. | GS | GS | GS | SS |
| Tennessee | A | G | G | G | SL | A | G | G | G | A |
| Texas | G | B | G | G | CE | (k) | B | G | B | (m) |
| Utah | G | A | GS | GS | AG | GS | GS | A | B | A |
| Vermont | CG | AT | GS | CG | CG | AT | CG | CG | BG | CE |
| Virginia | GB | G | GB | GB | GB | A | GB | B | GB | GB |
| Washington | G | B | G | (a-12) | (a-10) | CE | G | (a-12) | CE | (a-2) |
| West Virginia | CS | GS | GS | B | (a-8) | AT | GS | (a-13) | B | (a-2) |
| Wisconsin | A | A | GS | A | A | A | GS | CS | CE | B |
| Wyoming | A | A | G | G | (a-8) | G | GS | (a-12) | CE | A |
| American Samoa | GB | N.A. | GB | (a-12) | (a-4) | (a-3) | A | (a-12) | GB | G |
| Guam | GS | ... | GS | ... | CS | CS | GS | B | B | GS |
| No. Mariana Islands | G | A | GS | GS | C | GS | C | C | B | B |
| U.S. Virgin Islands | GS | GS | GS | GS | (a-24) | GS | GS | GS | GS | B |

*Appointed by:*
C — Cabinet Secretary
CG — Cabinet Secretary
A — Agency head
AB — Agency head
AG — Agency head
AGC — Agency head
AGS — Agency head
ALS — Agency head
ASH — Agency head
B — Board or commission
BG — Board
BGS — Board
BS — Board or commission
BA — Board or commission
CS — Civil Service
LS — Legislative Committee

*Approved by:*

Governor

Board
Governor
Governor & Council
Senate
Appropriate legislative committee
Senate president & House speaker

Governor
Governor & Senate
Senate
Agency head

Senate

(a) Chief administrative official or agency in charge of function:
(a-1) Lieutenant governor.
(a-2) Secretary of state.
(a-3) Attorney general.
(a-4) Treasurer.
(a-5) Adjutant general.
(a-6) Administration.
(a-7) Agriculture.
(a-8) Auditor.
(a-9) Banking.
(a-10) Budget.
(a-11) Civil rights.
(a-12) Commerce.
(a-13) Community affairs.
(a-14) Comptroller.
(a-15) Consumer affairs.
(a-16) Corrections.

## SELECTED STATE ADMINISTRATIVE OFFICIALS: METHODS OF SELECTION — Continued

| State or other jurisdiction | Emergency management | Employment services | Energy | Environmental protection | Finance | Fish & wildlife | General services | Health | Higher education | Highways |
|---|---|---|---|---|---|---|---|---|---|---|
| Alabama | G | CS | CS | B | G | CS | CS | B | B | G |
| Alaska | AG | AG | B | GB | AG | GB | AG | AG | B | GB |
| Arizona | G | A | A | GS | (a-14) | B | A | GS | B | A |
| Arkansas | GS | G | A | BG/BS | (a-6) | AB | GS | BG/B | BG/B | (a-49) |
| California | GS | GS | G | GS | G | G | GS | GS (n) | B (o) | (a-49) |
| Colorado | A | A | G | A | A | A | A | GS | GS | GS |
| Connecticut | GE | A | A | GE | GE | CS (p) | GE | GE | BG | (a-49) |
| Delaware | CG | CG | A | (a-35) | GS | CG | CG | CG | B | (a-49) |
| Florida | GS | GS | A | GS | CE (b) | GS | GS | GS | B | GOC |
| Georgia | G | A | CE | BG | G | A | A | A | B | B |
| Hawaii | A | CS | CS | CS | (q) | CS | (a-14) | GS | B | CS |
| Idaho | A | GS | A | GS | GS | B | ... | GS | B | (a-49) |
| Illinois | GS | GS | (a-42) | GS | (a-10) | (a-35) | (a-6) | GS | B | (a-49) |
| Indiana | G | G | LG | G | (a-10) | A | (a-6) | G | G | (a-49) |
| Iowa | GS | GS | GS | A | A | A | A | GS | N.O. | A |
| Kansas | (r) | (a-32) | B | C | N.A. | CS | (a-6) | GS | B | (a-49) |
| Kentucky | AG | AG | AG | G | G | G | ... | CG | B | CG |
| Louisiana | GS | A | CS | GS | GS | GS | GS | GS | B | GS |
| Maine | A | A | (a-38) | GLS | (a-6) | GLS | A | GLS | N.A. | (a-49) |
| Maryland | AG | A | G | GS | GS | ... | (a-6) | GS | G | AG |
| Massachusetts | G | CG | CG | CG | G | CG | G | CG | B | G |
| Michigan | GS | CS | (k) | GS | (a-10) | (s) | ... | GS | ... | (a-49) |
| Minnesota | GS | A | A | GS | GS | A | (a-6) | GS | B | GS |
| Mississippi | GS | GS | A | GS | (a-6) | GS | ... | BS | BS | (a-49) |
| Missouri | A | A | N.O. | A | AGS | (t) | A | GS | B | (a-49) |
| Montana | CP | CP | CP | GS | CP | GS | CP | GS | CP | GS |
| Nebraska | A | A | GS | GS | (u) | (v) | A | GS | B | (a-49) |
| Nevada | A | A | G | A | (a-14) | GD | (w) | | B | (a-49) |
| New Hampshire | G | GC | G | GC | (a-6) | BGC | GC | AGC | B | (a-49) |
| New Jersey | GS | A | A | GS | GS | B | (x) | GS | B | A |
| New Mexico | GS | (a-32) | GS | GS | GS | A | GS | GS | GS | A |
| New York | GS | GS | B | GS | CE | GS | G | GS | B | GS |
| North Carolina | G | G | A | G | G | G | G | G | B | A |
| North Dakota | A | G | A | A | A | G | G | G | B | (a-49) |
| Ohio | AG | GS | A | GS | A (y) | A | A | GS | B | GS |
| Oklahoma | GS | B | GS | B | GS | B | GS | B | B | B |
| Oregon | AG | GS | G | B | (a-4) | B | (a-6) | A | B | A |
| Pennsylvania | G | AG | AG | GS | G | B | GS | GS | AG | AG |
| Rhode Island | G | GS | A | GS | GS | GS | GS | GS | B (z) | (a-49) |
| South Carolina | A | B | A | B | B | B | A | GS | B | B |
| South Dakota | A | (a-37) | (a-48) | (a-35) | GS | GS | (a-6) | GS | B | (a-47) |
| Tennessee | A | G | A | G | G | B | G | G | B | (a-49) |
| Texas | A | B | ... | B | (a-14) | B | B | BG | B | (a-49) |
| Utah | A | GS | A | GS | AG | A | A | GS | B | (a-49) |
| Vermont | CG | GS | GS | CG | CG | CG | CG | CG | ... | (a-49) |
| Virginia | GB | GB | A | GB | GB | B | GB | GB | GB | GB |
| Washington | A | G | (a-23) | G | (a-10) | B | (a-6) | G | N.A. | (a-49) |
| West Virginia | GS | GS | GS | (a-22) | (a-6) | CS | C | GS | B (aa) | GS |
| Wisconsin | A | GS | A | A | A | A | (a-6) | A | N.A. | A |
| Wyoming | G | GS | A | GS | (a-8) | B | A | GS | B | GS |
| American Samoa | G | A | GB | GB | (a-4) | GB | G | GB | (a-18) | (a-49) |
| Guam | GS | GS | G | GS | GS | GS | GS | CS | B | GS |
| No. Mariana Islands | G | C | C | G | GS | C | GS | GS | B | C |
| U.S. Virgin Islands | GS | GS | GS | GS | GS | GS | GS | GS | GS | GS |

(a-17) Economic development.
(a-18) Education (chief state school officer).
(a-19) Election administration.
(a-20) Emergency management.
(a-21) Employment Services.
(a-22) Energy.
(a-23) Environmental protection.
(a-24) Finance.
(a-25) Fish and wildlife.
(a-26) General services.
(a-27) Health.
(a-28) Higher education.
(a-29) Highways.
(a-30) Information systems.
(a-31) Insurance.
(a-32) Labor.
(a-33) Licensing.

(a-34) Mental Health.
(a-35) Natural resources.
(a-36) Parks and recreation.
(a-37) Personnel.
(a-38) Planning.
(a-39) Post audit.
(a-40) Pre-audit.
(a-41) Public library development.
(a-42) Public utility regulation.
(a-43) Purchasing.
(a-44) Revenue.
(a-45) Social services.
(a-46) Solid waste management.
(a-47) State police.
(a-48) Tourism.
(a-49) Transportation.
(a-50) Welfare.

## SELECTED STATE ADMINISTRATIVE OFFICIALS: METHODS OF SELECTION — Continued

| State or other jurisdiction | Information systems | Insurance | Labor | Licensing | Mental health & retardation | Natural resources | Parks & recreation | Personnel | Planning | Post audit |
|---|---|---|---|---|---|---|---|---|---|---|
| Alabama | CS | G | G | N.O. | G | G | CS | B | (a-12) | LS |
| Alaska | AG | AG | GB | AG | AG | GB | AG | AG | ... | (a-8) |
| Arizona | A | GS | B | ... | G | GS | B | A | (a-10) | ... |
| Arkansas | GS | GS | GS | N.A. | A | G | GS | A | N.A. | ... |
| California | G | CE | AG | G | (bb) | GS | GS | GS | N.O. | N.O. |
| Colorado | G | BA | GS | A | A | GS | A | A | G | (a-8) |
| Connecticut | GE | GE | GE | CS | GE(cc) | CS | CS | GE | A | (a-8) |
| Delaware | GS | CE | GS | CG | CG (dd) | GS | CG | CG | CG | (a-8) |
| Florida | GS | GOC | GS | N.O. | A | GS | A | A | A | CE (b) |
| Georgia | GD | CE | CE | A | BG | BG | A | GS | (a-10) | (a-8) |
| Hawaii | CS | AG | GS | CS | G | GS | CS | GS | CS | CS |
| Idaho | (a-6) | GS | GS | GS | ... | B | B | GS | ... | (a-14) |
| Illinois | (a-6) | GS | GS | (a-9) | (a-45) | GS | (a-35) | (a-6) | ... | (a-8) |
| Indiana | G | G | G | G | A | G | A | G | N.O. | G |
| Iowa | A | GS | GS | N.O. | A | GS | A | A | N.O. | N.O. |
| Kansas | G | SE | GS | B | (ee) | GS | CS | C | N.A. | L |
| Kentucky | G | G | G | ... | CG | G | CG | G | G | (a-8) |
| Louisiana | A | CE | GS | ... | GS | GS | LGS | B | CS | CL |
| Maine | A | GLS | GLS | A | (a-45) | GLS | (a-35) | A | G | ... |
| Maryland | A | GS | GS | A | A (ff) | GS | A | A | GS | N.A. |
| Massachusetts | C | G | G | G | CG (gg) | CG | CG | CG | G | CE |
| Michigan | GS | GS | (a-12) | GS | CS | GS | CS | CS | ... | CL |
| Minnesota | GS | A | GS | A | GS (hh) | GS | A | (a-24) | N.A. | (a-8) |
| Mississippi | BS | SE | ... | ... | B | GS | GS | B | A | (a-8) |
| Missouri | A | GS | GS | A | A | GS | A | G | AGS | CE |
| Montana | A | CE | GS | CP | CP | GS | CP | CP | G | L |
| Nebraska | GS | GS | GS | A | A | GS | B | A | GS | (a-8) |
| Nevada | G | A | A | ... | (ii) | G | A | G | ... | ... |
| New Hampshire | GC | GC | GC | GC | AGC | GC | AGC | AGC | ... | (a-14) |
| New Jersey | A | GS | GS | ... | A (jj) | A | A | GS | A | (a-8) |
| New Mexico | GS | G | GS | G | ... | GS | N.A. | GD | N.A. | (a-8) |
| New York | G | GS | GS | (kk) | (ll) | (a-23) | GS | GS | GS | (a-14) |
| North Carolina | G | CE | CE | N.O. | A | G | A | G | N.A. | (a-8) |
| North Dakota | G | CE | G | ... | A | ... | G | A | ... | A |
| Ohio | G | GS | A | ... | GS (mm) | GS | A | A | GS | CE |
| Oklahoma | A | CE | CE | ... | B | (a-48) | (a-48) | GS | ... | ... |
| Oregon | A | GS | SE | GS | A | GOC | B | A | ... | SS |
| Pennsylvania | G | GS | GS | AG | AG | GS | A | G | G | (a-8) |
| Rhode Island | A | A | GS | CS | GS | GS | GS | A | A | N.A. |
| South Carolina | A | GS | GS | GS | B (nn) | B | GS | A | AB | B |
| South Dakota | GS | A | GS | ... | GS | GS | A | GS | ... | (a-8) |
| Tennessee | A | G | G | A | G | G | A | G | A | SL |
| Texas | B | G | B | B | B | B | B | ... | G | L |
| Utah | GS | GS | GS | AG | AB | GS | AG | GS | G | (a-8) |
| Vermont | CG | GS | GS | SS | CG | GS | CG | CG | ... | (a-8) |
| Virginia | B | B | GB | GB | GB | GB | GB | GB | (a-10) | (a-8) |
| Washington | G | SE | G | G | (a-45) | CE | G | G | (a-10) | N.A. |
| West Virginia | C | GS | GS | ... | GS | GS | GS | C | (a-17) | LS |
| Wisconsin | A | GS | GS | GS | A | GS | A | GS | ... | (a-8) |
| Wyoming | G | G | A | A | A | G | GS | A | G | (a-8) |
| American Samoa | (a-49) | G | N.A. | N.A. | (a-45) | AG | GB | A | (a-12) | G |
| Guam | GS | GS | GS | GS | GS | GS | GS | GS | GS | CE |
| No. Mariana Islands | C | CS | C | B | C | GS | C | GS | G | GS |
| U.S. Virgin Islands | G | SE | GS | GS | GS | GS | GS | GS | G | L |

(b) Effective Jan. 1, 2003 the positions of Commissioner & Treasurer, Banking, Comptroller, Finance, Insurance, Post audit, and Pre-audit merged into one Chief Financial Officer.

(c) Department abolished July 1, 2005; responsibilities transferred to office of Management and Budget, General Services and Department of State.

(d) Appointed by the House and approved by the Senate.

(e) In Maine, New Hampshire, Tennessee and West Virginia, the Presidents (or Speakers) of the Senate are next in line of succession to the Governorship. In Tennessee and West Virginia, the Speaker of the Senate bears the statutory title of Lieutenant Governor.

(f) The Governor has assigned the role of Secretary of State (GS) to the Lieutenant Governor.

(g) The auditor is a Constitutional office, but is appointed by the Senate and General Assembly in joint meeting as mandated in the New Jersey Constitution.

(h) Responsibilities shared between Co-Directors in Election Commission (G); appointed by the Governor, subject to approval by the Chairs of the State Republican and Democratic parties.

(i) Responsibilities shared between Secretary of State (CE); and Director, Bureau of Elections (CS).

(j) Responsibilities shared between Secretary of State (CE); Deputy Secretary of State for Elections, Office of Secretary of State (SS); and Chief Deputy Secretary of State, same office (A).

(k) Method not specified.

(l) The Rhode Island Economic Development Corporation is a quasi-public agency.

(m) Responsibilities shared between Secretary of State (G); and Division Director of Elections, Elections Division, Secretary of State (A).

(n) Responsibilities shared between Director of Health Care Services and Director of Public Health, both (GS).

(o) Responsibilities shared between Chancellor of California Community Colleges (B) and California Postsecondary Education Commission (B).

## SELECTED STATE ADMINISTRATIVE OFFICIALS: METHODS OF SELECTION — Continued

| State or other jurisdiction | Pre-audit | Public library development | Public utility regulation | Purchasing | Revenue | Social services | Solid waste mgmt. | State police | Tourism | Transportation | Welfare |
|---|---|---|---|---|---|---|---|---|---|---|---|
| Alabama | (a-14) | B | SE | CS | G | B | CS | G | G | (a-29) | (a-45) |
| Alaska | ... | AG | GB | AG | GB | GB | AG | AG | AG | GB | AG |
| Arizona | (a-14) | B | B | A | GS | GS | A | GS | GS | GS | GS |
| Arkansas | N.A. | GS | GS | A | A | GS | N.A. | GS | GS | BS | (a-45) |
| California | (a-14) | N.O. | GS | (a-26) | BS | GS | G | GS | N.O. | GS | AG |
| Colorado | (a-14) | BA | CS | CS | GS | GS | CS | A | CS | GS | GS |
| Connecticut | CE | CS | GB | CS | GE | GE | CS | GE | GE | GE | GE |
| Delaware | (a-8) | CG | CG | (a-26) | CG | GS (oo) | B | CG | CG | GS | CG |
| Florida | CE(b) | A | B | A | GOC | GS | A | A | N.A. | GS | A |
| Georgia | (a-8) | AB | CE | A | GS | GD | A | BG | A | (a-29) | A |
| Hawaii | CS | B | GS | GS | GS | GS | CS | ... | B | GS | CS |
| Idaho | (a-14) | B | GS | (a-6) | GS | (a-27) | ... | GS | A | B | A |
| Illinois | (a-14) | SS | GS | (a-6) | GS | GS | (a-23) | GS | (a-12) | GS | GS |
| Indiana | CE | G | G | A | G | G | A | G | LG | G | (a-45) |
| Iowa | CS | B | GS | A | GS | GS | CS | GS | CS | GS | (a-45) |
| Kansas | CS | GS | B | C | GS | GS | C | GS | C | GS | C |
| Kentucky | ... | G | G | G | G | G | AG | G | G | G | (a-45) |
| Louisiana | CS | BGS | BS | A | GS | GS | GS | GS | LGS | GS | CS |
| Maine | (a-14) | B | G | CS | A | GLS | CS | A/GLS | (a-17) | GLS | (a-45) |
| Maryland | A | A | GS | A | A | GS | A | GS | A | GS | (a-45) |
| Massachusetts | CE | B | G | CG | CG | CG | CG | CG | CG | G | CG |
| Michigan | ... | ... | GS | CS | CS | GS | CS | GS | ... | GS | (a-45) |
| Minnesota | (a-8) | N.A. | G (pp) | A | GS | GS (hh) | GS | A | A | GS | GS (hh) |
| Mississippi | (a-8) | B | GS | A | GS | GS | A | GS | A | B | GS |
| Missouri | A | B | GS | A | GS | GS | A | GS | A | B | A |
| Montana | L | CP | CE | CP | GS | GS | GS | CP | CP | GS | GS |
| Nebraska | A | B | B | A | GS | GS | A | GS | A | GS | GS |
| Nevada | ... | (qq) | G | A | G | G | ... | G | GD | B | (rr) |
| New Hampshire | (a-14) | AGC | GC | CS | GC | GC | AGC | AGC | AGC | GC | AGC |
| New Jersey | ... | ... | GS | GS | A | GS | A | GS | A | GS | A |
| New Mexico | N.A. | N.A. | G | N.A. | GS | N.A. | N.A. | GS | GS | GS | N.A. |
| New York | (a-14) | (a-18) | GS | (a-26) | GS | GS | (a-23) | GS | (a-17) | GS | (a-45) |
| North Carolina | (a-8) | A | G | A | G | A | A | G | A | G | A |
| North Dakota | ... | ... | CE | A | CE | G | A | G | G | G | G |
| Ohio | GS | B | BG | A | GS | (ss) | A | GS | LG | A | GS |
| Oklahoma | A | B | (tt) | A | GS | GS | A | A | B | B | GS |
| Oregon | (a-10) | B | GS | A | GS | GS | B | GS | A | GS | GS |
| Pennsylvania | (a-4) | G | GS | A | GS | GS | G | GS | G | GS | GS |
| Rhode Island | (a-14) | A | GS | A | GS | GS (uu) | (vv) | G | GS (l) | GS | GS |
| South Carolina | (a-14) | B | B | A | GS | GS | A | GS | GS | G | GS |
| South Dakota | CE | A | CE | A | GS | GS | A | A | GS | GS | (a-45) |
| Tennessee | A | A | SE | A | G | G | A | G | G | G | G |
| Texas | (a-14) | A | B | A | (a-14) | (k) | A | B | A | B | BG |
| Utah | AG | A | A | A | BS | GS | A | A | A | GS | GS |
| Vermont | (a-24) | CG | BG | CG | CG | GS | CG | GS | CG | GS | CG |
| Virginia | (a-14) | B | (ww) | A | GB | GB | (a-23) | GB | G | GB | (a-45) |
| Washington | (a-4) | (a-2) | (k) | (a-6) | G | G | G | G | N.A. | G | (a-34) |
| West Virginia | (a-8) | B | GS | CS | GS | C | B | GS | GS | (a-29) | GS |
| Wisconsin | A | A | GS | A | GS | A | A | A | GS | GS | A |
| Wyoming | (a-8) | A | G | A | G | GS | A | A | A | (a-29) | (a-45) |
| American Samoa | (a-4) | (a-18) | N.A. | A | (a-4) | GB | GB | GB | (a-12) | (a-29) | N.A. |
| Guam | GS | (k) | GS | GS | GS | GS | GS | GS | B | N.O. | GS |
| No. Mariana Islands | G | B | B | C | C | C | A | GS | GB | CS | A |
| U.S. Virgin Islands | GS | GS | GS | GS | GS | G | GS | GS | GS | GS | GS |

(p) Responsibilities shared between Director of Wildlife, Director of Inland Fisheries and Director of Marine Fisheries (CS).

(q) Responsibilities shared between Director of Budget and Finance (GS) and the Comptroller (GS).

(r) Responsibilities shared between Adjutant General (GS) and Deputy Director (C).

(s) Responsibilities shared between Director (GS), Chief of Fisheries (CS) and Chief of Wildlife (CS).

(t) Responsibilities shared between Administrator, Division of Fisheries, Department of Conservation; Administrator, Division of Wildlife, same department (AB).

(u) Responsibilities shared between State Tax Commissioner, Department of Revenue (GS); Administrator, Budget Division (A) and the Auditor of Public Accounts (CE).

(v) Responsibilities shared between Director, Game and Parks Commission (B), Division Administrator, Wildlife Division, Game and Parks Commission (A).

(w) Responsibilities shared between Director of Health and Human Services (G) and Division Administrator, Health (AG).

(x) Responsibilities shared between Director, Division of Purchase and Property, Dept. of Treasury (GS), and Director, Division of Property Management and Construction, Dept. of the Treasury (A).

(y) Responsibilities shared between Assistant Director, Office of Budget and Management (A) and Deputy Director, same office (A).

(z) This employee serves in a dual role as Commissioner of Higher Education and as the President of the Community College of Rhode Island.

(aa) Responsibilities shared between Community and Technical (B) and Higher Education Policy Commissioner (B).

## SELECTED STATE ADMINISTRATIVE OFFICIALS: METHODS OF SELECTION — Continued

(bb) Responsibilities shared between Director of Mental Health (GS) and Director of Developmental Services (GS).

(cc) Responsibilities shared between Commissioner of Mental Health (GE) and Commissioner of Retardation (GE).

(dd) Responsibilities shared between Director, Division of Substance Abuse and Mental Health Department of Health and Social Services (CG); and Director, Division of Developmental Disabilities Services, same department (CG).

(ee) Responsibilities shared between Director of Mental Health (C) and Director of Community Support (C).

(ff) Responsibilities shared between Executive Director, Mental Hygiene Administration (A); and Director, Developmental Disabilities Administration, Department of Health and Mental Hygiene (A).

(gg) Responsibilities shared between Commissioner, Department of Mental Retardation (CG); and Commissioner, Department of Mental Health, Executive Office of Human Services (CG).

(hh) Human/Social Services, Mental Health and Retardation and Welfare are under the Commissioner of Human Services (GS).

(ii) Responsibilities shared between Director of Health and Human Services (G) and Division Administrator, MHDS (G).

(jj) Responsibilities shared between Director, Division of Mental Health Services, Dept. of Human Services (A) and Director, Division of Developmental Disabilities, Dept. of Human Services (A).

(kk) Responsibilities shared between Secretary of State (GS) and Commissioner of State Education Department (B).

(ll) Responsibilities shared between Commissioner, Office of Mental Health, and Commissioner, Office of Mental Retardation and Developmental Disabilities, both (GS).

(mm) Responsibilities shared between Director, Dept. of Mental Retardation and Developmental Disabilities (GS) and Director, Department of Mental Health (GS).

(nn) Responsibilities shared between Director of Disabilities and Special Needs (B) and Director of Mental Health (B).

(oo) Responsibilities shared between Secretary of Health and Social Services (GS); and Secretary, Department of Services of Children, Youth and their Families (GS).

(pp) Responsibilities shared between the five Public Utility Commissioners (G).

(qq) Responsibilities shared between Director, Dept. of Cultural Affairs (G) and Division Administrator of Library and Archives (A).

(rr) Responsibilities shared between Director of Health and Human Services (G) and Division Administrator, Welfare and Support Services (AG).

(ss) Responsibilities shared between Director, OH Dept. of Job and Family Services (GS), Superintendent of Dept. of Education (B), Executive Director of Rehabilitation Services Commission (B), Director of Dept. of Aging (GS).

(tt) Responsibilities shared between General Administrator Public Utility Division, Corporation Commission (B); and 3 Commissioners, Corporation Commission (CE).

(uu) This position is filled by two employees: one, Stephen Costantino, is the Commissioner, Office of Health and Human Services; Sandra Powell serves as the Director of Human Services and reports to the Commissioner, Office of Health and Human Services.

(vv) Solid waste is managed by the Rhode Island Resource Recovery Corporation (RIRRC). Although not a department of the state government, RIRRC is a public corporation and a component of the State of Rhode Island for financial reporting purposes. To be financially self-sufficient, the agency earns revenue through the sale of recyclable products, methane gas royalties and fees for its services.

(ww) No single position. Functions are shared between Communication, Energy Regulation and Utility and Railroad Safety, all (B).

## Table 4.11
## SELECTED STATE ADMINISTRATIVE OFFICIALS: ANNUAL SALARIES

| State or other jurisdiction | Governor | Lieutenant governor | Secretary of state | Attorney general | Treasurer | Adjutant general | Admin. | Agriculture | Auditor | Banking |
|---|---|---|---|---|---|---|---|---|---|---|
| Alabama | $0 (c) | $134,592 | $85,248 | $160,002 | $85,248 | $91,014 | $119,500 | $84,655 | $85,248 | $157,380 |
| Alaska | 145,000 | 115,000 | (a-1) | 135,000 | 119,328 | 135,000 | 135,000 | 115,320 | 119,328 | 119,640 |
| Arizona | 95,000 | (a-2) | 70,000 | 90,000 | 70,000 | 134,000 | 160,000 | 102,260 | 128,785 | 119,000 |
| Arkansas | 86,890 | 41,896 | 54,305 | 72,408 | 54,305 | 105,940 | 144,435 | 104,840 | 54,305 | 126,078 |
| California | 173,987 | 130,490 | 130,490 | 151,127 | 139,189 | 176,468 | N.O. | 175,000 | 175,000 | 150,112 |
| Colorado | 90,000 | 68,500 | 68,500 | 80,000 | 68,500 | 146,040 | 146,040 | 146,040 | 140,000 | 128,004 |
| Connecticut | 150,000 | 110,000 | 110,000 | 110,000 | 110,000 | 162,617 | 160,000 | 118,000 | (d) | 128,935 |
| Delaware | 171,000 | 77,775 | 126,327 | 143,769 | 112,250 | 126,615 | . . . | 117,861 | 107,457 | 110,313 |
| Florida | 130,273 (e) | 124,851 | 140,000 | 128,972 | 128,972 | 157,252 | 140,000 | 128,972 | 135,000 | (a-4) |
| Georgia | 139,339 | 91,609 | 123,636 | 137,791 | 115,781 | 139,309 | 134,000 | 121,556 | 152,160 | 133,204 |
| Hawaii | 117,312 | 114,420 | . . . | 114,420 | 108,972 | 215,655 | (f) | 103,512 | 129,024 | 95,232 |
| Idaho | 115,348 | 30,400 | 93,756 | 103,984 | 93,756 | 134,118 | 83,200 | 106,620 | . . . | (a-24) |
| Illinois | 177,412 | 135,669 | 156,541 | 156,541 | 135,669 | 115,613 | 142,339 | 133,273 | 149,005 | 135,100 |
| Indiana | 107,881 | 84,031 | 72,974 | 87,790 | 72,974 | 129,293 | 105,000 | 99,001 | 72,974 | 104,562 |
| Iowa | 130,000 | 103,212 | 103,212 | 123,669 | 103,212 | 163,538 | 154,300 | 103,212 | 103,212 | 110,000 |
| Kansas | 99,636 | 54,000 | 86,003 | 98,901 | 86,003 | 106,392 | 114,000 | 110,000 | N.A. | 104,999 |
| Kentucky (g) | 151,643* | 113,615* | 113,615 | 113,615 | 113,615* | 139,456 | N.O. | 113,615 | 113,615 | 126,000 |
| Louisiana | 130,000 | 115,000 | 115,000 | 115,000 | 115,000 | 167,850 | 204,400 | 115,000 | 132,620 | 115,024 |
| Maine | 70,000 | (h) | 69,264 | 92,248 | 69,264 | 102,689 | 102,689 | 102,689 | 96,782 | 96,553 |
| Maryland | 150,000 | 125,000 | 87,500 | 125,000 | 125,000 | 130,560 (b) | 138,374 (b) | 130,050 (b) | . . . | 117,751 (b) |
| Massachusetts | 139,832 | 124,295 | 130,262 | 133,644 | 130,916 | 151,347 | 150,000 | 123,600 | 137,425 | 127,323 |
| Michigan | 159,300 (e) | 111,510 | 124,410 | 124,410 | 174,204 | 130,777 | 250,000 | 140,000 | 157,202 | 115,000 |
| Minnesota | 120,303 | 78,197 | 90,227 | 114,288 | (a-24) | 164,890 | 108,388 | 108,388 | 102,257 | 94,795 |
| Mississippi | 122,160 | 61,714 | 85,500 | 103,512 | 85,500 | 124,443 | 124,000 | 85,500 | 85,500 | 133,721 |
| Missouri | 133,821 | 86,484 | 107,746 | 116,437 | 107,746 | 90,112 | 123,967 | 120,000 | 107,746 | N.O. |
| Montana | 108,167 | 86,362 | 86,018 | 99,712 | (a-6) | 109,580 | 96,967 | 96,972 | 86,018 | 97,000 |
| Nebraska | 105,000 | 75,000 | 85,000 | 95,000 | 85,000 | 95,000 | 99,002 | 103,501 | 86,018 | 102,301 |
| Nevada | 141,000 | 60,000 | 97,000 | 133,000 | 97,000 | 117,030 | 115,847 | 107,465 | . . . | 97,901 |
| New Hampshire | 113,834 | (h) | 104,364 | 110,114 | 104,364 | 104,364 | 116,170 | 93,812 | . . . | 104,364 |
| New Jersey | 175,000 | 141,000 | (a-1) | 141,000 | 141,000 | 141,000 | . . . | 141,000 | 139,000 | 130,625 |
| New Mexico | 110,000 | 85,000 | 85,000 | 95,000 | 85,000 | 163,571 | 105,000 | 125,000 | 85,000 | 90,000 |
| New York | 179,000 (e) | 151,500 | 120,800 | 151,500 | 127,000 | 120,800 | 169,100 | 120,800 | 151,500 | 127,000 |
| North Carolina | 139,590 | 123,198 | 123,198 | 123,198 | 123,198 | 103,657 | 120,363 | 123,198 | 123,198 | 123,198 |
| North Dakota | 110,283 | 85,614 | 87,728 | 113,266 | 82,849 | 167,652 | . . . | 90,122 | 87,728 | 103,284 |
| Ohio | 148,886 | 78,041 | 109,554 | 109,986 | 109,986 | 116,397 | 127,400 | 121,784 | 109,985 | 100,485 |
| Oklahoma | 147,000 | 114,713 | 90,000 | 132,850 | 114,713 | 167,512 | 107,500 | 87,005 | 114,713 | 137,239 |
| Oregon | 93,600 | (a-2) | 72,000 | 77,200 | 72,000 | 167,160 | 182,184 | 136,320 | 140,964 | . . . |
| Pennsylvania(i) | 183,255* | 153,907* | 131,992* | 152,443 | 152,443 | 131,992* | 144,275 | 131,992* | 152,443 | 131,992* |
| Rhode Island (j) | 129,210 | 108,808 | 108,808 | 115,610 | 108,808 | 94,769 | 149,512 | (a-23) | 140,050 | 101,598 |
| South Carolina | 106,078 | 46,545 | 92,007 | 92,007 | 92,007 | 92,007 | 173,380 | 92,007 | N.A. | 101,101 |
| South Dakota | 98,031 | 120,000 | 78,363 | 97,928 | 78,363 | 100,000 | 90,000 | 90,000 | 98,345 | 89,250 |
| Tennessee | 170,340 (k) | 57,027 (h) | 182,800 | 167,976 | 182,880 | 152,400 | 182,880 | 152,400 | 182,880 | 152,400 |
| Texas | 150,000 | 7,200 (m) | 125,880 | 150,000 | (a-14) | 139,140 | . . . | 137,500 | 198,000 | 180,000 (n) |
| Utah | 109,470 | 104,000 | (a-1) | 98,509 | 104,000 | 101,608 | 116,355 | 101,608 | 104,000 | 113,235 |
| Vermont (l) | 142,542* | 60,507* | 90,376* | 108,202* | 90,376* | 87,090 | 115,606 | 115,606 | 90,376* | 127,254 |
| Virginia | 175,000 | 36,321 | 152,793 | 150,000 | 157,249 | 132,890 | 152,793 | 120,000 | 167,902 | 149,547 |
| Washington | 166,891 | 91,129 | 116,950 | 151,718 | 113,436 | 167,511 | 142,596 | 118,800 | 116,950 | 116,964 |
| West Virginia | 150,000 | (h) | 95,000 | 95,000 | 95,000 | 92,500 | 95,000 | 95,000 | 95,000 | 75,000 |
| Wisconsin | 144,423 | 76,261 | 68,556 | 140,147 | 68,556 | 121,500 | 125,500 | 120,000 | 111,000 | 103,325 |
| Wyoming | 105,000 | (a-2) | 92,000 | 137,150 | 92,000 | 118,930 | 142,771 | 107,588 | 92,000 | 100,002 |
| Guam | 90,000 | 85,000 | . . . | 105,286 | 52,492 | 68,152 | 88,915 | 60,850 | 100,000 | 88,915 |
| No. Mariana Islands | 70,000 | 65,000 | . . . | 80,000 | 40,800 (b) | . . . | 54,000 | 40,800 (b) | 80,000 | 40,800 (b) |
| U.S. Virgin Islands | 80,000 | 75,000 | (a-1) | 76,500 | 76,500 | 85,000 | 76,500 | 76,500 | 76,500 | 75,000 |

*Sources:* The Council of State Governments' survey of state personnel agencies and state websites, April 2012.

*Key:*

N.A.— Not available.

. . . — No specific chief administrative official or agency in charge of function.

(a) Chief administrative official or agency in charge of function:
(a-1) Lieutenant governor.
(a-2) Secretary of state.
(a-3) Attorney general.
(a-4) Treasurer.
(a-5) Adjutant general.
(a-6) Administration.
(a-7) Agriculture.
(a-8) Auditor.

(a-9) Banking.
(a-10) Budget.
(a-11) Civil rights.
(a-12) Commerce.
(a-13) Community affairs.
(a-14) Comptroller.
(a-15) Consumer affairs.
(a-16) Corrections.
(a-17) Economic development.
(a-18) Education (chief state school officer).
(a-19) Election administration.
(a-20) Emergency administration.
(a-21) Employment Services.
(a-22) Energy.
(a-23) Environmental protection.

## SELECTED STATE ADMINISTRATIVE OFFICIALS: ANNUAL SALARIES — Continued

| State or other jurisdiction | Budget | Civil rights | Commerce | Community affairs | Comptroller | Consumer affairs | Corrections | Economic development | Education | Election admin. |
|---|---|---|---|---|---|---|---|---|---|---|
| Alabama | $177,266 | N.O. | $162,232 | $91,014 | $131,633 | $100,198 | $123,500 | (a-13) | $190,000 | $67,378 |
| Alaska | 149,676 | 143,820 | 135,000 | (a-12) | 124,128 | (a-12) | 135,000 | (a-12) | 135,000 | 115,320 |
| Arizona | 140,000 | 123,651 | 300,000 | 98,133 | 117,702 | 135,000 | 160,000 | (a-12) | 85,000 | (a-2) |
| Arkansas | 88,957 | ... | (a-17) | N.A. | 110,486 | 115,634 | 133,033 | 91,800 | 224,400 | 83,637 |
| California | (a-24) | N.O. | N.O. | 138,528 | 139,189 | 175,000 | 225,000 | N.O. | 151,127 | 126,588 |
| Colorado | 156,465 | 124,572 | N.O. | 137,280 | 126,540 | 124,728 | 150,000 | 150,000 | 225,000 | 117,600 |
| Connecticut | 139,026 | 118,450 | 170,000 | 187,000 | 110,000 | 127,500 | 151,000 | 170,000 | 185,000 | 128,931 |
| Delaware | 145,911 | 78,469 | (a-2) | N.O. | 145,919 | 120,562 | 145,911 | 126,327 | 158,599 | 80,325 |
| Florida | 150,000 | 93,000 | 200,000 | 115,000 | (a-4) | 97,698 | 160,000 | 133,350 | 275,000 | 102,119 |
| Georgia | 155,000 | 105,202 | 125,000 | 146,795 | N.A. | 130,000 | 149,000 | 150,000 | 123,270 | 77,445 |
| Hawaii | 108,972 | 92,892 | 108,972 | ... | 108,972 | 92,760 | 103,512 | 103,512 | 142,500 | 75,000 |
| Idaho | 115,918 | 63,294 | 145,017 | ... | 93,756 | (a-3) | 123,676 | (a-12) | 93,756 | (a-2) |
| Illinois | 144,000 | 115,613 | 142,339 | (a-12) | 135,669 | (a-3) | 150,228 | (a-12) | 189,996 | 115,584 |
| Indiana | 126,000 | 88,000 | (a-17) | 115,267 | (a-8) | 92,000 | 115,000 | 150,000 | 87,790 | N.A. |
| Iowa | 130,000 | 97,460 | 100,000 | 93,658 | N.O. | 128,890 | 144,948 | 154,300 | 140,000 | 93,267 |
| Kansas | 98,000 | 76,476 | 103,000 | N.A. | 97,375 | 90,000 | 125,000 | 105,092 | 170,000 | (a-2) |
| Kentucky (g) | 148,719 | 117,822 | 137,865* | 113,474 | 106,152 | 86,928 | 93,324 | 250,000* | 225,000 | 65,100 |
| Louisiana | 114,296 | 82,347 | 320,000 | 102,000 | 204,400 | 89,000 | 136,719 | 320,000 | 275,000 | 109,803 |
| Maine | 90,355 | 69,409 | (a-17) | (a-17) | 90,355 | 96,553 | 102,689 | 102,689 | 102,689 | 83,574 |
| Maryland | 166,082 (b) | 110,699 (b) | 155,000 (b) | ... | 125,000 | 121,005 (b) | 166,082 (b) | 155,000 (b) | 195,000 | 109,372 (b) |
| Massachusetts | 92,700 | 117,266 | 150,000 | 139,050 | 154,669 | 139,050 | 140,000 | 150,000 | 154,500 | 130,916 |
| Michigan | 250,000 | 136,000 | 150,000 | N.O. | 128,000 | ... | 145,000 | ... | 183,945 | (o) |
| Minnesota | (a-24) | 108,388 | 108,388 | (a-17) | (a-24) | 110,350 | 108,388 | 108,388 | 108,388 | (a-2) |
| Mississippi | (a-6) | ... | (a-7) | 130,000 | (a-6) | 82,000 | 132,761 | 176,500 | 307,125 | 80,000 |
| Missouri | 102,000 | 67,078 | 120,000 | 93,787 | 95,288 | (a-3) | 120,000 | 120,000 | 185,400 | 65,196 |
| Montana | 94,000 | 69,300 | 96,984 | 72,382 | 87,213 | 69,433 | 98,426 | 105,000 | 104,635 | 69,640 |
| Nebraska | 132,500 | 76,126 | 127,500 | 80,538 | 101,500 | (a-3) | 125,002 | 127,500 | 207,500 | 81,407 |
| Nevada | (a-6) | 87,773 | 115,847 | ... | 97,000 | 97,901 | 108,850 | 117,030 | 113,295 | (p) |
| New Hampshire | 104,364 | 79,774 | 112,861 | ... | 104,364 | 86,229 | 116,170 | 86,131 | 112,861 | (a-2) |
| New Jersey | 133,507 | 124,000 | (a-17) | 141,000 | 141,000 | 136,000 | 141,000 | 186,600 | 141,000 | 115,000 |
| New Mexico | 109,000 | N.A. | 122,500 | N.A. | 100,000 | 80,642 | 106,000 | 122,500 | 125,000 | 85,000 |
| New York | 169,100 | 109,800 | 11 | 120,800 | 151,500 | 127,000 | 136,000 | 1 | 212,500 | (q) |
| North Carolina | (a-15) | 67,252 | 120,363 | N.O. | 153,319 | N.A. | N.A. | 101,702 | 123,198 | 117,397 |
| North Dakota | 110,952 | 84,000 | 135,000 | ... | 110,952 | 98,844 | 103,956 | 108,300 | 99,876 | 43,080 |
| Ohio | 150,405 | 96,408 | 116,397 | 90,002 | 150,405 | 100,006 | 127,400 | 127,400 | 185,016 | 109,985 |
| Oklahoma | 90,000 | 62,000 | 90,000 | N.A. | 100,000 | 105,000 | 132,309 | 90,000 | 124,373 | 105,665 |
| Oregon | 127,884 | 100,380 | 150,252 | N.A. | 127,884 | 150,252 | 164,928 | 150,252 | 72,000 | 110,556 |
| Pennsylvania (i) | 149,497 | 124,636 | 139,250* | 116,499 | N.A. | 112,548 | 146,579* | 139,250* | 142,310* | 98,015 |
| Rhode Island (j) | 154,151 | 81,363 | (a-9) | N.A. | 119,343 | (a-3) | 145,644 | 185,000 (r) | 203,000 | 137,573 |
| South Carolina | 124,331 | N.A. | 152,000 | N.A. | 92,007 | 99,777 | 144,746 | (a-12) | 92,007 | 84,375 |
| South Dakota | (a-24) | N.A. | (a-44) | (a-48) | (a-40) | 63,654 | 100,000 | 103,500 | 103,500 | 50,000 |
| Tennessee | 132,000 | 86,352 | (a-17) | (a-17) | 182,880 | 76,200 | 152,400 | 182,880 | 203,208 | 116,844 |
| Texas | 120,000 | 83,586 | ... | 129,250 | 150,000 | 108,516 | 186,300 | ... | 186,300 | (s) |
| Utah | 129,501 | 87,360 | 119,558 | 64,064 | 126,214 | 119,558 | 116,355 | 126,214 | 177,819 | 79,908 |
| Vermont (l) | (a-24) | 94,994 | 115,606 | 82,014 | (a-24) | 94,994 | 98,550 | 82,014 | 113,402 | (a-2) |
| Virginia | 157,500 | 76,745 | 160,433 | 124,335 | 140,671 | 99,316 | 150,000 | 260,500 | 175,467 | 104,000 |
| Washington | (a-24) | 92,148 | 142,596 | (a-12) | (a-24) | (a-3) | 147,000 | (a-12) | 117,972 | (a-2) |
| West Virginia | 97,416 | 55,000 | 95,000 | 95,000 | (a-8) | N.A. | 80,000 | (a-13) | 165,000 | (a-2) |
| Wisconsin | 123,739 | 100,247 | 121,000 | ... | 114,385 | 70,992 | 125,000 | 99,447 | 120,111 | 101,000 |
| Wyoming | 113,568 | 72,023 | 147,145 | (a-12) | (a-8) | (a-12) | 135,319 | (a-12) | 92,000 | 98,134 |
| Guam | 88,915 | ... | 88,915 | ... | 83,400 | 55,341 | 67,150 | 82,025 | 82,025 | 61,939 |
| No. Mariana Islands | 54,000 | 49,000 | 52,000 | 52,000 | 40,800 (b) | 52,000 | 40,800 (b) | 45,000 | 80,000 | 53,000 |
| U.S. Virgin Islands | 76,500 | 60,000 | 76,500 | (t) | 76,500 | 76,500 | 76,500 | 85,000 | 76,500 | 135,000 |

(a-24) Finance.
(a-25) Fish and wildlife.
(a-26) General services.
(a-27) Health.
(a-28) Higher education.
(a-29) Highways.
(a-30) Information systems.
(a-31) Insurance.
(a-32) Labor.
(a-33) Licensing.
(a-34) Mental Health.
(a-35) Natural resources.
(a-36) Parks and recreation.
(a-37) Personnel.
(a-38) Planning.

(a-39) Post audit.
(a-40) Pre-audit.
(a-41) Public library development.
(a-42) Public utility regulation.
(a-43) Purchasing.
(a-44) Revenue.
(a-45) Social services.
(a-46) Solid waste management.
(a-47) State police.
(a-48) Tourism.
(a-49) Transportation.
(a-50) Welfare.
(b) Salary ranges, top figure in ranges follow:
   Hawaii: Employment Services, $112,296; Energy, 112,296; Environmental Protection, $112,296; Fish and Wildlife, $112,296; Highways, $112,296;

## SELECTED STATE ADMINISTRATIVE OFFICIALS: ANNUAL SALARIES — Continued

| State or other jurisdiction | Emergency mgmt. | Employment services | Energy | Environ. protection | Finance | Fish & wildlife | General services | Health | Higher education | Highways |
|---|---|---|---|---|---|---|---|---|---|---|
| Alabama | $124,200 | $80,287 | $97,766 | $144,196 | $91,014 | $105,403 | $95,359 | $244,542 | $185,952 | $169,000 |
| Alaska | 115,320 | 143,820 | 158,303 | 135,000 | 115,320 | 135,000 | (a-43) | 135,000 | 320,000 | 119,328 |
| Arizona | 100,000 | 77,970 | 100,000 | 135,000 | (a-14) | 160,000 | 116,000 | 136,000 | 300,000 | 128,700 |
| Arkansas | 90,619 | 136,601 | 85,536 | 118,580 | (a-6) | 118,492 | 120,019 | 108,575 | 129,309 | 157,430 |
| California | 175,000 | 150,112 | 132,396 | 175,000 | 175,000 | 150,112 | 159,300 | (u) | (v) | (a-49) |
| Colorado | 105,000 | N.A. | 130,000 | 144,876 | 126,540 | 144,876 | 130,404 | 215,000 | 146,040 | 138,000 |
| Connecticut | 170,000 | 130,000 | 139,000 | 139,000 | 187,000 | (w) | 160,000 | 170,000 | 340,000 | 175,000 |
| Delaware | 81,652 | 95,115 | 95,205 | (a-35) | 145,911 | 97,564 | 107,100 | 168,300 | 100,499 | (a-49) |
| Florida | 140,000 | 133,350 | 90,000 | 140,000 | (a-4) | 129,430 | 140,000 | 140,000 | 200,000 | 128,000 |
| Georgia | 122,003 | 88,455 | 116,452 | 175,000 | 148,000 | 107,732 | N.A. | 175,000 | 425,000 | 100,000 |
| Hawaii | 90,048 | 78,888 (b) | 78,888 (b) | 78,888 (b) | (x) | 78,888 (b) | (a-14) | 108,972 | 427,512 | 78,888 (b) |
| Idaho | 122,982 | 111,945 | 82,825 | 112,340 | 102,731 | 130,000 | ... | 141,710 | 110,011 | (a-49) |
| Illinois | 128,920 | 142,339 | (a-42) | 133,273 | (a-10) | (a-35) | (a-6) | 150,228 | 193,800 | (a-49) |
| Indiana | 101,500 | 115,000 | 83,132 | 115,006 | (a-10) | 77,500 | (a-6) | 137,500 | 155,000 | (a-49) |
| Iowa | 112,070 | 140,000 | 154,300 | 110,656 | 121,285 | 116,168 | 121,285 | 130,000 | N.O. | 144,643 |
| Kansas | (y) | (a-32) | N.A. | 105,019 | N.A. | 73,320 | (a-6) | 190,000 | 197,000 | (a-49) |
| Kentucky (g) | 79,537 | N.A. | 137,865* | 102,900 | 137,865* | 134,352 | ... | 184,606 | 360,000 | 113,557 |
| Louisiana | 165,000 | 108,600 | 122,865 | 137,197 | 204,400 | 123,614 | 204,400 | 236,000 | 275,000 | 170,000 |
| Maine | 72,800 | N.A. | (a-38) | 102,689 | (a-6) | 102,689 | 86,902 | 109,220 | N.A. | (a-49) |
| Maryland | 127,500 (b) | 116,485 (b) | 130,050 (b) | (b) | 166,082 (b) | ... | (a-6) | 166,082 (b) | 127,500 (b) | 159,858 |
| Massachusetts | 133,900 | 150,000 | 120,000 | 130,000 | 150,000 | 126,690 | 125,000 | 142,363 | 206,000 | 145,000 |
| Michigan | 145,000 | 118,470 | 106,259 | 145,000 | 250,000 | (z) | ... | 145,000 | ... | (a-49) |
| Minnesota | 108,388 | 102,082 | 108,388 | 108,388 | 108,388 | 108,367 | (a-6) | 108,388 | 360,000 | 108,388 |
| Mississippi | 107,868 | 122,000 | 137,996 | 120,386 | (a-6) | 120,636 | ... | 200,000 | 341,250 | (a-49) |
| Missouri | 95,004 | 103,860 | N.O. | 91,303 | 105,372 | (aa) | 95,288 | 120,000 | 170,000 | (a-49) |
| Montana | 74,202 | 89,337 | 88,157 | 96,967 | 87,213 | 96,963 | 88,951 | (a-45) | 213,813 | (a-49) |
| Nebraska | 85,889 | 97,974 | 88,776 | 116,029 | (bb) | (cc) | 102,197 | 145,068 | 162,475 | (a-49) |
| Nevada | 86,757 | 127,721 | 99,397 | 112,275 | (a-14) | 117,030 | ... | (dd) | 23,660 (ee) | (a-49) |
| New Hampshire | 104,364 | 104,364 | 79,774 | 112,861 | (a-10) | 98,691 | (a-6) | 98,691 | 72,852 | (a-49) |
| New Jersey | 132,300 | 124,020 | 100,000 | 141,000 | 133,507 | 105,783 | (ff) | 141,000 | 86,793 | 124,110 |
| New Mexico | 115,000 | 95,000 | 100,000 | 105,000 | 125,000 | 100,000 | 105,000 | 122,500 | 125,000 | 105,000 |
| New York | 136,000 | 127,000 | 157,955 | 136,000 | 151,500 | 136,000 | 136,000 | 136,000 | 212,500 | 136,000 |
| North Carolina | 97,284 | 120,363 | 92,647 | 113,410 | 153,000 | 105,000 | 120,363 | 211,251 | 525,000 | 154,388 |
| North Dakota | 92,100 | 97,788 | 108,828 | 101,592 | 110,952 | 107,328 | 145,500 | 171,024 | 213,720 | (a-49) |
| Ohio | 100,901 | 127,400 | 90,002 | 127,400 | (gg) | 104,270 | 106,080 | 141,170 | 168,002 | 127,400 |
| Oklahoma | 75,705 | 93,190 | 90,000 | 119,008 | 108,000 | 116,986 | 108,000 | 194,244 | 394,983 | (a-49) |
| Oregon | N.A. | 150,252 | N.A. | 136,320 | (a-4) | 136,320 | (a-6) | 165,624 | 219,504 | 148,008 |
| Pennsylvania (i) | 135,003 | 120,001 | 115,013 | 146,579* | 149,497 | 119,257 | 139,250* | 146,579* | 116,167 | 130,602 |
| Rhode Island (j) | 88,177 | 130,152 | 75,154 | 108,460 | (a-44) | (a-23) | (a-6) | 134,975 | 265,000 (hh) | (a-49) |
| South Carolina | 97,000 | 134,227 | 84,307 | (ii) | 173,380 | 121,380 | N.A. | 144,746 | 100,907 | 143,000 |
| South Dakota | 73,181 | (a-37) | (a-48) | (a-35) | 120,000 | 104,000 | (a-6) | 104,000 | 323,000 | (a-47) |
| Tennessee | 92,028 | 152,400 | 111,768 | 152,400 | 182,880 | 152,400 | 152,400 | 170,004 | 186,732 | (a-49) |
| Texas | N.A. | 140,000 | ... | 145,200 | (a-14) | 143,000 | 126,500 | 183,750 | 186,300 | (a-49) |
| Utah | 69,493 | 129,688 | 86,112 | 116,938 | 122,845 | 119,558 | 113,235 | 194,813 | 129,688 | (a-49) |
| Vermont (l) | 80,018 | 93,995 | 95,992 | 92,997 | 89,669 | 88,005 | 89,357 | 115,606 | ... | (a-49) |
| Virginia | 120,383 | 128,100 | 92,400 | 157,729 | 160,433 | 130,977 | 148,293 | 191,906 | 182,490 | 198,450 |
| Washington | 122,412 | 137,304 | (a-23) | 137,304 | 158,160 | 136,776 | (a-6) | 137,304 | N.A. | (a-49) |
| West Virginia | 65,000 | 75,000 | 95,000 | (a-22) | (a-6) | 77,772 | 78,492 | 95,000 | (jj) | 92,500 |
| Wisconsin | 99,000 | 110,000 | 100,000 | 125,000 | 123,739 | 125,000 | 125,000 | 130,000 | 414,593 | (a-47) |
| Wyoming | 86,742 | 128,013 | 73,042 | 119,892 | (a-8) | 138,249 | 110,047 | 206,798 | 129,796 | 125,417 |
| Guam | 68,152 | 73,020 | 55,303 | 60,850 | 88,915 | 60,850 | 60,528 | 74,096 | 195,000 | 88,915 |
| No. Mariana Islands | 45,000 | 40,800 (b) | 45,000 | 58,000 | 54,000 | 40,800 (b) | 54,000 | 80,000 | 80,000 | 40,800 (b) |
| U.S. Virgin Islands | 71,250 | 76,500 | 69,350 | 76,500 | 76,500 | 76,500 | 76,500 | 76,500 | 76,500 | 65,000 |

Information Systems, $112,296; Licensing, 106,968; Parks and Recreation, $112,296; Planning, $119,160; Post-Audit, $112,296; Pre-Audit, $112,296; Solid Waste Management, $106,968; Welfare, $112,296.

Maryland: For these positions the salary in the chart is the actual salary and the following are the salary ranges: Adjutant General, $107,196–$143,270; Administration, $107,196–$143,270; Agriculture, $107,196–$143,270; Banking, $73,341–$117,751; Budget, $124,175–$166,082; Civil Rights, $86,161–$115,000; Commerce, $124,175–$166,082; Consumer Affairs, $78,233–$125,743; Corrections, $124,175–$166,082; Economic Development, $124,175–$166,082; Elections Administration, $86,161–$115,000; Emergency Management, $99,637–$133,112; Workforce Development, $92,640–$123,708; Energy, $99,637–$133,112; Environmental Protection, $115,356–$154,235; Finance, $124,175–$166,082; Health, $124,175–$166,082; Higher Education, $115,356–$154,235; Information Services, $124,175–$166,082; Insurance, $124,175–$166,082; Labor, $124,175–$166,082; Licensing, $86,161–$115,000; Mental Health

shared duties, $143,767–$237,562 (actual, $211,632) and $92,640–$123,708 (actual, $120,870); Natural Resources, $115,356–$154,235; Parks and Recreation, $86,161–$115,000; Personnel, $99,637–$133,112; Planning $107,196–$143,270; Pre-Audit, $92,640–$123,708; Public Library, $86,161–$115,000; Purchasing $80,160–$106,940; Revenue, $92,460–$123,708; Social Services, $124,175–$166,082; Solid Waste Management, $86,161–$115,000; State Police, $124,175–$166,082; Tourism, $92,640–$123,708; Transportation, $124,175–$166,082; Welfare, $124,175–$166,082.

Northern Mariana Islands: $49,266 top of range applies to the following positions: Treasurer, Banking, Comptroller, Corrections, Employment Services, Fish and Wildlife, Highways, Insurance, Mental Health and Retardation, Parks and Recreation, Purchasing, Social/Human Services, Transportation.

(c) Governor Bentley is not accepting a salary until the unemployment rate in Alabama drops.

## SELECTED STATE ADMINISTRATIVE OFFICIALS: ANNUAL SALARIES — Continued

| State or other jurisdiction | Info. systems | Insurance | Labor | Licensing | Mental health | Natural resources | Parks & recreation | Personnel | Planning | Post audit |
|---|---|---|---|---|---|---|---|---|---|---|
| Alabama | $122,232 | $91,014 | $91,014 | N.O. | $145,000 | $141,000 | $0 | $160,440 | (a-13) | $241,695 |
| Alaska | 119,640 | 124,128 | 135,000 | 111,144 | 84,156 | 135,000 | 115,320 | 119,640 | N.O. | (a-8) |
| Arizona | 131,387 | 115,650 | 126,069 | ... | 109,037 | 131,500 | 122,200 | 125,000 | 140,000 | ... |
| Arkansas | 128,542 | 120,258 | 117,308 | ... | 104,080 | 103,611 | 113,400 | 102,402 | ... | 170,900 |
| California | 175,000 | 139,189 | 175,000 | 150,112 | (kk) | 175,000 | 150,112 | 150,112 | N.O. | N.O. |
| Colorado | 156,000 | 120,000 | 146,040 | N.A. | 133,116 | 146,040 | 144,876 | N.A. | 138,000 | (a-8) |
| Connecticut | 158,000 | 143,000 | 130,000 | 104,954 | (ll) | 134,093 | 138,123 | 160,000 | 135,000 | (a-8) |
| Delaware | 158,559 | 107,457 | 117,861 | 112,972 | (mm) | 126,327 | 98,277 | 111,034 | 94,216 | (a-8) |
| Florida | 120,000 | 133,158 | 133,350 | N.A. | 120,000 | 140,000 | 105,000 | 100,000 | 115,000 | (a-4) |
| Georgia | 135,000 | 120,394 | 121,570 | 105,000 | 225,000 | 141,103 | 111,420 | 92,329 | (a-10) | (a-8) |
| Hawaii | 78,888 (b) | 95,232 | 103,512 | 75,144 (b) | 97,524 | 103,512 | 78,888 (b) | 103,512 | 83,724 (b) | 78,888 (b) |
| Idaho | (a-6) | 97,323 | 111,945 | 74,609 | ... | 112,798 | 86,320 | 95,680 | ... | (a-14) |
| Illinois | (a-6) | 135,081 | 124,090 | (a-9) | (a-45) | 133,273 | (a-35) | (a-6) | ... | (a-8) |
| Indiana | 108,813 | 92,500 | 99,180 | 96,393 | 98,910 | 105,000 | 80,378 | 111,657 | N.O. | 98,717 |
| Iowa | 133,182 | 106,623 | 112,070 | N.O. | 114,130 | 128,890 | 116,168 | 116,147 | N.O. | N.O. |
| Kansas | 130,000 | 86,003 | 102,000 | 60,706 | (nn) | 111,490 | 60,382 | 87,750 | N.A. | 115,296 |
| Kentucky (g) | 109,725 | 100,217 | 137,865* | ... | 103,950 | 95,445 | 111,000 | 137,865* | 148,719 | (a-8) |
| Louisiana | 167,000 | 115,000 | 137,000 | ... | 236,000 | 129,210 | 115,627 | 108,160 | 104,748 | N.A. |
| Maine | 96,553 | 88,545 | 102,689 | 98,737 | (a-45) | 102,689 | (a-35) | 90,355 | 77,521 | N.A. |
| Maryland | 166,082 (b) | (b) | 158,974 (b) | 100,581 (b) | (b)(oo) | 148,778 (b) | 115,000 (b) | 117,416 (b) | 124,848 (b) | N.A. |
| Massachusetts | 140,000 | 123,600 | 90,000 | 110,000 | (pp) | 150,000 | 130,000 | 142,127 | 150,000 | (a-8) |
| Michigan | 155,000 | 115,000 | 150,000 | 150,000 | 130,975 | 140,000 | 117,166 | 143,948 | ... | (a-8) |
| Minnesota | 120,000 | 97,217 | 108,388 | 78,571 | (a-45) | 108,388 | 108,367 | (a-24) | N.A. | (a-8) |
| Mississippi | 160,047 | 85,500 | ... | ... | 164,357 | 120,386 | 120,636 | 111,143 | 96,303 | (a-8) |
| Missouri | 110,000 | 120,000 | 120,000 | 80,000 | 113,878 | 120,000 | N.A. | 95,288 | 102,000 | 107,746 |
| Montana | 111,623 | 86,018 | 96,967 | 89,803 | 97,309 | 96,967 | 94,650 | 91,502 | 105,000 | 119,326 |
| Nebraska | 127,500 | 111,650 | 127,500 | 100,293 | 141,885 | 109,502 | 124,097 | 100,516 | 99,002 | (a-8) |
| Nevada | 123,783 | 117,030 | 88,799 | ... | (qq) | 127,721 | 107,465 | 97,474 | ... | ... |
| New Hampshire | 106,496 | 104,364 | 104,364 | 104,364 | 104,364 | 112,861 | 90,605 | 88,933 | ... | (a-14) |
| New Jersey | 130,380 | 130,000 | 141,000 | ... | (rr) | 125,000 | 102,000 | 141,000 | 95,000 | ... |
| New Mexico | 100,000 | 100,000 | 95,000 | 100,000 | ... | 95,986 | 92,860 | 118,000 | 73,245 | 85,000 |
| New York | 169,214 | 127,000 | 127,000 | (ss) | (tt) | 136,000 | 127,000 | 120,800 | 1 | 151,500 |
| North Carolina | 153,227 | 123,198 | 123,198 | N.O. | 145,000 | 120,363 | 106,974 | 120,363 | N.A. | (a-8) |
| North Dakota | 121,260 | 87,727 | 84,000 | ... | 95,220 | ... | 87,675 | 93,288 | ... | 96,600 |
| Ohio | 124,758 | 150,405 | 90,397 | (uu) | (vv) | 127,400 | 98,800 | 104,998 | 127,400 | (a-8) |
| Oklahoma | 160,000 | 126,713 | 105,053 | N.O. | 133,455 | 86,310 | 86,310 | 108,000 | N.O. | N.O. |
| Oregon | 134,220 | 150,252 | 72,000 | N.A. | 140,964 | N.A. | 136,320 | 110,556 | ... | 140,964 |
| Pennsylvania (i) | 136,998 | 131,922* | 146,579* | 105,018 | 125,184 | 139,250* | 116,675 | 139,013 | 135,003 | (a-8) |
| Rhode Island (j) | 137,604 | (a-9) | (a-21) | (ww) | 143,206 | (a-23) | (a-23) | 146,165 | 115,891 | N.A. |
| South Carolina | 123,750 | N.A. | 116,797 | 116,797 | (xx) | 121,380 | 112,504 | 116,984 | N.A. | 94,730 |
| South Dakota | 110,000 | 83,015 | 100,000 | N.A. | 95,000 | 100,000 | 82,995 | 97,000 | N.A. | (a-8) |
| Tennessee | 152,400 | 152,400 | 152,400 | 86,364 | 152,400 | 152,400 | 84,972 | 152,400 | N.A. | (a-14) |
| Texas | 175,000 | 163,800 | 140,000 | 135,000 | 163,200 | 145,200 | 143,000 | ... | 120,000 | (a-8) |
| Utah | 129,688 | 107,266 | 101,608 | 101,920 | 95,846 | 126,214 | 110,219 | 126,214 | (a-10) | (a-8) |
| Vermont (l) | 112,008 | 127,254 | 93,995 | 75,005 | 100,006 | 115,606 | 88,005 | 94,931 | ... | (a-8) |
| Virginia | 157,500 | 149,547 | 110,250 | 112,000 | 191,672 | 152,793 | 128,000 | 137,955 | (a-10) | (a-8) |
| Washington | 147,000 (yy) | 116,950 | 135,144 | 116,964 | (a-45) | 121,618 | 116,964 | 137,304 | (a-24) | N.A. |
| West Virginia | 109,999 | 92,500 | 70,000 | ... | 95,000 | 75,000 | 78,636 | 70,000 | (a-17) | 91,750 |
| Wisconsin | 130,000 | 117,500 | 85,608 | 110,500 | 110,500 | 125,000 | 110,000 | 104,287 | ... | (a-8) |
| Wyoming | 194,400 | 101,567 | 88,439 | 72,176 | 100,200 | 43,842 | 100,883 | 109,824 | 100,000 | (a-8) |
| Guam | 88,915 | 88,915 | 73,020 | 88,915 | 75,208 | 60,850 | 60,850 | 88,915 | 88,915 | 100,000 |
| No. Mariana Islands | 45,000 | 40,800 (b) | 45,000 | 45,360 | 40,800 (b) | 52,000 | 40,800 (b) | 60,000 | 45,000 | 80,000 |
| U.S. Virgin Islands | 71,250 | 75,000 | 76,500 | 76,500 | 70,000 | 76,500 | 76,500 | 76,500 | 76,500 | 55,000 |

(d) Responsibilities shared between John C. Geragosian, $147,790, and Robert M. Ward, $147,790.

(e) Florida Gov. Rick Scott does not collect his salary; Michigan Gov. Rick Snyder returns all but $1.00 of his salary; New York Gov. Andrew Cuomo has reduced his salary by 5 percent.

(f) There is no one single agency for Administration. The functions are divided among the Director of Budget and Finance, $108,972; Director of Human Resources Development, vacant; and the Comptroller, $108,972.

(g) Positions with asterisk have taken a 10 percent salary reduction in the reported salary upon request of the Governor in recognition of budget problems.

(h) In Maine, New Hampshire, Tennessee and West Virginia, the presidents (or speakers) of the Senate are next in line of succession to the governorship. In Tennessee and West Virginia, the speaker of the Senate bears the statutory title of lieutenant governor.

(i) The Pennsylvania entries with asterisks denote that 1.7 percent of the officeholders' salary is being repaid as part of the management pay freeze.

(j) A number of the employees receive a stipend for their length of service to the State (known as a longevity payment). This amount can vary significantly among employees and, depending on state turnover, can show dramatic changes in actual salaries from year to year.

(k) Governor Haslam returns his salary to the state.

(l) The officials who have voluntarily taken a five percent reduction in the annual salary set in statue are marked with an *.

(m) Lieutenant Governor receives additional pay when serving as acting governor.

(n) This agency is now a self-directed state agency.

(o) Responsibilites shared between Secretary of State Ruth Johnson, $112,410, and Bureau Director Christopher Thomas, $118,470.

## SELECTED STATE ADMINISTRATIVE OFFICIALS: ANNUAL SALARIES — Continued

| State or other jurisdiction | Pre-audit | Public library dvpmt. | Public utility reg. | Purchasing | Revenue | Social services | Solid waste mgmt. | State police | Tourism | Trans-portation | Welfare |
|---|---|---|---|---|---|---|---|---|---|---|---|
| Alabama | (a-14) | $107,737 | $103,490 | $90,725 | $91,014 | $140,000 | $113,479 | $105,403 | $91,014 | (a-29) | (a-45) |
| Alaska | N.O. | 115,320 | 107,280 | 138,624 | 135,000 | (a-27) | 124,128 | 135,000 | 107,280 | 135,000 | 115,320 |
| Arizona | (a-14) | 70,048 | 133,574 | 116,000 | 145,000 | 173,250 | 96,510 | 139,549 | 105,000 | 130,000 | 173,250 |
| Arkansas | N.A. | 99,886 | 116,501 | 100,442 | 127,959 | 147,321 | N.A. | 110,568 | 88,274 | (a-29) | (a-45) |
| California | (a-14) | N.O. | 138,528 | (a-26) | 150,112 | 203,616 | 150,112 | 186,336 | N.O. | 165,000 | 175,000 |
| Colorado | (a-14) | 112,548 | 114,948 | 99,600 | 146,040 | 150,000 | 114,948 | 135,000 | 100,000 | 151,840 | 150,000 |
| Connecticut | (a-14) | 113,525 | 137,686 | 124,537 | 170,000 | 170,000 | 127,707 | 170,000 | 130,000 | 175,000 | 170,000 |
| Delaware | (a-8) | 82,977 | 105,570 | (a-26) | 123,369 | (zz) | 175,000 | 147,087 | 91,805 | 136,629 | 113,884 |
| Florida | (a-4) | 95,545 | 125,000 | 135,000 | 120,000 | 140,000 | 93,680 | 127,500 | N.A. | 140,000 | 117,998 |
| Georgia | (a-8) | N.A. | 116,452 | 132,000 | 158,000 | 171,600 | 80,187 | 140,000 | 125,000 | 150,000 | 134,000 |
| Hawaii | 78,888 (b) | 114,000 | 90,060 | 85,524 | 108,972 | 103,512 | 75,144 (b) | ... | 194,352 | 108,972 | 78,888 (b) |
| Idaho | (a-14) | 93,808 | 92,167 | (a-6) | 85,447 | (a-27) | ... | 112,008 | 63,400 | 165,000 | 104,400 |
| Illinois | (a-14) | 99,516 | 100,860 | (a-6) | 142,390 | 150,228 | (a-23) | 132,566 | (a-12) | 150,228 | 142,339 |
| Indiana | 72,974 | 93,620 | 109,262 | 75,000 | 115,006 | 130,520 | 93,212 | 130,682 | 85,401 | 130,000 | (a-45) |
| Iowa | 105,373 | 133,182 | 125,008 | 110,750 | 148,500 | 150,000 | 110,656 | 125,000 | 96,658 | 140,005 | 121,285 |
| Kansas | 76,960 | 85,000 | 99,292 | 83,640 | 107,990 | 105,000 | 86,965 | 107,990 | 82,961 | 107,990 | 67,500 |
| Kentucky (g) | ... | 91,947 | 127,260 | 90,142 | 121,632 | | 79,739 | 111,352* | 111,352 | 137,865 | (a-45) |
| Louisiana | 101,337 | 107,000 | 130,000 | 146,400 | 124,446 | 129,995 | 102,000 | 134,351 | 107,000 | 170,000 | 87,630 |
| Maine | (a-14) | 90,667 | 117,104 | 68,752 | 96,553 | 109,220 | 74,297 | 96,553 | (a-17) | 102,689 | (a-45) |
| Maryland | 110,000 (b) | 115,000 (b) | 150,000 | (b) | 120,026 (b) | (b) | 114,167 (b) | 166,082 (b) | 114,444 (b) | 166,082 (b) | (a-45) |
| Massachusetts | (a-8) | 107,140 | 133,900 | 125,000 | 140,000 | 140,718 | 130,000 | 209,888 | 125,000 | 150,000 | 141,110 |
| Michigan | ... | ... | 113,612 | 124,500 | 118,470 | 140,000 | 112,404 | 145,000 | ... | 145,000 | (a-45) |
| Minnesota | (a-8) | N.A. | (aaa) | 104,358 | 108,388 | (a-34) | 108,388 | 108,388 | 108,388 | 108,388 | (a-34) |
| Mississippi | (a-8) | 108,000 | 141,505 | 79,633 | 108,185 | 130,000 | 78,008 | 138,115 | 85,748 | 144,354 | 130,000 |
| Missouri | 95,288 | 84,072 | 88,267 | 95,288 | 120,000 | 120,000 | 72,000 | 107,184 | 75,000 | 164,600 | 97,300 |
| Montana | 119,326 | 87,290 | 94,531 | 88,951 | 98,421 | 96,967 | 96,967 | 88,400 | 80,285 | 99,985 | (a-45) |
| Nebraska | 101,500 | 94,345 | 120,164 | 102,197 | 141,500 | 157,325 | 68,066 | 109,360 | 63,180 | 137,026 | (a-45) |
| Nevada | ... | (bbb) | 112,275 | 88,799 | 115,847 | 115,847 | (a-23) | 115,847 | 117,030 | 115,847 | (dd) |
| New Hampshire | (a-14) | 90,606 | 110,036 | 72,852 | 116,170 | 120,095 | 98,691 | 104,364 | 90,606 | 116,170 | 90,606 |
| New Jersey | ... | ... | 141,000 | 130,000(ccc) | 124,765 | (ddd) | 98,299 | 132,300 | 90,000 | 141,000 | 127,200 |
| New Mexico | 79,200 | 70,726 | 90,000 | 91,000 | 125,000 | 105,000 | 84,523 | 115,000 | 125,000 | 112,701 | 117,000 |
| New York | 151,500 | 212,500 | 127,000 | 136,000 | 127,000 | 136,000 | 136,000 | 121,860 | 1 | 136,000 | 136,000 |
| North Carolina | (a-8) | N.A. | 137,203 | 109,183 | 120,363 | 117,193 | 110,105 | 117,406 | 111,872 | 120,363 | N.A. |
| North Dakota | ... | ... | 90,120 | 72,408 | 95,212 | 148,452 | 80,400 | 89,436 | 102,972 | 128,184 | N.A. |
| Ohio | 150,405 | 96,990 | 124,509 | 106,080 | 127,400 | (eee) | 80,454 | 127,400 | 87,984 | 99,341 | 127,400 |
| Oklahoma | (a-14) | 85,850 | (fff) | 95,000 | 111,933 | 133,455 | 98,793 | 101,030 | 86,310 | 133,200 | 133,455 |
| Oregon | (a-10) | N.A. | N.A. | 100,380 | 150,252 | 140,964 | N.A. | 143,064 | N.A. | 165,276 | 140,964 |
| Pennsylvania (i) | (a-4) | 116,949 | 141,750 | 126,006 | 139,250* | 146,579* | 115,013 | 139,250* | N.A. | 146,579* | 146,579* |
| Rhode Island (j) | (a-14) | 124,420 | 125,071 | 121,409 | 156,876 | (ggg) | (hhh) | 148,937 | (a-17) | 130,000 | (a-45) |
| South Carolina | 92,007 | 89,555 | 160,272 | 109,323 | 130,063 | 144,746 | 151,942 | 143,000 | 112,504 | 146,000 | (a-45) |
| South Dakota | 78,363 | 70,298 | 91,390 | 48,098 | 90,000 | 104,800 | 83,843 | 84,500 | 85,000 | 93,000 | (a-45) |
| Tennessee | 107,280 | 121,920 | 152,400 | 71,424 | 152,400 | 152,400 | 88,272 | 180,840 | 152,400 | 152,400 | 152,400 |
| Texas | (a-14) | 104,500 | 120,000 | 116,748 | (a-14) | 168,000 | N.A. | 162,000 | N.A. | 192,500 | 210,000 |
| Utah | (a-24) | 110,219 | 104,395 | 113,235 | N.A. | 129,688 | 107,266 | 113,235 | 103,397 | 160,222 | 129,688 |
| Vermont (l) | (a-24) | 83,990 | 116,688 | 89,357 | 87,818 | 115,606 | 92,997 | 106,912 | 79,227 | 115,606 | 100,006 |
| Virginia | (a-14) | 139,535 | (iii) | 134,869 | 143,646 | 147,000 | 157,729 | 153,076 | 168,000 | 160,433 | 147,000 |
| Washington | (a-4) | (a-2) | 124,164 | (a-6) | 136,776 | 158,160 | (a-23) | 137,304 | N.A. | 158,160 | (a-45) |
| West Virginia | (a-8) | 72,000 | 90,000 | 98,928 | 92,500 | 83,652 | 78,500 | 85,000 | 70,000 | 99,999 | 95,000 |
| Wisconsin | (a-8) | 110,000 | 124,000 | 98,021 | 120,500 | 122,000 | 106,885 | 105,678 | 108,000 | 125,000 | 100,000 |
| Wyoming | (a-8) | 97,738 | 115,712 | 86,112 | 116,457 | 117,144 | 106,787 | 112,124 | 111,266 | (a-29) | (a-45) |
| Guam | 88,915 | 55,303 | 1,200 | 88,915 | 88,915 | 74,096 | 88,915 | 74,096 | 88,591 | N.O. | 74,096 |
| No. Mariana Islands | 54,000 | 45,000 | 80,000 | 40,800 (b) | 45,000 | 40,800 (b) | 54,000 | 54,000 | 70,000 | 40,800 (b) | 52,000 |
| U.S. Virgin Islands | 76,500 | 53,350 | 54,500 | 76,500 | 76,500 | 76,500 | 76,500 | 76,500 | 76,500 | 65,000 | 76,500 |

(p) Responsibilities shared between Secretary of State, $87,982; Deputy Secretary of State for Elections, $97,474; and Chief Deputy Secretary of State, $106,150.

(q) The statutory salary for each of the four members of the Board of Elections is $25,000, including the two co-chairs, Douglas A. Kellner and James A. Walsh.

(r) The Rhode Island Economic Development Corporation is a quasi-public agency.

(s) Responsibilities shared between Secretary of State, $125,880; and Division Director, $112,151.

(t) Responsibilities for St. Thomas, $74,400; St. Croix, $76,500; St. John, $74,400.

(u) Responsibilities shared between Director of Health Care Services, $165,000, and Director of Department of Public Health, $222,000.

(v) Responsibilities shared between Chancellor of California Community Colleges, $198,504, and California Post Secondary Education Commission (Vacant).

(w) Responsibilities shared between Director of Wildlife, $123,973, Director of Inland Fisheries, $107,210, and Director of Marine Fisheries, $121,133.

(x) Responsibilities shared between Director of Budget and Finance, $108,972, and Comptroller, $108,972.

(y) Responsibilities shared between Adjutant General, $106,394, and deputy director, $72,000.

(z) Responsibilities shared between Director, Dept. of Natural Resources, $140,000, and Chief, Fish, $88,477 and Chief, Wildlife, $104,283.

(aa) Responsibilities shared between Administrator, Division of Fisheries, Department of Conservation, $92,688; Administrator, Division of Wildlife, same department, $87,408.

## SELECTED STATE ADMINISTRATIVE OFFICIALS: ANNUAL SALARIES — Continued

(bb) Responsibilities shared between Auditor of Public Accounts— $85,000; Director of Administration—$132,500 and State Tax Commissioner—$141,500.

(cc) Responsibilities shared between Game & Parks Director— $124,097 and Wildlife Division Administrator—N.A.

(dd) Responsibilities shared between Director, Health and Human Services, $115,847, and Division Administrator, $106,150.

(ee) The Chancellor elected to receive a lower wage than authorized.

(ff) Responsibilities shared between Acting Director, Division of Purchase and Property, Dept. of the Treasury, $130,000 (acting), and Director, Division of Property Management and Construction, Dept. of the Treasury, $120,000.

(gg) Responsibilities shared between Assistant Director of Budget and Management, (vacant) and Deputy Director, Accounting, Office of Budget and Management, $98,072.

(hh) Serves a dual role as Commissioner of Higher Education and as the President of the Community College of Rhode Island.

(ii) Responsibilities shared between Commissioner Catherine Templeton $151,942, and Director Alvin Taylor, $121,380.

(jj) Responsibilities shared between Community and Technical Policy Commission, $134,000, and Higher Education Policy Commission, $200,000.

(kk) Responsibilities shared between Director of Mental Health, vacant and Director of Developmental Services, $165,000.

(ll) Responsibilities shared between Commissioner, Mental Health: $144,999, and Commissioner, Retardation: $150,000.

(mm) Responsibilities shared between Director, Division of Substance Abuse and Mental Health, Department of Health and Social Services, $142,290, and Director, Division of Developmental Disabilities Service, same department, $113,791.

(nn) Responsibilities shared between Interim Director of Mental Health, $58,756, and Director of Community Support, $74,000.

(oo) Responsibilities shared between Executive Director of Mental Hygiene Administration, $211,632, and Director of Developmental Disabilities Administration, $120,870.

(pp) Responsibilities shared between Commissioners Marcia Fowler, $132,532, and Elin M. Howe, $139,050.

(qq) Responsibilities shared between Director, Health and Human Services, $115,847, and Division Administrator, $112,275.

(rr) Responsibilities shared between Acting Assistant Commissioner Valerie Larosiliere, Division of Mental Health Services, Dept. of Human Services, $121,432, and position vacant but overseen by Deputy Commissioner Dawn Apgar, Division of Developmental Disabilities, Dept. of Human Services, $133,000.

(ss) Responsibilities shared between Commissioner, State Education Department, $212,500; Secretary of State, Department of State, $120,800.

(tt) Responsibilities shared between Commissioner of Office of Mental

Retardation and Developmental Disabilities, $136,000, and Commissioner of Office of Mental Health, $136,000.

(uu) Numerous licensing boards, too many to list.

(vv) Responsibilities shared between Director of Dept. of Mental Retardation and Developmental Disabilities, $126,089, and Director, Dept. of Mental Health, $116,397.

(ww) Varies by department.

(xx) Responsibilities shared between Director for Disabilities and Special Needs, $130,063, and Director of Mental Health, 155,787.

(yy) Responsibilities shared between Office of Chief Information Officer (Policy) Bharat Shyam, $147,157, and Consolidated Technology Services (Computing), Mike Ricchio, $142,596.

(zz) Function split between two cabinet positions: Secretary, Dept. of Health and Social Services: $145,911 (if incumbent holds a medical license, amount is increased by $12,000; if board-certified physician, a supplement of $3,000 is added) and Secretary, Dept. of Svcs. for Children, Youth and their Families, $131,427.

(aaa) Responsibilities shared between five commissioners with salaries of $88,448 for each.

(bbb) Responsibilities shared between Director, Department of Cultural Affairs, $106,150, and Division Administrator, Library and Archives, $97,474.

(ccc) Acting salary.

(ddd) Responsibilities shared between Commissioner, Department of Human Services, $141,000, and Commissioner, Department of Children and Families, $141,000.

(eee) Responsibilities shared between Director, Dept. of Job and Family Services, $127,400; Superintendent of Dept. of Education, $185,016; Executive Director of Rehabilitation Services Commission, $108,992 and Director of Dept. of Aging, $119,808.

(fff) Responsibilities shared between three Commissioners, $116,713, $114,713 and $109,250 and General Administrator, $90,000.

(ggg) Responsibilities shared between Commissioner, Office of Health and Human Services, $141,828, and Director of the Dept. of Human Service, $129,627, and reports to the Commissioner, Office of Health and Human Services.

(hhh) Solid waste is managed by the Rhode Island Resource Recovery Corporation (RIRRC). Although not a department of the state government, RIRRC is a public corporation and a component of the State of Rhode Island for financial reporting purposes. To be financially self-sufficient, the agency earns revenue through the sale of recyclable products, methane gas royalties and fees for its services.

(iii) Functions shared between Communications, William Irby, $142,425; Energy Regulation, William F. Stephens, $146,750; Utility and Railroad Safety.

# The Office of Lieutenant Governor: A Bedrock Principle

### By Julia Hurst

*The office of lieutenant governor is the proven method of gubernatorial succession in the states and territories, having stood the test of time and experience for more than 200 years. The few states that ever abolished the office of lieutenant governor have reinstated it. History reveals five principles to well-written succession law utilizing the office of lieutenant governor. Moreover, states and territories continue to capitalize on the value of this office with lieutenant governors garnering power and responsibility from the constitution, statute or gubernatorial appointment, or through personal initiative. The trend line for the growth and value of the office is seen through new studies and increasing pay rates, growth in duties and political roles, and anecdotally through press.*

## Introduction

National and homeland security directives and federal emergency preparedness circulars say continuity of government planning, which includes gubernatorial succession planning, is an essential duty of states. For more than 200 years, the office of lieutenant governor occupied by a statewide elected official has been the proven method of gubernatorial succession. The experience of states shows five key elements of effective succession law: a sufficiently deep and clearly delineated line of succession; clarity on resources available to successors during a succession; a thorough definition of when and under what circumstances a governor becomes "incapacitated"; and congruity of law for succession regardless of whether the succession occurs from physical vacancy, resignation, recall or impeachment. Beyond the succession role, a lieutenant governor is the second highest-ranking official in state or territorial government deriving powers four ways. Through the duties given this official, most states demonstrably leverage the office of lieutenant governor to improve the effectiveness and efficiency of state governance for the benefit of the state and its constituents.

## Succession Lineage

Every state and territorial constitution names an official who is first in line for gubernatorial succession. Gubernatorial succession may be caused by death, resignation, incapacitation (short-term or permanent), recall or impeachment (permitted in every state but Oregon). The rate of gubernatorial succession in the states between 2000 and 2010 shows an increase since 1900. The official first in line of gubernatorial succession is a lieutenant governor in 43 states and another official in seven states. Arizona, Oregon and Wyoming designate the secretary of state first in line, while Maine, New Hampshire, Tennessee and West Virginia rely on the senate president. Of these seven, Arizona, Tennessee and West Virginia saw efforts in recent years to establish the office of lieutenant governor as a statewide elected official. In Tennessee and West Virginia, the senate president statutorily is given the title of lieutenant governor. No state has abolished the office in the modern era, and of the few states that once abolished the office, every state has reinstated it.

## Succession Law

The increasing trend of gubernatorial successions has shown five key elements of well-written succession law. Generally, every state should specify which officials constitute the line of gubernatorial succession, in what order they form the line, how deep the line is and under what circumstances a person succeeds. Gubernatorial succession begins when the office is vacated prior to completion of a person's official term. The office may be vacated as a result of death, resignation, incapacitation, impeachment or recall. A leader may be incapacitated due to location (i.e. the official is out of the state or out of the country or in a war zone), physical ailment, unconscious state (i.e. the official is anesthetized or in a coma) or the inability to effectively function (i.e. the official is under federal indictment). State law also should specify whether succession could occur for a temporary basis, such as a temporary incapacitation. Law should define how incapacitation is determined and should specify if a declaration of incapacitation can be temporary or permanent. Indiana specifies a procedure that includes a finding of incapacitation involving both legislative leaders and the state supreme court. Gubernatorial succession law should detail when and how a succession due to incapacitation is enacted.

Once a line of gubernatorial succession has activated, state law should clarify whether successors become "acting" officials (i.e., is the "acting governor") or whether the successor fully assumes the title and office. Lawmakers should carefully consider whether resulting vacancies should be filled (i.e., such as a vacancy in the office of lieutenant governor) and, if so, how. In states in which the senate president has succeeded to governor, there have been questions about separation of power as the individual retained his or her senate post and became "acting governor." Law should specify whether the succeeding official retains any part or power of their previous position. In any case of gubernatorial succession, the law also should be clear on the length of service of the successor. In most states, a successor completes the remaining term of office. Some states, however, require a special election within a specified time period or at the next regularly scheduled statewide election if more than half the term of service remains.

State leaders also may review state code to ensure that statutes surrounding impeachment and recall provisions are not in conflict with constitutional and statutory language on gubernatorial succession. For example, the 2003 gubernatorial recall election of then-California Gov. Gray Davis brought to light an inconsistency with otherwise established gubernatorial succession. In the event of recall in California, the state supreme court ruled a new election for governor should be held simultaneously to the recall, negating gubernatorial succession as defined by the constitution. Recall law also may be reviewed to determine whether a governor and lieutenant governor elected on a ticket are recalled as a ticket, as is questioned in the 2012 recall effort in Wisconsin.

## Lieutenant Governor's Office

The shared duty of every lieutenant governor is to provide clarity in leadership and continuity in governance should a vacancy in the governor's office occur. All offices of lieutenant governor are generally accepted to have the power of "the bully pulpit." Nearly all lieutenant governors now put forth legislative packages or testify on proposals and budget actions both at the state and federal levels. Beyond this, a lieutenant governor may gar-

ner duties and authorities from the constitution, from statute, through gubernatorial appointment, through personal initiative or through a combination of these. Lieutenant governors generally may exercise any power not barred by constitution or law. These parameters mean the office of lieutenant governor is arguably the most diverse position across state governments. The office of lieutenant governor may be shaped in a state or territory to meet the greatest needs of the particular state on an ongoing basis and at pivotal moments in times of crisis.

Nearly half the lieutenant governors act as governor in various circumstances (i.e., some act as governor when the governor is out of state). Lieutenant governors are the only state officials with specific powers in both the legislative and executive branches. Nearly half the lieutenant governors preside over the state senates where they can cast tiebreaking votes. Just past the midway point in the 2012 General Assembly session, Virginia Lt. Gov. Bill Bolling had cast 10 tiebreaking votes on issues ranging from voting to eminent domain to drug screening some welfare recipients. Some lieutenant governors are directors of agencies or departments of state government. This may occur through statutory designation or through gubernatorial appointment. By statute, the South Carolina lieutenant governor leads the Office on Aging. In Colorado, Lt. Gov. Joseph Garcia is director of the Colorado Department for Higher Education through gubernatorial appointment.

## Gubernatorial Role

Governors and legislators have a role and responsibility in the evolution of the office of lieutenant governor in a state or territory. A governor may name the lieutenant governor to lead a department, to serve on the cabinet, to have a role in budget making, to be a liaison to the legislature and more. These actions may be taken formally or informally. Governors have used executive orders to delegate duties. Virginia Lt. Gov. Bill Bolling was named chief job creation officer via an executive order that detailed his role to co-chair the Economic Development Commission and to serve as a cabinet member coordinating state economic development efforts. Lieutenant governors may be named to chair or serve on commissions by the governor or the legislature, a role quantifiably acknowledged since 2002 in David Winder's report, "The Lieutenant Governor's Level of Activity in State Policymaking: Chairing Commissions as Key Factor."

The method of election of a lieutenant governor may impact the disposition of duties to the office by the governor. Eighteen states elect the lieutenant governor separately from the governor, while the remaining states elect the officials on a team ticket, though the ticket may be "an arranged marriage." In "an arranged marriage," an electorate chooses the candidate for each office in a primary election, caucus or convention and the results pair the officials as a team ticket at the general election. Officials who choose to run together on a team ticket may have a relationship that results in the lieutenant governor garnering a specific set of duties directly through gubernatorial appointment. Conversely, a lieutenant governor elected separately from a governor, and who may even be of the opposite party, may find power in being independent of the governor on issue positions and public statements.

## Legislative Role

Legislators also have a role in developing the office of lieutenant governor to its greatest effectiveness for a state or territory. Like a governor, legislators may name a lieutenant governor to chair or serve on a temporary or permanent commission. A legislature also may designate a lieutenant governor to lead an agency or department. The legislature, or voters themselves in some states, may place a referendum on the office's duties on a ballot. For example, a referendum passed in 1992 in Missouri established the "Office of Advocacy and Assistance for the Elderly" within the lieutenant governor's office.

## Diverse Office

The diverse means by which a lieutenant governor may obtain responsibilities leads to a diverse office across the states. It also means the office of lieutenant governor in a given state may have a portfolio of work that ranges from statutory roles to gubernatorially appointed tasks to items of personal initiative. The Indiana lieutenant governor, for example, presides over the state senate and can cast a tiebreaking vote. She manages five state agencies administering nearly $1 billion in programs and has more than 40 statutory duties covering 50 different sectors of government. These duties include leading the Indiana State Department of Agriculture, the Office of Energy Development, the Indiana Housing and Community Development Authority, the Office of Community and Rural Affairs, and the Office of Tourism Development, while chairing the state's Counter-Terrorism and Security Council.

The growth and effective use of the office is, in part, confirmed by the fact that the office of lieutenant governor was the only statewide elected office to see an increase in real income in the 30-year period ending in 2005, according to *State Legislator Compensation: A Trend Analysis*, published by The Council of State Governments in 2006. As an anecdotal measure, *USA Today* wrote in August 2005 that the office of lieutenant governor is a significant, visible and often controversial office. In a 2010 report, University of Virginia's Larry Sabato noted "It's twice as good to be lieutenant governor," pointing out lieutenant governors have a success rate twice as high as attorneys general at becoming governor.

## Political Players

In 2009, Sabato called the growing gubernatorial succession rate "Lieutenant Governor Mania." Data show approximately one in every four governors in the nation for the past 100 years first served as lieutenant governor. No office in the past 25 years had a better success rate of an officeholder becoming governor. When gubernatorial inaugurations were completed in January 2012, 14 of the sitting governors had first served as lieutenant governor, one more than the previous year. In this 2012 presidential election year, lieutenant governors are making presidential endorsements, serving as state chairs for presidential contenders, and several will have roles in party conventions. Lieutenant governors must always be ready for succession, should it occur, and their daily duties cover a range of state responsibilities and political roles that are a benefit to the states and their constituents.

## About the Author

**Julia Hurst** has 20 years of state government experience, having served as executive director of the National Lieutenant Governors Association since 2002. She formerly served as chief operating officer of The Council of State Governments, as chief of staff to a legislative caucus and spent time as a multi-state lobbyist in the fields of health care and telecommunications. For more, *visit www.nlga.us.*

## Table 4.12
## THE LIEUTENANT GOVERNORS, 2012

| State or other jurisdiction | Name and party | Method of selection | Length of regular term in years | Date of first service | Present term ends | Number of previous terms | Joint election of governor and lieutenant governor (a) |
|---|---|---|---|---|---|---|---|
| Alabama | Kay Ivey (R) | CE | 4 | 1/2011 | 1/2015 | ... | No |
| Alaska | Mead Treadwell (R) | CE | 4 | 12/2010 | 12/2014 | ... | Yes |
| Arizona | ...............................(b)................................ | | | | | | |
| Arkansas | Mark Darr (R) | CE | 4 | 1/2011 | 12/2015 | ... | No |
| California | Gavin Newson (D) | CE | 4 | 1/2011 | 1/2015 | ... | No |
| Colorado | Joseph Garcia (D) | CE | 4 | 1/2011 | 1/2015 | ... | Yes |
| Connecticut | Nancy Wyman (D) | CE | 4 | 1/2011 | 1/2015 | ... | Yes |
| Delaware | Matthew Denn (D) | CE | 4 | 1/2009 | 1/2013 | ... | No |
| Florida | Jennifer Carroll (R) | CE | 4 | 1/2011 | 1/2015 | ... | Yes |
| Georgia | Casey Cagle (R) | CE | 4 | 1/2007 | 1/2015 | 1 | No |
| Hawaii | Brian Schatz (D) | CE | 4 | 12/2010 | 12/2014 | ... | Yes |
| Idaho | Brad Little (R) | CE | 4 | 1/2009 (c) | 1/2015 | (c) | No |
| Illinois | Sheila Simon (D) | CE | 4 | 1/2011 | 1/2015 | ... | Yes |
| Indiana | Becky Skillman (R) | CE | 4 | 1/2005 | 1/2013 | 1 | Yes |
| Iowa | Kim Reynolds (R) | CE | 4 | 1/2011 | 1/2015 | ... | Yes |
| Kansas | Jeff Colyer (R) | CE | 4 | 1/2011 | 1/2015 | ... | Yes |
| Kentucky | Jerry Abramson (D) | CE | 4 | 12/2011 | 12/2015 | ... | Yes |
| Louisiana | Jay Dardenne (R) | CE | 4 | 11/2010 (d) | 1/2016 | 1 | No |
| Maine | ...............................(b)................................ | | | | | | |
| Maryland | Anthony Brown (D) | CE | 4 | 1/2007 | 1/2015 | 1 | Yes |
| Massachusetts | Tim Murray (D) | CE | 4 | 1/2007 | 1/2015 | 1 | Yes |
| Michigan | Brian Calley (R) | CE | 4 | 1/2011 | 1/2015 | ... | Yes |
| Minnesota | Yvonne Prettner Solon (D) | CE | 4 | 1/2011 | 1/2015 | ... | Yes |
| Mississippi | Tate Reeves (R) | CE | 4 | 1/2012 | 1/2016 | ... | Yes |
| Missouri | Peter Kinder (R) | CE | 4 | 1/2005 | 1/2013 | 1 | No |
| Montana | John Bohlinger (R) | CE | 4 | 1/2005 | 1/2013 | 1 | Yes (e) |
| Nebraska | Rick Sheehy (R) | CE | 4 | 1/2005 (f) | 1/2015 | (f) | Yes |
| Nevada | Brian Krolicki (R) | CE | 4 | 1/2007 | 1/2015 | 1 | No |
| New Hampshire | ...............................(b)................................ | | | | | | |
| New Jersey | Kim Guadagno (R) | CE | 4 | 1/2010 | 1/2014 | ... | Yes |
| New Mexico | John Sanchez (R) | CE | 4 | 1/2011 | 1/2015 | ... | Yes |
| New York | Robert Duffy (D) | CE | 4 | 1/2011 | 1/2015 | ... | Yes |
| North Carolina | Walter Dalton (D) | CE | 4 | 1/2009 | 1/2013 | ... | No |
| North Dakota | Drew Wrigley (R) | CE | 4 | 12/2010 (g) | 12/2014 | ... | Yes |
| Ohio | Mary Taylor (R) | SE | 4 | 1/2011 | 1/2015 | ... | Yes |
| Oklahoma | Todd Lamb (R) | CE | 4 | 1/2011 | 1/2015 | ... | No |
| Oregon | ...............................(b)................................ | | | | | | |
| Pennsylvania | Jim Cawley (R) | CE | 4 | 1/2011 | 1/2015 | ... | Yes |
| Rhode Island | Elizabeth H. Roberts (D) | SE | 4 | 1/2007 | 1/2015 | 1 | No |
| South Carolina | Glen McConnell (R) (o) | CE | 4 | 3/2012 (o) | 1/2015 | ... | No |
| South Dakota | Matt Michels (R) | CE | 4 | 1/2011 | 1/2015 | ... | Yes |
| Tennessee | Ron Ramsey (R) | (h) | 2 | 1/2007 | 1/2013 | 2 (h) | No |
| Texas | David Dewhurst (R) | CE | 4 | 1/2003 | 1/2015 | 2 | No |
| Utah | Greg Bell (R) | CE | 4 | 8/2009 | 1/2013 (i) | ... | Yes |
| Vermont | Phil Scott (R) | CE | 2 | 1/2011 | 1/2015 | ... | No |
| Virginia | William T. Bolling (R) | CE | 4 | 1/2006 | 1/2014 | 1 | No |
| Washington | Brad Owen (D) | CE | 4 | 1/1997 | 1/2013 | 3 | No |
| West Virginia | Jeffrey Kessler (j) | (k) | 2 | ... | ... | ... | No |
| Wisconsin | Rebecca Kleefisch (R) | CE | 4 | 1/2011 | 1/2015 | ... | Yes |
| Wyoming | ...............................(b)................................ | | | | | | |
| American Samoa | Ipulasi Aitofele Sunia (D) | CE | 4 | 4/2003 (l) | 1/2013 | 2(l) | Yes |
| Guam | Ray Tenorio (R) | CE | 4 | 1/2011 | 1/2015 | ... | Yes |
| No. Mariana Islands | Eloy Inos (D) (m)(n) | CE | 4 | 4/2009 (n) | 1/2015 (n) | (n) | Yes |
| Puerto Rico | ...............................(b)................................ | | | | | | |
| U.S. Virgin Islands | Gregory Francis (D) | SE | 4 | 1/2007 | 1/2015 | 1 | Yes |

See footnotes at end of table.

# THE LIEUTENANT GOVERNORS, 2012 — Continued

*Source:* The Council of State Governments, March 2012.

*Key:*

CE — Constitutional, elected by public.

SE — Statutory, elected by public.

... — Not applicable.

(a) The following also choose candidates for governor and lieutenant governor through a joint nomination process: Florida, Kansas, Maryland, Minnesota, Montana, North Dakota, Ohio, Utah, American Samoa, Guam, No. Mariana Islands, and U.S. Virgin Islands. For additional information see The National Lieutenant Governors Association website at *http://www.nlga.us*.

(b) No lieutenant governor.

(c) Brad Little was appointed by Governor Otter and confirmed by the state senate after Lieutenant Governor Ritsch won the U.S. Senate seat.

(d) Lieutenant Governor Dardenne won a special election in Nov. 2010 to replace Lieutenant Governor Mitch Landrieu after he left to become New Orleans mayor.

(e) Lieutenant Governor Bohlinger, a Republican, ran on a bipartisan ticket with Governor Brian Schweitzer, a Democrat, in 2004 and again in 2008.

(f) Lt. Governor Sheehy was appointed to the position of Lieutenant Governor January 24, 2005, by Governor Heineman.

(g) Lieutenant Governor Drew Wrigley was appointed by Gov. Jack Dalrymple, who moved from the office of lieutenant governor to governor when Gov. John Hoeven resigned to become a U.S. senator.

(h) In Tennessee, the President of the Senate and the Lieutenant Governor are one in the same. The legislature provided in statute the title of Lieutenant Governor upon the Senate President. The Senate President serves two-year terms, elected by the Senate on the first day of the first session of each two-year legislative term.

(i) Lieutenant Governor Gary Herbert was sworn in as governor on August 10, 2009 after Governor Huntsman resigned to accept President Obama's appointment as Ambassador to China. Utah law states that a replacement governor elevated in a term's first year will face a special election at the next regularly scheduled general election, November 2010, instead of serving the remainder of the term. Lt. Gov. Bell was named by Gov. Herbert in 2009 and together they won the 2010 special election to fill the regular term until 1/2013.

(j) Sen. Jeffrey Kessler was elected as Senate President on Nov. 14, 2011 to succeed Earl Ray Tomblin.

(k) In West Virginia, the President of the Senate and the Lieutenant Governor are one in the same. The legislature provided in statute the title of Lieutenant Governor upon the Senate President. The Senate President serves two-year terms, elected by the Senate on the first day of the first session of each two-year legislative term.

(l) Lt. Governor Sunia was appointed to the position of Lieutenant Governor in April 2003 by Governor Togiola Tulafono.

(m) Covenant Party.

(n) Lieutenant Governor Inos replaced Lieutenant Governor Villagomez after his resignation in 2009. Subsequently Governor Fitial and Lieutenant Governor Inos were elected to another term in the 2009 run-off election for the November 2009 general election. The current administration will serve a five-year term to change future CNMI elections to even-numbered years. The next election will occur in November 2014.

(o) As Senate President Pro Tem McConnell became Lieutenant Governor upon the resignation of Ken Ard in March 2011 following his indictment on ethics charges.

## Table 4.13
## LIEUTENANT GOVERNORS: QUALIFICATIONS AND TERMS

| State or other jurisdiction | Minimum age | State citizen (years) | U.S. citizen (years) (a) | State resident (years) (b) | Qualified voter (years) | Length of term (years) | Maximum consecutive terms allowed |
|---|---|---|---|---|---|---|---|
| Alabama | 30 | 7 | 10 | 7 | ... | 4 | 2 |
| Alaska | 30 | ★ | 7 | 7 | ★ | 4 | 2 |
| Arizona | ................(c)................ | | | | | | |
| Arkansas | 30 | 7 | ★ | 7 | ... | 4 | 2 |
| California | 18 | ★ | ★ | 5 | ★ | 4 | 2 |
| Colorado | 30 | ... | ★ | 2 | ... | 4 | 2 |
| Connecticut | 30 | ★ | ★ | ★ | ★ | 4 | ... |
| Delaware | 30 | ★ | 12 | 6 | ★ | 4 | 2 |
| Florida | 30 | ★ | ★ | 7 | ★ | 4 | 2 |
| Georgia | 30 | ★ | 15 | 6 | ★ | 4 | ... |
| Hawaii | 30 | 5 | ★ | 5 | ★ | 4 | 2 |
| Idaho | 30 | ... | ★ | 2 | ... | 4 | ... |
| Illinois | 25 | ... | ★ | 3 | ... | 4 | ... |
| Indiana | 30 | ★ | ★ | ★ | ★ | 4 | 2 |
| Iowa | 30 | ... | 2 | 2 | ... | 4 | ... |
| Kansas | ... | ... | ... | ... | ... | 4 | 2 |
| Kentucky | 30 | 6 | ★ | ★ | ★ | 4 | 2 |
| Louisiana | 25 | 5 | 5 | 5 | ... | 4 | ... |
| Maine | ................(c)................ | | | | | | |
| Maryland | 30 | ★ | ★ | ★ | ★ | 4 | 2 |
| Massachusetts | ... | ★ | ★ | ★ | ★ | 4 | ... |
| Michigan | 30 | ★ | ★ | 4 | 4 | 4 | 2 (d) |
| Minnesota | 25 | ... | ★ | 1 | ... | 4 | ... |
| Mississippi | 30 | ... | 20 | 5 | ★ | 4 | 2 |
| Missouri | 30 | 10 | 15 | 10 | ... | 4 | ... |
| Montana | 25 | 2 | ★ | 2 | ... | 4 | 2 (e) |
| Nebraska | 30 | 5 | ★ | 5 | ★ | 4 | 2 |
| Nevada | 25 | 2 | ★ | 2 | ★ | 4 | 2 |
| New Hampshire | ................(c)................ | | | | | | |
| New Jersey | 30 | ... | 20 | 7 | ... | 4 | 2 |
| New Mexico | 30 | ★ | ★ | 5 | ★ | 4 | 2 |
| New York | 30 | ★ | ★ | 5 | ★ | 4 | ... |
| North Carolina | 30 | ... | 5 | 2 | ... | 4 | 2 |
| North Dakota | 30 | 5 | ... | ... | ... | 4 | ... |
| Ohio | 18 | ... | ★ | ★ | ★ | 4 | 2 |
| Oklahoma | 31 | 10 | ★ | ★ | ★ | 4 | ... |
| Oregon | ................(c)................ | | | | | | |
| Pennsylvania | 30 | ★ | ★ | 7 | ★ | 4 | 2 |
| Rhode Island | 18 | ★ | ★ | ★ | ★ | 4 | 2 |
| South Carolina | 30 | 5 | 5 | 5 | ★ | 4 | 2 |
| South Dakota | 21 | 2 | ★ | 2 | ★ | 4 | 2 |
| Tennessee (f) | 30 | ★ | ★ | 3 | 1 | 2 | ... |
| Texas | 30 | ... | ★ | 5 | ... | 4 | ... |
| Utah | 30 | ★ | ★ | ★ | ★ | 4 | ... |
| Vermont | 18 | 4 | ★ | 4 | ★ | 2 | ... |
| Virginia | 30 | ... | ★ | 5 | 5 | 4 | ... |
| Washington | 18 | ★ | ★ | ★ | ★ | 4 | ... |
| West Virginia (g) | 25 | 1 | 1 | 1 | ★ | 2 | ... |
| Wisconsin | 18 | ★ | ★ | ★ | ★ | 4 | ... |
| Wyoming | ................(c)................ | | | | | | |
| American Samoa | 35 | (h) | ★ | 5 | ★ | 4 | 2 |
| Guam | 30 | ... | 5 | 5 | ★ | 4 | 2 |
| No. Mariana Islands | 35 | ★ | ★ | ★ | ★ | 4 | 2 |
| Puerto Rico | ................(c)................ | | | | | | |
| U.S. Virgin Islands | 30 | ... | 5 | 5 | 5 | 4 | 2 |

*Source*: The Council of State Governments' survey, January 2011.
*Note*: This table includes constitutional and statutory qualifications.
*Key*:
★ — Formal provision; number of years not specified.
... — No formal provision.
(a) In some states you must be a U.S. citizen to be an elector, and must be an elector to run.
(b) In some states you must be a state resident to be an elector, and must be an elector to run.
(c) No lieutenant governor.

(d) In 1993 a constitutional limit of two lifetime terms in the office was enacted.
(e) Eligible for eight out of 16 years.
(f) In Tennessee, the speaker of the Senate, elected from Senate membership, has statutory title of "lieutenant governor."
(g) In West Virginia, the President of the Senate and the Lieutenant Governor are one in the same. The legislature provided in statute the title of Lieutenant Governor upon the Senate President. The Senate President serves 2 year terms, elected by the Senate on the first day of the first session of each two year legislative term.
(h) Must be a U.S. national.

**Table 4.14**
# LIEUTENANT GOVERNORS: POWERS AND DUTIES

| State or other jurisdiction | Presides over Senate | Appoints committees | Breaks roll-call ties | Assigns bills | Authority for governor to assign duties | Member of governor's cabinet or advisory body | Serves as acting governor when governor out of state | Other duties (a) |
|---|---|---|---|---|---|---|---|---|
| Alabama | ★ | ★ | ★ | ★ | ... | ... | ★(b) | ... |
| Alaska | ... | ... | ... | ... | ★ | ★ | ... | (c) |
| Arizona | ............... (d) ............... | | | | | | | |
| Arkansas | ★ | ... | ★ | ... | ... | ... | ★ | ... |
| California | ★ | ... | ★ | ... | ★ | ★ | ★ | (c) |
| Colorado | ... | ... | ... | ... | ★ | ★ | ★ | (c) |
| Connecticut | ★ | ... | ★ | ... | ★ | ★ | ★ | ... |
| Delaware | ★ | ... | ★ | ... | ... | ... | ★ | (c) |
| Florida | ... | ... | ... | ... | ★ | ... | ★ | ... |
| Georgia | ★ | ★ | ... | ★ | ... | ... | ... | (c) |
| Hawaii | ... | ... | ... | ... | ★ | ... | ★ | (c) |
| Idaho | ★ | ... | ★ | ... | ★ | ... | ★ | ... |
| Illinois | ... | ... | ... | ... | ★ | ★ | ... | ... |
| Indiana | ★ | ... | ★ | ... | ... | ... | ★ | ... |
| Iowa | ... | (e) | ... | ... | ★ | (f) | (g) | ... |
| Kansas | ... | ... | ... | ... | ... | ★ | ... | ... |
| Kentucky | ... | ... | ... | ... | ★ | ... | (h) | (c) |
| Louisiana | ... | ... | ... | ... | ★ | ★ | ★ | ... |
| Maine | ............... (i) ............... | | | | | | | |
| Maryland | ... | ... | ... | ... | ★ | ★ | ★ | ... |
| Massachusetts | ... | ★ | ... | ... | ★ | ★ | ★ | (c) |
| Michigan | ★ | ... | ★ | ... | ★ | ★ | ★(j) | (c) |
| Minnesota | ... | ... | ... | ... | ★ | ... | ★ | (c) |
| Mississippi | ★ | ★ | ★ | ★ | ... | ... | ★ | (c) |
| Missouri | ★ | ... | ★ | ... | ★ | ... | ★ | (c) |
| Montana | ... | ... | ... | ... | ★ | ★ | ★ | ... |
| Nebraska | ★(k) | ... | ... | ... | ... | ... | ★ | ... |
| Nevada | ★ | ... | ★(l) | ... | ... | ... | ★ | ... |
| New Hampshire | ............... (i) ............... | | | | | | | |
| New Jersey | ... | ... | ... | ... | ★ | ★ | ★ | (c) |
| New Mexico | ★ | ... | ★ | ... | ... | ★ | ★ | ... |
| New York | ★ | ... | ★(m) | ... | ★ | ★ | ★ | ... |
| North Carolina | ★ | ... | ★ | ... | ★ | ★ | ★ | ... |
| North Dakota | ★ | ... | ... | ... | ... | ★ | ★ | ... |
| Ohio | ... | ... | ... | ... | ★ | ★ | ... | ... |
| Oklahoma | ★(n) | ... | ★ | ... | ... | ... | ★ | (c) |
| Oregon | ............... (d) ............... | | | | | | | |
| Pennsylvania | ★ | ... | ★ | ... | ... | ... | ... | ... |
| Rhode Island | ... | ... | ... | ... | ... | ... | ... | (c) |
| South Carolina | ★ | ★ | ★ | ★ | ... | ★ | ★ | (c) |
| South Dakota | ★ | ... | ★ | ... | ★ | ... | ... | (c) |
| Tennessee | ★ | ★ | ★ | ★ | ... | ... | ... | ... |
| Texas | ★ | ★ | ★ | ★ | ... | ... | ★ | (c) |
| Utah | ... | ... | ... | ... | ... | ★ | ... | ... |
| Vermont | ★ | ★(o) | ★ | ★(o) | ... | ★ | ★ | ... |
| Virginia | ★ | ... | ★ | ... | ... | ... | ... | ... |
| Washington | ★ | ★ | ★ | ... | ... | ... | ★ | ... |
| West Virginia | ★ | ★ | ... | ★ | ... | ... | ... | (c) |
| Wisconsin | ... | ... | ... | ... | ★ | ... | ... | ... |
| Wyoming | ............... (d) ............... | | | | | | | |
| American Samoa | ... | ... | ... | ... | ... | ... | ★ | ... |
| Guam | (u)(k) | ... | ... | ... | ★ | ★ | ★ | ... |
| No. Mariana Islands | ... | ... | ... | ... | ... | ★ | ★ | (c) |
| Puerto Rico | ............... (d) ............... | | | | | | | |
| U.S. Virgin Islands | ... | ... | ... | ... | ★(f) | ★ | ★ | ... |

See footnotes at end of table.

# LIEUTENANT GOVERNORS: POWERS AND DUTIES — Continued

*Sources*: The Council of State Governments, January 2011 and state constitutions and statutes. For additional information on the powers and duties visit the National Lieutenant Governors Association website at *http://www.nlga.us*.

Key:

★ — Provision for responsibility.

... — No provision for responsibility.

(a) Lieutenant governors may obtain duties through gubernatorial appointment, statute, the Constitution, direct democracy action, or personal initiative. Hence, an exhaustive list of duties is not maintained, but this chart provides examples which are not all inclusive.

(b) The lieutenant governor performs the duties of the governor in the event of the governor's death, impeachment, disability, or absence from the state for more than 20 days

(c) Alaska — The lieutenant governor bears these additional responsibilities: Alaska Historical Commission Chair; Alaska Workforce Investment Board; supervise the Division of Elections: supervise the certification process for citizen ballot initiative and referenda; provide constituent care and communications; lend support to governor's legislative and administrative initiatives; review, sign and file regulations; publish the Alaska Administrative Code and the Online Public Notice System; commission notaries public; regulate use of State Seal, co-chair Alaska Criminal Justice Working Group; member of Clemency Advisory Cmte.; represent Alaska on the Aerospace States Association (ASA), the National Association of Secretaries of State and the National Lieutenant Governors' Association. Arctic Winter Games; Experimental Program to Stimulate Competitive Research (EPSCoR), Chair; Project GRAD. California — Lieutenant governor also sits on the UC Board of Regents and the CSU Board of Trustees, serves as the chair of the Commission for Economic Development, chair of the State Lands Commission, member of the Ocean Protection Council, and as a member of the California Emergency Council. Colorado — Additional responsibilities include: Chair of the Colorado Commission of Indian Affairs (by statute); member of the Homeland Security and All-Hazards Senior Advisory Committee (Cabinet duty). Delaware — Serves as President of the Board of Pardons. Georgia — The Lieutenant Governor, by statute, is responsible for board, commission and committee appointments. In addition the Lieutenant Governor appoints conference committees, rules on germaneness, and must sign all acts of the General Assembly. Hawaii — Also serves as Secretary of State. Kentucky — In addition to the duties set forth by the Kentucky Constitution, state law also gives the lieutenant governor the responsibility to act as chair, or serve as a member, on various boards and commissions. Some of these include: the State Property and Buildings Commission, Kentucky Turnpike Authority, Kentucky Council on Agriculture, Board of the Kentucky Housing Corporation and the Appalachian Development Council. The governor also has the power to give the Lieutenant governor other specific job duties. Massachusetts — The lieutenant governor is a member of, and presides over, the Governor's Council, an elected body of 8 members which approves all judicial nominations. Michigan — The lieutenant governor serves as a member of the State Administrative Board; and represents the governor and the state at selected local, state, and national meetings. In addition the governor may delegate additional responsibilities. Minnesota — Serves as the Chair of the Capitol Area Architectural and Planning Board Committee. Mississippi — The lieutenant governor also appoints chairs of standing committees, appoints conferees to committees and is a member of the Legislative Budget Committee, chair of this committee every other year. Missouri — Other duties of the lieutenant governor include: Official Senior Advocate for State of Missouri and Advisor to Department of Elementary and Secondary Education on early childhood education and Parents-as-Teachers program. The lieutenant governor also serves on the following boards and commissions: Board of Fund Commissioners; Board of Public Buildings; Governor's Advisory Council for Veteran's (chair); Missouri Community Service Commission; Missouri Development Finance Board; Missouri Housing Development Commission; Missouri Rural Economic Development Council; Missouri Rural Economic Development Council; Missouri Senior Rx Program (chair); Missouri Tourism Commission (vice-chair); Personal Independence Commission (co-chair); Second State Capitol Commission; Statewide Safety Steering Committee; Veteran's Benefits Awareness Task Force (chair); Special Health, Psychological, and Social Needs of Minority Older Individuals Commission; Mental Health Task Force (chair); Missouri Energy Task Force. New Jersey — Governor Christie appointed Lieutenant Governor Guadagno to also serve as the secretary of state. Oklahoma — Lieutenant governor also serves on 10 boards and commissions including Tourism and School Land Commission. Rhode Island — Serves as Chair of a number of Advisory Councils including issues related to Emergency Management, Long Term Care and Small Business. Each year submits a legislative package to the General Assembly. South Carolina — The lieutenant governor heads the State Office on Aging; appoints members and chairs the South Carolina Affordable Housing Commission. South Dakota — The lieutenant governor also serves as the Chair of the Workers Compensation Advisory Commission and as a member of the Constitutional Revision Commission. Utah — The lieutenant governor serves as Secretary of State (Constitution); Chair of the Lieutenant Governor's Commission on Volunteers (statutory); Chair of the Lieutenant Governor's Commission on Civic and Character Education (statutory); Chair of the Utah Capitol Preservation Board (statutory); Chair (Governor's Cabinet). Direct cabinet oversight of following departments: 1. Utah Department of Public Safety and Homeland Security, 2. Utah Department of Transportation, 3. Utah Division of Water Rights, 4. Utah Division of Rural Affairs. West Virginia — The President of the Senate and the Lieutenant Governor are one in the same. The legislature provided in statute the title of Lieutenant Governor upon the Senate President. The Senate President serves 2 year terms, elected by the Senate on the first day of the first session of each two year legislative term. Northern Mariana Islands — The Lieutenant Governor is charged with overseeing administrative functions.

(d) No lieutenant governor; secretary of state is next in line of succession to governorship.

(e) Appoints all standing committees. Iowa — appoints some special committees.

(f) Presides over cabinet meetings in absence of governor.

(g) Only in emergency situations.

(h) The Kentucky Constitution specifically gives the lieutenant governor the power to act as governor, in the event the governor is unable to fulfill the duties of office.

(i) No lieutenant governor; senate president or speaker is next in line of succession to governorship.

(j) As defined in the state constitution, the lieutenant governor performs gubernatorial functions in the governor's absence. In the event of a vacancy in the office of governor, the lieutenant governor is first in line to succeed to the position.

(k) Unicameral legislative body. In Guam, that body elects own presiding officer.

(l) Except on final passage of bills and joint resolutions.

(m) With respect to procedural matters, not legislation.

(n) May preside over the Senate when desired.

(o) Appoints committees with the Pres. Pro Tem and one Senator on Committee on Committees. Committee on Committees assigns bills.

# Secretaries of State Open for Business: New Initiatives to Reduce Red Tape, Create State Business Culture for Success

### By Kay Stimson

*Can cutting red tape in state government really make a difference when it comes to job creation and business support? At a time when many states are seeking ways to encourage economic growth and stability, secretaries of state are making efforts to ensure that state filing and licensing offices are business-friendly and streamlined for success through business one-stops, fee reductions and other incentives.*

Iowa Secretary of State Matt Schultz wants to send a bold message to would-be entrepreneurs in his state: His office is open for business. As part of his efforts to create a more user-friendly business registration process, he proposed new legislation that would create an Iowa Start a Business Month. If the promotion gets the green light, his office would be able to waive or reduce the fees required to form a new business in the state. Schultz is convinced these incentives, coupled with efforts to streamline business registration and regulatory processes, will help boost commerce and cement the state's reputation as an incubator for successful companies.

"Iowa has very competitive fees already, but the idea is to let people know that we are serious about limiting the costs of starting a business and getting sole proprietors to take advantage of incorporating to protect their assets and reduce their liabilities," said Schultz. He also plans to use his office to gather information on the types of businesses that exist in Iowa so leaders can more accurately track the business sectors that are growing in the Cyclone State.

Meanwhile, Colorado Secretary of State Scott Gessler has taken the initiative to help attract out-of-state-companies looking to do business in his state. In August 2011, his office made it easier for out-of-state-companies to do business in Colorado by taking the filing process online. His office announced a corresponding "fee holiday" for these filings, allowing them to pay just $1 instead of the usual $125 fee for three months. The result? A slew of positive national publicity and a lot of interest from new business.

At a time when surveys by the U.S. Chamber of Commerce and other business trade associations show that small business owners are increasingly frustrated with government bureaucracy and over-regulation, secretaries of state are streamlining how businesses interact with state governments. Secretaries of state typically oversee business filing, reporting and licensing functions in states. It is an important time for states to be undergoing this transformation, they point out, because the economic downturn has made the creation and protection of jobs a priority at every level of government in almost every state. From reduced filing fees to new websites that connect businesses to multiple state agencies and eliminate bureaucratic confusion, the ultimate goal is to reduce the time and expense of dealing with state government agencies while creating a culture that is friendly to business creation and expansion.

"This is really an area where secretaries of state can reach out to state legislators and the business community to let them know how state business services offices are relevant to discussions on job growth, entrepreneurship and economic development," Iowa's Schultz said.

## Developing Incentives and Resources for Business

In Oregon, which is well-known for protecting the natural environment, Secretary of State Kate Brown is promoting her idea for maintaining the business environment. Brown has been leading the effort to develop Oregon's Central Business Registry into a one-stop, online resource for businesses. The idea is simple: Enable businesses to obtain or renew most, if not all, licenses, fees and permits required by state government from a single location. It also would include centralized payment processing and inquiries. In a state where the most recent unemployment rate of 8.9 percent is slightly higher than the national average, Brown's ultimate goal is to create jobs and put Oregonians back to work.

"By streamlining bureaucracy for businesses, we can actually contribute to the growth of Oregon's economy," said Brown, who hopes to use auditing tools to develop best practices on regulatory streamlining. "The easier and more convenient it is to navigate state government, the more we can encourage citizens to build their business here."

Brown is not alone in her efforts. Florida leaders hope to launch the state's business one-stop Web portal in 2012, making it one of more than a dozen states to offer such a site; others are Delaware, Kentucky, Michigan, Montana, Nebraska, North Carolina, Ohio, Oklahoma, South Carolina, Tennessee, Utah, Virginia and West Virginia. State agencies typically share the information obtained through these portals so business owners do not have to go from agency to agency. Secretaries of state say the enhanced features of one-stops are particularly helpful for small businesses, which can comprise up to 80 or 90 percent of all businesses in a state and are the source of many new jobs. They also point out that business one-stops can pay dividends for state governments.

"Our business one-stop has made it easier for businesses to navigate through the state agencies' requirements in a single location for establishing and running a business, resulting in increased compliance and fewer rejections of filings," said South Carolina Secretary of State Mark Hammond. "Now with data uniformity, we can better evaluate potential new system improvements that will benefit the business community and other taxpayers."

Similar to a business one-stop, Rhode Island Secretary of State A. Ralph Mollis has introduced an online, master business application for start-ups, which he dubbed Quick Start. Entrepreneurs looking to start businesses ranging from car dealerships to restaurants can find and complete in a single location every one of the more than 300 forms that state agencies can require. Quick Start has quickly become one of the most visited pages on the secretary of state's website. Mollis' office even worked with agencies to eliminate or consolidate their forms.

"Quick Start cuts red tape and paperwork," Mollis said. "Our goal is to make it easier to do business in Rhode Island."

West Virginia Secretary of State Natalie Tennant said minimizing regulatory hoops and making the business filing process faster and more convenient really can make an impact in today's conditions. Her office has seen the number of annual reports filed online nearly double as her office has made the process more efficient and added new resources to attract traffic. The improvements have reduced the time state employees spend dealing with noncompliant businesses that may or may not be paying attention to state deadlines and other requirements.

In fact, one of the most popular offerings on her website is a live, interactive chat helpline that allows business owners throughout West Virginia to communicate one-on-one with a business and licensing specialist. The service has enabled hundreds of new and seasoned business owners to log onto the Internet and get quick answers to their questions about filing with the state, along with additional tips and deadline reminders. The secretary of state's office also offers a four-minute tutorial video that takes business owners through the online filing process step-by-step.

"We want business owners to spend as little of their valuable time on paperwork as possible," said Tennant, "so they can get back to running their business and keeping our state's economy strong."

As part of their business outreach and incentive efforts, some secretaries of state are also making a concerted effort to tout the success of small businesses in their state. Ohio Secretary of State Jon Husted's office launched the Ohio Business Profile using a variety of social media platforms to raise awareness about Ohio companies that are creating interesting products, offering outstanding service, contributing to their local communities and employing Ohioans in the process. Tennessee Secretary of State Tre Hargett is using his office's website for similar purposes; he's launched a new program called Tennessee Business Spotlight.

## Working with State Legislators

Nearly all secretaries of state who oversee state business divisions say streamlining bureaucracy to assist business can be significantly aided by partnerships between the secretary of state's office and state legislators. In California, the state assembly allocated approximately $1.2 million in budgetary savings to the secretary of state's office to ensure speedier processing of business filings. A 2011 law in Kentucky requires a periodic assessment of the state's new business one-stop website to be delivered to the general assembly, the secretary of state and the governor. Most recently, Georgia Secretary of State Brian Kemp has approached legislators with a proposal to streamline how his state regulates various professions. Kemp's plan would decrease the amount of time currently required to issue new licenses and review deficient applications, so qualified Georgians can get to work and start new businesses sooner.

"Legislators can serve as a powerful conduit for communication between state agencies and the business communities they serve," said Oregon's Brown, who served in both the Oregon House of Representatives and Senate before becoming secretary of state. "If we can work together to develop legislation that helps business, solves agency issues or simply provides resources for state business registration and filing efficiency measures, we can make a big impact on the health of our state economy."

For his part, Iowa's Schultz hopes the legislature will work with him to establish Iowa Start a Business Month. If that venture is successful, he plans to look at other ways to increase the number of businesses registered in the state and new ways to conduct outreach with existing businesses.

"These are modern-day strategies for secretaries of state who want to help new businesses—as well as existing ones—weather uncertain financial conditions," said Schultz. "Reaffirming that your state is the right place to create a business, grow that business and maintain its base of operations is critical to remaining competitive."

## About the Author

**Kay Stimson** is director of communications and special projects for the National Association of Secretaries of State in Washington, D.C. A former television news reporter who covered the state legislatures in Maryland and South Carolina, she frequently writes about state and federal policy issues for lawmakers.

## Table 4.15
## THE SECRETARIES OF STATE, 2012

| State or other jurisdiction | Name and party | Method of selection | Length of regular term in years | Date of first service | Present term ends | Number of previous terms | Maximum consecutive terms allowed by constitution |
|---|---|---|---|---|---|---|---|
| Alabama | Beth Chapman (R) | E | 4 | 1/2007 | 1/2015 | 1 | 2 |
| Alaska | | | | ...(a)... | | | |
| Arizona | Ken Bennett (R) | E(b) | 4 | 1/2009 (b) | 1/2015 | (b) | 2 |
| Arkansas | Mark Martin (R) | E | 4 | 12/2010 | 12/2014 | ... | 2 |
| California | Debra Bowen (D) | E | 4 | 1/2007 | 1/2015 | 1 | 2 |
| Colorado | Scott Gessler (R) | E | 4 | 1/2011 | 1/2015 | ... | 2 |
| Connecticut | Denise Merrill (D) | E | 4 | 1/2011 | 1/2015 | ... | ... |
| Delaware | Jeffrey Bullock (D) | A (c) | ... | 1/2009 | ... | ... | ... |
| Florida | Kenneth Detzner (R) (e) | A | ... | 2/2012 | ... | (e) | 2 |
| Georgia | Brian Kemp (R) | E (d) | 4 | 1/2010 (d) | 1/2015 | (d) | ... |
| Hawaii | | | | ...(a)... | | | |
| Idaho | Ben Ysursa (R) | E | 4 | 1/2003 | 1/2015 | 2 | ... |
| Illinois | Jesse White (D) | E | 4 | 1/1999 | 1/2015 | 3 | ... |
| Indiana | Connie Lawson (R) (f) | E | 4 | 3/2012 (f) | 1/2015 | ... | 2 |
| Iowa | Matt Schultz (R) | E | 4 | 12/2010 | 12/2014 | ... | ... |
| Kansas | Kris Kobach (R) | E | 4 | 1/2011 | 1/2015 | ... | ... |
| Kentucky | Allison Lundergan Grimes (D) | E | 4 | 12/2011 | 12/2015 | ... | 2 |
| Louisiana | Tom Schedler (R) | E (g) | 4 | 11/2010 | 1/2012 | ... | ... |
| Maine | Charles Summers (R) | L | 2 | 1/2011 | 1/2013 | ... | 4 (h) |
| Maryland | John P. McDonough (D) | A | ... | 6/2008 | ... | ... | ... |
| Massachusetts | William Francis Galvin (D) | E | 4 | 1/1995 | 1/2015 | 4 | ... |
| Michigan | Ruth Johnson (R) | E | 4 | 1/2011 | 1/2015 | ... | 2 |
| Minnesota | Mark Ritchie (DFL) | E | 4 | 1/2007 | 1/2015 | 1 | ... |
| Mississippi | C. Delbert Hosemann, Jr.(R) | E | 4 | 1/2008 | 1/2012 | ... | ... |
| Missouri | Robin Carnahan (D) | E | 4 | 1/2005 | 1/2013 | 1 | ... |
| Montana | Linda McCulloch (D) | E | 4 | 1/2009 | 1/2013 | ... | (i) |
| Nebraska | John Gale (R) | E | 4 | 12/2000 (j) | 1/2015 | (j) | ... |
| Nevada | Ross Miller (D) | E | 4 | 1/2007 | 1/2015 | 1 | 2 |
| New Hampshire | William Gardner (D) | L | 2 | 12/1976 | 12/2012 | 17 | ... |
| New Jersey | | | | ...(a)(k)... | | | |
| New Mexico | Dianna Duran (R) | E | 4 | 12/2010 | 12/2014 | ... | 2 |
| New York | Cesar Perales (D) | A | ... | 5/2011 | ... | ... | ... |
| North Carolina | Elaine Marshall (D) | E | 4 | 1/1997 | 1/2013 | 2 | ... |
| North Dakota | Alvin A. Jaeger (R) | E | 4 | 1/1993 | 12/2014 | 5 | ... |
| Ohio | Jon Husted (R) | E | 4 | 1/2011 | 1/2015 | ... | 2 |
| Oklahoma | Glenn Coffee (R) | A | 4 | 1/2011 | 1/2015 | ... | ... |
| Oregon | Kate Brown (D) | E | 4 | 1/2009 | 1/2013 | ... | 2 |
| Pennsylvania | Carol Aichele (R) | A | ... | 1/2011 | ... | ... | ... |
| Rhode Island | Ralph Mollis (D) | E | 4 | 1/2007 | 1/2015 | 1 | 2 |
| South Carolina | Mark Hammond (R) | E | 4 | 1/2003 | 1/2015 | 2 | ... |
| South Dakota | Jason Gant (R) | E | 4 | 1/2011 | 1/2015 | ... | 2 |
| Tennessee | Tre Hargett (R) | L | 4 | 1/2009 | 1/2013 | ... | ... |
| Texas | Esperanza Andrade (R) | A | ... | 7/2008 | ... | ... | ... |
| Utah | | | | ...(a)... | | | |
| Vermont | Jim Condos (D) | E | 2 | 1/2011 | 1/2013 | ... | ... |
| Virginia | Janet Polarek (R) | A | ... | 1/2010 | ... | ... | ... |
| Washington | Sam Reed (R) | E | 4 | 1/2001 | 1/2013 | 2 | ... |
| West Virginia | Natalie Tennant (D) | E | 4 | 1/2009 | 1/2013 | ... | ... |
| Wisconsin | Douglas La Follette (D) | E | 4 | 1/1974 (l) | 1/2015 | 9 (l) | ... |
| Wyoming | Max Maxfield (R) | E | 4 | 1/2007 | 1/2015 | 1 | ... |
| American Samoa | | | | ...(a)... | | | |
| Guam | | | | ...(a)... | | | |
| No. Mariana Islands | | | | ...(a)... | | | |
| Puerto Rico | Kenneth McClintock (NPP) | A | ... | 1/2009 | ... | ... | ... |
| U.S. Virgin Islands | | | | ...(a)... | | | |

See footnotes at end of table.

# THE SECRETARIES OF STATE, 2012—Continued

*Source:* The Council of State Governments April 2012.

*Key:*

E — Elected by voters.

A — Appointed by governor.

L — Elected by legislature.

... — No provision for.

(a) No secretary of state; lieutenant governor performs functions of this office. See Tables 4.12 through 4.14.

(b) Ken Bennett was appointed by Gov. Brewer in January 2009 to fill her term after she was sworn in as governor; replacing Janet Napolitano who became the U.S. Secretary of Homeland Security. Bennett was elected to a full term in the 2010 general election.

(c) Appointed by the governor and confirmed by the Senate.

(d) Gov. Perdue appointed Brian Kemp on January 8, 2010 to replace Karen Handel after she resigned to run for the office of governor. Kemp was elected to a full term in the 2010 general election.

(e) Was appointed in Feb. 2012. He served previously in 2003 as the office transitioned from an elected position to an appointed one.

(f) Sen. Lawson was appointed March 16, 2012 to fill the position left vacant when Charlie White was dismissed Feb. 4, 2012 after his conviction on felony charges.

(g) Schedler was appointed and sworn in as secretary of state on November 22, 2010 after Jay Dardenne was elected to serve as lieutenant governor.

(h) Statutory term limit of 4 consecutive 2-year terms.

(i) Eligible for eight out of 16 years.

(j) Secretary Gale was appointed by Gov. Mike Johanns in December 2000 upon the resignation of Scott Moore. He was elected to full four-year terms in November 2002, 2006 and 2010.

(k) The secretary of state of New Jersey is an appointed position. Gov. Christie appointed Lt. Governor Kim Guadagno to serve as secretary of state for this term of office.

(l) Secretary La Follette was first elected in 1974 and served a 4-year term. He was elected again in 1982 and has been re-elected since. The present term ends in 2011.

## Table 4.16
## SECRETARIES OF STATE: QUALIFICATIONS FOR OFFICE

| State or other jurisdiction | Minimum age | U.S. citizen (years) (a) | State resident (years) (b) | Qualified voter (years) | Method of selection to office |
|---|---|---|---|---|---|
| Alabama | 25 | 7 | 5 | ★ | E |
| Alaska | ............ | ............ | (c) | ............ | ............ |
| Arizona | 25 | 10 | 5 | . . . | E |
| Arkansas | 18 | ★ | ★ | ★ | E |
| California | 18 | ★ | ★ | ★ | E |
| Colorado | 25 | ★ | 2 | . . . | E |
| Connecticut | 18 | ★ | ★ | ★ | E |
| Delaware | . . . | . . . | . . . | . . . | A |
| Florida | ............ | ............ | (d) | ............ | A |
| Georgia | 25 | 10 | 4 | ★ | E |
| Hawaii | ............ | ............ | (c) | ............ | ............ |
| Idaho | 25 | ★ | 2 | ★ | E |
| Illinois | 25 | ★ | 3 | . . . | E |
| Indiana | . . . | ★ | ★ | ★ | E |
| Iowa | 18 | ★ | . . . | . . . | E |
| Kansas | . . . | ★ | ★ | ★ | E |
| Kentucky | 30 | ★ | ★ | ★ | E |
| Louisiana | 25 | 5 | 5 | ★ | E |
| Maine | . . . | . . . | . . . | . . . | (e) |
| Maryland | . . . | . . . | . . . | . . . | A |
| Massachusetts | 18 | ★ | 5 | ★ | E |
| Michigan | 18 | ★ | ★ | ★ | E |
| Minnesota | 25 | ★ | 1 | ★ | E |
| Mississippi | 25 | ★ | 5 | ★ | E |
| Missouri | . . . | ★ | ★ | 2 | E |
| Montana | 25 | ★ | 2 | ★ | E |
| Nebraska | . . . | ★ | ★ | ★ | E |
| Nevada | 25 | 2 | 2 | . . . | E |
| New Hampshire | 18 | ★ | ★ | ★ | (e) |
| New Jersey | 18 | ★ | ★ | ★ | A |
| New Mexico | 30 | ★ | 5 | ★ | E |
| New York | 18 | ★ | ★ | . . . | A |
| North Carolina | 21 | ★ | ★ | ★ | E |
| North Dakota | 25 | ★ | 5 | 5 | E |
| Ohio | 18 | ★ | ★ | ★ | E |
| Oklahoma | 31 | ★ | ★ | 10 | A |
| Oregon | 18 | ★ | ★ | ★ | E |
| Pennsylvania | . . . | . . . | . . . | . . . | A |
| Rhode Island | 18 | ★ | 30 days | ★ | E |
| South Carolina | . . . | ★ | ★ | ★ | E |
| South Dakota | . . . | . . . | . . . | . . . | E |
| Tennessee | . . . | . . . | . . . | . . . | (e) |
| Texas | 18 | ★ | . . . | . . . | A |
| Utah | ............ | ............ | (c) | ............ | ............ |
| Vermont | 18 | ★ | ★ | ★ | E |
| Virginia | . . . | . . . | . . . | . . . | A |
| Washington | 18 | ★ | ★ | ★ | E |
| West Virginia | . . . | ★ | ★ | ★ | E |
| Wisconsin | 18 | ★ | ★ | ★ | E |
| Wyoming | 25 | ★ | 1 | ★ | E |
| American Samoa | ............ | ............ | (c) | ............ | ............ |
| Guam | ............ | ............ | (c) | ............ | ............ |
| No. Mariana Islands | ............ | ............ | (c) | ............ | ............ |
| Puerto Rico | . . . | 5 | 5 | . . . | A |
| U.S. Virgin Islands | ............ | ............ | (c) | ............ | ............ |

*Source:* The Council of State Governments, August 2011.

*Key:*
★ — Formal provision; number of years not specified.
. . . — No formal provision.
A — Appointed by governor.
E — Elected by voters.
(a) In some states you must be a U.S. citizen to be an elector, and must be an elector to run.

(b) In some states you must be a state resident to be an elector, and must be an elector to run.
(c) No secretary of state.
(d) As of January 1, 2003, the office of Secretary of State shall be an appointed position (appointed by the governor). It will no longer be a cabinet position, but an agency head and the Department of State shall be an agency under the governor's office.
(e) Chosen by joint ballot of state senators and representatives. In Maine and New Hampshire, every two years. In Tennessee, every four years.

## Table 4.17
## SECRETARIES OF STATE: ELECTION AND REGISTRATION DUTIES

| State or other jurisdiction | Election | | | | | | | | Registration | | | | |
|---|---|---|---|---|---|---|---|---|---|---|---|---|---|
| | Chief election officer | Determines ballot eligibility of political parties | Receives initiative and/or referendum petition | Files certificate of nomination or election | Supplies election ballots or materials to local officials | Files candidates' expense papers | Files other campaign reports | Conducts voter education programs | Registers charitable organizations | Registers corporations (a) | Processes and/or commissions notaries public | Registers securities | Registers trade names/marks |
| Alabama | ★ | ★ | ... | ★ | ★ | ★ | ★ | ★ | ★ | ★ | ★ | ... | ★ |
| Alaska (b) | ★ | ★ | ★ | ★ | ★ | ... | ... | ★ | ... | ... | ★ | ... | ... |
| Arizona | ★ | ★ | ★ | ★ | ... | ★ | ★ | ★ | ★ | ... | ★ | ... | ★ |
| Arkansas | ★ | ★ | ★ | ★ | ... | ★ | ★ | ★ | ... | ★ | ★ | ... | ★ |
| California | ★(c) | ★ | ★ | ★ | ★ | ★ | ★ | ★ | ★(d) | ★ | ★ | ... | ★ |
| Colorado | ★ | ★ | ★ | ★ | ... | ★ | ★ | ★ | ★ | ★ | ★ | ... | ★ |
| Connecticut | ★ | ★ | ... | ★ | ★ | ... | ... | ★ | ★ | ★ | ★ | ... | ★ |
| Delaware | ... | ... | ... | (e) | ... | ★ | (f) | ... | ★(g) | ... | ★ | ... | ★ |
| Florida | ★ | ★ | ... | ★ | ★ | ★ | ★ | ... | ★ | ★ | ... | ... | ★ |
| Georgia | ★ | ★ | ... | ★ | ★ | ★ | ★ | ★ | ★ | ★ | ... | ★ | ★ |
| Hawaii (b) | ... | ... | ... | ... | ★ | ★ | ★ | ★ | ... | ★ | ★ | ... | ★ |
| Idaho | ★ | ★ | ★ | ★ | ★ | ★ | ★ | ★ | ... | ★ | ★ | ★ | ★ |
| Illinois | ... | ... | ★ | (h) | ... | ... | ... | ★ | ★ | ★ | ★ | ★ | ★ |
| Indiana (i) | ★ | ★ | ... | ★ | ★ | ★ | ★ | ★ | ★ | ★ | ★ | ★ | ★ |
| Iowa | ★ | ★ | ... | ★ | ★ | ... | ... | ★ | ... | ★ | ★ | ... | ★ |
| Kansas | ★ | ★ | ... | ★ | ★ | ★ | ... | ★ | ★ | ★ | ★ | ... | ★ |
| Kentucky | ★ | ★ | ... | ★ | ... | ... | ... | ★ | ... | ★ | ★ | ... | ★ |
| Louisiana | ★ | ... | ... | ★ | ★ | ... | ... | ★ | ... | ★ | ★ | ... | ★ |
| Maine | ★ | ... | ★ | ★ | ★ | ... | ... | ★ | ... | ★ | ★ | ... | ★ |
| Maryland | ... | ★ | ★ | ★ | ... | ... | ... | ... | ★ | ★ | ★ | ... | ★ |
| Massachusetts | ★ | ★ | ★ | ★ | ★ | (f) | (f) | ★ | ... | ★ | ★ | ★ | ★ |
| Michigan | ★ | ★ | ★ | ★ | ... | ★ | ★ | ★ | ... | ... | ★ | ... | ★ |
| Minnesota | ★ | ★ | ... | ★ | ★ | ... | ... | ★ | ... | ★ | ★ | ... | ★ |
| Mississippi | ★ | ★ | ★ | ★ | ★ | ★ | ★ | ★ | ★ | ★ | ★ | ★ | ★ |
| Missouri | ★ | ★ | ★ | ★ | ... | ... | ... | ★ | ★ | ★ | ★ | ... | ★ |
| Montana | ★ | ★ | ★ | ★ | ★ | ... | ... | ★ | ★ | ★ | ★ | ... | ★ |
| Nebraska | ★ | ★ | ★ | ★ | ★ | ... | ... | ★ | ... | ★ | ★ | ... | ★ |
| Nevada (j) | ★ | ★ | ★ | ★ | ★ | ★ | ★ | ★ | ... | ★ | ★ | ★ | ★ |
| New Hampshire | ★ | ★ | ... | ★ | ★ | ★ | ★ | ★ | ... | ★ | ★ | ... | ★ |
| New Jersey | ★ | ★ | ★ | ★ | ★ | ★ | ★ | ★ | ... | ★ | ★ | ... | ★ |
| New Mexico | ★ | ★ | ... | ★ | ★ | ★ | ★ | ★ | ... | ... | ★ | ... | ★ |
| New York | ... | ... | ... | ... | ... | ... | ... | ... | ★ | ★ | ★ | ★ | ★ |
| North Carolina (k) | ... | ... | ... | ... | ... | ... | ... | ... | ★ | ★ | ★ | ... | ★ |
| North Dakota | ★ | ★ | ★ | ★ | ★ | ★ | ★ | ★ | ★ | ★ | ★ | ... | ★ |
| Ohio (l) | ★ | ★ | ★ | ★(m) | ★ | ★ | ★ | ... | ... | ★ | ★ | ... | ★ |
| Oklahoma | ... | ... | ★ | ★(n) | ... | ... | ... | ... | ★ | ★(n) | ★ | ... | ★ |
| Oregon | ★ | ★ | ★ | ★ | ★ | ★ | ★ | ★ | ★ | ★ | ★ | ★ | ★ |
| Pennsylvania | ★ | ★ | ... | ★ | ... | ... | ... | ★ | ★ | ★ | ★ | ... | ★ |
| Rhode Island (o) | ★ | ... | ... | ... | ★ | ... | ... | ★ | ... | ★ | ★ | ... | ★ |
| South Carolina | ... | ... | ... | ... | ... | ... | ... | ... | ★ | ★(p) | ★ | ... | ★ |
| South Dakota | ★ | ★ | ★ | ★ | ... | ★ | ★ | ★ | ... | ... | ★ | ... | ★ |
| Tennessee (q) | ... | ★ | ... | ★ | ★ | ... | ... | ★ | ★ | ★ | ★ | ... | ★ |
| Texas | ★ | ★ | ... | ★ | ★ | ... | ... | ★ | ★ | ★ | ★ | ... | ★ |
| Utah (b) | ★ | ★ | ★ | ★ | ★ | ★ | ★ | ★ | ... | ... | ... | ... | ... |
| Vermont (r) | ★ | ★ | ... | ★ | ★ | ★ | ... | ★ | ★ | ★ | ★ | ... | ★ |
| Virginia | ... | ... | ... | ... | ... | ... | ... | ★ | ★ | ... | ... | ★ | ★ |
| Washington | ★ | ★ | ★ | ★ | ... | ★ | ... | ★ | ★ | ★ | ★ | ... | ★ |
| West Virginia | ★ | ★ | ... | ★ | ... | ★ | ★ | ★ | ★ | ★ | ★ | ... | ★ |
| Wisconsin (s) | ... | ... | ... | ... | ... | ★ | ★ | ★ | ★ | ★ | ★ | ★ | ★ |
| Wyoming | ★ | ★ | ★ | ★ | (t) | ★ | ★ | ★ | ★ | ★ | ★ | ... | ★ |
| American Samoa (b) | ... | ... | ... | ★ | ... | ★ | ★ | ★ | ★ | ★ | ★ | ... | ... |
| Guam (b) | ... | ... | ... | ... | ... | ... | ... | ... | ... | ★ | ... | ... | ... |
| Puerto Rico | ... | ... | ... | ... | ... | ... | ... | ... | ★ | ★ | ★ | ★ | ★ |
| U.S. Virgin Islands (b) | ... | ... | ... | ... | ... | ... | ... | ... | ★ | ★(u) | ★ | ... | ★ |

See footnotes at end of table.

*Source:* The Council of State Governments, August 2011.
*Key:*
★ — Responsible for activity.
... — Not responsible for activity.

(a) Unless otherwise indicated, office registers domestic, foreign and non-profit corporations.

(b) No secretary of state. Duties indicated are performed by lieutenant governor. In Hawaii, election related responsibilities have been transferred to an independent Chief Election Officer. In U.S. Virgin Islands election duties are performed by Supervisor of Elections.

(c) Other election duties include: tallying votes from all 58 counties, testing and certifying voting systems, maintaining statewide voter registration database, publishing Voter Information Guide/State Ballot Pamphlet.

(d) This office does not register charitable trusts, but does register charitable organizations as nonprofit corporations; also limited partnerships, limited liability corporations, and domestic partners. Maintains the Advanced Health Care Directive Registry and Safe at Home Confidential Address Program.

(e) Files certificates of election for publication purposes only; does not file certificates of nomination.

(f) Federal candidates only.

(g) Incorporated organizations only.

(h) Office issues document, but does not receive it.

(i) Additional registration duties include securities enforcement and auto dealer registration and enforcement.

(j) Additional registration duties include: Issues annual State Business License, registers Domestic Partnerships, registers advanced directives for health care.

(k) Other election duties: administers the Electoral College. Other registration duties: Registers state legislative and executive branch lobbyists, and maintains secure online registry of advance health care directives.

(l) Supplies poll worker training materials to county boards of elections; certifies official form of the ballot to county boards of elections.

(m) Issues certificate of nomination or election to all statewide candidates and U.S. Representatives.

(n) Certifies U.S. Congressional election results to Washington, D.C. Also registers partnerships, limited liability companies, limited liability partnerships, limited liability companies and fictitious partnership names.

(o) Additional registration duties include: Non-resident landlord appointment of agent for service and Uniform Commercial Code.

(p) Also registers the Cable Franchise Authority.

(q) Appoints the Coordinator of Elections who performs the election duties indicated.

(r) Additional registration duties include: registers temporary officiants for civil marriages.

(s) Additional registration duties include: Issues authentications and apostilles.

(t) Materials not ballots.

(u) Both domestic and foreign profit; but only domestic non-profit.

## Table 4.18
## SECRETARIES OF STATE: CUSTODIAL, PUBLICATION AND LEGISLATIVE DUTIES

| State or other jurisdiction | Custodial | | | | Publication | | | | | Legislative | | | |
|---|---|---|---|---|---|---|---|---|---|---|---|---|---|
| | Archives state records and regulations | Files state agency rules and regulations | Administers uniform commercial code provisions | Files other corporate documents | State manual or directory | Session laws | State constitution | Statutes | Administrative rules and regulations | Opens legislative sessions (a) | Enrolls or engrosses bills | Retains copies of bills | Registers lobbyists |
| Alabama | ... | ... | ★ | ★ | ... | ★ | ★ | ★ | ... | ... | ★ | ★ | ... |
| Alaska (b) | ... | ★ | ... | ... | ... | ... | ★ | ... | ★ | ★ | ... | ★ | ... |
| Arizona | ★ | ★ | ★ | ... | ... | ... | ★ | ... | ★ | ... | ... | ★ | ★ |
| Arkansas (c) | ★ | ★ | ★ | ★ | ... | ★ | ... | ... | ★ | ... | ... | ★ | ★ |
| California | ★ | ★ | ★ | ★ | ★ | ... | ... | ... | ... | ... | (d) | ... | ★ |
| Colorado | ... | ★ | ★ | ★ | ... | ... | ★ | ... | ★ | ... | ... | ★ | ★ |
| Connecticut | ★(e) | ★ | ★ | ★ | ★ | ... | ... | ... | ... | S | ... | ★ | ★ |
| Delaware | ★ | ★ | ★ | ★ | ... | ... | ... | ... | ★ | ... | ... | ... | ... |
| Florida | ★ | ★ | ... | ★ | ... | ★ | ★ | ★ | ★ | ... | ... | ... | ... |
| Georgia | ★ | ★ | ... | ... | ★ | ... | ★ | ... | ★ | ... | ... | ... | ... |
| Hawaii (b) | ... | ★ | ... | ... | ... | ★ | ... | ★ | ★ | ... | ... | ★ | ... |
| Idaho | ... | ... | ★ | ... | ★ | ★ | ★ | ... | ... | ... | ... | ★ | ★ |
| Illinois | ★ | ★ | ★ | ★ | ★ | ★ | ★ | ... | ★ | H | ... | ★ | ★ |
| Indiana | ★ | ★ | ★ | ★ | ... | ... | ... | ... | ... | H | ... | ★ | ... |
| Iowa | ★ | ... | ★ | ★ | ... | ★ | ★ | ... | ... | ... | ★ | ★ | ... |
| Kansas | ... | ★ | ★ | ★ | ★ | ... | ... | ★ | ★ | ... | ... | ... | ★ |
| Kentucky | ★ | ... | ★ | ★ | ... | ... | ... | ... | ... | ... | ★ | ★ | ... |
| Louisiana | ★ | ... | ★ | ★ | ★ | ... | ★ | ... | ★ | ... | ★ | ★ | (f) |
| Maine | ★ | ★ | ★ | ★ | ... | ... | ★ | ... | ★ | ... | ... | ... | ... |
| Maryland | ... | ★ | ... | ... | ... | ★ | ... | ... | (g) | ... | ★ | ★ | ... |
| Massachusetts | ★ | ★ | ★ | ★ | ★ | ★ | ★ | ★ | ★ | ... | ... | ★ | ★ |
| Michigan | ★ | ★ | ★ | ... | ... | ★ | ★ | ★ | ★ | ... | ... | ... | ★ |
| Minnesota | ★ | ★ | ★ | ★ | ★ | ... | ... | ... | ... | H | ... | ... | ... |
| Mississippi | ... | ★ | ★ | ★ | ★ | ★ | ★ | ... | ★ | H | ... | ★ | ★ |
| Missouri | ★(h) | ★ | ★ | ★ | ★ | ... | ★ | ... | ★ | H | ★ | ★ | ... |
| Montana | ... | ★ | ★ | ★ | ... | ... | ★ | ... | ★ | H | ★ | ★ | ... |
| Nebraska | ★ | ★ | ★ | ★ | ... | ... | ... | ... | ★ | ... | ... | ★ | ... |
| Nevada | ★ | ★ | ★ | ★ | ... | ... | ... | ... | ... | ... | ... | ★ | ... |
| New Hampshire | ★ | ... | ★ | ★ | ★ | ... | ★ | ... | ... | ... | ★ | ★ | ★ |
| New Jersey | ★ | ... | ... | ... | ... | ... | ★ | ... | ... | ... | ... | ★ | ... |
| New Mexico | ... | ★ | ★ | ... | ★ | ★ | ★ | ... | ★ | H | ★ | ★ | ... |
| New York | ... | ★ | ★ | ... | ... | ★ | ★ | ... | ★ | ... | ... | ★ | ... |
| North Carolina | ★ | ★ | ★ | ... | ... | ★ | ★ | ... | ... | ... | ... | ... | ★ |
| North Dakota | ... | ... | ★ | ★ | ... | ... | ... | ... | ... | ... | ... | ★ | ★ |
| Ohio (i) | ... | ★ | ★ | ★ | ★ | ★ | ★ | ... | ... | ... | ... | ★ | ... |
| Oklahoma (j) | ... | ★ | ... | ★ | ... | ... | ... | ... | ★ | ... | ... | ★ | ... |
| Oregon | ★ | ★ | ★ | ★ | ★ | ... | ★ | ... | ★ | ... | ... | ★ | ... |
| Pennsylvania | ... | ... | ★ | ★ | ... | ... | ... | ... | ... | ... | ★ | ★ | ... |
| Rhode Island (k) | ★ | ★ | ★ | ★ | ... | ... | ★ | ... | ... | ... | ★ | ★ | ★ |
| South Carolina | ... | ... | ★ | ★ | ... | ... | ... | ★ | ... | ... | ... | ★ | ... |
| South Dakota | ★ | ★ | ★ | ★ | ★ | ... | ... | ... | ★ | H | ★ | ★ | ★ |
| Tennessee (l) | ★ | ★ | ★ | ★ | ★ | ★ | ... | ... | ★ | ... | ... | ... | ... |
| Texas | ★ | ★ | ★ | ★ | ... | ★ | ... | ... | ★ | ... | ... | ★ | ★ |
| Utah (b) | ... | ... | ★ | ★ | ... | ... | ... | ... | ... | ... | ... | ★ | ★ |
| Vermont (m) | ★ | ★ | ★ | ★ | ★ | ... | ★ | ... | ★ | H | ... | ★ | ★ |
| Virginia | ... | ... | ... | ... | ★ | ... | ... | ... | ... | ... | ... | ... | ★ |
| Washington | ★ | ... | ... | ★ | ★ | ... | ... | ... | ... | ... | ... | ★ | ... |
| West Virginia | ★ | ★ | ★ | ★ | ... | ... | ... | ... | ★ | ... | ... | ★ | ... |
| Wisconsin | ★ | ... | ... | ... | ... | ... | ... | ... | ... | ... | ... | ... | ... |
| Wyoming | ... | ★ | ★ | ★ | ... | ... | ★ | ... | ... | H | ... | ★ | ★ |
| American Samoa (b) | ... | ★ | ... | ★ | ... | ★ | ★ | ... | ★ | ... | ... | ... | ... |
| Guam (b) | ... | ... | ... | ... | ... | ... | ... | ★ | ... | ... | ... | ... | ... |
| Puerto Rico | ... | ★ | ★ | ★ | ... | ★ | ★ | ★ | ★ | ... | ... | ... | ... |
| U.S. Virgin Islands (b) | ... | ★ | ★ | ★ | ... | ... | ... | ... | ... | ... | ★ | ★ | ... |

See footnotes at end of table.

## SECRETARIES OF STATE: CUSTODIAL, PUBLICATION AND LEGISLATIVE DUTIES — Continued

*Source:* The Council of State Governments, August 2011.
*Key:*
★ — Responsible for activity.
... — Not responsible for activity.
(a) In this column only: ★ — Both houses; H — House; S — Senate.
(b) No secretary of state. Duties indicated are performed by lieutenant governor.
(c) Additional custodial duties for the Arkansas Secretary of State include serving as the caretaker for the Arkansas State Capitol Building and Grounds, including all custodial duties, HVAC system, building maintenance, historic preservation and conducting tours.
(d) Office does not enroll or engross bills but does chapter them.
(e) The secretary of state is keeper of public records, but the state archives is a department of the Connecticut State Library.
(f) Only registers political pollsters.
(g) Code of Maryland regulations.

(h) Also responsible for the State Library.
(i) Additional publication duties include: elections statistics, official roster of federal, state, and county officers and official roster of township and municipal officers. Additional legislative duties include :Distributing laws to specified state and local government agencies.
(j) Other custodial duties include: Effective Financing Statements identifying farm products that are subject to a security interest, UCC and mortgage documents pertaining to transmitting utilities and also railroads and files open meeting notices.
(k) Additional duties include administering oaths of office to general officers and legislators.
(l) Additional custodial duties include the Tennessee State Library and Archives, administrative law judges, charitable gaming regulation, service of process/summons, sports agent registration and temporary liens.
(m) Additional custodial duties include: records management, and certifying vital records.

# Pillars of Hope:
# Attorneys General Unite Against Human Trafficking

### By the National Association of Attorneys General

*More and more frequently, state and territorial attorneys general are at the forefront of dealing with great issues of the day, from combating human trafficking to enforcing consumer protection and cyberspace laws. With each year, attorneys general face additional challenges and legal landscapes. In 2012, attorneys general are shining a light on modern day slavery, as well as continuing to fight financial fraud. Additionally, Election Day 2012 will bring at least five new state attorneys general and another five who are seeking re-election.*

## Ending Modern Day Slavery

Human trafficking is a $32 billion global industry—the fastest-growing and second largest criminal activity in the world, tied with arms and after drug dealing. Each year, the U.S. Department of State produces the United Nations Trafficking in Persons Report. According to Secretary of State Hillary Rodham Clinton, it is estimated that between 12 million and 27 million human beings are trafficked across international borders into forced labor or sexual exploitation.

Today, international trade barriers have eased and Internet use has skyrocketed. These factors, among others, have helped make human trafficking—the forced or coerced transport and exploitation of human beings—much easier and more profitable.

"Human trafficking is the only crime I can think of where the victim is more likely to be prosecuted than the perpetrator," said Washington Attorney General Rob McKenna, the 2012 president of the National Association of Attorneys General, or NAAG. "It is aptly referred to as modern day slavery—the selling of another person's body through the use of force, fear or coercion."

In addition to the estimated 15,000–17,000 people smuggled into our country each year to work in fields, sweatshops, restaurants and the sex trade, hundreds of thousands of U.S. children are estimated to be at risk of commercial sexual exploitation. For example, police reports from around the country show that young people—many of whom are runaways or have been cast out of troubled homes—are coerced into prostitution and beaten when they have second thoughts.

Local prosecutors in Washington state charged a man in December 2011 for promising an 18-year-old woman with developmental disabilities a trip home for Thanksgiving if she agreed to prostitute herself. The man posted an advertisement on adult-services Backpage.com and then drove her to customers, taking the proceeds along the way.

Cases like these prompt law enforcement officials, including attorneys general, to seek more action in protecting victims caught in traffickers' clutches.

That is why McKenna announced in June 2011 his one-year NAAG presidential initiative would focus on human trafficking. "Pillars of Hope: Attorneys General Unite Against Human Trafficking" has four interlocking pieces with specific goals and deliverables. Those involved in the initiative are advocating to make the case by strengthening data and analyzing state laws, to hold traffickers accountable, to mobilize care for victims and to build public awareness.

McKenna established a Leadership Council to help him fulfill the initiative tasks. The council consists of attorneys general from California, Illinois, Indiana, Maine, Massachusetts, Michigan, New Mexico, Oregon and Texas. They have established a work program based on the four initiative pillars. Lexis-Nexis, along with the Polaris Project and Microsoft, serve as initiative partners.

## Pillar No. 1: Make the Case

Attorneys general often receive inquiries from reporters and others about the number of human trafficking cases in their states. Although data exist on trafficking cases tried by federal authorities, state-specific information is hard to find. No uniform database exists to capture an increasing number of cases being tried under state human trafficking statutes, or cases where traffickers are charged with related crimes such as pimping, kidnapping, or physical or sexual assault. The goal of the first pillar is to assess the extent of the problem in the United States and to analyze existing state laws and model criminal and civil statutes, as well as tools for evaluating the effectiveness of prevention strategies, law enforcement and victim services at the state level.

Promoting use of the National Human Trafficking Resource Center information to local authorities will help to quantify possible incidents and reporting them in a central location will assist in reaching the first pillar goal. The victim hotline, (888) 373-7888, also will be advertised to increase victims' access to services.

## Pillar No. 2: Hold Traffickers Accountable

Not all states have adopted a comprehensive set of human trafficking laws that provide the necessary tools to police and prosecutors. In addition, only a small number of states are actually using existing laws to prosecute traffickers. In order to assist state and local law enforcement, the second pillar encourages the implementation of criminal justice strategies such as conducting investigations to help identify individuals and organizations engaged in trafficking, supports the launch of a new FBI training program for local law enforcers, and spurs state program managers responsible for criminal justice statistics to participate in the FBI's effort to map trafficking offenses. The hope is that this process will ensure full implementation and compliance of human trafficking statutes and drive prosecutions in all 50 states.

Once the review of existing state anti-trafficking statutes and legislative templates is complete from the first pillar, a tool kit will be offered to attorneys general for adaptation in their states as appropriate. Each attorney general will determine which model criminal or civil statutes could be replicated in his or her state.

The U.S. Department of Justice's Bureau of Justice Assistance is addressing the lack of training for states in investigating human trafficking by funding and training 38 human trafficking task forces throughout the country. NAAG, through its training and research arm, National Attorneys General Training and Research Institute, received a sub-grant from the Upper Midwest Community Policing Institute[1] to assist in developing curriculum to train state and local prosecutors and judges on human trafficking prevention, investigation and prosecution. This grant is a reflection of our country's commitment to address human trafficking at every level.

In 2011, National Attorneys General Training and Research Institute worked with the Upper Midwest Community Policing Institute and the National Judicial College to hold a series of subject matter expert focus groups, develop the curriculum and present a few pilot trainings. Training courses will expand in 2012. Training state and local law enforcement, prosecutors and judges in how to tackle the largely unseen but virulent epidemic of human trafficking will create the environment in which states will be able to become full partners with their federal counterparts in combating this crime.

## Pillar No. 3: Rescue Victims

Through no fault of their own, victims of human trafficking are on society's fringes. They are sometimes runaways or don't speak English. They may have been brought into the country illegally and thus don't feel comfortable seeking out services for fear of being turned in to the police.

The objectives of third pillar include assembling a list of service provider networks in every state to ensure all identified victims of human trafficking have access to food, shelter and culturally appropriate services. It also will provide an inventory of advocacy organizations that assist with community awareness strategies at the state and local levels and will establish partnerships among service providers, victim advocates and law enforcement.

## Pillar No. 4: Reduce Demand

While it's difficult to imagine today, just two decades ago drunken driving was not recognized as a serious problem. Neither was the crime of domestic violence as appropriately emphasized as it is today. The fourth pillar aims to heighten public awareness and advocacy efforts to reduce the demand for human trafficking by changing public attitudes toward the commercial sex industry, its victims and those who buy and sell human beings.

Although numerous public awareness campaigns exist, few use proven metrics to demonstrate their effectiveness. Through "Pillars of Hope," the attorneys general will use proven messaging tactics via broadcast media, print and billboards. Many attorneys general planned programs in their states in conjunction with National Slavery and Human Trafficking Prevention month in January 2012. Special emphasis was made in targeting the commercial sex industry leading up to the February Super Bowl XLVI in Indianapolis. An outline of long-term strategies to reduce demand will be developed, including the creation of anti-trafficking content for placement in cyberspace.

NAAG membership voted in March to approve a resolution in support of the initiative principles, as already adopted by the Leadership Council. Other public officials at the state and local levels will be encouraged to sign it and act on it as well.

The attorneys general gathered for the Presidential Initiative Summit in March in Seattle. The conference convened experts representing academia, NGOs, state and federal government, and private industry to discuss progress in reaching the initiative goals and determining action for 2012 and 2013. Plans include the formation of a NAAG Committee on Human Trafficking by July 2012 to allow NAAG to continue its work on this issue in the years to come.

This heinous crime lurks in the shadows. It's time to bring it out into the light, to bring hope and resources to victims and to bring justice to traffickers and those who buy victims from them.

Many people don't enjoy the liberties promised by our founders. The goal of the "Pillars of Hope" initiative is to deliver on that promise by leading attorneys general across the nation in bringing hope and freedom to the victims of modern day slavery.

## Consumer Financial Protection Bureau Open for Business

State attorneys general have been one of the few law enforcers actively investigating predatory lending practices and fraud targeted at vulnerable consumers. Their actions continue into 2012 as they develop working relationships with the federal government's Consumer Financial Protection Bureau.

Created by the Dodd-Frank Wall Street Reform and Consumer Protection Act 2010 [P.L. 111-203], the bureau is independent within the Federal Reserve System and helps consumers with mortgages, credit cards and other consumer financial products and services. The Consumer Financial Protection Bureau officially launched July 2011 with President Obama nominating former Ohio Attorney General Richard Cordray to be the bureau's director that same month.

In October 2011, the U.S. Senate Committee on Banking, Housing and Urban Affairs voted 12-10 to send the Cordray nomination to the full Senate. A NAAG letter signed by 37 attorneys general in support of Cordray was sent.

"We are Attorneys General from across the country who represent a wide range of political interests. Some of us may disagree with aspects of

the Dodd-Frank legislation. But we are united in our belief that Mr. Cordray is very well qualified to carry out the responsibilities of this position," an Oct. 18, 2011 NAAG letter to Congress reads.

President Obama appointed Cordray to the position in January 2012.

The Consumer Financial Protection Bureau supervises banks, credit unions and financial companies and enforces federal consumer financial laws. In addition, the bureau promotes consumer financial education, and also gathers and analyzes information to better understand consumers, financial services providers and consumer financial markets.

The Consumer Financial Protection Bureau published four interim final rules in a July 2011 *Federal Register* that establishes its procedures and processes governing investigations, adjudicative hearings/administrative enforcement actions, disclosure of information and records to third parties, and state officials' notification to the bureau of enforcement actions they initiate.

One of the rules set forth procedures that state attorneys general and state regulators must follow before initiating a court, administrative or regulatory proceeding to enforce any provision of Dodd-Frank or Consumer Financial Protection Bureau regulations. The rule requires state officials to provide electronic and written notice to the financial protection bureau at least 10 days before initiating a proceeding, with an exception for emergency proceedings, allowing notice to the bureau to be delayed until up to 48 hours after the proceeding is initiated. Under the rule, the Consumer Financial Protection Bureau may intervene in a proceeding and, upon intervening, remove a state court proceeding to federal court. It also describes what information must be included in the notice to the Consumer Financial Protection Bureau, requires the bureau not to disclose the information in the notice to third parties, and provides that the notice requirements do not create a private right of action or defense.

## Joint Statement of Principles

State attorneys general have been working closely with the Consumer Financial Protection Bureau since its launch in 2011. As part of his 2010–11 Presidential Initiative on "America's Financial Recovery: Protecting Consumers As We Rebuild," then-NAAG President Roy Cooper of North Carolina convened a Presidential Initiative Working Group comprised of attorneys general and assistant attorneys general from Connecticut, Illinois, Indiana, Iowa, Michigan, New York, North Carolina and Washington. Their work continues today as the NAAG-CFPB Working Group.

The working group and the Consumer Financial Protection Bureau developed a Joint Statement of Principles on Consumer Financial Protection with the purpose of establishing and enhancing a lasting and productive partnership between the bureau and state attorneys general. Under the principles, the parties will seek to work together, develop joint training programs and share information about developments in federal consumer financial law where appropriate and to the greatest extent possible; share information, data and analysis about conduct and practices in consumer financial products and services markets; engage in regular consultation to identify mutual enforcement priorities; support each other to the fullest extent possible in the enforcement of the consumer financial and consumer protection laws, including joint and coordinated investigations; pursue legal remedies to foster transparency, competition and fairness in the financial products market across state lines; and develop a consistent and enduring framework to share investigatory information. The principles also state that both parties will work together to develop protocols and processes for sharing consumer complaint information and create and support technologies to enable data sharing.

In the latest federal action, the Financial Fraud Enforcement Task Force, as established by the U.S. Department of Justice, formed a consumer protection working group in January 2012 to address such issues as payday lenders, counterfeit goods, for-profit colleges, third-party payment processors and other issues. The attorneys general from Illinois, Indiana and North Carolina serve on this working group, which is co-chaired by leaders in the DOJ, Consumer Financial Protection Bureau and the Federal Trade Commission.

## Conclusion

Attorneys general and the Consumer Financial Protection Bureau have the greatest opportunity for collaboration around issues of enforcement. A successful partnership should have a profound impact on consumer financial markets by more effectively deterring unscrupulous lenders from deceptive practices, protecting consumers and ensuring greater compliance among lenders.

## Notes

[1] The UMCPI is one of eight regional institutes funded by the federal Community Oriented Policing Services (COPS).

## About the National Association of Attorneys General

The **National Association of Attorneys General**, *www.naag. org*, was founded in 1907 to help attorneys general fulfill the responsibilities of their office and to assist in the delivery of high quality legal services to the states and territorial jurisdictions.

The association provides a forum for the exchange of views and experiences on priority issues, fosters interstate cooperation on legal and law enforcement issues, conducts policy research and analysis of issues, improves the quality of legal services provided to the states and territories, and facilitates communication between its members and all levels of government. The association's members are the attorneys general of the 50 states and Washington, D.C., and the chief legal officers of the commonwealths of Puerto Rico (secretary of justice) and the Northern Mariana Islands, and the territories of American Samoa, Guam and the U.S. Virgin Islands.

This article was written by **Dan Sytman**, media relations manager, Washington Attorney General's Office, and NAAG Director of Communications **Marjorie Tharp**.

## Table 4.19
## THE ATTORNEYS GENERAL, 2012

| State or other jurisdiction | Name and party | Method of selection | Length of regular term in years | Date of first service | Present term ends | Number of previous terms | Maximum consecutive terms allowed |
|---|---|---|---|---|---|---|---|
| Alabama | Luther Strange (R) | E | 4 | 1/2011 | 1/2015 | 0 | 2 |
| Alaska | Michael Geraghty (R) | A | ... | 1/2012 | ... | 0 | ... |
| Arizona | Tom Horne (R) | E | 4 | 1/2011 | 1/2015 | 0 | 2 |
| Arkansas | Dustin McDaniel (D) | E | 4 | 1/2007 | 1/2015 | 1 | 2 |
| California | Kamala Harris (D) | E | 4 | 1/2011 | 1/2015 | 0 | 2 |
| Colorado | John W. Suthers (R) | E | 4 | 1/2005 (a) | 1/2015 | 1 (a) | 2 |
| Connecticut | George Jepsen (D) | E | 4 | 1/2011 | 1/2015 | 0 | ★ |
| Delaware | Joseph R. Biden III (D) | E | 4 | 1/2007 | 1/2015 | 1 | ★ |
| Florida | Pam Bondi (R) | E | 4 | 1/2011 | 1/2015 | 0 | 2 |
| Georgia | Sam Olens (R) | E | 4 | 1/2011 | 1/2015 | 0 | ★ |
| Hawaii | David Louie (D) | A | 4 (b) | 1/2011 | 1/2015 | 0 | ... |
| Idaho | Lawrence Wasden (R) | E | 4 | 1/2003 | 1/2015 | 2 | ★ |
| Illinois | Lisa Madigan (D) | E | 4 | 1/2003 | 1/2015 | 2 | ★ |
| Indiana | Greg Zoeller (R) | E | 4 | 1/2009 | 1/2013 | 0 | ★ |
| Iowa | Tom Miller (D) | E | 4 | 1/1979 (c) | 1/2015 | 7 (c) | ★ |
| Kansas | Derek Schmidt (R) | E | 4 | 1/2011 | 1/2015 | 0 | ★ |
| Kentucky | Jack Conway (D) | E | 4 | 12/2007 | 12/2015 | 0 | 2 |
| Louisiana | James D. Caldwell (D) | E | 4 | 1/2008 | 1/2016 | 0 | ★ |
| Maine | William J. Schneider (R) | L (d) | 2 | 1/2011 | 1/2013 | 0 | 4 |
| Maryland | Douglas F. Gansler (D) | E | 4 | 1/2007 | 1/2015 | 1 | ★ |
| Massachusetts | Martha Coakley (D) | E | 4 | 1/2007 | 1/2015 | 1 | 2 |
| Michigan | Bill Schuette (R) | E | 4 | 1/2011 | 1/2015 | 0 | 2 |
| Minnesota | Lori Swanson (D) | E | 4 | 1/2007 | 1/2015 | 1 | ★ |
| Mississippi | Jim Hood (D) | E | 4 | 1/2004 | 1/2016 | 1 | ★ |
| Missouri | Chris Koster (D) | E | 4 | 1/2009 | 1/2013 | 0 | ★ |
| Montana | Steve Bullock (D) | E | 4 | 1/2009 | 1/2013 | 0 | 2 |
| Nebraska | Jon Bruning (R) | E | 4 | 1/2003 | 1/2015 | 2 | ★ |
| Nevada | Catherine Cortez Masto (D) | E | 4 | 1/2007 | 1/2015 | 1 | 2 |
| New Hampshire | Michael Delaney (D) | A | 4 | 8/2009 | 8/2013 | 0 | ... |
| New Jersey | Jeffrey S. Chiesa (R) | A | 4 | 1/2012 | ... | 0 | ... |
| New Mexico | Gary King (D) | E | 4 | 1/2007 | 1/2015 | 1 | 2 (e) |
| New York | Eric Schneiderman (D) | E | 4 | 1/2011 | 1/2015 | 0 | ★ |
| North Carolina | Roy Cooper (D) | E | 4 | 1/2001 | 1/2013 | 2 | ★ |
| North Dakota | Wayne Stenehjem (R) | E | 4 (f) | 1/2001 | 12/2014 | 3 (f) | ★ |
| Ohio | Mike Dewine (R) | E | 4 | 1/2009 (i) | 1/2015 | 0 | 2 |
| Oklahoma | Scott Pruitt (R) | E | 4 | 1/2011 | 1/2015 | 0 | ★ |
| Oregon | John R. Kroger (D) | E | 4 | 1/2009 | 1/2013 | 0 | ★ |
| Pennsylvania | Linda L. Kelly (R) (g) | E | 4 | 5/2011 (g) | 1/2013 | 0 | 2 |
| Rhode Island | Peter Kilmartin (D) | E | 4 | 1/2011 | 1/2015 | 0 | 2 |
| South Carolina | Alan Wilson (R) | E | 4 | 1/2011 | 1/2015 | 0 | ★ |
| South Dakota | Martin J. Jackley (R) | E | 4 | 9/2009 (h) | 1/2015 | 1 | 2 (e) |
| Tennessee | Robert E. Cooper Jr. (D) | (i) | 8 | 10/2006 | 8/2014 | 0 | ... |
| Texas | Greg Abbott (R) | E | 4 | 1/2003 | 1/2015 | 2 | ★ |
| Utah | Mark Shurtleff (R) | E | 4 | 1/2001 | 1/2013 | 2 | ★ |
| Vermont | William H. Sorrell (D) | E | 2 | 5/1997 (j) | 1/2013 | 6 (j) | ★ |
| Virginia | Ken Cuccinelli (R) | E | 4 | 1/2010 | 1/2014 | 0 | (k) |
| Washington | Rob McKenna (R) | E | 4 | 1/2005 | 1/2013 | 1 | ★ |
| West Virginia | Darrell V. McGraw Jr. (D) | E | 4 | 1/1993 | 1/2013 | 4 | ★ |
| Wisconsin | J.B. Van Hollen (R) | E | 4 | 1/2007 | 1/2015 | 1 | ★ |
| Wyoming | Greg A. Phillips (D) | A (l) | ... | 3/2011 | ... | 0 | ... |
| Dist. of Columbia | Irvin Nathan (D) | A | ... | 1/2011 | ... | 0 | ... |
| American Samoa | Fepulea'i Afa Ripley Jr. (D) | A | 4 | 1/2007 | ... | 1 | ... |
| Guam | Lenny Rapadas | E | 4 | 1/2011 | 1/2015 | 0 | ... |
| No. Mariana Islands | Edward T. Buckingham | A | 4 | 8/2009 | ... | 0 | ... |
| Puerto Rico | Guillermo Somoza-Colombani | A | 4 | 12/2009 | ... | 0 | ... |
| U.S. Virgin Islands | Vincent Frazer | A | 4 | 1/2007 | 1/2011 | 0 | ... |

See footnotes at end of table.

# THE ATTORNEYS GENERAL, 2012—Continued

*Sources:* National Association of Attorneys General and The Council of State Governments, March 2012.

*Key:*

★ — No provision specifying number of terms allowed.

. . . — No formal provision, position is appointed or elected by governmental entity (not chosen by the electorate).

A — Appointed by the governor.

E — Elected by the voters.

L — Elected by the legislature.

N.A.— Not available.

(a) Appointed to fill unexpired term in January 2005 and elected to a full term in November 2006.

(b) Term runs concurrently with the governor.

(c) Attorney General Miller was elected in 1978, 1982, 1986, 1994, 1998, 2002, 2006 and 2010.

(d) Chosen biennially by joint ballot of state senators and representatives.

(e) After two consecutive terms , must wait four years and/or one full term before being eligible again.

(f) The term of the office of the elected official is four years, except that in 2004 the attorney general was elected for a term of two years.

(g) Appointed to fill Tom Corbett's unexpired term after he was elected to PA governor's office in May 2011.

(h) Appointed September 4, 2009 to fill Larry Long's unexpired term. AG Long resigned to accept a state judgeship.

(i) Appointed by judges of state Supreme Court.

(j) Appointed to fill unexpired term in May 1997. He was elected in 1998 to his first full term.

(k) Provision specifying individual may hold office for an unlimited number of terms.

(l) Must be confirmed by the Senate.

# Table 4.20
# ATTORNEYS GENERAL: QUALIFICATIONS FOR OFFICE

| State or other jurisdiction | Minimum age | U.S. citizen (years) (a) | State resident (years) (b) | Qualified voter (years) | Licensed attorney (years) | Membership in the state bar (years) | Method of selection to office |
|---|---|---|---|---|---|---|---|
| Alabama | 25 | 7 | 5 | ★ | ... | ... | E |
| Alaska | 18 | ★ | ... | ... | ★ | ★ | A |
| Arizona | 25 | 10 | 5 | ★ | 5 | ... | E |
| Arkansas | ... | ... | ★ | ★ | ... | ... | E |
| California | 18 | ★ | ★ | ★ | ★ | 5 | E |
| Colorado | 27 | ★ | 2 | ★ | ★ | ... | E |
| Connecticut | 18 | ★ | ★ | ★ | 10 | 10 | E |
| Delaware | ... | ... | ... | ... | ... | ... | E |
| Florida | 30 | ★ | 7 | ★ | ★ | 5 | E |
| Georgia | 25 | 10 | 4 | ★ | 7 | 7 | E |
| Hawaii | ... | 1 | 1 | ... | ★ | (d) | A |
| Idaho | 30 | ★ | 2 | ... | ★ | ★ | E |
| Illinois | 25 | ★ | 3 | ★ | ★ | ★ | E |
| Indiana | ... | 2 | 2 | ★ | 5 | ... | E |
| Iowa | 18 | ★ | ★ | ... | ... | ... | E |
| Kansas | ... | ... | ... | ... | ... | ... | E |
| Kentucky | 30 | ... | 2 (e) | ... | 8 | 2 | E |
| Louisiana | 25 | ★ | 5 | ★ | ★ | ★ | E |
| Maine | ... | ... | ... | ... | ★ | ★ | (f) |
| Maryland | ... | ★(g) | ★ | ★ | ★ | 10 | E |
| Massachusetts | 18 | ... | 5 | ★ | ... | ★ | E |
| Michigan | 18 | ★ | ★ | ... | ★ | ★ | E |
| Minnesota | 21 | ★ | 30 days | ★ | ... | ... | E |
| Mississippi | 26 | ★ | 5 | ★ | 5 | ★ | E |
| Missouri | ... | ★ | 1 | ... | ... | ... | E |
| Montana | 25 | ★ | 2 | ... | 5 | ★ | E |
| Nebraska | ... | ... | ★ | ... | ... | ... | E |
| Nevada | 25 | ★ | 2 | ★ | ... | ... | E |
| New Hampshire | ... | ★ | ★ | ... | ★ | ★ | A (h) |
| New Jersey | 18 | ... | ★ | ... | ... | ... | A |
| New Mexico | 30 | ★ | 5 | ★ | ★ | ... | E |
| New York | 30 | ★ | 5 | ... | (i) | ... | E |
| North Carolina | 21 | ★ | ★ | ★ | ★ | (i) | E |
| North Dakota | 25 | ★ | 5 | ★ | ★ | ★ | E |
| Ohio | 18 | ★ | ★ | ★ | ... | ... | E |
| Oklahoma | 31 | ★ | ★ | 10 | ... | ... | E |
| Oregon | 18 | ★ | ★ | ★ | ... | ... | E |
| Pennsylvania | 30 | ★ | ... | ... | ★ | ... | E |
| Rhode Island | 18 | ... | ... | ... | ★ | ★ | E |
| South Carolina | ... | ★ | 30 days | ★ | ★ | ★ | E |
| South Dakota | 18 | ★ | ★ | ★ | (i) | (i) | E |
| Tennessee | ... | ... | ... | ... | ... | ... | (j) |
| Texas | ... | ... | ★ | ... | (i) | (i) | E |
| Utah | 25 | ★ | 5 (e) | ★ | ★ | ★ | E |
| Vermont | 18 | ★ | ★ | ★ | ... | ... | E |
| Virginia | 30 | ★ | 1 (k) | ★ | ... | 5 (k) | E |
| Washington | 18 | ★ | ★ | ★ | ★ | ★ | E |
| West Virginia | 25 | ... | 5 | ★ | ... | ... | E |
| Wisconsin | ... | ★ | ★ | ... | ... | ... | E |
| Wyoming | ... | ★ | ★ | ★ | 4 | 4 | A (l) |
| Dist. of Columbia | ... | ... | ★ | ... | ★ | ★ | A |
| American Samoa | ... | ... | (c) | ... | (i) | (i) | A |
| Guam | ... | ... | ... | ... | ... | ... | A |
| No. Mariana Islands | ... | ... | 3 | ... | 5 | ... | A |
| Puerto Rico | ... | ★ | ... | ... | ★ | ★ | A |
| U.S. Virgin Islands | ... | ... | ★ | ★ | ★ | ★ | A |

*Sources:* The Council of State Governments' survey of attorneys general, November 2009 and state constitutions and statutes, January 2010. With updates from Web survey March 2012.

*Key:*

★ — Formal provision; number of years not specified.

... — No formal provision.

A — Appointed by governor.

E — Elected by voters.

(a) In some states you must be a U.S. citizen to be an elector, and must be an elector to run.

(b) In some states you must be a state resident to be an elector, and must be an elector to run.

(c) No statute specifically requires this, but the State Bar Act can be interpreted as making this a qualification.

(d) No period specified, all licensed attorneys are members of the state bar.

(e) State citizenship requirement.

(f) Chosen biennially by joint ballot of state senators and representatives.

(g) *Crosse v. Board of Supervisors of Elections* 243 Md. 555, 221 A.2d 431 (1966)–opinion rendered indicated that U.S. citizenship was, by necessity, a requirement for office.

(h) Appointed by the governor and confirmed by the governor and the executive council.

(i) Implied.

(j) Appointed by state supreme court.

(k) Same as qualifications of a judge of a court of record.

(l) Must be confirmed by the Senate.

## Table 4.21
## ATTORNEYS GENERAL: PROSECUTORIAL AND ADVISORY DUTIES

| State or other jurisdiction | Authority in local prosecutions: Authority to initiate local prosecutions | May intervene in local prosecutions | May assist local prosecutor | May supersede local prosecutor | Issues advisory opinions (a): To state executive officials | To legislators | To local prosecutors | On the constitutionality of bills or ordinances | Reviews legislation (b): Prior to passage | Before signing |
|---|---|---|---|---|---|---|---|---|---|---|
| Alabama | A | A,D | A,D | A | ★ | ★ | ★ | ... | ★ | ... |
| Alaska | (c) | (c) | (c) | (c) | ★ | ★ | ... | ★ | ★ | ★ |
| Arizona | A | A | A,B | A,F | ★ | ★ | ★ | ★ | (u) | (u) |
| Arkansas | ... | ... | ... | D | ★ | ★ | ★ | ★ | ... | ... |
| California | A,B,C,D,E,F | A,B,C,D,E,F | A,B,C,D,E,F | A,B,C,D,E,F,G | ★ | ★ | ★ | ★ | (v) | (v) |
| Colorado | A,F | B | D,F | B | ★ | ★ | ★ | ★ | ★ | ★ |
| Connecticut | ... | ... | ... | ... | ★ | (d) | ... | ★ | (e) | (e) |
| Delaware | A (f) | (f) | (f) | (f) | ★ | ★ | ★ | ★ | ★(g) | ★(g) |
| Florida | F | ... | D | ... | ★ | ★ | ★ | ... | ... | ... |
| Georgia | B,D,F,G | ... | A,D | ... | ★ | ★ | ★ | ... | ... | ... |
| Hawaii | A,B,C,D,E | A,B,C,D,E | A,B,C,D,E | A,B,C,D,E | ★ | ★ | ... | ★(h) | ★ | ★ |
| Idaho | B,D,F | ... | D | ... | ★ | ★ | ★ | ★ | ★ | ★ |
| Illinois | D,F | D,G | D | G | ★ | ★ | ★ | ... | (i) | (i) |
| Indiana | F | ... | D | ... | ★ | ★ | ★ | ★ | ... | ... |
| Iowa | D,F | D,F | D,F | D,E,F | ★ | ★ | ★ | ... | (j) | (j) |
| Kansas | A,B,C,D,F | A,D | D | A,F | ★ | ★ | ★ | ★ | ... | ... |
| Kentucky | D,F,G | B,D,G | D | B | ★ | ★ | ★ | ★ | ... | ... |
| Louisiana | D,E,G | D,E,G | D,E,G | E,G | ★ | ★ | ★ | ... | ★ | ★ |
| Maine | A | A | A | A | ★ | ★ | ... | ... | ... | ... |
| Maryland | B,F | D | D | ... | ★ | ★ | ★ | ★ | ★ | ★ |
| Massachusetts | A | A | A,D | A | ★ | ★(k) | ★ | ★ | (l) | (l) |
| Michigan | A | A | A | A | ★ | ★ | ★ | ★ | ... | ... |
| Minnesota | B,F | B,D,G | A,B,D,G | B | ★ | ★(k) | ★ | ... | ... | (l) |
| Mississippi | A,D,F | D,F | A,D,F | D,F | ★ | ★ | ★ | ... | ... | ... |
| Missouri | B,F,G | F | B,F | G | ★ | ★ | ★ | ... | (l) | (l) |
| Montana | D | E | E | E | ★ | ★(m) | ★ | ... | ... | ... |
| Nebraska | A,D,G | A,D,G | D | D | ★ | ★ | ★ | ★ | ... | ... |
| Nevada | D,F,G | D | ... | ... | ★ | ... | ★ | ★ | ... | ... |
| New Hampshire | A,E,F | A,E,F | A,D,E,F | A,E,F | ★ | ★ | ★ | ... | (n) | (n) |
| New Jersey | A,B,C,D | A,B,C,D | A,B,C,D | A,B,C,D | ★ | ★ | ★ | ★ | ★ | ★ |
| New Mexico | B,D,E,F | D,E,F | A,B,D,E,F | D,E,F,G | ★ | ★ | ★ | ★ | ★ | ★ |
| New York | B,F | B,D,F | D | B | ★ | ★(k) | ★ | ★ | ★ | ★ |
| North Carolina | ... | D | D | ... | ★ | ★ | ★ | ★ | ★ | ... |
| North Dakota | A,D,E,F,G | A,D,E,G | A,B,D,E,F,G | A,D,E,G | ★ | ★ | ★ | ★ | ... | ... |
| Ohio | F | D | D | F | ★ | (m) | ★ | ... | ... | ... |
| Oklahoma | A,B,C,D,E,F,G | A,B,C,D,E,F,G | A,B,C,D,E,F,G | A,B,C,D,E,F,G | ★ | ★ | ★ | ★ | ★ | ★ |
| Oregon | B,D,F | B,D | B,D | B | ★ | ★ | ★ | ... | ... | ★ |
| Pennsylvania | A,D,F | D,F | D,F | ... | ★ | ... | ... | ... | ... | ... |
| Rhode Island | A | A | A | A | ★ | ★ | ... | ... | ... | ... |
| South Carolina | A | A | A | A | ★ | (q) | ★ | ★ | ... | ... |
| South Dakota | A,B,D,E,F (p) | D,G (b) | A,B,D,E | D,F | ★ | ★ | ★ | ... | ★ | ... |
| Tennessee | D,F,G | D,F,G | D,F | ... | ★ | ★ | ★ | ★ | ... | ... |
| Texas | ... | ... | ... | ... | ... | ... | ★ | ★ | ... | ... |
| Utah | A,B,D,E,F,G | E,G | D,E | E | ★ | ★(q) | ★ | ★ | ★(l) | ★(l) |
| Vermont | A | A | A | E | ★ | ★ | ★ | ★ | ★ | ★ |
| Virginia | B,F | B,D,F | B,D,F | B | ★ | ★ | ★ | ★ | ★ | ★ |
| Washington | B,D,G | B,D,G | B,D,G | B,D,G | ★ | ★ | ★ | ... | (o) | (o) |
| West Virginia | (r) | ... | ... | ... | ★ | ★ | ★ | ★ | ... | ... |
| Wisconsin | B,C,D,F | B,C,D | D | B | ★ | ★ | ★ | ★ | (e) | (e) |
| Wyoming | B,D,F | B,D | B,D | G | ★ | ★ | ★ | ★(h) | ★ | ★ |
| Dist. of Columbia | F | D | D | F | ★ | ★ | (s) | ★ | ★ | ★ |
| American Samoa | A (t) | (t) | (t) | (t) | ★ | ... | (t) | (e) | (l) | (l) |
| Guam | A | A | A | A | ★ | ★ | ★ | ★ | (l) | B |
| No. Mariana Islands | A (t) | (t) | (t) | (t) | ★ | ★ | ... | ★ | ... | ... |
| Puerto Rico | A | (t) | (t) | (t) | ★ | ★ | ... | ... | ★ | ★ |
| U.S. Virgin Islands | A (t) | (t) | (t) | (t) | ★ | ... | ... | ★ | ★ | ★ |

See footnotes at end of table.

## ATTORNEYS GENERAL: PROSECUTORIAL AND ADVISORY DUTIES — Continued

*Source:* The Council of State Governments' survey of attorneys general, March 2011.

*Key:*
A — On own initiative.
B — On request of governor.
C — On request of legislature.
D — On request of local prosecutor.
E — When in state's interest.
F — Under certain statutes for specific crimes.
G — On authorization of court or other body.
★ — Has authority in area.
. . . — Does not have authority in area.

(a) Also issues advisory opinions to: Alabama—Designated heads of state departments, agencies, boards, and commissions; local public officials; and political subdivisions. Hawaii—Judges/judiciary as requested. Kansas—to counsel for local units of government. Montana—county and city attorneys, city commissioners. Wisconsin—corporation counsel.

(b) Also reviews legislation: Alabama—when requested by the governor. Alaska—after passage. Arizona—at the request of the legislature. Kansas—upon request of Legislator, no formal authority.

(c) The attorney general functions as the local prosecutor.

(d) To legislative leadership.

(e) Informally reviews bills or does so upon request.

(f) The attorney general prosecutes all criminal offenses in Delaware.

(g) Also at the request of agency or legislature.

(h) Bills, not ordinances.

(i) Review and track legislation that relates to the Office of Attorney General and the office mission.

(j) No requirements for review.

(k) To legislature as a whole, not individual legislators.

(l) Only when requested by governor or legislature.

(m) To either house of legislature, not individual legislators.

(n) Provides information when requested by the Legislature. Testifies for or against bills on the Attorney General's own initiative.

(o) May review legislation at request of clients or legislature.

(p) Certain statutes provide for concurrent jurisdiction with local prosecutors.

(q) Only when requested by legislature.

(r) Can be involved in local at request of local prosecutors. If requested by local authority, can participate in criminal prosecutions.

(s) The office of attorney general prosecutes local crimes to an extent. The office's Legal Counsel Division may issue legal advice to the office's prosecutorial arm. Otherwise, the office does not usually advise the OUSA, the district's other local prosecutor.

(t) The attorney general functions as the local prosecutor.

(u) Reviews enacted legislation only when there is a compelling need.

(v) May review legislation at any time but does not have a de jure role in approval of bills as to form or constitutionality; California has a separate Legislative Counsel to advise the legislature on bills.

## Table 4.22
## ATTORNEYS GENERAL: CONSUMER PROTECTION ACTIVITIES, SUBPOENA POWERS AND ANTITRUST DUTIES

| State or other jurisdiction | May commence civil proceedings | May commence criminal proceedings | Represents the state before regulatory agencies (a) | Administers consumer protection programs | Handles consumer complaints | Subpoena powers (b) | Antitrust duties |
|---|---|---|---|---|---|---|---|
| Alabama | ★ | ★ | ★ | ★ | ★ | ● | A,B,C |
| Alaska | ★ | ★ | ★ | ★ | ★ | ★ | A,B,C,D |
| Arizona | ★ | ... | ... | ★(c) | ★ | ★ | A,B,C,D |
| Arkansas | ★ | ... | ★ | ★ | ★ | ● | A,B |
| California | ★ | ★ | ★ | ★ | ★ | ★ | A,B,C,D |
| Colorado | ★ | ★ | ★ | ★ | ★ | ● | A,C,D |
| Connecticut | ★ | (d) | ★ | ★ | ★ | ● | A,B,D |
| Delaware | ★ | ★ | ★ | ★ | ★ | ★ | A,B,D |
| Florida | ★ | ... | ... | ★ | ★ | ★ | A,B,D |
| Georgia | ★ | ★ | ★ | ... | ... | ● | ... |
| Hawaii | ★ | ★ | ★ | ... | ★ | ★ | A,B,C,D |
| Idaho | ★ | ... | ★ | ★ | ★ | ● | A,B,D |
| Illinois | ★ | ... | ★ | ★ | ★ | ● | A,B,C |
| Indiana | ★ | ... | ★ | ★ | ★ | ★ | A,B |
| Iowa | ★ | ★ | ★ | ★ | ★ | ★ | B,C |
| Kansas | ★ | ★ | ★ | ★ | ★ | ★ | B,C,D |
| Kentucky | ★ | ★ | ★ | ★ | ★ | ★ | A,B,C,D |
| Louisiana | ★ | ★ | ★ | ★ | ★ | ★ | A,B,C |
| Maine | ★ | ★ | ★ | ★ | ★ | ★ | A,B,C |
| Maryland | ★ | ★(e) | ... | ★ | ★ | ★ | B,C,D |
| Massachusetts | ★ | ★ | ★ | ★ | ★ | ★ | A,B,C,D |
| Michigan | ★ | ★ | ★ | ★ | ★ | ★ | A,B,C,D |
| Minnesota | ★ | ... | ★ | ★ | ★ | ● | A,B,C |
| Mississippi | ★ | ★ | ... | ★ | ★ | ★ | A,B,C,D |
| Missouri | ★ | ★ | ★ | ★ | ★ | ★ | A,B,C,D |
| Montana | ★ | ★ | ... | ★ | ★ | ● | A,B |
| Nebraska | ★ | ★ | ★ | ★ | ★ | ★ | A,B,C,D |
| Nevada | ★ | ★ | ★ | ★ | ★ | ● | A,B,C,D |
| New Hampshire | ★ | ★ | ★ | ★ | ★ | ★ | A,B,C,D |
| New Jersey | ★ | ★ | ★ | ★ | ★ | ★ | A,B,C,D |
| New Mexico | ★ | ★ | ★ | ★ | ★ | ★ | A,B,C (g) |
| New York | ★ | ★ | ★ | ★ | ★ | ★ | A,B,C,D |
| North Carolina | ★ | ★(f) | ★ | ★ | ★ | ★ | A,B,C,D |
| North Dakota | ★ | ... | ★ | ★ | ★ | ★ | A,B,D |
| Ohio | ★ | ★ | ★ | ★ | ★ | ★ | A,B,C,D |
| Oklahoma | ★ | ★ | ★ | ★ | ★ | ★ | A,B,C,D |
| Oregon | ★ | ★(f) | ★ | ★ | ★ | ● | A,B,C,D |
| Pennsylvania | ★ | ★ | ★ | ★ | ★ | ● | A,B |
| Rhode Island | ★ | ★ | ... | ★ | ★ | ★ | A,B,C |
| South Carolina | ★(a) | ★(h) | ★ | ... | (i) | ● | A,B,C,D |
| South Dakota | ★ | ★ | ★ | ★ | ★ | ★ | A,B,C |
| Tennessee | ★ | (e)(f) | (f) | ★ | ... | ★ | B,C,D |
| Texas | ★ | ★ | ★ | ★ | ★ | ● | A,B,C,D |
| Utah | ★(j) | ★ | ★(j) | ... | ★(k) | ● | A (l),B,C,D (l) |
| Vermont | ★ | ★ | ★ | ★ | ★ | ★ | A,B,C |
| Virginia | ★ | (f) | ★ | ★(k) | ★(k) | ● | A,B,C,D |
| Washington | ★ | ... | ★ | ★ | ★ | ★ | A,B,D |
| West Virginia | ★ | ... | ★ | ★ | ★ | ★ | A,B,D |
| Wisconsin | ★ | ★ | ★ | ★ | ★ | ● | A,B,C (g) |
| Wyoming | ★ | ... | ★ | ★ | ★ | ● | A,B |
| Dist. of Columbia | ★ | ★(m) | ★ | ★ | ★ | ★ | A,B,C,D |
| American Samoa | ★ | ★ | ★ | ★ | ★ | ... | ... |
| Guam | ★ | ★ | ★ | ★ | ★ | ● | A,B,C,D |
| No. Mariana Islands | ★ | ★ | ★ | ★ | ★ | ★ | A,B |
| Puerto Rico | ★ | ★ | ... | ... | ... | ★ | A,B,C,D |
| U.S. Virgin Islands | ★ | ★ | ★ | ★ | ★ | ● | A |

See footnotes at end of table.

## ATTORNEYS GENERAL: CONSUMER PROTECTION ACTIVITIES, SUBPOENA POWERS AND ANTITRUST DUTIES — Continued

*Source:* The Council of State Governments' survey of attorneys general, March 2011.

*Key:*

A — Has parens patriae authority to commence suits on behalf of consumers in state antitrust damage actions in state courts.

B — May initiate damage actions on behalf of state in state courts.

C — May commence criminal proceedings.

D — May represent cities, counties and other governmental entities in recovering civil damages under federal or state law.

★ — Has authority in area.

... — Does not have authority in area.

(a) May represent state on behalf of: the "people" of the state; an agency of the state; or the state before a federal regulatory agency.

(b) In this column only: ★ broad powers and ● limited powers.

(c) The 49th Legislature, first regular session, established a statutory scheme that provided for a mortgage recovery fund to pay those harmed by dishonest loan originators. The attorney general is now authorized to try to recover from the dishonest loan originators the money that the fund paid out (See ARS 6-991.15).

(d) In certain cases only.

(e) May commence criminal proceedings with local district attorney.

(f) To a limited extent.

(g) May represent other governmental entities in recovering civil damages under federal or state law.

(h) When permitted to intervene.

(i) On a limited basis because the state has a separate consumer affairs department.

(j) Attorney general has exclusive authority.

(k) Attorney general handles legal matters only with no administrative handling of complaints.

(l) Opinion only, since there are no controlling precedents.

(m) In antitrust, not criminal proceedings.

## Table 4.23
## ATTORNEYS GENERAL: DUTIES TO ADMINISTRATIVE AGENCIES AND OTHER RESPONSIBILITIES

| State or other jurisdiction | Serves as counsel for state | Appears for state in criminal appeals | Issues official advice | Interprets statutes or regulations | Conducts litigation: On behalf of agency | Conducts litigation: Against agency | Prepares or reviews legal documents | Represents the public before the agency | Involved in rule-making | Reviews rules for legality |
|---|---|---|---|---|---|---|---|---|---|---|
| Alabama | A,B,C (a) | ★(a) | ★ | ★ | ★ | ★ | (b) | (b) | ★ | ★ |
| Alaska | A,B,C | ★ | ★ | ★ | ★ | ★ | ★ | ★ | ★ | ★ |
| Arizona | A,B,C | ★ | ★ | ★ | ★ | ★ | ★ | ... | ★ | ★ |
| Arkansas | A,B,C | ★ | ★ | ★ | ★ | ★ | ★ | ★ | ... | ... |
| California | A,B,C | ★ | ★ | ★ | ★ | ... | ★ | ... | ★ | ★ |
| Colorado | A,B,C | ★ | ★ | ★ | ★ | ★ | ★ | ★ | ★ | ★ |
| Connecticut | A,B,C | (b) | ★ | ★ | ★ | ★ | ★ | ★ | ★ | ★ |
| Delaware (f) | A,B,C | ★ | ★ | ★ | ★ | ★(g) | ★ | ★ | ★ | ★ |
| Florida | A,B,C | ★ | ★ | ★ | ★ | ... | ★ | ... | ... | ... |
| Georgia | A,B,C | ★ | ★ | ★ | ★ | ... | ★ | ... | ... | ★ |
| Hawaii | A,B,C | ★ | ★ | ★ | ★ | ★ | ★ | ★ | ★ | ★ |
| Idaho | A,B,C | ★(a) | ★ | ★ | ★ | ★ | ★ | ★ | ★ | ★ |
| Illinois | A,B,C | ★ | ... | ★ | ★ | ... | ★ | ... | ... | ... |
| Indiana | A,B,C | ★ | ★ | ★ | ★ | ... | ★ | ... | ★ | ★ |
| Iowa | A,B,C | ★ | ★ | ★ | ★ | ★ | ★ | ★ | ★ | ★ |
| Kansas | A,B,C | ★ | ★ | ★ | ★ | ★ | ★ | ... | ★ | ★ |
| Kentucky | A,B,C | ★ | ★ | ★ | ★ | ... | ... | ★ | ... | ... |
| Louisiana | A,B,C | ... | ★ | ★ | ★ | ... | ★ | ★ | ★ | ★ |
| Maine | A,B,C | ★ | ★ | ★ | ★ | ... | ★ | ... | ... | ... |
| Maryland | A,B,C | ★ | ★ | ★ | ★ | (b) | ★ | ★ | ★ | ★ |
| Massachusetts | A,B,C | (b)(c)(d) | ★ | ★ | ★ | ★ | ★ | ★ | ★ | ★ |
| Michigan | A,B,C | ★ | ★ | ★ | ★ | ★ | ★ | ★ | ★ | ★ |
| Minnesota | A,B,C | (c)(d) | ★ | ★ | (a) | ★ | ★ | ★ | ★ | ★ |
| Mississippi | A,B,C | ... | ★ | ★ | ★ | ... | ★ | ... | ... | ... |
| Missouri | A,B,C | ★ | ★ | ★ | ★ | ... | ★ | ★ | ★ | ★ |
| Montana (h) | A,B | ... | ★ | ★ | ★ | ... | ★ | ... | ... | ... |
| Nebraska | A,B,C | ★ | ★ | ★ | ★ | ★ | ★ | ... | ★ | ★ |
| Nevada | A,B,C | ★ | ★ | ★ | ★ | ... | ★ | ... | ★ | ★ |
| New Hampshire | A,B,C | ★ | ★ | ★ | ★ | ... | ★ | ★ | ★ | ... |
| New Jersey | A,B,C | ★ | ★ | ★ | ★ | ... | ★ | ... | ★ | ★ |
| New Mexico | A,B,C | ★ | ★ | ★ | ★ | ★ | ★ | ★ | ★ | ★ |
| New York | A,B,C | (b) | ... | ★ | ★ | (b) | ★ | (b) | ... | ... |
| North Carolina | A,B,C | ★ | ★ | ★ | ★ | ★ | ★ | (b) | ★ | ★ |
| North Dakota | A,B,C | ★ | ★ | ★ | ★ | ★ | ★ | ... | ★ | ★ |
| Ohio | A,B,C | ★ | ★ | ... | ★ | ... | ★ | ... | ... | ... |
| Oklahoma | A,B,C | ★ | ★ | ★ | ★ | ★ | ★ | ★ | ★ | ★ |
| Oregon | A,B | ★ | ★ | ★ | ★ | ... | ★ | ... | ★ | ★ |
| Pennsylvania | A,B | ... | ... | ... | ★ | ... | ★ | ... | ... | ★ |
| Rhode Island | A,B,C | ★ | ★ | ★ | ★ | ★ | ★ | ... | ... | ... |
| South Carolina | A,B,C | ★(d) | (a) | ★ | ★ | (b) | ★ | ... | ★ | ★ |
| South Dakota | A,B,C | ★ | ★ | ★ | ★ | ★ | ★ | ... | ... | ... |
| Tennessee | A,B,C | ★ | ★ | ★ | ★ | ... | ★ | (e) | (e) | ★ |
| Texas | A,B,C | ★(i) | ★ | ★ | ★ | ★ | ★ | ★ | ★ | ... |
| Utah | A,B,C | ★(a) | ★ | ★ | ★ | ★ | ★ | (b) | ★ | ★ |
| Vermont | A,B,C | ★ | ★ | ★ | ★ | ★ | ★ | ★ | ★ | ★ |
| Virginia | A,B,C | ★ | ★ | ★ | ★ | ★ | ★ | ★ | ★ | ★ |
| Washington | A,B,C | ★(k) | ★ | ★ | ★ | ★ | ★ | ★ | ★ | ★ |
| West Virginia | A,B,C | ★ | ★ | ★ | ★ | ★ | ★ | ... | (l) | (l) |
| Wisconsin | A,B,C | ★ | ★ | ★ | ★ | (b) | (b) | (b) | (b) | (b) |
| Wyoming | A,B,C | ★ | ★ | ★ | ★ | ★ | ★ | ... | ★ | ★ |
| Dist. of Columbia | A,B | ★(j) | ★ | ★ | ★ | ... | ★ | ... | ★ | ★ |
| American Samoa | A,B,C | ★(a) | ★ | ★ | ★ | ... | ★ | ... | ★ | ★ |
| Guam | A,B,C | ★ | ★ | ★ | (d) | ★ | ★ | (b) | ★ | ★ |
| No. Mariana Islands | A,B,C | ★ | ★ | ★ | ★ | ★ | ★ | ... | ★ | ★ |
| Puerto Rico | A,B,C | ★ | ★ | ★ | ★ | ... | ★ | ... | ★ | ★ |
| U.S. Virgin Islands | A,B | ★ | ★ | ★ | ★ | ★ | ★ | ★ | ... | ★ |

See footnotes at end of table.

## ATTORNEYS GENERAL: DUTIES TO ADMINISTRATIVE AGENCIES AND OTHER RESPONSIBILITIES — Continued

*Source:* The Council of State Governments' survey of attorneys general, March 2011.

*Key:*

A — Defend state law when challenged on federal constitutional grounds.

B — Conduct litigation on behalf of state in federal and other states' courts.

C — Prosecute actions against another state in U.S. Supreme Court.

★ — Has authority in area.

... — Does not have authority in area.

(a) Attorney general has exclusive jurisdiction.

(b) In certain cases only.

(c) When assisting local prosecutor in the appeal.

(d) Can appear on own discretion.

(e) Consumer Advocate Division represents the public in utility rate making hearings and rule making proceedings.

(f) Except as otherwise provided by statute, the Attorney General represents all state agencies and officials.

(g) Rarely.

(h) Most state agencies are represented by agency counsel who do not answer to the attorney general. The attorney general does provide representation for agencies in conflict situations and where the agency requires additional or specialized assistance.

(i) Primarily federal habeas corpus appeals only.

(j) However, OUSA handles felony cases and most major misdemeanors.

(k) Limited to federal death penalty habeas corpus.

(l) On request of agency. Office acts as legal counsel to any state agency on request and that can include reviewing legislation and drafting rules and regulations.

## Table 4.24
## THE TREASURERS, 2012

| State or other jurisdiction | Name and party | Method of selection | Length of regular term in years | Date of first service | Present term ends | Maximum consecutive terms allowed by constitution |
|---|---|---|---|---|---|---|
| Alabama .................... | Young Boozer (R) | E | 4 | 1/2011 | 1/2015 | 2 |
| Alaska (a)................... | Jerry Burnett | A | Governor's Discretion | 1/2009 | . . . | . . . |
| Arizona..................... | Doug Ducey (R) | E | 4 | 1/2011 | 1/2015 | 2 |
| Arkansas................... | Martha Shoffner (D) | E | 4 | 1/2007 | 1/2015 | 2 |
| California ................. | Bill Lockyer (D) | E | 4 | 1/2007 | 1/2015 | 2 |
| Colorado................... | Walker Stapleton (R) | E | 4 | 1/2011 | 1/2015 | 2 |
| Connecticut .............. | Denise L. Nappier (D) | E | 4 | 1/1999 | 1/2015 | ★ |
| Delaware ................. | Chip Flowers (D) | E | 4 | 1/2011 | 1/2015 | ★ |
| Florida (b) ............... | Jeff Atwater (R) | E | 4 | 1/2011 | 1/2015 | 2 |
| Georgia (c)................ | Thomas Hills | A | Pleasure of the Board | 9/2010 | . . . | . . . |
| Hawaii (d) ................ | Kalbert Young | A | Governor's Discretion | 12/2010 | . . . | . . . |
| Idaho........................ | Ron G. Crane (R) | E | 4 | 1/1999 | 1/2015 | ★ |
| Illinois...................... | Dan Rutherford (R) | E | 4 | 1/2011 | 1/2015 | ★ |
| Indiana..................... | Richard Mourdock (R) | E | 4 | 2/2007 | 2/2015 | (e) |
| Iowa ........................ | Michael L. Fitzgerald (D) Iowa | E | 4 | 1/1983 | 1/2015 | ★ |
| Kansas ..................... | Ron Estes (R) | E | 4 | 1/2011 | 1/2015 | ★ |
| Kentucky ................. | Todd Hollenbach (D) | E | 4 | 12/2007 | 12/2015 | 2 |
| Louisiana.................. | John N. Kennedy (R) | E | 4 | 1/2000 | 1/2016 | ★ |
| Maine....................... | Bruce Poliquin | L | 2 | 1/2011 | 1/2013 | 4 |
| Maryland ................. | Nancy K. Kopp (D) | L | 4 | 2/2002 | 2/2015 | ★ |
| Massachusetts .......... | Steve Grossman (D) | E | 4 | 1/2011 | 1/2015 | ★ |
| Michigan................... | Andy Dillon (D) (f) | A | Governor's Discretion | 1/2011 | . . . | . . . |
| Minnesota (g)........... | James Schowalter | A | Governor's Discretion | 1/2011 | . . . | . . . |
| Mississippi ............... | Lynn Fitch (R) | E | 4 | 1/2012 | 1/2016 | ★ |
| Missouri................... | Clint Zweifel (D) | E | 4 | 1/2009 | 1/2013 | 2 |
| Montana ................... | Janet Kelly | A | Governor's Discretion | 1/2005 | . . . | . . . |
| Nebraska .................. | Don Stenberg (R) | E | 4 | 1/2011 | 1/2015 | 2 |
| Nevada...................... | Kate Marshall (D) | E | 4 | 1/2007 | 1/2015 | 2 |
| New Hampshire ........ | Catherine Provencher | L | 2 | 1/2007 | 12/2012 | ★ |
| New Jersey ............... | Andrew P. Sidamon-Eristoff | A | Governor's Discretion | 2/2010 | . . . | . . . |
| New Mexico ............. | James B. Lewis (D) | E | 4 | 1/2007 | 1/2015 | 2 |
| New York.................. | Aida Brewer | A | Governor's Discretion | 2/2002 | . . . | . . . |
| North Carolina.......... | Janet Cowell (D) | E | 4 | 1/2009 | 1/2013 | ★ |
| North Dakota............ | Kelly L. Schmidt (R) | E | 4 | 1/2005 | 1/2013 | ★ |
| Ohio ........................ | Josh Mandel (R) | E | 4 | 1/2011 | 1/2015 | 2 |
| Oklahoma................. | Ken Miller (R) | E | 4 | 1/2011 | 1/2015 | ★ |
| Oregon..................... | Ted Wheeler (D) (h) | E | 4 | 3/2010 | 1/2015 | 2 |
| Pennsylvania............. | Robert McCord (D) | E | 4 | 1/2009 | 1/2013 | 2 |
| Rhode Island............. | Gina Raimondo (D) | E | 4 | 1/2011 | 1/2015 | 2 |
| South Carolina.......... | Curtis Loftis (R) | E | 4 | 1/2011 | 1/2015 | ★ |
| South Dakota ............ | Richard Sattgast (R) | E | 4 | 1/2011 | 1/2015 | 2 |
| Tennessee ................. | David H. Lillard Jr. | L | 2 | 1/2009 | 1/2013 | . . . |
| Texas (i)................... | Susan Combs (R) | E | 4 | 1/2007 | 1/2015 | ★ |
| Utah......................... | Richard K. Ellis (R) | E | 4 | 1/2009 | 1/2013 | ★ |
| Vermont.................... | Elizabeth Pearce (D) | E | 2 | 1/2011 | 1/2015 | ★ |
| Virginia.................... | Manju Ganeriwala | A | Governor's Discretion | 1/2009 | . . . | . . . |
| Washington............... | James L. McIntire (D) | E | 4 | 1/2009 | 1/2013 | ★ |
| West Virginia............ | John D. Perdue (D) | E | 4 | 1/1997 | 1/2013 | ★ |
| Wisconsin................. | Kurt Schuller (R) | E | 4 | 1/2011 | 1/2015 | ★ |
| Wyoming .................. | Joseph B. Meyer (R) | E | 4 | 1/2007 | 1/2015 | 2 |
| American Samoa ...... | Magalei Logovi'i | A | 4 | 1/2009 | . . . | . . . |
| Dist. of Columbia ..... | Lasana Mack | A | Pleasure of CFO | 8/2005 | N.A. | . . . |
| Guam ....................... | Rose T. Fejeran | CS | . . . | N.A. | . . . | . . . |
| No. Mariana Islands... | Antoinette S. Calvo | A | 4 | N.A. | N.A. | . . . |
| Puerto Rico.............. | Jesús F. Méndez Rodríguez | A | 4 | 1/2011 | N.A. | . . . |
| U.S. Virgin Islands .... | Laurel Payne | A | 4 | 2007 | N.A. | . . . |

*Sources:* National Association of State Treasurers and The Council of State Governments, April 2012.

*Key:*

★ — No provision specifying number of terms allowed.

. . . . — No formal provision, position is appointed or elected by governmental entity (not chosen by the electorate).

A — Appointed by the governor. (In the District of Columbia, the Treasurer is appointed by the Chief Financial Officer. In Georgia, position is appointed by the State Depository Board.)

E — Elected by the voters.

L — Elected by the legislature.

CS — Civil Service.

N.A. — Not available.

(a) The Deputy Commissioner of Department of Revenue performs this function.

(b) The official title of the office of state treasurer is Chief Financial Officer.

(c) The title is Director of the Office of Treasury and Fiscal Services.

(d) The Director of Finance performs this function.

(e) Eligible for eight out of any period of twelve years.

(f) Andy Dillon, former Speaker of the House of Representatives and a Democrat, was appointed by Governor Rick Snyder, a Republican.

(g) The Commissioner of Management and Budget performs this function.

(h) Wheeler was appointed as State Treasurer in March 2010 and had served as an interim designee. He was elected by Oregon voters in November 2010 to a full 4-year term.

(i) The Comptroller of Public Accounts performs this function.

**Table 4.25**
## TREASURERS: QUALIFICATIONS FOR OFFICE

| State or other jurisdiction | Minimum age | U.S. citizen (years) | State resident (years) | Qualified voter (years) |
|---|---|---|---|---|
| Alabama | 25 | 7 | 5 | ... |
| Alaska | ... | ... | ★ | ... |
| Arizona | 25 | 10 | 5 | ... |
| Arkansas | 21 | ★ | ★ | ... |
| California | 18 | ★ | ★ | ★ |
| Colorado | 25 | ★ | ★ | ★ |
| Connecticut | ... | ★ | ★ | ★ |
| Delaware | 18 | ★ | ★ | ★ |
| Florida | 30 | ★ | 7 | ★ |
| Georgia | ... | ... | ... | ... |
| Hawaii | ... | ★ | 5 | ... |
| Idaho | 25 | ★ | 2 | ... |
| Illinois | 25 | ★ | ★ | ... |
| Indiana | ... | ★ | ★ | ★ |
| Iowa | 18 | ... | ... | ... |
| Kansas | ... | ... | ... | ... |
| Kentucky | 30 | ★ | 6 | ★ |
| Louisiana | 25 | 5 | (a) | ★ |
| Maine | ... | ★ | ★ | ... |
| Maryland | ... | ... | ... | ... |
| Massachusetts | ... | ... | ★ | ... |
| Michigan | ... | ... | ... | ... |
| Minnesota | ... | ... | ... | ... |
| Mississippi | 25 | ★ | 5 | ★ |
| Missouri | ... | ★ | 5 | ★ |
| Montana | ... | ... | ... | ... |
| Nebraska | 19 | ★ | ★ | ★ |
| Nevada | 25 | ★ | ★ | ★ |
| New Hampshire | ... | ... | ... | ... |
| New Jersey | ... | ... | ★ | ... |
| New Mexico | 30 | ★ | ★ | ★ |
| New York | ... | ★ | ★ | N.A. |
| North Carolina | 21 | ★ | 1 | ★ |
| North Dakota | 25 | ★ | 5 | ★ |
| Ohio | 18 | ★ | ★ | ★ |
| Oklahoma | 31 | ★ | (b) | (c) |
| Oregon | 18 | ... | ★ | ... |
| Pennsylvania | ... | ... | ... | ... |
| Rhode Island | 18 | ★ | ★ | ★ |
| South Carolina | ... | ★ | ★ | ★ |
| South Dakota | ... | ... | ... | ... |
| Tennessee | ... | ... | ... | ... |
| Texas | 18 | ★ | ★ | ... |
| Utah | 25 | ★ | 5 | ★ |
| Vermont | ... | ★ | 2 | ... |
| Virginia | ... | ... | ... | ... |
| Washington | 18 | ★ | ... | ★ |
| West Virginia | 18 | 5 | 5 | ★ |
| Wisconsin | 18 | ★ | ★ | ★ |
| Wyoming | 25 | ★ | 1 | ★ |
| Dist. of Columbia | ... | ... | ... | ... |

*Source:* National Association of State Treasurers, March 2008 updated August 2011.

*Key:*
★ — Formal provision; number of years not specified.
... — No formal provision.
N.A. — Not applicable.

(a) Five years immediately preceding the date of qualification for office.
(b) For at least 10 years immediately preceding.
(c) Must be able to vote for at least 10 years immediately preceding election.

# Table 4.26
# RESPONSIBILITIES OF THE TREASURER'S OFFICE

| State or other jurisdiction | Cash management | Investment of retirement funds | Investment of trust funds | Deferred compensation | Management of bonded debt | Bond issuance | Debt service | Arbitrage rebate | Banking services | Unclaimed property | Archives for disbursement of documents | College savings | Collateral programs | Local government investment pool | Other |
|---|---|---|---|---|---|---|---|---|---|---|---|---|---|---|---|
| Alabama | ★ | ... | ... | ... | ★ | ... | ★ | ... | ★ | ★ | ... | ★ | ★ | ... | ... |
| Alaska | ★ | ★ | ★ | ... | ★ | ★ | ★ | ★ | ★ | ★ | ★ | ... | ... | ... | (a) |
| Arizona | ★ | ... | ★ | ... | ... | ... | ... | ★ | ★ | ... | ... | ... | ... | ★ | ... |
| Arkansas | ★ | ... | ★ | ... | ... | ... | ... | ... | ★ | ... | ... | ... | ... | ★ | ... |
| California | ★ | ... | ★ | ... | ★ | ★ | ★ | ★ | ★ | ... | ... | ... | ★ | ★ | ... |
| Colorado | ★ | ... | ... | ... | ... | ★ | ... | ... | ★ | ★ | ... | ... | ★ | ... | ... |
| Connecticut | ★ | ★ | ★ | ... | ★ | ★ | ★ | ★ | ★ | ★ | ... | ★ | ... | ★ | (b) |
| Delaware | ★ | ... | ... | ★ | ... | ★ | ★ | ★ | ★ | ... | ... | ★ | ★ | ★ | (c) |
| Florida | ★ | ... | ★ | ★ | ... | ... | ★ | ... | ★ | ★ | ... | ★ | ★ | ... | (d) |
| Georgia | ★ | ... | ... | ... | ... | ... | ★ | ... | ★ | ... | ... | ★ | ★ | ★ | ... |
| Hawaii | ★ | ★ | ... | ... | ★ | ★ | ★ | ★ | ... | ★ | ... | ★ | ★ | ... | ... |
| Idaho | ★ | ... | ... | ... | ... | ... | ... | ★ | ★ | ... | ... | ★ | ... | ★ | ... |
| Illinois | ★ | ... | ★ | ... | ... | ... | ★ | ★ | ★ | ★ | ... | ★ | ... | ★ | ... |
| Indiana | ★ | ... | ★ | ... | ★ | ... | ... | ★ | ★ | ... | ★ | ★ | ... | ★ | ... |
| Iowa | ★ | ★ | ... | ... | ★ | ... | ★ | ★ | ★ | ★ | ... | ★ | ★ | ... | ... |
| Kansas | ★ | ... | ... | ... | ... | ... | ... | ★ | ★ | ... | ... | ★ | ... | ... | (e) |
| Kentucky | ★ | ... | ... | ... | ... | ... | ... | ★ | ★ | ★ | ... | ★ | ... | ... | ... |
| Louisiana | ★ | ... | ★ | ... | ★ | ★ | ★ | ★ | ★ | ... | ... | ... | ★ | ... | (f) |
| Maine | ★ | ... | ★ | ... | ★ | ★ | ★ | ★ | ★ | ★ | ... | ... | ... | ... | (g) |
| Maryland | ★ | ... | ... | ... | ... | ★ | ★ | ... | ★ | ... | ... | ★ | ★ | ... | ... |
| Massachusetts | ★ | ★ | ★ | ★ | ★ | ★ | ★ | ★ | ★ | ★ | ... | ... | ★ | ★ | (h) |
| Michigan | ★ | ★ | ★ | ★ | ★ | ★ | ★ | ★ | ★ | ... | ★ | ... | ... | ... | ... |
| Minnesota | ★ | ... | ... | ... | ★ | ★ | ★ | ★ | ★ | ★ | ... | ★ | ... | ... | ... |
| Mississippi | ★ | ★ | ★ | ... | ★ | ★ | ★ | ★ | ★ | ... | ... | ★ | ★ | ... | ... |
| Missouri | ★ | ... | ★ | ... | ... | ... | ★ | ... | ★ | ★ | ... | ★ | ... | ... | (i) |
| Montana | ★ | ... | ... | ... | ★ | ★ | ★ | ★ | ★ | ... | ... | ... | ... | ... | ... |
| Nebraska | ★ | ... | ... | ... | ... | ... | ... | ★ | ★ | ... | ★ | ... | ... | ... | (j) |
| Nevada | ★ | ... | ★ | ... | ★ | ★ | ★ | ... | ★ | ★ | ... | ★ | ★ | ★ | ... |
| New Hampshire | ★ | ... | ★ | ... | ★ | ★ | ★ | ★ | ★ | ... | ★ | ... | ... | ... | ... |
| New Jersey | ★ | ★ | ... | ★ | ★ | ★ | ★ | ... | ★ | ★ | ... | ... | ★ | ... | ... |
| New Mexico | ★ | ... | ... | ... | ★ | ... | ... | ... | ★ | ★ | ... | ... | ★ | ... | ... |
| New York | ★ | ... | ... | ... | ... | ★ | ★ | ... | ★ | ★ | ... | ★ | ... | ... | (k) |
| North Carolina | ★ | ★ | ★ | ... | ★ | ★ | ★ | ★ | ★ | ... | ★ | ... | ★ | ... | ... |
| North Dakota | ★ | ... | ★ | ... | ... | ... | ... | ... | ★ | ... | ... | ... | ... | ... | ... |
| Ohio | ★ | ... | ★ | ... | ★ | ★ | ★ | ... | ★ | ★ | ... | ... | ★ | ... | ... |
| Oklahoma | ★ | ... | ★ | ... | ... | ★ | ... | ★ | ★ | ★ | ... | ★ | ★ | ... | ... |
| Oregon | ★ | ★ | ★ | ★ | ★ | ★ | ★ | ★ | ★ | ... | ★ | ★ | ★ | ★ | (l) |
| Pennsylvania | ★ | ★ | ★ | ... | ... | ★ | ★ | ★ | ★ | ... | ★ | ... | ★ | ... | ... |
| Rhode Island | ★ | ★ | ... | ... | ... | ★ | ★ | ★ | ... | ★ | ★ | ... | ... | ... | ... |
| South Carolina | ★ | ★ | ★ | ★ | ★ | ★ | ★ | ★ | ★ | ... | ★ | ★ | ★ | ★ | ... |
| South Dakota | ★ | ★ | ★ | ... | ... | ... | ... | ★ | ★ | ... | ... | ★ | ... | ... | (m) |
| Tennessee | ★ | ★ | ... | ★ | ... | ... | ... | ★ | ★ | ... | ... | ★ | ... | ... | ... |
| Texas | ★ | ... | ... | ... | ★ | ... | ... | ★ | ★ | ... | ★ | ★ | ★ | ★ | (n) |
| Utah | ★ | ... | ★ | ... | ★ | ★ | ★ | ★ | ★ | ... | ... | ... | ★ | ... | ... |
| Vermont | ★ | ★ | ★ | ★ | ★ | ★ | ★ | ★ | ★ | ... | ★ | ... | ... | ... | ... |
| Virginia | ★ | ... | ★ | ... | ★ | ★ | ★ | ★ | ★ | ★ | ... | ... | ★ | ... | (o) |
| Washington | ★ | ... | ★ | ... | ★ | ★ | ★ | ★ | ★ | ... | ... | ... | ★ | ... | ... |
| West Virginia | ★ | ... | ... | ... | ... | ★ | ... | ★ | ★ | ... | ★ | ★ | ... | ... | ... |
| Wisconsin | ... | ... | ... | ... | ... | ... | ... | ... | ★ | ... | ★ | ★ | ... | ... | ... |
| Wyoming | ★ | ... | ★ | ... | ★ | ★ | ★ | ★ | ★ | ★ | ... | ★ | ★ | ★ | ... |
| Dist. of Columbia | ★ | ★ | ★ | ★ | ★ | ★ | ★ | ★ | ★ | ★ | ... | ★ | ★ | ... | ... |

*Source:* The National Association of State Treasurers, March 2008.
*Key:*
★ — Responsible for activity.
... — Not responsible for activity.
(a) Revenue collection including oil and gas royalties and corporate income taxes; child support enforcement; permanent fund dividend eligibility.
(b) Second Injury Fund.
(c) General Fund account reconcilement; disbursements.
(d) State Accounting Disbursement, Fire Marshall, Insurance and Banking Consumer Services, Insurance Rehabilitation and Liquidation, Risk Management, Workers Compensation, Insurance Fraud, Insurance Agent and Agency Services.

(e) Municipal bond servicing.
(f) Social Security for Section 218 Agreements.
(g) Municipal Revenue Sharing.
(h) Massachusetts Municipal Depository Trust Funds for Cities and Towns.
(i) Investment of all state funds.
(j) Nebraska Child Support Payment Center.
(k) Linked Deposit Program.
(l) Legislation pending to move Unclaimed Property program to Treasurer's office.
(m) Treasurer is a member of the trust and retirement investment programs.
(n) Tax Administration/Collection.
(o) Risk Management.

# Transparency: It's Here to Stay

### By R. Kinney Poynter

*It could be argued that government is more transparent today than at any point in our country's history. From the example set by the American Recovery and Reinvestment Act, state financial managers have worked to implement legislation envisioning ever greater access by citizens to government spending data. Transparency websites were first a trend for just a few states; they are now the norm. With each passing legislative session, the federal government hones its focus—and its mandates—on the concept of transparency. But how much is too much? At what point on the spectrum does the risk inherent in sharing so much financial data outweigh the potential benefits? These are not easy questions to answer. Regardless, it looks like transparency is here to stay.*

## When Did Transparency Become Such a Big Deal, Anyway?

Lawmakers and citizens have long invoked the term transparency. Politicians seek to allay the fears of a suspicious public through assurances of accountability and transparency. Citizens cry for more transparency in the never-ending quest to hold elected and appointed leaders accountable for the management—and sometimes mismanagement—of the nation's affairs. In the past few years, however, technology and a lot of hard work have enabled extraordinary new levels of government transparency.

In the fall of 2008, the American economy suffered a blow the likes of which most in today's workforce have never experienced, and may never again, in their lifetimes. Lawmakers went into action to find ways to avert disaster; enter the American Recovery and Reinvestment Act of 2009. The act, which President Obama signed into law on Feb. 17, 2009, ultimately provided a whopping $862 billion to boost the American economy, with $280 billion going directly to the states. The Recovery Act injected an unprecedented amount of stimulus money into the economy and called for an unprecedented amount of transparency and accountability to support the expenditure of these enormous sums. The act also came with unprecedented expectations from Congress and citizens.

The Recovery Act did several new things. It established a Recovery Accountability and Transparency Board to facilitate transparency of the spending and to prevent and detect waste, fraud and abuse. It required state governors to certify that certain Recovery Act funds received and spent in their states were being used appropriately. The act also required quarterly reporting from grant recipients and the creation of a searchable online database, providing the public with never before experienced levels of access to government spending data.

Creating the new processes to enable quarterly reporting and support the searchable database was a daunting task. Initially, states were experiencing their worst economic and workforce situations since the Great Depression, and the timeframe to realize the reporting visions outlined in the Recovery Act were quite aggressive. Ultimately, representatives from all levels of government were able to come together to meet the challenge and establish a system to fulfill the requirements of the law. Quarterly reporting on Recovery Act funds came to pass beginning with the quarter ending Sept. 30, 2009, only seven months after the passage of the act—quite a feat considering the extraordinary amount of coordination required between federal, state and local governments, as well as other grant recipients. For the first time, states were reporting grant expenditures online, and government finance officials had pulled together to accomplish a task that many thought impossible.

## From Recovery to Accountability

President George W. Bush signed the Federal Financial Accountability and Transparency Act into law in 2006. The act required that information on federal awards be made available online. Although federal agencies had reported prime recipient information since Jan. 1, 2008, the requirement for sub-recipient information to be posted by Jan. 1, 2009, was never enforced. With the successes of the Recovery Act, fulfilling the aims of the Transparency Act again became a focus.

Building on the achievements of and lessons learned from implementing the Recovery Act, the U.S. Office of Management and Budget issued guidance in April and again in August 2010 on implementing the sub-recipient piece of the Federal Financial Accountability and Transparency Act. The act required reporting similar to that required by the Recovery Act, except that it applied to sub-grants and sub-contracts for first tier sub-awards, not grant expenditures. Also, unlike the Recovery Act, reporting responsibilities could not be delegated to sub-recipients. The Federal Financial Accountability and Transparency Act sub-recipient reporting began on Oct. 1, 2010.

## From Accountability to Transparency … and Beyond

In June 2011, House Resolution 2146, the Digital Accountability and Transparency Act was introduced by California Rep. Darrell Issa in an attempt to build on the successes of the Recovery Act. The Transparency Act essentially would continue the oversight established by the Recovery Act through the Recovery Accountability and Transparency Board and would require at least quarterly reporting of expenditure data for all grants and contracts. A companion measure has been introduced in the Senate.

The Transparency Act seeks to further several major pro-transparency reforms, including:

- Establishing a universal standard of recipient reporting of funds received from the federal government directly to an independent database.

- Collecting all agency expenditure data and combining it with data reported by recipients.

- Creating a Federal Accountability and Spending Transparency Board.

The implications of the Transparency Act will be huge for states. By some estimates, Recovery Act reporting only applied to about 50 percent of state funds; the Transparency Act would essentially require quarterly reporting of all funds. The number of state agencies and programs that will be required to report would increase drastically.

As deliberations on the Transparency Act occurred, President Obama issued an Executive Order to establish a Government Accountability and Transparency Board. This board will build on the lessons learned by the Recovery Accountability and Transparency Board and is charged with making recommendations aimed at enhancing transparency of federal spending and further advancing efforts to detect and remediate fraud, waste and abuse.

It is not yet certain if or when the Transparency Act will be signed into law or how it might be reconciled with the executive order creating the Government Accountability and Transparency Board. However, several associations representing state government financial managers are working together to secure amendments to the legislation to include some type of funding for state and local governments and state and local representation on the Federal Accountability and Spending Transparency Board.

## Other Federal Efforts

The creation of the Government Accountability and Transparency Board underscored the financial assistance community's need for an institutionalized, formal body to provide general coordination over federal grants and cooperative agreements. To address this gap, the U.S. Office of Management and Budget, on Oct. 27, 2011, created the Council on Financial Assistance Reform. In addition to representing the interests and perspectives of the financial assistance community, the council was tasked with identifying how to make it easier for recipients to learn about and apply for assistance, as well as to understand what benefits they, and the country as a whole, have received as a result.

## Build It and They Will Come

As these various transparency initiatives have evolved at the federal level, states have been making their own strides toward greater transparency. Prior to 2008, only a few states had pioneered websites providing expenditure data. Once the transparency train started rolling, however, it picked up steam quickly. Today, at least 40 states have websites that provide checkbook-level expenditure data, with some of them providing options to search by contractor, by activity or by other characteristics to provide the public with very specific, targeted information.

Each state's site is different, as the efforts have transpired in different ways. Some states mandated transparency websites by legislation. In other states, officials anticipated the trend and moved preemptively to establish a means of providing more transparency. Some websites were created using existing staff and in-house databases, while others were developed with assistance from contractors who developed huge statewide data warehouses to feed the searches. Whatever their form, state transparency initiatives have arrived.

Of course the existence of state expenditure data does not ensure that it will be used wisely, used correctly or even used at all. And, as several states have learned—the hard way—some will use the data to commit fraud.

As stewards of public resources, governmental financial managers understand the importance of transparency and accountability. Some, however, question the actual value of providing expenditure data on searchable websites, arguing that transparency sites are merely duplicating information that was already available to the public through other means. States are expending enormous sums to develop and maintain these sites at a time when they are under brutal economic stress. Leaders from California, for instance, recently decided to close their transparency portal. They affirmed their commitment to "keeping state government open and transparent while eliminating inefficiencies and unnecessary costs." A visit to the state's transparency website now presents visitors with a message directing them to several decentralized sources of existing information and data on government programs and spending.

Beyond costing states dollars and time, transparency websites also have presented interesting questions about privacy and security. What information should be excluded on state sites to protect the interests of citizens in their personal lives? Who is to be held accountable when information, available through transparency websites to anyone who cares to search for it, is used to commit costly crimes against state governments or even against individuals?

## A Buzzword No More

No matter what one thinks of the various initiatives aimed at providing clearer views of government spending, the public is demanding more accountability from its governments. Transparency is here to stay. The task for government financial managers now is to examine the various opportunities and work together to reach solutions to provide transparency in the most efficient, effective manner possible—all the while protecting privacy and security. No easy task, but as the old adage goes, "if it was easy, it would have been done a long time ago."

## About the Author

**R. Kinney Poynter** is the executive director of the National Association of State Auditors, Comptrollers and Treasurers.

**Table 4.27**
**THE STATE AUDITORS, 2012**

| State or other jurisdiction | State agency | Agency head | Title | Legal basis for office | Method of selection | Term of office | U.S. citizen | State resident | Maximum consecutive terms allowed |
|---|---|---|---|---|---|---|---|---|---|
| Alabama | Office of the Examiner of Public Accounts | Ronald L. Jones | Chief Examiner | S | LC | 7 yrs. | ★ | ... | None |
| Alaska | Division of Legislative Audit | Kris Curtis | Legislative Auditor | C,S | L | (a) | ... | ... | None |
| Arizona | Office of the Auditor General | Debra K. Davenport | Auditor General | S | LC | 5 yrs. | ... | ... | None |
| Arkansas | Division of Legislative Audit | Roger A. Norman | Legislative Auditor | S | LC | Indefinite | ★ | ★ | None |
| California | Bureau of State Audits | Elaine Howle | State Auditor | S | G | 4 yrs. | ★ | ... | None |
| Colorado | Office of the State Auditor | Dianne E. Ray | Colorado State Auditor | C,S | LC | 5 yrs. | ★ | ★ | None |
| Connecticut | Office of the Auditors of Public Accounts | John C. Geragosian and Robert M. Ward | State Auditors | C | L | 4 yrs. | ... | ... | None |
| Delaware | Office of the Auditor of Accounts | R. Thomas Wagner, Jr. | Auditor of Accounts | C | E | 4 yrs. | ★ | ★ | None |
| Florida | Office of the Auditor General | David W. Martin | Auditor General | C,S | L | (a) | ... | ... | None |
| Georgia | Department of Audits and Accounts | Russell W. Hinton | State Auditor | S | L | Indefinite | ... | ... | None |
| Hawaii | Office of the Auditor | Marion M. Higa | State Auditor | C | L | 8 yrs. | ... | ★ | None |
| Idaho | Legislative Services Office—Legislative Audits | April J. Renfro | Division Manager | S | LC | (b) | ... | ... | None |
| Illinois | Office of the Auditor General | William G. Holland | Auditor General | C,S | L | 10 yrs. | ... | ... | None |
| Indiana | State Board of Accounts | Bruce Hartman | State Examiner | S | G | 4 yrs. | ... | ... | None |
| Iowa | Office of the Auditor of State | David A. Vaudt | Auditor of State | C,S | E | 4 yrs. | ★ | ★ | None |
| Kansas | Legislative Division of Post Audit | Scott E. Frank | Legislative Post Auditor | S | LC | (b) | ... | ... | 2 |
| Kentucky | Office of the Auditor of Public Accounts | Adam Edelen | Auditor of Public Accounts | C,S | E | 4 yrs. | ★ | ★ | 2 |
| Louisiana | Office of the Legislative Auditor | Daryl G. Purpera | Temporary Legislative Auditor | S | L | (a) | ... | ... | None |
| Maine | Department of Audit | Neria R. Douglass | State Auditor | S | L | 4 | ... | ... | 2 |
| Maryland | Office of Legislative Audits | Bruce A. Myers | Legislative Auditor | S | ED | (a) | ... | ★ | None |
| Massachusetts | Office of the Auditor of the Commonwealth | Suzanne Bump | Auditor of the Commonwealth | C,S | E | 4 yrs. | ★ | ★ | None |
| Michigan | Office of the Auditor General | Thomas H. McTavish | Auditor General | C | L | 8 yrs. | ... | ★ | None |
| Minnesota | Office of the Legislative Auditor | James R. Nobles | Legislative Auditor | S | L | 6 yrs. | ★ | ★ | None |
| | Office of the State Auditor | Rebecca Otto | State Auditor | C | E | 4 yrs. | ★ | ★ | None |
| Mississippi | Office of the State Auditor | Stacey E. Pickering | State Auditor | C | E | 4 yrs. | ★ | ★ | None |
| Missouri | Office of the State Auditor | Thomas A. Schweich | State Auditor | C,S | E | 4 yrs. | ★ | ★ | None |
| Montana | Legislative Audit Division | Tori Hunthausen | Legislative Auditor | C,S | LC | 2 yrs. | ★ | ★ | None |
| Nebraska | Office of the Auditor of Public Accounts | Mike Foley | Auditor of Public Accounts | C | E | 4 yrs. | ★ | ★ | None |
| Nevada | Legislative Counsel Bureau, Audit Division | Paul Townsend | Legislative Auditor | S | LC | Indefinite | ... | ★ | None |
| New Hampshire | Legislative Budget Office | Jeffry Pattison | Legislative Budget Assistant | S | LC | 2 yrs. | ... | ... | None |
| New Jersey | Office of the State Auditor | Stephen Eells | State Auditor | C,S | L | 5 yr. term and until successor is appointed | ... | ★ | None |
| | Office of the State Comptroller | Matthew Boxer | State Comptroller | C | G | 6 yrs. | ... | ... | 2 |
| New Mexico | Office of the State Auditor | Hector H. Balderas | State Auditor | C,S | E | 4 yrs. | ★ | ★ | 2 |
| New York | Office of the State Comptroller, State Audit Bureau | Thomas P. DiNapoli | State Comptroller | C,S | E | 4 yrs. | ★ | ★ | None |
| North Carolina | Office of the State Auditor | Beth A. Wood | State Auditor | C | E | 4 yrs. | ★ | ★ | None |
| North Dakota | Office of the State Auditor | Robert R. Peterson | State Auditor | C,S | E | 4 yrs. | ★ | ★ | None |
| Ohio | Office of the Auditor of State | Dave Yost | Auditor of State | C,S | E | 4 yrs. | ★ | ... | 2 |

See footnotes at end of table.

# THE STATE AUDITORS, 2012 — Continued

| State or other jurisdiction | State agency | Agency head | Title | Legal basis for office | Method of selection | Term of office | U.S. citizen | State resident | Maximum consecutive terms allowed |
|---|---|---|---|---|---|---|---|---|---|
| Oklahoma | Office of the State Auditor and Inspector | Gary Jones | State Auditor and Inspector | C, S | E | 4 yrs. | ★ | ★ | None |
| Oregon | Secretary of State, Audits Division | Gary Blackmer | Director | C | SS | (c) | … | … | None |
| Pennsylvania | Department of the Auditor General | Jack Wagner | Auditor General | C, S | E | 4 yrs. | … | … | 2 |
| | Legislative Finance and Budget Cmte. | Philip R. Durgin | Executive Director | S | LC | (b) | … | … | None |
| Rhode Island | Office of the Auditor General | Dennis E. Hoyle | Acting Auditor General | S | LC | (b) | … | … | None |
| South Carolina | Legislative Audit Council | Perry K. Simpson | Director | S | LC | 4 yrs. | … | … | None |
| | Office of the State Auditor | Richard H. Gilbert, Jr. | Interim State Auditor | S | SB | Indefinite | … | … | None |
| South Dakota | Department of Legislative Audit | Martin L. Guindon | Auditor General | S | L | 8 yrs. | … | … | None |
| Tennessee | Comptroller of the Treasury, Dept. of Audit | Justin P. Wilson | Comptroller of the Treasury | C, S | L | 2 yrs. | … | … | None |
| Texas | Office of the State Auditor | John Keel | State Auditor | S | LC | (b) | ★ | … | None |
| Utah | Office of the State Auditor | Auston G. Johnson | State Auditor | C, S | E | 4 yrs. | ★ | ★ | None |
| Vermont | Office of the State Auditor | Thomas M. Salmon | State Auditor | C | E | 2 yrs. | … | ★ | None |
| Virginia | Office of the Auditor of Public Accounts | Walter J. Kucharski | Auditor of Public Accounts | C, S | L | 4 yrs. | … | … | None |
| Washington | Office of the State Auditor | Brian Sonntag | State Auditor | C, S | E | 4 yrs. | ★ | ★ | None |
| West Virginia | Office of the Legislative Auditor | Aaron Allred | Legislative Auditor | S | LC | (b) | … | ★ | None |
| Wisconsin | Legislative Audit Bureau | Joe Chrisman | State Auditor | S | GC | 6 yrs. | … | … | None |
| Wyoming | Department of Audit | Jeffrey C. Vogel | Director | S | E | 4 yrs. | … | … | None |
| Dist. Of Columbia | Office of the D.C. Auditor | Yolanda Branche | District of Columbia Auditor | S | | | … | … | |
| American Samoa | AS Territorial Auditor Office | Robert P. Dantini | Territorial Auditor | S | | | … | … | |
| Guam | Office of the Public Auditor | Doris Flores Brooks | Public Auditor | C, S | E | 4 yrs. | ★ | ★ | None |
| No. Mariana Islands | Office of the Public Auditor | Michael Pai | Public Auditor | C, S | GL | 6 yrs. | N.A. | N.A. | 2 |
| Puerto Rico | Office of the Comptroller of Puerto Rico | Yesmin M. Valdivieso-Galib | Comptroller of Puerto Rico | C | GL | 10 yrs. | ★ | ★ | 1 |

*Sources: Auditing in the States: A Summary,* 2009 edition, The National Association of State Auditors, Comptrollers and Treasurers and state websites, April 2012.

Key:
★ — Provision for.
… — No provision for.
E — Elected by the public.
G — Appointed by the governor.
L — Appointed by the legislature.
SS — Appointed by the secretary of state.
LC — Selected by legislative committee, commission or council.
ED — Appointed by the executive director of legislative services.
GC — Appointed by governor, secretary of state and treasurer.
GL — Appointed by the governor and confirmed by both chambers of the legislature.
SB — Appointed by state budget and control board.
C — Constitutional
S — Statutory
N.A. — Not applicable.
(a) Serves at the pleasure of the legislature.
(b) Serves at the pleasure of a legislative committee.
(c) Serves at the pleasure of the secretary of state.

## Table 4.28
## STATE AUDITORS: SCOPE OF AGENCY AUTHORITY

| State or other jurisdiction | Authority to audit all state agencies | Authority to audit local governments | Authority to obtain information | Authority to issue subpoenas | Authority to specify accounting principles for local governments | Investigations Agency investigates fraud, waste, abuse, and/or illegal acts | Agency operates a hotline |
|---|---|---|---|---|---|---|---|
| Alabama | ★ | ... | ★ | ★ | ★(a) | ★ | ... |
| Alaska | ★ | ... | ★ | ★ | ... | ★ | ... |
| Arizona | ★ | ... | ★ | ... | ... | ★ | ... |
| Arkansas | ★ | ★ | ★ | ★ | ... | ★ | ... |
| California | ★ | ★ | ★ | ★ | ... | ★ | ★ |
| Colorado | ★ | ★ | ★ | ★ | ★ | ★ | ... |
| Connecticut | ★ | ... | ★ | ... | ... | ★ | ★ |
| Delaware | ★ | ★ | ★ | ★ | ... | ★ | ★ |
| Florida | (b) | ★ | ★ | ... | ... | ★ | ... |
| Georgia | ★ | ★ | ★ | ★ | ★ | ★ | ... |
| Hawaii | ★ | ★ | ★ | ★ | ... | ★ | ... |
| Idaho | ... | ★ | ★ | ... | ... | ★ | ... |
| Illinois | ★ | ... | ★ | ★ | (c) | ★ | ... |
| Indiana | ★ | ★ | ★ | ★ | ★ | ★ | ... |
| Iowa | ★ | ★ | ★ | ★ | ... | ★ | ... |
| Kansas | ★ | ★ | ★ | ... | ... | ... | ... |
| Kentucky | ★ | ★ | ★ | ★ | ... | ★ | ★ |
| Louisiana | ★ | ★ | ★ | ... | ★ | ★ | ★ |
| Maine | ★ | ★ | ★ | ★ | ★ | ★ | ★ |
| Maryland | ★(b) | (d) | ★ | ... | ★ | ★ | ★ |
| Massachusetts | ★ | ★ | ★ | ★ | ... | ★ | ★ |
| Michigan | ★ | ... | ★ | ★ | ... | ★ | ... |
| Minnesota | | | | | | | |
|   Legislative Auditor | ★ | ... | ★ | ★ | ... | ★ | ... |
|   State Auditor | (e) | ★ | ★ | ★ | ★ | ★ | ... |
| Mississippi | ★ | ... | ★ | ★ | ★ | ★ | ★ |
| Missouri | ★ | ... | ★ | ★ | ... | ★ | ★ |
| Montana | ★ | ... | ★ | ... | ... | ★ | ★ |
| Nebraska | ★ | ★ | ★ | ... | ★ | ★ | ★ |
| Nevada | ★ | ★ | ★ | ... | ... | ★ | ... |
| New Hampshire | ★ | ... | ★ | ... | ... | ★ | ... |
| New Jersey | ★ | ... | ★ | ... | ... | ★ | ... |
| New Mexico | ★ | ★ | ★ | ★ | ★ | ★ | ★ |
| New York | ★ | ★ | ★ | ★ | ★ | ★ | ★ |
| North Carolina | ★ | ... | ★ | ★ | ... | ★ | ★ |
| North Dakota | (f) | ★ | ★ | ... | ★ | ★ | ★ |
| Ohio | ★ | ★ | ★ | ★ | ★ | ★ | ★ |
| Oklahoma | ★ | ★ | ★ | ★ | (g) | ★ | ★ |
| Oregon | ★ | ★ | ★ | ★ | ★ | ★ | ★ |
| Pennsylvania | (h) | ★ | ★ | ★ | ... | ★ | ★ |
| Rhode Island | ★ | ... | ★ | ★ | ★ | ★ | ... |
| South Carolina | | | | | | | |
|   Legislative Audit Council | ★ | ... | ★ | ... | ... | ★ | ★ |
|   State Auditor | (i) | ... | ★ | ... | ... | ★ | ... |
| South Dakota | ★ | ★ | ★ | ★ | ... | ★ | ... |
| Tennessee | ★ | ★ | ★ | ★ | ★ | ★ | ... |
| Texas | ★ | (j) | ★ | ... | ... | ★ | ★ |
| Utah | (k) | ★ | ★ | ★ | ★ | ★ | ★ |
| Vermont | ★ | ★ | ★ | ★ | (l) | ★ | ★ |
| Virginia | ★ | ... | ★ | ... | ★ | ★ | ... |
| Washington | ★ | ★ | ★ | ★ | ★ | ★ | ★ |
| West Virginia | N.A. | N.A. | N.A. | N.A. | N.A. | N.A. | N.A. |
| Wisconsin | ★ | ... | ★ | ★ | ... | ★ | ★ |
| Wyoming | ★ | ★ | ★ | ★ | ... | ★ | ... |
| Guam | ★ | ★ | ★ | ★ | ★ | ★ | ★ |
| No. Mariana Islands | ★ | N.A. | ★ | ★ | ★ | ★ | N.A. |
| Puerto Rico | N.A. | N.A. | N.A. | N.A. | N.A. | N.A. | N.A. |

See footnotes at end of table.

# STATE AUDITORS: SCOPE OF AGENCY AUTHORITY — Continued

*Source*: *Auditing in the States*, 2009 Edition, The National Association of State Auditors, Comptrollers and Treasurers.

*Key*:
★ — Provision for responsibility.
... — No provision for responsibility.
N.A. — Not available.
(a) Municipalities not covered.
(b) The legislature or legislative branch is excluded from audit authority.
(c) Audits of local governments conducted as directed by the General Assembly.
(d) Local school systems only.
(e) State agencies are audited by the Office of Legislative Auditor.

(f) The Bank of North Dakota, State Fair Association, and a few others are excluded from audit authority.
(g) County governments only.
(h) The legislative and judicial branches are excluded from audit authority.
(i) State's public colleges and universities and a few agencies are excluded from audit authority.
(j) The state auditor can conduct an audit or investigation of any entity receiving funds from the stated; also, certain political subdivisions of the state.
(k) State Retirement and Workers' Compensation Fund are excluded from audit authority.
(l) Local governments not receiving state money.

**Table 4.29**
**STATE AUDITORS: TYPES OF AUDITS**

| State or other jurisdiction | Financial statement | Single audit | Attestation engagements | Compliance only | Economy and efficiency | Program | Sunset | Performance measures | IT | Accounting and review services | Other audits |
|---|---|---|---|---|---|---|---|---|---|---|---|
| Alabama | ★ | ★ | | | | ★ | ★ | ★ | ★ | | |
| Alaska | ★ | ★ | | ★ | ★ | ★ | ★ | | ★ | ★ | |
| Arizona | ★ | ★ | ★ | ★ | | ★ | | | ★ | | (a) |
| Arkansas | ★ | ★ | ★ | | ★ | ★ | | ★ | ★ | | (b) |
| California | | ★ | | | ★ | ★ | | | ★ | | |
| Colorado | ★ | ★ | | ★ | ★ | ★ | | ★ | ★ | | |
| Connecticut | ★ | ★ | | ★ | ★ | ★ | | ★ | ★ | | (c) |
| Delaware | | ★ | ★ | ★ | ★ | | | | | | (d) |
| Florida | ★ | ★ | ★ | ★ | ★ | ★ | | ★ | ★ | | |
| Georgia | | ★ | ★ | ★ | ★ | ★ | ★ | ★ | ★ | ★ | (e) |
| Hawaii | ★ | ★ | ★ | ★ | ★ | ★ | | ★ | ★ | | |
| Idaho | ★ | ★ | | ★ | ★ | ★ | ★ | ★ | ★ | ★ | |
| Illinois | ★ | ★ | ★ | ★ | ★ | ★ | | ★ | ★ | | (f) |
| Indiana | ★ | ★ | ★ | ★ | ★ | ★ | | | ★ | | |
| Iowa | ★ | | | ★ | ★ | | | | ★ | | |
| Kansas | ★ | ★ | ★ | ★ | | ★ | | ★ | ★ | | |
| Kentucky | ★ | ★ | ★ | ★ | | ★ | | | ★ | ★ | |
| Louisiana | ★ | ★ | ★ | | ★ | | | ★ | ★ | | |
| Maine | ★ | ★ | ★ | ★ | | ★ | | | ★ | | (g) |
| Maryland | | | | | | | | | ★ | | |
| Massachusetts | | ★ | ★ | | | ★ | | ★ | ★ | ★ | (h) |
| Michigan | ★ | ★ | ★ | | ★ | ★ | | ★ | ★ | | |
| Minnesota | | | | | | | | | | | |
| Legislative Auditor | ★ | ★ | | ★ | | | | | ★ | | |
| State Auditor | ★ | ★ | | | ★ | | | | | | (i) |
| Mississippi | ★ | ★ | ★ | ★ | ★ | ★ | | | ★ | | (j) |
| Missouri | ★ | ★ | | ★ | | ★ | | | ★ | | |
| Montana | ★ | ★ | ★ | ★ | ★ | ★ | | ★ | ★ | | |
| Nebraska | ★ | ★ | ★ | ★ | | ★ | | ★ | ★ | | |
| Nevada | | ★ | | | ★ | ★ | | | ★ | | |
| New Hampshire | ★ | ★ | | ★ | ★ | ★ | | ★ | ★ | | |
| New Jersey | | | | | | | | | | | |
| State Auditor | ★ | ★ | | ★ | ★ | ★ | | | ★ | | |
| State Comptroller | | | | ★ | ★ | | | | ★ | | (k) |
| New Mexico | ★ | ★ | | ★ | | ★ | | ★ | ★ | | |
| New York | ★ | ★ | ★ | | ★ | ★ | | | ★ | ★ | |
| North Carolina | ★ | ★ | | | ★ | ★ | | ★ | ★ | | (l) |
| North Dakota | ★ | ★ | | | | ★ | | | ★ | ★ | |
| Ohio | ★ | ★ | ★ | ★ | ★ | ★ | | ★ | ★ | ★ | |

See footnotes at end of table.

# STATE AUDITORS: TYPES OF AUDITS — Continued

| State or other jurisdiction | Financial statement | Single audit | Attestation engagements | Compliance only | Economy and efficiency | Program | Sunset | Performance measures | IT | Accounting and review services | Other audits |
|---|---|---|---|---|---|---|---|---|---|---|---|
| Oklahoma | ★ | ★ | ★ | ... | ★ | ★ | ... | ... | ★ | ★ | (m) |
| Oregon | ★ | ★ | ★ | ... | ★ | ★ | ... | ★ | ★ | ... | ... |
| Pennsylvania | ★ | ★ | ★ | ★ | ★ | ★ | ... | ... | ★ | ... | ... |
| Rhode Island | ★ | ★ | ★ | ★ | ... | ... | ... | ... | ★ | ... | ... |
| South Carolina | | | | | | | | | | | |
| Legislative Audit Council | ... | ... | ... | ... | ★ | ★ | ... | ... | ... | ... | ... |
| State Auditor | ★ | ★ | ★ | ... | ... | ... | ... | ... | ... | ★ | ... |
| South Dakota | ★ | ★ | ★ | ★ | ★ | ... | ... | ★ | ★ | ★ | ... |
| Tennessee | ★ | ★ | ★ | ... | ★ | ★ | ★ | ★ | ★ | ★ | ... |
| Texas | ★ | ★ | ★ | ... | ★ | ... | ... | ★ | ... | ★ | (n) |
| Utah | ★ | ★ | ... | ★ | ★ | ... | ... | ★ | ★ | ★ | ... |
| Vermont | ★ | ★ | ... | ★ | ★ | ... | ... | ★ | ★ | ... | ... |
| Virginia | ★ | ★ | ★ | ... | ... | ★ | ... | ★ | ★ | ... | (o) |
| Washington | N.A. | ★ | ★ | ★ | ★ | N.A. | ★ | ★ | ★ | ★ | N.A. |
| West Virginia | N.A. | N.A. | N.A. | N.A. | N.A. | N.A. | N.A. | N.A. | N.A. | N.A. | N.A. |
| Wisconsin | ★ | ★ | ... | ... | ★ | ★ | ... | ... | ... | ... | ... |
| Wyoming | ... | ... | ... | ★ | ★ | ... | ... | ★ | ... | ★ | ... |
| Guam | ... | ... | ... | ... | ★ | ★ | ... | ... | ... | ... | ... |
| No. Mariana Islands | ★ | ★ | ★ | ... | ★ | ★ | ... | ... | ... | ★ | ★ |
| Puerto Rico | N.A. | N.A. | N.A. | N.A. | N.A. | N.A. | N.A. | N.A. | N.A. | N.A. | N.A. |

*Sources: Auditing in the States: A Summary*, 2009 edition. The National Association of State Auditors, Comptrollers and Treasurers and state constitutions and statutes. Updated December 2011.

*Key:*
★ – Provision for responsibility.
... – No provision for responsibility.
N.A. – Not available.
(a) Internal control and compliance reviews.
(b) Investigations, assessments related to high risk.
(c) Agreed-upon procedures.
(d) Delaware contracts out financial statement and IT audits.
(e) Desk reviews.
(f) Agreed-upon procedures.
(g) Investigative or forensic audits.
(h) Privatization audits.
(i) Internal control and compliance audits.
(j) Agreed-upon procedures.
(k) School district forensic audits.
(l) Internal control reviews; studies.
(m) Investigations (reviews).
(n) Special projects, feasibility studies.
(o) Cash receipts audits at local courts.

**Table 4.30**
**THE STATE COMPTROLLERS, 2012**

| State | Agency or office | Name | Title | Legal basis for office | Method of selection | Approval or confirmation, if necessary | Date of first service | Present term ends | Length of term | Elected comptroller's maximum consecutive terms | Civil service or merit system employee |
|---|---|---|---|---|---|---|---|---|---|---|---|
| Alabama | Office of the State Comptroller | Thomas L. White, Jr. | State Comptroller | S | (c) | AG | 1/2010 | (b) | (b) | ... | ★ |
| Alaska | Division of Finance | Scot Arehart | Director of Finance | S | (a) | AG | NA | (a) | (a) | ... | ... |
| Arizona | General Accounting Office | D. Clark Partridge | State Comptroller | S | (d) | AG | 4/2002 | ... | (b) | ... | ... |
| Arkansas | Dept. of Finance and Administration | Richard A. Weiss | Chief Fiscal Officer, Director | S | G | ... | 5/2002 | (a) | (a) | ... | ... |
| California | Office of the State Controller | John Chiang (D) | State Controller | C | E | ... | 1/2007 | 1/2015 | 4 yrs. | 2 terms | ★ |
| Colorado | Office of the State Controller | David J. McDermott | State Controller | S | (d) | AG | 4/2008 | (b) | (g) | ... | ... |
| Connecticut | Office of the Comptroller | Kevin P Lembo (D) | Comptroller | C | E | AG | 1/2011 | 1/2015 | 4 yrs. | unlimited | ... |
| Delaware | Dept. of Finance | Thomas J. Cook | Secretary of Finance | S | E | AS | 3/2010 | (a) | (a) | ... | ... |
| Florida | Dept. of Financial Services | Jeff Atwater (R) | Chief Financial Officer | C,S | E | ... | 1/2011 | 1/2015 | 4 yrs. | 2 terms | ... |
| Georgia | State Accounting Office | Greg S. Griffin | State Accounting Officer | S | G | ... | 8/2008 | (a) | (a) | ... | ... |
| Hawaii | Dept. of Accounting and General Services | Dean H. Seki | Acting State Comptroller | S | G | AS | NA | 12/2014 | 4 yrs. | ... | ★ |
| Idaho | Office of State Controller | Donna Jones (R) | State Controller | C | E | ... | 1/2007 | 1/2015 | 4 yrs. | 2 terms | ... |
| Illinois | Office of the State Comptroller | Judy Baar Topinka (R) | State Comptroller | C | E | ... | 1/2011 | 1/2015 | 4 yrs. | unlimited | ... |
| Indiana | Office of the Auditor of State | Tim Berry (R) | Auditor of State | C | E | ... | 1/2007 | 1/2015 | 4 yrs. | 2 terms | ... |
| Iowa | State Accounting Enterprise | Calvin McKelvogue | Chief Operating Officer | S | (g) | AS | 5/2004 | N.A. | (a) | ... | ... |
| Kansas | Office of Management, Analysis and Standards | Martin Eckhardt | Director | S | (d) | ... | 2011 | N.A. | (b) | ... | ★ |
| Kentucky | Office of the Controller | Edgar C. Ross | Controller | S | (f) | AG | 6/1975 | N.A. | (i) | ... | ... |
| Louisiana | Division of Administration | Afranie Adomako | Director | S | G | ... | N.A. | N.A. | ... | ... | ... |
| Maine | Office of the State Controller | Terry Bram | State Controller | S | (f) | AG | 5/2010 | N.A. | (i) | ... | Exempt |
| Maryland | Office of the Comptroller of the Treasury | Peter Franchot (D) | State Comptroller | C | E | AG | 1/2007 | 1/2015 | 4 yrs. | unlimited | ... |
| Massachusetts | Office of the Comptroller | Martin J. Benison | State Comptroller | S | G | ... | 1/1999 | 1/2015 | (j) | unlimited | ... |
| Michigan | Office of Financial Management | Michael J. Moody | Director | S | SBD | SBD | 8/2002 | N.A. | (k) | ... | ★ |
| Minnesota | Department of Finance | James Schowalter | Commissioner | S | G | AS | 1/2011 | (a) | (a) | ... | ... |
| Mississippi | Dept. of Finance and Administration | Max Arinder | Executive Director | C,S | G | AS | 1/2011 | N.A. | (a) | ... | ... |
| Missouri | Division of Accounting | Stacy Neal | Director of Accounting | S | (d) | ... | 5/2011 | N.A. | (g) | ... | ... |
| Montana | State Accounting Division | Paul Christofferson | Administrator | S | (m) | ... | 6/2004 | N.A. | (b) | ... | ... |
| Nebraska | Accounting Division | Wes Mohling | Acting State Accounting Administrator | C | (d) | ... | 1/2012 | N.A. | (b) | ... | ★ |
| Nevada | Office of the State Controller | Kim Wallin (D) | State Controller | C | E | ... | 1/2007 | 1/2015 | (b) | 2 terms | ... |
| New Hampshire | Division of Accounting Services | Edgar R. Carter | Comptroller | S | G | ... | 1/2011 | 1/2015 | 4 yrs. | ... | ... |
| New Jersey | Office of Management and Budget | Matthew Boxer | Director | S | G | AS | 1/2008 | (b) | (a) | ... | ... |

See footnotes at end of table.

# THE STATE COMPTROLLERS, 2012—Continued

| State | Agency or office | Name | Title | Legal basis for office | Method of selection | Approval or confirmation, if necessary | Date of first service | Present term ends | Length of term | Elected comptroller's maximum consecutive terms | Civil service or merit system employee |
|---|---|---|---|---|---|---|---|---|---|---|---|
| New Mexico | Dept. of Finance and Administration, Financial Control Division | Ricky Bejarano | State Controller and Director | S | G | ... | 10/2011 | 1/2015 | 4 yrs. | unlimited | ★ |
| New York | Office of the State Comptroller | Thomas P. DiNapoli | State Comptroller | C,S | E | ... | 1/2007 | 1/2015 | 4 yrs. | unlimited | ... |
| North Carolina | Office of the State Controller | David McCoy | State Controller | S | G | GA | 8/2008 | 7/2013 | 7 yrs. | unlimited | ... |
| North Dakota | Office of Management and Budget | Pam Sharp | Director | S | G | ... | 1/2003 | (a) | (a) | unlimited | ... |
| Ohio | Office of Budget and Management | Timothy S. Keen | Director | S | G | AS | 1/2011 | 1/2015 | (a) | ... | ... |
| Oklahoma | Office of State Finance | Lynne Bajema | State Comptroller | S | (e) | AG | 4/2012 | N.A. | (h) | ... | ... |
| Oregon | State Controller's Division | Joy Sebastian | Acting State Controller | S | (d) | AG | 10/2011 | (b) | (g) | ... | ... |
| Pennsylvania | Comptroller Operations | Anna Maria Kiehl | Chief Accounting Officer | S | SBD | AG | 12/2008 | 12/2011 | (a) | ... | ★ |
| Rhode Island | Office of Accounts and Control | Marc Leonetti | State Controller | C,S | (d) | ... | 6/2008 | N.A. | (b) | ... | ... |
| South Carolina | Office of the Comptroller General | Richard Eckstrom (R) | Comptroller General | C,S | E | ... | 1/2003 | 1/2015 | 4 yrs. | unlimited | ... |
| South Dakota | Office of the State Auditor | Steve Barnett (R) | State Auditor | C | E | ... | 1/2011 | 1/2015 | 4 yrs. | 2 terms | ... |
| Tennessee | Division of Accounts | Jan I. Sylvis | Chief of Accounts | S | (f) | ... | 12/1995 | N.A. | (b) | ... | ... |
| Texas | Office of the Comptroller of Public Accounts | Susan Combs (R) | Comptroller of Public Accounts | C,S | E | ... | 1/2007 | 1/2015 | 4 yrs. | unlimited | ... |
| Utah | Division of Finance | John Reidhead | Director | S | (d) | AG | 9/2005 | N.A. | (g) | ... | ... |
| Vermont | Dept. of Finance and Management | James Reardon | Commissioner | S | G | AS | 2/2005 | N.A. | (a) | ... | ★ |
| Virginia | Department of Accounts | David A.Von Moll | State Comptroller | S | G | GA | 11/2001 | (a) | (a) | ... | ... |
| Washington | Office of Financial Management | Marty Brown | Director | C | G | ... | 1/1999 | (a) | (a) | ... | ... |
| West Virginia | Office of the State Auditor | Glen B. Gainier III (D) | State Auditor | C | E | ... | 1/1993 | 1/2013 | 4 yrs. | unlimited | ... |
| | Finance Division, Office of the State Comptroller | Ross Taylor | State Comptroller and Finance Director | S | (d) | AG | 10/2005 | N.A. | (g) | ... | ... |
| Wisconsin | State Controller's Office | Steve Censky | State Controller | S | CS | ... | 8/2007 | N.A. | (b) | ... | ★ |
| Wyoming | Office of the State Auditor | Cynthia Cloud | State Auditor | C,S | E | ... | 1/2011 | 1/2015 | 4 yrs. | 2 terms | ... |

*Source: Comptrollers: Technical Activities and Functions,* 2008 edition, National Association of State Auditors, Comptrollers and Treasurers. April 2012.

Key:
★ – Yes, provision for.
... – No provision for.
C – Constitutional.
S – Statutory.
N.A. – Not applicable.
E – Elected by the public.
G – Appointed by the Governor.
CS – Civil Service.
AG – Approved by the Governor.
AS – Approved/confirmed by the Senate.
SBD – Approved by State Budget Director.
GA – Confirmed by the General Assembly.
SDB – Confirmed by State Depository Board.

(a) Serves at the pleasure of the governor.
(b) Indefinite.
(c) Appointed by the Director of the Dept. of Finance (merit system position).
(d) Appointed by the head of the department of administration or administrative services.
(e) Appointed by the head of finance, department or agency.
(f) Appointed by the head of financial and administrative services.
(g) Serves at the pleasure of the head of the department of administration or administrative services.
(h) Serves at the pleasure of the head of the finance department or agency.
(i) Serves at the pleasure of the head of the financial and administrative services.
(j) Appointed by the governor for a term coterminous with the governor.
(k) Two-year renewable contractual term; classified executive service.
(l) As of July 1, 2005, the responsibility for accounting and financial reporting in Georgia was transferred to the newly-created State Accounting Office.
(m) Classified position.

## Table 4.31
## STATE COMPTROLLERS: QUALIFICATIONS FOR OFFICE

| State | Minimum age | U.S. citizen (years) | State resident (years) (b) | Education years or degree | Professional experience and years | Professional certification and years | Other qualifications | No specific qualifications for office |
|---|---|---|---|---|---|---|---|---|
| Alabama | ★ | ★ | ★ | ★, B.S. | ★, 6 yrs. | ... | ... | ... |
| Alaska | ... | ... | ... | ... | ... | ... | ... | ★ |
| Arizona | ... | ★, 1 yr. | ★, 1 yr. | ★, B.S. | ★, 7–10 yrs. | ★(a) | ... | ... |
| Arkansas | 30 | ... | ... | ... | ★ | ... | ... | ... |
| California | ★ | ... | ... | ... | ... | ... | (b) | ... |
| Colorado | ... | ... | ... | ★(i) | ★, 6yrs. | ★, CPA | ... | ... |
| Connecticut | ... | ... | ★ | ... | ... | ... | ... | ... |
| Delaware | ... | ... | ... | ... | ... | ... | ... | ★ |
| Florida | 30 | ... | ★, 7 yrs. | ... | ... | ... | ... | ... |
| Georgia | ... | ... | ... | ... | ... | ... | ... | ★ |
| Hawaii | ... | ... | 30 days | ... | ... | ... | ... | ★ |
| Idaho | 25 | ★(j) | ★, 2 yrs. | ... | ... | ... | ... | ... |
| Illinois | 25 | ★ | ★, 3 yrs. | ... | ... | ... | ... | ... |
| Indiana | ... | ... | ★(j) | ... | ... | ... | ... | ... |
| Iowa | ... | ... | ... | ... | ... | ... | ... | ★ |
| Kansas | ... | ... | ... | ... | ... | ... | ... | ★ |
| Kentucky | ... | ... | ... | ... | ... | ... | (c) | ★ |
| Louisiana | ... | ... | ... | ... | ... | ... | ... | ★ |
| Maine | ... | ... | ... | ... | ... | ... | (d) | ★ |
| Maryland | 18 | ★ | ★ | ... | ... | ... | ... | ... |
| Massachusetts | ... | ... | ... | ★(k) | ★, 7 yrs. | ... | ... | ... |
| Michigan | ... | ... | ... | ★(l) | ★, 2 yrs. | (l) | (l) | ... |
| Minnesota | ... | ... | ... | ... | ... | ... | ... | ★ |
| Mississippi | ... | ... | ... | ★(k) | ★, 10 yrs. | ★, CPA | (e) | ... |
| Missouri | ... | ... | ... | ... | ... | ... | ... | ★ |
| Montana | ... | ... | ... | ★(p) | ★, 5 yrs. | ★, CPA | ... | ★ |
| Nebraska | ... | ... | ... | ★(m) | ★(n) | ★, CPA | ... | ... |
| Nevada | 25 | ★ | ★, 2 yrs. | ... | ... | ... | ... | ... |
| New Hampshire | ... | ... | ... | ... | ... | ... | (f) | ★ |
| New Jersey | ... | ... | ... | ... | ... | ... | ... | ★ |
| New Mexico | 30 | ★ | 5 | N.A. | N.A. | N.A. | N.A. | N.A. |
| New York | 30 | ★ | ★, 5 yrs. | ... | ... | ... | ... | ... |
| North Carolina | ... | ... | ... | ★ | ★ | ... | (g) | ... |
| North Dakota | ... | ... | ... | ... | ... | ... | ... | ... |
| Ohio | ... | ... | ... | ... | ... | ... | ... | ★ |
| Oklahoma | ... | ★ | ★ | ★(q) | ★, 5 yrs. | ... | ... | ★ |
| Oregon | ... | ... | ... | ... | ... | ... | ... | ★ |
| Pennsylvania | ... | ... | ... | ... | ... | ... | ... | ★ |
| Rhode Island | ... | ★ | ★ | ★(h) | ★ | ★, CPA | ... | ... |
| South Carolina | 18 | ★ | ★ | ... | ... | ... | ... | ... |
| South Dakota | ★ | ★ | ★, 1 yr. | ... | ... | ... | ... | ... |
| Tennessee | ... | ... | ... | ★ | ★, 7 yrs. | ★, CPA | ... | ... |
| Texas | 18 | ★(j) | ★, 1 yr. | ... | ... | ... | ... | ... |
| Utah | ... | ... | ... | ★ | ★, 6 yrs. | ★, CPA | ... | ... |
| Vermont | ... | ... | ... | ... | ... | ... | ... | ★ |
| Virginia | ... | ... | ... | ... | ... | ... | ... | ★ |
| Washington | ★ | ★, Whole life | ★ | ★ | ★ | ★ | ... | ... |
| West Virginia- | | | | | | | | |
| Office of State Auditor | 25 | ★ | ★ | ... | ... | ... | ... | ... |
| Division of Finance, Office of State Comptroller | ... | ★ | ★ | ★, B.S., B.A. | ★, 4 yrs. | ... | ... | ... |
| Wisconsin | ... | ... | ... | ★(o) | ... | ★, CPA | ... | ... |
| Wyoming | ... | ★ | ... | ... | ... | ... | ... | ... |

*Source: Comptrollers: Technical Activities and Functions,* 2008 Edition, The National Association of State Auditors, Comptrollers and Treasurers. December 2011.

*Key:*

★ — Formal provision.
... — No formal provision.
N.A. — Not applicable.
(a) Any of those mentioned or CFE, CPM, etc.
(b) 18 yrs. At time of election or appointment and a citizen of the state.
(c) The Kentucky Revised Statutes state that "The state controller shall be a person qualified by education and experience for the position and held in high esteem in the accounting community."
(d) There are no educational or professional mandates, yet the appointed official is generally qualified by a combination of experience and education.

(e) At least 5 yrs. experience in high level management.
(f) Education and relevant experience.
(g) Qualified by education and experience for the position.
(h) Master's degree in accounting, finance or business management or public administration.
(i) 5 yrs. or college degree.
(j) Years not specified.
(k) Master's degree.
(l) Bachelor's degree no professional certification required, but CPA certification is considered desirable. Financial management experience, knowledge of GAAP and good communication skills are other qualifications.
(m) 4 yrs. with major in accounting.
(n) 3 yrs. directing the work of others.
(o) Bachelor's degree in accounting.

Table 4.32
## STATE COMPTROLLERS: DUTIES AND RESPONSIBILITIES

| State | Comprehensive annual financial report (CAFR) | Disbursement of state funds | Payroll processing | Pre-auditing of payments | Post-auditing of payments | Operation of statewide financial management system | Management of state travel policies |
|---|---|---|---|---|---|---|---|
| Alabama | N.A. | N.A. | N.A. | N.A. | N.A. | N.A. | N.A. |
| Alaska | N.A. | N.A. | N.A. | N.A. | N.A. | N.A. | N.A. |
| Arizona | ... | ... | ... | ... | ... | ... | ★ |
| Arkansas | N.A. | N.A. | N.A. | N.A. | N.A. | N.A. | N.A. |
| California | N.A. | N.A. | N.A. | N.A. | N.A. | N.A. | N.A. |
| Colorado | ★ | ... | ★ | ... | ★ | ★ | ★ |
| Connecticut | N.A. | N.A. | N.A. | N.A. | N.A. | N.A. | N.A. |
| Delaware | ★ | ... | ... | ★ | ... | ★ | ★ |
| Florida | ★ | ★ | ★ | ★ | ★ | ★ | ★ |
| Georgia | N.A. | N.A. | N.A. | N.A. | N.A. | N.A. | N.A. |
| Hawaii | ★ | ★ | ★ | ★ | ★ | ★ | ★ |
| Idaho | ★ | ★ | ★ | ... | ★ | ... | ★ |
| Illinois | ★ | ★ | ★ | ... | ★ | ★ | ★ |
| Indiana | N.A. | N.A. | ★ | ★ | ... | ★ | N.A. |
| Iowa | ★ | ★ | ★ | ... | ... | ... | ★ |
| Kansas | N.A. | N.A. | N.A. | N.A. | N.A. | N.A. | N.A. |
| Kentucky | ★ | ★ | ★ | ... | ★ | ★ | ★ |
| Louisiana | N.A. | N.A. | N.A. | N.A. | N.A. | N.A. | N.A. |
| Maine | ★ | ★ | ★ | ★ | ★ | ★ | ★ |
| Maryland | ★ | ★ | ★ | ★ | ★ | ★ | ★ |
| Massachusetts | ★ | N.A. | N.A. | N.A. | N.A. | N.A. | N.A. |
| Michigan | ★ | ★ | ★ | ... | ... | ★ | ★ |
| Minnesota | N.A. | ★ | N.A. | N.A. | N.A. | N.A. | N.A. |
| Mississippi | ★ | ★ | ★ | ★ | ★ | ★ | ★ |
| Missouri | ... | ★ | ★ | ... | ... | ★ | ★ |
| Montana | ★ | ★ | ★ | ... | ... | ★ | ★ |
| Nebraska | N.A. | N.A. | N.A. | N.A. | N.A. | N.A. | N.A. |
| Nevada | ★ | ★ | ★ | ... | ... | ★ | ★ |
| New Hampshire | N.A. | N.A. | N.A. | N.A. | N.A. | N.A. | N.A. |
| New Jersey | ★ | ★ | ★ | ... | ... | ★ | ★ |
| New Mexico | ★ | ★ | ★ | ★ | ... | ... | ★ |
| New York | ★ | ★ | ★ | ★ | ★ | ★ | ★ |
| North Carolina | ... | ... | ★ | ... | ... | ★ | ★ |
| North Dakota | N.A. | N.A. | N.A. | N.A. | N.A. | N.A. | N.A. |
| Ohio | ★ | ★ | ★ | ★ | ★ | ... | ★ |
| Oklahoma | ★ | ★ | ... | ★ | ★ | ... | ★ |
| Oregon | ★ | ... | ★ | ... | ... | ★ | ★ |
| Pennsylvania | ★ | ★ | ★ | ★ | ★ | ★ | ★ |
| Rhode Island | ★ | N.A. | N.A. | N.A. | N.A. | N.A. | N.A. |
| South Carolina | ★ | ★ | ★ | ★ | ★ | ★ | ★ |
| South Dakota | N.A. | N.A. | N.A. | N.A. | N.A. | N.A. | N.A. |
| Tennessee | ★ | ★ | ★ | ... | ★ | ★ | ★ |
| Texas | ★ | ★ | ★ | ★ | ★ | ★ | ★ |
| Utah | ★ | ... | ★ | ... | ★ | ★ | ★ |
| Vermont | N.A. | N.A. | N.A. | N.A. | N.A. | N.A. | N.A. |
| Virginia | N.A. | N.A. | N.A. | N.A. | N.A. | N.A. | N.A. |
| Washington | ★ | ... | ... | ... | ... | ★ | ★ |
| West Virginia | ★ | ★ | ★ | ★ | ★ | ... | ★ |
| Wisconsin | ... | ★ | ★ | ... | ... | ★ | ★ |
| Wyoming | ★ | ★ | ★ | ... | ... | ★ | ... |

*Source: Comptrollers: Technical Activities and Functions, 2008 Edition,*
The National Association of State Auditors, Comptrollers and Treasurers.

*Key:*
★ — Formal provision.
. . . — No formal provision.
N.A. — Not available

# Chapter Five

# STATE JUDICIAL BRANCH

# Governing the State Judiciaries:
# Exercising Leadership and Other Challenges

David B. Rottman and Shelley S. Miller[1]

*State courts in 2011 continued to face acute problems associated with contention over judicial selection, unrealistic budget allocations and attacks on the legitimacy of the state court's role as arbiter of the constitutionality of state laws. Sound leadership is a key ingredient to overcoming these and other pressing challenges. Steps taken to strengthen and reinvigorate judicial leadership were among the more newsworthy developments of 2011. Those steps included efforts to enlist new understandings of what compels people to obey the law in order to better guide court management and court reform.*

## Supporting Judicial Leadership

However selected, as a category, judicial leaders face fundamental challenges inherent in their positions. Chief justices of state supreme courts, for example, serve terms and are selected by methods that differ dramatically among the states. At one extreme, 13 states appoint chief justices for life, until age 70, or to indefinite terms. At the other extreme, seven states require the chief justice seat to rotate annually or biannually such that no chief justice holds successive terms of office. In the remaining states, chief justices serve fixed terms ranging from three to 14 years.[2] A lack of continuity in leaders is even more pronounced at the trial court level, where short, nonconsecutive terms for presiding judges prevail.

The manner in which chief justices are selected varies almost as greatly as the length of their terms. Some are elected to the position by the state's voters, some by choice of their peers on the supreme court, others by gubernatorial appointment or seniority, and, as previously noted, some rotate into the position. Each method of selection carries implications for the status of a chief justice as a leader.

Whatever the term length and selection method, nearly all chief justices stand at the apex of a loosely organized hierarchy for policymaking and administration. The authority to have the final say on cases is clearly delineated through the appellate process. Whether a chief justice has authority to decide administrative matters or set policy for the court system is less clear cut. Moreover, core court functions are often responsibilities shared by state and local court leaders. Consequently, state-level judicial leaders may have limited ability to move forcefully on many policy and management issues.

Short terms of office for judicial leaders and limited authority to make management decisions for trial courts have not always been problematic. Judicial leadership, however, has undergone a qualitative change in recent decades. Judicial leaders traditionally held limited responsibilities. For the most part, as chief justices they presided as the first among equals in deciding cases on appeal. Most decisions affecting the administration of justice occurred locally. In recent decades state court systems have centralized, making state supreme courts, in the words of the longest-serving chief justice, Randall Shepard of Indiana, "the boards of directors of state court systems." Leadership demands grew during the 1980s and 1990s as judicial leaders were sought as important contributors to programs responding to social and economic problems, such as domestic violence, mortgage foreclosure, child welfare, and substance abuse. As a result, the leadership challenges at both the state and local levels expanded for judges. A gap opened between what chief justices were expected to do and what they had the capacity to accomplish.[3]

To identify ways to overcome these challenges, the Harvard Kennedy School of Government collaborated with the National Center for State Courts in convening an "Executive Session on Court Leadership in the 21st Century." Executive Sessions bring together individuals of independent standing who take joint responsibility for rethinking and improving society's response to an issue. After three years of meetings, the Executive Session concluded its work in 2011. More than a dozen papers will be published throughout 2012 to transmit fresh ideas on how judicial leadership can be more effective for courts and other parts of the justice system. The first two papers in the "Perspectives on State Court Leadership" series were published in early 2012.

In the first paper, "A Case for Court Governance Principles,"[4] Chief Justice Christine Durham of the Utah Supreme Court and Utah State Court Administrator Dan Becker propose a new approach to court governance that focuses on 11 unifying principles. The first eight principles reference necessary elements for preserving a well-managed court system:

- A well-defined governance structure for policy decision-making and administration for the entire court system;
- Meaningful input from all court levels into the decision-making process;
- Selection of judicial leadership based on competency, not seniority or rotation;
- Commitment to transparency and accountability;
- A focus on policy level issues, delegation with clarity to administrative staff, and a commitment to evaluation;
- Open communication on decisions and how they are reached;
- Clear, well-understood and well-respected roles and responsibilities among the governing entity, presiding judges, court administrators, boards of judges, and court committees; and
- A system that speaks with a single voice.

The remaining principles govern how the court system relates to the rest of state government:

- Authority to allocate resources and spend appropriated funds independent of the legislative and executive branches;
- Positive institutional relationships that foster trust among other branches and constituencies; and
- The judicial branch should govern and administer operations that are core to the process of adjudication.[5]

The second paper, "Herding Lions: Shared Leadership of State Trial Courts,"[6] focuses on the positive aspects of the inherent tensions present in most contemporary state court systems.[7] Retired Phoenix trial judge Barbara Mundell and Texas Chief Justice Wallace Jefferson note how standardization and centralization of court governance result in significant tensions between local courts and the statewide court administration. Instead of principles, Mundell and Jefferson propose a new approach to court governance based on recognition of the collective responsibility of all courts within a state for the quality of justice administered. They urge that leadership be shared across the different levels of court structure and that local innovation be encouraged

and, where effective, replicated statewide. Recognizing the benefits of a healthy tension between the local and state levels, they propose specific initiatives that "stand to create a more cohesive sense of court mission and shared leadership on the part of the chief justice, the state administrative office, presiding judges, trial judges, and court personnel."

### Judicial Evaluation Programs

Most judges—nearly 90 percent—run in a popular election to obtain or retain their office. Unlike other elected officials, judges frequently participate in performance evaluation programs. In nearly half of the states—20 in 2011—formal, ongoing judicial performance evaluation programs exist for some or all trial judges. Similar programs at the appellate level are being planned. The evaluation results are used for purposes that range from judicial self-improvement, internal court administrative decisions on retention and advancement in office, planning judicial education programs and, in seven states, as information for voters when deciding on election day whether a judge should be retained in office. The latter use is part of the Missouri Plan, in which a nominating commission selects three candidates for an open judgeship, the governor selects one of the three for the post, and the judge subsequently runs against their own record when voters are asked if "Judge X should be retained in office."

The primary method for evaluation in all uses is the distribution of evaluation surveys to attorneys, court personnel, litigants, and others who have appeared before a judge in a case. Research published in 2011 raises questions about the integrity of surveys now being used in Judicial Performance Evaluation programs. Specifically, at least some existing surveys appear to hold a potential for biases based on gender, ethnicity, and race that places female and minority group judges at a disadvantage.[8] A new survey explicitly designed to minimize the potential for bias was used for the first time in 2011 in Illinois, where the purpose of the Judicial Performance Evaluation is purely self-improvement. This was done, in part, by devising questions that focus respondents on specific behavior on the part of a judge in the courtroom. Five performance areas are covered in the survey: *Legal Ability, Impartiality, Professionalism, Communications Skills, and Management Skills.*

The initial round of performance evaluations using the new Illinois survey provides reassurance that the survey is unbiased. Even if the potential for bias can be contained, state judicial performance evaluation programs can be criticized for being over-reliant on survey-based assessments, and should be complemented with data collected using other methods. A number of states already supplement their survey results with interviews of the judge being evaluated, review of statistics on workload and timeliness, and a review of the clarity of written opinions and orders.

A step taken in Utah during 2011 promises a new non-survey-based option for building a multi-method approach to evaluating judicial performance. The Utah Judicial Performance Commission developed a pilot program to be launched in the 2012 elections that will provide additional information to guide decisions on whether a judge will be recommended for retention. Trained volunteer observers are assigned to various judges' courtrooms to use the principles of procedural fairness to record the behaviors they observe and their personal reactions to those behaviors.[9] The three key principles being evaluated are neutrality (neutral, principled decision-making), respect (treating people with courtesy and politeness and respecting their rights), and voice (providing an opportunity for litigants and others to tell their side of the story in their own words).

The Utah Legislature mandated that the Utah Judicial Performance Evaluation Commission must provide observers with "a list of principles and standards used to evaluate the behavior observed."[10] In implementing that requirement, the commission relied on an article on "Procedural Justice and the Courts," by Yale law professor and social psychologist Tom Tyler, originally published in the official periodical of the American Judges Association.

### Procedural Fairness

Utah's courtroom observation initiative is only one instance in which court leaders have looked to the academic field of procedural fairness for guidance. Procedural fairness, sometimes referred to as procedural justice, is a field of social psychology that is increasingly relevant for application in the criminal justice system as an evidence-based practice. The core idea of procedural fairness is that, in assessing the fairness of a decision by an authority figure, people care more about the fairness of the process they experience than they do about the favorability of the outcome.

People are more likely to be satisfied, and comply, with court decisions if they perceive procedural fairness characterized their experience in court. This may seem counterintuitive in light of what we believe we know about human nature, but decades of compelling research findings attest to its veracity.

Defendants and litigants perceive procedural fairness when they experience respect (being treated with dignity and having their rights respected), neutrality (an honest and impartial decision-maker who bases decisions on facts), participation (the opportunity to express their viewpoint to the decision-maker in their own words), and trustworthiness (decision-makers who are sincerely concerned about people and are benevolent). There is a broad movement in United States criminal justice policy toward a focus on what evidence shows courts, police, and correctional authorities can do to promote voluntary compliance with the law.[11]

The implications of the procedural fairness perspective for the courts are immense. David B. Rottman, a researcher at the National Center for State Courts, referred to procedural fairness as "the organizing theory for which 21st century court reform has been waiting."[12] Previous periods of court reform also were guided by then-prevailing theories on what made organizations succeed. For the most part, the policy implications of those theories led court leaders to make courts more efficient. While welcome, no clear evidence suggests that such reforms have resonated with the public in a manner that increases support for the courts. Procedural fairness differs in that its expression in court policies and procedures has a demonstrable ability both to build public support for the courts and promote law-abiding behavior.

Procedural fairness also suggests methods for helping judges to improve their performance on the bench. Programs that videotape judges are using procedural fairness as the standard for how a judge should behave on the bench. When viewing the tape, the judge compares his/her own behavior, either on his/her own or with a facilitator, to litigant expectations of procedural fairness. In doing so, judges can see where their behavior on the bench conveys a lack of respect, neutrality, participation or trustworthiness. They can then take corrective action.[13]

A website launched in early 2012 offers the state court community a comprehensive resource on the application of procedural fairness—or procedural justice—in the courts. That website and blog, *www. proceduralfairness.org*, is a collaborative effort by judges, researchers, and university professors who share a belief that an emphasis on procedural fairness can make judges and court managers more effective decision-makers, improve compliance with court orders, and increase public satisfaction with the court system. The site provides resources to judges and court administrators on issues of procedural fairness.

## *The Continuing Debate on How Judges Should be Selected*

Lawsuits in federal court and legislative initiatives continued contention over the question of how judges should be selected. Nearly all states elect their judges in even years. Wisconsin is an exception. The hotly contested 2011 Wisconsin Supreme Court election, which is nonpartisan in nature, offers possible insight into what might happen in November 2012. Few, if any, recent judicial elections attracted the level of national interest prompted by Wisconsin's 2011 Supreme Court election. Sitting Supreme Court Justice David T. Prosser ran for re-election against three challengers. This was the first election in which the state's judicial candidates had the option of receiving public financing under the terms of the 2009 Impartial Justice bill, which replaced an earlier system that had been unable to generate realistic levels of funding. Interest in the result was considerable because the provision of public financing has been touted as one way to stem the dominance some see in campaign expenditures by special interests.

Justice Prosser and general election challenger JoAnne Kloppenburg both chose to receive public financing. Although both candidates accepted public funding in the general election, their stated motivations appeared to be slightly different. For Kloppenburg, the move allowed voters to "be confident that the justice they elect is truly independent and impartial."[14] Prosser, perhaps more realistically, admitted "if [he] had not accepted the public financing scheme [he] would have been roasted alive."[15] The new law did not curtail interest group spending in the primary or general election. Special interest spending was close to $3.6 million in the general election.[16] The race quickly became a referendum on the union battle that placed Wisconsin in the national spotlight because the state's Supreme Court will likely have the last word on the constitutionality of the legislation enacted earlier in the year. The final tally of a statewide recount certified Prosser's narrow defeat of Kloppenburg by approximately 7,000 votes. Interest in the result was considerable because the often-challenged provisions of public financing have been touted as one way to stem the dominance some see in campaign expenditures by special interests. Indeed, two federal lawsuits were filed challenging the constitutionality of Wisconsin's public financing program soon after the passage of the 2009 bill.[17]

North Carolina also experienced challenges to its public campaign financing provisions. Two Greensboro-based political action committees run by North Carolina Right to Life President Barbara Holt filed suit to enjoin the North Carolina Board of Elections from enforcing the state's public financing law for judicial elections.[18] The suit, filed in September, 2011, claims that the matching funds provision of the North Carolina system has chilled plaintiffs' willingness to engage in protected political speech.[19] This is not the first time North Carolina Right to Life has sought to overturn the public financing statute.[20] In 2006, it filed a similar lawsuit but saw that suit dismissed by the District Court, and the Fourth Circuit affirmed.[21] The most recent case is still active in the U.S. District Court for the Eastern District of North Carolina.

The fate of public financing in judicial elections rests, in all likelihood, on the fate of court challenges to the constitutionality of public financing provisions. In *McComish v. Bennett*, which invalidated the Arizona Clean Elections Act, the U.S. Supreme Court reversed the Ninth Circuit's unanimous holding that the law was constitutional. By promoting public financing, the Act endeavored to discourage the manipulation of candidates and electoral outcomes by private interests. The Supreme Court justified its decision by ruling the Act placed a substantial burden on the political speech of independent groups wishing to provide monetary support to a candidate, and that the state's interest in controlling corruption is not sufficiently compelling to justify the restriction under First Amendment scrutiny.[22] On the one hand, the *McComish* ruling is relatively narrow and recognizes public financing as a vital element of elections. The decision, however, overturned provisions that would provide additional funding for candidates who accepted the preset amount of money from the public funding pool and were outspent by their opponents or interest groups.[23]

It remains to be seen to what extent judicial elections will be treated differently with regard to public financing. Justice Anthony Kennedy brought out in his separate opinion in *Nevada Commission on Ethics v. Carrigan*, "The differences between the role of political bodies in formulating and enforcing public policy, on the one hand, and the role of courts in adjudicating individual disputes according to law, on the other, may call for a different understanding of the responsibilities attendant upon holders of those respective offices and of the legitimate restrictions that can be imposed upon them."[24]

Litigation over what judicial candidates can say and do continues to evolve. In May, 2011, the U.S. Supreme Court denied certiorari for two petitions seeking to overturn decisions that supported restrictions on how judges could campaign for office. In *Siefert v. Alexander*, the Seventh Circuit upheld Wisconsin's public endorsement and personal solicitation bans and struck down its party affiliation ban. In *Bauer v. Shepard*, the Seventh Circuit found a challenge to prior provisions of the Indiana Code of Judicial Conduct unripe and upheld the lower court's finding that commits, recusal, partisan activities, and solicitation clauses were constitutional. Recently, the string of victories for supporters of the Canons continued when in March 2012 the Eighth Circuit Court of Appeals, sitting *en banc*, upheld the constitutionality of the endorsement and personal solicitation provisions of Minnesota's Code of Judicial Conduct in *Wersal v. Sexton*. The ruling came fourteen months after oral arguments were heard and also declared the challenge to the "solicitation for a political organization" unripe.

## Prospects for 2012 and Beyond

Sound leadership is a precious commodity at any time, but especially so during a time of inadequate budgets and efforts in some states and nationally by politicians to diminish public support for the legitimacy of court decisions. Judicial leaders face constraints that are not found in the other branches. The completion of the Harvard Kennedy School of Government Executive Session on State Court Leaders in the 21st Century may prove to be an important milestone for the state courts. The Executive Session represented a rare moment when judges, court administrators, representatives of other branches of government, and university faculty devoted significant sustained attention to the manner in which the state courts are governed and on that basis, proposed new directions. Very little is written about the leadership role of judges and much of what is known on the topic is part of an oral tradition. The Executive Session paper series, along with advances in the area of procedural fairness, provide an avenue to sustain and enhance the leadership of the judiciary as well as public support of the judiciary. These developments are crucial at a time when the judiciary faces so many challenges on various fronts.

## Notes

[1] The authors are grateful for the research and editorial assistance provided by Natch Greyes.

[2] National Center for State Courts, State Court Organization 2004, Williamsburg, Virginia: National Center for State Courts, 2006. (Table 4).

[3] *The Role of State Court Leaders in Supporting Public Policy that Affects the Administration of Justice: A Conference Report and Profiles of State Inter-Branch Initiatives*. Philadelphia, PA: The Pew Center on the States and the National Center for State Courts, 2008. (Available in the NCSC Library.)

[4] See Christine M. Durham & Daniel J. Becker, "A Case for Court Governance Principles," in Executive Session for State Court Leaders in the 21st Century (2012).

[5] Id.

[6] See Barbara Rodriguez Mundell & Wallace B. Jefferson, "Herding Lions: Shared Leadership of State Trial Courts," in Executive Session for State Court Leaders in the 21st Century (2012).

[7] Id.

[8] Rebecca Gill et al., "Are judicial performance evaluations fair to women and minorities?," 45 *L. & Soc. Rev.* 731, (2011).

[9] This makes Utah the third state holding retention elections (the others are Alaska and Colorado) to incorporate the results of courtroom observations into the decision on whether to recommend that a serving judge be retained in office for another term.

[10] Utah Code Ann. 78A-12-203(3).

[11] Tom R. Tyler, *Why People Cooperate: The Role of Social Motivations*. Princeton University Press, 2011.

[12] David B. Rottman, "Procedural Fairness as a Court Reform Agenda," 44 *Court Review* 32 (2009).

[13] See Steve Leben, "Considering Procedural Fairness Concepts in the Courts of Utah" 30–32 (2011), available at *http://www.proceduralfairness.org/~/media/Microsites/Files/procedural-fairness/Utah%20Courts%20and%20Procedural%20Fairness%2009-2011.ashx*.

[14] Steven Elbow, "Supreme Court Race Could See Deluge of Special Interest Spending," *The Capital Times* (Feb. 16, 2011, 6:30 A.M.), *http://host.madison.com/ct/news/local/govt-and-politics/elections/article_ad10b24c-8339-5fc1-a29c-0b7aae956207.html*.

[15] Id.

[16] Press Release, Brennan Center for Justice, "Final Numbers: Special Interest Spending Near $3.6 Million in Wisconsin" (Apr. 6, 2011), *http://www.brennancenter.org/content/resource/final_numbers_special_interest_spending_near_3.6_million_in_wisconsin/*.

[17] In a lawsuit brought in 2009, Wisconsin Right to Life argues that the law violates the First Amendment because it has a chilling effect on speech. In another suit brought in 2009, Jefferson County Circuit Judge Randy Koschnick, who unsuccessfully ran for a Supreme Court vacancy, and the Washington, D.C.-based Center for Competitive Politics claim that the law unconstitutionally favors candidates who receive public funding over those who do not, and therefore violates free speech and equal protection guarantees.

[18] *North Carolina Right to Life v. Leake*, No. 5:11-cv-00 472-FL (E.D.N.C. filed Sept. 9, 2011). Chris Bagley, Group wants N.C. judicial funding ended, *Triangle Bus. J.* (September 13, 2011), *http://www.bizjournals.com/triangle/news/ 2011/09/12/group-wants-nc-judicial-funding-ended.html*; Tom Breen, "Groups seek to overturn NC campaign spending law," Associated Press, September 13, 2011, available at *http://www.chron.com/news/article/Groups-seek-to-over turn-NC-campaign-spending-law-2168288.php*.

[19] Bagley, *supra* note xix; Breen, *supra* note xix.

[20] Bagley, *supra* note xix; Breen, *supra* note xix.

[21] Bagley, *supra* note xix; Breen, *supra* note xix.

[22] *Arizona Free Enter. Club's Freedom Club PAC v. Bennett*, 131 S. Ct. 2806, 180 L. Ed. 2d 664 (2011) (Kagan, J, dissenting at 2830).

[23] Court Cases: *Arizona Free Enterprise Club v. Bennett*, Brennan Center for Justice (June 27, 2011), *http://www. brennancenter.org/content/resource/mccomish_v._bennett/* (quoting McComish at 29).

[24] *Nev. Comm'n on Ethics v. Carrigan*, 131 S.Ct. 2343, 2353 (2011).

## About the Authors

**David B. Rottman** is a principal research consultant at the National Center for State Courts in Williamsburg, Va. His current research concerns public opinion on the courts, the effectiveness of problem-solving courts, and aspects of judicial selection. He also directs a project dedicated to increasing awareness of the work of state supreme courts. He has authored books on community justice, social inequality, and modern Ireland, as well as articles and book chapters on a wide variety of court-related topics. He has a doctorate in sociology from the University of Illinois at Urbana.

**Shelley S. Miller** is a research analyst at the National Center for State Courts. She works on projects related to access to justice and judicial selection. She holds a J.D. from the William and Mary School of Law.

# Using Evidence-based Practices in Sentencing Criminal Offenders

## By Matthew Kleiman

*The fields of medicine, education, child welfare, mental health, probation and corrections have all been influenced by evidence-based practices. In essence, evidence-based practices are a set of guidelines — based upon rigorous research, evaluations and meta-analysis — that have proved effective in improving decision making and outcomes. In the medical world, for example, evidence-based practice refers to the "conscientious, explicit, and judicious use of current best evidence in making decisions about the care of individual patients."[1] Only recently, however, has this approach spilled over into state courts in the form of providing decision-making tools for judges at the time of criminal sentencing.*

Judges confront one of the most difficult decisions they have to make during criminal sentencing — the determination of what loss of liberty is appropriate for an offender and society. Evidence-based practices in sentencing hold the promise of improving judicial decision making, which can lead to enhanced public safety (reductions in offender recidivism rates) and to efficient use of scarce criminal justice resources. This essay will discuss the changing landscape of criminal sentencing; detail the risks, needs and responsivity principles of evidence-based sentencing; describe the application of evidence-based sentencing in Virginia and Wisconsin; and discuss issues important for implementation.

## The Changing Landscape of Sentencing

Over the past four decades, criminal sentencing policy has undertaken several paradigm shifts that have shaped judicial discretion and judicial sentencing practices. Beginning in the mid-1970s, research concluded that programs, treatment and interventions aimed at changing offender behavior did not work. This overt criticism, along with a rising violent crime rate, provided the impetus for the adoption of policies that replaced the rehabilitative model of sentencing with a punitive approach that emphasized retribution and determinate sentencing. The new model of sentencing emphasized punishment through incarceration and general deterrence through the adoption of "tough on crime" policies, such as mandatory minimum sentences, truth in sentencing, determinate sentencing and three strikes laws. This led to a dramatic increase in the incarceration rate.

Between 1920 and the mid-1970s, the U.S. imprisonment rate remained constant at 110 per 100,000 people. With the change in sentencing philosophy

in the mid to late 1970s, the imprisonment rate began to steadily increase to the current rate of 500 people per 100,000. As a result, between 1974 and 2005 the number of inmates in federal and state prisons increased from roughly 215,000 to more than 1.5 million.[2] To accommodate this rapid growth, states responded by building new prisons, which greatly increased the amount of state resources devoted to corrections. For example, expenditures on corrections increased by 200 percent between 1985 and 2004, while expenditures for higher education only increased 3 percent during the same period.[3]

In recent years, the budgetary challenges confronting state governments and a growing body of literature supporting the effectiveness of treatment in reducing recidivism have resulted in the swing in sentencing philosophy back toward rehabilitation. Missouri's Chief Justice Ray Price said "[t]here is a better way. We need to move from anger-based sentencing that ignores cost and effectiveness to evidence-based sentencing that focuses on results — sentencing that assesses each offender's risk and then fits that offender with the cheapest and most effective rehabilitation that he or she needs."[4]

## Evidence-based Sentencing

Evidence-based sentencing refers to judges using information about offender risk, needs and responsivity to inform the most appropriate sentence for a convicted offender. This information, provided to judges prior to sentencing, improves judicial decision-making by identifying sentences and treatments that are most effective and cost efficient in reducing an offender's future risk to the community. The information, based upon empirical investigations of past cases, quantifies the risk of an offender committing future criminal acts and the specific treatment likely to prevent reoffending.[5] It provides guidance about the level of supervision and the type of interventions that are most likely to reduce future criminality.

As a risk-reduction strategy, evidence-based sentencing helps sort out which offenders should receive incarceration, intensive supervised probation, diversion, inpatient care, vocational training, etc. The *risk* and *needs* information is not intended to limit judicial discretion, but instead to better inform judicial decision-making by identifying *who* to target, *what* to target and *how* to target to ensure the lowest levels of recidivism and the best possibility of offender change. Evidence-based sentencing is guided by the principles of risk, needs and responsivity.[6]

The *risk* principle requires that the level of supervision and treatment match an offender's likelihood of reoffending. Higher-risk cases require more intervention, structure, supervision and resources. Focusing supervision and treatment resources on lower-risk offenders can lead to wasted resources and, in some cases, may actually increase recidivism rates.[7] In short, the risk principle tells us who to target.[8] While risk assessment is a valuable tool for classifying offenders according to their risk to reoffend, the risk component alone does not provide guidance for offender treatment and supervision.[9]

The *needs* principle stresses that offender criminogenic needs be assessed and, where a need exists, targeted with treatment and interventions. Criminogenic needs are dynamic — or changeable — risk factors most associated with criminal behavior. The dynamic risk factors most strongly associated with recidivism are a history of antisocial attitudes, antisocial peers, antisocial personality pattern and a history of antisocial behavior. Additional risk factors include substance abuse, family/marital relationships, lack of achievement in education/employment and a lack of pro-social recreational activities.[10] Assessing criminogenic needs informs judges of what types of treatment services should be targeted. Chief Justice Michael Wolff, of Missouri, commented that in order to "reduce recidivism, the punishment should fit the offender as well as the crime."[11]

The *responsivity* principle contends that any treatment intervention should be tailored to the offender's learning style, motivation, developmental stage and cognitive abilities. The treatment intervention also should use cognitive social learning strategies. The responsivity principle addresses the question of how to target offenders to ensure successful interventions that reduce future criminality.

Recent meta-analyses have confirmed that a significant relationship exists between the adherence to the risk, needs and responsivity principles and reductions in recidivism.[12] Programs that directly target criminogenic factors are more effective in reducing recidivism than those that do not.[13] Judge Roger Warren, former President of the National Center for State Courts and retired California Judge, highlighted these findings, saying there is "a voluminous body of solid research showing that certain 'evidence-based' sentencing and corrections practices do work and can reduce crime rates as effectively as prisons and at much lower costs."[14] Providing the risk, needs and responsivity information to judges can potentially allow them to divert low-risk offenders from prison settings, order treatment conditions that match an offender's risk factors and make better informed pretrial release decisions.

A National Working Group on the use of offender risk and needs assessment information recommended that "judges have offender assessment information available to inform their decisions regarding risk management and reduction."[15] The group concluded that the incorporation of risk, needs and responsivity principles into sentencing has several advantages, including improved public safety, a reduction in prison admissions resulting from recidivism, less reliance on costly incarceration by reserving prison beds for serious and violent offenders, a reduction in subjective sentencing decisions through the use of scientifically based decision tools, a focus on offender accountability to elicit behavioral changes, and a reduction in social, economic and family costs associated with inappropriate interventions targeted at low-risk offenders.[16]

Evidence-based sentencing is a relatively new idea for state trial courts. Lessons learned from probation and corrections are finally beginning to influence criminal sentencing in the courtroom. Currently, a growing number of jurisdictions are providing risk, needs and responsivity information to judges prior to sentencing. States that have begun to use or explore the use of evidence-based sentencing include Alabama, Arizona, California, Colorado, Idaho, Iowa, Missouri, Texas, Virginia, Washington and Wisconsin. A brief description of the implementation of a risk assessment tool in Virginia and of a pilot program in Wisconsin follows.

## Virginia Nonviolent Risk Assessment

In 1994, Virginia abolished parole and adopted truth-in-sentencing guidelines for people convicted of a felony. At the request of the general assembly, the Virginia Criminal Sentencing Commission developed a method for diverting 25 percent of nonviolent, prison-bound offenders into alternative sanctions using an empirically based risk assessment instrument. An instrument identified which offenders, otherwise recommended for incarceration by the sentencing guidelines, have the lowest probability of being convicted of another felony crime. These offenders are recommended for some form of less restrictive, alternative punishment.

The Virginia risk assessment recommendation represents a nonbinding supplement to the pre-existing sentencing guidelines and is given to judges prior to the sentencing of drug, fraud and larceny offenders. The instrument was designed to assess an offender's risk to public safety, not gauge the needs of individual offenders and, as such, does not recommend any specific type or form of alternative punishment. An evaluation by the National Center for State Courts found that the risk assessment instrument was effective in identifying low-risk candidates for diversion. It also reduced use of prison and jail and produced cost-savings of between $2.9 million and $3.6 million for the Commonwealth of Virginia without jeopardizing the safety of its citizens.[17]

## Wisconsin: Assess, Inform, and Measure Pilot Program

The pilot project, Wisconsin Assess, Inform and Measure—or AIM—which began in the fall of 2006, is intended to provide judges with valid and reliable information to help inform sentencing decisions. The AIM process is based upon the principles of risk, needs and responsivity.

The AIM model has two stated goals:

1. Provide the sentencing court with a valid risk, needs and unique characteristic (responsivity) and community intervention assessment, while creating a feedback loop that provides information on the success of court dispositions and community interventions in promoting offender success and public safety.

2. Put into practice and evaluate a process that offers the court reliable information that will have value in the sentencing process. It may lead to the safe diversion of some people who may have otherwise received jail or prison time to community-based supervision and treatment.

Eight pilot counties—Bayfield, Dane, Eau Claire, Iowa, La Crosse, Marathon, Milwaukee and Portage—participated in the AIM Project. The pilot counties ranged from small, one judge courts to large urban jurisdictions. The AIM program grew directly out of concerns by members of the Wisconsin Planning and Policy Advisory Committee that jail and prison may not be the best method for changing people's behavior and ensuring safety for the community. Committee members questioned whether the number of individuals being incarcerated was too large and how effective this type of sanction was in changing people's behavior.

To foster participation in the AIM project, each of the pilot counties was given latitude in selecting their own target populations (Class F, G, H, I felonies; operating while under the influence offenders; misdemeanor repeat offenders), assessment tools (COMPAS; LSI-R), and the point at which the assessment would be conducted (bond hearing or pre-sentence). Despite the variations, judges in each jurisdiction received information about the current charges, criminal history, risk assessment, needs assessment, responsivity and community-based program availability. Unlike the risk assessment in Virginia, the AIM report identifies relevant resources in the community that are appropriate for the particular offender's risk and needs profile, should the judge decide to keep the offender in the community. Wisconsin is considering expanding the AIM program statewide.[18]

## Conclusion

In a speech to the American Bar Association's Annual Meeting, U.S. Supreme Court Associate Justice Anthony Kennedy, commenting on American sentencing, said "[o]ur resources are misspent, our punishments too severe, our sentences too long."[19] Evidence-based sentencing applies risk, needs and responsivity principles to begin to redress Kennedy's concerns. The use of these instruments provides judges with information to better inform sentencing decisions, which can lead to more effective and efficient use of scarce resources, reduction in offender recidivism and reduced prison admissions.

The continued diffusion, adoption and utilization of evidence-based practices by trial court judges is contingent on educating judges and justice system stakeholders (prosecutors, defense bar, policymakers) about the theory and use of risk- and needs-assessment information.[20] Educational sessions should highlight the science and research behind the risk, needs and responsivity principles and the interpretation and use of assessment information. The National Working Group suggests that judges and other stakeholders need to understand "that 'high risk' does not necessarily translate to 'need to incarcerate.' They also need to understand what dynamic risk factors are and … recognize that RNA (risk and needs assessment) tools are intended to enhance, not replace, judicial decision making."[21] Finally, judges and stakeholders should be exposed to the latest research on what works. Wolff, Missouri's chief justice, proclaims that "[w]e must pay particular attention to which sentences make recidivism more likely, which sentences are ineffectual at reducing recidivism, and which programs and punishment-treatment regimes have the best outcomes."[22]

## Notes

[1] Sackett, D., Rosenberg, W.M.C., Gray, J.A.M., Haynes, R.B., Richardson, W.S. (1996). "Evidence-based Medicine — What it is and what it isn't." *British Medical Journal* 312. *http://www.bmj.com/cgi/content/full/312/7023/71.*

[2] Warren, Roger K. (2009). "Evidence-Based Practices and Sentencing: The Application of Principles of Evidence-Based Practice to State Sentencing Practice and Policy." *University of San Francisco Law Review* 43: 585–634.

[3] Ibid.

[4] Price, Ray, Jr. (2010). State of the Judiciary. *http://www.courts.mo.gov/page.jsp?id=36875.*

[5] Extensive research has shown that actuarial algorithms are more accurate and consistent than subjective clinical judgment or human decision-makers. See for example, Grove, W.M., & Meehl, P.E. (1996). "Comparative Efficiency of Informal (Subjective, Impressionistic) and Formal (Mechanical, Algorithmic) Prediction Procedures: the Clinical-Statistical Controversy." *Psychology, Public Policy, and Law*; Meehl, P.E. (1996). *Clinical versus statistical prediction: A theoretical analysis and a review of the evidence.* Northvale, NJ: Jason Aronson. (Original work published 1954).

[6] The risk, needs , responsivity framework derives from the arena of correctional programming. See, Andrews, D., & Bonta, J. (2006). *The Psychology of Criminal Conduct, 4th Ed.* Cincinnati: Anderson.

[7] Lowenkamp, C., & Latessa, E. (2004) "Understanding the Risk Principle: How and Why Correctional Interventions Can Harm Low-risk Offenders." *Topics in Community Corrections.*

[8] Duran, L., & D'Amora, D. (2011) "Responsivity in the Risk/Need Framework" (PPT presentation). 2011 Justice and Mental Health Collaboration Program National Training and Technical Assistance Event. Washington, D.C.: The Council of State Governments. *http://consensusproject.org/documents/0000/0935/Risk_Need_Slides.pdf.*

[9] Actuarial risk assessment uses an explicit set of factors that correlate with re-offending to classify offenders into groups that re-offend at similar rates within-group, but at different rates between groups. Traditionally, the types of

factors used include the offender's criminal history, the nature of the offense, social variables like the offender's age, educational and employment history, and history of substance abuse. See Domurad, F. (1999). "So You Want to Develop Your Own Risk Assessment Instrument." In *Topics in Community Corrections: NIC Annual Report 2009: Classification and Risk Assessment.* Longmont, CO: National Institute of Corrections.

[10] Andrews, D.A., Bonta, J., & Wormith, J.S. (2006). "The Recent Past and Near Future of Risk and/or Need Assessment." *Crime & Delinquency*, (52), 1, 7–27.

[11] Wolff, M.A., (2008). Brennan Lecture Evidence-Based Judicial Discretion: Promoting Public Safety through State Sentencing Reform (November 2008). *New York University Law Review*, Vol. 83, No. 5; Saint Louis U. Legal Studies Research Paper No. 2008-14.

[12] Andrews, D. & Bonta, J. (2006). *The Psychology of Criminal Conduct, 4th Ed.* Cincinnati: Anderson.

[13] Cullen, F.T., & Gendreau, P. (2000). Assessing correctional rehabilitation: Policy, practice, and prospects. In J. Horney (Ed.), *NIJ criminal justice 2000: Changes in decision making and discretion in the criminal justice system* (pp. 109–175). Washington, D.C.: U.S. Department of Justice, National Institute of Justice.

[14] Warren, R.K. (2009). "Arming the Courts with Research: 10 Evidence-Based Sentencing Initiatives to Control Crime and Reduce Costs." The Pew Center on the States.

[15] The National Working Group was chaired by Alabama's Chief Justice Sue Bell Cobb. Members included an appellate court justice and representatives from parole, public defense, prosecution, probation, court administration, and academia. See, Casey, P.M., Warren, R.K., and Elek, J.K. (2011). *Using Offender Risk and Needs Assessment Information at Sentencing: Guidance for Courts from a National Working Group.* Williamsburg, VA: National Center for State Courts.

[16] Ibid.

[17] See, Ostrom, B., Kleiman, M., Cheesman, F., Hansen, R., & Kauder, N. (2002). *Offender Risk Assessment in Virginia.* National Center for State Courts.

[18] See, Tallarico, S., Cheesman, F.C., Kirven, M., & Kleiman, M. (2011). *Effective Justice Strategies in Wisconsin.* A Report to the Director of State Courts and the Wisconsin Supreme Court, Planning and Policy Advisory Committee, Effective Justice Strategies Subcommittee.

[19] Kennedy, A.M., (August 14, 2003). Speech at the American Bar Association Annual Meeting: An Address by Anthony M. Kennedy, Associate Justice, Supreme Court of the United States.

[20] The National Center for State Courts, in collaboration with the National Judicial College and the Crime and Justice Institute, has developed a model national judicial educational curriculum. The curriculum, "Evidence-Based Sentencing to Improve Public Safety and Reduce Recidivism," is available at *http://www.ncsconline.org/csi.*

[21] Casey, P.M., Warren, R.K., & Elek, J.K. (2011). *Using Offender Risk and Needs Assessment Information at Sentencing: Guidance for Courts from a National Working Group.* Williamsburg, VA: National Center for State Courts, p. 21.

[22] Wolff, M.A., (2008). Brennan Lecture Evidence-Based Judicial Discretion: Promoting Public Safety through State Sentencing Reform (November 2008). *New York University Law Review*, Vol. 83, No. 5; Saint Louis U. Legal Studies Research Paper No. 2008-14.

---

## About the Author

**Matthew Kleiman** is a senior court research associate with the National Center for State Courts in Williamsburg, Va. His work has focused on: the use of risk and needs information at the time of sentencing; assessments of consistency and fairness in criminal sentencing; the development and implementation of a set of court specific performance measures (CourTools); and the development of statewide resource assessment models for judicial officers, court staff, and public defender and prosecutor attorneys and staff. He holds a doctorate in political science and is the co-author of a recent Temple University Press book on court culture — *Trial Courts as Organizations*.

# Table 5.1
# STATE COURTS OF LAST RESORT

| State or other jurisdiction | Name of court | Justices chosen (a) At large | By district | No. of judges (b) | Term (in years) (c) | Chief Justice Method of selection | Term of office for chief justice |
|---|---|---|---|---|---|---|---|
| Alabama | S.C. | ★ | | 9 | 6 | Non-partisan popular election | 6 years |
| Alaska | S.C. | ★ | | 5 | 10 | By court | 3 years |
| Arizona | S.C. | ★ | | 5 | 6 | By court | 5 years |
| Arkansas | S.C. | ★ | | 7 | 8 | Non-partisan popular election | 8 years |
| California | S.C. | ★ | | 7 | 12 | Appointed by governor | 12 years |
| Colorado | S.C. | ★ | | 7 | 10 | By court | Indefinite |
| Connecticut | S.C. | ★ | | 7 | 8 | Gubernatorial appointment from Judicial Nominating Commission with consent of legislature | 8 years |
| Delaware | S.C. | ★ | | 5 | 12 | Appointed by governor | 12 years |
| Florida | S.C. | (d) | | 7 | 6 | By court | 2 years |
| Georgia | S.C. | ★ | | 7 | 6 | By court | 2 years |
| Hawaii | S.C. | ★ | | 5 | 10 | Gubernatorial appointment from Judicial Nominating Commission with consent of legislature | 10 years |
| Idaho | S.C. | ★ | | 5 | 6 | By court | 4 years |
| Illinois | S.C. | | ★ | 7 | 10 | By court | 3 years |
| Indiana | S.C. | ★ | | 5 | 10 (e) | Judicial Nominating Commission appointment | 5 years |
| Iowa | S.C. | ★ | | 7 | 8 | By court | 8 years |
| Kansas | S.C. | ★ | | 7 | 6 | Rotation by seniority | Indefinite |
| Kentucky | S.C. | | ★ | 7 | 8 | By court | 4 years |
| Louisiana | S.J.C. | | ★ | 7 | 10 | By seniority of service | Duration of service |
| Maine | S.J.C. | ★ | | 7 | 7 | Appointed by governor | 7 years |
| Maryland | C.A. | | ★ | 7 | 10 | Appointed by governor | Indefinite |
| Massachusetts | S.J.C. | ★ | | 7 | To age 70 | Appointed by governor (f) | To age 70 |
| Michigan | S.C. | ★ | | 7 | 8 | By court | 2 years |
| Minnesota | S.C. | ★ | | 7 | 6 | Gubernatorial appointment | 6 years |
| Mississippi | S.C. | | ★ | 9 | 8 | By seniority of service | Duration of service |
| Missouri | S.C. | ★ | | 7 | 12 | By court | 2 years |
| Montana | S.C. | ★ | | 7 | 8 | Non-partisan popular election | 8 years |
| Nebraska | S.C. | | ★(g) | 7 | 6 (h) | Appointed by governor from Judicial Nominating Commission | Duration of service |
| Nevada | S.C. | ★ | | 5 | 6 | Rotation | 2 years (i) |
| New Hampshire | S.C. | ★ | | 5 | 5 | Seniority | 5 years |
| New Jersey | S.C. | ★ | | 7 | 7 (j) | Gubernatorial appointment with consent of the legislature | Duration of service |
| New Mexico | S.C. | ★ | | 5 | 8 | By court | 2 years |
| New York | C.A. | ★ | | 7 | 14 | Appointed by governor from Judicial Nomination Commission | 14 years |
| North Carolina | S.C. | ★ | | 7 | 8 | Non-partisan popular election | 8 years |
| North Dakota | S.C. | ★ | | 5 | 10 | By Supreme and district court judges | 5 years (k) |
| Ohio | S.C. | ★ | | 7 | 6 | Popular election (l) | 6 years |
| Oklahoma | S.C. | | ★ | 9 | 6 | By court | Duration of service |
| Oklahoma | C.C.A. | | ★ | 5 | 6 | By court | 5 years |
| Oregon | S.C. | ★ | | 7 | 6 | By court | 6 years |
| Pennsylvania | S.C. | ★ | | 7 | 10 | Seniority | Duration of term |
| Rhode Island | S.C. | ★ | | 5 | Life | Appointed by governor from Judicial Nominating Commission | Life |
| South Carolina | S.C. | ★ | | 5 | 10 | Legislative appointment | 10 years |

See footnotes at end of table.

# STATE COURTS OF LAST RESORT—Continued

| State or other jurisdiction | Name of court | Justices chosen (a) At large | Justices chosen (a) By district | No. of judges (b) | Term (in years) (c) | Chief justice Method of selection | Term of office for chief justice |
|---|---|---|---|---|---|---|---|
| South Dakota | S.C. | ★(m) | ★(m) | 5 | 8 | By court | 4 years |
| Tennessee | S.C. | ★ | | 5 | 8 | By court | 4 years |
| Texas | S.C. | ★ | | 9 | 6 | Partisan election | 6 years |
| Texas | C.C.A. | ★ | | 9 | 6 | Partisan election | 6 years (n) |
| Utah | S.C. | ★ | | 5 | 10 (o) | By court | 4 years |
| Vermont | S.C. | ★ | | 5 | 6 | Appointed by governor from Judicial Nomination Commission with consent of the legislature | 6 years |
| Virginia | S.C. | ★ | | 7 | 12 | Seniority | 4 years |
| Washington | S.C. | ★ | | 9 | 6 | By court | 4 years |
| West Virginia | S.C.A. | ★ | | 5 | 12 | Seniority | 1 year |
| Wisconsin | S.C. | ★ | | 7 | 10 | Seniority | Until declined |
| Wyoming | S.C. | ★ | | 5 | 8 | By court | 4 years |
| Dist. of Columbia | C.A. | ★ | | 9 | 15 | Judicial Nominating Commission appointment | 4 years |
| Puerto Rico | S.C. | ★ | | 7 | To age 70 | Gubernatorial appointment with consent of the legislature | To age 70 |

*Sources: State Court Organization, 2004,* U.S. Department of Justice Statistics, National Center for State Courts, March 2012.

*Key:*
★ — Yes
S.C. — Supreme Court
S.C.A. — Supreme Court of Appeals
S.J.C. — Supreme Judicial Court
C.A. — Court of Appeals
C.C.A. — Court of Criminal Appeals
H.C. — High Court

(a) See Table 5.6, entitled, "Selection and Retention of Appellate Court Judges," for more detail.
(b) Number includes chief justice.
(c) The initial term may be shorter. See Table 5.6, entitled, "Selection and Retention of Appellate Court Judges," for more detail.
(d) Regional (5), Statewide (2), Regional based on District of Appeal.
(e) Initial term is two years; retention 10 years.

(f) Chief Justice, in the appellate courts, is a separate judicial office from that of an Associate Justice. Chief Justices are appointed, until age 70, by the governor with the advice and consent of the Executive (governor's) Council.
(g) Chief justice chosen statewide; associate judges chosen by district.
(h) More than three years for first election and every six years thereafter.
(i) The term may be split between eligible justices.
(j) Followed by tenure. All judges are subject to gubernatorial reappointment and consent by the Senate after and initial seven-year term; thereafter, they may serve until mandatory retirement at age 70.
(k) Or expiration of term, whichever is first.
(l) Party affiliation is not included on the ballot in the general election, but candidates are chosen through partisan primary nominations.
(m) Initially chosen by district; retention determined statewide.
(n) Presiding judge of Court of Criminal Appeals.
(o) The initial term of appointment is until the next general election immediately following the third year from the time of the initial appointment.

## Table 5.2
## STATE INTERMEDIATE APPELLATE COURTS AND GENERAL TRIAL COURTS: NUMBER OF JUDGES AND TERMS

| State or other jurisdiction | Intermediate appellate court | | | General trial court | | |
|---|---|---|---|---|---|---|
| | Name of court | 2009 No. of judges | Term (years) | Name of court | 2009 No. of judges | Term (years) |
| Alabama | Court of Criminal Appeals | 5 | 6 | Circuit Court | 144 | 6 |
| | Court of Civil Appeals | 5 | 6 | | | |
| Alaska | Court of Appeals | 3 | 8 | Superior Court | 50 | 6 (a) |
| Arizona | Court of Appeals | 22 | 6 | Superior Court | 174 | 4 |
| Arkansas | Court of Appeals | 12 | 8 | Chancery/Probate Court and Circuit Court | 118 | 6 |
| California | Courts of Appeal | 105 | 12 | Superior Court | 2,022 | 6 |
| Colorado | Court of Appeals | 19 | 8 | District Court | 153 | 6 (b) |
| Connecticut | Appellate Court | 9 | 8 | Superior Court | 201 | 8 |
| Delaware | ... | ... | ... | Superior Court | 19 | 12 |
| | | | | Court of Chancery | 5 | 12 |
| Florida | District Courts of Appeals | 62 | 6 | Circuit Court | 599 | 6 |
| Georgia | Court of Appeals | 12 | 6 | Superior Court | 205 | 4 |
| Hawaii | Intermediate Court of Appeals | 6 | 10 | Circuit Court | 48 | 10 |
| Idaho | Court of Appeals | 4 | 6 | District Court | 43 | 4 |
| Illinois | Appellate Court | 54 | 10 | Circuit Court | 517 | 6 |
| Indiana | Court of Appeals | 15 | 12 (c) | Superior Court, Probate Court and Circuit Court | 315 | 6 |
| Iowa | Court of Appeals | 9 | 6 | District Court | 350 (d) | 6 (e) |
| Kansas | Court of Appeals | 12 | 4 | District Court | 246 (f) | 4 |
| Kentucky | Court of Appeals | 14 | 8 | Circuit Court | 95 | 8 |
| Louisiana | Courts of Appeal | 53 (g) | 10 | District Court | 236 | 6 |
| Maine | ... | ... | ... | Superior Court | 17 | 7 |
| Maryland | Court of Special Appeals | 13 | 10 | Circuit Court | 153 | 15 |
| Massachusetts | Appeals Court | 25 (h) | To age 70 | Superior Court | 82 | To age 70 |
| Michigan | Court of Appeals | 28 | 6 | Circuit Court | 221 | 6 |
| Minnesota | Court of Appeals | 19 | 6 | District Court | 289 | 6 |
| Mississippi | Court of Appeals | 10 | 8 | Circuit Court | 51 | 4 |
| Missouri | Court of Appeals | 32 | 12 | Circuit Court | 369 (i) | 6 (j) |
| Montana | ... | ... | ... | District Court | 43 (k) | 6 |
| Nebraska | Court of Appeals | 6 | 3 (l) | District Court | 55 | 6 (m) |
| Nevada | ... | ... | ... | District Court | 72 | 6 |
| New Hampshire | ... | ... | ... | Superior Court | 25 | To age 70 |
| New Jersey | Appellate Division of Superior Court | 32 | 7 (n) | Superior Court | 411 | 7 (o) |
| New Mexico | Court of Appeals | 10 | 8 | District Court | 88 | 6 |
| New York | Appellate Division of Supreme Court | 56 | 5 (p) | Supreme Court | 326 | 14 |
| | Appellate Terms of Supreme Court | (q) | | County Court | 129 | 10 |
| North Carolina | Court of Appeals | 15 | 8 | Superior Court | 111 (r) | 8 (s) |
| North Dakota | Temporary Court of Appeals | 3 (ff) | 1 (gg) | District Court | 44 | 6 |
| Ohio | Courts of Appeals | 69 | 6 | Court of Common Pleas | 394 | 6 |

See footnotes at end of table.

# STATE INTERMEDIATE APPELLATE COURTS AND GENERAL TRIAL COURTS: NUMBER OF JUDGES AND TERMS — Continued

| State or other jurisdiction | Intermediate appellate court | | | General trial court | | |
|---|---|---|---|---|---|---|
| | Name of court | 2009 No. of judges | Term (years) | Name of court | 2009 No. of judges | Term (years) |
| Oklahoma | Court of Appeals | 12 | 6 | District Court | 241 (t) | 4 (u) |
| Oregon | Court of Appeals | 10 | 6 | Circuit Court | 173 | 6 |
| | | | | Tax Court | 1 | 6 |
| Pennsylvania | Superior Court | 15 (v) | 10 | Court of Common Pleas | 439 (x) | 10 |
| | Commonwealth Court | 9 (w) | 10 | | | |
| Rhode Island | ... | | Life | Superior Court | 27 (y) | Life |
| South Carolina | Court of Appeals | 9 | 6 | Circuit Court | 46 | 6 (aa) |
| South Dakota | ... | | ... | Circuit Court | 41 | 8 |
| Tennessee | Court of Appeals | 12 | 8 | Chancery Court | 34 | 8 |
| | Court of Criminal Appeals | 12 | 8 | Circuit Court | 95 | 8 |
| | | | | Criminal Court | 33 | 8 |
| | | | | Probate Court | 2 | 8 |
| Texas | Courts of Appeals | 80 | 6 | District Court | 449 | 4 |
| Utah | Court of Appeals | 7 | 6 (aa) | District Court | 109(bb) | 6 (cc) |
| Vermont | ... | | | Superior Court, District Court & Family Court | 30 | 6 (cc) |
| Virginia | Court of Appeals | 11 | 8 | Circuit Court | 157 | 8 |
| Washington | Courts of Appeal | 24 | 6 | Superior Court | 188 | 4 |
| West Virginia | ... | | ... | Circuit Court | 70 | 8 |
| Wisconsin | Court of Appeals | 16 | 6 | Circuit Court | 248 | 6 |
| Wyoming | ... | | ... | District Court | 21 | 6 |
| Dist. of Columbia | ... | | ... | Superior Court | 62 | 15 |
| Puerto Rico | Circuit Court of Appeals | 39 | 16 | Court of First Instance | 326 (dd) | 12 (ee) |

*Sources: State Court Organization, 2004,* U.S. Department of Justice Statistics, update from the National Center for State Courts, March 2012.

Key:

... — Court does not exist in jurisdiction or not applicable.

(a) The initial term for Superior Court judges is three years.

(b) The initial term for District Court, Denver Probate Court, Denver Juvenile Court and County Court judges is two years.

(c) Two years initial; 10 years retention.

(d) The number of District Court judges includes associate judges and magistrates.

(e) The initial term for District Court judges is at least one year. Associate judges serve a term of four years with an initial term of at least one year, and magistrate judges serve a term of four years.

(f) The number of District Court judges includes magistrates.

(g) The Courts of Appeal have 55 authorized judicial positions.

(h) The Appeals Court has 25 authorized judicial positions. The judges of the Appeals Court are assisted by the services on recall of several retired judges.

(i) The number of Circuit Court judges includes associate judges.

(j) Associate Circuit judges serve a term of four years.

(k) Four of those judges serve the Water Court.

(l) More than three years for first election and retention is every six years thereafter.

(m) The initial term is for three years but not more than five years.

(n) Followed by tenure. All judges are subject to gubernatorial reappointment and consent by the Senate after an initial seven-year term; thereafter, they may serve until mandatory retirement at age 70.

(o) After an initial seven-year term, the reapportionment term for Superior and Tax Court judges is open-ended until mandatory retirement age at age 70.

(p) Or duration.

(q) Appellate Terms of the Supreme Court have been established within the First and Second Departments of the Appellate Division. Data for the Appellate Terms are not included in the information presented here.

(r) The number of Superior Court judges includes special judges.

(s) Special judges serve a term of four years.

(t) The number of District Court judges includes associate judges and special judges.

(u) District and associate judges serve four-year terms; special judges serve at pleasure.

(v) The Superior Court has 15 authorized judicial positions. The judges of the Superior Court are assisted by senior judges specially appointed by the Supreme Court.

(w) The judges of the Commonwealth Court are assisted by senior judges specially appointed by the Supreme Court. Also, senior Common Pleas Court judges occasionally serve on the Commonwealth Court.

(x) Includes both active and senior judges.

(y) The number of judges includes magistrates.

(z) Four to five judges are currently working as active retired judges.

(aa) The initial term of appointment is until the next general election immediately following the third year from the time of the initial appointment.

(bb) Effective 2011, the Family, District, and Probate Courts were combined into the Superior Court.

(cc) The initial term of appointment is until the next general election immediately following the third year from the time of the initial appointment.

(dd) The number of Court of First Instance judges includes Municipal Division judges.

(ee) Municipal judges serve a term of eight years.

(ff) The Supreme Court may provide for the assignment of active or retired District Court judges, retired justices of the Supreme Court, and lawyers, to serve on three-judge panels.

(gg) Assignments are for a specified time, not to exceed one year or the completion of one or more cases on the docket of the Supreme Court.

## Table 5.3
## QUALIFICATIONS OF JUDGES OF STATE APPELLATE COURTS AND GENERAL TRIAL COURTS

| State or other jurisdiction | Residency requirement State | | Local | | Minimum age | | Legal credentials | |
|---|---|---|---|---|---|---|---|---|
| | A | T | A | T | A | T | A | T |
| Alabama | 1 yr. | 1 yr. | ... | 1 yr. | ... | 18 | 10 years state bar | 5 years state bar |
| Alaska | 5 yrs. | 5 yrs. | ... | ... | ... | ... | 8 years practice | 5 years practice |
| Arizona | 10 yrs. (a) | 5 yrs. | (b) | 1 yr. | (e) | 30 | (c) | (d) |
| Arkansas | 2 yrs. | ... | (b) | ... | 30 | ... | 8 years practice | 6 years licensed in state |
| California | ★ | ... | ... | ... | ... | ... | 10 years state bar | 10 years state bar |
| Colorado | ★ | ★ | ... | ★ | ... | ... | 5 years state bar | 5 years state bar |
| Connecticut | ★ | ★ | ... | ... | ... | ... | Licensed attorney | Member of the bar |
| Delaware | ★ | ★ | ... | ★ | ... | ... | "Learned in law" | "Learned in law" |
| Florida | ★(f) | ★ | ★(f) | ★(g) | ... | ... | 10 years state bar | 5 years state bar |
| Georgia | ★ | 3 yrs. | ... | ... | ... | 30 | 7 years state bar | 7 years state bar |
| Hawaii | ★ | ★ | ... | ... | ... | 30 | 10 years state bar | 10 years state bar |
| Idaho | 2 yrs. | 1 yr. | ... | ... | 30 | ... | 10 years state bar | 10 years state bar |
| Illinois | ★ | ★ | ★ | ★ | ... | ... | Licensed attorney | ... |
| Indiana | ★ | 1 yr. | ... | ★ | ... | ... | 10 years state bar (h) | ... |
| Iowa | ★ | ★ | ... | ★ | ... | ... | Licensed attorney | Admitted to state bar |
| Kansas | ... | ... | ... | ... | 30 | 30 | 10 years active and continuous practice (i) | 5 years state bar |
| Kentucky | 2 yrs. | 2 yrs. | 2 yrs. | 2 yrs. | ... | ... | 8 years state bar and licensed attorney | 8 years state bar |
| Louisiana | 1 yr. | 1 yr. | 1 yr. | 1 yr. | ... | ... | 10 years state bar | 5 years state bar |
| Maine | ... | ... | ... | ... | ... | ... | "Learned in law" | "Learned in law" |
| Maryland | 5 yrs. | 5 yrs. | 6 mos. | 6 mos. | 30 | 30 | State bar member | State bar member |
| Massachusetts | ... | ... | ... | ... | ... | ... | ... | ... |
| Michigan | ★ | ★ | ... | ... | ... | ... | State bar member and 5 years practice | State bar member |
| Minnesota | 30 days | 30 days | ... | 30 days | ... | ... | Licensed attorney | Licensed attorney |
| Mississippi | 5 yrs. | 5 yrs. | ★(j) | ... | 30 | 26 | 5 years state bar | 5 years practice |
| Missouri | 9 yrs. (k) | 3 yrs. (k) | ... | ★(k) | 30 | 30 | State bar member | State bar member |
| Montana | 2 yrs. | 2 yrs. | ... | ... | ... | ... | 5 years state bar | 5 years state bar |
| Nebraska | 3 yrs. | ★ | ★ | ★ | 30 | 30 | 5 years practice | 5 years practice |
| Nevada | 2 yrs. | 2 yrs. | ... | ... | 25 | 25 | State bar member (l) | 2 years state bar member and 10 years practice |
| New Hampshire | ... | ... | ... | ... | ... | ... | 10 years practice | ... |
| New Jersey | ... | (m) | ... | (m) | ... | ... | Admitted to practice in state for at least 10 years | 10 years practice of law |
| New Mexico | 3 yrs. | 3 yrs. | ... | ★ | 35 | 35 | 10 years practice | 6 years active practice |
| New York | ★ | ★ | ... | ... | ... | 18 | 10 years state bar | 10 years state bar |
| North Carolina | ... | ★ | ... | (n) | ... | ... | State bar member | State bar member |
| North Dakota | ★ | ★ | ... | ★ | ... | ... | License to practice law | State bar member |
| Ohio | ★ | ★ | ... | ★ | ... | ... | 6 years practice | 6 years practice |
| Oklahoma | ★ | (o) | 1 yr. | ★ | 30 | ... | 5 years state bar | (p) |
| Oregon | 3 yrs. | 3 yrs. | ... | 1 yr. | ... | ... | State bar member | State bar member |
| Pennsylvania | 1 yr. | ★ | ... | 1 yr. | ... | 21 | State bar member | State bar member |
| Rhode Island | ... | ... | ... | ... | 21 | ... | License to practice law | State bar member |
| South Carolina | 5 yrs. | 5 yrs. | ... | (q) | 32 | 32 | 8 years state bar | 8 years state bar |
| South Dakota | ★ | ★ | ★ | ★ | ... | ... | State bar member | State bar member |
| Tennessee | 5 yrs. | 5 yrs. | ★(r) | 1 yr. | 35 | 30 | License to practice law | License to practice law |
| Texas | ★ | ... | ... | 2 yrs. | 35 | 25 | (s) | (t) |
| Utah | 5 yrs. | 3 yrs. | ... | ★ | 30 | 25 | State bar member | State bar member |
| Vermont | ... | ... | ... | ... | ... | ... | 5 years state bar | 5 years state bar |
| Virginia | ... | ★ | ... | ★ | ... | ... | 5 years state bar | 5 years state bar |
| Washington | 1 yr. | 1 yr. | 1 yr. | 1 yr. | ... | ... | State bar member | State bar member |
| West Virginia | 5 yrs. | ★ | ... | ★ | 30 | 30 | 10 years state bar | 5 years state bar |
| Wisconsin | 10 days | 10 days | 10 days | 10 days | ... | ... | 5 years state bar | 5 years state bar |
| Wyoming | 3 yrs. | 2 yrs. | ... | ... | 30 | 28 | 9 years practice | ... |
| Dist. of Columbia | N.A. | N.A. | 90 days | 90 days | ... | ... | 5 years practice | 5 years state bar (u) |
| Puerto Rico | 5 yrs. | ... | ... | ... | ... | ... | 10 years practice | 7 years state bar |

See footnotes at end of table.

# QUALIFICATIONS OF JUDGES OF STATE APPELLATE COURTS
## AND GENERAL TRIAL COURTS — Continued

*Sources: State Court Organization, 2004*, U.S. Department of Justice Statistics, update from the National Center for State Courts, March 2012.

*Key:*

A — Judges of courts of last resort and intermediate appellate courts.

T — Judges of general trial courts.

★ — Provision; length of time not specified.

... — No specific provision.

N.A.— Not applicable.

(a) For Court of Appeals, five years.

(b) No local residency requirement stated for Supreme Court. Local residency required for Court of Appeals.

(c) Supreme Court—ten years state bar, Court of Appeals—five years state bar.

(d) Admitted to the practice of law in Arizona for five years.

(e) Court of Appeals minimum age is 30.

(f) The candidate must be a resident of the district at the time of the original appointment.

(g) Circuit Court judge must reside within the territorial jurisdiction of the court.

(h) In the Supreme Court and the Court of Appeals, five years service as a general jurisdiction judge may be substituted.

(i) Relevant legal experience, such as being a member of a law faculty or sitting as a judge, may qualify under the 10-year requirement.

(j) Must reside within the district.

(k) At the appellate level must have been a state voter for nine years. At the general trial court level must have been a state voter for three years and resident of the circuit for one year.

(l) Minimum of two years state bar member and at least 15 years of legal practice.

(m) For Superior Court: out of a total of 441 authorized judgeships there are 283 restricted Superior Court judgeships that require residence within the particular county of assignment at time of appointment and reappointment; there are 158 unrestricted judgeships for which assignment of county is made by the chief justice.

(n) Resident judges of the Superior Court are required to have local residency, but special judges are not.

(o) District and associate judges must be state residents for six months if elected, and associate judges must be county residents.

(p) District Court: Judges must be a state bar member for four years or a judge of a court of record. Associate judges must be a state bar member for two years or a judge of a court of record.

(q) Circuit judges must be county electors and residents of the circuit.

(r) Supreme Court: One justice from each of three divisions and two seats at large; no more than two may be from any grand division. Court of Appeals and Court of Criminal Appeals: Must reside in the grand division served.

(s) Ten years practicing law or a lawyer and judge of a court of record at least 10 years.

(t) District Court: Judges must have been practicing lawyers or judges of a court in this state, or both combined, for four years.

(u) Superior Court: Judge must also be an active member of the unified District of Columbia bar and have been engaged, during the five years immediately preceding the judicial nomination, in the active practice of law as an attorney in the District, been on the faculty of a law school in the District, or been employed by either the United States or District of Columbia government.

**Table 5.4**
## COMPENSATION OF JUDGES OF APPELLATE COURTS AND GENERAL TRIAL COURTS

| State or other jurisdiction | Appellate courts | | | | | | General trial courts | Salary |
|---|---|---|---|---|---|---|---|---|
| | Court of last resort | Chief Justice salaries | Associate Justice salaries | Intermediate appellate court | Chief/Presiding salaries | Judges salaries | | |
| **Eastern Region** | | | | | | | | |
| Connecticut | Supreme Court | $175,645 | $162,520 | Appellate Court | $160,722 | $152,637 | Superior courts | $146,780 |
| Delaware | Supreme Court | 194,750 | 185,050 | ... | ... | ... | Superior courts | 168,850 |
| Maine | Supreme Judicial Court | 138,138 | 119,476 | ... | ... | ... | Superior courts | 111,969 |
| Maryland | Court of Appeals | 181,352 | 162,352 | Court of Special Appeals | 152,552 | 149,552 | Circuit courts | 140,352 |
| Massachusetts | Supreme Judicial Court | 151,239 | 145,984 | Appellate Court | 140,358 | 135,087 | Superior courts | 129,694 |
| New Hampshire | Supreme Court | 151,477 | 146,917 | ... | ... | ... | Superior courts | 137,084 |
| New Jersey | Supreme Court | 192,795 | 185,482 | Appellate division of | 175,534 | 175,534 | Superior courts | 165,000 |
| New York | Court of Appeals | 156,000 | 151,200 | Appellate divisions of | 148,000 | 144,000 | Supreme courts | 136,700 |
| Pennsylvania | Supreme Court | 195,138 | 189,620 | Superior Court | 184,432 | 178,914 | Courts of common pleas | 164,602 |
| Rhode Island | Supreme Court | 182,300 | 165,726 | ... | ... | ... | Superior courts | 149,207 |
| Vermont | Supreme Court | 135,421 | 129,230 | ... | ... | ... | Superior/District/Family | 122,867 |
| Regional averages | | 166,821 | 156,898 | | 159,753 | 155,456 | | 141,981 |
| **Midwestern Region** | | | | | | | | |
| Illinois | Supreme Court | 209,344 | 209,344 | Court of Appeals | 197,032 | 197,032 | Circuit courts | 180,802 |
| Indiana | Supreme Court | 153,295 | 153,295 | Court of Appeals | 149,015 | 149,015 | Circuit courts | 127,280 |
| Iowa | Supreme Court | 170,850 | 163,200 | Court of Appeals | 153,000 | 147,900 | District courts | 137,700 |
| Kansas | Supreme Court | 139,310 | 135,905 | Court of Appeals | 134,750 | 131,518 | District courts | 120,037 |
| Michigan | Supreme Court | 164,610 | 164,610 | Court of Appeals | 151,441 | 151,441 | Circuit courts | 139,919 |
| Minnesota | Supreme Court | 160,579 | 145,981 | Court of Appeals | 144,429 | 137,552 | District courts | 129,124 |
| Nebraska | Supreme Court | 142,760 | 142,760 | Court of Appeals | 135,622 | 135,622 | District courts | 132,053 |
| North Dakota | Supreme Court | 133,968 | 130,228 | ... | ... | ... | District courts | 119,330 |
| Ohio | Supreme Court | 150,850 | 141,600 | Court of Appeals | 132,000 | 132,000 | Courts of common pleas | 121,350 |
| South Dakota | Supreme Court | 120,173 | 118,173 | ... | ... | ... | Circuit courts | 110,377 |
| Wisconsin | Supreme Court | 152,495 | 144,495 | Court of Appeals | 136,316 | 136,316 | Circuit courts | 128,600 |
| Regional averages | | 154,385 | 149,963 | | 148,178 | 146,488 | | 131,507 |
| **Southern Region** | | | | | | | | |
| Alabama | Supreme Court | (a) | (b) | Court of Criminal Appeals | (c) | (d) | Circuit courts | (e) |
| Arkansas | Supreme Court | 156,864 | 145,204 | Court of Appeals | 142,969 | 140,732 | Circuit courts | 136,257 |
| Florida | Supreme Court | 157,976 | 157,976 | District Court of Appeals | 150,077 | 150,077 | Circuit courts | 142,178 |
| Georgia | Supreme Court | 167,210 | 167,210 | Court of Appeals | 166,186 | 166,186 | Superior courts | (f) |
| Kentucky | Supreme Court | 140,504 | 135,504 | Court of Appeals | 133,044 | 130,044 | Circuit courts | 124,620 |
| Louisiana | Supreme Court | 157,050 | 149,572 | Court of Appeals | 149,570 | 142,477 | District courts | 136,544 |
| Mississippi | Supreme Court | 115,390 | 112,530 | Court of Appeals | 108,130 | 105,050 | Chancery courts | 104,170 |
| Missouri | Supreme Court | 139,534 | 137,034 | Court of Appeals | 128,207 | 128,207 | Circuit courts | 120,484 |
| North Carolina | Supreme Court | 140,932 | 137,249 | Court of Appeals | 135,061 | 131,531 | Superior courts | 124,382 |
| Oklahoma | Supreme Court | 147,000 | 137,655 | Court of Appeals | 132,825 | 130,410 | District courts | 124,373 |
| South Carolina | Supreme Court | 144,029 | 137,171 | Court of Appeals | 135,799 | 133,741 | Circuit courts | 130,312 |
| Tennessee | Supreme Court | 172,980 | 167,976 | Court of Appeals | 164,892 | 162,396 | Chancery courts | 156,792 |
| Texas | Supreme Court | 152,500 | 150,000 | Court of Appeals | (e) | (g) | District courts | (h) |
| Virginia | Supreme Court (i) | 195,104 | 183,839 | Court of Appeals (j) | 171,383 | 168,322 | Circuit courts | 158,134 |
| West Virginia | Supreme Court | 136,000 | 136,000 | ... | ... | ... | Circuit courts | 126,000 |
| Regional averages | | 151,648 | 146,780 | | 141,955 | 138,484 | | 129,770 |

See footnotes at end of table.

# COMPENSATION OF JUDGES OF APPELLATE COURTS AND GENERAL TRIAL COURTS—Continued

| State or other jurisdiction | Appellate courts | | | | | | General trial courts | |
|---|---|---|---|---|---|---|---|---|
| | Court of last resort | Chief Justice salaries | Associate Justice salaries | Intermediate appellate court | Chief/Presiding salaries | Judges salaries | | Salary |
| **Western Region** | | | | | | | | |
| Alaska................ | Supreme Court | 192,936 | 192,372 | Court of Appeals | 181,752 | 181,752 | Superior courts | 177,888 |
| Arizona............... | Supreme Court | 160,000 | 155,000 | Court of Appeals | 150,000 | 150,000 | Superior courts | 145,000 |
| California............ | Supreme Court | 228,856 | 218,237 | Court of Appeals | ... | 204,599 | Superior court | 178,789 |
| Colorado............. | Supreme Court | 142,708 | 139,660 | Court of Appeals | 137,201 | 134,128 | District courts | 128,598 |
| Hawaii............... | Supreme Court | 156,727 | 151,118 | Intermediate Court | 145,532 | 139,924 | Circuit courts | 136,127 |
| Idaho................ | Supreme Court | 121,006 | 119,506 | Court of Appeals | 118,506 | 118,506 | District courts | 112,043 |
| Montana............. | Supreme Court | 122,686 | 121,434 | ... | ... | ... | District courts | 113,928 |
| Nevada.............. | Supreme Court | 170,000 | 170,000 | ... | ... | ... | District courts | 160,000 |
| New Mexico......... | Supreme Court | 125,691 | 123,691 | Court of Appeals | 119,406 | 117,506 | District courts | 111,631 |
| Oregon.............. | Supreme Court | 128,556 | 125,688 | Court of Appeals | 125,688 | 122,820 | Circuit courts | 114,468 |
| Utah................ | Supreme Court | 147,350 | 145,350 | Court of Appeals | 140,750 | 138,750 | District courts | 132,150 |
| Washington.......... | Supreme Court | 164,221 | 164,221 | Court of Appeals | 156,328 | 156,328 | Superior courts | 148,832 |
| Wyoming............. | Supreme Court | 131,500 | 131,500 | ... | 107,769 | 105,923 | District courts | 125,200 |
| Regional averages... | | 151,853 | 148,981 | | | | | 126,769 |
| Regional averages w/o California... | | 135,000 | 133,167 | | 138,293 | 142,749 | | 131,128 |
| Dist. of Columbia.... | Court of Appeals | 180,000 | 179,500 | ... | ... | ... | Superior courts | 169,300 |
| American Samoa..... | High Court | 125,000 | 119,000 | ... | ... | ... | District courts | 97,000 |
| Guam............... | Supreme Court | 133,000 | 131,000 | ... | ... | ... | Superior courts | 112,486 |
| No. Mariana Islands.. | Commonwealth Supreme Court | 130,000 | 126,000 | ... | ... | ... | Superior courts | 120,000 |
| Puerto Rico.......... | Supreme Court | 125,000 | 120,000 | Appellate Court | 105,000 | 105,000 | Superior courts | 90,000 |
| U.S. Virgin Islands... | Territorial Court | 186,300 | 181,300 | ... | ... | ... | ... | ... |

*Source:* National Center for State Courts, July 1, 2011.

*Note:* Compensation is shown rounded to the nearest thousand, and is reported according to most recent legislation, even though laws may not yet have taken effect. There are other non-salary forms of judicial compensation that can be a significant part of a judge's compensation package. It should be noted that many of these can be important to judges or attorneys who might be interested in becoming judges or justices. These include retirement, disability, and death benefits, expense accounts, vacation, holiday, and sick leave and various forms of insurance coverage.

*Key:*
(a) Salary range is between $161,002–$201,252.
(b) Salary range is between $160,003–$200,007.
(c) Salary range is between $159,503–$199,378.
(d) Salary range is between $159,003–$198,753.
(e) Salary range is between $119,949–$149,936.
(f) Salary range is between $120,252–$190,452.
(g) Salary range is between $137,500–$145,000.
(h) Salary range is between $125,000–$140,000.
(i) Plus $13,500 in lieu of travel, lodging, and other expenses.
(j) Plus $6,500 in lieu of travel, lodging, and other expenses.

## Table 5.5
## SELECTED DATA ON COURT ADMINISTRATIVE OFFICES

| State or other jurisdiction | Title | Established | Appointed by (a) | Salary |
|---|---|---|---|---|
| Alabama | Administrative Director of Courts | 1971 | CJ (b) | (g) |
| Alaska | Administrative Director | 1959 | CJ (b) | 190,372 |
| Arizona | Administrative Director of Courts | 1960 | SC | (h) |
| Arkansas | Director, Administrative Office of the Courts | 1965 | CJ (c) | 108,230 |
| California | Administrative Director of the Courts | 1960 | JC | (i) |
| Colorado | State Court Administrator | 1959 | SC | 137,201 |
| Connecticut | Chief Court Administrator (d) | 1965 | CJ | 168,783 |
| Delaware | Director, Administrative Office of the Courts | 1971 | CJ | 126,550 |
| Florida | State Courts Administrator | 1972 | SC | 134,879 |
| Georgia | Director, Administrative Office of the Courts | 1973 | JC | 144,473 |
| Hawaii | Administrative Director of the Courts | 1959 | CJ (b) | 129,073 |
| Idaho | Administrative Director of the Courts | 1967 | SC | 118,506 |
| Illinois | Administrative Director of the Courts | 1959 | SC | 197,032 |
| Indiana | Executive Director, Division of State Court Administration | 1975 | CJ | 115,440 |
| Iowa | Court Administrator | 1971 | SC | 154,300 |
| Kansas | Judicial Administrator | 1965 | CJ | 120,037 |
| Kentucky | Administrative Director of the Courts | 1976 | CJ | 124,620 |
| Louisiana | Judicial Administrator | 1954 | SC | 142,447 |
| Maine | Court Administrator | 1975 | CJ | 111,969 |
| Maryland | State Court Administrator | 1955 | CJ (b) | 142,287 |
| Massachusetts | Chief Justice for Administration & Management | 1978 | SC | 140,358 |
| Michigan | State Court Administrator | 1952 | SC | (j) |
| Minnesota | State Court Administrator | 1963 | SC | (k) |
| Mississippi | Court Administrator | 1974 | SC | 89,960 |
| Missouri | State Courts Administrator | 1970 | SC | 118,450 |
| Montana | State Court Administrator | 1975 | SC | 96,990 |
| Nebraska | State Court Administrator | 1972 | CJ | 116,389 |
| Nevada | Director, Office of Court Administration | 1971 | SC | 123,783 |
| New Hampshire | Director of the Administrative Office of the Court | 1980 | SC | 117,820 |
| New Jersey | Administrative Director of the Courts | 1948 | CJ | 175,534 |
| New Mexico | Director, Administrative Office of the Courts | 1959 | SC | 123,325 |
| New York | Chief Administrator of the Courts | 1978 | CJ | 147,600 |
| North Carolina | Director, Administrative Office of the Courts | 1965 | CJ | 126,738 |
| North Dakota | Court Administrator (h) | 1971 | CJ | 106,428 |
| Ohio | Administrative Director of the Courts | 1955 | SC | (l) |
| Oklahoma | Administrative Director of the Courts | 1967 | SC | 130,410 |
| Oregon | Court Administrator | 1971 | SC | (m) |
| Pennsylvania | Court Administrator | 1968 | SC | 178,914 |
| Rhode Island | State Court Administrator | 1969 | CJ | (n) |
| South Carolina | Director of Court Administration | 1973 | CJ | 123,453 |
| South Dakota | State Court Administrator | 1974 | SC | 100,000 |
| Tennessee | Director | 1963 | SC | 156,792 |
| Texas | Administrative Director of the Courts (i) | 1977 | SC | 130,000 |
| Utah | Court Administrator | 1973 | SC | 132,150 |
| Vermont | Court Administrator | 1967 | SC | 122,867 |
| Virginia | Executive Secretary to the Supreme Court | 1952 | SC | 176,738 |
| Washington | Administrator for the Courts | 1957 | SC (e) | 142,800 |
| West Virginia | Administrative Director of the Supreme Court of Appeals | 1975 | SC | 135,000 |
| Wisconsin | Director of State Courts | 1978 | SC | 136,316 |
| Wyoming | Court Coordinator | 1974 | SC | 110,000 |
| Dist. of Columbia | Executive Officer, Courts of D.C. | 1971 | (f) | 174,000 |
| American Samoa | Administrator/Comptroller | N.A | N.A. | N.A. |
| Guam | Administrative Director of Superior Court | N.A. | CJ | 120,000 (o) |
| No. Mariana Islands | Director of Courts | N.A. | N.A. | N.A. |
| Puerto Rico | Administrative Director of the Courts | 1952 | CJ | N.A. |
| U.S. Virgin Islands | Court/Administrative Clerk | N.A. | N.A. | 118,500 |

*Source:* National Center for State Courts, July 1, 2011.

*Note:* Compensation shown is rounded to the nearest thousand, and is reported according to most recent legislation, even though laws may not yet have taken effect. Other information from State Court Administrator websites.

*Key:*
SC — State court of last resort.
CJ — Chief justice or chief judge of court of last resort.
JC — Judicial council.
N.A. — Not available.
(a) Term of office for all court administrators is at pleasure of appointing authority.
(b) With approval of Supreme Court.

(c) With approval of Judicial Council.
(d) Administrator is an associate judge of the Supreme Court.
(e) Appointed from list of five submitted by governor.
(f) Joint Committee on Judicial Administration.
(g) Salary range is between $100,197 and $152,618.
(h) Salary range is between $109,000 and $179,000.
(i) Salary range is between $192,084 and $211,272.
(j) Salary range is between $109,704 and $148,123.
(k) Salary range is between $97,322 and $150,816.
(l) Salary range is between $125,000 and $145,000.
(m) Salary range is between $98,124 and $159,744.
(n) Salary range is between $114,118 and $137,604.
(o) After supplements: $149,000.

## Table 5.6
# SELECTION AND RETENTION OF APPELLATE COURT JUDGES

| State or other jurisdiction | Name of court | Type of court | Method of selection Unexpired term | Method of selection Full term | Method of retention | Geographic basis for selection |
|---|---|---|---|---|---|---|
| Alabama | Supreme Court | SC | GU | PE | PE | SW |
| | Court of Civil Appeals | IA | GU | PE | PE | SW |
| | Court of Criminal Appeals | IA | GU | PE | PE | SW |
| Alaska | Supreme Court | SC | GN | GN | RE (a) | SW |
| | Court of Appeals | IA | GN | GN | RE (a) | SW |
| Arizona | Supreme Court | SC | GN | GN | RE | SW |
| | Court of Appeals | IA | GN | GN | RE | DS |
| Arkansas | Supreme Court | SC | GU | NP | NP | SW |
| | Court of Appeals | IA | GU | NP | NP | DS |
| California | Supreme Court | SC | GU | GU | RE | SW |
| | Courts of Appeal | IA | GU | GU | RE | DS |
| Colorado | Supreme Court | SC | GN | GN | RE | SW |
| | Court of Appeals | IA | GN | GN | RE | SW |
| Connecticut | Supreme Court | SC | GNL | GNL | GNL | SW |
| | Appellate Court | IA | GNL | GNL | GNL | SW |
| Delaware | Supreme Court | SC | GNL | GNL | GNL | SW |
| Florida | Supreme Court | SC | GN | GN | RE | DS and SW (b) |
| | District Courts of Appeal | IA | GN | GN | RE | DS |
| Georgia | Supreme Court | SC | GN | NP | NP | SW |
| | Court of Appeals | IA | GN | NP | NP | SW |
| Hawaii | Supreme Court | SC | GNL | GNL | JN | SW |
| | Intermediate Court of Appeals | IA | GNL | GNL | JN | SW |
| Idaho | Supreme Court | SC | GN | NP | NP | SW |
| | Court of Appeals | IA | GN | NP | NP | SW |
| Illinois | Supreme Court | SC | CS | PE | RE | DS |
| | Appellate Court | IA | SC | PE | RE | DS |
| Indiana | Supreme Court | SC | GN | GN | RE | SW |
| | Court of Appeals | IA | GN | GN | RE | DS |
| | Tax Court | IA | GN | GN | RE | SW |
| Iowa | Supreme Court | SC | GN | GN | RE | SW |
| | Court of Appeals | IA | GN | GN | RE | SW |
| Kansas | Supreme Court | SC | GN | GN | RE | SW |
| | Court of Appeals | IA | GN | GN | RE | SW |
| Kentucky | Supreme Court | SC | GN | NP | NP | DS |
| | Court of Appeals | IA | GN | NP | NP | DS |
| Louisiana | Supreme Court | SC | CS (c) | PE (d) | PE (d) | DS |
| | Courts of Appeal | IA | SC (c) | PE (d) | PE (d) | DS |
| Maine | Supreme Judicial Court | SC | GL | GL | GL | SW |
| Maryland | Court of Appeals | SC | GNL | GNL | RE | DS |
| | Court of Special Appeals | IA | GNL | GNL | RE | DS |
| Massachusetts | Supreme Judicial Court | SC | (e) | GNE (f) | (g) | SW |
| | Appeals Court | IA | (e) | GNE (f) | (g) | SW |
| Michigan | Supreme Court | SC | GU | NP (h) | NP (h) | SW |
| | Court of Appeals | IA | GU | NP (h) | NP (h) | DS |
| Minnesota | Supreme Court | SC | GU | NP | NP | SW |
| | Court of Appeals | IA | GU | NP | NP | SW |
| Mississippi | Supreme Court | SC | GU | NP | NP | DS |
| | Court of Appeals | IA | GU | NP | NP | DS |
| Missouri | Supreme Court | SC | GN | GN | RE | SW |
| | Court of Appeals | IA | GN | GN | RE | DS |
| Montana | Supreme Court | SC | GNL | NP | NP (i) | SW |
| Nebraska | Supreme Court | SC | GN | GN | RE | SW and DS (j) |
| | Court of Appeals | IA | GN | GN | RE | DS |
| Nevada | Supreme Court | SC | GN | NP | NP | SW |

See footnotes at end of table.

## SELECTION AND RETENTION OF APPELLATE COURT JUDGES — Continued

| State or other jurisdiction | Name of court | Type of court | Method of selection | | Method of retention | Geographic basis for selection |
|---|---|---|---|---|---|---|
| | | | Unexpired term | Full term | | |
| New Hampshire | Supreme Court | SC | GE | GE | (k) | SW |
| New Jersey | Supreme Court | SC | GL | GL | GL | SW |
| | Superior Court, Appellate Div. | IA | GL | GL (l) | GL (l) | SW |
| New Mexico | Supreme Court | SC | GN | PE | RE | SW |
| | Court of Appeals | IA | GN | PE | RE | SW |
| New York | Court of Appeals | SC | GNL | GNL | GNL | SW |
| | Supreme Court, Appellate Div. | IA | GN | GN | GN | SW (m) |
| North Carolina | Supreme Court | SC | GU | NP | NP | SW |
| | Court of Appeals | IA | GU | NP | NP | SW |
| North Dakota | Supreme Court | SC | GN (n) | NP | NP | SW |
| | Temporary Court of Appeals | IA | (w) | SC (x) | (w) | SW |
| Ohio | Supreme Court | SC | GU | PE (o) | PE (o) | SW |
| | Courts of Appeals | IA | GU | PE (o) | PE (o) | DS |
| Oklahoma | Supreme Court | SC | GN | GN | RE | DS |
| | Court of Criminal Appeals | SC | GN | GN | RE | DS |
| | Court of Civil Appeals | IA | GN | GN | RE | DS |
| Oregon | Supreme Court | SC | GU | NP | NP | SW |
| | Court of Appeals | IA | GU | NP | NP | SW |
| Pennsylvania | Supreme Court | SC | GL | PE | RE | SW |
| | Superior Court | IA | GL | PE | RE | SW |
| | Commonwealth Court | IA | GL | PE | RE | SW |
| Rhode Island | Supreme Court | SC | GN | GN | (p) | SW |
| South Carolina | Supreme Court | SC | LA | LA | LA | SW |
| | Court of Appeals | IA | LA | LA | LA | SW |
| South Dakota | Supreme Court | SC | GN | GN | RE | DS and SW (q) |
| Tennessee | Supreme Court | SC | GN | GN | RE | SW |
| | Court of Appeals | SC | GN | GN | RE | SW |
| | Court of Criminal Appeals | IA | GN | GN | RE | SW |
| Texas | Supreme Court | SC | GU | PE | PE | SW |
| | Court of Criminal Appeals | SC | GU | PE | PE | SW |
| | Courts of Appeals | IA | GU | PE | PE | DS |
| Utah | Supreme Court | SC | GNL | GNL | RE | SW |
| | Court of Appeals | IA | GNL | GNL | RE | SW |
| Vermont | Supreme Court | SC | GNL | GNL | LA | SW |
| Virginia | Supreme Court | SC | GU (r) | LA | LA | SW |
| | Court of Appeals | IA | GU (r) | LA | LA | SW |
| Washington | Supreme Court | SC | GU | NP | NP | SW |
| | Courts of Appeals | IA | GU | NP | NP | DS |
| West Virginia | Supreme Court of Appeals | SC | GU (s) | PE | PE | SW |
| Wisconsin | Supreme Court | SC | GN | NP | NP | SW |
| | Court of Appeals | IA | GN | NP | NP | DS |
| Wyoming | Supreme Court | SC | GN | GN | RE | SW |
| District of Columbia | Court of Appeals | SC | (t) | (t) | (t) | SW (u) |
| Puerto Rico | Supreme Court | SC | GL | GL | (v) | SW |
| | Court of Appeals | IA | GL | GL | GL | SW |

See footnotes at end of table.

# SELECTION AND RETENTION OF APPELLATE COURT JUDGES — Continued

*Source:* Bureau of Justice Statistics, *State Court Organization, 2004* NCJ 212351, Update from the National Center for State Courts, March 2012.

*Key:*
SC — Court of last resort
IA — Intermediate appellate court
N/S — Not stated
N.A. — Not applicable
AP — At pleasure
CS — Court selection
DS — District
DU — Duration of service
GE — Gubernatorial appointment with approval of elected executive council
GL — Gubernatorial appointment with consent of the legislature
GN — Gubernatorial appointment from judicial nominating commission
GNE — Gubernatorial appointment from judicial nominating commission with approval of elected executive council
GNL — Gubernatorial appointment from judicial nominating commission with consent of the legislature
GU — Gubernatorial appointment
ID — Indefinite
JN — Judicial nominating commission appoints
LA — Legislative appointment
NP — Non-partisan election
PE — Partisan election
RE — Retention election
SC — Court of last resort appoints
SCJ — Chief justice/judge of the court of last resort appoints
SN — Seniority
SW — Statewide

(a) A judge must run for a retention election at the next election, immediately following the third year from the time of initial appointment.

(b) Five justices are selected by region (based on the District Courts of Appeal) and two justices are selected statewide.

(c) The person selected by the Supreme Court is prohibited from running for that judgeship; an election is held within one year to serve the remainder of the term.

(d) Louisiana uses a blanket primary, in which all candidates appear with party labels on the primary ballot. The two top vote-getters compete in the general election.

(e) There are no expired judicial terms. A judicial term expires upon the death, resignation, retirement, or removal of an incumbent.

(f) The Executive (Governor's) Council is made up of nine people elected by geographical area and presided over by the Lieutenant Governor.

(g) There is no retention process. Judges serve during good behavior to age 70.

(h) Candidates may be nominated by political parties and are elected on a nonpartisan ballot.

(i) If the justice/judge is unopposed, a retention election is held.

(j) Chief Justices are selected statewide while Associate Justices are selected by district.

(k) There is no retention process. Judges serve during good behavior to age 70.

(l) All Superior Court judges, including Appellate Division judges, are subject to gubernatorial reappointment and consent by the Senate after an initial seven-year term. Among all the judges, the Chief Justice designates the judges of the Appellate Division.

(m) The Presiding Judge of each Appellate Division must be a resident of the department.

(n) The Governor may appoint from a list of names or call a special election at his discretion.

(o) Party affiliation is not included on the ballot in the general election, but candidates are chosen through partisan primary nominations.

(p) There is no retention process. Judges serve during good behavior for a life tenure.

(q) Initial selection is by district, but retention selection is statewide.

(r) Gubernatorial appointment is for interim appointments.

(s) Appointment is effective only until the next election year; the appointee may run for election to any remaining portion of the unexpired term.

(t) Initial appointment is made by the President of the United States and confirmed by the Senate. Six months prior to the expiration of the term of office, the judge's performance is reviewed by the tenure commission. Those found "well qualified" are automatically reappointed. If a judge is found to be "qualified" the President may nominate the judge for an additional term (subject to Senate confirmation). If the President does not wish to reappoint the judge, the District of Columbia Nomination Commission compiles a new list of candidates.

(u) The geographic basis of selection is the District of Columbia.

(v) There is no retention process. Judges serve during good behavior to age 70.

(w) The Supreme Court may provide for the assignment of active or retired District Court judges, retired justices of the Supreme Court, and lawyers, to serve on three-judge panels.

(x) There is neither a retention process nor unexpired terms. Assignments are for a specified time, not to exceed one year or the completion of one or more cases on the docket of the Supreme Court.

## Table 5.7
## SELECTION AND RETENTION OF TRIAL COURT JUDGES

| State or other jurisdiction | Name of Court | Types of court | Method of selection | | Method of retention | Geographic basis for selection |
|---|---|---|---|---|---|---|
| | | | Unexpired term | Full term | | |
| Alabama...................... | Circuit | GJ | GU (a) | PE | PE | Circuit |
| | District | LJ | GU (a) | PE | PE | County |
| | Municipal | LJ | MU | MU | RA | Municipality |
| | Probate | LJ | GU | PE | PE | County |
| Alaska ......................... | Superior | GJ | GN | GN | RE (b) | State (c) |
| | District | LJ | GN | GN | RE (d) | District |
| | Magistrate's Division | N.A. | PJ | PJ | PJ | District |
| Arizona ...................... | Superior | GJ | GN or VA (e) | GN or NP (f) | NP or RE (f) | County |
| | Justice of the Peace | LJ | CO | PE | PE | Precinct |
| | Municipal | LJ | CC (g) | CC (g) | CC (g) | Municipality |
| Arkansas ..................... | Circuit | GJ | GU (h) | NP | NP | Circuit |
| | District | LJ | GU | NP | NP | District |
| | City | LJ | LD | LD | LD | City |
| California.................... | Superior | GJ | GU | NP | NP (i) | County |
| Colorado ..................... | District | GJ | GN | GN | RE | District |
| | Denver Probate | GJ | GN | GN | RE | District |
| | Denver Juvenile | GJ | GN | GN | RE | District |
| | Water | GJ | SC (j) | SC (j) | RE | District |
| | County | LJ | GN | GN (k) | RE | County |
| | Municipal | LJ | MU | MU | RA | Municipality |
| Connecticut ................ | Superior | GJ | GNL | GNL | GNL | State |
| | Probate | LJ | PE | PE | PE | District |
| Delaware..................... | Superior | GJ | GNL | GNL | GNL | State |
| | Chancery | LJ | GNL | GNL | GNL | State |
| | Justice of the Peace | LJ | GNL (l) | GNL (l) | GU | County |
| | Family | LJ | GNL | GNL | GNL | County |
| | Common Pleas | LJ | GNL | GNL | GNL | County |
| | Alderman's | LJ | LD | CC | LD | Town |
| Florida........................ | Circuit | GJ | GN | NP | NP | Circuit |
| | County | LJ | GN | NP | NP | County |
| Georgia ....................... | Superior | GJ | GN | NP | NP | Circuit |
| | Juvenile | LJ | CS (m) | CS (m) | CS (m) | County/Circuit |
| | Civil | LJ | GU | PE | PE | County |
| | State | LJ | GU | NP | NP | County |
| | Probate | LJ | GU | PE (n) | PE (n) | County |
| | Magistrate | LJ | LD | LD (o) | LD (o) | County |
| | Municipal/of Columbus | LJ | MA | Elected | Elected | Municipality |
| | County Recorder's | LJ | LD | LD | LD | County |
| | Municipal/City of Atlanta | LJ | MU | MU | LD | Municipality |
| Hawaii ........................ | Circuit | GJ | GNL | GNL | JN | State |
| | District | LJ | SCJ (p) | SCJ (p) | JN | Circuit |
| Idaho .......................... | District | GJ | GN | NP | NP | District |
| | Magistrate's Division | LJ | JN (q) | JN (q) | RE | County |
| Illinois........................ | Circuit | GJ | SC | PE | RE | Circuit/County (r) |
| | Associate Division | N.A. | SC | PE | RE | Circuit/County (r) |
| Indiana ....................... | Superior | GJ | GU | PE (s) | PE (s) | County |
| | Circuit | GJ | GU | PE (t) | PE (t) | County |
| | Probate | GJ | GU | PE | PE | County |
| | County | LJ | GU | PE | PE | County |
| | City | LJ | GU | PE | PE | Municipality |
| | Town | LJ | GU | PE | PE | Municipality |
| | Small Claims/Marion County | LJ | GU | PE | PE | Township |
| Iowa............................ | District | GJ | GN (u) | GN (u) | RE (u) | District |
| Kansas ........................ | District | GJ | GN and PE(v) | GN and PE (v) | RE and PE (v) | District |
| | Municipal | LJ | MU | MU | MU | City |
| Kentucky..................... | Circuit | GJ | GN | NP | NP | Circuit |
| | District | LJ | GN | NP | NP | District |
| Louisiana .................... | District | GJ | SC (w) | PE | PE | District |
| | Juvenile & Family | GJ | SC (w) | PE | PE | District |
| | Justice of the Peace | LJ | SC (w) | PE(x) | PE | Ward |
| | Mayor's | LJ | MA | LD | LD | City |
| | City & Parish | LJ | SC (w) | PE | PE | Ward |

See footnotes at end of table.

# SELECTION AND RETENTION OF TRIAL COURT JUDGES — Continued

| State or other jurisdiction | Name of Court | Types of court | Method of selection Unexpired term | Method of selection Full term | Method of retention | Geographic basis for selection |
|---|---|---|---|---|---|---|
| Maine | Superior | GJ | GL | GL | GL | State |
| | District | GJ | GL | GL | GL | State and District (y) |
| | Probate | LJ | GU | PE | PE | County |
| Maryland | Circuit | GJ | GNL | GNL | NP | County |
| | District | LJ | GNL | GNL | RA | District |
| | Orphan's | LJ | GU | PE (z) | PE (z) | County |
| Massachusetts | Superior | GJ | (aa) | GNE (bb) | (cc) | State |
| | District | LJ | (aa) | GNE (bb) | (cc) | State |
| | Probate & Family | LJ | (aa) | GNE (bb) | (cc) | State |
| | Juvenile | LJ | (aa) | GNE (bb) | (cc) | State |
| | Housing | LJ | (aa) | GNE (bb) | (cc) | State |
| | Boston Municipal | LJ | (aa) | GNE (bb) | (cc) | State |
| | Land | LJ | (aa) | GNE (bb) | (cc) | State |
| Michigan | Circuit | GJ | GU | NP | NP | Circuit |
| | Claims | GJ | GU | NP | NP | Circuit |
| | District | LJ | GU | NP | NP | District |
| | Probate | LJ | GU | NP | NP | District and Circuit |
| | Municipal | LJ | LD | NP | NP | City |
| Minnesota | District | GJ | GN | NP | NP | District |
| Mississippi | Circuit | GJ | GU | NP | NP | District |
| | Chancery | LJ | GU | NP | NP | District |
| | County | LJ | GU | NP | NP | County |
| | Municipal | LJ | LD | LD | LD | Municipality |
| | Justice | LJ | LD | PE | PE | District in County |
| Missouri | Circuit | GJ | GU and GN (dd) | PE and GN (ee) | PE and RE (ff) | Circuit/County (gg) |
| | Municipal | LJ | LD | LD | LD | City |
| Montana | District | GJ | GN | NP | NP | District |
| | Workers' Compensation | GJ | GN | GN | RA | State |
| | Water | GJ | SCJ (hh) | SCJ (hh) | SCJ (ii) | State |
| | Justice of the Peace | LJ | CO | NP | NP | County |
| | Municipal | LJ | MU | NP | NP | City |
| | City | LJ | CC | NP | NP | City |
| Nebraska | District | GJ | GN | GN | RE | District |
| | Separate Juvenile | LJ | GN | GN | RE | District |
| | County | LJ | GN | GN | RE | District |
| | Workers' Compensation | LJ | GN | GN | RE | District |
| Nevada | District | GJ | GN | NP | NP | District |
| | Justice | LJ | CO | NP | NP | Township |
| | Municipal | LJ | CC | NP | NP | City |
| New Hampshire | Superior | GJ | GE | GE | (jj) | State |
| | District | LJ | GE | GE | (jj) | District |
| | Probate | LJ | GE | GE | (jj) | County |
| New Jersey | Superior | GJ | GL | GL | GL | County |
| | Tax | LJ | GL | GL | GL | State |
| | Municipal | LJ | MA or MU (kk) | MA or MU (kk) | MU | Municipality |
| New Mexico | District | GJ | GN | PE | RE | District |
| | Magistrate | LJ | GU | PE | PE | County |
| | Metropolitan/Bernalillo County | LJ | GN | PE | RE | County |
| | Municipal | LJ | MU | PE | PE | City |
| | Probate | LJ | CO | PE | PE | County |
| New York | Supreme | GJ | GL | PE | PE | District |
| | County | GJ | GL | PE | PE | County |
| | Claims | GJ | GNL | GNL | GU | State |
| | Surrogates' | LJ | GNL | PE | PE | County |
| | Family | LJ | GNL and MU (ll) | PE and MU (ll) | PE and MU (ll) | County and NYC |
| | District | LJ | (mm) | PE | PE | District |
| | City | LJ | Elected | Elected | LD | City |
| | NYC Civil | LJ | MA (nn) | PE | PE | City |
| | NYC Criminal | LJ | MA | MA | MA | City |
| | Town & Village Justice | LJ | LD | LD | LD | Town or Village |
| North Carolina | Superior | GJ | GU | NP | NP | District |
| | District | LJ | GU | NP | NP | District |

See footnotes at end of table.

## SELECTION AND RETENTION OF TRIAL COURT JUDGES — Continued

| State or other jurisdiction | Name of Court | Types of court | Method of selection | | Method of retention | Geographic basis for selection |
|---|---|---|---|---|---|---|
| | | | Unexpired term | Full term | | |
| **North Dakota** ............. | District | GJ | GN | NP | NP | District |
| | Municipal | LJ | MA | NP | NP | City |
| **Ohio** .............................. | Common Pleas | GJ | GU | PE (oo) | PE (oo) | County |
| | Municipal | LJ | GU | PE (oo) | PE (oo) | County/City |
| | County | LJ | GU | PE (oo) | PE (oo) | County |
| | Claims | LJ | SCJ | SCJ | SCJ | N.A. |
| | Mayor's | LJ | Elected | PE | PE | City/Village |
| **Oklahoma** ................... | District | GJ | GN (pp) | NP (pp) | NP (pp) | District |
| | Municipal Not of Record | LJ | MM | MM | MM | Municipality |
| | Municipal of Record | LJ | MU | MU | MU | Municipality |
| | Workers' Compensation | LJ | GN | GN | GN | State |
| | Tax Review | LJ | SCJ | SCJ | SCJ | District |
| **Oregon** ...................... | Circuit | GJ | GU | NP | NP | District |
| | Tax | GJ | GU | NP | NP | State |
| | County | LJ | CO | NP | NP | County |
| | Justice | LJ | GU | NP | NP | County |
| | Municipal | LJ | CC | CC/Elected | CC/Elected | (qq) |
| **Pennsylvania** .............. | Common Pleas | GJ | GL | PE | RE | District |
| | Philadelphia Municipal | LJ | GL | PE | RE | City/County |
| | Magisterial District Judges | LJ | GL | PE | PE | District |
| | Philadelphia Traffic | LJ | GL | PE | RE | City/County |
| **Rhode Island** ............. | Superior | GJ | GN | GN | (rr) | State |
| | Workers' Compensation | LJ | GN | GN | (rr) | State |
| | District | LJ | GN | GN | (rr) | State |
| | Family | LJ | GN | GN | (rr) | State |
| | Probate | LJ | CC | CC or MA | RA | Town |
| | Municipal | LJ | CC | CC or MA | CC or MA | Town |
| | Traffic Tribunal | LJ | GN | GN | (rr) | State |
| **South Carolina** ........... | Circuit | GJ | LA and GN (ss)(tt) | LA and GN (tt) | LA and GL (tt) | Circuit and State (tt) |
| | Family | LJ | LA | LA | LA | Circuit |
| | Magistrate | LJ | GL | GL | GL | County |
| | Probate | LJ | GU | PE | PE | County |
| | Municipal | LJ | CC | CC | CC | District |
| **South Dakota** ............. | Circuit | GJ | GN | NP | NP | Circuit |
| | Magistrate | LJ | PJS | PJS | PJS | Circuit |
| **Tennessee** .................... | Circuit | GJ | GU | PE (uu) | PE | District |
| | Chancery | GJ | GU | PE (uu) | PE | District |
| | Criminal | GJ | GU | PE (uu) | PE | District |
| | Probate | GJ | (vv) | PE (uu) | PE | District |
| | Juvenile | LJ | (vv) | PE (uu) | PE | County |
| | Municipal | LJ | LD | LD (uu) | LD | Municipality |
| | General Sessions | LJ | MU | PE (uu) | PE | County |
| **Texas** ........................... | District | GJ | GL | PE | PE | District |
| | Constitutional County | LJ | CO | PE | PE | County |
| | Probate | LJ | CO | PE | PE | County |
| | County at Law | LJ | CO | PE | PE | County |
| | Justice of the Peace | LJ | CO | PE | PE | Precinct |
| | Municipal | LJ | CC | LD | LD | Municipality |
| **Utah** ........................... | District | GJ | (ww) | GNL | RE | District |
| | Justice | LJ | MM (xx) | MM (xx) | RE and RA (yy) | County/Municipality |
| | Juvenile | LJ | (ww) | GNL | RE | District |
| **Vermont** ...................... | Superior (zz) | GJ | GNL | GNL | LA | State |
| | Judicial Bureau | LJ | PJ | PJ | AP | State |
| **Virginia** ....................... | Circuit | GJ | GU | LA | LA | Circuit |
| | District | LJ | CS (aaa) | LA | LA | District |
| **Washington** ................. | Superior | GJ | GU | NP | NP | County |
| | District | LJ | CO | NP | NP | District |
| | Municipal | LJ | CC | MA/CC | MA/CC (bbb) | Municipality |
| **West Virginia** .............. | Circuit | GJ | GU | PE | PE | Circuit |
| | Magistrate | LJ | PJ | PE | PE | County |
| | Municipal | LJ | LD | LD | LD | Municipality |
| | Family | LJ | GU | PE | PE | Circuit |

See footnotes at end of table.

## SELECTION AND RETENTION OF TRIAL COURT JUDGES — Continued

| State or other jurisdiction | Name of Court | Types of court | Method of selection | | Method of retention | Geographic basis for selection |
|---|---|---|---|---|---|---|
| | | | Unexpired term | Full term | | |
| **Wisconsin**.................. | Circuit | GJ | GU | NP | NP | District |
| | Municipal | LJ | MU (ccc) | NP | NP | Municipality |
| **Wyoming**.................. | District | GJ | GN | GN | RE | District |
| | Circuit | LJ | GN | GN | RE | Circuit |
| | Municipal | LJ | MA | MA | LD | Municipality |
| **Dist. of Columbia**....... | Superior | GJ | (ddd) | (ddd) | (ddd) | State (eee) |
| **Puerto Rico** ............... | First Instance | GJ | GL | GL | GL | State |

*Source:* Bureau of Justice Statistics, *State Court Organization, 2004* NCJ 212351, Update from the National Center for State Courts, March 2012.

*Key:*
GJ — General jurisdiction court
LJ — Limited jurisdiction court
N/S — Not stated
N.A. — Not applicable
AP — At pleasure
CA — Court administrator appointment
CC — City or town council/commission appointment
CO — County board/commission appointment
CS — Court selection
DU — Duration of service
GE — Gubernatorial appointment with approval of elected executive council
GL — Gubernatorial appointment with consent of the legislature
GN — Gubernatorial appointment from judicial nominating commission
GNE — Gubernatorial appointment from judicial nominating commission with approval of elected executive council
GNL — Gubernatorial appointment from judicial nominating commission with consent of the legislature
GU — Gubernatorial appointment
JN — Judicial nominating commission appoints
LA — Legislative appointment
LD — Locally determined
MA — Mayoral appointment
MC — Mayoral appointment with consent of city council
MM — Mayoral appointment with consent of governing municipal body
MU — Governing municipal body appointment
NP — Non-partisan election
PE — Partisan election
PJ — Presiding judge of the general jurisdiction court appoints
PJS — Presiding judge of the general jurisdiction court appoints with approval of the court of last resort
RA — Reappointment
RE — Retention election
SC — Court of last resort appoints
SCJ — Chief justice/judge of the court of last resort appoints
VA — Varies
(a) The counties of Baldwin, Jefferson, Lauderdale, Madison, Mobile, Shelby, Talladega, and Tuscaloosa use gubernatorial appointment from the recommendations of the Judicial Nominating Commission.
(b) A judge must run for retention at the next election immediately following the third year from the time of the initial appointment.
(c) Judges are selected on a statewide basis, but run for retention on a district-wide basis.
(d) Judges must run for retention at the first general election held more than one year after appointment.
(e) Maricopa and Pima counties use the gubernatorial appointment from the Judicial Nominating Commission process. The method for submitting names for the other 13 counties varies.
(f) Maricopa and Pima counties use the gubernatorial appointment from the Judicial Nominating Commission process. The other 13 counties hold non-partisan elections.
(g) Municipal court judges are usually appointed by the city or town council except in Yuma, where judges are elected.
(h) The office can be held until December 31 following the next general election and then the judge must run in a non-partisan election for the remainder of the term.
(i) If unopposed for reelection, incumbent's name does not appear on the ballot unless a petition was filed not less than 83 days before the election date indicating that a write-in campaign will be conducted for the office.

An unopposed incumbent is not declared elected until the election date. This is for the general election; different timing may apply for the primary election (see Elec. Code §8203).
(j) Judges are chosen by the Supreme Court from among District Court judges.
(k) The mayor appoints Denver County Court judges.
(l) The Magistrate Screening Commission recommends candidates.
(m) Juvenile Court judges are appointed by Superior Court judges in all but one county, in which juvenile judges are elected. Associate judges (formerly referees) must be a member of the state bar or law school graduates. They serve at the pleasure of the judge(s).
(n) Probate judges are selected in non-partisan elections in 66 of 159 counties.
(o) Magistrate judges are selected in non-partisan elections in 41 of 159 counties.
(p) Selection occurs by means of Chief Justice appointment from the Judicial Nominating Commission with consent of the Senate.
(q) The Magistrate Commission consists of the administrative judge, three mayors and two electors appointed by the governor, and two attorneys (nominated by the district bar and appointed by the state bar). There is one commission in each district.
(r) There exists a unit less than county in Cook County.
(s) Non-partisan elections are used in the Superior Courts in Allen and Vanderburgh counties. Nominating commissions are used in St. Joseph County and in some courts in Lake County. In those courts that use the nominating commission process for selection; retention elections are used as the method of retention.
(t) Non-partisan elections are used in the Circuit Courts in Vanderburgh County.
(u) This applies to district judges only. Associate judges are selected by the district judges and retention is by a retention election. Magistrates are selected and retained by appointment from the County Judicial Magistrate Nominating Commission. The County Judicial Magistrate Nominating Commission consists of three members appointed by the county board and two elected by the county bar, presided over by a District Court judge.
(v) Seventeen districts use gubernatorial appointment from the Judicial Nominating Commission for selection and retention elections for retention. Fourteen districts use partisan elections for selection and retention.
(w) Depending on the amount of time remaining, selection may be by election following a Supreme Court appointment.
(x) Louisiana uses a blanket primary in which all candidates appear with party labels on the primary ballot. The top two vote-getters compete in the general election.
(y) At least one judge who is a resident of the county in which the district lies must be appointed from each of the 13 districts.
(z) Two exceptions are Hartford and Montgomery counties where Circuit Court judges are assigned.
(aa) There are no expired judicial terms. A judicial term expires upon the death, resignation, retirement, or removal of an incumbent.
(bb) The Executive (Governor's) Council is made up of eight people elected by geographical area and presided over by the lieutenant governor.
(cc) There is no retention process. Judges serve during good behavior to age 70.
(dd) Gubernatorial appointment occurs in partisan circuits; gubernatorial appointment from Judicial Nominating Commission takes place in non-partisan circuits.
(ee) Partisan elections occur in some circuits; gubernatorial appointment from the Judicial Nominating Commission with a non-partisan election takes place in others.
(ff) Partisan elections take place in some circuits; retention elections occur in other circuits.
(gg) Associate circuit judges are selected on a county basis.

## SELECTION AND RETENTION OF TRIAL COURT JUDGES — Continued

(hh) Selection occurs through Chief Justice appointment from Judicial Nominating Commission.

(ii) Other judges are designated by the District Court judges.

(jj) There is no retention process. Judges serve during good behavior to age 70.

(kk) In multi-municipality, joint, or countywide municipal courts, selection is by gubernatorial appointment with consent of the Senate.

(ll) Mayoral appointment occurs in New York City.

(mm) The appointment is made by the County Chief Executive Officer with confirmation by District Board of Supervisors.

(nn) Housing judges are appointed by the Chief Administrator of the courts.

(oo) Party affiliation is not included on the ballot in the general election, but candidates are chosen through partisan primary nominations.

(pp) This applies to district and associate judges; special judges are selected by the district judges.

(qq) The geographic basis for selection is the municipality for those judges that are elected. Judges that are either appointed or are under contract may be from other cities.

(rr) There is no retention process. Judges serve during good behavior for a life tenure.

(ss) The governor may appoint a candidate if the unexpired term is less than one year.

(tt) In addition to Circuit Court judges, the Circuit Court has masters-in-equity whose jurisdiction is in matters referred to them in the Circuit Court. Masters-in-equity are selected by gubernatorial appointment from the Judicial Merit Selection Commission, retained by gubernatorial appointment with the consent of the Senate, and the geographic basis for selection is the state.

(uu) Each county legislative body has the discretion to require elections to be non-partisan.

(vv) The selection method used to fill an unexpired term is established by a special legislative act.

(ww) There are no expired terms; each new judge begins a new term.

(xx) Appointment is by the local government executive with confirmation by the local government legislative body (may be either county or municipal government).

(yy) County judges are retained by retention election; municipal judges are reappointed by the city executive.

(zz) Effective 2011, the Family, District, Environmental and Probate Courts were combined into the Superior Court.

(aaa) Circuit Court judges appoint.

(bbb) Full-time municipal judges must stand for non-partisan election.

(ccc) A permanent vacancy in the office of municipal judge may be filled by temporary appointment of the municipal governing body or jointly by the governing bodies of all municipalities served by the judge.

(ddd) The Judicial Nomination Commission nominates for Presidential appointment and Senate confirmation. Not less than six months prior to the expiration of the term of office, the judge's performance is reviewed by the Commission on Judicial Disabilities and Tenure. A judge found "well qualified" is automatically reappointed for a new term of 15 years; a judge found "qualified" may be renominated by the President (and subject to Senate confirmation). A judge found "unqualified" is ineligible for reappointment or if the President does not wish to reappoint a judge, the Nomination Commission compiles a new list of candidates.

(eee) The geographic basis for selection is the District of Columbia.

# Table 5.8
## JUDICIAL DISCIPLINE: INVESTIGATING AND ADJUDICATING BODIES

| State or other jurisdiction | Investigating body | Adjudicating body | Appeals from adjudication are filed with: | Final disciplining body | Point at which reprimands are made public |
|---|---|---|---|---|---|
| Alabama | Judicial Inquiry Committee | Court of the Judiciary | Supreme Court | Court of the Judiciary | Filing of the complaint with the Court of the Judiciary |
| Alaska | Committee on Judicial Conduct | Supreme Court | N.A. | Supreme Court | Filing of recommendation with Supreme Court |
| Arizona | Commission on Judicial Conduct | Commission on Judicial Conduct | Discretionary with Supreme Court | Supreme Court | Within 15 days of formal charges being brought, unless a motion for reconsideration is filed |
| Arkansas | Judicial Discipline and Disability Commissions | Commission | Supreme Court | Supreme Court | At disposition of case |
| California | Commission on Judicial Performance | Commission on Judicial Performance | Supreme Court has discretionary review | Commission on Judicial Performance | Upon commission determination (a) |
| Colorado | Committee on Judicial Discipline | Commission on Judicial Discipline | No appeal | Supreme Court | Adjudication |
| Connecticut | Judicial Review Council | Judicial Review Council; Supreme Court | Supreme Court | Supreme Court | Public censure is issued at between 10 and 30 days after notice to the judge, provided that if the judge appeals, there is an automatic stay of disclosure. |
| Delaware | Preliminary Committee of the Court on the Judiciary; Investigatory Committee of the Court on the Judiciary | Council on Probate Judicial Conduct; Court on the Judiciary | Supreme Court; No appeal | Supreme Court; Court on the Judiciary | Upon issuance of opinion and imposition of sanction |
| Florida | Judicial Qualifications Commission | Judicial Qualifications Commission (b) | No appeal | Supreme Court (c) | Filing of formal charges by Committee with Supreme Court Clerk |
| Georgia | Judicial Qualifications Commission | Supreme Court | No appeal | Supreme Court | Formal Hearing |
| Hawaii | Commission on Judicial Conduct | Commission on Judicial Conduct | No appeal | Supreme Court | Imposition of public discipline by Supreme Court |
| Idaho | Judicial Council | Supreme Court | Supreme Court | Supreme Court | Filing with Supreme Court |
| Illinois | Judicial Inquiry Board | Courts Commission | No appeal | Courts Commission | Filing of decision by Courts Commission |
| Indiana | Judicial Qualifications Committee | Supreme Court | No appeal | Supreme Court | Institution of Formal Proceedings |
| Iowa | Judicial Qualifications Commission | Judicial Qualifications Commission | Supreme Court | Supreme Court | Referral by the commission to the Supreme Court recommending formal sanction |
| Kansas | Commission on Judicial Qualifications | Supreme Court | Supreme Court | Supreme Court | Reprimand is published by Supreme Court if approved by Supreme Court. |
| Kentucky | Judicial Conduct Committee | Judicial Conduct Committee | Supreme Court | Judicial Conduct Committee | Once formal charges are filed, and the judge has made a response to those charges |
| Louisiana | Judiciary Commission | Supreme Court | No appeal | Supreme Court | The lodging of the record of proceedings and a recommendation by the Judiciary Commission to the Supreme Court |
| Maine | Committee on Judicial Responsibility and Disability | Supreme Judicial Court | No appeal | Supreme Judicial Court | Filing of report to Supreme Judicial Court |

See footnotes at end of table.

# JUDICIAL DISCIPLINE: INVESTIGATING AND ADJUDICATING BODIES — Continued

| State or other jurisdiction | Investigating body | Adjudicating body | Appeals from adjudication are filed with: | Final disciplining body | Point at which reprimands are made public |
|---|---|---|---|---|---|
| Maryland | Commission on Judicial Disabilities | Court of Appeals | N.A. | Court of Appeals | Unless confidential, upon filing of a response (or expiration of the time for filing a response) with the Commission |
| Massachusetts | Commission on Judicial Conduct | Supreme Judicial Court | No appeal | Supreme Judicial Court | After final of formal charges with the Supreme Judicial Court |
| Michigan | Judicial Tenure Commission | Supreme Court | Supreme Court | Supreme Court | Filing of formal complaint by commission with Supreme Court |
| Minnesota | Board of Judicial Standards | Supreme Court | No appeal | Supreme Court | Filing of formal charges by Committee with Supreme Court |
| Mississippi | Commission on Judicial Performance | Supreme Court | No appeal | Supreme Court | Recommendation of Commission to Supreme Court |
| Missouri | Commission on Retirement, Removal and Discipline | Commission on Retirement, Removal and Discipline | Supreme Court | Supreme Court | Filing of recommendation by Committee to Supreme Court |
| Montana | Judicial Standards Commission | Supreme Court | No appeal | Supreme Court | Filing of record by Committee with Supreme Court |
| Nebraska | Commission on Judicial Qualification | Supreme Court | No appeal | Supreme Court | Commission may issue a public reprimand |
| Nevada | Commission on Judicial Discipline | Commission on Judicial Discipline | Supreme Court | Commission on Judicial Discipline | Discretion of the Commission, upon filing of report by Committee and service upon judge |
| New Hampshire | Supreme Court Committee on Judicial Conduct | | No appeal | Supreme Court | On issuance of reprimand (d) |
| New Jersey | Advisory Committee on Judicial Conduct | Supreme Court | No appeal | Supreme Court | When reprimand is filed by Supreme Court |
| New Mexico | Judicial Standards Commission | Supreme Court | No appeal | Supreme Court | Filing of record by Commission with Supreme Court |
| New York | Commission on Judicial Conduct | Commission on Judicial Conduct | Court of Appeals | Commission on Judicial Conduct and Court of Appeals | After a hearing at which a judge is admonished, censured, removed or retired, and after the judge is served |
| North Carolina | Judicial Standards Commission | Supreme Court | No appeal | Supreme Court | Upon recommendation of Commission to Supreme Court |
| North Dakota | Commission on Judicial Conduct | Supreme Court | No appeal | Supreme Court | At formal hearing |
| Ohio | Board of Commissioners on Grievance and Discipline (e) | Board of Commissioners on Grievance and Discipline | Supreme Court | Supreme Court | Adjudication |
| Oklahoma | Court on the Judiciary Trial Division Council; Council on Judicial Complaints | Court on the Judiciary Trial Division; Council on Judicial Complaints | Court on the Judiciary Division; no appeal from Council on Judicial Complaints | Court on the Judiciary Appellate Division | Filing with clerk of the Appellate Court |
| Oregon | Commission of Judicial Fitness and Disability (f) | Supreme Court | No appeal | Supreme Court | (g) |
| Pennsylvania | Judicial Conduct Board | Court of Judicial Discipline | Supreme Court | Supreme Court | Once a final decision has been made |
| Rhode Island | Commission on Judicial Tenure and Discipline | Supreme Court | No appeal | Supreme Court | Unless private, after the commission files its recommendation with the Chief Justice |

See footnotes at end of table.

## JUDICIAL DISCIPLINE: INVESTIGATING AND ADJUDICATING BODIES — Continued

| State or other jurisdiction | Investigating body | Adjudicating body | Appeals from adjudication are filed with: | Final disciplining body | Point at which reprimands are made public |
|---|---|---|---|---|---|
| South Carolina | Commissioners on Judicial Conduct | Supreme Court | No appeal | Supreme Court | Adjudication |
| South Dakota | Judicial Qualifications Commission | Supreme Court | No appeal | Supreme Court | Filing with the Supreme Court |
| Tennessee | Court of the Judiciary | Court of the Judiciary | Supreme Court, then General Assembly | Supreme Court or General Assembly | Filing of complaint in Appellate Court Clerk's office |
| Texas | State Commission on Judicial Conduct | Supreme Court, Commission on Judicial Conduct, or review tribunal consisting of Justices of Courts of Appeals | Supreme Court | Supreme Court, Commission on Judicial Conduct, or review tribunal consisting of Justices of Courts of Appeals | When issued by the Commission |
| Utah | Judicial Conduct Commission | Judicial Conduct Commission | Supreme Court | Supreme Court | 10 days after filing appeal |
| Vermont | Judicial Conduct Board | Supreme Court | Supreme Court | Supreme Court | Filing of formal charges by Board with Supreme Court |
| Virginia | Judicial Inquiry and Review Commission | Supreme Court | Supreme Court | Supreme Court | Filing of formal complaint by Committee with Supreme Court |
| Washington | Commission on Judicial Conduct | Supreme Court | No appeal | Commission on Judicial Conduct or Supreme Court | Beginning of fact finding hearing by Committee |
| West Virginia | Judicial Investigation Committee and Judicial Hearing Board | Judicial Hearing Board (JHB) | JHB recommends to SCA (i) | Supreme Court of Appeals (h) | Upon decision by Supreme Court of Appeals |
| Wisconsin | Judicial Commission | Supreme Court (i) | No appeal | Supreme Court | Filing of petitioner formal complaint by Judicial Commission w/Supreme Court |
| Wyoming | Commission on Judicial Conduct and Ethics | Supreme Court | No appeal | Supreme Court | Upon the recommendation of the Conduct and Ethics Commission and Order of the Supreme Court |
| Dist. of Columbia | Commission on Judicial Disabilities and Tenure | Commission on Judicial Disabilities and Tenure | Federal judge panel: 3 appointments by Chief Justice of Supreme Court | Commission on Judicial Disabilities and Tenure | Filing of order with D.C. Court of Appeals (j) |
| Puerto Rico | Disciplinary and Removal from office for health reasons | Supreme Court | No appeal | Supreme Court | Filing of formal complaint to the Discipline Commission |

*Source:* Bureau of Justice Statistics, *State Court Organization, 2004* NCJ 212351, update from the National Center for State Courts, March 2012.

*Key:*

N.A.— Not applicable

(a) In cases involving more serious misconduct, the commission may issue a public admonishment or public censure. The nature and impact of the misconduct generally determine the level of discipline. Both public admonishments and public censures are notices sent to the judge describing the improper conduct and stating the findings made by the commission. These notices are also made available to the press and the general public.

(b) The Judicial Qualifications Commission investigates and makes recommendations to the Supreme Court for discipline or removal.

(c) The Supreme Court power of removal is alternative and cumulative to the power of impeachment and suspension by the Governor and Senate.

(d) The Supreme Court Committee on Judicial Conduct may admonish, reprimand or order conditions, and the Supreme Court may impose formal discipline.

(e) Initial review is carried out by a panel of three commissioners.

(f) Technically, the Commission of Judicial Fitness and Disability does not adjudicate disciplinary matters. It hears the evidence and makes recommendations to the Supreme Court, which must review the records, or any stipulation for discipline and can hear additional evidence. Technically, then, there is no appeal. The Supreme Court orders any discipline, including any stipulated sanction.

(g) In Oregon, the allegations become public when the Commission issues a notice of public hearing, generally 14 days in advance of the hearing (although it can be less in the public interest). The actual complaint is not made public then, but the notice includes the general nature of the allegations. In a disciplinary case (but not a disability case), the Commission hearing, the evidence received there, and the Commission's decisions and recommendations are public. The Supreme Court decision is public when the Court files its opinion. There is no reprimand or other sanction until the Supreme Court decision.

(h) The final disciplining body is the same for both the Commission and Judicial Hearing Board.

(i) The Judicial Conduct and Disability Panel, through an ad hoc three-judge panel (two must be Court of Appeals judges, one can be a retired, reserve judge or Court of Appeals judge appointed as a hearing examiner) makes a report to the Supreme Court.

(j) This only applies in cases of removal or involuntary retirement wherein the Chief Justice appoints a three-member federal judge panel to review commission's order of removal.

# Chapter Six

# ELECTIONS

# Election Issues Continue to Challenge States

## By R. Doug Lewis

*Even though the nation has more than 200 years experience in conducting elections, changes mandated by federal and state laws, combined with technological changes and major shifts within society, mean that states need immediate policy and budget responses. The cost to states and local governments for election administration is likely to be high for the next three years, but some of that can be mitigated with legislative action to grant reprieve from outdated laws and practices.*

The aftermath of the 2000 presidential election helped ensure election administration and voter registration issues would be at the forefront of policymakers' minds for the next decade. The federal government has spent about $4 billion on the elections process since 2000.

States had to spend from their budgets to comply with new federal mandates, as well as added mandates of their own for election reform issues during the past 10 years. This has made elections more expensive for both the states and their local election jurisdictions.

States face policy decisions about how to best handle a potential tidal wave of additional costs related to elections during the next three or four fiscal years—but some policy initiatives can streamline the elections process. Understanding the nature of some of the initiatives and the reasons for election costs can assist policymakers in shaping election budget initiatives.

### Take Laws Off the Books, Delete Some Mandates

States responded to the 2000 presidential election with new initiatives and a renewed emphasis on the basics of voter registration and election administration. Significant savings can be made within state and local election budgets if state legislatures will review the election code and revamp legal mandates and administrative requirements to fit current conditions.

Society has changed considerably since most state election codes were developed, and state governments have not adjusted the mandates to reflect new technologies and social habits. For instance, many states still require advertising election notices in newspapers when the public no longer relies on printed news as its principal source of information. Many of the requirements for sample ballots, voter information and voter publications could be better served, and at a lower cost, by allowing publishing

on websites and/or electronic distribution rather than printed or mailed. For a complete list of recommended changes, policymakers can engage the local election administrators within each state or contact the Election Center in Houston.

### Voting Equipment Needs to Be Replaced

Congress in 2002 passed the Help America Vote Act, which provided assistance to states to comply with federal elections laws and set minimum standards for the administration of federal elections. The act also forced almost all states to buy new voting equipment within a narrow band of time. States that had used lever voting machines—some in use continuously for more than 60 years—were "encouraged" by the federal government to get rid of the units. States and local governments that were using punch-card voting machines, which had been used for 25 years or more in some locations, also discontinued the use of those devices.

The most expensive election problem facing the states and local governments now is almost all of that equipment will need to be replaced soon. It will begin as early as 2013 for some and will affect almost all before the 2016 election. History has taught us that making major changes to voting equipment should occur well before a presidential election year so voters and election administrators have experience with the equipment before the year in which the largest number of voters will participate. Some factors affecting this area are included here since they are not readily apparent to budget and political authorities.

### Maintenance Costs Are Higher

Both lever machines and punch-card machines were relatively low cost devices to maintain and to store. The types of voting machines that comply with the Help America Vote Act requirements means states have been changing to either optical scan or direct recording equipment. Direct recording machines are sometimes called "touchscreen units," but the terms are not synonymous, since touchscreen units are a type of DRE, but not all DREs are touchscreens. The costs of purchasing, maintaining, storing and programming these types of machines, and/or software maintenance, mean that the cost of elections for states making the switch from older technologies to newer technologies has been dramatically increased from previous budgets.

Neither lever machines nor punch-card machines required any special storage facilities, so the normal governmental storage facilities could be used for those kinds of voting units. The newer versions of voting equipment all require specialized storage facilities for environmental, maintenance and security reasons. This has greatly increased the cost of elections for local jurisdictions since the cost of such storage facilities is considerably more expensive than the old days of placing units in county barns or unairconditioned facilities. Additionally, pest control is necessary since the newer devices are adversely affected by rodents and insects, so facilities have to have better barriers to pests.

Maintenance costs are also higher since not only do the newer voting devices need environmentally controlled facilities, but they also need continuous electrical connection to maintain their internal batteries. State and local governments have had to upgrade the expectations of the types of employees who can handle and work with the equipment. Employees with competent technical skills are more expensive—and not always as available in sufficient numbers—than the previous generations of employees who staffed elections. Training costs also are higher for both the full-time employees, non-technical staff and poll workers who handle the precinct-based elections.

## Software Upgrades and Software Maintenance Are Added Costs

Software upgrades and software maintenance agreements have added tremendously to the cost of elections for state and local governments. In periods of financial difficulties or recession, governments have deferred software and hardware maintenance and software and hardware upgrades. The cost-cutting sounds like a prudent measure until policymakers and budget authorities discover the errors that such decisions can cause in the ensuing elections. This is because the known problems updates would have corrected were not fixed due to a lack of funding.

## Security-related Costs Are Higher

One additional factor has driven the cost of elections significantly. The cost to secure the voting equipment so that only known and approved individuals have access to it has been a new phenomenon for most of the jurisdictions in America. It was not that the machines were unsecured before, but there were fewer ways to alter the voting equipment in the past.

Voting equipment now must be secured in a much more elaborate process than in previous budget histories for state and local governments. Video monitoring systems, electronic and controlled access systems, witnessed access to software, equipment, control devices and ballots—even the delivery of equipment to polling sites—have become more complicated and expensive.

## Mandated Changes in the Business Model

Because the changes required by the Help America Vote Act are relatively new, there have been no new budget patterns for state and local governments to follow. Even the industry itself had no experience with the kind of consequences resulting from the legislative changes forced upon the election process. Old pricing models weren't working and voting equipment manufacturers began to reduce the number of employees serving states and local governments. Industry consolidation has been a concern for policymakers and election administrators as well.

A combination of a weak economy paired with massive legislative changes has meant some of the voting systems companies simply ceased to operate or merged with other larger companies. The full impact of that is still not known, but clearly there are fewer choices for governments and prices are considerably higher—and will be for the immediate future.

## Obsolescence Accelerates Need to Replace Voting Equipment

One of the unfortunate realities of modern voting equipment is that not even the manufacturers can force electronics suppliers to have the same parts available seven, 10 or 12 years later. Finding parts to repair the voting units can be difficult, if not impossible. Contracts can be written to have manufacturers provide these parts and supplies into the distant future, but that drives up the costs of the units at purchase time and for maintenance contracts. For actual cost of ownership issues, it is likely to be less expensive to purchase new voting equipment every eight to 12 years than to try to maintain older equipment past its prime.

Some states are exploring options with vendors willing to design voting software that can run on Commercial Off The Shelf (COTS) hardware, but even this software will be designed to accommodate COTS equipment available at the time of the purchase. While equipment may become effectively obsolete, the software may also be out of date within a period of years, but it is more likely that software can be updated to accommodate then current COTS equipment. The unknown in this example is whether the cost of software will increase to equal the expense of new hardware.

## Technical Skills Are the Wave of the Future

It is clear that all of government is moving to a more technology-based workplace, but election workers will need to be especially skilled. States that cannot make adjustments in requirements for greater technological skills and training, which can be costly, may need to look at the model developed in Georgia, where the state contracted with Kennesaw State University to handle all the programming and maintenance of its electronic voting devices. This model is likely to be adopted by other states as programming for vote tabulation and vote reporting software becomes more difficult, and mission critical, and as hardware becomes more expensive to repair.

Additionally, the shorter life cycles of much of the voting equipment is likely to mean that it will be necessary to have permanent staff within each state (such as the Georgia & KSU model) who know how and why the technology has to be designed according to certain practices, with appropriate security safeguards, and how best to achieve accurate elections. Only the largest jurisdictions within states will likely be able to accomplish this on their own.

States are faced with unchartered territory in much of the post-Help America Vote Act era. Legal policy is a factor, but so is the changing nature of society itself. This combination of changes means that governors and legislatures will be faced with finding new solutions, even though the nation has had elections for more than 200 years. And for the foreseeable future, those new answers appear to be dramatically more expensive, which means that streamlining the process within each state becomes more important than ever. The budget wave will begin as early as 2013 for many states.

## About the Author

**Doug Lewis**, a certified elections/registration administrator (CERA), is executive director of The Election Center, a nonpartisan, nonprofit organization representing the nation's election officials. He has been called on by Congress, federal agencies, state legislatures, and national and worldwide news media for solutions to voting issues.

## Table 6.1
## STATE EXECUTIVE BRANCH OFFICIALS TO BE ELECTED: 2012–2016

| State or other jurisdiction | 2012 | 2013 | 2014 | 2015 | 2016 |
|---|---|---|---|---|---|
| Alabama | ... | ... | G, LG, AG, AR, A, SS, T | ... | ... |
| Alaska | ... | ... | G, LG | ... | ... |
| Arizona | (a) | ... | G, AG, SS, SP, T (a) | ... | (a) |
| Arkansas | ... | ... | G, LG, AG, A, SS, T (b) | ... | ... |
| California | ... | ... | G, LG, AG, C, CI, SS, SP, T (c) | ... | ... |
| Colorado | ... | ... | G, LG, AG, SS, T | ... | ... |
| Connecticut | ... | ... | G, LG, AG, C, SS, T | ... | ... |
| Delaware | G, LG, CI | ... | AG, A, T | ... | G, LG, CI |
| Florida | ... | ... | G, LG, AG, AR, CFO | ... | ... |
| Georgia | ... | ... | G, LG, AG, AR, CI, SS, SP (d) | ... | ... |
| Hawaii | ... | ... | G, LG | ... | ... |
| Idaho | ... | ... | G, LG, AG, C, SS, SP, T | ... | ... |
| Illinois | ... | ... | G, LG, AG, C, SS, T | ... | ... |
| Indiana | G, LG, AG, SP | ... | A, SS, T | ... | G, LG, AG, SP |
| Iowa | ... | ... | G, LG, AG, AR, A, SS, T | ... | ... |
| Kansas | ... | ... | G, LG, AG, CI, SS, T | ... | ... |
| Kentucky | ... | ... | ... | G, LG, AG, AR, A, SS, T | ... |
| Louisiana | ... | ... | ... | G, LG, AG, AR, CI, SS, T | ... |
| Maine (e) | ... | ... | G | ... | ... |
| Maryland | ... | ... | G, LG, AG, C | ... | ... |
| Massachusetts | (f) | ... | G, LG, AG, A, SS, T | ... | (f) |
| Michigan | (f) | ... | G, LG, AG, SS (f) | ... | ... |
| Minnesota | G (g) | ... | G, LG, AG, A, SS | ... | ... |
| Mississippi | ... | ... | A | G, LG, AG, AR, A, CI, SS, T | G, LG, AG, SS, T |
| Missouri | G, LG, AG, SS, T | ... | ... | ... | G, LG, AG, SS, T |
| Montana | G, LG, AG, A, SS, SP | ... | G, LG, AG, A, SS, T | ... | G, LG, AG, A, SS, SP |
| Nebraska | G, LG, AG, A, SS, SP | ... | G, LG, AG, C, SS, T | ... | ... |
| Nevada | G | ... | G | ... | G |
| New Hampshire | G | ... | G | ... | ... |
| New Jersey | ... | G, LG | ... | ... | ... |
| New Mexico | ... | ... | ... | ... | ... |
| New York | ... | ... | G, LG, AG, A, SS, T (h) | ... | ... |
| North Carolina | G, LG, AG, AR, A, CI, SS, SP, T (i) | ... | G, LG, AG, C | ... | G, LG, AG, AR, A, CI, SS, SP, T (i) |
| North Dakota | G, LG, A, CI, SP, T (j) | ... | ... | ... | G, LG, A, CI, SP, T (j) |
| Ohio | ... | ... | AG, AR, SS (j)(k) | ... | ... |
| Oklahoma | ... | ... | G, LG, AG, A, CI, SP, T (l) | ... | (l) |
| Oregon | AG, SS, T (m) | ... | G, SP | ... | AG, SS, T (m) |
| Pennsylvania | AG, A, T | ... | G, LG | ... | AG, A, T |
| Rhode Island | ... | ... | G, LG, AG, SS, T | ... | ... |
| South Carolina | ... | ... | G, LG, AG, AR, C, SS, SP, T (n) | ... | ... |
| South Dakota | (o) | ... | G, LG, AG, A, SS, SP, T (o) | ... | (o) |
| Tennessee | ... | ... | G | ... | ... |
| Texas | (p) | ... | G, LG, AG, AR, C (p) | ... | (p) |
| Utah | G, LG, AG, A, T | ... | ... | ... | G, LG, AG, A, T |
| Vermont | G, LG, AG, A, SS, T | ... | G, LG, AG, A, SS, T | ... | G, LG, AG, A, SS, T |

See footnotes at end of table.

# STATE EXECUTIVE BRANCH OFFICIALS TO BE ELECTED: 2012–2016—Continued

| State or other jurisdiction | 2012 | 2013 | 2014 | 2015 | 2016 |
|---|---|---|---|---|---|
| Virginia | ... | G, LG, AG | ... | ... | ... |
| Washington | G, LG, AG, A, CI, SS, SP, T (q) | ... | ... | ... | G, LG, AG, A, CI, SS, SP, T (q) |
| West Virginia | G, AG, AR, A, SS, T | ... | ... | ... | G, AG, AR, A, SS, T |
| Wisconsin | ... | SP | G, LG, AG, SS, T | ... | ... |
| Wyoming | ... | ... | G, A, SS, SP, T | ... | ... |
| American Samoa | G, LG | ... | ... | ... | G, LG |
| Guam | ... | ... | G, LG, AG, A | ... | ... |
| No. Mariana Islands | ... | ... | G, LG (r) | ... | ... |
| Puerto Rico | G | ... | ... | ... | G |
| U.S. Virgin Islands | ... | ... | G, LG | ... | ... |
| **Totals for year** | | | | | |
| Governor | 14 | 2 | 38 | 3 | 13 |
| Lieutenant Governor | 10 | 2 | 33 | 3 | 10 |
| Attorney General | 10 | 1 | 31 | 3 | 10 |
| Agriculture | 2 | 0 | 7 | 3 | 2 |
| Auditor | 8 | 0 | 16 | 2 | 8 |
| Chief Financial Officer | 0 | 0 | 1 | 0 | 0 |
| Comptroller | 0 | 0 | 9 | 0 | 0 |
| Comm. of Insurance | 4 | 0 | 4 | 2 | 4 |
| Secretary of State | 7 | 0 | 26 | 3 | 7 |
| Supt. of Public Inst. or Comm. of Education | 5 | 1 | 9 | 0 | 5 |
| Treasurer | 9 | 0 | 24 | 3 | 9 |

*Sources:* The Council of State Governments' survey and state election administration offices and websites, March 2012.

*Note:* This table shows the executive branch officials up for election in a given year. Footnotes indicate other offices (e.g., commissioners of labor, public service, etc.) also up for election in a given year. The data contained in this table reflect information available at press time.

*Key:*
... – No regularly scheduled elections of state executive officials.
G – Governor
LG – Lieutenant Governor
AG – Attorney General
AR – Agriculture
A – Auditor
C – Comptroller/Controller
CFO – Chief Financial Officer
CI – Commissioner of Insurance
SS – Secretary of State
SP – Superintendent of Public Instruction or Commissioner of Education
T – Treasurer

(a) Corporation commissioners (5)—4-year terms, 2012–2016—3 seats, 2014–2 seats, 2016–3 seats. State Mine Inspector—4-year term, 2014 election.
(b) Commissioner of State Lands.
(c) Five (5) Board of Equalization members are elected to serve 4-year concurrent terms that will expire January 2014.
(d) Commissioner of Labor—4-year term, 2014.
(e) In Maine the legislature elects constitutional officers (AG, SS, T) in even-numbered years for 2-year terms; the auditor was elected by the legislature in 2008 and will serve a 4-year term.

(f) Michigan State University trustees (8)—8-year terms, 2012–2, 2014–2, 2016–2, 2018–2; University of Michigan regents (8)—8-year terms, 2012–2, 2014–2, 2016–2, 2018–2. Wayne State University governors (8)—8-year terms, 2012–2, 2014–2, 2016–2, 2018–2; State Board of Education (8)—8-year terms, 2012–2, 2014–2, 2016–2, 2018–2.
(g) Minnesota Governor Scott Walker will face a recall election on June 5, 2012. His Democratic challenger will be chosen in the May 8 primary.
(h) Commissioner of Public Lands—4-year term, 2014.
(i) Commissioner of Labor elected in 2012.
(j) There are 3 Public Service Commissioners. One is up for election every two years. (3)—6-year terms, 2012–1, 2014–1, 2016–1.
(k) Tax Commissioner.
(l) Corporation Commissioners (3)—6-year terms, 2012–1, 2014–1, 2016–1; Commissioner of Labor—2014, 4-year term.
(m) Commissioner of the Bureau of Labor and Industries.
(n) Adjutant general—4-year term.
(o) The title is Commissioner of School and Public Lands; Public Utility Commissioners (3)—6-year terms, 2012–2, 2014–1, 2016–2. The terms are typically staggered, but one commissioner was appointed to fill a vacancy in 2011, and can only serve until the next general election at which time he may run for the remainder of the unexpired term.
(p) Commissioner of General Land Office—4-year term, 2014; railroad commissioners (3)—6-year terms, 2012–1, 2014–1, 2016–1.
(q) Commissioner of Public Lands.
(r) The current governor and lieutenant governor are serving a 5-year term to change future CNMI elections to even-numbered years.

# Table 6.2
## STATE LEGISLATURE MEMBERS TO BE ELECTED: 2012–2016

| State or other jurisdiction | Total legislators Senate | Total legislators House/Assembly | 2012 Senate | 2012 House/Assembly | 2013 Senate | 2013 House/Assembly | 2014 Senate | 2014 House/Assembly | 2015 Senate | 2015 House/Assembly | 2016 Senate | 2016 House/Assembly |
|---|---|---|---|---|---|---|---|---|---|---|---|---|
| Alabama | 35 | 105 | ... | ... | ... | ... | 35 | 105 | ... | ... | ... | ... |
| Alaska | 20 | 40 | 19 (a) | 40 | ... | ... | 9 | 40 | ... | ... | 10 | 40 |
| Arizona | 30 | 60 | 30 | 60 | ... | ... | 30 | 60 | ... | ... | 30 | 60 |
| Arkansas | 35 | 100 | 35 (a) | 100 | ... | ... | 18 | 100 | ... | ... | 17 | 100 |
| California | 40 | 80 | 20 | 80 | ... | ... | 20 | 80 | ... | ... | 20 | 80 |
| Colorado | 35 | 65 | 20 (b) | 65 | ... | ... | 18 | 65 | ... | ... | 17 | 65 |
| Connecticut | 36 | 151 | 36 | 151 | ... | ... | 36 | 151 | ... | ... | 36 | 151 |
| Delaware | 21 | 41 | 21 (a) | 41 | ... | ... | 10 | 41 | ... | ... | 11 | 41 |
| Florida | 40 | 120 | 40 (a) | 120 | ... | ... | 20 (c) | 120 | ... | ... | 20 (d) | 120 |
| Georgia | 56 | 180 | 56 | 180 | ... | ... | 56 | 180 | ... | ... | 56 | 180 |
| Hawaii | 25 | 51 | 25 (a) | 51 | ... | ... | 12 | 51 | ... | ... | 13 | 51 |
| Idaho | 35 | 70 | 35 | 70 | ... | ... | 35 | 70 | ... | ... | 35 | 70 |
| Illinois | 59 | 118 | 59 (a) | 118 | ... | ... | 20 | 118 | ... | ... | 20 | 118 |
| Indiana | 50 | 100 | 25 | 100 | ... | ... | 25 | 100 | ... | ... | 25 | 100 |
| Iowa | 50 | 100 | 25 (c) | 100 | ... | ... | 25 (d) | 100 | ... | ... | 25 (c) | 100 |
| Kansas | 40 | 125 | 40 | 125 | ... | ... | 40 | 125 | ... | ... | 40 | 125 |
| Kentucky | 38 | 100 | 19 (d) | 100 | ... | ... | 19 (c) | 100 | ... | ... | 19 (d) | 100 |
| Louisiana | 39 | 105 | ... | ... | ... | ... | ... | ... | 39 | 105 | ... | ... |
| Maine | 35 | 151 | 35 | 151 | ... | ... | 35 | 151 | ... | ... | 35 | 151 |
| Maryland | 47 | 141 | ... | ... | ... | ... | 47 | 141 | ... | ... | ... | ... |
| Massachusetts | 40 | 160 | 40 | 160 | ... | ... | 40 | 160 | ... | ... | 40 | 160 |
| Michigan | 38 | 110 | ... | 110 | ... | ... | 38 | 110 | ... | ... | ... | 110 |
| Minnesota | 67 | 134 | ... | 134 | ... | ... | 67 | 134 | ... | ... | ... | 134 |
| Mississippi | 52 | 122 | ... | 122 | ... | ... | ... | ... | 52 | 122 | ... | ... |
| Missouri | 34 | 163 | 17 (d) | 163 | ... | ... | 17 (c) | 163 | ... | ... | 17 (d) | 163 |
| Montana | 50 | 100 | 25 | 100 | ... | ... | 25 | 100 | ... | ... | 25 | 100 |
| Nebraska | 49 | U | 25 (d) | U | ... | ... | 24 (c) | U | ... | ... | 25 (d) | U |
| Nevada | 21 | 42 | 10 | 42 | ... | ... | 11 | 42 | ... | ... | 10 | 42 |
| New Hampshire | 24 | 400 | 24 | 400 | ... | ... | 24 | 400 | ... | ... | 24 | 400 |
| New Jersey | 40 | 80 | ... | ... | 40 | 80 | ... | ... | ... | 80 | ... | ... |
| New Mexico | 42 | 70 | 42 | 70 | ... | ... | 42 | 70 | ... | ... | 42 | 70 |
| New York | 62 | 150 | 62 | 150 | ... | ... | 62 | 150 | ... | ... | 62 | 150 |
| North Carolina | 50 | 120 | 50 | 120 | ... | ... | 50 | 120 | ... | ... | 50 | 120 |
| North Dakota | 47 | 94 | 25 (c)(e) | 47 | ... | ... | 24 (d) | 47 | ... | ... | 23 (c) | 47 |
| Ohio | 33 | 99 | 16 (c) | 99 | ... | ... | 17 (d) | 99 | ... | ... | 16 (c) | 99 |
| Oklahoma | 48 | 101 | 24 (d) | 101 | ... | ... | 24 (c) | 101 | ... | ... | 24 (d) | 101 |
| Oregon | 30 | 60 | 16 (f) | 60 | ... | ... | 15 | 60 | ... | ... | 15 | 60 |
| Pennsylvania | 50 | 203 | 25 (d) | 203 | ... | ... | 25 (c) | 203 | ... | ... | 25 (d) | 203 |
| Rhode Island | 38 | 75 | 38 | 75 | ... | ... | 38 | 75 | ... | ... | 38 | 75 |
| South Carolina | 46 | 124 | 46 | 124 | ... | ... | ... | 124 | ... | ... | 46 | 124 |

See footnotes at end of table.

# STATE LEGISLATURE MEMBERS TO BE ELECTED: 2012–2016—Continued

| State or other jurisdiction | Total legislators | | 2012 | | 2013 | | 2014 | | 2015 | | 2016 | |
|---|---|---|---|---|---|---|---|---|---|---|---|---|
| | Senate | House/Assembly | Senate | House/Assembly | Senate | House/Assembly | Senate | House/Assembly | Senate | House/Assembly | Senate | House/Assembly |
| South Dakota | 35 | 70 | 35 | 70 | … | … | 35 | 70 | … | … | 35 | 70 |
| Tennessee | 33 | 99 | 16 (c) | 99 | … | … | 17 (d) | 99 | … | … | 16 (c) | 99 |
| Texas | 31 | 150 | 31 (a) | 150 | … | … | 16 | 150 | … | … | 15 | 150 |
| Utah | 29 | 75 | 16 (g) | 75 | … | … | 14 | 75 | … | … | 15 | 75 |
| Vermont | 30 | 150 | 30 | 150 | … | … | 30 | 150 | … | … | 30 | 150 |
| Virginia | 40 | 100 | … | … | … | 100 | … | … | 40 | 100 | … | … |
| Washington | 49 | 98 | 26 (c)(h) | 98 | … | … | 24 (d) | 98 | … | … | 25 (c) | 98 |
| West Virginia | 34 | 100 | 17 | 100 | … | … | 17 | 100 | … | … | 17 | 100 |
| Wisconsin | 33 | 99 | 16 (c) | 99 | … | … | 17 (d) | 99 | … | … | 16 (c) | 99 |
| Wyoming | 30 | 60 | 15 (c) | 60 | … | … | 15 (d) | 60 | … | … | 15 (c) | 60 |
| Dist. of Columbia | 13 | U | 6 | U | … | … | 7 | U | … | … | 6 | U |
| American Samoa | 18 | 20 | (i) | 20 | … | … | (i) | 20 | … | … | (i) | 20 |
| Guam | 15 | U | 15 | U | … | … | 15 | U | … | … | 15 | U |
| No. Mariana Islands | 9 | 18 | … | … | 6 | 18 | … | … | 3 | 18 | … | … |
| Puerto Rico (j) | 31 | 54 | 31 | 54 | … | … | … | … | … | … | 27 | 51 |
| U.S. Virgin Islands | 15 | U | 15 | U | … | … | 15 | U | … | … | 15 | U |
| State Totals | 1,971 | 5,411 | 1,227 | 4,711 | 40 | 180 | 1,196 | 4,957 | 131 | 417 | 1,095 | 4,641 |
| Totals | 2,072 | 5,503 | 1,294 | 4,785 | 46 | 198 | 1,233 | 4,977 | 134 | 435 | 1,158 | 4,712 |

*Source:* The Council of State Governments' survey, April 2012.

*Note:* This table shows the number of elections in a given year. As a result of redistricting, states may adjust some elections. The data compiled in this table reflect information avaible at press time. See the Chapter 3 table entitled, '"The Legislators: Numbers, Terms, and Party Affiliations," for specific information on legislative terms.

*Key:*

… — No regularly scheduled elections

U — Unicameral legislature

(a) All Senate seats are up for election to reflect reapportionment redistricting that occurs at the start of each decade.

Alaska: One Senate district saw minimal change due to reapportionment and is not on the ballot in 2012.

Illinois: The Senate operates on a ten-year election cycle. All 59 senators are elected in each year ended in a "2" (following the redistricting based upon the decennial census). Senate districts are then divided into three groups. Each group of senators is elected to one of the following schedules: terms of four years, four years and two years; terms of two years, four years and four years; and terms of four years, two years and four years.

(b) There would normally be 17 Senate seats on the ballot in Colorado this year. However, there are three seats that are currently held by senators appointed to fill a mid-term vacancy, and they must run for a full term this election year.

(c) Even-numbered Senate districts.

(d) Odd-numbered Senate districts.

(e) North Dakota: There are also elections for two odd-numbered districts whose boundaries were changed due to redistricting.

(f) Oregon: There is currently a vacant Senate seat. The elected candidate will fill the remainder of the existing term of two years.

(g) There would normally be 15 Senate seats on the ballot in Utah this year, but there is one additional seat currently held by a senator appointed to fill a mid-term vacancy, and he must run for a full term this election year.

(h) There would normally be 25 Senate seats on the ballot in Washington this year, but there is one additional seat currently held by a senator appointed to fill a mid-term vacancy, and he must run for a full term this election year.

(i) In American Samoa, Senators are not elected by popular vote. They are selected by county council of chiefs.

(j) If in the general election more than 2/3 of the members of either house are elected from one party or from a single ticket, as both are defined by law, the numbers shall be increased in accordance with Article III Section 7 of the Puerto Rico Constitution.

## Table 6.3
## METHODS OF NOMINATING CANDIDATES FOR STATE OFFICES

| State or other jurisdiction | Methods of nominating candidates |
|---|---|
| Alabama | Primary election; however, the state executive committee or other governing body of any political party may choose instead to hold a state convention for the purpose of nominating candidates. Submitting a petition to run as an independent or third-party candidate or an independent nominating procedure. |
| Alaska | Primary election. Petition for no-party candidates. |
| Arizona | Candidates who are members of a recognized party are nominated by an open primary election. Candidates who are not members of a recognized political party may file petitions to appear on the general election ballot. A write-in option is also available. |
| Arkansas | Primary election, convention and petition. |
| California | Primary election or independent nomination procedure. |
| Colorado | Primary election, convention or by petition. |
| Connecticut | Convention/primary election. Major political parties hold state conventions (convening not earlier than the 68th day and closing not later than the 50th day before the date of the primary) for the purpose of endorsing candidates. If no one challenges the endorsed candidate, no primary election is held. However, if anyone (who received at least 15 percent of the delegate vote on any roll call at the convention) challenges the endorsed candidate, a primary election is held to determine the party nominee for the general election. |
| Delaware | Primary election for Democrats and primary election and convention for Republicans.. |
| Florida | Primary election. Minor parties may nominate their candidate in any manner they deem proper. |
| Georgia | Primary election. |
| Hawaii | Primary election. |
| Idaho | Primary election and convention. New political parties hold a convention to nominate candidates to be placed on a general election ballot. |
| Illinois | Primary election. The primary election nominates established party candidates. New political parties and independent candidates go directly to the general election file based on a petition process. |
| Indiana | Primary election, convention and petition. The governor is chosen by a primary. All other state officers are chosen at a state convention, unless the candidate is an independent. Any party that obtains between 2 percent and 8 percent of the vote for secretary of state may hold a convention to select a candidate. |
| Iowa | Primary election, convention and petition. |
| Kansas | Candidates for the two major parties are nominated by primary election. Candidates for minor parties are nominated for the general election at state party conventions. Independent candidates are nominated for the general election by petition. |
| Kentucky | Primary election. A slate of candidates for governor and lieutenant governor that receives the highest number of its party's votes but which number is less than 40 percent of the votes cast for all slates of candidates of that party, shall be required to participate in a runoff primary with the slate of candidates of the same party receiving the second highest number of votes. |
| Louisiana | Candidates may qualify for any office they wish, regardless of party affiliation, by completing the qualifying document and paying the appropriate qualifying fee; or a candidate may file a nominating petition. |
| Maine | Primary election or non-party petition. |
| Maryland | Primary election, convention and petition. Unaffiliated candidates or candidates affiliated with non-recognized political parties may run for elective office by collecting the requisite number of signatures on a petition. The required number equals 1 percent of the number of registered voters eligible to vote for office. Only recognized non-principal political parties may nominate its candidate by a convention in accordance with its by laws. (At this time, Maryland has four non-principal parties: Libertarian, Green, Constitution and Populist.) |
| Massachusetts | Primary election. |
| Michigan | Governor, State House, State Senate use primary election. Lieutenant Governor runs as the running mate to gubernatorial candidate, not separately, and is selected through the convention process. Secretary of State and Attorney general candidates are chosen at convention. Nominees for State Board of Education, University of Michigan Regents, Michigan State University Trustees and Wayne State University Governors are nominated by convention. Minor parties nominate candidates to all partisan offices by convention. |
| Minnesota | Primary election. Candidates for minor parties or independent candidates are by petition. They must have the signatures of 2,000 people who will be eligible to vote in the next general election. |
| Mississippi | Primary election, petition (for independent candidates), independent nominating procedures (third-party candidate). |
| Missouri | Primary election. |
| Montana | Primary election and independent nominating procedure. |
| Nebraska | Primary election. |
| Nevada | Primary election. Independent candidates are nominated by petition for the general election. Minor parties nominated by petition or by party. |
| New Hampshire | Primary election. Minor parties by petition. |
| New Jersey | Primary election. Independent candidates are nominated by petition for the general election. |

See footnotes at end of table.

# METHODS OF NOMINATING CANDIDATES FOR STATE OFFICES — Continued

| State or other jurisdiction | Methods of nominating candidates |
|---|---|
| New Mexico | Statewide candidates petition to go to convention and are nominated in a primary election. District and legislative candidates petition for primary ballot access. |
| New York | Primary election/petition. |
| North Carolina | Primary election. Newly recognized parties just granted access submit their first nominees by convention. All established parties use primaries. |
| North Dakota | Convention/primary election. Political parties hold state conventions for the purpose of endorsing candidates. Endorsed candidates are automatically placed on the primary election ballot, but other candidates may also petition their name on the ballot. |
| Ohio | Primary election, petition and by declaration of intent to be a write-in candidate. |
| Oklahoma | Primary election. |
| Oregon | Primary election Minor parties hold conventions. |
| Pennsylvania | Primary election, and petition. Nomination petitions filed by major party candidates to access primary ballot. Nomination papers filed by minor party and independent candidates to access November ballot. |
| Rhode Island | Primary election. |
| South Carolina | Primary election for Republicans and Democrats; party conventions held for minor parties. Candidates can have name on ballot via petition. |
| South Dakota | Convention, petition and independent nominating procedure. |
| Tennessee | Primary election/petition. |
| Texas | Primary election/convention. Minor parties without ballot access nominate candidates for the general election after qualifying for ballot access by petition. |
| Utah | Convention, primary election and petition. |
| Vermont | Primary election. Major parties by primary, minor parties by convention, independents by petition. |
| Virginia | Primary election, convention and petition. |
| Washington | Primary election. |
| West Virginia | Primary election, convention, petition and independent nominating procedure. |
| Wisconsin | Primary election/petition. Candidates must file nomination papers (petitions) containing the minimum number of signatures required by law. Candidates appear on the primary ballot for the party they represent. The candidate receiving the most votes in each party primary goes on to the November election. |
| Wyoming | Primary election. |
| Dist. of Columbia | Primary election. Independent and minor party candidates file by nominating petition. |
| American Samoa | Individual files petition for candidacy with the chief election officer. Petition must be signed by statutorily-mandated number of qualified voters. |
| Guam | Individual files petition for candidacy with the chief election officer. Petition must be signed by statutorily-mandated number of qualified voters. |
| No. Mariana Islands | Candidates are all nominated by petition. Candidates seeking the endorsement of recognized political parties must also include in their submitted petition submission a document signed by the recognized political parties' chairperson/president and secretary attesting to such nomination. Recognized political parties may, or may not, depending on their by-laws and party rules conduct primaries separate from any state election agency participation. |
| Puerto Rico | Primary election and convention. |
| U.S. Virgin Islands | Primary election. |

*Sources*: The Council of State Governments' survey of state election administration offices, January 2007, and state websites, December 2010.

*Note*: The nominating methods described here are for state offices; procedures may vary for local candidates. Also, independent candidates may have to petition for nomination.

## Table 6.4
## ELECTION DATES FOR NATIONAL AND STATE ELECTIONS
### (Formulas and dates of state elections)

| State or other jurisdiction | Type of primary | National (a) Primary | National (a) General | State (b) Primary | State (b) Runoff | State (b) General |
|---|---|---|---|---|---|---|
| Alabama | Open | March, 2nd T<br>March 13, 2012 | Nov., ★<br>Nov. 6, 2012 | June, 1st T<br>June 3, 2014 | 6th T AP<br>July 15, 2014 | Nov., ★<br>Nov. 4, 2014 |
| Alaska | Rep: Semi-Closed<br>Dem: Open | (c) Rep: March 6, 2012<br>Dem: April 10–April 14, 2012 | Nov., ★<br>Nov. 6, 2012 | Aug., 4th T<br>Aug. 28, 2012 | … | Nov., ★<br>Nov. 6, 2012 |
| Arizona | Semi-Closed | (d)<br>Feb. 28, 2012 | Nov., ★<br>Nov. 6, 2012 | 10th T Prior<br>Aug. 28, 2012 | … | Nov., ★<br>Nov. 6, 2012 |
| Arkansas | Open | T 3 wks. prior to runoff<br>May 22, 2012 | Nov., ★<br>Nov. 6, 2012 | T 3 wks. prior to runoff<br>May 22, 2012 | June, 2nd T<br>June 12, 2012 | Nov., ★<br>Nov. 6, 2012 |
| California | Rep: Closed<br>Dem: Semi-Closed | June ★<br>June 5, 2012 | Nov., ★<br>Nov. 6, 2012 | June ★<br>June 5, 2012 (e) | … | Nov., ★<br>Nov. 6, 2012 |
| Colorado | Closed | (c) Rep: Feb. 7, 2012<br>Dem: March 6, 2012 | Nov., ★<br>Nov. 6, 2012 | June, last T<br>June 26, 2012 | … | Nov., ★<br>Nov. 6, 2012 |
| Connecticut | Closed | April, 4th T<br>April 24, 2012 | Nov., ★<br>Nov. 6, 2012 | Aug., 2nd T<br>Aug. 14, 2012 | … | Nov., ★<br>Nov. 6, 2012 |
| Delaware | Closed | April, 4th T<br>April 24, 2012 | Nov., ★<br>Nov. 6, 2012 | Sept., 2nd T after 1st M<br>Sept. 11, 2012 | … | Nov., ★<br>Nov. 6, 2012 |
| Florida | Closed | (f)<br>Jan. 31, 2012 | Nov., ★<br>Nov. 6, 2012 | 12th T prior to General<br>Aug. 14, 2012 | … | Nov., ★<br>Nov. 6, 2012 |
| Georgia | Open | (g)<br>March 6, 2012 | Nov., ★<br>Nov. 6, 2012 | July, last T<br>July 31, 2012 | 3rd T AP<br>Aug. 21, 2012 | Nov., ★<br>Nov. 6, 2012 |
| Hawaii | Rep: Closed<br>Dem: Open | (c) Rep: March 7, 2012<br>Dem: March 13, 2012 | Nov., ★<br>Nov. 6, 2012 | Aug., 2nd S<br>Aug. 11, 2012 | … | Nov., ★<br>Nov. 6, 2012 |
| Idaho | Rep: Closed<br>Dem: Semi-Closed | (c) Rep: March 6, 2012<br>Dem: April 14, 2012 | Nov., ★<br>Nov. 6, 2012 | May, 3rd T<br>May 15, 2012 | … | Nov., ★<br>Nov. 6, 2012 |
| Illinois | Semi-Closed | March, 3rd T<br>March 20, 2012 | Nov., ★<br>Nov. 6, 2012 | March, 3rd T<br>March 20, 2012 | … | Nov., ★<br>Nov. 6, 2012 |
| Indiana | Open | May, ★<br>May 8, 2012 | Nov., ★<br>Nov. 6, 2012 | May, ★<br>May 8, 2012 | … | Nov., ★<br>Nov. 6, 2012 |
| Iowa | Closed | (c)(h)<br>Jan. 3, 2012 | Nov., ★<br>Nov. 6, 2012 | June, ★<br>June 5, 2012 | … | Nov., ★<br>Nov. 6, 2012 |
| Kansas | Rep: Closed<br>Dem: Open | (c) Rep: March 10, 2012<br>Dem: April 14, 2012 | Nov., ★<br>Nov. 6, 2012 | Aug., 1st T<br>Aug. 7, 2012 | … | Nov., ★<br>Nov. 6, 2012 |
| Kentucky | Closed | May, 1st T after 3rd M<br>May 22, 2012 | Nov., ★<br>Nov. 6, 2012 | May, 1st T after 3rd M<br>May 22, 2012 | | Nov., ★<br>Nov. 6, 2012 |
| Louisiana | Closed | March, 3rd S after 1st T<br>March 24, 2012 | Nov., ★<br>Nov. 6, 2012 | Oct., 2nd to last S (i)<br>Oct. 24, 2015 | (i) | (i) Nov., 4th S AP<br>Nov. 21, 2015 |
| Maine | Closed | (c) Rep: Feb. 4–11, 2012<br>Dem: March 11, 2012 | Nov., ★<br>Nov. 6, 2012 | June, 2nd T<br>June 12, 2012 | … | Nov., ★<br>Nov. 6, 2012 |

See footnotes at end of table.

# ELECTION DATES FOR NATIONAL AND STATE ELECTIONS
## (Formulas and dates of state elections)

| State or other jurisdiction | Type of primary | National (a) Primary | National (a) General | State (b) Primary | State (b) Runoff | State (b) General |
|---|---|---|---|---|---|---|
| Maryland | Closed | April, 1st T<br>April 3, 2012 | Nov., ★<br>Nov. 6, 2012 | June, last T<br>June 24, 2014 | ... | Nov., ★<br>Nov. 4, 2014 |
| Massachusetts | Semi-Closed | March, 1st T<br>March 6, 2012 | Nov., ★<br>Nov. 6, 2012 | 7th T Prior<br>Sept. 6, 2012 (j) | ... | Nov., ★<br>Nov. 6, 2012 |
| Michigan | Open | Feb. 4th T<br>Feb. 28, 2012 | Nov., ★<br>Nov. 6, 2012 | Aug., ★<br>Aug. 7, 2012 | ... | Nov., ★<br>Nov. 6, 2012 |
| Minnesota | Open | (c)(k) Rep: Feb. 7, 2012<br>Dem: March 6, 2012 | Nov., ★<br>Nov. 6, 2012 | Aug., 2nd T<br>Aug. 14, 2012 | ... | Nov., ★<br>Nov. 6, 2012 |
| Mississippi | Open | March, 2nd T<br>March 13, 2012 | Nov., ★<br>Nov. 6, 2012 | Aug., ★<br>Aug. 4, 2015 | 3rd T AP<br>Aug. 25, 2015 | Nov., ★<br>Nov. 3, 2015 |
| Missouri | Open | (c) Rep: March 17, 2012<br>Dem: Feb. 7, 2012 | Nov., ★<br>Nov. 6, 2012 | Aug., ★<br>Aug. 7, 2012 | ... | Nov., ★<br>Nov. 6, 2012 |
| Montana | Open | June, ★<br>June 5, 2012 | Nov., ★<br>Nov. 6, 2012 | June, ★<br>June 5, 2012 | ... | Nov., ★<br>Nov. 6, 2012 |
| Nebraska | Semi-Closed | May, 1st T after 2nd M<br>May 15, 2012 | Nov., ★<br>Nov. 6, 2012 | May, 1st T after 2nd M<br>May 15, 2012 | ... | Nov., ★<br>Nov. 6, 2012 |
| Nevada | Closed | (c) Rep: Feb. 18, 2012<br>Dem: Jan. 21, 2012 | Nov., ★<br>Nov. 6, 2012 | June, 2nd T<br>June 12, 2012 | ... | Nov., ★<br>Nov. 6, 2012 |
| New Hampshire | Semi-Closed (l) | Set by Secretary of State<br>Jan. 10, 2012 | Nov., ★<br>Nov. 6, 2012 | Sept., 2nd T<br>Sept. 11, 2012 | ... | Nov., ★<br>Nov. 6, 2012 |
| New Jersey | Closed | June, ★<br>June 5, 2012 | Nov., ★<br>Nov. 6, 2012 | June, ★<br>June 4, 2013 | ... | Nov., ★<br>Nov. 5, 2013 |
| New Mexico | Closed | June, 1st T<br>June 5, 2012 | Nov., ★<br>Nov. 6, 2012 | June, 1st T<br>June 5, 2012 | ... | Nov., ★<br>Nov. 6, 2012 |
| New York | Closed | (l)<br>April 24, 2012 | Nov., ★<br>Nov. 6, 2012 | Sept., 1st T after 2nd M<br>Sept. 13, 2012 (l) | ... | Nov., ★<br>Nov. 6, 2012 |
| North Carolina | Semi-Closed (m) | May, ★<br>May 8, 2012 | Nov., ★<br>Nov. 6, 2012 | May, ★<br>May 8, 2012 | 7 wks AP<br>June 26, 2012 | Nov., ★<br>Nov. 6, 2012 |
| North Dakota | Rep: Closed<br>Dem: Open | (c)(n) Rep: March 6, 2012<br>Dem: June 5, 2012 | Nov., ★<br>Nov. 6, 2012 | June, 2nd T<br>June 12, 2012 | ... | Nov., ★<br>Nov. 6, 2012 |
| Ohio | Semi-Closed | March, ★<br>March 6, 2012 | Nov., ★<br>Nov. 6, 2012 | March, ★<br>March 6, 2012 | ... | Nov., ★<br>Nov. 6, 2012 |
| Oklahoma | Closed | March, 1st T<br>March 6, 2012 | Nov., ★<br>Nov. 6, 2012 | June, last T<br>June 26, 2012 | Aug., 4th T<br>Aug. 28, 2012 | Nov., ★<br>Nov. 6, 2012 |
| Oregon | Closed | May, 3rd T<br>May 15, 2012 | Nov., ★<br>Nov. 6, 2012 | May, 3rd T<br>May 15, 2012 | ... | Nov., ★<br>Nov. 6, 2012 |
| Pennsylvania | Closed | April, 4th T<br>April 24, 2012 | Nov., ★<br>Nov. 6, 2012 | April, 4th T<br>April 24, 2012 | ... | Nov., ★<br>Nov. 6, 2012 |

See footnotes at end of table.

# ELECTION DATES FOR NATIONAL AND STATE ELECTIONS
## (Formulas and dates of state elections)

| State or other jurisdiction | Type of primary | National (a) Primary | National (a) General | State (b) Primary | State (b) Runoff | State (b) General |
|---|---|---|---|---|---|---|
| Rhode Island | Semi-Closed | April, 4th T<br>April 24, 2012 | Nov., ★<br>Nov. 6, 2012 | Sept., 2nd T after 1st M<br>Sept. 11, 2012 | ... | Nov., ★<br>Nov. 6, 2012 |
| South Carolina | Open | Rep: Jan. 21, 2012<br>Dem: (o) | Nov., ★<br>Nov. 6, 2012 | June, 2nd T<br>June 12, 2012 | 2nd T AP<br>June 26, 2012 | Nov., ★<br>Nov. 6, 2012 |
| South Dakota | Rep: Closed<br>Dem: Open | June, ★<br>June 5, 2012 | Nov., ★<br>Nov. 6, 2012 | June, ★<br>June 5, 2012 | 3rd T AP<br>June 26, 2012 | Nov., ★<br>Nov. 6, 2012 |
| Tennessee | Open | March, 1st T<br>March 6, 2012 | Nov., ★<br>Nov. 6, 2012 | Aug., 1st TH<br>Aug. 2, 2012 | ... | Nov., ★<br>Nov. 6, 2012 |
| Texas | Open | (p)<br>May 29, 2012 | Nov., ★<br>Nov. 6, 2012 | (p)<br>May 29, 2012 | (p)<br>July 31, 2012 | Nov., ★<br>Nov. 6, 2012 |
| Utah | Rep: Closed<br>Dem: Open | (CA) Dem: March 13, 2012<br>Rep: Primary: June 26, 2012 | Nov., ★<br>Nov. 6, 2012 | June, 4th T<br>June 26, 2012 | ... | Nov., ★<br>Nov. 6, 2012 |
| Vermont | Open | March, 1st T<br>March 6, 2012 | Nov., ★<br>Nov. 6, 2012 | Aug., 4th T<br>Aug. 28, 2012 | ... | Nov., ★<br>Nov. 6, 2012 |
| Virginia | Open | March, 1st T<br>March 6, 2012 | Nov., ★<br>Nov. 6, 2012 | June, 2nd T<br>June 11, 2013 | ... | Nov., ★<br>Nov. 5, 2013 |
| Washington | Rep: Closed<br>Dem: Semi-Closed | (c)(q) Rep: March 3, 2012<br>Dem: April 15, 2012 | Nov., ★<br>Nov. 6, 2012 | Aug., 1st T<br>Aug. 7, 2012 | ... | Nov., ★<br>Nov. 6, 2012 |
| West Virginia | Semi-Closed | May, 2nd T<br>May 8, 2012 | Nov., ★<br>Nov. 6, 2012 | May, 2nd T<br>May 8, 2012 | ... | Nov., ★<br>Nov. 6, 2012 |
| Wisconsin | Open | April, 1st T<br>April 3, 2012 | Nov., ★<br>Nov. 6, 2012 | (r)<br>May 8, 2012 (r) | ... | (r)<br>June 5, 2012 (r) |
| Wyoming | Closed | (c) Rep: March 6, 2012<br>Dem: April 14, 2012 | Nov., ★<br>Nov. 6, 2012 | Aug., 1st T after 3rd M<br>Aug. 21, 2012 | ... | Nov., ★<br>Nov. 6, 2012 |
| Dist. of Columbia | Closed | April, 1st T<br>April 3, 2012 | Nov., ★<br>Nov. 6, 2012 | April, 1st T<br>April 3, 2012 | ... | Nov., ★<br>Nov. 6, 2012 |
| American Samoa | Open | (c) Dem: March 6, 2012<br>Rep: April 13, 2012 | Nov., ★<br>Nov. 6, 2012 | (s) | 14 days after General<br>Nov. 20, 2012 | Nov., ★<br>Nov. 6, 2012 |
| Guam | Closed | (c) Rep: March 10, 2012<br>Dem: May 5, 2012 | Nov., ★<br>Nov. 6, 2012 | Sept., 1st S<br>Sept. 1, 2012 | ... | Nov., ★<br>Nov. 6, 2012 |
| No. Marianas Islands | Closed | (c)<br>March 10, 2012 | Nov., ★<br>Nov. 6, 2012 | NA<br>NA | ... | Nov., ★<br>Nov. 6, 2012 |
| Puerto Rico | Rep: Closed<br>Dem: Open | Rep: March 18, 2012 (Primary)<br>Dem: June 3, 2012 (Caucus) | Nov., ★<br>Nov. 6, 2012 | (t)<br>March 18, 2012 (t) | ... | Nov., ★<br>Nov. 6, 2012 |
| U.S. Virgin Islands | N.A. | (c) Rep: March 10, 2012<br>Dem: June 3, 2012 | Nov., ★<br>Nov. 6, 2012 | Sept., 2nd S<br>Sept. 8, 2012 | 14 days AP<br>Sept. 22, 2012 | Nov., ★<br>Nov. 6, 2012 |

See footnotes at end of table.

# ELECTION DATES FOR NATIONAL AND STATE ELECTIONS
## (Formulas and dates of state elections)

*Source:* The Council of State Governments, April 2012.

*Note:* This table describes the basic formulas for determining when national and state elections will be held. For specific information on a particular state, the reader is advised to contact the state election administration office. All dates provided are based on the state election formula and dates are subject to change.

*Key:*

★ — First Tuesday after first Monday.
... — No provision.
M — Monday.
T — Tuesday.

TH — Thursday.
S — Saturday.
Prior — Prior to general election.
AP — After primary.

*Key:* Column 1:

(a) National refers to presidential elections.
(b) State refers to election in which a state executive official or legislator is to be elected. See Table 6.1, State Officials to be Elected.
(c) The dates for presidential caucuses are set by the political parties.
(d) The Arizona governor can use his or her proclamation powers to move the state's primary to a date on which the event would have an impact on the nomination.
(e) In June 2010, California voters approved Proposition 410. State primary elections will now be open to all registered voters and the top two vote getters in every race — no matter their party affiliations — will advance to the November general election.
(f) The date of the presidential primary is selected by the Presidential Preference Primary Date Selection Committee. It may be no earlier than the first Tuesday in January and no later than the first Tuesday in March in the year of the presidential preference primary.
(g) The Secretary of State has the authority to set the date of the presidential primary election. Currently held in March, the presidential primary could be held as late as June 14.
(h) Iowa does not have a presidential primary. The Iowa Caucuses mark the beginning of the presidential candidate selection process by choosing delegates to the next level of political party conventions.
(i) Louisiana has an open primary which requires all candidates, regardless of party affiliation, to appear on a single ballot. If a candidate receives over 50 percent of the vote in the primary, that candidate is elected to the office. If no candidate receives a majority vote, then a single election is held between the two candidates receiving the most votes. For national elections, the first vote is held on the first Saturday in October of even-numbered years with the general election held on the first Tuesday after

the first Monday in November. For state elections, the election is held on the second to last Saturday in October with the runoff being held on the fourth Saturday after first election. Local elections vary depending on the location and the year.

(j) The date of the 2012 primary election day was moved from Sept. 18 to Thursday, Sept. 6 after Secretary of State William Galvin recommended the change to avoid a conflict with the Jewish holiday Rosh Hashanah.

(k) Parties must notify the Secretary of State's Office in writing prior to Dec. 1st the year preceding the date of the election of their intentions to hold a preference primary election.

(l) Date for national primary set by statute for 2012 only per Chapter 17, § 8–100 (2012). Date for state primary moved for 2012 to avoid conflict with observance of September 11.

(m) Unaffiliated voters, by state statute and with permission of a party, may vote in a party primary. Currently both the Democratic and Republican parties allow this.

(n) On one designated day, following presidential nominating contests in the states of Iowa and New Hampshire and prior to the first Wednesday in March in every presidential election year, every political party entitled to a separate column may conduct a presidential preference caucus. Before August 15 of the odd-numbered year immediately preceding the presidential election year, the secretary of state shall designate the day after consulting with and taking recommendations from the two political parties casting the greatest vote for president of the United States at the most recent general elections when the office of president appeared on the ballot.

(o) The South Carolina Democratic Party did not hold a publicly-conducted presidential primary in 2012.

(p) The date of the 2012 primary and runoff elections were delayed by a federal court, due to repeated delays in the redistricting process.

(q) The Washington Legislature voted to suspend the 2012 presidential primary for budgetary reasons, replacing it with caucuses. The primary is expected to return in 2016.

(r) Wisconsin will hold a recall election on June 5, 2012 for the governor, lieutenant governor, and four senate seats. The primary for the recall election will be held on May 8. The regularly scheduled primary will be held on Aug. 14, 2012, with the general election to be held on Nov. 6, 2012.

(s) American Samoa does not conduct primary elections.

(t) Scheduled gubernatorial primary elections were not held in Puerto Rico because neither major party's candidate was challenged.

## Table 6.5
## POLLING HOURS: GENERAL ELECTIONS

| State or other jurisdiction | Polls open | Polls close | Notes on hours (a) |
|---|---|---|---|
| Alabama | 7 a.m. | 7 p.m. | |
| Alaska | 7 a.m. | 8 p.m. | |
| Arizona | 6 a.m. | 7 p.m. | |
| Arkansas | 7:30 a.m. | 7:30 p.m. | |
| California | 7 a.m. | 8 p.m. | |
| Colorado | 7 a.m. | 7 p.m. | |
| Connecticut | 6 a.m. | 8 p.m. | |
| Delaware | 7 a.m. | 8 p.m. | |
| Florida | 7 a.m. | 7 p.m. | |
| Georgia | 7 a.m. | 7 p.m. | |
| Hawaii | 7 a.m. | 6 p.m. | |
| Idaho | 8 a.m. | 8 p.m. | Clerk has the option of opening all polls at 7 a.m. Idaho is in two time zones—MST and PST. |
| Illinois | 6 a.m. | 7 p.m. | |
| Indiana | 6 a.m. | 6 p.m. | |
| Iowa | 7 a.m. | 9 p.m. | Hours for school and city elections: polls open at 7 a.m. or noon (depending upon choice of county auditor, with legal limitations on opening the polls at noon). |
| Kansas | 7 a.m. | 7 p.m. | Counties may choose to open polls as early as 6 a.m. and close as late as 8 p.m. Several western counties are on Mountain time. |
| Kentucky | 6 a.m. | 6 p.m. | Counties may be either in Eastern or Central time zones. |
| Louisiana | 6 a.m. | 8 p.m. | |
| Maine | Between 6 and 10 a.m. | 8 p.m. | Applicable opening time depends on variables related to the size of the precinct. |
| Maryland | 7 a.m. | 8 p.m. | Anyone in line at 8 p.m. will be allowed to vote. |
| Massachusetts | 7 a.m. | 8 p.m. | |
| Michigan | 7 a.m. | 8 p.m. | Eastern time zone and Central time zone. |
| Minnesota | 7 a.m. | 8 p.m. | Towns outside of the Twin Cities metro area with less than 500 inhabitants may have a later time for the polls to open as long as it is not later than 10 a.m. |
| Mississippi | 7 a.m. | 7 p.m. | |
| Missouri | 6 a.m. | 7 p.m. | Those individuals in line at 7 p.m. will be allowed to vote. |
| Montana | 7 a.m. | 8 p.m. | Polling places with fewer than 400 registered electors must open no later than noon and until 8 p.m. or until all registered electors in any precinct have voted. |
| Nebraska | 7 a.m MST/8 a.m. CST | 7 p.m. MST/8 p.m. CST | |
| Nevada | 7 a.m. | 7 p.m. | |
| New Hampshire | No later than 11 a.m. | No earlier than 7 p.m. | Polling hours vary from town to town. The hours of 11 a.m. to 7 p.m. are by statute. |
| New Jersey | 6 a.m. | 8 p.m. | |
| New Mexico | 7 a.m. | 7 p.m. | |
| New York | 6 a.m. | 9 p.m. | |
| North Carolina | 6:30 a.m. | 7:30 p.m. | |
| North Dakota | Between 7 and 9 a.m. | Between 7 and 9 p.m. | Counties must have polls open by 9 a.m., but can choose to open as early as 7 a.m. Polls remain open until 7 p.m., but can be open as late as 9 p.m. The majority of polls in the state are open from 8 a.m. to 7 p.m. in their respective time zones (CST and MST). |
| Ohio | 6:30 a.m. | 7:30 p.m. | |
| Oklahoma | 7 a.m. | 7 p.m. | |
| Oregon | 7 a.m. | 8 p.m. | Oregon's polls (County Clerk's office and dropsites) are open from 7 a.m. to 8 p.m. |
| Pennsylvania | 7 a.m. | 8 p.m. | |
| Rhode Island | Between 7 and 9 a.m | 8 p.m. | |
| South Carolina | 7 a.m. | 7 p.m. | |
| South Dakota | 7 a.m. | 7 p.m. | Local time. |
| Tennessee | 7 a.m. (as early as 6 a.m.) | 7 p.m. CST/ 8 p.m. EST | Poll hours are set by each county election commission. Polling places shall be open a minimum of 10 hours but no more than 13 hours. All polling locations in the Eastern time zone shall close at 8 p.m. and those in the Central time zone shall close at 7 p.m. Polls may open as early as 6 a.m. |
| Texas | 7 a.m. | 7 p.m. | |
| Utah | 7 a.m. | 8 p.m. | |
| Vermont | Between 5 and 10 a.m. | 7 p.m. | The opening time for polls is set by local boards of civil authority. |

See footnotes at end of table.

## POLLING HOURS: GENERAL ELECTIONS — Continued

| State or other jurisdiction | Polls open | Polls close | Notes on hours (a) |
|---|---|---|---|
| Virginia | 6 a.m. | 7 p.m. | |
| Washington | NA | NA | Washington has a vote-by-mail only system. Ballots must be post-marked by election day if mailed, and, if voters choose to drop their ballot in the ballot drop box or deliver it to their county auditor, they don't need a stamp, but it must be in the box or delivered by 8:00 p.m. on election day. |
| West Virginia | 6:30 a.m. | 7:30 p.m. | |
| Wisconsin | Between 7 and 9 a.m. | 8 p.m. | In cities with a population of 10,000 or more, the polls must open at 7:00 a.m. In cities, towns and villages with populations of 10,000, the polls may open any time between 7:00 a.m. and 9:00 a.m. |
| Wyoming | 7 a.m. | 7 p.m. | |
| Dist. of Columbia | 7 a.m. | 8 p.m. | |
| American Samoa | 6 a.m | 6 p.m. | Election proclamation issued by Chief Election Officer contains a statement of time and place for each territorial election. |
| Guam | 7 a.m. | 8 p.m. | |
| No. Mariana Islands | 7 a.m. | 7 p.m. | Elections are held on six separate islands. At the close of the polls, ballots are flown to Saipan where they are tabulated at election headquarters. |
| Puerto Rico | 8 a.m. | 3 p.m. | |
| U.S. Virgin Islands | 7 a.m. | 7 p.m. | |

*Sources:* The Council of State Governments' survey, January 2007 and state election websites, April 2012.

*Note:* Hours for primary, municipal and special elections may differ from those noted.

*Key:*
(a) In all states, voters standing in line when the polls close are allowed to vote; however, provisions for handling those voters vary across jurisdictions.

# Table 6.6
# VOTER REGISTRATION INFORMATION

| State or other jurisdiction | Closing date for registration bfr. gen. election (days) | Early voting allowed (a) | Voter ID Required (b) | Persons eligible for absentee voting (c) | Absentee voting Cut-off for receiving absentee ballots | Absentee votes signed by witness or notary (d) | Residency requirements (e) | Registration in other places prohibited (f) | Provision for felons Voting rights revoked | Method/process or provision for restoration | Provision regarding mental competency |
|---|---|---|---|---|---|---|---|---|---|---|---|
| Alabama | 10 | No | Yes | B,D,O,P,S,T | (g) | N or 2 W | S, 1 day | ★ | ★ | ● | ★ |
| Alaska | 30 | Yes | Yes | No excuse required | 8 p.m. Election Day | N or 1 W | S, D, 30 | ★ | ★ | ● | ★ |
| Arizona | 29 | Yes | Yes | No excuse required | 7 p.m. Election Day | ... | S, C, 29 | ★ | ★ | ● | ★ |
| Arkansas | 30 | Yes | Yes | B,D,O,P,T | 7:30 p.m. Election Day | ... | C, 30 | ★ | ★ | ★ | ★ |
| California | 15 | Yes | No | No excuse required | 8 p.m. Election Day | ... | S | ... | ... | ... | ★ |
| Colorado | 29 | Yes | Yes | No excuse required | 7 p.m. Election Day | ... | S, P, 30 | ★ | ★ | ★ | ★ |
| Connecticut | (h)(i) | No | Yes | B,D,E,O,P,R,T | 8 p.m. Election Day | ... | S, T | ★ | ★ | ★ | ... |
| Delaware | 20 | No | Yes | B,D,E,O,P,R,S,T | 8 p.m. Election Day | N | S | ★ | ★ | ● | ★ |
| Florida | 29 | Yes | Yes | No excuse required | 7 p.m. Election Day | ... | S, C | ... | ★ | ● | ★ |
| Georgia | 30 (i) | Yes | Yes | No excuse required | Close of polls | ... | S, C | ... | ★ | ★ | ★ |
| Hawaii | 30 | Yes | Yes | No excuse required | 6 p.m. Election Day | ... | S | ★ | ★ | ★ | ★ |
| Idaho | Election Day (j) | Yes | Yes | No excuse required | 8 p.m. Election Day | ... | S, C, 30 | ★ | ★ | ★ | ★ |
| Illinois | 28 (k) | Yes | No | No excuse required | Close of polls on Election Day (l) | ... | S, P, 30 | ★ | ★ | ★ | ★ |
| Indiana | 29 | Yes | No | A | Close of polls | ... | S, P, 30 | ★ | ★ | ★ | ★ |
| Iowa | Election Day (j) | Yes | No | No excuse required | Postmarked by Election Day (m) | ... | S | ★ | ★ | ★ | ★ |
| Kansas | 21 | Yes | Yes | No excuse required | Close of polls | ... | S | ★ | ★ | ★ | ★ |
| Kentucky | 29 | No | Yes | A | 6 p.m. Election Day | ... | S, P, 28 | ★ | ★ | ★ | ★ |
| Louisiana | 30 | Yes | Yes | A | 4:30 Election Day (n) | N or W | S, C, P, 30 | ★ | ★ | ★ | ★ |
| Maine | Election Day (j) | Yes | No | No excuse required | 8 p.m. Election Day | N or W | S, M | ★ | ... | ★ | ★ |
| Maryland | 21 | Yes | No | No excuse required | 8 p.m. Election Day (o) | ... | S, 21 | ★ | ★ | ★ | ★ |
| Massachusetts | 20 | No | No | B,D,O,P,R,T | Close of polls (p) | ... | S | ... | ★ | ★ | ★ |
| Michigan | 30 | No | No | B,C,D,O,P,R,T | 8 p.m. Election Day | ... | S, M, 30 | ★ | ★ | ★ | ★ |
| Minnesota | Election Day (j) | No | No (q) | B,D,O,P,R,T | Election Day | N or W | S, 20 | ★ | ★ | ★ | ★ |
| Mississippi | 30 | No | Yes *** (r) | A | 5 p.m. day before election | N (s) | S, C, 30 | ★ | ★ | ● | ★ |
| Missouri | 28 | No | Yes | B,D,O,P,R,T | Close of polls | N (t) | S | ★ | ★ | ★ | ★ |
| Montana | Election Day (j) | Yes | No | No excuse required | Close of polls | ... | S, 30 | ★ | ★ | ★ | ★ |
| Nebraska | (u) | No | No | No excuse required | Close of polls | ... | S | ★ | ★ | ● | ★ |
| Nevada | (v) | Yes | No | B,D,E,O,P,R,T | Close of polls | ... | S, C, 30; P, 10 (w) | ★ | ★ | ★ | ... |
| New Hampshire | Election Day (j) | No | Yes | B,D,E,O,P,R,T | (x) | ... | S | ★ | ★ | ★ | ... |
| New Jersey | 21 | No | No | No excuse required | 8 p.m. Election Day | W or N | S, C, 30 | ★ | ★ | ★ | ★ |
| New Mexico | 28 | Yes | No | No excuse required | 7 p.m. Election Day | ... | S | ★ | ★ | ★ | ★ |
| New York | (y) | No | No | B,D,O,P,T | Postmarked day before election | W | S, C, 30 | ★ | ★ | ★ | ★ |
| North Carolina | (j) | Yes | No | No excuse required | 5 p.m. day before election | ... | S, C, 30 | ★ | ★ | ★ | ★ |
| North Dakota | (z) | Yes | Yes | No excuse required | Postmarked day before election; | ... | S, P, 30 | (z) | ★ | ★ | ★ |
| Ohio | 30 | Yes | Yes | No excuse required | Close of polls (aa) | ... | S, 30 | ★ | ★ | ★ | ... |
| Oklahoma | 24 | Yes | Yes | No excuse required | 7 p.m. Election Day | N (bb) | S | ★ | ★ | ★ | ★ |
| Oregon | 21 | No | No | No excuse required | 8 p.m. Election Day | ... | S | ★ | ★ | ★ | ★ |
| Pennsylvania | 30 | No | Yes (cc) | B,C,D,O,P,R,S,T | 5 p.m. Friday before election | ... | S, D, 30 | ★ | ★ | ● | ... |
| Rhode Island | 30 (i) | Yes | Yes (cc) | B,D,O,P,R,T | 9 p.m. Election Day | N or 2 W (dd) | S, C | ★ | ★ | ★ | ★ |
| South Carolina | 30 | No | Yes** | A | 5 p.m. Election Day | N or W (ee) | S, C, P | ★ | ★ | ★ | ★ |

See footnotes at end of table.

# VOTER REGISTRATION INFORMATION — Continued

| State or other jurisdiction | Closing date for registration bfr. gen. election (days) (a) | Early voting allowed (a) | Voter ID Required (b) | Persons eligible for absentee voting (c) | Absentee voting Cut-off for receiving absentee ballots | Absentee votes signed by witness or notary (d) | Residency requirements (e) | Registration in other places prohibited (f) | Provision for felons Voting rights revoked | Method/process or provision for restoration | Provision regarding mental competency |
|---|---|---|---|---|---|---|---|---|---|---|---|
| South Dakota......... | 15 | Yes | Yes | No excuse required | Close of polls | (ff) | S | ★ | ★ | ★ | ★ |
| Tennessee............. | 30 | Yes | Yes | A | Close of polls | W | S | ★ | ★ | ● | ★ |
| Texas.................... | 30 | Yes | Yes** | B,C,D,O,P,S,T | Close of polls | ... | S,C | ... | ★ | ● | ★ |
| Utah..................... | (gg) | Yes | Yes | No excuse required | Noon on day of canvass | ... | S,30 | ★ | ★ | ★ | ★ |
| Vermont................ | 6 | Yes | No | No excuse required | Close of polls | ... | S,C | ... | ... | ... | ★ |
| Virginia................. | 22 | No | Yes | B,D,O,P,R,S,T | Close of polls | W | S | ★ | ★ | ★ | ★ |
| Washington........... | (hh) | No | Yes | No excuse required | Postmarked on or bfr. Election Day | ... | S,30 | ★ | ★ | ... | ★ |
| West Virginia......... | 21 | Yes | No | B,D,E,O,P,S,T (ii) | (jj) | W | S,C,30 | ★ | ★ | ... | ★ |
| Wisconsin.............. | Election Day (j) | Yes | Yes* | No excuse required | Close of polls | ... | S,P,28 | ... | ★ | ● | ★ |
| Wyoming................ | Election Day (j) | Yes | No | No excuse required | 7 p.m. Election Day | ... | S,P | ★ | ★ | ★ | ★ |
| Dist. of Columbia... | Election Day (j) | No | No | No excuse required | (kk) | ... | D,30 | ★ | ★ | ... | ★ |
| American Samoa... | 30 | N.A. | N.A. | A | 1:30 p.m. Election Day | ... | T | ★ | N.A. | N.A. | N.A. |
| Guam..................... | 10 | No | No | B,D,F,O,P,S,T | Close of Polls | N (ll) | T | ★ | ★ | N.A. | ★ |
| No. Mariana Islands......... | 60 | Yes | N.A. | B,D,E,O,P,S,T | 14 days after election | N (ll) | T,120 | ★ | ★ | ... | ★ |
| Puerto Rico........... | 50 | Yes | Yes | B,O,P,S,T | (mm) | ... | T (oo) | ★ | ... | ... | ★ |
| U.S. Virgin Islands............. | 30 | No | Yes | A | 14 days before election | Affidavit | T,P,90 | ★ | ★ | ★ | ★ |

*Source:* The Council of State Governments survey of state election websites, May 2012.

*Note:* Previous editions of this chart contained a column for "Automatic cancellation of registration for failure to vote for ___ years." However, the National Voter Registration Act requires a confirmation notice prior to any cancellation and thus effectively bans any automatic cancellation of voter registration. In addition, all states and territories except Puerto Rico and the U.S. Virgin Islands allow mail-in registration.

Key:
★ — Provision exists.
. . . — No state provision.
● — Limited voting restoration.
N.A. — Information not available at press time.

(a) Column 2: Early voting is usually done in person on the same equipment as that used on Election Day. An excuse is not required.

(b) Voter identification laws include both photo or non-photo identification requirements: *Blocked pending state judicial review. **Photo identification requirement blocked pending pre-clearance by the U.S. Department of Justice under Section 5 of the Voting Rights Act, but other voter ID provisions remain in effect. ***Photo identification requirement blocked pending pre-clearance by the U.S. Department of Justice under Section 5 of the Voting Rights Act, no voter ID provisions currently in effect.

(c) Persons eligible for absentee voting: A — All of these; B — Absent on business; C — Senior citizen; D — Disabled persons; E — Not absent, but prevented by employment from registering; M/O — No absentee registration (or municipality in PA); O — Out of state; P — Out of precinct (or municipality in PA); R — Absent for religious reasons; S — Students; T — Temporarily out of jurisdiction.

(d) Absentee votes must be signed by: N — Notary or W — Witness. Numbers indicated the number of signatures required.

(e) Key for residency requirements: S — State, C — County, D — District, M — Municipality, P — Precinct, T — Town. Numbers represent the number of days before an election for which one must be a resident.

(f) State provision prohibiting registration or claiming the right to vote in another state or jurisdiction.

(g) An absentee ballot returned by mail must be postmarked no later than the day prior to the election and received by the Absentee Election Manager no later than noon on Election Day. If hand-delivered, the ballot must be in the office of the Absentee Election Manager by the close of business (but no later than 5 p.m.) on the day prior to the election.

(h) For primary, must be postmarked five days before election or registration may be completed in person by noon on the last business day before election. For general, must be postmarked 14 days before election or registration may be completed in person by the seventh day before election.

(i) The 5th Monday before a general primary, general election, or presidential preference primary; the 5th day after the date of the call for all other special primaries and special elections.

(j) Connecticut will have election-day registration starting in 2013.

Idaho—25 days before the election or election-day registration at precincts.

Iowa—10 days before the election or election-day registration.

Maine—By mail, 21 days before the election. In-person, up to and including Election Day.

Montana—30 days before the election or election-day registration.

Minnesota—21 days before an election or election-day registration at polling precincts.

New Hampshire—Received by city or town clerk 10 days before election or election-day registration at precincts.

North Carolina—25 days; people may register and vote on the same day at Early Voting sites during Early Voting periods (19 to 3 days before the day of the election, whether it is the Primary or General Election). Same Day Registration cannot be used on Election Day.

Rhode Island—Election-day registration is available, but voters who do so can vote only for the offices of President and Vice President, not in state or local races.

Wisconsin—By mail, 20 days before the election, or completed in the local voter registration office by 5:00 p.m. one day before election, or election-day registration at polling precincts.

Wyoming—30 days before or election-day registration at polling precincts.

District of Columbia—Postmarked 30 days before election day by mail; after 30th day before the election, can register in person but can no longer change party affiliation; Election Day registration.

# VOTER REGISTRATION INFORMATION—Continued

a period from close of registration for a primary or election and until 14th day before the primary or election. If a voter who registers during this time period wishes to vote at that first election occurring after grace period, he/she must do so by grace period voting (at the discretion of the election authority a grace period registrant may vote by mail).

(k) Closing date for registration before general election is 28 days before. Illinois now has grace period registration which allows for registration of voters and change of address during a period from close of registration for a primary or election and until 14th day before the primary or election. If a voter who registers during this time period wishes to vote at that first election occurring after grace period, he/she must do so by grace period voting (at the discretion of the election authority a grace period registrant may vote by mail).

(l) Mailed absentee ballots must be postmarked no later than midnight on the night prior to the election, and must be received within 14 days of the election.

(m) An absentee ballot must be returned before the polls are closed on election day; or if the ballot is mailed, the envelope must be postmarked before Election Day. Timely postmarked ballots are considered on time if the ballot is received before noon on Monday following Election Day. However, if the canvass of votes for the election is required by law to be held earlier, the ballot must be received by the time set for the canvass of votes. The canvass of votes for the school election and some city elections will be held on Thursday or Friday after the election.

(n) 8:00 pm on Election Day for military personnel, people residing outside of U.S., and those who are hospitalized.

(o) Must be mailed on or before Election Day and it must be received by the local board of elections by 10 am on the 2nd Friday following the election.

(p) If mailed from outside the U.S., must be postmarked on Election Day and must be received 10 days after election.

(q) Minnesota voters will consider a constitutional amendment in November 2012 that would require the use of photo identification at the polls. Governor Mark Dayton vetoed a similar measure last year.

(r) Mississippi voters approved a constitutional amendment in November 2011 that requires the use of photo identification at the polls.

(s) Disabled voters do not need to have an absentee ballot notarized, but it must be witnessed.

(t) All absentee ballots must be notarized with the exception of the following: Missouri residents outside the U.S., including military on active duty and their immediate family members; permanently disabled voters and those voting absentee due to illness or physical disability; and caregivers.

(u) In person by 6 p.m. on the 2nd Friday before election or postmarked by the 3rd Friday before the election.

(v) By mail or at the Department of Motor Vehicles, 30 days before the election. In person, 20 days before the election.

(w) Must have continuously resided in the state and county at least 30 days and in precinct at least 10 days before election.

(x) In person: day before election. By mail: day of election.

(y) Postmarked at least 25 days before the election, and received at least 20 days before the election.

(z) No Voter registration.

(aa) Ballots from in-country voters must be received by close of polls; ballots returned from outside the United States must be received within 10 days of Election Day.

(bb) All absentee ballots must notarized with the following exceptions: Physically incapacitated voters and voters who care for physically incapacitated persons (ballot affidavit must be witnessed by two people); voters in a nursing home; overseas voters.

(cc) Voter ID provisions passed by the Pennsylvania General Assembly in 2012 will be in effect for the November 2012 general election.

(dd) All absentee ballots must be notarized or signed by two witnesses with the following exceptions: military and overseas voters.

(ee) All absentee ballots must be notarized or signed by one witness, with the exception of qualified voters under the Uniformed and Overseas Citizens Absentee Voters Act.

(ff) Absentee ballot applications (not absentee ballots) are required to be notarized or submitted with a copy of the voter's photo identification.

(gg) Must be postmarked 30 days before an election if mailed. May register in person the 15th day before an election, but will be only be eligible to vote on Election Day, not in early voting.

(hh) Thirty days before the election if mailed or 15 days before the election if delivered in-person to the local voter registration office.

(ii) Because West Virginia offers an early voting period, unless a voter seeks to vote absentee by mail because of illness or disability, the ballot must be mailed to an out-of-county address.

(jj) Received by mail by the day after the election or postmarked by Election Day and received by the start of the canvass.

(kk) Postmarked by Election Day, received 10 days after election.

(ll) Notary public or commissioned officer authorized to administer oath for Armed Services personnel.

(mm) 30 days after receipt of ballot for voters on the mainland, 45 days after receipt of ballot for voters residing outside of the United States.

(nn) Absentee ballot applications (not absentee ballots) are required to be certified by various officials, depending on the reason for voting absentee, such as a college registrar, employer, or medical official.

(oo) According to Electoral Law the voter must have a permanent residence in Puerto Rico to be a qualified elector.

## Table 6.7
## VOTING STATISTICS FOR GUBERNATORIAL ELECTIONS BY REGION

| State or other jurisdiction | Date of last election | Primary election — Republican | Democrat | Independent and third party | Other | Total votes | General election — Republican | Percent | Democrat | Percent | Independent and third party | Percent | Other | Percent | Total votes |
|---|---|---|---|---|---|---|---|---|---|---|---|---|---|---|---|
| **Eastern Region** | | | | | | | | | | | | | | | |
| Connecticut | 2010 | .......... | 73,961 | (a) | 0 | 102,933 | 560,874 | 49.0 | 567,278 (b) | 49.5 | 17,629 | 1.5 | 18 | 0.0 | 1,145,799 |
| Delaware | 2008 | 28,972 | 122,936 | | 0 | 254,343 | 126,662 | 32.0 | 266,861 | 67.5 | 0 | 0.0 | 1,681 | 0.4 | 395,204 |
| Maine | 2010 | 131,407 | 480,523 | | 0 | 759,315 | 218,065 | 38.1 | 109,387 | 19.1 | 242,690 | 42.4 | 2,624 | 0.5 | 572,766 |
| Maryland | 2010 | 278,792 | 358,145 | | 0 | 576,801 | 776,319 | 41.8 | 1,044,961 | 56.2 | 34,574 | 1.9 | 2,026 | 0.1 | 1,857,880 |
| Massachusetts | 2010 | 218,656 | 57,558 | | 0 | 185,649 | 964,866 | 42.0 | 1,112,283 | 48.4 | 217,290 | 9.5 | 2,600 | 0.1 | 2,297,039 |
| New Hampshire | 2010 | 128,091 | 209,304 | | 0 | 543,519 | 205,616 | 45.0 | 240,346 | 52.6 | 10,089 | 2.2 | 537 | 0.1 | 456,588 |
| New Jersey | 2009 | 334,215 | (c) | | 0 | | 1,174,445 | 48.5 | 1,087,731 | 44.9 | 161,508 | 6.7 | 0 | 0.0 | 2,423,684 |
| New York | 2010 | 479,684 | | 19,051 | 0 | 498,735 | 1,548,184 (d) | 33.3 | 2,911,721 (d) | 62.6 | 194,447 | 4.2 | 0 | 0.0 | 4,654,352 |
| Pennsylvania | 2010 | 852,416 | 1,021,068 | | 0 | 1,873,484 | 2,172,763 | 54.5 | 1,814,788 | 45.5 | 0 | 0.0 | 0 | 0.0 | 3,987,551 |
| Rhode Island | 2010 | 18,182 | 73,142 (c) | | 0 | 91,324 | 114,911 | 33.6 | 78,896 | 23.0 | 148,483 | 43.4 | 0 | 0.0 | 342,290 |
| Vermont | 2010 | 28,868 | 73,576 | 369 | 0 | 102,813 | 115,212 | 47.7 | 119,543 | 49.5 | 6,190 | 2.6 | 660 | 0.3 | 241,605 |
| Regional total | | 2,499,283 | 2,470,213 | 19,420 | 0 | 4,988,916 | 7,977,917 | 43.4 | 9,353,795 | 50.9 | 1,032,900 | 5.6 | 10,146 | 0.1 | 18,374,758 |
| **Midwestern Region** | | | | | | | | | | | | | | | |
| Illinois | 2010 | 767,485 | 915,726 | 5,086 | 0 | 1,688,297 | 1,713,385 | 45.9 | 1,745,219 | 46.8 | 271,142 | 7.3 | 243 | 0.0 | 3,729,989 |
| Indiana | 2008 | 350,390 | 1,151,951 | | 0 | 1,502,341 | 1,563,885 | 57.8 | 1,082,463 | 40.0 | 28 | 0.0 | 57,376 | 2.1 | 2,703,752 |
| Iowa | 2010 | 227,525 | 58,827 | | 0 | 286,352 | 592,494 | 52.8 | 484,798 | 43.2 | 38,014 | 3.4 | 6,707 | 0.6 | 1,122,013 |
| Kansas | 2010 | 321,080 | 74,754 (c) | | 0 | 395,834 | 530,760 | 63.3 | 270,166 | 32.2 | 37,857 | 4.5 | 7 | 0.0 | 838,790 |
| Michigan | 2010 | 1,048,384 | 528,822 | | 0 | 1,577,206 | 1,874,834 | 58.1 | 1,287,320 | 39.9 | 63,907 | 2.0 | 27 | 0.0 | 3,226,088 |
| Minnesota | 2010 | 130,408 | 442,137 | 17,714 | 0 | 590,259 | 910,462 | 43.2 | 919,232 | 43.6 | 275,463 | 13.1 | 1,864 | 0.1 | 2,107,021 |
| Nebraska | 2010 | 170,090 | 57,463 (c) | | 0 | 227,553 | 360,645 | 73.9 | 127,343 | 26.1 | 0 | 0.0 | 0 | 0.0 | 487,988 |
| North Dakota | 2008 | 50,226 | 38,784 | | 18 | 89,028 | 235,009 | 74.4 | 74,279 | 23.5 | 6,404 | 2.0 | 0 | 0.0 | 315,692 |
| Ohio | 2010 | 746,719 (c) | 630,785 (c) | 5,331 | 0 | 1,382,835 | 1,889,186 | 49.0 | 1,812,059 | 47.0 | 150,591 | 3.9 | 633 | 0.0 | 3,852,469 |
| South Dakota | 2010 | 83,817 | (c) | 2,437 | 0 | 83,817 | 195,046 | 61.5 | 122,037 | 38.5 | 0 | 0.0 | 59 | 0.0 | 317,083 |
| Wisconsin | 2010 | 618,828 | 235,762 | | 0 | 857,027 | 1,128,941 | 52.3 | 1,004,303 | 46.5 | 25,671 | 2.2 | 0 | 0.0 | 2,133,244 |
| Regional total | | 4,514,952 | 4,135,011 | 30,568 | 18 | 8,680,549 | 9,978,600 | 50.3 | 8,929,219 | 45.0 | 869,077 | 4.4 | 66,916 | 0.3 | 19,843,812 |
| **Southern Region** | | | | | | | | | | | | | | | |
| Alabama | 2010 | 492,897 (e) | 318,330 | | 0 | 811,227 | 860,272 | 57.9 | 625,052 | 42.1 | 0 | 0.0 | 0 | 0.0 | 1,485,324 |
| Arkansas | 2010 | (c) | (c) | | 0 | (c) | 262,784 | 33.6 | 503,336 | 64.4 | 14,513 | 1.9 | 700 | 0.1 | 781,333 |
| Florida | 2010 | 1,294,438 | 871,335 | | 0 | 2,165,773 | 2,619,335 | 48.9 | 2,557,785 | 47.7 | 123,831 | 2.3 | 58,784 | 1.1 | 5,359,735 |
| Georgia | 2010 | 680,499 | 395,467 | | 0 | 1,075,966 | 1,365,832 | 53.0 | 1,107,011 | 43.0 | 103,194 | 4.0 | 124 | 0.0 | 2,576,161 |
| Kentucky | 2011 | 142,108 | (c) | | 0 | 142,108 | 294,034 | 35.3 | 464,245 | 55.7 | 74,860 | 9.0 | 0 | 0.0 | 833,139 |
| Louisiana | 2011 | 673,239 | 288,161 | 12,528 | 49,235 | 1,023,163 | 673,239 (f) | 65.8 | 288,161 (f) | 28.2 | 12,528 | 1.2 | 49,235 | 4.8 | 1,023,163 |
| Mississippi | 2011 | 289,788 | 412,530 (g) | | 0 | 702,318 | 544,851 | 61.0 | 348,617 | 39.0 | 0 | 0.0 | 0 | 0.0 | 893,468 |
| Missouri | 2008 | 395,885 | 358,016 | | 1,729 | 755,630 | 1,136,364 | 39.5 | 1,680,611 | 58.4 | 0 | 0.0 | 60,803 | 2.1 | 2,877,778 |
| North Carolina | 2008 | 504,973 | 1,494,998 | | 0 | 1,999,971 | 2,001,168 | 46.9 | 2,146,189 | 50.3 | 0 | 0.0 | 121,584 | 2.8 | 4,268,941 |
| Oklahoma | 2010 | 249,069 | 263,688 | | 0 | 512,757 | 625,506 | 60.4 | 409,261 | 39.6 | 0 | 0.0 | 0 | 0.0 | 1,034,767 |
| South Carolina | 2010 | 422,251 (h) | 189,348 | | 0 | 611,599 | 690,525 | 51.4 | 630,534 | 46.9 | 20,114 | 1.5 | 3,025 | 0.2 | 1,344,198 |
| Tennessee | 2010 | 725,408 | 284,894 (c) | | 0 | 1,010,302 | 1,041,545 | 65.0 | 529,851 | 33.1 | 30,092 | 1.9 | 61 | 0.0 | 1,601,549 |
| Texas | 2010 | 1,484,542 | 680,548 | | 0 | 2,165,090 | 2,737,481 | 55.0 | 2,106,395 | 42.3 | 128,727 | 2.6 | 7,267 | 0.1 | 4,979,870 |
| Virginia | 2009 | (a) | 319,168 | | 0 | 319,168 | 1,163,523 | 58.7 | 818,901 | 41.3 | 0 | 0.0 | 0 | 0.0 | 1,982,424 |
| West Virginia | 2011 | 81,019 (a) | 354,849 | | 0 | 435,868 | 141,656 | 47.1 | 149,202 | 49.6 | 10,069 | 3.3 | 157 | 0.1 | 301,084 |
| Regional total | | 7,436,116 | 6,231,332 | 12,528 | 50,964 | 13,730,940 | 16,158,115 | 52.0 | 14,365,151 | 45.4 | 517,928 | 1.8 | 301,740 | 0.8 | 31,342,934 |

See footnotes at end of table.

# VOTING STATISTICS FOR GUBERNATORIAL ELECTIONS BY REGION—Continued

| State or other jurisdiction | Date of last election | Primary election Republican | Democrat | Independent and third party | Other | Total votes | General election Republican | Percent | Democrat | Percent | Independent and third party | Percent | Other | Percent | Total votes |
|---|---|---|---|---|---|---|---|---|---|---|---|---|---|---|---|
| **Western Region** | | | | | | | | | | | | | | | |
| Alaska (j) | 2010 | 107,982 | 46,427 | 0 | 0 | 154,409 | 151,318 | 59.1 | 96,519 | 37.7 | 7,457 | 2.9 | 898 | 0.4 | 256,192 |
| Arizona | 2010 | 585,851 | 286,565 | 4,485 | 0 | 876,901 | 938,934 | 54.3 | 733,935 | 42.5 | 54,850 | 3.2 | 362 | 0.0 | 1,728,081 |
| California (k) | 2010 | 2,377,079 | 2,395,287 | 85,097 | 0 | 4,857,463 | 4,127,391 | 40.9 | 5,428,149 | 53.8 | 539,282 | 5.3 | 363 | 0.0 | 10,095,185 |
| Colorado | 2010 | 390,108 | 303,245 (c) | 2,246 | 0 | 695,599 | 199,034 | 11.1 | 912,005 | 51.0 | 676,605 | 37.8 | 86 | 0.0 | 1,787,730 |
| Hawaii | 2010 | 44,599 | 236,607 | 679 | 0 | 281,885 | 157,311 | 41.1 | 222,724 | 58.2 | 2,548 | 0.7 | 0 | 0.0 | 382,583 |
| Idaho | 2010 | 167,617 | 27,412 | 0 | 0 | 195,029 | 267,483 | 59.1 | 148,680 | 32.9 | 36,372 | 8.0 | 0 | 0.0 | 452,535 |
| Montana | 2008 | 81,526 | 175,043 | 0 | 0 | 256,569 | 158,268 | 32.5 | 318,670 | 65.5 | 0 | 0.0 | 9,796 | 2.0 | 486,734 |
| Nevada | 2010 | 175,040 | 114,391 | 0 | 0 | 289,431 | 382,350 | 53.4 | 298,171 | 41.6 | 23,777 | 3.3 | 12,231 | 1.7 | 716,529 |
| New Mexico | 2010 | 122,269 | 109,318 | 0 | 0 | 231,587 | 321,219 | 53.3 | 280,614 | 46.5 | 0 | 0.0 | 994 | 0.2 | 602,827 |
| Oregon | 2010 | 314,087 | 374,404 | 0 | 0 | 688,491 | 694,287 | 47.8 | 716,525 | 49.3 | 39,523 | 2.7 | 3,213 | 0.2 | 1,453,548 |
| Utah | 2010 | (a) | | | | | 412,151 | 64.1 | 205,246 | 31.9 | 25,909 | 4.0 | 1 | 0.0 | 643,307 |
| Washington | 2008 | 695,116 | 712,952 | 10,884 | 23,505 | 1,442,457 | 1,404,124 | 46.8 | 1,598,738 | 53.2 | 0 | 0.0 | 0 | 0.0 | 3,002,862 |
| Wyoming | 2010 | 105,760 | 22,851 | 0 | 0 | 128,611 | 123,780 | 65.7 | 43,240 | 22.9 | 5,362 | 2.8 | 16,081 | 8.5 | 188,463 |
| Regional total | | 5,167,034 | 4,804,502 | 103,391 | 23,505 | 10,098,432 | 9,337,650 | 42.8 | 11,003,216 | 50.5 | 1,411,685 | 6.5 | 44,025 | 0.2 | 21,796,576 |
| Regional total without California | | 2,789,955 | 2,409,215 | 18,294 | 23,505 | 5,240,969 | 5,210,259 | 44.5 | 5,575,067 | 47.6 | 872,403 | 7.5 | 43,662 | 0.4 | 11,701,391 |
| American Samoa (l) | 2008 | N.A. | N.A. | N.A. | N.A. | | 0 | 0.0 | 6,590 | 56.5 | 5,084 | 43.5 | 0 | 0.0 | 11,674 |
| U.S. Virgin Islands | 2010 | N.A. | 14,046 | N.A. | 0 | 14,046 | 0 | 0.0 | 17,535 | 56.3 | 13,580 | 43.6 | 45 | 0.1 | 31,160 |
| Puerto Rico | 2008 | N.A. | N.A. | N.A. | N.A. | | 1,025,945 | 52.8 | 801,053 | 41.3 | 53,690 | 2.8 | 60,975 | 3.1 | 1,941,663 |

*Sources:* The Council of State Governments' survey of election administration offices, November 2009, and state elections websites, March 2012.

*Key:*

N.A. — Not applicable.

(a) Candidate nominated by convention.

(b) Democratic vote includes 26,308 from the Working Families Party.

(c) Candidate ran unopposed.

(d) Democratic vote includes 146,648 from the Independent Party and 154,843 from the Working Families Party. The Republican vote includes 232,281 from the Conservative Party and 25,821 from the Taxpayers Party.

(e) In the Republican primary in Alabama, a runoff was held because no candidate received more than 50% of the vote. The vote total in the runoff election was 465,736.

(f) Louisiana has an open primary which requires all candidates, regardless of party affiliation, to appear on a single ballot. If a candidate receives over 50 percent of the vote in the primary, he is elected to the office. If no candidate receives a majority vote, then a single election is held between the two candidates receiving the most votes. In the October 22, 2011 primary election Governor Bobby Jindal (R) received 65.8 percent of the vote, the four Democrats received 28.2 percent of the vote and the other five candidates received the remaining 6 percent of the vote. No runoff election was required.

(g) In the Democratic primary in Mississippi, a runoff was held because no candidate received more than 50% of the vote. The vote total in the runoff election was 323,284.

(h) In the Republican primary in South Carolina, a runoff was held because no candidate received more than 50% of the vote. The vote total in the runoff election was 359,334.

(i) A special election was held on October 4, 2011 to fill the office of governor, which became vacant after the resignation of Governor Joe Manchin, who was elected to the U.S. Senate in 2010. State Senate President Earl Ray Tomblin, first in the line of succession, became governor on November 15, 2010. In January 2011, the West Virginia Supreme Court of Appeals ruled that a special election must be held so that the governor would be in place by November 15, 2011, one year after Manchin's resignation.

(j) The Democratic Primary combines the candidates from the Democratic Party, the Libertarian Party, and the Alaskan Independence Party.

(k) California became an open primary state after passage of Proposition 14 in the June 2010 election. The top two vote-getters in primary races for congressional, state legislative and statewide offices, regardless of political party, will be in a face-off in the general election.

(l) The results displayed in the table are from the Nov. 18, 2008 runoff election.

## Table 6.8
## VOTER TURNOUT FOR PRESIDENTIAL ELECTIONS BY REGION: 2000, 2004 AND 2008
### (In thousands)

| State or other jurisdiction | 2008 Voting age population (a) | 2008 Number registered | 2008 Number voting (b) | 2004 Voting age population (a) | 2004 Number registered | 2004 Number voting (b) | 2000 Voting age population (a) | 2000 Number registered | 2000 Number voting (b) |
|---|---|---|---|---|---|---|---|---|---|
| U.S. Total............................. | 227,719 | 189,391 | 128,628 | 208,247 | 170,937 | 122,501 | 205,410 | 156,420 | 105,587 |
| **Eastern Region** | | | | | | | | | |
| Connecticut.......................... | 2,682 | 2,210 | 1,645 | 2,574 | 1,823 | 1,579 | 2,499 | 1,874 | 1,460 |
| Delaware ............................ | 659 | 602 | 391 | 594 | 554 | 376 | 582 | 505 | 328 |
| Maine .................................. | 1,037 | 1,000 | 731 | 1,042 | 957 | 741 | 968 | 882 | 652 |
| Maryland ............................ | 4,259 | 3,429 | 2,632 | 3,922 | 3,070 | 2,396 | 3,925 | 2,715 | 2,024 |
| Massachusetts ................... | 5,016 | 4,220 | 3,103 | 4,931 | 3,973 | 2,927 | 4,749 | 4,009 | 2,734 |
| New Hampshire ................ | 1,017 | 864 | 708 | 991 | 856 | 684 | 911 | 857 | 569 |
| New Jersey ......................... | 6,622 | 5,379 | 3,868 | 6,669 | 5,009 | 3,612 | 6,245 | 4,711 | 3,187 |
| New York............................. | 14,884 | 12,031 | 7,675 | 14,206 | 11,837 | 7,448 | 13,805 | 11,263 | 6,960 |
| Pennsylvania ..................... | 9,646 | 8,730 | 5,995 | 9,404 | 8,367 | 5,770 | 9,155 | 7,782 | 4,912 |
| Rhode Island...................... | 824 | 701 | 470 | 803 | 709 | 437 | 753 | 655 | 409 |
| Vermont.............................. | 489 | 454 | 325 | 490 | 445 | 312 | 460 | 427 | 294 |
| Regional total ................... | 47,135 | 39,620 | 27,543 | 45,626 | 37,600 | 26,282 | 44,052 | 35,680 | 23,529 |
| **Midwestern Region** | | | | | | | | | |
| Illinois................................ | 9,653 | 7,790 | 5,578 | 9,519 | 7,499 | 5,274 | 8,983 | 7,129 | 4,742 |
| Indiana............................... | 4,758 | 4,515 | 2,751 | 4,420 | 4,163 | 2,468 | 4,448 | 4,001 | 2,180 |
| Iowa ................................... | 2,276 | 2,076 | 1,537 | 2,212 | 2,107 | 1,522 | 2,165 | 1,841 | 1,314 |
| Kansas ................................ | 2,079 | 1,750 | 1,264 | 2,038 | 1,694 | 1,188 | 1,983 | 1,624 | 1,072 |
| Michigan............................. | 7,624 | 7,471 | 5,044 | 7,541 | 7,164 | 4,839 | 7,358 | 6,861 | 4,233 |
| Minnesota........................... | 3,937 | 3,200 | 2,910 | 3,823 | 2,977 | 2,828 | 3,547 | 3,265 | 2,439 |
| Nebraska............................. | 1,328 | 1,157 | 801 | 1,257 | 1,160 | 778 | 1,234 | 1.085 | 697 |
| North Dakota..................... | 496 | (d) | 317 | 487 | (d) | 316 | 477 | (c) | 288 |
| Ohio.................................... | 8,715 | 8,163 | 5,698 | 8,604 | 7,973 | 5,426 | 8,433 | 7,538 | 4,702 |
| South Dakota.................... | 599 | 508 | 382 | 573 | 502 | 395 | 543 | 471 | 316 |
| Wisconsin .......................... | 4,280 | 3,405 (d) | 2,983 | 4,119 | 2,957 (d) | 2,997 | 3,930 | (d) | 2,599 |
| Regional total ................... | 45,745 | 40,035 | 24,174 | 44,593 | 38,196 | 28,031 | 43,101 | 33,815 | 24,582 |
| **Southern Region** | | | | | | | | | |
| Alabama ............................ | 3,504 | 2,841 | 2,100 | 3,252 | 2,597 | 1,883 | 3,333 | 2,529 | 1,666 |
| Arkansas............................. | 2,134 | 1,686 | 1,087 | 1,951 | 1,686 | 1,055 | 1,929 | 1,556 | 922 |
| Florida ............................... | 14,207 | 11,248 | 8,358 | 12,539 | 10,301 | 7,610 | 11,774 | 8,753 | 5,963 |
| Georgia............................... | 7,013 | 5,266 | 3,924 | 6,080 | 4,249 | 3,285 | 5,893 | 3,860 | 2,583 |
| Kentucky............................. | 3,237 | 2,907 | 1,827 | 3,012 | 2,819 | 1,796 | 2,993 | 2,557 | 1,544 |
| Louisiana............................ | 3,213 | 2,945 | 1,961 | 3,249 | 2,923 | 1,957 | 3,255 | 2,730 | 1,766 |
| Mississippi ......................... | 2,150 | 1,873 | 1,290 | 2,014 | 1,865 | 1,140 | 2,047 | 1,740 | 994 |
| Missouri.............................. | 4,453 | 4,181 | 2,925 | 4,297 | 4,194 | 2,731 | 4,105 | 3,861 | 2,360 |
| North Carolina.................. | 6,843 | 6,226 | 4,311 | 6,453 | 5,527 | 3,501 | 5,797 | 5,122 | 2,915 |
| Oklahoma........................... | 2,717 | 2,184 | 1,463 | 2,515 | 2,143 | 1,464 | 2,531 | 2,234 | 1,234 |
| South Carolina................. | 3,347 | 2,554 | 1,921 | 3,214 | 2,315 | 1,618 | 2,977 | 2,157 | 1,386 |
| Tennessee .......................... | 4,685 | 3,978 | 2,600 | 4,284 | 3,532 | 2,437 | 4,221 | 3,181 | 2,076 |
| Texas .................................. | 17,281 | 13,575 | 8,077 | 16,071 | 13,098 | 7,411 | 14,479 | 12,365 | 6,408 |
| Virginia.............................. | 5,885 | 5,044 | 3,724 | 5,194 | 4,528 | 3,195 | 5,263 | 3,770 | 2,790 |
| West Virginia.................... | 1,424 | 1,212 | 713 | 1,406 | 1,169 | 744 | 1,416 | 1,068 | 648 |
| Regional total ................... | 82,093 | 67,720 | 46,281 | 75,531 | 62,946 | 41,827 | 72,013 | 57,483 | 35,255 |
| **Western Region** | | | | | | | | | |
| Alaska................................. | 501 | 496 | 326 | 460 | 472 | 313 | 436 | 474 | 286 |
| Arizona............................... | 4,668 | 2,987 | 2,321 | 3,800 | 2,643 | 2,038 | 3,625 | 2,173 | 1,532 |
| California .......................... | 27,169 | 23,209 | 13,214 | 22,075 | 16,557 | 12,589 | 21,461 | 15,707 | 11,142 |
| Colorado............................. | 3,668 | 3,209 | 2,401 | 3,246 | 2,890 | 2,130 | 3,067 | 2,274 | 1,741 |
| Hawaii ............................... | 997 | 691 | 454 | 873 | 647 | 429 | 909 | 637 | 368 |
| Idaho.................................. | 1,091 | 862 | 655 | 996 | 798 | 613 | 921 | 728 | 502 |
| Montana ............................ | 738 | 668 | 490 | 680 | 596 | 450 | 668 | 698 | 411 |
| Nevada............................... | 1,905 | 1,208 | 968 | 1,580 | 1,094 | 830 | 1,390 | 898 | 609 |
| New Mexico ....................... | 1,469 | 1,193 | 830 | 1,318 | 1,105 | 756 | 1,263 | 973 | 599 |
| Oregon................................ | 2,884 | 2,154 | 1,828 | 2,665 | 2,120 | 1,837 | 2,530 | 1,944 | 1,534 |
| Utah.................................... | 1,828 | 1,433 | 905 | 1,522 | 1,278 | 928 | 1,465 | 1,123 | 771 |
| Washington........................ | 4,932 | 3,630 | 3,037 | 4,596 | 3,508 | 2,883 | 4,368 | 3,336 | 2,487 |
| Wyoming............................. | 397 | 276 | 255 | 370 | 246 | 244 | 358 | 220 | 214 |
| Regional total ................... | 52,247 | 42,016 | 30,620 | 44,181 | 33,954 | 26,040 | 42,461 | 31,185 | 22,196 |
| Regional total without California ......... | 25,078 | 18,807 | 17,406 | 22,106 | 17,397 | 13,451 | 21,000 | 15,478 | 11,054 |
| Dist. of Columbia............. | 474,572 | 427 | 267 | 435 | 384 | 228 | 411 | 354 | 202 |

*Sources*: U.S. Congress, Clerk of the House, Statistics of the Presidential and Congressional Election, 2004, U.S. Census Bureau, Current Population Survey, December 2008. The Council of State Governments' survey of election officials, January 2009. 2000 data provided by the Federal Election Commission.

*Key*:
(a) Estimated population, 18 years old and over. Includes armed forces in each state, aliens, and institutional population.
(b) Number voting is number of ballots cast in presidential race.
(c) Information not available.
(d) No statewide registration required. Excluded from totals for persons registered.

# 2011 Ballot Propositions

## By John G. Matsusaka

*Voters in nine states approved 21 of 34 ballot propositions in 2011. The number of propositions was down significantly from 183 in 2010, but comparable to previous odd-year elections. Perhaps the highest profile contest was an Ohio referendum on a law limiting collective bargaining by public employees. The fate of tax and borrowing proposals in several states provides a temperature reading on the electorate's fiscal attitude.*

## Overview

Voters decided 34 ballot propositions in nine states in 2011, approving 62 percent of them, roughly consistent with past patterns. See Table A. The number of propositions was down from 183 in 2010, but comparable to the average of 30 over the last four odd-year elections.

Propositions that qualify for the ballot by citizen petition—initiatives and referendums—usually garner the most attention, and this year was no exception.[1] The highest profile measure was Ohio's Issue 2, a referendum that proposed to repeal an existing law limiting collective bargaining by public employees. Another referendum, Maine's Question 1, proposed to roll back a new law that ended the state's system of same-day voter registration. Voters agreed with petitioners in both cases and repealed the existing laws.

Voters also considered 10 initiatives, new laws proposed by petition, including a proposal to increase taxes in Colorado, proposals to permit more gambling in Maine, and a proposal to abolish state-run liquor stores and allow more competition in liquor distribution in Washington. Voters rejected the Colorado and Maine initiatives, and overall approved only 50 percent of the initiatives. The remaining 21 propositions were placed on the ballot by state legislatures, and voters approved 67 percent of them.

## Initiative Trends

Initiatives historically have been the highest profile and highest impact propositions, and the most contentious. Advocates see the initiative process as offering citizens an opportunity to wrest control of

## Table A: State-by-State Totals for 2011

| State | Initiatives | Referendums | Legislative measures | Constitutional convention | Total | Notable issues |
|---|---|---|---|---|---|---|
| Arkansas.................. | ... | ... | 1 (1) | ... | 1 (1) | $575 billion highway bonds |
| Colorado (a)............ | 1 (0) | ... | ... | ... | 1 (0) | Income and sales tax increase |
| Louisiana (b).......... | ... | ... | 6 (4) | ... | 6 (4) | Tobacco taxes, eminent domain |
| Maine (c) ................ | 2 (0) | 1 (1) | 1 (0) | ... | 4 (1) | Same-day registration, gambling |
| Mississippi .............. | 3 (2) | ... | ... | ... | 3 (2) | Abortion ban, ban on real estate transfer taxes |
| New Jersey .............. | ... | ... | ... | 1 (1) | 1 (1) | Gambling |
| Ohio (d).................. | 1 (1) | 1 (0) | 1 (0) | ... | 3 (1) | Public employee collective bargaining |
| Texas....................... | ... | ... | 10 (7) | ... | 10 (7) | Bonding authority |
| Washington.............. | 3 (2) | ... | 2 (2) | ... | 5 (4) | State liquor stores, long-term health care |
| Total........................ | 10 (5) | 2 (1) | 21 (14) | 1 (1) | 34 (21) | |

*Source:* Initiative & Referendum Institute (*www.iandrinstitute.org*).
*Note:* The table reports the total number of propositions during 2011. Except as noted below, all propositions appeared on the ballot Nov. 8. The main entry is the number of propositions appearing, and the number approved is in parentheses. A referendum in which the original law is *retained* is considered to have been approved; Maine reports in the opposite way on its website.

*Key:*
(a) Colorado initiative election was Nov. 1.
(b) Louisiana includes five measures from Oct. 22 (three approved) and one measure from Nov. 19 (approved).
(c) Voters repealed the existing law in the Maine referendum (a vote "yes" in this state).
(d) Voters repealed the existing law in the Ohio referendum (a vote "no" in this state).

## Figure A: Number of Initiatives by Decade

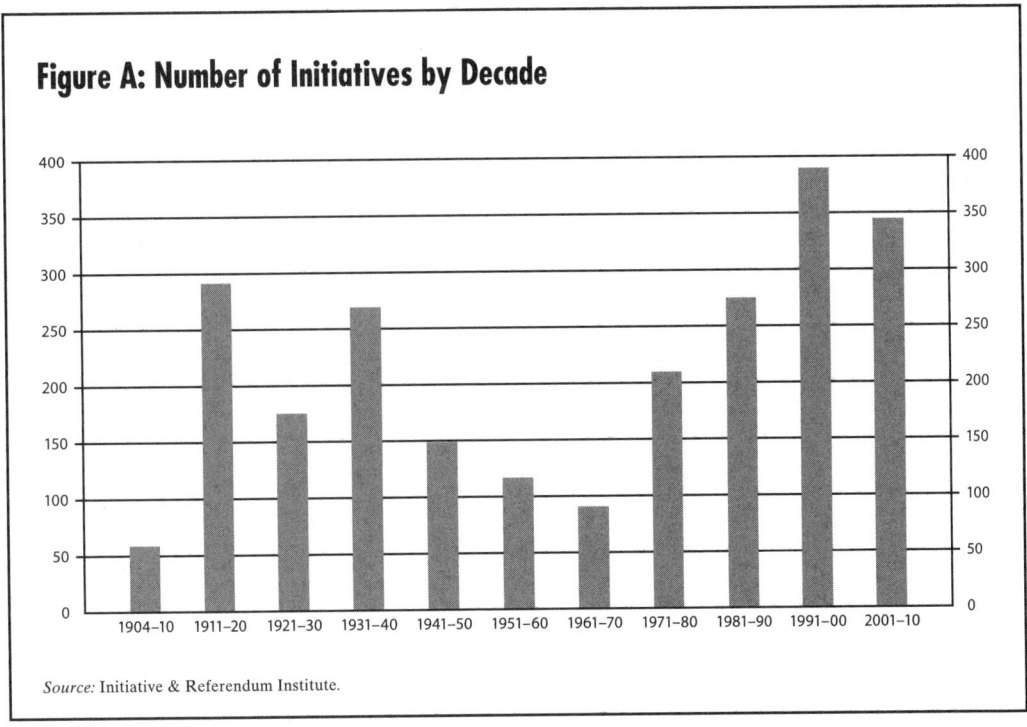

*Source:* Initiative & Referendum Institute.

government from the special interests they believe dominate the legislature, while opponents see the process as a tool that perversely increases the influence of wealthy and organized interest groups. South Dakota was the first state to adopt the process, in 1898, followed by Utah in 1900 and Oregon in 1902. By 1918, 19 states had adopted the process, and adoption has continued at the rate of about one state every 20 years since then; Mississippi was the latest adopter in 1992, bringing the number of states that allow initiatives to 24.[2]

The 10 initiatives in 2011 is the second-highest number of initiatives to appear in an odd year in the 100-plus year history of the process, exceeded only by the 18 initiatives in 2005. It remains to be seen if this signals the start of another burst of initiative activity over the next few years. Figure A shows the number of initiatives by decade, beginning in 1904 when the first initiatives were decided in Oregon.

Initiatives were used extensively in the second, third and fourth decades of the 20th century. Much of that activity arose from tension between the new urban majorities in many states and the rural interests that controlled the legislature. Initiative activity tailed off in the middle decades of the century, with only 89 measures from 1961 to 1970.

Beginning in the late 1970s, initiative use picked up again, following California's Proposition 13 in 1978 that set off a national tax revolt. Each successive decade set a new record for the number of initiatives, peaking with 389 from 1991 to 2000.

One interesting landmark of 2011 was Mississippi's approval of Initiative 27, which requires a photo ID to vote, and Initiative 31, which bans the use of eminent domain to transfer property for use by private parties. These are the first initiatives to be approved in Mississippi since the state adopted the process in 1992. Now all 24 states that permit initiatives have approved at least one measure.

### Issues

#### Public Employee Unions

As the scope of unfunded liabilities in public employee pension funds has become more widely recognized, compensation and the political power of public unions has emerged as a political issue. That was clear in 2009 and 2010 with a drawn-out battle in Wisconsin between the Republican governor and legislature and Democratic groups associated with the unions. The battle included passage of new laws limiting collective bargaining rights; it spilled over to judicial elections and culminated in a series of recall elections.

In terms of ballot propositions, conservative groups have placed a number of propositions on ballots over the last few years trying to curtail the power of unions, with mixed success. For example, in 2010, Arizona, South Carolina and Utah voters approved measures requiring secret ballots for union elections, while in 2008, Colorado and Oregon voters rejected measures that would have prohibited the use of union dues for political purposes without member consent.

Ohio's Issue 2, a referendum placed on the ballot by a union-backed petition drive, gave voters the option to repeal Senate Bill 5, approved by the Republican-controlled legislature in March 2011. Senate Bill 5 limited collective bargaining with public employee unions over topics such as the number of employees overall and on duty, employer contributions to pensions and health care costs; allowed workers to not pay union dues; prohibited strikes by public employees; and required workers to contribute more for their pensions and health care. Supporters of Senate Bill 5 argued that controlling public employee costs was critical for closing the budget deficit and that performance-based pay for teachers would improve education in the state.

Opponents of Senate Bill 5 argued that the law sought to undermine unions and the middle class, and ran ads claiming that Senate Bill 5 endangered public safety by preventing firefighters and other public employees from negotiating for more workers. Labor groups spent a remarkable $42 million opposing Senate Bill 5, compared to $12 million spent by its proponents. With more than $54 million in total spending, the campaign surrounding Issue 2 appears to have been one of the most expensive in state history.

On Election Day, voters repealed Senate Bill 5 by a decisive 62-28 margin. Such a crushing defeat may give union opponents pause before advancing similar laws in the future.

### Bonds and Budgets

Many states require voter authorization for bond issues. Since the onset of the financial crisis, legislators have been cautious about proposing new bond issues; voters approved only $2 billion in new bonds in 2010 compared to $13 billion in 2008 and $43 billion in 2006. Bucking the trend, the Texas legislature asked voters to approve three bond-related measures in 2011. Proposition 2 proposed to authorize $6 billion on a rolling basis for water bonds; Proposition 3 proposed to increase higher education bonding authority from $125 million per year to $350 million per year; and Proposition 5 proposed to allow counties to issue bonds for redevelopment projects in blighted areas. Proposition 2 passed 52-48 and Proposition 3 passed 55-45, somewhat narrow margins for bond elections, and Proposition 5 failed 40-60. These results suggest that a healthy proportion of Texas voters are averse to additional debt issues. In contrast, Arkansas voters overwhelmingly approved—by a margin of 81-19—renewal of a $575 million bond program for construction and maintenance of highways.

Budget stabilization—or so-called "rainy day"—funds continue to be a popular subject for ballot propositions. Voters considered six measures concerning such funds during 2009–10, as states sought to insulate themselves from turmoil in financial markets and revenue volatility, and considered two more in 2011. Louisiana voters rejected Amendment 4 that would have made it easier for the state to divert revenue from the budget stabilization fund by a 49-51 margin, while Washington voters by a 66-33 margin approved SJR 8206 that required larger contributions to the fund in years of extraordinary revenue growth.

### Abortion

Many initiatives have proposed laws relating to abortion over the years. Perhaps most common have been proposals to require parental notification or consent when a minor seeks an abortion. Proposals to significantly curtail or ban abortion have been much rarer—the Initiative and Referendum Institute Historical Database reveals only five proposals in the past 100 years to entirely ban abortion—in part because it is doubtful that states have the authority to take such an action. A recent strategy by pro-life groups has been to propose a constitutional amendment that defines a "person" as a human being from the point of conception. Colorado voters rejected two such initiatives by huge margins, one in 2008 and one in 2010. In 2011, Mississippi voters rejected another "personhood" amendment, Initiative 26, by a smaller but still decisive margin, 42-58. The prospects for passage of such amendments in the future anywhere in the country appear dim.

### Gambling

Gambling is a perennially popular topic for ballot propositions, with 11 gambling-related measures appearing from 2008 to 2010. In 2011, voters con-

# Table B: Complete List of Statewide Ballot Propositions in 2011

| State | Type | Result | Short description |
|---|---|---|---|
| **Arkansas** | | | |
| Question | L/ST | Approved 81-19 | $575 million bonds for highways. |
| **Colorado** | | | |
| Prop 203 (Nov. 1) | I/ST | Failed 37-62 | Increases income and sales taxes for five years. |
| **Louisiana** | | | |
| Amendment 1 (Oct. 22) | L/CA | Approved 70-30 | Makes permanent existing 4-cents/pack tobacco tax. |
| Amendment 2 (Oct. 22) | L/CA | Approved 59-41 | Diverts revenue to state pension funds. |
| Amendment 3 (Oct. 22) | L/CA | Approved 53-47 | Prohibits diversion of money from Patient's Compensation Fund. |
| Amendment 4 (Oct. 22) | L/CA | Failed 49-51 | Removes provision regarding mineral revenue in rainy day fund. |
| Amendment 5 (Oct. 22) | L/CA | Failed 48-52 | Makes explicit an existing implicit tax law exemption for New Orleans. |
| Amendment 1 (Nov. 19) | L/CA | Approved 81-19 | Prohibits new taxes on real estate transfers. |
| **Maine** | | | |
| Question 1 | R/ST | Failed 40-60 (a) | Voters repealed existing law banning same-day voter registration. |
| Question 2 | I/ST | Failed 45-55 | Allows slot machines at race tracks. |
| Question 3 | I/ST | Failed 37-63 | Authorizes casino in Lewiston. |
| Question 4 | L/ST | Approved 53-47 | Changes year of redistricting. |
| **Mississippi** | | | |
| Initiative 26 | I/CA | Failed 42-58 | Bans abortion by defining "person" as human from moment of fertilization. |
| Initiative 27 | I/CA | Approved 62-38 | Requires photo identification to vote. |
| Initiative 31 | I/CA | Approved 73-27 | Bans transfer to private parties of property taken by eminent domain. |
| **New Jersey** | | | |
| Public Question 1 | Advisory | Approved 64-36 | Allows sports betting if permitted by federal law. |
| **Ohio** | | | |
| Issue 1 | L/CA | Failed 38-62 | Increases from 70 to 75 years as maximum age for judge to take office. |
| Issue 2 | R/ST | Failed 38-62 (b) | Voters repealed existing law limiting public worker collective bargaining. |
| Issue 3 | I/CA | Approved 66-34 | Prohibits government from requiring participation in a health care system. |
| **Texas** | | | |
| Prop 1 | L/CA | Approved 83-17 | Property tax exemption for spouse of disabled veteran. |
| Prop 2 | L/CA | Approved 52-48 | $6 billion bonds for Texas Water Development Board. |
| Prop 3 | L/CA | Approved 55-45 | Increases higher education bonding authority. |
| Prop 4 | L/CA | Failed 40-60 | Authorizes local government development bonds. |
| Prop 5 | L/CA | Approved 58-42 | Allows cities to contract with each for services with new taxes. |
| Prop 6 | L/CA | Approved 52-48 | Allows greater withdrawals from permanent school fund. |
| Prop 7 | L/CA | Failed 48-52 | Authorizes El Paso to create conservation districts. |
| Prop 8 | L/CA | Failed 47-53 | Lowers taxes for land devoted to water stewardship. |
| Prop 9 | L/CA | Approved 57-43 | Allows governor to grant pardon in certain circumstance. |
| Prop 10 | L/CA | Approved 56-34 | Allows office holders to run for office without resigning current office. |
| **Washington** | | | |
| I-1125 | I/ST | Failed 47-53 | Requires vehicle fund revenue to be used only for transportation. |
| I-1163 | I/ST | Approved 65-35 | Increases regulation of long-term health care workers. |
| I-1183 | I/ST | Approved 59-41 | Closes state liquor stores. |
| SJR 8205 | L/CA | Approved 73-27 | Deletes inoperative voter registration provision. |
| SJR 8206 | L/CA | Approved 67-33 | Increases contribution to rainy day fund when revenue growth is high. |

*Source:* Initiative & Referendum Institute.
   *Note:* Unless another date is given, a proposition appeared on the Nov. 8 ballot. Under results, "Approved 81-19" means the proposition was approved with 81 percent in favor and 19 percent against.
   *Key:*
CA — Constitutional amendment
I — Initiative
L — Legislative measure

R — Referendum
ST — Statute
Advisory — Advisory measure
(a) In Maine, a "yes" vote is to repeal the existing law, so the outcome was 60 percent yes and 40 percent no.
(b) In Ohio, a "yes" vote is to retain the law, so the outcome was 38 percent yes and 62 percent no.

sidered three gambling measures. Maine voters rejected Question 2, which would have allowed slot machines at horse tracks, and Question 3, which would have allowed a casino in the city of Lewiston. The vote in Maine may not reflect an anti-gambling sentiment so much as a view that the one casino and one racino already authorized for the state are enough. New Jersey voters, in contrast, approved by a 64-36 margin an advisory measure to legalize sports betting if permitted by federal law.

### Government Liquor Stores

Washington voters approved I-1183 by a 59-41 margin, closing down all state-run liquor stores, licensing private parties to sell alcohol if their stores measure at least 10,000 square feet, and allowing retailers to buy directly from distilleries rather than distributors. The campaign for I-1183 was funded by the grocery industry, led by a $22.5 million contribution from Costco Wholesale. The opposition campaign was financed by wine and liquor distributors who feared that other states might consider repealing their laws prohibiting retailers from purchasing directly from distilleries. The opposition campaign focused on safety implications of the measure. This vote is a surprising about-face by the electorate after it rejected two similar proposals in 2010. One important change is that the previous initiatives would have permitted minimarts and gas stations to sell liquor and would have deregulated beer distribution, neither of which were included in I-1183.

## Notes

[1] This article uses referend*ums* instead of referend*a* as the plural, following the *Oxford English Dictionary* and common practice.

[2] For detailed information on initiative adoption and provisions and a discussion of views pro and con about the process, see John G. Matsusaka, *For the Many or the Few: The Initiative, Public Policy, and American Democracy* (University of Chicago Press, 2004) and M. Dane Waters, *Initiative and Referendum Almanac* (Carolina Academic Press, 2003).

## About the Author

**John G. Matsusaka** is the Charles F. Sexton Chair in American Enterprise in the Marshall School of Business, Gould School of Law, and Department of Political Science, and president of the Initiative & Referendum Institute, all at the University of Southern California. He is the author of *For the Many or the Few: The Initiative, Public Policy, and American Democracy* (University of Chicago Press, 2004).

## Table 6.9
## STATEWIDE INITIATIVE AND REFERENDUM

| State or other jurisdiction | Changes to constitution | | | Changes to statutes | | | |
|---|---|---|---|---|---|---|---|
| | Initiative | | Referendum | Initiative | | Referendum | |
| | Direct (a) | Indirect (a) | Legislative (b) | Direct (c) | Indirect (c) | Legislative | Citizen petition (d) |
| Alabama | ... | ... | ★ | ... | ... | ★ | ... |
| Alaska | ... | ... | ★ | ★ | ... | ... | ★ |
| Arizona | ★ | ... | ★ | ★ | ... | ★ | ★ |
| Arkansas | ★ | ... | ★ | ★ | ... | ... | ★ |
| California | ★ | ... | ★ | ★ | ... | ★ | ... |
| Colorado | ★ | ... | ★ | ★ | ... | ★ | ... |
| Connecticut | ... | ... | ★ | ... | ... | ... | ... |
| Delaware | ... | ... | ★ | ... | ... | ★ | ... |
| Florida | ★ | ... | ★ | ... | ... | ... | ... |
| Georgia | ... | ... | ★ | ... | ... | ★ | ... |
| Hawaii | ... | ... | ★ | ... | ... | ... | ... |
| Idaho | ... | ... | ★ | ★ | ... | ★ | ★ |
| Illinois | ★ | ... | ★ | ... | ... | ... | ... |
| Indiana | ... | ... | ★ | ... | ... | ★ | ... |
| Iowa | ... | ... | ★ | ... | ... | ... | ... |
| Kansas | ... | ... | ★ | ... | ... | ... | ... |
| Kentucky | ... | ... | ★ | ... | ... | ★ | ★ |
| Louisiana | ... | ... | ★ | ... | ... | ... | ... |
| Maine | ... | ... | ★ | ... | ★ | ★ | ★ |
| Maryland | ... | ... | ★ | ... | ... | ... | ★ |
| Massachusetts | ... | ★ | ★ | ... | ★ | ★ | ★ |
| Michigan | ★ | ... | ★ | ... | ★ | ★ | ★ |
| Minnesota | ... | ... | ★ | ... | ... | ... | ... |
| Mississippi | ... | ★ | ★ | ... | ★ | ... | ... |
| Missouri | ★ | ... | ★ | ★ | ... | ★ | ★ |
| Montana | ★ | ... | ★ | ★ | ... | ★ | ★ |
| Nebraska | ★ | ... | ★ | ★ | ... | ... | ★ |
| Nevada | ★ | ... | ★ | ★ | ★ | ... | ★ |
| New Hampshire | ... | ... | ★ | ... | ... | ... | ... |
| New Jersey | ... | ... | ★ | ... | ... | ... | ... |
| New Mexico | ... | ... | ★ | ... | ... | ... | ... |
| New York | ... | ... | ★ | ... | ... | ★ | ... |
| North Carolina | ... | ... | ★(f) | ... | ... | ... | ... |
| North Dakota | ★ | ... | ★ | ★ | ... | ★ | ★ |
| Ohio | ★ | ... | ... | ... | ★ | ... | ★ |
| Oklahoma | ★ | ... | ★ | ★ | ... | ★ | ★ |
| Oregon | ★ | ... | ★ | ★ | ... | ★ | ★(e) |
| Pennsylvania | ... | ... | ★ | ... | ... | ... | ... |
| Rhode Island | ... | ... | ★ | ... | ... | ... | ... |
| South Carolina | ... | ... | ★ | ... | ... | ... | ... |
| South Dakota | ★ | ... | ★ | ★ | ... | ★ | ★ |
| Tennessee | ... | ... | ★ | ... | ... | ★ | ... |
| Texas | ... | ... | ... | ... | ... | ... | ... |
| Utah | ... | ... | ★ | ★ | ★ | ... | ★ |
| Vermont | ... | ... | ★ | ... | ... | ★ (limited) | ... |
| Virginia | ... | ... | ★ | ... | ... | ... | ... |
| Washington | ... | ... | ... | ★ | ★ | ★ | ★ |
| West Virginia | ... | ... | ★ | ... | ... | ★ | ... |
| Wisconsin | ... | ... | ★ | ... | ... | ... | ... |
| Wyoming | ... | ... | ★ | ... | ★ | ... | ★ |
| American Samoa | ... | ... | ★ | ... | ... | ... | ... |
| No. Mariana Islands ... | ★ | ★ | ★ | ★ | ★ | ★ | ★ |
| Puerto Rico | ... | ... | ★ | ... | ... | ★ | ... |
| U.S. Virgin Islands | ★ | ... | ★ | ... | ... | ★ | ... |

See footnotes at end of table.

## STATEWIDE INITIATIVE AND REFERENDUM — Continued

*Source*: The Council of State Governments' survey of state election administration offices, January 2007 and state websites December 2010.

*Note*: This table summarizes state provisions for initiatives and referenda. Initiatives may propose constitutional amendments or develop state legislation and may be formed either directly or indirectly. The direct initiative allows a proposed measure to be placed on the ballot after a specific number of signatures have been secured on a citizen petition. The indirect initiative must be submitted to the legislature for a decision after the required number of signatures has been secured on a petition and prior to placing the proposed measure on the ballot. Referendum refers to the process whereby a state law or constitutional amendment passed by the legislature may be referred to the voters before it goes into effect. Three forms of referenda exist: (1) citizen petition, whereby the people may petition for a referendum on legislation which has been considered by the legislature; (2) submission by the legislature (designated in table as "Legislative"), whereby the legislature may voluntarily submit laws to the voters for their approval; and (3) constitutional requirement, whereby the state constitution may require that certain questions be submitted to the voters.

*Key*:
★ — State Provision.
... — No state provision.

(a) See Table 1.3, "Constitutional Amendment Procedure: By Initiative," for more detail.

(b) See Table 1.2, "Constitutional Amendment Procedure: By the Legislature," for more detail.

(c) See Chapter 6 tables on State Initiatives, for more detail.

(d) See Chapter 6 tables on State Referendums, for more detail.

(e) No provision for statewide referenda initiated by citizen petition. There are several county/local referenda that can be initiated by citizen petition.

(f) Only the legislature can make statutory changes while in session. Proposed constitutional changes must be passed by the legislature and then are submitted to the citizens to be voted on.

# Table 6.10
## STATE INITIATIVES: REQUESTING PERMISSION TO CIRCULATE A PETITION

| State or other jurisdiction | Applied to (a) | | Signatures required to request a petition (b) | | Request submitted to | Request form furnished by (c) | Restricted subject matter (d) | Individual responsible for petition | | Financial contributions reported (e) | Deposits required (f) |
|---|---|---|---|---|---|---|---|---|---|---|---|
| | Const. amdt. | Statute | Const. amdt. | Statute | | | | Title | Summary | | |
| Alabama | ... | ... | ... | 100 | LG | SBE | Y | LG | LG | Y | $100 |
| Alaska | ... | D | 15% (g) | 10% (g) | SS | SS | N | (h) | (h) | Y | ... |
| Arizona | D | D | 10% | 8% | AG | SP | N | AG | AG | Y | ... |
| Arkansas | D | D | ... | ... | AG | ... | Y | AG | AG | N (i) | ... |
| California | D | D | ... | ... | AG | ... | Y | ... | ... | Y | $200 (i) |
| Colorado | D | D | 5% (j) | 5% (j) | SS | SS | N | (k) | (k) | Y | N |
| Connecticut | ... | ... | ... | ... | ... | ... | ... | ... | ... | ... | ... |
| Delaware | D | ... | ... | ... | SS | SP | N | SP | SP | Y | N |
| Florida | D | ... | ... | ... | ... | ... | N | SP | SP | Y | N |
| Georgia | ... | ... | ... | ... | ... | ... | ... | ... | ... | ... | ... |
| Hawaii | ... | ... | ... | ... | SS | SP | N | AG | AG | Y | N |
| Idaho | ... | D | ... | 20 | SS | SP | Y | AG | AG | Y | N |
| Illinois | D | ... | ... | ... | ... | ... | Y | ... | ... | Y | N |
| Indiana | ... | ... | ... | ... | ... | ... | ... | ... | ... | ... | ... |
| Iowa | ... | ... | ... | ... | ... | ... | ... | ... | ... | ... | ... |
| Kansas | ... | ... | ... | ... | ... | ... | ... | ... | ... | ... | ... |
| Kentucky | ... | ... | ... | ... | ... | ... | ... | ... | ... | ... | ... |
| Louisiana | ... | I | ... | 5 (l) | SS | SS | Y | P | SS | Y | N |
| Maine | ... | I | ... | 3 (m) | SS (n) | SBE | Y | ... | ... | Y | N |
| Maryland | ... | ... | ... | ... | SS (n) | SBE | Y | ... | ... | ... | ... |
| Massachusetts | I | I | 10 | 10 | AG | SS | Y | AG | AG | Y | N |
| Michigan | ... | ... | ... | ... | ... | ... | Y | SP | SP | Y | ... |
| Minnesota | I | ... | 12% | ... | SP | SP | ... | ... | ... | ... | ... |
| Mississippi | I | ... | ... | ... | SS | SP | Y | AG | AG | Y | N |
| Missouri | D | D | ... | ... | SS | SP | Y | SS, AG | SS, AG | Y | ... |
| Montana | D | D | ... | ... | (x) | SP | Y | AG | AG | Y | N |
| Nebraska | D | D | ... | ... | SS | SP | Y | SP | SP | Y | N |
| Nevada | ... | ... | ... | ... | SS | SS | Y | P, SP | P, SP | ... | ... |
| New Hampshire | ... | ... | ... | ... | ... | ... | ... | ... | ... | ... | ... |
| New Jersey | ... | ... | ... | ... | ... | ... | ... | ... | ... | ... | ... |
| New Mexico | ... | ... | ... | ... | ... | ... | ... | ... | ... | ... | ... |
| New York | ... | ... | ... | ... | ... | ... | ... | ... | ... | ... | ... |
| North Carolina | D | D | 4% (o) | 2% (o) | SS | SP | N | SS, AG | SS | Y (e) | N |
| North Dakota | D | I | 1,000 | 1,000 | AG | (p) | N (q) | (p) | (p) | Y | N |
| Ohio | D | D | 15% | 8% | SS | O | N | P | P | Y | ... |
| Oklahoma | D | D | ... | ... | SS | SS | N | AG | AG | Y | ... |
| Oregon | D | D | 8% (r) | 6% (r) | SS | SS | N | AG | AG | Y | N |
| Pennsylvania | ... | ... | ... | ... | ... | ... | ... | ... | ... | ... | N |
| Rhode Island | ... | ... | ... | ... | ... | ... | ... | ... | ... | ... | ... |
| South Carolina | ... | ... | ... | ... | ... | ... | ... | ... | ... | ... | ... |

See footnotes at end of table.

# STATE INITIATIVES: REQUESTING PERMISSION TO CIRCULATE A PETITION—Continued

| State or other jurisdiction | Applied to (a) | | Signatures required to request a petition (b) | | Request submitted to | Request form furnished by (c) | Restricted subject matter (d) | Individual responsible for petition | | Financial contributions reported (e) | Deposits required (f) |
|---|---|---|---|---|---|---|---|---|---|---|---|
| | Const. amdt. | Statute | Const. amdt. | Statute | | | | Title | Summary | | |
| South Dakota............ | D | D | (s) | 5 EV | SS | SS | Y | SP | SP | Y | N |
| Tennessee ............... | ... | ... | ... | ... | ... | ... | ... | ... | ... | ... | ... |
| Texas...................... | ... | ... | ... | ... | ... | ... | ... | ... | ... | ... | ... |
| Utah........................ | ... | D.I | ... | 5 SP | LG | LG | N | SP | SP | Y | N |
| Vermont.................. | ... | ... | ... | ... | ... | ... | ... | ... | ... | ... | ... |
| Virginia................... | ... | ... | ... | ... | ... | ... | ... | ... | ... | ... | ... |
| Washington............. | ... | D.I | ... | (i) | SS | SP | N | AG | AG | N | $5 |
| West Virginia.......... | ... | ... | ... | ... | ... | SS | ... | ... | ... | ... | ... |
| Wisconsin ............... | ... | I | ... | ... | ... | ... | ... | ... | ... | ... | ... |
| Wyoming ................. | ... | ... | ... | 100 | SS | SS | Y | SS | AG, SS | Y | $500 |
| American Samoa ...... | ... | ... | ... | ... | ... | ... | ... | ... | ... | ... | ... |
| No. Mariana Islands ... | D | I | 50% | 20% | AG | AG | Y | SP | SP | Y | N |
| Puerto Rico............. | D | ... | ... | (u) | SBE | (v) | N | (v) | (v) | Y | $500 |
| U.S. Virgin Islands...... | D | ... | 41% (w) | ... | SBE | SBE | Y | SBE | SBE | Y | N |

*Source:* The Council of State Governments' survey of state election administration offices, July 2011.

*Key:*

... — Not applicable
D — Direct initiative
I — Indirect initiative
EV — Eligible voters
LG — Lieutenant Governor
SS — Secretary of State
SBE — State Board of Elections
N — No

AG — Attorney General
O — Other
P — Proponent
ST — State
SP — Sponsor
Y — Yes

(a) An initiative may provide a constitutional amendment or develop a new statute, and may be formed either directly or indirectly. The direct initiative allows a proposed measure to be placed on the ballot after a specific number of signatures have been secured on a petition. The indirect initiative must first be submitted to the legislature for decision after the required number of signatures have been secured on a petition, prior to placing the proposed measure on the ballot.

(b) Prior to circulating a statewide petition, a request for permission to do so must first be submitted to a specified state officer.

(c) The form on which the request for petition is submitted may be the responsibility of the sponsor or may be furnished by the state.

(d) Restrictions may exist regarding the subject matter to which an initiative may be applied. The majority of these restrictions pertain to the dedication of state revenues and appropriations, and laws that maintain the preservation of public peace, safety, and health. In Illinois, amendments are restricted to "structural and procedural subjects contained in" the legislative article.

(e) In some states, a list of financial contributors and the amount of their contributions must be submitted to the specified state officer with whom the petition is filed. In North Dakota, must report any contributions and/or expenditures in excess of $100. Must also report the gross total of all contributions

received and gross totals of all expenditures made. Must give total cash on hand in the filer's account at the start and close of a reporting period.

(f) A deposit may be required after permission to circulate a petition has been granted. This amount is refunded when the completed petition has been filed correctly.

(g) The number of signatures required to request permission to circulate a petition in 2012: Constitutional amendment, 259,212; statute, 172,808.

(h) The proponent and sponsor are responsible for the title and summary.

(i) No report required at time of filing request, but later if any money is raised, $200 deposit required.

(j) Five percent of all votes cast for Secretary of State at last election; governor in preceding election.

(k) Title Setting Board—secretary of state, attorney general, director of legislative legal services.

(l) The name and address of five voters.

(m) Three percent of last vote for governor—in 2012, 55,736.

(n) Secretary of state accepts and turns over to State Board of Elections.

(o) Percentage of resident population of the state at the last federal decennial census.

(p) Petitioners must prepare the summary and submit it to the Ohio Attorney General, who then must certify whether the summary fully and accurately describes the proposal.

(q) Such restrictions apply to referendums, but not initiatives.

(r) Constitutional amendment, 116,283; Statute, 87,213.

(s) Number of signatures required to request a petition for a constitutional amendment, 10% of the total votes cast in the last gubernatorial election.

(t) Statute requires 240,229.

(u) Ten percent district and 41 percent territorial.

(v) Office of the Supervisor of Elections Titling Board.

(w) District wide 10%, territory wide 41%.

(x) Legislative Services Division.

## Table 6.11
## STATE INITIATIVES: CIRCULATING THE PETITION

| State or other jurisdiction | Basis for signatures (see key below) Const. amdt. | Basis for signatures (see key below) Statute | Maximum time period allowed for petition circulation (a) | Can signatures be removed from petition (b) | Completed petition filed with | Days prior to election Const. amdt. | Days prior to election Statute |
|---|---|---|---|---|---|---|---|
| Alabama | ... | ... | ... | ... | ... | ... | ... |
| Alaska | 15% VG | 10% TV from 3/4 ED | 1 yr. | Y | LG | ... | 4 mos. |
| Arizona | 10% VG | 10% VG | 2 yr. | Y | SS | 4 mos. | 4 mos. |
| Arkansas | 8% VG | 8% VG | ... | N | SS | 120 days | 120 days |
| California | 8% VG | 5% VG | 150 days | Y | (c) | 131 days | 131 days |
| Colorado | 5% VSS | 5% VSS | 6 mos. (3 mos prior to election) | Y | SS | 90 days | 90 days |
| Connecticut | ... | ... | ... | ... | ... | ... | ... |
| Delaware | ... | ... | ... | ... | ... | ... | ... |
| Florida | 8% VEP, 8% from 1/2 CD | 8% VEP, 8% from 1/2 CD | ... | N | SS | Feb. 1 (d) | ... |
| Georgia | ... | ... | ... | ... | ... | ... | ... |
| Hawaii | ... | ... | ... | ... | ... | ... | ... |
| Idaho | ... | 6% EV | (e) | Y | SS | ... | 4 mos. |
| Illinois | 8% VG | ... | 18 mos. prior to election | Y | SBE | 6 mos. | ... |
| Indiana | ... | ... | ... | ... | ... | ... | ... |
| Iowa | ... | ... | ... | ... | ... | ... | ... |
| Kansas | ... | ... | ... | ... | ... | ... | ... |
| Kentucky | ... | ... | ... | ... | ... | ... | ... |
| Louisiana | ... | 10% VG | 1 yr. | ... | SS | ... | (f) |
| Maine | ... | ... | ... | ... | ... | ... | ... |
| Maryland | ... | ... | ... | ... | ... | ... | ... |
| Massachusetts | 3% VG, no more than 25% from 1 county | 3% VG, no more than 25% from 1 county (g) | From 1st Wed. in Sept. to 1st Wed. in Dec. (i) | Y (h) | SS (i) | (g) | (j) |
| Michigan | 10% VG | 8% VG | 180 days | N (k) | SS | 120 days | 160 days |
| Minnesota | ... | ... | ... | ... | ... | ... | ... |
| Mississippi | 12% VG | ... | 1 yr. | Y | SS (c) | 90 days prior to LS | ... |
| Missouri | 8% VG, 8% each from 2/3 CD | 5% VG, 5% each from 2/3 CD | Approx. 18 mos. | Y | SS | 6 mos. | 6 mos. |
| Montana | 10% VG and 10% in 40 of the SLD | 5% VG and 5% in 34 of the SLD | (l) | Y | SS | (l) | (l) |
| Nebraska | 10% EV | 7% EV | (m) | Y | SS | 4 mos. | 4 mos. |
| Nevada | 10% TV | 10% TV | ... | Y | SS | 90 days | 30 days prior to LS |
| New Hampshire | ... | ... | ... | ... | ... | ... | ... |
| New Jersey | ... | ... | ... | ... | ... | ... | ... |
| New Mexico | ... | ... | ... | ... | ... | ... | ... |
| New York | ... | ... | ... | ... | ... | ... | ... |
| North Carolina | 4% resident population | 2% resident population | ... | ... | ... | ... | ... |
| North Dakota | 10% VG, 5% each from 1/2 counties | 3% VG, 1.5% each from 1/2 counties | 1 yr. | N | SS | 90 days | 90 days |
| Ohio | ... | ... | ... | Y | SS | 90 days | (n) |
| Oklahoma | 15% VH | 8% VG | 90 days | Y | SS | 60 days | 60 days |
| Oregon | 8% VG | 6% VG | ... | Y (o) | SS | 4 mos. | 4 mos. |
| Pennsylvania | ... | ... | ... | ... | ... | ... | ... |
| Rhode Island | ... | ... | ... | ... | ... | ... | ... |
| South Carolina | ... | ... | ... | ... | ... | ... | ... |

See footnotes at end of table.

# STATE INITIATIVES: CIRCULATING THE PETITION — Continued

| State or other jurisdiction | Basis for signatures (see key below) | | Maximum time period allowed for petition circulation (a) | Can signatures be removed from petition (b) | Completed petition filed with | Days prior to election | |
|---|---|---|---|---|---|---|---|
| | Const. amdt. | Statute | | | | Const. amdt. | Statute |
| **South Dakota** | 10% VG | 5% VG | (p) | N | SS | ... | ... |
| **Tennessee** | ... | ... | ... | ... | ... | ... | ... |
| **Texas** | ... | ... | ... | ... | ... | ... | ... |
| **Utah** | ... | 10% VG, 10% each from 26 of 29 senate districts (q) | 1 yr. | Y | LG | ... | June 1 |
| **Vermont** | ... | ... | ... | ... | ... | ... | ... |
| **Virginia** | ... | ... | ... | ... | ... | ... | ... |
| **Washington** | ... | 8% VG | 6 to 9 mos. | N | SS | ... | ... |
| **West Virginia** | ... | ... | ... | ... | ... | ... | (r) |
| **Wisconsin** | ... | ... | ... | ... | ... | ... | ... |
| **Wyoming** | ... | 15% TV, from 2/3 counties | 18 mos. | Y | SS | ... | 120 days |
| **American Samoa** | ... | ... | (s) | ... | ... | ... | ... |
| **No. Mariana Islands** | ... | ... | ... | Y | ... | ... | ... |
| **Puerto Rico** | ... | ... | ... | ... | ... | ... | ... |
| **U.S. Virgin Islands** | ... | 10 % ED | 180 days | Y | SS | ... | 6 mos. |

*Source:* The Council of State Governments' survey of state election administration offices, July 2011.

Key:
... – Not applicable.
VG — Total votes cast for the position of governor in the last election.
EV — Eligible voters.
VH — Total votes cast for the office receiving the highest number of votes in last general election.
TV — Total voters in last election.
VSS — Total votes cast for all candidates for the office of secretary of state at the previous general election.
VEP — Total votes cast in the state as a whole on the last presidential election.
ED — Election district.
CD — Congressional district.
SBE — State Board of Elections.
SLD — State legislative district.
LG — Lieutenant Governor.
SS — Secretary of State.
LS — Legislative session.
Y — Yes.
N — No.
T — Tuesday.
(a) The petition circulation period begins when petition forms have been approved and provided to sponsors. Sponsors are those individuals granted permission to circulate a petition, and are therefore responsible for the validity of each signature on a given petition.
(b) Should an individual wish to remove his/her name from a petition, a request to do so must be submitted in writing to the state officer with whom the petition is filed.
(c) County elections officials.
(d) February 1 of the general election year.
(e) Eighteen months from receipt of ballot title or April 30 of year of election on initiative, whichever occurs first.
(f) To be placed on November ballot, petitions must be submitted to SS by 5 p.m. on 50th day after convening of Legislature in 1st regular session, or by 5 p.m. on 25th day in 2nd regular session.
(g) First Wednesday in December.
(h) Should an individual wish to remove his/her name from a petition, a request to do so must be submitted in writing to the local election official before the petition is submitted for certification of signatures.
(i) Petitions first must be submitted to local municipal clerks for signature certification.
(j) After legislative inaction, petitions must be filed no later than the 1st Wednesday in July, signed by not less than 1/2 of 1 percent of the last vote cast for governor.
(k) Not after petition has been filed.
(l) No maximum, but petitions must be submitted to the county election administrators at least four weeks before the third Friday in July. This is the deadline for county election administrator to file the petitions with the Secretary of State after their review of signatures.
(m) Constitutional amendment–276 days; Amend or create a statute–291 days.
(n) Ten days prior to commencement of General Assembly session for initial filing; second petition must be filed within 90 days after General Assembly takes no action, fails to enact or pass amended form; the petition is filed with the secretary of state.
(o) Only by the chief petitioners before submitting signatures for verification. Signatures many not be removed once the signatures have been submitted to the Secretary of State.
(p) No more than 18 months preceding the election date specified on the petition.
(q) Five percent in both categories for indirect.
(r) Initiatives to the legislature must be turned in 10 days before the legislature convenes If the legislature does not act, the initiative goes to the next General Election ballot.
(s) Until 120 days before the date of the election.

# Table 6.12
## STATE INITIATIVES: PREPARING THE INITIATIVE TO BE PLACED ON THE BALLOT

| State or other jurisdiction | Signatures verified by: (a) | Within how many days after filing | Number of days to amend/appeal a petition that is: Incomplete (b) | Not accepted (c) | Penalty for falsifying petition (denotes fine, jail term) | Petition certified by: (d) |
|---|---|---|---|---|---|---|
| Alabama | Division of Elections | ... | ... | ... | Class B misdemeanor | LG |
| Alaska | County recorder | 60 days | ... | ... | Class 1 misdemeanor | SS |
| Arizona | SS | 10 days (e) | ... | ... | ... | SS |
| Arkansas | County clerk | 30 days | 30 days | 30 days | Felony or misdemeanor (depending on severity) | SS |
| California | County clerk | 30 days | ... | ... | ... | SS |
| Colorado | SS | 30 days | 10 days | ... | (f) | SS |
| Connecticut | ... | ... | ... | ... | ... | ... |
| Delaware | ... | ... | ... | ... | ... | ... |
| Florida | Supervisor of elections | N.A. | N.A. | N.A. | First degree misdemeanor | SS |
| Georgia | ... | ... | ... | ... | ... | ... |
| Hawaii | ... | ... | ... | ... | ... | ... |
| Idaho | County clerk | 60 days | ... | 10 days | $5,000, 2 yrs. | SS |
| Illinois | SBE (g) | ... | (h) | (h) | Class 3 felony | SBE |
| Indiana | ... | ... | ... | ... | ... | ... |
| Iowa | ... | ... | ... | ... | ... | ... |
| Kansas | ... | ... | ... | ... | ... | ... |
| Kentucky | ... | ... | ... | ... | ... | ... |
| Louisiana | ... | ... | ... | ... | ... | ... |
| Maine | Registrar of voters | ... | ... | ... | ... | SS |
| Maryland | ... | ... | ... | ... | ... | ... |
| Massachusetts | Local board of registrar | 2 weeks | ... | ... | $1,000, 1 yr. | SS |
| Michigan | SS | Approx. 60 days | ... | ... | $500, 90 days | BSC |
| Minnesota | ... | ... | ... | ... | ... | ... |
| Mississippi | Circuit clerk | ... | 10 days | 10 days | $1,000, 1 yr. | CC |
| Missouri | County clerk | 63 days | 10 days | 10 days | Class A misdemeanor | SS |
| Montana | County election administrators | 4 weeks | 10 days | 10 days | $500, 6 mos. | SS |
| Nebraska | County clerk | 40 days | ... | ... | ... | SS |
| Nevada | County clerk | (i) | 5 days (j) | ... | ... | SS |
| New Hampshire | ... | ... | ... | ... | ... | ... |
| New Jersey | ... | ... | ... | ... | ... | ... |
| New Mexico | ... | ... | ... | ... | ... | ... |
| New York | ... | ... | ... | ... | ... | ... |
| North Carolina | ... | ... | ... | ... | ... | ... |
| North Dakota | SS | 35 days | ... | ... | (k) | SS |
| Ohio | County board of elections | 10 days | 10 days | 20 days | 5th degree felony | SS |
| Oklahoma | SS | 30 days | 10 days | ... | $1,000, 1 yr. | SS |
| Oregon | County clerk | 30 days | (l) | ... | (m) | SS |
| Pennsylvania | ... | ... | ... | ... | ... | ... |
| Rhode Island | ... | ... | ... | ... | ... | ... |
| South Carolina | ... | ... | ... | ... | ... | ... |

See footnotes at end of table.

# STATE INITIATIVES: PREPARING THE INITIATIVE TO BE PLACED ON THE BALLOT—Continued

| State or other jurisdiction | Signatures verified by: (a) | Within how many days after filing | Number of days to amend/appeal a petition that is: | | Penalty for falsifying petition (denotes fine, jail term) | Petition certified by: (d) |
|---|---|---|---|---|---|---|
| | | | Incomplete (b) | Not accepted (c) | | |
| South Dakota | SS | ... | ... | ... | Class 1 misdemeanor | SBE |
| Tennessee | ... | ... | ... | ... | ... | ... |
| Texas | ... | ... | ... | ... | ... | ... |
| Utah | County clerk | 30 days | ... | 14 days | Class A misdemeanor | LG |
| Vermont | ... | ... | ... | ... | ... | ... |
| Virginia | ... | ... | ... | ... | ... | ... |
| Washington | SS | (n) | 5 days | 5 | Fine or imprisonment | SS |
| West Virginia | ... | ... | ... | ... | ... | ... |
| Wisconsin | ... | ... | ... | ... | ... | ... |
| Wyoming | SS | 60 days | 30 days | 30 days | $1,000, 1 yr. | SS |
| American Samoa | ... | ... | ... | ... | ... | ... |
| No. Mariana Islands | Election Commission | (o) | 30 days (p) | 119 days | (q) | AG |
| Puerto Rico | Office of the Supervisor of Elections | 15 days | 3 days | ... | ... | SBE |
| U.S. Virgin Islands | Office of the Supervisor of Elections | 15 days | 7 days | ... | ... | Office of the Supervisor of Elections |

*Source:* The Council of State Governments' survey of state election administration offices, January 2007 and state websites March 2010.

Key:
... — Not applicable.
CC — Circuit Clerk.
SS — Secretary of State.
LG — Lieutenant Governor.
BSC — Board of State Canvassers.
SBE — State Board of Elections.

(a) The validity of the signatures, as well as the correct number of required signatures must be verified before the initiative is allowed on the ballot.

(b) If an insufficient number of signatures is submitted, sponsors may amend the original petition by filing additional signatures within a given number of days after filing. If the necessary number of signatures has not been submitted by this date, the petition is declared void.

(c) In some cases, the state officer will not accept a valid petition. In such a case, sponsors may appeal this decision to the Supreme Court, where the sufficiency of the petition will be determined. If the petition is determined to be sufficient, the initiative is required to be placed on the ballot.

(d) A petition is certified for the ballot when the required number of signatures has been submitted by the filing deadline, and are determined to be valid.

(e) Removal of petition and ineligible signatures by Secretary of State's office fifteen days (A.R.S. § 19-121.01), certification by County Recorder ten days after receipt from secretary of State's office (A.R.S. § 19-121.02).

(f) Secretary conducts hearing, then turns over to the attorney general for investigation/possible criminal prosecution.

(g) State Board of Elections and County Clerks or Municipal Boards of Election Commissioners. Individual petition sheets must be from a single jurisdiction. The SBE verifies that all signatures are from a single jurisdiction and the County Clerks or Municipal Boards verify the signatures against their registration files.

(h) Amendments are not permitted. Judicial review must be sought within ten days after determination be State Board of Elections.

(i) 1. Within four days county clerk totals the number of signatures and forwards to the secretary of state. 2. The secretary of state immediately notifies county clerks if they are to proceed or not proceed with the signature verification. 3. If ordered by the secretary of state, the county clerks verify signatures within nine days (excluding weekends and holidays).

(j) In Nevada, appeal must be within 5 working days after SS determines the petition is not sufficient.

(k) Any violations discovered will be reported to the attorney general for investigation and prosecution.

(l) Additional signatures may be submitted if signatures were turned in prior to deadline for submitting signatures.

(m) Whether a penalty is assessed would be based upon what information on the petition was falsified.

(n) Signatures must be verified by not later than the 3rd Tuesday following the primary.

(o) Within 90 days before the date of election.

(p) 30 days if submitted 150 days before the date of the election. No amendment/appeal if submitted 120 days before the date of election.

(q) Subject to statute governing fraud and perjury.

# Table 6.13
## STATE INITIATIVES: VOTING ON THE INITIATIVE

| State or other jurisdiction | Ballot (a) Title by: | Ballot (a) Summary by: | Election where initiative voted on | Effective date of approved initiative (b) Const. amdt. | Effective date of approved initiative (b) Statute | Days to contest election results (c) | Can an approved initiative be: Amended? | Can an approved initiative be: Vetoed? | Can an approved initiative be: Repealed? | Can a defeated initiative be refiled? |
|---|---|---|---|---|---|---|---|---|---|---|
| Alabama | … | … | … | … | … | … | … | … | … | … |
| Alaska | LG | LG | GE, PR or SP | 30 days (d) | 90 days (d) | 10 | Y | N | Y | N |
| Arizona | SS,AG | LC | GE | … | IM(e) | 5 | (f) | N | N | Y |
| Arkansas | AG | AG | GE | 30 days | 30 days | 20 | Y | N | Y | Y |
| California | AG | AG | GE, PR or SP | 1 day | IM | 5 (d) | Y (g) | N | Y (g) | Y |
| Colorado | TB (h) | (h) | GE, Odd year | 30 days | 30 days | 10 | N (i) | N (i) | N (i) | |
| Connecticut | … | … | … | … | … | … | … | … | … | … |
| Delaware | … | … | … | … | … | … | … | … | … | … |
| Florida | SP | SP | GE | (j) | … | 10 | Y (k) | N | Y (k) | Y |
| Georgia | … | … | … | … | … | … | … | … | … | … |
| Hawaii | … | … | … | … | … | … | … | … | … | … |
| Idaho | AG | AG | GE | … | 30 days | 20 | Y | N | Y | Y |
| Illinois | | SS (l) | GE | … | … | 30 | (m) | … | … | Y |
| Indiana | … | … | … | … | … | … | … | … | … | … |
| Iowa | … | … | … | … | … | … | … | … | … | … |
| Kansas | … | … | … | … | … | … | … | … | … | … |
| Kentucky | … | … | … | … | … | … | … | … | … | … |
| Louisiana | … | … | … | … | … | … | … | … | … | … |
| Maine | Sponsor, SS | (n) | REG or SP | … | 30 days (e) | 5 | Y | N | Y | |
| Maryland | … | … | … | … | … | … | … | … | … | after 2 biennial elections |
| Massachusetts | AG | AG | GE | 30 days | 30 days | 10 | Y | Y | Y | Y |
| Michigan | BSC | BSC | GE | 45 days | 10 days | 2 (o) | Y | N | Y | Y |
| Minnesota | … | … | … | … | … | … | … | … | … | … |
| Mississippi | AG | AG | GE | 30 days | … | … | N | N | N | Y |
| Missouri | SS,AG | SS,AG | GE | 30 days | IM | 30 (o) | Y | N | Y | Y |
| Montana | AG | AG | GE | Jul. 1 | Oct. 1 | 1 yr. | Y | N | Y | Y |
| Nebraska | AG | AG | GE | 10 days | 10 days | 40 | Y | N | Y | N (p) |
| Nevada | SS,AG | SS,AG | GE | (q) | (q) | 14 | (r) | (r) | (r) | Y |
| New Hampshire | … | … | … | … | … | … | … | … | … | … |
| New Jersey | … | … | … | … | … | … | … | … | … | … |
| New Mexico | … | … | … | … | … | … | … | … | … | … |
| New York | … | … | … | … | … | … | … | … | … | … |
| North Carolina | … | … | … | … | … | … | … | … | … | … |
| North Dakota | SS,AG | SS | PR or GE | 30 days | 30 days | 14 | (s) | N | (s) | Y |
| Ohio | Ohio Ballot Board | (t) | GE | 30 days | 30 days | 15 | (u) | N | N | Y |
| Oklahoma | AG | P | GE or SP | IM | IM | 40 | Y | Y | Y | after 3 yrs. |
| Oregon | AG | AG | GE | 30 days | 30 days | … | Y | Y | Y | Y |
| Pennsylvania | … | … | … | … | … | … | … | … | … | … |
| Rhode Island | … | … | … | … | … | … | … | … | … | … |
| South Carolina | … | … | … | … | … | … | … | … | … | … |

See footnotes at end of table.

## STATE INITIATIVES: VOTING ON THE INITIATIVE—Continued

| State or other jurisdiction | Ballot (a) | | Election where initiative voted on | Effective date of approved initiative (b) | | Days to contest election results (c) | Can an approved initiative be: | | | Can a defeated initiative be refiled? |
|---|---|---|---|---|---|---|---|---|---|---|
| | Title by: | Summary by: | | Const. amdt. | Statute | | Amended? | Vetoed? | Repealed? | |
| South Dakota | AG | AG | GE | 1 day | 1 day | ... | Y | N | N | Y |
| Tennessee | ... | ... | ... | ... | ... | ... | ... | ... | ... | ... |
| Texas | ... | ... | ... | ... | ... | ... | ... | ... | ... | ... |
| Utah | LLS | LLS | GE | ... | 5 days (v) | 40 | Y | N | N | after 2 yrs. |
| Vermont | ... | ... | ... | ... | ... | ... | ... | ... | ... | ... |
| Virginia | AG | AG | GE | ... | 30 days | 10 days | Y (w) | N | Y (w) | Y |
| Washington | AG | AG | GE | ... | 30 days | 10 days | Y (w) | N | Y (w) | Y |
| West Virginia | ... | ... | ... | ... | ... | ... | ... | ... | ... | ... |
| Wisconsin | ... | ... | ... | ... | ... | ... | ... | ... | ... | ... |
| Wyoming | SS | SS, AG | GE 120 days after LS | ... | 90 days | 15 after Canvass | Y | N | after 2 yrs. | after 5 yrs. |
| American Samoa | ... | ... | ... | ... | ... | ... | ... | ... | ... | ... |
| No. Mariana Islands | AG | AG | GE | (x) | (x) | 30 | ... | ... | ... | Y |
| Puerto Rico | LC | AG, LLS | GE | IM | IM | ... | Y | ... | ... | Y |
| U.S. Virgin Islands | Office of Supervisor of Elections | Office of Supervisor of Elections | Any election | IM | IM | 7 | (r) | ... | (r) | Y |

*Sources:* The Council of State Governments' survey of state election administration offices, January 2007 and state websites, March 2010.

*Key:*

PR — Primary election.
... — Not applicable.
LG — Lieutenant Governor.
SS — Secretary of State.
AG — Attorney General.
P — Proponent.
LC — Legislative Council.
LLS — Legislative Legal Services.
BSC — Board of State Canvassers.
SBE — State Board of Elections.
GE — General election.
REG — Regular election.
SP — Special election.
IM — Immediately.
LS — Legislative session.
TB — Title Board.
Y — Yes.
N — No.
w/i — Within.

(a) In some states, the ballot title and summary will differ from that on the petition.

(b) A majority of the popular vote is required to enact a measure. In Massachusetts and Nebraska, apart from satisfying the requisite majority vote, the measure must receive, respectively, 30% and 35% of the total votes cast in favor. An initiative approved by the voters may be put into effect immediately after the approving votes have been canvassed. In California and Nebraska, the measure may specify an enacting date. In Colorado, measures take effect from the date of proclamation by governor, but no later than 30 days after votes have been canvassed and certified by secretary of state. In Nebraska, 10 days after completion of canvass by the State Board of Canvassers.

(c) Individuals may contest the results of a vote on an initiative within a certain number of days after the election including the measure proposed.

(d) After certification of election.

(e) Upon governor's proclamation.

(f) Initiative can be amended by three-fourths of the members of each house of the legislature (AZ Constitution Article 4, Part 1, Section14.

(g) By vote only.

(h) Ballot title: Drafted by Legislative Council of the General Assembly, then finalized by three board members called the Title Board. Summary by: Legislative Council of the General Assembly.

(i) If it is statutory it can be changed by the legislature.

(j) It is effective the first Tuesday after the first Monday in January following election unless specified in the amendment.

(k) Amendments or repeal must be voted on by the voters.

(l) Subject to approval of the Attorney General.

(m) Changing a constitutional amendment would require another constitutional amendment.

(n) Revisor of Statutes.

(o) After election is certified.

(p) Not on next ballot.

(q) Constitutional amendment—after passed twice by the voters it becomes effective upon the completion of the canvass of votes by the Supreme Court on the fourth Tuesday of November following the election. Statute—effective on the date approved by the governor or the canvass of the vote by the Supreme Court.

(r) It cannot be amended or repealed within three years from the date it takes effect.

(s) A measure approved by the electors may not be amended or repealed by the legislative assembly for seven years from its effective date, except by a two-thirds vote of the members elected to each house.

(t) No summary, but the Ohio Ballot Board prescribes the ballot language. Also explanations and arguments for and against the proposal may be prepared by the petitioner and the person(s) appointed by the governor or, if appropriate, the General Assembly. The Ohio Ballot Board must prepare any missing explanation or argument.

(u) Initiate constitutional amendment proposed by petition cannot be vetoed: cannot be amended or repealed except by another constitutional amendment. Initiated statute cannot be vetoed by the governor, but may be amended or repealed after its effective date via legislation or another initiative.

(v) Effective date may be written in the initiative, otherwise it takes place within five days after governor's proclamation.

(w) An initiative may be challenged in court as to constitutionality. No act, law or bill approved by a majority of the electors voting thereon shall be amended or repealed by the legislature within a period of two years following such enactment. Such enactment may be amended or repealed at any general regular or special election by direct vote of the people thereon.

(x) Effective upon approval by voters and certification of election result by Election Commission: usually 15 days after date of election or later if there is an election contest.

## Table 6.14
## STATE REFERENDUMS: REQUESTING PERMISSION TO CIRCULATE A CITIZEN PETITION

| State or other jurisdiction | Citizen petition (a) | Signatures required to request a petition (b) | Request submitted to: | Request forms furnished by: (c) | Restricted subject matter (d) | Individual responsible for petition Title | Individual responsible for petition Summary | Financial contributions reported (e) | Deposit required (f) |
|---|---|---|---|---|---|---|---|---|---|
| Alabama | ... | ... | ... | ... | ... | ... | ... | ... | ... |
| Alaska | Y | 100 | LG | DV | Y | LG | LG | Y | $100 |
| Arizona | Y | 5% VG | SS | SS | Y | P | P | Y | N |
| Arkansas | Y | 8% | AG | SP | N | SP | AG | Y | N |
| California | Y | ... | AG | ... | Y | AG | AG | N | $200 |
| Colorado | ... | ... | ... | ... | ... | ... | ... | ... | ... |
| Connecticut | ... | ... | ... | ... | ... | ... | ... | ... | ... |
| Delaware | ... | ... | ... | ... | ... | ... | ... | ... | ... |
| Florida | ... | ... | ... | ... | ... | ... | ... | ... | ... |
| Georgia | ... | ... | ... | ... | ... | ... | ... | ... | ... |
| Hawaii | ... | ... | ... | ... | ... | ... | ... | ... | ... |
| Idaho | Y | 20 | SS | SP | N | AG | AG | Y | N |
| Illinois | Y | ... | ... | ... | Y | ... | ... | ... | ... |
| Indiana | (g) | Varies | SS | SS | Y | Varies | ... | ... | ... |
| Iowa | ... | ... | ... | ... | ... | ... | ... | ... | ... |
| Kansas | ... | ... | ... | ... | ... | ... | ... | ... | ... |
| Kentucky | Y | ... | SS | ... | Y | ... | ... | ... | ... |
| Louisiana | ... | ... | ... | ... | ... | ... | ... | ... | ... |
| Maine | Y | 5 (h) | SS | SS | Y | SP, SS | SS (i) | Y | ... |
| Maryland | Y | (j) | ... | ... | Y | SP | SP | Y | N |
| Massachusetts | Y | 10 | SS | SS | Y | AG | AG | Y | N |
| Michigan | Y | ... | ... | ... | Y | SP | SP | Y | N |
| Minnesota | ... | ... | ... | ... | ... | ... | ... | ... | ... |
| Mississippi | ... | ... | ... | ... | ... | ... | ... | ... | ... |
| Missouri | Y | ... | ... | SP | Y | SS, AG | (l) | Y | N |
| Montana | Y | (k) | LS, SS, AG | SP | Y | AG | AG | Y | N |
| Nebraska | Y | ... | SS | ... | Y | SP | SP | Y | N |
| Nevada | Y | ... | SS | SS | Y | P, SP | P, SP | Y | N |
| New Hampshire | ... | ... | ... | ... | ... | ... | ... | ... | ... |
| New Jersey | ... | ... | ... | ... | ... | ... | ... | ... | ... |
| New Mexico | ... | ... | ... | ... | ... | ... | ... | ... | ... |
| New York | ... | ... | ... | ... | ... | ... | ... | ... | ... |
| North Carolina | ... | ... | ... | ... | ... | ... | ... | ... | ... |
| North Dakota | Y | (m) | SS | SP | N | SS, AG | SS | Y | N |
| Ohio | Y | ... | SS, AG | PE | Y | PE | PE (n) | Y | N |
| Oklahoma | Y | (o) | SS | (j) | N | P | P | Y | N |
| Oregon | Y | 4% or 58,142 | SS | SS | Y (p) | AG | AG | Y | N |
| Pennsylvania | ... | ... | ... | ... | ... | ... | ... | ... | ... |
| Rhode Island | ... | ... | ... | ... | ... | ... | ... | ... | ... |
| South Carolina | ... | ... | ... | ... | ... | ... | ... | ... | ... |
| South Dakota | Y | 5% EV | SS (q) | SP | N | AG | AG | Y | N |
| Tennessee | ... | ... | ... | ... | ... | ... | ... | ... | ... |
| Texas | ... | ... | ... | ... | ... | ... | ... | ... | ... |
| Utah | Y | 5 SP | LG | LG | Y (r) | SP | SP | Y | ... |
| Vermont | ... | ... | ... | ... | ... | ... | ... | ... | ... |
| Virginia | ... | ... | ... | ... | ... | ... | ... | ... | ... |
| Washington | Y | 120,114 | SS | SS | Y (p) | AG | AG | N | $5.00 |
| West Virginia | Y | varies | ... | SS | Y | ... | ... | N | N |
| Wisconsin | ... | ... | ... | ... | ... | ... | ... | ... | ... |
| Wyoming | Y | 100 | SS | SS | Y | SS | SS | Y | $500 |
| American Samoa | ... | ... | ... | ... | ... | ... | ... | ... | ... |
| No. Mariana Islands | Y | ... | ... | ... | Y | SP | AG | Y | N |
| Puerto Rico | Y | 10% district/ 41% territorial | Other | SBE | N | SP | Other | Y | N |
| U.S. Virgin Islands | ... | ... | L | L | N | L | L | N | N |

See footnotes at end of table.

# STATE REFERENDUMS: REQUESTING PERMISSION TO CIRCULATE A CITIZEN PETITION—Continued

*Source*: The Council of State Governments' survey of state election administration offices, July 2011.

*Key*:

... — Not applicable.

EV — Eligible voters.

VG — Total votes cast for the position of governor in last election.

LG — Lieutenant Governor.

LS — Legislative services.

L — Legislature.

SS — Secretary of State.

SBE — State Board of Elections.

DV — Division of Elections.

AG — Attorney General.

P — Proponent.

PE — Petitioner.

ST — State.

SP — Sponsor.

Y — Yes.

N — No.

(a) Three forms of referenda exist: citizen petition, submission by the legislature, and constitutional requirement. This table outlines the steps necessary to enact a citizen's petition.

(b) Prior to circulating a statewide petition, a request for permission to do so must first be submitted to a specified state officer. Some states require such signatures to only be those of eligible voters.

(c) The form on which the request for petition is submitted may be the responsibility of the sponsor or may be furnished by the state.

(d) Restrictions may exist regarding the subject matter to which a referendum may be applied. The majority of these restrictions pertain to the dedication of state revenues and appropriations, and laws that maintain the preservation of public peace, safety and health. In Kentucky, referenda are only permitted for the establishment of soil and water and watershed conservation districts.

(e) In some states, a list of individuals who contribute financially to the referendum campaign must be submitted to the specified state officer with whom the petition is filed.

(f) A deposit may be required after permission to circulate a petition has been granted. This amount is refunded when the completed petition has been filed correctly.

(g) A referendum can only be placed on the ballot if authorized by a state law. As a result, a county or town election board cannot print any referendum on the ballot unless the legislature has already passed a law to permit the referendum. Therefore, each statute is different.

(h) The name and address of five voters.

(i) Revisor of statutes.

(j) Petition sponsor may submit proposed petition summary for approval to State Administrator of Elections but a formal request to circulate a petition is not required.

(k) No specific requirement to request a petition. Legislative Services receives the request and reviews it, and then the sponsor submits it to the Secretary of State and Attorney General for petition format review and legal and constitutional sufficiency review.

(l) State auditor writes the fiscal note.

(m) Two percent of resident population of state at the last federal decennial census.

(n) Petitioners must prepare the summary, and submit it to the Ohio Attorney General, who then must certify whether the summary fully and accurately describes the proposal.

(o) Five percent of legal voters based upon the total number of votes cast at the last general election for the state office receiving the highest number of votes at such election.

(p) No bills with an emergency clause.

(q) Do not have to request permission to circulate but must follow certain steps for this process.

(r) May not challenge laws passed by two-thirds of each house of the legislature.

## Table 6.15
## STATE REFERENDUMS: CIRCULATING THE CITIZEN PETITION

| State or other jurisdiction | Basis for signatures | Maximum time period allowed for petition circulation (a) | Can signatures be removed from petition (b) | Completed petition filed: With | Completed petition filed: Days after legislative session |
|---|---|---|---|---|---|
| Alabama | ... | ... | ... | ... | ... |
| Alaska | 10% TV, from 3/4 ED | w/i 90 days of LS | Y | ... | 90 days after LS |
| Arizona | 5% VG | w/i 90 days after LS | Y | SS | 90 days |
| Arkansas | 6% VG | ... | N | SS | 90 days |
| California | 5% VG | 90 days | Y | (c) | ... |
| Colorado | ... | ... | ... | ... | ... |
| Connecticut | ... | ... | ... | ... | ... |
| Delaware | ... | ... | ... | ... | ... |
| Florida | ... | ... | ... | ... | ... |
| Georgia | ... | ... | ... | ... | ... |
| Hawaii | ... | ... | ... | ... | ... |
| Idaho | 6% EV | w/i 60 days after LS | Y | SS | 60 days |
| Illinois | 8% VG (d) | ... | Y | SBE | ... |
| Indiana | ... | ... | ... | ... | ... |
| Iowa | ... | ... | ... | ... | ... |
| Kansas | ... | ... | ... | ... | ... |
| Kentucky | 5% VG | ... | ... | SS | 4 mos. |
| Louisiana | ... | ... | ... | ... | ... |
| Maine | 10% VG | 90 days of LS (e) | ... | SS | 90 days |
| Maryland | 3% VG | (f) | Y | SS | ... |
| Massachusetts | 1.5% VG for emergency 2% or immediate suspension | 90 days | Y (g) | SS | 90 days after signed by governor |
| Michigan | 5% VG | 90 days after LS | N | SS | 90 days |
| Minnesota | ... | ... | ... | ... | ... |
| Mississippi | ... | ... | ... | ... | ... |
| Missouri | 5% VG, from 2/3 ED | w/i 90 days after LS | Y | SS | 90 days |
| Montana | 5% EV and 5% from 34 of 100 ED | (h) | Y | SS | 6 mos. |
| Nebraska | 5% EV | ... | Y | SS | 90 days |
| Nevada | 10% EV last GE | (i) | Y | SS | 120 prior to next GE |
| New Hampshire | ... | ... | ... | ... | ... |
| New Jersey | ... | ... | ... | ... | ... |
| New Mexico | ... | ... | ... | ... | ... |
| New York | ... | ... | ... | ... | ... |
| North Carolina | ... | ... | ... | ... | ... |
| North Dakota | 2% total population | 90 days | N | SS | (j) |
| Ohio | 6% VG, 3% each from 1/2 counties | 90 days | Y | SS | 90 days |
| Oklahoma | 5% VH | w/i 90 days of LS | Y | SS | 90 days |
| Oregon | 4% VG | w/i 90 days of LS | Y (k) | SS | 90 days |
| Pennsylvania | ... | ... | ... | ... | ... |
| Rhode Island | ... | ... | ... | ... | ... |
| South Carolina | ... | ... | ... | ... | ... |
| South Dakota | 5% VG | w/i 90 days of LS | N | SS | 90 days |
| Tennessee | ... | ... | ... | ... | ... |
| Texas | ... | ... | ... | ... | ... |
| Utah | 10% VG | 40 days after LS | Y | CC | 40 days |
| Vermont | ... | ... | ... | ... | ... |
| Virginia | ... | ... | ... | ... | ... |
| Washington | 4% VG | Approx. 90 days | N | SS | 90 days |
| West Virginia | ... | ... | ... | ... | ... |
| Wisconsin | ... | ... | ... | ... | ... |
| Wyoming | 15% TV, from 2/3 county | 18 months | N | SS | 90 days |
| American Samoa | ... | ... | ... | ... | ... |
| No. Mariana Islands | ... | Up to 120 days before election | Y | AG | ... |
| Puerto Rico | ... | ... | ... | ... | ... |
| U.S. Virgin Islands | No. of registered voters | 180 days | ... | ... | ... |

See footnotes at end of table.

# STATE REFERENDUMS: CIRCULATING THE CITIZEN PETITION — Continued

*Source:* The Council of State Governments' survey of state election administration offices, July 2011.

*Key:*

... — Not applicable.

VG — Total votes cast for the position of governor in the last election.

EV — Eligible voters.

TV — Total voters in the last general election.

VH — Total votes cast for the office receiving the highest number of votes in last general election.

VSS — Total votes cast for all candidates for the office of secretary of state at the previous general election.

ED — Election district.

GE — General election.

LS — Legislative session.

LG — Lieutenant governor.

SBE — State Board of Elections.

SS — Secretary of state.

AG — Attorney general.

CC — County clerk.

Y — Yes.

N — No.

w/i — Within.

(a) The petition circulation period begins when petition forms have been approved and provided to or by the sponsors. Sponsors are those individuals granted permission to circulate a petition, and are therefore responsible for the validity of each signature on a given petition.

(b) Should an individual wish to remove his/her name from a petition, a request to do so must first be submitted in writing to the state officer with whom the petition is filed.

(c) County elections office.

(d) Referenda are advisory only.

(e) Request for petition must be submitted within 10 days of adjournment of legislative session.

(f) No signature may be collected until the final action of the General Assembly. Session ends the second Monday in April. One third of the signatures must be submitted not later than May 31. The remaining signatures are due no later than June 30th.

(g) Should an individual wish to remove his/her name from a petition, a request to do so must first be submitted in writing to the local election official prior to the petition being submitted for certification of signatures.

(h) No specific beginning date for circulation of petitions, so there is no maximum time period. There is an ending deadline of 6 months after legislative session.

(i) Not later than the third Tuesday in May of even-numbered years.

(j) Within 90 days after the legislation is filed in the Secretary of State's office.

(k) Only by the chief petitioners before submitting signatures before verification. Signatures may not be removed once the signatures have been submited to the secretary of state for verification.

## Table 6.16
## STATE REFERENDUMS: PREPARING THE CITIZEN PETITION REFERENDUM TO BE PLACED ON BALLOT

| State or other jurisdiction | Signatures verified by: (a) | Within how many days after filing | No. of days to amend/ appeal petition that is: Incomplete (b) | No. of days to amend/ appeal petition that is: Not accepted (c) | Penalty for falsifying petition (denotes fine, jail term) | Petition certified by: (d) |
|---|---|---|---|---|---|---|
| Alabama | ... | ... | ... | ... | ... | ... |
| Alaska | Division of elections | 60 | 10 | 10 | Class B misdemeanor | LG |
| Arizona | County recorder | (e) | ... | ... | Class 1 misdemeanor | SS |
| Arkansas | SS | 30 | ... | 30 | Class D felony | SS |
| California | County clerk | 8 | ... | ... | Felony or misdemeanor (depending on severity) | SS |
| Colorado | ... | ... | ... | ... | ... | ... |
| Connecticut | ... | ... | ... | ... | ... | ... |
| Delaware | ... | ... | ... | ... | ... | ... |
| Florida | ... | ... | ... | ... | ... | ... |
| Georgia | ... | ... | ... | ... | ... | ... |
| Hawaii | ... | ... | ... | ... | ... | ... |
| Idaho | County clerk | ... | ... | ... | $5,000, 2 yrs. | SS |
| Illinois | State Board of Elections | varies | ... | ... | Class 3 felony | SBE |
| Indiana | County clerk | ... | ... | ... | ... | ... |
| Iowa | ... | ... | ... | ... | ... | ... |
| Kansas | ... | ... | ... | ... | ... | ... |
| Kentucky | ... | ... | ... | ... | ... | ... |
| Louisiana | ... | ... | ... | ... | ... | ... |
| Maine | Registrars of voters | 30 | ... | ... | ... | SS |
| Maryland | Local Board of Elections | 20 | ... | ... | Misdemeanor (f) | SS, SBE |
| Massachusetts | Local boards of registrars | 14 | ... | ... | $1,000, 1 year | SS |
| Michigan | SS | Approx. 60 | ... | ... | $500, 90 days | BSC |
| Minnesota | ... | ... | ... | ... | ... | ... |
| Mississippi | ... | ... | ... | ... | ... | ... |
| Missouri | County clerk | (g) | ... | 10 | Class A misdemeanor | SS |
| Montana | County election administrators | 28 | 10 | 10 | $500, 6 mos. | SS |
| Nebraska | County clerk | 40 | ... | ... | ... | SS |
| Nevada | County clerk | (h) | 5 | ... | ... | SS |
| New Hampshire | ... | ... | ... | ... | ... | ... |
| New Jersey | ... | ... | ... | ... | ... | ... |
| New Mexico | ... | ... | ... | ... | ... | ... |
| New York | ... | ... | ... | ... | ... | ... |
| North Carolina | ... | ... | ... | ... | ... | ... |
| North Dakota | SS | 35 | ... | 20 | (i) | SS |
| Ohio | County board of elections | 10 | 10 | ... | 5th degree felony | SS |
| Oklahoma | SS | ... | 10 | ... | $1,000, 1 year | SS |
| Oregon | SS, county clerk | ... | ... | ... | (j) | SS |
| Pennsylvania | ... | ... | ... | ... | ... | ... |
| Rhode Island | ... | ... | ... | ... | ... | ... |
| South Carolina | ... | ... | ... | ... | ... | ... |
| South Dakota | SS | ... | ... | ... | Class 1 misdemeanor | SS |
| Tennessee | ... | ... | ... | ... | ... | ... |
| Texas | ... | ... | ... | ... | ... | ... |
| Utah | County clerks | 55 (k) | ... | 10 | Class A misdemeanor | LG |
| Vermont | ... | ... | ... | ... | ... | ... |
| Virginia | ... | ... | ... | ... | ... | ... |
| Washington | SS | (l) | ... | 10 | Class C felony (possible) | SS |
| West Virginia | ... | ... | ... | ... | ... | ... |
| Wisconsin | ... | ... | ... | ... | ... | ... |
| Wyoming | SS | 60 | 60 | 60 | $1,000, 1 yr. | SS |
| American Samoa | ... | ... | ... | ... | ... | ... |
| No. Mariana Islands | AG | ... | (m) | (m) | (n) | AG |
| Puerto Rico | ... | ... | ... | ... | ... | ... |
| U.S. Virgin Islands | Supervisor of Elections | 15 | ... | ... | ... | Supervisor of Elections. |

See footnotes at end of table.

## STATE REFERENDUMS: PREPARING THE CITIZEN PETITION REFERENDUM TO BE PLACED ON BALLOT— Continued

*Sources*: The Council of State Governments' survey of state election administration offices, January 2007 and state websites, March 2010.

*Key*:

... — Not applicable.

SS — Secretary of State.

LG — Lieutenant Governor.

BSC — Board of State Canvassers.

SBE — State Board of Elections.

(a) The validity of the signatures, as well as the correct number of required signatures must be verified before the referendum is allowed on the ballot.

(b) If an insufficient number of signatures are submitted, sponsors may amend the original petition by filing additional signatures within a given number of days after filing. If the necessary number of signatures have not been submitted by this date, the petition is declared void.

(c) In some cases, the state officer will not accept a valid petition. In such cases, sponsors may appeal this decision to the Supreme Court, where the sufficiency of the petition will be determined. If the petition is determined to be sufficient, the referendum is required to be placed on the ballot.

(d) A petition is certified for the ballot when the required number of signatures have been submitted by the filing deadline, and are determined to be valid.

(e) In Arizona, the secretary of state has 15 days to count signatures and to complete random sample; the county recorder then has 10 days to verify signatures.

(f) Misdemeanor, punishable by a $10–$250 fine or 30 days—six months in jail, or both.

(g) In Missouri, must be certified as sufficient or insufficient by the 13th Tuesday prior to the general election.

(h) 1. Within four days county clerks count total number of signatures and forward to the secretary of state. 2. The secretary of state immediately notifies county clerks if they are to proceed or not proceed with the signature verification. 3. If ordered by the secretary of state, the county clerks verify signatures within nine days (excluding weekends and holidays).

(i) Any violations discovered will be reported to the attorney general for investigation and prosecution.

(j) Whether a penalty is assessed would be based upon what information on the petition was falsified.

(k) After the end of the legislative session.

(l) Not later than the third Tuesday following the primary election.

(m) Incomplete: 30 or more days if submitted 150 days before date of the election; none if submitted 120 days before date of election. Not accepted: If submitted 119 days or less before the election.

(n) Subject to statute governing fraud or perjury.

## Table 6.17
## STATE REFERENDUMS: VOTING ON THE CITIZEN PETITION REFERENDUM

| State or other jurisdiction | Ballot (a) Title by: | Ballot (a) Summary by: | Election where referendum voted on | Effective date of approved referendum (b) | Days to contest election results (c) |
|---|---|---|---|---|---|
| Alabama | ... | ... | ... | ... | ... |
| Alaska | LG | LG | 1st statewide election 180 days after LS | 30 days | 10 |
| Arizona | SS, AG | LC | GE | (d) | 5 |
| Arkansas | AG | ... | GE | ... | 20 |
| California | AG | AG | GE or PR | 1 day | 5 (e) |
| Colorado | ... | ... | ... | ... | ... |
| Connecticut | ... | ... | ... | ... | ... |
| Delaware | ... | ... | ... | ... | ... |
| Florida | ... | ... | ... | ... | ... |
| Georgia | ... | ... | ... | ... | ... |
| Hawaii | ... | ... | ... | ... | ... |
| Idaho | AG | AG | GE | 30 days | 20 (e) |
| Illinois | ... | ... | GE | Advisory only | 30 |
| Indiana | ... | ... | ... | ... | ... |
| Iowa | ... | ... | ... | ... | ... |
| Kansas | ... | ... | ... | ... | ... |
| Kentucky | ... | ... | GE or SP | IM | ... |
| Louisiana | ... | ... | ... | ... | ... |
| Maine | ... | ... | GE or statewide election more than 60 days after filing | 30 days | 5 |
| Maryland | SS | LSS | GE | (f) | ... |
| Massachusetts | SS, AG | AG | GE more than 60 days after filing | 30 days | 10 |
| Michigan | BSC | BSC | GE | 10 days | 2 (e) |
| Minnesota | ... | ... | ... | ... | ... |
| Mississippi | ... | ... | ... | ... | ... |
| Missouri | SS, AG | SS | GE | IM | 30 |
| Montana | AG | AG | GE | (g) | 1 yr. |
| Nebraska | AG | AG | GE | ... | ... |
| Nevada | SS, AG | SS, AG | GE | Nov., 4th Tues. | 14 |
| New Hampshire | ... | ... | ... | ... | ... |
| New Jersey | ... | ... | ... | ... | ... |
| New Mexico | ... | ... | ... | ... | ... |
| New York | ... | ... | ... | ... | ... |
| North Carolina | ... | ... | ... | ... | ... |
| North Dakota | SS, AG | SS | PR | 30 days | 14 (e) |
| Ohio | ... | ... | GE more than 60 days after filing | IM | 15 (h) |
| Oklahoma | LLS, AG | LLS | GE or SP | ... | ... |
| Oregon | AG | AG | GE (i) | 30 days | 40 |
| Pennsylvania | ... | ... | ... | ... | ... |
| Rhode Island | ... | ... | ... | ... | ... |
| South Carolina | ... | ... | ... | ... | ... |
| South Dakota | AG | AG | GE | 1 day | ... |
| Tennessee | ... | ... | ... | ... | ... |
| Texas | ... | ... | ... | ... | ... |
| Utah | LLS | LLS | GE | 5 days | 40 |
| Vermont | ... | ... | ... | ... | ... |
| Virginia | ... | ... | ... | ... | ... |
| Washington | AG | AG | GE | 30 days | 10 |
| West Virginia | ... | ... | ... | ... | ... |
| Wisconsin | ... | ... | ... | ... | ... |
| Wyoming | SS | SS, AG | GE more than 120 days after LS | 90 days | 15 |
| American Samoa | ... | ... | ... | ... | ... |
| No. Mariana Islands | AG | AG | GE or special election if specified | (j) | 30 days |
| Puerto Rico | ... | ... | ... | ... | ... |
| U.S. Virgin Islands | ... | ... | ... | ... | ... |

See footnotes at end of table.

# STATE REFERENDUMS: VOTING ON THE CITIZEN PETITION REFERENDUM — Continued

*Sources*: The Council of State Governments' survey of state election administration offices, January 2007 and state websites, March 2010.

*Key*:

... — Not applicable.

LG — Lieutenant Governor.
AG — Attorney General.
SS — Secretary of State.
BSC — Board of State Canvassers.
LC — Legislative Counsel.
LSS — Legislative Legal Services.
SBE — State Board of Elections.

GE — General election.
PR — Primary election.
REG — Regular election.
SP — Special election.
IM — Immediately.
LS — Legislative session.

(a) In some states, the ballot title and summary will differ from that on the petition.

(b) A majority of the popular vote is required to enact a measure in every state. In Arizona, a referendum approved by the voters becomes effective upon the governor's proclamation. In Nebraska, a referendum may be put into effect immediately after the approving votes have been canvassed by the Board of State Canvassers and upon the governor's proclamation. In Massachusetts the measure must also receive at lease 30 percent of the total ballots cast in the last election. In Oklahoma, put into effect upon certification of election results by state election board. In Utah, after proclamation by governor and date specified in petition.

(c) Individuals may contest the results of a vote on a referendum within a certain number of days after the election including this matter. In Alaska, five days to request recount with appeal to the court within five days after recount.

(d) Upon proclamation of the governor after the canvas. (AZ Const. Article 4, Part 1, Section 13).

(e) After election is certified.

(f) After the certification of election results. Depends on date Board of State Canvassers meets. They must meet within 35 days after General Election.

(g) Unless specifically provided by the legislature in an act referred by it to the people or until suspended by a petition signed by at least 15% of the qualified electors in a majority of the legislative representative districts, an act referred to the people is in effect as provided by law until it is approved or rejected at the election. An act that is rejected is repealed effective the date the result of the canvass is filed by the secretary of state under 13-27-503. An act referred to the people that was in effect at the time of the election and is approved by the people remains in effect. An act that was suspended by a petition and is approved by the people is effective the date the result of the canvass is filed by the secretary of state under 13-27-503. An act referred by the legislature that contains an effective date following the election becomes effective on that date if approved by the people. An act that provides no effective date and whose substantive provisions were delayed by the legislature pending approval at an election and that is approved is effective October 1 following the election.

(h) After election is certified or if recount conducted, 10 days after recount.

(i) Special election can be held at the request of the Legislative Assembly.

(j) Upon approval by voters and certification of election results by Election Commission, usually 15 days after date of election if no contest.

## Table 6.18
## STATE RECALL PROVISIONS

| State or other jurisdiction | Provision for recall | Officials subject to recall | Constitutional and statutory citations for recall of state officials | Constitutional or statutory language |
|---|---|---|---|---|
| Alabama | No | | | |
| Alaska | Yes | All (a) | Const. Art., 11 § 8; AS § 15.45.470 et seq. | All elected public officials in the State, except judicial officers, are subject to recall by the voters of the State or political subdivision from which elected. |
| Arizona | Yes | All | Const. Art. 8, § 1-6; ARS § 19-201–19-234 | Every public officer in the state of Arizona, holding an elective office, either by election or appointment, is subject to recall from such office by the qualified electors of the electoral district from which candidates are elected to such office. |
| Arkansas | No | | | |
| California | Yes | All | Const. Art. 2, § 13-19; CA Election Code § 11000–11386 | Recall is the power of the electors to remove an elective officer. Recall of a state officer is initiated by delivering to the Secretary of State a petition alleging reason for recall. Sufficiency of reason is not reviewable. |
| Colorado | Yes | All | Const. Art. 21, § 1; CRS § 1-12-101–1-12-122, 23-17-120.5, 31-4-501-505 | Every elective public officer of the state of Colorado may be recalled from office at any time by the registered electors entitled to vote for a successor of such incumbent through the procedure and in the manner herein provided for, which procedure shall be known as the recall, and shall be in addition to and without excluding any other method of removal by law. |
| Connecticut | No | | | |
| Delaware | No | | | |
| Florida | No | | | |
| Georgia | Yes | All | Const. Art. 2, § 2.4; GA Code § 21-4-1 et seq. | The General Assembly is hereby authorized to provide by general law for the recall of public officials who hold elective office. The procedures, grounds, and all other matters relative to such recall shall be provided for in such law. |
| Hawaii | No | | | |
| Idaho | Yes | All (a) | Const. Art 6, § 6; ID Code § 34-1701–34-1715 | Every public officer in the state of Idaho, excepting the judicial officers, is subject to recall by the legal voters of the state or of the electoral district from which he is elected. The legislature shall pass the necessary laws to carry this provision into effect. |
| Illinois (b) | Yes | (b) | Const. Art 3, § 7 | The recall of the Governor may be proposed by a petition signed by a number of electors equal in number to at least 15% of the total votes cast for Governor in the preceding gubernatorial election, with at least 100 signatures from each of at least 25 separate counties. A petition shall have been signed by the petitioning electors not more than 150 days after an affidavit has been filed with the State Board of Elections providing notice of intent to circulate a petition to recall the Governor. The affidavit may be filed no sooner than 6 months after the beginning of the Governor's term of office. The affidavit shall have been signed by the proponent of the recall petition, at least 20 members of the House of Representatives, and at least 10 members of the Senate, with no more than half of the signatures of members of each chamber from the same established political party. |
| Indiana | No | | | |

See footnotes at end of table.

## STATE RECALL PROVISIONS — Continued

| State or other jurisdiction | Provision for recall | Officials subject to recall | Constitutional and statutory citations for recall of state officials | Constitutional or statutory language |
|---|---|---|---|---|
| Iowa | No | | | |
| Kansas | Yes | All (a) | Const. Art. 4, § 3; KSA § 25-4301–25-4331 | All elected public officials in the State, except judicial officers, shall be subject to recall by voters of the state or political subdivision from which elected. Procedures and grounds for recall shall be prescribed by law. |
| Kentucky | No | | | |
| Louisiana | Yes | All (a) | Const. Art. 10, § 26; LRS § 18:1300.1–18:1300.17 | The legislature shall provide by general law for the recall by election of any state, district, parochial, ward, or municipal officer except judges of the courts of record. The sole issue at a recall election shall be whether the official shall be recalled. |
| Maine | No | | | |
| Maryland | No | | | |
| Massachusetts | No | | | |
| Michigan | Yes | All (a) | Const. Art. 2, § 8; MCL § 168.951–168.975 | Laws shall be enacted to provide for the recall of all elective officers except judges of courts of record upon petition of electors equal in number to 25 percent of the number of persons voting in the last preceding election for the office of governor in the electoral district of the officer sought to be recalled. The sufficiency of any statement of reasons or grounds procedurally required shall be a political rather than a judicial question. |
| Minnesota | Yes | (c) | Const. Art. 8, § 6; MS § 211C.01 et. seq. | A state officer other than a judge may be subject to recall for serious malfeasance or nonfeasance during the term of office in the performance of the duties of the office or conviction during the term of office for a serious crime. |
| Mississippi | No | | | |
| Missouri | No | | | |
| Montana | Yes | All | Mont. Code § 2-16-601–2-16-635 | Every person holding a public office of the state or any of its political subdivisions, either by election or appointment , is subject to recall from such office. |
| Nebraska | No | | | |
| Nevada | Yes | All | Const. Art. 2, § 9; NRS § 294A.006, Chapter 306 | Every public officer in the State of Nevada is subject, as herein provided, to recall from office by the registered voters of the state, or of the county, district, or municipality which he represents. |
| New Hampshire | No | | | |
| New Jersey | Yes | All | Const. Art. 1, § 2; NJRS § 19:27A-1–19:27A-18 | The people reserve unto themselves the power to recall, after at least one year of service, any elected official in this State or representing this State in the United States Congress. |
| New Mexico | No | | | |
| New York | No | | | |
| North Carolina | No | | | |
| North Dakota | Yes | All (d) | Const. Art. 3, § 1 and 10; ND Century Code § 16. 1-01-09.1 | Any elected official of the state, of any county or of any legislative or county commissioner district shall be subject to recall by petition of electors equal in number to twenty-five percent of those who voted at the preceding general election for the office of governor in the state, county, or district in which the official is to be recalled. |

See footnotes at end of table.

## STATE RECALL PROVISIONS — Continued

| State or other jurisdiction | Provision for recall | Officials subject to recall | Constitutional and statutory citations for recall of state officials | Constitutional or statutory language |
|---|---|---|---|---|
| Ohio .......................... | No | | | |
| Oklahoma................... | No | | | |
| Oregon....................... | Yes | All (d) | Const. Art. 2, § 18; ORS § 249.865–249.880 | Every public official in Oregon is subject, as herein provided, to recall by the electors of the state or of the electoral district from which the public official is elected. |
| Pennsylvania ............. | No | | | |
| Rhode Island............. | Yes | (e) | Const. Art. 4, § 1 | Recall is authorized in the case of a general officer who has been indicted or informed against for a felony, convicted of a misdemeanor, or against whom a finding of probable cause of violation of the code of ethics has been made by the ethics commission. |
| South Carolina.......... | No | | | |
| South Dakota............ | No | | | |
| Tennessee ................. | No | | | |
| Texas.......................... | No | | | |
| Utah ........................... | No | | | |
| Vermont...................... | No | | | |
| Virginia...................... | No (f) | | | |
| Washington................ | Yes | All (a) | Const. Art. 1, Sec. 33-34; WRC § 29.82-010–29.82.220 | Every elective public officer of the state of Washington except judges of courts of record is subject to recall and discharge by the legal voters of the state, or of the political subdivision of the state, from which he was elected whenever a petition demanding his recall, . . . is filed with the officer with whom a petition for nomination, or certificate for nomination, to such office must be filed under the laws of this state, and the same officer shall call a special election as provided by the general election laws of this state and the result determined as therein provided. |
| West Virginia............. | No | | | |
| Wisconsin ................. | Yes | All | Const. Art. 13, § 12; Wisc. Stat. § 9.10 | The qualified electors of the state, of any congressional, judicial or legislative district or of any county may petition for the recall of any incumbent elective officer after the first year of the term for which the incumbent was elected, by filing a petition with the filing officer with whom the nomination petition is filed, demanding the recall of the incumbent. |
| Wyoming ................... | No | | | |
| No. Mariana Islands... | Yes | All | N.A. | N.A. |
| Puerto Rico............... | Yes | All | N.A. | N.A. |
| U.S. Virgin Islands..... | Yes | All | Constitutional and statutory citations exist. | N.A. |

*Sources*: The Council of State Governments, state constitutions and statutes, May 2012.
*Note*: This table refers only to officials elected to statewide office. Many local governments allow recall of elected officials.
N.A. — Not available
(a) Except judicial.

(b) Illinois allows for recall of the governor.
(c) State executive officers, legislators, and judicial officers.
(d) Except for U.S. Congress.
(e) Governor, Lieutenant Governor, Secretary of State, Treasurer, and Attorney General.
(f) Virginia permits a recall trial, not a recall election.

# Table 6.19
## STATE RECALL PROVISIONS: APPLICABILITY TO STATE OFFICIALS AND PETITION CIRCULATION

| State or other jurisdiction | Officers to whom recall is applicable (a) | No. of times recall can be attempted | Recall may be initiated after official has been in office | Recall may not be initiated with days remaining in term | Basis for signatures (b) (see key below) Statewide officers | Others | Maximum time allowed for petition circulation (c) |
|---|---|---|---|---|---|---|---|
| Alabama | ... | ... | ... | ... | ... | ... | ... |
| Alaska | All but judicial officers | ... | 120 days | 180 | 25% VO | 25% VO | ... |
| Arizona | All elected officials | 1 (d) | 6 mos./5 days legislators | ... | 25% VO (e) | 25% VO (e) | 120 days |
| Arkansas | ... | ... | ... | ... | ... | ... | ... |
| California | All elected officials | (f) | 90 days | 6 mos. | 12% VO, 1% from 5 counties | 20% VO | 160 days |
| Colorado | All elected officials | (g) | 6 mos. | 6 mos. | 25% VO | 25% VO | 60 days |
| Connecticut | ... | ... | ... | ... | ... | ... | ... |
| Delaware | ... | ... | ... | ... | ... | ... | ... |
| Florida | ... | ... | ... | ... | ... | ... | ... |
| Georgia | All state level officials, county and city elected officials | ... | 180 days | 180 | 15% EV (h), 1/15 from each congressional district | 30% EV (h) | (i) |
| Hawaii | ... | ... | ... | ... | ... | ... | ... |
| Idaho | All but judicial officers | (d) | ... | ... | 20% EVg | 50% VO | 60 days |
| Illinois | Governor | ... | 90 days | ... | 15% VO from 25 counties | 20 state Rep. and 10 state Sen. | 150 days |
| Indiana | ... | ... | ... | ... | ... | ... | ... |
| Iowa | ... | ... | ... | ... | ... | ... | ... |
| Kansas | All but judicial officers | 1 | 120 days | 180 | 40% VO | 40% VO | 90 days |
| Kentucky | ... | ... | ... | ... | ... | ... | ... |
| Louisiana | All but judicial officers | (j) | 1 day | 6 mos. | 33 1/3% EV (k) | 33 1/3% EV (k) | 180 days |
| Maine | ... | ... | ... | ... | ... | ... | ... |
| Maryland | ... | ... | ... | ... | ... | ... | ... |
| Massachusetts | All but judicial officers | No limit | 6 mos. | 6 mos. | 25% VG in district | 25% VG in district | 90 days |
| Michigan | All state level officials | No limit | ... | 6 mos. | 25% VO | 25% VO | 90 days |
| Minnesota | ... | ... | ... | ... | ... | ... | ... |
| Mississippi | ... | ... | ... | ... | ... | ... | ... |
| Missouri | ... | ... | ... | ... | ... | ... | ... |
| Montana | All state level officers & elected officials | (l) | 2 mos. | ... | 10% EV | (m) | 3 mos. |
| Nebraska | Elected officials from political subdivisions | (n) | 6 mos. | ... | ... | 35–45% VO | ... |
| Nevada | All officers | (d) | 6 mos. (o) | 6 mos. | 25% VO in given jurisdiction | 25% VO in given jurisdiction | 90 days |
| New Hampshire | ... | ... | ... | ... | ... | ... | ... |
| New Jersey | All elected officials | (p) | (q) | (r) | 25% VO in given jurisdiction | 25% VO in given jurisdiction | (s) |
| New Mexico | ... | ... | ... | ... | ... | ... | ... |
| New York | ... | ... | ... | ... | ... | ... | ... |
| North Carolina | ... | ... | ... | ... | ... | ... | ... |
| North Dakota | All elected state officials | 1 | ... | 190 | 25% EVg | 25% EV | 90 days |
| Ohio | ... | ... | ... | ... | ... | ... | ... |
| Oklahoma | ... | ... | ... | ... | ... | ... | ... |
| Oregon | All elected state officials | No limit | 180 days (t) | ... | 15% (u) | 15% (u) | 90 days |
| Pennsylvania | ... | ... | ... | ... | ... | ... | ... |
| Rhode Island | Gov., lt. gov., atty. gen., sec. of state, treasurer | ... | 6 mos. | ... | 15% VO | 25% VO in given jurisdiction | 90 days |
| South Carolina | ... | ... | ... | ... | 15% VO | ... | ... |

See footnotes at end of table.

# STATE RECALL PROVISIONS: APPLICABILITY TO STATE OFFICIALS AND PETITION CIRCULATION — Continued

| State or other jurisdiction | Officers to whom recall is applicable (a) | No. of times recall can be attempted | Recall may be initiated after official has been in office | Recall may not be initiated with days remaining in term | Basis for signatures (b) (see key below) Statewide officers | Basis for signatures (b) (see key below) Others | Maximum time allowed for petition circulation (c) |
|---|---|---|---|---|---|---|---|
| South Dakota | ... | ... | ... | ... | ... | ... | ... |
| Tennessee | ... | ... | ... | ... | ... | ... | ... |
| Texas | ... | ... | ... | ... | ... | ... | ... |
| Utah | ... | ... | ... | ... | ... | ... | ... |
| Vermont | ... | ... | ... | ... | ... | ... | ... |
| Virginia | ... | ... | ... | 180 | 25% VO | 35% VO | (v) |
| Washington | All but judges of courts of record | ... | IM | ... | ... | ... | ... |
| West Virginia | ... | ... | 1 yr. | ... | 25% VG (w) | 25% VG (w) | 60 days |
| Wisconsin | All elected officials | 1 | ... | ... | ... | ... | ... |
| Wyoming | ... | ... | ... | ... | 40% EV (y) | ... | ... |
| American Samoa | ... | (x) | ... | ... | ... | ... | ... |
| No. Mariana Islands | All elected officials | ... | 180 days | ... | ... | ... | ... |
| Puerto Rico | ... | Unlimited | 1 year | ... | ... | ... | (z) |
| U.S. Virgin Islands | All elected officials | ... | ... | 365 | ... | Registered electors | 180 days |

*Source:* The Council of State Governments, June 2011.

*Key:*

... — Not applicable.
All — All elective officials.
VO — Number of votes cast in the last election for the office or official being recalled.
EVg — Number of eligible voters in the last general election for governor.
EV — Eligible voters.
VG — Total votes cast for the position of governor in the last election.
VP — Total votes cast for position of president in last presidential election.
IM — Immediately.

(a) An elective official may be recalled by qualified voters entitled to vote for the recalled official's successor. An appointed official may be recalled by qualified voters entitled to vote for the successor(s) of the elective officer(s) authorized to appoint an individual to the position.

(b) Signature requirements for recall of those other than state elective officials are based on votes in the jurisdiction to which the said official has been elected.

(c) The petition circulation period begins when petition forms have been approved and provided to sponsors. Sponsors are those individuals granted permission to circulate a petition, and are therefore responsible for the validity of each signature on a given petition.

(d) Additional recall attempts can be made provided that the state treasury is reimbursed the cost of the previous recall attempt(s). The specific reason for recalling on one petition cannot be the basis for a second recall petition during the current term of office.

(e) 25% of the number of votes cast at the preceding general election for all candidates for the office held by the officer, even if the officer was not elected at that election, divided by the number of offices that were being filled at that election. (A.R.S.§ 19-201).

(f) Open ended.

(g) One attempt unless a second petition is circulated and valid signatures gathered are at least 50% of votes cast for all candidates in last election.

(h) Eligible voters for office at last general election to fill office.

(i) For any statewide office, 90 days. Any officer holding an office other than statewide office and for whom no less than 5,000 signatures are required for the recall petition, 45 days. Any officer holding an office other than statewide office and for whom less than 5,000 are required, 30 days.

(j) Unlimited. Once every 18 months.

(k) Basis for signatures 33 1/3 percent if over 1,000 eligible voters; 40 percent if under 1,000 eligible voters.

(l) No recall petition may be filed against an officer for whom a recall election has been held for a period of 2 years during his term of office unless the state or political subdivisions financing such recall election is first reimbursed for all expenses of the preceding election.

(m) 15-20 percent of eligible voters depending on the office.

(n) If voted on, no recall for one year.

(o) For legislators, anytime after 10 days from the beginning of the first legislative session after their election.

(p) An elected official sought to be recalled who is not recalled as the result of a recall election shall not again be subject to recall until after having served one year of a term calculated from the date of the recall election.

(q) The recall drive may not commence before the 50th day preceding the completion of the elected official's first year of the current term.

(r) No election to recall an elected official shall be held after the date occurring six months prior to the general election or regular election for that office, as appropriate, in the final year of the official's term.

(s) The maximum time allowed for petition circulation is 320 days for a governor or 160 days for other elected officials.

(t) Unless it is a state senator or representative and then it is anytime after fifth day from the beginning of legislative session or after election of legislator.

(u) 15 percent of the total number of votes cast in the public officer's electoral district for all candidates for governor at the last election at which a candidate for governor was elected to a full term.

(v) Statewide officials 270 days; others 180 days.

(w) At least 25 percent of the vote case for the office of governor at the last election within the same district or territory as that of the officeholder being recalled.

(x) Not more than once a year or not during the first six months in office.

(y) Grounds for recall must be stated and must be signed by 40% of voters represented by the elected official.

(z) Until 120 days before the election.

## Table 6.20
## STATE RECALL PROVISIONS: PETITION REVIEW, APPEAL AND ELECTION

| State or other jurisdiction | Signatures verified (a) by: | Days to amend/appeal a petition that is: Incomplete (b) | Not accepted (c) | Penalty for falsifying petition (denotes fines, jail time) | Days allowed for petition to be certified (d) | Days to step down after certification (e) | Voting on the recall (f) Election held | Election type | Days to contest election results (g) |
|---|---|---|---|---|---|---|---|---|---|
| Alabama | ... | ... | ... | ... | ... | ... | ... | ... | ... |
| Alaska | Division of Elections | 20 | 20 | Class B misdemeanor | 30 | 1 | 60–90 days after cert. | GE, PR, SP | 10 |
| Arizona | County recorder | ... | ... | Class 1 misdemeanor | 70 | 5 | (h) | (i) | 5 |
| Arkansas | ... | ... | ... | ... | ... | ... | ... | ... | ... |
| California | County clerk/registrar of voters | 10 | 10 | ... | 10 | (j) | 60–80 days after cert. | GE | 5 |
| Colorado | SS | ... | 15 (k) | ... | 10 | 5 | 45–75 days after cert. | SP or GE | 10 |
| Connecticut | ... | ... | ... | ... | ... | ... | ... | ... | ... |
| Delaware | ... | ... | ... | ... | ... | ... | ... | ... | ... |
| Florida | ... | ... | ... | ... | ... | ... | ... | ... | ... |
| Georgia | Registrar of voters | ... | ... | Misdemeanor | 30–45 | ... | 30–45 days after cert. | SP | 5 |
| Hawaii | ... | ... | ... | ... | ... | ... | ... | ... | ... |
| Idaho | County clerk | 30 | ... | $5,000, 2 yrs. | 10 | 5 | 45+ days after cert. (l) | SP, PR, GE (l) | 20 (m) |
| Illinois | SBE | ... | ... | ... | ... | ... | 100 days after cert. | SP | ... |
| Indiana | ... | ... | ... | ... | ... | ... | ... | ... | ... |
| Iowa | ... | ... | ... | ... | ... | ... | ... | ... | ... |
| Kansas | County clerk | ... | ... | Class B misdemeanor; up to $1,000, up to one year, or both. | 30 | Next day | 60–90 days after cert. | SP | 5 (m) |
| Kentucky | ... | ... | ... | ... | ... | ... | ... | ... | ... |
| Louisiana | Registrar of voters | (n) | (n) | ... | 15–20 days | (o) | (p) | ... | (q) |
| Maine | ... | ... | ... | ... | ... | ... | ... | ... | ... |
| Maryland | ... | ... | ... | ... | ... | ... | ... | ... | ... |
| Massachusetts | ... | ... | ... | ... | ... | ... | ... | ... | ... |
| Michigan | SS, local election officials (r) | 90 | ... | $500, 90 days | 35 | 5 | (s) | SP | 2 (m) |
| Minnesota | SS | ... | ... | Felony | 10 | ... | (t) | GE | 7 |
| Mississippi | ... | ... | ... | ... | ... | ... | ... | ... | ... |
| Missouri | ... | ... | ... | ... | ... | ... | ... | ... | ... |
| Montana | County election administrators | 10 | 10 | $500 or six months in county jail, or both. | (u) | 5 | (v) | SP or GE (dd)(v) | 12 mos. |
| Nebraska | County clerk | ... | ... | ... | 15 | 5 | 30–45 days after cert. | SP | 40 |
| Nevada | County clerk, registrar of voters | 5 | ... | Misdemeanor | (w) | 5 | (x) | SP | (y) |
| New Hampshire | ... | ... | ... | ... | ... | ... | ... | ... | ... |
| New Jersey | Recall elections official | ... | ... | Crime of the 4th degree | 10 | 5 | (z) | SP or GE | (aa) |
| New Mexico | ... | ... | ... | ... | ... | ... | ... | ... | ... |
| New York | ... | ... | ... | ... | ... | ... | ... | ... | ... |
| North Carolina | ... | ... | ... | ... | ... | ... | ... | ... | ... |
| North Dakota | SS | ... | ... | ... | 30 | 10 | 50–60 | ... | 14 (bb) |
| Ohio | ... | ... | ... | ... | ... | ... | ... | ... | ... |
| Oklahoma | ... | ... | ... | ... | ... | ... | ... | ... | ... |
| Oregon | County clerk | (cc) | ... | (dd) | 10 | 5 | w/i 35 days after resignation period | SP | 40 |
| Pennsylvania | ... | ... | ... | ... | ... | ... | ... | ... | ... |
| Rhode Island | SBE | w/i 90 days | ... | ... | 90 | ... | ... | SP | ... |
| South Carolina | ... | ... | ... | Misdemeanor and/or felony | ... | ... | ... | ... | ... |

See footnotes at end of table.

# STATE RECALL PROVISIONS: PETITION REVIEW, APPEAL AND ELECTION — Continued

| State or other jurisdiction | Signatures verified (a) by: | Days to amend/appeal a petition that is: Incomplete (b) | Not accepted (c) | Penalty for falsifying petition (denotes fines, jail time) | Days allowed for petition to be certified (d) | Days to step down after certification (e) | Voting on the recall (f) Election held | Election type | Days to contest election results (g) |
|---|---|---|---|---|---|---|---|---|---|
| South Dakota | … | … | … | … | … | … | … | … | … |
| Tennessee | … | … | … | … | … | … | … | … | … |
| Texas | … | … | … | … | … | … | … | … | … |
| Utah | … | … | … | … | … | … | … | … | … |
| Vermont | … | … | … | … | … | … | … | … | … |
| Virginia | … | … | … | … | … | … | … | … | 3 |
| Washington | SS | 30 | … | Class B felony or misdemeanor | not specified | … | 45–60 days after cert. (ee) | SP | … |
| West Virginia | … | … | … | … | … | … | 6 weeks after cert. | GE or PR | 3 (ff) |
| Wisconsin | SBE | … | … | Class 1 felony—$10,000, 3 yrs. prison, or both. | 31 | 10 | … | … | … |
| Wyoming | … | … | … | … | … | … | … | … | … |
| American Samoa | … | 150 days | … | Statute governs fraud or perjury | 15 days | … | (gg) | GE, SP | 30 |
| No. Mariana Islands | AG | … | … | … | … | … | … | … | … |
| Puerto Rico | … | … | … | … | … | … | … | … | … |
| U.S. Virgin Islands | Office of the Supervisor of Elections | … | … | … | 10 | IM | … | GE | 5 |

*Source:* The Council of State Governments, May 2012.

Key:
… — Not applicable.
SBE — State Board of Elections.
SS — Secretary of State.
SP — Special election.
GE — General election.
PR — Primary election.
IM — Immediate and automatic removal from office.
w/i — Within.
N.A. — Information not available.

(a) The validity of the signatures, as well as the correct number of required signatures must be verified before the recall is allowed on the ballot.
(b) If an insufficient number of signatures are submitted, sponsors may amend the original petition by filing additional signatures within a given number of days. If the necessary number of signatures have not been submitted by this date, the petition is declared void.
(c) In some cases, the state officer will not accept a valid petition. In such a case, sponsors may appeal this decision to the Supreme Court, where the sufficiency of the petition will be determined. When this is declared, the recall is required to be placed on the ballot.
(d) A petition is certified for the ballot when the required number of signatures has been submitted by the filing deadline, and are determined to be valid.
(e) The official to whom a recall is proposed has a certain number of days to step down from his position before a recall election is initiated, if he desires to do so.
(f) A majority of the popular vote is required to recall an official in each state.
(g) Individuals may contest the results of a vote on a recall within a certain number of days after the results are certified. In Alaska, an appeal to courts must be filed within five days of the recount.
(h) The election order is issued within 15 days if the officer does not resign within five days after certification.

(i) To be held on the next consolidated election date pursuant to § 16-204 that is 90 days or more after the order calling the election (A.R.S. § 19-209(A)).
(j) Prior to election being called.
(k) After determination of sufficiency.
(l) In Idaho, the dates on which elections may be conducted are the first Tuesday in February, the fourth Tuesday in May, the first Tuesday in August, or the Tuesday following the first Monday in November. In addition, an emergency election may be called upon motion of the governing board of a political subdivision. Recall elections conducted by any political subdivision shall be held on the nearest of these dates which falls more than 45 days after the clerk of the political subdivision orders that the recall election shall be held.
(m) After election is certified. In Michigan, if a petition is filed against a local officer, a recount can be requested up to 6 days after certification of recall election.
(n) The Registrar of Voters shall honor the written request of any voter who either desires to have his handwritten signature stricken from or added to the petition at any time prior to certification of the petition, or within five days after receipt of such signed petition, whichever is earlier.
(o) Election returns are certified on the fifth day after the election, and the office is immediately vacant.
(p) The local registrar of voters sends the original certified recall petition to the governor, who issues, within 15 days, a proclamation calling a special election, placing the special election on the next regularly scheduled election date.
(q) Not later than 4:30 p.m. of the 30th day after the official promulgation of the results of the election. Promulgation is on or before the 12th day after the election.
(r) Secretary of state if filed on the state level; county or local clerks if filed on county level.
(s) Under Michigan's consolidated elections, the recall election is held on the next fixed election date that falls at least 95 days after the recall petition is filed.
(t) An election will not be held in the last 6 mos. of a term after certification.
(u) County election administrators have 30 days; sponsor has three mos. to submit the petition from the date of certification.
(v) A special election is called unless the filing is within 90 days of a general election.

# STATE RECALL PROVISIONS: PETITION REVIEW, APPEAL AND ELECTION—Continued

(w) Within four days, county clerks count signature totals and forward to the Secretary of State. The Secretary of State immediately notifies the clerks if they are to proceed with signature verification.

(x) In Nevada, a recall election is held 10–20 days after the Secretary of State completes notification of the petition sufficiency; unless a complaint is filed, the clerk shall issue a call for the election which is to be held within 30 days after the issuance of the call.

(y) Five days after recount is completed or 14 days after the election if no recount is demanded.

(z) New Jersey Permanent Statutes, 19:27A-13: In the case of an office which is ordinarily filled at the general election, a recall election shall be held at the next general election occurring at least 55 days following the fifth business day after service of certification, unless it was indicated in the notice of intention to recall that the recall election shall be held at a special election in which case the recall election official shall order and fix the date for holding the recall election to be the next Tuesday occurring during the period beginning with the 55th day and ending on the 61st day following the fifth business day after service of the certification of the petition.

(aa) New Jersey Permanent Statutes, 19:27A-16.

(bb) Fourteen days after the canvass board has certified the results.

(cc) Chief petitioners may submit additional signatures if the deadline for submitting signatures has not passed.

(dd) Whether a penalty is assessd would depend on what information on the petition was falsified.

(ee) If possible to be held on a regularly scheduled election; cannot be held between the primary and general.

(ff) Business days.

(gg) The election is held at the next regular general election or at a special election set forth in the recall petition.

# Chapter Seven

# STATE FINANCE

# State Budgets in 2011 and 2012:
# Recovery Begins for States, but Fiscal Conditions
# Remain Below Pre-Recession Levels

## By Brian Sigritz

*Fiscal conditions began to improve for states in the 2011 fiscal year. State revenue collections grew by 6.4 percent and state general fund spending increased by 4 percent following two consecutive years of declines. Additionally, the number of states making midyear budget cuts dropped from 39 states in fiscal 2010 to 19 states in fiscal 2011. In the 2012 fiscal year, states are expected to continue their recent improvement with both state revenues and state spending projected to grow. Fiscal conditions, however, remain below pre-recession levels in many states even with the recent increases. States will have to continue to make difficult decisions in the 2013 fiscal year and beyond as they contend with increased spending demands, slowly recovering revenue collections, uncertainty regarding future federal funding and long-term liabilities including pensions and retiree health care costs.*

## Introduction

The 2011 fiscal year marked a turning point for state finances following two of the most challenging years for state budgets since the Great Depression. After a revenue decline of 8 percent in the 2009 fiscal year, and an additional 2.5 percent in the 2010 fiscal year, state revenues grew by 6.4 percent in 2011.[1] State spending also experienced a turnaround with general fund spending growing 4 percent in the 2011 fiscal year. This followed a 3.8 percent decline in general fund spending in 2009 and a 5.7 percent decline in 2010, which marked the first time in the 34 year history of the National Association of State Budget Officers' *Fiscal Survey of States* that general fund spending declined two years in a row.[2] While the 2010 fiscal year saw 45 states with general fund expenditures below 2009 levels, 38 states enacted a 2011 fiscal year budget with general fund spending levels above those of the 2010 fiscal year.[3] Perhaps not surprisingly, the number of states making midyear budget cuts also declined in 2011 with 19 states making midyear cuts, compared to 43 states in 2009 and 39 states in 2010.[4]

Both state revenues and state spending are projected to continue to grow in the 2012 fiscal year, although at slower rates than witnessed in 2011. According to governors' enacted budgets, state revenues are expected to increase 1.6 percent in 2012,[5] while general fund expenditures are expected to increase 2.9 percent.[6] Additionally, the vast majority of states have assumed at least moderate budget

growth, with 43 states enacting a 2012 fiscal year budget with general fund spending levels above the 2011 fiscal year.[7]

Although fiscal conditions have improved, states still face a difficult budgetary environment. Revenues, spending and balances all remain well below pre-recession levels. Total state general fund revenues in 2012 are forecast to be nearly $21 billion, or 3.1 percent, below general fund revenue collections in fiscal 2008. Similarly, state general fund spending remains more than $20 billion, or 3.1 percent, below its 2008 fiscal year level. Total state balance levels have declined from a high of $69 billion in the 2006 fiscal year to $41.2 billion in the 2012 fiscal year. Furthermore, in 2012 states had to contend with a $43 billion dropoff in temporary federal aid provided through the *American Recovery and Reinvestment Act of 2009*.[8] All these factors, along with increased spending demands and uncertainty surrounding future federal funding levels, continue to present states with significant fiscal challenges.

## The Current State Fiscal Condition
### *Revenues in Fiscal 2011*

State revenues began a slow recovery in the 2011 fiscal year. After declining sharply by 8 percent in the 2009 fiscal year[9] and an additional 2.5 percent in the 2010 fiscal year, state revenues grew by 6.4 percent in 2011.[10] Sales, personal income and corporate income tax revenues all experienced gains in the 2011 fiscal year. Individually, sales tax collections grew by 4.8 percent, personal income tax collections rose by 9.7 percent and corporate income tax collections were 9.4 percent higher than 2010 fiscal year levels. In nominal dollars, sales tax revenues increased by $9.4 billion, personal income tax grew by $22.9 billion and corporate income tax collections rose by $3.7 billion.[11] Further indication of the improving revenue outlook can be seen in the fact that 2011 fiscal year revenue collections from all sources[12] were higher than projections in 32 states, on target in nine states and lower than budgeted amounts in only nine states. This contrasts sharply from the 2010 fiscal year, when revenues were lower than anticipated in 36 states, on target in another two states and higher than projections in only 12 states.[13]

### Revenues in Fiscal 2012

Revenue collections are expected to continue to grow in the 2012 fiscal year, although likely at a slower rate than the 2011 fiscal year. State revenues are expected to increase 1.6 percent, or $10.4 billion, in the 2012 year, according to governors' enacted budgets.[14] The latest data from the Nelson A. Rockefeller Institute of Government indicates that state revenues are growing as forecasted. According to the Rockefeller Institute, state tax revenues grew by 6.1 percent in the first quarter of the 2012 fiscal year—third quarter of calendar year 2011—compared to the same quarter of the 2011 fiscal year. Additionally, preliminary figures for October and November 2011 show state revenues growing by 5.2 percent compared to the same time period in 2010.[15]

While encouraging, the revenue growth figures do not tell the entire story. For one, revenue growth has trended downward so far in 2012. First quarter growth rate of 6.1 percent in the 2012 fiscal year is considerably lower than the last quarter of the 2011 fiscal year, which saw 11.1 percent growth. Secondly, even if 2012 revenues grow at their projected level, state revenues will still be 3.1 percent below the 2008 fiscal year. In nominal dollars, revenues are projected to be $659.4 billion in 2012 compared to $680.2 billion in 2008, a decline of more than $20 billion. Revenue totals similar to the 2012 fiscal year haven't been seen since the 2007 fiscal year.[16]

### Tax and Fee Changes in Fiscal 2012

In response to significant reductions in revenue, states enacted $23.9 billion in tax and fee increases in the 2010 fiscal year, marking the highest dollar amount attributable to tax and fee changes since NASBO's *Fiscal Survey of States* began tracking this data in

1979. In the 2011 fiscal year, states enacted an additional $6.2 billion in tax and fee increases. In the 2012 fiscal year, however, states enacted an aggregate decrease of $584.1 million in new taxes and fees. The decrease in net taxes and fees in 2012 is the first time since 2007 that states did not enact an increase.[17]

The largest enacted reduction in taxes and fees in the 2012 fiscal year came in corporate income taxes, declining by $1.3 billion. Of this, $1.1 billion is the result of the replacement of the Michigan Business Tax with a 6 percent corporate income tax. Overall, 13 states decreased corporate income taxes, while four states increased them. States also enacted a net decrease of $690.5 million in sales taxes in the 2012 fiscal year. Much of the change was due to the expiration of a temporary sales tax in North Carolina.

While states enacted an overall net reduction of nearly $600 million in taxes and fees, not all types of revenue experienced a decline. For example, personal income taxes experienced a net increase of $571 million, with much of this due to changes in Michigan and Connecticut. Other revenue sources that experienced a net increase include cigarette and tobacco taxes ($58.1 million), motor fuel taxes ($8.7 million), alcohol taxes ($97.1 million), other taxes ($557.1 million), and fees ($81.9 million).[18]

### State Spending in 2011

Similar to what occurred with state revenue, state spending experienced a turnaround in the 2011 fiscal year. Spending from state funds—general funds and other state funds combined—grew for the first time since fiscal 2008. It should be noted though that the level of growth was significantly lower than the historical average. Additionally, federal funds to states continued to grow in the 2011 fiscal year. The federal funds growth rate, however, was much lower in 2011 than 2010 due to the winding down of American Recovery and Reinvestment Act, or Recovery Act, funds. This combination of modest growth in state funds and declining federal funds growth meant that state resources continued to be constrained in 2011.

Looking in greater detail at the 2011 fiscal year, general fund spending is estimated to be $636.3 billion, a 2.8 percent increase from 2010. General funds serve as the primary source for financing state operations. General funds typically receive their revenue from broad-based state taxes such as sales and personal income taxes.

The majority of program areas saw increased general fund spending in the 2011 fiscal year. Elementary and secondary education, higher education, Medicaid, corrections and transportation all experienced increased general fund spending, while public assistance and the "all other"[19] category saw relatively minor declines.[20] By far, the largest growth area in general fund spending was Medicaid, growing 13.5 percent. The large increase in state general fund Medicaid spending is attributable to a combination of factors, including increased enrollment, the winding down of temporary Medicaid funds provided through the Recovery Act, and maintenance of effort requirements included in the Recovery Act. Elementary and secondary education remained the largest category of general fund expenditures in 2011, accounting for 35 percent of general fund expenditures. Medicaid represented 17.4 percent and higher education accounted for 11.5 percent. Combined, Medicaid and education comprised 64 percent of total state general fund spending. Other categories of general fund spending included corrections at 7.4 percent, public assistance at 1.8 percent, transportation at 0.5 percent and all other spending at 26.5 percent.[21]

Federal funds to states increased by 4 percent in the 2011 fiscal year, much lower than the 2009 and 2010 fiscal years, which saw growth rates of 19.3 and 19.4 percent respectively. Federal fund spending grew from $552.7 billion in the 2010 fiscal year to an estimated $574.8 billion in the 2011 fiscal year.[22] All spending categories of federal funds, with the exception of corrections, experienced at least a modest increase in 2011. Medicaid accounted for the largest share of state spending from federal funds at 43.5 percent. Elementary and secondary education at 12.7 percent and transportation at 7.2 percent represented the next largest shares.[23]

Total state expenditures—general funds, federal funds, other state funds and bonds combined—grew by an estimated 4.1 percent in the 2011 fiscal year to $1.69 trillion.[24] Medicaid remained the largest component of total state spending in the 2011 fiscal year, representing 23.6 percent of total state expenditures. As recently as the 2008 fiscal year, elementary and secondary education represented a larger share of total state expenditures than Medicaid. In 2011, K–12 education represented 20.1 percent of total state expenditures. Other categories of total state expenditures include higher education at 10.1 percent, transportation at 7.6 percent, corrections at 3.1 percent, public assistance at 1.6 percent and all other spending at 33.9 percent.[25]

Finally, the passage of the Recovery Act in February 2009 produced a shift in the funding sources for state expenditures. Federal funds have grown from representing 26.3 percent of total state expenditures in the 2008 fiscal year to 34.1 percent in estimated expenditures in the 2011 fiscal year, while general funds have gone from representing 45.9 percent of total state spending in fiscal 2008 to 37.7 percent in fiscal 2011.[26] General funds, however, will likely make up a larger component of total state expenditures in the 2012 fiscal year as states deal with the rapid decline of Recovery Act funds.

### State Spending in 2012

According to appropriated budgets, general fund expenditures are expected to increase by 2.9 percent in the 2012 fiscal year. General fund spending is estimated to be $666.6 billion in 2012, an $18.5 billion increase from the 2011 fiscal year.[27] Forty-three states enacted a 2012 fiscal year budget with general fund spending levels above 2011.[28] By comparison, as recently as fiscal 2010, 45 states enacted general fund budgets with lower levels of spending.[29] The 2012 fiscal year general fund spending is expected to remain well below pre-recession levels, even after assuming a 2.9 percent growth from the 2011 fiscal year. Specifically, general fund spending will remain $20 billion, or 3.1 percent, below its peak level in 2008. Furthermore, 29 states enacted a 2012 fiscal year budget with lower general fund spending than they had in the 2008 fiscal year.[30]

### Budget Cuts

The number of states forced to make midyear budget cuts declined significantly in the 2011 fiscal year. While 43 states made midyear cuts totaling $31.3 billion in the 2009 fiscal year, and 39 states made midyear cuts totaling $18.3 billion in the 2010 fiscal year, only 19 states made midyear cuts totaling $7.4 billion in 2011. While the number of states forced to make midyear budget cuts was reduced in half from 2010 to 2011, states still made significant cuts. Education was one area that experienced widespread cuts, with 18 states making midyear cuts to higher education and 17 states making midyear cuts to K–12. Other program areas that were cut midyear include corrections (16 states), Medicaid (12 states), public assistance (11 states), and transportation (seven states).[31]

The number of states making midyear budget cuts has decreased even further so far in the 2012 fiscal year, with only two states reporting midyear cuts through December. The decrease in the number of states making midyear budget cuts is likely attributable to improved revenue collections and more accurate revenue projections. Through December,

15 states were exceeding revenue projections, while 22 states were on target, and only seven states were seeing revenues coming in lower than projections; not all states were able to provide preliminary 2012 fiscal year data.[32]

### Balances

Total balances include both ending balances as well as the amounts in states' budget stabilization funds. Combined, these reserves reflect the funds states may use to respond to unforeseen circumstances after budget obligations have been met. Forty-eight states currently have either a budget stabilization fund or a "rainy day" fund, with about three-fifths of the states having limits on the size of these funds.[33]

Balances have fallen since the start of the recession as states have turned to them in response to declining revenue levels. In the 2012 fiscal year, balances are projected to be 6.2 percent of expenditures at $41.2 billion, considerably less than the 2008 fiscal year when balances were 8.6 percent of expenditures, or $59.1 billion. As recently as the 2006 fiscal year, balances were at record high levels of 11.5 percent of expenditures, $69 billion. The informal rule-of-thumb is that balances should be at least 5 percent of expenditures. While the 50-state average balance level of 6.2 percent for the 2012 fiscal year may seem like a significant cushion, two states—Alaska and Texas—represent nearly half of total balance levels. When those two states are removed, total balance levels drop to 3.7 percent of expenditures. Over the past 34 years, balances have averaged 5.8 percent of general fund expenditures.[34]

### Looking Ahead

Even with the recent improvement in the national economy, states are likely to continue to face tight fiscal conditions for a number of years to come. While revenues have increased for most states, overall state revenues remain nearly $21 billion, or 3.1 percent, less than prerecession levels. Typically, state tax revenues lag movements in the national economy and can remain weak for several years after a recession ends. For example, it took state revenues at least five years to fully recover after the past two recessions.[35] Similar to state revenues, state general fund spending remains more than $20 billion, or 3.1 percent, less than the 2008 fiscal year. This is even after factoring in the 2012 fiscal year's projected 2.9 percent growth, the second consecutive year that general fund spending has increased. States also continue to face increased spending demands in areas such as Medicaid and public assistance due to the lingering impacts of the recent economic downturn and are being asked to maintain adequate funding levels in areas such as education.

Looking forward, states are concerned that general fund revenues will not have fully recovered enough to meet increased spending demands, as well as to replace the recently expired federal Recovery Act funds. States also face uncertainties regarding national economic growth, health care reform and future federal funding levels, and also must deal with long-term liabilities including pensions and retiree health care costs. All these factors combined mean that states are likely to face austere budgets for at least the next several years and will have to continue to reassess the roles and responsibilities of state government by making difficult decisions regarding funding levels and priorities.

Although conditions have improved and states will continue to meet their obligations, they face a challenging fiscal road ahead.

## Notes

[1] National Association of State Budget Officers, *The Fiscal Survey of States*, (December 2011), 4–5.
[2] *The Fiscal Survey of States*, (December 2011), 2.
[3] *The Fiscal Survey of States*, (December 2011), 3.
[4] *The Fiscal Survey of States*, (December 2011), 8.
[5] The Fiscal Survey of States, (December 2011), 44.
[6] See note 2 above.
[7] See note 3 above.
[8] National Association of State Budget Officers, *Summary: Fall 2011 Fiscal Survey of States*, (November 2011), 1–4.
[9] *The Fiscal Survey of States*, (December 2010), 4.
[10] *The Fiscal Survey of States*, (December 2011), 4–5.
[11] *The Fiscal Survey of States*, (December 2011), 47.
[12] "All Sources" includes revenues from sales, personal income, corporate income, gaming taxes, and all other taxes and fees.
[13] *The Fiscal Survey of States*, (December 2011), 45.
[14] *The Fiscal Survey of States*, (December 2011), 5-6
[15] Nelson A. Rockefeller Institute of Government, *State Revenue Report*, (January 2012), 1.
[16] *Summary: Fall 2011 Fiscal Survey of States*, (November 2011), 2.
[17] *The Fiscal Survey of States*, (December 2011), 50.
[18] *The Fiscal Survey of States*, (December 2011), 49, 53.
[19] "All Other" spending in states includes the Children's Health Insurance Program (CHIP), institutional and community care for the mentally ill and developmentally disabled, public health programs, employer contributions to pensions and health benefits, economic development, environmental projects, state police, parks and recreation, housing, and general aid to local governments.
[20] National Association of State Budget Officers, *2010 State Expenditure Report,* (Fall 2011), 6.
[21] *2010 State Expenditure Report*, (Fall 2011), 9.

[22] *2010 State Expenditure Report*, (Fall 2011), 7.

[23] See note 21 above.

[24] See note 22 above.

[25] See note 21 above.

[26] See note 22 above.

[27] See note 14 above.

[28] See note 3 above.

[29] *The Fiscal Survey of States*, (December 2010), 3.

[30] *Summary: Fall 2011 Fiscal Survey of States*, (November 2011), 1.

[31] *The Fiscal Survey of States*, (December 2011), 10.

[32] See note 13 above.

[33] National Association of State Budget Officers, *Budget Processes in the States*, (Summer 2008), 67–69.

[34] *The Fiscal Survey of States*, (December 2011), 55–56.

[35] Nelson A. Rockefeller Institute of Government, *Fiscal Features: What Will Happen to State Budgets When the Money Runs Out?*, (February 2009), 2.

## About the Author

**Brian Sigritz** is the Director of State Fiscal Studies at the National Association of State Budget Officers (NASBO). He received his M.P.A. from the George Washington University and his B.A. from St. Bonaventure University. Prior to working at NASBO, Sigritz worked for the Ohio Senate and the Ohio House of Representatives.

## Table 7.1
## FISCAL 2010 STATE GENERAL FUND, ACTUAL, BY REGION
### (In millions of dollars)

| State | Beginning balance | Revenues | Adjustments | Total resources | Expenditures | Adjustments | Ending balance | Budget stabilization fund |
|---|---|---|---|---|---|---|---|---|
| U.S. totals* ................... | $10,181 | $609,870 | . . . | $638,354 | $623,394 | . . . | $8,014 | $21,034 |
| **Eastern Region** | | | | | | | | |
| Connecticut ................. | 0 | 17,689 | 0 | 17,689 | 17,208 | 0 | 481 | 0 |
| Delaware* ................... | 379 | 3,235 | 0 | 3,614 | 3,077 | 0 | 537 | 186 |
| Maine (a) ...................... | 26 | 2,693 | 202 | 2,921 | 2,849 | 71 | 0 | 0 |
| Maryland (b) ................ | 87 | 12,891 | 795 | 13,773 | 13,429 | 0 | 344 | 612 |
| Massachusetts (c)........ | 1,017 | 30,310 | 0 | 31,327 | 30,424 | 0 | 903 | 670 |
| New Hampshire ............ | 9 | 1,398 | 28 | 1,436 | 1,405 | -45 | 75 | 9 |
| New Jersey* (d) .......... | 614 | 28,144 | 526 | 29,284 | 28,480 | 0 | 804 | 0 |
| New York* (e)............. | 1,948 | 52,556 | 0 | 54,504 | 52,202 | 0 | 2,302 | 1,206 |
| Pennsylvania (f)........... | -2,030 | 26,523 | 2,854 | 27,346 | 27,641 | 0 | -294 | 1 |
| Rhode Island (g)......... | -61 | 3,017 | -74 | 2,881 | 2,864 | -1 | 18 | 112 |
| Vermont........................ | 0 | 1,038 | 52 | 1,090 | 1,088 | 2 | -0 | 57 |
| Regional totals............ | 1,988 | 179,494 | 4,381 | 185,864 | 180,665 | 29 | 5,171 | 2,854 |
| **Midwestern Region** | | | | | | | | |
| Illinois (h).................... | 2,094 | 25,254 | 5,261 | 32,609 | 25,165 | 6,991 | 453 | 0 |
| Indiana (i) ................... | 964 | 12,321 | 371 | 13,656 | 12,877 | -52 | 831 | 0 |
| Iowa (j) ........................ | 0 | 5,634 | 0 | 5,634 | 5,298 | 48 | 287 | 422 |
| Kansas ......................... | 50 | 5,191 | 0 | 5,241 | 5,268 | 0 | -27 | 0 |
| Michigan (k)................. | 177 | 6,506 | 1,209 | 7,892 | 7,705 | 0 | 187 | 2 |
| Minnesota (l) ............... | 447 | 14,620 | 0 | 15,067 | 14,627 | 0 | 440 | 0 |
| Nebraska (m) ............... | 424 | 3,207 | -21 | 3,610 | 3,313 | 0 | 297 | 467 |
| North Dakota (n)........ | 362 | 1,241 | 295 | 1,898 | 1,585 | 0 | 313 | 325 |
| Ohio.............................. | 735 | 24,950 | 0 | 25,685 | 25,175 | 0 | 510 | 0 |
| South Dakota (o)........ | 0 | 1,110 | 22 | 1,132 | 1,132 | 0 | 0 | 107 |
| Wisconsin (p) ............. | 90 | 12,132 | 742 | 12,963 | 12,824 | 68 | 71 | 0 |
| Regional totals............ | 5,342 | 112,165 | 7,879 | 125,386 | 114,969 | 7,055 | 3,362 | 1,323 |
| **Southern Region** | | | | | | | | |
| Alabama (q)................. | 105 | 6,484 | 162 | 6,751 | 7,457 | -778 | 72 | 0 |
| Arkansas...................... | 0 | 4,323 | 0 | 4,323 | 4,323 | 0 | 0 | 0 |
| Florida ......................... | 631 | 22,165 | 0 | 22,796 | 21,223 | 0 | 1,573 | 275 |
| Georgia* (r) ............... | 1,738 | 15,216 | 156 | 17,110 | 15,971 | 0 | 1,138 | 116 |
| Kentucky (s)............... | 40 | 8,331 | 234 | 8,604 | 8,452 | 72 | 80 | 0 |
| Louisiana (t)............... | 782 | 7,174 | 619 | 8,575 | 8,683 | 0 | -108 | 644 |
| Mississippi .................. | 8 | 4,491 | 0 | 4,499 | 4,320 | 175 | 5 | 257 |
| Missouri (u)................. | 311 | 6,774 | 670 | 7,755 | 7,570 | 0 | 185 | 260 |
| North Carolina............ | 92 | 18,657 | 0 | 18,750 | 18,513 | 0 | 237 | 150 |
| Oklahoma (v)............... | 26 | 5,166 | -30 | 5,163 | 5,119 | 2 | 42 | 373 |
| South Carolina*.......... | 121 | 5,242 | 0 | 5,363 | 5,117 | 0 | 245 | 111 |
| Tennessee (w) ............. | 77 | 9,732 | 195 | 10,004 | 9,451 | 314 | 240 | 453 |
| Texas........................... | 2,427 | 38,371 | 118 | 40,916 | 39,465 | -82 | 1,533 | 7,693 |
| Virginia........................ | 161 | 14,758 | 0 | 14,919 | 14,787 | 0 | 132 | 295 |
| West Virginia (x)......... | 481 | 3,758 | 1 | 4,240 | 3,677 | 11 | 552 | 556 |
| Regional totals............ | 7,000 | 170,642 | 2,123 | 179,766 | 174,126 | -287 | 5,926 | 11,183 |
| **Western Region** | | | | | | | | |
| Alaska (y)..................... | 0 | 5,617 | 18 | 5,635 | 6,603 | 461 | -1,429 | 10,364 |
| Arizona (z).................. | -481 | 6,460 | 1,866 | 7,846 | 7,852 | 0 | -6 | 0 |
| California* ................... | -5,375 | 87,041 | 228 | 81,894 | 87,237 | 0 | -5,342 | -6,113 |
| Colorado* (aa)............ | 443 | 6,410 | 0 | 6,853 | 6,716 | 0 | 137 | 133 |
| Hawaii ......................... | -37 | 4,852 | 0 | 4,816 | 4,838 | 0 | -22 | 63 |
| Idaho (bb) .................. | 0 | 2,265 | 71 | 2,336 | 2,507 | -171 | 0 | 31 |
| Montana (cc)............... | 393 | 1,627 | 6 | 2,026 | 1,716 | -1 | 311 | 0 |
| Nevada......................... | 212 | 3,007 | 143 | 3,362 | 3,212 | -163 | 314 | 0 |
| New Mexico* .............. | 479 | 4,799 | 653 | 5,930 | 5,358 | 0 | 572 | 278 |
| Oregon (dd) ............... | 0 | 5,982 | 0 | 5,982 | 6,371 | 0 | -390 | 216 |
| Utah (ee)..................... | 22 | 4,193 | 220 | 4,435 | 4,441 | 22 | -28 | 210 |
| Washington (ff)........... | 189 | 13,571 | 715 | 14,475 | 15,036 | 0 | -561 | 95 |
| Wyoming (gg) ............. | 5 | 1,745 | 0 | 1,750 | 1,750 | 0 | 0 | 398 |
| Regional totals............ | -4,150 | 147,568 | 3,920 | 147,339 | 153,635 | 148 | (6,445) | 5,674 |
| Regional totals without California.... | (1,225) | 60,527 | 3,692 | 65,445 | 66,398 | 148 | (1,102) | (439) |
| Puerto Rico (hh)......... | 0 | 7,670 | 2,500 | 10,170 | 10,170 | 0 | 0 | 0 |

See footnotes at end of table.

# FISCAL 2010 STATE GENERAL FUND, ACTUAL, BY REGION — Continued
## (In millions of dollars)

*Source:* National Association of State Budget Officers. *The Fiscal Survey of the States* (December 2011).

*Note:* NA Indicates data not available. *In these states, the ending balance includes the balance in the budget stabilization fund.

NA — Indicates data are not available.

... — Not applicable.

(a) Revenue & Expenditure adjustments reflect legislatively authorized transfers.

(b) Revenue adjustments reflect a $13.0 million reimbursement from the reserve for Sustainable Community Tax Credits, $6.0 million reimbursement from the reserve for Biotechnology Tax Credits, and transfers of $775.6 million from other special funds.

(c) Includes Budgeted Fund balances.

(d) Transfers from other funds and budget vs. GAAP adjustments.

(e) Total expenditures are not adjusted for the impact of delaying the end-of-year school aid payment ($2.06 billion) from March 2010 to the statutory deadline of June 1, 2010, which was done to carry forward the FY 2010 budget shortfall into FY 2011. The ending balance includes $1.2 billion in rainy day reserve funds, $96 million in a community projects fund, $73 million reserved for debt reduction and $21 million reserved for litigation risks. The ending balance also includes a reserve of $905 million for deferred payments, a result of deferring more payments than were needed to carry forward the FY 2010 budget shortfall, which was used when the deferred payments were made during the first quarter of FY 2011.

(f) Revenues include $755 million transferred from the Rainy Day fund. Revenue adjustments include a $5.0 million adjustment to the beginning balance, $150.4 million in prior year lapses, $1,776.7 million in Enhanced Federal Medical Assistance Percentage and $921.4 million in State Fiscal Stabilization Funds.

(g) Opening balance includes a deficit of $62.3 million and re-appropriations of $1.0 million from the prior year. Adjustments to revenues reflect a transfer to the Budget Stabilization Fund.

(h) Revenue adjustment accounted for by the sum of transfers in plus pension obligation note proceeds. Expenditure adjustment is accounted for by the sum of the statutory transfers out plus repayment of the pension obligation notes.

(i) Revenue Adjustment: Transfer from General Fund to Rainy Day Fund; Expenditure Adjustments: Local Option Income Tax Distributions; PTRF Adjust for Abstracts.

(j) Expenditure adjustments include $48.3 million which was credited from the ending balance of the General Fund to the Senior Living Trust Fund. This completes all funding of the Senior Living Trust Fund.

(k) Fiscal 2010 revenue adjustments include the impact of federal and state law changes ($279.3 million); revenue sharing law changes ($528.4 million); and deposits from state restricted revenues ($401.6 million).

(l) Ending balance includes cash flow account of $266 million and appropriations carried forward of $106.7 million.

(m) Revenue adjustments are transfers between the General Fund and other funds. Among others, this includes a $112 million transfer from the General Fund to the Property Tax Credit Cash Fund as well as a $105 million transfer to the General Fund from the Cash Reserve Fund (Rainy Day Fund).

(n) Revenue adjustments are a $295.0 million transfer from the permanent oil tax trust fund to the general fund.

(o) Adjustments in Revenues: $21.8 million was from one-time receipts.

(p) Revenue adjustments include Transfers in General Fund, $418.8 million; Other Revenue, $297.7 million; Tribal Gaming, $25.1 million. Expenditure adjustments include Designation for Continuing Balances, $78.5 million; and Unreserved Designated Balance, -$10.6 million.

(q) Revenue Adjustments include an increase for a transfer from the General Fund Rainy Day Account of $161.6 million. Expenditure adjustments include a reduction due to across the board percentage cuts of $695.8 million, and a reduction of $81.9 million for reversions and other adjustments.

(r) Agency surplus returned.

(s) Revenue includes $105.5 million in Tobacco Settlement funds. Adjustment for Revenues includes $66.2 million that represents appropriation balances carried over from the prior fiscal year, and $167.4 million from fund transfers into the General Fund. Adjustment to Expenditures represents appropriation balances forwarded to the next fiscal year.

(t) Actuals (FY 2009–2010) reflect the Legislative Auditors reviewed revenues and expenditures made per the fiscal status summary presented to the Joint Legislative Committee on the Budget (JLCB) on January 21, 2011, as required by Louisiana Revised Statue 39:75 A.(3)(a). Revenue — State General Fund (SGF) revenues estimated to be $7,173.7 million; Act 122 of 2009 allowed the use of $86.2 million of Budget Stabilization Fund (BSF); Act 51 of 2010 used $198.4 million of BSF; Act 20 used $782.3 million of the Fiscal Year 2007–2008 surplus; Act 226 of 2009 transferred $13.5 million from the various funds of SGF; Act 226 of 2009 transferred $13.5 million from the Rapid Response Fund, $75.6 million from the Insure Louisiana Program Fund, and $3.9 million from the Incentive Fund to the SGF; $42.8 million was carried forward from prior years SGF appropriations to FY 10–11; and Act 51 of 2010 appropriated $115 million from the Amnesty Fund.

(u) Revenue adjustments are transfers from other funds into the general revenue fund, including $370.7 million from the enhanced FMAP authorized in the American Recovery and Reinvestment Act of 2009.

(v) Revenue adjustment represents the difference in cash flow. $1.6 million expenditure adjustment is amount paid in interest on funds borrowed for cash management until action was taken by the legislature on budget shortfall.

(w) Adjustments (Revenues): 109.0 million transfer from debt service fund unexpended appropriations; $103.4 million transfer from Rainy Day Fund; -$17.3 million transfer to dedicated revenue reserves. Adjustments (Expenditures): $69.9 million transfer to capital outlay projects fund. $13.1 million transfer to state office buildings and support facilities fund; $230.8 million transfer to reserves for dedicated revenue appropriations. Ending Balance $239.4 million reserve for appropriations 2010–2011; $0.3 million undesignated balance.

(x) Fiscal Year 2010 Beginning balance includes $432.6 million in Reappropriations, Unappropriated Surplus Balance of $22.2 million, and FY 2009 13th month expenditures of $26.0 million. Expenditures include Regular, Surplus and Reappropriated funds and $26.0 million of 31 day prior year expenditures. Revenue adjustments are prior year redeposits. Expenditure adjustment represents the amount transferred to the Rainy Day Fund. The ending balance is mostly the historically carried forward reappropriation amounts that will remain and be reappropriated to the next fiscal year, the 13th month expenditures and unappropriated surplus balance.

(y) Revenue adjustments: $17.8 million reappropriation and carry forward. Expenditure adjustments: $401.6 million Constitutional Budget Reserve savings deposit plus net of ($1,057.4) million Public Education Fund draw and $1,117.0 Public Education Fund forward funding. Rainy Day = $9,166.1 million CBR + $1,197.5.

(z) Adjustments to revenue include fund transfers, county transfer, proceeds from asset sales lease back and lottery bond revenues.

(aa) Colorado's ending reserve statutory requirement per Section 24-75-2011, CRS is the rainy day fund balance.

(bb) In order to help balance the FY 2010 budget there was $71 million transferred from various dedicated funds to the General Fund. The Legislature also approved a General Fund reduction of $187.6 million that was distributed among all General Fund agencies.

(cc) Adjustments to Revenues and Expenditures reflect prior year revenue collected, prior year expenditures made, and other minor adjustments to tie to the CAFR.

(dd) Rainy Day Fund balance includes normal RDF (primarily General Fund) plus an Education Stability Fund (primarily Lottery Funds). Balances in RDF & ESF may include donations.

(ee) Includes transfers from previous year balance, to/from Rainy Day Fund, and special revenue funds.

(ff) Fund transfers between General Fund and other accounts, and balancing to the final audited ending balance.

(gg) WY budgets on a biennial basis. To arrive at annual figures assumptions and estimates were required.

(hh) The General Fund Budget included an allocation of $1.0 million to facilitate the orderly implementation of certain expense reduction measures adopted by the Government of Puerto Rico pursuant to Act 7 of March 8, 2009. This allocation covered the cost of transitioning public employees to non-government sectors by proving re-training vouchers, self employment opportunities, relocation and salary subsidies alternatives. On the other hand, the General Fund Budget also included an allocation from the Local Stabilization Fund of $1.5 billion to cover payroll and operating expenses that were expected to be reduced through fiscal year 2010, but whose savings will not be realized in such fiscal year. The Local Stabilization Fund is funded with proceeds from the bonds issued by the Sales Tax Financing Corporation.

## Table 7.2
## FISCAL 2011 STATE GENERAL FUND, PRELIMINARY ACTUAL, BY REGION
(In millions of dollars)

| State | Beginning balance | Revenues | Adjustments | Resources | Expenditures | Adjustments | Ending balance | Budget stabilization fund |
|---|---|---|---|---|---|---|---|---|
| U.S. totals ..................... | $8,334 | $649,047 | ... | $676,868 | $648,095 | ... | $18,925 | $24,154 |
| **Eastern Region** | | | | | | | | |
| Connecticut ................. | 0 | 18,083 | 0 | 18,083 | 17,845 | 0 | 238 | 0 |
| Delaware* ..................... | 537 | 3,531 | 0 | 4,069 | 3,271 | 0 | 798 | 186 |
| Maine (a)...................... | 7 | 2,896 | 86 | 2,990 | 2,873 | 98 | 19 | 72 |
| Maryland (b)................. | 344 | 13,537 | 347 | 14,228 | 13,238 | 0 | 990 | 624 |
| Massachusetts (c)........ | 903 | 33,075 | 0 | 33,978 | 32,078 | 0 | 1,901 | 1,379 |
| New Hampshire .......... | 75 | 1,384 | 4 | 1,462 | 1,302 | 125 | 36 | 9 |
| New Jersey* (d) .......... | 804 | 28,180 | 735 | 29,718 | 29,025 | 0 | 693 | 0 |
| New York* (e)............. | 2,302 | 54,447 | 0 | 56,749 | 55,373 | 0 | 1,376 | 1,206 |
| Pennsylvania (f).......... | -294 | 26,347 | 3,160 | 29,213 | 28,321 | -182 | 1,073 | 0 |
| Rhode Island (g)......... | 18 | 3,083 | -81 | 3,021 | 2,959 | -3 | 65 | 130 |
| Vermont (h) ................ | 0 | 1,157 | 71 | 1,228 | 1,162 | 66 | 0 | 54 |
| Regional totals............ | 4,696 | 185,720 | 4,332 | 194,739 | 181,406 | 104 | 7,189 | 3,660 |
| **Midwestern Region** | | | | | | | | |
| Illinois (i)...................... | 453 | 28,306 | 7,951 | 36,710 | 25,933 | 9,806 | 971 | 276 |
| Indiana (j) ................... | 831 | 13,384 | -54 | 14,161 | 13,050 | -12 | 1,124 | 57 |
| Iowa (k)....................... | 0 | 5,840 | -6 | 5,834 | 5,283 | 69 | 482 | 437 |
| Kansas ......................... | -27 | 5,790 | 0 | 5,763 | 5,727 | 0 | 36 | 0 |
| Michigan (l)................. | 187 | 7,248 | 1,455 | 8,891 | 8,630 | 0 | 260 | 2 |
| Minnesota (m) ............ | 440 | 15,826 | 0 | 16,265 | 15,540 | 0 | 725 | 9 |
| Nebraska (n) ............... | 297 | 3,494 | 33 | 3,824 | 3,322 | 0 | 502 | 313 |
| North Dakota.............. | 313 | 1,532 | 865 | 2,710 | 1,651 | 62 | 997 | 386 |
| Ohio............................ | 510 | 27,763 | 0 | 28,274 | 27,429 | 0 | 845 | 0 |
| South Dakota (o)........ | 0 | 1,163 | -15 | 1,148 | 1,148 | 0 | 0 | 107 |
| Wisconsin (p).............. | 26 | 12,912 | 642 | 13,580 | 13,565 | -70 | 86 | 0 |
| Regional totals............ | 3,030 | 123,258 | 10,871 | 137,160 | 121,278 | 9,855 | 6,028 | 1,587 |
| **Southern Region** | | | | | | | | |
| Alabama (q)................. | 72 | 6,909 | 0 | 6,981 | 7,356 | -414 | 38 | 0 |
| Arkansas...................... | 0 | 4,479 | 0 | 4,479 | 4,479 | 0 | 0 | 0 |
| Florida ......................... | 1,573 | 22,914 | 0 | 24,487 | 24,054 | 0 | 433 | 279 |
| Georgia* (r) ................ | 1,138 | 16,559 | 498 | 18,195 | 17,064 | 0 | 1,131 | 445 |
| Kentucky (s)................ | 80 | 8,859 | 197 | 9,136 | 8,789 | 57 | 290 | 0 |
| Louisiana* (t).............. | -108 | 7,770 | 106 | 7,768 | 7,731 | 50 | -13 | 647 |
| Mississippi (u)............. | 5 | 4,600 | 0 | 4,605 | 4,528 | 0 | 76 | 176 |
| Missouri (v)................. | 185 | 7,176 | 723 | 8,084 | 7,705 | 0 | 379 | 247 |
| North Carolina............ | 237 | 19,157 | 0 | 19,394 | 18,503 | 307 | 584 | 296 |
| Oklahoma (w)............. | 42 | 5,750 | -33 | 5,759 | 5,417 | 249 | 93 | 249 |
| South Carolina*......... | 246 | 5,633 | 0 | 5,879 | 5,167 | 0 | 712 | 0 |
| Tennessee (x) .............. | 240 | 10,519 | 431 | 11,189 | 10,508 | 310 | 372 | 284 |
| Texas........................... | 1,533 | 40,515 | -407 | 41,641 | 41,149 | -608 | 1,100 | 5,041 |
| Virginia........................ | 161 | 14,758 | 0 | 14,919 | 14,787 | 0 | 132 | 295 |
| West Virginia (y)........ | 552 | 4,064 | 0 | 4,616 | 3,772 | 51 | 793 | 659 |
| Regional totals............ | 5,956 | 179,662 | 1,515 | 177,610 | 187,132 | 2 | 6,120 | 8,618 |
| **Western Region** | | | | | | | | |
| Alaska (z)..................... | 0 | 5,307 | 0 | 5,307 | 6,075 | 17 | -785 | 11,065 |
| Arizona (aa)................. | -6 | 7,250 | 1,131 | 8,376 | 8,372 | 0 | 3 | 0 |
| California* ................... | -5,343 | 94,781 | 574 | 90,012 | 91,480 | -262 | -1,206 | -1,976 |
| Colorado* (bb) ........... | 137 | 7,235 | 0 | 7,373 | 6,921 | 0 | 451 | 157 |
| Hawaii ......................... | -22 | 5,117 | 0 | 5,095 | 4,969 | 0 | 126 | 10 |
| Idaho* (cc) .................. | 0 | 2,445 | 74 | 2,519 | 2,384 | 66 | 69 | 0 |
| Montana (dd).............. | 311 | 1,783 | -1 | 2,092 | 1,747 | 5 | 340 | 0 |
| Nevada........................ | 314 | 3,186 | 110 | 3,609 | 3,337 | 47 | 225 | 0 |
| New Mexico* .............. | 278 | 5,164 | 38 | 5,480 | 5,203 | 0 | 277 | 235 |
| Oregon........................ | -390 | 6,532 | 0 | 6,142 | 6,107 | 0 | 35 | 16 |
| Utah (ee)..................... | -28 | 4,562 | 190 | 4,724 | 4,710 | 14 | 0 | 204 |
| Washington (ff)........... | -561 | 14,648 | 652 | 14,739 | 14,823 | 0 | -84 | 0 |
| Wyoming (gg) ............. | 0 | 1,567 | 0 | 1,567 | 1,562 | 0 | 5 | 572 |
| Regional totals............ | -5,310 | 159,577 | 2,768 | 157,035 | 157,690 | -113 | -544 | 10,283 |
| Regional totals without California.... | -33 | -33,632 | 2,827 | -24,329 | -26,877 | -9 | -376 | 11,532 |
| Puerto Rico (hh).......... | 0 | 8,134 | 1,016 | 9,150 | 9,150 | 0 | 0 | 0 |

See footnotes at end of table.

# FISCAL 2011 STATE GENERAL FUND, PRELIMINARY ACTUAL, BY REGION — Continued
## (In millions of dollars)

*Source:* National Association of State Budget Officers. *The Fiscal Survey of the States* (December 2011).

*In these states, the ending balance includes the balance in the budget stabilization fund.

... — Not applicable.

(a) Revenue & Expenditure adjustments reflect legislatively authorized transfers. Beginning balance differs from FY 10 ending balance due to Controller's year-end adjustments.

(b) Revenue adjustments reflect a $5.2 million reimbursement from the reserve for Sustainable Community Tax Credits, $8 million reimbursement from the reserve for Biotechnology Tax Credits, and transfers of $333.9 million from other special funds.

(c) Includes Budgeted Fund balances.

(d) Balances targeted to be lapsed.

(e) Total expenditures are adjusted to reflect the impact of delaying the end-of-year school aid payment ($2.06 billion) from March 2010 to the statutory deadline of June 1, 2010, which was done to carry forward the FY 2010 budget shortfall FY 2011. The ending balance includes $1.2 billion in rainy day reserve funds, $136 million in a community projects fund, $13 million reserved for debt reduction and $21 million reserved for litigation risks.

(f) Revenue adjustments include a $0.25 million adjustment to the beginning balance, $93.7 million in prior year lapsed, $1,756.5 million in Enhanced Federal Medical Assistance Percentage, $921.4 million in federal State Fiscal Stabilization Funds and $387.8 million in federal Education Jobs Funds. Expenditure adjustment reflects $181.5 million in current year lapses. The year-end transfer to the Rainy Day Fund (25 percent of the ending balance) was suspended for FY 2011.

(g) Opening balance includes a surplus of $17.7 million and re-appropriations of $3.4 million from the prior year and prior period adjustments. Adjustments to revenues reflect a transfer to the Budget Stabilization Fund and the adjustments to expenditures are the appropriations from FY 2010.

(h) Transfer to Human Services Caseload Reserve and other transactions.

(i) Revenue adjustment accounted for by the sum of inter-fund borrowing, short term borrowing, pension obligation note proceeds, tobacco securitization proceeds and statutory transfers in. Expense adjustment is accounted for by the sum of repayment of our short term borrowing, FY 2011 pension payment and statutory transfers out.

(j) Revenue adjustments: Transfer from Rainy Day Fund to General Fund; Expenditure adjustments: Local Option Income Tax Distributions, PTRF Adjust for Abstracts.

(k) Revenues are based upon the March 2011 REC, adjustments to revenues include $15.4 million increase due to the passage of the Tax Relief Act of 2010, and also due to tax legislation passed during the 2011 Legislative Session. Adjustments to expenditures are due to legislative changes passed during the 2011 Legislative Session that changed appropriation levels.

(l) Fiscal 2011 revenue adjustments include the impact of federal and state law changes ($275.8 million); revenue sharing law changes ($514.9 million); and deposits from state restricted revenues ($664.3 million).

(m) Ending balance includes cash flow account of $266 million.

(n) Revenue adjustments are transfers between the General Fund and other funds. Among others, this includes a $112 million transfer from the General Fund to the Property Tax Credit Cash Fund as well as a $154 million transfer to the General Fund from the Cash Reserve Fund (Rainy Day Fund).

(o) Adjustments in Revenues: $9.9 million addition to revenue in from one-time receipts; $26.1 million decrease to revenue in a one-time refund of taxes.

(p) Revenue adjustments include Transfers out of General Fund, -$148 million; Other Revenue, $632.4 million; Tribal Gaming, $24.7 million. Expenditures adjustments include Designation for Continuing Balances, $8.2 million; and Unreserved Designated Balance, -$78.5 million.

(q) Expenditure Adjustments are a reduction due to across the board percentage cuts.

(r) Agency surplus returned.

(s) Revenue includes $99.8 million in Tobacco Settlement funds. Adjustment for Revenues includes $72.0 million that represents appropriation balances carried over from the prior fiscal year, and $125.1 million from fund transfers into the General Fund. Adjustment to Expenditures represents appropriation balances forwarded to the next fiscal year and budgeted balances to be expended in the next fiscal year.

(t) Actuals (FY 10–11) reflect revenues and expenditures on the fiscal status report presented to the JLCB on October 28, 2011. Per Revised Statute 39:75A.(3)(a), the actual amounts will not be finalized until the first JLCB after the publication of the Comprehensive Annual Financial Report. Revenues—prior year deficit, $107.97 million, which was solved by Executive Revenues—prior year deficit, and $107.97 million, which was solved by Executive Order reductions during FY 2010–2011; State General Fund revenues were $7,770.0 million; adjusted revenues include refund of debt service expenditure of $3.7 million; Act 633 of 2010 and Acts 52 and 378 of 2011 transferred $55.87 million to the SGF; $46.4 million was carried forward from prior years to FY 2010–2011. Adjusted Expenditures—Fiscal Year 2010–2011 carry forward expenditure of Interim Emergency Board (IEB), $1.1 million; carry forward of operating expenditures of $16.6 million; and carry forward of Capital Outlay expenditures, $32.6 million.

(u) General Fund Ending Balance and Rainy Day Fund are before splits. Rainy Day Fund Balance not inclusive of $15 million for Ayers court settlement.

(v) Revenue adjustments include transfers from other funds into the general revenue fund, including $562.4 million from enhanced FMAP authorized in the American Recovery and Reinvestment Act of 2009.

(w) Revenue adjustment represents the difference in cash flow. $249.2 million expenditure adjustment is amount deposited into the Rainy Day fund from surplus revenues.

(x) Adjustments (Revenues): $92.9 million transfer from debt service fund unexpended appropriations; $181.4 million transfer from TennCare Reserve; -$28.1 million transfer to TennCare Trust Fund; $169.5 million transfer from Rainy Day Fund; $15.0 million transfer from reserves for dedicated revenue appropriations. Adjustments (Expenditures): $291.7 million transfer to capital outlay projects fund; 13.1 million transfer to state office buildings and support facilities fund; $4.7 million transfer to reserves for dedicated revenue appropriations. Ending Balance $371.3 million reserve for appropriations 2011–2012; $0.2 million undesignated balance.

(y) Fiscal Year 2011 Beginning balance includes $418.7 million in Reappropriations, Unappropriated Surplus Balance of $102.6 million, and FY 2010 13th month expenditures of $30.6 million. Expenditures include Regular, Surplus and Reappropriated funds and $30.6 million of 31 day prior year expenditures. Revenue adjustments are prior year redeposits. Expenditure adjustment represents the amount transferred to the Rainy Day Fund. The ending balance is mostly the historically carried forward reappropriation amounts that will remain and be reappropriated to the next fiscal year, the 13th month expenditures and unappropriated surplus balance.

(z) Revenue adjustments: $21.4 million reappropriation and carry forward. Expenditure adjustments: Net of ($1,114.3) million Public Education Fund draw and $1,131.0 million Public Education Fund forward funding. Rainy Day = $10,016.8 million CBR + $1,048.6 million SBR.

(aa) Adjustments to revenue include fund transfers, VLT shift, county transfer, and temporary 1 percent sales tax increase.

(bb) Colorado's ending reserve statutory requirement per Section 24-75-201.1, CRS is the rainy day fund balance. Note that FY 2010–2011 contains a $294.4 million transfer (per the June 2011 OSPB forecast) from the GF to the State Education Fund ($226.9 million) and public School Fund ($67.5 million) per SB11-230 (source: footnote E and F to Table 1 on page 7 in the OSPB September 2011 forecast).

(cc) The remainder of the rainy day fund balances were transferred to the General Fund for FY 2011; this included $30.1 million from the Budget Stabilization Fund and $48.8 million from the Economic Recovery Reserve Fund. There was an additional $1.5 million transferred to the General Fund from various other dedicated accounts and $1 million was transferred to the Disaster Recovery Fund/Military Division.

## FISCAL 2011 STATE GENERAL FUND, PRELIMINARY ACTUAL, BY REGION — Continued
### (In millions of dollars)

(dd) Adjustments to Revenues and Expenditures reflect prior year revenue collected, prior year expenditures made, and other minor adjustments to tie to the preliminary unaudited ending fund balance for FY 2011.

(ee) Includes transfers from previous year balance, to/from Rainy Day Fund, and special revenue funds.

(ff) Fund transfers between General Fund and other accounts.

(gg) WY budgets on a biennial basis. To arrive at annual figures assumptions and estimates were required.

(hh) Included $1.0 billion from the Local Stabilization Fund to cover operational expenses expected to be reduced through the fiscal year 2011.

## Table 7.3
## FISCAL 2012 STATE GENERAL FUND, APPROPRIATED, BY REGION
### (In millions of dollars)

| State or other jurisdiction | Beginning balance | Revenues | Adjustments | Resources | Expenditures | Adjustments | Ending balance | Budget stabilization fund |
|---|---|---|---|---|---|---|---|---|
| **U.S. totals** ..................... | $18,010 | $659,445 | . . . | $687,817 | $666,572 | . . . | $15,624 | $30,175 |
| **Eastern Region** | | | | | | | | |
| Connecticut ................. | 0 | 18,789 | 0 | 18,789 | 18,708 | 0 | 81 | 0 |
| Delaware* ..................... | 798 | 3,423 | 0 | 4,221 | 3,575 | 0 | 646 | 186 |
| Maine (a) ..................... | 19 | 2,946 | 79 | 3,044 | 3,039 | 5 | 1 | 46 |
| Maryland (b) ............... | 990 | 13,910 | 249 | 15,149 | 14,749 | 0 | 400 | 682 |
| Massachusetts ............. | 1,901 | 32,253 | 0 | 34,154 | 32,533 | 0 | 1,622 | 1,275 |
| New Hampshire .......... | 9 | 1,381 | -11 | 1,379 | 1,248 | 137 | -5 | 9 |
| New Jersey* ................. | 693 | 29,339 | 0 | 30,032 | 29,393 | 0 | 639 | 0 |
| New York*(c) .............. | 1,376 | 57,293 | 0 | 58,669 | 56,932 | 0 | 1,737 | 1,306 |
| Pennsylvania (d) ......... | 1,073 | 26,571 | 63 | 27,706 | 27,149 | 140 | 418 | 140 |
| Rhode Island (e) ......... | 65 | 3,246 | -91 | 3,220 | 3,170 | -5 | 55 | 149 |
| Vermont (f) ................. | 0 | 1,191 | 30 | 1,221 | 1,236 | -15 | 0 | 58 |
| Regional totals ............ | 6,924 | 190,342 | 319 | 197,584 | 191,732 | 262 | 5,594 | 3,851 |
| **Midwestern Region** | | | | | | | | |
| Illinois (g) ................... | 971 | 31,589 | 1,866 | 34,151 | 29,188 | 4,561 | 402 | 276 |
| Indiana ........................ | 1,124 | 13,889 | 0 | 15,014 | 13,855 | 0 | 1,159 | 61 |
| Iowa (h) ....................... | 0 | 6,355 | -77 | 6,277 | 5,998 | 0 | 279 | 596 |
| Kansas ......................... | 36 | 6,045 | 0 | 6,080 | 6,073 | 0 | 8 | 0 |
| Michigan (i) ................. | 260 | 7,550 | 900 | 8,709 | 8,271 | 427 | 11 | 258 |
| Minnesota (j) .............. | 725 | 16,481 | 0 | 17,206 | 16,733 | 0 | 473 | 0 |
| Nebraska (k) ............... | 502 | 3,591 | -253 | 3,841 | 3,468 | 240 | 132 | 421 |
| North Dakota .............. | 997 | 1,442 | 495 | 2,933 | 1,993 | 0 | 941 | 386 |
| Ohio ............................ | 845 | 27,173 | 0 | 28,018 | 27,863 | 0 | 155 | 247 |
| South Dakota (l) ......... | 0 | 1,165 | -13 | 1,153 | 1,150 | 0 | 3 | 107 |
| Wisconsin (m) ............. | 86 | 13,297 | 674 | 14,058 | 14,166 | -182 | 73 | 0 |
| Regional totals ............ | 5,546 | 128,577 | 3,592 | 137,440 | 128,758 | 5,046 | 3,636 | 2,352 |
| **Southern Region** | | | | | | | | |
| Alabama (n) ................. | 38 | 7,064 | 293 | 7,395 | 7,357 | 0 | 38 | 0 |
| Arkansas ...................... | 0 | 4,479 | 0 | 4,479 | 4,479 | 0 | 0 | 0 |
| Florida ......................... | 433 | 24,309 | 0 | 24,742 | 23,384 | 0 | 1,358 | 495 |
| Georgia* ...................... | 1,131 | 17,208 | 0 | 18,338 | 17,208 | 0 | 1,131 | 445 |
| Kentucky (o) ............... | 133 | 8,974 | 153 | 9,260 | 9,230 | 30 | 0 | 122 |
| Louisiana (p) ............... | 0 | 8,264 | 0 | 8,264 | 8,261 | 0 | 3 | 647 |
| Mississippi ................... | 7 | 4,622 | 0 | 4,628 | 4,628 | 0 | 0 | 87 |
| Missouri (q) ................. | 379 | 7,295 | 396 | 8,071 | 7,971 | 0 | 100 | 250 |
| North Carolina ............ | 583 | 19,175 | 124 | 19,882 | 19,683 | 124 | 75 | 296 |
| Oklahoma .................... | 93 | 5,846 | 0 | 5,938 | 5,578 | 0 | 361 | 0 |
| South Carolina* (r) ..... | 712 | 5,489 | 0 | 6,201 | 5,677 | 108 | 416 | 288 |
| Tennessee (s) ............... | 372 | 10,979 | -27 | 11,323 | 11,238 | 73 | 12 | 311 |
| Texas ............................ | 1,100 | 39,508 | 4,331 | 44,939 | 44,153 | 0 | 786 | 5,882 |
| Virginia ........................ | 265 | 16,294 | 0 | 16,559 | 16,557 | 0 | 2 | 304 |
| West Virginia (t) .......... | 793 | 4,016 | 0 | 4,809 | 4,080 | 0 | 729 | 820 |
| Regional totals ............ | 6,039 | 183,522 | 5,270 | 194,828 | 189,484 | 335 | 5,011 | 9,947 |
| **Western Region** | | | | | | | | |
| Alaska (u) .................... | 0 | 7,300 | 0 | 7,300 | 7,371 | -33 | -38 | 11,981 |
| Arizona (v) ................... | -332 | 7,375 | 1,288 | 8,331 | 8,318 | 0 | 14 | 0 |
| California .................... | -1,206 | 88,456 | 0 | 87,250 | 85,937 | 0 | 1,313 | 543 |
| Colorado*(w) .............. | 157 | 7,268 | 0 | 7,424 | 7,163 | 0 | 261 | 261 |
| Hawaii ......................... | 126 | 5,518 | 0 | 5,644 | 5,599 | 0 | 45 | 6 |
| Idaho (x) ...................... | 0 | 2,494 | 38 | 2,532 | 2,529 | 0 | 3 | 0 |
| Montana ...................... | 340 | 1,786 | 0 | 2,125 | 1,824 | 0 | 302 | 0 |
| Nevada ......................... | 225 | 2,983 | 60 | 3,268 | 3,105 | 0 | 163 | 0 |
| New Mexico* .............. | 235 | 5,431 | 0 | 5,667 | 5,431 | 0 | 235 | 263 |
| Oregon (y) ................... | 35 | 6,704 | -35 | 6,704 | 7,078 | 0 | -375 | 61 |
| Utah (z) ....................... | 0 | 4,677 | 123 | 4,800 | 4,781 | 12 | 7 | 204 |
| Washington (aa) ........... | -84 | 15,324 | -16 | 15,224 | 15,776 | 0 | -542 | 136 |
| Wyoming (bb) ............. | 5 | 1,567 | 0 | 1,572 | 1,572 | 0 | 0 | 571 |
| Regional totals ............ | -499 | 156,883 | 1,458 | 157,841 | 156,484 | -21 | 1,388 | 14,026 |
| Regional totals without California .... | -707 | 68,427 | . . . | 70,591 | 70,547 | . . . | 75 | 13,483 |
| Puerto Rico (cc) .......... | 0 | 8,650 | 610 | 9,260 | 9,260 | 0 | . . . | 0 |

See footnotes at end of table.

# FISCAL 2012 STATE GENERAL FUND, APPROPRIATED, BY REGION — Continued
## (In millions of dollars)

*Source:* National Association of State Budget Officers. *The Fiscal Survey of the States* (December 2011).

Key:

*In these states, the ending balance includes the balance in the budget stabilization fund.

NA — Indicates data are not available.

... — Not applicable.

(a) Revenue & Expenditure adjustments reflect legislatively authorized transfers.

(b) Revenue adjustments reflect a $13.3 million reimbursement from the reserve for Sustainable Community Tax Credits, $8 million reimbursement from the reserve for Biotechnology Tax Credits, and transfers of $227.7 million from other special funds.

(c) The ending balance includes $1.3 billion in rainy day reserve funds, $346 reserved to cover costs of potential retroactive labor settlements with certain unions, $51 million in a community projects fund, $13 million reserved for debt reduction and $21 million reserved for litigation risks.

(d) Revenue adjustments include $62.7 million in prior year lapses. Expenditure adjustment reflects a transfer of $139.5 million (25 percent of ending balance) to the Rainy Day Fund.

(e) Opening balance includes a surplus of $60.8 million and re-appropriations of $4.5 million from the prior year. Adjustments to revenues reflect a transfer to the Budget Stabilization Fund and the adjustments to expenditures are the appropriations from FY 2011.

(f) Transfer from Human Services Caseload Reserve and other transactions.

(g) Revenue adjustment accounted for by statutory transfers in. Expenditure adjustment is accounted for by statutory transfers out.

(h) Revenues are based upon the March 2011 REC, adjustments to revenues include $119.3 million increase due to the passage of the Tax Relief Act of 2010, and also to legislation adjusting revenues passed during the 2011 Legislative Session. Expenditures are based upon appropriations passed during the 2011 Legislative Session.

(i) FY 2012 revenue adjustments include the impact of federal and state law changes (-$288.3 million); revenue sharing law changes ($477.8 million); deposits from state restricted revenues ($622.5 million); sale of properties ($6.5 million); and deposits from state restricted revenues ($558.8 million). Also, the fiscal 2012 enacted expenditures include $427.4 million of one-time spending financed from one-time revenues.

(j) Ending balance includes cash flow account of $95 million.

(k) Revenue adjustments are transfers between the General Fund and other funds. Among others, this includes a $110 million transfer from the General Fund to the Property Tax Credit Cash Fund as well as a $37 million transfer to the General Fund from the Cash Reserve Fund (Rainy Day Fund). Revenue adjustments also include a $25 million transfer from the General Fund for the University of Nebraska Innovation Campus to jump-start significant new investment in research infrastructure. Expenditure adjustments are appropriations ($235.3 million) of the unexpected balance of appropriations from the prior fiscal year and a small amount ($5 million) reserved for supplemental/deficit appropriations).

(l) Adjustments in Revenues: $1.0 million addition to revenue is from one-time receipts; $13.6 million decrease to revenue is a budgeted one-time refund of taxes.

(m) Revenue adjustments include Other Revenue, $647.9 million; Tribal Gaming, $26.5 million. Expenditure adjustments include Compensation Reserve, $28.8 million; Transfers to other funds, $27.5 million; Other legislation, $65.0 million; and Lapses, -$303.0 million.

(n) Revenue Adjustments include one-time revenues of $293.1 million.

(o) Revenue includes $102.7 million in Tobacco Settlement funds. Adjustment for Revenues includes $29.8 million that represents appropriation balances carried over from the prior fiscal year, and $122.7 million from fund transfers into the General Fund. Adjustment to Expenditures represents appropriation balances forwarded and to the next fiscal year and budgeted balances to be expended in the next fiscal year.

(p) The recommended Executive Budget for FY 2011–2012 reflects the Official Revenue Forecast from June 21, 2010, meeting of the Revenue Estimating Conference for State General Fund.

(q) Revenue adjustments include transfers from other funds into the general revenue fund, including $68 million from enhanced FMAP authorized in the American Recovery and Reinvestment Act of 2009 and $209.3 million from enhanced FMAP authorized in the Education Jobs and Medicaid Assistance Act.

(r) Rainy day fund includes general fund and capital reserves. Expenditure Adjustment includes FY 2010–2011 Capital Reserve Appropriations transferred to State agencies for expenditure.

(s) Adjustments (Revenues): -$27.4 million transfer to Rainy Day Fund. Adjustments (Expenditures): $55.4 million transfer to capital outlay projects fund; $13.1 million transfer to state office buildings and support facilities fund; $4.6 million transfer to reserves for dedicated revenue appropriations. Ending Balance: $11.1 million reserve for capital outlay 2012–2013. $0.5 million undesignated balance.

(t) Fiscal Year 2012, Beginning balance includes $425.6 million in Reappropriations, Unappropriated Surplus Balance of $338.8 million, and FY 2011 13 month expenditures of $28.6M. Revenues are FY 12's Official General Revenue Estimate. Expenditures include FY 12 Regular General Revenue and FY 12 Surplus Appropriations.

(u) Revenue adjustments: none. Expenditure adjustments: Net of ($1,127.3) million Public Education Fund draw and $1,094.0 million Public Education Fund forward funding. Rainy Day = $10,589.0 million CBR + $1,392.4 million SBR.

(v) Adjustments to revenue include fund transfers, VLT shift, county transfer, temporary 1 percent sales tax increase, and revenue from the tax recovery program. At the time FY 12 budget was enacted, the beginning balance (i.e. FY 2011 ending balance) was estimated to be -$332 million. Thanks to much stronger-than-expected revenue performance, FY 2011 ended with a positive balance.

(w) Colorado's ending reserve statutory requirement per Section 24-75-2011, CRS is the rainy day fund balance. Current forecast shows FY 2011–2012 slightly below the required ending balance (GF reserve) of 4 percent (by $18.3 million GF). See Table 1 line 21 in the FY 11–12 column, of the September 2011 OSPB forecast.

(x) Transfers for FY 2012 included $38 million from various dedicated funds; house concurrent resolution 25 gave the Governor the authority to delay the implementation of the next phase of the Grocery Tax Credit ($15 million); and it was estimated that there would be an additional $19.7 million in revenue from the Tax Compliance Initiative. The Revenue estimate was also reduced by $91.5 million to set the budgets for FY 2012.

(y) Revenue adjustment transfers prior biennium ending GF balance to Rainy Day Fund (which can be up to 1 percent of total budgeted appropriation). Oregon budgets on a biennial basis. The constitution requires the state to be balanced at the end of the first fiscal year does not necessarily translate into a budget gap.

(z) Includes transfers from previous year balance and special revenue funds.

(aa) Fund transfers from previous year balance and special revenue funds.

(bb) WY budgets on a biennial basis. To arrive at annual figures assumptions and estimates were required.

(cc) Includes $610 million from the Local Stabilization Fund to cover operational expenses.

## Table 7.4
## FISCAL 2011 STATE TAX COLLECTIONS COMPARED WITH PROJECTIONS
## USED IN ADOPTING FISCAL 2011 BUDGETS, BY REGION
(In millions of dollars)

| State or other jurisdiction | Sales tax Original estimate | Sales tax Current estimate | Personal income tax Original estimate | Personal income tax Current estimate | Corporate income tax Original estimate | Corporate income tax Current estimate | Revenue collection (a) |
|---|---|---|---|---|---|---|---|
| U.S. totals ..................... | $209,057 | $207,883 | $247,956 | $259,947 | $42,919 | $43,068 | — |
| **Eastern Region** | | | | | | | |
| Connecticut................. | 3,165 | 3,342 | 6,683 | 7,220 | 663 | 784 | H |
| Delaware ..................... | NA | NA | 849 | 997 | 79 | 168 | H |
| Maine.......................... | 972 | 976 | 1,393 | 1,415 | 193 | 209 | H |
| Maryland ..................... | 3,667 | 3,656 | 6,292 | 6,643 | 514 | 571 | H |
| Massachusetts ............. | 4,897 | 4,905 | 10,704 | 11,576 | 1,397 | 1,951 | H |
| New Hampshire .......... | NA | NA | NA | NA | 261 | 248 | L |
| New Jersey ................. | 8,353 | 8,236 | 9,855 | 10,536 | 2,455 | 2,382 | T |
| New York..................... | 10,775 | 10,782 | 36,897 | 36,210 | 5,714 | 5,279 | H |
| Pennsylvania ............... | 8,337 | 8,590 | 10,125 | 10,436 | 1,847 | 2,132 | H |
| Rhode Island.............. | 787 | 813 | 938 | 1,021 | 119 | 85 | L |
| Vermont....................... | 321 | 326 | 527 | 553 | 66 | 90 | H |
| Regional totals.......... | 41,274 | 41,274 | 84,263 | 86,607 | 13,308 | 13,899 | — |
| **Midwestern Region** | | | | | | | |
| Illinois.......................... | 6,385 | 6,833 | 9,625 | 12,261 | 1,900 | 1,983 | T |
| Indiana......................... | 6,438 | 6,218 | 4,547 | 4,586 | 819 | 705 | H |
| Iowa ............................ | 2,267 | 2,395 | 3,202 | 3,435 | 369 | 386 | T |
| Kansas ........................ | 2,273 | 2,253 | 2,595 | 2,710 | 231 | 225 | H |
| Michigan...................... | 6,261 | 6,499 | 5,538 | 6,222 | 2,191 | 2,060 | H |
| Minnesota.................... | 4,492 | 4,403 | 7,342 | 7,529 | 799 | 925 | H |
| Nebraska ..................... | 1,365 | 1,373 | 1,630 | 1,735 | 185 | 155 | H |
| North Dakota.............. | 599 | 782 | 334 | 428 | 119 | 147 | H |
| Ohio............................. | 7,267 | 7,578 | 7,568 | 8,120 | 132 | 237 | H |
| South Dakota.............. | 671 | 710 | NA | NA | NA | NA | H |
| Wisconsin ................... | 4,321 | 4,109 | 6,432 | 6,701 | 808 | 853 | T |
| Regional totals............ | 42,339 | 43,153 | 48,813 | 53,727 | 7,553 | 7,676 | — |
| **Southern Region** | | | | | | | |
| Alabama ...................... | 1,887 | 1,920 | 2,553 | 2,794 | 414 | 333 | L |
| Arkansas...................... | 2,087 | 2,056 | 2,203 | 2,270 | 344 | 351 | T |
| Florida ........................ | 16,824 | 16,638 | NA | NA | 2,180 | 1,875 | L |
| Georgia........................ | 5,254 | 5,098 | 7,282 | 7,659 | 602 | 670 | H |
| Kentucky ..................... | 2,919 | 2,896 | 3,300 | 3,418 | 235 | 301 | H |
| Louisiana..................... | 2,402 | 2,627 | 2,466 | 2,449 | 372 | 283 | L |
| Mississippi ................... | 1,765 | 1,791 | 1,353 | 1,383 | 393 | 448 | H |
| Missouri....................... | 1,746 | 1,760 | 4,522 | 4,640 | 310 | 386 | H |
| North Carolina............. | 5,691 | 5,872 | 9,543 | 9,735 | 1,018 | 1,014 | L |
| Oklahoma.................... | 1,584 | 1,668 | 1,703 | 1,832 | 172 | 274 | H |
| South Carolina............. | 2,137 | 2,245 | 2,046 | 2,396 | 120 | 183 | H |
| Tennessee ................... | 6,249 | 6,475 | 186 | 189 | 1,476 | 1,518 | H |
| Texas .......................... | 22,500 | 20,600 | NA | NA | NA | NA | L |
| Virginia........................ | 2,881 | 2,969 | 9,588 | 9,746 | 793 | 767 | T |
| West Virginia............... | 1,174 | 1,196 | 1,586 | 1,689 | 214 | 307 | H |
| Regional totals............ | 77,100 | 75,811 | 48,331 | 50,200 | 8,643 | 8,710 | — |
| **Western Region** | | | | | | | |
| Alaska.......................... | NA | NA | NA | NA | 669 | 615 | H |
| Arizona........................ | 3,602 | 3,467 | 2,471 | 2,864 | 446 | 560 | H |
| California (b)................ | 27,044 | 27,140 | 47,127 | 50,027 | 10,897 | 9,963 | H |
| Colorado (c)................ | 1,933 | 2,044 | 4,604 | 4,496 | 368 | 394 | T |
| Hawaii ......................... | 2,496 | 2,496 | 1,349 | 1,231 | 37 | 51 | H |
| Idaho........................... | 989 | 972 | 1,171 | 1,153 | 133 | 169 | H |
| Montana ...................... | 61 | 65 | 762 | 816 | 97 | 119 | H |
| Nevada......................... | 849 | 815 | NA | NA | NA | NA | T |
| New Mexico ................. | 1,740 | 1,797 | 1,055 | 1,055 | 220 | 180 | H |
| Oregon......................... | NA | NA | 5,781 | 5,524 | 331 | 469 | L |
| Utah............................. | 1,430 | 1,556 | 2,229 | 2,248 | 217 | 267 | T |
| Washington.................. | 7,768 | 6,501 | NA | NA | NA | NA | L |
| Wyoming ..................... | 433 | 439 | NA | NA | NA | NA | H |
| Regional totals............ | 48,345 | 47,292 | 66,549 | 69,414 | 13,415 | 12,787 | — |
| Regional totals without California.... | 21,301 | 20,152 | 19,422 | 19,387 | 2,518 | 2,824 | — |
| Puerto Rico ................. | 604 | 555 | 2,812 | 2,348 | 1,667 | 1,566 | T |

See footnotes at end of table.

## FISCAL 2011 STATE TAX COLLECTIONS COMPARED WITH PROJECTIONS USED IN ADOPTING FISCAL 2011 BUDGETS, BY REGION—Continued
### (In millions of dollars)

*Source:* National Association of State Budget Officers. *The Fiscal Survey of the States* (December 2011).

*Note:* Unless otherwise noted, original estimates reflect the figures used when the fiscal 2011 budget was adopted, and current estimates reflect preliminary actual tax collections.

*Key:*

H — Revenues higher than estimates.

L — Revenues lower than estimates.

T — Revenues on target.

NA — Indicates data are not available because, in most cases, these states do not have that type of tax.

(a) Refers to whether actual fiscal 2011 collections of Sales, Personal Income and Corporate taxes were higher than, lower than, or on target with original estimates.

(b) Compared to projection at 2010–2012 Budget Act.

(c) On target relative to the basis for the final appropriation authorized by the General Assembly during the 2011 Legislative Session.

## Table 7.5
## COMPARISON OF TAX COLLECTIONS IN FISCAL 2010, FISCAL 2011, AND ENACTED FISCAL 2012, BY REGION
### (In millions of dollars)

| State or other jurisdiction | Sales tax | | | Personal income tax | | | Corporate income tax | | |
|---|---|---|---|---|---|---|---|---|---|
| | Fiscal 2010 | Fiscal 2011 | Fiscal 2012 | Fiscal 2010 | Fiscal 2011 | Fiscal 2012 | Fiscal 2010 | Fiscal 2011 | Fiscal 2012 |
| U.S. totals (a) ............... | $198,448 | $207,883 | $207,351 | $237,048 | $259,947 | $273,591 | $39,373 | $43,068 | $43,026 |
| **Eastern Region** | | | | | | | | | |
| Connecticut ................. | 3,204 | 3,342 | 3,798 | 6,586 | 7,220 | 8,457 | 667 | 784 | 708 |
| Delaware ..................... | NA | NA | NA | 853 | 997 | 1,054 | 88 | 168 | 138 |
| Maine.......................... | 954 | 976 | 1,013 | 1,298 | 1,415 | 1,446 | 175 | 209 | 180 |
| Maryland (b)............... | 3,523 | 3,656 | 4,164 | 6,178 | 6,643 | 6,688 | 689 | 571 | 623 |
| Massachusetts ............. | 4,612 | 4,905 | 5,095 | 10,110 | 11,576 | 11,595 | 1,600 | 1,951 | 1,850 |
| New Hampshire .......... | NA | NA | NA | NA | NA | NA | 259 | 248 | 259 |
| New Jersey .................. | 7,898 | 8,236 | 8,539 | 10,323 | 10,536 | 11,132 | 2,275 | 2,382 | 2,543 |
| New York..................... | 9,871 | 10,782 | 11,173 | 34,752 | 36,210 | 39,059 | 5,371 | 5,279 | 6,101 |
| Pennsylvania............... | 8,029 | 8,590 | 8,788 | 9,969 | 10,436 | 11,000 | 1,791 | 2,132 | 2,232 |
| Rhode Island............... | 803 | 813 | 847 | 898 | 1,021 | 1,010 | 147 | 85 | 121 |
| Vermont....................... | 311 | 326 | 337 | 498 | 553 | 595 | 63 | 90 | 78 |
| Regional totals (a)....... | 39,205 | 41,626 | 43,754 | 81,465 | 86,607 | 92,036 | 13,125 | 13,899 | 14,833 |
| **Midwestern Region** | | | | | | | | | |
| Illinois......................... | 6,308 | 6,833 | 6,586 | 9,430 | 12,261 | 16,500 | 1,649 | 1,983 | 2,853 |
| Indiana........................ | 5,915 | 6,218 | 6,518 | 3,876 | 4,586 | 4,774 | 592 | 705 | 687 |
| Iowa ........................... | 2,293 | 2,395 | 2,470 | 3,236 | 3,435 | 3,615 | 389 | 386 | 432 |
| Kansas ........................ | 1,858 | 2,253 | 2,386 | 2,418 | 2,710 | 2,727 | 225 | 225 | 226 |
| Michigan...................... | 6,177 | 6,499 | 6,646 | 5,532 | 6,222 | 6,798 | 1,864 | 2,060 | 1,065 |
| Minnesota.................... | 4,177 | 4,403 | 4,647 | 6,531 | 7,529 | 7,774 | 664 | 925 | 852 |
| Nebraska ..................... | 1,290 | 1,373 | 1,425 | 1,515 | 1,735 | 1,758 | 154 | 155 | 200 |
| North Dakota (f) ........ | 610 | 782 | 756 | 302 | 428 | 266 | 88 | 147 | 62 |
| Ohio............................ | 6,995 | 7,578 | 7,869 | 7,479 | 8,120 | 8,147 | 100 | 237 | 220 |
| South Dakota.............. | 652 | 710 | 720 | NA | NA | NA | NA | NA | NA |
| Wisconsin (c)............... | 3,944 | 4,109 | 4,270 | 6,089 | 6,701 | 6,868 | 835 | 853 | 881 |
| Regional totals (a)....... | 40,219 | 43,153 | 44,293 | 46,408 | 53,727 | 59,227 | 6,560 | 7,676 | 7,478 |
| **Southern Region** | | | | | | | | | |
| Alabama....................... | 1,852 | 1,920 | 2,022 | 2,586 | 2,794 | 2,785 | 415 | 333 | 321 |
| Arkansas...................... | 1,966 | 2,056 | 2,162 | 2,091 | 2,270 | 2,277 | 362 | 351 | 359 |
| Florida ........................ | 16,015 | 16,638 | 17,436 | NA | NA | NA | 1,790 | 1,875 | 2,112 |
| Georgia........................ | 4,865 | 5,098 | 5,333 | 7,016 | 7,659 | 7,979 | 685 | 670 | 685 |
| Kentucky ..................... | 2,794 | 2,896 | 3,031 | 3,155 | 3,418 | 3,470 | 238 | 301 | 237 |
| Louisiana..................... | 2,363 | 2,627 | 2,672 | 2,212 | 2,449 | 2,815 | 175 | 283 | 255 |
| Mississippi .................. | 1,781 | 1,791 | 1,817 | 1,340 | 1,383 | 1,389 | 403 | 448 | 432 |
| Missouri....................... | 1,732 | 1,760 | 1,823 | 4,434 | 4,640 | 4,815 | 288 | 386 | 331 |
| North Carolina............. | 5,565 | 5,872 | 5,293 | 9,048 | 9,735 | 9,800 | 1,198 | 1,014 | 1,000 |
| Oklahoma.................... | 1,516 | 1,668 | 1,747 | 1,655 | 1,832 | 1,830 | 168 | 274 | 203 |
| South Carolina............ | 2,191 | 2,245 | 2,251 | 2,171 | 2,396 | 2,323 | 110 | 183 | 187 |
| Tennessee (g) .............. | 6,158 | 6,475 | 6,658 | 173 | 189 | 201 | 1,400 | 1,518 | 1,548 |
| Texas .......................... | 19,600 | 20,600 | 22,200 | NA | NA | NA | NA | NA | NA |
| Virginia........................ | 3,083 | 2,969 | 3,116 | 9,088 | 9,746 | 10,330 | 807 | 767 | 832 |
| West Virginia............... | 1,143 | 1,196 | 1,227 | 1,542 | 1,689 | 1,742 | 237 | 307 | 178 |
| Regional totals (a)....... | 72,624 | 75,811 | 78,788 | 46,511 | 50,200 | 51,756 | 8,276 | 8,710 | 8,680 |
| **Western Region** | | | | | | | | | |
| Alaska.......................... | NA | NA | NA | NA | NA | NA | 528 | 615 | 640 |
| Arizona (d).................. | 3,423 | 3,467 | 3,666 | 2,416 | 2,864 | 2,671 | 413 | 560 | 687 |
| California (e) .............. | 26,741 | 27,140 | 19,009 | 44,852 | 50,027 | 50,408 | 9,115 | 9,963 | 9,012 |
| Colorado...................... | 1,825 | 2,044 | 1,888 | 4,084 | 4,496 | 4,666 | 372 | 394 | 403 |
| Hawaii ........................ | 2,316 | 2,496 | 2,590 | 1,528 | 1,231 | 1,487 | 59 | 51 | 51 |
| Idaho .......................... | 956 | 972 | 1,044 | 1,062 | 1,153 | 1,205 | 97 | 169 | 136 |
| Montana ...................... | 66 | 65 | 61 | 718 | 816 | 809 | 88 | 119 | 115 |
| Nevada........................ | 784 | 815 | 833 | NA | NA | NA | NA | NA | NA |
| New Mexico ................ | 1,634 | 1,797 | 1,810 | 957 | 1,055 | 1,095 | 125 | 180 | 283 |
| Oregon........................ | NA | NA | NA | 4,943 | 5,524 | 5,839 | 359 | 469 | 430 |
| Utah............................ | 1,403 | 1,556 | 1,522 | 2,105 | 2,248 | 2,394 | 258 | 267 | 280 |
| Washington.................. | 6,840 | 6,501 | 7,649 | NA | NA | NA | NA | NA | NA |
| Wyoming ..................... | 413 | 439 | 455 | NA | NA | NA | NA | NA | NA |
| Regional totals (a)....... | 46,401 | 47,292 | 40,527 | 62,665 | 69,414 | 70,574 | 11,414 | 12,787 | 12,037 |
| Regional totals without California (a)... | 19,660 | 20,152 | 21,518 | 17,813 | 19,387 | 20,166 | 2,299 | 2,824 | 3,025 |
| Puerto Rico ................. | 539 | 555 | 680 | 2,575 | 2,348 | 2,109 | 1,678 | 1,566 | 1,515 |

See footnotes at end of table.

## COMPARISON OF TAX COLLECTIONS IN FISCAL 2010, FISCAL 2011, AND ENACTED FISCAL 2012, BY REGION—Continued
### (In millions of dollars)

*Source:* National Association of State Budget Officers. *The Fiscal Survey of the States* (December 2011).

*Note:* Unless otherwise noted, fiscal 2010 figures reflect actual tax collections, 2011 figures reflect preliminary actual tax collections estimates, and fiscal 2012 figures reflect the estimates used in enacted budgets.

*Key:*

NA — Indicates data are not available because, in most cases, these states do not have that type of tax.

(a) Totals include only those states with data for all years.

(b) FY 2010 corporate income tax collections include $129.0 million of extraordinary income from the sale of Constellation Energy.

(c) FY 2011 Preliminary Actuals from September 2, Legislative Fiscal Bureau memorandum to the Joint Committee on Finance; FY 2012 estimates from LFB Comparative Summary of Act 32, Table 7.

(d) FY 2011 and FY 2012 Sales Tax amounts do not include the temporary 1 cent sales tax (passed in May 2010), which generated $835 million in FY 2011 and est. $901 million in FY 2012.

(e) It is too early to judge our 2011–2012 revenues.

(f) North Dakota reduced Personal Income Tax and Corporate Income Tax rates for FY 2012.

(g) Sales tax, personal income tax, and corporate income tax are shared with local governments.

# Table 7.6
## TOTAL STATE EXPENDITURES: CAPITAL INCLUSIVE, BY REGION
### (In millions of dollars)

| State | Actual fiscal 2009 | | | | | Actual fiscal 2010 | | | | | Estimated fiscal 2011 | | | | |
|---|---|---|---|---|---|---|---|---|---|---|---|---|---|---|---|
| | General fund | Federal funds | Other state funds | Bonds | Total | General fund | Federal funds | Other state funds | Bonds | Total | General fund | Federal funds | Other state funds | Bonds | Total |
| **U.S. totals** | $659,449 | $462,980 | $400,059 | $35,928 | $1,558,416 | $619,093 | $552,655 | $411,691 | $37,931 | $1,621,370 | $636,257 | $574,760 | $434,599 | $41,480 | $1,687,096 |
| **Eastern Region** | | | | | | | | | | | | | | | |
| Connecticut (a) | 11,496 | 1,860 | 4,090 | 1,852 | 19,298 | 11,851 | 2,567 | 3,457 | 1,819 | 19,694 | 11,969 | 2,520 | 3,675 | 2,381 | 20,545 |
| Delaware | 3,296 | 1,256 | 3,908 | 281 | 8,741 | 3,077 | 1,607 | 3,783 | 253 | 8,720 | 3,271 | 1,848 | 3,090 | 203 | 8,412 |
| Maine | 3,020 | 2,778 | 2,184 | 110 | 8,092 | 2,866 | 3,151 | 2,159 | 81 | 8,257 | 2,858 | 3,000 | 2,191 | 122 | 8,171 |
| Maryland | 14,353 | 7,759 | 8,759 | 1,062 | 31,933 | 13,442 | 9,825 | 8,766 | 1,071 | 33,104 | 13,262 | 10,621 | 9,830 | 1,082 | 34,795 |
| Massachusetts | 29,662 | 3,305 | 14,107 | 1,568 | 48,642 | 27,582 | 3,932 | 17,037 | 1,873 | 50,424 | 28,468 | 3,739 | 17,719 | 1,835 | 51,761 |
| New Hampshire | 1,438 | 1,680 | 1,687 | 171 | 4,976 | 1,380 | 2,072 | 1,876 | 138 | 5,466 | 1,322 | 1,938 | 2,042 | 133 | 5,435 |
| New Jersey (b) | 30,825 | 11,384 | 3,437 | 1,641 | 47,287 | 28,926 | 13,687 | 3,482 | 1,669 | 47,764 | 29,322 | 13,518 | 3,694 | 1,701 | 48,235 |
| New York (c) | 54,607 | 34,668 | 29,144 | 3,153 | 121,572 | 54,262 | 40,834 | 30,578 | 3,263 | 128,937 | 53,313 | 44,707 | 31,163 | 3,582 | 132,765 |
| Pennsylvania | 27,085 | 20,825 | 13,735 | 999 | 62,644 | 24,942 | 27,669 | 13,842 | 1,655 | 68,108 | 25,142 | 29,977 | 14,409 | 561 | 70,089 |
| Rhode Island (d) | 3,001 | 2,271 | 1,933 | 149 | 7,354 | 2,864 | 2,813 | 2,032 | 101 | 7,810 | 2,974 | 3,085 | 2,121 | 112 | 8,292 |
| Vermont | 773 | 1,475 | 2,015 | 56 | 4,319 | 774 | 1,865 | 1,954 | 74 | 4,667 | 822 | 1,864 | 2,055 | 86 | 4,827 |
| Regional totals | 179,556 | 89,261 | 84,999 | 11,042 | 364,858 | 171,966 | 110,022 | 88,966 | 11,997 | 382,951 | 172,723 | 116,817 | 91,989 | 11,798 | 393,327 |
| **Midwestern Region** | | | | | | | | | | | | | | | |
| Illinois | 29,788 | 14,262 | 13,539 | 151 | 57,740 | 26,301 | 16,050 | 17,410 | 892 | 60,653 | 22,902 | 16,185 | 15,296 | 1,839 | 56,222 |
| Indiana (e) | 13,036 | 9,060 | 3,525 | 98 | 25,719 | 12,915 | 10,333 | 3,245 | 169 | 26,662 | 13,037 | 10,596 | 3,309 | 100 | 27,042 |
| Iowa | 5,904 | 5,201 | 6,329 | 43 | 17,477 | 5,302 | 6,174 | 6,050 | 111 | 17,637 | 5,348 | 6,088 | 6,534 | 568 | 18,538 |
| Kansas | 6,064 | 3,795 | 3,800 | 301 | 13,960 | 5,269 | 5,188 | 3,270 | 318 | 14,045 | 5,727 | 3,865 | 4,824 | 362 | 14,778 |
| Michigan (f) | 8,506 | 17,074 | 20,004 | 242 | 45,826 | 7,696 | 19,541 | 20,254 | 267 | 47,758 | 8,386 | 22,415 | 19,018 | 201 | 50,020 |
| Minnesota | 17,555 | 7,563 | 4,181 | 599 | 29,898 | 15,425 | 9,389 | 4,573 | 746 | 30,133 | 16,478 | 9,468 | 5,289 | 847 | 32,082 |
| Nebraska | 3,329 | 2,566 | 3,258 | 0 | 9,153 | 3,313 | 2,973 | 3,320 | 0 | 9,606 | 3,322 | 3,220 | 3,260 | 0 | 9,802 |
| North Dakota | 1,240 | 1,362 | 1,329 | 10 | 3,941 | 1,585 | 1,852 | 1,388 | 20 | 4,845 | 1,585 | 1,801 | 1,567 | 21 | 4,974 |
| Ohio | 28,160 | 11,462 | 17,131 | 1,040 | 57,793 | 25,412 | 14,236 | 16,864 | 1,128 | 57,640 | 27,649 | 14,431 | 17,217 | 1,017 | 60,314 |
| South Dakota | 1,154 | 1,397 | 921 | 77 | 3,549 | 1,132 | 1,729 | 892 | 67 | 3,820 | 1,148 | 1,671 | 912 | 50 | 3,781 |
| Wisconsin | 12,744 | 9,709 | 15,989 | 0 | 38,442 | 12,824 | 11,532 | 15,730 | 0 | 40,086 | 13,565 | 12,236 | 17,043 | 0 | 42,844 |
| Regional totals | 127,480 | 83,451 | 90,006 | 2,561 | 303,498 | 117,174 | 98,997 | 92,996 | 3,718 | 312,885 | 119,147 | 101,976 | 94,269 | 5,005 | 320,397 |
| **Southern Region** | | | | | | | | | | | | | | | |
| Alabama (g) | 7,285 | 7,246 | 4,613 | 593 | 19,737 | 6,588 | 8,692 | 4,913 | 391 | 20,584 | 6,507 | 9,067 | 4,910 | 359 | 20,843 |
| Arkansas | 4,380 | 5,425 | 8,337 | 51 | 18,193 | 4,223 | 6,894 | 8,716 | 89 | 19,922 | 4,442 | 7,026 | 8,782 | 83 | 20,333 |
| Florida | 23,662 | 19,725 | 15,245 | 2,042 | 60,674 | 21,216 | 22,763 | 16,725 | 1,345 | 62,049 | 24,046 | 24,999 | 20,096 | 1,377 | 70,518 |
| Georgia | 16,476 | 11,473 | 11,083 | 1,151 | 40,183 | 14,575 | 14,647 | 10,058 | 1,161 | 40,441 | 15,954 | 14,217 | 8,326 | 669 | 39,166 |
| Kentucky | 9,031 | 8,233 | 6,796 | 0 | 24,060 | 8,450 | 10,477 | 7,014 | 0 | 25,941 | 8,787 | 9,763 | 6,978 | 0 | 25,528 |
| Louisiana | 9,490 | 10,996 | 6,966 | 592 | 28,044 | 9,061 | 11,859 | 7,573 | 641 | 29,134 | 7,951 | 12,406 | 9,237 | 580 | 30,174 |
| Mississippi | 4,802 | 7,794 | 4,419 | 367 | 17,382 | 4,278 | 8,731 | 4,855 | 419 | 18,283 | 4,344 | 9,578 | 5,589 | 266 | 19,777 |
| Missouri (h) | 8,402 | 8,484 | 7,252 | 89 | 24,227 | 7,565 | 10,919 | 6,330 | 712 | 25,526 | 7,616 | 10,294 | 6,371 | 447 | 24,728 |
| North Carolina | 19,652 | 15,108 | 11,957 | 600 | 47,317 | 18,512 | 17,162 | 12,583 | 488 | 48,745 | 18,503 | 17,605 | 14,543 | 473 | 51,124 |
| Oklahoma | 6,817 | 9,708 | 4,922 | 188 | 21,635 | 6,225 | 10,362 | 4,455 | 565 | 21,607 | 6,475 | 10,048 | 5,267 | 277 | 22,067 |
| South Carolina | 5,812 | 7,068 | 7,704 | 182 | 20,766 | 5,146 | 7,691 | 7,380 | 85 | 20,302 | 5,080 | 12,844 | 7,767 | 0 | 25,691 |
| Tennessee (i) | 11,921 | 11,032 | 5,629 | 490 | 29,072 | 9,914 | 12,951 | 5,484 | 100 | 28,449 | 11,227 | 13,930 | 5,554 | 193 | 30,904 |
| Texas | 41,779 | 32,728 | 16,411 | 1,378 | 92,296 | 39,465 | 36,672 | 15,924 | 1,060 | 93,121 | 40,541 | 35,901 | 16,742 | 1,259 | 94,443 |
| Virginia | 15,020 | 6,772 | 13,539 | 1,632 | 36,963 | 14,989 | 9,327 | 15,001 | 1,456 | 40,773 | 16,435 | 9,832 | 14,839 | 1,364 | 42,470 |
| West Virginia | 3,901 | 3,824 | 12,592 | 130 | 20,447 | 3,682 | 4,475 | 12,122 | 77 | 20,356 | 3,793 | 4,638 | 12,998 | 63 | 21,492 |
| Regional totals | 188,430 | 165,616 | 137,465 | 9,485 | 500,996 | 173,889 | 193,622 | 139,133 | 8,589 | 515,233 | 181,701 | 202,148 | 147,999 | 7,410 | 539,528 |

See footnotes at end of table.

# TOTAL STATE EXPENDITURES: CAPITAL INCLUSIVE, BY REGION — Continued
## (In millions of dollars)

| State | Actual fiscal 2009 | | | | | Actual fiscal 2010 | | | | | Estimated fiscal 2011 | | | | |
|---|---|---|---|---|---|---|---|---|---|---|---|---|---|---|---|
| | General fund | Federal funds | Other state funds | Bonds | Total | General fund | Federal funds | Other state funds | Bonds | Total | General fund | Federal funds | Other state funds | Bonds | Total |
| **Western Region** | | | | | | | | | | | | | | | |
| Alaska............ | 7,176 | 3,007 | 2,054 | 345 | 12,582 | 5,626 | 2,925 | 1,208 | 0 | 9,759 | 8,878 | 3,174 | 1,643 | 228 | 13,923 |
| Arizona............ | 9,239 | 10,240 | 6,768 | 982 | 27,229 | 9,079 | 10,655 | 6,891 | 1,055 | 27,680 | 8,676 | 10,499 | 9,654 | 435 | 29,264 |
| California......... | 90,940 | 73,090 | 23,844 | 7,602 | 195,476 | 87,237 | 89,088 | 23,514 | 6,250 | 206,089 | 91,480 | 91,459 | 31,219 | 13,195 | 227,353 |
| Colorado (j)....... | 7,722 | 6,447 | 14,637 | 0 | 28,806 | 7,326 | 9,223 | 14,515 | 0 | 31,064 | 6,984 | 8,813 | 12,665 | 0 | 28,462 |
| Hawaii............ | 5,375 | 1,919 | 3,958 | 570 | 11,822 | 4,838 | 2,391 | 3,045 | 674 | 10,948 | 4,969 | 2,554 | 3,117 | 582 | 11,222 |
| Idaho............ | 2,724 | 2,305 | 1,258 | 29 | 6,316 | 2,338 | 2,573 | 1,455 | 27 | 6,393 | 2,388 | 3,014 | 1,621 | 27 | 7,050 |
| Montana (k)....... | 1,753 | 1,827 | 1,946 | 0 | 5,526 | 1,628 | 2,285 | 2,136 | 0 | 6,049 | 1,701 | 2,380 | 2,083 | 0 | 6,164 |
| Nevada............ | 3,777 | 2,525 | 2,935 | 255 | 9,492 | 3,050 | 2,792 | 2,318 | 124 | 8,284 | 3,401 | 2,642 | 2,284 | 222 | 8,549 |
| New Mexico....... | 6,080 | 4,843 | 3,873 | 583 | 15,379 | 5,258 | 5,429 | 3,953 | 606 | 15,246 | 5,203 | 5,716 | 3,910 | 0 | 14,829 |
| Oregon............ | 5,889 | 5,914 | 12,465 | 255 | 24,523 | 6,371 | 8,378 | 17,336 | 469 | 32,554 | 6,107 | 9,334 | 17,507 | 507 | 33,455 |
| Utah (l)........... | 4,817 | 2,963 | 3,736 | 43 | 11,559 | 4,441 | 3,607 | 4,550 | 2,393 | 14,991 | 4,710 | 3,954 | 4,662 | 46 | 13,372 |
| Washington....... | 14,617 | 8,146 | 8,775 | 2,176 | 33,714 | 15,036 | 9,238 | 7,284 | 2,029 | 33,587 | 14,825 | 8,543 | 7,037 | 2,025 | 32,430 |
| Wyoming.......... | 3,874 | 1,426 | 1,340 | 0 | 6,640 | 3,836 | 1,430 | 2,391 | 0 | 7,657 | 3,364 | 1,737 | 2,940 | 0 | 8,041 |
| Regional totals...... | 163,983 | 124,652 | 87,589 | 12,840 | 389,064 | 156,064 | 150,014 | 90,596 | 13,627 | 410,301 | 162,686 | 153,819 | 100,342 | 17,267 | 434,114 |
| Regional totals without California.... | 73,043 | 51,562 | 63,745 | 5,238 | 193,588 | 68,827 | 60,926 | 67,082 | 7,377 | 204,212 | 71,206 | 62,360 | 69,123 | 4,072 | 206,761 |

*Source:* National Association of State Budget Officers, *State Expenditure Report 2010* (December 2011).

*Note:* State funds refers to general funds plus other state fund spending. State spending from bonds is excluded. Total funds refers to funding from all sources—general fund, federal funds, other state funds and bonds. Small dollar amounts, when rounded, cause an aberration in the percentage increase. In these instances, the actual dollar amounts should be consulted to determine the exact percentage increase.

*Key:*

(a) Bonds data is based on bond allocations by the State Bond Commission.

(b) In some cases 2009 Actuals have been updated to reflect corrections/changes.

(c) Prior to the submission of the FY 2011 Executive Budget, the Division of the Budget adjusted their methodology for reporting certain State and Federal funds to be comparable with the fund structure reported by the State's funding classification. Total expenditures are not adjusted for the impact of delaying the end-of-year school aid payment ($2.06 billion) from March 2010 to the statutory deadline of June 1, 2010, which was done to carry forward the FY 2010 budget shortfall into FY 2011. General State Charges are counted centrally in the General Fund, and by agency, as Fringe Benefits, in other funds.

(d) Commencing in fiscal 2009, federal expenditures for Medicaid are inclusive of "pass-through" financing for qualifying LEA-administered special education expenditures.

(e) Expenditure figures for "2009 Actual and 2010 Actual—Elementary and Secondary Education (General Funds)" increased in part due to HEA 1001 (2008), the Governor's property tax reform legislation whereby the state assumed the responsibility for funding 100% for the K–12 tuition support formula.

(f) Figures reflect K–12 education, the Michigan Department of Education, adult education and pre-school. Employer contributions to current employees' pensions and health benefits are reported for Department of Education employees but excluded for employees of K–12 schools. General fund revenue support decreased for fiscal 2010 and 2011 as support from other sources in the State School Aid Fund increased, largely due to federal ARRA funding for K–12 and other education programs. Actual ARRA expenditures will be recorded with the fiscal 2011 annual financial report.

(g) Federal funds received directly by local school systems are not reported at the state budget level.

(h) Principal and interest payments on bonds are included in total expenditures. Capital expenditures are not reported separately but are included in total expenditures.

(i) Tennessee collects personal income tax on income from dividends on stocks and interest on certain bonds. Tax revenue estimates do not include federal funds and other departmental revenues. However, federal funds and other departmental revenues are included in the budget as funding sources for the general fund, along with state tax revenues.

(j) School personnel are paid at the school district level—state costs for employer contributions to employee pensions and health benefits only reflect Colorado Dept. of Education personnel. Funds library-related programs across the state.

(k) For fiscal 2010, general fund decreased and federal funds increased due to ARRA enhanced FMAP rate.

(l) All numerical information presented represents bond "expenditures." All bond information included in the report is for General Obligation bonds. Not included in the report is State Building Ownership Authority (SBOA) Revenue Bonds or Board of Regents Revenue Bonds.

# Table 7.7
## ELEMENTARY AND SECONDARY EDUCATION EXPENDITURES, BY STATE AND REGION
### (In millions of dollars)

| State | Actual fiscal 2009 | | | | | Actual fiscal 2010 | | | | | Estimated fiscal 2011 | | | | |
|---|---|---|---|---|---|---|---|---|---|---|---|---|---|---|---|
| | General fund | Federal funds | Other state funds | Bonds | Total | General fund | Federal funds | Other state funds | Bonds | Total | General fund | Federal funds | Other state funds | Bonds | Total |
| U.S. totals .............. | $232,080 | $56,437 | $40,477 | $5,394 | $334,388 | $218,548 | $70,678 | $40,034 | $2,971 | $335,294 | $220,708 | $74,104 | $39,220 | $3,356 | $337,388 |
| **Eastern Region** | | | | | | | | | | | | | | | |
| Connecticut............ | 2,672 | 441 | 4 | 642 | 3,759 | 2,393 | 861 | 4 | 700 | 3,958 | 2,439 | 834 | 4 | 390 | 3,667 |
| Delaware................. | 1,163 | 150 | 524 | 234 | 2,071 | 1,117 | 242 | 531 | 188 | 2,078 | 1,092 | 243 | 575 | 150 | 2,060 |
| Maine...................... | 1,201 | 218 | 3 | 0 | 1,422 | 1,171 | 276 | 10 | 0 | 1,457 | 1,132 | 298 | 9 | 0 | 1,439 |
| Maryland................. | 5,548 | 904 | 13 | 0 | 6,465 | 5,330 | 1,610 | 24 | 0 | 6,964 | 4,985 | 1,751 | 448 | 0 | 7,184 |
| Massachusetts......... | 4,454 | 1,189 | 636 | 0 | 6,279 | 4,302 | 1,484 | 731 | 0 | 6,517 | 4,275 | 1,261 | 658 | 0 | 6,194 |
| New Hampshire....... | 0 | 168 | 898 | 48 | 1,114 | 0 | 193 | 795 | 50 | 1,038 | 0 | 201 | 933 | 57 | 1,191 |
| New Jersey.............. | 10,416 | 832 | 18 | 0 | 11,266 | 9,559 | 2,156 | 16 | 0 | 11,731 | 10,719 | 1,112 | 18 | 0 | 11,849 |
| New York (a).......... | 19,435 | 3,559 | 3,108 | 7 | 26,109 | 19,119 | 4,255 | 2,969 | 20 | 26,363 | 18,146 | 6,090 | 3,277 | 9 | 27,522 |
| Pennsylvania........... | 9,629 | 2,101 | 632 | 0 | 12,362 | 9,119 | 3,766 | 629 | 0 | 13,514 | 8,914 | 3,777 | 754 | 0 | 13,445 |
| Rhode Island........... | 826 | 213 | 16 | 6 | 1,061 | 803 | 260 | 17 | 20 | 1,100 | 846 | 299 | 26 | 4 | 1,175 |
| Vermont (b)............ | 48 | 119 | 1,309 | 11 | 1,487 | 49 | 181 | 1,301 | 10 | 1,541 | 55 | 183 | 1,305 | 7 | 1,550 |
| Regional totals........ | 55,392 | 9,894 | 7,161 | 948 | 73,395 | 52,962 | 15,284 | 7,027 | 988 | 76,261 | 52,603 | 16,049 | 8,007 | 617 | 77,276 |
| **Midwestern Region** | | | | | | | | | | | | | | | |
| Illinois.................... | 7,442 | 3,050 | 44 | 0 | 10,536 | 7,328 | 3,690 | 42 | 0 | 11,060 | 6,901 | 4,127 | 47 | 0 | 11,075 |
| Indiana (c).............. | 5,695 | 1,476 | 51 | 0 | 7,222 | 7,155 | 1,377 | 104 | 0 | 8,636 | 7,256 | 1,105 | 149 | 0 | 8,510 |
| Iowa........................ | 2,598 | 425 | 56 | 0 | 3,079 | 2,239 | 533 | 280 | 0 | 3,052 | 2,531 | 568 | 123 | 0 | 3,222 |
| Kansas..................... | 3,147 | 420 | 115 | 0 | 3,682 | 2,710 | 736 | 138 | 0 | 3,584 | 3,019 | 612 | 248 | 0 | 3,879 |
| Michigan (d)........... | 85 | 2,179 | 10,968 | 0 | 13,232 | 51 | 2,857 | 10,638 | 1 | 13,546 | 42 | 2,891 | 10,770 | 0 | 13,703 |
| Minnesota................ | 6,931 | 642 | 41 | 7 | 7,621 | 5,339 | 1,157 | 43 | 1 | 6,540 | 6,090 | 1,173 | 46 | 1 | 7,310 |
| Nebraska.................. | 1,064 | 270 | 59 | 0 | 1,393 | 1,071 | 380 | 57 | 0 | 1,508 | 1,040 | 500 | 63 | 0 | 1,603 |
| North Dakota........... | 363 | 121 | 39 | 0 | 523 | 388 | 124 | 39 | 0 | 551 | 543 | 232 | 44 | 0 | 819 |
| Ohio (e)................... | 6,950 | 1,698 | 2,597 | 6 | 11,251 | 6,712 | 2,111 | 2,831 | 0 | 11,661 | 6,727 | 2,254 | 1,661 | 3 | 10,645 |
| South Dakota........... | 381 | 198 | 12 | 0 | 591 | 388 | 196 | 3 | 0 | 587 | 388 | 242 | 2 | 0 | 632 |
| Wisconsin................ | 5,623 | 1,327 | 204 | 0 | 7,154 | 5,946 | 1,131 | 198 | 0 | 7,275 | 6,249 | 926 | 232 | 0 | 7,407 |
| Regional totals........ | 40,279 | 11,806 | 14,186 | 13 | 66,284 | 39,327 | 14,292 | 14,373 | 1 | 68,000 | 40,786 | 14,630 | 13,385 | 4 | 68,805 |
| **Southern Region** | | | | | | | | | | | | | | | |
| Alabama (f)............. | 3,912 | 857 | 178 | 0 | 4,947 | 3,582 | 1,241 | 179 | 0 | 5,002 | 3,718 | 1,597 | 188 | 0 | 5,503 |
| Arkansas.................. | 1,949 | 494 | 774 | 0 | 3,217 | 1,852 | 699 | 876 | 0 | 3,427 | 1,943 | 786 | 794 | 0 | 3,523 |
| Florida (g).............. | 8,698 | 1,878 | 1,276 | 0 | 11,852 | 8,224 | 3,257 | 1,214 | 0 | 12,695 | 9,159 | 3,876 | 1,217 | 0 | 14,252 |
| Georgia................... | 7,348 | 1,775 | 13 | 105 | 9,241 | 6,587 | 3,036 | 16 | 298 | 9,937 | 7,067 | 2,812 | 17 | 171 | 10,067 |
| Kentucky................. | 4,017 | 707 | 15 | 0 | 4,739 | 3,840 | 1,169 | 11 | 0 | 5,020 | 3,917 | 1,080 | 11 | 0 | 5,008 |
| Louisiana................. | 3,410 | 1,058 | 387 | 0 | 4,855 | 3,224 | 1,229 | 828 | 0 | 5,281 | 3,205 | 1,539 | 955 | 0 | 5,699 |
| Mississippi.............. | 2,148 | 645 | 311 | 4 | 3,108 | 1,906 | 739 | 485 | 0 | 3,130 | 1,907 | 803 | 440 | 0 | 3,150 |
| Missouri.................. | 3,019 | 888 | 1,321 | 0 | 5,228 | 2,559 | 1,578 | 1,289 | 0 | 5,426 | 2,647 | 1,457 | 1,349 | 0 | 5,453 |
| North Carolina........ | 8,142 | 1,263 | 135 | 0 | 9,540 | 7,487 | 1,503 | 429 | 0 | 9,419 | 7,262 | 1,549 | 549 | 0 | 9,360 |
| Oklahoma................ | 1,740 | 731 | 833 | 0 | 3,304 | 1,438 | 845 | 634 | 0 | 2,917 | 1,542 | 874 | 689 | 0 | 3,105 |
| South Carolina........ | 2,150 | 765 | 678 | 0 | 3,593 | 1,920 | 943 | 611 | 0 | 3,474 | 1,832 | 705 | 561 | 0 | 3,098 |
| Tennessee................ | 3,967 | 929 | 46 | 0 | 4,942 | 3,661 | 1,337 | 33 | 0 | 5,031 | 3,645 | 1,963 | 70 | 0 | 5,678 |
| Texas (h)................. | 19,081 | 6,233 | 3,987 | 43 | 29,344 | 16,228 | 7,029 | 3,996 | 39 | 27,292 | 16,516 | 6,287 | 4,047 | 14 | 26,864 |
| Virginia................... | 5,678 | 844 | 665 | 0 | 7,187 | 4,853 | 1,335 | 641 | 0 | 6,829 | 4,832 | 1,288 | 579 | 0 | 6,699 |
| West Virginia.......... | 1,795 | 345 | 13 | 23 | 2,176 | 1,728 | 386 | 11 | 23 | 2,148 | 1,750 | 420 | 13 | 23 | 2,206 |
| Regional totals........ | 77,054 | 19,412 | 10,632 | 175 | 107,273 | 69,089 | 26,326 | 11,253 | 360 | 107,028 | 70,942 | 27,036 | 11,479 | 208 | 109,665 |

See footnotes at end of table.

# ELEMENTARY AND SECONDARY EDUCATION EXPENDITURES, BY STATE AND REGION — Continued
## (In millions of dollars)

| State | Actual fiscal 2009 | | | | | Actual fiscal 2010 | | | | | Estimated fiscal 2011 | | | | |
|---|---|---|---|---|---|---|---|---|---|---|---|---|---|---|---|
| | General fund | Federal funds | Other state funds | Bonds | Total | General fund | Federal funds | Other state funds | Bonds | Total | General fund | Federal funds | Other state funds | Bonds | Total |
| **Western Region** | | | | | | | | | | | | | | | |
| Alaska | 1,076 | 196 | 78 | 0 | 1,350 | 1,138 | 203 | 84 | 0 | 1,425 | 1,280 | 255 | 10 | 0 | 1,545 |
| Arizona | 3,954 | 971 | 1,457 | 96 | 6,478 | 3,275 | 1,664 | 1,067 | 90 | 6,096 | 3,594 | 1,328 | 421 | 90 | 5,433 |
| California | 31,476 | 9,843 | 737 | 3,977 | 46,033 | 31,269 | 7,805 | 86 | 1,278 | 40,438 | 32,717 | 8,503 | 92 | 3,347 | 44,659 |
| Colorado (i) | 3,215 | 535 | 3,653 | 0 | 7,403 | 3,240 | 629 | 3,809 | 0 | 7,678 | 2,963 | 888 | 3,535 | 0 | 7,386 |
| Hawaii (j) | 2,272 | 207 | 44 | 0 | 2,523 | 1,349 | 317 | 44 | 0 | 1,710 | 1,336 | 323 | 52 | 1 | 1,712 |
| Idaho | 1,360 | 218 | 151 | 0 | 1,729 | 1,166 | 291 | 296 | 0 | 1,753 | 1,232 | 322 | 104 | 1 | 1,658 |
| Montana (k) | 661 | 145 | 66 | 0 | 872 | 568 | 207 | 137 | 0 | 912 | 618 | 252 | 63 | 0 | 933 |
| Nevada | 1,413 | 463 | 140 | 0 | 2,016 | 1,270 | 352 | 155 | 0 | 1,777 | 1,239 | 416 | 150 | 0 | 1,805 |
| New Mexico | 2,524 | 402 | 17 | 0 | 2,943 | 2,547 | 669 | 1 | 0 | 3,217 | 2,323 | 593 | 1 | 0 | 2,917 |
| Oregon | 2,745 | 631 | 484 | 0 | 3,860 | 2,435 | 737 | 604 | 0 | 3,776 | 2,321 | 826 | 600 | 0 | 3,747 |
| Utah (l) | 2,293 | 552 | 165 | 0 | 3,010 | 2,271 | 499 | 62 | 0 | 2,832 | 2,322 | 447 | 83 | 0 | 2,852 |
| Washington | 6,334 | 1,067 | 712 | 185 | 8,298 | 6,496 | 1,200 | 236 | 247 | 8,179 | 6,321 | 1,097 | 254 | 122 | 7,794 |
| Wyoming | 7 | 92 | 794 | 0 | 893 | 7 | 93 | 795 | 0 | 895 | 6 | 80 | 831 | 0 | 917 |
| Regional totals | 59,330 | 15,322 | 8,498 | 4,258 | 87,408 | 57,031 | 14,666 | 7,376 | 1,615 | 80,688 | 58,272 | 15,330 | 6,196 | 3,560 | 83,358 |
| Regional totals without California | 27,854 | 5,479 | 7,761 | 281 | 41,375 | 25,762 | 6,861 | 7,290 | 337 | 40,250 | 36,555 | 6,827 | 6,104 | 213 | 38,699 |

*Source:* National Association of State Budget Officers. *State Expenditure Report 2010* (December 2011).

Key:

(a) Total expenditures are not adjusted for the impact of delaying the end-of-year school aid payment ($2.06 billion) from March 2010 to the statutory deadline of June 1, 2010, which was done to carry forward the FY 2010 budget shortfall into FY 2011.

(b) Fiscal 2009 Other State Funds figures were restated from last year's survey to correct a double counting issue with transfers.

(c) Expenditure figures for "2009 Actual and 2010 Actual — Elementary and Secondary Education (General Funds)" increased in part due to HEA 1001 (2008), the Governor's property tax reform legislation whereby the state assumed the responsibility for funding 100% of the K–12 tuition support formula.

(d) Figures reflect K–12 education, the Michigan Department of Education, adult education and preschool. Employer contributions to current employees' pensions and health benefits are reported for Department of Education employees but excluded for employees of K–12 schools. General fund revenue support decreased for fiscal 2010 and 2011, as support from other revenue sources in the State School Aid Fund increased, largely due to federal ARRA funding for K–12 and other education programs. Actual ARRA expenditures will be recorded with the fiscal 2011 annual financial report.

(e) Other state funds includes capital spending for the state's school building program. During FY 2008–2011 bond funds were replaced with tobacco securitization proceeds.

(f) Federal funds received directly by local school systems are not reported at the state budget level.

(g) State appropriations to school districts for operational costs include funding intended to be expended by school districts for contributions to current employees' pensions, employee health benefits, and for the operational cost of libraries.

(h) Decreases in state support from 2009 to 2010–11 should not be interpreted as a decrease in total funding for public education because state funding for 2009 includes a one-time, thirteenth payment of approximately $1.76 billion. Additionally, these amounts do not reflect revenue generated by local tax collections, which impact the state's share of funding.

(i) School personnel are paid at the school district level — state costs for employer contributions to employee pensions and health benefits only reflect Colorado Dept. of Education personnel. Funds library-related programs across the state.

(j) Employer contributions to current employees' pensions and health benefits: general fund amounts are budgeted centrally (except for Elementary and Secondary Education and Higher Education) and reported in "All Other State Expenditures." For non-general funds, employer contributions are shown in each functional area.

(k) For fiscal 2010, general funds decreased and other state funds increased as a result of natural resource bonus payments (namely Otter Creek – approximately $81 million offset to general fund). Additionally, for fiscal 2010 and fiscal 2011, and to a lesser extent fiscal 2009, federal funds increased and general funds decreased due to ARRA SFSF and JOBS bill.

(l) Included with the General Fund is the Education Fund (income tax revenue) which in Utah is restricted by the Utah state constitution for the sole use of public and higher education.

# Table 7.8
# MEDICAID EXPENDITURES BY STATE AND REGION
## (In millions of dollars)

| State | Actual fiscal 2009 | | | | Actual fiscal 2010 | | | | Estimated fiscal 2011 | | | |
|---|---|---|---|---|---|---|---|---|---|---|---|---|
| | General fund | Federal funds | Other state funds | Total | General fund | Federal funds | Other state funds | Total | General fund | Federal funds | Other state funds | Total |
| U.S. totals | $107,716 | $206,479 | $27,268 | $341,463 | $97,540 | $233,633 | $30,674 | $361,847 | $110,672 | $249,807 | $38,092 | $398,571 |
| **Eastern Region** | | | | | | | | | | | | |
| Connecticut (a) | 3,852 | 0 | 1,530 | 5,382 | 3,855 | 0 | 1,145 | 5,000 | 4,466 | 0 | 1,127 | 5,593 |
| Delaware | 494 | 497 | 0 | 991 | 538 | 539 | 0 | 1,077 | 481 | 777 | 0 | 1,258 |
| Maine | 499 | 1,734 | 183 | 2,416 | 383 | 1,801 | 175 | 2,359 | 439 | 1,694 | 205 | 2,338 |
| Maryland | 2,580 | 2,821 | 217 | 5,618 | 2,400 | 3,629 | 324 | 6,353 | 2,005 | 4,098 | 558 | 6,661 |
| Massachusetts | 8,679 | 0 | 0 | 8,679 | 9,462 | 0 | 0 | 9,462 | 10,440 | 0 | 0 | 10,440 |
| New Hampshire | 421 | 706 | 191 | 1,318 | 385 | 797 | 180 | 1,362 | 395 | 831 | 145 | 1,371 |
| New Jersey | 4,734 | 4,640 | 134 | 9,508 | 4,230 | 5,485 | 136 | 9,851 | 4,111 | 6,007 | 136 | 10,254 |
| New York | 8,568 | 19,102 | 3,370 | 31,040 | 7,689 | 21,310 | 3,429 | 32,428 | 6,296 | 26,060 | 4,669 | 37,025 |
| Pennsylvania | 6,488 | 9,596 | 1,701 | 17,785 | 6,029 | 11,096 | 1,625 | 18,750 | 5,523 | 12,188 | 1,716 | 19,427 |
| Rhode Island (b) | 726 | 1,100 | 5 | 1,831 | 715 | 1,234 | 7 | 1,956 | 806 | 1,234 | 7 | 2,047 |
| Vermont | 175 | 707 | 219 | 1,101 | 147 | 834 | 229 | 1,210 | 177 | 855 | 253 | 1,285 |
| Regional totals | 37,216 | 40,903 | 7,550 | 85,669 | 35,833 | 46,725 | 7,250 | 89,808 | 35,139 | 53,744 | 8,816 | 97,699 |
| **Midwestern Region** | | | | | | | | | | | | |
| Illinois | 4,345 | 7,563 | 2,440 | 14,348 | 3,327 | 8,397 | 2,571 | 14,295 | 3,341 | 9,560 | 3,320 | 16,221 |
| Indiana | 1,225 | 3,986 | 384 | 5,595 | 1,186 | 4,554 | 432 | 6,172 | 1,292 | 4,879 | 432 | 6,603 |
| Iowa | 588 | 1,889 | 655 | 3,132 | 602 | 2,165 | 522 | 3,289 | 403 | 2,331 | 843 | 3,577 |
| Kansas | 820 | 1,522 | 81 | 2,423 | 713 | 1,860 | 70 | 2,643 | 790 | 1,828 | 125 | 2,743 |
| Michigan (c) | 1,554 | 7,359 | 1,629 | 10,542 | 1,451 | 8,435 | 1,683 | 11,569 | 1,440 | 8,743 | 1,821 | 12,004 |
| Minnesota | 3,046 | 4,118 | 0 | 7,164 | 2,745 | 4,748 | 67 | 7,560 | 3,156 | 4,848 | 61 | 8,065 |
| Nebraska | 577 | 1,009 | 22 | 1,608 | 532 | 1,095 | 22 | 1,649 | 507 | 1,085 | 21 | 1,613 |
| North Dakota | 166 | 384 | 4 | 554 | 193 | 467 | 2 | 662 | 225 | 501 | 2 | 728 |
| Ohio | 10,241 | 1,464 | 175 | 11,880 | 8,611 | 3,024 | 658 | 12,293 | 10,777 | 2,590 | 598 | 13,965 |
| South Dakota | 239 | 529 | 0 | 768 | 225 | 604 | 0 | 829 | 267 | 611 | 0 | 878 |
| Wisconsin | 1,157 | 3,920 | 972 | 6,049 | 1,367 | 4,742 | 759 | 6,868 | 1,413 | 5,071 | 787 | 7,271 |
| Regional totals | 23,958 | 33,743 | 6,362 | 64,063 | 20,952 | 40,091 | 6,719 | 67,829 | 23,611 | 42,047 | 8,010 | 73,668 |
| **Southern Region** | | | | | | | | | | | | |
| Alabama (d) | 622 | 3,567 | 859 | 5,048 | 315 | 3,957 | 1,037 | 5,309 | 345 | 3,851 | 1,086 | 5,282 |
| Arkansas | 657 | 2,625 | 295 | 3,577 | 602 | 3,209 | 179 | 3,990 | 635 | 3,424 | 119 | 4,178 |
| Florida | 3,522 | 9,892 | 2,788 | 16,202 | 2,823 | 11,984 | 3,817 | 18,624 | 3,978 | 12,081 | 3,721 | 19,780 |
| Georgia | 1,830 | 5,365 | 424 | 7,619 | 1,663 | 5,832 | 389 | 7,884 | 1,731 | 5,793 | 520 | 8,044 |
| Kentucky | 1,020 | 4,045 | 337 | 5,402 | 811 | 4,499 | 383 | 5,693 | 911 | 4,537 | 360 | 5,808 |
| Louisiana | 1,114 | 4,793 | 262 | 6,169 | 798 | 5,634 | 484 | 6,916 | 658 | 5,353 | 1,088 | 7,099 |
| Mississippi | 314 | 3,256 | 737 | 4,307 | 139 | 3,199 | 849 | 4,187 | 168 | 3,395 | 901 | 4,464 |
| Missouri | 1,427 | 5,603 | 1,588 | 8,618 | 1,422 | 6,196 | 1,168 | 8,786 | 1,531 | 6,389 | 1,050 | 8,970 |
| North Carolina | 2,766 | 7,690 | 1,363 | 11,819 | 2,319 | 8,113 | 1,364 | 11,796 | 2,466 | 7,660 | 1,172 | 11,298 |
| Oklahoma | 960 | 2,432 | 439 | 3,831 | 739 | 2,586 | 360 | 3,685 | 960 | 2,675 | 457 | 4,092 |
| South Carolina | 589 | 3,354 | 634 | 4,577 | 529 | 3,521 | 546 | 4,596 | 726 | 3,870 | 522 | 5,118 |
| Tennessee (e) | 2,588 | 4,514 | 287 | 7,389 | 1,632 | 6,227 | 322 | 8,181 | 2,152 | 6,252 | 275 | 8,679 |
| Texas | 6,819 | 14,135 | 62 | 21,016 | 6,701 | 16,086 | 86 | 22,873 | 7,887 | 16,936 | 58 | 24,881 |
| Virginia | 2,903 | 3,176 | 0 | 6,079 | 2,590 | 3,963 | 1 | 6,554 | 2,977 | 4,197 | 0 | 7,174 |
| West Virginia | 309 | 1,885 | 239 | 2,433 | 252 | 2,100 | 211 | 2,563 | 307 | 2,239 | 240 | 2,786 |
| Regional totals | 27,440 | 76,332 | 10,314 | 114,086 | 23,335 | 87,106 | 11,195 | 121,637 | 27,432 | 88,652 | 11,569 | 127,653 |

See footnotes at end of table.

# MEDICAID EXPENDITURES BY STATE AND REGION — Continued
## (In millions of dollars)

| State | Actual fiscal 2009 | | | | Actual fiscal 2010 | | | | Estimated fiscal 2011 | | | |
|---|---|---|---|---|---|---|---|---|---|---|---|---|
| | General fund | Federal funds | Other state funds | Total | General fund | Federal funds | Other state funds | Total | General fund | Federal funds | Other state funds | Total |
| **Western Region** | | | | | | | | | | | | |
| Alaska | 329 | 682 | 7 | 1,018 | 341 | 823 | 7 | 1,171 | 373 | 871 | 14 | 1,258 |
| Arizona | 1,239 | 5,971 | 762 | 7,972 | 1,187 | 5,608 | 868 | 7,663 | 1,290 | 5,848 | 1,044 | 8,182 |
| California | 11,707 | 27,990 | 538 | 40,235 | 10,319 | 27,968 | 738 | 39,025 | 12,573 | 36,814 | 5,573 | 54,960 |
| Colorado | 1,355 | 2,176 | 522 | 4,053 | 1,120 | 2,533 | 1,115 | 4,768 | 1,269 | 2,807 | 1,435 | 5,511 |
| Hawaii (f) | 447 | 884 | 0 | 1,331 | 499 | 957 | 0 | 1,456 | 606 | 1,180 | 0 | 1,786 |
| Idaho | 331 | 1,013 | 97 | 1,441 | 288 | 1,069 | 111 | 1,468 | 299 | 1,311 | 194 | 1,804 |
| Montana (g) | 142 | 642 | 57 | 841 | 137 | 728 | 65 | 930 | 152 | 741 | 72 | 965 |
| Nevada | 526 | 856 | 139 | 1,521 | 465 | 944 | 107 | 1,516 | 487 | 974 | 135 | 1,596 |
| New Mexico | 641 | 2,430 | 115 | 3,186 | 567 | 2,683 | 113 | 3,363 | 539 | 2,342 | 115 | 2,996 |
| Oregon | 711 | 2,425 | 369 | 3,505 | 808 | 3,037 | 404 | 4,249 | 918 | 3,408 | 557 | 4,883 |
| Utah | 265 | 1,215 | 243 | 1,723 | 229 | 1,370 | 185 | 1,784 | 258 | 1,419 | 238 | 1,915 |
| Washington | 3,528 | 3,633 | 62 | 7,223 | 3,754 | 3,870 | 108 | 7,732 | 3,825 | 3,943 | 141 | 7,909 |
| Wyoming | 220 | 317 | 0 | 537 | 196 | 363 | 0 | 559 | 226 | 336 | 0 | 562 |
| Regional totals | 21,441 | 50,234 | 2,772 | 74,586 | 19,910 | 51,953 | 3,714 | 75,684 | 22,815 | 61,994 | 9,518 | 94,327 |
| Regional totals without California | 9,734 | 22,244 | 2,234 | 34,351 | 9,591 | 23,985 | 2,976 | 36,659 | 10,242 | 25,180 | 3,945 | 39,367 |

*Source:* National Association of State Budget Officers. *State Expenditure Report 2010* (December 2011).

*Note:* States were asked to report Medicaid expenditures as follows: General funds: all general funds appropriated to the Medicaid agency and any other agency which are used for direct Medicaid matching purposes under Title XIX. Other state funds: other funds and revenue sources used as Medicaid match, such as local funds and provider taxes, fees, donations, assessments (as defined by the Centers for Medicare and Medicaid Services). Federal funds: all federal matching funds provided pursuant to Title XIX.

*Key:*

(a) Medicaid appropriation is "gross funded" — Federal funds are deposited directly to the State Treasury. Connecticut's FMAP is currently at 50 percent, excluding enhanced FMAP available under ARRA ($403 million in fiscal 2009 and $539 million in fiscal 2010 and $481 million in fiscal 2011). Excludes state portion of Qualified Medicare Beneficiaries and School Based Child Health as those expenditures are netted out of federal Medicaid reimbursement. Other State funds in fiscal 2009 and fiscal 2010 includes retroactive adjustments for facilities at the Department of Developmental Services, which were claimed under the Medicaid program. Medicaid figures exclude medical assistance under the State Administered General Assistance Program. Amounts for that purpose were $188 million in fiscal 2009 and $182 million in fiscal 2010.

(b) Commencing in fiscal 2009, federal expenditures for Medicaid are inclusive of "pass-through" financing for qualifying LEA-administered special education expenditures.

(c) Other state funds include local funds of $102.0 million, and provider taxes of $888.0 million for fiscal 2009; local funds of $98.0 million and provider taxes of $725.0 million for fiscal 2010; and local funds of

$85.1 million and provider taxes of $885.1 million for fiscal 2011. The fluctuation in provider assessment funds is due to the 2.6 percentage point rate increase in the regular FMAP rate between fiscal 2010 and fiscal 2011 at the same time that federal ARRA/FMAP funding ($1,042.0 million for fiscal 2009, $1,220.2 million for fiscal 2010, and $627.3 million for fiscal 2011). Public health and community and institutional care for mentally and developmentally disabled persons are partially reported in the Medicaid totals.

(d) Fiscal 2009 through fiscal 2011 Other State Funds includes provider taxes in the amounts of $59 million, $270 million, and $312million, respectively.

(e) Regarding premium revenue: fiscal 2009 totals $77 million, fiscal 2010 totals $221 million, and fiscal 2011 totals $263 million. Regarding Certified Public Expenditures—Local fund from Hospitals: fiscal 2009 totals $248 million, fiscal 2010 totals $312 million, and fiscal 2011 totals $221 million. Regarding Nursing Home Tax: fiscal 2009 totals $84 million, fiscal 2010 totals $87 million, and fiscal 2011 totals $87 million. Regarding ICF/MR 6 percent Gross Receipts Tax: fiscal 2009 totals $21 million, fiscal 2010 totals $12 million, and fiscal 2011 totals $12 million. Regarding Intergovernmental Transfers: fiscal 2009 totals $0 million, fiscal 2010 totals $0 million, and fiscal 2011 totals $0 million.

(f) Employer contributions to current employees' pensions and health benefits: general fund amounts are budgeted centrally (except for Elementary and Secondary Education and Higher Education) and reported in "All Other State Expenditures." For non-general funds, employer contributions are shown in each functional area.

(g) For fiscal 2010, general fund decreased and federal funds increased due to ARRA enhanced FMAP rate.

# Post-Recession State Tax Revenues
# and Taxation of Digitized Transactions

## By William F. Fox and LeAnn Luna

*State tax performance since 2008 shows that effects of recessions on revenues can last five years or more. Policymakers planning for potential revenue shortfalls must consider relatively long time periods. This article addresses two key revenue policy issues. First, it provides a brief summary of state tax revenue performance during the past several years, with a focus on how collections stand relative to their previous peak. This section shows the relative revenue performance for state governments in aggregate since 2008. Second, it describes key sales tax issues associated with the dramatic movement towards digitization and identifies some policy options.*

## Revenues are Recovering from the Deep Recession

State tax revenues are rebounding from the worst fiscal recession in modern history. Although regional performance varies considerably, overall state tax revenues expanded rapidly in 2011, and growth continued nearly as strongly into 2012. Last year, inflation-adjusted tax revenue growth was the third fastest since 1998 and 2012 would be the fourth fastest if growth is sustained at the first quarter's level throughout the year. (see Figure A) After revenues declined by 10.2 percent between 2008 and 2010, 2011 revenues of $755.2 billion are only $26.6 billion under the peak reached in 2008 and are just shy of 2007 collections.[1]

The decline in revenues is much greater when inflation is taken into account.[2] Real revenues fell by 15.4 percent between 2007—the peak in real revenues—and 2010, and they ended last year $91.5 billion below the peak (or 11.4 percent lower than peak real revenues). The 2012 fiscal year nominal revenues for the sum of the states will surely exceed the 2008 maximum, but revenues will remain much lower in inflation-adjusted terms. Only seven states anticipate a revenue decline in 2012, though more than one-half of states expect nominal revenues to rise by less than 5 percent.[3]

States differ widely in the recovery of revenue. (see Figure B).[4] After one year of upturn, nominal 2011 revenue exceeded 2008 collections in only 16 states. Only North Dakota and Oregon had more revenue in 2011 than in 2008 after inflation is taken into account. As a general rule, revenues have recovered better in the upper Midwest, mid-Atlantic and New England regions. Revenues are further from their peak in the Southeast. The

biggest declines relative to 2008 are in Alaska, Louisiana, South Carolina and Georgia, whose 2011 revenues are 85 percent of their peak or less.

States have tried a variety of policy responses to the revenue reductions, with rate increases being an important component in some states. Eleven states raised their sales tax rate and seven increased their personal income tax rate since 2008. Six of the 16 states that had higher revenues in 2011 than in 2008 increased one of these two tax rates. Interestingly, five states, including New Mexico, North Carolina, Ohio,[5] Oklahoma, and Rhode Island, reduced their personal income tax rate between 2008 and 2011 despite having less revenue than in 2008.[6] Both North Carolina and Utah raised their sales tax rates as they lowered their personal income tax rate. North Dakota lowered its income tax rate and Oregon raised its rate.

The corporate income tax experienced the largest revenue decline between 2008 and 2010, followed by the personal income and general sales taxes. Revenue from each tax grew in 2011, but was still lower than in 2008. (see Figure C) For example, sales tax revenue declined by 7.4 percent in the recession, but was only 2.3 percent below its peak in 2011. During 2012, aggregate state sales and personal income tax revenue will likely exceed their 2008 peak,, but corporate income taxes will continue to lag significantly behind pre-recession levels.

## Sales Taxation of Digital Goods and Web-Exabled Transactions[7]

Technological advances are changing the way businesses do business. For example, payroll software was once typically delivered via disk or DVD and downloaded onto company computers for use. Today, that software is more typically downloaded electronically and installed on company desktop computers, installed on a central server accessed by company employees from their desktops or increasingly accessed by users from the "cloud." Call centers and help desks no longer need a brick-and-mortar location to provide services. Customers calling an 800 number could be routed to desks of employees working from home or to centers located anywhere in the world, depending on call volume, time of day, etc.

These changes in delivery methods have profound effects on the sales and use taxation of digital products and services..

## Taxation of Digital Products and Services

Digital products typically consumed by businesses may be subject to sales and use tax if the transaction involves (1) the sale of software, (2) data processing, data storage or canned information, or (3) the digital equivalent to tangible personal property (i.e., "digital goods"). The Streamlined Sales Tax Agreement defines "specified digital products" as electronically transferred "digital audio-visual works" (e.g., movies), "digital audio works" (e.g., ringtones, music) and "digital books."[8]

States take several different approaches to taxing software depending on the type of software and how it is delivered. First, some states have never taxed software. Second, some states tax standardized or custom software delivered by a physical medium—such as DVDs—as tangible personal property.[9] Third, most states tax standardized or canned software, whether delivered by physical medium or downloaded remotely, as a sale of a tangible product. On the other hand, custom software is often classified as a service and taxed accordingly, depending on

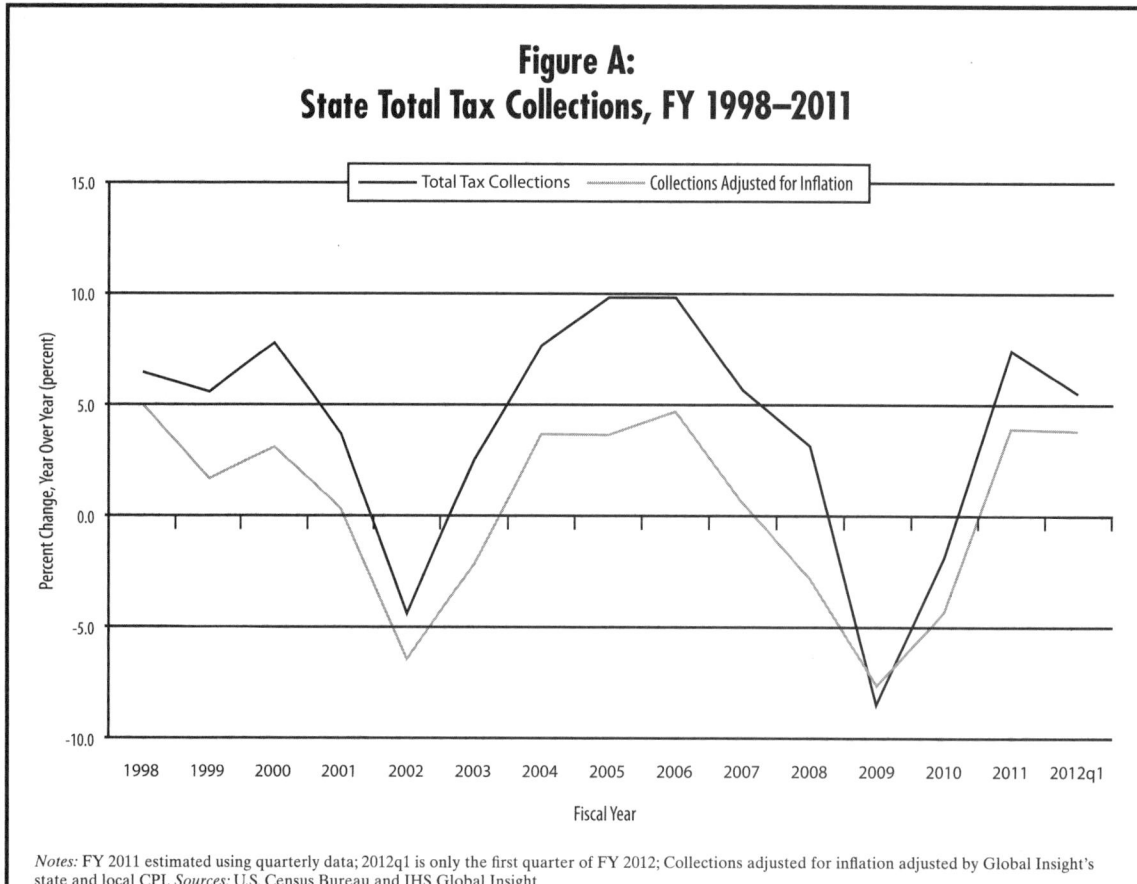

## Figure A:
## State Total Tax Collections, FY 1998–2011

*Notes:* FY 2011 estimated using quarterly data; 2012q1 is only the first quarter of FY 2012; Collections adjusted for inflation adjusted by Global Insight's state and local CPI. *Sources:* U.S. Census Bureau and IHS Global Insight

the state's taxation of such services in general. Data services can be taxed as information services or as telecommunication services.

Digitized transactions create two unique sourcing issues. The first is determining where the taxable transaction, or consumption of the product or service, occurs. Once a transaction is properly sited to a particular state, the next step is determining whether the seller has nexus in that state and therefore a sales tax collection obligation. In general, software applications or digital goods will be taxed in the state where they are accessed or downloaded by the user, but exceptions do exist and the taxability becomes more complicated when multiple users are located in several jurisdictions.[10]

States will often tax hosted services (see discussion of cloud computing below) based on where the customer receives the benefit of the service, the principal place of business or at the point of delivery.

The Streamlined Sales Tax Agreement uses the following hierarchy to determine where to source digital transactions. The "best" approach is to use the address provided by the customer's instructions. The "next best" approach is to use the address the seller has for the customer in the seller's records (e.g., ship to address or billing address).[11] Third, is to use the customer's address obtained during the sale, and finally, to use the address of the seller's server.

## Cloud Computing

Much of the recent growth in digital products is in "cloud computing." The U.S. National Institute for Standards and Technology developed the following definition of cloud computing.[12]

Cloud computing is a model for enabling ubiquitous, convenient, on-demand network access to a shared pool of configurable computing resources

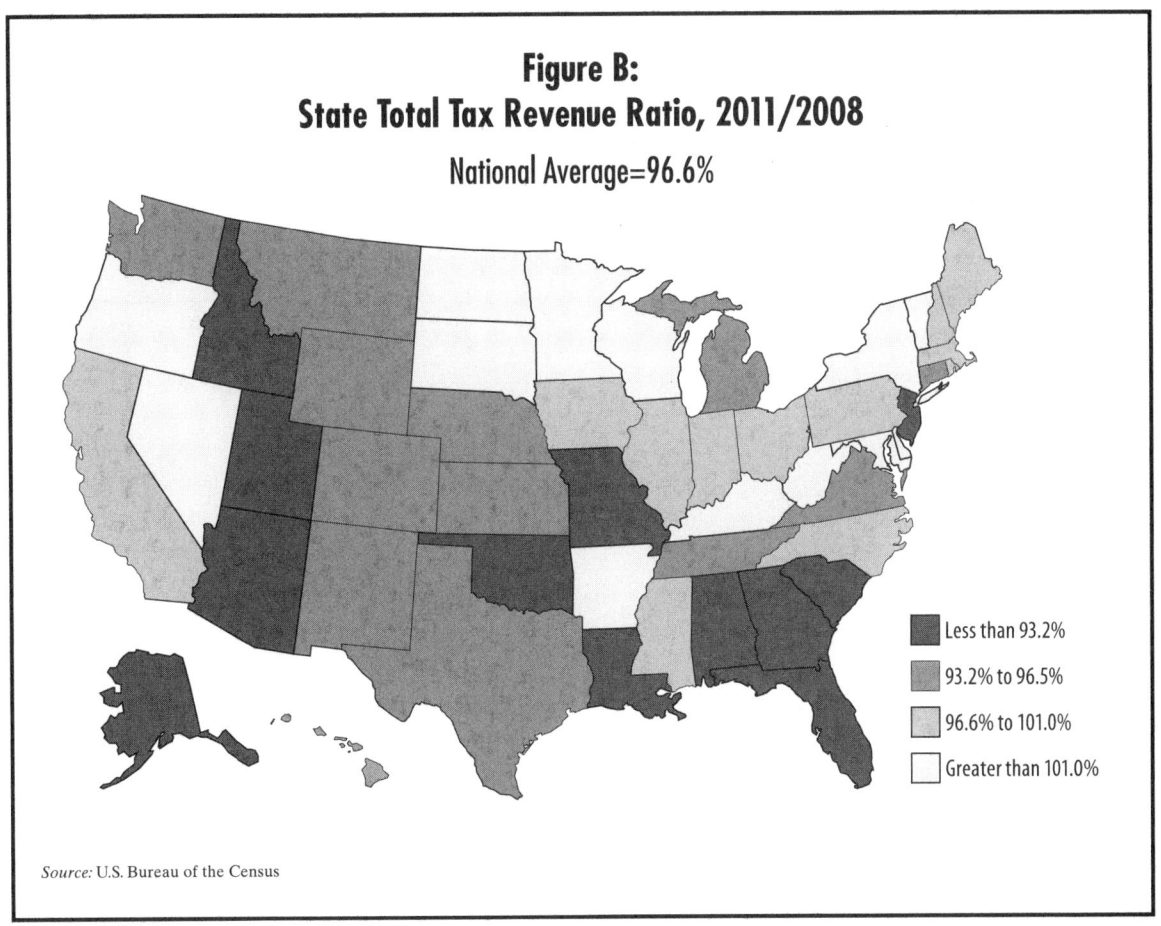

**Figure B:**
**State Total Tax Revenue Ratio, 2011/2008**

National Average=96.6%

Less than 93.2%

93.2% to 96.5%

96.6% to 101.0%

Greater than 101.0%

*Source:* U.S. Bureau of the Census

(e.g., networks, servers, storage, applications, and services) that can be rapidly provisioned and released with minimal management effort or service provider interaction.

## Types of Services in the Cloud

For sales tax purposes, cloud computing is best thought of as an alternate delivery method of electronic products and services rather than as a novel set of products. The transaction can take many forms, but with all of them, clients remotely access computing services by linking to a server that is often located in a state other than where the services are consumed. Infrastructure as a service provides clients access to data storage and computing services, such as data backup and storage to business and individual clients. Software as a service vendors provide access to common programs and applications, such as online tax preparation programs. Platform as a Service provides tools to software developers.

## Problems with Taxing Services in the Cloud

Delivery of services through cloud computing creates several interrelated problems. A sales tax collection obligation arises on the part of the seller in the state in which consumption occurs if the seller/taxpayer has *physical* presence in that state.[13] For cloud computing, attributing consumption to a particular state can be complicated. Computing services are sold by businesses that can be located anywhere to customers that can access them from anywhere from servers often maintained by third parties. For example, a company headquartered in California may purchase server space and cloud-based software from a company in Pennsylvania. The software company in Pennsylvania contracts hosting services from a third party with servers in Florida, Illinois and Washington. Employees of the California-headquartered company may access the software across the country by connecting to the servers via the Internet directly or by routing

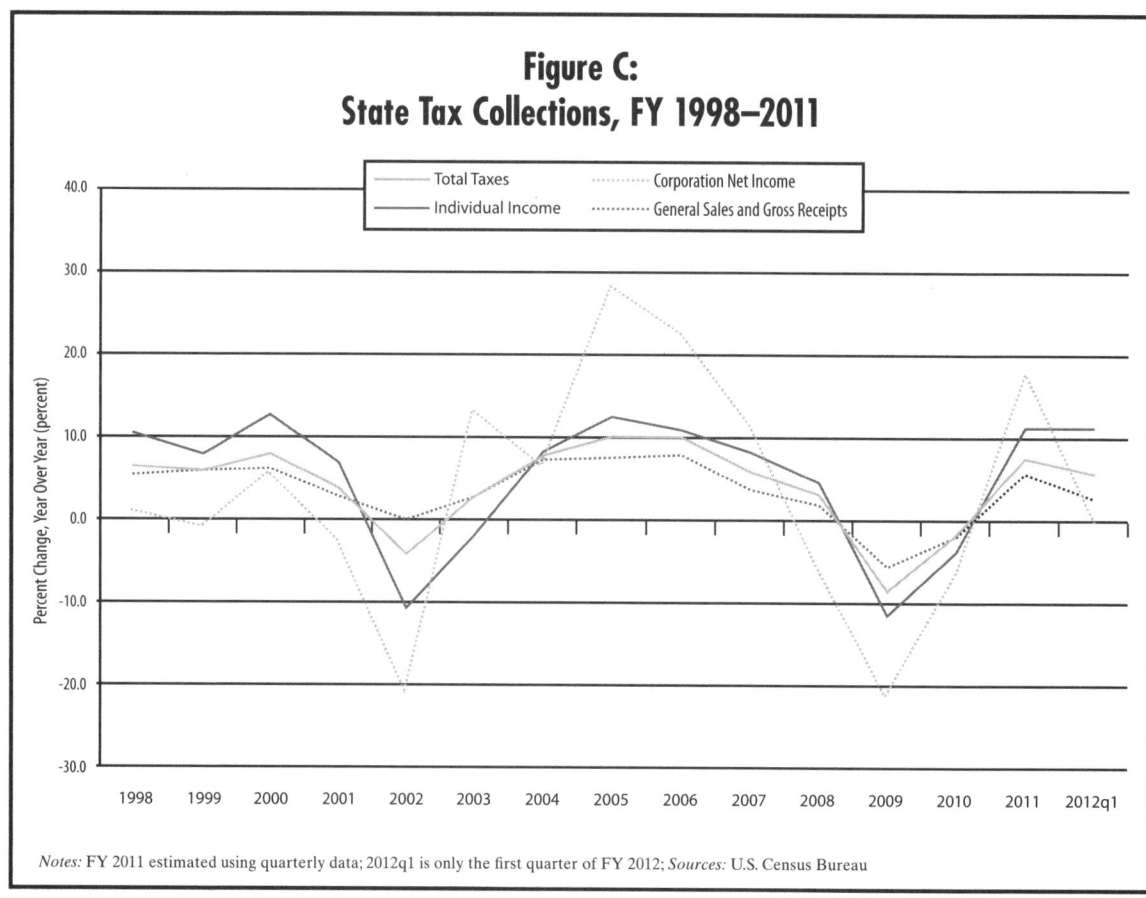

**Figure C:
State Tax Collections, FY 1998–2011**

*Notes:* FY 2011 estimated using quarterly data; 2012q1 is only the first quarter of FY 2012; *Sources:* U.S. Census Bureau

the transaction through the client company's main server in California. A number of questions must be addressed to determine if and where the transaction would be taxable. If the transaction is the sale of a digital product, in which state does the sale take place? Options include where the server is located, the location of the consumer when the software was accessed or the billing address for the parent company. If the sale is deemed to be a service, in which state are the services consumed? Does it matter if the software is licensed on a monthly or annual basis or on a per-use basis? Once it can be determined where the services were consumed, in which states does the software company have nexus and therefore a sales tax collection obligation?[14] One guiding practice is that in recent years, states have asserted nexus based on the activities of third-party vendors whose activities benefit the seller.

The sales tax treatment of cloud computing often follows the taxation of analogous products delivered by other means. The first step is to determine what type of good or service is being provided. Most transactions can be characterized as access to services, infrastructure or software. For example, infrastructure as a service, analogous to data storage or processing services, is often taxed consistent with such services offered in a more traditional delivery method. As a result, states differ in how they tax infrastructure as a service. Connecticut, Ohio and Texas tax data storage and processing services if the *customer* is located in the state.[15] On the other hand, Florida treats the transaction as a rental of the computer, or access to infrastructure, and taxes the transaction based on where the *server* is located. Servers located in another state and therefore not "rented" in Florida are not taxed.

Software as a service and platform as a service provide software services to users without transferring the software to customer computers either via DVD or download. Whether a client accesses canned software through download or the cloud, the nature of the service is the same. Sourcing the transaction, however, is difficult. Assume a California company hosts software that it makes available to clients located in New York and Pennsylvania. Does the transfer and taxable sale occur in California or the state where the clients access the software? Pennsylvania, Kansas and Utah treat the "sale" as occurring in California and therefore not subject to sales or use tax at all. New York takes a different approach and subjects the transaction to New York sales/use tax, even though the software remains housed at all times in California, and then looks to the seller's nexus to determine whether New York can impose a sales tax collection obligation on the seller.

Electronic commerce combines information services delivered over telecommunication networks and can be classified for sales tax purposes under either umbrella. Some states tax telecommunication services but not information services. Further, cloud computing services are often bundled, with clients receiving access to applications and platforms, data storage and support for a flat fee. In many states, the storage—a service—may not be taxable, but the access to applications—access to software—is taxed. Because the provider charges a flat fee, however, the proper amount of tax may not be remitted to the state.

Recent rulings rely on the "true object test" to make a taxability determination on the bundled transaction.[16] States may also split the transaction into its component parts and assign a part of the purchase price to each function. Massachusetts held that fees charged for access to a database were nontaxable but "add-ons" were deemed taxable use of the software. Thus, a customer can search a database tax-free, but when new tools are purchased, it becomes software subject to sales tax.[17]

Court battles can result from disagreement over which components are taxable and where. In one example, the taxpayer separately stated charges for hardware, software and a service that collects, manipulates and transmits data so that only parts of the transaction were taxable.[18] The department of revenue concluded the entire transaction was taxable because the transmission of data was equivalent to a taxable communication service. But the court ruled in favor of the taxpayer, acknowledging the validity of separating the system into its parts.[19]

## Click-Through Nexus Laws

States have taken a number of approaches to collecting sales tax due on other forms of remote transactions. In 1982, the *Quill* decision provided the bright line physical presence nexus standard regarding sales and use tax, though federal legislation requiring use tax collection by remote sellers has also been recently introduced.[20] New York was the first state to enact click-through nexus—also known as "the Amazon Law"—in 2008, asserting nexus for vendors with certain third-party e-commerce relationships. The law seems to target large e-commerce venders such as Amazon.com and Overstock.com to enforce use taxes on their e-commerce sales.[21] The constitutionality of some of the Amazon laws remains unclear.[22] And in *Amazon.com LLC v. N.Y.*

*Dep't of Taxation & Fin. (N.Y. App. Div. Nov. 4, 2010)*, the appellate court remanded the case back to trial court to determine whether in-state representatives were soliciting business or merely advertising on Amazon's behalf.

Arkansas, California, Connecticut, Illinois, New York, North Carolina, Rhode Island Texas and Vermont have enacted click-through nexus statutes.[23] Click-through nexus legislation is under consideration in several states—including Arizona, Massachusetts, Michigan, Mississippi and South Carolina. Colorado and Oklahoma—require greater use tax reporting and a number of other states have asserted click through nexus authority without specific legislation.

As an indication of the stakes in this controversy, both Amazon and Overstock have often responded to newly enacted click through statutes by ending nexus-creating affiliate programs in those states.

## Notes

[1]Revenue data are taken from the U.S. Bureau of the Census. Note that the 2011 data are estimated from the quarterly tax collections data and the earlier years are taken from the annual tax collections. Some differences exist between these two data series. For example, the quarterly data are generally based on cash received during the year and the annual data allow for adjustments such as for accruals.

[2]Revenues were adjusted using the state and local government deflator that is prepared by the U.S. Bureau of Economic Analysis.

[3]See, NCSL Fiscal Brief: Projected State Tax Growth in FY 2012 and Beyond, Dec. 6, 2011.

[4]Figure B compares all states with 2008 revenue, though the year may not have been the peak revenues in every case.

[5]Ohio's rate decrease was enacted in 2006.

[6]In addition, several states temporarily raised their rate and lowered it back by 2011.

[7]Much of this section is drawn from presentations by staff from Ernst & Young and Deloitte.

[8]As new technologies develop, this definition will likely evolve. For example, is an iPhone application considered a "specified digital product"?

[9]Digital goods as defined by the Streamlined Sales Tax Agreement are taxed as tangible property if the state elects to do so. Further, some states impose sales tax on the sale of streaming digital products. For example, Washington taxes streamed digital goods, but New Jersey does not.

[10]The simplest example is of a network license bought by a company headquartered in one state, but with employees who are authorized to use that software scattered across the country.

[11]This will likely not be very accurate as the billing address may be the corporate headquarters and not where the service is actually being used.

[12]*http://csrc.nist.gov/publications/nistpubs/800-145/SP800-145.pdf*

[13]See Quill Corp. v. North Dakota, 501 U.S. 298 (1992).

[14]For a helpful discussion of the often conflicting state approaches to the taxation of cloud computing, see Houghton, Kendall, and Luongo, Maryann, "No Improved Visibility for Cloud Computing Taxation," *State Tax Notes*, (July 4, 2011), 69–74.

[15]Martin I. Eisenstein and Barbara J. Slote. "Let the Sunshine In: The Age of Cloud Computing." State Tax Notes, (Nov. 28, 2011), 573–582.

[16]The test is also called the "real object test," "the essence of the transaction test," and the "essence of the relationship test." (BNA State Tax portfolio)

[17]See Revenue Information Bulletin 11-010 (May 23, 2011).

[18]See *Qualcomm, Inc. v. Department of Revenue*, Washington Supreme Court (March 10, 2011).

[19]The court looked at the true object and found the service to be an information service rather than a telecommunication service.

[20]The Main Street Fairness Act (see also S. 1452), H.R. 2701; The Marketplace Equity Act, H.R. 3179; and The Marketplace Fairness Act, S. 1832.

[21]Basis for the law originates in *Scripto, Inc. v. Carson* (362 U.S. 207 1960), which addressed agency nexus and dealt with live agents.

[22]See "Lobbying Congress: 'Amazon' Laws in the Lands of Lincoln and Mt. Rushmore," by Edward Zelinksy, State Tax Notes, May 23, 2011, pp. 557–567.

[23]Vermont's law is only in effect if 15 other states enact an Amazon law. California's law was stayed until 2012, subject to passage of a federal bill.

## About the Authors

**William F. Fox** is a Chancellor's Professor, the William B. Stokely Distinguished Professor of Business and the Director of the Center for Business and Economic Research at the University of Tennessee. He has served as a consultant in more than 25 countries and 10 U.S. states on a wide range of public policy issues.

**LeAnn Luna** is an associate professor and holds a joint appointment between the Department of Accounting and Information Management and the Center for Business and Economic Research at the University of Tennessee. Earlier in her career, Luna amassed nearly a decade of corporate experience that included positions with an international accounting firm and private industry.

# Amazon and the States: New Momentum for States to Recoup Sales Taxes on E-Commerce Transactions

By Sujit M. CanagaRetna

## Rising E-Commerce Transactions and Declining State Revenues

The reach of the Internet into the lives of Americans, particularly in the area of commerce, continues in near-limitless fashion and will, undoubtedly, expand even further in the future. The Internet, however, has exposed a gaping structural chasm in state tax and revenue systems that will only continue to widen unless policymakers, primarily at the federal level, initiate remedial action. Specifically, the exponential growth in Internet-based e-commerce transactions in the past few years has eroded the sales tax revenues of state and local governments given the prohibition on these governments recouping sales taxes on e-commerce purchases. This latter development continues to be a major structural flaw that corrodes state tax and revenue systems. Hence, even when the revenue flows in state and local governments improve to more robust levels from the depths they plunged into during the Great Recession, the inability for all states to uniformly levy sales taxes on e-commerce transactions will result in state and local governments hemorrhaging billions of dollars in revenue every year.

## Limits on States Collecting Sales Taxes on E-Commerce Transactions

The genesis for the prohibition on states universally collecting sales taxes on e-commerce transactions may be traced to a 1992 U.S. Supreme Court ruling, Quill Corporation v. North Dakota, which held that an online retailer is only required to collect sales tax on a transaction if the retailer has a physical presence in the state of the purchasing customer. So, a company like Amazon, an online operation, is not required to collect sales taxes on purchases, while a company like Best Buy, which also has a thriving online operation, is required to levy sales taxes on online purchases, given that practically every state is home to a Best Buy retail outlet. Consequently, states are largely unable to collect sales taxes on a sizable sector of the economy—e-commerce transactions—that has experienced stratospheric growth in the last decade.

## Exponential Growth in E-Commerce Sales

In fact, the U.S. Department of Commerce estimated total e-commerce sales for 2011 at $194.3 billion, an increase of 16.1 percent over 2010. Given that total retail sales in 2011 increased 7.9 percent from 2010, e-commerce sales increasing by twice the rate clearly demonstrates the rising importance of this sector of the economy. Forrester Research, the technology and market research company, estimates that by 2014, U.S. e-commerce sales will expand to nearly $250 billion. Even as a proportion of total sales, e-commerce transactions (adjusted) have seen steady growth. In the fourth quarter of 2011, they accounted for 4.8 percent of total sales in contrast to the fourth quarter of 2002, when they amounted to a mere 1.6 percent, a stark reflection of the growing clout of e-commerce. Figure A shows the escalating importance of e-commerce as a proportion of total retail sales between 2002 and 2011.

## Estimates on State and Local Government Sales Tax Losses Related to E-Commerce Sales

To a large extent, the more than $194 billion in e-commerce transactions in 2011 occurred without online retailers collecting sales taxes on behalf of state and local governments. In fact, the University of Tennessee's Center for Business and Economic Research estimates that, in 2012, states will lose between $11.4 billion and $12.65 billion from untaxed online sales. The center has been studying this issue for nearly 15 years and, in its most recent study—April 2009, estimated the state and local government sales tax losses arising from e-commerce for 46 states and the District of Columbia using both a baseline forecast and an optimistic forecast for e-commerce growth. According to the baseline case, the Center for Business and Economic Research estimated that annual national state and local sales tax losses on e-commerce will grow to $11.4 billion by 2012, for a six-year total loss of $52 billion. For the more optimistic growth case scenario, the center estimated losses to reach $12.65 billion by 2012 and an aggregate loss of $56.3 billion.

Under the baseline estimates carried out by the center, the losses to states—large and small—remain substantial. For instance, for the six-year period 2007-12, Florida is projected to lose $3.7 billion as a result of not collecting sales taxes on e-commerce transactions, while Texas' losses are projected to reach $4 billion for the same period. California is estimated to lose the largest amount—$8.7 billion. Even smaller states like Mississippi ($616.5 million) and South Carolina ($569.3 million) are estimated to experience significant losses. Indiana is estimated to lose $893 million over the six-year review period while Tennessee, which does not have a personal income tax, is estimated to lose $1.9 billion in potential sales tax revenues. Table A provides details on total state and local sales and use tax revenue losses from e-commerce sales and sales as a percentage of 2007 sales and use tax collections, 2007-12.

## Federal Actions Stymie States from Collecting Sales Taxes on E-Commerce Transactions

In addition to the 1992 U.S. Supreme Court Quill decision that prevents states from capturing sales tax revenues on e-commerce purchases, federal legislation, The Internet Tax Freedom Act, enacted in 1998—and extended on three subsequent occa-sions, through 2014—imposes a moratorium on any new taxes on e-commerce transactions in an effort "to promote and preserve the commercial, educational, and informational potential of the Internet." These twin federal actions continue to stymie state efforts to collect taxes on e-commerce transactions at a time of unprecedented fiscal stress at the state level, a time when every dollar in state revenue remains critically important.

## Leveling the Playing Field: Online versus Main Street Purchases

In fact, state policymakers often make the point that recouping taxes on e-commerce purchases is not introducing a new tax, but simply leveling the playing field, i.e., placing online retailers on an equal footing with their "bricks-and-mortar" counterparts regarding the collection of sales taxes. Former Mississippi Gov. Haley Barbour reinforced this viewpoint and, in his farewell address in January 2012, stated that "[G]ood public policy says it is past time that our 'bricks-and-mortar' merchants on Main Street and in our shopping centers get a level playing field with Amazon and the Internet." Only Congressional action, however, can remove federal obstacles on states collecting sales taxes on e-commerce purchases, a move that not only equalizes business opportunities for both online

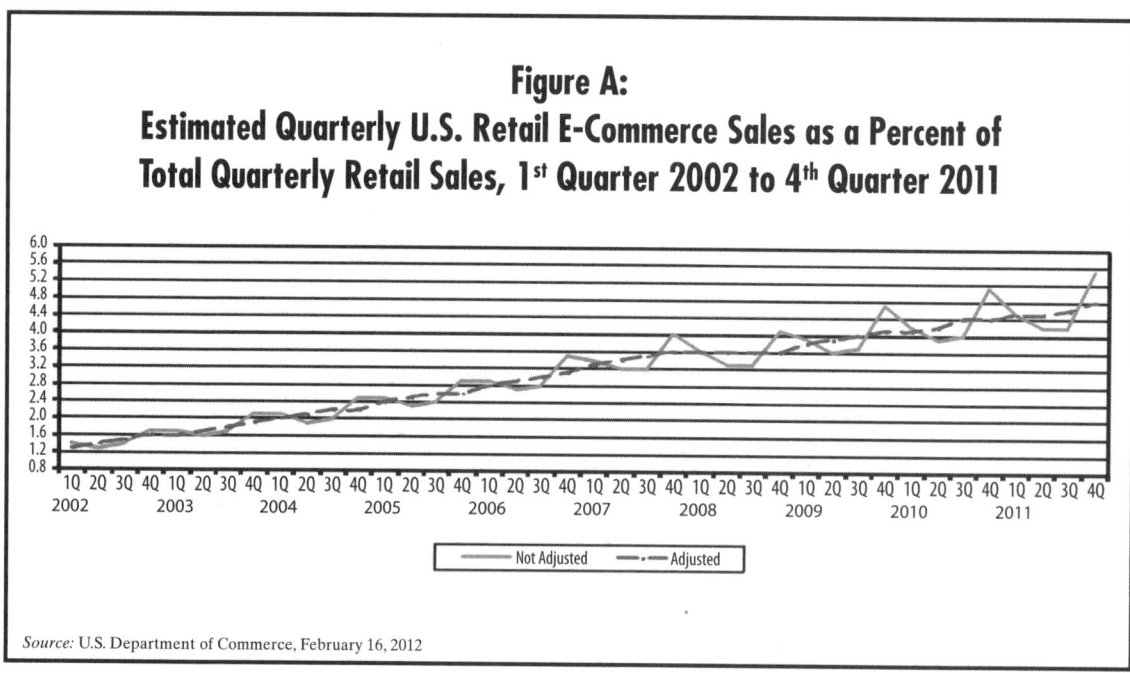

## Figure A:
## Estimated Quarterly U.S. Retail E-Commerce Sales as a Percent of Total Quarterly Retail Sales, 1st Quarter 2002 to 4th Quarter 2011

*Source:* U.S. Department of Commerce, February 16, 2012

# Table A:
# Total State and Local Sales and Use Tax Revenue Losses from E-Commerce Sales, and Sales as a Percentage of Total 2007 Sales and Use Tax Collections, 2007–12

| State or other jurisdiction | 2007 | | 2008 | | 2009 | | 2010 | | 2011 | | 2012 | | Total |
|---|---|---|---|---|---|---|---|---|---|---|---|---|---|
| | Amount | Percent | Amount | Percent | Amount | Percent | Amount | Percent | Amount | Percent | Amount | Percent | |
| Alabama | $108.30 | 2.7% | $115.50 | 2.8% | $103.90 | 2.6% | $128.90 | 3.2% | $151.60 | 3.7% | $170.40 | 4.2% | $778.60 |
| Alaska | 1.00 | 0.6 | 1.00 | 0.6 | 0.90 | 0.5 | 1.10 | 0.7 | 1.30 | 0.8 | 1.50 | 0.9 | 6.80 |
| Arizona | 235.20 | 3.0 | 250.80 | 3.2 | 225.60 | 2.9 | 279.80 | 3.6 | 329.00 | 4.2 | 369.80 | 4.7 | 1690.30 |
| Arkansas | 72.40 | 1.9 | 77.20 | 2.1 | 69.50 | 1.8 | 86.20 | 2.3 | 101.30 | 2.7 | 113.90 | 3.0 | 520.40 |
| California | 1211.20 | 3.0 | 1291.60 | 3.2 | 1162.10 | 2.8 | 1441.10 | 3.5 | 1694.40 | 4.1 | 1904.50 | 4.7 | 8704.80 |
| Colorado | 109.90 | 2.3 | 117.10 | 2.4 | 105.40 | 2.2 | 130.70 | 2.7 | 153.70 | 3.1 | 172.70 | 3.5 | 789.50 |
| Connecticut | 40.60 | 1.3 | 43.20 | 1.4 | 38.90 | 1.3 | 48.30 | 1.6 | 56.70 | 1.9 | 63.80 | 2.1 | 291.50 |
| Florida | 511.20 | 2.2 | 545.10 | 2.4 | 490.40 | 2.1 | 608.20 | 2.7 | 715.10 | 3.1 | 803.80 | 3.5 | 3673.90 |
| Georgia | 260.90 | 2.5 | 278.20 | 2.7 | 250.30 | 2.4 | 310.40 | 3.0 | 365.00 | 3.5 | 410.30 | 3.9 | 1875.20 |
| Hawaii | 38.20 | 1.6 | 40.70 | 1.7 | 36.60 | 1.5 | 45.40 | 1.9 | 53.40 | 2.2 | 60.00 | 2.5 | 274.20 |
| Idaho | 29.50 | 2.3 | 31.30 | 2.5 | 28.30 | 2.2 | 35.10 | 2.8 | 41.20 | 3.2 | 46.40 | 3.6 | 211.90 |
| Illinois | 322.30 | 3.5 | 343.70 | 3.8 | 309.30 | 3.4 | 383.50 | 4.2 | 450.90 | 4.9 | 506.80 | 5.6 | 2316.60 |
| Indiana | 124.20 | 2.3 | 132.50 | 2.4 | 119.20 | 2.2 | 147.80 | 2.7 | 173.80 | 3.2 | 195.30 | 3.6 | 892.80 |
| Iowa | 56.40 | 2.4 | 60.10 | 2.6 | 54.10 | 2.3 | 67.10 | 2.9 | 78.90 | 3.4 | 88.70 | 3.8 | 405.30 |
| Kansas | 90.90 | 3.1 | 96.90 | 3.3 | 87.20 | 2.9 | 108.10 | 3.6 | 127.10 | 4.3 | 142.90 | 4.8 | 653.20 |
| Kentucky | 69.90 | 2.2 | 74.60 | 2.3 | 67.10 | 2.1 | 83.20 | 2.6 | 97.80 | 3.0 | 109.90 | 3.4 | 502.50 |
| Louisiana | 251.80 | 3.8 | 268.50 | 4.0 | 241.60 | 3.6 | 299.60 | 4.5 | 352.20 | 5.3 | 395.90 | 5.9 | 1809.50 |
| Maine | 20.40 | 1.9 | 21.70 | 2.1 | 19.60 | 1.9 | 24.30 | 2.3 | 28.50 | 2.7 | 32.10 | 3.0 | 146.60 |
| Maryland | 117.10 | 2.3 | 124.90 | 2.4 | 112.40 | 2.2 | 139.30 | 2.7 | 163.80 | 3.2 | 184.10 | 3.6 | 841.60 |
| Massachusetts | 83.50 | 2.0 | 89.00 | 2.1 | 80.10 | 1.9 | 99.30 | 2.4 | 116.80 | 2.8 | 131.30 | 3.1 | 600.00 |
| Michigan | 90.00 | 1.1 | 96.00 | 1.2 | 86.30 | 1.1 | 107.10 | 1.3 | 125.90 | 1.6 | 141.50 | 1.8 | 646.70 |
| Minnesota | 149.60 | 3.0 | 159.60 | 3.1 | 143.60 | 2.8 | 178.00 | 3.5 | 209.30 | 4.1 | 235.30 | 4.6 | 1075.30 |
| Mississippi | 85.80 | 2.1 | 91.50 | 2.9 | 82.30 | 2.6 | 102.10 | 3.2 | 120.00 | 3.8 | 134.90 | 4.3 | 616.50 |
| Missouri | 134.00 | 2.6 | 142.90 | 2.7 | 128.60 | 2.5 | 159.40 | 3.1 | 187.50 | 3.6 | 210.70 | 4.1 | 963.00 |
| Nebraska | 39.00 | 2.3 | 41.60 | 2.4 | 37.40 | 2.2 | 46.40 | 2.7 | 54.60 | 3.1 | 61.30 | 3.5 | 280.40 |
| Nevada | 107.40 | 3.2 | 114.60 | 3.4 | 108.10 | 3.1 | 127.80 | 3.8 | 150.30 | 4.5 | 168.90 | 5.0 | 772.10 |
| New Jersey | 128.80 | 1.5 | 137.30 | 1.7 | 123.50 | 1.5 | 153.20 | 1.8 | 180.10 | 2.2 | 202.50 | 2.4 | 925.50 |
| New Mexico | 76.60 | 2.7 | 81.70 | 2.9 | 73.50 | 2.6 | 91.10 | 3.3 | 107.20 | 3.8 | 120.50 | 4.3 | 550.50 |
| New York | 550.40 | 2.8 | 586.90 | 3.0 | 528.10 | 2.7 | 654.90 | 3.3 | 770.00 | 3.9 | 865.50 | 4.4 | 3955.70 |
| North Carolina | 136.00 | 1.8 | 145.00 | 2.0 | 130.40 | 1.8 | 161.80 | 2.2 | 190.20 | 2.6 | 213.80 | 2.9 | 977.10 |
| North Dakota | 9.80 | 1.5 | 10.40 | 1.5 | 9.40 | 1.4 | 11.60 | 1.7 | 13.60 | 2.0 | 15.30 | 2.3 | 70.10 |
| Ohio | 195.80 | 2.1 | 208.80 | 2.3 | 187.90 | 2.0 | 233.00 | 2.5 | 274.00 | 3.0 | 307.90 | 3.3 | 1407.50 |
| Oklahoma | 89.50 | 2.6 | 95.50 | 2.8 | 85.90 | 2.5 | 106.50 | 3.1 | 125.30 | 3.6 | 140.80 | 4.1 | 643.50 |
| Pennsylvania | 220.00 | 2.5 | 234.60 | 2.6 | 211.00 | 2.4 | 261.70 | 3.0 | 307.70 | 3.5 | 345.90 | 3.9 | 1580.90 |
| Rhode Island | 18.50 | 2.1 | 19.70 | 2.3 | 17.70 | 2.0 | 22.00 | 2.5 | 25.80 | 3.0 | 29.00 | 3.3 | 132.70 |
| South Carolina | 79.20 | 2.4 | 84.50 | 2.5 | 76.00 | 2.3 | 94.20 | 2.8 | 110.80 | 3.3 | 124.50 | 3.7 | 569.30 |
| South Dakota | 18.90 | 1.8 | 20.20 | 2.0 | 18.20 | 1.8 | 22.50 | 2.2 | 26.50 | 2.6 | 29.80 | 2.9 | 136.10 |
| Tennessee | 261.30 | 3.0 | 278.60 | 3.2 | 250.70 | 2.9 | 310.90 | 3.6 | 365.50 | 4.3 | 410.80 | 4.8 | 1877.70 |
| Texas | 553.60 | 1.9 | 590.30 | 2.0 | 531.10 | 1.8 | 658.60 | 2.3 | 774.40 | 2.6 | 870.40 | 3.0 | 3978.30 |
| Utah | 56.30 | 2.3 | 60.00 | 2.4 | 54.00 | 2.2 | 66.90 | 2.7 | 78.70 | 3.2 | 88.50 | 3.6 | 404.30 |
| Vermont | 16.00 | 2.6 | 17.00 | 2.7 | 15.30 | 2.5 | 19.00 | 3.0 | 22.30 | 3.6 | 25.10 | 4.0 | 114.80 |
| Virginia | 131.60 | 2.4 | 140.40 | 2.5 | 126.30 | 2.3 | 156.60 | 2.8 | 184.10 | 3.3 | 207.00 | 3.7 | 946.00 |
| Washington | 179.30 | 1.9 | 191.20 | 2.1 | 172.00 | 1.8 | 213.30 | 2.3 | 250.80 | 2.7 | 281.90 | 3.0 | 1288.70 |
| West Virginia | 32.20 | 2.5 | 34.30 | 2.6 | 30.90 | 2.4 | 38.30 | 2.9 | 45.00 | 3.5 | 50.60 | 3.9 | 231.40 |
| Wisconsin | 90.40 | 2.0 | 96.40 | 2.2 | 86.70 | 2.0 | 107.60 | 2.4 | 126.50 | 2.9 | 142.10 | 3.2 | 649.70 |
| Wyoming | 18.20 | 2.0 | 19.40 | 2.2 | 17.50 | 1.9 | 21.60 | 2.4 | 25.40 | 2.8 | 28.60 | 3.2 | 130.70 |
| Dist. of Columbia | 22.60 | 2.8 | 24.10 | 3.0 | 21.70 | 2.7 | 26.90 | 3.3 | 31.60 | 3.9 | 35.50 | 4.4 | 162.50 |
| Total | 7245.60 | 2.4 | 7726.30 | 2.6 | 6951.40 | 2.3 | 8620.40 | 2.9 | 10135.80 | 3.4 | 11392.70 | 3.8 | 52072.20 |

*Sources:* "State and Local Government Sales Tax Revenue Losses from Electronic Commerce," The University of Tennessee, April 12, 2009

retailers and bricks-and-mortar retailers, but also permits states to repair one of the major structural flaws in their tax systems. As Indiana Gov. Mitch Daniels noted in January 2012, "[T]he only complete answer to this problem is a federal solution that treats all retailers and all states the same."1

## Amazon's Dominant Role in E-Commerce

In assessing the major players in the tens of billions of dollar e-commerce trade, Amazon.com vaults to the top. Amazon.com, the multinational e-commerce company founded in 1994 by Jeff Bezos (the site went online in 1995), is the largest online retailer in the United States and, for that reason alone, garners the most attention in the ongoing debate with states over sales tax collections. In fact, in 2011, Amazon's e-commerce net sales were more than four and a half times the amount of one of its major rivals, Staples, Inc.— $48.1 billion compared to $11 billion. According to estimates by 24/7 Wall St., the financial news and opinion publication, about $1 billion of the amount states lose from e-commerce is related to transactions on Amazon.

## Impetus for Online Retailers Blocking States From Collecting Sales Taxes

For a number of years, online retailers like Amazon (with net sales that rose over 40 percent to more than $48.1 billion in 2011 from $34.2 billion in 2010), Overstock.com and diamond Internet retailer Blue Nile, have resisted collecting sales taxes on behalf of state and local governments on the e-commerce transactions occurring through their websites. The primary force behind this resistance is the increased retail costs that come with applying a sales tax, a move that would make the online retailer less competitive compared to a similar purchase made at a bricks-and-mortar store. Furthermore, online retailers contend that they are not required to collect sales taxes because: (1) they usually do not have a physical presence, or nexus, in the state; (2) they are not always directly involved in the transaction since they often deploy local affiliates, i.e., partner sites, local businesses, blogs or nonprofits, that earn commissions by advertising or linking to an online retailer's products; and (3) the warehouses processing the e-commerce purchases are owned

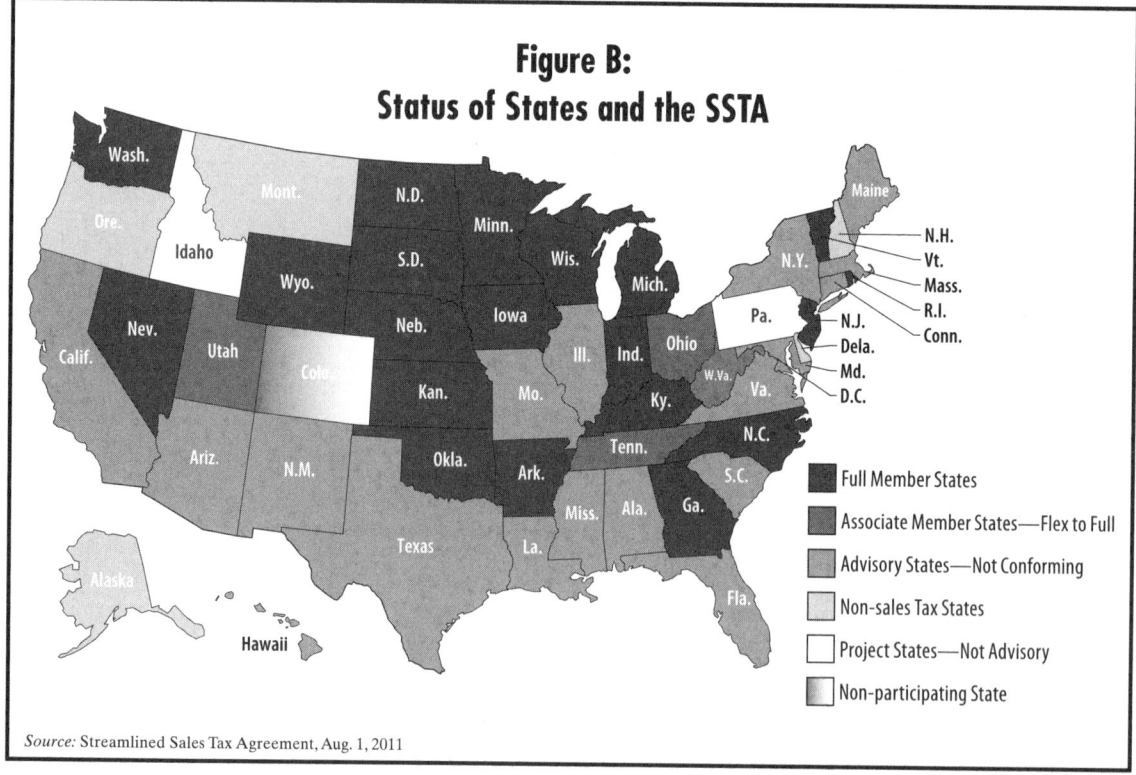

**Figure B:
Status of States and the SSTA**

- Full Member States
- Associate Member States—Flex to Full
- Advisory States—Not Conforming
- Non-sales Tax States
- Project States—Not Advisory
- Non-participating State

*Source:* Streamlined Sales Tax Agreement, Aug. 1, 2011

by subsidiaries and not directly by the online retailer. Amazon does collect sales taxes in five states: Washington, where it is based; Kansas and North Dakota, where it has call centers; Kentucky, where it processes returns; and New York, where the legislature passed a law in 2008 to require the tax, although Amazon is protesting this law in court. Similarly, Overstock.com, another major Web-based retailer, collects sales taxes from customers in its home state of Utah.

## States Fight Back: Streamlined Sales Tax Agreement

Given the lack of a federal solution to this vexing revenue problem for some two decades, states have been forced to act unilaterally on securing even a portion of the sales taxes on e-commerce purchases. These efforts have gathered momentum in recent years as states sought to identify every possible revenue source during the lean years of the Great Recession. One of the strategies states have adopted includes the formation of the Streamlined Sales and Use Tax Agreement in fall 1999, an effort to collect taxes on the burgeoning e-commerce transactions occurring within their borders. The agreement seeks to simplify the rules that govern the collection of sales taxes in more than 8,000 different jurisdictions across the country. Specifically, the agreement intends to minimize the costs and administrative burdens placed on retailers that collect sales taxes, particularly retailers operating in multiple states. The agreement also works toward ensuring that the administration of the sales tax in one state is similar to any other state. In addition, while the agreement encourages remote sellers selling over the Internet and by mail order to collect sales taxes from customers living in states that have enacted conforming legislation, it also levels the playing field so that local bricks-and-mortar stores, online shops and mail-order retailers operate under the same rules. State fiscal experts anticipate that once federal legislation is introduced to remove the barriers on states collecting sales taxes on e-commerce transactions, states that have adopted the Streamlined Sales and Use Tax Agreement could immediately begin compelling online retailers to collect sales taxes on their behalf. As of Aug. 1, 2011, 24 states had enacted conforming legislation complying with the agreement, though a number of the larger states, including California, Florida, Illinois, New York, Pennsylvania and Texas, have not signed on as full member states.

## States Fight Back: Forwarding Tax Bills to Online Retailers

Another state strategy involves forwarding tax bills to Amazon for uncollected sales taxes. For instance, in September 2010, based on an audit of e-commerce transactions within the state, Texas Comptroller Susan Combs sent the company a bill for $269 million for uncollected sales taxes, including interest and penalties, for the period December 2005 to December 2009. Combs maintained that, "[I]f you have a presence in the state of Texas, you are required to pay sales taxes, just like any other business that has a presence in the state." In response, Amazon emphasized that its Irving, Texas, location did not represent a company storefront—since it was owned by a subsidiary—and that it did not constitute the kind of physical presence the state's sales tax laws require. Combs' office indicated that Texas loses an estimated $600 million in e-commerce sales taxes every year. In response to the tax bill from Texas, Amazon announced the closure of its Irving distribution center—one it had operated since 2005—and decided to relocate to another state with a more hospitable tax environment.

## States Fight Back: Affiliate Marketers and "Click Through" Laws

Yet another strategy adopted by a handful of states involves claiming nexus via in-state affiliates that sell products on well-known websites such as Amazon. Tapping local affiliates to collect sales taxes on online transactions through an out-of-state online retailer's website takes the form of so-called "click through" laws. Local affiliates are offered a referral fee by the out-of-state-online retailer, such as Amazon, for every purchase that originates at the local affiliate's site and then proceeds to the online retailer's site. The click through provision in these state laws said that the local affiliate represented a sufficient physical presence, a designation that required the online retailer to collect sales taxes on the purchase. In response to the click through legislation requiring affiliates to collect sales taxes, Amazon terminated its affiliate programs in Arkansas, Colorado, Illinois, North Carolina and Rhode Island.

## Multiple States Clinch Agreements with Amazon

Several other developments related to Amazon and the states surfaced in late 2011 and the first quarter of 2012. In December 2011, Virginia Gov.

Bob McDonnell announced that Amazon would open two distribution centers that would generate 1,350 jobs in the state. In late February 2012, in a victory for traditional brick-and-mortar retailers, McDonnell announced an agreement with Amazon in which the company agreed to collect and pay sales tax on online purchases made by Virginians. The Virginia General Assembly had been considering legislation to close the so-called Amazon loophole. In January 2012, Amazon, which currently operates three warehouses in Indiana and has announced plans to open a fourth, reached an agreement with the state to begin collecting Indiana sales taxes on online purchases shipped to the state on Jan. 1, 2014, or 90 days from the enactment of a federal law, whichever comes first. Amazon had clinched similar agreements with Tennessee and South Carolina. In early 2012, Amazon also approached Florida officials regarding building two $200 million distribution centers that would hire 2,500-3,000 Floridians in exchange for a delay in collecting sales taxes until 2014.

## Change in Strategy Propelled by Amazon v. California

In the first half of 2011, Amazon engaged in a bitter battle with California on the state's effort to require out-of-state retailers to collect sales taxes on online purchases if the company had affiliates, offices, workers or other ties to the state. In fact, Amazon channeled millions of dollars to place the issue before California voters via a ballot referendum and wiped out all references to California-based affiliates on its website. Amazon suddenly relented and decided to enter into a deal with California, presumably on the grounds that the damage to its reputation was mounting. In September 2011, California Gov. Jerry Brown signed an agreement with Amazon that will require the company to begin collecting sales taxes on online purchases after a one-year grace period. This represented a complete turnaround in Amazon's strategy on this issue not only with California, but also with other states.

The California agreement signaled a radical change in strategy on Amazon's part in dealing with the states. The company had previously engaged in acrimonious battles with states, and analysts contend that Amazon executives concluded that the company's brand name could suffer irreparable harm if these legal entanglements continued. In addition, Amazon had often pitted states against each other, dangling the promise of thousands of jobs at distribution facilities to states that offered sales tax exemptions and threatening to leave states that did not, a strategy that imperiled the company's reputation, particularly with customers. Hence, the agreement signed with California was a radical departure in the company's approach to dealing with states regarding the sales tax issue and signaled an inclination to work collaboratively with state officials to resolve this nettlesome issue in a mutually beneficial manner.

## Amazon Explores Retail Establishments

Finally, there is strong speculation that Amazon intends to launch a chain of small, boutique stores in key cities across the country, starting in Seattle, stocked with the company's high margin, high-end items, including the growing line of Amazon exclusives, Kindle e-readers, Kindle Fire and accessories such as cases, screen protectors and USB adapters. If the Amazon boutique store concept spreads across the country, along with an increasing number of Amazon-owned distribution centers in numerous states, the constraints of the Quill decision will not be as severe to states if the status quo prevails regarding federal legislation.

## Amazon Radically Changes Its Strategy in Dealing with States

The donnybrook between states seeking to require companies to collect sales taxes on online purchases and the efforts by companies like Amazon to block these state collection efforts often has been venomous and frequently litigated in court. As described above, this thrust and parry has gone on for a number of years now. While Amazon's decision to reach an agreement with California in September 2011 constituted an important shift in the company's strategy vis-à-vis states on the sales tax issue, Amazon's wholehearted support of legislation that emerged in the U.S. Senate a few months later further confirmed this transformation.

In November 2011, a bipartisan group of 10 U.S. senators introduced The Marketplace Fairness Act. The bill, which was immediately referred to the U.S. Senate Finance Committee, establishes a system for states and localities to collect sales taxes on online purchases, the kind of federal initiative that states have sought for some time. While the legislation had been previously introduced, these efforts did not have the force of bipartisan support and, equally importantly, did not have the support of the nation's largest online retailer, Amazon.

In a Nov. 9, 2011, press release, Paul Misener, Amazon's vice president for Global Public Policy noted, "[A]mazon strongly supports enactment of the Enzi-Durbin-Alexander bill and will work with Congress, retailers, and the states to get this bipartisan legislation passed. It's a win-win resolution—and as analysts have noted, Amazon offers customers the best prices with or without sales tax."2 Amazon's support for the federal legislation remains a transformational move and the bipartisan nature of the proposed bill enhances the likelihood of its passage, twin developments that were never achieved previously. It appears that Amazon made the calculation that it was better to pursue a national solution to this obstacle and avoid rancorous legal wrangles with states that had the potential to not only seriously tarnish the company's brand name, but also lead to customer losses. If this bill becomes law, it will not only permit states to compel out-of-state retailers to collect sales tax at the time of the online purchase and remit those taxes on behalf of customers, but also will expedite collection on behalf of third-party sellers. Furthermore, the proposed legislation will authorize states to recoup additional revenue without new taxes or federal spending and will facilitate compliance with state sales tax laws for consumers and small retailers. The bipartisan action at the Congressional level and Amazon's positive response not only represents a sea change in the decade-plus long saga of states trying to collect taxes on online purchases, but these developments also represent real potential for both repairing and bolstering state tax and revenue systems in the future.

## Conclusion

While states can afford to be cautiously optimistic about the action at the federal level and the enthusiastic support for this measure by Amazon, the enactment of The Marketplace Fairness Act into law is still far from a done deal. Given that 2012 is an election year and the toxic political climate in Washington, D.C., continues, public and private officials at all levels of government will need to invest a significant amount of political capital to secure passage. Nevertheless, states can rest assured that the progress made on leveling the playing field between online purchases and brick-and-mortar purchases in the last year has been the most impressive since the 1992 Quill decision.

## Notes

[1]"State, *Amazon.com*, reach sales tax agreement" Media Release, Office of the Governor, Indiana, January 9, 2012. *http://www.in.gov/activecalendar/EventList.aspx?view=EventDetails&eventid=50510&information_id=101251&type=&syndicate=syndicate*

[2]"Amazon Strongly Supports Enactment Of Enzi-Durbin-Alexander Federal Online Sales Tax Bill," Press Release, November 9, 2011. *http://www.thestreet.com/story/11305878/1/amazon-strongly-supports-enactment-of-enzi-durbin-alexander-federal-online-sales-tax-bill.html*

## About the Author

**Sujit M. CanagaRetna** is senior fiscal analyst at The Council of State Governments' Southern office, the Southern Legislative Conference in Atlanta, Ga., where he researches, analyzes and writes on state fiscal and economic development trends. He also tracks legislative issues and policy developments in Mississippi, North Carolina and Tennessee. CanagaRetna frequently testifies before state legislatures and other audiences across the country on topics affecting state finances. He is regularly interviewed by different media outlets (television, radio and print) on issues affecting state finances. CanagaRetna also has staffed state legislative delegations to a number of countries, including England, Scotland, Thailand, Indonesia and China. He has a bachelor's degree from Bennington College in Vermont and master's degrees in International Affairs and Public Administration from Columbia University in New York. Prior to joining CSG in March 1998, CanagaRetna worked for the New York City Comptroller's Office for nearly six years.

## Table 7.9
## STATE TAX AMNESTY PROGRAMS, 1982–Present

| State or other jurisdiction | Amnesty period | Legislative authorization | Major taxes covered | Accounts receivable included | Collections ($ millions) (a) | Installment arrangements permitted (b) |
|---|---|---|---|---|---|---|
| Alabama | 1/20/84–4/1/84 | No (c) | All | No | 3.2 | No |
| | 2/1/09–5/15/09 | Yes | Ind. Income, Corp. Income, Business, Sales & Use | N.A. | 8.1 | N.A. |
| Arizona | 11/22/82–1/20/83 | No (c) | All | No | 6.0 | Yes |
| | 1/1/02–2/28/02 | Yes | Individual Income | No | N.A. | No |
| | 9/1/03–10/31/03 | Yes | All (t) | N.A. | 73.0 | Yes |
| | 5/1/09–6/1/09 | N.A. | All | N.A. | 32.0 | N.A. |
| Arkansas | 9/1/87–11/30/87 | Yes | All | No | 1.7 | Yes |
| | 7/1/04–12/31/04 | Yes | All | N.A. | N.A. | No |
| California | 12/10/84–3/15/85 | Yes | Individual Income | Yes | 154.0 | Yes |
| | | Yes | Sales | No | 43.0 | Yes |
| | 2/1/05–3/31/05 | Yes | Income, Franchise, Sales | N.A. | N.A. | Yes |
| Colorado | 9/16/85–11/15/85 | Yes | All | No | 6.4 | Yes |
| | 6/1/03–6/30/03 | N.A. | All | N.A. | 18.4 | Yes |
| | 10/1/11–11/15/11 | Yes | All | No | … | No |
| Connecticut | 9/1/90–11/30/90 | Yes | All | Yes | 54.0 | Yes |
| | 9/1/95–11/30/95 | Yes | All | Yes | 46.2 | Yes |
| | 9/1/02–12/2/02 | N.A. | All | N.A. | 109.0 | N.A. |
| | 5/1/09–6/25/09 | Yes | All | No | 40.0 | No |
| Delaware | 9/1/09–10/30/09 | Yes | All | Yes | N.A. | Yes |
| Florida | 1/1/87–6/30/87 | Yes | Intangibles | No | 13.0 | No |
| | 1/1/88–6/30/88 | Yes (d) | All | No | 8.4 (d) | No |
| | 7/1/03–10/31/03 | Yes | All | N.A. | 80.0 | N.A. |
| | 7/1/10–9/30/10 | Yes | All | Yes | … | Yes |
| Georgia | 10/1/92–12/5/92 | Yes | All | Yes | 51.3 | No |
| Hawaii | 5/27/09–6/26/09 | N.A. | All | No | 14.0 | No |
| Idaho | 5/20/83–8/30/83 | No (c) | Individual Income | No | 0.3 | No |
| Illinois | 10/1/84–11/30/84 | Yes | All (u) | Yes | 160.5 | No |
| | 10/1/03–11/17/03 | Yes | All | N.A. | 532.0 | N.A. |
| | 10/1/10–11/8/10 | Yes | All | Yes | 314 (y) | No |
| Indiana | 9/15/05–11/15/05 | N.A. | All | N.A. | 255.0 | Yes |
| Iowa | 9/2/86–10/31/86 | Yes | All | Yes | 35.1 | N.A. |
| | 9/4/07–10/31/07 | Yes | All | Yes | N.A. | N.A. |
| Kansas | 7/1/84–9/30/84 | Yes | All | No | 0.6 | No |
| | 10/1/03–11/30/03 | Yes | All | Yes | 53.7 | N.A. |
| | 9/1/10–10/15/10 | Yes | All | Yes | … | No |
| Kentucky | 9/15/88–9/30/88 | Yes (c) | All | No | 100.0 | No |
| | 8/1/02–9/30/02 | Yes (c) | All | No | 100.0 | No |
| Louisiana | 10/1/85–12/31/85 | Yes | All | No | 1.2 | Yes (f) |
| | 10/1/87–12/15/87 | Yes | All | No | 0.3 | Yes (f) |
| | 10/1/98–12/31/98 | Yes | All | No (q) | 1.3 | No |
| | 9/1/01–10/30/01 | Yes | All | Yes | 192.9 | No |
| | 9/1/09–10/31/09 | Yes | All | … | 303.7 | … |
| Maine | 11/1/90–12/31/90 | Yes | All | Yes | 29.0 | Yes |
| | 9/1/03–11/30/03 | Yes | All | N.A. | 37.6 | N.A. |
| | 9/1/09–11/30/09 | Yes | All | Yes | 16.2 | No |
| | 9/1/10–11/30/10 | Yes | Tax Receivables Reduction Initiative | Yes | 16.2 | No |
| Maryland | 9/1/87–11/2/87 | Yes | All | Yes | 34.6 (g) | No |
| | 9/1/01–10/31/01 | Yes | All | Yes | 39.2 | No |
| | 9/1/09–10/31/09 | Yes | Income, Withholding, Sales & Use | Yes | 9.6 | Yes |
| Massachusetts | 10/17/83–1/17/84 | Yes | All | Yes | 86.5 | Yes (h) |
| | 10/1/02–11/30/02 | Yes | All | Yes | 96.1 | Yes |
| | 1/1/03–2/28/03 | Yes | All | Yes | 11.2 | N.A. |
| | 4/1/10–6/1/10 (x) | Yes | All | Yes | 32.6 | No |
| Michigan | 5/12/86–6/30/86 | Yes | All | Yes | 109.8 | No |
| | 5/15/02–6/30/02 | Yes | All | Yes | N.A. | N.A. |
| | 5/15/11–6/30/11 | Yes | All | Yes | … | No |
| Minnesota | 8/1/84–10/31/84 | Yes | All | Yes | 12.1 | No |
| Mississippi | 9/1/86–11/30/86 | Yes | All | No | 1.0 | No |
| | 9/1/04–12/31/04 | Yes | All | No | 7.9 | No |

See footnotes at end of table.

# STATE TAX AMNESTY PROGRAMS, 1982–Present — Continued

| State or other jurisdiction | Amnesty period | Legislative authorization | Major taxes covered | Accounts receivable included | Collections ($ millions) (a) | Installment arrangements permitted (b) |
|---|---|---|---|---|---|---|
| Missouri........................ | 9/1/83–10/31/83 | No (c) | All | No | 0.9 | No |
| | 8/1/02–10/31/02 | Yes | All | Yes | 76.4 | N.A. |
| | 8/1/03–10/31/03 | Yes | All | Yes | 20.0 | N.A. |
| Nebraska ...................... | 8/1/04–10/31/04 | Yes | All | No | 7.5 | No |
| Nevada.......................... | 2/1/02–6/30/02 | N.A. | All | N.A. | 7.3 | N.A. |
| | 7/1/08–10/28/08 | No | Sales, Business, License | Yes | ... | No |
| | 7/1/10–10/1/10 | Yes | All | Yes | ... | No |
| New Hampshire ........... | 12/1/97–2/17/98 | Yes | All | Yes | 13.5 | No |
| | 12/1/01–2/15/02 | Yes | All | Yes | 13.5 | N.A. |
| New Jersey ................... | 9/10/87–12/8/87 | Yes | All | Yes | 186.5 | Yes |
| | 3/15/96–6/1/96 | Yes | All | Yes | 359.0 | No |
| | 4/15/02–6/10/02 | Yes | All | Yes | 276.9 | N.A. |
| | 5/4/09–6/15/09 | Yes | All | N.A. | 725.0 | N.A. |
| New Mexico ................. | 8/15/85–11/13/85 | Yes | All (i) | No | 13.6 | Yes |
| | 8/16/99–11/12/99 | Yes | All | Yes | 45.0 | Yes |
| | 6/7/10–9/30/10 | Yes | All | No | ... | Yes |
| New York...................... | 11/1/85–1/31/86 | Yes | All (j) | Yes | 401.3 | Yes |
| | 11/1/96–1/31/97 | Yes | All | Yes | 253.4 | Yes (o) |
| | 11/18/02–1/31/03 | Yes | All | Yes | 582.7 | Yes (s) |
| | 10/1/05–3/1/06 | N.A. | Income, Corporate | N.A. | 349.0 | N.A. |
| New York City ............. | 10/20/03–1/23/04 | Yes | All (v) | Yes (w) | ... | No |
| | 1/15/10–3/15/10 | Yes | ... | Yes | 56.5 | No |
| North Carolina............. | 9/1/89–12/1/89 | Yes | All (k) | Yes | 37.6 | No |
| North Dakota............... | 9/1/83–11/30/83 | No (c) | All | No | 0.2 | Yes |
| | 10/1/03–1/31/04 | Yes | N.A. | N.A. | 6.9 | N.A. |
| Ohio............................. | 10/15/01–1/15/02 | Yes | All | No | 48.5 | No |
| | 1/1/06–2/15/06 | Yes | All | No | 63.0 | No |
| Oklahoma..................... | 7/1/84–12/31/84 | Yes | Income, Sales | Yes | 13.9 | No (l) |
| | 8/15/02–11/15/02 | N.A. | All (r) | Yes | N.A. | N.A. |
| | 9/15/08–11/14/08 | Yes | All | Yes | 81.0 | Yes |
| Oregon......................... | 10/1/09–11/19/09 | Yes | Personal, Corporate, Inheritance | N.A. | N.A. | N.A. |
| Pennsylvania ............... | 10/13/95–1/10/96 | Yes | All | Yes | N.A. | No |
| | 4/26/10–6/18/10 | Yes | All | Yes | 261.0 | No |
| Rhode Island............... | 10/15/86–1/12/87 | Yes | All | No | 0.7 | Yes |
| | 4/15/96–6/28/96 | Yes | All | Yes | 7.9 | Yes |
| | 7/15/06–9/30/06 | N.A. | All | Yes | 6.5 | Yes |
| South Carolina............. | 9/1/85–11/30/85 | Yes | All | Yes | 7.1 | Yes |
| | 10/15/02–12/2/02 | Yes | All | Yes | 66.2 | N.A. |
| South Dakota............... | 4/1/99–5/15/99 | Yes | All | Yes | 0.5 | N.A. |
| Texas............................ | 2/1/84–2/29/84 | No (c) | All (m) | No | 0.5 | No |
| | 3/11/04–3/31/04 | No (c) | All (m) | No | N.A. | No |
| | 6/15/07–8/15/07 | No (c) | All (m) | No | N.A. | No |
| Vermont........................ | 5/15/90–6/25/90 | Yes | All | Yes | 1 (e) | No |
| | 7/20/09–8/31/09 | Yes | All | N.A. | 2.2 | N.A. |
| Virginia........................ | 2/1/90–3/31/90 | Yes | All | Yes | 32.2 | No |
| | 9/2/03–11/3/03 | Yes | All | Yes | 98.3 | N.A. |
| | 10/7/09–12/5/09 | Yes | All | Yes | 102.1 | No |
| Washington................... | 2/1/11–4/30/11 | N.A. | N.A. | N.A. | ... | N.A. |
| West Virginia............... | 10/1/86–12/31/86 | Yes | All | Yes | 15.9 | Yes |
| | 9/1/04–10/31/04 | Yes | All | N.A. | 10.4 | Yes |
| Wisconsin ..................... | 9/15/85–11/22/85 | Yes | All | Yes (n) | 27.3 | Yes |
| | 6/15/98–8/14/98 | Yes | All | Yes | 30.9 | N.A. |
| Dist. of Columbia ........ | 7/1/87–9/30/87 | Yes | All | Yes | 24.3 | Yes |
| | 7/10/95–8/31/95 | Yes | All (p) | Yes | 19.5 | Yes (p) |
| | 8/2/10–9/30/10 | Yes | All (p) | Yes | 20.8 | No |
| No. Mariana Islands .... | 9/30/05–3/30/06 | Yes | All | N.A. | N.A. | N.A. |

See footnotes at end of table.

# STATE TAX AMNESTY PROGRAMS, 1982–Present — Continued

*Source:* The Federation of Tax Administrators, March 2012.

*Key:*

N.A. — Not available.

(a) Where applicable, figure includes local portions of certain taxes collected under the state tax amnesty program.

(b) "No" indicates requirement of full payment by the expiration of the amnesty period. "Yes" indicates allowance of full payment after the expiration of the amnesty period.

(c) Authority for amnesty derived from pre-existing statutory powers permitting the waiver of tax penalties.

(d) Does not include intangibles tax and drug taxes. Gross collections totaled $22.1 million, with $13.7 million in penalties withdrawn.

(e) Preliminary figure.

(f) Amnesty taxpayers were billed for the interest owed, with payment due within 30 days of notification.

(g) Figure includes $1.1 million for the separate program conducted by the Department of Natural Resources for the boat excise tax.

(h) The amnesty statute was construed to extend the amnesty to those who applied to the department before the end of the amnesty period, and permitted them to file overdue returns and pay back taxes and interest at a later date.

(i) The severance taxes, including the six oil and gas severance taxes, the resources excise tax, the corporate franchise tax, and the special fuels tax were not subject to amnesty.

(j) Availability of amnesty for the corporation tax, the oil company taxes, the transportation and transmissions companies tax, the gross receipts oil tax and the unincorporated business tax restricted to entities with 500 or fewer employees in the United States on the date of application. In addition, a taxpayer principally engaged in aviation, or a utility subject to the supervision of the State Department of Public Service was also ineligible.

(k) Local taxes and real property taxes were not included.

(l) Full payment of tax liability required before the end of the amnesty period to avoid civil penalties.

(m) Texas does not impose a corporate or individual income tax. In practical effect, the amnesty was limited to the sales tax and other excises.

(n) Waiver terms varied depending upon the date the tax liability was assessed.

(o) Installment arrangements were permitted if applicant demonstrated that payment would present a severe financial hardship.

(p) Does not include real property taxes. All interest was waived on tax payments made before July 31, 1995. After this date, only 50 percent of the interest was waived.

(q) Exception for individuals who owed $500 or less.

(r) Except for property and motor fuel taxes.

(s) Multiple payments could be made so long as the required balance was paid in full no later than March 15, 2003.

(t) All taxes except property, estate and unclaimed property.

(u) Does not include the motor fuel use tax.

(v) All NYC taxes administered by the NYC Dept. of Finance are covered except for Real Estate Tax. NYC Sales & Use Tax & NYC Resident Personal Income Tax also are not covered because they are administered by the NYS Dept. of Taxation & Finance.

(w) Taxpayers under audit as of 3/10/03 are ineligible; Taxpayers with an existing installment agreement are ineligible; Taxpayers under criminal investigation are ineligible; Taxpayers party to an administrative or court proceeding must withdraw as a condition.

(x) The Massachusetts Department of Revenue was required to hold an amnesty to end before June 30, 2010.

(y) In Illinois, the 2010 Amnesty called collected a total of $717 million, $314 million for the state GF and the rest for local governments.

## Table 7.10
## STATE EXCISE TAX RATES
(As of January 1, 2012)

| State or other jurisdiction | General sales and gross receipts tax (percent) | Cigarettes (cents per pack of 20) | Distilled spirits Excise tax rate ($ per gallon) | Distilled spirits Sales taxes applied | Motor fuel excise tax rates (cents per gallon) (a) Gasoline | Motor fuel excise tax rates (cents per gallon) (a) Diesel | Motor fuel excise tax rates (cents per gallon) (a) Gasohol |
|---|---|---|---|---|---|---|---|
| Alabama | 4.0 | 42.5 (b) | (c) | Yes | 18.0 (e)(g) | 19.0 (e)(g) | 18.0 (e)(g) |
| Alaska | 0.0 | 200 | 12.80 (d) | ... | 8.0 | 8.0 | 8.0 |
| Arizona | 6.6 | 200 | 3.00 (d) | Yes | 19.0 (g) | 27.0 (g) | 19.0 (g) |
| Arkansas | 6.0 | 115 | 2.50 (k) | Yes | 21.8 (g) | 22.8 (g) | 21.8 (g) |
| California | 7.25 (h) | 87 | 3.30 (d) | Yes | 41.2 (g)(i) | 38.0 (g)(i) | 41.2 (g)(i) |
| Colorado | 2.9 | 84 | 2.28 | Yes | 22.0 | 20.5 | 22.0 |
| Connecticut | 6.35 | 340 | 4.50 (d) | Yes | 25.0 | 46.2 | 25.0 |
| Delaware | 0.0 | 160 | 5.46 (d) | ... | 23.0 (g) | 22.0 (g) | 23.0 (g) |
| Florida | 6.0 | 133.9 (j) | 6.50 (k) | Yes | 16.6 (g)(l) | 30.0 (g)(l) | 16.6 (g)(l) |
| Georgia | 4.0 | 37 | 3.79 (d) | Yes | 20.4 (g) | 21.8 (g) | 20.4 (g) |
| Hawaii | 4.0 | 320 | 5.98 | Yes | 17.0 (e)(g) | 17.0 (e)(g) | 17.0 (e)(g) |
| Idaho | 6.0 | 57 | (c) | Yes | 26.0 (g)(n) | 26.0 (g)(n) | 26.0 (g)(n) |
| Illinois | 6.25 | 98 (b) | 8.55 (d) | Yes | 20.1 (e)(f)(g) | 22.6 (e)(f)(g) | 20.1 (e)(f)(g) |
| Indiana | 7.0 | 99.5 | 2.68 (d) | Yes | 18.0 (f)(g) | 16.0 (f)(g) | 18.0 (f)(g) |
| Iowa | 6.0 | 136 | (c) | Yes | 22.0 (g) | 23.5 (g) | 20.0 (g) |
| Kansas | 6.3 | 79 | 2.50 (d) | ... | 24.0 | 26.0 | 24.0 |
| Kentucky | 6.0 | 60 (o) | 1.92 (d) | Yes (k) | 27.8 (f)(g)(p) | 24.8 (f)(g)(p) | 27.8 (f)(g)(p) |
| Louisiana | 4.0 | 36 | 2.50 (d) | Yes | 20.0 | 20.0 | 20.0 |
| Maine | 5.0 | 200 | (c) | Yes | 30.0 (q) | 31.2 (q) | 30.0 (q) |
| Maryland | 6.0 | 200 | 1.50 | Yes | 23.5 | 24.25 | 23.5 |
| Massachusetts | 6.25 | 251 | 4.05 (d) | Yes | 21.0 | 21.0 | 21.0 |
| Michigan | 6.0 | 200 | (c) | Yes | 19.0 (g) | 15.0 (g) | 19.0 (g) |
| Minnesota | 6.875 | 123 (r) | 5.03 (d) | Yes | 28.1 (g)(q) | 28.1 (g)(q) | 28.1 (g)(q) |
| Mississippi | 7.0 | 68 | (c) | Yes | 18.4 (g) | 18.4 (g) | 18.4 (g) |
| Missouri | 4.225 | 17 (b) | 2.00 | Yes | 17.3 (g) | 17.3 (g) | 17.3 (g) |
| Montana | 0.0 | 170 | (c) | ... | 27.0 | 27.75 | 27.0 |
| Nebraska | 5.5 | 64 | 3.75 | Yes | 27.6 (g)(q) | 27.0 (g)(q) | 27.6 (g)(q) |
| Nevada | 6.85 (u) | 80 | 3.60 (d) | Yes | 23.805 (e)(g) | 27.75 (e)(g) | 23.805 (e)(g) |
| New Hampshire | 0.0 | 168 | (c) | ... | 19.625 (g) | 19.625 (g) | 19.625 (g) |
| New Jersey | 7.0 | 270 | 5.50 | Yes | 14.5 (g) | 17.5 (g) | 14.5 (g) |
| New Mexico | 5.125 | 166 | 6.06 | Yes | 18.875 (g) | 22.875 (g) | 18.875 (g) |
| New York | 4.0 | 435 (b) | 6.44 (d) | Yes | 25.8 (g) | 24.05 (g) | 25.8 (g) |
| North Carolina | 4.75 | 45 | (c) | Yes (k) | 39.15 (g)(p) | 39.15 (g)(p) | 39.15 (g)(p) |
| North Dakota | 5.0 | 44 | 2.50 (d) | ... | 23.0 | 23.0 | 23.0 |
| Ohio | 5.5 | 125 | (c) | Yes | 28.0 (g) | 28.0 (g) | 28.0 (g) |
| Oklahoma | 4.5 | 103 | 5.56 (d) | Yes | 17.0 (g) | 14.0 (g) | 17.0 (g) |
| Oregon | 0.0 | 118 | (c) | ... | 30.0 (e) | 30.0 (e) | 30.0 (e) |
| Pennsylvania | 6.0 | 160 | (c) | Yes | 31.2 (g) | 38.1 (g) | 31.2 (g) |
| Rhode Island | 7.0 | 346 | 3.75 | Yes | 33.0 (g) | 33.0 (g) | 33.0 (g) |
| South Carolina | 6.0 | 57 | 2.72 (d) | Yes | 16.75 (g) | 16.75 (g) | 16.75 (g) |
| South Dakota | 4.0 | 153 | 3.93(d) | Yes | 24.0 (e)(g) | 24.0 (e)(g) | 22.0 (e)(g) |
| Tennessee | 7.0 | 62 (b)(o) | 4.40 (d) | Yes | 21.4 (e)(g) | 18.4 (e)(g) | 21.4 (e)(g) |
| Texas | 6.25 | 141 | 2.40 (d) | Yes | 20.0 | 20.0 | 20.0 |
| Utah | 5.95 (v) | 170 | (c) | Yes | 24.5 | 24.5 | 24.5 |
| Vermont | 6.0 | 262 | (c)(d) | ... | 26.13 (g) | 29.0 (g) | 24.98 (g) |
| Virginia | 5.0 (t) | 30 (b) | (c) | Yes | 17.5 (e)(s) | 17.5 (e)(s) | 17.5 (e)(s) |
| Washington | 6.5 | 302.5 | (c) | Yes (k) | 37.5 (g) | 37.5 (g) | 37.5 (g) |
| West Virginia | 6.0 | 55 | (c) | Yes | 33.4 (g) | 33.4 (g) | 33.4 (g) |
| Wisconsin | 5.0 | 252 | 3.25 | Yes | 32.9 (g) | 32.9 (g) | 32.9 (g) |
| Wyoming | 4.0 | 60 | (c) | Yes | 14.0 (g) | 14.0 (g) | 14.0 (g) |
| Dist. of Columbia | 6.0 | 250 (m) | 1.50 (d) | Yes | 23.5 | 23.5 | 23.5 |

See footnotes at end of table.

## STATE EXCISE TAX RATES — Continued
### (As of January 1, 2012)

*Source:* Compiled by The Federation of Tax Administrators from various sources, January 2012.

*Key:*

. . . — Tax is not applicable.

(a) The tax rates listed are fuel excise taxes collected by distributor/supplier/retailers in each state. Additional taxes may apply to motor carriers. Carrier taxes are coordinated by the International Fuel Tax Association.

(b) Counties and cities may impose an additional tax on a pack of cigarettes in Alabama, 1¢ to 6¢; Illinois, 10¢ to 15¢; Missouri, 4¢ to 7¢; New York City, $1.50; Tennessee, 1¢; and Virginia, 2¢ to 15¢.

(c) In 18 states, the government directly controls the sales of distilled spirits. Revenue in these states is generated from various taxes, fees and net liquor profits.

(d) Other taxes in addition to excise taxes for the following states: Alaska, under 21 percent—$2.50/gallon; Arkansas, under 5 percent—$0.50/gallon, under 21 percent—$1.00/gallon, $0.20/case and 3 percent off- 14 percent on-premise retail taxes; California, over 50 percent—$6.60/gallon; Connecticut, under 7 percent—$2.05/gallon; Delaware, under 25 percent—$3.64/gallon; Florida under 17.259%—$2.25/gallon, over 55.780%—$9.53/gallon and 6.67 cents/ounce on-premise retail tax; Georgia, $0.83/gallon local tax; Illinois, under 20 percent—$1.39/gallon, $2.68/gallon in Chicago and $2.00/gallon in Cook County; Indiana, under 15 percent—$0.47/gallon; Kansas, 8 percent off- and 10 percent on-premise retail tax; Kentucky, under 6 percent—$0.25/gallon, $0.05/case and 11 percent wholesale tax; Louisiana, under 6 percent—$0.32/gallon; Massachusetts, under 15 percent—$1.10/gallon, over 50 percent alcohol—$4.05/proof gallon, 0.57 percent on private club sales; Minnesota, $0.01/bottle (except miniatures) and 9 percent sales tax; Nevada, under 14 percent—$0.70/gallon and under 21 percent—$1.30/gallon; New York, under 24 percent—$2.54/gallon, $1.00/gallon New York City; North Dakota, 7 percent state sales tax; Oklahoma, 13.5 percent on-premise; South Carolina, $5.36/case and 9 percent surtax additional 5 percent on-premise tax; South Dakota, under 14 percent—$0.93/gallon, 2 percent wholesale tax; Tennessee, $0.15/case and 15 percent on-premise, under 7 percent—$1.10/gallon; Texas, 14 percent on-premise and $0.05/drink on airline sales; Vermont, 10% on-premise sales tax; and District of Columbia, 8 percent off- and 10 percent on-premise sales tax.

(e) Tax rates do not include local option taxes. In Alabama, 1–3 cents; Hawaii, 8.8 to 18.0 cents; Illinois, 5 cents in Chicago and 6 cents in Cook County (gasoline only); Nevada, 4 to 9 cents; Oregon, 1 to 3 cents; South Dakota and Tennessee, one cent; and Virginia, 2 percent.

(f) Carriers pay an additional surcharge: Illinois, 21.0 cents (gasoline), 19.5 cents (diesel); Indiana, 11 cents; Kentucky, 2 percent (gasoline), 4.7 percent (diesel).

(g) Other taxes and fees; Alabama—inspection fee; Arizona—Diesel rate specified is the fuel use tax rate on large trucks. Small vehicles are subject to the 18 cents tax rate and leaking underground storage tax (LUST); Arkansas—environmental fee; California—Includes pre-paid sales tax; Delaware—plus 0.9 percent GRT; Florida—sales tax added to excise; Georgia—sales tax added to excise; Hawaii—sales tax additional; Idaho—clean water tax; Illinois—sales tax additional, environmental fee and leaking underground storage tax (LUST); Indiana—sales tax additional; Iowa—environmental fee; Kentucky—environmental fee; Michigan—sales tax additional; Minnesota—inspection fee; Mississippi—environmental fee; Missouri—inspection fee; Nebraska—petroleum fee; Nevada—inspection fee and clean-up fee; New Hampshire—oil discharge cleanup fee; New Jersey—petroleum fee; New Mexico—petroleum loading fee; New York—sales tax applicable and petroleum tax; North Carolina—inspection tax; Ohio—plus 3 cents commercial; Oklahoma—environmental fee; Pennsylvania—oil franchise tax; Rhode Island—leaking underground storage tank tax (LUST); South Carolina—inspection fee and leaking underground storage tank tax (LUST); South Dakota—inspection fee; Tennessee—petroleum tax and environmental fee; Vermont—petroleum cleanup fee and transportation fee; Washington—0.5 percent privilege tax; West Virginia—sales tax added to excise; Wisconsin—petroleum inspection fee; Wyoming—license tax.

(h) Tax rate may be adjusted annually according to a formula based on balances in the unappropriated general fund and the school foundation fund.

(i) California gasoline subject to 2.25 percent sales tax. Diesel subject to 9 percent sales tax.

(j) Includes a $1 per pack surcharge.

(k) Sales tax is applied to on-premise sales only.

(l) Local taxes for gasoline and gasohol vary from 10.8 cents to 18.9 cents. Plus a 1.0 cent per gallon pollution tax.

(m) Imposes an in lieu cigarette sales tax calculated every March 31. The current rate is 36 cents.

(n) Tax rate is reduced by the percentage of ethanol used in blending (reported rate assumes the maximum 10 percent ethanol).

(o) Dealers pay an additional enforcement and administrative fee of 0.1 cent per pack in Kentucky and .05 cent in Tennessee.

(p) Tax rate is based on the average wholesale price and is adjusted quarterly. The actual rates are: Kentucky, 9 percent and North Carolina, 17.5 cents plus 7 percent.

(q) Portion of the rate is adjustable based on maintenance costs, sales volume, cost of fuel to state government, or inflation.

(r) In addition, Minnesota imposes an in lieu cigarette sales tax determined annually by the Department of Revenue. The current rate is 37 cents through July 31, 2012.

(s) Large trucks pay an additional 3.5 cents.

(t) Includes statewide tax of 1.0 percent levied by local governments in Virginia.

(u) Nevada sales tax rate is scheduled to fall to 6.5 percent on July 1, 2013.

(v) Includes a statewide tax of 1.25 percent levied by local governments in Utah. Food sales subject to local taxes.

## Table 7.11
## FOOD AND DRUG SALES TAX EXEMPTIONS
## (As of January 1, 2012)

| State or other jurisdiction | Tax rate (percentage) | Exemptions | | |
|---|---|---|---|---|
| | | Food (a) | Prescription drugs | Nonprescription drugs |
| Alabama | 4.0 | ... | ★ | ... |
| Alaska | 0.0 | ... | ... | ... |
| Arizona | 6.6 | ★ | ★ | ... |
| Arkansas | 6.0 | 1.5% (d) | ★ | ... |
| California (c) | 7.25 | ★ | ★ | ... |
| Colorado | 2.9 | ★ | ★ | ... |
| Connecticut | 6.35 | ★ | ★ | ... |
| Delaware | 0.0 | ... | ... | ... |
| Florida | 6.0 | ★ | ★ | ★ |
| Georgia | 4.0 | ★(d) | ★ | ... |
| Hawaii | 4.0 | ... | ★ | ... |
| Idaho | 6.0 | ... | ★ | ... |
| Illinois | 6.25 | 1% | 1% | 1% |
| Indiana | 7.0 | ★ | ★ | ... |
| Iowa | 6.0 | ★ | ★ | ... |
| Kansas | 6.3 | ... | ★ | ... |
| Kentucky | 6.0 | ★ | ★ | ... |
| Louisiana | 4.0 | ★(d) | ★ | ... |
| Maine | 5.0 | ★ | ★ | ... |
| Maryland | 6.0 | ★ | ★ | ★ |
| Massachusetts | 6.25 | ★ | ★ | ... |
| Michigan | 6.0 | ★ | ★ | ... |
| Minnesota | 6.875 | ★ | ★ | ★ |
| Mississippi | 7.0 | ... | ★ | ... |
| Missouri | 4.225 | 1.225% | ★ | ... |
| Montana | 0.0 | ... | ★ | ... |
| Nebraska | 5.5 | ★ | ★ | ... |
| Nevada | 6.85 (e) | ★ | ★ | ... |
| New Hampshire | 0.0 | ... | ... | ★ |
| New Jersey | 7.0 | ★ | ★ | ★ |
| New Mexico | 5.125 | ★ | ★ | ... |
| New York | 4.0 | ★ | ★ | ★ |
| North Carolina | 4.75 | ★(d) | ★ | ... |
| North Dakota | 5.0 | ★ | ★ | ... |
| Ohio | 5.5 | ★ | ★ | ... |
| Oklahoma | 4.5 | ... | ★ | ... |
| Oregon | 0.0 | ... | ... | ... |
| Pennsylvania | 6.0 | ★ | ★ | ★ |
| Rhode Island | 7.0 | ★ | ★ | ★ |
| South Carolina | 6.0 | ★ | ★ | ... |
| South Dakota | 4.0 | ... | ★ | ... |
| Tennessee | 7.0 | 5.5% | ★ | ... |
| Texas | 6.25 | ★ | ★ | ★ |
| Utah | 5.95 (d) | 1.75% (d) | ★ | ... |
| Vermont | 6.0 | ★ | ★ | ★ |
| Virginia | 5.0 (b) | 2.5% (b) | ★ | ★ |
| Washington | 6.5 | ★ | ★ | ... |
| West Virginia | 6.0 | 2% (f) | ★ | ... |
| Wisconsin | 5.0 | ★ | ★ | ... |
| Wyoming | 4.0 | ★ | ★ | ... |
| Dist. of Columbia | 6.0 | ★ | ★ | ★ |

*Source:* Compiled by FTA from various sources, January 2012.
*Key:*
★ — Indicates exempt from tax, blank indicates subject to general sales tax rate.
(a) Some states tax food, but allow a rebate or income tax credit to compensate poor households. They are: Hawaii, Idaho, Kansas, Oklahoma and South Dakota.
(b) Includes statewide 1.0% tax levied by local governments in Virginia.

(c) The tax rate may be adjusted annually according to a formula based on balances in the unappropriated general fund and the school foundation fund.
(d) Includes statewide tax of 1.25 percent levied by local governments in Utah. Food sales subject to local taxes.
(e) Nevada sales tax rate is scheduled to fall to 6.5% on July 1, 2013.
(f) West Virginia tax rate on food scheduled to decrease to 1% on July 1, 2012.

## Table 7.12
## STATE INDIVIDUAL INCOME TAXES
### (Tax rates for tax year 2012—as of January 1, 2012)

| State or other jurisdiction | Tax rate range (in percents) Low | High | Number of brackets | Income brackets Lowest | Highest | Personal exemptions Single | Married | Dependents | Federal income tax deductible |
|---|---|---|---|---|---|---|---|---|---|
| Alabama | 2.0 – | 5.0 | 3 | 500 (b) – | 3,001 (b) | 1,500 | 3,000 | 500 (e) | ★ |
| Alaska | | | | (No state income tax) | | | | | ... |
| Arizona | 2.59 – | 4.54 | 5 | 10,000 (b) – | 150,001 (b) | 2,100 | 4,200 | 2,100 | ... |
| Arkansas (a) | 1.0 – | 7 | 6 | 3,899 – | 32,700 | 23 (c) | 46 (c) | 23 (c) | ... |
| California (a) | 1.00 – | 9.3 (f) | 6 | 7,316 – | 48,029 (b) | 102 (c) | 204 (c) | 315 (c) | ... |
| Colorado | 4.63 | | 1 | Flat rate | | 3,700 (d) | 7,400 (d) | 3,700 (d) | ... |
| Connecticut | 3.0 – | 6.7 | 6 | 10,000 (b) – | 250,000 (b) | 13,000 (g) | 24,000 (g) | 0 | ... |
| Delaware | 2.2 – | 6.75 | 6 | 5,000 – | 60,001 | 110 (c) | 220 (c) | 110 (c) | ... |
| Florida | | | | (No state income tax) | | | | | ... |
| Georgia | 1.0 – | 6.0 | 6 | 750 (h) – | 7,001 (h) | 2,700 | 5,400 | 3,000 | ... |
| Hawaii | 1.4 – | 11.0 | 12 | 2,400 (b) – | 200,001 (b) | 1,040 | 2,080 | 1,040 | ... |
| Idaho (a) | 1.6 – | 7.8 | 8 | 1,338 (b) – | 26,760 (h) | 3,700 (d) | 7,400 (d) | 3,700 (d) | ... |
| Illinois | 5.0 | | 1 | Flat rate | | 2,000 | 4,000 | 2,000 | ... |
| Indiana | 3.4 | | 1 | Flat rate | | 1,000 | 2,000 | 2,500 (i) | ... |
| Iowa (a) | 0.36 – | 8.98 | 9 | 1,439 – | 66,105 | 40 (c) | 80 (c) | 40 (c) | ★ |
| Kansas | 3.5 – | 6.45 | 3 | 15,000 (b) – | 30,001 (b) | 2,250 | 4,500 | 2,250 | ... |
| Kentucky | 2.0 – | 6.0 | 6 | 3,000 – | 75,001 | 20 (c) | 40 (c) | 20 (c) | ... |
| Louisiana | 2.0 – | 6.0 | 3 | 12,500 (b) – | 50,001 (b) | 4,500 (j) | 9,000 (j) | 1,000 | ★ |
| Maine (a) | 2.0 – | 8.5 | 4 | 5,100 (b) – | 20,350 (b) | 2,850 | 5,700 | 2,850 | ... |
| Maryland | 2.0 – | 5.50 | 7 | 1,000 – | 500,001 | 3,200 | 6,400 | 3,200 | ... |
| Massachusetts (a) | 5.3 | | 1 | Flat rate | | 4,400 | 8,800 | 1,000 | ... |
| Michigan (a) | 4.35 | | 1 | Flat rate | | 3,600 | 7,200 | 4,200 (k) | ... |
| Minnesota (a) | 5.35 – | 7.85 | 3 | 23,670 (l) – | 77,731 (l) | 3,700 (d) | 7,400 (d) | 3,700 (d) | ... |
| Mississippi | 3.0 – | 5.0 | 3 | 5,000 – | 10,001 | 6,000 | 12,000 | 1,500 | ... |
| Missouri | 1.5 – | 6.0 | 10 | 1,000 – | 9,001 | 2,100 | 4,200 | 1,200 | ★ (m) |
| Montana (a) | 1.0 – | 6.9 | 7 | 2,700 – | 16,000 | 2,190 | 4,380 | 2,190 | ★ (m) |
| Nebraska (a) | 2.56 – | 6.84 | 4 | 2,400 (b) – | 27,001 (b) | 123 (c) | 246 (c) | 123 (c) | ... |
| Nevada | | | | (No state income tax) | | | | | ... |
| New Hampshire | | | | (State income tax of 5% on dividends and interest income only.) | | | | | ... |
| New Jersey | 1.4 – | 8.97 | 6 | 20,000 (n) – | 500,000 (n) | 1,000 | 2,000 | 1,500 | ... |
| New Mexico | 1.7 – | 4.9 | 4 | 5,500 (o) – | 16,001 (o) | 3,700 (d) | 7,400 (d) | 3,700 (d) | ... |
| New York | 4.0 – | 8.82 | 8 | 8,000 (b) – | 1,000,000 (b) | 0 | 0 | 1,000 | ... |
| North Carolina | 6.0 – | 7.75 | 3 | 12,750 (p) – | 60,000 (p) | 1,150 | 2,300 | 1,150 | ... |
| North Dakota (a) | 1.51 – | 3.99 | 5 | 35,300 (q) – | 388,350 (q) | 3,700 (d) | 7,400 (d) | 3,700 (d) | ... |
| Ohio (a) | 0.587 – | 5.925 | 9 | 5,100 – | 204,200 | 1,650 (r) | 3,300 (r) | 1,650 (r) | ... |
| Oklahoma | 0.5 – | 5.25 | 7 | 1,000 (s) – | 8,701 (v) | 1,000 | 2,000 | 1,000 | ... |
| Oregon (a) | 5.0 – | 9.9 | 4 | 2,000 (b) – | 125,000 (b) | 183 (c) | 366 (c) | 183 (c) | ★ (m) |
| Pennsylvania | 3.07 | | 1 | Flat rate | | None | | | ... |
| Rhode Island (a) | 3.75 – | 6.0 | 3 | 57,150 – | 129,900 | 3,650 | 7,300 | 3,650 | ... |
| South Carolina (a) | 0.0 – | 7.0 | 6 | 2,800 – | 14,000 | 3,700 (d) | 7,400 (d) | 3,700 (d) | ... |
| South Dakota | | | | (No state income tax) | | | | | ... |
| Tennessee | | | | (State income tax 6% on dividends and interest income only.) | | 1,250 | 2,500 | 0 | ... |
| Texas | | | | (No state income tax) | | | | | ... |
| Utah | 5.0 | | 1 | Flat rate | | (t) | (t) | (t) | ... |
| Vermont (a) | 3.55 – | 8.95 | 5 | 35,300 (u) – | 388,350 (u) | 3,700 (d) | 7,400 (d) | 3,700 (d) | ... |
| Virginia | 2.0 – | 5.75 | 4 | 3,000 – | 17,001 | 930 | 1,860 | 930 | ... |
| Washington | | | | (No state income tax) | | | | | ... |
| West Virginia | 3.0 – | 6.5 | 5 | 10,000 – | 60,000 | 2,000 | 4,000 | 2,000 | ... |
| Wisconsin (a) | 4.6 – | 7.75 | 5 | 10,570 (v) – | 232,660 (v) | 700 | 1,400 | 700 | ... |
| Wyoming | | | | (No state income tax) | | | | | ... |
| Dist. of Columbia | 4.0 – | 9.0 | 4 | 10,000 – | 350,000 | 1,675 | 3,350 | 1,675 | ... |

See footnotes at end of table.

# STATE INDIVIDUAL INCOME TAXES—Continued
## (Tax rates for tax year 2012—as of January 1, 2012)

*Source:* The Federation of Tax Administrators from various sources, January 2012.

*Key:*

★ — Yes

... — No

(a) Seventeen states have statutory provision for automatically adjusting to the rate of inflation the dollar values of the income tax brackets, standard deductions, and/or personal exemptions. Massachusetts, Michigan, and Nebraska index the personal exemption only. Oregon does not index the income brackets for $125,000 and over. Because the inflation adjustments for 2012 are not yet available in most cases, the table reports the 2011 amounts.

(b) For joint returns, taxes are twice the tax on half the couple's income.

(c) The personal exemption takes the form of a tax credit instead of a deduction.

(d) These states use the personal exemption amounts provided in the federal Internal Revenue Code.

(e) In Alabama, the per-dependent exemption is $1,000 for taxpayers with state AGI of $20,000 or less, $500 with AGI from $20,001 to $100,000, and $300 with AGI over $100,000.

(f) California imposes an additional 1% tax on taxable income over $1 million, making the maximum rate 10.3% over $1 million.

(g) Connecticut's personal exemption incorporates a standard deduction. An additional tax credit is allowed ranging from 75% to 0% based on state adjusted gross income. Exemption amounts are phased out for higher income taxpayers until they are eliminated for households earning over $71,000.

(h) The Georgia income brackets reported are for single individuals. For married couples filing jointly, the same tax rates apply to income brackets ranging from $1,000, to $10,000.

(i) In Indiana, includes an additional exemption of $1,500 for each dependent child.

(j) The amounts reported for Louisiana are a combined personal exemption-standard deduction.

(k) In Michigan, includes an additional exemption of $600 for children age 18 and under. Tax rate scheduled to decrease to 4.25% on 10/1/13.

(l) The income brackets reported for Minnesota are for single individuals. For married couples filing jointly, the same tax rates apply to income brackets ranging from $34,590, to $137,431.

(m) The deduction for federal income tax is limited to $5,000 for individuals and $10,000 for joint returns in Missouri and Montana, and to $5,950 for all filers in Oregon.

(n) The New Jersey rates reported are for single individuals. For married couples filing jointly, the tax rates also range from 1.4% to 8.97%, with seven brackets and the same high and low income ranges.

(o) The income brackets reported for New Mexico are for single individuals. For married couples filing jointly, the same tax rates apply to income brackets ranging from $8,000, to $24,000.

(p) The income brackets reported for North Carolina are for single individuals. For married taxpayers filing jointly, the same tax rates apply to income brackets ranging from $21,250, to $100,000.

(q) The income brackets reported for North Dakota are for single individuals. For married couples filing jointly, the same tax rates apply to income brackets ranging from $59,100, to $388,350.

(r) Ohio provides an additional tax credit of $20 per exemption. 2012 tax rates and brackets reported.

(s) The income brackets reported for Oklahoma are for single persons. For married persons filing jointly, the same tax rates apply to income brackets ranging from $2,000, to $15,000.

(t) Utah provides a tax credit equal to 6% of the federal personal exemption amounts (an applicable standard deduction).

(u) Vermont's income brackets reported are for single individuals. For married taxpayers filing jointly, the same tax rates apply to income brackets ranging from $59,050, to $388,350.

(v) The Wisconsin income brackets reported are for single individuals. For married taxpayers filing jointly, the same tax rates apply to income brackets ranging from $14,090, to $310,210.

## Table 7.13
## STATE PERSONAL INCOME TAXES: FEDERAL STARTING POINTS
(As of January 1, 2012)

| State or other jurisdiction | Relation to Internal Revenue Code | Federal tax base used as a starting point to calculate state taxable income |
|---|---|---|
| Alabama | ... | ... |
| Alaska | | —————No state income tax ————— |
| Arizona | 1/1/2011 | Adjusted gross income |
| Arkansas | ... | ... |
| California | 1/1/2009 | Adjusted gross income |
| Colorado | Current | Taxable income |
| Connecticut | Current | Adjusted gross income |
| Delaware | Current | Adjusted gross income |
| Florida | | —————No state income tax ————— |
| Georgia | 1/1/2011 | Adjusted gross income |
| Hawaii | 12/31/2010 | Adjusted gross income |
| Idaho | 1/1/2011 | Taxable income |
| Illinois | Current | Adjusted gross income |
| Indiana | 1/1/2011 | Adjusted gross income |
| Iowa | 1/1/2011 | Adjusted gross income |
| Kansas | Current | Adjusted gross income |
| Kentucky | 12/31/2006 | Adjusted gross income |
| Louisiana | Current | Adjusted gross income |
| Maine | 12/31/2010 | Adjusted gross income |
| Maryland | Current | Adjusted gross income |
| Massachusetts | 1/1/2005 | Adjusted gross income |
| Michigan | Current (a) | Adjusted gross income |
| Minnesota | 4/14/2011 | Taxable income |
| Mississippi | ... | ... |
| Missouri | Current | Adjusted gross income |
| Montana | Current | Adjusted gross income |
| Nebraska | Current | Adjusted gross income |
| Nevada | | —————No state income tax ————— |
| New Hampshire | | ————— On interest and dividends only————— |
| New Jersey | ... | ... |
| New Mexico | Current | Adjusted gross income |
| New York | Current | Adjusted gross income |
| North Carolina | 1/1/2011 | Taxable income |
| North Dakota | Current | Taxable income |
| Ohio | 3/7/2011 | Adjusted gross income |
| Oklahoma | Current | Adjusted gross income |
| Oregon | 12/31/2010 | Taxable income |
| Pennsylvania | ... | ... |
| Rhode Island | Current | Adjusted gross income |
| South Carolina | 12/31/2010 | Taxable income |
| South Dakota | | —————No state income tax ————— |
| Tennessee | | ————— On interest and dividends only————— |
| Texas | | —————No state income tax ————— |
| Utah | Current | Adjusted gross income |
| Vermont | 1/1/2010 | Taxable income |
| Virginia | 12/31/2010 | Adjusted gross income |
| Washington | | —————No state income tax ————— |
| West Virginia | 12/31/2010 | Adjusted gross income |
| Wisconsin | 12/31/2010 | Adjusted gross income |
| Wyoming | | —————No state income tax ————— |
| Dist. of Columbia | Current | Adjusted gross income |

*Source:* Compiled by the Federation of Tax Administrators from various sources. January 2012.

*Key:*
... — State does not employ a federal starting point.
Current — Indicates state has adopted the Internal Revenue Code as currently in effect. Dates indicate state has adopted IRC as amended to that date.
(a) Michigan's taxpayers can choose to use either current or 1/1/1996 federal law.

## Table 7.14
## RANGE OF STATE CORPORATE INCOME TAX RATES
### (For tax year 2012, as of January 1, 2012)

| State or other jurisdiction | Tax rate (percent) | Tax brackets Lowest | Tax brackets Highest | Number of brackets | Financial institution tax rates (percent) (a) | Federal income tax deductible |
|---|---|---|---|---|---|---|
| Alabama | 6.5 | -------- Flat Rate --------- | | 1 | 6.5 | ★ |
| Alaska | 1.0–9.4 | 9,999 | 90,000 | 10 | 1.0–9.4 | ... |
| Arizona | 6.968 (b) | -------- Flat Rate --------- | | 1 | 6.968 (b) | ... |
| Arkansas | 1.0–6.5 | 3,000 | 100,001 | 6 | 1.0–6.5 | ... |
| California | 8.84 (c) | -------- Flat Rate --------- | | 1 | 10.84 (c) | ... |
| Colorado | 4.63 | -------- Flat Rate --------- | | 1 | 4.63 | ... |
| Connecticut | 7.5 (d) | -------- Flat Rate --------- | | 1 | 7.5 (d) | ... |
| Delaware | 8.7 | -------- Flat Rate --------- | | 1 | 8.7–1.7 (e) | ... |
| Florida | 5.5 (f) | -------- Flat Rate --------- | | 1 | 5.5 (f) | ... |
| Georgia | 6.0 | -------- Flat Rate --------- | | 1 | 6.0 | ... |
| Hawaii | 4.4–6.4 (g) | 25,000 | 100,001 | 3 | 7.92 (g) | ... |
| Idaho | 7.6 (h) | -------- Flat Rate --------- | | 1 | 7.6 (h) | ... |
| Illinois | 9.5 (i) | -------- Flat Rate --------- | | 1 | 9.5 (i) | ... |
| Indiana | 8.5 (j) | -------- Flat Rate --------- | | 1 | 8.5 | ... |
| Iowa | 6.0–12.0 | 25,000 | 250,001 | 4 | 5.0 | ★(k) |
| Kansas | 4.0 (l) | -------- Flat Rate --------- | | 1 | 2.25 (l) | ... |
| Kentucky | 4.0–6.0 | 50,000 | 100,001 | 3 | (a) | ... |
| Louisiana | 4.0–8.0 | 25,000 | 200,001 | 5 | 4.0–8.0 | ★ |
| Maine | 3.5–8.93 | 25,000 | 250,000 | 4 | 1.0 (m) | ... |
| Maryland | 8.25 | -------- Flat Rate --------- | | 1 | 8.25 | ... |
| Massachusetts | 8.0 (n) | -------- Flat Rate --------- | | 1 | 9.0 (n) | ... |
| Michigan | 6 | -------- Flat Rate --------- | | 1 | (a) | ... |
| Minnesota | 9.8 (o) | -------- Flat Rate --------- | | 1 | 9.8 (o) | ... |
| Mississippi | 3.0–5.0 | 5,000 | 10,001 | 3 | 3.0–5.0 | ... |
| Missouri | 6.25 | -------- Flat Rate --------- | | 1 | 7.0 | ★(k) |
| Montana | 6.75 (p) | -------- Flat Rate --------- | | 1 | 6.75 (p) | ... |
| Nebraska | 5.58–7.81 | 100,000 | | 2 | (a) | ... |
| Nevada | ------------------------------- No corporate income tax ------------------------------- | | | | | |
| New Hampshire | 8.5 (q) | -------- Flat Rate --------- | | 1 | 8.5 (q) | ... |
| New Jersey | 9.0 (r) | -------- Flat Rate --------- | | 1 | 9.0 (r) | ... |
| New Mexico | 4.8–7.6 | 500,000 | 1 million | 3 | 4.8–7.6 | ... |
| New York | 7.1 (s) | -------- Flat Rate --------- | | 1 | 7.1 (s) | ... |
| North Carolina | 6.9 | -------- Flat Rate --------- | | 1 | 6.9 (t) | ... |
| North Dakota | 1.7–5.2 | 25,000 | 50,001 | 3 | 7.0 (b) | ★ |
| Ohio | ----------------------------------------- (u) ----------------------------------------- | | | | | ... |
| Oklahoma | 6.0 | -------- Flat Rate --------- | | 1 | 6.0 | ... |
| Oregon | 6.6–7.6 (v) | 250,001 | | 2 | 6.6–7.6 (v) | ... |
| Pennsylvania | 9.99 | -------- Flat Rate --------- | | 1 | (a) | ... |
| Rhode Island | 9.0 (b) | -------- Flat Rate --------- | | 1 | 9.0 (b) | ... |
| South Carolina | 5.0 | -------- Flat Rate --------- | | 1 | 4.5 (w) | ... |
| South Dakota | ... | ... | | ... | 6.0–0.25% (b) | ... |
| Tennessee | 6.5 | -------- Flat Rate --------- | | 1 | 6.5 | ... |
| Texas | ----------------------------------------- (x) ----------------------------------------- | | | | | ... |
| Utah | 5.0 (b) | -------- Flat Rate --------- | | ... | 5.0 (b) | ... |
| Vermont (b) | 6.0–8.5 (b) | 10,000 | 25,000 | 3 | (a) | ... |
| Virginia | 6.0 | -------- Flat Rate --------- | | 1 | 6.0 | ... |
| Washington | ------------------------------- No corporate income tax ------------------------------- | | | | | |
| West Virginia | 7.5 (y) | -------- Flat Rate --------- | | 1 | 7.5 (y) | ... |
| Wisconsin | 7.9 | -------- Flat Rate --------- | | 1 | 7.9 | ... |
| Wyoming | ------------------------------- No corporate income tax ------------------------------- | | | | | |
| Dist. of Columbia | 9.975 (b) | -------- Flat Rate --------- | | 1 | 9.975 (b) | ... |

See footnotes at end of table.

## RANGE OF STATE CORPORATE INCOME TAX RATES — Continued
### (For tax year 2012, as of January 1, 2012)

*Source:* Compiled by the Federation of Tax Administrators from various sources January 2012.

Key:

★ — Yes

... — No

(a) Rates listed are the corporate income tax rate applied to financial institutions or excise taxes based on income. Some states have other taxes based upon the value of deposits or shares.

(b) Minimum tax is $50 in Arizona, $100 in District of Columbia, $50 in North Dakota (banks), $500 in Rhode Island, $200 per location in South Dakota (banks), $100 in Utah, $250 in Vermont.

(c) The minimum corporation franchise tax in California is $800. The additional alternative minimum tax is levied at a 6.65% rate.

(d) Connecticut's tax is the greater of the 7.5% tax on net income, a 0.31% tax on capital stock and surplus (maximum tax of $1 million), or $250 (the minimum tax). Plus, an additional 20% surtax applies for tax years 2012 and 2013.

(e) The Delaware Bank marginal rate decreases over 4 brackets ranging from $20 to $650 million in taxable income. Building and loan associations are taxed at a flat 8.7%.

(f) An exemption of $5,000 is allowed. Florida's Alternative Minimum Tax rate is 3.3%.

(g) Hawaii taxes capital gains at 4%. Financial institutions pay a franchise tax of 7.92% of taxable income (in lieu of the corporate income tax and general excise taxes).

(h) Idaho's minimum tax on a corporation is $20. The $10 Permanent Building Fund Tax must be paid by each corporation in a unitary group filing a combined return. Taxpayers with gross sales in Idaho under $100,000, and with no property or payroll in Idaho, may elect to pay 1% on such sales (instead of the tax on net income).

(i) The Illinois rate of 9.5% is the sum of a corporate income tax rate of 7.0% plus a replacement tax of 2.5%.

(j) The Indiana tax rate is scheduled to decrease to 8% on July 1, 2012.

(k) 50% of the federal income tax is deductible.

(l) In addition to the flat 4% corporate income tax, Kansas levies a 3.0% surtax on taxable income over $50,000. Banks pay a privilege tax of 2.25% of net income, plus a surtax of 2.125% (2.25% for savings and loans, trust companies, and federally chartered savings banks) on net income in excess of $25,000.

(m) The state franchise tax on financial institutions is either (1) the sum of 1% of the Maine net income of the financial institution for the taxable year, plus 8¢ per $1,000 of the institution's Maine assets as of the end of its taxable year, or (2) 39¢ per $1,000 of the institution's Maine assets as of the end of its taxable year.

(n) Business and manufacturing corporations pay an additional tax of $2.60 per $1,000 on either taxable Massachusetts tangible property or taxable net worth allocable to the state (for intangible property

corporations). The minimum tax for both corporations and financial institutions is $456.

(o) In addition, Minnesota levies a 5.8% tentative minimum tax on Alternative Minimum Taxable Income.

(p) Montana levies a 7% tax on taxpayers using water's edge combination. The minimum tax per corporation is $50; the $50 minimum applies to each corporation included on a combined tax return. Taxpayers with gross sales in Montana of $100,000 or less may pay an alternative tax of 0.5% on such sales, instead of the net income tax.

(q) New Hampshire's 8.5% Business Profits Tax is imposed on both corporations and unincorporated associations with gross income over $50,000. In addition, New Hampshire levies a Business Enterprise Tax of 0.75% on the enterprise base (total compensation, interest and dividends paid) for businesses with gross income over $150,000 or base over $75,000.

(r) In New Jersey small businesses with annual entire net income under $100,000 pay a tax rate of 7.5%; businesses with income under $50,000 pay 6.5%. The minimum Corporation Business Tax is based on New Jersey gross receipts. It ranges from $500 for a corporation with gross receipts less than $100,000, to $2,000 for a corporation with gross receipts of $1 million or more.

(s) New York's General business corporate rate shown. Corporations may also be subject to AMT tax at 1.5% (3% banks), or a capital stocks tax. A minimum tax ranges from $25 to $5,000, depending on receipts ($250 minimum for banks). Certain qualified New York manufacturers pay 6.5%. Small business taxpayers in New York pay rates of 6.5%, 7.1%, and 4.35% on 3 brackets of entire net income up to $390,000.

(t) In North Carolina financial institutions are also subject to a tax equal to $30 per one million in assets.

(u) Ohio no longer levies a tax based on income (except for a particular subset of corporations), but instead imposes a Commercial Activity Tax (CAT) equal to $150 for gross receipts sitused to Ohio of between $150,000 and $1 million, plus 0.26% of gross receipts over $1 million. Banks continue to pay a franchise tax of 1.3% of net worth. For those few corporations for whom the franchise tax on net worth or net income still applies, a litter tax also applies.

(v) Oregon's minimum tax for C corporations depends on the Oregon sales of the filing group. The minimum tax ranges from $150 for corporations with sales under $500,000, up to $100,000 for companies with sales of $100 million or above.

(w) South Carolina taxes savings and loans at a 6% rate.

(x) Texas imposes a Franchise Tax, otherwise known as margin tax, imposed on entities with more than $1,000,000 total revenues at rate of 1%, or 0.5% for entities primarily engaged in retail or wholesale trade, on lesser of 70% of total revenues or 100% of gross receipts after deductions for either compensation or cost of goods sold.

(y) West Virginia's corporate rate is scheduled for reduction as follows: 7.75% after 2011, 7.0% after 2012, 6.5% after 2013.

## Table 7.15
## STATE SEVERANCE TAXES: 2012

| State | Title and application of tax (a) | Rate |
|---|---|---|
| **Alabama** ........... | Iron Ore Mining Tax | $.03/ton. |
| | Forest Products Severance Tax | Varies by species and ultimate use. |
| | Oil and Gas Conservation & Regulation of Production Tax | 2% of gross value at point of production, of all oil and gas produced. 1% of the gross value (for a 5-year period from the date production begins) for well, for which the initial permit issued by the Oil and Gas Board is dated on or after July 1, 1996 and before July 1, 2002, except a replacement well for which the initial permit was dated before July 1, 1996. |
| ............................... | Oil and Gas Privilege Tax on Production | 8% of gross value at point of production; 4% of gross value at point of incremental production resulting from a qualified enhanced recovery project; 4% if wells produce 25 bbl. or less oil per day or 200,000 cu. ft. or less gas per day; 6% of gross value at point of production for certain on-shore and off-shore wells. A 50% rate reduction for wells permitted by the oil and gas board on or after July 1, 1996 and before July 1, 2002 for 5 years from initial production, except for replacement wells for which the initial permit was dated before July 1, 1996. |
| | Coal and Lignite Severance Tax | $.20/ton in addition to coal severance tax. |
| | Local Solid Minerals Tax | Varies by county. |
| | Uniform Natural Minerals Tax | $.10/ton. |
| **Alaska** ........... | Cost Recovery Fisheries Assessment (b) | Elective; currently no assessments in place. |
| | Dive Fishery Management Assessment (b) | Elective; currently 7% of value for select dive fishery species in select management regions. |
| | Fisheries Business Tax | Tax based on unprocessed value of fishery resources processed in or exported from the state. 1% of value for shore-based processing in developing fisheries; 3% of value for floating processing in developing fisheries or shore-based processing in established fisheries; 4.5% of value for salmon cannery processing in established fisheries; 5% of value for floating processing in established fisheries. |
| | Fishery Resource Landing Tax | Tax based on unprocessed value of fishery resources processed outside and first landed in the state. 1% of value for developing fisheries; 3% of value for established fisheries. |
| | Mining License Tax | Up to 7% of net income and royalties received in connection with mining properties and activities in Alaska. New mining operations other than sand and gravel exempt for 3 1/2 years after production begins. |
| | Petroleum Profits Tax (PPT) | 22.5% net value at wellhead (excludes capital costs, operating costs and other qualified expenditures) minus credits. Additional 0.25% surcharge for each dollar that net value exceeds $40 per barrel; surcharge cannot exceed 25% of the monthly production tax value of taxable oil and gas. Conservation surcharge of 4 cents per barrel; plus another 1 cent per barrel surcharge if there is less than $50 million in the Hazardous Release Fund. |
| | Salmon Enhancement Tax (b) | Elective; 2% or 3% of value for salmon sold in or exported from select aquaculture regions. |
| | Seafood Development Tax (b) | Elective; currently 1% of value for select commercial fish species in select seafood development regions. |
| | Seafood Marketing Assessment (b) | Elective; currently 0.3% of value for all commercial fish species. |
| **Arizona** ........... | Severance Tax | 2.5% of net severance base for mining (metalliferous minerals); $1.51/1000 board ft. ($2.13 for ponderosa pine) for timbering. 3.125% for oil and gas production and nonmetal mining. |
| **Arkansas** ........... | Natural Resources Severance Tax | Separate rate for each substance. |
| | Oil and Gas Conservation Tax | Natural gas 0.3 of $.01 cent per MCF; crude oil 4% to 5% depending on production levels. |
| | Oil and Gas Conservation Assessment | Maximum 43 mills/bbl. of oil and 9 mills per MCF produced of gas. |
| **California** ........... | Oil and Gas Production Assessment | Rate determined annually by Department of Conservation. |
| **Colorado** ........... | Severance Tax (c) | Taxable years commencing prior to July 1, 1999, 2.25% of gross income exceeding $11 million for metallic minerals and taxable years commencing after July 1, 1999, 2.25% of gross income exceeding $19 million for metallic minerals; on or after July 1, 1999, $.05/ton for each ton exceeding 625,000 tons each quarter for molybdenum ore; 2% to 5% based on gross income for oil, gas, $CO_2$, and coalbed methane; after July 1, 1999, $.36/ton adjusted by the producers' prices index for each ton exceeding 300,000 tons each quarter for coal; and 4% of gross proceeds on production exceeding 15,000 tons per day for oil shale. |
| | Oil and Gas Conservation Levy | Maximum 1.5 mills/$1 of market value at wellhead. (d) |

See footnotes at end of table.

## STATE SEVERANCE TAXES: 2012—Continued

| State | Title and application of tax (a) | Rate |
|---|---|---|
| Florida | Oil, Gas and Sulfur Production Tax | 5% of gross value for small well oil, and 8% of gross value for all other, and an additional 12.5% for escaped oil; the gas base rate ($0.171) times the gas base adjustment rate each fiscal year for gas; and the sulfur base rate ($2.43) times the sulfur base rate adjustment each fiscal year for sulfur. |
| | Solid Minerals Tax (e) | 8% of the value of the minerals severed, except phosphate rock (rate computed annually at $1.95/ton plus year 2010 surcharge rate of $1.38/ton) and heavy minerals (rate computed annually at a base rate of $1.34/ton times the base rate adjustment). Yet solid minerals, except phosphate rock and heavy minerals, upon which the sales tax is ultimately paid to the state are exempt from severance tax. |
| Idaho | Ore Severance Tax | 1% of net value. |
| | Oil and Gas Production Tax | Maximum of 5 mills/bbl. of oil and 5 mills/50,000 cu. ft. of gas. (f) |
| | Additional Oil and Gas Production Tax | 2% of market value at site of production. |
| Illinois | Timber Fee | 4% of purchase price (g). |
| Indiana | Petroleum Production Tax (h) | 1% of value or $.24 per barrel for oil or $.03 per 1000 cu. ft. of gas, whichever is greater. |
| Kansas | Severance Tax (i) | 8% of gross value of oil and gas, less property tax credit of 3.67%; $1/ton of coal. |
| | Oil and Gas Conservation Tax | 91.00 mills/bbl. crude oil or petroleum marketed or used each month; 12.9 mills/1,000 cu. ft. of gas sold or marketed each month. |
| | Mined-Land Conservation & Reclamation Tax | $50, plus per ton fee of between $.03 and $.10. |
| Kentucky | Oil Production Tax | 4.5% of market value. |
| | Coal Severance Tax | 4.5% of gross value, less transportation expenses. |
| | Natural Resource Severance Tax (j) | 4.5% of gross value, less transportation expenses. |
| Louisiana | Natural Resources Severance Tax | Rate varies according to substance. |
| | Oil Field Site Restoration Fee | Rate varies according to type of well and production. |
| | Freshwater Mussel Tax | 5% of revenues from the sale of whole freshwater mussels, at the point of first sale. |
| Maine | Mining Excise Tax | The greater of a tax on facilities and equipment or a tax on gross proceeds. |
| Maryland | Mine Reclamation Surcharge | $.17/ton of coal removed by open-pit, strip or deep mine methods. Of the $.15, $.06 is remitted to the county from which the coal was removed. |
| Michigan | Gas and Oil Severance Tax | 5% (gas), 6.6% (oil) and 4% (oil from stripper wells and marginal properties) of gross cash market value of the total production. Maximum additional fee of 1% of gross cash market value on all oil and gas produced in state in previous year. |
| Minnesota | Taconite and Iron Sulfides | $2.38 per ton of concentrates or pellets. |
| | Direct Reduced Iron (k) | $2.38 per ton of concentrates plus an additional $.03 per ton for each 1% that the iron content exceeds 72%. |
| Mississippi | Oil and Gas Severance Tax | 6% of value at point of gas production; 3% of gross value of occluded natural gas from coal seams at point of production for well's first five years; also, maximum 35 mills/bbl. oil or 4 mills/1,000 cu. ft. gas (Oil and Gas Board maintenance tax). 6% of value at point of oil production; 3% of value at production when enhanced oil recovery method used. |
| | Timber Severance Tax | Varies depending on type of wood and ultimate use. |
| | Salt Severance Tax | 3% of value of entire production in state. |
| Montana | Coal Severance Tax | Varies from 3% to 15% depending on quality of coal and type of mine. |
| | Metalliferous Mines License Tax (l) | Progressive rate, taxed on amounts in excess of $250,000. For concentrate shipped to smelter, mill or reduction work, 1.81%. Gold, silver or any platinum group metal shipped to refinery, 1.6%. |
| | Oil or Gas Conservation Tax | Maximum 0.3% on the market value of each barrel of crude petroleum oil or 10,000 cu. ft. of natural gas produced, saved and marketed or stored within or exported from the state. (m) |
| | Oil and Natural Gas Production Tax | Varies from 0.5% to 14.8% according to the type of well and type of production. |
| | Micaceous Minerals License Tax | $.05/ton. |
| | Cement License Tax (n) | $.22/ton of cement, $.05/ton of cement, plaster, gypsum or gypsum products. |
| | Resource Indemnity Trust Tax | $25 plus 0.5% of gross value greater than $5,000. For talc, $25 plus 4% of gross value greater than $625. For coal, $25 plus 0.40% of gross value greater than $6,250. For vermiculite, $25 plus 2% of gross value greater than $1,250. For limestone, $25 plus 10% of gross value greater than $250. For industrial garnets, $25 plus 1% of gross value greater than $2,500.00. |

See footnotes at end of table.

# STATE SEVERANCE TAXES: 2012—Continued

| State | Title and application of tax (a) | Rate |
|---|---|---|
| Nebraska | Oil and Gas Severance Tax | 3% of value of nonstripper oil and natural gas; 2% of value of stripper oil. |
| | Oil and Gas Conservation Tax | Maximum 15 mills/$1 of value at wellhead, as of January 1, 2000 (f). |
| | Uranium Tax | 2% of gross value over $5 million. The value of the uranium severed subject to tax is the gross value less transportation and processing costs. |
| Nevada | Minerals Extraction Tax | Between 2% and 5% of net proceeds of each geographically separate extractive operation, based on ratio of net proceeds to gross proceeds of whole operation. |
| | Oil and Gas Conservation Tax | $50/mills/bbl. of oil and 50 mills/50,000 cu. ft. of gas. |
| New Hampshire | Refined Petroleum Products Tax | 0.1% of fair market value. |
| | Excavation Tax | $.02 per cubic yard of earth excavated. |
| | Timber Tax | 10% of stumpage value at the time of cutting. |
| New Mexico | Resources Excise Tax (o) | Potash .5%, molybdenum .125%, all others .75% of value. |
| | Severance Tax (o) | Potash 2.5%, copper .5%, timber .125% of value. Pumice, gypsum, sand, gravel, clay, fluorspar and other non-metallic minerals, .125% of value. Gold, silver .20%; Lead, zinc, thorium, molybdenum, manganese, rare earth and other .125% of value. |
| | Oil and Gas Severance Tax | 3.75% of value of oil, other liquid hydrocarbons, natural gas and carbon dioxide. |
| | Oil and Gas Emergency School Tax | 3.15% of value of oil, other liquid hydrocarbons and carbon dioxide. 4% of value of natural gas. |
| | Natural Gas Processor's Tax | $0.0220/Mmbtu tax on volume. |
| | Oil and Gas Ad Valorem Production Tax | Varies, based on property tax in district of production. |
| | Oil and Gas Conservation Tax (p) | 0.19% of value. |
| North Carolina | Oil and Gas Conservation Tax | Maximum 5 mills/barrel of oil and 0.5 mill/1,000 cu. ft. of gas.. |
| | Primary Forest Product Assessment Tax | $.50/1,000 board ft. for softwood sawtimber, $.40/1,000 board ft. for hardwood sawtimber, $.20/cord for softwood pulpwood, $.12/cord hardwood pulpwood. |
| North Dakota | Oil Gross Production Tax | 5% of gross value at well. |
| | Gas Gross Production Tax | $.04/1000 cu.ft. of gas produced (the rate is subject to a gas rate adjustment each fiscal year). For FY05, the rate was 10.37 cents per mcf. |
| | Coal Severance Tax | $.375/ton plus $.02/ton. (q) |
| | Oil Extraction Tax | 6.5% of gross value at well (with exceptions due to production volumes and and production incentives for enhanced recovery projects). |
| Ohio | Resource Severance Tax | $.10/bbl. of oil; $.025/1,000 cu. ft. of natural gas; $.04/ton of salt; $.02/ton of sand, gravel, limestone and dolomite; $.10/ton of coal; and $0.01/ton of clay, sandstone or conglomerate, shale, gypsum or quartzite. |
| Oklahoma | Oil, Gas and Mineral Gross Production Tax and Petroleum Excise Tax (r) | Rate: 0.75% levied on asphalt and metals. 7% (if greater than $2.10 mcf) 4% (if greater than $1.75 mcf, but less than $2.10 mcf) 1% (if less than $1.75 mcf) casinghead gas and natural gas as well as 0.95% being levied on crude oil, casinghead gas and natural gas. Oil Gross Production Tax is now a variable rate tax, beginning with January 1999 production, at the following rates based on the average price of Oklahoma oil: a) If the average price equals or exceeds $17/bbl, the tax shall be 7%; b) If the average price is less than $17/bbl, but is equal to or exceeds $14/bbl, the tax shall be 4%; c) If the average price is less than $14/bbl, the tax shall be 1%. |
| Oregon | Forest Products Harvest Tax | $3.5750/1000 board ft. harvested from public and private land. (rate is for 2009 harvests). |
| | Oil and Gas Production Tax | 6% of gross value at well. |
| | STF Severance Tax— Eastern Oregon Forestland Option | $3.70/1000 board ft. harvested from land under the Small Tract Forestland Option. |
| | STF Severance Tax— Western Oregon Forestland Option | $4.74/1000 board ft. harvested from land under the Small Tract Forestland Option. |
| Pennsylvania | Natural Gas Severance Tax | Annual $50,000 per-well fee. Local fees and taxes determined by county. |
| South Carolina | Forest Renewal Tax | Softwood products: 50 cents per 1,000 board feet or 25 cents per cord. Hardwood products: 25 cents per 1,000 board feet or 7 cents per cord. |
| South Dakota | Precious Metals Severance Tax | $4 per ounce of gold severed plus additional tax depending on price of gold; 10% on net profits or royalties from sale of precious metals, and 8% of royalty value. |
| | Energy Minerals Severance Tax (s) | 4.5% of taxable value of any energy minerals. |
| | Conservation Tax | 2.4 mills of taxable value of any energy minerals. |

See footnotes at end of table.

# STATE SEVERANCE TAXES: 2012 — Continued

| State | Title and application of tax (a) | Rate |
|---|---|---|
| **Tennessee** | Oil and Gas Severance Tax | 3% of sales price. |
| | Coal Severance Tax (t) | $.50/ton (effective 7/1/09). |
| | Mineral Tax | Up to $0.15 per ton, rate set by county legislative body. |
| **Texas** | Natural Gas Production Tax | 7.5% of market value of gas. Condensate Production Tax: 4.6% of market value of gas. |
| | Crude Oil Production Tax | 4.6% of market value or $.046/bbl. |
| | Sulphur Production Tax | $1.03/long ton or fraction thereof. |
| | Cement Production Tax | $0.55 per ton or $.0275/100 lbs. or fraction of 100 pounds of taxable cement. |
| | Oil-Field Cleanup Regulatory Fees | 5/8 of $.01/barrel; 1/15 of $.01/1000 cubic feet of gas. (u) |
| | Oyster Sales Fee | $1 per 300 lb. barrel of oysters taken from Texas waters. |
| **Utah** | Mining Severance Tax | 2.6% of taxable value for metals or metalliferous minerals sold or otherwise disposed of. |
| | Oil and Gas Severance Tax | 3% of value for the first $13 per barrel of oil, 5% from $13.01 and above; 3% of value for first $1.50/mcf, 5% from $1.51 and above; and 4% of taxable value of natural gas liquids. |
| | Oil and Gas Conservation Fee | .002% of market value at wellhead. |
| **Virginia** | Forest Products Tax | $1.15 per 1000 feet B.M. of pine lumber and 1000 board feet of pine logs. $0.475 collected per cord of pine pulpwood. |
| | Coal Surface Mining Reclamation Tax | Varies depending on balance of Coal Surface Mining Reclamation Fund. |
| **Washington** | Uranium and Thorium Milling Tax (tax reported as inactive) | $0.05/per pound. |
| | Enhanced Food Fish Tax | 0.09% to 5.62% of value (depending on species) at point of landing. |
| | Timber Excise Tax | 5% of stumpage value for harvests on public and private lands. |
| **West Virginia** | Natural Resource Severance Taxes | Coal: State rate is greater of 5% or $.75 per ton (4.65% for state purposes and .35% for distribution to local governments). Special state rates for coal from new low seam mines. For seams between 37″ and 45″ the rate is greater of 2% or $.75/ton (1.65% for state purposes and .35% for distribution to local governments). For seams less than 37″ the rate is greater of 1% or $.75/ton (.65% for state purposes and .35% for distribution to local governments). For coal from gob, refuse piles, or other sources of waste coal, the rate is 2.5% (distributed to local governments). Additional tax for workers' compensation debt reduction is $.56/ton. Two special reclamation taxes at $.07/clean ton and $.02/clean ton. Limestone or sandstone, quarried or mined, and other natural resources: 5% of gross value. Natural gas: 5% of gross value (10% of net tax distributed to local governments), additional tax for workers' compensation debt reduction is $.047/mcf of natural gas produced. Oil: 5% of gross value (10% of net tax distributed to local governments). Sand, gravel or other mineral products not quarried or mined: 5% of gross value. Timber: 1.22%, additional tax for workers' compensation debt reduction is 2.78%. |
| **Wisconsin** | Mining Net Proceeds Tax | Progressive net proceeds tax ranging from 3% to 15% is imposed on the net proceeds from mining metalliferous minerals. The tax brackets are annually adjusted for inflation based on the change in the GNP deflator. |
| | Oil and Gas Severance Tax | 7% of market value of oil or gas at the mouth of the well. |
| | Forest Crop Law Severance Tax | 10% of stumpage. |
| | Managed Forest Law Yield Tax | 5% yield tax. This tax will be waived for the first five years of most MFL land. |
| **Wyoming** | Severance Taxes | Severance Tax is defined as an excise tax imposed on the present and continuing privilege of removing, extracting, severing or producing any mineral in this state. Except as otherwise provided by W.S. 39-14-205. The total Severance Tax on crude oil, lease condensate or natural gas shall be six percent (6%). Stripper oil is taxed at four percent (4%). Surface coal is taxed at seven percent (7%). Underground coal is taxed at three and three-fourths percent (3.75%). Trona is taxed at four percent (4%). Bentonite, sand and gravel, and all other minerals are taxed at two percent (2%). Uranium (4%). |

See footnotes at end of table.

# STATE SEVERANCE TAXES: 2012—Continued

*Source:* The Council of State Governments, 2012.

*Note:* Severance tax collection totals may be found in the Chapter Seven table entitled "State Government Revenue, By Type of Tax."

*Key:*

(a) Application of tax is same as that of title unless otherwise indicated by a footnote.

(b) Tax rates and applicability for these severance taxes determined by a vote of the appropriate association within the seafood industry, by the Alaska Seafood Marketing Institute, or by the Department of Revenue. Proceeds from these elective assessments are customarily appropriated for benefit of the seafood industry.

(c) Metallic minerals, molybdenum ore, coal, oil shale, oil, gas, $CO_2$, and coalbed methane.

(d) As of July 1, 2004, set at .0005 mill/$1.

(e) Clay, gravel, phosphate rock, lime, shells, stone, sand, heavy minerals and rare earths.

(f) Actual rate set by administrative actions. Idaho—Current conservation rate is 5 mills (.005); Nebraska—Current conservation rate is 3 mills (.003).

(g) Buyer deducts amount from payment to grower; amount forwarded to Department of Natural Resources.

(h) Petroleum, oil, gas and other hydrocarbons.

(i) Coal, oil and gas.

(j) Coal and oil excepted.

(k) Production is considered commercial when it exceeds 50,000 tons annually. There is a six-year phase-in of the tax. In years one and two, the rate is zero. In year three, it is 25% of the statutory rate and 50% and 75% in years four and five respectively. An Aggregate Materials Tax is imposed by resolution of of county boards. It is not required that any county impose the tax, which is $.10/cubic yard or $.07/ton on materials produced in the county.

(l) Metals, precious and semi-precious stones and gems.

(m) The maximum rate of 0.3% is split between the Oil or Gas Conservation Tax and the Oil, Gas and Coal Natural Resource Account Fund. Currently the Oil or Gas Conservation Tax is .18% and the Oil, Gas and Coal Natural Resource Account Fund tax rate is .08%.

(n) Cement and gypsum or allied products.

(o) Natural resources except oil, natural gas, liquid hydrocarbons or carbon dioxide.

(p) Oil, coal, gas, liquid hydrocarbons, geothermal energy, carbon dioxide and uranium.

(q) Rate reduced by 50 percent if burned in cogeneration facility using renewable resources as fuel to generate at least 10 percent of its energy output. Coal shipped out of state is subject to the $.02/ton tax and 30% of the $.375/ton tax. The coal may be subject to up to the $.375/ton tax at the option of the county in which the coal is mined.

(r) Asphalt and ores bearing lead, zinc, jack, gold, silver, copper or petroleum or other crude oil or other mineral oil, natural gas or casing-head gas and uranium ore.

(s) Any mineral fuel used in the production of energy, including coal, lignite, petroleum, oil, natural gas, uranium and thorium.

(t) Counties and municipalities also authorized to levy severance taxes on sand, gravel, sandstone, chert and limestone at a rate up to $.15/ton.

(u) Fees will not be collected when Oil-Field Cleanup Fund reaches $20 million, but will again be collected when fund falls below $10 million.

# Table 7.16
## STATE GOVERNMENT TAX REVENUE, BY SELECTED TYPES OF TAX: 2010
### (In thousands of dollars)

| State | Total taxes | Sales and gross receipts | Licenses | Individual income | Corporation net income | Severance | Property taxes | Death and gift | Documentary and stock transfer | Other |
|---|---|---|---|---|---|---|---|---|---|---|
| United States | $702,221,472 | $343,620,371 | $50,358,297 | $235,961,745 | $36,808,525 | $11,077,494 | $14,176,457 | $3,890,364 | $4,234,610 | $2,093,609 |
| Alabama | 8,185,563 | 4,234,238 | 492,844 | 2,589,249 | 428,245 | 90,538 | 319,999 | 96 | 30,354 | 0 |
| Alaska | 4,517,927 | 258,005 | 142,849 | 0 | 643,068 | 3,355,049 | 118,870 | 86 | 0 | 0 |
| Arizona | 10,199,338 | 6,192,335 | 369,150 | 2,416,324 | 413,193 | 33,372 | 774,613 | 351 | 0 | 0 |
| Arkansas | 7,279,215 | 3,704,634 | 333,841 | 2,091,082 | 385,365 | 65,147 | 647,944 | 89 | 26,275 | 24,838 |
| California | 104,840,520 | 38,578,241 | 8,123,248 | 45,646,436 | 9,114,589 | 24,409 | 3,353,597 | 0 | 0 | 0 |
| Colorado | 8,586,401 | 3,515,780 | 549,111 | 4,089,948 | 360,003 | 71,436 | 0 | 123 | 0 | 0 |
| Connecticut | 12,285,994 | 5,368,695 | 374,048 | 5,768,846 | 507,752 | 61 | 0 | 167,977 | 98,615 | 0 |
| Delaware | 2,769,731 | 462,914 | 1,257,425 | 853,107 | 142,417 | 0 | 0 | 231 | 52,875 | 762 |
| Florida | 31,498,998 | 26,241,172 | 2,124,726 | 0 | 1,793,200 | 71,000 | 700 | 3,300 | 1,252,500 | 12,400 |
| Georgia | 14,782,779 | 6,516,066 | 467,750 | 7,016,412 | 684,701 | 0 | 86,228 | 0 | 11,622 | 0 |
| Hawaii | 4,837,862 | 3,044,380 | 145,952 | 1,527,790 | 79,853 | 0 | 0 | 0 | 39,887 | 0 |
| Idaho | 2,951,703 | 1,506,829 | 268,003 | 1,068,754 | 98,327 | 6,730 | 0 | 282 | 0 | 2,778 |
| Illinois | 27,511,933 | 14,901,490 | 2,405,779 | 8,510,000 | 1,360,000 | 0 | 50,962 | 243,379 | 40,323 | 0 |
| Indiana | 13,796,427 | 8,490,450 | 704,694 | 3,868,093 | 597,347 | 1,426 | 1,206 | 133,211 | 0 | 0 |
| Iowa | 6,809,344 | 3,185,571 | 700,707 | 2,650,037 | 192,138 | 0 | 0 | 68,358 | 12,533 | 0 |
| Kansas | 6,492,996 | 2,962,674 | 304,342 | 2,687,542 | 352,419 | 102,878 | 74,745 | 8,396 | 0 | 0 |
| Kentucky | 9,531,108 | 4,677,297 | 441,918 | 3,154,488 | 383,815 | 317,146 | 516,170 | 37,202 | 3,072 | 0 |
| Louisiana | 8,757,557 | 4,842,797 | 425,575 | 2,286,500 | 393,036 | 758,469 | 49,426 | 1,754 | 0 | 0 |
| Maine | 3,489,953 | 1,666,914 | 248,270 | 1,303,370 | 175,292 | 0 | 45,713 | 31,210 | 19,184 | 0 |
| Maryland | 15,223,923 | 6,257,681 | 740,264 | 6,200,292 | 891,392 | 0 | 774,109 | 173,460 | 127,401 | 59,324 |
| Massachusetts | 20,050,292 | 6,773,581 | 859,728 | 10,128,035 | 1,834,859 | 0 | 4,549 | 221,379 | 166,989 | 61,172 |
| Michigan | 22,205,870 | 12,435,171 | 1,357,502 | 5,531,349 | 631,895 | 0 | 2,065,215 | 0 | 121,632 | 0 |
| Minnesota | 17,208,877 | 7,882,903 | 1,055,697 | 6,458,111 | 721,742 | 63,106 | 765,742 | 148,422 | 152,970 | 0 |
| Mississippi | 6,268,804 | 4,074,607 | 408,756 | 1,352,481 | 316,331 | 23,290 | 24,378 | 40 | 0 | 1,379 |
| Missouri | 9,708,463 | 4,528,599 | 595,866 | 4,326,507 | 206,936 | 90,832 | 29,538 | 246 | 8,361 | 12,408 |
| Montana | 2,142,809 | 532,013 | 308,933 | 714,814 | 93,225 | 253,649 | 236,830 | 48 | 0 | 3,297 |
| Nebraska | 3,809,266 | 1,897,901 | 226,944 | 1,514,831 | 154,332 | 3,473 | 1,168 | 67 | 10,550 | 0 |
| Nevada | 5,835,963 | 4,274,994 | 572,427 | 0 | 0 | 182,752 | 363,218 | 0 | 57,462 | 385,110 |
| New Hampshire | 2,124,984 | 801,949 | 262,684 | 82,365 | 499,669 | 0 | 393,796 | 0 | 84,470 | 0 |
| New Jersey | 25,927,891 | 11,307,452 | 1,388,521 | 10,322,943 | 2,047,474 | 0 | 3,908 | 581,624 | 275,969 | 0 |
| New Mexico | 4,413,988 | 2,337,528 | 194,203 | 956,600 | 125,100 | 654,752 | 59,624 | 8 | 0 | 86,173 |
| New York | 63,529,354 | 20,911,997 | 1,541,769 | 34,751,382 | 3,895,349 | 0 | 0 | 866,377 | 311,230 | 1,251,250 |
| North Carolina | 21,517,254 | 9,433,591 | 1,536,012 | 9,133,689 | 1,294,314 | 1,464 | 0 | 83,980 | 34,204 | 0 |
| North Dakota | 2,645,695 | 948,778 | 166,119 | 303,764 | 88,347 | 1,136,553 | 2,125 | 9 | 0 | 0 |
| Ohio | 23,583,596 | 12,245,348 | 3,243,554 | 7,886,802 | 142,318 | 10,550 | 0 | 55,024 | 0 | 0 |
| Oklahoma | 7,079,985 | 2,953,081 | 906,188 | 2,224,783 | 216,400 | 743,686 | 0 | 22,702 | 11,321 | 1,824 |
| Oregon | 7,289,362 | 957,241 | 887,011 | 4,945,538 | 353,589 | 12,742 | 25,092 | 98,034 | 10,115 | 0 |
| Pennsylvania | 30,169,122 | 15,464,898 | 2,546,905 | 9,352,287 | 1,648,956 | 0 | 55,363 | 728,713 | 347,108 | 24,892 |
| Rhode Island | 2,568,851 | 1,404,981 | 93,364 | 909,674 | 121,668 | 0 | 2,046 | 30,131 | 6,895 | 92 |
| South Carolina | 7,312,534 | 4,017,383 | 433,497 | 2,673,000 | 148,500 | 0 | 9,317 | 73 | 30,764 | 0 |

See footnotes at end of table.

# STATE GOVERNMENT TAX REVENUE, BY SELECTED TYPES OF TAX: 2010
## (In thousands of dollars) — Continued

| State | Total taxes | Sales and gross receipts | Licenses | Individual income | Corporation net income | Severance | Property taxes | Death and gift | Documentary and stock transfer | Other |
|---|---|---|---|---|---|---|---|---|---|---|
| South Dakota.......... | 1,304,487 | 1,072,409 | 192,193 | 0 | 31,157 | 8,410 | 0 | 143 | 175 | 0 |
| Tennessee.............. | 10,513,788 | 8,027,796 | 1,167,316 | 172,459 | 901,617 | 2,251 | 0 | 81,091 | 124,226 | 37,032 |
| Texas.................. | 39,399,251 | 31,119,148 | 6,542,886 | 0 | 0 | 1,737,136 | 0 | 81 | 0 | 0 |
| Utah.................. | 5,092,415 | 2,262,675 | 389,896 | 2,104,641 | 245,980 | 89,162 | 0 | 61 | 0 | 0 |
| Vermont.............. | 2,511,387 | 845,336 | 106,558 | 489,107 | 85,178 | 0 | 941,894 | 14,165 | 24,808 | 4,341 |
| Virginia............... | 16,411,055 | 5,871,652 | 655,193 | 8,659,470 | 789,655 | 1,882 | 31,181 | 5,670 | 289,488 | 106,864 |
| Washington........... | 16,106,154 | 12,849,019 | 933,241 | 0 | 0 | 20,905 | 1,822,278 | 81,720 | 398,991 | 0 |
| West Virginia......... | 4,655,034 | 2,219,017 | 192,606 | 1,446,852 | 366,245 | 417,230 | 5,051 | 100 | 7,933 | 0 |
| Wisconsin............. | 14,368,569 | 6,686,839 | 833,180 | 5,791,991 | 851,537 | 5,004 | 142,653 | 872 | 44,308 | 12,185 |
| Wyoming ............. | 2,117,100 | 874,321 | 139,052 | 0 | 0 | 721,002 | 377,209 | 28 | 0 | 5,488 |

*Source:* U.S. Census Bureau, 2010 Annual Survey of State Government Finances. For information on sampling and nonsampling errors and definitions, see *http://www.census.gov/govs/state/how_data_collected. html*. Data users who create their own estimates from this table should cite the U.S. Census Bureau as the source of the original data only.

*Note:* Detail may not add to total due to rounding.

**Table 7.17**
**STATE GOVERNMENT SALES AND GROSS RECEIPTS TAX REVENUE: 2010**
**(In thousands of dollars)**

| State | Total | General sales or gross receipts | Selective sales taxes Total | Motor fuels | Insurance premiums | Public utilities | Tobacco products | Alcoholic beverages | Amusements | Pari-mutuels | Other |
|---|---|---|---|---|---|---|---|---|---|---|---|
| United States | $343,620,371 | $224,229,136 | $119,391,235 | $36,563,396 | $15,768,805 | $14,536,619 | $16,781,991 | $5,507,914 | $6,390,981 | $149,166 | $23,692,363 |
| Alabama | 4,234,238 | 2,097,434 | 2,136,804 | 558,476 | 259,169 | 812,367 | 137,401 | 167,285 | 115 | 2,104 | 199,887 |
| Alaska | 258,005 | 0 | 258,005 | 23,834 | 51,374 | 4,085 | 70,147 | 38,939 | 8,920 | 0 | 60,706 |
| Arizona | 6,192,335 | 4,409,603 | 1,782,732 | 796,560 | 437,975 | 21,406 | 338,473 | 65,418 | 12,179 | 285 | 110,436 |
| Arkansas | 3,704,634 | 2,615,290 | 1,089,344 | 466,482 | 144,237 | 0 | 250,841 | 45,315 | 8,787 | 4,725 | 168,957 |
| California | 38,578,241 | 31,197,154 | 7,381,087 | 3,163,694 | 2,180,786 | 745,467 | 922,986 | 311,242 | 0 | 15,541 | 41,371 |
| Colorado | 3,515,780 | 2,050,445 | 1,465,335 | 602,347 | 189,786 | 12,536 | 203,064 | 36,209 | 98,567 | 528 | 322,298 |
| Connecticut | 5,368,695 | 3,145,579 | 2,223,116 | 498,177 | 203,955 | 279,575 | 385,636 | 48,197 | 420,224 | 7,062 | 380,290 |
| Delaware | 462,914 | 0 | 462,914 | 112,889 | 69,568 | 58,263 | 131,712 | 16,446 | 0 | 116 | 73,920 |
| Florida | 26,241,172 | 18,537,000 | 7,704,172 | 2,266,814 | 667,800 | 3,079,200 | 389,267 | 590,423 | 148,604 | 11,460 | 550,604 |
| Georgia | 6,516,066 | 4,864,691 | 1,651,375 | 854,360 | 274,367 | 0 | 227,180 | 169,019 | 0 | 0 | 126,449 |
| Hawaii | 3,044,380 | 2,316,434 | 727,946 | 86,370 | 108,646 | 157,661 | 105,523 | 44,074 | 0 | 0 | 225,672 |
| Idaho | 1,506,829 | 1,126,671 | 380,158 | 230,377 | 72,602 | 2,138 | 48,724 | 7,882 | 0 | 899 | 17,536 |
| Illinois | 14,901,490 | 8,842,231 | 6,059,259 | 1,339,228 | 344,144 | 1,781,022 | 581,817 | 230,394 | 514,533 | 7,034 | 1,261,087 |
| Indiana | 8,490,450 | 5,941,044 | 2,549,406 | 759,959 | 176,426 | 198,988 | 484,686 | 41,563 | 873,166 | 4,546 | 10,072 |
| Iowa | 3,185,571 | 2,121,842 | 1,063,729 | 437,763 | 88,571 | 0 | 232,573 | 14,488 | 279,413 | 3,913 | 7,008 |
| Kansas | 2,962,674 | 2,150,270 | 812,404 | 424,703 | 138,768 | 385 | 106,181 | 111,405 | 454 | 13 | 30,495 |
| Kentucky | 4,677,297 | 2,794,057 | 1,883,240 | 655,245 | 125,063 | 66,787 | 299,541 | 111,074 | 187 | 0 | 625,343 |
| Louisiana | 4,842,797 | 2,579,946 | 2,262,851 | 587,995 | 532,643 | 8,828 | 135,927 | 55,331 | 667,151 | 5,268 | 269,708 |
| Maine | 1,666,914 | 989,645 | 677,269 | 241,687 | 105,811 | 28,816 | 149,067 | 16,864 | 28,173 | 2,447 | 104,404 |
| Maryland | 6,257,681 | 3,753,778 | 2,503,903 | 722,597 | 391,569 | 124,075 | 405,915 | 29,874 | 23,446 | 1,541 | 804,886 |
| Massachusetts | 6,773,581 | 4,625,682 | 2,147,899 | 654,649 | 310,589 | 23,480 | 579,854 | 71,887 | 3,190 | 2,098 | 502,152 |
| Michigan | 12,435,171 | 9,012,729 | 3,422,442 | 967,728 | 257,510 | 27,698 | 1,007,873 | 140,586 | 101,815 | 6,239 | 912,993 |
| Minnesota | 7,882,903 | 4,426,608 | 3,456,295 | 832,291 | 335,839 | 58 | 428,767 | 75,051 | 34,382 | 637 | 1,749,270 |
| Mississippi | 4,074,607 | 2,849,099 | 1,225,508 | 393,363 | 194,020 | 1,970 | 156,558 | 41,208 | 155,123 | 0 | 283,266 |
| Missouri | 4,528,599 | 2,919,117 | 1,609,482 | 721,917 | 270,053 | 0 | 106,163 | 32,785 | 390,931 | 0 | 87,633 |
| Montana | 532,013 | 0 | 532,013 | 204,390 | 65,048 | 50,622 | 88,034 | 31,920 | 52,414 | 86 | 39,499 |
| Nebraska | 1,897,901 | 1,306,702 | 591,199 | 298,805 | 45,463 | 57,806 | 52,487 | 27,002 | 6,691 | 149 | 102,796 |
| Nevada | 4,274,994 | 2,559,489 | 1,715,505 | 292,804 | 234,253 | 23,025 | 110,345 | 39,380 | 864,252 | 0 | 151,446 |
| New Hampshire | 801,949 | 0 | 801,949 | 147,805 | 75,172 | 85,201 | 237,988 | 12,865 | 147 | 1,591 | 241,180 |
| New Jersey | 11,307,452 | 7,898,165 | 3,409,287 | 535,281 | 509,305 | 938,945 | 759,742 | 126,367 | 296,125 | 0 | 243,522 |
| New Mexico | 2,337,528 | 1,718,795 | 618,733 | 227,633 | 122,703 | 28,236 | 37,926 | 39,337 | 58,654 | 36 | 104,208 |
| New York | 20,911,997 | 10,568,466 | 10,343,531 | 1,613,229 | 1,430,125 | 891,406 | 1,351,332 | 224,621 | 690 | 22,472 | 4,809,656 |
| North Carolina | 9,433,591 | 5,856,993 | 3,576,598 | 1,551,660 | 507,038 | 398,661 | 273,946 | 294,532 | 15,678 | 0 | 535,083 |
| North Dakota | 948,778 | 603,740 | 345,038 | 151,050 | 35,894 | 34,002 | 23,875 | 7,368 | 8,387 | 291 | 84,171 |
| Ohio | 12,245,348 | 7,253,496 | 4,991,852 | 1,727,242 | 432,925 | 1,144,976 | 886,875 | 93,643 | 0 | 8,370 | 697,821 |
| Oklahoma | 2,953,081 | 1,968,309 | 984,772 | 431,151 | 148,708 | 31,899 | 248,472 | 90,066 | 13,908 | 1,319 | 19,249 |
| Oregon | 957,241 | 0 | 957,241 | 403,284 | 72,876 | 43,780 | 239,254 | 16,252 | 187 | 3,014 | 178,594 |
| Pennsylvania | 15,464,898 | 8,029,797 | 7,435,101 | 2,020,099 | 778,175 | 1,292,373 | 1,090,892 | 297,638 | 1,231,127 | 17,460 | 707,337 |
| Rhode Island | 1,404,981 | 798,481 | 606,500 | 123,805 | 62,148 | 95,318 | 137,501 | 11,924 | 0 | 1,476 | 174,328 |
| South Carolina | 4,017,383 | 2,833,839 | 1,183,544 | 521,215 | 125,334 | 31,479 | 35,257 | 148,942 | 35,326 | 0 | 285,991 |

See footnotes at end of table.

# STATE GOVERNMENT SALES AND GROSS RECEIPTS TAX REVENUE: 2010—Continued
## (In thousands of dollars)

| State | Total | General sales or gross receipts | Selective sales taxes Total | Motor fuels | Insurance premiums | Public utilities | Tobacco products | Alcoholic beverages | Amusements | Pari-mutuels | Other |
|---|---|---|---|---|---|---|---|---|---|---|---|
| South Dakota | 1,072,409 | 742,363 | 330,046 | 125,223 | 63,285 | 3,514 | 67,747 | 14,766 | 26 | 377 | 55,108 |
| Tennessee | 8,027,796 | 6,130,877 | 1,896,919 | 824,795 | 555,163 | 10,328 | 290,438 | 117,516 | 0 | 0 | 98,679 |
| Texas | 31,119,148 | 19,663,374 | 11,455,774 | 3,043,495 | 1,307,847 | 765,596 | 1,388,765 | 809,234 | 37,564 | 10,279 | 4,092,994 |
| Utah | 2,262,675 | 1,638,906 | 623,769 | 351,449 | 103,119 | 28,817 | 58,676 | 41,260 | 0 | 0 | 40,448 |
| Vermont | 845,336 | 311,140 | 534,196 | 99,278 | 55,825 | 12,363 | 70,058 | 20,552 | 0 | 0 | 276,120 |
| Virginia | 5,871,652 | 3,543,210 | 2,328,442 | 882,919 | 414,165 | 158,487 | 175,581 | 182,381 | 112 | 0 | 514,797 |
| Washington | 12,849,019 | 9,607,285 | 3,241,734 | 1,196,688 | 405,923 | 448,251 | 426,265 | 282,555 | 0 | 2,049 | 480,003 |
| West Virginia | 2,219,017 | 1,095,687 | 1,123,330 | 391,995 | 114,537 | 171,895 | 114,128 | 9,398 | 0 | 3,282 | 318,095 |
| Wisconsin | 6,686,839 | 3,944,260 | 2,742,579 | 972,979 | 146,886 | 350,580 | 704,156 | 53,792 | 333 | 306 | 513,547 |
| Wyoming | 874,321 | 789,413 | 84,908 | 25,617 | 25,617 | 4,254 | 26,375 | 1,644 | 0 | 153 | 1,248 |

*Source:* U.S. Census Bureau, 2010 Annual Survey of State Government Finances. For information on sampling and nonsampling errors and definitions, *see http://www.census.gov/govs/state/how_data_collected. html.* Data users who create their own estimates from this table should cite the U.S. Census Bureau as the source of the original data only.

*Note:* Detail may not add to total due to rounding.

## Table 7.18
## STATE GOVERNMENT LICENSE TAX REVENUE: 2010
(In thousands of dollars)

| State | Total license tax revenue | Motor vehicle license revenue | Occupation and business license, NEC | Corporation license | Motor vehicle operator's license | Hunting and fishing license | Public utility license | Alcoholic beverage license | Amusement license | Other license taxes |
|---|---|---|---|---|---|---|---|---|---|---|
| United States ............. | $50,358,297 | $2,376,844 | $12,636,215 | $9,921,925 | $20,962,965 | $1,500,349 | $962,445 | $440,659 | $623,624 | $933,271 |
| Alabama...................... | 492,844 | 19,148 | 126,525 | 108,682 | 200,285 | 20,810 | 13,525 | 3,868 | 0 | 1 |
| Alaska........................ | 142,849 | 0 | 43,543 | 228 | 63,692 | 24,059 | 346 | 2,475 | 2 | 8,504 |
| Arizona...................... | 369,150 | 23,701 | 113,170 | 9,456 | 176,095 | 28,156 | 9,241 | 5,444 | 0 | 3,887 |
| Arkansas..................... | 333,841 | 16,871 | 113,194 | 24,504 | 139,582 | 26,715 | 8,647 | 2,931 | 464 | 933 |
| California................... | 8,123,248 | 270,344 | 4,065,097 | 52,916 | 3,108,956 | 91,440 | 449,195 | 51,423 | 15,027 | 18,850 |
| Colorado..................... | 549,111 | 20,937 | 42,176 | 13,881 | 379,611 | 68,562 | 16,040 | 6,045 | 828 | 1,031 |
| Connecticut.................. | 374,048 | 37,251 | 95,303 | 23,901 | 196,778 | 8,442 | 0 | 7,757 | 66 | 4,550 |
| Delaware..................... | 1,257,425 | 4,356 | 277,882 | 767,478 | 47,375 | 2,970 | 6,699 | 1,409 | 436 | 148,820 |
| Florida....................... | 2,124,726 | 310,101 | 219,401 | 238,147 | 1,282,832 | 15,143 | 31,638 | 8,583 | 15,000 | 3,881 |
| Georgia...................... | 467,750 | 42,648 | 74,279 | 33,318 | 282,516 | 24,135 | 23 | 1,327 | 269 | 9,235 |
| Hawaii....................... | 145,952 | 241 | 21,682 | 1,461 | 100,575 | 378 | 20,325 | 0 | 0 | 1,290 |
| Idaho......................... | 268,003 | 7,676 | 63,088 | 1,923 | 120,275 | 34,035 | 35,451 | 1,399 | 315 | 3,841 |
| Illinois....................... | 2,405,779 | 92,484 | 409,868 | 322,868 | 1,446,595 | 39,606 | 25,780 | 11,952 | 48,554 | 8,072 |
| Indiana...................... | 704,694 | 214,505 | 41,033 | 10,206 | 393,350 | 20,682 | 0 | 11,502 | 5,444 | 7,972 |
| Iowa.......................... | 700,707 | 14,428 | 110,012 | 33,072 | 466,982 | 28,663 | 12,171 | 11,803 | 16,464 | 7,112 |
| Kansas ....................... | 304,342 | 18,222 | 28,850 | 45,343 | 174,932 | 24,987 | 6,621 | 2,811 | 25 | 2,551 |
| Kentucky .................... | 441,918 | 16,537 | 116,665 | 74,724 | 198,783 | 24,716 | 0 | 5,885 | 271 | 4,337 |
| Louisiana .................... | 425,575 | 12,758 | 105,938 | 156,648 | 109,388 | 27,252 | 10,911 | 0 | 0 | 2,680 |
| Maine ........................ | 248,270 | 8,400 | 106,915 | 8,211 | 94,633 | 15,886 | 0 | 4,711 | 722 | 8,792 |
| Maryland .................... | 740,264 | 28,554 | 166,317 | 93,086 | 433,777 | 15,384 | 0 | 1,118 | 23 | 2,005 |
| Massachusetts............... | 859,728 | 104,298 | 249,807 | 25,137 | 362,053 | 5,222 | 0 | 3,006 | 423 | 109,782 |
| Michigan..................... | 1,357,502 | 51,712 | 154,820 | 20,752 | 877,844 | 50,601 | 24,260 | 14,264 | 0 | 163,249 |
| Minnesota.................... | 1,055,697 | 46,189 | 332,015 | 7,955 | 557,733 | 58,140 | 779 | 1,788 | 1,174 | 49,924 |
| Mississippi................... | 408,756 | 33,255 | 93,219 | 112,064 | 124,437 | 14,176 | 8,543 | 2,815 | 6,144 | 14,103 |
| Missouri...................... | 595,866 | 17,215 | 143,270 | 91,566 | 265,623 | 32,248 | 20,970 | 4,890 | 1,766 | 18,318 |
| Montana...................... | 308,933 | 8,500 | 97,429 | 2,925 | 142,189 | 44,503 | 7 | 2,053 | 4,669 | 6,658 |
| Nebraska..................... | 226,944 | 10,858 | 74,505 | 14,989 | 79,479 | 17,247 | 0 | 3,508 | 184 | 26,174 |
| Nevada....................... | 572,427 | 20,136 | 207,331 | 65,226 | 158,987 | 8,806 | 0 | 0 | 107,312 | 4,629 |
| New Hampshire............. | 262,684 | 12,122 | 54,630 | 40,201 | 131,100 | 10,018 | 10,049 | 3,704 | 140 | 720 |
| New Jersey................... | 1,388,521 | 50,345 | 434,587 | 227,497 | 578,968 | 13,484 | 4,172 | 10,399 | 66,807 | 2,262 |
| New Mexico.................. | 194,203 | 3,705 | 25,186 | 9,071 | 121,770 | 25,372 | 1,332 | 3,534 | 16 | 4,233 |
| New York..................... | 1,541,769 | 136,785 | 220,000 | 59,899 | 965,000 | 75,629 | 34,047 | 49,000 | 0 | 1,393 |
| North Carolina.............. | 1,536,012 | 127,096 | 199,421 | 621,546 | 548,379 | 16,331 | 15,507 | 15,507 | 281 | 7,732 |
| North Dakota................ | 166,119 | 4,040 | 59,486 | 0 | 87,145 | 14,906 | 4 | 257 | | 0 |
| Ohio.......................... | 3,243,554 | 89,456 | 795,721 | 1,387,449 | 832,589 | 38,661 | 33,179 | 38,882 | 4,417 | 23,200 |
| Oklahoma.................... | 906,188 | 15,916 | 108,388 | 46,198 | 579,380 | 19,969 | 5 | 1,169 | 121,596 | 13,567 |
| Oregon....................... | 887,011 | 28,501 | 284,278 | 15,284 | 496,097 | 44,549 | 5,615 | 3,390 | 2,727 | 6,570 |
| Pennsylvania ................ | 2,546,905 | 60,995 | 796,930 | 538,905 | 800,432 | 70,733 | 61,214 | 16,333 | 182,899 | 18,464 |
| Rhode Island................ | 93,364 | 626 | 32,097 | 4,264 | 53,385 | 2,253 | 0 | 109 | 427 | 203 |
| South Carolina.............. | 433,497 | 51,121 | 128,629 | 71,033 | 147,405 | 17,231 | 0 | 7,740 | 2,093 | 8,245 |

See footnotes at end of table.

# STATE GOVERNMENT LICENSE TAX REVENUE: 2010—Continued
## (In thousands of dollars)

| State | Total license tax revenue | Motor vehicle license revenue | Occupation and business license, NEC | Corporation license | Motor vehicle operator's license | Hunting and fishing license | Public utility license | Alcoholic beverage license | Amusement license | Other license taxes |
|---|---|---|---|---|---|---|---|---|---|---|
| South Dakota.............. | 192,193 | 3,611 | 87,747 | 3,911 | 52,822 | 28,236 | 0 | 378 | 124 | 15,364 |
| Tennessee................. | 1,167,316 | 45,118 | 271,796 | 551,412 | 249,577 | 32,362 | 7,372 | 1,161 | 296 | 8,222 |
| Texas........................ | 6,542,886 | 101,229 | 730,635 | 3,866,846 | 1,542,188 | 98,700 | 24,684 | 68,416 | 8,238 | 101,950 |
| Utah.......................... | 389,896 | 13,806 | 43,906 | 3,581 | 292,359 | 28,418 | 0 | 1,936 | 0 | 5,890 |
| Vermont..................... | 106,558 | 7,241 | 16,641 | 1,700 | 72,214 | 6,585 | 0 | 381 | 37 | 1,759 |
| Virginia..................... | 655,193 | 58,743 | 162,137 | 54,145 | 339,581 | 24,432 | 0 | 11,700 | 86 | 4,369 |
| Washington................ | 933,241 | 66,666 | 241,255 | 25,834 | 463,075 | 35,222 | 18,059 | 12,676 | 7,061 | 63,393 |
| West Virginia............. | 192,606 | 3,900 | 42,849 | 2,585 | 86,691 | 16,653 | 21,976 | 17,538 | 200 | 214 |
| Wisconsin.................. | 833,180 | 42,309 | 183,214 | 18,231 | 471,556 | 71,686 | 39,565 | 1,682 | 597 | 4,340 |
| Wyoming .................. | 139,052 | 2,188 | 23,348 | 11,666 | 65,895 | 35,955 | 0 | 0 | 0 | 0 |

*Source:* U.S. Census Bureau, 2010 Annual Survey of State Government Finances. For information on sampling and nonsampling errors and definitions, see *http://www.census.gov/govs/state/how_data_collected.html*. Data users who create their own estimates from this table should cite the U.S. Census Bureau as the source of the original data only.

*Note:* Detail may not add to total due to rounding.

## Table 7.19
## SUMMARY OF FINANCIAL AGGREGATES, BY STATE: 2010
(In millions of dollars)

| State | Revenue | | | | Expenditure | | | | Total debt outstanding at end of fiscal year | Total cash and security holdings at end of fiscal year |
|---|---|---|---|---|---|---|---|---|---|---|
| | Total | General | Utilities & liquor store | Insurance trust (a) | Total | General | Utilities & liquor store | Insurance trust | | |
| United States ......... | 2,035,700 | 1,563,629 | 21,617 | 450,455 | 1,942,822 | 1,593,134 | 28,791 | 320,897 | 1,113,355 | 3,329,533 |
| Alabama.................. | 26,824 | 22,990 | 252 | 3,582 | 27,700 | 24,016 | 242 | 3,442 | 8,785 | 34,218 |
| Alaska..................... | 12,375 | 11,036 | 19 | 1,320 | 10,997 | 9,733 | 108 | 1,157 | 6,381 | 60,083 |
| Arizona................... | 32,842 | 26,324 | 30 | 6,488 | 33,016 | 27,982 | 32 | 5,001 | 13,956 | 41,841 |
| Arkansas................. | 19,595 | 16,221 | 0 | 3,374 | 17,354 | 15,150 | 0 | 2,204 | 4,261 | 23,210 |
| California ............... | 278,495 | 196,643 | 4,053 | 77,799 | 257,249 | 210,359 | 3,850 | 43,040 | 148,929 | 480,484 |
| Colorado................. | 27,991 | 19,931 | 0 | 8,060 | 27,661 | 21,818 | 28 | 5,816 | 16,710 | 58,034 |
| Connecticut ............ | 26,840 | 21,924 | 29 | 4,887 | 27,437 | 21,600 | 526 | 5,311 | 30,216 | 38,297 |
| Delaware ................ | 7,976 | 7,234 | 15 | 727 | 7,827 | 6,917 | 125 | 784 | 5,515 | 12,860 |
| Florida ................... | 91,653 | 71,341 | 21 | 20,291 | 81,629 | 68,482 | 98 | 13,049 | 40,404 | 164,426 |
| Georgia.................. | 44,878 | 36,480 | 7 | 8,392 | 44,482 | 36,710 | 44 | 7,728 | 13,789 | 68,961 |
| Hawaii.................... | 11,566 | 9,627 | 0 | 1,938 | 11,178 | 9,710 | 5 | 1,463 | 7,701 | 13,951 |
| Idaho...................... | 8,859 | 6,727 | 118 | 2,015 | 8,514 | 7,119 | 91 | 1,304 | 3,872 | 16,364 |
| Illinois.................... | 73,275 | 55,674 | 0 | 17,601 | 75,270 | 59,248 | 0 | 16,022 | 61,412 | 112,452 |
| Indiana................... | 35,575 | 29,802 | 0 | 5,773 | 35,474 | 30,503 | 0 | 4,971 | 23,635 | 53,585 |
| Iowa ...................... | 21,265 | 17,113 | 214 | 3,938 | 19,109 | 16,306 | 147 | 2,655 | 5,140 | 30,041 |
| Kansas.................... | 16,546 | 14,215 | 0 | 2,330 | 16,584 | 14,176 | 0 | 2,408 | 6,478 | 15,977 |
| Kentucky ................ | 26,993 | 22,862 | 0 | 4,131 | 29,098 | 24,193 | 51 | 4,854 | 14,393 | 35,941 |
| Louisiana................ | 32,188 | 27,441 | 11 | 4,736 | 33,615 | 29,561 | 6 | 4,049 | 17,443 | 52,142 |
| Maine..................... | 9,539 | 8,248 | 0 | 1,291 | 9,024 | 7,930 | 4 | 1,091 | 6,034 | 15,977 |
| Maryland ................ | 37,394 | 31,185 | 124 | 6,085 | 37,488 | 32,110 | 851 | 4,526 | 24,475 | 52,115 |
| Massachusetts ......... | 50,472 | 42,209 | 211 | 8,052 | 51,731 | 41,784 | 266 | 9,680 | 73,940 | 88,582 |
| Michigan................. | 65,972 | 52,667 | 780 | 12,524 | 63,918 | 51,510 | 635 | 11,772 | 32,146 | 75,389 |
| Minnesota............... | 39,887 | 31,462 | 0 | 8,425 | 37,943 | 31,642 | 119 | 6,182 | 11,683 | 52,479 |
| Mississippi.............. | 20,979 | 17,427 | 257 | 3,294 | 20,023 | 17,500 | 207 | 2,315 | 6,468 | 27,785 |
| Missouri.................. | 33,916 | 26,112 | 0 | 7,804 | 30,772 | 25,795 | 0 | 4,977 | 20,421 | 62,767 |
| Montana ................. | 7,141 | 6,009 | 68 | 1,065 | 7,052 | 6,005 | 76 | 971 | 4,374 | 16,033 |
| Nebraska ................ | 10,063 | 8,676 | 0 | 1,387 | 9,584 | 8,816 | 0 | 769 | 2,330 | 12,538 |
| Nevada ................... | 14,053 | 9,937 | 84 | 4,032 | 12,935 | 9,478 | 86 | 3,371 | 4,436 | 23,762 |
| New Hampshire ...... | 7,828 | 6,222 | 514 | 1,092 | 7,706 | 6,351 | 437 | 918 | 8,347 | 11,588 |
| New Jersey ............. | 66,740 | 51,183 | 881 | 14,677 | 67,971 | 49,249 | 2,745 | 15,978 | 60,958 | 102,728 |
| New Mexico ............ | 17,567 | 14,011 | 0 | 3,556 | 17,996 | 15,890 | 14 | 2,092 | 8,740 | 39,950 |
| New York................ | 195,460 | 139,966 | 7,427 | 48,067 | 174,308 | 137,997 | 11,705 | 24,606 | 129,530 | 304,452 |
| North Carolina........ | 57,467 | 44,058 | 0 | 13,410 | 52,190 | 43,014 | 55 | 9,121 | 18,853 | 83,941 |
| North Dakota.......... | 6,118 | 5,415 | 0 | 703 | 5,134 | 4,688 | 0 | 446 | 2,198 | 13,848 |
| Ohio....................... | 89,664 | 57,508 | 779 | 31,377 | 76,731 | 57,371 | 470 | 18,890 | 31,177 | 172,456 |
| Oklahoma................ | 23,692 | 19,486 | 491 | 3,714 | 22,640 | 19,233 | 546 | 2,861 | 9,963 | 32,346 |
| Oregon................... | 28,703 | 19,001 | 421 | 9,282 | 26,978 | 20,560 | 243 | 6,175 | 13,510 | 61,257 |
| Pennsylvania .......... | 83,287 | 63,884 | 1,511 | 17,892 | 87,285 | 69,402 | 1,479 | 16,404 | 44,738 | 118,685 |
| Rhode Island........... | 8,809 | 7,088 | 28 | 1,694 | 8,211 | 6,352 | 159 | 1,700 | 9,498 | 15,362 |
| South Carolina........ | 28,868 | 21,512 | 1,689 | 5,667 | 28,927 | 22,810 | 1,940 | 4,177 | 15,771 | 33,751 |
| South Dakota.......... | 4,493 | 3,974 | 0 | 518 | 4,429 | 3,988 | 0 | 441 | 3,483 | 11,404 |
| Tennessee ............... | 29,720 | 25,517 | 0 | 4,202 | 29,675 | 26,324 | 2 | 3,349 | 5,835 | 36,508 |
| Texas...................... | 120,390 | 99,924 | 0 | 20,466 | 119,605 | 102,373 | 0 | 17,232 | 42,034 | 249,830 |
| Utah....................... | 16,022 | 13,228 | 237 | 2,558 | 16,263 | 14,183 | 174 | 1,906 | 6,478 | 25,385 |
| Vermont.................. | 6,001 | 5,331 | 45 | 626 | 5,726 | 5,172 | 75 | 479 | 3,493 | 6,586 |
| Virginia.................. | 46,357 | 37,103 | 559 | 8,695 | 43,457 | 38,154 | 455 | 4,848 | 24,967 | 69,947 |
| Washington............. | 44,299 | 33,711 | 579 | 10,009 | 46,238 | 36,469 | 547 | 9,222 | 27,478 | 72,786 |
| West Virginia.......... | 13,564 | 11,561 | 82 | 1,921 | 12,343 | 10,767 | 70 | 1,505 | 7,144 | 17,684 |
| Wisconsin .............. | 48,088 | 30,845 | 0 | 17,243 | 38,590 | 31,678 | 7 | 6,905 | 22,319 | 88,918 |
| Wyoming ................ | 7,411 | 5,586 | 82 | 1,744 | 5,757 | 4,957 | 71 | 729 | 1,514 | 19,829 |

Source: U.S. Census Bureau, 2010 Annual Survey of State Government Finances. For information on sampling and nonsampling errors and definitions, see http://www.census.gov/govs/state/how_data_collected.html. Data users who create their own estimates from this table should cite the U.S. Census Bureau as the source of the original data only.

Note: Detail may not add to total due to rounding. Data presented are statistical in nature and do not represent an accounting statement. Therefore, a difference between an individual government's total revenue and expenditure does not necessarily indicate a budget surplus or deficit.

Key:
(a) Within insurance trust revenue, net earnings of state retirement systems is a calculated statistic (the item code in the data file is X08), and thus can be positive or negative. Net earnings is the sum of earnings on investments plus gains on investments minus losses on investments. The change made in 2002 for asset valuation from book to market value in accordance with Statement 34 of the Governmental Accounting Standards Board is reflected in the calculated statistics.

## Table 7.20
## NATIONAL TOTALS OF STATE GOVERNMENT FINANCES FOR SELECTED YEARS: 2006–2010

| Item | 2010 | 2009 | 2008 | 2007 | 2006 |
|---|---|---|---|---|---|
| **Revenue total** | $2,035,699,790 | $1,137,574,359 | $1,580,143,198 | $1,995,125,717 | $1,774,648,692 |
| General revenue | 1,563,628,659 | 1,495,730,319 | 1,511,123,496 | 1,451,715,159 | 1,391,133,672 |
| Taxes | 702,221,472 | 715,496,219 | 781,788,125 | 757,470,540 | 715,973,170 |
| Intergovernmental revenue | 575,561,683 | 495,623,675 | 442,360,639 | 427,029,937 | 419,640,660 |
| From Federal Government | 555,296,681 | 475,952,532 | 419,760,229 | 406,934,021 | 398,200,459 |
| Public welfare | 315,517,460 | 281,119,147 | 240,821,188 | 230,884,476 | 224,406,166 |
| Education | 105,404,764 | 82,425,828 | 74,228,387 | 73,414,986 | 72,376,901 |
| Highways | 42,969,373 | 36,529,755 | 35,722,176 | 35,196,031 | 34,187,690 |
| Employment security administration | 4,972,238 | 4,455,882 | 3,952,385 | 3,932,896 | 4,380,567 |
| Other | 82,461,627 | 67,957,875 | 61,736,565 | 60,062,060 | 62,849,135 |
| From local government | 20,265,002 | 19,671,143 | 22,600,410 | 20,095,916 | 21,440,201 |
| Charges and miscellaneous revenue | 285,845,504 | 284,610,425 | 286,974,732 | 267,214,682 | 255,519,842 |
| Liquor stores revenue | 6,494,993 | 6,376,562 | 6,128,282 | 5,799,273 | 5,475,237 |
| Utility revenue | 15,121,578 | 16,471,341 | 16,521,947 | 16,735,684 | 15,816,555 |
| Insurance trust revenue (a) | 450,454,560 | -381,003,863 | 46,369,473 | 520,875,601 | 362,223,228 |
| Employee retirement | 351,444,857 | -446,723,542 | -11,968,317 | 457,613,822 | 295,602,816 |
| Unemployment compensation | 75,037,579 | 41,976,470 | 34,359,648 | 34,063,242 | 36,863,504 |
| Worker compensation | 16,591,538 | 16,458,342 | 18,574,527 | 19,785,182 | 21,906,234 |
| Other | 7,380,586 | 7,284,867 | 5,403,615 | 9,413,355 | 7,850,674 |
| **Expenditure and debt redemption** | 2,054,344,041 | 1,931,791,457 | 1,813,059,431 | 1,709,950,197 | 1,631,438,503 |
| Debt redemption | 111,521,897 | 104,930,318 | 77,377,412 | 75,141,138 | 76,905,629 |
| Expenditure total | 1,942,822,144 | 1,826,861,139 | 1,735,682,019 | 1,634,809,059 | 1,554,532,874 |
| General expenditure | 1,593,134,279 | 1,555,918,037 | 1,504,121,032 | 1,422,830,665 | 1,349,968,143 |
| Education | 570,958,895 | 567,103,565 | 546,875,379 | 514,123,945 | 483,476,753 |
| Intergovernmental expenditure | 316,843,198 | 324,495,673 | 315,461,936 | 301,091,116 | 280,090,982 |
| State institutions of higher education | 214,040,896 | 206,794,634 | 197,623,181 | 180,793,485 | 169,883,923 |
| Other education | 356,917,999 | 360,308,931 | 349,252,198 | 333,330,460 | 313,592,830 |
| Public welfare | 462,726,745 | 438,394,913 | 411,158,050 | 392,796,499 | 376,675,058 |
| Intergovernmental expenditure | 59,519,344 | 59,183,863 | 58,263,287 | 57,343,557 | 54,858,307 |
| Cash assistance, categorical program | 29,362,783 | 28,936,340 | 28,438,340 | 30,553,638 | 30,310,961 |
| Cash assistance, other | 6,000,585 | 6,155,806 | 5,591,135 | 4,689,487 | 4,516,397 |
| Other public welfare | 427,363,377 | 403,302,767 | 377,128,575 | 357,553,374 | 341,847,700 |
| Highways | 110,840,105 | 107,077,164 | 107,368,119 | 103,201,172 | 100,841,813 |
| Intergovernmental expenditure | 17,914,186 | 16,453,767 | 16,535,299 | 14,868,267 | 15,495,306 |
| Regular state highway facilities | 102,596,494 | 98,838,841 | 98,952,922 | 95,863,536 | 93,964,195 |
| State toll highways/facilities | 8,243,611 | 8,238,323 | 8,415,197 | 7,337,636 | 6,877,618 |
| Health and hospitals | 123,616,348 | 119,302,427 | 114,598,642 | 106,194,836 | 96,663,369 |
| Hospitals | 63,807,295 | 56,957,190 | 53,749,062 | 48,982,511 | 45,960,293 |
| Health | 59,809,053 | 62,345,237 | 60,849,580 | 57,212,325 | 50,703,076 |
| Natural resources | 21,506,591 | 22,585,813 | 22,523,830 | 22,038,266 | 20,036,460 |
| Corrections | 48,452,750 | 50,380,985 | 49,880,748 | 46,485,220 | 42,793,514 |
| Financial administration | 22,102,980 | 22,493,411 | 23,156,673 | 22,586,446 | 21,676,940 |
| Employment security administration | 5,075,538 | 4,533,861 | 4,053,723 | 3,962,040 | 4,551,037 |
| Police protection | 13,809,518 | 13,646,171 | 13,594,279 | 12,856,160 | 12,220,732 |
| Interest on general debt | 45,397,738 | 45,201,558 | 44,722,795 | 41,589,474 | 38,231,722 |
| Veterans' services | 475,960 | 423,542 | 399,051 | 375,475 | 992,146 |
| Utility expenditure | 23,547,443 | 26,539,464 | 24,945,908 | 24,530,299 | 24,922,440 |
| Insurance trust expenditure | 320,896,739 | 239,228,987 | 201,670,429 | 182,783,985 | 175,304,033 |
| Employee retirement | 166,648,918 | 154,899,467 | 148,145,152 | 136,201,600 | 127,501,115 |
| Unemployment compensation | 134,908,383 | 65,974,092 | 35,470,883 | 28,854,007 | 28,008,860 |
| Other | 19,339,438 | 18,355,428 | 18,054,394 | 17,728,378 | 19,794,058 |
| **Total expenditure by character and object** | 1,942,822,144 | 1,826,861,139 | 1,735,682,019 | 1,634,809,059 | 1,554,532,874 |
| Direct expenditure | 1,457,276,564 | 1,335,539,268 | 1,256,672,350 | 1,174,624,949 | 1,122,267,668 |
| Current operation | 933,729,010 | 896,785,732 | 863,425,561 | 807,565,330 | 774,002,589 |
| Capital outlay | 117,356,157 | 116,577,726 | 112,252,280 | 110,043,905 | 103,253,138 |
| Construction | 100,625,378 | 97,526,425 | 92,346,205 | 90,788,297 | 85,712,794 |
| Other capital outlay | 16,730,779 | 19,051,301 | 19,906,075 | 19,255,608 | 17,540,344 |
| Assistance and subsidies | 37,805,604 | 35,702,856 | 32,603,424 | 30,651,647 | 29,564,773 |
| Interest on debt | 47,489,054 | 47,243,967 | 46,720,656 | 43,580,082 | 40,143,135 |
| Insurance benefits and repayments | 320,896,739 | 239,228,987 | 201,670,429 | 182,783,985 | 175,304,033 |
| Intergovernmental expenditure | 485,545,580 | 491,321,871 | 479,009,669 | 460,184,110 | 432,265,206 |
| **Cash and security holdings at end of fiscal year** | 3,329,533,245 | 3,098,673,552 | 3,787,863,671 | 3,874,644,404 | 3,443,236,625 |
| Insurance trust | 2,218,828,655 | 2,041,713,773 | 2,688,131,631 | 2,827,944,398 | 2,495,133,155 |
| Unemployment fund balance | -17,632,312 | 9,820,731 | 38,489,823 | 39,795,912 | 35,053,864 |
| Debt offsets | 499,290,334 | 489,510,744 | 461,987,514 | 430,156,267 | 390,865,042 |

*Source:* U.S. Census Bureau, 2004–2010 Census of Governments. For information on sampling and nonsampling errors and definitions, see *http://www.census.gov/govs/state/how_data_collected.html.* Data users who create their own estimates from this table should cite the U.S. Census Bureau as the source of the original data only.

*Key:*
(a) Within insurance trust revenue, net earnings of state retirement systems is a calculated statistic (the item code in the data file is X08), and thus can be positive or negative. Net earnings is the sum of earnings on investments plus gains on investments minus losses on investments. The change made in 2002 for asset valuation from book to market value in accordance with Statement 34 of the Governmental Accounting Standards Board is reflected in the calculated statistics.

## Table 7.21
## STATE GENERAL REVENUE, BY SOURCE AND BY STATE: 2010 (In thousands of dollars)

| State | Total general revenue (a) | Taxes Total (b) | Sales and gross receipts Total (b) | General | Motor fuels | Licenses Total (b) | Motor vehicle | Individual income | Corporation net income | Intergovernmental revenue | Charges and miscellaneous general revenue |
|---|---|---|---|---|---|---|---|---|---|---|---|
| United States ........ | $1,563,628,659 | $702,221,472 | $343,620,371 | $224,229,136 | $36,563,396 | $50,358,297 | $20,962,965 | $235,961,745 | $36,808,525 | $575,561,683 | $285,845,504 |
| Alabama............. | 22,989,680 | 8,185,563 | 4,234,238 | 2,097,434 | 558,476 | 492,844 | 200,285 | 2,589,249 | 428,245 | 9,369,725 | 5,434,392 |
| Alaska................ | 11,035,812 | 4,517,927 | 258,005 | 0 | 23,834 | 142,849 | 63,692 | 0 | 643,068 | 2,961,501 | 3,556,384 |
| Arizona.............. | 26,324,126 | 10,199,338 | 6,192,335 | 4,409,603 | 796,560 | 369,150 | 176,095 | 2,416,324 | 413,193 | 12,577,215 | 3,547,573 |
| Arkansas............ | 16,221,062 | 7,279,215 | 3,704,634 | 2,615,250 | 466,482 | 333,841 | 139,582 | 2,091,082 | 385,365 | 5,978,147 | 2,963,700 |
| California .......... | 196,643,170 | 104,840,520 | 38,578,241 | 31,197,154 | 3,163,694 | 8,123,248 | 3,108,956 | 45,646,436 | 9,114,589 | 67,805,353 | 23,997,297 |
| Colorado............ | 19,930,978 | 8,586,401 | 3,515,780 | 2,050,445 | 602,347 | 549,111 | 379,611 | 4,089,948 | 360,003 | 6,371,099 | 4,973,478 |
| Connecticut ....... | 21,924,404 | 12,285,994 | 5,368,695 | 3,145,579 | 498,177 | 374,048 | 196,778 | 5,768,846 | 507,752 | 6,229,831 | 3,408,579 |
| Delaware ........... | 7,233,570 | 2,769,731 | 462,914 | 0 | 112,889 | 1,257,425 | 47,375 | 853,107 | 142,417 | 2,035,019 | 2,428,820 |
| Florida .............. | 71,341,309 | 26,241,172 | 26,241,172 | 18,537,000 | 2,266,814 | 2,124,726 | 1,282,832 | 0 | 1,793,200 | 25,447,682 | 14,394,629 |
| Georgia ............. | 36,479,685 | 14,782,779 | 6,516,066 | 4,864,691 | 854,360 | 467,750 | 282,516 | 7,016,412 | 684,701 | 16,193,428 | 5,503,478 |
| Hawaii............... | 9,627,041 | 4,837,862 | 3,044,380 | 2,316,434 | 86,370 | 145,952 | 100,575 | 1,527,790 | 79,853 | 2,592,047 | 2,197,132 |
| Idaho................. | 6,726,503 | 2,951,703 | 1,506,829 | 1,126,671 | 230,377 | 268,003 | 120,275 | 1,068,754 | 98,327 | 2,672,926 | 1,101,874 |
| Illinois............... | 55,674,264 | 27,511,933 | 14,901,490 | 8,842,231 | 1,339,228 | 2,405,779 | 1,446,595 | 8,510,000 | 1,360,000 | 19,345,760 | 8,816,571 |
| Indiana.............. | 29,801,851 | 13,796,427 | 8,490,450 | 5,941,044 | 759,959 | 704,694 | 393,350 | 3,868,093 | 597,347 | 10,400,713 | 5,604,711 |
| Iowa .................. | 17,113,161 | 6,809,344 | 3,185,571 | 2,121,842 | 437,763 | 700,707 | 466,982 | 2,650,037 | 192,138 | 6,743,091 | 3,560,726 |
| Kansas............... | 14,215,169 | 6,492,996 | 2,962,674 | 2,150,270 | 424,703 | 304,342 | 174,932 | 2,687,542 | 352,419 | 4,624,104 | 3,098,069 |
| Kentucky ........... | 22,861,951 | 9,531,108 | 4,677,297 | 2,794,057 | 655,245 | 441,918 | 198,783 | 3,154,488 | 383,815 | 9,149,028 | 4,181,815 |
| Louisiana ........... | 27,440,627 | 8,757,557 | 4,842,797 | 2,579,946 | 587,995 | 425,575 | 109,388 | 2,286,500 | 393,036 | 13,255,001 | 5,428,069 |
| Maine ................ | 8,247,985 | 3,489,953 | 1,666,914 | 989,645 | 241,687 | 248,270 | 94,633 | 1,303,370 | 175,292 | 3,212,892 | 1,545,140 |
| Maryland ........... | 31,184,749 | 15,223,923 | 6,257,681 | 3,753,778 | 722,597 | 740,264 | 433,777 | 6,200,292 | 891,392 | 10,534,111 | 5,426,715 |
| Massachusetts ..... | 42,208,719 | 20,050,292 | 6,773,581 | 4,625,682 | 654,649 | 859,728 | 362,053 | 10,128,035 | 1,834,859 | 13,326,217 | 8,832,210 |
| Michigan............ | 52,667,317 | 22,205,870 | 12,435,171 | 9,012,729 | 967,728 | 1,357,502 | 877,844 | 5,531,349 | 631,895 | 19,527,609 | 10,933,838 |
| Minnesota........... | 31,462,337 | 17,208,877 | 7,882,903 | 4,426,608 | 832,291 | 1,055,697 | 557,733 | 6,458,111 | 721,742 | 10,024,802 | 4,228,658 |
| Mississippi ......... | 17,427,242 | 6,268,804 | 4,074,607 | 2,849,099 | 393,363 | 408,756 | 124,437 | 1,352,481 | 316,331 | 8,807,805 | 2,350,633 |
| Missouri ............ | 26,111,659 | 9,708,463 | 4,528,599 | 2,919,117 | 721,917 | 595,866 | 265,623 | 4,326,507 | 206,936 | 11,798,319 | 4,604,877 |
| Montana ............ | 6,008,627 | 2,142,809 | 532,013 | 0 | 204,390 | 308,933 | 142,189 | 714,814 | 93,225 | 2,504,673 | 1,361,145 |
| Nebraska ........... | 8,675,960 | 3,809,266 | 1,897,901 | 1,306,702 | 298,805 | 226,944 | 79,479 | 1,514,831 | 154,332 | 3,202,752 | 1,663,942 |
| Nevada .............. | 9,937,131 | 5,835,963 | 4,274,994 | 2,559,489 | 292,804 | 572,427 | 158,987 | 0 | 0 | 2,917,112 | 1,184,056 |
| New Hampshire ... | 6,221,852 | 2,124,984 | 801,949 | 0 | 147,805 | 262,684 | 131,100 | 82,365 | 499,669 | 2,360,687 | 1,736,181 |
| New Jersey ......... | 51,182,545 | 25,927,891 | 11,307,452 | 7,898,165 | 535,281 | 1,388,521 | 578,968 | 10,322,943 | 2,047,474 | 15,476,911 | 9,777,743 |
| New Mexico ....... | 14,010,955 | 4,413,988 | 2,337,528 | 1,718,795 | 227,633 | 194,203 | 121,770 | 956,600 | 125,100 | 6,247,462 | 3,349,505 |
| New York ........... | 139,965,783 | 63,529,354 | 20,911,997 | 10,568,466 | 1,613,229 | 1,541,769 | 965,000 | 34,751,382 | 3,895,349 | 55,725,570 | 20,710,859 |
| North Carolina.... | 44,057,698 | 21,517,254 | 9,433,591 | 5,856,993 | 1,551,660 | 1,536,012 | 548,379 | 9,133,689 | 1,294,314 | 15,698,831 | 6,841,613 |
| North Dakota...... | 5,415,249 | 2,645,695 | 948,778 | 603,740 | 151,050 | 166,119 | 87,145 | 303,764 | 88,347 | 1,741,931 | 1,027,623 |
| Ohio .................. | 57,507,853 | 23,583,596 | 12,245,348 | 7,253,496 | 1,727,242 | 3,243,554 | 832,589 | 7,886,802 | 142,318 | 22,461,873 | 11,462,384 |
| Oklahoma........... | 19,486,441 | 7,079,985 | 2,953,081 | 1,968,309 | 431,151 | 906,188 | 579,380 | 2,224,783 | 216,400 | 8,007,066 | 4,399,390 |
| Oregon............... | 19,000,510 | 7,289,362 | 957,241 | 0 | 403,284 | 887,011 | 496,097 | 4,945,538 | 353,589 | 6,857,718 | 4,853,430 |
| Pennsylvania ...... | 63,884,140 | 30,169,122 | 15,464,898 | 8,029,797 | 2,020,099 | 2,546,905 | 800,432 | 9,352,287 | 1,648,956 | 21,338,641 | 12,376,377 |
| Rhode Island....... | 7,087,779 | 2,568,851 | 1,404,981 | 798,481 | 123,805 | 93,364 | 53,385 | 909,674 | 121,668 | 2,966,972 | 1,551,956 |
| South Carolina.... | 21,511,929 | 7,312,534 | 4,017,383 | 2,833,839 | 521,215 | 433,497 | 147,405 | 2,673,000 | 148,500 | 7,933,502 | 6,265,893 |

See footnotes at end of table.

# STATE GENERAL REVENUE, BY SOURCE AND BY STATE: 2010 (In thousands of dollars)—Continued

| State | Total general revenue (a) | Taxes Total (b) | Sales and gross receipts Total (b) | General | Motor fuels | Licenses Total (b) | Motor vehicle | Individual income | Corporation net income | Intergovernmental revenue | Charges and miscellaneous general revenue |
|---|---|---|---|---|---|---|---|---|---|---|---|
| South Dakota | 3,974,366 | 1,304,487 | 1,072,409 | 742,363 | 125,223 | 192,193 | 52,822 | 0 | 31,157 | 1,794,047 | 875,832 |
| Tennessee | 25,517,396 | 10,513,788 | 8,027,796 | 6,130,877 | 824,795 | 1,167,316 | 249,577 | 172,459 | 901,617 | 11,371,391 | 3,632,217 |
| Texas | 99,923,805 | 39,399,251 | 31,119,148 | 19,663,374 | 3,043,495 | 6,542,886 | 1,542,188 | 0 | 0 | 41,450,202 | 19,074,352 |
| Utah | 13,227,809 | 5,092,415 | 2,262,675 | 1,638,906 | 351,449 | 389,896 | 292,359 | 2,104,641 | 245,980 | 4,373,886 | 3,761,508 |
| Vermont | 5,330,512 | 2,511,387 | 845,336 | 311,140 | 99,278 | 106,558 | 72,214 | 489,107 | 85,178 | 1,904,907 | 914,218 |
| Virginia | 37,103,065 | 16,411,055 | 5,871,652 | 3,543,210 | 882,919 | 655,193 | 339,581 | 8,659,470 | 789,655 | 9,779,654 | 10,912,356 |
| Washington | 33,710,587 | 16,106,154 | 12,849,019 | 9,607,285 | 1,196,688 | 933,241 | 463,075 | 0 | 0 | 11,176,371 | 6,428,062 |
| West Virginia | 11,561,249 | 4,655,034 | 2,219,017 | 1,095,687 | 391,995 | 192,606 | 86,691 | 1,446,852 | 366,245 | 4,426,116 | 2,480,099 |
| Wisconsin | 30,845,174 | 14,368,569 | 6,686,839 | 3,944,260 | 972,979 | 833,180 | 471,556 | 5,791,991 | 851,537 | 10,403,378 | 6,073,227 |
| Wyoming | 5,585,873 | 2,117,100 | 874,321 | 789,413 | 25,617 | 139,052 | 65,895 | 0 | 0 | 2,456,605 | 1,012,168 |

*Source:* U.S. Census Bureau, 2010 Annual Survey of State Government Finances. For information on sampling and nonsampling errors and definitions, see *http://www.census.gov/govs/state/how_data_collected. html*. Data users who create their own estimates from this table should cite the U.S. Census Bureau as the source of the original data only.

*Note:* Detail may not add to total due to rounding.
*Key:*
(a) Total general revenue equals total taxes plus intergovernmental revenue plus charges and miscellaneous revenue.
(b) Total includes other taxes not shown separately in this table.

## Table 7.22
## STATE EXPENDITURE, BY CHARACTER AND OBJECT AND BY STATE: 2010 (In thousands of dollars)

| State | Intergovernmental expenditures | Direct expenditures | | Capital outlay | | | Assistance and subsidies | Interest on debt | Insurance benefits and repayments | Exhibit: Total salaries and wages |
| | | Total | Current operation | Total | Construction | Other | | | | |
|---|---|---|---|---|---|---|---|---|---|---|
| United States | $485,545,580 | $1,457,276,564 | $933,729,010 | $117,356,157 | $100,625,378 | $16,730,779 | $37,805,604 | $47,489,054 | $320,896,739 | $243,209,352 |
| Alabama | 6,604,013 | 21,095,674 | 14,664,600 | 2,074,629 | 1,458,024 | 616,605 | 542,260 | 372,648 | 3,441,537 | 4,444,987 |
| Alaska | 1,655,467 | 9,341,496 | 6,432,078 | 1,243,983 | 1,077,686 | 166,297 | 206,563 | 302,291 | 1,156,581 | 1,700,062 |
| Arizona | 9,179,514 | 23,836,077 | 16,019,332 | 1,628,186 | 1,376,612 | 251,574 | 589,282 | 598,023 | 5,001,254 | 3,180,343 |
| Arkansas | 4,791,989 | 12,561,722 | 9,071,256 | 820,631 | 727,042 | 93,589 | 317,052 | 148,633 | 2,204,150 | 1,435,136 |
| California | 90,517,531 | 166,731,160 | 104,288,872 | 9,671,465 | 8,421,316 | 1,250,149 | 3,018,863 | 6,711,987 | 43,039,973 | 30,443,984 |
| Colorado | 7,177,794 | 20,483,070 | 11,977,651 | 1,557,328 | 1,357,710 | 199,618 | 293,792 | 838,541 | 5,815,758 | 3,899,829 |
| Connecticut | 4,877,144 | 22,560,180 | 13,910,437 | 1,369,979 | 1,180,336 | 189,643 | 510,668 | 1,457,931 | 5,311,165 | 4,209,442 |
| Delaware | 1,235,608 | 6,591,218 | 4,705,128 | 664,509 | 529,645 | 134,864 | 148,935 | 288,297 | 784,349 | 2,266,215 |
| Florida | 18,478,449 | 63,150,664 | 41,739,275 | 5,065,101 | 4,457,168 | 607,933 | 1,939,348 | 1,358,255 | 13,048,685 | 8,780,315 |
| Georgia | 10,747,620 | 33,734,588 | 21,390,574 | 2,793,411 | 2,537,550 | 255,861 | 1,123,773 | 698,998 | 7,727,832 | 5,414,833 |
| Hawaii | 156,881 | 11,021,511 | 8,269,694 | 858,437 | 667,859 | 190,578 | 121,968 | 308,715 | 1,462,697 | 2,510,083 |
| Idaho | 2,022,896 | 6,491,179 | 4,092,661 | 780,434 | 687,550 | 92,884 | 140,819 | 173,576 | 1,303,689 | 1,049,380 |
| Illinois | 15,383,259 | 59,886,415 | 34,637,195 | 4,946,938 | 4,608,448 | 338,490 | 1,163,189 | 3,117,469 | 16,021,624 | 8,760,873 |
| Indiana | 9,705,254 | 25,768,940 | 16,602,413 | 2,309,906 | 1,948,360 | 361,546 | 885,573 | 999,723 | 4,971,325 | 4,242,570 |
| Iowa | 4,528,319 | 14,580,269 | 9,552,390 | 1,602,122 | 1,424,871 | 177,251 | 519,909 | 250,384 | 2,655,464 | 2,377,335 |
| Kansas | 4,176,958 | 12,406,991 | 8,429,435 | 1,019,106 | 858,728 | 160,378 | 208,907 | 341,160 | 2,408,383 | 3,580,372 |
| Kentucky | 5,078,845 | 24,018,686 | 15,726,860 | 2,042,584 | 1,755,769 | 286,815 | 796,931 | 598,107 | 4,854,204 | 3,805,359 |
| Louisiana | 6,658,397 | 26,957,089 | 18,602,304 | 2,555,452 | 2,178,021 | 377,431 | 692,542 | 1,057,848 | 4,048,943 | 4,479,744 |
| Maine | 1,338,300 | 7,686,022 | 5,742,514 | 388,794 | 317,017 | 71,777 | 208,643 | 255,152 | 1,090,919 | 777,356 |
| Maryland | 8,592,779 | 28,894,849 | 19,291,377 | 2,468,058 | 2,029,753 | 438,305 | 1,576,304 | 1,032,742 | 4,526,368 | 4,776,435 |
| Massachusetts | 9,107,584 | 42,623,277 | 26,026,862 | 2,622,632 | 2,403,413 | 219,219 | 788,798 | 3,504,595 | 9,680,390 | 5,159,661 |
| Michigan | 19,410,018 | 44,507,633 | 27,686,548 | 2,467,151 | 2,120,729 | 346,422 | 1,389,817 | 1,191,657 | 11,772,460 | 6,608,060 |
| Minnesota | 10,427,657 | 27,515,070 | 18,126,213 | 1,601,649 | 1,261,074 | 340,575 | 1,052,501 | 552,335 | 6,182,372 | 5,198,408 |
| Mississippi | 5,272,442 | 14,750,211 | 10,623,947 | 1,349,926 | 985,886 | 364,040 | 225,858 | 235,282 | 2,315,198 | 2,405,967 |
| Missouri | 6,227,630 | 24,543,886 | 16,269,207 | 1,921,291 | 1,691,370 | 229,921 | 556,509 | 819,964 | 4,976,915 | 3,789,775 |
| Montana | 1,334,478 | 5,717,902 | 3,716,530 | 755,124 | 679,480 | 75,644 | 104,786 | 170,356 | 971,106 | 960,080 |
| Nebraska | 2,192,338 | 7,392,155 | 5,558,502 | 805,358 | 739,863 | 65,495 | 162,136 | 97,340 | 768,819 | 2,282,049 |
| Nevada | 3,703,574 | 9,230,935 | 4,720,519 | 695,708 | 637,606 | 58,102 | 241,249 | 202,908 | 3,370,551 | 1,566,615 |
| New Hampshire | 1,261,454 | 6,444,333 | 4,498,632 | 466,297 | 403,311 | 62,986 | 158,458 | 403,400 | 917,546 | 939,903 |
| New Jersey | 11,940,861 | 56,030,506 | 32,569,027 | 4,076,105 | 3,403,811 | 672,294 | 1,244,291 | 2,163,480 | 15,977,603 | 10,110,123 |
| New Mexico | 4,308,854 | 13,687,184 | 9,821,223 | 1,176,386 | 1,054,733 | 121,653 | 257,950 | 339,592 | 2,092,033 | 2,698,519 |
| New York | 54,318,363 | 119,989,175 | 77,948,983 | 10,523,619 | 8,712,411 | 1,811,208 | 1,577,775 | 5,333,051 | 24,605,747 | 18,011,598 |
| North Carolina | 13,429,946 | 38,759,945 | 25,469,694 | 3,073,825 | 2,442,335 | 631,490 | 492,672 | 602,425 | 9,121,329 | 8,537,894 |
| North Dakota | 1,245,686 | 3,888,444 | 2,592,852 | 579,222 | 513,142 | 66,080 | 156,277 | 114,460 | 445,633 | 960,305 |
| Ohio | 18,373,625 | 58,356,997 | 31,234,792 | 4,469,090 | 4,085,563 | 383,527 | 2,238,769 | 1,524,668 | 18,889,678 | 8,463,707 |

See footnotes at end of table.

# STATE EXPENDITURE, BY CHARACTER AND OBJECT AND BY STATE: 2010 (In thousands of dollars) — Continued

| State | Intergovernmental expenditures | Direct expenditures | | Capital outlay | | | Assistance and subsidies | Interest on debt | Insurance benefits and repayments | Exhibit: Total salaries and wages |
|---|---|---|---|---|---|---|---|---|---|---|
| | | Total | Current operation | Total | Construction | Other | | | | |
| Oklahoma.............. | 4,546,446 | 18,093,532 | 11,699,718 | 2,612,664 | 2,316,848 | 295,816 | 407,391 | 513,113 | 2,860,646 | 3,119,210 |
| Oregon.................. | 5,864,882 | 21,113,272 | 12,373,948 | 1,586,078 | 1,188,562 | 397,516 | 532,852 | 445,471 | 6,174,923 | 4,324,126 |
| Pennsylvania........ | 18,615,065 | 68,670,221 | 40,946,259 | 7,506,718 | 6,655,387 | 851,331 | 2,075,982 | 1,736,913 | 16,404,349 | 8,072,449 |
| Rhode Island........ | 1,124,458 | 7,086,745 | 4,433,723 | 397,007 | 352,440 | 44,567 | 126,623 | 429,472 | 1,699,920 | 1,096,055 |
| South Carolina...... | 5,369,519 | 23,557,601 | 15,988,611 | 1,746,611 | 1,477,833 | 268,778 | 939,767 | 705,380 | 4,177,232 | 3,565,618 |
| South Dakota........ | 737,190 | 3,692,007 | 2,372,787 | 669,853 | 623,019 | 46,834 | 82,220 | 126,229 | 440,918 | 899,706 |
| Tennessee............ | 6,664,828 | 23,010,544 | 16,885,663 | 1,624,918 | 1,394,196 | 230,722 | 908,426 | 242,670 | 3,348,867 | 3,595,113 |
| Texas................... | 27,461,315 | 92,143,573 | 64,866,427 | 6,677,238 | 5,398,443 | 1,278,795 | 2,197,332 | 1,170,209 | 17,232,367 | 15,638,657 |
| Utah.................... | 3,027,680 | 13,235,277 | 8,508,997 | 1,925,320 | 1,716,958 | 208,362 | 640,114 | 255,337 | 1,905,509 | 2,653,421 |
| Vermont............... | 1,518,129 | 4,207,905 | 3,172,930 | 232,531 | 206,139 | 26,392 | 169,004 | 154,143 | 479,297 | 735,396 |
| Virginia............... | 10,959,394 | 32,497,756 | 22,321,955 | 2,673,089 | 2,208,354 | 464,735 | 1,583,940 | 1,070,371 | 4,848,401 | 6,233,732 |
| Washington........... | 9,798,444 | 36,439,578 | 21,151,809 | 3,334,280 | 2,796,818 | 537,462 | 1,564,475 | 1,166,932 | 9,222,082 | 6,715,521 |
| West Virginia........ | 2,382,633 | 9,960,418 | 6,984,904 | 1,004,272 | 868,504 | 135,768 | 198,482 | 267,268 | 1,505,492 | 1,731,700 |
| Wisconsin............ | 10,253,124 | 28,336,691 | 17,474,054 | 2,328,873 | 2,120,395 | 208,478 | 652,245 | 976,323 | 6,905,196 | 4,292,114 |
| Wyoming.............. | 1,760,946 | 3,995,991 | 2,537,648 | 592,269 | 567,290 | 24,979 | 73,584 | 63,230 | 729,260 | 709,217 |

*Source:* U.S. Census Bureau, 2010 Annual Survey of State Government Finances. For information on sampling and nonsampling errors and definitions, see *http://www.census.gov/govs/state/how_data_collected. html.* Data users who create their own estimates from this table should cite the U.S. Census Bureau as the source of the original data only.

*Note:* Detail may not add to total due to rounding.

## Table 7.23
## STATE GENERAL EXPENDITURE, BY FUNCTION AND BY STATE: 2010 (In thousands of dollars)

| State | Total general expenditures (a) | Education | Public welfare | Highways | Hospitals | Natural Resources | Health | Corrections | Financial administration | Employment security administration | Police |
|---|---|---|---|---|---|---|---|---|---|---|---|
| United States | 1,593,134,279 | 570,958,895 | 462,726,745 | 110,840,105 | 63,807,295 | 21,506,591 | 59,809,053 | 48,452,750 | 22,102,980 | 5,075,538 | 13,809,518 |
| Alabama | 24,016,434 | 10,555,436 | 6,032,533 | 1,514,572 | 2,043,064 | 328,307 | 608,732 | 551,544 | 240,457 | 96,504 | 188,062 |
| Alaska | 9,732,818 | 2,303,781 | 1,799,862 | 1,447,216 | 55,371 | 420,565 | 300,110 | 270,536 | 204,201 | 44,014 | 98,362 |
| Arizona | 27,982,432 | 8,806,846 | 9,211,757 | 2,117,105 | 61,538 | 273,975 | 1,934,704 | 1,061,067 | 361,941 | 86,825 | 239,436 |
| Arkansas | 15,149,561 | 6,701,746 | 4,212,448 | 944,806 | 768,757 | 265,673 | 246,348 | 268,953 | 385,661 | 40,798 | 62,786 |
| California | 210,359,200 | 70,303,564 | 63,848,655 | 13,326,933 | 11,010,832 | 4,146,716 | 7,276,827 | 7,956,461 | 3,462,041 | 530,621 | 1,623,171 |
| Colorado | 21,817,530 | 9,090,749 | 5,078,892 | 1,380,546 | 574,482 | 329,406 | 1,201,265 | 985,100 | 440,078 | 68,157 | 131,730 |
| Connecticut | 21,599,844 | 6,623,768 | 6,029,549 | 1,084,512 | 1,438,938 | 151,634 | 901,328 | 682,065 | 373,772 | 115,757 | 208,817 |
| Delaware | 6,917,204 | 2,432,264 | 1,656,504 | 521,987 | 55,963 | 80,377 | 396,381 | 261,950 | 209,442 | 17,466 | 105,368 |
| Florida | 68,482,499 | 23,043,590 | 20,880,282 | 5,382,114 | 881,388 | 1,264,096 | 3,686,342 | 2,504,397 | 666,405 | 152,426 | 441,041 |
| Georgia | 36,710,385 | 16,985,461 | 9,886,063 | 2,175,074 | 864,088 | 463,137 | 1,063,229 | 1,432,460 | 423,959 | 118,718 | 303,865 |
| Hawaii | 9,710,283 | 3,254,387 | 1,960,542 | 468,922 | 609,893 | 104,865 | 545,908 | 206,695 | 108,059 | 5,693 | 34,211 |
| Idaho | 7,119,304 | 2,761,322 | 1,784,787 | 813,816 | 52,078 | 190,429 | 181,764 | 223,624 | 170,187 | 44,057 | 52,218 |
| Illinois | 59,248,050 | 17,282,643 | 18,857,634 | 5,956,960 | 1,182,220 | 276,785 | 2,397,263 | 1,301,450 | 625,243 | 154,013 | 439,341 |
| Indiana | 30,502,869 | 14,214,891 | 7,996,960 | 2,656,946 | 165,690 | 309,419 | 582,108 | 669,218 | 262,582 | 122,462 | 244,963 |
| Iowa | 16,306,414 | 5,946,941 | 4,662,116 | 1,796,979 | 1,083,134 | 302,230 | 265,724 | 289,856 | 188,945 | 49,949 | 88,139 |
| Kansas | 14,175,566 | 5,917,771 | 3,341,973 | 1,176,849 | 1,075,513 | 210,172 | 233,815 | 341,998 | 237,973 | 29,089 | 108,573 |
| Kentucky | 24,192,556 | 9,325,602 | 7,191,181 | 1,972,134 | 1,180,426 | 344,184 | 729,353 | 511,528 | 254,875 | 96,677 | 190,640 |
| Louisiana | 29,560,930 | 9,060,789 | 6,436,385 | 2,064,808 | 2,286,599 | 757,490 | 639,275 | 774,510 | 376,015 | 94,206 | 356,710 |
| Maine | 7,929,528 | 2,097,101 | 2,908,167 | 585,393 | 55,546 | 167,101 | 473,951 | 145,588 | 146,934 | 21,818 | 78,290 |
| Maryland | 32,110,165 | 11,685,818 | 8,772,071 | 2,193,278 | 509,503 | 489,701 | 1,888,732 | 1,392,836 | 552,277 | 60,464 | 465,444 |
| Massachusetts | 41,784,126 | 11,879,337 | 13,772,343 | 1,948,609 | 486,992 | 398,124 | 1,054,843 | 1,203,611 | 538,157 | 62,477 | 624,631 |
| Michigan | 51,510,080 | 22,777,372 | 14,469,837 | 2,643,742 | 2,478,235 | 302,828 | 1,117,685 | 1,684,525 | 392,473 | 205,112 | 305,370 |
| Minnesota | 31,641,587 | 11,743,700 | 10,727,038 | 2,365,578 | 237,638 | 560,261 | 642,730 | 508,658 | 298,918 | 76,412 | 369,120 |
| Mississippi | 17,500,003 | 5,581,577 | 5,181,703 | 1,407,717 | 1,065,703 | 245,289 | 423,719 | 366,733 | 93,540 | 101,668 | 101,959 |
| Missouri | 25,794,601 | 8,949,863 | 7,312,995 | 2,326,314 | 1,471,659 | 367,173 | 1,375,621 | 723,521 | 191,506 | 33,229 | 210,649 |
| Montana | 6,004,791 | 1,824,149 | 1,305,718 | 734,164 | 47,333 | 235,500 | 166,217 | 184,888 | 197,455 | 27,061 | 47,282 |
| Nebraska | 8,815,674 | 3,268,458 | 2,281,071 | 663,162 | 258,220 | 257,134 | 442,495 | 237,884 | 105,740 | 40,787 | 89,027 |
| Nevada | 9,478,097 | 4,032,431 | 1,942,891 | 707,462 | 232,222 | 117,580 | 227,264 | 298,822 | 92,637 | 83,492 | 93,531 |
| New Hampshire | 6,350,744 | 2,003,098 | 1,909,365 | 560,500 | 53,102 | 59,138 | 89,808 | 114,567 | 85,108 | 43,776 | 59,539 |
| New Jersey | 49,248,529 | 16,525,685 | 13,806,299 | 2,905,213 | 2,258,908 | 652,579 | 1,340,661 | 1,563,653 | 817,945 | 191,043 | 465,469 |
| New Mexico | 15,890,396 | 5,519,109 | 4,390,919 | 882,437 | 918,976 | 218,155 | 535,037 | 413,725 | 238,306 | 11,992 | 149,580 |
| New York | 137,996,674 | 39,107,606 | 49,595,770 | 4,644,815 | 5,761,923 | 497,352 | 8,895,513 | 3,266,368 | 2,105,278 | 346,324 | 1,034,695 |
| North Carolina | 43,013,853 | 18,644,909 | 11,417,170 | 3,045,230 | 1,529,760 | 556,843 | 1,705,764 | 1,436,294 | 355,811 | 205,053 | 520,263 |
| North Dakota | 4,688,497 | 1,765,141 | 828,652 | 594,876 | 64,361 | 243,232 | 126,901 | 72,657 | 64,107 | 8,316 | 27,013 |
| Ohio | 57,370,930 | 22,051,876 | 16,882,487 | 3,258,502 | 2,572,584 | 381,711 | 2,309,442 | 1,605,846 | 840,531 | 326,926 | 285,131 |

See footnotes at end of table.

# STATE GENERAL EXPENDITURE, BY FUNCTION AND BY STATE: 2010 (In thousands of dollars)—Continued

| State | Total general expenditures (a) | Education | Public welfare | Highways | Hospitals | Natural Resources | Health | Corrections | Financial administration | Employment security administration | Police |
|---|---|---|---|---|---|---|---|---|---|---|---|
| Oklahoma | 19,233,124 | 7,761,989 | 5,412,442 | 1,920,884 | 231,730 | 247,539 | 788,653 | 587,482 | 248,573 | 77,904 | 175,579 |
| Oregon | 20,559,825 | 7,341,838 | 5,423,746 | 1,759,045 | 1,477,147 | 415,965 | 459,211 | 754,369 | 478,615 | 69,785 | 170,477 |
| Pennsylvania | 69,401,526 | 21,357,846 | 21,609,686 | 7,434,147 | 3,278,971 | 692,230 | 2,736,804 | 1,874,225 | 1,211,654 | 138,474 | 878,283 |
| Rhode Island | 6,352,238 | 1,768,009 | 2,329,603 | 293,947 | 57,913 | 41,543 | 190,318 | 174,958 | 144,956 | 22,497 | 77,150 |
| South Carolina | 22,809,855 | 7,775,952 | 6,083,219 | 1,249,688 | 1,435,197 | 224,572 | 1,023,050 | 460,351 | 693,890 | 84,597 | 173,906 |
| South Dakota | 3,988,279 | 1,303,153 | 977,597 | 531,186 | 63,984 | 156,994 | 134,121 | 110,189 | 102,889 | 22,505 | 33,527 |
| Tennessee | 26,324,459 | 8,973,778 | 10,038,634 | 1,595,076 | 472,403 | 264,510 | 1,129,326 | 758,842 | 283,027 | 114,815 | 209,416 |
| Texas | 102,372,521 | 46,704,736 | 29,017,233 | 5,830,910 | 4,047,211 | 888,625 | 2,753,187 | 3,691,934 | 978,159 | 223,460 | 818,673 |
| Utah | 14,183,072 | 6,124,277 | 2,680,789 | 1,595,689 | 930,644 | 166,172 | 395,171 | 302,043 | 252,931 | 20,898 | 131,464 |
| Vermont | 5,172,036 | 2,300,338 | 1,404,798 | 387,389 | 20,152 | 69,882 | 156,962 | 125,326 | 47,284 | 23,015 | 74,486 |
| Virginia | 38,153,971 | 14,023,259 | 8,727,177 | 2,779,737 | 3,219,295 | 237,522 | 956,154 | 1,496,231 | 561,675 | 138,666 | 645,815 |
| Washington | 36,469,427 | 14,817,620 | 8,546,635 | 3,147,410 | 1,892,729 | 789,477 | 1,733,220 | 1,063,830 | 418,468 | 249,676 | 315,411 |
| West Virginia | 10,767,434 | 3,931,867 | 3,042,614 | 1,157,005 | 121,617 | 236,900 | 291,129 | 270,717 | 172,601 | 30,272 | 72,880 |
| Wisconsin | 31,677,742 | 11,091,896 | 8,325,974 | 2,317,321 | 1,160,327 | 681,853 | 764,473 | 1,131,141 | 296,601 | 112,148 | 135,435 |
| Wyoming | 4,956,616 | 1,613,556 | 733,979 | 571,400 | 5,336 | 423,646 | 290,415 | 137,524 | 103,098 | 33,444 | 52,590 |

*Source:* U.S. Census Bureau, 2010 Annual Survey of State Government Finances. For information on sampling and nonsampling errors and definitions, see *http://www.census.gov/govs/state/how_data_collected. html.* Data users who create their own estimates from this table should cite the U.S. Census Bureau as the source of the original data only.

*Note:* Detail may not add to total due to rounding.
*Key:*
(a) Total includes other expenditures not shown separately in this table.

## Table 7.24
## STATE DEBT OUTSTANDING AT END OF FISCAL YEAR, BY STATE: 2010
(In thousands of dollars)

| State | Total | Long-term total | Short-term | Net long-term total (a) |
|---|---|---|---|---|
| United States .......................... | $1,113,354,521 | $1,098,645,730 | $8,354,323 | $599,355,396 |
| Alabama................................ | 8,785,245 | 8,758,844 | 27,964 | 6,944,646 |
| Alaska.................................. | 6,380,597 | 6,230,707 | 149,724 | 2,285,301 |
| Arizona................................ | 13,956,433 | 13,913,824 | 42,436 | 8,957,581 |
| Arkansas............................... | 4,260,547 | 4,260,547 | 0 | 1,929,708 |
| California .............................. | 148,929,107 | 148,840,107 | 34,000 | 114,739,983 |
| Colorado............................... | 16,709,540 | 16,157,918 | 541,562 | 3,906,970 |
| Connecticut............................ | 30,215,550 | 29,620,782 | 585,141 | 16,124,297 |
| Delaware .............................. | 5,515,150 | 5,515,150 | 0 | 2,900,946 |
| Florida ................................ | 40,403,855 | 40,373,594 | 31,347 | 30,084,393 |
| Georgia................................ | 13,788,833 | 13,669,833 | 81,908 | 10,696,435 |
| Hawaii.................................. | 7,700,654 | 7,700,654 | 0 | 6,183,575 |
| Idaho................................... | 3,872,453 | 3,862,240 | 8,993 | 448,189 |
| Illinois................................. | 61,411,694 | 61,395,941 | 14,846 | 31,401,609 |
| Indiana................................ | 23,634,564 | 22,934,548 | 1,099,568 | 2,709,786 |
| Iowa ................................... | 5,140,385 | 5,140,385 | 0 | 1,351,539 |
| Kansas ................................ | 6,478,228 | 6,478,228 | 5,000 | 3,497,792 |
| Kentucky .............................. | 14,393,269 | 14,353,329 | 17,099 | 7,797,588 |
| Louisiana.............................. | 17,442,967 | 17,427,245 | 18,254 | 8,698,405 |
| Maine.................................. | 6,034,227 | 6,034,227 | 0 | 1,385,443 |
| Maryland.............................. | 24,474,671 | 24,401,532 | 71,991 | 11,832,438 |
| Massachusetts ......................... | 73,939,716 | 73,844,949 | 132,324 | 34,371,800 |
| Michigan............................... | 32,146,344 | 31,875,754 | 316,712 | 14,825,528 |
| Minnesota.............................. | 11,682,878 | 11,677,209 | 5,524 | 5,018,984 |
| Mississippi ............................ | 6,467,833 | 6,444,509 | 38,815 | 4,825,390 |
| Missouri................................ | 20,421,226 | 20,382,275 | 32,917 | 5,567,547 |
| Montana............................... | 4,373,930 | 4,373,810 | 880 | 881,680 |
| Nebraska............................... | 2,330,277 | 2,328,682 | 1,690 | 431,436 |
| Nevada................................. | 4,435,774 | 4,435,774 | 0 | 3,118,023 |
| New Hampshire ....................... | 8,347,216 | 8,278,458 | 69,447 | 2,220,196 |
| New Jersey ............................ | 60,958,345 | 60,932,220 | 25,308 | 39,620,405 |
| New Mexico ........................... | 8,739,878 | 8,497,512 | 45,290 | 3,428,670 |
| New York.............................. | 129,529,501 | 129,037,349 | 475,986 | 68,735,592 |
| North Carolina........................ | 18,853,155 | 18,793,371 | 174,991 | 8,107,401 |
| North Dakota.......................... | 2,198,282 | 2,196,058 | 1,098 | 773,270 |
| Ohio.................................... | 31,177,155 | 30,659,677 | 914,262 | 16,464,819 |
| Oklahoma.............................. | 9,963,419 | 9,939,558 | 10,319 | 5,229,918 |
| Oregon................................. | 13,510,005 | 13,510,005 | 60,000 | 9,925,422 |
| Pennsylvania .......................... | 44,737,622 | 44,231,898 | 969,508 | 20,745,043 |
| Rhode Island.......................... | 9,498,115 | 9,440,814 | 42,002 | 2,762,940 |
| South Carolina........................ | 15,770,780 | 15,413,129 | 235,907 | 10,682,249 |
| South Dakota.......................... | 3,483,142 | 3,480,990 | 1,831 | 700,784 |
| Tennessee ............................. | 5,835,113 | 5,181,420 | 457,939 | 1,436,656 |
| Texas................................... | 42,033,571 | 33,464,210 | 1,382,778 | 21,787,994 |
| Utah.................................... | 6,477,933 | 6,435,980 | 33,776 | 2,991,511 |
| Vermont................................ | 3,492,873 | 3,404,538 | 85,456 | 1,085,054 |
| Virginia................................ | 24,966,916 | 24,860,393 | 109,730 | 10,630,303 |
| Washington............................ | 27,478,320 | 27,478,320 | 0 | 17,881,025 |
| West Virginia.......................... | 7,144,323 | 7,144,323 | 0 | 3,014,167 |
| Wisconsin.............................. | 22,318,551 | 22,318,551 | 0 | 8,105,426 |
| Wyoming .............................. | 1,514,359 | 1,514,359 | 0 | 109,539 |

*Source:* U.S. Census Bureau, 2010 Annual Survey of State Government Finances. For information on sampling and nonsampling errors and definitions, see *http://www.census.gov/govs/state/how_data_collected.html.* Data users who create their own estimates from this table should cite the U.S. Census Bureau as the source of the original data only.

*Note:* Detail may not add to total due to rounding.
*Key:*
(a) Long-term debt outstanding minus long-term debt offsets.

## Table 7.25
## NUMBER AND MEMBERSHIP OF STATE PUBLIC EMPLOYEE-RETIREMENT SYSTEMS BY STATE: FISCAL YEAR 2010

| State | Number of systems | Membership Total | Membership Active members | Membership Inactive members | Total beneficiaries receiving periodic benefit payments |
|---|---|---|---|---|---|
| United States........................ | 222 | 17,455,648 | 12,984,720 | 4,470,928 | 6,994,538 |
| Alabama............................. | 4 | 258,209 | 229,024 | 29,185 | 108,008 |
| Alaska ................................ | 4 | 48,359 | 39,761 | 8,598 | 35,880 |
| Arizona .............................. | 4 | 468,493 | 254,956 | 213,537 | 117,813 |
| Arkansas ............................ | 6 | 162,799 | 133,997 | 28,802 | 61,963 |
| California ........................... | 5 | 1,902,986 | 1,379,919 | 523,067 | 802,270 |
| Colorado ............................ | 2 | 368,961 | 201,046 | 167,915 | 88,819 |
| Connecticut ........................ | 6 | 123,469 | 109,932 | 13,537 | 74,099 |
| Delaware............................. | 1 | 44,910 | 42,507 | 2,403 | 24,098 |
| Florida................................ | 1 | 633,098 | 557,585 | 75,513 | 302,987 |
| Georgia .............................. | 9 | 581,625 | 360,992 | 220,633 | 145,612 |
| Hawaii ............................... | 1 | 75,833 | 69,353 | 6,480 | 43,533 |
| Idaho ................................. | 2 | 77,263 | 67,071 | 10,192 | 33,703 |
| Illinois............................... | 6 | 798,787 | 489,942 | 308,845 | 299,337 |
| Indiana .............................. | 8 | 290,630 | 236,149 | 54,481 | 116,187 |
| Iowa.................................. | 4 | 236,258 | 170,398 | 65,860 | 98,125 |
| Kansas ............................... | 1 | 204,155 | 160,831 | 43,324 | 73,164 |
| Kentucky............................ | 6 | 336,874 | 223,344 | 113,530 | 132,708 |
| Louisiana ........................... | 14 | 306,740 | 211,063 | 95,677 | 140,297 |
| Maine ................................ | 1 | 58,584 | 50,482 | 8,102 | 35,846 |
| Maryland............................ | 2 | 252,860 | 200,613 | 52,247 | 117,380 |
| Massachusetts...................... | 13 | 266,236 | 197,664 | 68,572 | 121,410 |
| Michigan ............................ | 6 | 333,642 | 305,668 | 27,974 | 268,728 |
| Minnesota ........................... | 8 | 513,902 | 282,533 | 231,369 | 161,103 |
| Mississippi.......................... | 4 | 295,003 | 165,644 | 129,359 | 82,082 |
| Missouri ............................. | 10 | 278,007 | 227,535 | 50,472 | 128,633 |
| Montana............................. | 9 | 74,961 | 53,866 | 21,095 | 32,804 |
| Nebraska ............................ | 5 | 90,525 | 65,475 | 25,050 | 17,836 |
| Nevada .............................. | 2 | 114,478 | 102,640 | 11,838 | 43,985 |
| New Hampshire ................... | 2 | 57,711 | 50,517 | 7,194 | 25,897 |
| New Jersey.......................... | 7 | 580,345 | 509,009 | 71,336 | 256,850 |
| New Mexico ........................ | 5 | 158,847 | 118,088 | 40,759 | 61,721 |
| New York ........................... | 2 | 970,756 | 847,689 | 123,067 | 517,528 |
| North Carolina .................... | 6 | 625,891 | 485,460 | 140,431 | 219,199 |
| North Dakota ...................... | 2 | 34,448 | 30,461 | 3,987 | 14,200 |
| Ohio.................................. | 5 | 1,247,261 | 683,186 | 564,075 | 398,976 |
| Oklahoma ........................... | 6 | 166,145 | 151,839 | 14,306 | 91,057 |
| Oregon .............................. | 1 | 214,374 | 176,750 | 37,624 | 111,160 |
| Pennsylvania....................... | 3 | 531,361 | 400,559 | 130,802 | 292,297 |
| Rhode Island ...................... | 1 | 40,279 | 32,885 | 7,394 | 25,293 |
| South Carolina .................... | 4 | 388,134 | 219,259 | 168,875 | 120,501 |
| South Dakota ...................... | 2 | 52,860 | 39,186 | 13,674 | 21,279 |
| Tennessee........................... | 1 | 244,711 | 214,711 | 30,000 | 112,133 |
| Texas................................. | 7 | 1,548,108 | 1,331,443 | 216,665 | 457,357 |
| Utah.................................. | 6 | 140,038 | 105,106 | 34,932 | 44,146 |
| Vermont ............................. | 3 | 32,516 | 24,896 | 7,620 | 12,990 |
| Virginia ............................. | 1 | 376,778 | 342,609 | 34,169 | 148,496 |
| Washington......................... | 6 | 293,089 | 248,897 | 44,192 | 131,554 |
| West Virginia ...................... | 1 | 91,887 | 73,561 | 18,326 | 51,733 |
| Wisconsin........................... | 1 | 415,646 | 267,293 | 148,353 | 150,671 |
| Wyoming............................ | 6 | 46,816 | 41,326 | 5,490 | 21,090 |

*Source:* 2010 Survey of Public-Employee Retirement Systems. Data users who create their own estimates using data from this report should cite the U.S. Census Bureau as the source of the original data only. The data in this table are based on information from public records and contain no confidential data. Although the data in this table come from a census of retirement systems and are not subject to sampling error, the census results do contain nonsampling error. Additional information on nonsampling error, and response rates may be found at *http://www. census.gov/govs/retire/how_data_collected.html.*

*Note:* Detail may not add to total due to rounding.

## Table 7.26
## FINANCES OF STATE-ADMINISTERED EMPLOYEE RETIREMENT SYSTEMS, BY STATE: FISCAL YEAR 2010
### (In thousands of dollars)

| State and level of government | Total receipts | Employee contributions | Government contributions Total | From state government | From local government | Earnings on investments (a) | Total payments | Benefits | Withdrawals | Other payments |
|---|---|---|---|---|---|---|---|---|---|---|
| United States......... | $387,275,709 | $33,009,625 | $64,650,956 | $35,386,653 | $29,264,303 | $289,615,128 | $173,453,369 | $163,505,281 | $3,494,033 | $6,454,055 |
| Alabama.................. | 3,852,895 | 517,973 | 1,151,009 | 917,264 | 233,745 | 2,183,913 | 2,447,362 | 2,344,387 | 55,470 | 47,505 |
| Alaska .................... | 1,320,571 | 180,272 | 326,472 | 150,515 | 175,957 | 813,827 | 877,633 | 839,698 | 3,472 | 34,463 |
| Arizona ................. | 5,898,431 | 1,053,580 | 1,121,716 | 195,555 | 926,161 | 3,723,135 | 2,980,600 | 2,627,998 | 184,020 | 168,582 |
| Arkansas .............. | 2,961,721 | 170,149 | 671,877 | 245,559 | 426,318 | 2,119,695 | 1,251,299 | 1,157,579 | 12,767 | 80,953 |
| California ............... | 61,706,055 | 5,757,226 | 10,839,366 | 4,476,519 | 6,362,847 | 45,109,463 | 25,466,815 | 24,232,265 | 552,113 | 682,437 |
| Colorado ................ | 7,067,141 | 618,432 | 947,133 | 305,942 | 641,191 | 5,501,576 | 3,321,058 | 3,004,875 | 156,553 | 159,630 |
| Connecticut ........... | 4,972,369 | 335,393 | 1,334,570 | 1,295,276 | 39,294 | 3,302,406 | 2,818,111 | 2,792,941 | 24,612 | 558 |
| Delaware................. | 751,619 | 53,129 | 167,607 | 133,859 | 33,748 | 530,883 | 466,451 | 438,207 | 3,486 | 24,758 |
| Florida.................... | 18,214,881 | 23,416 | 3,150,760 | 687,182 | 2,463,578 | 15,040,705 | 6,443,688 | 6,088,727 | 2,821 | 352,140 |
| Georgia .................. | 8,030,266 | 558,182 | 1,379,589 | 847,096 | 532,493 | 6,092,495 | 4,190,695 | 4,058,545 | 61,358 | 70,792 |
| Hawaii.................... | 2,203,063 | 169,394 | 513,209 | 384,043 | 129,166 | 1,520,460 | 838,438 | 792,313 | 3,669 | 42,456 |
| Idaho ..................... | 1,547,338 | 178,462 | 285,328 | 113,822 | 171,506 | 1,083,548 | 607,507 | 558,344 | 0 | 49,163 |
| Illinois................... | 17,455,293 | 1,762,328 | 4,794,044 | 3,962,224 | 831,820 | 10,898,921 | 8,506,564 | 7,982,207 | 151,067 | 373,290 |
| Indiana .................. | 4,512,967 | 338,148 | 1,379,128 | 1,003,421 | 375,707 | 2,795,691 | 1,840,972 | 1,709,285 | 50,249 | 81,438 |
| Iowa ...................... | 3,589,354 | 321,346 | 507,530 | 86,714 | 420,816 | 2,760,478 | 1,488,933 | 1,422,753 | 43,413 | 22,767 |
| Kansas ................... | 2,286,386 | 282,205 | 521,552 | 367,170 | 154,382 | 1,482,629 | 1,206,454 | 1,119,947 | 43,363 | 43,144 |
| Kentucky................ | 3,311,151 | 552,832 | 945,966 | 623,394 | 322,572 | 1,812,353 | 2,971,710 | 2,862,175 | 37,586 | 71,949 |
| Louisiana .............. | 5,569,555 | 771,842 | 1,515,571 | 1,357,189 | 158,382 | 3,282,142 | 3,176,436 | 2,968,466 | 105,410 | 102,560 |
| Maine .................... | 1,465,319 | 158,963 | 342,000 | 326,627 | 15,373 | 964,356 | 704,769 | 650,834 | 23,096 | 30,839 |
| Maryland................ | 6,101,334 | 535,581 | 1,346,630 | 1,240,458 | 106,172 | 4,219,123 | 2,468,104 | 2,467,294 | 34 | 776 |
| Massachusetts........ | 7,043,873 | 1,167,716 | 1,547,243 | 1,399,712 | 147,531 | 4,328,914 | 3,850,809 | 3,806,418 | 5,078 | 39,313 |
| Michigan ............... | 7,751,964 | 489,101 | 1,750,457 | 447,903 | 1,302,554 | 5,512,406 | 5,328,093 | 5,037,138 | 41,547 | 249,408 |
| Minnesota.............. | 7,059,976 | 730,547 | 847,896 | 193,052 | 654,844 | 5,481,533 | 3,352,569 | 3,233,583 | 52,775 | 66,211 |
| Mississippi............. | 3,438,548 | 441,787 | 762,023 | 277,954 | 484,069 | 2,234,738 | 1,764,933 | 1,643,224 | 73,668 | 48,041 |
| Missouri ................ | 6,927,718 | 749,698 | 1,285,311 | 462,277 | 823,034 | 4,892,709 | 3,380,400 | 2,913,138 | 66,437 | 400,825 |
| Montana................. | 1,190,141 | 161,381 | 221,606 | 102,119 | 119,487 | 807,154 | 534,170 | 485,157 | 18,770 | 30,243 |
| Nebraska................ | 1,274,503 | 162,173 | 200,694 | 68,306 | 132,388 | 911,636 | 433,217 | 367,493 | 34,281 | 31,443 |
| Nevada .................. | 3,492,294 | 126,605 | 1,281,916 | 193,575 | 1,088,341 | 2,083,773 | 1,357,369 | 1,302,032 | 20,271 | 35,066 |
| New Hampshire .... | 991,224 | 150,140 | 271,431 | 47,296 | 224,135 | 569,653 | 525,863 | 494,367 | 21,851 | 9,645 |
| New Jersey............. | 11,932,043 | 1,712,182 | 1,973,507 | 1,907,886 | 65,621 | 8,246,354 | 7,387,688 | 7,192,773 | 145,881 | 49,034 |
| New Mexico........... | 3,802,129 | 476,772 | 610,233 | 408,276 | 201,957 | 2,715,124 | 1,455,793 | 1,319,982 | 61,517 | 74,294 |
| New York ............... | 41,349,298 | 423,660 | 3,275,765 | 1,732,464 | 1,543,301 | 37,649,873 | 13,685,726 | 13,052,660 | 17,071 | 615,995 |
| North Carolina....... | 10,806,291 | 1,184,700 | 781,602 | 507,602 | 274,000 | 8,839,989 | 4,103,446 | 3,977,240 | 108,512 | 17,694 |
| North Dakota........ | 507,989 | 66,169 | 71,286 | 17,911 | 53,375 | 370,534 | 223,905 | 204,759 | 6,499 | 12,647 |
| Ohio....................... | 25,512,455 | 2,832,514 | 3,205,641 | 1,813,094 | 1,392,547 | 19,474,300 | 11,072,895 | 10,264,097 | 390,121 | 418,677 |
| Oklahoma.............. | 3,771,032 | 406,154 | 1,033,129 | 535,821 | 497,308 | 2,331,749 | 1,720,151 | 1,612,307 | 43,186 | 64,658 |
| Oregon .................. | 8,019,724 | 13,601 | 433,269 | 77,587 | 355,682 | 7,572,854 | 3,283,086 | 2,915,569 | 25,692 | 341,825 |
| Pennsylvania.......... | 12,809,156 | 1,320,184 | 824,183 | 538,692 | 285,491 | 10,664,789 | 7,623,191 | 7,279,893 | 38,470 | 304,828 |
| Rhode Island.......... | 1,355,798 | 171,327 | 340,581 | 219,693 | 120,888 | 843,890 | 847,686 | 816,964 | 9,777 | 20,945 |
| South Carolina ...... | 4,667,557 | 641,199 | 952,698 | 300,565 | 652,133 | 3,073,660 | 2,447,555 | 2,283,684 | 90,998 | 72,873 |
| South Dakota ....... | 566,404 | 98,639 | 97,745 | 35,686 | 62,059 | 370,020 | 362,074 | 329,239 | 29,148 | 3,687 |
| Tennessee............... | 3,749,071 | 255,049 | 836,722 | 343,058 | 493,669 | 2,657,295 | 1,607,964 | 1,535,187 | 36,423 | 36,354 |
| Texas...................... | 18,651,474 | 3,235,937 | 3,966,175 | 2,321,371 | 1,644,804 | 11,449,362 | 10,150,229 | 9,481,373 | 452,074 | 216,782 |
| Utah....................... | 2,823,929 | 35,660 | 665,235 | 665,235 | 0 | 2,123,034 | 958,446 | 942,338 | 5,661 | 10,447 |
| Vermont ................. | 575,644 | 58,867 | 65,007 | 63,431 | 1,576 | 451,770 | 223,510 | 203,727 | 3,833 | 15,950 |
| Virginia .................. | 8,384,837 | 26,498 | 1,834,686 | 505,681 | 1,329,005 | 6,523,653 | 3,447,436 | 3,035,274 | 93,086 | 319,076 |
| Washington............ | 7,462,249 | 519,182 | 961,745 | 883,595 | 78,150 | 5,981,366 | 3,014,906 | 2,743,114 | 53,975 | 217,817 |
| West Virginia ........ | 1,940,274 | 170,352 | 571,794 | 404,637 | 167,157 | 1,198,128 | 823,812 | 798,473 | 16,724 | 8,615 |
| Wisconsin............... | 15,148,669 | 736,689 | 632,706 | 169,374 | 463,332 | 13,779,274 | 4,075,566 | 3,797,615 | 0 | 277,951 |
| Wyoming................ | 1,451,736 | 106,333 | 107,608 | 22,971 | 84,637 | 1,237,795 | 337,282 | 317,623 | 16,148 | 3,511 |

Source: 2010 Survey of Public-Employee Retirement Systems. Data users who create their own estimates using data from this report should cite the U.S. Census Bureau as the source of the original data only. The data in this table are based on information from public records and contain no confidential data. Although the data in this table come from a census of retirement systems and are not subject to sampling error, the census results do contain nonsampling error. Additional information on nonsampling error, and response rates may be found at http://www.census.gov/govs/ retire/how_data_collected.html.

Note: Detail may not add to total due to rounding.
Key:
(a) The total of "net earnings" is a calculated statistic (the item code in the data file is X08), and thus can be positive or negative. Net earnings is the sum of earnings on investments plus gains on investments minus losses on investments. The change made in 2002 for asset valuation from book to market value in accordance with Statement 34 of the Governmental Accounting Standards Board is reflected in the calculated statistics.

## Table 7.27
## NATIONAL SUMMARY OF STATE PUBLIC EMPLOYEE RETIREMENT SYSTEM FINANCES: SELECTED YEARS, 2007–2010*

| | Amount (in thousands of dollars) | | | | Percentage distribution | | | |
|---|---|---|---|---|---|---|---|---|
| | 2009–2010* | 2008–2009 | 2007–2008 | 2006–2007 | 2009–2010 | 2008–2009 | 2007–2008 | 2006–2007 |
| **Total Receipts** .......................... | 387,275,709 | -414,603,147 | 24,501,829 | 489,404,135 | 100.0% | 100.0% | 100.0% | 100.0% |
| Employee contributions..................... | 33,009,625 | 33,354,133 | 31,905,999 | 29,323,427 | 33.8% | 34.4% | 33.2% | 33.7% |
| Government contributions ................ | 64,650,956 | 63,498,578 | 64,307,264 | 57,765,406 | 66.2% | 65.6% | 66.8% | 66.3% |
| State government contributions.... | 35,386,653 | 34,602,633 | 36,019,351 | 31,675,999 | 36.2% | 35.7% | 37.4% | 36.4% |
| Local government contributions ... | 29,264,303 | 28,895,945 | 28,287,913 | 26,089,407 | 30.0% | 29.8% | 29.4% | 30.0% |
| Earnings on investments (a).............. | 289,615,128 | -511,455,858 | -71,711,434 | 402,315,302 | 100.0% | 100.0% | 100.0% | 100.0% |
| **Total Payments..........................** | 173,453,369 | 164,180,706 | 158,370,519 | 149,284,184 | 100.0% | 100.0% | 100.0% | 100.0% |
| Benefits.............................................. | 163,505,281 | 154,003,213 | 144,794,017 | 131,679,735 | 94.3% | 93.8% | 91.4% | 88.2% |
| Withdrawals....................................... | 3,494,033 | 3,344,173 | 3,360,646 | 4,562,127 | 2.0% | 2.0% | 2.1% | 3.1% |
| Other payments................................. | 6,454,055 | 6,833,320 | 10,215,856 | 13,042,322 | 3.7% | 4.2% | 6.5% | 8.7% |
| **Total cash and investment holdings........** | 2,220,230,277 | 2,006,306,305 | 2,617,063,172 | 2,772,082,282 | 100.0% | 100.0% | 100.0% | 100.0% |
| **Cash and short-term investments ...........** | 80,223,779 | 86,447,690 | 82,365,777 | 91,889,276 | 3.6% | 4.3% | 3.1% | 3.3% |
| **Total securities ..............................** | 1,820,101,684 | 1,643,682,453 | 2,159,598,947 | 2,379,153,634 | 82.0% | 81.9% | 82.5% | 85.8% |
| Government securities ....................... | 191,186,104 | 182,207,267 | 185,421,948 | 222,463,385 | 8.6% | 9.1% | 7.1% | 8.0% |
| Federal government............................ | 189,937,858 | 181,469,946 | 184,428,997 | 221,263,987 | 8.6% | 9.0% | 7.0% | 8.0% |
| United States Treasury ....................... | 130,478,129 | 126,644,894 | 117,442,647 | 138,308,828 | 5.9% | 6.3% | 4.5% | 5.0% |
| Federal agency................................... | 59,459,729 | 54,825,052 | 66,986,350 | 82,955,159 | 2.7% | 2.7% | 2.6% | 3.0% |
| State and local government ............... | 1,248,246 | 737,321 | 992,951 | 1,199,398 | 0.1% | 0.0% | 0.0% | 0.0% |
| **Nongovernmental securities.....................** | 1,628,915,580 | 1,461,475,186 | 1,974,176,999 | 2,156,690,249 | 73.4% | 72.8% | 75.4% | 77.8% |
| Corporate bonds ............................... | 350,635,793 | 339,440,158 | 424,001,200 | 363,109,402 | 15.8% | 16.9% | 16.2% | 13.1% |
| Corporate stocks ............................... | 767,686,738 | 673,547,616 | 941,308,968 | 1,056,169,226 | 34.6% | 33.6% | 36.0% | 38.1% |
| Mortgages ......................................... | 9,489,129 | 11,099,573 | 16,221,239 | 16,801,440 | 0.4% | 0.6% | 0.6% | 0.6% |
| Funds held in trust ........................... | 32,239,305 | 28,039,993 | 36,103,622 | 43,943,975 | 1.5% | 1.4% | 1.4% | 1.6% |
| Foreign and international................... | 362,028,456 | 317,285,825 | 407,064,028 | 446,388,358 | 16.3% | 15.8% | 15.6% | 16.1% |
| Other nongovernmental securities .... | 106,836,159 | 92,062,021 | 149,477,942 | 230,277,848 | 4.8% | 4.6% | 5.7% | 8.3% |
| **Other investments..........................** | 319,904,814 | 276,176,162 | 375,098,448 | 301,039,372 | 14.4% | 13.8% | 14.3% | 10.9% |
| Real property .................................... | 87,584,970 | 88,428,263 | 99,271,409 | 95,276,289 | 3.9% | 4.4% | 3.8% | 3.4% |
| Miscellaneous investments ................ | 232,319,844 | 187,747,899 | 275,827,039 | 205,763,083 | 10.5% | 9.4% | 10.5% | 7.4% |

*Source:* 2010–2006 Survey of Public-Employee Retirement Systems. Data users who create their own estimates using data from this report should cite the U.S. Census Bureau as the source of the original data only. The data in this table are based on information from public records and contain no confidential data. Although the data in this table come from a census of retirement systems and are not subject to sampling error, the census results do contain nonsampling error. Additional information on nonsampling error, and response rates may be found at *http://www.census. gov/govs/retire/how_data_collected.html.*

*Note:* Detail may not add to total due to rounding.

*Key:*
*Data in this report refer to fiscal years that ended between July 1, 2009, and June 30, 2010 (FY2010), and do not reflect data for the entire calendar year of 2010.

(a) The total of "net earnings" is a calculated statistic (the item code in the data file is X08), and thus can be positive or negative. Net earnings is the sum of earnings on investments plus gains on investments minus losses on investments. The change made in 2002 for asset valuation from book to market value in accordance with Statement 34 of the Governmental Accounting Standards Board is reflected in the calculated statistics.

# Chapter Eight

# STATE MANAGEMENT AND ADMINISTRATION

# State Business Incentives

## By Jennifer Burnett

*Since the Great Recession, states have been faced with high levels of unemployment, an increased demand for safety net services and a shrinking revenue base. Although the past year has brought some improvements, the number one question on state policy-makers' minds continues to be: "What can we do to encourage job growth?" Traditionally, a key policy lever for development and job creation strategies was—and remains—tax and financial incentive programs designed to encourage new firms to start up or existing firms to grow or relocate.*

Over the past three decades, states have developed various incentive programs designed to encourage economic activity in order to create, retain or expand business opportunities. In addition to tax and financial incentives, some states have used customized, company-specific incentives to engage in bidding wars with other states, making interstate competition for industries and businesses increasingly intense.

### Trends in the Use of Tax and Financial Incentives

From the 1970s into the late 1980s and early 1990s, the number of states providing tax and financial incentives to businesses and the types of incentives being offered increased significantly. Over the past 10 years, the number of states offering incentives of varying degrees and types has become relatively stable.

In 1977, at least 28 states offered tax concessions or credits to businesses for equipment and machinery, goods in transit, manufacturers' inventories, raw materials in manufacturing and job creation. In 1998, the number of states offering those incentives had grown to 42; by 2008 that count stood at 44 states.

The number of states offering an excise tax exemption in 2008 stood at 28—nearly triple the 10 states offering it in 1977. That year, 21 states offered a corporate income tax exemption and 19 states offered a personal income tax exemption; by 2010, the number of states offering these exemptions grew to 41 and 37, respectively.

Similarly, the number of states with financial incentive programs also increased over the past three decades. In 1977, fewer than 20 states offered special low-interest loans for building construction, equipment, machinery, plant expansion and establishment of industrial plants in areas of high unemployment. By 1998, more than 40 states offered those incentives—a number that remained essentially the same over the next decade.

During the past 10 years in particular, export promotion for small and medium-sized enterprises has become an increasingly important component of state economic development strategies. Nearly half the states responding to a CSG survey reported providing grants to small businesses as part of their export assistance portfolios.

The "New Energy Economy" has emerged alongside export promotion as a key focus of state economic development programs, with as many as 39 states developing policies and making explicit investments to advance green economic development as part of their Great Recession recovery strategies.

All 50 states, the District of Columbia and Puerto Rico offer two or more types of incentives for renewable energy. Similarly, 48 states, the District of Columbia and Puerto Rico offer at least one type of incentive for energy efficiency.

### Criticisms of Effectiveness

While incentives are in use in every state and Puerto Rico, researchers and state policymakers have questioned the effectiveness, impact and true costs of those programs, especially in the current fiscal environment of austerity measures and years of big budget gaps. Although incentives continue to be a popular economic tool in many states, some state leaders are increasingly critical of programs that pull revenue away from a shrinking tax base without clear evidence of a payback.

One of the criticisms applied to an incentive-focused development strategy is that incentives are a zero-sum game because they create bidding wars among states. One state luring business away from

# Table A: State-by-State Tax Incentives Offered in 2010

| State or other jurisdiction | Corporate Income Tax Exemption | Personal Income Tax Exemption | Excise Tax Exemption | Tax Exemption or Moratorium on Land, Capital Improvements | Tax Exemption or Moratorium on Equipment, Machinery | Inventory Tax Exemption on Goods in Transit (Freeport) | Tax Exemption on Manufacturers' Inventories | Sales/Use Tax Exemption on New Equipment | Tax Exemption on Raw Materials Used in Manufacturing | Tax Incentive for Creation of Jobs | Tax Incentive for Industrial Investment | Tax Credits for Use of Specified State Products | Tax Stabilization Agreements for Specified Industries | Tax Exemption to Encourage Research and Development | Accelerated Depreciation of Industrial Equipment |
|---|---|---|---|---|---|---|---|---|---|---|---|---|---|---|---|
| Alabama | ★ | ★ | ★ | ★ | ★ | ★ | ★ | ★ | ★ | ★ | ★ | | | ★ | ★ |
| Alaska | | ★ | ★ | ★ | | | | ★ | ★ | | | ★ | | ★ | ★ |
| Arizona | ★ | ★ | | ★ | ★ | ★ | ★ | ★ | ★ | ★ | ★ | | | ★ | ★ |
| Arkansas | ★ | | ★ | ★ | ★ | ★ | ★ | ★ | ★ | ★ | ★ | ★ | | ★ | ★ |
| California | | ★ | ★ | ★ | ★ | ★ | ★ | ★ | ★ | ★ | ★ | | | ★ | ★ |
| Colorado | ★ | | ★ | | ★ | ★ | ★ | ★ | ★ | ★ | ★ | | | | |
| Connecticut | ★ | | ★ | ★ | ★ | ★ | ★ | ★ | ★ | ★ | ★ | | ★ | ★ | ★ |
| Delaware | ★ | ★ | ★ | ★ | ★ | ★ | ★ | ★ | ★ | ★ | ★ | | | ★ | ★ |
| Florida | ★ | ★ | ★ | ★ | ★ | ★ | ★ | ★ | ★ | ★ | ★ | | | ★ | ★ |
| Georgia | | | | ★ | ★ | ★ | ★ | ★ | ★ | ★ | ★ | | | ★ | ★ |
| Hawaii | ★ | ★ | ★ | | | ★ | ★ | ★ | ★ | ★ | ★ | | ★ | ★ | ★ |
| Idaho | ★ | | | | | ★ | ★ | ★ | ★ | ★ | ★ | | | ★ | ★ |
| Illinois | ★ | ★ | ★ | ★ | | ★ | ★ | ★ | ★ | ★ | ★ | | | ★ | ★ |
| Indiana | ★ | ★ | | | ★ | ★ | ★ | ★ | ★ | ★ | ★ | | | ★ | ★ |
| Iowa | ★ | ★ | ★ | ★ | ★ | ★ | ★ | ★ | ★ | ★ | ★ | | | ★ | ★ |
| Kansas | ★ | ★ | | | ★ | ★ | ★ | ★ | ★ | ★ | ★ | | | ★ | ★ |
| Kentucky | ★ | ★ | | ★ | ★ | ★ | ★ | ★ | ★ | ★ | ★ | ★ | | ★ | ★ |
| Louisiana | ★ | ★ | | ★ | ★ | ★ | ★ | ★ | ★ | ★ | ★ | | ★ | ★ | ★ |
| Maine | ★ | ★ | | ★ | ★ | ★ | ★ | ★ | ★ | ★ | ★ | | | ★ | ★ |
| Maryland | ★ | ★ | ★ | ★ | ★ | ★ | ★ | ★ | ★ | ★ | ★ | | | ★ | ★ |
| Massachusetts | ★ | ★ | ★ | ★ | ★ | ★ | ★ | ★ | ★ | ★ | ★ | | ★ | ★ | ★ |
| Michigan | ★ | ★ | | ★ | ★ | ★ | ★ | ★ | ★ | ★ | ★ | | ★ | ★ | ★ |
| Minnesota | ★ | | ★ | ★ | ★ | ★ | ★ | ★ | ★ | ★ | ★ | | ★ | ★ | ★ |
| Mississippi | ★ | ★ | | ★ | ★ | ★ | ★ | ★ | ★ | ★ | ★ | | | ★ | ★ |
| Missouri | ★ | ★ | ★ | ★ | ★ | ★ | ★ | ★ | ★ | ★ | ★ | | | ★ | ★ |
| Montana | ★ | ★ | | ★ | ★ | ★ | ★ | ★ | ★ | ★ | ★ | ★ | ★ | ★ | ★ |
| Nebraska | | ★ | | ★ | ★ | ★ | ★ | ★ | ★ | ★ | ★ | | | ★ | ★ |
| Nevada | ★ | ★ | ★ | | ★ | ★ | ★ | ★ | ★ | ★ | | | | | ★ |
| New Hampshire | | ★ | | | ★ | ★ | ★ | ★ | ★ | | | | | | ★ |
| New Jersey | ★ | | | ★ | ★ | ★ | ★ | ★ | ★ | ★ | ★ | | | ★ | |
| New Mexico | ★ | ★ | | ★ | ★ | ★ | ★ | ★ | ★ | ★ | ★ | | | ★ | ★ |
| New York | ★ | ★ | ★ | ★ | ★ | ★ | ★ | ★ | ★ | ★ | ★ | | | ★ | |
| North Carolina | ★ | | | ★ | ★ | ★ | ★ | ★ | ★ | ★ | ★ | | | ★ | |
| North Dakota | ★ | | ★ | ★ | ★ | ★ | ★ | ★ | ★ | ★ | ★ | | | ★ | ★ |
| Ohio | ★ | ★ | | ★ | ★ | ★ | ★ | ★ | ★ | ★ | ★ | | | ★ | ★ |
| Oklahoma | ★ | ★ | ★ | ★ | ★ | ★ | ★ | ★ | ★ | ★ | ★ | ★ | ★ | ★ | ★ |
| Oregon | | ★ | ★ | ★ | ★ | ★ | ★ | ★ | ★ | | ★ | | | ★ | ★ |
| Pennsylvania | ★ | ★ | ★ | ★ | ★ | ★ | | ★ | ★ | ★ | ★ | ★ | ★ | ★ | ★ |
| Rhode Island | | | ★ | ★ | ★ | ★ | ★ | ★ | ★ | ★ | ★ | ★ | ★ | ★ | ★ |
| South Carolina | ★ | ★ | ★ | ★ | ★ | ★ | ★ | ★ | ★ | ★ | ★ | | | ★ | ★ |
| South Dakota | ★ | ★ | ★ | ★ | | ★ | ★ | ★ | ★ | ★ | ★ | | | ★ | ★ |
| Tennessee | ★ | ★ | ★ | ★ | | ★ | ★ | ★ | ★ | ★ | ★ | | | ★ | ★ |
| Texas | ★ | ★ | | ★ | ★ | ★ | ★ | ★ | ★ | ★ | ★ | | | ★ | ★ |
| Utah | | | | | ★ | ★ | ★ | ★ | ★ | ★ | ★ | | | | ★ |
| Vermont | | | ★ | | ★ | ★ | ★ | ★ | ★ | ★ | ★ | | ★ | | ★ |
| Virginia | ★ | ★ | ★ | ★ | ★ | ★ | ★ | ★ | ★ | ★ | ★ | | ★ | ★ | ★ |
| Washington | ★ | ★ | ★ | | ★ | ★ | ★ | ★ | ★ | ★ | ★ | | | ★ | |
| West Virginia | ★ | ★ | ★ | ★ | ★ | ★ | ★ | ★ | ★ | ★ | ★ | ★ | | ★ | ★ |
| Wisconsin | ★ | ★ | | | ★ | ★ | ★ | ★ | ★ | ★ | ★ | | | ★ | ★ |
| Wyoming | ★ | ★ | | | | ★ | ★ | | ★ | | | | | | |
| State Totals | 41 | 38 | 29 | 40 | 44 | 49 | 47 | 49 | 50 | 45 | 45 | 8 | 12 | 42 | 41 |
| Puerto Rico | ★ | ★ | ★ | ★ | ★ | ★ | ★ | ★ | ★ | ★ | ★ | ★ | ★ | ★ | ★ |

*Data Source: Site Selection Magazine.*
*Note:* Table appeared in *State Business Incentives: Trends and Options for the Future,* 2011, Jennifer Burnett, The Council of State Governments.

another with the promise of tax benefits does not create new economic activity; it simply transfers existing activity into another geographic location.

Some studies have shown that a company's decision to locate in a particular state has less to do with the incentives offered and more to do with the pre-existing assets of a state, such as workforce education levels, transportation capacity and access, housing affordability, and a geography appropriate for the firm's needs.

In addition, some argue that incentives are used inappropriately to correct weak spots in the economic climate, tax or regulatory infrastructure of a state. Instead, they argue, state policymakers should engage in strategic planning to improve their overall business climates, including initiating a review and analysis of regulatory barriers, tax codes, business permitting systems, workers' compensation systems and labor relations.

## Making Incentives Pay

Given the significant amount of funding at stake—in some cases, upward of half a billion dollars per state economic development program per year—many states are now using a number of strategies to ensure their investments are paying off, including:

- **Specify qualifications for a tax break**—States often require companies to meet certain criteria—such as wages paid, jobs created, health insurance and other benefits provided, capital investment made, and taxes created—to qualify for a tax break or incentive. Forty-three states have a rule for at least one of their incentive programs that addresses this type of qualification. Some states provide additional or stand-alone incentives for firms that create jobs in a particularly high-growth area or jobs that pay a high wage. In New Mexico, for example, an eligible employer may receive a tax credit for each new high-wage job it creates under the High Wage Jobs Tax Credit. The credit amount equals 10 percent of the wages and benefits paid for each new job created.

- **Strengthen the approval process**—In Texas, for example, the governor, lieutenant governor and speaker of the house must OK all projects that receive money from the state's Enterprise Fund. In Wyoming, the state's economic development staff does extensive diligence on each project and follows development of those projects throughout its life. As required by the state's constitution, the investments are with the governmental entities rather than companies directly and should the

endeavor fail, the governmental entity retains the assets created.

- **Public disclosure and online accountability**—One strategy states increasingly are employing is the use of online transparency and accountability systems. These systems provide the public with company-specific information on the amount of the tax subsidy, comparisons on the number of jobs promised and the number of jobs actually created, wage levels for employees, and the company's compliance record with various state rules and regulations.

  *Show Us the Subsidies*, a December 2010 report by the group Good Jobs First, singled out Illinois, Ohio and Wisconsin as having some of the most robust online disclosure systems in the nation. The report also found that 37 states provided online recipient disclosure for at least one key subsidy program, which is a significant improvement over 2007 when only about 23 states were doing so.

- **Clawbacks**—Some states penalize businesses that don't comply with the requirements of the tax incentive. Minnesota, for example, has an especially strong clawback law. First, all state and local subsidy agreements must contain clawback provisions. Second, the granting jurisdiction in Minnesota can recapture all or part of a subsidy, with interest, and any company that does not meet its contractual commitment also can be barred from future tax incentives. Currently, at least 37 states use some form of clawback provision, either written into their statutes or defined by program guidelines.

- **Post-Performance Awards**—Providing incentive-based awards after a firm has met the criteria for an award ensures the state will see the return it specifies and creates more of a backend accountability system. It also provides a true incentive for businesses to perform in the manner they have promised. If businesses cannot perform in that manner, states do not have to chase a business for reimbursement for a promise unfulfilled. In Utah, all state incentives are awarded on a post-performance basis so that companies must meet specific milestones, including generation of new state tax revenue, before incentives are disbursed.

Other common mechanisms states use include placing sunset provisions in statute so tax incentive programs cannot continue without additional legislative action and closely monitoring programs using performance audits. For example, in Nevada, audits

# Table B: State-by-State Financial Incentives Offered in 2010

| State or other jurisdiction | State-Sponsored Industrial Development Authority | Privately Sponsored Development Credit Corporation | State Authority or Agency Revenue Bond Financing | State Authority or Agency General Obligation Bond Financing | State Loans on Building Construction | State Loans for Equipment, Machinery | State Loan Guarantees for Building Construction | State Loan Guarantees for Equipment, Machinery | State Financing Aid for Existing Plant Expansion | State Matching Funds for City and/or County Industrial/Financing Programs | State Incentive for Establishing Industrial Plants in Areas of High Unemployment |
|---|---|---|---|---|---|---|---|---|---|---|---|
| Alabama | ★ | ★ | ★ | | ★ | ★ | | | ★ | | ★ |
| Alaska | ★ | ★ | ★ | ★ | ★ | ★ | ★ | ★ | ★ | ★ | ★ |
| Arizona | | | | | ★ | ★ | ★ | ★ | ★ | | ★ |
| Arkansas | ★ | ★ | ★ | ★ | ★ | ★ | ★ | ★ | ★ | | ★ |
| California | ★ | ★ | ★ | ★ | ★ | ★ | ★ | ★ | ★ | | ★ |
| Colorado | ★ | ★ | | | ★ | ★ | ★ | ★ | ★ | ★ | ★ |
| Connecticut | ★ | ★ | ★ | ★ | ★ | ★ | ★ | ★ | ★ | | ★ |
| Delaware | ★ | ★ | | | ★ | ★ | | | ★ | ★ | ★ |
| Florida | | | ★ | | ★ | ★ | | | ★ | | ★ |
| Georgia | ★ | ★ | ★ | | | | | | | | |
| Hawaii | ★ | | ★ | ★ | ★ | ★ | | | | | |
| Idaho | | ★ | | | | | | | | | |
| Illinois | ★ | ★ | ★ | | ★ | ★ | | ★ | ★ | | ★ |
| Indiana | ★ | ★ | ★ | | ★ | ★ | ★ | ★ | ★ | | ★ |
| Iowa | ★ | ★ | ★ | | ★ | ★ | ★ | ★ | ★ | ★ | ★ |
| Kansas | | | ★ | ★ | | | | | ★ | ★ | ★ |
| Kentucky | ★ | ★ | ★ | ★ | ★ | ★ | | | ★ | ★ | ★ |
| Louisiana | | ★ | ★ | ★ | ★ | ★ | ★ | ★ | ★ | ★ | ★ |
| Maine | ★ | | ★ | | ★ | ★ | ★ | ★ | ★ | | ★ |
| Maryland | ★ | | ★ | | ★ | ★ | ★ | ★ | ★ | ★ | ★ |
| Massachusetts | ★ | ★ | ★ | | ★ | ★ | | ★ | ★ | | ★ |
| Michigan | ★ | ★ | ★ | | ★ | ★ | | | ★ | | ★ |
| Minnesota | ★ | ★ | ★ | ★ | ★ | ★ | | | ★ | ★ | ★ |
| Mississippi | ★ | ★ | ★ | ★ | ★ | ★ | ★ | ★ | ★ | | ★ |
| Missouri | ★ | ★ | ★ | | ★ | ★ | ★ | ★ | ★ | | ★ |
| Montana | | ★ | ★ | ★ | ★ | ★ | ★ | ★ | ★ | | |
| Nebraska | ★ | ★ | ★ | ★ | ★ | ★ | ★ | ★ | | ★ | ★ |
| Nevada | | ★ | ★ | ★ | | | | | | | ★ |
| New Hampshire | ★ | ★ | ★ | | | | ★ | ★ | ★ | | |
| New Jersey | ★ | | ★ | | ★ | ★ | ★ | ★ | ★ | | ★ |
| New Mexico | ★ | ★ | ★ | ★ | ★ | ★ | ★ | ★ | ★ | ★ | ★ |
| New York | ★ | ★ | ★ | ★ | ★ | ★ | ★ | ★ | ★ | | ★ |
| North Carolina | ★ | | | | | | | | | | ★ |
| North Dakota | | ★ | ★ | ★ | ★ | ★ | ★ | ★ | ★ | ★ | ★ |
| Ohio | ★ | ★ | ★ | | ★ | ★ | | | ★ | ★ | ★ |
| Oklahoma | ★ | | ★ | ★ | ★ | ★ | ★ | ★ | ★ | ★ | ★ |
| Oregon | ★ | ★ | ★ | ★ | ★ | ★ | ★ | ★ | ★ | ★ | ★ |
| Pennsylvania | ★ | ★ | ★ | ★ | ★ | ★ | ★ | ★ | ★ | ★ | ★ |
| Rhode Island | ★ | ★ | ★ | ★ | ★ | ★ | ★ | ★ | ★ | ★ | ★ |
| South Carolina | ★ | ★ | ★ | | | | | | ★ | | ★ |
| South Dakota | ★ | | ★ | ★ | ★ | ★ | | | ★ | ★ | |
| Tennessee | | | ★ | ★ | ★ | ★ | ★ | ★ | ★ | ★ | ★ |
| Texas | ★ | ★ | ★ | ★ | ★ | ★ | ★ | ★ | ★ | ★ | |
| Utah | ★ | ★ | | | | | | | | | ★ |
| Vermont | ★ | ★ | ★ | | ★ | ★ | ★ | ★ | ★ | ★ | |
| Virginia | ★ | ★ | ★ | | ★ | ★ | | ★ | ★ | ★ | ★ |
| Washington | ★ | ★ | ★ | | | ★ | | ★ | ★ | ★ | ★ |
| West Virginia | ★ | ★ | ★ | | ★ | ★ | ★ | ★ | ★ | ★ | ★ |
| Wisconsin | ★ | | ★ | | ★ | ★ | | | ★ | | |
| Wyoming | ★ | ★ | ★ | | ★ | ★ | ★ | ★ | ★ | ★ | |
| State Totals | 42 | 39 | 45 | 24 | 41 | 42 | 30 | 34 | 44 | 27 | 43 |
| Puerto Rico | ★ | ★ | ★ | ★ | ★ | ★ | ★ | ★ | ★ | ★ | ★ |

*Data Source: Site Selection Magazine.*
*Note: Table appeared in State Business Incentives: Trends and Options for the Future, 2011, Jennifer Burnett, The Council of State Governments.*

are conducted for all incentives to affirm that the agreed upon number of workers have been hired or trained and pay levels are consistent with the incentive agreement.

## To Learn More

Check out the newest edition of *State Business Incentives: Trends and Options for the Future* to learn more. It includes an interactive comparative database of state incentive programs. *http://knowledgecenter.csg.org/drupal/content/state-business-incentives-trends-and-options-future*.

## About the Author

**Jennifer Burnett** joined CSG in 2006. She coordinates the research efforts at CSG, including requests for information from members, and manages the collection, analysis and presentation of data, particularly public access to interactive online databases. Her areas of expertise are fiscal, economic and government operational policy, including labor, state budget and tax policy and performance management. Burnett created and manages *States Perform*, a website that provides users with access to interactive, customizable and up-to-date comparative performance measurement data for states and territories in six key areas.

Prior to joining CSG, Burnett was a research associate at the University of Kentucky Center for Business and Economic Research and a legislative aide for a member of Canadian Parliament.

She holds bachelor's degrees in economics and finance from the University of Kentucky, a master's degree from the Patterson School of Diplomacy and International Commerce at the University of Kentucky and a Juris Doctor from the Salmon P. Chase College of Law.

# States Turn to Commissions, Task Forces for Transportation Funding Solutions

## By Sean Slone

*Many states face an ever-widening chasm between how much they have available to spend on transportation infrastructure and how much it actually costs to maintain and improve that infrastructure. There are numerous reasons for this, including the decline of existing revenue sources due to increased fuel efficiency, inflation and other factors. Absent a consensus on how to move forward, a number of states in 2011 turned to transportation funding task forces and blue ribbon commissions, diverse groups of stakeholders charged with making recommendations as to how these states could come up with the needed funds to meet their infrastructure needs in the years ahead. While their recommendations aren't always heeded immediately by policymakers, task forces and commissions can play an important role during a time of tough decisions and political divisions.*

### The Year of the Commission

When it comes to transportation funding policy, 2011 was something like the year of the commission/task force/blue ribbon/citizens' panel. As this is written in March 2012, we won't know definitively for a while whether their work will translate into policy action this year. But it may be worth taking a look at what's happened so far in four states—Iowa, Maryland, Pennsylvania and Washington—that had such a panel to assess their transportation needs. As other states seek to assess their own needs, officials may find value in evaluating other states' findings and experiences, their specific recommendations and panel members' thoughts on whether the process itself was a worthwhile endeavor.

Common themes emerge from the reports and discussions with members of these panels:

- States face substantial unmet transportation funding needs.

- State transportation systems face severe cutbacks unless funding solutions are found.

- Many state governments can choose from an extensive menu of revenue options, none of which are politically or economically easy to swallow and some of which would provide only temporary, stopgap solutions. States also are looking to provide more revenue options that localities can enact to help fund transportation.

- States are eager to explore more sustainable, user-fee based, long-term solutions such as a rev-enue mechanism based on vehicle miles traveled and expanded tolling. But more work is required at the state and federal levels to make them a reality.

- States are interested in working with the private sector to finance transportation, but remain wary of giving up too much in the process.

- State officials face a public skeptical of government and of the need for additional tax revenues for infrastructure investment. The push is on in some states with initiatives to assure the public that revenues intended for transportation will be used for that purpose and that state government is doing what it can to modernize, streamline and increase the efficiency of transportation systems and government agencies.

- Transportation funding commissions are valuable, members say, because they can bring a diverse group of stakeholders together, allow them to hear different perspectives and allow them to spend time on an issue for which policymakers seldom have time.

- While appointing commissions is often derided as a "kick-the-can-down-the-road" approach to public policy or as a delay tactic when the policy options are politically unpalatable, it also can provide politicians some political cover when a diverse group reaches consensus on some of those unpalatable ideas. But a diverse commission's recommendations also can put pressure on policymakers to take action.

- Commissions see urgency in policymakers taking action on transportation. Impending political shifts, deteriorating infrastructure and escalating costs all add to that sense of urgency.
- Some recommendations may take longer—in some cases, much longer—than one policy cycle or legislative session to accomplish. Ensuring commission reports and recommendations are written so that they have an extended shelf life should be a key goal for those who draft them.
- Commission members advise that recommendations should be both practical and aspirational. Aim high, but expect the political process to grind slowly and bring things back to earth. Hope that half-measures and stopgap solutions will be enough to temporarily stem the tide.

While the findings and recommendations of these commissions include remarkable similarities, each state faces its own unique challenges. But it's also clear from talking with commission members that each state has found unique value in having gone through this exercise. Whether that will translate into policy action is another question. Even the most practical, well-reasoned solutions can come up against strong political headwinds and harsh economic and budgetary realities. Nevertheless, here's what four states learned from the process of assessing their transportation needs and the options available to them.

## Pennsylvania's Transportation Funding Advisory Commission

Pennsylvania faces $3.5 billion in unmet transportation funding needs, a gap that is projected to more than double to $7.2 billion by 2020 unless the state can come up with a plan to address the situation. The reasons for the widening gap are laid out in a report issued in 2011 by a Transportation Funding Advisory Commission empaneled by Gov. Tom Corbett:

- A projected decline in fuel tax revenue over the next decade as a result of increased vehicle fuel efficiency driven by federal CAFÉ (corporate average fuel economy) standards;
- The impact of inflation which increases the cost of asphalt, steel, concrete and other materials by about 3 percent each year and reduces buying power; and
- A 66 percent increase in the portion of the Motor License Fund devoted to the Pennsylvania State Police over the last decade.

Among the policy changes recommended by the commission to fill the gap:

- Indexing all vehicle and driver fees to the Consumer Price Index, a measure of inflation;
- Uncapping the Oil Company Franchise Tax over five years;
- Increasing traffic fines;
- Increasing vehicle registration fees, with the revenue designated for local use;
- Implementing various modernization and cost-saving measures, including putting registration on a biennial schedule and driver license renewal on an eight-year cycle;
- Dedicating 2 percent of existing sales tax revenue to transit; and
- Consolidating and regionalizing transit delivery.

The commission said such a plan could add approximately $2.5 billion within five years for highways, bridges and transit, still far short of the $3.5 billion required to meet immediate needs. The commission recommended that the state legislature pass enabling legislation so local governments can have the option of raising taxes to support transportation investment, as well as legislation that would allow the state to enter into public-private partnerships to accelerate the maintenance, improvement and expansion of infrastructure. The commission also recommended expanding the state's authority to toll all interstates, along with studying whether different kinds of transportation usage-based charges—such as one based on vehicle miles traveled—might be feasible in the state in the future.[1]

In producing their final report, commission members aimed to offer recommendations that were both practical for the immediate future and more farsighted, said the panel's chairman, Pennsylvania Transportation Secretary Barry Schoch.

But some in the legislature have criticized Corbett for not showing leadership by jumping on the commission's recommendations immediately or putting forward a plan of his own to meet the state's transportation needs.[2] He said in February 2012 that those needs are too large to even be considered as part of the state budget and need to be considered separately.[3] Still, Schoch said the governor's reticence does nothing to diminish the work of the commission and simply reflects a common problem for many of the nation's chief executives.

"We produced a good blueprint and one that (the governor) has in my dialogue with him taken very seriously and sees a lot of good recommendations out of it," Schoch said. "The issue for him, like any governor, is that this is just one of the many silos he has to deal with. ... He's got the entire gamut of state services and he's got an incredibly difficult—like most governors do right now—general fund problem because revenues are flat or down and mandated costs and pension costs are rising."

With the scope of the challenges in perspective, Schoch said it's of little wonder that the commission's recommendations haven't been quickly embraced and adopted.

"As the governor and I both say, you don't get into this problem overnight, you don't get out of it overnight," Schoch said. "The idea that you're just going to wave a wand and solve it all in a year is just far-fetched."

Nevertheless, Schoch expects the commission's recommendations to still be valid for years to come. And despite what may be a long road ahead for Pennsylvania's efforts to meet its transportation needs, Schoch said he would advise any state to form a commission like his to start working on solutions.

"One of the biggest difficulties that you face in getting something passed is getting a consistent message in front of the media, the legislature and the public," he said. "If you don't do one of these (commissions), if you don't take the time to come up with a reasonable plan to tell people how you would charge them, how you'd invest it and what the results would be, you'll never get that consistent message. And I think that's a sure way to fail."[4]

### Connecting Washington Task Force

In Washington state, it was called the Connecting Washington Task Force, a 31-member panel of business, local government, labor and environmental leaders appointed by Gov. Chris Gregoire in July 2011 to develop a 10-year strategy for maintaining and improving the state's transportation system.

The panel's January 2012 report laid out the challenges the state faces in the years ahead. They include, among other things, a lack of funding for maintenance and operations or for future improvements. While fuel tax increases in 2003 and 2005 allowed the state to issue bonds to pay for more than 400 transportation projects around the state, the revenues generated by those increases are fully committed to debt service and remaining revenue is not sufficient to meet current needs.

The task force recommended a series of actions state officials could take to raise additional revenues and stretch available dollars:

- Focus investments in areas such as system preservation, strategic mobility improvements, system efficiency and safety.

- Invest $21 billion in state funding over a decade to preserve the transportation system and make strategic investments in the corridors that hold the most promise for job creation and economic growth. Interestingly, the task force noted that closer to $50 billion is actually needed to fully address the objectives they identified, but they proposed the lower level of investment due to the state's challenging economic conditions.

- Consider a series of new potential funding options to pay for the needed investments, including fee increases that could be enacted by a simple majority vote of the legislature and tax increases that would require either a two-thirds vote of the legislature or a majority vote of the people on a ballot measure.

- Expand funding options that can be enacted at the local level, including local option fuel and property taxes, tolling and parking fees.

- Begin making the transition to more sustainable funding sources for transportation, which could include direct user fees based on miles traveled, wear-and-tear on roadways or other direct impact on the transportation system. This, the panel said, would allow the system to be managed and funded as a statewide transportation utility with rates based on use.[5]

But Gregoire quickly nixed the idea of a gas tax increase in the task force's report because it was unlikely to win public support during the challenging economic climate. She proposed instead a $1.50 fee per barrel of oil refined in the state, since that would only have to go before the legislature. The fee, it was estimated, could raise $3.6 billion in transportation funds during the next decade, a fraction of the $21 billion the task force said was actually needed.

"A lot of the work that we did in that Connecting Washington (Task Force) did not come to fruition in the legislature this year," said state Rep. Judy Clibborn, a member of the task force who chairs the House Transportation Committee in Olympia. "The barrel fee was controversial. It would have been challenged in court. Some people said it was a tax. Some people said it was a fee. It got wrapped around a whole bunch of axles. The gas tax was never a player because we would have had to go to the people (in the initiative process). And so what we did this year is raise a few internal fees."[6]

The fee increases, which include an 80 percent hike for driver's licenses, are projected to raise an estimated $52 million next year and an average of $80 million annually during the next decade,[7] an even smaller fraction of what the task force said was needed.

Despite the disappointments, Clibborn is convinced the task force's report and recommendations will have a shelf life that extends well beyond the current policy cycle. She believes the task force had value because it allowed a diverse group of stakeholders to come together to hear different perspectives on the transportation issues the state faces.

"When you get the right caliber of people around the table and they have enough 'oomph' in their communities, they are saying things to each other that they won't hear if they're just sitting at home," she said. "The people who would come in and say 'We only want bike lanes' were hearing that if we don't have freight (mobility), we don't have jobs."[8]

## Iowa's Transportation 2020 Citizen Advisory Commission

In March 2011, Iowa Gov. Terry Branstad established the Governor's Transportation 2020 Citizen Advisory Commission, which worked for five months holding public meetings around the state to gather citizen input about the state's transportation needs and potential funding options.[9]

The commission's report offered a series of recommendations, including generating a minimum of $215 million in revenue per year through a combination of efficiency savings and increased revenue. Specifically, the commission called for an increase in state fuel tax rates across the board by 8 to 10 cents, which would generate an estimated $184 million–$230 million.[10]

As in Pennsylvania and Washington, however, adoption of the commission's recommendations appears to have been at least temporarily delayed by a reluctant governor and legislature.

"I think if the governor would have come out right away and just said, 'I think the legislature should take a very hard, serious look at this and I think that their findings are very credible,' I would almost bet you that we would have had a bill passed out of the legislature by now," said Rep. David Tjepkes, who chairs the House Transporta-

tion Committee and was an ex-officio member of the commission. "He did not say, 'Oh no, I'm opposed to those.' He said, 'Before we consider (new revenues), we need to make sure that the department (of transportation) is exploring all the potential efficiencies that they can derive from their budget. …' That exercise in Iowa has in fact been going forward."

Tjepkes noted that Branstad is keeping an open mind about transportation revenue options and he predicted that a gas tax increase could get folded into a larger discussion on tax policy. He remains optimistic that the commission's recommendations will hold sway and Iowa policymakers will recognize the urgency of the situation and move forward to adopt them.

"I think legislators need to do their jobs, step up to the plate and do what (voters) sent us to the capitol to do and that's to govern," he said.[11]

## Maryland's Blue Ribbon Commission on Transportation Funding

A 28-member commission representing state, county and local governments, as well as various transportation, economic and environmental interests, came together in Maryland starting in 2010 and continuing through 2011. While noting that no single funding source will be sufficient due to the magnitude of the state's investment needs and obligations, the commission recommended Maryland raise approximately $870 million in new net annual revenues for transportation primarily from revenue sources that are directly related to transportation. The commission selected from a menu of revenue options that were assessed at various levels. They ultimately recommended, among other things, a 15-cent per gallon increase in gas and special fuel taxes phased in over three years with an indexing mechanism added in the fourth year that would put both a floor and a ceiling on the tax level. This, they estimated, would produce $491 million in net new revenues.[12]

It then came as something of a surprise to some when Gov. Martin O'Malley, instead of proposing the recommended gas tax increase, proposed a 6 percent sales tax on the retail price of motor fuel.[13] While that was an idea on the commission's full menu of revenue options included in an appendix to the report, it was ultimately not recommended even though it was estimated the sales tax could bring in as much as $613 million annually.

But the commission's chairman, Gus Bauman, said he didn't have a problem with the governor's choice because the sales tax would still bear some resemblance to a user fee.

"What I am more concerned about is not which tax or fee is used in what amount to get what we need, but will the money be protected and used only for transportation purposes," said Bauman, an attorney who focuses on land use and environmental issues for the Washington, D.C.-based law firm, Beveridge and Diamond.[14]

Maryland is one of at least 19 states with a dedicated Transportation Trust Fund into which revenues flow that are supposed to be used for transportation purposes.[15]

"What's happened over the past decade is a lot of money has been diverted to general fund uses by the state," Bauman said. "We have to put the 'trust' back in the Transportation Trust Fund. In my opinion, there is no way you can get the public to agree to higher fees and taxes on transportation-related activities such as pumping gasoline without a guarantee that the money will then be used for transportation purposes by the state."

So the commission also recommended a constitutional amendment to prohibit transfer from the fund for non-transportation purposes, except in declared fiscal emergencies.

As of this writing, the jury is still out on whether either O'Malley's sales tax plan or the constitutional amendment will be successful in 2012. But regardless of what happens this year, Bauman believes the commission's work will have a lasting impact. He said the report was ultimately strengthened by the way the commission members went about their work.

"I made clear to the group from the outset that our goal here … is that we should be both practical and aspirational," he said. "(The commission's recommendations) need to be not crazy nor beyond the pale of ever being adopted. But at the same time they have to be somewhat aspirational, telling the elected folks in Annapolis these are the things that a government ought to be doing so that they can have something to shoot for."

Ultimately, Bauman believes the process produced a report that policymakers should find invaluable.

"We were able to devote time to a subject that no elected official ever has time to devote to," he said. "And (with) a broad-ranging group, it can be said that this is something that is politically possible. You can take these recommendations and you can apply them because this is politically viable."[16]

## Conclusion

While the political viability of most recommendations is still in question in all four of these states, the usefulness of this exercise is not. America's transportation needs and how to fund them going forward are large enough problems to warrant all the hours of public hearings, all the input from diverse stakeholders and all the hundreds of pages of final reports they can produce. Unfortunately, the problems are also large enough that policymakers can choose to ignore both the practical and aspirational recommendations of such commissions for both practical and political reasons. But commissions and task forces can be an important part of eventually reaching solutions to these seemingly intractable, unsolvable problems even when those solutions seem—for the moment—a bridge too far.

## Notes

[1] Pennsylvania Governor's Transportation Funding Advisory Report. Final Report. August 2011. Accessed from: *ftp://ftp.dot.state.pa.us/public/pdf/TFAC/TFAC%20Final %20Report%20-%20Spread%20Version.pdf.*

[2] "Governor Tom Corbett on funding for transportation." PAMatters.com. Video recorded February 23, 2012. Accessed from: *http://www.pamatters.com/2012/02/23/governor-tom-corbett-on-funding-for-transportation/.*

[3] Paul Nussbaum. "Corbett says road, bridge and transit problems too big for Pa. budget." *Philadelphia Inquirer.* February 9, 2012. Accessed from: *http://www.philly.com/philly/ news/politics/state/20120209_Corbett_says_road_bridge_ and_transit_problems_too_big_for_Pa_budget.html.*

[4] Barry Schoch. Telephone interview. March 2012.

[5] Connecting Washington Task Force. "Strategic Transportation Investments to Strengthen Washington's Economy and Create Jobs." January 6, 2012. Accessed from: *http:// www.governor.wa.gov/priorities/transportation/connect/ final_report.pdf.*

[6] Rep. Judy Clibborn. Telephone interview. March 2012.

[7] Jonathan Kaminsky. "Wash. Lawmakers push driving-related fee hikes." *The Seattle Times.* February 6, 2012. Accessed from: *http://seattletimes.nwsource.com/html/localnews/ 2017442774_apwaxgrtransportationfunding1stldwritethru. html.*

[8] Clibborn.

[9] Iowa Department of Transportation. "2011 Road Use Tax Fund (RUTF) Study." December 30, 2011. Accessed from: *http://www.iowadot.gov/pdf_files/RUTFStudy2011.pdf.*

[10] Ibid.

[11] Rep. David Tjepkes. Telephone interview. March 2012.

[12] Blue Ribbon Commission on Maryland Transportation Funding. "Final Report to the Governor and Maryland General Assembly by the Blue Ribbon Commission on Transportation Funding." November 1, 2011. Accessed from: *http://www.mdot.maryland.gov/Office%20of%20Planning*

*%20and%20Capital%20Programming/Blue_Ribbon/Docu ments/BRC_Final_Report_Nov_01_2011.pdf.*

[13] Aaron C. Davis. "O'Malley proposes 6% sales tax on gas." *The Washington Post.* January 30, 2012. Accessed from: *http://www.washingtonpost.com/local/md-politics/omalley-proposes-6percent-sales-tax-on-gas/2012/01/30/gIQAiaU rdQ_story.html.*

[14] Gus Bauman. Telephone interview. March 2012.

[15] National Conference of State Legislatures and American Association of State Highway and Transportation Officials. "Transportation Governance and Finance: A 50-State Review of State Legislatures and Departments of Transportation." May 2011. Accessed from: *http://www.ncsl.org/docu ments/transportation/FULL-REPORT.pdf.*

[16] Bauman.

---

## About the Author

**Sean Slone** is the senior transportation policy analyst at The Council of State Governments. He staffs CSG's Transportation Policy Task Force and writes about transportation policy for CSG publications, such as *Capitol Ideas* magazine, the Capitol Comments blog and Capitol Research policy materials. He is the author of two CSG national reports: *Transportation and Infrastructure Finance* (2009) and *Shovel-Ready or Not? State Stimulus Successes on the Road to Recovery* (2010). His work also appeared in the 2010 and 2011 volumes of *The Book of the States*.

# Puerto Rico Pursues a Pro-Growth Agenda to Tackle Fiscal and Economic Woes

## By Douglas Holtz-Eakin

*Since 2006, Puerto Rico has suffered one of the worst recessions of its history while simultaneously facing severe fiscal distress. Reforms made by Gov. Luis G. Fortuño, elected in 2008, have controlled the largest proportional deficit among the states. Puerto Rico's pro-growth reform agenda has since been touted as a model for addressing fiscal and economic problems at the state and federal level.*

## Introduction

Puerto Rico entered what would become a prolonged recession in March 2006, nearly two years before the downturn in the rest of the United States. By the time Fortuño became governor in January 2009, the gross national product was projected to decline 3.4 percent that year and another 2 percent in 2010.[1] In addition to the nation's economic malaise, the territory government was suffering severe budgetary distress.

The onset of the global economic and financial crisis worsened the economic outlook and further jeopardized the territory's fiscal outlook. The island's economy was already in recession, and the territory government had a long record of deficit spending. From 2006 to 2009, Puerto Rico's budgeted operating expenses exceeded the actual revenue collected by more than 50 percent, a gap bigger than any state in the country. The budgetary authority failed to accurately embed the recession in its forecasts and, as a result, consistently overestimated economic growth and tax receipts. The immense structural deficit that developed was disguised with stopgap measures instead of the requisite fundamental reforms.

Following Fortuño's gubernatorial election on a platform of change, the Puerto Rican government began serious economic reforms to address its weak economy and budgetary crisis. These reforms included reducing the government payroll; enacting a flatter, simplified personal income tax code; reducing corporate tax rates to increase competitiveness; cracking down on tax evasion; reforming the unemployment insurance system to incentivize a timely return to employment; taking comprehensive steps to cut waste and streamline government services; and enacting measures to diversify sources of energy. These measures have been controversial at times, but also generally have been supported by economists, who frequently cite the need for comprehensive reform to remedy budgetary problems at the federal level.

## Limited Government and Pro-Growth Policies in Puerto Rico

When Fortuño took office, the territory's fiscal situation was precarious. It was running a $3.3 billion budget deficit representing 44 percent of revenues. As a matter of reality, the territory government had very limited options to close the budget gap—reduce outlays, increase revenues or borrow the budgetary deficit. Realistically, the third option was restricted because of previous and imminent downgrades in the Puerto Rican government's credit rating, which stood just one step above junk. Moreover, access to credit markets was limited during the global financial crisis.

Beginning immediately upon taking office, Fortuño acted to stabilize the fiscal emergency and enact pro-growth reforms to bolster the economy. The history of poor forecasts by the Planning Board (the agency tasked with economic planning) had yielded little relationship between budget projections and fiscal and economic reality. The Fortuño administration implemented an aggressive plan in the form of four legislative measures, enforced by the Puerto Rico Fiscal Stabilization and Reconstruction Board, to close the deficit, stabilize the island's finances and boost economic development. First, Puerto Rico, which previously employed a far greater percentage of its population than most states, managed to reduce its payroll costs by 17 percent and transition to 401k plans for all government workers, one of the first states or territories to do so.

Having reduced spending, the government stabilized its finances by improving oversight of the tax system and increasing revenue—without adding economic hardship to businesses or individuals.

To accomplish this, Fortuño pushed for comprehensive, pro-growth tax reform. This reform was one of the most fundamental tenets of Fortuño's overall plan to bring the deficit under control and restart the economy. The previous tax system, which closely mirrored that of the United States federal government, has been replaced by a new code with a top tax rate of 30 percent on household incomes of more than $250,000. This rate is lower than the U.S. federal income tax, nearly every western European country and many Latin American countries. In addition to reducing rates, the code has been simplified through the elimination or scale back of tax expenditures. Tax reform at the individual level achieved two objectives: It reduced the amount of economic activity undertaken for purely tax-based motives, broadened the tax base by eliminating unneeded exemptions and deductions, and used the broader tax base to reduce tax rates and improve incentives. These income tax cuts will provide an estimated average $1.2 billion in tax relief annually by the time of full implementation.

Perhaps more importantly for the overall economy, Puerto Rico also reduced corporate tax rates to increase economic competitiveness, attract jobs and increase revenue. The existing tax rate of 41 percent was among the highest corporate tax rates in the hemisphere. Effective Jan. 1, 2011, the top rate dropped from 41 percent to 30 percent. The previous seven-tier corporate income brackets were simplified into three lower rates of 20, 25 and 30 percent. By 2014, the top bracket will be lowered further to 25 percent.

Several economic studies show that low corporate tax rates create a better business environment for existing companies and startup entities. One study by the Organization for Economic Cooperation and Development found that a 10 percentage point reduction in tax rates results in a 7 percent increase in investment. The same study also estimated that such a reduction increases productivity growth an additional 0.5 percentage points over its trend. These two effects combine to have a powerful impact on productivity, which over long periods is the basic building block of higher standards of living.[2]

Third, the administration embedded a housing initiative within its comprehensive pro-growth strategy. This initiative cut property and capital gains taxes for buyers, sellers and investors and created a new rental initiative, exempting residential rental income from income taxes for 10 years. In 2011, both new home sales and existing home sales increased, a striking contrast to the largely depressed housing market in the rest of the country.

Fourth, to diversify sources of energy, the island's public utility, Puerto Rico Electric Power Authority (PREPA), is expanding its liquefied natural gas terminal capacity while expanding its natural gas distribution pipelines. With around two-thirds of its energy coming from oil, the government recognized the value of diversifying away from increasingly volatile oil prices, which left the bulk of the island's energy needs at the mercy of global economic conditions.

The combination of dramatically cutting the size of the government workforce, moving employees to a defined contribution pension plan, turning over toll roads and airport to private operators and taking steps to diversify its sources of energy sends a message from Puerto Rico to would-be investors and businesses that the island has permanently changed to be more business-friendly. The reforms were undertaken not only to reduce the massive budgetary deficit, but also to promote economic growth simultaneously.

## Result of Reforms: Puerto Rico's Fiscal and Economic Rebound

In the recession, Puerto Rico's economic output fell by more than 10 percent from peak to trough in 2010, a decline that more than offset previous growth that decade. The Puerto Rican economy, however, has largely stabilized and showed positive growth in the final months of 2011.

In December 2011, Puerto Rico's Economic Activity Index registered its first positive year-over-year growth since March 2006, at 0.5 percent.[3] After five years of negative GNP growth, the economy is expected to grow in 2012, albeit at a modest 0.7 percent rate. The unemployment rate, which reached a peak of 16.6 percent in May 2010, fell to 15.1 percent by the beginning of 2012.[4] This marks a more than 9 percent decrease in the number of unemployed Puerto Ricans since May 2010.

A total of 14,716 new corporations were created in 2011, reflecting a 14 percent increase compared to 2010. The reduced rates in the corporate tax code were just one piece of a comprehensive plan to make Puerto Rico a more business friendly environment.

While the Puerto Rican economy remains far from its potential, it is showing broad indications of an upturn.

The fiscal situation also has stabilized. The budget deficit of $3.3 billion when Fortuño took office has been reduced from 44 percent of revenues to 7 percent. The deficit has shrunk from $3.3 billion to $610 million, and the island is on track to close the budget gap next fiscal year. Originally ranked last among the states for having the highest proportional deficit, Puerto Rico is now ranked number 15.

Despite reductions in tax rates, general fund net revenues actually increased in 2011 due to the positive effects of tax reform. General fund net revenues increased by 12 percent, from $6.9 billion in 2010 to $7.7 billion in 2011, one sign that the fundamental tax reforms initiated and passed by Fortuño elicited the desired results.

Both Moody's and Standard and Poor's ratings agencies released improved credit ratings for Puerto Rico, noting their positive outlook for Puerto Rico's credit and economic performance. Moody's raised Puerto Rico's credit rating from Baa3 to Baa1, up two notches, while Standard and Poor's upgraded Puerto Rico from BBB- to BBB, the first credit rating upgrade by S&P in the U.S. since 2009.

The Puerto Rican economy remains below full potential. Nevertheless, the reforms the government passed have put the territory government on a more fiscally sustainable path moving forward and made Puerto Rico more economically competitive. While unemployment is still far too high, the governor's economic and fiscal plans have laid the groundwork for economic growth. Its reforms have essentially averted near disaster and the credit upgrades are a good indication of its improved standing and positive economic and fiscal outlook moving forward.

## Notes

[1] Puerto Rico Planning Board, "Press Release: The Board Revises Economic Figures for Fiscal Year 2008 and Updates Forecasts for Fiscal Years 2009 and 2010" (2009), at: *http://www.gdb-pur.com/communications/PressReleases/2009-02-10-ComunicadoJP-ing.pdf*.

[2] Jens Arnold and Cyrille Schwellnus, "Do corporate taxes reduce productivity and investment at the firm level? Cross-country evidence from the Amadeus dataset" (2008), OECD Economics Department Working Paper No. 641, September 30, 2008, at: *http://www.cepii.fr/anglaisgraph/workpap/summaries/2008/wp08-19.htm*.

[3] Government Development Bank for Puerto Rico, "Economic Activity Index for the month of December 2011," (2012), at: *http://www.gdb-pur.com/documents/2011-12-GDB-EAI-FINAL-GS.pdf*.

## About the Author

**Douglas Holtz-Eakin** is the president of the American Action Forum, a think tank based in Washington, D.C. He has served in a variety of policy positions including chief economist of the President's Council of Economic Advisers from 2001 to 2002, and the sixth director of the nonpartisan Congressional Budget Office from 2003 to 2005.

## Table 8.1
## SUMMARY OF STATE GOVERNMENT EMPLOYMENT: 1953–2010

| Year (October) | Employment (in thousands) Total, full-time and part-time | | | Full-time equivalent | | | Monthly payrolls (in millions of dollars) | | | Average monthly earnings of full-time employees | | |
|---|---|---|---|---|---|---|---|---|---|---|---|---|
| | All | Education | Other | All | Education | Other | All | Education | Other | All | Education | Other |
| 1953 | 1,082 | 294 | 788 | 966 | 211 | 755 | $278.6 | $73.5 | $205.1 | $289 | $320 | $278 |
| 1954 | 1,149 | 310 | 839 | 1,024 | 222 | 802 | 300.7 | 78.9 | 221.8 | 294 | 325 | 283 |
| 1955 | 1,199 | 333 | 866 | 1,081 | 244 | 837 | 325.9 | 88.5 | 237.4 | 302 | 334 | 290 |
| 1956 | 1,268 | 353 | 915 | 1,136 | 250 | 886 | 366.5 | 108.8 | 257.7 | 321 | 358 | 309 |
| 1957 (April) | 1,300 | 375 | 925 | 1,153 | 257 | 896 | 372.5 | 106.1 | 266.4 | 320 | 355 | 309 |
| 1958 | 1,408 | 406 | 1,002 | 1,259 | 284 | 975 | 446.5 | 123.4 | 323.1 | 355 | 416 | 333 |
| 1959 | 1,454 | 443 | 1,011 | 1,302 | 318 | 984 | 485.4 | 136.0 | 349.4 | 373 | 427 | 352 |
| 1960 | 1,527 | 474 | 1,053 | 1,353 | 332 | 1,021 | 524.1 | 167.7 | 356.4 | 386 | 439 | 365 |
| 1961 | 1,625 | 518 | 1,107 | 1,435 | 367 | 1,068 | 586.2 | 192.4 | 393.8 | 409 | 482 | 383 |
| 1962 | 1,680 | 555 | 1,126 | 1,478 | 389 | 1,088 | 634.6 | 201.8 | 432.8 | 429 | 518 | 397 |
| 1963 | 1,775 | 602 | 1,173 | 1,558 | 422 | 1,136 | 696.4 | 230.1 | 466.3 | 447 | 545 | 410 |
| 1964 | 1,873 | 656 | 1,217 | 1,639 | 460 | 1,179 | 761.1 | 257.5 | 503.6 | 464 | 560 | 427 |
| 1965 | 2,028 | 739 | 1,289 | 1,751 | 508 | 1,243 | 849.2 | 290.1 | 559.1 | 484 | 571 | 450 |
| 1966 | 2,211 | 866 | 1,344 | 1,864 | 575 | 1,289 | 975.2 | 353.0 | 622.2 | 522 | 614 | 483 |
| 1967 | 2,335 | 940 | 1,395 | 1,946 | 620 | 1,326 | 1,105.5 | 406.3 | 699.3 | 567 | 666 | 526 |
| 1968 | 2,495 | 1,037 | 1,458 | 2,085 | 694 | 1,391 | 1,256.7 | 477.1 | 779.6 | 602 | 687 | 544 |
| 1969 | 2,614 | 1,112 | 1,501 | 2,179 | 746 | 1,433 | 1,430.5 | 554.5 | 876.1 | 655 | 743 | 597 |
| 1970 | 2,755 | 1,182 | 1,573 | 2,302 | 803 | 1,499 | 1,612.2 | 630.3 | 981.9 | 700 | 797 | 605 |
| 1971 | 2,832 | 1,223 | 1,609 | 2,384 | 841 | 1,544 | 1,741.7 | 681.5 | 1,060.2 | 731 | 826 | 686 |
| 1972 | 2,957 | 1,267 | 1,690 | 2,487 | 867 | 1,619 | 1,936.6 | 746.9 | 1,189.7 | 778 | 871 | 734 |
| 1973 | 3,013 | 1,280 | 1,733 | 2,547 | 887 | 1,660 | 2,158.2 | 822.2 | 1,336.0 | 843 | 952 | 805 |
| 1974 | 3,155 | 1,357 | 1,798 | 2,653 | 929 | 1,725 | 2,409.5 | 932.7 | 1,476.9 | 906 | 1,023 | 855 |
| 1975 | 3,271 | 1,400 | 1,870 | 2,744 | 952 | 1,792 | 2,652.7 | 1,021.7 | 1,631.1 | 964 | 1,080 | 909 |
| 1976 | 3,343 | 1,434 | 1,910 | 2,799 | 973 | 1,827 | 2,893.7 | 1,111.5 | 1,782.1 | 1,031 | 1,163 | 975 |
| 1977 | 3,491 | 1,484 | 2,007 | 2,903 | 1,005 | 1,898 | 3,194.6 | 1,234.4 | 1,960.1 | 1,096 | 1,237 | 1,031 |
| 1978 | 3,539 | 1,508 | 2,032 | 2,966 | 1,016 | 1,950 | 3,483.0 | 1,332.9 | 2,150.2 | 1,167 | 1,311 | 1,102 |
| 1979 | 3,699 | 1,577 | 2,122 | 3,072 | 1,046 | 2,026 | 3,869.3 | 1,451.4 | 2,417.9 | 1,257 | 1,399 | 1,193 |
| 1980 | 3,753 | 1,599 | 2,154 | 3,106 | 1,063 | 2,044 | 4,284.7 | 1,608.0 | 2,676.6 | 1,373 | 1,523 | 1,305 |
| 1981 | 3,726 | 1,603 | 2,123 | 3,087 | 1,063 | 2,024 | 4,667.5 | 1,768.0 | 2,899.5 | 1,507 | 1,671 | 1,432 |
| 1982 | 3,747 | 1,616 | 2,131 | 3,083 | 1,051 | 2,032 | 5,027.7 | 1,874.0 | 3,153.7 | 1,625 | 1,789 | 1,551 |
| 1983 | 3,816 | 1,666 | 2,150 | 3,116 | 1,072 | 2,044 | 5,345.5 | 1,989.0 | 3,357.0 | 1,711 | 1,850 | 1,640 |
| 1984 | 3,898 | 1,708 | 2,190 | 3,177 | 1,091 | 2,086 | 5,814.9 | 2,178.0 | 3,637.0 | 1,825 | 1,991 | 1,740 |
| 1985 | 3,984 | 1,764 | 2,220 | 2,990 | 945 | 2,046 | 6,328.6 | 2,433.7 | 3,884.9 | 1,935 | 2,155 | 1,834 |
| 1986 | 4,068 | 1,800 | 2,267 | 3,437 | 1,256 | 2,181 | 6,801.4 | 2,583.4 | 4,226.9 | 2,052 | 2,263 | 1,956 |
| 1987 | 4,115 | 1,804 | 2,310 | 3,491 | 1,264 | 2,227 | 7,297.8 | 2,758.3 | 4,539.5 | 2,161 | 2,396 | 2,056 |
| 1988 | 4,236 | 1,854 | 2,381 | 3,606 | 1,309 | 2,297 | 7,842.3 | 2,928.6 | 4,913.7 | 2,260 | 2,490 | 2,158 |
| 1989 | 4,365 | 1,925 | 2,440 | 3,709 | 1,360 | 2,349 | 8,443.1 | 3,175.0 | 5,268.1 | 2,372 | 2,627 | 2,259 |
| 1990 | 4,503 | 1,984 | 2,519 | 3,840 | 1,418 | 2,432 | 9,083.0 | 3,426.0 | 5,657.0 | 2,472 | 2,732 | 2,359 |
| 1991 | 4,521 | 1,999 | 2,522 | 3,829 | 1,375 | 2,454 | 9,437.0 | 3,550.0 | 5,887.0 | 2,479 | 2,530 | 2,433 |
| 1992 | 4,595 | 2,050 | 2,545 | 3,856 | 1,384 | 2,472 | 9,828.0 | 3,774.0 | 6,054.0 | 2,562 | 2,607 | 2,521 |
| 1993 | 4,673 | 2,112 | 2,562 | 3,891 | 1,436 | 2,455 | 10,288.2 | 3,999.3 | 6,288.9 | 2,722 | 3,034 | 2,578 |
| 1994 | 4,694 | 2,115 | 2,579 | 3,917 | 1,442 | 2,475 | 10,666.3 | 4,176.8 | 6,489.3 | 2,776 | 3,073 | 2,640 |
| 1995 | 4,719 | 2,120 | 2,598 | 3,971 | 1,469 | 2,502 | 10,926.5 | 4,173.3 | 6,753.2 | 2,854 | 3,138 | 2,725 |
| 1996 | (a) | (a) | (a) | (a) | (a) | (a) | (a) | (a) | (a) | (a) | (a) | (a) |
| 1997 (March) | 4,733 | 2,114 | 2,619 | 3,987 | 1,484 | 2,503 | 11,413.1 | 4,372.0 | 7,041.1 | 2,968 | 3,251 | 2,838 |
| 1998 (March) | 4,758 | 2,173 | 2,585 | 3,985 | 1,511 | 2,474 | 11,845.2 | 4,632.1 | 7,213.1 | 3,088 | 3,382 | 2,947 |
| 1999 (March) | 4,818 | 2,229 | 2,588 | 4,034 | 1,541 | 2,493 | 12,564.1 | 4,957.0 | 7,607.7 | 3,236 | 3,544 | 3,087 |
| 2000 (March) | 4,877 | 2,259 | 2,618 | 4,083 | 1,563 | 2,520 | 13,279.1 | 5,255.3 | 8,023.8 | 3,374 | 3,692 | 3,219 |
| 2001 (March) | 4,985 | 2,329 | 2,656 | 4,173 | 1,615 | 2,559 | 14,136.3 | 5,620.7 | 8,515.6 | 3,521 | 3,842 | 3,362 |
| 2002 (March) | 5,072 | 2,414 | 2,658 | 4,223 | 1,659 | 2,564 | 14,837.8 | 5,996.6 | 8,841.2 | 3,657 | 4,007 | 3,479 |
| 2003 (March) | 5,043 | 2,413 | 2,630 | 4,191 | 1,656 | 2,534 | 15,116.4 | 6,154.4 | 8,962.0 | 3,751 | 4,115 | 3,566 |
| 2004 (March) | 5,041 | 2,432 | 2,609 | 4,188 | 1,673 | 2,515 | 15,477.5 | 6,411.8 | 9,065.7 | 3,845 | 4,256 | 3,631 |
| 2005 (March) | 5,078 | 2,459 | 2,620 | 4,209 | 1,684 | 2,525 | 16,061.6 | 6,668.9 | 9,392.6 | 3,966 | 4,390 | 3,745 |
| 2006 (March) | 5,128 | 2,493 | 2,635 | 4,251 | 1,708 | 2,542 | 16,769.4 | 6,960.9 | 9,808.6 | 4,098 | 4,505 | 3,883 |
| 2007 (March) | 5,200 | 2,538 | 2,663 | 4,307 | 1,740 | 2,566 | 17,418.9 | 7,418.9 | 10,369.9 | 4,276 | 4,670 | 4,063 |
| 2008 (March) | 5,270 | 2,593 | 2,677 | 4,363 | 1,780 | 2,582 | 18,725.9 | 7,883.2 | 10,842.7 | 4,445 | 4,853 | 4,222 |
| 2009 (March) | 5,346 | 2,649 | 2,697 | 4,408 | 1,814 | 2,594 | 19,424.8 | 8,278.6 | 11,146.3 | 4,565 | 5,007 | 4,320 |
| 2010 (March) | 5,326 | 2,669 | 2,656 | 4,378 | 1,824 | 2,554 | 19,579.1 | 8,516.5 | 11,062.6 | 4,620 | 5,111 | 4,342 |

*Source:* U.S. Census Bureau, 1953–2010 Census of Governments. For information on sampling and nonsampling errors and definitions, see *http://www.census.gov/govs/apes/how_data_collected.html.* Data users who create their own estimates from this table should cite the U.S. Census Bureau as the source of the original data only.

*Note:* Detail may not add to totals due to rounding.

*Key:*
(a) Due to a change in the reference period, from October to March, the October 1996 Annual Survey of Government Employment and Payroll was not concluded. This change in collection period was effective beginning with the March 1997 survey.

## Table 8.2
## EMPLOYMENT AND PAYROLLS OF STATE AND LOCAL GOVERNMENTS BY FUNCTION: MARCH 2010

| Functions | All employees, full-time and part-time (in thousands) | | | March payrolls (in millions of dollars) | | | Average March earnings of full-time employees |
|---|---|---|---|---|---|---|---|
| | Total | State government | Local government | Total | State government | Local government | |
| All functions............................................ | 19,599 | 5,326 | 14,274 | 70,404,452 | 19,579,083 | 50,825,369 | 4,388 |
| Education: | | | | | | | |
| Higher education ................................. | 3,121 | 2,511 | 611 | 9,532,184 | 7,915,424 | 1,616,760 | 5,156 |
| Instructional personnel only.......... | 1,113 | 819 | 295 | 4,424,062 | 3,563,562 | 860,500 | 6,991 |
| Elementary/Secondary schools.......... | 7,917 | 64 | 7,853 | 26,601,268 | 226,761 | 26,374,507 | 4,019 |
| Instructional personnel only.......... | 5,355 | 45 | 5,311 | 20,968,824 | 182,281 | 20,786,543 | 4,509 |
| Libraries.............................................. | 189 | 1 | 188 | 432,268 | 1,604 | 430,664 | 3,697 |
| Other Education ................................. | 94 | 94 | 0 | 374,295 | 374,295 | 0 | 4,379 |
| | | | | | | | |
| Selected functions: | | | | | | | |
| Streets and Highways.......................... | 547 | 235 | 311 | 2,144,687 | 983,372 | 1,161,315 | 4,108 |
| Public Welfare .................................... | 535 | 241 | 294 | 1,934,703 | 875,357 | 1,059,347 | 3,835 |
| Hospitals.............................................. | 1,077 | 438 | 638 | 4,519,168 | 1,837,466 | 2,681,702 | 4,598 |
| Police protection................................. | 1,010 | 109 | 901 | 4,885,047 | 560,646 | 4,324,401 | 5,297 |
| Police Officers............................... | 728 | 69 | 659 | 3,968,811 | 409,612 | 3,559,198 | 5,709 |
| Fire protection.................................... | 421 | 0 | 421 | 1,946,790 | 0 | 1,946,790 | 5,852 |
| Firefighters only............................ | 388 | 0 | 388 | 1,815,861 | 0 | 1,815,861 | 5,920 |
| Natural Resources............................... | 204 | 155 | 49 | 743,109 | 575,972 | 167,136 | 4,229 |
| Correction............................................ | 743 | 477 | 267 | 2,997,222 | 1,914,624 | 1,082,598 | 4,105 |
| Social Insurance ................................. | 92 | 92 | 0 | 363,996 | 361,358 | 2,637 | 4,137 |
| Financial Admin. ................................ | 423 | 169 | 254 | 1,694,288 | 706,917 | 987,372 | 4,391 |
| Judicial and Legal .............................. | 450 | 181 | 269 | 2,051,389 | 901,239 | 1,150,151 | 4,865 |
| Other Government Admin. ................ | 419 | 59 | 359 | 1,213,841 | 245,287 | 968,554 | 4,468 |
| Utilities................................................ | 517 | 38 | 480 | 2,508,005 | 227,689 | 2,280,316 | 5,111 |
| State Liquor stores ................................. | 12 | 12 | 0 | 29,968 | 29,968 | 0 | 3,366 |
| Other and unallocable.......................... | 1,830 | 451 | 1,379 | 6,432,223 | 1,841,104 | 4,591,119 | 4,252 |

Source: U.S. Census Bureau, 2010 Annual Survey of Public Employment and Payroll. For information on sampling and nonsampling errors and definitions, see http://www.census.gov/govs/apes/how_data_collected.html.

Data users who create their own estimates from this table should cite the U.S. Census Bureau as the source of the original data only.
    Note: Detail may not add to total due to rounding.

## Table 8.3
## STATE AND LOCAL GOVERNMENT EMPLOYMENT, BY STATE: MARCH 2010

| State or other jurisdiction | All employees (full-time and part-time) | | | Full-time equivalent employment | | |
|---|---|---|---|---|---|---|
| | Total | State | Local | Total | State | Local |
| United States ..................... | 19,599,463 | 5,325,575 | 14,273,888 | 16,581,617 | 4,377,777 | 12,203,840 |
| Alabama............................. | 320,163 | 107,657 | 212,506 | 287,128 | 89,632 | 197,496 |
| Alaska................................. | 63,248 | 29,943 | 33,305 | 54,449 | 26,689 | 27,760 |
| Arizona............................... | 344,014 | 82,890 | 261,124 | 294,885 | 66,807 | 228,078 |
| Arkansas............................. | 198,363 | 72,401 | 125,962 | 175,661 | 63,484 | 112,177 |
| California ........................... | 2,164,724 | 490,791 | 1,673,933 | 1,785,534 | 410,653 | 1,374,881 |
| Colorado............................. | 339,696 | 96,875 | 242,821 | 273,277 | 71,064 | 202,213 |
| Connecticut........................ | 224,781 | 78,563 | 146,218 | 187,486 | 63,199 | 124,287 |
| Delaware ............................ | 57,031 | 31,194 | 25,837 | 49,238 | 26,022 | 23,216 |
| Florida................................ | 1,014,698 | 213,910 | 800,788 | 907,973 | 184,465 | 723,508 |
| Georgia............................... | 583,617 | 154,017 | 429,600 | 517,438 | 124,115 | 393,323 |
| Hawaii................................. | 89,569 | 73,634 | 15,935 | 73,200 | 58,121 | 15,079 |
| Idaho.................................. | 102,589 | 28,533 | 74,056 | 78,101 | 21,940 | 56,161 |
| Illinois................................ | 791,221 | 158,587 | 632,634 | 639,845 | 131,352 | 508,493 |
| Indiana................................ | 411,647 | 116,572 | 295,075 | 344,813 | 89,549 | 255,264 |
| Iowa ................................... | 231,664 | 66,631 | 165,033 | 178,662 | 51,328 | 127,334 |
| Kansas ................................ | 246,429 | 54,727 | 191,702 | 202,484 | 43,824 | 158,660 |
| Kentucky ............................ | 284,908 | 98,127 | 186,781 | 242,473 | 80,714 | 161,759 |
| Louisiana............................ | 316,159 | 104,325 | 211,834 | 277,376 | 88,720 | 188,656 |
| Maine.................................. | 95,898 | 28,077 | 67,821 | 72,424 | 21,130 | 51,294 |
| Maryland ............................ | 343,184 | 93,930 | 249,254 | 302,531 | 88,318 | 214,213 |
| Massachusetts ..................... | 384,039 | 116,404 | 267,635 | 329,246 | 95,354 | 233,892 |
| Michigan............................. | 590,868 | 186,890 | 403,978 | 476,915 | 145,606 | 331,309 |
| Minnesota........................... | 352,903 | 98,437 | 254,466 | 279,290 | 79,941 | 199,349 |
| Mississippi.......................... | 214,073 | 64,226 | 149,847 | 192,991 | 56,858 | 136,133 |
| Missouri.............................. | 384,529 | 104,263 | 280,266 | 324,533 | 88,818 | 235,715 |
| Montana ............................. | 73,116 | 26,219 | 46,897 | 58,430 | 20,375 | 38,055 |
| Nebraska ............................ | 145,606 | 37,717 | 107,889 | 121,394 | 32,560 | 88,834 |
| Nevada................................ | 133,543 | 35,105 | 98,438 | 114,144 | 28,345 | 85,799 |
| New Hampshire ................... | 88,634 | 26,111 | 62,523 | 72,990 | 19,470 | 53,520 |
| New Jersey .......................... | 598,457 | 176,993 | 421,464 | 510,786 | 152,003 | 358,783 |
| New Mexico ........................ | 146,792 | 56,530 | 90,262 | 128,475 | 48,160 | 80,315 |
| New York............................ | 1,399,811 | 287,708 | 1,112,103 | 1,224,337 | 251,150 | 973,187 |
| North Carolina.................... | 646,533 | 174,022 | 472,511 | 549,207 | 146,409 | 402,798 |
| North Dakota...................... | 60,301 | 24,658 | 35,643 | 44,588 | 18,139 | 26,449 |
| Ohio ................................... | 733,646 | 187,678 | 545,968 | 607,305 | 139,907 | 467,398 |
| Oklahoma........................... | 250,608 | 88,750 | 161,858 | 216,870 | 70,501 | 146,369 |
| Oregon................................ | 248,318 | 83,083 | 165,235 | 198,374 | 65,369 | 133,005 |
| Pennsylvania ...................... | 719,343 | 208,973 | 510,370 | 599,674 | 168,268 | 431,406 |
| Rhode Island....................... | 58,012 | 23,422 | 34,590 | 49,490 | 18,694 | 30,796 |
| South Carolina.................... | 284,462 | 89,741 | 194,721 | 251,990 | 77,071 | 174,919 |
| South Dakota...................... | 61,680 | 18,771 | 42,909 | 46,232 | 14,310 | 31,922 |
| Tennessee ........................... | 371,970 | 99,984 | 271,986 | 328,925 | 82,871 | 246,054 |
| Texas.................................. | 1,635,413 | 364,638 | 1,270,775 | 1,452,324 | 317,912 | 1,134,412 |
| Utah ................................... | 186,798 | 65,293 | 121,505 | 141,356 | 51,291 | 90,065 |
| Vermont.............................. | 49,785 | 16,644 | 33,141 | 40,490 | 14,408 | 26,082 |
| Virginia............................... | 520,087 | 157,827 | 362,260 | 443,079 | 124,709 | 318,370 |
| Washington......................... | 428,063 | 155,147 | 272,916 | 350,449 | 122,772 | 227,677 |
| West Virginia....................... | 117,323 | 47,613 | 69,710 | 101,724 | 39,375 | 62,349 |
| Wisconsin ........................... | 384,869 | 105,621 | 279,248 | 286,316 | 72,428 | 213,888 |
| Wyoming ............................ | 61,091 | 15,723 | 45,368 | 50,813 | 13,577 | 37,236 |
| District of Columbia............ | 45,187 | 0 | 45,187 | 43,902 | 0 | 43,902 |

*Source:* U.S. Census Bureau, 2010 Annual Survey of Public Employment and Payroll. For information on sampling and nonsampling errors and definitions, see http://www.census.gov/govs/apes/how_data_collected.html.

Data users who create their own estimates from this table should cite the U.S. Census Bureau as the source of the original data only.

*Note:* Statistics for local governments are estimates subject to sampling variation.

## Table 8.4
## STATE AND LOCAL GOVERNMENT PAYROLLS AND AVERAGE EARNINGS
## OF FULL-TIME EMPLOYEES, BY STATE: MARCH 2010

| State or other jurisdiction | Amount of payroll (in thousands of dollars) | | | Percentage of March payroll | | Average earnings of full-time state and local government employees (dollars) | | |
|---|---|---|---|---|---|---|---|---|
| | Total | State government | Local governments | State government | Local government | All | Education employees | Other |
| United States ....... | $70,404,452 | $19,579,083 | $50,825,369 | 28% | 72% | $4,388 | $4,243 | $4,546 |
| Alabama.............. | 991,486 | 357,087 | 634,399 | 36% | 64% | 3,497 | 3,461 | 3,534 |
| Alaska.................. | 267,655 | 134,205 | 133,450 | 50% | 50% | 5,077 | 4,783 | 5,328 |
| Arizona............... | 1,182,750 | 277,539 | 905,212 | 23% | 77% | 4,163 | 3,780 | 4,600 |
| Arkansas............. | 564,781 | 232,717 | 332,064 | 41% | 59% | 3,290 | 3,403 | 3,143 |
| California ........... | 9,766,915 | 2,247,814 | 7,519,101 | 23% | 77% | 5,774 | 5,453 | 6,043 |
| Colorado.............. | 1,169,714 | 347,659 | 822,055 | 30% | 70% | 4,321 | 4,121 | 4,724 |
| Connecticut......... | 944,643 | 341,537 | 603,105 | 36% | 64% | 5,253 | 5,105 | 5,448 |
| Delaware ............ | 202,396 | 105,247 | 97,149 | 52% | 48% | 4,287 | 4,830 | 3,861 |
| Florida ............... | 3,491,351 | 705,846 | 2,785,505 | 20% | 80% | 3,965 | 3,540 | 4,339 |
| Georgia................ | 1,795,002 | 460,261 | 1,334,741 | 26% | 74% | 3,520 | 3,655 | 3,340 |
| Hawaii................. | 304,525 | 229,207 | 75,318 | 75% | 25% | 4,181 | 3,864 | 4,481 |
| Idaho................... | 271,395 | 88,917 | 182,479 | 33% | 67% | 3,625 | 3,357 | 3,920 |
| Illinois................. | 2,942,253 | 646,734 | 2,295,519 | 22% | 78% | 4,806 | 4,578 | 5,092 |
| Indiana................ | 1,217,636 | 338,133 | 878,133 | 28% | 72% | 3,667 | 3,714 | 3,601 |
| Iowa .................... | 719,139 | 255,180 | 463,959 | 35% | 65% | 4,255 | 4,126 | 4,418 |
| Kansas ................ | 695,095 | 177,786 | 517,309 | 26% | 74% | 3,541 | 3,483 | 3,623 |
| Kentucky ............ | 802,449 | 309,681 | 492,767 | 39% | 61% | 3,370 | 3,279 | 3,513 |
| Louisiana............. | 990,737 | 368,080 | 622,657 | 37% | 63% | 3,672 | 3,573 | 3,766 |
| Maine.................. | 259,153 | 84,683 | 174,470 | 33% | 67% | 3,691 | 3,558 | 3,896 |
| Maryland ............ | 1,484,423 | 410,955 | 1,073,468 | 28% | 72% | 5,030 | 5,326 | 4,705 |
| Massachusetts ...... | 1,554,116 | 466,624 | 1,087,492 | 30% | 70% | 4,865 | 4,699 | 5,054 |
| Michigan............. | 2,128,503 | 704,751 | 1,423,751 | 33% | 67% | 4,800 | 4,910 | 4,649 |
| Minnesota............ | 1,237,917 | 404,158 | 833,759 | 33% | 67% | 4,702 | 4,631 | 4,788 |
| Mississippi .......... | 602,328 | 195,955 | 406,373 | 33% | 67% | 3,147 | 3,138 | 3,157 |
| Missouri............... | 1,113,759 | 302,459 | 811,300 | 27% | 73% | 3,524 | 3,562 | 3,481 |
| Montana ............. | 203,656 | 77,974 | 125,683 | 38% | 62% | 3,677 | 3,582 | 3,777 |
| Nebraska ............ | 446,045 | 120,579 | 325,466 | 27% | 73% | 3,856 | 3,680 | 4,048 |
| Nevada................ | 557,819 | 135,776 | 422,042 | 24% | 76% | 5,084 | 4,513 | 5,555 |
| New Hampshire ... | 280,123 | 84,226 | 195,896 | 30% | 70% | 4,011 | 3,827 | 4,279 |
| New Jersey .......... | 2,730,092 | 844,503 | 1,885,589 | 31% | 69% | 5,540 | 5,639 | 5,424 |
| New Mexico ......... | 455,676 | 184,145 | 271,532 | 40% | 60% | 3,644 | 3,582 | 3,714 |
| New York............. | 6,363,026 | 1,360,116 | 5,002,910 | 21% | 79% | 5,354 | 5,184 | 5,492 |
| North Carolina..... | 2,010,446 | 556,942 | 1,453,503 | 28% | 72% | 3,739 | 3,554 | 3,936 |
| North Dakota....... | 163,846 | 70,985 | 92,861 | 43% | 57% | 3,772 | 3,918 | 3,583 |
| Ohio ................... | 2,494,714 | 651,902 | 1,842,812 | 26% | 74% | 4,302 | 4,336 | 4,265 |
| Oklahoma............ | 714,989 | 265,474 | 449,515 | 37% | 63% | 3,351 | 3,264 | 3,364 |
| Oregon................ | 848,998 | 289,734 | 559,264 | 34% | 66% | 4,408 | 4,251 | 4,550 |
| Pennsylvania ....... | 2,524,003 | 760,014 | 1,763,989 | 30% | 70% | 4,364 | 4,528 | 4,172 |
| Rhode Island........ | 243,560 | 95,959 | 147,600 | 39% | 61% | 5,085 | 5,192 | 4,973 |
| South Carolina..... | 886,991 | 286,281 | 600,710 | 32% | 68% | 3,576 | 3,674 | 3,469 |
| South Dakota....... | 150,224 | 54,379 | 95,845 | 36% | 64% | 3,396 | 3,284 | 3,534 |
| Tennessee ............ | 1,119,779 | 307,540 | 812,239 | 27% | 73% | 3,472 | 3,318 | 3,629 |
| Texas................... | 5,344,915 | 1,328,253 | 4,016,662 | 25% | 75% | 3,746 | 3,651 | 3,885 |
| Utah.................... | 526,993 | 215,405 | 311,589 | 41% | 59% | 3,962 | 3,992 | 3,929 |
| Vermont............... | 156,038 | 66,246 | 89,793 | 42% | 58% | 3,983 | 3,802 | 4,290 |
| Virginia............... | 1,744,005 | 530,599 | 1,213,407 | 30% | 70% | 4,037 | 3,988 | 4,103 |
| Washington.......... | 1,754,719 | 577,896 | 1,176,823 | 33% | 67% | 5,297 | 5,243 | 5,332 |
| West Virginia........ | 335,962 | 137,746 | 198,215 | 41% | 59% | 3,354 | 3,642 | 2,998 |
| Wisconsin ........... | 1,188,772 | 326,643 | 862,129 | 27% | 73% | 4,394 | 4,439 | 4,336 |
| Wyoming ............. | 202,442 | 55,549 | 146,893 | 27% | 73% | 4,171 | 4,223 | 4,125 |
| Dist. of Columbia.. | 256,499 | 0 | 256,499 | 0% | 100% | 5,900 | 5,358 | 6,028 |

*Source:* U.S. Census Bureau, 2010 Annual Survey of Public Employment and Payroll. For information on sampling and nonsampling errors and definitions, see *http://www.census.gov/govs/apes/how_data_collected.html.*

Data users who create their own estimates from this table should cite the U.S. Census Bureau as the source of the original data only.
*Note:* Statistics for local governments are estimates subject to sampling variation.

## Table 8.5
## STATE GOVERNMENT EMPLOYMENT (FULL-TIME EQUIVALENT) FOR SELECTED FUNCTIONS, BY STATE: 2010

| | | Selected functions | | | | | | | | | | |
|---|---|---|---|---|---|---|---|---|---|---|---|---|
| | | Education | | | | | | | | | Financial and other | Judicial |
| State | All functions | Higher education (a) | Other education (b) | Highways | Public welfare | Hospitals | Corrections | Police protection | Natural resources | governmental administration | and legal administration |
| United States ....... | 4,377,777 | 1,685,920 | 138,122 | 230,370 | 235,934 | 409,195 | 472,306 | 106,864 | 140,242 | 218,126 | 176,496 |
| Alabama .............. | 89,632 | 38,385 | 2,969 | 4,649 | 4,342 | 12,070 | 5,487 | 1,641 | 2,220 | 3,089 | 3,534 |
| Alaska.................. | 26,689 | 5,467 | 3,418 | 3,089 | 1,897 | 247 | 1,942 | 676 | 2,387 | 1,917 | 1,441 |
| Arizona................ | 66,807 | 28,597 | 3,024 | 2,673 | 4,625 | 667 | 9,702 | 2,048 | 2,063 | 3,733 | 1,958 |
| Arkansas.............. | 63,484 | 25,783 | 1,455 | 3,416 | 4,120 | 6,762 | 5,191 | 1,211 | 2,032 | 2,772 | 1,598 |
| California ............ | 410,653 | 158,064 | 4,360 | 21,061 | 4,025 | 41,653 | 61,710 | 11,924 | 15,134 | 27,907 | 6,677 |
| Colorado.............. | 71,064 | 37,409 | 1,297 | 3,093 | 2,268 | 5,241 | 7,345 | 1,507 | 1,718 | 2,512 | 4,140 |
| Connecticut .......... | 63,199 | 18,696 | 2,397 | 2,950 | 5,789 | 6,756 | 7,220 | 1,868 | 740 | 3,933 | 4,820 |
| Delaware ............. | 26,022 | 8,029 | 338 | 1,556 | 1,552 | 1,712 | 2,876 | 999 | 500 | 1,218 | 1,715 |
| Florida ............... | 184,465 | 54,145 | 3,092 | 7,648 | 10,043 | 3,852 | 30,712 | 4,372 | 9,767 | 8,861 | 19,970 |
| Georgia................ | 124,115 | 53,623 | 3,097 | 5,585 | 8,500 | 7,376 | 19,234 | 2,041 | 4,211 | 4,496 | 3,631 |
| Hawaii................. | 58,121 | 9,692 | 27,519 | 854 | 489 | 4,297 | 2,377 | 0 | 1,094 | 1,476 | 2,454 |
| Idaho................... | 21,940 | 8,328 | 417 | 1,637 | 1,655 | 717 | 1,940 | 438 | 1,830 | 1,520 | 495 |
| Illinois................ | 131,352 | 62,054 | 2,052 | 6,818 | 9,311 | 11,127 | 11,128 | 3,679 | 3,501 | 7,297 | 2,634 |
| Indiana................ | 89,549 | 56,645 | 1,101 | 4,007 | 4,704 | 2,451 | 6,796 | 1,957 | 2,309 | 2,814 | 1,399 |
| Iowa ................... | 51,328 | 22,874 | 1,191 | 2,405 | 3,063 | 7,901 | 3,214 | 1,001 | 1,647 | 1,625 | 2,188 |
| Kansas ................ | 43,824 | 19,549 | 648 | 3,225 | 2,240 | 3,071 | 3,406 | 1,110 | 808 | 2,611 | 2,082 |
| Kentucky ............. | 80,714 | 37,208 | 1,993 | 4,534 | 5,745 | 5,001 | 4,138 | 2,271 | 2,970 | 3,106 | 5,235 |
| Louisiana ............ | 88,720 | 29,764 | 5,208 | 4,786 | 5,855 | 14,667 | 7,006 | 1,711 | 4,445 | 4,850 | 1,650 |
| Maine.................. | 21,130 | 7,298 | 230 | 2,191 | 3,024 | 461 | 1,176 | 587 | 966 | 1,511 | 668 |
| Maryland ............. | 88,318 | 27,102 | 2,048 | 4,710 | 6,578 | 4,313 | 12,597 | 2,380 | 2,090 | 5,068 | 5,127 |
| Massachusetts ...... | 95,354 | 31,206 | 1,184 | 3,550 | 7,004 | 6,545 | 6,179 | 6,266 | 1,259 | 5,656 | 9,307 |
| Michigan.............. | 145,606 | 74,299 | 555 | 2,916 | 10,795 | 18,756 | 15,133 | 2,606 | 3,959 | 5,764 | 1,432 |
| Minnesota............ | 79,941 | 36,830 | 3,962 | 4,763 | 2,936 | 4,886 | 4,204 | 1,000 | 3,096 | 3,918 | 3,359 |
| Mississippi ........... | 56,858 | 18,807 | 1,602 | 3,416 | 2,991 | 11,661 | 3,340 | 1,195 | 3,150 | 1,843 | 721 |
| Missouri............... | 88,818 | 28,475 | 1,743 | 6,118 | 7,604 | 11,067 | 12,475 | 2,435 | 2,500 | 4,045 | 4,021 |
| Montana .............. | 20,375 | 7,201 | 385 | 2,103 | 1,644 | 610 | 1,337 | 489 | 1,517 | 1,396 | 682 |
| Nebraska ............. | 32,560 | 12,533 | 638 | 2,142 | 2,516 | 3,949 | 2,906 | 777 | 2,143 | 1,059 | 753 |
| Nevada ................ | 28,345 | 10,128 | 134 | 1,807 | 1,682 | 1,434 | 3,670 | 841 | 979 | 2,344 | 734 |
| New Hampshire ... | 19,470 | 6,833 | 324 | 1,886 | 1,500 | 729 | 1,178 | 505 | 388 | 1,183 | 961 |
| New Jersey .......... | 152,003 | 33,838 | 21,734 | 6,277 | 8,992 | 18,486 | 9,482 | 4,345 | 2,022 | 6,788 | 13,601 |
| New Mexico ......... | 48,160 | 19,073 | 1,037 | 2,276 | 1,823 | 7,567 | 4,033 | 734 | 1,099 | 1,428 | 3,245 |
| New York............. | 251,150 | 52,997 | 4,363 | 12,130 | 4,892 | 43,935 | 31,840 | 6,489 | 3,346 | 17,395 | 21,661 |
| North Carolina..... | 146,409 | 59,122 | 2,258 | 10,911 | 1,211 | 19,469 | 21,175 | 3,470 | 4,605 | 4,722 | 7,080 |
| North Dakota....... | 18,139 | 8,849 | 284 | 1,012 | 531 | 921 | 756 | 190 | 793 | 879 | 563 |
| Ohio .................... | 139,907 | 69,657 | 2,336 | 6,905 | 2,741 | 15,159 | 15,470 | 2,561 | 2,775 | 8,212 | 2,921 |
| Oklahoma............. | 70,501 | 30,339 | 1,973 | 3,002 | 6,882 | 2,612 | 5,351 | 1,976 | 1,954 | 2,414 | 2,911 |
| Oregon................. | 65,369 | 22,966 | 716 | 3,890 | 8,164 | 5,455 | 5,503 | 1,404 | 2,574 | 5,213 | 3,195 |
| Pennsylvania ........ | 168,268 | 58,960 | 4,130 | 14,793 | 11,964 | 11,694 | 18,867 | 6,629 | 6,651 | 11,242 | 3,072 |
| Rhode Island........ | 18,694 | 5,599 | 1,050 | 747 | 1,221 | 737 | 1,585 | 313 | 424 | 1,418 | 1,152 |
| South Carolina..... | 77,071 | 29,334 | 3,098 | 4,855 | 4,323 | 6,970 | 7,444 | 1,936 | 2,144 | 4,400 | 768 |
| South Dakota....... | 14,310 | 5,225 | 382 | 1,002 | 1,082 | 970 | 884 | 304 | 1,070 | 798 | 630 |
| Tennessee ............. | 82,871 | 33,722 | 2,210 | 4,204 | 8,057 | 5,242 | 6,988 | 1,640 | 3,911 | 4,242 | 2,473 |
| Texas................... | 317,912 | 126,190 | 4,970 | 14,225 | 23,032 | 31,411 | 44,785 | 6,553 | 11,059 | 9,395 | 5,729 |
| Utah.................... | 51,291 | 24,294 | 1,143 | 1,612 | 2,894 | 6,941 | 3,084 | 771 | 1,328 | 2,792 | 1,597 |
| Vermont............... | 14,408 | 5,099 | 528 | 1,013 | 1,305 | 298 | 1,050 | 710 | 558 | 1,200 | 663 |
| Virginia................ | 124,709 | 54,586 | 2,910 | 7,610 | 2,824 | 14,757 | 13,941 | 2,936 | 2,199 | 5,066 | 3,643 |
| Washington........... | 122,772 | 55,470 | 2,041 | 5,926 | 9,454 | 10,668 | 9,585 | 2,157 | 5,063 | 4,526 | 1,995 |
| West Virginia........ | 39,375 | 13,335 | 1,305 | 5,101 | 3,325 | 1,840 | 3,339 | 1,015 | 1,958 | 2,302 | 1,492 |
| Wisconsin ............ | 72,428 | 38,292 | 1,032 | 1,408 | 1,937 | 3,349 | 10,172 | 896 | 2,277 | 3,452 | 2,160 |
| Wyoming .............. | 13,577 | 3,949 | 241 | 1,853 | 783 | 735 | 1,353 | 300 | 1,009 | 718 | 559 |

*Source:* U.S. Census Bureau, 2010 Annual Survey of Public Employment and Payroll. For information on sampling and nonsampling errors and definitions, see http://www.census.gov/govs/apes/how_data_collected.html. Data users who create their own estimates from this table should cite the U.S. Census Bureau as the source of the original data only.

*Key:*
(a) Includes instructional and other personnel.
(b) Includes instructional and other personnel in elementary and secondary schools.

## Table 8.6
## STATE GOVERNMENT PAYROLLS FOR SELECTED FUNCTIONS, BY STATE: MARCH 2010
(In thousands of dollars)

| State | All functions | Education | | Highways | Public welfare | Hospitals | Corrections | Police protection | Natural resources | Financial and other governmental administration | Judicial and legal administration |
|---|---|---|---|---|---|---|---|---|---|---|---|
| | | Higher education (a) | Other education (b) | | Selected functions | | | | | | |
| United States ...... | $19,579,083 | $7,915,424 | $601,056 | $983,372 | $875,357 | $1,837,466 | $1,914,624 | $560,646 | $575,972 | $952,204 | $901,239 |
| Alabama.............. | 357,087 | 165,996 | 11,161 | 13,720 | 15,168 | 48,773 | 17,716 | 6,277 | 8,615 | 13,782 | 15,004 |
| Alaska................ | 134,205 | 28,527 | 14,003 | 16,842 | 7,886 | 1,310 | 9,201 | 3,928 | 12,135 | 10,002 | 8,165 |
| Arizona.............. | 277,539 | 131,632 | 9,902 | 11,120 | 14,705 | 2,664 | 36,276 | 10,557 | 8,073 | 14,756 | 9,087 |
| Arkansas............ | 232,717 | 104,393 | 5,188 | 12,431 | 12,867 | 24,183 | 15,741 | 4,461 | 6,893 | 10,280 | 5,540 |
| California .......... | 2,247,814 | 854,221 | 19,831 | 130,550 | 15,474 | 274,109 | 362,135 | 78,388 | 71,368 | 120,804 | 41,849 |
| Colorado............ | 347,659 | 190,496 | 6,296 | 14,554 | 10,424 | 21,339 | 31,340 | 8,091 | 9,176 | 11,749 | 21,175 |
| Connecticut........ | 341,537 | 99,222 | 13,478 | 16,750 | 31,497 | 40,049 | 36,292 | 10,745 | 3,803 | 20,686 | 23,626 |
| Delaware ............ | 105,247 | 37,225 | 1,822 | 4,909 | 5,172 | 5,625 | 10,557 | 5,736 | 1,846 | 4,457 | 7,514 |
| Florida............... | 705,846 | 266,009 | 10,192 | 31,083 | 29,955 | 11,679 | 93,674 | 17,030 | 31,488 | 31,821 | 78,831 |
| Georgia............... | 460,261 | 242,288 | 12,563 | 16,805 | 25,400 | 18,232 | 47,885 | 7,725 | 12,826 | 17,856 | 15,692 |
| Hawaii................. | 229,207 | 48,911 | 94,885 | 3,487 | 1,801 | 19,580 | 9,514 | 0 | 4,706 | 5,430 | 10,221 |
| Idaho.................. | 88,917 | 33,231 | 1,997 | 5,180 | 5,343 | 2,145 | 7,910 | 1,685 | 8,085 | 6,724 | 3,685 |
| Illinois............... | 646,734 | 272,194 | 10,240 | 37,973 | 48,732 | 55,504 | 61,005 | 24,463 | 14,343 | 36,487 | 22,294 |
| Indiana.............. | 339,133 | 222,240 | 4,082 | 12,858 | 15,356 | 7,693 | 20,644 | 8,040 | 8,177 | 11,741 | 9,228 |
| Iowa ................... | 255,180 | 117,057 | 5,795 | 10,676 | 13,175 | 41,927 | 14,083 | 6,317 | 8,049 | 7,667 | 10,445 |
| Kansas................ | 177,786 | 91,042 | 2,640 | 11,579 | 7,095 | 9,702 | 10,351 | 4,776 | 3,147 | 9,584 | 8,842 |
| Kentucky ............ | 309,681 | 157,501 | 8,166 | 14,907 | 18,077 | 21,009 | 11,222 | 8,993 | 9,305 | 12,752 | 18,547 |
| Louisiana............ | 368,080 | 130,304 | 21,992 | 18,922 | 21,397 | 56,767 | 27,140 | 9,151 | 18,087 | 20,680 | 7,227 |
| Maine.................. | 84,683 | 29,513 | 895 | 7,859 | 10,267 | 2,036 | 5,013 | 2,708 | 4,273 | 6,477 | 3,107 |
| Maryland............ | 410,955 | 143,388 | 9,297 | 20,531 | 25,737 | 17,649 | 51,227 | 12,194 | 10,113 | 23,445 | 26,928 |
| Massachusetts ..... | 466,624 | 145,938 | 6,568 | 18,246 | 34,701 | 27,742 | 30,765 | 34,111 | 6,803 | 27,607 | 47,471 |
| Michigan............ | 704,751 | 355,940 | 2,851 | 13,956 | 48,405 | 86,810 | 82,480 | 11,637 | 18,018 | 29,246 | 9,861 |
| Minnesota........... | 404,158 | 200,635 | 22,035 | 22,348 | 11,092 | 21,300 | 18,105 | 4,811 | 14,359 | 18,791 | 17,742 |
| Mississippi .......... | 195,955 | 77,675 | 5,086 | 9,832 | 9,669 | 34,708 | 8,907 | 3,893 | 9,421 | 6,729 | 4,213 |
| Missouri.............. | 302,459 | 116,477 | 5,599 | 21,520 | 19,723 | 33,832 | 32,488 | 9,773 | 7,944 | 14,103 | 14,755 |
| Montana ............. | 77,974 | 26,667 | 1,511 | 9,027 | 5,699 | 2,017 | 5,369 | 1,356 | 5,846 | 5,454 | 2,965 |
| Nebraska ............ | 120,579 | 48,931 | 2,388 | 7,936 | 7,428 | 14,166 | 9,357 | 3,440 | 7,221 | 4,025 | 3,589 |
| Nevada............... | 135,776 | 52,556 | 669 | 8,132 | 6,206 | 6,923 | 16,765 | 4,384 | 4,516 | 10,307 | 4,758 |
| New Hampshire .. | 84,226 | 32,774 | 1,367 | 6,865 | 5,810 | 3,004 | 4,962 | 2,580 | 1,748 | 5,188 | 4,079 |
| New Jersey ......... | 844,503 | 209,345 | 124,922 | 35,095 | 44,192 | 77,382 | 54,837 | 30,157 | 11,132 | 32,428 | 78,019 |
| New Mexico ........ | 184,145 | 70,108 | 4,151 | 8,282 | 6,253 | 30,049 | 13,769 | 4,390 | 4,675 | 6,181 | 13,778 |
| New York ........... | 1,360,116 | 275,658 | 21,911 | 49,813 | 23,134 | 216,638 | 166,865 | 48,837 | 17,584 | 82,407 | 136,943 |
| North Carolina.... | 556,942 | 229,675 | 9,118 | 36,348 | 4,312 | 78,406 | 64,886 | 18,318 | 16,294 | 20,699 | 32,127 |
| North Dakota...... | 70,985 | 36,916 | 1,019 | 4,118 | 1,616 | 2,672 | 2,602 | 869 | 2,785 | 3,288 | 2,598 |
| Ohio ................... | 651,902 | 317,237 | 11,554 | 30,960 | 14,765 | 71,927 | 66,691 | 12,625 | 11,501 | 41,294 | 17,189 |
| Oklahoma........... | 265,474 | 125,399 | 7,345 | 10,114 | 20,444 | 8,017 | 17,021 | 8,381 | 6,678 | 9,019 | 12,806 |
| Oregon............... | 289,734 | 115,239 | 2,949 | 16,903 | 27,821 | 24,668 | 22,542 | 6,894 | 10,001 | 21,426 | 14,190 |
| Pennsylvania ....... | 760,014 | 302,222 | 17,382 | 55,167 | 46,027 | 40,664 | 80,517 | 36,998 | 29,041 | 47,326 | 22,033 |
| Rhode Island....... | 95,959 | 27,033 | 5,098 | 3,525 | 6,174 | 4,031 | 8,855 | 2,112 | 2,269 | 7,123 | 6,408 |
| South Carolina.... | 286,281 | 130,080 | 11,130 | 15,004 | 11,979 | 20,769 | 21,069 | 6,885 | 6,536 | 14,698 | 3,751 |
| South Dakota....... | 54,379 | 20,817 | 1,388 | 3,791 | 3,586 | 3,103 | 2,794 | 1,102 | 4,199 | 3,350 | 2,740 |
| Tennessee ........... | 307,540 | 128,584 | 7,832 | 13,193 | 25,106 | 24,454 | 19,989 | 6,987 | 14,226 | 17,030 | 12,624 |
| Texas.................. | 1,328,253 | 604,515 | 22,135 | 56,896 | 70,983 | 155,022 | 127,609 | 26,362 | 49,648 | 40,756 | 28,816 |
| Utah................... | 215,405 | 110,851 | 4,752 | 6,841 | 10,128 | 26,297 | 10,828 | 3,287 | 5,006 | 12,516 | 7,137 |
| Vermont.............. | 66,246 | 24,858 | 2,347 | 4,232 | 5,540 | 1,286 | 4,481 | 4,523 | 2,747 | 4,743 | 2,824 |
| Virginia.............. | 530,599 | 259,426 | 12,665 | 31,914 | 10,747 | 56,982 | 43,090 | 13,274 | 9,549 | 20,882 | 17,219 |
| Washington......... | 577,896 | 258,778 | 9,563 | 31,383 | 38,689 | 61,542 | 41,417 | 11,640 | 21,598 | 21,887 | 11,101 |
| West Virginia....... | 137,746 | 57,229 | 5,170 | 15,240 | 8,586 | 4,807 | 8,902 | 4,078 | 6,474 | 7,262 | 6,339 |
| Wisconsin ........... | 326,643 | 172,526 | 4,943 | 7,104 | 7,887 | 13,812 | 42,943 | 4,309 | 9,408 | 15,745 | 13,257 |
| Wyoming ............ | 55,549 | 15,945 | 1,186 | 7,579 | 3,127 | 2,464 | 4,795 | 1,367 | 4,238 | 3,511 | 2,901 |

*Source:* U.S. Census Bureau, 2010 Annual Survey of Public Employment and Payroll. For information on sampling and nonsampling errors and definitions, see *http://www.census.gov/govs/apes/how_data_collected.html.* Data users who create their own estimates from this table should cite the U.S. Census Bureau as the source of the original data only.

*Key:*
(a) Includes instructional and other personnel.
(b) Includes instructional and other personnel in elementary and secondary schools.

## Table 8.7
## STATE EMPLOYEES: PAID HOLIDAYS**

| State or other jurisdiction | Major holidays (a) | Martin Luther King's Birthday (b) | Lincoln's Birthday | President's Day (c) | Washington's Birthday (c) | Good Friday | Memorial Day (d) | Columbus Day (e) | Veteran's Day | Day after Thanksgiving | Day before or after Christmas | Day before or after New Year's | Election Day (f) | Other (g) |
|---|---|---|---|---|---|---|---|---|---|---|---|---|---|---|
| Alabama | ★ | ★(h) | ... | ... | ★(i) | ... | ★ | ★ | ★ | (k) | (k) | ... | ... | ★ |
| Alaska | ★ | ★ | ... | ★ | ... | ... | ★ | ... | ★ | ... | ... | ... | ... | ★ |
| Arizona | ★ | ★ | ... | ★ | ... | ... | ★ | ★ | ★ | ... | ... | ... | ... | ... |
| Arkansas | ★ | ★(h) | ... | ... | ★(i) | ... | ★ | ... | ★ | (k) | Before | ... | ... | ★ |
| California | ★ | ★ | ... | ★ | ... | ... | ★ | ... | ★ | ★ | ... | ... | ... | ★ |
| Colorado | ★ | ★ | ... | ★ | ... | ... | ★ | ★ | ★ | ... | ... | ... | ... | ★ |
| Connecticut | ★ | ★ | ★ | ... | ★ | ★ | ★ | ★ | ★ | ... | ... | ... | ... | ... |
| Delaware | ★ | ★ | ... | ★ | ... | ★ | ★ | ★ | ★ | ★ | ... | ... | ★ | ... |
| Florida | ★ | ★ | ... | ... | ... | ... | ★ | ... | ★ | ★ | ... | ... | ... | ★ |
| Georgia | ★ | ★ | ... | ... | (l) | ... | ★ | ★ | ★ | (l) | (l) | ... | ... | ★ |
| Hawaii | ★ | ★ | ... | ★ | ... | ★ | ★ | ... | ★ | ... | ... | ... | ★ | ★ |
| Idaho | ★ | ★ | ... | ★ | ... | ... | ★ | ★ | ★ | ... | ... | ... | ... | ... |
| Illinois | ★ | ★ | ★ | ... | ★ | ... | ★ | ★ | ★ | ★ | ... | ... | ★ | ... |
| Indiana | ★ | ★ | (m) | ... | (m) | ★ | ★ | ★ | ★ | (m) | (m) | ... | ★ | ... |
| Iowa | ★ | ★ | ... | ... | ... | ... | ★ | ... | ★ | ★ | ... | ... | ... | ★ |
| Kansas | ★ | ★ | ... | ... | ... | ... | ★ | ... | ★ | ★ | ... | ... | ... | ★ |
| Kentucky | ★ | ★ | ... | ... | ... | ★(n) | ★ | ... | ★ | ★ | ★ | ★ | ★(t) | ... |
| Louisiana | ★ | ★ | ... | ... | ... | ★ | ★ | ... | ★ | ... | ... | ... | ★(u) | ★ |
| Maine | ★ | ★ | ... | ★ | ... | ... | ★ | ★ | ★ | ★ | ... | ... | ... | ★ |
| Maryland | ★ | ★ | ... | ★ | ... | ... | ★ | ★ | ★ | ★(aa) | ... | ... | ★ | ★ |
| Massachusetts | ★ | ★ | ... | ... | ★ | ... | ★ | ★ | ★ | ... | ... | ... | ... | ★ |
| Michigan | ★ | ★ | ... | ★ | ... | ... | ★ | ... | ★ | ★ | ★ | ★ | ★(z) | ... |
| Minnesota | ★ | ★ | ... | ★ | ... | ... | ★ | ... | ★ | ★ | ... | ... | ... | ★ |
| Mississippi | ★ | ★(h) | ... | ... | ★ | ... | ★(v) | ... | ★ | (k) | (k) | ... | ... | ★ |
| Missouri | ★ | ★ | ★ | ... | ★ | ... | ★ | ★ | ★ | (k) | ... | ... | ... | ★ |
| Montana | ★ | ★ | ... | ★ | ... | ... | ★ | ★ | ★ | ... | ... | ... | ★ | ... |
| Nebraska | ★ | ★ | ... | ★ | ... | ... | ★ | ★ | ★ | ... | ... | ... | ... | ★ |
| Nevada | ★ | ★ | ... | ★ | ... | ... | ★ | ... | ★ | ★ | ... | ... | ... | ★ |
| New Hampshire | ★ | ★ | ... | ★ | ... | ... | ★ | ... | ★ | ★ | ... | ... | ★ | ... |
| New Jersey | ★ | ★ | ... | ★ | ... | ★ | ★ | ★ | ★ | (k) | ... | ... | ★ | ... |
| New Mexico | ★ | ★ | (o) | ... | ... | ... | ★ | ... | ★ | (o) | ... | ... | (w) | ... |
| New York | ★ | ★ | (j) | ... | ★ | ... | ★ | ★ | ★ | ... | ... | ... | (j) | ... |
| North Carolina | ★ | ★ | ... | ... | ... | ★ | ★ | ... | ★ | ★ | (x) | ... | ... | ★ |
| North Dakota | ★ | ★ | ... | ★ | ... | ★ | ★ | ★ | ★ | ... | (p) | ... | ... | ... |
| Ohio | ★ | ★ | ... | ★ | ... | ... | ★ | ★ | ★ | ... | ... | ... | ... | ... |
| Oklahoma | ★ | ★ | ... | ★ | ... | ... | ★ | ... | ★ | ★ | (k) | ... | ... | ... |
| Oregon | ★ | ★ | ... | ★ | ... | ... | ★ | ... | ★ | (k) | (k) | (k) | ... | ... |
| Pennsylvania | ★ | ★ | ... | ★ | ... | ... | ★ | ★ | ★ | ★ | ... | ... | ... | ... |
| Rhode Island | ★ | ★ | ... | ... | ★ | ... | ★ | ★ | ★ | ★ | ... | ... | ... | ★ |
| South Carolina | ★ | ★ | ... | ★ | ... | ... | ★ | ... | ★ | ★ | ★ | ... | ... | ★ |
| South Dakota | ★ | ★ | ... | ★ | ... | (k) | ★ | (y) | ★ | (k) | ... | ... | ... | ... |
| Tennessee | ★ | ★ | ... | ★ | ... | ★ | ★ | (q) | ★ | (q) | (k) | ... | ... | ★ |
| Texas | ★ | ★ | ... | ★ | (r) | ... | ★ | ★ | ★ | ★ | ★ | ... | ... | ★ |
| Utah | ★ | ★ | ... | ★ | ... | ... | ★ | ★ | ★ | ... | ... | ... | ... | ★ |
| Vermont | ★ | ★ | ... | ★ | ... | ... | ★ | (cc) | ★ | (g) | ... | ... | ... | ★ |
| Virginia | ★ | ★ | ... | ... | ★ | ... | ★ | ★ | ★ | ★ | (k) | (k) | ... | ★ |
| Washington | ★ | ★ | ... | ★ | ... | ... | ★ | ... | ★ | ★ | ... | ... | ... | ★ |
| West Virginia | ★ | ★ | ... | ★ | ... | ... | ★ | ★ | ★ | ★ | (s) | (s) | ★ | ★ |
| Wisconsin | ★ | ★ | ... | ... | ... | ... | ★ | ... | ... | ... | ... | ★ | ★ | ... |
| Wyoming | ★ | ★ | ... | ★ | ... | ... | ★ | ... | ★ | ... | ... | ... | ... | ... |
| Dist. of Columbia | ★ | ★ | ... | ... | ★ | ... | ★ | ★ | ★ | ... | ... | ... | ... | ★ |
| American Samoa | ★ | ★ | ... | ★ | ... | ★ | ★ | ★ | ★ | ... | ... | ... | ... | ★ |
| Guam | ★ | ★ | ... | ... | ... | ★ | ★ | ★ | ★ | ... | ... | ★ | ... | ★ |
| No. Mariana Islands | ★ | ... | ... | ★ | ... | ★ | ★ | ★ | ★ | ... | ... | ... | ... | ★ |
| Puerto Rico | ★ | ... | ... | ★ | ... | ★ | ★ | ★ | ★ | ... | ... | ... | ... | ★ |
| U.S. Virgin Islands | ★ | ★ | ... | ★ | ... | ★ | ★ | ★ | ★ | ... | ... | (bb) | ... | ★ |

See footnotes at end of table.

## STATE EMPLOYEES: PAID HOLIDAYS** — Continued

**Holidays in addition to any other authorized paid personal leave granted state employees.

*Source:* The Council of State Governments' survey of state personnel office websites, March 2011.

*Note:* In some states, the governor may proclaim additional holidays or select from a number of holidays for observance by state employees. In some states, the list of paid holidays is determined by the personnel department at the beginning of each year; as a result, the number of holidays may change from year to year. Number of paid holidays may also vary across some employee classifications. If a holiday falls on a weekend, generally employees get the day preceding or following.

*Key:*

★ — Paid holiday granted.

... — Paid holiday not granted.

(a) New Year's Day, Independence Day, Labor Day, Thanksgiving Day and Christmas Day.

(b) Third Monday in January.

(c) Generally, third Monday in February; Washington's Birthday or President's Day. In some states the holiday is called President's Day or Washington-Lincoln Day. Most frequently, this day recognizes George Washington and Abraham Lincoln.

(d) Last Monday in May in all states indicated, except Vermont where holiday is observed on May 30. Generally, states follow the federal government's observance (last Monday in May) rather than the traditional Memorial Day (May 30).

(e) Second Monday in October.

(f) General election day only, unless otherwise indicated. In Indiana, primary and general election days.

(g) Additional holidays:

Alabama — Mardi Gras Day (or personal leave day) (Tuesday before Ash Wednesday), Confederate Memorial Day (fourth Monday in April), Jefferson Davis' Birthday (first Monday in June).

Alaska — Seward's Day (last Monday in March), Alaska Day (October 18).

Arkansas — Employee's birthday.

California — César Chávez Day (March 31), one personal holiday.

Colorado — Requests for César Chávez Day (March 31) in lieu of another holiday within the same fiscal year will be considered.

Delaware — Return Day, after noon (Thursday after a general election) in Sussex County only.

Florida — One personal day is granted every July 1. This personal day does not accrue.

Georgia — Confederate Memorial Day (fourth Monday in April).

Hawaii — Prince Jonah Kuhio Kalanianaole Day (March 26), King Kamehameha Day (June 11), Statehood Day (third Friday in August).

Iowa — Additionally, two unscheduled holidays are added to vacation accrual.

Kansas — One discretionary holiday that can be used any time during the calendar year.

Louisiana — Mardi Gras Day (Tuesday before Ash Wednesday), Inauguration Day (every four years, in Baton Rouge only).

Maine — Patriot's Day (third Monday in April).

Maryland — Service reduction day in 2011 (May 27) for all state agencies, except for those providing 24/7 service.

Massachusetts — Patriot's Day (third Monday in April), Evacuation Day (March 17 — Suffolk County only), Bunker Hill Day (June 17 — Suffolk County only).

Minnesota — One floating holiday.

Mississippi — Confederate Memorial Day (last Monday in April).

Missouri — Harry Truman's Birthday (May 8).

Nebraska — Arbor Day (last Friday in April).

Nevada — Nevada Day (last Friday in October).

New Hampshire — Employees who are employed on a full-time basis are eligible for Floating Holidays.

Rhode Island — Victory Day (second Monday in August).

South Carolina — Confederate Memorial Day (May 10).

Texas — The following are partial staffing state holidays where state offices are scheduled to be open: Confederate Heroes Day (January 19), Texas Independence Day (March 2), San Jacinto Day (April 21), Emancipation Day (June 19) and Lyndon Johnson's Birthday (August 27). The following are optional holidays that a state employee may observe in lieu of any state holiday on which the employee's agency is required to be open: Rosh Hashanah, Yom Kippur, Good Friday and César Chávez Day (March 31).

Utah — Pioneer Day (July 24) and each employee may select one additional day, called Personal Preference Day, to be scheduled pursuant to rules adopted by the Department of Human Resource Management.

Vermont — Town Meeting Day (first Tuesday in March), Bennington Battle Day (August 16), most state offices will be closed the day after Thanksgiving.

Virginia — Lee-Jackson Day (Friday preceding the third Monday in January); state offices will close at noon on November 21 in observance of Thanksgiving and will also close on Friday, Nov. 23, 2012.

Washington — One floating holiday.

West Virginia — West Virginia Day (third Friday in June).

District of Columbia — Presidential Inauguration Day (January 20) and District of Columbia Emancipation Day (April 16).

American Samoa — Easter Monday and Flag Day.

Guam — Liberation Day (July 21), All Souls' Day (November 2) and Our Lady of Camarin Day (December 8).

Northern Mariana Islands — Covenant Day, Citizenship Day and Constitution Day.

Puerto Rico — Three Kings Day (January 6), Birthday of Eugenio Maria de Hostos (second Monday in January), Emancipation Day (March 22), Jose de Diego Day (third Monday in April), Birthday of Luis Munoz Rivera (third Monday in July), Constitution Day (July 25), Birthday of José Celso Barbosa (July 27), Discovery of Puerto Rico Day (November 19).

U.S. Virgin Islands — Three Kings Day (January 6), Holy Thursday (April 8), Organic Act Day (June 21), Emancipation Day (July 2), Supplication Day (July 28), Local Thanksgiving and Hamilton Jackson Day.

(h) Also, celebrated as Robert E. Lee's Birthday.

(i) In Alabama, celebrated as George Washington's and Thomas Jefferson's Birthday. In Arkansas, celebrated as George Washington's Birthday and Daisy Gaston Bates Day.

(j) Floating holiday; Employee may choose either to work on that day or to take it off. If an employee works on the floating holiday, they may take another day off at any time within one year with supervisory approval.

(k) At the discretion of the governor. In South Carolina, the day after Christmas is an established holiday.

(l) In Georgia, Robert E. Lee's Birthday is observed on the day after Thanksgiving, and Washington's Birthday is observed the day before Christmas.

(m) In Indiana, Lincoln's Birthday is observed on the day after Thanksgiving, and Washington's Birthday is observed the day before Christmas.

(n) In Kentucky, half day.

(o) In New Mexico, President's Day is observed on the day after Thanksgiving.

(p) In North Dakota, offices close on Tuesday, December 25, 2012, for Christmas.

(q) In Tennessee, at the governor's discretion Columbus Day may be observed the day after Thanksgiving.

(r) In Texas, a state employee may observe Good Friday in lieu of any state holiday on which the employee's agency is required to be open.

(s) Half day on Christmas Eve and New Year's Eve if they fall on Monday, Tuesday, Wednesday or Thursday. West Virginia — includes Friday.

(t) Up to four hours.

(u) General Election Day is a state holiday the first Tuesday after the first Monday in November in even-numbered years.

(v) Also celebrated as Jefferson Davis' Birthday.

(w) Employees are allowed up to two hours paid administrative leave to vote.

(x) Three days when Christmas Day falls on Tuesday, Wednesday or Thursday; two days when Christmas Day falls on Friday or Monday.

(y) Celebrated as Native American's Day.

(z) Election Day approved beginning in 2006 (even years only) with the exception of employees who work in 24/7 shifts. Those employees receive four hours of annual leave each year in lieu of the paid Election Day.

(aa) Observed as American Indian Heritage Day.

(bb) Observed as Boxing Day.

(cc) Columbus Day is a floating holiday in 2012 and state offices will be open.

# Chapter Nine

# SELECTED
# STATE POLICIES
# AND PROGRAMS

# Elections, Greater Federal Grant Scrutiny and Ongoing Disasters Continue to Test Management System

### By Beverly Bell

*Almost 60 years of federal record-keeping passed before this country reached its highest number of major disaster declarations, 81 in 2010. It took only one more year to shatter that record, with 99 in 2011. State emergency management handled the growing number of events even as the average operating budget slid for the second year in a row. While Congressional scrutiny over federal spending persisted in Washington, D.C., state emergency management showed the initiative and proposed a substantial restructuring of related federal grants, one that promotes flexibility and accountability. The backdrop to all of this is national elections, which can turn every issue—including better preparation for the next disaster in order to save lives and protect property—into a political football.*

## One Record After Another

As experts continue to debate the causes and frequency of disasters, the economic impact of disasters is on the rise. Citing research from the World Bank and The Organisation for Economic Co-operation and Development, *The Economist* gives several reasons for the increase: development in previously uninhabited regions, elimination of natural barriers, which means more exposed property, and repeated rebuilding even though areas have been devastated over and over again. The result? Five of the world's costliest disasters from a financial perspective have occurred in the past four years. Without significant policy change and dedicating more resources to prevention, there's nothing to indicate that the trend will reverse.

For its part, the United States experienced more than its share of disasters in 2011. Devastating tornadoes ripped through Alabama and Joplin, Mo., killing an estimated 400 people. Hurricane Irene and Tropical Storm Lee caused serious flooding all along the East Coast. A 5.8 magnitude earthquake struck Virginia, Washington, D.C., and several eastern seaboard states; record winter snowstorms hit Alaska and massive wildfires ravaged Texas. In fact, 2011 marked the largest number of fire management assistance declarations at 114. Texas accounted for most of these with 55. The total is almost 33 percent higher than the previous record of 86 in 2006, when fire ravaged the western United States, the Southwest and the Great Plains.

The decade from 2001–2010 had the most presidential declarations since the Federal Emergency Management Agency started tracking the numbers in 1953, averaging almost 60 a year. A presidential declaration is the highest designation a disaster can receive from the federal government. It indicates the severity and destruction of an event and makes available the greatest amount of federal assistance.

The record-setting pace continued at the state level as well. In the National Emergency Management Association 2012 Biennial Report,[1] states[2] reported 250 gubernatorial emergencies in the 2011 fiscal year[3], a 39 percent increase over the 180 gubernatorial emergencies in the 2009 fiscal year, when the last update was published. The number of events that required a significant commitment of state resources, but did not result in a declared state of emergency, also jumped. In the 2011 fiscal year, there were 258 events, compared to 122 events in 2009, which represents a 111 percent increase. Given the rising number of events, it's not surprising that states requested federal disaster or emergency declarations 242 times in the 2011 fiscal year, which is almost 2.5 times the 97 requested in 2009.

## The Role of Emergency Management

Emergency management manages all these disasters at the state level. It is one of the most crucial functions of state government when a disaster strikes, acting as the central coordination point for all resources and assistance provided during disasters and emergencies, including acts of terrorism. It also has the overarching responsibility of saving lives, protecting property and helping citizens recover once a disaster has occurred. Typically, emergency management comes to the forefront once an event has taken place. In reality, much of the work comes before—in the form of disaster drills and exercises, hazard mitigation programs, public warning tests and preparedness education.

Emergency management includes four main parts, referred to as the "Four Pillars":

- Mitigation—Activities that reduce or eliminate the degree of risk to human life and property;

- Preparedness—Pre-disaster activities to develop and maintain a capability to respond rapidly and effectively to emergencies and disasters;

- Response—Activities to assess and contain the immediate effects of disasters, provide life support to victims and deliver emergency services; and

- Recovery—Activities to restore damaged facilities and equipment, and support the economic and social revitalization of affected areas to their pre-emergency status.

On the state level, these four elements encompass many different aspects, from planning and implementation to training and exercising. A state emergency manager will interact with all sectors of the population, including other state agencies, elected officials, local jurisdictions, all public safety personnel, the private sector and the general public.

## State Emergency Management Organizational Structures/Budgets

2011 ushered in one of the largest class of new governors in this country, with 27 never having held the top state executive spot. This resulted in 17 newly appointed emergency management directors. Some state emergency management agencies also experienced reorganization. Currently, the emergency management agency is located within the department of public safety in 12 states; within the military department under the auspices of the adjutant general in 18 states; and within the governor's office in nine states. Eight states have it in a combined emergency management/homeland security agency.

Regardless of agencies' organizational structure for daily operations, emergency management ranks high among governors' priorities. While the state emergency management director is an appointed

position in all 50 states, the director is appointed by the governor in 33—or nearly two-thirds—of states.

Even though state emergency management is handling more disasters and emergencies, their budgets remain relatively flat. Agency operating budgets for the 2012 fiscal year range up to about $47 million. Twenty states saw their emergency management budgets shrink from the 2011 fiscal year. The average 2012 budget is $5,987,294 and the median is $2,826,624, which are both down from the previous year.

## State Homeland Security Offices Also Evolving

Like emergency management, the state homeland security function has seen organizational changes. There is no one common structure, however, and responsibilities also vary. In some cases, state homeland security directors manage grants and budgets; in other cases, they have very limited roles.

In 18 states, a combined emergency management/ homeland security office oversees daily operations of the homeland security function. Four states have the day-to-day operations in a homeland security agency or office. Five states run it out of the governor's office. Ten states have it in the adjutant general/military affairs department and 12 states keep the homeland security function in their public safety department.

All states have a designated homeland security point of contact to the federal government and this position has become a critical component of a governor's staff. Currently, 14 states assign the homeland security responsibility to their homeland security director. In another 21 states, either the emergency management director or a combined emergency management/homeland security director is the primary point of contact. Seven states have the adjutant general serving in this capacity. Only two public safety secretaries/commissioners are in this role. The remaining states have other arrangements.

To fund their homeland security function, states rely on federal grants, state appropriations, a combination of the two and other sources. Fifteen states receive 100 percent of funding for their state homeland security office from federal grants. Only New Hampshire uses 100 percent state money for this function. Forty states receive at least 60 percent of funding from the federal government. This is only a slight increase from last year, when it was 39 states. On average, states rely on almost 76 percent federal funding to pay for their homeland security function, 18 percent state appropriations and 6 percent from other sources.

# Table A: State Emergency Management: Agency Structure, Budget and Staffing

| State or other jurisdiction | Position appointed | Appointed/ selected by | Organizational structure | Agency operating budget FY 2012 | Full-time employee positions |
|---|---|---|---|---|---|
| Alabama | ★ | G | Stand Alone Agency | $1,229,167 | 97 |
| Alaska | ★ | G | Adjutant General/Military Affairs | $2,400,900 | 62 (b) |
| Arizona | ★ | ADJ | Adjutant General/Military Affairs | $2,693,820 | 61 |
| Arkansas | ★ | G | Governor's Office | $2,136,729 | 100 (b) |
| California (c) | ★ | G | Combined Homeland Security/Emerg. Mgt. | $36,888,000 | 548 (b) |
| Colorado | ★ | ED | Department of Local Affairs | $640,000 | 29 |
| Connecticut | ... | PSS | Combined Homeland Security/Emerg. Mgt. | $5,500,000 | 35 (b) |
| Delaware | | | ........(a)........ | | |
| Florida | ★ | G | Governor's Office | $46,843,050 | 150 |
| Georgia | ★ | G | Governor's Office | $2,722,853 | 114 (b) |
| Hawaii | ★ | G | Adjutant General/Military Affairs | $2,640,170 | 62 (b) |
| Idaho | ★ | ADJ | Adjutant General/Military Affairs | $1,466,700 | 66 (b) |
| Illinois | ★ | G | Governor's Office | $34,141,500 | 220 |
| Indiana | ★ | G | Combined Homeland Security/Emerg. Mgt. | $12,851,000 | 243 (b) |
| Iowa | ★ | G | Adjutant General/Military Affairs | $2,873,799 | 144 (b) |
| Kansas | ★ | G | Adjutant General/Military Affairs | $1,068,389 | 46 |
| Kentucky | ★ | G | Adjutant General/Military Affairs | $2,091,700 | 107 |
| Louisiana | ★ | G | Governor's Office | $15,400,276 | 122 (b) |
| Maine | ★ | G | Adjutant General/Military Affairs | $1,013,831 | 30 (b) |
| Maryland | ★ | G | Adjutant General/Military Affairs | $1,500,000 | 70 |
| Massachusetts | ★ | G | Public Safety | $4,506,189 | 84 |
| Michigan | ★ | G | State Police | $4,848,400 | 126 (b) |
| Minnesota | ★ | PSS | Public Safety | $6,792,000 | 74 (b) |
| Mississippi | ★ | G | Governor's Office | $4,850,362 | 188 |
| Missouri | ★ | PSS | Public Safety | $2,851,248 | 65 |
| Montana | ... | ADJ | Adjutant General/Military Affairs | $1,505,000 | 23 (b) |
| Nebraska | ★ | ADJ | Adjutant General/Military Affairs | $931,578 | 37 |
| Nevada | ★ | PSS | Public Safety | $486,970 | 33 (b) |
| New Hampshire | ★ | G | Public Safety | $5,215,510 | 43 (b) |
| New Jersey | ★ | G | State Police | $1,986,691 | 341 |
| New Mexico | ★ | G | Combined Homeland Security/Emerg. Mgt. | $2,802,000 | 62 (b) |
| New York | ★ | G | Combined Homeland Security/Emerg. Mgt. | $8,809,000 | 403 (b) |
| North Carolina | ★ | G | Public Safety | $8,388,740 | 175 (b) |
| North Dakota | ★ | ADJ | Adjutant General/Military Affairs | $8,618,759 | 63 (b) |
| Ohio | ★ | PSS | Public Safety | $6,046,752 | 97 |
| Oklahoma | ★ | G | Governor's Office | $651,179 | 22 |
| Oregon | ★ | ADJ | Adjutant General/Military Affairs | $3,277,804 | 40 |
| Pennsylvania | ★ | G | Governor's Office | $10,930,000 | 188 |
| Rhode Island | ★ | G | Adjutant General/Military Affairs | $2,115,407 | 28 (b) |
| South Carolina | ★ | ADJ | Adjutant General/Military Affairs | $2,322,350 | 57 |
| South Dakota | ★ | PSS | Public Safety | $627,324 | 19 |
| Tennessee | ★ | G | Adjutant General/Military Affairs | $5,200,000 | 112 |
| Texas | ★ | PSS | State Police | $4,140,693 | 223 |
| Utah | ★ | PSS | Public Safety | $945,000 | 65 (b) |
| Vermont | ★ | PSS | Public Safety | $2,753,143 | 23 |
| Virginia | ★ | G | Public Safety | $7,106,773 | 148 (b) |
| Washington | ★ | ADJ | Adjutant General/Military Affairs | $3,645,847 | 90 (b) |
| West Virginia | ★ | G | Public Safety | $5,340,945 | 53 (b) |
| Wisconsin | ★ | G | Adjutant General/Military Affairs | $9,876,325 | 53 |
| Wyoming | | | ........(d)........ | | |
| Dist. of Columbia | ★ | M | Combined Homeland Security/Emerg. Mgt. | $2,000,000 | 56 (b) |
| Guam | ★ | G | Combined Homeland Security/Emerg. Mgt. | $0 | 10 |
| No. Mariana Islands | ★ | G | Governor's Office | $416,720 | 26 |
| U.S. Virgin Islands | ★ | G | Combined Homeland Security/Emerg. Mgt. | $5,248,675 | 94 (b) |

*Source:* The National Emergency Management Association, March 2012.

*Key:*
★ — Yes
... — No
G — Governor
ADJ — Adjutant General
ED — Executive Director, Dept. of Local Affairs
M — Mayor
PSS — Public Safety Secretary/Commissioner/Director
PSS — Public Safety Secretary/Commissioner/Director

(a) Not a member of NEMA, and is not represented in the survey data.
(b) Includes homeland security and emergency management positions.
(c) After the survey was completed, California underwent a reorganization and is now organized under the Governor's Office.
(d) Wyoming is currently a NEMA member, but was not at the time of the survey.

## The Next Iteration of Grant Funding

Given the federal government's current economic environment with continued concern over the debt and deficit spending, Congress is still closely scrutinizing all outlays. State homeland security and emergency management grants are part of this analysis. To tackle the uncertain future of grant funding, a group of emergency management and homeland security professionals from across the country put forward a proposal in 2012—even before that of the president or Congress—suggesting a comprehensive restructuring of these grants while providing grantees with increased flexibility and Congress with more accountability on how the funds are spent. Previous grants were reorganized into three allocations from the U.S. Department of Homeland Security: a new homeland security cadre grant, a project-based investment and innovation grant and Emergency Management Performance Grants (EMPG).

## EMPG'S Impact Quantified

EMPG is a core state emergency management funding mechanism and the lifeblood of emergency management throughout the United States. It's the only source of federal money directed to state and local governments for planning, training, exercises and personnel for all-hazards emergency preparedness.

In 2011, the emergency management community issued a report on EMPG, outlining the impact of the grant at the state and local levels. This report was updated and provided to Congress in early 2012. *Emergency Management Performance Grants: Providing Returns on a Nation's Investment* quantifies the thousands of local and state warnings systems, operational, special needs and evacuation plans, training and educational classes, full-scale exercises, mutual aid agreements and outreach campaigns that are possible in this country because of EMPG dollars. What is also significant about EMPG is that while the initial 2011 fiscal year federal investment was $340 million, state and local government contributed at least another $340 million because of the 50-50 match required by the program. Even as budgets have faced serious challenges in recent years and some have supported the federal government providing a higher portion, state government has stood behind the match, believing that every level of government has a responsibility in building emergency management capacity nationwide.

The fear is that if EMPG is cut, states will not be able to provide the match and would lose irreplaceable dollars. Investments made thus far in terrorism-preparedness programs, response equipment, planning efforts and training will be jeopardized without adequate money to sustain them. States already have seen ramifications at the local emergency management level. Because local emergency management programs can't provide their EMPG cost share, they're turning down grant funding, which puts local agencies across the country at risk and seriously compromises that vital first rung of response capability.

## More Deliverables for PPD-8

Last year, President Barack Obama signed Presidential Policy Directive-8, known as PPD-8, National Preparedness, which provided a broad outline for the nation to prevent, protect, mitigate, respond and recover from the most significant threats to the country. Replacing Homeland Security Presidential Directive 8, known as HSPD-8, under President George W. Bush, it also represented the first time the federal government worked to develop a National Preparedness Goal as called for in HSPD-8 and the 2006 Post Katrina Emergency Management Reform Act.

Since then, several milestones related to PPD-8 have been reached, including the release of the goal, which spells out the necessary capabilities, a description of a National Preparedness System with required resources and tools, a status report on national preparedness and an outline with specifics on roles and responsibilities in reaching a state of preparedness.

Many PPD-8 components are having a real effect on states because these elements partially determine how states can invest certain federal grants and report their actions/results related to those grant expenditures. This approach is part of the administration's overall pursuit of performance metrics, requiring specific outcomes based on investment and programmatic goals.

## Nation's Mutual Aid System

The Emergency Management Assistance Compact, known as EMAC, a mutual aid agreement that allows support across state lines when a disaster occurs, continues to demonstrate its importance to the nation's disaster management system. Many states experienced severe flooding after Hurricane Irene and Tropical Storm Lee roared up the east coast in August 2011. As a result, 1,126 personnel from 25 states were deployed under EMAC to New York, New Jersey, Virginia, Maryland, Massachusetts,

# Table B: Homeland Security Structures

| State or other jurisdiction | State homeland security advisor | Homeland security organizations | |
|---|---|---|---|
| | Designated homeland security advisor | Day-to-day operations under | Full-time employee positions |
| Alabama | Homeland Security Director | Homeland Security (stand-alone office) | 16 |
| Alaska | Dual Title–Emerg. Mgt./Homeland Security Director | Adjutant General/Military Affairs | 62 (b) |
| Arizona | Homeland Security Director | Homeland Security (stand-alone office) | 16 |
| Arkansas | Dual Title–Emerg. Mgt./Homeland Security Director | Governor's Office | 100 (b) |
| California (c) | Dual Title–Emerg. Mgt./Homeland Security Director | Combined Emerg. Mgt./Homeland Security Office | 548 (b) |
| Colorado | Executive Director of the Dept. of Public Safety | Public Safety | 33.5 |
| Connecticut | Emergency Management Director | Combined Emerg. Mgt./Homeland Security Office | 35 (b) |
| Delaware | ...............................................................(a)........................................................ | | |
| Florida | Florida Dept. of Law Enforcement | Florida Dept. of Law Enforcement | 35 |
| Georgia | Dual Title–Emerg. Mgt./Homeland Security Director | Combined Emerg. Mgt./Homeland Security Office | 114 (b) |
| Hawaii | Adjutant General | Adjutant General/Military Affairs | 62 (b) |
| Idaho | Dual Title–Emerg. Mgt./Homeland Security Director | Adjutant General/Military Affairs | 66 (b) |
| Illinois | Dual Title–Emerg. Mgt./Homeland Security Director | Combined Emerg. Mgt./Homeland Security Office | 5 |
| Indiana | Dual Title–Emerg. Mgt./Homeland Security Director | Combined Emerg. Mgt./Homeland Security Office | 243 (b) |
| Iowa | Dual Title–Emerg. Mgt./Homeland Security Director | Combined Emerg. Mgt./Homeland Security Office | 144 (b) |
| Kansas | Adjutant General | Adjutant General/Military Affairs | 0 |
| Kentucky | Homeland Security Director | Governor's Office | 14 |
| Louisiana | Dual Title–Emerg. Mgt./Homeland Security Director | Governor's Office | 122 (b) |
| Maine | Adjutant General | Combined Emerg. Mgt./Homeland Security Office | 30 (b) |
| Maryland | Homeland Security Advisor | Homeland Security (stand-alone office) | 3 |
| Massachusetts | Dual Title–Emerg. Mgt./Homeland Security Director | Public Safety | 8 |
| Michigan | State Police Superintendent/Director/Commissioner | State Police | 126 (b) |
| Minnesota | Dual Title–Emerg. Mgt./Homeland Security Director | Public Safety | 74 (b) |
| Mississippi | Homeland Security Director | Public Safety | 19 |
| Missouri | Public Safety Secretary/Commissioner | Public Safety | 16 |
| Montana | Emergency Management Director | Adjutant General/Military Affairs | 23 (b) |
| Nebraska | Lieutenant Governor | Combined Emerg. Mgt./Homeland Security Office | 1 |
| Nevada | Dual Title–Emerg. Mgt./Homeland Security Director | Combined Emerg. Mgt./Homeland Security Office | 33 (b) |
| New Hampshire | Dual Title–Emerg. Mgt./Homeland Security Director | Combined Emerg. Mgt./Homeland Security Office | 43 (b) |
| New Jersey | Homeland Security Director | Homeland Security (stand-alone office) | 105 |
| New Mexico | Dual Title–Emerg. Mgt./Homeland Security Director | Combined Emerg. Mgt./Homeland Security Office | 62 (b) |
| New York | Dual Title–Emerg. Mgt./Homeland Security Director | Combined Emerg. Mgt./Homeland Security Office | 403 (b) |
| North Carolina | Public Safety Secretary/Commissioner | Combined Emerg. Mgt./Homeland Security Office | 175 (b) |
| North Dakota | Homeland Security Director | Adjutant General/Military Affairs | 63 (b) |
| Ohio | Homeland Security Director | Public Safety | 19 |
| Oklahoma | Homeland Security Director | Public Safety | 14 |
| Oregon | Adjutant General | Adjutant General/Military Affairs | 2 |
| Pennsylvania | State Police Superintendent/Director/Commissioner | Governor's Office | 5 |
| Rhode Island | Adjutant General | Adjutant General/Military Affairs | 28 (b) |
| South Carolina | State Police Superintendent/Director/Commissioner | State Police | 20 |
| South Dakota | Homeland Security Director | Public Safety | 3 |
| Tennessee | Homeland Security Director | Public Safety | 26 |
| Texas | Homeland Security Director | Public Safety | 40 |
| Utah | Dual Title–Emerg. Mgt./Homeland Security Director | Public Safety | 65 (b) |
| Vermont | Homeland Security Director | Public Safety | 7 |
| Virginia | Homeland Security Secretary | Combined Emerg. Mgt./Homeland Security Office | 148 (b) |
| Washington | Adjutant General | Adjutant General/Military Affairs | 90 (b) |
| West Virginia | Dual Title–Emerg. Mgt./Homeland Security Director | Combined Emerg. Mgt./Homeland Security Office | 53 (b) |
| Wisconsin | Adjutant General | Adjutant General/Military Affairs | 0 |
| Wyoming | ...............................................................(d)........................................................ | | |
| Dist. of Columbia | Dual Title–Emerg. Mgt./Homeland Security Director | Combined Emerg. Mgt./Homeland Security Office | 56 (b) |
| Guam | Homeland Security Director | Combined Emerg. Mgt./Homeland Security Office | 12 |
| No. Mariana Islands | Homeland Security Director | Governor's Office | 8 |
| U.S. Virgin Islands | Dual Title–Emerg. Mgt./Homeland Security Director | Combined Emerg. Mgt./Homeland Security Office | 94 (b) |

*Source:* The National Emergency Management Association, March 2012.

(a) Not a member of NEMA and is not represented in the survey data.

(b) Includes homeland security and emergency management positions.

(c) After the survey was completed, California underwent a reorganization and is now organized under the Governor's Office.

(d) Wyoming is currently a NEMA member, but was not at the time of the survey.

Delaware, Connecticut, Vermont and Pennsylvania. This included 86 missions in a seven-week period and more than $13 million in estimated costs for requested resources. Earlier in the year, almost 950 personnel were deployed under the compact in response to the floods and tornados in Missouri, North Dakota, Nebraska, South Dakota, Mississippi, Alabama and Tennessee.

As part of its normal procedure for a larger event, EMAC conducted an after-action review and issued a report on the August disasters. It focused on four main operational components of the process: activation; the request and offer; response-mobilization, deployment and de-mobilization; and reimbursement. The document identified what worked well and those areas that need improvement. These recommendations will become part of EMAC's long-term work plan.

## Impact of Elections

In national election years, all issues can become political. This is certainly a consideration for 2012, when elections for president, all 435 seats in the U.S. House of Representatives, 33 U.S. Senate seats and governor in 11 states as well as two territories will be held. New faces in Washington and in the governor's mansions could result in more changes for emergency management and homeland security as national and state leaders revise current strategies or develop new ones.

To encourage a productive discussion about emergency management and homeland security before the November elections, the National Emergency Management Association—which represents state emergency management directors in all 50 states, the District of Columbia and the territories—is meeting with presidential campaign representatives. The purpose is to learn candidates' positions regarding all hazards, emergency preparedness and homeland security.

## Possible Changes to Declaration Process

Under current federal law, only a governor has the authority after a disaster to request either an emergency or major declaration from the president, which, if granted, allows federal assistance. In 2011, however, FEMA announced its support to allow a tribal government, if it chooses, to make a separate declaration request directly to the president without going through the state. The modification requires an amendment to the Robert T. Stafford Disaster Relief and Emergency Relief Act (42 U.S.C. 5121 et seq.), which is the legislation that guides the declaration

process. The proposal also raises a number of issues related to the cost-share requirements; population guidelines and overall criteria.

Besides the tribal proposition, another possible change is underway. The U.S. Department of Agriculture has issued a suggested rule that would allow a county to initiate a declaration of an agriculture-related disaster directly to the USDA, removing the governor from the process. There are concerns that both of these changes could erode a governor's authority.

## Notes

[1] *NEMA 2012 Biennial Report*, National Emergency Management Association, March 2012.

[2] In this section, "states" refer to two territories, the District of Columbia, and 48 states that responded a National Emergency Management Association 2012 survey about emergency management organizations, funding and other issues.

[3] FY11 refers to the federal fiscal year, which is October 1, 2010 through September 30, 2011.

## About the Author

**Beverly Bell** is the senior policy analyst for the National Emergency Management Association, an affiliate of The Council of State Governments. In her position, she coordinates and conducts research, interacts with the states on changing federal policy and acts as an information clearinghouse for emergency management and homeland security issues.

# States Making Early Steps in Journey Toward Common Core State Standards Implementation

## By Tim Weldon

*Ensuring students are academically prepared for postsecondary education was the spark leading the National Governors Association and Council of Chief State School Officers in 2005 to push for a consistent, clear understanding of what students are expected to learn—known as the common core state standards. Because states historically have set their own academic standards, the nation has been faced with a patchwork of academic expectations. The knowledge and skills in reading, writing and math that a student was expected to have at each grade level in one state could be significantly different from those in another. This inconsistency of standards became a serious problem whenever a family moved from one state to another. Students could easily be forced to repeat material they had already learned or, even worse, face a learning gap in which they had not yet learned material that had already been covered in the state to which their families moved.*

*Upon the release of the common core state standards in June 2010, 46 states, the District of Columbia and the U.S. Virgin Islands adopted the standards in almost rapid fire succession. It is critical to note that a state formally adopting common core state standards, doesn't mark an end as much as a beginning. The focus in states that have adopted common core state standards now shifts to successful implementation, and the challenges they are likely to encounter along the way.*

Less than 40 years ago, nearly 75 percent of the jobs in the U.S. could be filled by workers with no more than a high school diploma.[1] Manufacturing, farming and construction work, among many others, typically required no formal education beyond 12th grade. But as technology has advanced and critical problem-solving skills became inseparably linked with most occupations, so too has the level of education required for most jobs that were once classified as unskilled. As a result, a new norm related to the level of education needed for the jobs of the future is rapidly developing.

The Georgetown University Center on Education and the Workplace projects that by 2018, nearly three-fourths of all jobs in the U.S. will require some college. One-third of those jobs will require a bachelor's or graduate degree, and another 12 percent an associate degree from a two- or four-year college.[1] Those filling the 17 percent of jobs that require some college, but not a postsecondary degree, will need to have strong math, reading and writing skills to be college-ready.

Most high school graduates today do not meet all college-readiness benchmarks. According to a 2010 analysis of data from the National Center for Education Statistics, only 24 percent of ACT-tested high school graduates met college benchmark scores in all four academic subjects: English, math, reading and science.[2]

Adoption and full implementation of common core state standards is widely viewed as a significant policy statement to ensure more students graduate from high school with college- and career-readiness skills to be successful once they graduate. The designers of the standards, led by the Council of Chief State School Officers and the National Governors Association in consultation with teachers, parents, experts and administrators, intended them to be aligned with college and work expectations. Those standards:

- Include rigorous content *and* application of knowledge through higher-order skills;
- Build upon strengths and lessons of current state standards;

- Are informed by top-performing countries so all students are prepared to succeed in the global economy and society; and
- Are evidence- and research-based.[3]

Although most states were quick to adopt the common core state standards, experts point out that adoption is merely a first step. Successful implementation of the standards is the key to achieving the goal of college- and career-readiness. A report issued by the Center for Education Policy concludes that in many states, it will take until 2013 or later to fully implement the more complex changes associated with the new academic standards.[4] Legislators and elected and appointed state education leaders must make many critical decisions soon to ensure successful implementation of the standards in a timely fashion.

## Assessment

Assessing student progress is costly but mandatory under the provisions of the No Child Left Behind Act of 2001. Even in states that have received federal waivers from accountability provisions of the law, it remains vitally important for local, state and federal education leaders to know if students are learning the skills required to be college- and career-ready. Current state assessments already are considered obsolete by many education experts; therefore new assessments must be put in place aligned to the new common core state standards.

The SMARTER Balanced Assessment Consortium and the Partnership for Assessment of Readiness for College and Careers received federal Race to the Top funding to work with states to create a new generation of student assessments. States adopting common core state standards have joined one or both of these consortia. Both are developing traditional summative assessments, which are given to students at the end of the school year to test their achievement. The consortia also include formative assessments, which teachers can give throughout the year to determine whether students are progressing as they should.

Using one of these common assessments can result in a potential savings for states, because the cost of designing and scoring student tests will be spread over multiple states rather than each state being required to create, administer and score its own, unique assessment. The test results also will provide a reliable measure to compare student achievement among multiple states giving the same assessment. The current patchwork of state assessments makes this data comparison impossible.

## Accountability

One of the primary purposes of end-of-year student assessments is to provide a basis for accountability for schools and local school districts. These assessments must provide a transparent means to tell the public, local education leaders, and state and federal policymakers to what extent students are learning the knowledge and skills they are supposed to learn. Data from the testing provide vital information about where improvement is needed.

The Council of Chief State School Officers, which represents state school chiefs, suggests policymakers should adopt accountability systems that include high school graduation requirements, accreditation criteria for individual schools and districts, policies related to grade promotion (e.g. expectations for students to advance from one grade to the next), and state evaluation of school and district performance.[5]

## Teachers and the Common Core Standards

In order for common core state standards or other similar college- and career-ready academic standards to be successful, policymakers must consider how to ensure teachers and education leaders are adequately trained and whether they possess knowledge about what is included in the more rigorous standards, and how they can ensure their students are able to meet the new expectations. This will require an investment in innovative and comprehensive professional development programs for teachers and administrators. In many cases, changes in teaching and learning may be required. New evaluation systems for educators will, in some cases, need to be developed along with curriculum materials and other resources that are linked to common core state standards.

In many cases, this means K–12 and postsecondary education policymakers will have to collaborate to ensure the new standards provide a seamless transition so students have the knowledge and skills to be successful in postsecondary education without having to take remedial courses. Some of the higher education policy changes that may be necessary include aligning the academic content of teacher education programs with the common core state standards. Teacher pre-service programs at postsecondary colleges of education should become incubators where future teachers are introduced to these more rigorous standards and prepared to teach to them upon graduation. State policymakers also should consider aligning college admission requirements and the first-year undergraduate core curriculum with the new standards.

## Kentucky Leads the Way in College-Ready Standards

In February 2010, Kentucky's Board of Education took the monumental step of adopting the common core state standards. What made the decision monumental was that the standards hadn't even been finalized or released to the public at the time Kentucky provisionally adopted them. It would be another four months before the standards were unveiled. Yet Kentucky education leaders were confident the standards would set the benchmark for college- and career-readiness standards.

One year earlier, the Kentucky legislature enacted Senate Bill 1, designed to raise the quality of elementary and postsecondary education in the state. The bill called for the development and implementation of revisions to Kentucky's academic content standards. This paved the way for the adoption one year later of common core state standards by the state's education leadership.

Kentucky is widely viewed as leading the nation in the standards' implementation. The implementation of the common core state standards has given Kentucky an opportunity to prepare students with content that is more focused and coherent and demands a deeper level of learning. Establishing specific expectations for preschool through grade 12 and also aligning standards with postsecondary institutions' expectations will result in a seamless approach to learning from the time a child enters school until he or she graduates from college.

In February 2011, the Kentucky Department of Education developed Kentucky's College and Career Readiness Delivery Plan, a collaboration with higher education officials which specifies the strategies for increasing the number of students that are college- and career-ready. One of the Plan's goals is to increase the percentage of students who graduate college- and career-ready from Kentucky high schools from 34 percent at the Plan's inception to 67 percent by 2015. The second goal is to increase the percentage of high school freshmen who graduate from 76 percent in 2010 to 90 percent in 2015.

The Kentucky Department of Education and the state's Council on Postsecondary Education have placed a strong emphasis on increasing pathways for students through acceleration and intervention supports. This includes expanding advanced placement and dual credit opportunities with increased rigor and STEM—science, technology, engineering and math—coursework aligned to college- and career-ready expectations.

Within one month of adoption of common core state standards, the Kentucky Department of Education provided local school districts with a contrast in Kentucky's former standards and the newly adopted ones. State education leadership also worked closely with district and school leaders to ensure the provisions of common core state standards were understood and being implemented properly on the local level.

Beginning with the 2011–12 school year, teachers and administrators began to design new learning experiences for students based on the more rigorous common core state standards. According to department of education staff, year two of common core state standards implementation is designed to integrate the components of teacher and leader professional growth and effectiveness system, along with strategies for implementing the standards and the valid use of data.

## Notes

[1] Anthony Carnevale, et al. "Help Wanted: Projections of Jobs and Education Requirements Through 2018." Georgetown University Center on Education and the Workforce. (2010) Accessed at *http://www9.georgetown.edu/grad/gppi/hpi/cew/pdfs/FullReport.pdf* on January 11, 2012.

[2] Alliance for Excellent Education. "Accelerating the College and Career Readiness of the Nation's Students." (2010) Accessed at *http://www.all4ed.org/files/Nation_cs.pdf* on January 11, 2012.

[3] The Common Core State Standards Initiative. "Introduction to the Common Core State Standards." (June 2, 2010) Accessed at *http://www.corestandards.org/assets/ccssi-introduction.pdf* on January 11, 2012.

[4] Kober, Nancy and Diane Stark Rentner. "States Progress and Challenges in Implementing Common Core State Standards." The Center on Education Policy. (January 2011) Accessed at *http://www.cep-dc.org/index.cfm?DocumentTopicID=1* on January 11, 2012.

[5] Council of Chief State School Officers. "Accountability Systems." Accessed at *http://www.ccsso.org/Resources/Programs/Accountability_Systems.html* on January 19, 2012.

## About the Author

**Tim Weldon** is an education policy analyst at The Council of State Governments. He is a former television and newspaper journalist and high school social studies teacher. He holds an M.S. degree in secondary education curriculum.

## Table 9.1
## NUMBER AND TYPES OF PUBLIC ELEMENTARY AND SECONDARY SCHOOLS, BY STATE OR JURISDICTION: SCHOOL YEAR 2010–11

| State or other jurisdiction | Total number of schools (a) | Type of school | | | | Charter | Magnet (b) | Title I (c) | Title I schoolwide (c) |
|---|---|---|---|---|---|---|---|---|---|
| | | Regular | Special education | Vocational education | Alternative education | | | | |
| Reporting states (d)..... | 98,817 | 88,929 | 2,206 | 1,485 | 6,197 | 5,274 | 2,722 | 66,646 | 48,990 |
| Alabama........................ | 1,600 | 1,372 | 41 | 72 | 115 | n/a | 30 | 924 | 897 |
| Alaska.......................... | 509 | 441 | 3 | 3 | 62 | 27 | 19 | 366 | 335 |
| Arizona........................ | 2,265 | 1,880 | 21 | 217 | 77 | 519 | N.R. | 1,764 | 1,224 |
| Arkansas...................... | 1,110 | 1,069 | 4 | 26 | 11 | 40 | 38 | 810 | 710 |
| California .................... | 10,124 | 8,526 | 147 | 86 | 1,365 | 908 | 282 | 6,028 | 4,878 |
| Colorado...................... | 1,796 | 1,694 | 8 | 6 | 88 | 168 | 24 | 658 | 447 |
| Connecticut.................. | 1,157 | 1,046 | 54 | 16 | 41 | 18 | 54 | 532 | 186 |
| Delaware ..................... | 214 | 183 | 19 | 6 | 6 | 29 | 3 | 171 | 155 |
| Florida ........................ | 4,131 | 3,468 | 182 | 53 | 428 | 458 | 414 | 2,935 | 2,649 |
| Georgia ....................... | 2,449 | 2,265 | 66 | 1 | 117 | 67 | 78 | 1,566 | 1,399 |
| Hawaii.......................... | 289 | 285 | 3 | 0 | 1 | 31 | n/a | 205 | 183 |
| Idaho........................... | 748 | 637 | 15 | 11 | 85 | 40 | 2 | 547 | 519 |
| Illinois........................ | 4,361 | 4,012 | 146 | 53 | 150 | 50 | 104 | 3,272 | 1,575 |
| Indiana........................ | 1,936 | 1,862 | 34 | 28 | 12 | 60 | 26 | 1,460 | 1,095 |
| Iowa ........................... | 1,436 | 1,390 | 6 | 0 | 40 | 7 | n/a | 978 | 519 |
| Kansas ........................ | 1,378 | 1,365 | 10 | 1 | 2 | 25 | 36 | 1,148 | 804 |
| Kentucky ..................... | 1,554 | 1,249 | 10 | 126 | 169 | n/a | 41 | 1,090 | 1,040 |
| Louisiana ..................... | 1,471 | 1,265 | 34 | 6 | 166 | 78 | 72 | 1,245 | 1,207 |
| Maine.......................... | 631 | 601 | 3 | 27 | 0 | n/a | 1 | 526 | 400 |
| Maryland ..................... | 1,449 | 1,322 | 40 | 24 | 63 | 44 | 90 | 412 | 312 |
| Massachusetts .............. | 1,829 | 1,748 | 23 | 39 | 19 | 63 | N.R. | 1,017 | 521 |
| Michigan...................... | 3,877 | 3,257 | 279 | 62 | 279 | 300 | 464 | 2,836 | 1,672 |
| Minnesota.................... | 2,392 | 1,641 | 277 | 11 | 463 | 176 | 73 | 854 | 284 |
| Mississippi................... | 1,083 | 925 | 3 | 90 | 65 | 0 | 20 | 877 | 837 |
| Missouri ...................... | 2,410 | 2,172 | 65 | 66 | 107 | 53 | 30 | 1,165 | 622 |
| Montana ...................... | 827 | 821 | 2 | 0 | 4 | n/a | n/a | 692 | 430 |
| Nebraska ..................... | 1,096 | 1,067 | 24 | 0 | 5 | n/a | n/a | 524 | 298 |
| Nevada ........................ | 645 | 598 | 12 | 1 | 34 | 34 | 24 | 374 | 328 |
| New Hampshire ........... | 480 | 480 | 0 | 0 | 0 | 14 | n/a | 415 | 119 |
| New Jersey .................. | 2,607 | 2,355 | 71 | 56 | 125 | 76 | N.A. | 1,488 | 416 |
| New Mexico ................. | 851 | 803 | 6 | 2 | 40 | 81 | N.A. | 750 | 728 |
| New York ..................... | 4,757 | 4,576 | 124 | 29 | 28 | 170 | N.R. | 4,418 | 2,535 |
| North Carolina............. | 2,567 | 2,449 | 30 | 1 | 87 | 99 | 106 | 2,044 | 1,909 |
| North Dakota............... | 516 | 468 | 33 | 10 | 5 | n/a | n/a | 303 | 93 |
| Ohio ........................... | 3,758 | 3,621 | 59 | 72 | 6 | 339 | n/a | 2,913 | 2,116 |
| Oklahoma.................... | 1,785 | 1,775 | 4 | 0 | 6 | 18 | n/a | 1,191 | 1,049 |
| Oregon........................ | 1,296 | 1,252 | 2 | 0 | 42 | 108 | n/a | 600 | 446 |
| Pennsylvania ............... | 3,233 | 3,125 | 9 | 86 | 13 | 145 | 52 | 2,373 | 1,491 |
| Rhode Island............... | 317 | 297 | 3 | 11 | 6 | 16 | n/a | 232 | 129 |
| South Carolina............. | 1,214 | 1,144 | 10 | 39 | 21 | 44 | 104 | 1,000 | 942 |
| South Dakota............... | 710 | 658 | 11 | 4 | 37 | n/a | n/a | 601 | 350 |
| Tennessee ................... | 1,784 | 1,730 | 15 | 17 | 22 | 29 | 32 | 1,480 | 1,398 |
| Texas........................... | 8,732 | 7,635 | 26 | 0 | 1,017 | 561 | 219 | 6,802 | 6,508 |
| Utah........................... | 1,016 | 875 | 87 | 6 | 48 | 78 | 24 | 288 | 224 |
| Vermont....................... | 320 | 304 | 0 | 15 | 1 | n/a | n/a | 243 | 183 |
| Virginia........................ | 2,175 | 1,882 | 55 | 49 | 189 | 4 | 131 | 741 | 442 |
| Washington.................. | 2,338 | 1,898 | 104 | 16 | 320 | n/a | n/a | 1,518 | 1,205 |
| West Virginia................ | 757 | 691 | 3 | 31 | 32 | n/a | n/a | 366 | 366 |
| Wisconsin .................... | 2,238 | 2,131 | 9 | 7 | 91 | 207 | 4 | 1,535 | 547 |
| Wyoming ..................... | 360 | 333 | 3 | 0 | 24 | 3 | n/a | 185 | 91 |
| Dist. of Columbia ........ | 228 | 204 | 10 | 4 | 10 | 97 | 7 | 184 | 177 |
| Dept. of Defense (DoDEA) ................. | 191 | 191 | 0 | 0 | 0 | 0 | 0 | N.A. | N.A. |
| Bureau of Indian Education ..... | 173 | 173 | 0 | 0 | 0 | n/a | N.A. | 173 | 173 |
| American Samoa ......... | 28 | 27 | 0 | 1 | 0 | N.A. | N.A. | N.A. | N.A. |
| Guam.......................... | 40 | 40 | 0 | 0 | 0 | N.A. | N.A. | n/a | n/a |
| No. Mariana Islands .... | 30 | 30 | 0 | 0 | 0 | n/a | n/a | 0 | n/a |
| Puerto Rico.................. | 1,473 | 1,411 | 24 | 30 | 8 | n/a | n/a | 1,456 | 1,371 |
| U.S. Virgin Islands....... | 32 | 31 | 0 | 1 | 0 | n/a | n/a | N.A. | N.A. |

See footnotes at end of table.

# NUMBER AND TYPES OF PUBLIC ELEMENTARY AND SECONDARY SCHOOLS,
## BY STATE OR JURISDICTION: SCHOOL YEAR 2010–11—Continued

*Source:* U.S. Department of Education, National Center for Education Statistics, Common Core of Data (CCD), "Public Elementary/Secondary School Universe Survey," 2007–08, Version 1a.

*Note:* Every school is assigned a school type based on its instructional emphasis: numbers and types of schools may differ from those published by state. A school may also be included under the Charter, Magnet, and/or Title I statuses, which are independent of one another and of school type.

*Key:*

N.A. — Not available.

n/a — Not applicable. Some states/jurisdictions do not have charter school authorization and some states/jurisdictions do not designate magnet schools.

N.R. — Reporting standards not met. Data reported for less than 80 percent of schools in the state of jurisdiction.

(a) Total number of operating schools excludes schools also reported by the Bureau of Indian Education (BIE). The numbers of operating schools shared with BIE include two in Arizona, one in Michigan, and eight in North Dakota.

(b) Arizona, Massachusetts, New Jersey, and New Mexico have magnet schools but were not able to provide data that indicate school's magnet status. Total includes suppressed data due to unmet reporting standards.

(c) Schools eligible for Title I schoolwide programs are also included in the count of all Title I eligible schools. A Title 1 eligible school is one in which the percentage of children from low-income families is at least as high as the percentages of children from low-income families served by the local education agency (LEA) as a whole or because 35 percent or more of the children in the school are from low-income families. A schoolwide Title I eligible school has a percentage of low-income students that is at least 40 percent.

(d) "Reporting states" totals include the 50 states and the District of Columbia. A "reporting states" total, and not a "United States" total, is shown if data for any item in the table were not available for some, but not more than 15 percent, of all schools in the United States.

## Table 9.2
## TOTAL NUMBER OF STUDENTS IN MEMBERSHIP IN OPERATING PUBLIC AND SECONDARY SCHOOLS, BY SCHOOL TYPE, AND STATE OR JURISDICTION: SCHOOL YEAR 2010–11

| State or other jurisdiction | Total number of students (a) | Type of school | | | | Charter | Magnet (b) | Title I (c) | Title I schoolwide (c) |
|---|---|---|---|---|---|---|---|---|---|
| | | Regular | Special education | Vocational education | Alernative education | | | | |
| **Reporting states (d)......** | 49,212,583 | 48,291,615 | 191,677 | 164,074 | 565,217 | 1,789,496 | 2,057,769 | 33,471,665 | 24,862,616 |
| Alabama...................... | 749,815 | 746,003 | 984 | 26 | 2,802 | n/a | 15,662 | 452,560 | 439,402 |
| Alaska........................ | 132,104 | 113,484 | 585 | 786 | 17,249 | 5,751 | 6,951 | 74,829 | 66,954 |
| Arizona....................... | 1,070,020 | 1,056,796 | 910 | 2,209 | 10,105 | 124,467 | N.A. | 1,023,950 | 651,532 |
| Arkansas..................... | 482,114 | 480,303 | 224 | 0 | 1,587 | 10,209 | 21,668 | 322,613 | 275,471 |
| California.................... | 6,207,959 | 6,005,125 | 25,467 | 4,470 | 172,897 | 363,916 | 284,446 | 3,722,019 | 3,119,140 |
| Colorado..................... | 842,864 | 827,731 | 1,064 | 778 | 13,291 | 74,685 | 10,638 | 239,656 | 183,487 |
| Connecticut.................. | 559,912 | 543,392 | 2,712 | 10,643 | 3,165 | 5,139 | 22,982 | 251,815 | 88,169 |
| Delaware ..................... | 128,935 | 119,134 | 1,455 | 7,195 | 1,151 | 9,525 | 2,106 | 102,887 | 91,422 |
| Florida........................ | 2,643,282 | 2,581,668 | 17,894 | 3,983 | 39,737 | 155,227 | 447,497 | 2,160,615 | 1,892,529 |
| Georgia....................... | 1,677,067 | 1,663,442 | 10,097 | n/a | 3,528 | 41,981 | 72,661 | 1,019,836 | 911,468 |
| Hawaii........................ | 179,601 | 179,409 | 78 | n/a | 114 | n/a | 8,289 | 121,108 | 104,039 |
| Idaho......................... | 275,859 | 270,907 | 112 | 0 | 4,840 | 15,330 | 1,017 | 205,701 | 191,085 |
| Illinois........................ | 2,082,202 | 2,064,025 | 9,555 | 428 | 8,194 | 43,089 | 75,252 | 1,613,536 | 813,434 |
| Indiana........................ | 1,047,232 | 1,045,416 | 612 | 0 | 1,204 | 22,472 | 12,942 | 784,111 | 584,149 |
| Iowa .......................... | 484,849 | 481,650 | 557 | n/a | 2,642 | 298 | n/a | 318,190 | 174,136 |
| Kansas ....................... | 480,074 | 479,451 | 486 | 1 | 136 | 4,618 | 14,629 | 362,109 | 268,299 |
| Kentucky ..................... | 673,128 | 665,064 | 597 | 0 | 7,467 | n/a | 36,931 | 566,112 | 530,013 |
| Louisiana..................... | 695,772 | 658,227 | 997 | 0 | 36,548 | 29,199 | 40,542 | 594,172 | 566,860 |
| Maine......................... | 183,477 | 183,427 | 50 | 0 | n/a | n/a | 103 | 152,922 | 106,282 |
| Maryland..................... | 852,202 | 831,573 | 4,200 | 8,188 | 8,241 | 14,492 | 81,050 | 183,151 | 139,970 |
| Massachusetts ............... | 955,563 | 911,866 | 4,730 | 35,384 | 3,583 | 28,422 | N.A. | 494,068 | 256,257 |
| Michigan...................... | 1,557,672 | 1,495,750 | 27,062 | 1,314 | 33,546 | 111,984 | 213,508 | 1,262,993 | 704,210 |
| Minnesota.................... | 837,930 | 807,005 | 15,528 | 174 | 15,223 | 37,253 | 36,998 | 324,783 | 97,072 |
| Mississippi................... | 490,526 | 490,526 | n/a | n/a | n/a | n/a | 4,378 | 477,623 | 443,868 |
| Missouri...................... | 918,639 | 908,337 | 3,921 | 4,504 | 1,877 | 20,076 | 14,630 | 400,420 | 222,448 |
| Montana ...................... | 141,693 | 141,577 | 34 | n/a | 82 | n/a | n/a | 113,661 | 68,959 |
| Nebraska ..................... | 298,500 | 297,911 | 589 | n/a | 0 | n/a | n/a | 138,568 | 73,886 |
| Nevada........................ | 437,149 | 432,471 | 839 | 236 | 3,603 | 14,074 | 35,672 | 256,960 | 224,845 |
| New Hampshire ............. | 194,001 | 194,001 | n/a | n/a | n/a | 983 | n/a | 165,115 | 35,757 |
| New Jersey................... | 1,352,815 | 1,319,636 | 6,580 | 24,548 | 2,051 | 24,591 | N.A. | 800,173 | 248,241 |
| New Mexico .................. | 336,005 | 331,126 | 681 | 281 | 3,917 | 15,290 | N.A. | 293,324 | 282,323 |
| New York...................... | 2,734,955 | 2,668,188 | 25,284 | 35,073 | 6,410 | 54,443 | N.R. | 2,614,438 | 1,454,547 |
| North Carolina.............. | 1,488,321 | 1,478,603 | 2,739 | 277 | 6,702 | 42,141 | 69,500 | 1,102,689 | 1,009,791 |
| North Dakota................ | 94,273 | 93,691 | 17 | n/a | 565 | n/a | n/a | 49,682 | 15,836 |
| Ohio .......................... | 1,753,046 | 1,745,614 | 5,641 | 905 | 886 | 97,537 | n/a | 1,317,787 | 909,015 |
| Oklahoma..................... | 659,828 | 658,502 | 254 | n/a | 1,072 | 6,585 | n/a | 431,449 | 369,670 |
| Oregon........................ | 553,617 | 547,851 | 132 | n/a | 5,634 | 20,372 | n/a | 220,645 | 171,333 |
| Pennsylvania ................ | 1,763,859 | 1,743,583 | 1,134 | 18,344 | 798 | 90,613 | 26,478 | 1,243,690 | 742,229 |
| Rhode Island................ | 142,575 | 139,261 | 146 | 1,783 | 1,385 | 3,971 | n/a | 117,125 | 59,489 |
| South Carolina.............. | 724,911 | 723,328 | 813 | 0 | 770 | 16,390 | 79,630 | 599,310 | 544,065 |
| South Dakota................ | 125,883 | 123,650 | 236 | 22 | 1,975 | n/a | n/a | 91,064 | 45,757 |
| Tennessee .................... | 987,422 | 984,153 | 1,796 | 18 | 1,455 | 6,517 | 18,337 | 801,374 | 737,028 |
| Texas.......................... | 4,935,473 | 4,856,643 | 1,970 | n/a | 76,860 | 165,326 | 191,597 | 3,897,469 | 3,689,658 |
| Utah........................... | 585,552 | 574,798 | 6,194 | 4 | 4,556 | 39,862 | 11,100 | 138,502 | 105,139 |
| Vermont....................... | 85,144 | 85,131 | n/a | 0 | 13 | n/a | n/a | 61,613 | 44,713 |
| Virginia....................... | 1,250,206 | 1,247,696 | 377 | 0 | 2,133 | 348 | 131,339 | 334,691 | 198,558 |
| Washington................... | 1,043,472 | 990,425 | 4,553 | 679 | 47,815 | n/a | n/a | 679,354 | 526,328 |
| West Virginia................ | 282,879 | 281,823 | 142 | 12 | 902 | n/a | n/a | 107,119 | 107,119 |
| Wisconsin.................... | 872,164 | 866,602 | 206 | 726 | 4,630 | 36,863 | 1,581 | 559,884 | 196,745 |
| Wyoming ..................... | 88,779 | 87,673 | 7 | n/a | 1,099 | 258 | n/a | 41,455 | 20,647 |
| Dist. of Columbia ......... | 71,263 | 67,967 | 1,436 | 1,083 | 777 | 26,910 | 2,843 | 62,745 | 59,242 |
| **DoDDS:** | | | | | | | | | |
| DoDs Overseas (d) ... | N.A. | N.A. | n/a | n/a | n/a | n/a | n/a | N.A. | N.A. |
| **Bureau of Indian Education ......** | 41,962 | 41,962 | n/a | n/a | n/a | n/a | N.A. | 41,962 | n/a |
| American Samoa .......... | N.A. | N.A. | n/a | N.A. | n/a | N.A. | N.A. | N.A. | N.A. |
| Guam.......................... | 31,618 | 31,618 | n/a | n/a | n/a | N.A. | N.A. | n/a | n/a |
| No. Mariana Islands ..... | 11,105 | 11,105 | n/a | n/a | n/a | n/a | n/a | n/a | n/a |
| Puerto Rico.................. | 473,735 | 454,120 | 2,316 | 16,950 | 349 | n/a | n/a | 472,235 | 442,844 |
| U.S. Virgin Islands........ | 15,495 | 15,495 | n/a | 0 | n/a | n/a | 1,399 | N.A. | N.A. |

See footnotes at end of table.

# TOTAL NUMBER OF STUDENTS IN MEMBERSHIP IN OPERATING PUBLIC AND SECONDARY SCHOOLS, BY SCHOOL TYPE, AND STATE OR JURISDICTION: SCHOOL YEAR 2010–11— Continued

*Source:* U.S. Department of Education, National Center for Education Statistics, Common Core of Data (CCD), "Public Elementary/Secondary School Universe Survey," 2010–11, Version 1a.

*Note:* Numbers and types of schools may differ from those published by states. A school may also be included under the Charter, Magnet, and/or Title I statuses, which are independent of one another and of school type.

*Key:*

N.A. — Not available.

n/a — Not applicable. Membership reported as not applicable or some states do not have charter school authorization and some states do not designate magnet schools.

N.R. — Reporting standards not met. Data reported for less than 80 percent of schools in the state or jurisdiction

(a) Membership is the count of students enrolled on October 1 of the reported school year. Individual state total number of students is included only if the state or jurisdiction reports data for regular, special education, vocational education, and alternative education school types.

(b) Total includes suppressed data due to unmet reporting standards.

(c) Schools eligible for Title I schoolwide programs are also included in the count of all Title I eligible schools.

(d) "Reporting states" totals include the 50 states and the District of Columbia. A "reporting states" total, and not a "United States" total, is shown if data for any item in the table were not available for some, but not more than 15 percent, of all schools in the United States.

Table 9.3
PUBLIC HIGH SCHOOL NUMBER OF GRADUATES, NUMBER OF HIGH SCHOOL DROPOUTS
FOR GRADES 9–12, AND HIGH SCHOOL EVENT DROPOUT RATE FOR GRADES 9–12,
BY GENDER AND STATE OR JURISDICTION: SCHOOL YEAR 2008–09

| | | | High school dropouts (b) | | | |
| | Number of graduates (a) | | Male | | Female | |
| State or other jurisdiction | Male | Female | Number of dropouts | Dropout rate (c) | Number of dropouts | Dropout rate (c) |
|---|---|---|---|---|---|---|
| Reporting states (d) | 1,286,199 | 1,329,709 | 267,370 | 3.6 | 198,154 | 2.7 |
| Alabama | 20,207 | 21,826 | 1,987 | 1.8 | 1,326 | 1.2 |
| Alaska | 3,966 | 4,042 | 1,602 | 7.6 | 1,302 | 6.4 |
| Arizona | 30,459 | 31,843 | 12,733 | 7.9 | 9,845 | 6.4 |
| Arkansas | 14,091 | 13,965 | 3,305 | 4.7 | 2,327 | 3.5 |
| California | N.A. | N.A. | N.A. | N.A. | N.A. | N.A. |
| Colorado | 23,227 | 24,232 | 8,075 | 6.7 | 6,496 | 5.6 |
| Connecticut | 17,270 | 17,696 | 3,508 | 3.9 | 1,876 | 2.2 |
| Delaware | 3,862 | 3,977 | 1,202 | 6.2 | 754 | 4.0 |
| Florida | 72,427 | 77,639 | 11,687 | 3.0 | 8,549 | 2.3 |
| Georgia | 41,306 | 44,857 | 11,691 | 5.1 | 7,768 | 3.4 |
| Hawaii | 6,026 | 5,482 | 1,496 | 5.4 | 1,071 | 4.2 |
| Idaho | 8,371 | 8,436 | 747 | 1.8 | 592 | 1.5 |
| Illinois | 63,901 | 66,193 | 35,414 | 11.5 | 27,568 | 8.6 |
| Indiana | 30,229 | 32,083 | 3,192 | 2.0 | 2,099 | 1.4 |
| Iowa | 16,857 | 17,069 | 2,761 | 3.6 | 2,020 | 2.7 |
| Kansas | 14,973 | 14,729 | 1,683 | 2.4 | 1,130 | 1.7 |
| Kentucky | 20,200 | 20,987 | 2,940 | 2.9 | 2,184 | 2.3 |
| Louisiana | 16,544 | 19,077 | 7,263 | 8.2 | 5,006 | 5.5 |
| Maine | 6,403 | 6,390 | 1,204 | 4.0 | 885 | 3.2 |
| Maryland | 28,217 | 30,087 | N.A. | N.A. | N.A. | N.A. |
| Massachusetts | 32,388 | 32,870 | 5,039 | 3.4 | 3,542 | 2.5 |
| Michigan | 54,787 | 57,297 | 11,994 | 4.4 | 8,321 | 3.2 |
| Minnesota | 30,059 | 29,626 | 2,982 | 2.1 | 2,138 | 1.6 |
| Mississippi | 11,225 | 13,228 | 3,465 | 5.0 | 2,378 | 3.4 |
| Missouri | 31,392 | 31,577 | 6,777 | 4.7 | 5,157 | 3.7 |
| Montana | 5,089 | 4,988 | 1,288 | 5.6 | 984 | 4.5 |
| Nebraska | 9,682 | 9,819 | 1,313 | 2.8 | 865 | 2.0 |
| Nevada | N.A. | N.A. | N.A. | N.A. | N.A. | N.A. |
| New Hampshire | 7,434 | 7,323 | 670 | 2.0 | 445 | 1.4 |
| New Jersey | 47,721 | 47,364 | 3,975 | 1.8 | 2,944 | 1.4 |
| New Mexico | 8,745 | 9,186 | 2,697 | 5.4 | 2,095 | 4.4 |
| New York | 88,242 | 92,352 | 21,408 | 4.9 | 15,237 | 3.6 |
| North Carolina | 41,247 | 43,600 | 13,387 | 6.2 | 8,990 | 4.3 |
| North Dakota | 3,646 | 3,586 | 406 | 2.6 | 351 | 2.4 |
| Ohio | 59,687 | 60,141 | 12,469 | 4.3 | 10,508 | 3.8 |
| Oklahoma | 18,649 | 18,570 | 2,450 | 2.7 | 2,012 | 2.3 |
| Oregon | 16,864 | 17,151 | 3,257 | 3.7 | 2,579 | 3.2 |
| Pennsylvania | 64,759 | 65,483 | 7,620 | 2.6 | 5,559 | 2.0 |
| Rhode Island | 4,864 | 5,164 | 1,233 | 5.2 | 853 | 3.7 |
| South Carolina | 18,141 | 20,792 | 4,055 | 3.8 | 2,986 | 2.9 |
| South Dakota | 4,058 | 4,065 | 376 | 1.9 | 307 | 1.6 |
| Tennessee | 29,651 | 30,717 | 5,398 | 3.7 | 3,718 | 2.6 |
| Texas | 131,773 | 132,468 | 22,595 | 3.4 | 18,924 | 3.0 |
| Utah | 15,000 | 15,358 | N.A. | N.A. | N.A. | N.A. |
| Vermont | N.A. | N.A. | N.A. | N.A. | N.A. | N.A. |
| Virginia | 38,014 | 40,395 | 5,484 | 2.9 | 3,833 | 2.1 |
| Washington | 30,056 | 31,876 | 8,497 | 5.1 | 6,557 | 4.1 |
| West Virginia | 8,818 | 8,872 | 1,947 | 4.5 | 1,497 | 3.7 |
| Wisconsin | 32,919 | 32,491 | 3,941 | 2.7 | 2,471 | 1.8 |
| Wyoming | 2,753 | 2,740 | 157 | 1.1 | 105 | 0.8 |
| District of Columbia | 1,498 | 2,019 | 629 | 7.6 | 545 | 5.9 |
| DoDDS: DoDs Overseas (e) | N.A. | N.A. | N.A. | N.A. | N.A. | N.A. |
| DDESS: DoDs Domestic (e) | N.A. | N.A. | N.A. | N.A. | N.A. | N.A. |
| Bureau of Indian Education | N.A. | N.A. | N.A. | N.A. | N.A. | N.A. |
| American Samoa | N.A. | N.A. | N.A. | N.A. | N.A. | N.A. |
| Guam | N.A. | N.A. | N.A. | N.A. | N.A. | N.A. |
| No. Mariana Islands | N.A. | N.A. | N.A. | N.A. | N.A. | N.A. |
| Puerto Rico | N.A. | N.A. | N.A. | N.A. | N.A. | N.A. |
| U.S. Virgin Islands | 397 | 543 | 256 | 10.4 | 131 | 4.8 |

See footnotes at end of table.

# PUBLIC HIGH SCHOOL NUMBER OF GRADUATES, NUMBER OF HIGH SCHOOL DROPOUTS FOR GRADES 9–12, AND HIGH SCHOOL EVENT DROPOUT RATE FOR GRADES 9–12, BY GENDER AND STATE OR JURISDICTION: SCHOOL YEAR 2008–09—Continued

*Source:* U.S. Department of Education, National Center for Education Statistics, Common Core of Data (CCD), "NCES Common Core of Data State Dropout and Completion Data File," School Year 2008–09, Version 1a; and "NCES Common Core of Data Local Education Agency Universe Survey Dropout and Completion Restricted-Use Data File," School Year 2008–09, Version 1a.

*Key:*

N.A. — Not available. State or jurisdiction did not report graduate counts or dropout counts by gender.

(a) Graduate counts were calculated using district-level data. Totals may differ from graduate counts on other tables due to different reporting levels. Graduation rates were not calculated due to missing data at the school district level.

(b) Ungraded dropouts are prorated by NCES into grades based on the graded dropout counts to calculate numerators for dropout rates. Ungraded student enrollments are prorated by NCES into grades based on graded enrollments to calculate denominators for dropout rates.

(c) The event dropout rate is defined as the count of dropouts from a given school year divided by the count of student enrollments within the same grade span at the beginning of the same school year.

(d) Reporting states totals include any of the 50 states and the District of Columbia that reported all data elements.

(e) DoDDS and DDESS are the Department of Defense Overseas Dependent Elementary and Secondary Schools and the Department of Defense Domestic Dependent Elementary and Secondary Schools, respectively.

## Table 9.4
## TOTAL REVENUES, PERCENTAGE DISTRIBUTION, AND REVENUES PER PUPIL FOR PUBLIC ELEMENTARY AND SECONDARY SCHOOLS, BY SOURCE AND STATE OR JURISDICTION: FISCAL YEAR 2009

| State or other jurisdiction | Revenues (in thousands of dollars) | | | | Percentage distribution | | |
|---|---|---|---|---|---|---|---|
| | Total | Local (a) | State | Federal | Local (a) | State | Federal |
| United States (b) .............. | $593,061,181 | $259,250,999 | $277,079,518 | $56,730,664 | 43.7 | 46.7 | 9.6 |
| Alabama............................ | 7,239,083 | 2,295,475 | 4,166,018 | 777,591 | 31.7 | 57.5 | 10.7 |
| Alaska............................... | 2,262,964 | 488,356 | 1,459,658 | 314,949 | 21.6 | 64.5 | 13.9 |
| Arizona............................. | 9,771,972 | 4,040,008 | 4,594,648 | 1,137,316 | 41.3 | 47.0 | 11.6 |
| Arkansas........................... | 4,823,956 | 1,583,147 | 2,684,309 | 556,500 | 32.8 | 55.6 | 11.5 |
| California ......................... | 70,687,012 | 20,895,829 | 40,605,913 | 9,185,270 | 29.6 | 57.4 | 13.0 |
| Colorado........................... | 8,353,849 | 4,105,376 | 3,670,240 | 578,233 | 49.1 | 43.9 | 6.9 |
| Connecticut....................... | 9,871,755 | 5,588,751 | 3,842,177 | 440,826 | 56.6 | 38.9 | 4.5 |
| Delaware ........................... | 1,755,133 | 517,796 | 1,094,909 | 142,428 | 29.5 | 62.4 | 8.1 |
| Florida.............................. | 26,322,090 | 14,579,923 | 9,047,588 | 2,694,579 | 55.4 | 34.4 | 10.2 |
| Georgia............................. | 18,017,477 | 8,548,478 | 7,780,725 | 1,688,274 | 47.4 | 43.2 | 9.4 |
| Hawaii (c)......................... | 2,689,757 | 91,889 | 2,205,032 | 392,837 | 3.4 | 82.0 | 14.6 |
| Idaho................................ | 2,243,784 | 504,812 | 1,509,815 | 229,156 | 22.5 | 67.3 | 10.2 |
| Illinois.............................. | 26,512,711 | 16,041,221 | 7,324,750 | 3,146,741 | 60.5 | 27.6 | 11.9 |
| Indiana............................. | 12,569,782 | 6,172,042 | 4,964,928 | 1,432,813 | 49.1 | 39.5 | 11.4 |
| Iowa ................................. | 5,519,854 | 2,530,666 | 2,545,360 | 443,827 | 45.8 | 46.1 | 8.0 |
| Kansas.............................. | 5,757,927 | 1,980,973 | 3,323,346 | 453,608 | 34.4 | 57.7 | 7.9 |
| Kentucky........................... | 6,641,128 | 2,107,627 | 3,802,150 | 731,351 | 31.7 | 57.3 | 11.0 |
| Louisiana.......................... | 8,099,981 | 3,095,662 | 3,740,262 | 1,264,057 | 38.2 | 46.2 | 15.6 |
| Maine................................ | 2,575,516 | 1,202,765 | 1,127,032 | 245,719 | 46.7 | 43.8 | 9.5 |
| Maryland........................... | 13,097,508 | 6,703,926 | 5,698,735 | 694,847 | 51.2 | 43.5 | 5.3 |
| Massachusetts .................... | 15,102,480 | 7,790,028 | 6,036,202 | 1,276,250 | 51.6 | 40.0 | 8.5 |
| Michigan........................... | 19,585,635 | 6,427,004 | 10,904,987 | 2,253,644 | 32.8 | 55.7 | 11.5 |
| Minnesota.......................... | 10,542,303 | 2,995,407 | 6,914,839 | 632,057 | 28.4 | 65.6 | 6.0 |
| Mississippi......................... | 4,360,702 | 1,350,375 | 2,334,355 | 675,972 | 31.0 | 53.5 | 15.5 |
| Missouri............................ | 10,042,753 | 5,783,128 | 3,425,716 | 833,909 | 57.6 | 34.1 | 8.3 |
| Montana............................ | 1,595,197 | 622,089 | 774,091 | 199,017 | 39.0 | 48.5 | 12.5 |
| Nebraska........................... | 3,455,794 | 1,961,810 | 1,213,317 | 280,666 | 56.8 | 35.1 | 8.1 |
| Nevada.............................. | 4,450,741 | 2,654,134 | 1,362,123 | 434,484 | 59.6 | 30.6 | 9.8 |
| New Hampshire .................. | 2,717,115 | 1,566,547 | 1,003,249 | 147,318 | 57.7 | 36.9 | 5.4 |
| New Jersey ........................ | 25,283,290 | 13,717,006 | 10,525,550 | 1,040,733 | 54.3 | 41.6 | 4.1 |
| New Mexico ....................... | 3,820,116 | 575,152 | 2,675,916 | 569,047 | 15.1 | 70.0 | 14.9 |
| New York........................... | 55,558,190 | 26,991,217 | 25,346,556 | 3,220,417 | 48.6 | 45.6 | 5.8 |
| North Carolina................... | 13,322,946 | 3,515,648 | 8,401,249 | 1,406,049 | 26.4 | 63.1 | 10.6 |
| North Dakota..................... | 1,102,479 | 532,990 | 408,004 | 161,484 | 48.3 | 37.0 | 14.6 |
| Ohio ................................. | 22,956,215 | 10,352,625 | 10,917,974 | 1,685,617 | 45.1 | 47.6 | 7.3 |
| Oklahoma.......................... | 5,729,610 | 1,916,378 | 3,042,487 | 770,745 | 33.0 | 53.1 | 13.5 |
| Oregon.............................. | 6,145,206 | 2,357,357 | 3,117,303 | 670,547 | 38.0 | 50.7 | 9.7 |
| Pennsylvania ..................... | 25,632,072 | 13,843,699 | 9,920,340 | 1,868,034 | 54.0 | 38.7 | 7.3 |
| Rhode Island...................... | 2,232,149 | 1,199,044 | 817,590 | 215,514 | 53.7 | 36.6 | 9.0 |
| South Carolina................... | 7,702,962 | 3,260,758 | 3,679,907 | 762,297 | 42.0 | 47.8 | 9.9 |
| South Dakota..................... | 1,241,892 | 628,359 | 410,179 | 203,354 | 50.6 | 33.0 | 16.4 |
| Tennessee .......................... | 8,283,928 | 3,539,325 | 3,809,467 | 935,135 | 42.7 | 46.0 | 11.3 |
| Texas................................ | 46,962,119 | 21,974,171 | 19,973,129 | 5,014,820 | 46.8 | 42.5 | 10.7 |
| Utah................................. | 4,542,690 | 1,589,970 | 2,387,698 | 565,022 | 35.0 | 52.6 | 12.4 |
| Vermont............................ | 1,571,006 | 121,922 | 1,346,300 | 102,785 | 7.8 | 85.7 | 6.5 |
| Virginia............................. | 14,964,444 | 7,746,272 | 6,303,648 | 914,524 | 51.8 | 42.1 | 6.1 |
| Washington........................ | 11,903,510 | 3,371,667 | 7,146,394 | 1,385,449 | 28.3 | 60.0 | 11.6 |
| West Virginia..................... | 3,281,385 | 976,347 | 1,938,999 | 366,038 | 29.8 | 59.1 | 11.2 |
| Wisconsin ......................... | 10,832,105 | 4,720,471 | 4,809,185 | 1,302,449 | 43.6 | 44.4 | 12.0 |
| Wyoming .......................... | 1,675,896 | 620,095 | 945,167 | 110,634 | 37.0 | 56.4 | 6.6 |
| Dist. of Columbia (c)......... | 1,651,014 | 1,475,283 | n/a. | 175,732 | 89.4 | n/a. | 10.6 |
| American Samoa ............... | 79,922 | 209 | 11,282 (d) | 68,432 | 0.3 | 14.1 | 85.6 |
| Guam................................ | 262,823 | 212,652 | n/a. | 50,170 | 80.9 | n/a. | 19.1 |
| No. Mariana Islands .......... | 65,538 | 225 | 34,602 (d) | 30,711 | 0.3 | 52.8 | 46.9 |
| Puerto Rico ....................... | 3,542,658 | 3,787 | 2,462,725 (d) | 1,076,147 | 0.1 | 69.5 | 30.4 |
| U.S. Virgin Islands ............. | 243,079 | 203,042 | n/a. | 40,037 | 83.5 | n/a. | 16.5 |

*Source:* U.S. Department of Education, National Center for Education Statistics, Common Core of Data (CCD), "National Public Education Financial Survey (NPEFS)," fiscal year 2009, Version 1a.

*Note:* Detail may not sum to totals because of rounding.

*Key:*

n/a.— Not applicable.

(a) Local revenues include intermediate revenues from education agencies with fundraising capabilities that operate between the state and local government levels.

(b) U.S. totals include the 50 states and the District of Columbia.

(c) Both the District of Columbia and Hawaii have only one school district each; therefore, neither is comparable to other states. Local revenues in Hawaii consist almost entirely of student fees and charges for services, such as food services, summer school, and student activities.

(d) Reported state revenue data are revenues received from the central government of the jurisdiction.

## Table 9.5
## TOTAL EXPENDITURES FOR PUBLIC ELEMENTARY AND SECONDARY EDUCATION: FISCAL YEAR 2009

| State or other jurisdiction | Expenditures (in thousands of dollars) | | | | | |
|---|---|---|---|---|---|---|
| | Total | Current for elementary/ secondary education (a) | Facilities acquisitions and construction | Replacement equipment | Other programs (b) | Interest on debt |
| United States (c).......... | $610,109,923(d)(e) | $518,997,430(d) | $59,175,475(e) | $6,706,440(d)(e) | $8,539,329(d)(e) | $16,691,228(e) |
| Alabama....................... | 7,866,617 | 6,683,843 | 877,252 | 49,894 | 115,007 | 140,621 |
| Alaska......................... | 2,359,510 | 2,006,114 | 287,076 | 17,428 | 7,966 | 40,926 |
| Arizona....................... | 10,451,060(d)(e) | 8,625,276(d) | 100,802 | 241,789(d)(e) | 51,625(e) | 531,568 |
| Arkansas..................... | 4,862,688(d) | 4,240,839(d) | 406,241 | 67,197 | 28,502 | 119,909 |
| California..................... | 72,059,482(d) | 60,080,929(d) | 8,656,312 | 188,550(d) | 1,235,054 | 1,898,637 |
| Colorado...................... | 8,732,152 | 7,187,267 | 889,650 | 159,106 | 56,266 | 439,864 |
| Connecticut................. | 9,904,492(d)(e) | 8,708,294(d) | 786,749 | 106,917(d)(e) | 146,086(e) | 156,445 |
| Delaware ..................... | 1,834,876 | 1,518,786 | 251,203 | 6,884 | 20,920 | 46,083 |
| Florida ........................ | 29,197,311(d) | 23,328,028(d) | 4,419,080 | 104,181 | 510,550 | 8,325,471 |
| Georgia........................ | 18,989,232(d) | 15,976,945(d) | 2,526,583 | 188,185 | 36,743 | 260,776 |
| Hawaii (f)..................... | 2,423,593 | 2,225,437 | 58,408 | 11,456 | 25,231 | 103,060 |
| Idaho........................... | 2,370,488(d) | 1,957,740(d) | 316,766 | 35,557 | 4,266 | 56,159 |
| Illinois......................... | 27,273,680(d) | 23,495,271(d) | 2,320,911 | 563,384 | 165,318 | 728,796 |
| Indiana........................ | 11,069,893(d) | 9,680,895(d) | 719,031 | 210,120 | 142,523 | 317,325 |
| Iowa ........................... | 5,517,616 | 4,731,463 | 575,588 | 101,740 | 27,506 | 81,318 |
| Kansas ........................ | 5,389,538 | 4,805,310 | 238,116 | 171,535 | 6,268 | 168,308 |
| Kentucky ..................... | 6,839,799 | 5,886,890 | 602,921 | 111,400 | 86,735 | 151,852 |
| Louisiana..................... | 8,269,661(d) | 7,276,651(d) | 751,473 | 77,581 | 54,859 | 109,097 |
| Maine........................... | 2,579,168(d) | 2,350,447(d) | 121,441 | 34,862 | 27,881 | 44,537 |
| Maryland...................... | 12,753,441(d) | 11,591,965(d) | 888,193 | 100,702 | 25,038 | 147,544 |
| Massachusetts .............. | 15,081,541(d) | 13,942,586(d) | 781,961 | 11,738 | 65,704 | 279,552 |
| Michigan...................... | 19,897,270 | 17,217,584 | 1,224,195 | 245,198 | 339,221 | 871,072 |
| Minnesota.................... | 11,332,655(d) | 9,270,281(d) | 1,063,806 | 152,020 | 422,034 | 424,514 |
| Mississippi .................. | 4,402,170(d) | 3,967,232(d) | 207,916 | 125,646 | 28,517 | 72,858 |
| Missouri....................... | 10,466,632 | 8,827,224 | 884,834 | 244,419 | 195,440 | 314,714 |
| Montana ...................... | 1,624,979 | 1,436,062 | 135,449 | 26,486 | 9,036 | 17,946 |
| Nebraska ..................... | 3,579,827(d) | 3,053,575 | 353,115 | 96,850(d) | 3,242(d) | 73,045 |
| Nevada........................ | 4,550,664 | 3,606,035 | 610,473 | 23,096 | 22,291 | 288,769 |
| New Hampshire ........... | 2,655,947 | 2,490,623 | 80,835 | 31,673 | 7,225 | 45,591 |
| New Jersey .................. | 25,623,867(d) | 23,589,224 | 1,323,431 | 108,620(d) | 249,594 | 352,997 |
| New Mexico ................. | 3,912,992 | 3,186,252 | 705,386 | 16,986 | 4,229 | 138 |
| New York ..................... | 54,766,076(d) | 48,635,363(d) | 2,506,573 | 402,086 | 2,103,039 | 1,119,015 |
| North Carolina............. | 14,242,947 | 12,470,470 | 1,378,025 | 315,281 | 72,203 | 6,967 |
| North Dakota............... | 1,046,126 | 928,528 | 62,369 | 33,007 | 9,129 | 13,093 |
| Ohio............................ | 22,901,610 | 19,397,511 | 2,157,673 | 398,678 | 470,118 | 477,631 |
| Oklahoma.................... | 5,622,898 | 5,082,062 | 397,548 | 75,010 | 12,794 | 55,484 |
| Oregon........................ | 6,624,906 | 5,529,831 | 759,605 | 43,463 | 23,268 | 268,739 |
| Pennsylvania ............... | 26,001,339 | 21,831,816 | 2,121,265 | 347,610 | 599,517 | 1,101,131 |
| Rhode Island................ | 2,259,628(d) | 2,139,317(d) | 12,424 | 13,099 | 57,046 | 37,742 |
| South Carolina............. | 8,378,028 | 6,626,763 | 1,238,106 | 79,569 | 74,810 | 358,781 |
| South Dakota............... | 1,273,677 | 1,080,054 | 122,935 | 44,364 | 3,630 | 22,694 |
| Tennessee .................... | 8,645,029(d) | 7,768,052(d) | 520,396 | 115,717 | 65,622 | 175,242 |
| Texas........................... | 52,980,125(d) | 40,688,181(d) | 8,904,438 | 388,719 | 303,178 | 2,695,608 |
| Utah............................ | 4,754,524 | 3,638,775 | 798,010 | 93,445 | 104,773 | 119,521 |
| Vermont....................... | 1,501,278 | 1,413,329 | 37,285 | 27,237 | 10,119 | 13,308 |
| Virginia........................ | 15,155,776(d) | 13,505,290 | 1,148,766 | 270,144 | 77,601 | 153,975 |
| Washington.................. | 12,226,885(d) | 9,940,056(d) | 1,708,236 | 103,000 | 57,389 | 418,204 |
| West Virginia............... | 3196,380(d) | 3,059,420(d) | 31,914 | 51,443(d) | 41,145 | 12,458 |
| Wisconsin .................... | 11,135,130 | 9,696,228 | 476,816 | 154,630 | 301,023 | 506,432 |
| Wyoming ..................... | 1,650,665 | 1,268,407 | 325,198 | 47,312 | 7,289 | 2,460 |
| Dist. of Columbia (f).... | 1,865,053(d) | 1,352,905(d) | 402,716 | 71,424 | 24,754 | 13,254 |
| American Samoa ......... | 71,468 | 65,436 | 2,150 | 1,902 | 1,980 | 0 |
| Guam .......................... | 265,065(e) | 235,711 | 17,254 | 5,545 | 0 | 6,555(e) |
| No. Mariana Islands .... | 65,766(d) | 62,787(d) | 215 | 1,188 | 1,576 | 0 |
| Puerto Rico.................. | 4,026,886(d)(e) | 3,502,757(d) | 334,939(e) | 82,173 | 101,921 | 5,096 |
| U.S. Virgin Islands ....... | 207,633(d) | 201,326(d) | 3,963 | 666(d) | 1,677 | 0 |

See footnotes at end of table.

# TOTAL EXPENDITURES FOR PUBLIC ELEMENTARY AND SECONDARY EDUCATION: FISCAL YEAR 2009
## —Continued

*Source:* U.S. Department of Education, National Center for Education Statistics, Common Core of Data (CCD), "National Public Education Financial Survey (NPEFS)," fiscal year 2009, Version 1a.

*Note:* Detail may not sum to totals because of rounding.

(a) Include instruction, instruction-related, support services, and other elementary/secondary current expenditures, but exclude expenditures on capital outlay, other programs, and interest on long-term debt.

(b) Includes expenditures for community services, adult education, community colleges, private schools, and other programs that are not part of public elementary and secondary education.

(c) U.S. totals include the 50 states and the District of Columbia.

(d) Value affected by redistribution of reported values to correct for missing data items and/or to distribute state direct support expenditures.

(e) Value contains imputation for missing data.

(f) Both the District of Columbia and Hawaii have only one school district each; therefore, neither is comparable to other states.

## Table 9.6
## CURRENT EXPENDITURES AND PERCENTAGE DISTRIBUTION FOR PUBLIC ELEMENTARY AND SECONDARY EDUCATION, BY FUNCTION AND STATE OR JURISDICTION: FISCAL YEAR 2009

| State or other jurisdiction | Total | Instruction and instruction related (b) | Student support (c) | Administration (d) | Operations (e) | Instruction and instruction related (b) | Student support (c) | Admin. (d) | Ops. (e) |
|---|---|---|---|---|---|---|---|---|---|
| | | Current expenditures (in thousands of dollars) (a) | | | | Percentage distribution | | | |
| United States (f) | $518,997,430(g) | $341,333,417(g) | $28,104,003(g) | $56,205,466(g) | $93,354,543(g) | 65.8 | 5.4 | 10.8 | 18.0 |
| Alabama | 6,683,843 | 4,209,460 | 373,911 | 720,345 | 1,380,127 | 63.0 | 5.6 | 10.8 | 20.6 |
| Alaska | 2,006,114 | 1,236,883 | 161,052 | 224,715 | 383,464 | 61.7 | 8.0 | 11.2 | 19.1 |
| Arizona | 8,625,276(g) | 5,437,417(g) | 530,369(g) | 923,845(g) | 1,733,645(g) | 63.0 | 6.1 | 10.7 | 20.1 |
| Arkansas | 4,240,839(g) | 2,798,792(g) | 210,994(g) | 431,139(g) | 799,914(g) | 66.0 | 5.0 | 10.2 | 18.9 |
| California | 60,080,929(g) | 39,870,809(g) | 3,067,163(g) | 7,134,964(g) | 10,007,994(g) | 66.4 | 5.1 | 11.9 | 16.7 |
| Colorado | 7,187,267 | 4,536,864 | 334,618 | 1,119,177 | 1,196,607 | 63.1 | 4.7 | 15.6 | 16.6 |
| Connecticut | 8,708,294(g) | 5,714,525(g) | 539,182(g) | 877,466(g) | 1,577,120(g) | 65.6 | 6.2 | 10.1 | 18.1 |
| Delaware | 1,518,786 | 943,160 | 76,345 | 183,543 | 315,737 | 62.1 | 5.0 | 12.1 | 20.8 |
| Florida | 23,328,028(g) | 15,617,921(g) | 1,087,761(g) | 2,146,232(g) | 4,476,114(g) | 66.9 | 4.7 | 9.2 | 19.2 |
| Georgia | 15,976,945(g) | 10,821,624(g) | 766,374(g) | 1,699,692(g) | 2,689,254(g) | 67.7 | 4.8 | 10.6 | 16.8 |
| Hawaii (h) | 2,225,437 | 1,457,641 | 211,127 | 223,022 | 333,647 | 65.5 | 9.5 | 10.0 | 15.0 |
| Idaho | 1,957,740(g) | 1,273,409(g) | 113,401(g) | 196,274(g) | 374,656(g) | 65.0 | 5.8 | 10.0 | 19.1 |
| Illinois | 23,495,271(g) | 14,897,532(g) | 1,508,922(g) | 3,027,032(g) | 4,061,785(g) | 63.4 | 6.4 | 12.9 | 17.3 |
| Indiana | 9,680,895(g) | 6,010,358(g) | 451,616(g) | 1,091,532(g) | 2,127,390(g) | 62.1 | 4.7 | 11.3 | 22.0 |
| Iowa | 4,731,463 | 3,111,969 | 268,931 | 543,224 | 807,340 | 65.8 | 5.7 | 11.5 | 17.1 |
| Kansas | 4,805,310 | 3,127,431 | 276,623 | 543,474 | 857,782 | 65.1 | 5.8 | 11.3 | 17.9 |
| Kentucky | 5,886,890 | 3,796,829 | 260,815 | 588,775 | 1,240,471 | 64.5 | 4.4 | 10.0 | 21.1 |
| Louisiana | 7,276,651(g) | 4,612,957(g) | 334,256(g) | 813,512(g) | 1,515,927(g) | 63.4 | 4.6 | 11.2 | 20.8 |
| Maine | 2,350,447(g) | 1,527,457(g) | 147,738(g) | 241,229(g) | 434,023 | 65.0 | 6.3 | 10.3 | 18.5 |
| Maryland | 11,591,965(g) | 7,744,425(g) | 529,879(g) | 1,203,579(g) | 2,114,082 | 66.8 | 4.6 | 10.4 | 18.2 |
| Massachusetts | 13,942,586(g) | 9,734,532(g) | 956,365(g) | 1,073,285 | 2,178,404 | 69.8 | 6.9 | 7.7 | 15.6 |
| Michigan | 17,217,584 | 10,663,874 | 1,306,870 | 2,152,661 | 3,094,179 | 61.9 | 7.6 | 12.5 | 18.0 |
| Minnesota | 9,270,281(g) | 6,467,005(g) | 247,591(g) | 995,876(g) | 1,559,809(g) | 69.8 | 2.7 | 10.7 | 16.8 |
| Mississippi | 3,967,232(g) | 2,509,877(g) | 186,883(g) | 435,199(g) | 835,274(g) | 63.3 | 4.7 | 11.0 | 21.1 |
| Missouri | 8,827,224 | 5,710,394 | 414,203 | 986,285 | 1,716,343 | 64.7 | 4.7 | 11.2 | 19.4 |
| Montana | 1,436,062 | 917,809 | 81,182 | 152,746 | 284,325 | 63.9 | 5.7 | 10.6 | 19.8 |
| Nebraska | 3,053,575 | 2,069,593 | 112,011 | 307,745 | 564,226 | 67.8 | 3.7 | 10.1 | 18.5 |
| Nevada | 3,606,035 | 2,331,320 | 173,167 | 446,466 | 655,081 | 64.7 | 4.8 | 12.4 | 18.2 |
| New Hampshire | 2,490,623 | 1,678,766 | 173,945 | 243,606 | 394,306 | 67.4 | 7.0 | 9.8 | 15.8 |
| New Jersey | 23,589,224 | 14,686,274 | 2,187,782 | 2,253,314 | 4,461,854 | 62.3 | 9.3 | 9.6 | 18.9 |
| New Mexico | 3,186,252 | 1,933,201 | 324,958 | 362,062 | 566,032 | 60.7 | 10.2 | 11.4 | 17.8 |
| New York | 48,635,363(g) | 35,005,524(g) | 1,629,616(g) | 4,191,181(g) | 7,809,042(g) | 72.0 | 3.4 | 8.6 | 16.1 |
| North Carolina | 12,470,470 | 8,372,971 | 572,903 | 1,301,261 | 2,223,336 | 67.1 | 4.6 | 10.4 | 17.8 |
| North Dakota | 928,528 | 570,648 | 38,023 | 111,595 | 208,262 | 61.5 | 4.1 | 12.0 | 22.4 |
| Ohio | 19,397,511 | 12,310,607 | 1,180,645 | 2,555,132 | 3,351,127 | 63.5 | 6.1 | 13.2 | 17.3 |
| Oklahoma | 5,082,062 | 3,092,681 | 342,773 | 563,608 | 1,083,001 | 60.9 | 6.7 | 11.1 | 21.3 |
| Oregon | 5,529,831 | 3,457,726 | 397,276 | 781,815 | 893,015 | 62.5 | 7.2 | 14.1 | 16.1 |
| Pennsylvania | 21,831,816 | 14,053,422 | 1,086,621 | 2,419,772 | 4,272,001 | 64.4 | 5.0 | 11.1 | 19.6 |
| Rhode Island | 2,139,317(g) | 1,350,162(g) | 266,637(g) | 203,333(g) | 319,186(g) | 63.1 | 12.5 | 9.5 | 14.9 |
| South Carolina | 6,626,763 | 4,263,993 | 487,739 | 682,779 | 1,192,252 | 64.3 | 7.4 | 10.3 | 18.0 |
| South Dakota | 1,080,054 | 671,377 | 61,302 | 131,806 | 215,569 | 62.2 | 5.7 | 12.2 | 20.0 |
| Tennessee | 7,768,052(g) | 5,327,093(g) | 321,372 | 746,738 | 1,372,849 | 68.6 | 4.1 | 9.6 | 17.7 |
| Texas | 40,688,181(g) | 26,535,438(g) | 1,971,160(g) | 4,363,881(g) | 7,817,702(g) | 65.2 | 4.8 | 10.7 | 19.2 |
| Utah | 3,638,775 | 2,510,179 | 138,666 | 344,254 | 645,675 | 69.0 | 3.8 | 9.5 | 17.7 |
| Vermont | 1,413,329 | 937,989 | 103,821 | 163,303 | 208,216 | 66.4 | 7.3 | 11.6 | 14.7 |
| Virginia | 13,505,290 | 9,100,777 | 655,441 | 1,235,758 | 2,513,315 | 67.4 | 4.9 | 9.2 | 18.6 |
| Washington | 9,940,056(g) | 6,425,796(g) | 660,150 | 1,134,446 | 1,719,663 | 64.6 | 6.6 | 11.4 | 17.3 |
| West Virginia | 3,059,420(g) | 1,948,448(g) | 113,038(g) | 285,772(g) | 712,161(g) | 63.7 | 3.7 | 9.3 | 23.3 |
| Wisconsin | 9,696,228 | 6,406,522 | 448,911 | 1,259,262 | 1,581,533 | 66.1 | 4.6 | 13.0 | 16.3 |
| Wyoming | 1,268,407 | 829,548 | 73,057 | 142,376 | 223,426 | 65.4 | 5.8 | 11.2 | 17.6 |
| Dist. of Columbia (h) | 1,352,905 | 712,407 | 138,818 | 245,382 | 256,298 | 52.7 | 10.3 | 18.1 | 18.9 |
| American Samoa | 65,436 | 36,109 | 1,799 | 8,514 | 19,014 | 55.2 | 2.7 | 13.0 | 29.1 |
| Guam | 235,711 | 142,016 | 26,318 | 20,738 | 46,639 | 60.3 | 11.2 | 8.8 | 19.8 |
| No. Mariana Islands | 62,787(g) | 33,763(g) | 7,857(g) | 8,674(g) | 12,493(g) | 53.8 | 12.5 | 13.8 | 19.9 |
| Puerto Rico | 3,502,757(g) | 1,906,650(g) | 227,299(g) | 500,594(g) | 868,215(g) | 54.4 | 6.5 | 14.3 | 24.8 |
| U.S. Virgin Islands | 201,326(g) | 12,231(g) | 11,687(g) | 36,440(g) | 31,968(g) | 60.2 | 5.8 | 18.1 | 15.9 |

See footnotes at end of table.

## CURRENT EXPENDITURES AND PERCENTAGE DISTRIBUTION FOR PUBLIC ELEMENTARY AND SECONDARY EDUCATION, BY FUNCTION AND STATE OR JURISDICTION: FISCAL YEAR 2009 — Continued

*Source:* U.S. Department of Education, National Center for Education Statistics, Common Core of Data (CCD), "National Public Education Financial Survey (NPEFS)," fiscal year 2009, Version 1a.

*Note:* Detail may not sum to totals because of rounding.

(a) Include instruction, instruction-related, support services, and other elementary/secondary current expenditures, but exclude expenditures on capital outlay, other programs, and interest on long-term debt.

(b) Include current expenditures for classroom instruction (including teachers and teaching assistants), libraries, in-service teacher training, curriculum development, student assessment and instruction technology.

(c) Include attendance and social work, guidance, health, psychological services, speech pathology, audiology, and other student support services.

(d) Include general administration, school administration, and other support services.

(e) Include operations and maintenance, student transportation, food services, and enterprise operations.

(f) U.S. totals include the 50 states and the District of Columbia.

(g) Value affected by redistribution of reported expenditure values to correct for missing data items, and/or to distribute state direct support expenditures.

(h) Both the District of Columbia and Hawaii have only one school district each; therefore, neither is comparable to other states.

## Table 9.7
## CURRENT INSTRUCTION AND INSTRUCTION-RELATED EXPENDITURES FOR PUBLIC ELEMENTARY AND SECONDARY EDUCATION, BY OBJECT AND STATE OR JURISDICTION: FISCAL YEAR 2009

| State or other jurisdiction | Current instruction and instruction-related expenditures (in thousands of dollars)(a) | | | | | | |
|---|---|---|---|---|---|---|---|
| | Total | Salaries | Employee benefits | Purchased services | Tuition to out-of-state and private schools | Instructional supplies | Other |
| United States (b) ...... | $316,345,253 (c) | $213,460,836 (c) | $71,021,533 (c) | $12,717,008 (c) | $4,521,684 (c) | $13,330,592 (c) | $1,293,601 (c) |
| Alabama.................... | 3,897,501 | 2,538,697 | 995,729 | 103,225 | 2,220 | 245,035 | 12,595 |
| Alaska...................... | 1,123,574 | 605,310 | 394,576 | 58,449 | 189 | 55,816 | 9,234 |
| Arizona..................... | 5,205,607 (c) | 3,901,008 (c) | 842,989 (c) | 227,016 (c) | 40,985 | 164,888 (c) | 28,721 (c) |
| Arkansas................... | 2,462,105 (c) | 1,716,716 (c) | 448,615 (c) | 79,542 (c) | 11,180 | 187,295 (c) | 18,755 (c) |
| California ................. | 35,942,432 (c) | 24,365,952 (c) | 7,573,923 (c) | 1,580,419 (c) | 795,996 | 1,622,480 (c) | 3,662 (c) |
| Colorado................... | 4,141,866 | 2,970,930 | 686,311 | 105,025 | 41,608 | 277,943 | 60,049 |
| Connecticut.............. | 5,441,636 (c) | 3,444,804 (c) | 1,330,077 (c) | 176,677 (c) | 357,872 | 124,644 (c) | 7,562 (c) |
| Delaware .................. | 925,411 | 595,657 | 262,135 | 12,515 | 6,510 | 38,954 | 9,640 |
| Florida ..................... | 14,104,997 (c) | 8,945,024 (c) | 2,693,246 (c) | 1,860,387 (c) | 1,027 | 499,287 (c) | 106,025 (c) |
| Georgia..................... | 10,013,104 (c) | 7,143,976 (c) | 2,045,123 (c) | 220,2654 (c) | 6,211 | 559,662 (c) | 37,868 (c) |
| Hawaii (d) ................ | 1,384,466 | 868,444 | 342,919 | 78,083 | 5,573 | 80,934 | 8,513 |
| Idaho........................ | 1,192,267 (c) | 826,522 (c) | 267,652 (c) | 43,233 (c) | 1,152 | 53,322 (c) | 387 (c) |
| Illinois..................... | 13,813,130 (c) | 9,200,780 (c) | 3,281,007 (c) | 567,610 (c) | 119,052 | 488,519 (c) | 156,162 (c) |
| Indiana..................... | 5,652,947 (c) | 3,710,506 (c) | 1,639,628 (c) | 89,559 | 2,230 | 207,784 | 3,241 |
| Iowa ........................ | 2,897,898 | 2,085,292 | 624,587 | 68,150 | 23,680 | 92,264 | 3,925 |
| Kansas ..................... | 2,902,869 | 2,131,867 | 539,367 | 81,429 | 2,640 | 129,984 | 17,581 |
| Kentucky .................. | 3,486,673 | 2,497,941 | 785,432 | 59,333 | 235 | 130,493 | 13,239 |
| Louisiana.................. | 4,218,540 (c) | 2,886,091 (c) | 955,367 (c) | 99,390 (c) | 3,884 | 264,081 (c) | 9,727 (c) |
| Maine ....................... | 1,414,747 (c) | 899,047 | 370,583 (c) | 27,829 | 74,471 | 37,798 | 5,018 |
| Maryland .................. | 7,147,477 (c) | 4,715,495 | 1,773,297 (c) | 195,810 | 272,921 | 181,503 | 8,452 |
| Massachusetts .......... | 9,072,483 (c) | 5,471,801 | 2,666,870 (c) | 55,222 | 641,755 | 221,577 | 15,257 |
| Michigan................... | 984,371 | 6,092,786 | 2,813,156 | 636,710 | 108 | 281,953 | 19,018 |
| Minnesota................. | 6,042,279 (c) | 3,890,743 (c) | 1,613,032 (c) | 271,994 (c) | 62,591 | 188,940 (c) | 14,980 (c) |
| Mississippi ............... | 2,327,535 (c) | 1,628,918 (c) | 494,848 (c) | 55,192 (c) | 5,671 | 133,566 (c) | 9,340 (c) |
| Missouri.................... | 5,304,123 (c) | 3,742,157 | 998,610 | 165,813 (c) | 9,162 | 368,880 | 19,500 (c) |
| Montana ................... | 862,843 | 571,819 | 162,073 | 56,989 | 785 | 67,157 | 4,020 |
| Nebraska .................. | 1,982,560 | 1,370,628 | 450,345 | 65,351 | 12,071 | 73,012 | 11,153 |
| Nevada...................... | 2,142,723 | 1,423,181 | 523,471 | 40,499 | 1,536 | 149,253 | 4,783 |
| New Hampshire ........ | 1,600,157 | 1,001,599 | 383,562 | 40,757 | 128,751 | 41,445 | 3,044 |
| New Jersey ................ | 13,929,759 | 9,060,869 | 3,315,778 | 357,623 | 629,357 | 445,953 | 120,179 |
| New Mexico .............. | 1,837,760 | 1,262,435 | 392,632 | 70,535 | 0 | 111,597 | 562 |
| New York .................. | 33,644,194 (c) | 21,827,433 (c) | 9,072,740 (c) | 1,693,593 (c) | 297,344 | 748,286 (c) | 4,798 (c) |
| North Carolina.......... | 7,900,594 | 5,851,080 | 1,439,719 | 277,171 | 0 | 332,459 | 165 |
| North Dakota............ | 541,896 | 386,587 | 113,367 | 15,378 | 952 | 22,990 | 2,622 |
| Ohio ........................ | 11,049,442 | 7,302,475 | 2,425,988 | 524,224 | 208,157 | 433,361 | 155,238 |
| Oklahoma................. | 2,908,376 | 2,059,086 | 584,338 | 41,863 | 0 | 214,302 | 8,787 |
| Oregon...................... | 3,218,961 | 1,948,924 | 938,113 | 130,335 | 24,545 | 160,368 | 16,677 |
| Pennsylvania ............ | 13,201,013 | 8,725,192 | 2,993,434 | 679,050 | 251,452 | 524,087 | 27,798 |
| Rhode Island ............ | 1,280,778 (c) | 825,840 (c) | 339,836 (c) | 10,398 (c) | 80,151 | 23,305 (c) | 1,249 (c) |
| South Carolina.......... | 3,826,821 | 2,719,581 | 786,959 | 129,052 | 893 | 164,399 | 25,938 |
| South Dakota............ | 626,773 | 4,217,872 | 118,218 | 29,718 | 7,409 | 48,323 | 1,322 |
| Tennessee ................. | 4,874,867 (c) | 3,368,417 | 963,177 | 86,883 | 438 (c) | 439,768 | 16,185 |
| Texas........................ | 24,415,370 (c) | 18,866,604 (c) | 2,872,423 (c) | 774,806 (c) | 48,971 | 1,630,930 (c) | 221,635 (c) |
| Utah......................... | 2,352,270 | 1,500,840 | 613,409 | 56,716 | 558 | 173,676 | 7,070 |
| Vermont.................... | 881,722 | 551,703 | 194,306 | 47,566 | 63,095 | 22,899 | 2,203 |
| Virginia.................... | 8,194,326 | 5,737,097 | 1,973,692 | 172,917 | 6,248 | 299,201 | 5,172 |
| Washington............... | 5,981,819 (c) | 4,050,112 | 1,339,697 | 316,146 | 15,135 (c) | 221,773 | 38,956 |
| West Virginia ........... | 1,825,237 (c) | 1,140,047 (c) | 552,394 (c) | 33,997 (c) | 1,158 | 97,080 (c) | 561 (c) |
| Wisconsin ................. | 5,935,538 | 3,711,184 | 1,802,495 | 97,994 | 112,628 | 198,213 | 13,025 |
| Wyoming................... | 745,889 | 504,324 | 176,771 | 25,481 | 996 | 37,273 | 1,042 |
| Dist. of Columbia(d).. | 624,116 (c) | 395,532 (c) | 53,516 (c) | 23,093 (c) | 140,129 | 10,883 (c) | 963 (c) |
| American Samoa ...... | 32,737 | 19,841 | 3,331 | 1,901 | 0 | 4,097 | 3,568 |
| Guam ....................... | 135,903 | 97,490 | 28,715 | 1,491 | 0 | 8,046 | 160 |
| No. Mariana Islands . | 28,625 (c) | 24,460 (c) | 3,161 (c) | 774 (c) | 0 | 130 (c) | 100 (c) |
| Puerto Rico............... | 1,738,493 (c) | 1,335,281 (c) | 205,139 (c) | 27,028 | 0 | 64,423 | 106,622 |
| U.S. Virgin Islands .... | 116,671 | 82,799 | 26,253 | 6,607 | 0 | 1,012 | 0 |

See footnotes at end of table.

## CURRENT INSTRUCTION AND INSTRUCTION-RELATED EXPENDITURES FOR PUBLIC ELEMENTARY AND SECONDARY EDUCATION, BY OBJECT AND STATE OR JURISDICTION: FISCAL YEAR 2009 — Continued

*Source:* U.S. Department of Education, National Center for Education Statistics, Common Core of Data (CCD), "National Public Education Financial Survey (NPEFS)," fiscal year 2009, Version 1a.

*Note:* Detail may not sum to totals due to rounding.

(a) Include expenditures for activities related to the interaction between teachers and students, including salaries and benefits for teachers and teacher aides, textbooks, supplies, and purchased services. These expenditures also include expenditures relating to extracurricular and cocurricular activities.

(b) U.S. totals include the 50 states and the District of Columbia.

(c) Value affected by redistribution of reported values to correct for missing data items, and/or to distribute state direct support expenditures.

(d) Both the District of Columbia and Hawaii have only one school district each; therefore, neither is comparable to other states.

**Table 9.8**

**AVERAGE UNDERGRADUATE TUITION AND FEES AND ROOM AND BOARD RATES IN INSTITUTIONS OF HIGHER EDUCATION, BY CONTROL OF INSTITUTION AND STATE: 2008–2009 AND 2009–2010**

| State or other jurisdiction | Public 4-year 2008–2009 Total | Public 4-year 2008–2009 Tuition (in-state) | Public 4-year 2009–2010 Total | Public 4-year 2009–2010 Tuition (in-state) | Public 4-year 2009–2010 Room | Public 4-year 2009–2010 Board | Out-of-state tuition and required fees 2009–10 | Private 4-year 2008–2009 Total | Private 4-year 2008–2009 Tuition | Private 4-year 2009–2010 Total | Private 4-year 2009–2010 Tuition (b) | Private 4-year 2009–2010 Room | Private 4-year 2009–2010 Board | Public 2-year In-state 2008–09 | Public 2-year In-state 2009–10 | Public 2-year Out-of-state 2009–10 |
|---|---|---|---|---|---|---|---|---|---|---|---|---|---|---|---|---|
| United States | $14,262 | $6,312 | $15,014 | $6,695 | $4,565 | $3,754 | $18,451 | $32,090 | $22,852 | $32,790 | $23,210 | $5,249 | $4,331 | $2,136 | $2,285 | $6,075 |
| Alabama | 12,183 | 5,554 | 13,052 | 6,061 | 3,572 | 3,420 | 15,202 | 20,997 | 13,997 | 23,234 | 15,896 | 3,655 | 3,682 | 2,826 | 2,834 | 6,141 |
| Alaska | 12,970 | 5,008 | 13,281 | 5,246 | 4,545 | 3,490 | 15,246 | 28,514 | 19,194 | 29,412 | 19,765 | 4,400 | 5,247 | 3,289 | 3,900 | 4,300 |
| Arizona | 14,098 | 5,589 | 15,710 | 6,720 | 5,417 | 3,573 | 20,116 | 24,939 | 16,430 | 29,383 | 17,389 | 7,892 | 4,102 | 1,610 | 1,652 | 7,129 |
| Arkansas | 14,098 | 5,589 | 15,710 | 6,720 | 5,417 | 3,573 | 20,116 | 24,939 | 16,430 | 29,383 | 17,389 | 7,892 | 4,102 | 1,610 | 1,652 | 7,129 |
| California | 15,679 | 5,266 | 17,652 | 6,240 | 5,849 | 5,563 | 24,319 | 36,779 | 25,780 | 37,832 | 26,397 | 6,378 | 5,057 | 586 | 719 | 5,413 |
| Colorado | 14,250 | 5,693 | 15,056 | 6,188 | 4,533 | 4,335 | 23,567 | 28,702 | 18,757 | 28,765 | 18,808 | 5,544 | 4,414 | 2,198 | 2,446 | 7,443 |
| Connecticut | 17,358 | 7,883 | 18,331 | 8,375 | 5,361 | 4,595 | 23,348 | 42,142 | 30,768 | 43,780 | 31,878 | 6,576 | 5,326 | 2,983 | 3,199 | 9,559 |
| Delaware | 17,199 | 8,306 | 18,383 | 9,026 | 5,564 | 3,793 | 21,598 | 21,033 | 12,554 | 21,852 | 12,951 | 4,558 | 4,342 | 2,684 | 2,816 | 6,524 |
| Florida | 11,487 | 3,293 | 11,659 | 3,452 | 4,827 | 3,380 | 13,798 | 27,694 | 18,808 | 28,352 | 19,116 | 5,072 | 4,164 | 2,106 | 2,480 | 9,064 |
| Georgia | 11,532 | 4,261 | 12,552 | 4,839 | 4,335 | 3,378 | 18,158 | 30,587 | 21,211 | 30,323 | 20,717 | 5,496 | 4,110 | 1,904 | 2,324 | 7,380 |
| Hawaii | 13,358 | 5,326 | 14,182 | 5,943 | 4,112 | 4,126 | 17,755 | 22,780 | 12,232 | 22,948 | 12,405 | 4,538 | 6,006 | 1,757 | 1,955 | 6,589 |
| Idaho | 10,403 | 4,610 | 10,895 | 4,883 | 2,798 | 3,214 | 14,376 | 11,937 | 6,491 | 12,670 | 6,650 | 2,013 | 4,006 | 2,240 | 2,420 | 6,939 |
| Illinois | 18,228 | 9,860 | 19,355 | 10,443 | 4,706 | 4,206 | 24,179 | 32,223 | 22,443 | 33,272 | 23,166 | 5,600 | 4,507 | 2,520 | 2,670 | 8,342 |
| Indiana | 14,976 | 6,920 | 15,590 | 7,306 | 4,188 | 4,097 | 22,397 | 31,099 | 23,152 | 31,722 | 23,468 | 4,237 | 4,017 | 2,930 | 3,090 | 6,306 |
| Iowa | 13,828 | 6,434 | 14,174 | 6,712 | 3,707 | 3,754 | 20,054 | 23,680 | 17,186 | 23,019 | 16,392 | 2,969 | 3,657 | 3,418 | 3,549 | 4,595 |
| Kansas | 11,999 | 5,733 | 12,578 | 6,052 | 3,206 | 3,320 | 15,745 | 23,877 | 17,563 | 25,067 | 18,414 | 3,124 | 3,529 | 2,090 | 2,212 | 3,548 |
| Kentucky | 13,213 | 6,843 | 14,228 | 7,165 | 3,693 | 3,371 | 16,121 | 23,744 | 16,876 | 23,779 | 16,984 | 3,377 | 3,418 | 2,930 | 3,026 | 10,299 |
| Louisiana | 10,380 | 4,079 | 10,873 | 4,282 | 3,701 | 2,890 | 11,839 | 32,303 | 23,736 | 32,781 | 24,043 | 4,917 | 3,821 | 1,703 | 1,849 | 3,929 |
| Maine | 16,162 | 8,045 | 17,020 | 8,504 | 4,169 | 4,347 | 21,586 | 34,553 | 24,854 | 34,871 | 25,090 | 4,850 | 4,931 | 3,273 | 3,303 | 5,853 |
| Maryland | 16,112 | 7,252 | 16,407 | 7,321 | 5,150 | 3,937 | 18,857 | 38,528 | 28,560 | 39,750 | 29,361 | 6,130 | 4,258 | 3,061 | 3,099 | 7,399 |
| Massachusetts | 17,103 | 8,207 | 17,819 | 9,221 | 5,553 | 3,045 | 20,584 | 43,490 | 32,051 | 45,087 | 33,160 | 6,745 | 5,181 | 3,252 | 3,522 | 7,991 |
| Michigan | 17,034 | 9,075 | 17,852 | 9,638 | 4,171 | 4,043 | 26,696 | 22,847 | 15,528 | 23,170 | 15,524 | 3,727 | 3,920 | 2,254 | 2,312 | 5,011 |
| Minnesota | 15,097 | 8,284 | 15,730 | 8,728 | 3,596 | 3,406 | 12,805 | 31,439 | 23,572 | 31,927 | 23,814 | 4,297 | 3,816 | 4,611 | 4,791 | 5,381 |
| Mississippi | 11,093 | 4,953 | 11,583 | 5,046 | 3,742 | 2,795 | 12,668 | 19,256 | 13,211 | 19,666 | 13,563 | 2,953 | 3,150 | 1,769 | 1,837 | 3,657 |
| Missouri | 14,056 | 6,925 | 14,368 | 7,047 | 4,287 | 3,035 | 14,813 | 26,353 | 18,481 | 27,106 | 18,766 | 4,343 | 3,997 | 2,458 | 2,406 | 4,651 |
| Montana | 11,970 | 5,461 | 12,399 | 5,612 | 3,122 | 3,665 | 17,578 | 22,945 | 16,082 | 23,438 | 16,471 | 3,156 | 3,811 | 3,082 | 3,121 | 7,972 |
| Nebraska | 12,652 | 5,883 | 13,265 | 6,229 | 3,486 | 3,550 | 14,969 | 23,809 | 17,156 | 24,895 | 17,778 | 3,599 | 3,518 | 2,212 | 2,248 | 3,054 |
| Nevada | 12,824 | 3,316 | 13,682 | 3,559 | 5,689 | 4,434 | 15,219 | 26,207 | 16,299 | 25,768 | 15,651 | 5,538 | 4,579 | 1,920 | 2,010 | 8,198 |
| New Hampshire | 19,228 | 10,183 | 20,492 | 10,958 | 5,554 | 3,980 | 22,026 | 36,681 | 26,681 | 37,766 | 27,344 | 5,975 | 4,448 | 5,999 | 6,296 | 13,817 |
| New Jersey | 20,727 | 10,366 | 21,591 | 10,680 | 7,061 | 3,851 | 21,075 | 36,908 | 26,135 | 38,071 | 26,933 | 6,036 | 5,102 | 3,195 | 3,388 | 6,122 |
| New Mexico | 11,261 | 4,414 | 11,809 | 4,655 | 3,892 | 3,262 | 13,880 | 24,977 | 16,249 | 22,210 | 13,413 | 4,281 | 4,516 | 1,273 | 1,338 | 3,493 |
| New York | 14,878 | 5,098 | 16,147 | 5,720 | 6,278 | 4,149 | 13,167 | 38,526 | 27,539 | 40,115 | 28,646 | 6,857 | 4,612 | 3,520 | 3,724 | 6,725 |
| North Carolina | 11,354 | 4,376 | 11,874 | 4,559 | 4,072 | 3,243 | 16,411 | 30,890 | 22,838 | 32,252 | 23,788 | 4,357 | 4,107 | 1,404 | 1,639 | 7,054 |
| North Dakota | 11,426 | 5,780 | 11,891 | 5,968 | 2,616 | 3,307 | 14,837 | 15,749 | 10,799 | 16,419 | 11,227 | 2,271 | 2,921 | 4,116 | 3,873 | 8,500 |
| Ohio | 16,567 | 8,043 | 17,133 | 8,058 | 5,033 | 4,042 | 20,187 | 31,592 | 23,514 | 32,751 | 24,115 | 4,360 | 4,276 | 3,155 | 3,014 | 6,728 |

See footnotes at end of table.

## AVERAGE UNDERGRADUATE TUITION AND FEES AND ROOM AND BOARD RATES IN INSTITUTIONS OF HIGHER EDUCATION, BY CONTROL OF INSTITUTION AND STATE: 2008–2009 AND 2009–2010—Continued

| State or other jurisdiction | Public 4-year | | | | | | | Private 4-year | | | | | | Public 2-year, tuition and required fees | | |
|---|---|---|---|---|---|---|---|---|---|---|---|---|---|---|---|---|
| | 2008–2009 | | 2009–2010 | | | | | 2008–2009 | | 2009–2010 | | | | In-state 2008–09 | In-state 2009–10 | Out-of-state 2009–10 |
| | Total | Tuition (in-state) | Total | Tuition (in-state) | Room | Board | Out-of-state tuition and required fees 2009–10 | Total | Tuition | Total | Tuition (b) | Room | Board | | | |
| Oklahoma.............. | 12,355 | 5,011 | 11,444 | 4,955 | 3,384 | 3,106 | 13,538 | 24,747 | 17,399 | 25,811 | 18,105 | 3,896 | 3,810 | 2,533 | 2,423 | 6,003 |
| Oregon................. | 15,183 | 6,274 | 15,629 | 6,941 | 4,900 | 3,789 | 21,656 | 33,898 | 25,397 | 35,090 | 26,260 | 4,494 | 4,337 | 2,942 | 3,220 | 6,456 |
| Pennsylvania......... | 18,147 | 10,148 | 19,017 | 10,550 | 4,948 | 3,519 | 20,273 | 38,131 | 28,224 | 39,574 | 29,317 | 5,617 | 4,640 | 3,300 | 3,454 | 10,246 |
| Rhode Island......... | 17,289 | 7,663 | 18,509 | 8,435 | 6,075 | 3,999 | 24,642 | 38,951 | 28,305 | 40,295 | 29,420 | 6,065 | 4,810 | 3,090 | 3,376 | 9,008 |
| South Carolina....... | 16,137 | 8,985 | 16,788 | 9,439 | 4,597 | 2,751 | 22,062 | 25,311 | 18,502 | 26,156 | 19,000 | 3,581 | 3,575 | 3,355 | 3,477 | 7,224 |
| South Dakota........ | 11,357 | 5,748 | 12,022 | 6,128 | 2,665 | 3,229 | 7,820 | 21,666 | 15,730 | 22,207 | 16,024 | 2,848 | 3,335 | 3,945 | 4,357 | 4,583 |
| Tennessee ............ | 12,057 | 5,682 | 12,748 | 6,048 | 3,628 | 3,072 | 18,991 | 27,316 | 19,598 | 27,925 | 19,965 | 4,304 | 3,657 | 2,778 | 2,941 | 11,460 |
| Texas.................. | 13,222 | 6,023 | 13,764 | 6,350 | 3,890 | 3,524 | 16,823 | 29,399 | 21,275 | 30,636 | 22,178 | 4,620 | 3,837 | 1,473 | 1,512 | 4,061 |
| Utah................... | 10,301 | 4,236 | 10,109 | 4,532 | 2,627 | 2,950 | 13,545 | 13,658 | 6,765 | 14,098 | 6,992 | 3,551 | 3,555 | 2,571 | 2,734 | 7,566 |
| Vermont............... | 19,688 | 11,339 | 20,735 | 12,008 | 5,510 | 3,216 | 28,503 | 36,143 | 26,815 | 37,677 | 28,046 | 5,157 | 4,473 | 4,684 | 4,876 | 9,652 |
| Virginia............... | 14,850 | 7,427 | 15,616 | 7,795 | 4,322 | 3,498 | 22,512 | 26,997 | 19,412 | 27,247 | 19,365 | 4,082 | 3,801 | 2,665 | 2,853 | 7,266 |
| Washington........... | 14,153 | 5,688 | 15,189 | 6,032 | 4,561 | 4,596 | 21,058 | 33,698 | 25,201 | 35,132 | 26,184 | 4,763 | 4,185 | 2,841 | 3,025 | 5,861 |
| West Virginia......... | 12,128 | 4,708 | 12,426 | 4,899 | 3,948 | 3,579 | 14,623 | 18,561 | 11,365 | 17,761 | 10,490 | 3,517 | 3,754 | 2,785 | 2,847 | 7,694 |
| Wisconsin ............ | 12,400 | 6,552 | 13,190 | 6,963 | 3,675 | 2,551 | 17,982 | 30,050 | 22,556 | 30,805 | 22,879 | 4,122 | 3,804 | 3,521 | 3,543 | 8,680 |
| Wyoming .............. | 10,556 | 3,057 | 10,952 | 3,162 | 3,466 | 4,324 | 9,498 | 11,325 | 11,325 | ... | ... | ... | ... | 2,009 | 2,120 | 5,393 |
| Dist. of Columbia ... | ... | 3,140 | ... | 5,370 | ... | ... | 12,300 | 36,636 | 25,232 | 37,357 | 25,713 | 7,694 | 3,949 | ... | ... | ... |

*Source:* U.S. Department of Education, National Center for Education Statistics, 2008–09 and 2009–10 Integrated Postsecondary Education Data System (IPEDS), Fall 2008, Fall 2009, Spring 2009, and Spring 2010. (This table was prepared October 2010.) U.S. Department of Education.

*Note:* Data are for the entire academic year and are average charges. In-state tuition and fees were weighted by the number of full-time-equivalent undergraduates, but were not adjusted to reflect student residency. Out-of-state tuition and fees were weighted by the number of first-time freshmen attending the institution in fall 2008 from out of state. Room and board are based on full-time students. Degree-granting institutions grant associate's or higher degrees and participate in Title IV federal financial aid programs. Some data have been revised from previously published figures. Detail may not sum to totals because of rounding.

*Key:*

... — Not applicable

# Table 9.9
## DEGREE GRANTING INSTITUTIONS AND BRANCHES, BY TYPE AND CONTROL OF INSTITUTION, 2010–2011

| State or other jurisdiction | Total | All public institutions | Public 4-year institutions | | | | | Public 2-year | All not-for-profit institutions | Not-for-profit 4-year institutions | | | | | Not-for-profit 2-year | For profit institutions | | |
|---|---|---|---|---|---|---|---|---|---|---|---|---|---|---|---|---|---|---|
| | | | Total | Doctoral (a) | Master's (b) | Baccalaureate (c) | Special focus (d) | | | Total | Doctoral (a) | Master's (b) | Baccalaureate (c) | Special focus (d) | | Total | 4-year | 2-year |
| United States (e) | 4,409 | 1,676 | 652 | 165 | 261 | 181 | 45 | 1,024 | 1,629 | 1,537 | 105 | 344 | 532 | 556 | 92 | 1,104 | 530 | 574 |
| Alabama | 75 | 39 | 14 | 4 | 9 | 1 | 0 | 25 | 19 | 19 | 1 | 2 | 10 | 6 | 0 | 17 | 10 | 7 |
| Alaska | 7 | 5 | 3 | 1 | 2 | 0 | 0 | 2 | 1 | 1 | 0 | 1 | 0 | 0 | 0 | 1 | 1 | 0 |
| Arizona | 84 | 24 | 4 | 3 | 0 | 0 | 1 | 20 | 11 | 11 | 0 | 2 | 2 | 7 | 0 | 49 | 31 | 18 |
| Arkansas | 51 | 33 | 11 | 1 | 5 | 4 | 1 | 22 | 12 | 12 | 0 | 1 | 9 | 2 | 0 | 6 | 4 | 2 |
| California | 454 | 148 | 35 | 9 | 19 | 5 | 2 | 113 | 146 | 141 | 15 | 26 | 21 | 79 | 5 | 160 | 73 | 87 |
| Colorado | 85 | 27 | 12 | 5 | 2 | 5 | 0 | 15 | 12 | 11 | 1 | 3 | 3 | 4 | 1 | 46 | 26 | 20 |
| Connecticut | 46 | 21 | 9 | 1 | 4 | 4 | 0 | 12 | 19 | 18 | 3 | 6 | 6 | 3 | 1 | 6 | 4 | 2 |
| Delaware | 11 | 5 | 2 | 1 | 1 | 0 | 0 | 3 | 5 | 4 | 1 | 1 | 1 | 1 | 1 | 1 | 1 | 0 |
| Florida | 223 | 43 | 33 | 11 | 2 | 19 | 1 | 10 | 57 | 56 | 4 | 11 | 21 | 20 | 1 | 123 | 55 | 68 |
| Georgia | 132 | 67 | 27 | 4 | 13 | 9 | 1 | 40 | 34 | 32 | 2 | 4 | 18 | 8 | 2 | 31 | 18 | 13 |
| Hawaii | 20 | 10 | 4 | 1 | 0 | 3 | 0 | 6 | 6 | 6 | 0 | 2 | 1 | 3 | 0 | 4 | 3 | 1 |
| Idaho | 15 | 7 | 4 | 1 | 1 | 2 | 0 | 3 | 4 | 4 | 0 | 1 | 2 | 1 | 0 | 4 | 3 | 1 |
| Illinois | 181 | 60 | 12 | 5 | 7 | 0 | 0 | 48 | 84 | 80 | 6 | 16 | 22 | 36 | 4 | 37 | 23 | 14 |
| Indiana | 109 | 29 | 15 | 5 | 6 | 4 | 0 | 14 | 41 | 40 | 6 | 9 | 15 | 10 | 1 | 39 | 20 | 19 |
| Iowa | 66 | 19 | 3 | 2 | 1 | 0 | 0 | 16 | 34 | 33 | 0 | 5 | 19 | 9 | 1 | 13 | 12 | 1 |
| Kansas | 67 | 33 | 8 | 3 | 4 | 0 | 1 | 25 | 24 | 22 | 0 | 6 | 13 | 3 | 2 | 10 | 5 | 5 |
| Kentucky | 76 | 24 | 8 | 2 | 5 | 1 | 0 | 16 | 26 | 26 | 1 | 3 | 14 | 8 | 0 | 26 | 16 | 10 |
| Louisiana | 74 | 39 | 17 | 4 | 9 | 1 | 3 | 22 | 10 | 10 | 1 | 2 | 4 | 3 | 0 | 25 | 5 | 20 |
| Maine | 32 | 15 | 8 | 1 | 1 | 6 | 0 | 7 | 15 | 12 | 1 | 3 | 5 | 3 | 3 | 2 | 0 | 2 |
| Maryland | 61 | 29 | 13 | 3 | 8 | 1 | 1 | 16 | 22 | 22 | 1 | 4 | 7 | 10 | 0 | 10 | 5 | 5 |
| Massachusetts | 124 | 30 | 14 | 3 | 7 | 2 | 2 | 16 | 83 | 80 | 9 | 14 | 25 | 32 | 3 | 11 | 7 | 4 |
| Michigan | 107 | 45 | 15 | 7 | 7 | 1 | 0 | 30 | 50 | 50 | 1 | 9 | 23 | 17 | 0 | 12 | 10 | 2 |
| Minnesota | 113 | 43 | 12 | 1 | 8 | 3 | 0 | 31 | 36 | 35 | 0 | 9 | 11 | 15 | 1 | 34 | 29 | 5 |
| Mississippi | 40 | 24 | 9 | 4 | 4 | 0 | 1 | 15 | 9 | 9 | 0 | 3 | 4 | 2 | 0 | 7 | 5 | 2 |
| Missouri | 138 | 34 | 13 | 4 | 6 | 3 | 0 | 21 | 58 | 54 | 2 | 12 | 12 | 28 | 4 | 46 | 22 | 24 |
| Montana | 23 | 18 | 6 | 2 | 1 | 3 | 0 | 12 | 5 | 4 | 0 | 1 | 2 | 1 | 1 | 0 | 0 | 0 |
| Nebraska | 43 | 15 | 7 | 1 | 3 | 2 | 1 | 8 | 19 | 16 | 0 | 3 | 8 | 5 | 3 | 9 | 5 | 4 |
| Nevada | 25 | 7 | 6 | 2 | 0 | 4 | 0 | 1 | 3 | 3 | 0 | 0 | 1 | 2 | 0 | 15 | 8 | 7 |
| New Hampshire | 29 | 12 | 5 | 1 | 2 | 2 | 0 | 7 | 15 | 13 | 2 | 2 | 6 | 3 | 2 | 2 | 0 | 2 |
| New Jersey | 66 | 33 | 14 | 3 | 9 | 1 | 1 | 19 | 25 | 25 | 3 | 9 | 3 | 10 | 0 | 8 | 4 | 4 |
| New Mexico | 44 | 28 | 8 | 2 | 4 | 1 | 1 | 20 | 3 | 3 | 0 | 2 | 1 | 0 | 0 | 13 | 8 | 5 |
| New York | 302 | 78 | 43 | 6 | 20 | 13 | 4 | 35 | 180 | 164 | 17 | 36 | 31 | 80 | 16 | 44 | 18 | 26 |
| North Carolina | 139 | 75 | 16 | 6 | 6 | 3 | 1 | 59 | 45 | 44 | 2 | 5 | 28 | 9 | 1 | 19 | 14 | 5 |
| North Dakota | 21 | 14 | 8 | 2 | 1 | 4 | 1 | 6 | 6 | 5 | 0 | 1 | 1 | 3 | 1 | 1 | 1 | 0 |
| Ohio | 215 | 60 | 36 | 10 | 1 | 22 | 3 | 24 | 75 | 68 | 3 | 18 | 24 | 23 | 7 | 80 | 22 | 58 |
| Oklahoma | 60 | 29 | 17 | 2 | 6 | 7 | 2 | 12 | 14 | 14 | 2 | 3 | 5 | 4 | 0 | 17 | 9 | 8 |
| Oregon | 60 | 26 | 9 | 3 | 3 | 2 | 1 | 17 | 24 | 24 | 2 | 3 | 8 | 11 | 0 | 10 | 5 | 5 |
| Pennsylvania | 262 | 61 | 44 | 4 | 16 | 22 | 2 | 17 | 118 | 105 | 7 | 30 | 36 | 32 | 13 | 83 | 11 | 72 |
| Rhode Island | 13 | 3 | 2 | 1 | 1 | 0 | 0 | 1 | 10 | 10 | 1 | 4 | 1 | 4 | 0 | 0 | 0 | 0 |
| South Carolina | 75 | 33 | 13 | 3 | 4 | 5 | 1 | 20 | 24 | 22 | 0 | 4 | 14 | 4 | 2 | 18 | 11 | 7 |

See footnotes at end of table.

# DEGREE GRANTING INSTITUTIONS AND BRANCHES, BY TYPE AND CONTROL OF INSTITUTION, 2010–2011 — Continued

| State or other jurisdiction | Total | All public institutions | Public 4-year: Total | Public 4-year: Doctoral (a) | Public 4-year: Master's (b) | Public 4-year: Baccalaureate (c) | Public 4-year: Special focus (d) | Public 2-year | All not-for-profit institutions | Not-for-profit 4-year: Total | Not-for-profit 4-year: Doctoral (a) | Not-for-profit 4-year: Master's (b) | Not-for-profit 4-year: Baccalaureate (c) | Not-for-profit 4-year: Special focus (d) | Not-for-profit 2-year | For profit: Total | For profit: 4-year | For profit: 2-year |
|---|---|---|---|---|---|---|---|---|---|---|---|---|---|---|---|---|---|---|
| South Dakota | 25 | 12 | 7 | 2 | 0 | 3 | 2 | 5 | 8 | 7 | 0 | 1 | 3 | 3 | 1 | 5 | 5 | 0 |
| Tennessee | 109 | 22 | 9 | 4 | 5 | 0 | 0 | 13 | 47 | 45 | 2 | 10 | 17 | 16 | 2 | 40 | 22 | 18 |
| Texas | 252 | 108 | 45 | 11 | 21 | 5 | 8 | 63 | 57 | 53 | 4 | 16 | 17 | 16 | 4 | 87 | 30 | 57 |
| Utah | 41 | 12 | 7 | 2 | 2 | 3 | 0 | 5 | 4 | 3 | 1 | 1 | 1 | 0 | 1 | 25 | 19 | 6 |
| Vermont | 24 | 6 | 5 | 1 | 2 | 2 | 0 | 1 | 17 | 16 | 0 | 5 | 8 | 3 | 1 | 1 | 1 | 0 |
| Virginia | 129 | 39 | 15 | 6 | 6 | 3 | 0 | 24 | 38 | 38 | 1 | 7 | 20 | 10 | 0 | 52 | 28 | 24 |
| Washington | 85 | 43 | 16 | 2 | 6 | 6 | 2 | 27 | 23 | 22 | 0 | 10 | 3 | 9 | 1 | 19 | 11 | 8 |
| West Virginia | 46 | 23 | 13 | 1 | 1 | 10 | 1 | 10 | 9 | 9 | 0 | 2 | 6 | 1 | 0 | 14 | 3 | 11 |
| Wisconsin | 84 | 31 | 14 | 2 | 9 | 3 | 0 | 17 | 29 | 28 | 0 | 10 | 10 | 8 | 1 | 24 | 21 | 3 |
| Wyoming | 11 | 8 | 1 | 1 | 0 | 0 | 0 | 7 | 0 | 0 | 0 | 0 | 0 | 0 | 0 | 3 | 3 | 0 |
| Dist. of Columbia | 20 | 2 | 2 | 0 | 1 | 0 | 1 | 0 | 14 | 14 | 1 | 2 | 10 | 0 | 0 | 4 | 4 | 0 |
| U.S. Service Academies | 5 | 5 | 5 | 0 | 0 | 5 | 0 | 0 | n/a | n/a | n/a | n/a | n/a | n/a | n/a | n/a | n/a | n/a |
| American Samoa | 1 | 1 | 0 | 0 | 0 | 0 | 0 | 1 | 0 | 0 | 0 | 0 | 0 | 0 | 0 | 0 | 0 | 0 |
| Federated States of Micronesia | 1 | 1 | 0 | 0 | 0 | 0 | 0 | 1 | 0 | 0 | 0 | 0 | 0 | 0 | 0 | 0 | 0 | 0 |
| Guam | 3 | 2 | 1 | 0 | 1 | 0 | 0 | 1 | 1 | 1 | 0 | 0 | 0 | 1 | 0 | 0 | 0 | 0 |
| Marshall Islands | 1 | 1 | 0 | 0 | 0 | 0 | 0 | 1 | 0 | 0 | 0 | 0 | 0 | 0 | 0 | 0 | 0 | 0 |
| No. Mariana Islands | 1 | 1 | 1 | 0 | 0 | 1 | 0 | 0 | 0 | 0 | 0 | 0 | 0 | 0 | 0 | 0 | 0 | 0 |
| Palau | 1 | 1 | 0 | 0 | 0 | 0 | 0 | 1 | 0 | 0 | 0 | 0 | 0 | 0 | 0 | 0 | 0 | 0 |
| Puerto Rico | 80 | 18 | 14 | 1 | 1 | 9 | 3 | 4 | 45 | 41 | 2 | 5 | 22 | 12 | 4 | 17 | 17 | 0 |
| U.S. Virgin Islands | 1 | 1 | 1 | 0 | 0 | 1 | 0 | 0 | 0 | 0 | 0 | 0 | 0 | 0 | 0 | 0 | 0 | 0 |

*Source:* U.S. Department of Education, National Center for Education Statistics, 2010–11 Integrated Postsecondary Education Data System (IPEDS), Fall 2010.

n/a = Not applicable

(a) Institutions that award at least 20 doctor's degrees per year.

(b) Institutions that award at least 50 master's degrees per year.

(c) Institutions that primarily emphasize undergraduate education.

(d) Four-year institutions that award degrees primarily in single fields of study, such as medicine, business, fine arts, theology, and engineering. Includes some institutions that have 4-year programs, but have not reported sufficient data to identify program category. Also, includes institutions classified as 4-year under the IPEDS system, which had been classified as 2-year in the Carnegie Classification system because they primarily award an associate's degree.

(e) U.S. totals include the District of Columbia and U.S. Service Schools.

# Table 9.10
## AVERAGE SALARY OF FULL-TIME FACULTY ON 9-MONTH CONTRACTS: 2009–2010

| State or other jurisdiction | Total | Public institutions — All public institutions | Public 4-year Total | Public 4-year Doctoral (a) | Public 4-year Master's (b) | Public 4-year Other | Public 2-year | Not-for-profit — All not-for-profit | NFP 4-year Total | NFP 4-year Doctoral (a) | NFP 4-year Master's (b) | NFP 4-year Other | Not-for-profit 2-year | For-profit institutions |
|---|---|---|---|---|---|---|---|---|---|---|---|---|---|---|
| United States | $74,625 | $72,183 | $76,153 | $82,244 | $68,176 | $61,513 | $62,265 | $80,593 | $80,744 | $97,732 | $67,976 | $66,184 | $45,731 | $54,842 |
| Alabama | 63,395 | 64,994 | 69,596 | 74,579 | 59,380 | 68,661 | 53,376 | 54,793 | 54,793 | 68,322 | 54,226 | 48,349 | n/a | 24,226 |
| Alaska | 70,760 | 71,403 | 71,335 | 72,465 | 70,567 | n/a | 79,991 | 55,619 | 55,619 | n/a | 55,619 | n/a | n/a | n/a |
| Arizona | 76,399 | 76,729 | 81,227 | 81,593 | n/a | 51,729 | 68,259 | 56,630 | 56,630 | n/a | 42,969 | 65,276 | n/a | 82,929 |
| Arkansas | 54,663 | 54,848 | 59,296 | 65,468 | 51,972 | 55,151 | 43,820 | 53,608 | 53,608 | n/a | 56,463 | 51,495 | n/a | n/a |
| California | 89,690 | 88,011 | 91,779 | 106,873 | 78,974 | 73,197 | 83,684 | 96,616 | 96,711 | 105,869 | 81,287 | 93,001 | 64,586 | 67,920 |
| Colorado | 69,185 | 68,250 | 72,137 | 78,708 | 58,474 | 56,673 | 50,118 | 76,085 | 76,085 | 77,478 | 76,546 | 53,637 | n/a | 48,928 |
| Connecticut | 90,321 | 83,084 | 87,823 | 99,890 | 76,851 | n/a | 68,850 | 97,966 | 97,966 | 112,294 | 85,483 | 76,537 | n/a | 45,225 |
| Delaware | 88,007 | 88,505 | 94,579 | 98,068 | 67,987 | n/a | 62,317 | 83,488 | 83,488 | 64,584 | 103,373 | n/a | n/a | n/a |
| Florida | 69,160 | 67,966 | 70,775 | 76,554 | 66,565 | 57,985 | 53,183 | 72,558 | 72,558 | 85,613 | 68,290 | 55,009 | n/a | 92,469 |
| Georgia | 68,420 | 67,151 | 69,182 | 82,950 | 58,313 | 51,765 | 47,303 | 72,011 | 72,023 | 98,605 | 63,201 | 56,498 | 35,000 | n/a |
| Hawaii | 78,970 | 81,036 | 86,718 | 91,616 | 71,594 | 69,640 | 68,213 | 68,480 | 68,480 | n/a | 65,596 | 86,446 | n/a | n/a |
| Idaho | 58,357 | 59,104 | 61,158 | 63,161 | 61,365 | 48,055 | 48,241 | 50,859 | 50,859 | n/a | 50,447 | 51,176 | n/a | n/a |
| Illinois | 76,844 | 71,870 | 74,809 | 80,202 | 63,558 | n/a | 66,575 | 84,351 | 84,525 | 101,715 | 66,512 | 59,604 | 39,416 | 33,370 |
| Indiana | 70,229 | 69,462 | 73,399 | 78,789 | 59,571 | 54,480 | 44,060 | 71,857 | 72,011 | 89,867 | 61,718 | 60,729 | 43,283 | 41,085 |
| Iowa | 67,913 | 72,580 | 82,260 | 86,781 | 65,584 | n/a | 53,095 | 60,021 | 60,021 | 61,336 | 59,043 | 60,515 | n/a | n/a |
| Kansas | 62,813 | 65,410 | 72,428 | 78,594 | 58,586 | 66,164 | 49,869 | 46,545 | 46,920 | n/a | 49,925 | 41,667 | 37,815 | 60,734 |
| Kentucky | 60,082 | 61,391 | 66,277 | 78,226 | 59,543 | n/a | 48,856 | 54,885 | 54,885 | 63,399 | 48,785 | 56,432 | n/a | n/a |
| Louisiana | 63,584 | 61,972 | 64,612 | 72,786 | 56,273 | 59,333 | 49,280 | 71,406 | 71,406 | 84,609 | 63,394 | 57,747 | n/a | 21,571 |
| Maine | 71,261 | 68,209 | 71,807 | 79,449 | 74,961 | 57,521 | 55,223 | 76,309 | 76,379 | 59,011 | 53,365 | 87,179 | 70,705 | n/a |
| Maryland | 75,087 | 72,793 | 76,330 | 82,184 | 68,358 | n/a | 65,944 | 82,984 | 82,984 | 105,776 | 69,969 | n/a | n/a | 57,576 |
| Massachusetts | 92,335 | 74,583 | 80,247 | 89,736 | 70,783 | n/a | 60,046 | 100,193 | 100,221 | 114,694 | 81,918 | 80,408 | 42,846 | 61,796 |
| Michigan | 78,811 | 81,410 | 82,667 | 86,299 | 70,080 | 55,497 | 75,813 | 63,853 | 63,853 | 47,522 | 63,248 | 64,915 | n/a | n/a |
| Minnesota | 70,307 | 71,382 | 78,161 | 93,673 | 70,056 | 59,197 | 61,151 | 68,338 | 68,371 | 67,270 | 64,155 | 71,687 | 42,993 | 42,230 |
| Mississippi | 54,953 | 55,163 | 59,811 | 61,951 | 50,733 | n/a | 48,607 | 53,086 | 53,086 | n/a | 57,948 | 40,108 | 51,111 | n/a |
| Missouri | 66,607 | 63,821 | 66,776 | 73,245 | 58,358 | 56,936 | 54,486 | 72,146 | 72,423 | 89,555 | 56,112 | 51,970 | n/a | 57,576 |
| Montana | 56,825 | 58,510 | 61,245 | 64,293 | 54,585 | 48,415 | 42,452 | 46,058 | 47,381 | n/a | 46,190 | 48,222 | 34,248 | n/a |
| Nebraska | 65,774 | 68,749 | 74,212 | 85,125 | 64,289 | n/a | 50,927 | 57,872 | 57,924 | 70,704 | 53,665 | 47,815 | 41,732 | 46,922 |
| Nevada | 79,986 | 80,427 | 81,873 | 89,657 | n/a | 66,295 | 63,398 | 63,854 | 63,854 | n/a | 63,854 | n/a | 42,993 | 58,360 |
| New Hampshire | 79,431 | 77,204 | 84,032 | 92,936 | 70,384 | 80,136 | 54,120 | 83,005 | 83,005 | 100,625 | 69,209 | 61,142 | n/a | 52,470 |
| New Jersey | 91,058 | 89,403 | 97,021 | 104,707 | 90,141 | n/a | 70,224 | 95,303 | 95,303 | 110,531 | 73,149 | 65,602 | n/a | n/a |
| New Mexico | 62,567 | 62,508 | 68,555 | 74,081 | 56,252 | 44,980 | 48,298 | 77,244 | 77,244 | n/a | 77,244 | n/a | n/a | 25,482 |
| New York | 84,784 | 82,814 | 82,814 | 96,306 | 79,747 | 72,862 | 69,854 | 90,853 | 91,081 | 102,177 | 73,538 | 79,528 | 50,241 | 40,996 |
| North Carolina | 68,053 | 65,373 | 78,123 | 83,660 | 69,019 | 68,324 | 47,331 | 76,717 | 76,891 | 102,319 | 55,655 | 55,059 | 38,929 | 90,410 |
| North Dakota | 58,355 | 59,901 | 61,838 | 67,630 | 55,653 | 47,535 | 46,191 | 66,025 | 66,891 | 49,990 | 60,231 | 44,349 | n/a | n/a |
| Ohio | 70,423 | 72,538 | 75,783 | 78,322 | n/a | 58,276 | 59,533 | 66,025 | 66,066 | 76,908 | 60,231 | 65,347 | 58,334 | 35,862 |
| Oklahoma | 61,291 | 61,393 | 64,954 | 74,881 | 55,835 | 47,938 | 47,649 | 60,850 | 60,850 | 78,729 | 56,982 | 42,679 | n/a | n/a |
| Oregon | 67,065 | 66,312 | 69,343 | 73,552 | 55,402 | 56,994 | 61,941 | 69,395 | 69,395 | 59,066 | 72,570 | 70,506 | n/a | n/a |
| Pennsylvania | 79,084 | 76,860 | 80,024 | 87,393 | 76,694 | 63,991 | 59,890 | 81,593 | 81,835 | 96,604 | 69,144 | 73,920 | 44,023 | 38,183 |
| Rhode Island | 83,902 | 73,372 | 73,955 | 83,955 | 65,200 | n/a | 62,212 | 90,538 | 90,538 | 94,211 | 85,411 | 117,764 | n/a | n/a |
| South Carolina | 59,911 | 61,712 | 69,333 | 76,889 | 63,140 | 53,408 | 46,308 | 52,543 | 52,786 | n/a | 53,120 | 52,364 | 41,027 | 111,136 |

See footnotes at end of table.

# AVERAGE SALARY OF FULL-TIME FACULTY ON 9-MONTH CONTRACTS, 2009–2010—Continued

| State or other jurisdiction | Total | Public institutions | | | | | | Not-for-profit institutions | | | | | | For-profit institutions |
|---|---|---|---|---|---|---|---|---|---|---|---|---|---|---|
| | | All public institutions | 4-year | | | | Public 2-year | All not-for-profit | 4-year | | | | Not-for-profit 2-year | |
| | | | Total | Doctoral (a) | Master's (b) | Other | | | Total | Doctoral (a) | Master's (b) | Other | | |
| South Dakota | 56,359 | 58,192 | 60,538 | 61,177 | 61,914 | 41,645 | 44,986 | 48,523 | 48,523 | n/a | 46,856 | 49,357 | n/a | 45,265 |
| Tennessee | 63,539 | 61,233 | 65,841 | 67,612 | 58,191 | n/a | 46,497 | 68,209 | 68,209 | 91,880 | 52,961 | 55,637 | n/a | 42,944 |
| Texas | 70,018 | 68,676 | 75,324 | 80,637 | 61,774 | 52,587 | 54,011 | 76,428 | 76,716 | 88,491 | 66,259 | 59,181 | 31,361 | 65,205 |
| Utah | 72,095 | 64,944 | 67,948 | 76,569 | 59,416 | 58,960 | 49,955 | 91,513 | 91,874 | 95,027 | 67,786 | n/a | 56,163 | n/a |
| Vermont | 71,869 | 72,528 | 72,528 | 78,697 | 64,726 | 57,878 | n/a | 71,247 | 74,255 | n/a | 79,512 | 58,510 | 43,154 | n/a |
| Virginia | 72,597 | 74,432 | 79,044 | 83,296 | 64,617 | 66,271 | 57,503 | 66,665 | 66,665 | 66,355 | 67,253 | 66,301 | n/a | n/a |
| Washington | 68,322 | 67,918 | 74,163 | 82,430 | 67,524 | 56,105 | 55,770 | 70,181 | 70,181 | 72,639 | 69,849 | 67,444 | n/a | 49,267 |
| West Virginia | 57,809 | 59,415 | 61,736 | 73,001 | 57,915 | 51,131 | 45,870 | 46,922 | 46,922 | 49,707 | 46,319 | 46,471 | n/a | n/a |
| Wisconsin | 69,370 | 71,121 | 70,926 | 80,632 | 58,695 | 92,789 | 71,496 | 62,639 | 62,639 | 74,097 | 57,017 | 55,348 | n/a | n/a |
| Wyoming | 70,106 | 70,106 | 79,487 | 79,487 | n/a | n/a | 59,133 | n/a | n/a | n/a | n/a | n/a | n/a | n/a |
| Dist. of Columbia | 88,096 | 77,787 | 77,787 | n/a | 76,409 | 92,224 | n/a | 91,090 | 91,090 | 91,843 | 79,748 | n/a | n/a | 53,529 |
| U.S. Service Academies | 118,643 | 118,643 | 118,643 | n/a | n/a | 118,643 | n/a | n/a | n/a | n/a | n/a | n/a | n/a | n/a |
| American Samoa | 28,862 | 28,862 | n/a | n/a | n/a | n/a | 28,862 | n/a | n/a | n/a | n/a | n/a | n/a | n/a |
| Federated States of Micronesia | 19,849 | 19,849 | n/a | n/a | n/a | n/a | 19,849 | n/a | n/a | n/a | n/a | n/a | n/a | n/a |
| Guam | 57,874 | 57,874 | 64,240 | n/a | 64,240 | n/a | 48,975 | n/a | n/a | n/a | n/a | n/a | n/a | n/a |
| Marshall Islands | 26,150 | 26,150 | n/a | n/a | n/a | n/a | 26,150 | n/a | n/a | n/a | n/a | n/a | n/a | n/a |
| No. Mariana Islands | 41,979 | 41,979 | 41,979 | n/a | n/a | 41,979 | n/a | n/a | n/a | n/a | n/a | n/a | n/a | n/a |
| Palau | 17,079 | 17,079 | n/a | n/a | n/a | n/a | 17,079 | n/a | n/a | n/a | n/a | n/a | n/a | n/a |
| Puerto Rico | 64,042 | 64,507 | 64,507 | 69,567 | n/a | n/a | n/a | 34,826 | 34,826 | 36,109 | 33,819 | n/a | n/a | n/a |
| U.S. Virgin Islands | 63,318 | 63,318 | 63,318 | n/a | 63,318 | 59,447 | n/a | n/a | n/a | n/a | n/a | n/a | n/a | n/a |

*Source:* U.S. Department of Education, National Center for Education Statistics, 2009–10 Integrated Postsecondary Education Data System (IPEDS), Winter 2009–10. (This table was prepared August 2010.)

*Note:* Degree-granting institutions grant associate's or higher degrees and participate in Title IV federal financial aid programs. Data include imputations for nonrespondent institutions.

*Key:*
n/a — Not applicable
(a) Institutions that awarded 20 or more doctor's degrees during the previous academic year.
(b) Institutions that awarded 20 or more master's degrees, but fewer than 20 doctor's degrees, during the previous academic year.

# Long-Term Care and Supports:
# A Tool for Targeting State Improvement

### By Enid Kassner

*A high-performing system of long-term care services and supports must address four critical dimensions: affordability/access; choice of setting/provider; quality of life and care; and support for family caregivers. A recent scorecard assessed the states on 25 indicators within these dimensions and found marked differences in performance. States can use these findings to target system improvements.*

## Introduction

*The Cook County Almshouse ... was the only public institution at any jurisdictional level specifically established to provide long-term refuge for the most extremely destitute people in the Chicago area. These were people with chronic physical illnesses or disabilities, mental illness or retardation, [or] elderly people. ... [T]he almshouse was regarded as a refuge of last resort. The number of residents peak[ed] ... [at] ... about 4,300 in January 1932. ...*

*Encyclopedia of Chicago[1]*

Throughout most of the 20th century, caring for older family members and people with disabilities was not a major public policy concern. In 1900, life expectancy at birth in the United States was just 49.2 years, compared to 77.5 years in 2003.[2] Most women did not work outside the home and older relatives often lived with their children when they could no longer care for themselves. Older people who had no one to care for them ended up in publicly run "almshouses" or private "old age homes"[3] as a last resort. But over the course of the 20th century, the population age 65 and older increased 11-fold and the share of the older population increased from 1-in-25 to 1-in-8 Americans.[4]

In the early 20th century, people with physical disabilities were less likely to be accepted as part of the American mainstream than they are today, often lacking full access to public education and career opportunities. For example, although Franklin D. Roosevelt was stricken with polio as an adult and was unable to walk without assistance, he was almost never photographed in his wheelchair. Through the 1930s, someone disabled at a young age or born to a family with few economic resources may well have had a future in an almshouse.

When Medicare and Medicaid were enacted in 1965, they were designed to address, respectively, the health care needs of the elderly and the poor. Nursing home coverage was added, almost as an afterthought, to the Medicaid program with no anticipation as to how the cost of this coverage would soar in the following decades. Although much has changed in the years since Medicaid's enactment—in terms of demographics, societal expectations and the health care delivery system—the nation's system of services and supports for older people and adults with physical disabilities bears the imprint of policies enacted for a society that is now obsolete.

Today, older people and working-age adults with physical disabilities prefer to remain in their own home or in small-group settings that have a homelike feel. Some states have made enormous strides in reducing public spending for long-term care services and supports for nursing homes, which is a costly and undesirable option for most. Although steady progress has occurred throughout the nation, change has been hampered at times by resistance among institutional providers who derive revenue from publicly provided services, and by Medicaid rules themselves, which continue to favor institutional care as the first-line service for people who need assistance.

The AARP Public Policy Institute, with support from The Commonwealth Fund and The SCAN Foundation, set out to develop a method for evaluating states' systems of long-term care support and services for the elderly, adults with physical disabilities and family caregivers by articulating a vision of how a high-performing system would look. Then came the painstaking task of determining what data were available to measure performance in a way that would be meaningful, unambiguous, available for all states and replicable. The goal was to take a multidimensional look at the long-term care support and services system from the perspective of consumers and their families.

## Vision of a High-Performing System

The project, referred to as the *Scorecard*, first defined the characteristics of a high-performing system for older people, adults with physical disabilities and family caregivers. It then measured and ranked the states on four critical dimensions:

**Affordability and Access**—*In a high performing long-term support and services system, consumers can easily find and afford the services they need and a safety net is in place for those who cannot afford services.*[5] Measures of affordability and access include the affordability of nursing home and home care services for private pay patients, the reach of private long-term care insurance, the breadth of the state's Medicaid program, and an assessment of the state's access and navigation system. These navigation systems are variously referred to as "single entry point," "no wrong door," or "Aging and Disability Resource Center."

**Choice of Setting and Provider**—*A person- and family-centered approach to long-term services and supports places high value on allowing consumers to exercise choice and control over where they receive services and who provides them.*[6] Measures of choice included the extent to which the state has balanced its expenditures for long-term care toward home and community-based services, as opposed to nursing homes; the ability of participants in public programs to direct their services and choose their provider; the availability of home care workers and alternative residential settings in the state; and the percentage of nursing home residents with comparatively low care needs.

**Quality of Life and Quality of Care**—*Services maximize positive outcomes and consumers are treated with respect. Personal preferences are honored when possible.*[7] Quality of life was measured by looking at survey data regarding life satisfaction among people with disabilities and the relative percentage of working-age adults with disabilities who are employed. Quality of care in nursing homes and home health care also was measured.

**Support for Family Caregivers**—*The needs of family caregivers are assessed and addressed so they can continue in their caregiving role without being overburdened.*[8] Because family caregivers play such a substantial role in providing long-term care and support, this component was considered

of equal importance to the other elements of a high-performing system. Measures included legal and system supports for family caregivers, state laws on the ability of nurses to delegate certain health maintenance tasks to home care workers, and the extent to which caregivers believe they receive the support they need.

Every state was ranked on each of the 25 indicators (except for a handful of instances in which missing data prevented a state ranking) and on each of the four dimensions. The states also were ranked for overall system performance.

## *Scorecard* Purpose

The *Scorecard* was designed to help state policymakers and private sector service providers evaluate the strengths and weaknesses of their state's long-term care system. The goal of the project was to enable policymakers and other stakeholders to target improvement efforts on low-performance areas and learn from the actions taken in higher-ranking states.

States were ranked relative to each other. Even the top-performing state falls short of the overall vision of high performance. Moreover, the highest rank on any indicator illustrates the best that any state performed at the time the data were collected—not the best a state could possibly perform. While the most recently available data were used for every indicator, state performance may have changed in the intervening years.

The *Scorecard* illustrates meaningful differences among the states on a broad range of performance measures. In many cases, a four- or six-fold difference separated top and bottom states. In some areas, the range was even broader.

Because the *Scorecard* looked at the long-term care system from a wide range of needs that consumers experience, its indicators span areas that are subject to varying degrees of state control. For example, the private pay cost of services is important to system users, but is an area that is difficult for states to directly control. Measures of life satisfaction are influenced by myriad factors, some of which have nothing to do with state policy or even the individual's needs as a person with a disability. Other areas are influenced by a combination of factors. For example, quality of care is determined largely by private providers, but public oversight, monitoring and regulation can affect it. Yet there are numerous areas of performance that are directly controlled by state laws and policies. States have a major role in determining who is eligible to receive services, what services are provided, and how family caregivers will be supported.

The *Scorecard* measured the reach of both the state's overall Medicaid, as well as its Medicaid long-term care services and support programs for people with disabilities who have low incomes; the functions performed by the state's Aging and Disability Resource Center or single entry point system; the balancing of each state's Medicaid system toward home and community-based services; the proportion of consumers who are able to direct their own services; the state's tools and policies to facilitate choice (such as programs to divert or transition long-term care users from nursing homes into the community-based settings they choose); legal and system supports for family caregivers (such as laws that extend family and medical leave to working caregivers or prevent employment discrimination); and the number of health maintenance tasks (from a list of 16) that nurses may delegate to home care workers.

## Major Findings

States that ranked in the top quartile of performance tended to rank high across all dimensions, as illustrated in Figure A.[9] Conversely, states in the bottom quartile generally ranked low across all dimensions. Even so, no state ranked in the top quartile across all 25 indicators and every state in the bottom quartile ranked in the top on at least one indicator. Thus, every state has areas of both strength and weakness.

However, across *all* states, the private pay cost of long-term care and support was determined to be unaffordable for middle-income people. This emphasizes the importance of the public safety net. Many families in the United States rely on family caregivers for the majority of the services they receive, and then exhaust their life savings paying for care when they need more help than their families can provide. Only after they have impoverished themselves, they may turn to the public safety net as a last resort.

The *Scorecard* found that Medicaid was a leading indicator for state performance. States that ranked high on the performance of their Medicaid systems for providing both access to and choice in services tended to rank well overall. This finding is not surprising, as Medicaid is the primary source of payment for long-term care and support. States that have improved their Medicaid systems generally have embraced a philosophy that supports choice

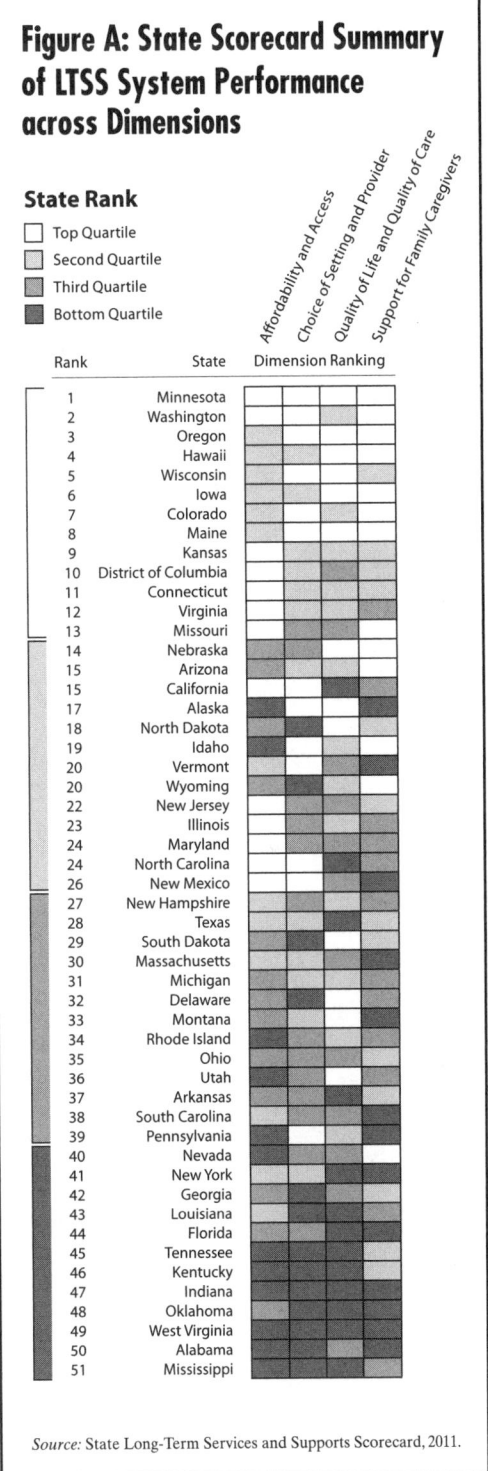

## Figure A: State Scorecard Summary of LTSS System Performance across Dimensions

**State Rank**

- ☐ Top Quartile
- ☐ Second Quartile
- ☐ Third Quartile
- ■ Bottom Quartile

*Source:* State Long-Term Services and Supports Scorecard, 2011.

and control among people with disabilities. States that have adopted person- and family-centered policies designed to enhance choice and control among people who need assistance with daily activities look different than those states that have let outdated policies languish.

Also of note was the finding that states that ranked well on providing support for family caregivers, in general, ranked high overall. Family caregivers are the backbone of the nation's long-term care system. The economic value of their contributions equaled some $450 billion in 2009, an amount that exceeded Medicaid spending on long-term care and support by a factor of four.[10]

Gaps in data prevented the research team from developing measures in critical areas. Areas that could be included in future versions of the *Scorecard* include home and community-based services quality, state spending for respite services, measures of coordination and integration among health care and long-term care, and the availability of housing and transportation options for people with disabilities.

## Steps to Improve State Performance

The U.S. has come a long way from the days when people with physical or cognitive disabilities were segregated from public life. With the tremendous growth of the aging population, both public and private sectors have made strides in developing the infrastructure necessary to support the ability of people to age in their homes and communities. But as the *Scorecard* reveals, progress is uneven across the states and across the various dimensions of a complex long-term care and support system.

For the foreseeable future, Medicaid will continue to be the default public system for long-term care. Because it consumes such a large share of state budgets, generally second only to public education, policymakers often are concerned that it is growing out of control. Although the cost of long-term care is high, analysis of Medicaid spending trends reveals that the costs associated with it are not the driver in rising Medicaid budgets. Between 1997 and 2007, Medicaid spending on long-term care increased 80 percent, whereas non-long-term care spending increased 102 percent.[11] In particular, use of nursing homes declined substantially and disability rates among residents increased. Had nursing home use remained constant between 1994 and 2004, there would have been nearly three-quarters of a million more nursing home residents by 2004.[12]

The good news is that states that make the effort to move away from institutionally based long-term care systems toward the home and community-based systems that consumers prefer will, over time, see slower growth in public spending compared to states that continue to rely on nursing homes.[13] In general, states can serve three people in home and community-based settings for the cost of maintaining one person in a nursing home.[14]

With the passage of the Patient Protection and Affordable Care Act, states were offered a host of new tools to improve their long-term care systems through Medicaid. Several provisions specifically address system balancing, including:

***Community First Choice*** offers states a 6 percentage point increase in federal matching funds if they offer person-centered home and community-based care, including attendant services. States may not impose waiting lists and must offer services statewide. Depending on the income eligibility used, states have the option to provide services to individuals with disability levels lower than those required for institutional care, provided beneficiaries' incomes do not exceed 150 percent of the federal poverty level.

***Balancing Incentives Payment Program*** directs the greatest financial incentives to states that have the least balanced systems. These five-year grants provide either a two or five percentage point increase in federal matching funds to qualifying states. In return, states must implement certain structural changes. These include developing a single entry point system, adopting conflict-free case management services and implementing a uniform method for determining eligibility. States also must increase the percentage of their Medicaid long-term care dollars that go toward home and community-based services by the end of the grant period. It is notable that the structural reforms, such as single entry point systems and standardized assessments, are factors measured by the LTSS *Scorecard*.

Other federal funding for system improvement approved through the Affordable Care Act included new "Money Follows the Person" grants designed to move people from nursing homes into home and community-based settings, as well as expanded grants to establish or expand Aging and Disability Resource Centers. The Affordable Care Act included provisions for states to establish "health homes"—a team of professionals that provide person-centered, integrated health care. These could be used to improve coordination of services for people with both long-term care needs and chronic health conditions. It also established the Federal Coordinated Health Care Office, which is charged with improving the integration of benefits.

## Conclusion

The flexibility states have to craft their own long-term care systems results in both challenges and opportunities. States that endeavor to improve their systems can learn from the creative approaches demonstrated by states that scored high on the *Scorecard* and that were highlighted in that report for their promising practices. Yet this same flexibility results in glaring disparities in the support available to frail older people, low-income people with disabilities and family caregivers. What the *Scorecard* demonstrated was that all states have some areas of strength on which to build, but also challenges to overcome.

The highest-ranked state, Minnesota, scored in the top quartile in 15 of 25 indicators and was ranked in the top five states on 11 indicators. Yet it had several low scores in the area of home health care services. Rather than resting on their laurels, state officials in Minnesota have taken a keen interest in improving their performance on home health measures.

In a different situation, Tennessee ranked in the fourth quartile on three of four dimensions, with 13 of 25 indicators in the bottom tier. Yet despite these challenges, the state is dedicated to improving the balance of its long-term care toward home and community-based services. After being ranked dead last in Medicaid balancing in a 2008 AARP report,[15] Tennessee implemented a Medicaid managed long-term care program. The *Scorecard* found the state's share of public long-term care dollars going toward home and community-based services had increased to 26 percent, bringing it into the third quartile. While still below the national average of 37 percent, it represents progress and a commitment to change that is commendable.

A key factor in state success is the philosophy that guides its public policy decisions. States that embrace the importance of older people and people with disabilities having dignity, choice, autonomy and control will have a head start on crafting programs and policies that facilitate these features. While the almshouses of the 18th and 19th centuries no longer exist, our nation still has a long way to go to achieve the vision of a high-performing long-term care system as articulated in the *Scorecard*. But the *Scorecard* can be used as an effective tool for states to target low-performing areas for improvement. Our intent is to repeat the *Scorecard* approximately every three years so that we can measure progress over time: state by state, and as a nation overall.

## Notes

[1] Encyclopedia of Chicago, Accessed on the Web at *http://encyclopedia.chicagohistory.org/pages/1735.html.*

[2] Laura B. Shrestha, *Life Expectancy in the United States,* CRS Report for Congress, Washington, D.C. August 16, 2006. Accessed on the Web at *http://aging.senate.gov/crs/aging1.pdf.*

[3] Accessed on the Web at *Pegasus.cc.ucsf.edu/~oetjen/HLTC.ppt.*

[4] U.S. Department of Commerce, *Sixty Five Plus in the United States,* May 1995. Accessed on the Web at *http://www.census.gov/population/socdemo/statbriefs/agebrief.html.*

[5] Susan C. Reinhard, Enid Kassner, Ari Houser, and Robert Mollica. *Raising Expectations: A State Scorecard on Long-Term Services and Supports for Older Adults, People with Physical Disabilities, and Family Caregivers*, AARP, The Commonwealth Fund, and The SCAN Foundation, September 2011.

[6] Ibid.

[7] Ibid.

[8] Ibid.

[9] Ibid.

[10] Lynn Feinberg, Susan C. Reinhard, Ari Houser, and Rita Choula. *Valuing the Invaluable: 2011 Update*, AARP, June 2011.

[11] Robert L. Mollica, Enid Kassner, Lina Walker, and Ari Houser. *Taking the Long View: Investing in Medicaid Home and Community-Based Services is Cost-Effective,* AARP, March 2009.

[12] Donald L. Redfoot and Ari Houser. *More Older People with Disabilities Living in the Community: Trends From the National Long-Term Care Survey 1984–2004,* AARP, September 2010.

[13] Stephen H. Kaye, Mitchell P. LaPlante, and Charlene Harrington. "Do Noninstitutional Long-Term Care Services Reduce Medicaid Spending?," *Health Affairs,* January/February 2009: 262–272.

[14] Enid Kassner, Susan Reinhard, Wendy Fox-Grage, Ari Houser, and Jean Accius. *A Balancing Act: State Long-Term Care Reform,* AARP, July 2008.

[15] Ibid.

## About the Author

**Enid Kassner**, MSW, is director of Independent Living/Long-Term Services and Supports for the AARP Public Policy Institute. She has nearly 30 years of experience in the field of aging as a policy analyst, researcher, author, lobbyist and speaker on a broad range of issues, including long-term services and supports, Medicaid and long-term care insurance.

# Medicaid Spending:
# States Face Budget Dilemma After ARRA Bailout

By Debra Miller

*Medicaid is the stuff of nightmares for state budgeters. With the Great Recession, Medicaid enrollment expanded as unemployment increased. Overall health care costs also continued to swell, although recent data indicate that the health spending growth rate may have slowed somewhat. The American Recovery and Reinvestment Act of 2009 provided an enhanced federal matching rate for state Medicaid programs in recognition of the counter-cyclical nature of the program—just when state revenues contract, the demand for more spending in Medicaid increases. The enhanced Medicaid matching rates ended during the 2011 fiscal year and states face difficult budget decisions that pit Medicaid against other state policy priorities.*

Medicaid, the largest health insurance program in the nation, is jointly financed by state and federal governments. The federal government establishes matching rates for each state each year, setting the percentage of overall costs paid by the federal government—between 50 and 83 percent—based on a state's per capita income compared to the nation's per capita income. The American Recovery and Reinvestment Act provided all states with enhanced matching rates for their Medicaid programs in recognition of the fiscal issues states faced in the Great Recession.

A 2011 Council of State Governments' report analyzed the value of the Medicaid matching rate to states before, during and after Recovery Act funding. The report interpreted Medicaid matching rates in a straightforward way: For every dollar a state spends for Medicaid, it calculated how many federal dollars flowed to the state through the federal match. On average, states gained $1.07 additional match for each state dollar spent under the Recovery Act enhanced rates, as the average federal return on a state dollar rose from $1.61 in 2008 to $2.68 in late 2010.[1] The additional match for states ranged from 56 cents in Alaska to $2.39 in Mississippi.

But states lost the last of the enhanced federal match on June 30, 2011, and reverted back to the pre-recession calculation of Medicaid matching rates. When CSG reviewed Medicaid match rates for 2012, it found that for 20 states, the rate was lower than the pre-recession rate in the 2008 fiscal year. The rate increased for 17 states and remained the same for 13 states and the District of Columbia. Regardless of whether states were winners or losers in the comparison of 2008 and 2012 match

rates, all had to cope with the loss of the enhanced matching rates available from the Recovery Act.

## Medicaid State Spending Increases 2007–11

All states except Maine, Nebraska and North Carolina experienced growth in Medicaid expenditures during the Great Recession years. Using Medicaid expenditure data collected each year by the National Association of State Budget Officers, Figure A compares 2007 Medicaid expenditures to estimated expenditures for 2011, the most recent data available.[2] Expenditures for 2007 were adjusted to 2011 dollars using Consumer Price Index data from the U.S. Bureau of Labor Statistics. Expenditure data displayed in Figure A include all sources—federal, state general fund and other state funds.

Colorado led the states with growth of 94 percent over the four-year period, meaning the Medicaid budget in that state nearly doubled. Funding for the expansion was provided by a new provider tax on Colorado hospitals. Medicaid budgets in Idaho, California and Hawaii grew by about 50 percent. The national average increase for the 2007 to 2011 period was 20.4 percent. Twenty states exceeded the national average growth.

## Medicaid Expenditures Grow, 2007–11, Despite Decreased State General Funds

Just how much the enhanced federal Medicaid match under the Recovery Act benefited states is apparent in Figure B. Only 10 states allocated more state general funds to Medicaid from 2007 to 2011, even while overall Medicaid expenditures grew for all but three states. In other words, states' Medicaid expenditures continued to grow in all

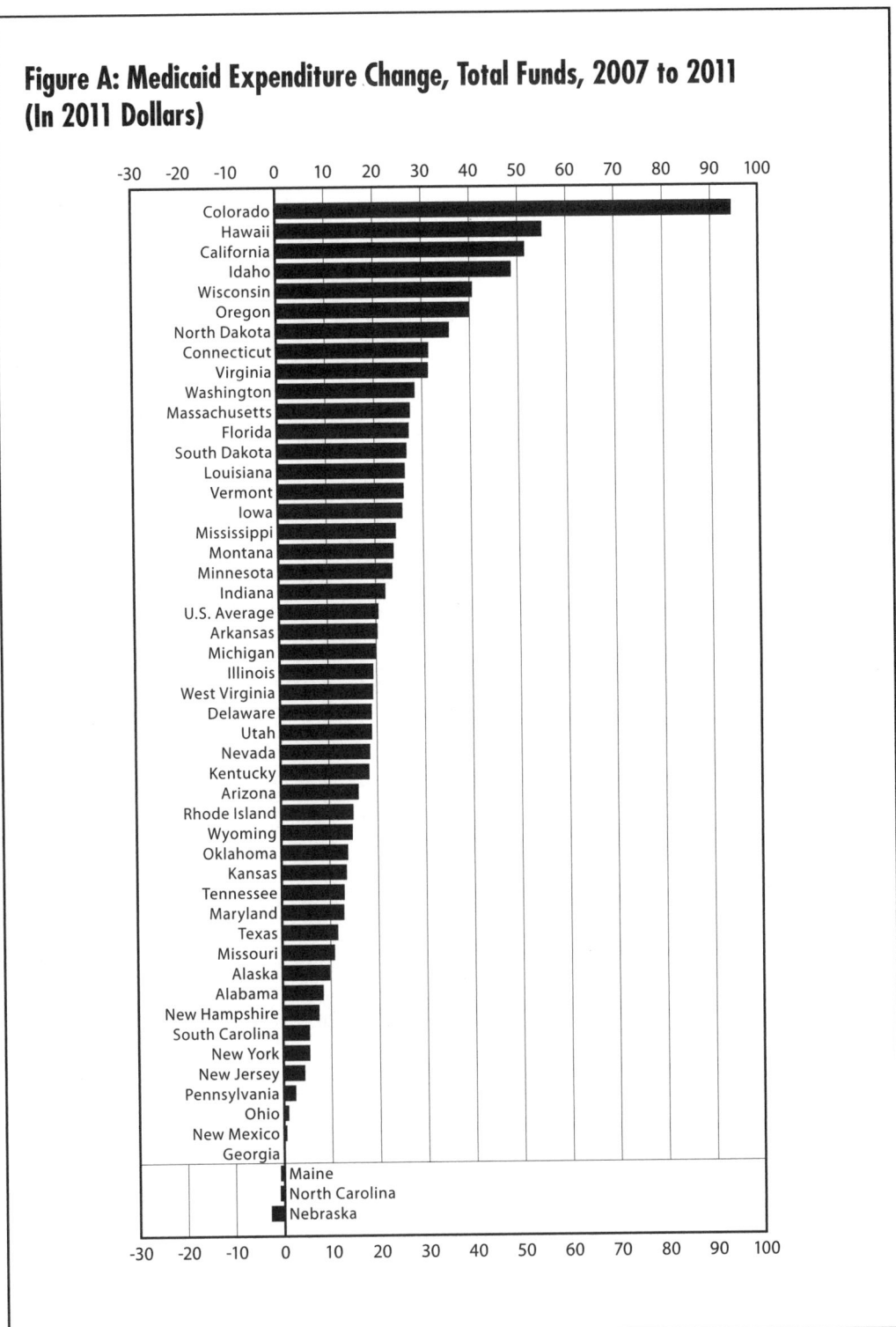

Figure A: Medicaid Expenditure Change, Total Funds, 2007 to 2011 (In 2011 Dollars)

## Figure B: Medicaid Expenditure Change, State General Funds, 2007 to 2011 (In 2011 Dollars)

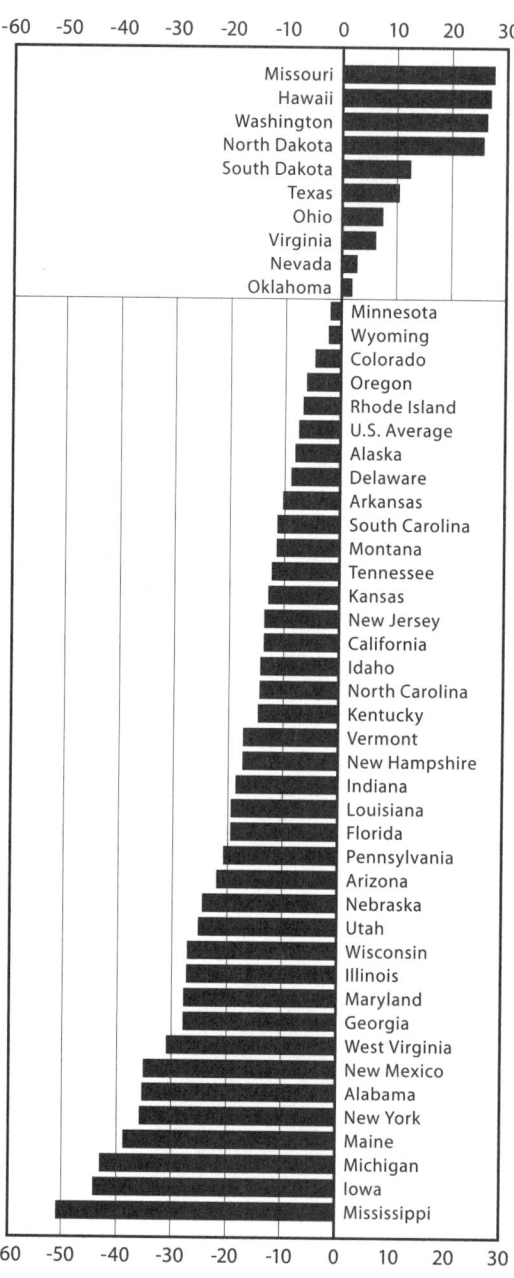

*Note:* Connecticut and Massachusetts are not included. Federal funds are deposited directly into state treasuries, resulting in a co-mingling of federal and state funds.

# Table A: Medicaid Expenditures by State and Region (In Millions of Dollars)

| State | Actual expenditures 2007 (adjusted to 2011 dollars) | | | | Estimated expenditures 2011 | | | | Expenditure change 2007 to 2011 | | | | Medicaid expenditures as percent of total expenditures 2011 |
|---|---|---|---|---|---|---|---|---|---|---|---|---|---|
| | General fund | Federal funds | Other state funds | Total | General fund | Federal funds | Other state funds | Total | General fund | Federal funds | Other state funds | Total | |
| U.S. totals .............. | $119,586 | $182,187 | $29,255 | $331,029 | $110,672 | $249,807 | $38,092 | $398,571 | -7.5% | 37.1% | 30.2% | 20.4% | 23.6% |
| **Eastern Region** | | | | | | | | | | | | | |
| Connecticut (a)....... | $3,420 | $0 | $841 | $4,260 | $4,466 | $0 | $1,127 | $5,593 | 30.6 | n.a. | 34.0 | 31.3 | 27.2 |
| Delaware ................ | 527 | 532 | 0 | 1,059 | 481 | 777 | 0 | 1,258 | -8.8 | 46.2 | n.a. | 18.8 | 16.2 |
| Maine...................... | 716 | 1,456 | 183 | 2,355 | 439 | 1,694 | 205 | 2,338 | -38.7 | 16.4 | 11.8 | -0.7 | 28.6 |
| Maryland................ | 2,776 | 3,011 | 125 | 5,912 | 2,005 | 4,098 | 558 | 6,661 | -27.8 | 36.1 | 347.2 | 12.7 | 21.6 |
| Massachusetts (a).... | 8,192 | 0 | 0 | 8,192 | 10,440 | 0 | 0 | 10,440 | 27.4 | n.a. | n.a. | 27.4 | 20.2 |
| New Hampshire ..... | 477 | 629 | 170 | 1,277 | 395 | 831 | 145 | 1,371 | -17.3 | 32.1 | -14.9 | 7.4 | 25.2 |
| New Jersey ............. | 4,752 | 4,941 | 140 | 9,832 | 4,111 | 6,007 | 136 | 10,254 | -13.5 | 21.6 | -2.8 | 4.3 | 21.9 |
| New York............... | 9,783 | 21,554 | 3,801 | 35,138 | 6,296 | 26,060 | 4,669 | 37,025 | -35.6 | 20.9 | 22.8 | 5.4 | 29.1 |
| Pennsylvania.......... | 6,963 | 10,243 | 1,773 | 18,978 | 5,523 | 12,188 | 1,716 | 19,427 | -20.7 | 19.0 | -3.2 | 2.4 | 31.1 |
| Rhode Island ......... | 864 | 920 | 0 | 1,784 | 806 | 1,234 | 7 | 2,047 | -6.7 | 34.1 | n.a. | 14.8 | 24.7 |
| Vermont.................. | 214 | 603 | 204 | 1,021 | 177 | 855 | 253 | 1,285 | -17.2 | 41.7 | 24.0 | 25.9 | 26.6 |
| Regional totals ....... | 35,907 | 40,877 | 7,113 | 83,896 | 35,139 | 53,744 | 8,816 | 97,699 | -2.1 | 31.5 | 23.9 | 16.5 | n.a. |
| **Midwestern Region** | | | | | | | | | | | | | |
| Illinois................... | 4,595 | 6,484 | 2,534 | 13,613 | 3,341 | 9,560 | 3,320 | 16,221 | -27.3 | 47.4 | 31.0 | 19.2 | 28.9 |
| Indiana................... | 1,585 | 3,382 | 450 | 5,417 | 1,292 | 4,879 | 432 | 6,603 | -18.5 | 44.3 | -4.0 | 21.9 | 24.4 |
| Iowa....................... | 721 | 1,595 | 532 | 2,848 | 403 | 2,331 | 843 | 3,577 | -44.1 | 46.2 | 58.6 | 25.6 | 19.3 |
| Kansas.................... | 906 | 1,421 | 93 | 2,420 | 790 | 1,828 | 125 | 2,743 | -12.8 | 28.6 | 34.0 | 13.3 | 18.6 |
| Michigan................ | 2,523 | 5,671 | 1,825 | 10,019 | 1,440 | 8,743 | 1,821 | 12,004 | -42.9 | 54.2 | -0.2 | 19.8 | 24.0 |
| Minnesota.............. | 3,217 | 3,320 | 0 | 6,537 | 3,156 | 4,848 | 61 | 8,065 | -1.9 | 46.0 | n.a. | 23.4 | 25.1 |
| Nebraska ............... | 672 | 964 | 22 | 1,658 | 507 | 1,085 | 21 | 1,613 | -24.5 | 12.5 | -3.2 | -2.7 | 16.5 |
| North Dakota ......... | 179 | 354 | 4 | 537 | 225 | 501 | 2 | 728 | 25.7 | 41.7 | -53.9 | 35.6 | 14.6 |
| Ohio....................... | 10,036 | 2,555 | 1,248 | 13,839 | 10,777 | 2,590 | 598 | 13,965 | 7.4 | 1.4 | -52.1 | 0.9 | 23.2 |
| South Dakota.......... | 238 | 456 | 0 | 693 | 267 | 611 | 0 | 878 | 12.4 | 34.1 | n.a. | 26.6 | 23.2 |
| Wisconsin............... | 1,940 | 3,076 | 159 | 5,175 | 1,413 | 5,071 | 787 | 7,271 | -27.2 | 64.9 | 393.5 | 40.5 | 17.0 |
| Regional totals........ | 26,612 | 29,277 | 6,867 | 62,756 | 23,611 | 42,047 | 8,010 | 73,668 | -11.3 | 43.6 | 16.6 | 17.4 | n.a. |
| **Southern Region** | | | | | | | | | | | | | |
| Alabama.................. | 533 | 3,371 | 974 | 4,878 | 345 | 3,851 | 1,086 | 5,282 | -35.2 | 14.2 | 11.5 | 8.3 | 25.3 |
| Arkansas................. | 707 | 2,492 | 277 | 3,476 | 635 | 3,424 | 119 | 4,178 | -10.2 | 37.4 | -57.0 | 20.2 | 20.5 |
| Florida................... | 4,935 | 8,995 | 1,627 | 15,557 | 3,978 | 12,081 | 3,721 | 19,780 | -19.4 | 34.3 | 128.7 | 27.1 | 28.0 |
| Georgia................... | 2,399 | 4,852 | 792 | 8,042 | 1,731 | 5,793 | 520 | 8,044 | -27.8 | 19.4 | -34.3 | 0.0 | 20.5 |
| Kentucky................ | 1,065 | 3,371 | 480 | 4,916 | 911 | 4,537 | 360 | 5,808 | -14.5 | 34.6 | -24.9 | 18.2 | 22.8 |
| Louisiana................ | 816 | 4,359 | 448 | 5,623 | 658 | 5,353 | 1,088 | 7,099 | -19.3 | 22.8 | 142.8 | 26.2 | 23.5 |
| Mississippi.............. | 342 | 2,796 | 458 | 3,595 | 168 | 3,395 | 901 | 4,464 | -50.8 | 21.4 | 96.8 | 24.2 | 22.6 |
| Missouri.................. | 1,200 | 4,342 | 2,560 | 8,102 | 1,531 | 6,389 | 1,050 | 8,970 | 27.6 | 47.2 | -59.0 | 10.7 | 36.3 |
| North Carolina....... | 2,875 | 6,674 | 1,836 | 11,385 | 2,466 | 7,660 | 1,172 | 11,298 | -14.2 | 14.8 | -36.2 | -0.8 | 22.1 |
| Oklahoma .............. | 943 | 2,325 | 335 | 3,603 | 960 | 2,675 | 457 | 4,092 | 1.8 | 15.1 | 36.3 | 13.6 | 18.5 |
| South Carolina ....... | 818 | 3,322 | 715 | 4,855 | 726 | 3,870 | 522 | 5,118 | -11.2 | 16.5 | -27.0 | 5.4 | 19.9 |
| Tennessee............... | 2,451 | 4,955 | 290 | 7,695 | 2,152 | 6,252 | 275 | 8,679 | -12.2 | 26.2 | -5.1 | 12.8 | 28.1 |
| Texas ..................... | 7,148 | 13,423 | 1,773 | 22,345 | 7,887 | 16,936 | 58 | 24,881 | 10.3 | 26.2 | -96.7 | 11.4 | 26.3 |
| Virginia.................. | 2,806 | 2,665 | 0 | 5,470 | 2,977 | 4,197 | 0 | 7,174 | 6.1 | 57.5 | n.a. | 31.2 | 16.9 |
| West Virginia.......... | 444 | 1,678 | 218 | 2,340 | 307 | 2,239 | 240 | 2,786 | -30.8 | 33.4 | 10.1 | 19.1 | 13.0 |
| Regional totals........ | 32,257 | 72,630 | 12,907 | 117,794 | 27,432 | 88,652 | 11,569 | 127,653 | -15.0 | 22.1 | -10.4 | 8.4 | n.a. |
| **Western Region** | | | | | | | | | | | | | |
| Alaska.................... | 406 | 712 | 29 | 1,147 | 373 | 871 | 14 | 1,258 | -8.1 | 22.4 | -52.2 | 9.7 | 9.0 |
| Arizona................... | 1,652 | 4,813 | 596 | 7,061 | 1,290 | 5,848 | 1,044 | 8,182 | -21.9 | 21.5 | 75.3 | 15.9 | 28.0 |
| California................ | 14,541 | 21,067 | 698 | 36,305 | 12,573 | 36,814 | 5,573 | 54,960 | -13.5 | 74.8 | 698.9 | 51.4 | 24.2 |
| Colorado................. | 1,330 | 1,406 | 101 | 2,837 | 1,269 | 2,807 | 1,435 | 5,511 | -4.6 | 99.6 | 1,322.3 | 94.3 | 19.4 |
| Hawaii.................... | 477 | 668 | 7 | 1,152 | 606 | 1,180 | 0 | 1,786 | 26.9 | 76.6 | -100.0 | 55.0 | 15.9 |
| Idaho...................... | 348 | 774 | 92 | 1,214 | 299 | 1,311 | 194 | 1,804 | -14.1 | 69.5 | 110.4 | 48.6 | 25.6 |
| Montana ................. | 171 | 553 | 55 | 780 | 152 | 741 | 72 | 965 | -11.3 | 33.9 | 30.1 | 23.7 | 15.7 |
| Nevada................... | 474 | 759 | 115 | 1,349 | 487 | 974 | 135 | 1,596 | 2.7 | 28.3 | 17.4 | 18.4 | 18.7 |
| New Mexico ........... | 829 | 2,106 | 48 | 2,982 | 539 | 2,342 | 115 | 2,996 | -35.0 | 11.2 | 140.9 | 0.5 | 20.2 |
| Oregon................... | 977 | 2,087 | 429 | 3,493 | 918 | 3,408 | 557 | 4,883 | -6.1 | 63.3 | 30.0 | 39.8 | 14.6 |
| Utah ...................... | 345 | 1,068 | 200 | 1,612 | 258 | 1,419 | 238 | 1,915 | -25.2 | 32.9 | 19.2 | 18.8 | 14.3 |
| Washington............. | 3,028 | 3,132 | 0 | 6,160 | 3,825 | 3,943 | 141 | 7,909 | 26.3 | 25.9 | n.a. | 28.4 | 24.4 |
| Wyoming................ | 231 | 259 | 0 | 490 | 226 | 336 | 0 | 562 | -2.2 | 29.6 | n.a. | 14.6 | 7.0 |
| Regional totals........ | 24,811 | 39,404 | 2,368 | 66,582 | 22,815 | 61,994 | 9,518 | 94,327 | -8.0 | 57.3 | 301.9 | 41.7 | n.a. |
| Regional totals w/o California..... | 10,270 | 18,337 | 1,671 | 30,277 | 10,242 | 25,180 | 3,945 | 39,367 | -0.3 | 37.3 | 136.1 | 30.0 | n.a. |

*Source:* Medicaid expenditures as percent of total expenditures: Numbers are percents for FY 2010 actual expenditures (including all state and federal funds) from National Association of State Budget Officers. "State Expenditure Report: Examining Fiscal 2009–2011 State Spending." http://www.nasbo.org/LinkClick.aspx?fileticket=C3LJlSFxbdo%3d&tabid=38.

*Key:*
(a) Medicaid appropriations are "gross funded"—federal funds are deposited directly to the state treasuries.
(b) Inflation adjustment (1.0849) from Consumer Price Index, U.S. Bureau of Labor Statistics.

but three states between 2007 and 2011 without increased investment from states' general funds. In the three states where overall Medicaid expenditures fell—Maine, Nebraska and North Carolina—so did state general funds.

While the average drop in state general fund expenditures in the four-year period was 7.5 percent, Mississippi dropped its state general fund expenditures for Medicaid by 50 percent over the four-year period. Thirteen states' general fund expenditure for Medicaid dropped by 25 percent or more as the enhanced federal Medicaid match backfilled the decreased state funding.

## Medicaid Pressure on State Budgets, 2012 and Beyond

The old conventional wisdom among state budget experts was that expenditures for primary and secondary—or K–12—education required the biggest piece of a state's budget pie. According to NASBO data, Medicaid expenditures as a percent of state budgets increased from 22.3 percent of actual expenditures in 2010 to 23.6 percent of estimated expenditures in 2011, and on average, surpassed K–12 education spending, which averaged 20.1 percent of state expenditures.[3]

Twenty states' Medicaid budget share in 2011 exceeded the national average of 23.6 percent. Missouri was the highest at 36.3 percent, followed by Pennsylvania at 31.1 percent. Alaska and Wyoming spent less than 10 percent of their expenditures on Medicaid in 2011—Wyoming spent just 7 percent, and Alaska 9 percent.

This analysis brings into sharp focus the dilemma of state decision-makers following the loss of the enhanced federal Medicaid match. In order for states to maintain current expenditure levels of Medicaid in the future, given the decreased share of federal funding, they must increase state match from state general funds or develop other state funding mechanisms. States also are searching for a way to institute Medicaid cost-containment, even as they anticipate the possible added expenses of Medicaid expansion called for under federal health care reform if the U.S. Supreme Court does not overturn it.

## Conclusion

The growth of state Medicaid funding during the recession is not surprising, given the constant pressure of increasing health care costs coupled with rising Medicaid enrollment that was the direct result of the unprecedented rise in unemployment.

The enhanced federal Medicaid match provided states a lifeline, just as Congress intended. A state that continued to allocate the same state dollars in Medicaid match was able to grow its Medicaid budget painlessly given that the enhanced federal match provided more funding than before, leading to an increase in overall state Medicaid expenditures. Other states were able to meet Medicaid budgets with reduced state funding, allowing investment in other policy priorities. Now states are faced with backfilling the temporary Recovery Act funds even as slow economic recovery provides few new dollars to address other state policy priorities.

## Notes

[1] Debra Miller, "States Face Medicaid Match Loss After Recovery Act Expires." *CSG Capitol Research*, March 2011. http://knowledgecenter.csg.org/drupal/system/files/States_Face_Medicaid_Match_Loss_After_Recovery_Act_Expires_0.pdf.

[2] The Council of State Governments. *The Book of the States: 2010* and *2011*. Table 7.8.

[3] National Association of State Budget Officers. *State Expenditure Report 2010 (Fiscal 2009–2011 Data)*. http://www.nasbo.org/publications-data/state-expenditure-report/state-expenditure-report-2010-fiscal-2009-2011-data.

## About the Author

**Debra Miller** is director of health policy at the national headquarters of The Council of State Governments. She staffs the Health Policy Task Force, coordinates CSG's health policy academies and regularly writes for CSG publications. She has over 30 years of experience in health and human services and has served on a number of gubernatorial and legislative task forces on issues related to health, children and poverty, including the CHIP Advisory Council in Kentucky.

# The Call to Leadership:
# Medicaid as a Driver in Health Care Reform

### By Matt Salo

*The challenges facing today's Medicaid program are more significant than at any time in the program's history. Medicaid directors are struggling to finance the current health care safety net while simultaneously attempting to drive significant reforms in the broader health care system. To better assist them, the National Association of Medicaid Directors was created to serve and represent them in their efforts to guide the program through an uncertain future.*

## Medicaid's Visibility

Despite covering more than 60 million individuals at a combined state and federal cost of $420 billion in 2011, Medicaid remains poorly understood and appreciated by the general public and federal policymakers. It is truly the nation's health care safety net, yet it remains in the shadow of Medicare for a variety of reasons, including the heterogeneity of its beneficiaries and the wide variation in program design from state to state.

Unlike Medicare, which is generally understood as a program for the elderly, Medicaid's impact is truly "birth to earth." Medicaid pays for more than 40 percent of all births in this country and for the majority of long-term services and supports. It is also the largest funding source for practically all expensive, specialty services such as HIV/AIDS treatment and mental/behavioral health. It covers the entire spectrum of children and adults with physical, developmental and intellectual disabilities. This makes Medicaid hard to simplify or categorize.

Also unlike Medicare, Medicaid's program design can vary widely from state to state. Some state programs cover practically the entire population in capitated managed care arrangements, while others have almost no managed care. Some states have expanded coverage for residents with relatively high income levels, while in other states, working families can only be covered at miniscule income levels, and childless adults have no access to the program, regardless of income.

## Challenges

Despite all the state variation, one common theme unites the directors: the desire to provide the best possible health care to their beneficiaries within the constraints of often crushing budgetary pressures. These two goals, of improving health care and reducing costs, often can be diametrically opposed, and this lies at the heart of the challenge of administering Medicaid today.

Medicaid directors face multiple challenges in administering the program. These can basically be categorized into short term, intermediate and long term. While general statements may apply to most states, there are always outliers and exceptions.

## Short-term Challenges

In the short term, states are still struggling with the repercussions of the state revenue collapse that started in 2007. The past few years have seen states facing multiple consecutive budget windows in which 5, 10, 15, even as much as 25 percent reductions in spending are commonplace.

These budgetary challenges do not come with easy solutions. While the American Recovery and Reinvestment Act provided more than $100 billion in direct relief to beleaguered state Medicaid budgets, that funding is now gone. As a result, state spending on Medicaid is expected to increase by nearly 50 percent from 2010 to 2012, according to the Centers for Medicare & Medicaid Services actuaries.

The traditional tools states have used to weather budgetary challenges are poorly suited to deficits of this magnitude. Traditionally, states needing to make significant budgetary reductions in Medicaid have looked to cuts in eligibility, services and reimbursement rates, as reducing any of those three categories generally leads to less spending, at least in the short term.

Federal law, specifically the maintenance of effort provision contained in the Affordable Care Act, however, prohibits states from reducing eligibility levels or coverage in any way. While the merits of this restriction can be debated, it undeniably limits state options to reduce costs.

Similarly, as states look to reduce reimbursement rates as a means of achieving short-term Medicaid savings, they are challenged by the fact that Medicaid is the least generous payer for everything within the health care system. From prescription drugs and nursing home beds to hospitalizations and physicians, Medicaid's baseline rates are generally so low that significant savings are difficult to achieve from reducing reimbursement rates alone. For example, the average state's payment rate for primary care physicians is about 70 percent of the Medicare rate, which in turn is roughly 70 percent of what the private market pays.

Finally, there is limited ability to achieve significant savings through eliminating or reducing benefits. The so-called optional benefits within Medicaid can be categorized one of two ways: those that can be cut with little impact to beneficiary's health, such as podiatry, adult dental, vision or chiropractics, and those that simply cannot be cut without severely impacting the health care safety net, such as prescription drugs or long-term services and supports. Unfortunately, there's simply not enough savings to be found in cutting the first category and cutting the second is generally unthinkable.

## Intermediate Challenges

Unfortunately, at the same time that states are struggling to balance their budgets, they also are planning and preparing for the fundamental changes the Affordable Care Act will bring to Medicaid. While the law contains many components, the two primary impacts on states will be the largest expansion in the program's history, scheduled to begin Jan. 1, 2014, and the fundamental overhaul of how Medicaid eligibility works and the resulting changes to the eligibility, claims process and information systems currently in place.

The expansion will bring an estimated 17 million individuals into Medicaid, on top of its current coverage and growth trends. While this newly eligible group will be 100 percent federally funded in the beginning, the state exposure to costs increases gradually over the next decade. The other key factor will be absorbing the so-called "woodwork effect," as the 13 million adults and children currently eligible for Medicaid but not enrolled begin to show up in the system. The Affordable Care Act provides no enhanced federal match at all for this population, and depending on demographics, it could represent a cohort significantly sicker, and therefore more expensive, than the general expansion population.

Further complicating this effort will be the necessity to address the challenges of providing access to the newly insured population. Not only will Medicaid be facing huge increases in beneficiaries, but tens of millions of individuals will have newly subsidized private coverage through the insurance exchanges. Reimbursement rates will have to be sufficient to attract the appropriate levels of providers in both programs, but no amount of reimbursement will be able to summon providers from thin air where they currently do not exist.

Another near term challenge will be Congressional efforts to reduce the federal deficit by reforming entitlement programs. While it is clear that some form of Medicaid, Medicare and Social Security reform is necessary, Medicaid directors worry that such efforts could have unintended consequences. Medicaid directors are concerned that Congress may see the simplest approach to saving federal dollars is to shift costs to the states without addressing any of the underlying structural barriers to improving health care. Efforts to reduce or eliminate provider taxes or simply reduce every state's federal matching rate could have the effect of eliminating tens or hundreds of billions of dollars from the system without reducing any of Medicaid's current obligations or entitlements.

## Long-term Challenges

The final challenge is one of sustainability. Regardless of the fate of state cost-containment efforts, federal deficit reduction efforts or the Affordable Care Act, the future of Medicaid rests on two separate trend lines: the expected growth in state revenues and the continued reliance of an aging nation on Medicaid for the entirety of its long-term care financing.

Aside from unpaid, informal caregiving and out-of-pocket expenses, Medicaid is by far the dominant funding source for the nation's long-term care bills. As the population needing services grows—100,000 dual eligibles are added to the rolls every month, so too does Medicaid's obligations. While states have made significant strides in rebalancing the system to include a whole spectrum of non-institutional care options, they also have succeeded in massively increasing the number of people served and reducing the sense of urgency for any other payer to step in and provide relief. This is unsustainable in the face of states' historic capacity to finance the program.

Over the past 30 years, state revenues have grown on average by 6.5 percent per year, while Medicaid's growth has been about 7 percent. This slow growth has led to Medicaid's taking almost 50 years to become close to 25 percent of the average state budget. Once the economy improves, however, reliable forecasts project Medicaid to grow at more than 7 percent, with state revenues stabilizing around 4.5 percent. The increasing disparity between the growth in state revenues and the growth in Medicaid enrollments poses the greatest threat to the program's sustainability that we have ever seen.

## Solutions

In the short term, cuts in program spending are inevitable. In the long term, however, fundamental program reform is equally inevitable. Medicaid directors are seizing the opportunity to turn the battleship of cost and quality in the U.S. health care system around. This will involve completely rethinking the delivery system and the incentives inherent in the fee-for-service payment model. The future of Medicaid is in managed care, although this will include a full spectrum of models, ranging from fully capitated for-profit managed care entities on one end to an in-house, managed fee-for-service model using health homes or medical homes on the other. But there is no question that the current incentives in the system which deliver quantity as opposed to quality must end.

While the Medicaid program, which is ultimately 56 different state and territorial programs, is perhaps not the ideal lever for fundamentally rethinking the entirety of the U.S. health care system, it is the lever we have and the one we will use. Most importantly, the state Medicaid budget crisis brings a sense of urgency to this issue that is significantly greater than that faced by any other payer or entity.

The National Association of Medicaid Directors' goal is to help its members as they steer the nation's largest health insurance program through difficult and uncertain times. While these obstacles seem insurmountable, it is our goal to help equip the directors with the tools and the support they need to mount sustained challenges to the challenges that lie ahead.

## NAMD History

The National Association of Medicaid Directors is the only organization in the country that represents each of the 56 state and territorial Medicaid programs. The association was incorporated in January 2011 with the goal of giving the nation's state Medicaid directors a stronger collective voice

and a more robust platform from which to share best practices and help each state build a stronger Medicaid program.

While Medicaid directors have been working in states since the creation of the program in 1965, they were represented for decades by a larger umbrella group, the American Public Human Services Association. They shared equal billing with a variety of state social services agencies, such as Temporary Assistance for Needy Families, child welfare and Supplemental Nutrition Assistance Program or SNAP, formerly called food stamps. While state Medicaid directors had a home in that organization, few felt it was sufficiently focused on supporting them and their issues, thus the movement toward independence began to take shape.

The need for this change for the Medicaid program also was driven by several external factors, including its growing importance in political discussions at both the state and the federal level, its inexorable growth in terms of the number of people covered by the program and total expenditures, and the practical aspect of Medicaid's movement away from being a welfare program in favor of a more mainstream health insurance program.

The executive committee laid the groundwork in the summer of 2010 to formally withdraw from the American Public Human Services Association and began the process of achieving independent status. The National Association of Medicaid Directors was formally created by January 2011 as a stand-alone 501(c)(3) and a formal affiliate of the National Governors Association.

## Vision

The new association was created with the primary goal of creating a more powerful, effective organization to better serve its members. This is especially critical as states struggle through difficult budgetary times, prepare for the implementation of the Affordable Care Act and address other challenges to the program's sustainability, both at the state and federal level.

The National Association of Medicaid Directors' vision is to ensure the voices of all state Medicaid directors are being heard. Only then can the needs of all state Medicaid directors be met. This will require building consensus. While that may not be easy, it is necessary to effectively influence the development of federal legislation, as well as regulations and other forms of guidance from the administration.

But the association will not focus entirely on policy development or federal advocacy. In recognizing that not every challenge can be resolved at the national or federal level, the association also will play a strong role in developing technical assistance and best practices to educate and inform all states. Medicaid is so large and complex that even veteran directors will be challenged by the multitude of reforms anticipated in the Affordable Care Act. The association aims to help all directors become more efficient and effective, utilizing tools such as timely analysis of federal developments, member-to-member networking and knowledge development, as well as issue briefs highlighting promising practices and lessons learned.

## NAMD Structure

The association created a formal committee structure to help guide both its internal policymaking process and inform the best practices work. Every director is a member of one of four standing committees: Eligibility and Access, Health Information Technology and Systems, Care Management and Integration, and Delivery System and Payment Reform. These committees meet regularly and are not only the convening area for internal discussions key to the program's future, but also the focal point for external conversations about Medicaid's role in the broader health policy and political landscape.

The work of the four committees has been robust, producing comprehensive analysis and consensus comments on a number of key federal regulations on managed care, pharmaceutical pricing, and long-term services and supports, as well as working extensively with the Centers for Medicare & Medicaid Services to guide implementation of the Affordable Care Act, including the conversion to the new Medicaid eligibility rules and the interface with the health insurance exchanges.

The full membership convenes twice annually, at a spring state-only meeting and a fall conference that welcomed almost 850 attendees in its inaugural year. These events offer the members opportunities for robust peer-to-peer learning and sharing of best practices.

## About the Author

**Matt Salo** was named executive director of the National Association of Medicaid Directors (NAMD) in February 2011. The newly formed association represents all 56 of the nation's state and territorial Medicaid Directors, and provides them with a strong unified voice in national discussions as well as a locus for technical assistance and best practices.

Matt formerly spent 12 years at the National Governors Association, where he worked on the Governors' health care and human services reform agendas, and spent the five years prior to that as a health policy analyst working for the state Medicaid directors as part of the American Public Human Services Association. Matt also spent two years as a substitute teacher in the public school system in Alexandria, Virginia, and holds a B.A. in Eastern Religious Studies from the University of Virginia.

## Table 9.11
## HEALTH INSURANCE COVERAGE STATUS BY STATE FOR ALL PEOPLE, BY REGION: 2010
## (In thousands)

| State or other jurisdiction | Total | Covered and not covered by health insurance during the year | | | |
|---|---|---|---|---|---|
| | | Covered | Percent | Not covered | Percent |
| **United States** ................................. | 306,110 | 256,206 | 83.7 | 49,904 | 16.3 |
| **Eastern Region** | | | | | |
| Connecticut.................................. | 3,497 | 3,113 | 89.0 | 384 | 11.0 |
| Delaware ..................................... | 881 | 782 | 88.7 | 99 | 11.3 |
| Maine.......................................... | 1,285 | 1,164 | 90.6 | 121 | 9.4 |
| Maryland ..................................... | 5,727 | 4,979 | 86.9 | 747 | 13.1 |
| Massachusetts ............................. | 6,616 | 6,246 | 94.4 | 370 | 5.6 |
| New Hampshire ........................... | 1,302 | 1,168 | 89.7 | 134 | 10.3 |
| New Jersey ................................... | 8,672 | 7,334 | 84.6 | 1,338 | 15.4 |
| New York...................................... | 19,289 | 16,403 | 85.0 | 2,886 | 15.0 |
| Pennsylvania ............................... | 12,453 | 11,085 | 89.0 | 1,368 | 11.0 |
| Rhode Island................................ | 1,048 | 928 | 88.6 | 119 | 11.4 |
| Vermont....................................... | 622 | 563 | 90.5 | 59 | 9.5 |
| Regional total ............................. | 61,390 | 53,764 | 87.6 | 7,626 | 12.6 |
| **Midwestern Region** | | | | | |
| Illinois......................................... | 12,901 | 10,986 | 85.2 | 1,914 | 14.8 |
| Indiana........................................ | 6,359 | 5,505 | 86.6 | 855 | 13.4 |
| Iowa ............................................ | 2,962 | 2,597 | 87.7 | 366 | 12.3 |
| Kansas ........................................ | 2,757 | 2,407 | 87.3 | 350 | 12.7 |
| Michigan...................................... | 9,772 | 8,500 | 87.0 | 1,271 | 13.0 |
| Minnesota.................................... | 5,186 | 4,678 | 90.2 | 509 | 9.8 |
| Nebraska ..................................... | 1,788 | 1,551 | 86.7 | 237 | 13.3 |
| North Dakota............................... | 635 | 552 | 86.9 | 83 | 13.1 |
| Ohio............................................ | 11,349 | 9,795 | 86.3 | 1,554 | 13.7 |
| South Dakota............................... | 806 | 701 | 87.0 | 105 | 13.0 |
| Wisconsin .................................... | 5,610 | 5,084 | 90.6 | 526 | 9.4 |
| Regional total .............................. | 60,126 | 52,356 | 87.1 | 7,770 | 12.9 |
| **Southern Region** | | | | | |
| Alabama....................................... | 4,672 | 3,951 | 84.6 | 720 | 15.4 |
| Arkansas...................................... | 2,880 | 2,341 | 81.3 | 539 | 18.7 |
| Florida......................................... | 18,531 | 14,677 | 79.2 | 3,854 | 20.8 |
| Georgia........................................ | 9,832 | 7,927 | 80.6 | 1,905 | 19.4 |
| Kentucky ..................................... | 4,292 | 3,653 | 85.1 | 640 | 14.9 |
| Louisiana ..................................... | 4,432 | 3,545 | 80.0 | 886 | 20.0 |
| Mississippi .................................. | 2,929 | 2,311 | 78.9 | 618 | 21.1 |
| Missouri....................................... | 5,979 | 5,143 | 86.0 | 835 | 14.0 |
| North Carolina............................. | 9,248 | 7,673 | 83.0 | 1,575 | 17.0 |
| Oklahoma.................................... | 3,673 | 3,049 | 83.0 | 624 | 17.0 |
| South Carolina............................. | 4,526 | 3,596 | 79.4 | 930 | 20.6 |
| Tennessee .................................... | 6,311 | 5,381 | 85.3 | 930 | 14.7 |
| Texas ........................................... | 25,154 | 18,973 | 75.4 | 6,181 | 24.6 |
| Virginia........................................ | 7,771 | 6,675 | 85.9 | 1,096 | 14.1 |
| West Virginia................................ | 1,807 | 1,564 | 86.5 | 244 | 13.5 |
| Regional total ............................. | 112,037 | 90,460 | 80.7 | 21,577 | 19.3 |
| **Western Region** | | | | | |
| Alaska.......................................... | 693 | 568 | 82.0 | 125 | 18.0 |
| Arizona........................................ | 6,703 | 5,420 | 80.9 | 1,283 | 19.1 |
| California...................................... | 37,223 | 30,014 | 80.6 | 7,209 | 19.4 |
| Colorado...................................... | 5,050 | 4,393 | 87.0 | 656 | 13.0 |
| Hawaii ......................................... | 1,257 | 1,160 | 92.3 | 97 | 7.7 |
| Idaho........................................... | 1,531 | 1,238 | 80.8 | 294 | 19.2 |
| Montana ...................................... | 971 | 795 | 81.9 | 176 | 18.1 |
| Nevada......................................... | 2,639 | 2,076 | 78.7 | 563 | 21.3 |
| New Mexico ................................. | 2,015 | 1,580 | 78.4 | 435 | 21.6 |
| Oregon......................................... | 3,777 | 3,165 | 83.8 | 612 | 16.2 |
| Utah............................................. | 2,829 | 2,443 | 86.4 | 386 | 13.6 |
| Washington.................................. | 6,723 | 5,797 | 86.2 | 927 | 13.8 |
| Wyoming ..................................... | 537 | 444 | 82.7 | 93 | 17.3 |
| Regional total .............................. | 71,949 | 59,094 | 82.1 | 12,855 | 17.9 |
| Regional total without California.................... | 34,725 | 29,079 | 83.7 | 5,646 | 16.3 |
| Dist. of Columbia........................ | 608 | 532 | 87.5 | 76 | 12.5 |

*Source:* U.S. Census Bureau, Current Population Survey, 2011 Annual Social and Economic Supplement. URL: *http://www.census.gov/hhes/www/cpstables/032011/health/toc.htm.* A joint effort between the Bureau of Labor Statistics and the Census Bureau.
*Note:* Unrelated individuals under 15 are included.

## Table 9.12
## NUMBER AND PERCENT OF CHILDREN UNDER 19 YEARS OF AGE, AT OR BELOW
## 200 PERCENT OF POVERTY, BY HEALTH INSURANCE COVERAGE, STATE AND REGION: 2010
(In thousands)

| State or other jurisdiction | Total children under 19 years, all income levels | At or below 200 percent of poverty | | | | | |
|---|---|---|---|---|---|---|---|
| | | Number | Percent | Health insurance coverage | | | |
| | | | | With | | Without | |
| | | | | Number | Percent | Number | Percent |
| United States ..................... | 78,857 | 33,150 | 42.0 | 27,942 | 35.4 | 5,207 | 6.6 |
| **Eastern Region** | | | | | | | |
| Connecticut ........................ | 852 | 196 | 23.0 | 164 | 19.2 | 33 | 3.8 |
| Delaware .......................... | 223 | 79 | 35.7 | 67 | 29.9 | 13 | 5.7 |
| Maine .............................. | 287 | 107 | 37.1 | 101 | 35.2 | 5 | 1.8 |
| Maryland .......................... | 1,409 | 416 | 29.5 | 353 | 25.0 | 63 | 4.5 |
| Massachusetts ................... | 1,545 | 514 | 33.3 | 484 | 31.3 | 30 | 1.9 |
| New Hampshire ................ | 303 | 69 | 22.9 | 66 | 21.7 | 4 | 1.2 |
| New Jersey ........................ | 2,191 | 637 | 29.1 | 529 | 24.1 | 109 | 5.0 |
| New York.......................... | 4,700 | 2,086 | 44.4 | 1,854 | 39.4 | 233 | 4.9 |
| Pennsylvania .................... | 2,990 | 1,077 | 36.0 | 958 | 32.0 | 119 | 4.0 |
| Rhode Island..................... | 240 | 100 | 41.5 | 89 | 37.0 | 11 | 4.5 |
| Vermont............................ | 130 | 46 | 35.6 | 41 | 31.7 | 5 | 3.9 |
| Regional total .................. | 14,870 | 5,327 | 35.8 | 4,706 | 31.6 | 625 | 4.2 |
| **Midwestern Region** | | | | | | | |
| Illinois.............................. | 3,384 | 1,423 | 42.0 | 1,206 | 35.6 | 217 | 6.4 |
| Indiana.............................. | 1,723 | 760 | 44.1 | 665 | 38.6 | 95 | 5.5 |
| Iowa ................................. | 754 | 282 | 37.4 | 251 | 33.2 | 31 | 4.1 |
| Kansas .............................. | 743 | 302 | 40.6 | 260 | 35.0 | 41 | 5.5 |
| Michigan........................... | 2,503 | 976 | 39.0 | 893 | 35.7 | 83 | 3.3 |
| Minnesota......................... | 1,306 | 447 | 34.3 | 402 | 30.8 | 45 | 3.5 |
| Nebraska ........................... | 477 | 168 | 35.2 | 147 | 30.7 | 21 | 4.4 |
| North Dakota..................... | 153 | 51 | 33.1 | 46 | 30.4 | 4 | 2.7 |
| Ohio.................................. | 2,843 | 1,164 | 41.0 | 987 | 34.7 | 177 | 6.2 |
| South Dakota..................... | 209 | 90 | 43.1 | 77 | 36.9 | 13 | 6.2 |
| Wisconsin ......................... | 1,369 | 447 | 32.7 | 412 | 30.1 | 35 | 2.6 |
| Regional total .................. | 15,464 | 6,110 | 39.5 | 5,346 | 34.5 | 762 | 4.9 |
| **Southern Region** | | | | | | | |
| Alabama............................ | 1,165 | 649 | 55.7 | 576 | 49.5 | 73 | 6.2 |
| Arkansas........................... | 742 | 373 | 50.2 | 319 | 43.0 | 53 | 7.2 |
| Florida ............................. | 4,197 | 1,891 | 45.1 | 1,369 | 32.6 | 522 | 12.4 |
| Georgia............................. | 2,717 | 1,217 | 44.8 | 1,000 | 36.8 | 217 | 8.0 |
| Kentucky .......................... | 1,066 | 464 | 43.5 | 411 | 38.5 | 53 | 5.0 |
| Louisiana.......................... | 1,225 | 538 | 43.9 | 466 | 38.1 | 72 | 5.8 |
| Mississippi ....................... | 825 | 477 | 57.8 | 423 | 51.3 | 54 | 6.5 |
| Missouri............................ | 1,517 | 647 | 42.7 | 544 | 35.9 | 103 | 6.8 |
| North Carolina.................. | 2,425 | 1,064 | 43.9 | 837 | 34.5 | 226 | 9.3 |
| Oklahoma.......................... | 976 | 431 | 44.2 | 369 | 37.9 | 62 | 6.4 |
| South Carolina.................. | 1,154 | 464 | 40.2 | 384 | 33.3 | 80 | 6.9 |
| Tennessee ......................... | 1,565 | 709 | 45.3 | 623 | 39.8 | 86 | 5.5 |
| Texas ................................ | 7,293 | 3,676 | 50.4 | 2,875 | 39.4 | 801 | 11.0 |
| Virginia............................. | 2,016 | 665 | 33.0 | 580 | 28.8 | 85 | 4.2 |
| West Virginia..................... | 410 | 168 | 40.9 | 155 | 37.7 | 13 | 3.2 |
| Regional total .................. | 29,293 | 13,433 | 45.8 | 10,931 | 37.3 | 2,500 | 8.5 |
| **Western Region** | | | | | | | |
| Alaska............................... | 194 | 66 | 34.0 | 56 | 29.0 | 10 | 5.0 |
| Arizona............................. | 1,811 | 919 | 50.7 | 727 | 40.1 | 192 | 10.6 |
| California ......................... | 9,964 | 4,392 | 44.1 | 3,728 | 37.4 | 664 | 6.7 |
| Colorado........................... | 1,312 | 477 | 36.4 | 389 | 29.6 | 88 | 6.7 |
| Hawaii .............................. | 312 | 129 | 41.2 | 123 | 39.5 | 5 | 1.7 |
| Idaho................................ | 441 | 197 | 44.7 | 166 | 37.6 | 31 | 7.1 |
| Montana ............................ | 229 | 102 | 44.4 | 86 | 37.5 | 16 | 7.0 |
| Nevada.............................. | 706 | 306 | 43.4 | 245 | 34.6 | 62 | 8.8 |
| New Mexico ...................... | 545 | 289 | 53.1 | 229 | 42.1 | 60 | 11.0 |
| Oregon.............................. | 906 | 386 | 42.6 | 320 | 35.3 | 66 | 7.3 |
| Utah.................................. | 921 | 305 | 33.1 | 236 | 25.7 | 68 | 7.4 |
| Washington....................... | 1,629 | 599 | 36.8 | 555 | 34.1 | 44 | 2.7 |
| Wyoming .......................... | 143 | 50 | 34.9 | 43 | 30.0 | 7 | 4.9 |
| Regional total .................. | 19,113 | 8,217 | 42.9 | 6,903 | 36.1 | 1,313 | 6.8 |
| Regional total without California......... | 9,149 | 3,825 | 41.8 | 3,175 | 34.7 | 649 | 7.0 |
| Dist. of Columbia.............. | 119 | 63 | 53.3 | 56 | 47.2 | 7 | 6.1 |

*Source:* U.S. Census Bureau, Current Population Survey, 2010 Annual Social and Economic Supplement. URL: *http://www.census.gov/hhes/www/* *cpstables/032009/health/h10_000.htm*. A joint effort between the Bureau of Labor Statistics and the Census Bureau.

# Table 9.13
## REVENUES USED BY STATES FOR HIGHWAYS, BY REGION: 2009

| State or other jurisdiction | Beginning balance total (a) | Highway-user revenues (b): Motor-fuel taxes | Motor-vehicle and motor-carrier taxes | Road and crossing tolls | Total | Appropriations from general funds (c) | Other state imposts | Miscellaneous | Bond proceeds (d) | Payments from other governments — Federal funds: Federal Hwy. Administration | Other agencies | From local government | Total receipts |
|---|---|---|---|---|---|---|---|---|---|---|---|---|---|
| United States........... | 64,609,388 | 30,696,156 | 22,146,885 | 7,704,701 | 60,547,742 | 7,308,616 | 5,113,180 | 8,393,216 | 21,119,139 | 34,553,020 | 1,869,305 | 3,658,387 | 142,562,602 |
| **Eastern Region** | | | | | | | | | | | | | |
| Connecticut............ | 330,928 | 253,744 | 128,590 | 161 | 382,495 | 0 | 57,134 | 76,421 | 855,838 | 481,421 | 11,498 | 24,376 | 1,889,183 |
| Delaware................ | 450,402 | 65,927 | 67,674 | 254,158 | 387,759 | 57,427 | 0 | 24,861 | 237,261 | 174,991 | 7,347 | 0 | 889,646 |
| Maine.................... | 58,374 | 231,369 | 54,849 | 132,842 | 419,060 | 0 | 0 | 32,961 | 88,695 | 149,719 | 5,774 | 0 | 696,209 |
| Maryland............... | 1,243,969 | 564,787 | 577,737 | 275,715 | 1,418,239 | 78,578 | 0 | 72,097 | 847,599 | 480,481 | 8,594 | 0 | 2,905,587 |
| Massachusetts......... | 1,356,303 | 588,395 | 317,559 | 380,423 | 1,286,377 | 115,401 | 0 | 232,764 | 440,199 | 670,745 | 6,312 | 0 | 2,751,798 |
| New Hampshire...... | 1,457,529 | 131,461 | 121,482 | 104,788 | 357,731 | 0 | 0 | 137,108 | 30,000 | 158,874 | 15,981 | 5,889 | 705,583 |
| New Jersey............. | 1,913,221 | 281,555 | 462,054 | 1,152,093 | 1,895,702 | 0 | 0 | 329,361 | 2,741,519 | 595,762 | 19,208 | 0 | 5,581,552 |
| New York............... | 226,694 | 1,204,390 | 896,954 | 1,187,354 | 3,288,698 | 588,465 | 0 | 680,519 | 1,856,058 | 1,614,690 | 26,247 | 38,051 | 8,072,728 |
| Pennsylvania.......... | 3,634,656 | 1,256,277 | 446,579 | 793,886 | 2,496,742 | 844,963 | 0 | 650,843 | 1,203,050 | 1,467,701 | 30,564 | 30,364 | 6,724,227 |
| Rhode Island.......... | 92,471 | 47,993 | 21,974 | 10,630 | 80,597 | 0 | 0 | 56,011 | 52,985 | 183,538 | 6,062 | 0 | 379,193 |
| Vermont................ | 9,455 | 53,004 | 100,560 | | 153,564 | 13,439 | 0 | 17,765 | 15,200 | 145,265 | 20,594 | 1,104 | 366,391 |
| Regional total........ | 10,774,002 | 4,678,902 | 3,196,012 | 4,292,050 | 12,166,964 | 1,698,273 | 57,134 | 2,310,711 | 8,368,404 | 6,123,187 | 158,181 | 99,784 | 30,962,097 |
| **Midwestern Region** | | | | | | | | | | | | | |
| Illinois.................. | 2,002,261 | 844,383 | 857,823 | 665,687 | 2,367,893 | 540,802 | 280 | 39,799 | 780,000 | 1,232,205 | 27,020 | 829 | 4,988,828 |
| Indiana (d)............ | 394,256 | 793,884 | 214,744 | 149,246 | 1,157,874 | 496 | 82,900 | 285,138 | 415,850 | 1,084,642 | 8,813 | 32,503 | 3,068,214 |
| Iowa..................... | 253,268 | 411,494 | 443,471 | 0 | 854,965 | 51,074 | 219,101 | 25,743 | 0 | 429,706 | 93,095 | 0 | 1,673,684 |
| Kansas.................. | 727,574 | 331,620 | 92,967 | 79,589 | 504,176 | 29,032 | 276,305 | 38,251 | 77,425 | 425,981 | 8,610 | 48,780 | 1,408,560 |
| Michigan............... | 896,710 | 803,857 | 732,352 | 33,660 | 1,569,869 | 91,718 | 71,767 | 115,145 | 326,513 | 1,037,570 | 23,476 | 17,096 | 3,253,154 |
| Minnesota............. | 948,757 | 533,873 | 392,029 | 0 | 925,902 | 0 | 205,425 | 102,022 | 174,500 | 614,941 | 42,337 | 204,630 | 2,269,757 |
| Nebraska............... | 135,931 | 305,979 | 61,157 | 0 | 367,136 | 49,439 | 151,801 | 37,018 | 0 | 261,746 | 9,935 | 474,428 | 1,351,503 |
| North Dakota......... | 93,732 | 130,590 | 75,306 | 0 | 205,896 | 6,064 | 0 | 674 | 0 | 238,923 | 8,148 | 28,678 | 488,383 |
| Ohio..................... | 1,500,300 | 1,600,371 | 713,338 | 186,824 | 2,500,533 | 21,433 | 0 | 427,729 | 528,450 | 1,138,720 | 36,122 | 99,985 | 4,752,972 |
| South Dakota......... | 110,826 | 106,644 | 2,974 | 0 | 109,618 | 0 | 53,153 | 39,293 | 0 | 221,603 | 10,978 | 11,414 | 446,059 |
| Wisconsin.............. | 471,646 | 771,167 | 479,059 | 0 | 1,250,226 | 58,507 | 0 | 81,401 | 281,118 | 792,103 | 88,355 | 96,881 | 2,648,591 |
| Regional total........ | 7,535,261 | 6,633,862 | 4,065,220 | 1,115,006 | 11,814,088 | 848,565 | 1,060,732 | 1,192,213 | 2,583,856 | 7,478,140 | 356,889 | 1,015,224 | 26,349,705 |
| **Southern Region** | | | | | | | | | | | | | |
| Alabama................ | 363,835 | 697,010 | 167,725 | 0 | 864,735 | 98,825 | 47,670 | 8,930 | 0 | 735,944 | 39,704 | 3,460 | 1,799,268 |
| Arkansas............... | 273,216 | 392,517 | 148,689 | 0 | 541,206 | 54,662 | 5,198 | 21,628 | 0 | 390,773 | 46,256 | 14,074 | 1,073,797 |
| Florida.................. | 2,762,547 | 1,535,672 | 783,253 | 1,001,075 | 3,320,000 | 251,573 | 111,955 | 257,381 | 12,570 | 1,802,075 | 185,733 | 257,663 | 6,198,950 |
| Georgia................. | 1,368,660 | 836,561 | 184,748 | 19,491 | 1,040,800 | 232,193 | 0 | 100,201 | 988,863 | 1,166,196 | 51,778 | 35,043 | 3,615,074 |
| Kentucky............... | 411,644 | 534,759 | 493,689 | 0 | 1,028,448 | 4,875 | 0 | 306,884 | 361,152 | 533,913 | 12,131 | 0 | 2,247,403 |
| Louisiana.............. | 2,664,683 | 596,301 | 181,504 | 38,730 | 816,535 | 306,341 | 53,131 | 39,590 | 432,129 | 893,001 | 93,041 | 104,405 | 2,637,567 |
| Mississippi............ | 260,905 | 368,623 | 144,108 | 0 | 512,731 | 0 | 41,755 | 6,341 | 0 | 528,559 | 22,084 | 53,965 | 1,215,875 |
| Missouri............... | 1,052,560 | 677,287 | 287,087 | 0 | 964,374 | 6,875 | 266,774 | 181,437 | 145,570 | 844,571 | 33,184 | 33,611 | 2,496,750 |
| North Carolina....... | 1,059,348 | 1,384,845 | 599,849 | 2,106 | 1,986,800 | 0 | 454,122 | 51,469 | 0 | 1,031,606 | 16,197 | 29,343 | 3,573,805 |
| Oklahoma............. | 516,115 | 68,218 | 90,710 | 206,431 | 365,359 | 223,333 | 294,181 | 135,670 | 35,000 | 752,190 | 13,851 | 34,720 | 1,848,927 |
| South Carolina....... | 426,229 | 501,363 | 172,839 | 12,374 | 686,576 | 141 | 2,726 | 29,958 | 0 | 412,014 | 12,689 | 0 | 1,178,824 |
| Tennessee............. | 1,580,878 | 703,203 | 316,467 | 36 | 1,019,706 | 0 | 57,667 | 47,480 | 0 | 690,779 | 44,525 | 0 | 1,860,157 |
| Texas.................... | 6,622,599 | 1,113,441 | 1,824,260 | 413,599 | 3,351,300 | 25,737 | 39,631 | 1,498,760 | 2,046,412 | 2,511,426 | 43,641 | 154,993 | 9,671,400 |
| Virginia................ | 2,104,707 | 630,807 | 574,348 | 20,545 | 1,225,700 | 235,119 | 689,244 | 178,454 | 0 | 660,702 | 29,452 | 80,772 | 3,099,443 |
| West Virginia......... | 293,543 | 381,091 | 242,378 | 53,673 | 677,142 | 17,889 | 3,494 | 42,283 | 134,108 | 475,433 | 20,356 | 439 | 1,371,144 |
| Regional total........ | 21,761,469 | 10,421,698 | 6,211,654 | 1,768,060 | 18,401,412 | 1,457,563 | 2,067,548 | 2,906,466 | 4,155,804 | 13,429,182 | 664,622 | 802,488 | 43,888,384 |

See footnotes at end of table.

# REVENUES USED BY STATES FOR HIGHWAYS, BY REGION: 2009 — Continued

| State or other jurisdiction | Beginning balance total (a) | Highway-user revenues (b) | | | | Appropriations from general funds (c) | Other state imposts | Miscellaneous | Bond proceeds (d) | Payments from other governments | | | Total receipts |
|---|---|---|---|---|---|---|---|---|---|---|---|---|---|
| | | Motor-fuel taxes | Motor-vehicle and motor-carrier taxes | Road and crossing tolls | Total | | | | | Federal funds | | From local government | |
| | | | | | | | | | | Federal Hwy. Administration | Other agencies | | |
| **Western Region** | | | | | | | | | | | | | |
| Alaska | 0 | 7,331 | 36,190 | 21,409 | 64,930 | 337,300 | 0 | 26,205 | 162,160 | 335,810 | 9,070 | 0 | 935,475 |
| Arizona | 1,618,788 | 459,283 | 236,636 | 0 | 695,919 | 0 | 692,836 | 136,338 | 734,593 | 569,708 | 39,436 | 10,587 | 2,879,417 |
| California | 15,282,246 | 5,239,858 | 5,937,943 | 344,450 | 11,522,251 | 2,328,686 | 786,048 | 940,005 | 3,547,924 | 2,604,757 | 106,112 | 1,545,518 | 23,381,301 |
| Colorado | 2,981,290 | 460,840 | 808,979 | 0 | 1,269,819 | 0 | 0 | 34,028 | 0 | 800,380 | 23,452 | 34,668 | 2,162,347 |
| Hawaii | 313,164 | 78,223 | 87,917 | 0 | 166,140 | 0 | 0 | 20,110 | 126,033 | 217,025 | 3,107 | 0 | 532,415 |
| Idaho | 133,042 | 196,529 | 142,531 | 0 | 339,060 | 0 | 0 | 16,131 | 179,086 | 289,894 | 38,751 | 6,248 | 869,170 |
| Montana | 54,652 | 92,861 | 105,845 | 0 | 198,706 | 3,468 | 6,488 | 58,037 | 0 | 359,321 | 34,951 | 2,559 | 663,530 |
| Nevada | 471,261 | 436,131 | 205,863 | 649 | 642,643 | 46 | 0 | 114,097 | 0 | 323,713 | 11,347 | 0 | 1,091,846 |
| New Mexico | 658,553 | 175,942 | 215,268 | 0 | 391,210 | 53,781 | 11,619 | 80,082 | 0 | 303,617 | 63,532 | 0 | 903,841 |
| Oregon | 1,625,367 | 266,419 | 262,278 | 0 | 528,697 | 53,364 | 13,718 | 96,800 | 352,204 | 392,394 | 129,758 | 5,015 | 1,571,950 |
| Utah | 719,820 | 329,243 | 111,175 | 1,221 | 441,639 | 178,367 | 276,001 | 24,635 | 398,000 | 313,124 | 86,338 | 96,701 | 1,814,805 |
| Washington | 1,038,818 | 1,163,235 | 411,664 | 161,856 | 1,736,755 | 0 | 49,002 | 311,443 | 507,276 | 741,909 | 100,807 | 39,595 | 3,486,787 |
| Wyoming | 58,840 | 32,415 | 37,221 | 0 | 69,636 | 112,759 | 73,705 | 45,613 | 0 | 270,189 | 39,567 | 0 | 611,469 |
| Regional total | 24,955,841 | 8,938,310 | 8,599,510 | 529,585 | 18,067,405 | 3,067,771 | 1,909,417 | 1,903,524 | 6,007,276 | 7,521,841 | 686,228 | 1,740,891 | 40,904,353 |
| Regional total w/o California | 9,673,595 | 3,698,452 | 2,661,567 | 185,135 | 6,545,154 | 739,085 | 1,123,369 | 963,519 | 2,459,352 | 4,917,084 | 580,116 | 195,373 | 17,523,052 |
| Dist. of Columbia | 24,203 | 23,384 | 74,489 | 0 | 97,873 | 236,944 | 18,349 | 100,302 | 0 | 670 | 3,385 | 0 | 457,523 |

*Source:* U.S. Department of Transportation, Federal Highway Administration, *Highway Statistics, 2009,* (March 2011).

*Note:* Detail may not add to totals due to rounding. This table was compiled from reports of state authorities.

*Key:*
(a) Any differences between beginning balances and the closing balances on last year's table are the result of accounting adjustments, inclusion of funds not previously reported, etc.

(b) Amounts shown represent only those highway user revenues that were expended on state or local roads.

(c) Amounts shown represent gross general fund appropriations for highways reduced by the amount of highway-user revenues placed in the State General Fund.

(d) Amount shown represents original and refunding issues.

# Table 9.14
## STATE DISBURSEMENTS FOR HIGHWAYS, BY REGION: 2009

| State or other jurisdiction | Capital outlay total (a) | Maintenance and services total (a) | Administration research and planning | Highway law enforcement and safety | Interest | Bond retirement | Total disbursements | Total end-of-year balances (b) |
|---|---|---|---|---|---|---|---|---|
| United States .......... | $65,102,982 | $20,762,054 | $9,247,068 | $8,266,048 | $6,304,759 | $8,008,423 | $117,691,336 | $63,361,485 |
| **Eastern Region** | | | | | | | | |
| Connecticut.............. | 659,277 | 112,391 | 330,181 | 14,724 | 240,989 | 785,778 | 2,143,340 | 44,654 |
| Delaware.................. | 334,746 | 108,347 | 93,621 | 78,641 | 13,884 | 81,887 | 711,126 | 628,922 |
| Maine...................... | 299,913 | 220,807 | 24,331 | 34,678 | 24,388 | 23,310 | 627,427 | 102,349 |
| Maryland.................. | 1,428,578 | 386,165 | 94,376 | 120,696 | 127,452 | 131,493 | 2,288,760 | 1,349,636 |
| Massachusetts.......... | 752,115 | 397,205 | 252,735 | 180,837 | 463,792 | 292,395 | 2,339,395 | 1,297,809 |
| New Hampshire........ | 223,252 | 208,415 | 63,564 | 68,464 | 18,200 | 21,210 | 603,105 | 1,522,007 |
| New Jersey.............. | 1,594,245 | 616,875 | 166,289 | 398,271 | 819,041 | 475,764 | 4,070,485 | 3,272,562 |
| New York................. | 2,760,761 | 1,396,630 | 312,265 | 410,993 | 572,659 | 645,046 | 6,098,355 | 868,670 |
| Pennsylvania........... | 3,459,225 | 1,730,356 | 455,090 | 574,136 | 203,885 | 110,962 | 6,533,654 | 3,380,119 |
| Rhode Island........... | 150,197 | 109,307 | 30,902 | 27,347 | 31,126 | 35,946 | 384,825 | 82,964 |
| Vermont.................. | 155,222 | 86,297 | 33,892 | 57,939 | 4,281 | 1,494 | 339,125 | 23,921 |
| Regional total.......... | 11,817,531 | 5,372,795 | 1,857,246 | 1,966,726 | 2,519,697 | 2,605,285 | 26,139,280 | 12,573,613 |
| **Midwestern Region** | | | | | | | | |
| Illinois..................... | 2,852,653 | 788,154 | 250,695 | 257,528 | 265,281 | 237,633 | 4,651,944 | 1,606,572 |
| Indiana (e).............. | 1,579,927 | 121,813 | 382,857 | 3,259 | 268,440 | 130,658 | 2,486,954 | 182,096 |
| Iowa........................ | 680,583 | 188,138 | 69,381 | 122,057 | | - | 1,060,159 | 205,454 |
| Kansas.................... | 744,351 | 166,668 | 69,844 | 79,841 | 87,614 | 9,950 | 1,158,268 | 672,259 |
| Michigan................. | 1,272,105 | 295,922 | 122,088 | 253,184 | 110,073 | 98,820 | 2,152,192 | 972,041 |
| Minnesota............... | 848,952 | 437,633 | 134,999 | 155,139 | 28,171 | 57,906 | 1,662,800 | 821,976 |
| Nebraska................. | 426,708 | 175,214 | 28,024 | 78,146 | | | 708,092 | 89,063 |
| North Dakota........... | 298,716 | 37,687 | 20,547 | 24,002 | 2,063 | 3,255 | 386,270 | 104,477 |
| Ohio........................ | 1,787,355 | 610,980 | 310,377 | 280,582 | 70,859 | 413,885 | 3,474,038 | 1,400,814 |
| South Dakota........... | 311,973 | 70,820 | 41,389 | 35,078 | | | 459,260 | 57,036 |
| Wisconsin................ | 1,193,332 | 224,807 | 182,919 | 106,177 | 111,546 | 136,834 | 1,955,615 | 571,143 |
| Regional total.......... | 11,996,655 | 3,117,836 | 1,613,120 | 1,394,993 | 944,047 | 1,088,941 | 20,155,592 | 6,682,931 |
| **Southern Region** | | | | | | | | |
| Alabama.................. | 951,106 | 160,406 | 184,536 | 147,659 | | 12,450 | 1,456,157 | 194,501 |
| Arkansas................. | 530,273 | 173,946 | 32,604 | 98,227 | 20,803 | 52,685 | 908,538 | 274,795 |
| Florida.................... | 4,443,504 | 925,110 | 238,818 | 420,253 | 399,962 | 231,180 | 6,658,827 | 1,767,617 |
| Georgia................... | 2,100,782 | 213,370 | 428,314 | 196,855 | 181,076 | 272,551 | 3,392,948 | 1,478,147 |
| Kentucky................. | 1,488,876 | 376,354 | 17,984 | 84,310 | 118,863 | 133,390 | 2,219,777 | 136,840 |
| Louisiana................ | 2,973,935 | 327,469 | 52,723 | 80,226 | 3,542 | 37,981 | 3,475,876 | 1,822,620 |
| Mississippi.............. | 707,655 | 127,600 | 73,253 | 36,874 | 27,462 | 65,044 | 1,037,888 | 175,746 |
| Missouri.................. | 1,474,105 | 526,300 | 71,924 | 204,395 | 114,698 | 84,890 | 2,476,312 | 703,008 |
| North Carolina......... | 1,989,813 | 693,956 | 324,030 | 359,568 | 44,955 | 99,835 | 3,512,157 | 973,927 |
| Oklahoma............... | 966,335 | 179,039 | 129,140 | 107,307 | 99,221 | 66,555 | 1,547,597 | 600,169 |
| South Carolina......... | 645,602 | 359,292 | 90,710 | 94,268 | 31,862 | 84,027 | 1,305,761 | 251,976 |
| Tennessee............... | 1,018,307 | 321,511 | 262,296 | 36,560 | | | 1,638,674 | 1,504,648 |
| Texas...................... | 5,364,789 | 1,285,943 | 288,814 | 777,356 | 713,907 | 989,181 | 9,419,990 | 6,410,788 |
| Virginia................... | 1,091,029 | 1,240,877 | 366,911 | 191,353 | 95,775 | 231,204 | 3,217,149 | 1,631,867 |
| West Virginia........... | 841,764 | 289,994 | 95,672 | 38,549 | 31,684 | 101,263 | 1,398,926 | 255,078 |
| Regional total.......... | 26,587,875 | 7,201,167 | 2,657,729 | 2,873,760 | 1,883,810 | 2,462,236 | 43,666,577 | 18,181,727 |

See footnotes at end of table.

# STATE DISBURSEMENTS FOR HIGHWAYS, BY REGION: 2009—Continued

| State or other jurisdiction | Capital outlay total (a) | Maintenance and services total (a) | Administration research and planning | Highway law enforcement and safety | Interest | Bond retirement | Total disbursements | Total end-of-year balances (b) |
|---|---|---|---|---|---|---|---|---|
| **Western Region** | | | | | | | | |
| Alaska | 578,918 | 240,030 | 56,202 | 37,597 | 6,832 | 14,123 | 933,702 | 1 |
| Arizona | 1,216,653 | 142,088 | 267,085 | 196,566 | 134,422 | 212,065 | 2,168,879 | 1,507,657 |
| California | 5,849,124 | 2,737,812 | 1,409,389 | 1,039,052 | 311,202 | 1,057,400 | 12,403,979 | 16,867,942 |
| Colorado | 841,307 | 227,847 | 220,400 | 136,748 | 57,460 | 108,040 | 1,591,802 | 3,237,538 |
| Hawaii | 276,618 | 55,781 | 80,042 | 9,390 | 17,610 | 27,445 | 466,886 | 341,396 |
| Idaho | 485,090 | 104,496 | 29,477 | 37,988 | - | 22,852 | 679,903 | 112,065 |
| Montana | 435,888 | 107,326 | 56,018 | 49,888 | 6,910 | 9,070 | 665,100 | 10,295 |
| Nevada | 738,746 | 137,254 | 134,787 | 115,459 | 37,578 | 51,420 | 1,215,245 | 342,453 |
| New Mexico | 528,164 | 152,547 | 235,146 | 23,535 | 96,213 | 74,500 | 1,110,105 | 289,957 |
| Oregon | 684,589 | 213,796 | 129,515 | 94,779 | 60,282 | 34,365 | 1,217,796 | 1,802,796 |
| Utah | 911,965 | 241,536 | 247,548 | 55,702 | 46,058 | 112,491 | 1,615,300 | 679,392 |
| Washington | 1,724,834 | 626,597 | 201,921 | 190,781 | 182,638 | 128,190 | 3,054,961 | 718,188 |
| Wyoming | 429,025 | 83,146 | 51,443 | 43,084 | 0 | 0 | 606,698 | 59,073 |
| Regional total | 14,700,921 | 5,070,256 | 3,118,973 | 2,030,569 | 957,205 | 1,851,961 | 27,730,356 | 25,968,753 |
| Regional total without California | 8,851,797 | 2,332,444 | 1,709,584 | 991,517 | 646,003 | 794,561 | 15,326,377 | 9,100,811 |
| Dist. of Columbia | 285,947 | 52,589 | 30,251 | - | - | 100,322 | 469,109 | 12,617 |

*Source:* U.S. Department of Transportation, Federal Highway Administration, Highway Statistics, 2009, (March 2011).

*Note:* Detail may not add to totals due to rounding. This table was compiled from reports of state authorities.

*Key:*
(a) Includes state administered and local roads and streets.
(b) Amounts shown represent both reserves for current highway work and reserves for debt service.

**Table 9.15**
**PUBLIC ROAD LENGTH MILES BY OWNERSHIP: 2009**

| State or other jurisdiction | Rural mileage | | | | | | Urban mileage | | | | | | Total rural & urban mileage |
|---|---|---|---|---|---|---|---|---|---|---|---|---|---|
| | State highway agency | County | Town, township & municipal (a) | Other jurisdictions (b) | Federal agency (c) | Total rural roads | State highway agency | County | Town, township & municipal (a) | Other jurisdictions (b) | Federal agency (c) | Total urban roads | |
| **Total** | 632,497 | 1,591,651 | 580,001 | 49,052 | 123,811 | 2,977,013 | 152,091 | 197,866 | 721,843 | 6,533 | 7,807 | 1,086,140 | 4,063,153 |
| **United States total** | 631,473 | 1,591,651 | 577,944 | 49,052 | 123,789 | 2,973,909 | 148,533 | 197,866 | 711,834 | 6,533 | 7,799 | 1,072,565 | 4,046,475 |
| **Eastern Region** | | | | | | | | | | | | | |
| Connecticut | 1,289 | 0 | 4,658 | 285 | 14 | 6,246 | 2,430 | 0 | 12,607 | 60 | 64 | 15,161 | 21,407 |
| Delaware | 3,082 | 0 | 103 | 44 | 84 | 3,313 | 2,256 | 0 | 683 | 4 | 51 | 2,994 | 6,307 |
| Maine | 7,511 | 0 | 12,032 | 132 | 167 | 19,843 | 990 | 0 | 1,983 | 18 | 4 | 2,995 | 22,838 |
| Maryland | 3,101 | 10,396 | 406 | 134 | 33 | 14,071 | 2,051 | 10,815 | 4,291 | 126 | 107 | 17,389 | 31,459 |
| Massachusetts | 753 | 1 | 6,832 | 367 | 27 | 7,981 | 2,242 | 2 | 25,591 | 277 | 85 | 28,196 | 36,177 |
| New Hampshire | 3,207 | | 7,697 | 48 | 146 | 11,098 | 765 | | 4,138 | 5 | 0 | 4,908 | 16,006 |
| New Jersey | 455 | 1,987 | 3,831 | 585 | 422 | 7,279 | 1,870 | 4,453 | 24,712 | 423 | 100 | 31,558 | 38,837 |
| New York | 9,936 | 15,903 | 39,383 | 526 | 368 | 66,116 | 5,033 | 4,444 | 37,731 | 807 | 416 | 48,431 | 114,546 |
| Pennsylvania | 28,848 | 20 | 43,451 | 3,398 | 767 | 76,484 | 11,014 | 270 | 33,564 | 352 | 88 | 45,288 | 121,772 |
| Rhode Island | 316 | 0 | 871 | 0 | 27 | 1,214 | 793 | | 4,363 | 3 | 29 | 5,187 | 6,401 |
| Vermont | 2,451 | 0 | 10,210 | 210 | 142 | 13,013 | 178 | 0 | 1,221 | 0 | 25 | 1,424 | 14,436 |
| Regional total | 60,902 | 28,291 | 129,367 | 5,762 | 2,204 | 226,526 | 29,501 | 19,952 | 150,708 | 2,154 | 954 | 203,269 | 429,795 |
| **Midwestern Region** | | | | | | | | | | | | | |
| Illinois | 10,914 | 14,048 | 72,552 | 406 | 224 | 98,144 | 5,110 | 2,297 | 33,697 | 305 | 24 | 41,433 | 139,577 |
| Indiana (d) | 8,841 | 57,084 | 2,975 | 0 | 0 | 68,901 | 2,334 | 9,015 | 15,431 | 1 | 0 | 26,780 | 95,680 |
| Iowa | 7,936 | 88,477 | 6,031 | 449 | 100 | 102,993 | 956 | 1,045 | 9,162 | 174 | 19 | 11,355 | 114,348 |
| Kansas | 9,619 | 111,878 | 5,245 | 178 | 939 | 127,859 | 750 | 1,460 | 10,480 | 60 | 0 | 12,750 | 140,609 |
| Michigan | 7,060 | 74,178 | 2,949 | 43 | 1,562 | 85,791 | 2,598 | 15,078 | 18,183 | 0 | 0 | 35,859 | 121,650 |
| Minnesota | 10,538 | 42,409 | 60,625 | 4,041 | 0 | 117,613 | 1,355 | 2,467 | 16,772 | 32 | 0 | 20,626 | 138,239 |
| Nebraska | 9,551 | 60,281 | 17,010 | 216 | 160 | 87,218 | 402 | 666 | 5,275 | 0 | 71 | 6,414 | 93,633 |
| North Dakota | 7,167 | 10,072 | 66,140 | 23 | 1,543 | 84,945 | 217 | | 1,682 | 0 | 0 | 1,899 | 86,844 |
| Ohio | 14,253 | 25,717 | 36,722 | 1,063 | 505 | 78,260 | 5,005 | 3,270 | 36,321 | 73 | 44 | 44,713 | 122,973 |
| South Dakota | 7,608 | 35,004 | 33,507 | 928 | 2,170 | 79,217 | 228 | 304 | 2,267 | 131 | 2 | 2,932 | 82,149 |
| Wisconsin | 9,730 | 19,221 | 62,770 | 12 | 839 | 92,572 | 2,040 | 1,495 | 18,679 | 57 | 0 | 22,271 | 114,843 |
| Regional total | 103,343 | 540,532 | 369,735 | 7,309 | 8,117 | 1,026,036 | 20,928 | 35,042 | 167,341 | 830 | 90 | 224,231 | 1,250,267 |
| **Southern Region** | | | | | | | | | | | | | |
| Alabama | 8,751 | 60,214 | 5,429 | 169 | 827 | 75,390 | 2,187 | 520 | 18,622 | 0 | 606 | 21,935 | 97,325 |
| Arkansas | 15,012 | 65,661 | 4,781 | 0 | 2,173 | 87,627 | 1,418 | 479 | 9,794 | 1 | 493 | 12,185 | 99,812 |
| Florida | 5,968 | 29,308 | 3,185 | 0 | 1,905 | 40,366 | 6,116 | 40,496 | 34,258 | 0 | 150 | 81,020 | 121,386 |
| Georgia | 13,995 | 62,740 | 3,652 | 238 | 2,398 | 83,023 | 3,989 | 22,214 | 11,018 | 61 | 1,328 | 38,609 | 121,632 |
| Kentucky | 25,148 | 37,968 | 2,227 | 263 | 774 | 66,380 | 2,429 | 1,645 | 8,302 | 50 | 157 | 12,583 | 78,963 |
| Louisiana | 13,196 | 28,666 | 2,513 | 3 | 618 | 44,996 | 3,481 | 4,060 | 8,776 | 14 | 9 | 16,340 | 61,335 |
| Mississippi | 9,507 | 51,109 | 2,517 | 84 | 741 | 63,958 | 1,393 | 2,090 | 7,479 | 14 | 50 | 11,025 | 74,983 |
| Missouri | 30,796 | 69,383 | 5,172 | 0 | 1,415 | 106,767 | 2,842 | 3,731 | 16,923 | 0 | 97 | 23,592 | 130,360 |
| North Carolina | 62,890 | 0 | 4,930 | 748 | 3,106 | 71,674 | 16,576 | 0 | 16,492 | 0 | 361 | 33,429 | 105,103 |
| Oklahoma | 11,089 | 77,949 | 7,083 | 1,100 | 47 | 97,268 | 1,191 | 2,130 | 12,625 | 110 | 1 | 16,057 | 113,325 |
| South Carolina | 30,268 | 16,889 | 324 | 191 | 2,169 | 49,840 | 11,154 | 3,379 | 1,887 | 2 | 0 | 16,422 | 66,262 |
| Tennessee | 10,855 | 52,815 | 4,358 | 323 | 1,242 | 69,594 | 3,016 | 4,979 | 15,638 | 10 | 13 | 23,657 | 93,251 |
| Texas | 66,419 | 132,961 | 12,781 | 7 | 831 | 212,999 | 13,648 | 12,671 | 66,948 | 138 | 723 | 93,405 | 306,404 |
| Virginia | 47,723 | 61 | 499 | 24 | 2,079 | 50,386 | 10,380 | 1,630 | 11,046 | 15 | 723 | 23,795 | 74,181 |
| West Virginia | 31,448 | 0 | 897 | 53 | 834 | 33,232 | 3,062 | 0 | 2,271 | 33 | 0 | 5,366 | 38,598 |
| Regional total | 383,089 | 685,036 | 60,301 | 3,199 | 21,603 | 1,153,228 | 82,679 | 99,245 | 240,803 | 445 | 4,057 | 427,229 | 1,580,457 |

See footnotes at end of table.

## PUBLIC ROAD LENGTH MILES BY OWNERSHIP: 2009—Continued

| State or other jurisdiction | Rural mileage | | | | | | Urban mileage | | | | | | Total rural & urban mileage |
|---|---|---|---|---|---|---|---|---|---|---|---|---|---|
| | State highway agency | County | Town, township & municipal (a) | Other jurisdictions (b) | Federal agency (c) | Total rural roads | State highway agency | County | Town, township & municipal (a) | Other jurisdictions (b) | Federal agency (c) | Total urban roads | |
| **Western Region** | | | | | | | | | | | | | |
| Alaska | 4,994 | 2,418 | 1,522 | 1,750 | 2,614 | 13,299 | 641 | 1,146 | 263 | 16 | 353 | 2,419 | 15,718 |
| Arizona | 5,774 | 15,359 | 3,276 | 202 | 12,911 | 37,522 | 981 | 2,804 | 18,613 | 185 | 334 | 22,917 | 60,439 |
| California | 10,808 | 51,882 | 4,163 | 3,017 | 11,960 | 81,831 | 4,384 | 13,292 | 70,973 | 51 | 1,343 | 90,043 | 171,874 |
| Colorado | 7,702 | 51,517 | 2,406 | 648 | 6,648 | 68,921 | 1,399 | 4,665 | 13,234 | 15 | 32 | 19,345 | 88,266 |
| Hawaii | 580 | 1,323 | 0 | 48 | 101 | 2,052 | 366 | 1,919 | 0 | 16 | 17 | 2,318 | 4,370 |
| Idaho | 4,604 | 15,475 | 142 | 14,320 | 7,897 | 42,437 | 341 | 145 | 2,721 | 2,524 | 11 | 5,743 | 48,180 |
| Montana | 10,497 | 44,917 | 1,352 | 338 | 13,448 | 70,552 | 299 | 4 | 2,771 | 0 | 0 | 3,075 | 73,626 |
| Nevada | 4,758 | 19,901 | 234 | 695 | 1,974 | 27,561 | 627 | 2,196 | 4,451 | 4 | 4 | 7,283 | 34,844 |
| New Mexico | 10,991 | 36,019 | 1,370 | 215 | 11,796 | 60,392 | 960 | 3,515 | 3,517 | 0 | 1 | 7,992 | 68,384 |
| Oregon | 6,693 | 30,292 | 1,712 | 545 | 6,992 | 46,234 | 853 | 2,864 | 9,078 | 84 | 14 | 12,894 | 59,127 |
| Utah | 4,782 | 22,273 | 2,476 | 0 | 4,201 | 33,732 | 1,058 | 1,610 | 8,261 | 0 | 218 | 11,146 | 44,878 |
| Washington | 5,737 | 33,694 | 2,250 | 10,170 | 8,465 | 60,316 | 1,325 | 6,175 | 15,447 | 49 | 194 | 23,189 | 83,505 |
| Wyoming | 6,332 | 14,181 | 695 | 810 | 3,383 | 25,392 | 412 | 427 | 1,595 | 211 | 69 | 2,713 | 28,105 |
| Regional total | 84,319 | 339,155 | 21,248 | 34,180 | 92,536 | 571,438 | 13,584 | 40,788 | 149,942 | 3,114 | 1,878 | 209,306 | 780,774 |
| Regional total w/o California | 73,507 | 287,086 | 17,199 | 31,163 | 79,000 | 487,955 | 9,191 | 27,513 | 79,252 | 3,063 | 1,258 | 120,277 | 608,262 |
| Dist. of Columbia | 0 | 0 | 0 | 0 | 0 | 0 | 1,391 | 0 | 0 | 23 | 91 | 1,505 | 1,505 |
| Puerto Rico | 1,024 | 0 | 2,057 | 0 | 22 | 3,104 | 3,558 | 0 | 10,009 | 0 | 7 | 13,574 | 16,678 |

*Source:* U.S. Department of Transportation, Federal Highway Administration, *Highway Statistics, 2009.*

Key:
... — Not applicable.
(a) Prior to 1999, municipal was included with other jurisdictions.
(b) Includes state park, state toll, other state agency, other local agency and other roadways not identified by ownership.
(c) Roadways in federal parks, forests, and reservations that are not part of the state and local highway systems.
(d) Excludes 788 miles of federal agency-owned roads.

Table 9.16
## APPORTIONMENT OF FEDERAL FUNDS ADMINISTERED BY THE FEDERAL HIGHWAY ADMINISTRATION BY REGION: FISCAL YEAR 2010 (In thousands of dollars)

| State or other jurisdiction | Interstate maintenance | National highway system | Surface transportation program | Bridge program | Congestion mitigation & air quality improvement | Highway safety improvement program | Appalachian development highway system |
|---|---|---|---|---|---|---|---|
| Total........................ | $7,040,519 | $8,704,980 | $9,010,263 | $5,726,448 | $2,372,787 | $1,502,675 | $470,000 |
| United States Total... | 7,040,519 | 8,549,974 | 9,010,263 | 5,726,448 | 2,372,787 | 1,502,675 | 470,000 |
| **Eastern Region** | | | | | | | |
| Connecticut............. | 70,173 | 64,704 | 82,578 | 177,451 | 45,739 | 12,460 | 0 |
| Delaware ................. | 10,589 | 63,680 | 43,003 | 14,340 | 11,702 | 7,175 | 0 |
| Maine...................... | 32,511 | 35,634 | 38,399 | 34,056 | 10,287 | 6,307 | 0 |
| Maryland................. | 102,006 | 115,036 | 125,507 | 128,095 | 55,487 | 19,363 | 13,696 |
| Massachusetts .......... | 89,098 | 90,290 | 112,758 | 205,603 | 65,711 | 15,268 | 0 |
| New Hampshire ....... | 23,005 | 45,784 | 39,830 | 26,303 | 10,797 | 6,620 | 0 |
| New Jersey .............. | 134,269 | 194,985 | 196,995 | 235,880 | 107,653 | 27,244 | 0 |
| New York................. | 219,727 | 249,362 | 296,405 | 522,834 | 189,706 | 44,987 | 9,399 |
| Pennsylvania........... | 228,758 | 241,422 | 272,982 | 532,787 | 109,255 | 42,701 | 111,768 |
| Rhode Island............ | 12,193 | 52,765 | 37,611 | 83,232 | 10,245 | 6,251 | 0 |
| Vermont................... | 21,545 | 50,744 | 41,856 | 37,862 | 11,349 | 6,958 | 0 |
| Regional average ...... | 85,807 | 109,491 | 117,084 | 181,677 | 57,085 | 17,758 | 12,260 |
| **Midwestern Region** | | | | | | | |
| Illinois...................... | 306,813 | 261,610 | 338,729 | 169,267 | 111,127 | 52,727 | 0 |
| Indiana..................... | 211,206 | 213,613 | 242,223 | 91,274 | 49,685 | 33,020 | 0 |
| Iowa........................ | 87,348 | 126,963 | 121,787 | 71,427 | 11,171 | 20,333 | 0 |
| Kansas ..................... | 70,530 | 98,458 | 110,402 | 48,416 | 9,827 | 21,089 | 0 |
| Michigan.................. | 177,500 | 222,131 | 282,047 | 132,034 | 77,305 | 45,384 | 0 |
| Minnesota................. | 122,756 | 151,811 | 190,205 | 43,747 | 32,646 | 29,990 | 0 |
| Nebraska.................. | 51,198 | 88,946 | 76,246 | 27,902 | 10,559 | 13,502 | 0 |
| North Dakota........... | 35,954 | 99,817 | 48,616 | 13,236 | 10,801 | 9,254 | 0 |
| Ohio........................ | 281,303 | 246,549 | 308,456 | 208,863 | 99,864 | 45,563 | 22,703 |
| South Dakota........... | 49,852 | 96,331 | 62,810 | 15,143 | 12,357 | 12,771 | 0 |
| Wisconsin ................ | 128,223 | 218,572 | 209,186 | 29,129 | 28,202 | 35,404 | 0 |
| Regional average ..... | 138,426 | 165,891 | 180,973 | 77,313 | 41,231 | 29,003 | 2,064 |
| **Southern Region** | | | | | | | |
| Alabama................... | 131,657 | 148,409 | 171,792 | 86,252 | 12,023 | 33,785 | 117,500 |
| Arkansas.................. | 97,382 | 121,568 | 125,680 | 79,890 | 12,518 | 23,440 | 0 |
| Florida .................... | 352,758 | 504,803 | 539,351 | 149,575 | 14,344 | 92,297 | 0 |
| Georgia ................... | 293,814 | 270,085 | 345,553 | 89,386 | 71,483 | 59,007 | 11,849 |
| Kentucky ................. | 136,321 | 155,284 | 146,401 | 85,465 | 14,250 | 24,444 | 39,081 |
| Louisiana................. | 121,325 | 113,260 | 137,216 | 228,236 | 11,637 | 24,458 | 0 |
| Mississippi .............. | 85,629 | 125,209 | 121,839 | 66,514 | 11,431 | 25,535 | 5,019 |
| Missouri................... | 184,968 | 207,283 | 223,455 | 158,699 | 23,981 | 39,929 | 0 |
| North Carolina......... | 188,798 | 221,564 | 253,020 | 156,065 | 53,912 | 39,868 | 32,922 |
| Oklahoma................ | 115,769 | 150,073 | 165,888 | 94,405 | 11,860 | 30,694 | 4 |
| South Carolina......... | 131,951 | 132,536 | 173,403 | 69,171 | 12,840 | 35,143 | 7,174 |
| Tennessee ................ | 188,204 | 191,807 | 206,055 | 70,539 | 38,423 | 36,967 | 24,658 |
| Texas ...................... | 630,130 | 794,503 | 843,434 | 206,626 | 159,567 | 132,142 | 0 |
| Virginia................... | 203,571 | 199,071 | 243,839 | 137,829 | 57,160 | 38,069 | 38,091 |
| West Virginia............ | 74,230 | 74,821 | 80,964 | 83,953 | 14,806 | 16,253 | 36,139 |
| Regional average ..... | 195,767 | 227,352 | 251,859 | 117,507 | 34,682 | 43,469 | 20,829 |
| **Western Region** | | | | | | | |
| Alaska...................... | 90,106 | 106,251 | 91,612 | 37,605 | 25,448 | 15,603 | 0 |
| Arizona.................... | 157,595 | 190,727 | 181,335 | 28,676 | 55,162 | 35,950 | 0 |
| California ................ | 583,434 | 738,463 | 811,930 | 558,734 | 475,106 | 136,379 | 0 |
| Colorado.................. | 106,037 | 142,205 | 133,659 | 41,594 | 43,446 | 21,581 | 0 |
| Hawaii .................... | 11,204 | 55,225 | 38,463 | 34,184 | 10,426 | 6,393 | 0 |
| Idaho....................... | 58,499 | 78,061 | 61,213 | 27,654 | 13,316 | 11,746 | 0 |
| Montana .................. | 91,664 | 121,937 | 68,790 | 20,721 | 14,732 | 13,947 | 0 |
| Nevada..................... | 77,442 | 86,032 | 79,756 | 17,322 | 31,855 | 14,327 | 0 |
| New Mexico ............. | 94,711 | 113,914 | 81,068 | 16,839 | 11,857 | 15,245 | 0 |
| Oregon..................... | 88,019 | 111,957 | 109,996 | 100,737 | 19,218 | 18,995 | 0 |
| Utah ........................ | 101,882 | 70,192 | 75,708 | 14,901 | 12,159 | 11,028 | 0 |
| Washington............... | 111,642 | 127,683 | 143,203 | 172,532 | 37,385 | 22,168 | 0 |
| Wyoming ................. | 62,398 | 106,337 | 39,763 | 13,325 | 10,873 | 6,724 | 0 |
| Regional average ...... | 125,741 | 157,614 | 147,423 | 83,448 | 58,537 | 25,391 | 0 |
| Regional average without California... | 87,600 | 109,210 | 92,047 | 43,841 | 23,823 | 16,142 | 0 |
| Dist. of Columbia...... | 2,823 | 61,505 | 37,247 | 30,141 | 10,097 | 6,190 | 0 |
| American Samoa ...... | 0 | 5,283 | 0 | 0 | 0 | 0 | 0 |
| Guam ...................... | 0 | 13,670 | 0 | 0 | 0 | 0 | 0 |
| No. Mariana Islands... | 0 | 4,914 | 0 | 0 | 0 | 0 | 0 |
| Puerto Rico (b)........ | 0 | 117,721 | 0 | 0 | 0 | 0 | 0 |
| U.S. Virgin Islands..... | 0 | 13,418 | 0 | 0 | 0 | 0 | 0 |

*Source:* U.S. Department of Transportation, Federal Highway Administration, Highway Statistics, 2009 (October 2010).

*Note:* Apportioned pursuant to the Safe, Accountable, Flexible, Efficient Transportation Act: A Legacy for Users (SAFETEA-LU). Does not include funds from the Mass Transit Account of the Highway Trust Fund.

(a) Does not include funds from the following programs: emergency relief,

## APPORTIONMENT OF FEDERAL FUNDS ADMINISTERED BY THE FEDERAL HIGHWAY ADMINISTRATION BY REGION: FISCAL YEAR 2010 (In thousands of dollars)

| State or other jurisdiction | Recreation trails | Metropolitan planning | Railroad highway crossings | Coordinated border infrastructure | Safe routes to school | Equity bonus (a) | Total (b) |
|---|---|---|---|---|---|---|---|
| Total........................... | $84,160 | $303,967 | $220,000 | $210,000 | $180,000 | $2,692,857 | $38,518,656 |
| United States ............ | 84,160 | 303,967 | 220,000 | 210,000 | 180,000 | 2,692,857 | 38,363,650 |
| **Eastern Region** | | | | | | | |
| Connecticut.............. | 1,037 | 4,300 | 1,301 | 0 | 2,017 | 36,592 | 498,352 |
| Delaware ................. | 885 | 1,520 | 1,100 | 0 | 1,000 | 7,361 | 162,355 |
| Maine...................... | 1,817 | 1,520 | 1,206 | 12,677 | 1,000 | 0 | 175,412 |
| Maryland ................. | 1,159 | 6,492 | 2,262 | 0 | 3,148 | 24,101 | 596,354 |
| Massachusetts .......... | 1,238 | 8,507 | 2,347 | 0 | 3,456 | 11,991 | 606,268 |
| New Hampshire........ | 1,460 | 1,520 | 1,100 | 333 | 1,000 | 8,200 | 165,951 |
| New Jersey .............. | 1,280 | 11,706 | 3,644 | 0 | 5,066 | 72,578 | 991,301 |
| New York................. | 2,888 | 23,408 | 6,342 | 27,536 | 10,322 | 66,361 | 1,669,277 |
| Pennsylvania ............ | 2,211 | 12,396 | 7,068 | 0 | 6,720 | 76,037 | 1,644,105 |
| Rhode Island............ | 875 | 1,520 | 1,100 | 0 | 1,000 | 0 | 206,791 |
| Vermont................... | 1,166 | 1,520 | 1,100 | 8,485 | 1,000 | 513 | 184,096 |
| Regional average ..... | 1,456 | 6,764 | 2,597 | 4,457 | 3,248 | 27,612 | 627,297 |
| **Midwestern Region** | | | | | | | |
| Illinois.................... | 1,769 | 14,701 | 10,157 | 0 | 7,554 | 94,568 | 1,369,022 |
| Indiana.................... | 1,409 | 5,150 | 7,264 | 0 | 3,806 | 107,261 | 965,912 |
| Iowa ....................... | 1,308 | 1,683 | 5,045 | 0 | 1,694 | 17,232 | 465,991 |
| Kansas .................... | 1,148 | 1,823 | 6,159 | 0 | 1,647 | 6,135 | 375,633 |
| Michigan.................. | 3,908 | 9,932 | 7,522 | 28,298 | 5,992 | 64,447 | 1,056,502 |
| Minnesota................ | 3,151 | 4,094 | 6,000 | 4,181 | 2,907 | 41,516 | 633,005 |
| Nebraska.................. | 1,051 | 1,520 | 3,452 | 0 | 1,024 | 9,646 | 285,045 |
| North Dakota........... | 1,120 | 1,520 | 3,479 | 10,495 | 1,000 | 8,338 | 243,629 |
| Ohio........................ | 1,880 | 11,038 | 8,566 | 0 | 6,577 | 100,313 | 1,341,675 |
| South Dakota........... | 1,056 | 1,520 | 2,306 | 0 | 1,000 | 16,351 | 271,497 |
| Wisconsin ................ | 2,792 | 4,291 | 5,437 | 0 | 3,072 | 78,409 | 742,717 |
| Regional average ..... | 1,872 | 5,207 | 5,944 | 3,907 | 3,298 | 49,474 | 704,603 |
| **Southern Region** | | | | | | | |
| Alabama ................... | 1,490 | 2,931 | 4,369 | 0 | 2,739 | 46,544 | 759,490 |
| Arkansas.................. | 1,399 | 1,520 | 3,788 | 0 | 1,622 | 34,866 | 503,673 |
| Florida .................... | 2,041 | 20,336 | 8,632 | 0 | 9,725 | 225,478 | 1,919,342 |
| Georgia.................... | 1,698 | 7,564 | 8,024 | 0 | 5,631 | 139,735 | 1,303,829 |
| Kentucky.................. | 1,452 | 2,365 | 3,600 | 0 | 2,356 | 48,800 | 659,819 |
| Louisiana................. | 1,447 | 3,828 | 4,252 | 0 | 2,588 | 36,210 | 684,458 |
| Mississippi............... | 1,311 | 1,520 | 3,409 | 0 | 1,848 | 23,065 | 472,328 |
| Missouri.................. | 1,545 | 4,666 | 5,807 | 0 | 3,318 | 68,476 | 922,396 |
| North Carolina......... | 1,719 | 5,678 | 6,200 | 0 | 5,034 | 88,794 | 1,053,573 |
| Oklahoma................. | 1,362 | 2,240 | 5,121 | 0 | 2,097 | 32,682 | 612,191 |
| South Carolina......... | 1,222 | 2,829 | 4,160 | 0 | 2,434 | 56,858 | 629,722 |
| Tennessee ................ | 1,516 | 4,476 | 4,615 | 0 | 3,405 | 67,789 | 838,455 |
| Texas ...................... | 2,997 | 22,337 | 16,975 | 55,859 | 15,219 | 337,934 | 3,217,725 |
| Virginia................... | 1,415 | 7,116 | 4,487 | 0 | 4,291 | 78,752 | 1,013,690 |
| West Virginia............ | 1,280 | 1,520 | 1,975 | 0 | 1,000 | 39,682 | 426,625 |
| Regional average ..... | 1,593 | 6,062 | 5,694 | 3,724 | 4,220 | 88,378 | 1,001,154 |
| **Western Region** | | | | | | | |
| Alaska...................... | 1,931 | 1,520 | 1,100 | 1,421 | 1,000 | 55,892 | 429,490 |
| Arizona.................... | 1,615 | 5,900 | 2,671 | 10,157 | 3,612 | 75,660 | 749,060 |
| California ................ | 4,680 | 45,321 | 15,618 | 26,560 | 22,580 | 182,640 | 3,601,446 |
| Colorado.................. | 1,710 | 4,851 | 3,126 | 0 | 2,660 | 26,506 | 527,375 |
| Hawaii ..................... | 853 | 1,520 | 1,100 | 0 | 1,000 | 3,077 | 163,445 |
| Idaho....................... | 1,707 | 1,520 | 1,690 | 1,481 | 1,000 | 26,738 | 284,624 |
| Montana .................. | 1,521 | 1,520 | 1,787 | 7,763 | 1,000 | 37,363 | 382,744 |
| Nevada..................... | 1,308 | 2,531 | 1,100 | 0 | 1,456 | 23,120 | 336,248 |
| New Mexico ............. | 1,167 | 1,520 | 1,589 | 1,880 | 1,122 | 25,359 | 366,271 |
| Oregon..................... | 1,548 | 2,983 | 3,091 | 0 | 1,963 | 15,711 | 474,219 |
| Utah........................ | 1,591 | 2,639 | 1,533 | 0 | 1,718 | 19,161 | 312,512 |
| Washington.............. | 1,824 | 6,498 | 4,023 | 12,973 | 3,577 | 13,924 | 657,331 |
| Wyoming ................. | 1,377 | 1,520 | 1,100 | 0 | 1,000 | 12,904 | 257,319 |
| Regional average ..... | 1,756 | 6,142 | 3,041 | 4,787 | 3,361 | 39,850 | 657,083 |
| Regional average without California... | 1,513 | 2,877 | 1,993 | 2,973 | 1,759 | 27,951 | 411,720 |
| Dist. of Columbia...... | 825 | 1,520 | 1,100 | 0 | 1,000 | 915 | 153,363 |
| American Samoa ....... | 0 | 0 | 0 | 0 | 0 | 0 | 5,283 |
| Guam ...................... | 0 | 0 | 0 | 0 | 0 | 0 | 13,670 |
| No. Mariana Islands... | 0 | 0 | 0 | 0 | 0 | 0 | 4,914 |
| Puerto Rico (b)......... | 0 | 0 | 0 | 0 | 0 | 0 | 117,721 |
| U.S. Virgin Islands..... | 0 | 0 | 0 | 0 | 0 | 0 | 13,418 |

federal lands highway programs, Commonwealth of Puerto Rico highway programs, high priority projects, Woodrow Wilson Bridge, National Byways, construction of ferry terminal facilities, and intelligent vehicle-system, among others. These funds are distributed from the Highway Trust Fund.

(b) Under SAFETEA-LU, Puerto Rico received a stand-alone authorization of $217,665,552.

# Reentry Evolution:
# The Federal Role in Supporting State and Local Efforts

By Warren T. Hansen

*Individuals released from prison and jail and who are on community supervision have complex needs. If those needs are not met, the likelihood of their successful transition to the community is reduced, which can pose a threat to public safety. Despite the fiscal challenges many state governments have faced in recent years, policymakers and community stakeholders are increasingly aware that, in many cases, the cycle of reoffending can be broken if the right tools and approaches are used. With continued federal support and strong state and local leadership, the chance for meaningful and lasting change is within reach.*

In recent years, state governments across the country have been working to reduce the costs of their corrections systems. From 1988 to 2008, state spending on corrections has risen faster than spending on nearly any other state budget item—increasing from about $12 billion to $52 billion a year nationally.[1] As many states deal with budget shortfalls, the level of spending on corrections is simply unsustainable.

This tremendous fiscal investment also has failed to result in the types of public safety outcomes expected, as evidenced in part by the fact that many states' recidivism rates remain stubbornly high. Since 2005, more than 650,000 inmates have been released from state prisons each year.[2] Yet, according to a previous U.S. Department of Justice study, nearly 50 percent of individuals are reincarcerated within three years.[3]

In recent years, state policymakers across the country have scrutinized more closely the effectiveness of their public safety investments in hopes of generating better outcomes. Research on criminogenic risk is helping to provide the answers they need to develop more effective and efficient policies and practices at the state and local levels.[4] This research provides some of the best guidance for those working to reduce recidivism. To continue building on that knowledge, however, state policymakers will need to develop and strengthen meaningful collaborations with those working in the field of reentry, including corrections, law enforcement, probation and parole officials, as well as leaders from community-based organizations.

## Reentry Growing Pains

In the past decade, there has been a sea change in how government officials and community leaders are seeking to reduce the number of crimes committed by people under supervision or released from prisons and jails and to facilitate their success in communities. What once fell to a relatively small number of corrections managers, jail administrators, and scattered service providers has become a major priority for state officials. The result has been an exponential growth in the number of individuals, organizations, and government agencies whose mission includes assisting people who have been incarcerated or who are on probation and parole as they work to become law-abiding, contributing members of families and communities.

Rapid growth in the field has resulted in difficult implementation challenges. Many government officials and community leaders, under pressure to launch and administer a reentry program, have sought help wherever they could find it. A smattering of tools and guides could be found on the Internet, but practitioners and policymakers have been uncertain as to which ones were most credible or relevant. The online information also has been incomplete. As a result, a jurisdiction implementing a program may not have been aware of the keys to reentry program success in another jurisdiction, and therefore could not benefit from the knowledge sprinkled throughout the field.

Evaluations of the outcomes of different types of reentry programs were similarly difficult to aggregate and understand. State and local leaders have found it difficult to compile studies and identify best practices for implementing an initiative. Even when specific policy recommendations were uncovered, how to put them into action in a particular jurisdiction often has been unclear. The field also lacked a unified research agenda to address gaps in this knowledge base. There was no single center that compiled and developed reliable information, or served as a forum for facilitated exchanges among experts and peers eager to share problems or valuable solutions.

Congress recognized that for states to reduce recidivism rates, they would require more resources than their government agencies and community groups could muster on their own. Better coordination between the states and the federal government also was needed to begin systematically addressing the needs of individuals who have been under correctional control.

## A Strong Federal Commitment

Congress's passage of the Second Chance Act (SCA) in 2008 was a milestone celebrated by states, counties, and the reentry field. The SCA authorizes federal grants to government agencies and nonprofit organizations to provide a wide range of services and vital support to individuals on probation or parole, or returning to the community from prisons, jails, and juvenile facilities. Permissible uses include employment assistance, substance abuse treatment, housing support, family programming, mentoring, victims' aide, and other services that can help reduce recidivism. Between 2009 and 2011, Congress appropriated $208 million for nearly 400 grant programs in 48 states.

In addition to its grant programs, the SCA also authorized the creation of the National Reentry Resource Center (NRRC), a clearinghouse that provides educational resources, training and technical assistance to states, tribes, territories, local governments, service agencies, nonprofit organizations, and corrections institutions committed to working on prison and jail reentry. Following a competitive process, The Council of State Governments (CSG) Justice Center was selected by the Bureau of Justice Assistance, U.S. Department of Justice, to coordinate the NRRC in October 2009.

The CSG Justice Center, through the NRRC and in partnership with experts from across the nation, serves as the training and technical assistance provider for all grantees around the country. In this capacity, the Justice Center hosts an annual conference to facilitate networking and the exchange of promising approaches and research developments. It also coordinates a website that compiles the latest news, research, and funding opportunities in reentry, and distributes a monthly newsletter to more than 10,000 people nationwide.[5] The Justice Center regularly hosts webinars that provide opportunities for learning about the most effective reentry programs, policies, and practices.

One of the CSG Justice Center's primary objectives for the resource center is to help policymakers and practitioners interested in reentry identify, understand, and integrate evidence-based practices into their efforts. In partnership with the Urban Institute, the CSG Justice Center is developing a database that offers easy access to important research on a wide variety of reentry programs and practices. This online tool will be launched on the NRRC website in 2012. Practitioners and researchers will find information on the reentry strategies that have demonstrated effectiveness and those that require additional research.

## The Summit on Public Safety

After passage of this landmark legislation, congressional leaders built on this momentum by looking for strategic ways to advance the reentry field. After the U.S. House Commerce, Justice and Science Appropriations Subcommittee held a series of hearings on reentry and recidivism-reduction in 2009, the CSG Justice Center and its partner organizations helped convene the National Summit on Justice Reinvestment and Public Safety on January 27, 2010, in Washington, D.C.[6] Supported by members of Congress on both sides of the aisle and with the leadership of Rep. Frank Wolf (R-VA) and Sen. Sheldon Whitehouse (D-RI), the goal of this summit was to highlight data-driven, fiscally responsible policies and practices that increase public safety.

Four themes emerged from the summit, each based on the promising approaches some states were taking to reduce recidivism and make better investments in public safety:[7]

1. **Focus on Individuals Most Likely to Reoffend:** By using validated risk assessment tools, officials can more accurately determine the likelihood of individuals' committing a new crime and tailor supervision levels and intervention programs to individuals' needs.

2. **Base Programs on Science and Ensure Quality:** Officials should draw on research when designing programs, including how they identify the desired outcomes for participants and the means for measuring progress.

3. **Implement Effective Community Supervision Policies and Practices:** Supervision and services should be concentrated at the times when most people commit new crimes or violate their conditions of supervision (soon after release from a correctional facility or at the start of supervision), and in places where these individuals can be

found. In addition, policies and practices must provide parole and probation officers with a broad range of options for swift and certain sanctions that are proportionate to the violation and appropriate for the individual under supervision.

4. **Apply Place-Based Strategies:** Local law enforcement and community corrections officers should explore how to best allocate resources in communities where people released from prison or jail disproportionly return. This will allow these criminal justice agencies to better coordinate with community-based agencies delivering health, employment, and other social services that can help an individual adjust after his or her incarceration and improve public safety outcomes.

## An All-States Working Forum on Recidivism

To carry out many of the goals articulated in the public safety report and further expand the field's knowledge, congressional and federal agency partners encouraged the CSG Justice Center to convene a national forum on recidivism-reduction in December 2011. The forum brought together three-person teams from each of the 50 states, with teams composed of the heads of departments of corrections, legislative leaders, judges, and governors' staff, to develop plans for reducing recidivism in their states.

Participants heard from leaders across the country about recent advances and how efforts to reduce recidivism have progressed since the public safety summit, including:

- U.S. Sen. Rob Portman (R-OH), one of the original authors of the Second Chance Act, talked about how Ohio would save $46 million through the 2015 fiscal year because of legislation passed by the Ohio General Assembly and signed by Gov. John Kasich. Drawing from the principles identified at the January 2010 summit, Ohio's legislation focuses community-based intensive treatment and supervision slots on people that benefit most from monitoring and support.[8]

- U.S. Rep. Chaka Fattah (D-PA), ranking member of a subcommittee of the U.S. House Appropriations Committee, praised the strong partnership between the federal government, state agencies, and community organizations in finding innovative policies to address recidivism, even in difficult fiscal times.

- North Carolina state Rep. W. David Guice spoke about his state's legislation that policymakers expect to result in $560 million in averted corrections costs and cumulative savings over a six-year period. These savings are expected to allow the state to reinvest more than $4 million annually to expand community-based behavioral health treatment programs for people on supervision.[9]

- Senior officials from the Bureau of Justice Assistance, the Association of State Correctional Administrators, the Public Welfare Foundation and the Pew Center on the States met with and provided support to the teams.[10]

In addition, the state teams gathered individually to discuss strategies for lowering rates of reoffending among individuals with criminal histories. This unprecedented convening of leaders across systems provided an opportunity for creative problem solving and resource sharing. As a result of the forum, all teams have set measurable goals for reducing recidivism or identified ways to improve upon existing goals; designed plans to achieve those goals by drawing on the strongest research and experiences from the field; and identified benchmarks that state and federal policymakers can use to track progress.

To assist in this effort, Denise O'Donnell, director of the Bureau of Justice Assistance, announced that her agency would make technical assistance available for all 50 states. Coordinated by the National Reentry Resource Center, each state team will work with a grantee coach to develop and enhance their state's recidivism-reduction plan.

The Bureau of Justice Assistance also announced at the forum its release of another round of solicitations for Second Chance Act demonstration sites in March 2012. The grant program will fund selected states up to $1 million to achieve statewide recidivism-reduction goals, giving these states a chance to test strategies and make more effective investments in public safety.

As the forum highlighted, although many states have been reforming their corrections systems because of dramatic and enduring budget cuts, the field was ready to achieve real change if given the right tools and supports. A strong sense of accountability and commitment to strategies that are research-based was already driving the field forward. The launch of the National Reentry Resource Center, coupled with significant investments by the federal government and major phil-anthropic entities to complement state and local efforts, has created a structure for systemic change. Seeing an opportunity to function more cost-effectively while increasing public safety, dozens of states have taken advantage of resources for reducing recidivism. As more states experience success, the knowledge base for effective policy will grow and the impact will surely spread across the country.

## Notes

[1] National Association of State Budget Officers, *Fiscal Year 1988 State Expenditure Report*, Washington, D.C.: National Association of State Budget Officers, 1989, 71, *http://www.nasbo.org/Publications/StateExpenditureReport/StateExpenditureReportArchives/tabid/107/Default.aspx*; National Association of State Budget Officers, *Fiscal Year 2008 State Expenditure Report*, Washington, D.C.: National Association of State Budget Officers, 2009, 54, *http://www.nasbo.org/Publications/StateExpenditureReport/tabid/79/Default.aspx*.

[2] Guerino, Paul, Paige M. Harrison, and William J. Sabol. *Prisoners in 2010*. Washington, D.C.: U.S. Department of Justice, Office of Justice Programs, Bureau of Justice Statistics, December 2011, 5.

[3] Patrick A. Langan and David J. Levin. *Recidivism of Prisoners Released in 1994, NCJ 193427*. Washington, D.C.: U.S. Department of Justice, Bureau of Justice Statistics, 2002, 1. A more recent study conducted by the Pew Center on the States' Public Safety Performance Project confirms that many states continue to struggle with high recidivism rates. Pew Center on the States, *State of Recidivism: The Revolving Door of America's Prisons*. Washington, D.C.: The Pew Charitable Trusts, April 2011.

[4] In particular, the "Risk-Need-Responsivity" (RNR) model examines how supervision, services, and other interventions can be matched to individuals' objectively assessed risk factors for committing a future crime in order to decrease individuals' likelihood of reoffending. See Andrews, Donald A., James Bonta, and Robert D. Hoge, "Classification for Effective Rehabilitation: Rediscovering Psychology," *Criminal Justice and Behavior* 17, no. 1 (1990): 19–52.

[5] Information on subscribing to the newsletter and feature articles can be accessed at *www.nationalreentryresourcecenter.org*.

[6] The summit was conducted in partnership with The Pew Center on the States, with additional support from the Bureau of Justice Assistance, U.S. Department of Justice; and the Public Welfare Foundation. For other partners and supporters of the justice reinvestment efforts in many states, see *http://justicereinvestment.org/about/funders*.

[7] Clement, Marshall, Matthew Schwarzfeld, and Michael Thompson. *The National Summit on Justice Reinvestment and Public Safety: Addressing Recidivism, Crime, and Corrections Spending*. New York: The Council of State Governments Justice Center, January 2011, 6–7, *http://justicereinvestment.org/summit/report*.

[8] See a summary of this effort at *http://justicereinvestment.org/states/ohio*.

[9] For more information, visit *http://justicereinvestment.org/states/north_carolina*.

[10] For videos of each panel discussion and the conference agenda, with a description of the presentations and a list of expert presenters and moderators, visit *http://www.nationalreentryresourcecenter.org/forum-on-reentry-and-recidivism*.

## About the Author

**Warren T. Hansen** is a public affairs manager for The Council of State Governments Justice Center in the Washington, D.C. office. He has a B.A. in history and government & politics from the University of Maryland. He has worked on two state political campaigns, was a public information officer for the Maryland State Comptroller and served as a press secretary for a member of Congress.

## Table 9.17
## TRENDS IN STATE PRISON POPULATION BY REGION, 2000, 2009 and 2010

| State or other jurisdiction | Total state prison population | | | Average annual change 2000–2009 | Percent change 2009–2010 |
|---|---|---|---|---|---|
| | December 31, 2010 | December 31, 2009 | December 31, 2000 | | |
| **United States**........................ | 1,543,206 | 1,550,196 | 1,331,278 | 1.7% | -0.5% |
| Federal............................ | 190,641 | 187,886 | 125,044 | 4.6 | 1.5 |
| State ................................ | 1,352,565 | 1,362,310 | 1,206,234 | 1.4 | -0.7 |
| **Eastern Region** | | | | | |
| Connecticut (a).................... | 13,308 | 13,466 | 13,155 | 0.3 | -1.2 |
| Delaware (a) ...................... | 3,961 | 3,971 | 3,937 | 0.1 | -0.3 |
| Maine................................. | 1,942 | 1,980 | 1,635 | 2.2 | -1.9 |
| Maryland............................ | 22,275 | 21,868 | 22,490 | -0.3 | 1.9 |
| Massachusetts (b) .............. | 10 | 10,070 | 9,479 | 0.7 | -0.9 |
| New Hampshire ................. | 2,761 | 2,731 | 2,257 | 2.1 | 1.1 |
| New Jersey (c)..................... | 25,007 | 25,382 | 29,784 | -1.8 | -1.5 |
| New York............................ | 56,461 | 58,455 | 70,199 | -2.0 | -3.4 |
| Pennsylvania....................... | 51,075 | 51,316 | 36,844 | 3.7 | -0.5 |
| Rhode Island (a) ................ | 2,086 | 2,220 | 1,966 | 1.4 | -6.0 |
| Vermont (a)........................ | 1,649 | 1,724 | 1,313 | 3.1 | -4.4 |
| Regional total..................... | 180,535 | 193,183 | 193,059 | N.A. | -1.7 |
| **Midwestern Region** | | | | | |
| Illinois (c)........................... | 48,418 | 45,161 | 45,281 | 0.0 | 7.2 |
| Indiana............................... | 28,012 | 28,788 | 19,811 | 4.2 | -2.7 |
| Iowa (d).............................. | 9,388 | 8,813 | 7,955 | 1.1 | 6.5 |
| Kansas (d) .......................... | 9,051 | 8,641 | 8,344 | 0.4 | 4.7 |
| Michigan............................ | 44,113 | 45,478 | 47,718 | -0.5 | -3.0 |
| Minnesota.......................... | 9,796 | 9,986 | 6,238 | 5.4 | -1.9 |
| Nebraska............................ | 4,498 | 4,392 | 3,816 | 1.6 | 2.4 |
| North Dakota ..................... | 1,487 | 1,486 | 994 | 4.6 | 0.1 |
| Ohio (d).............................. | 51,712 | 51,606 | 45,833 | 1.3 | 0.2 |
| South Dakota...................... | 3,431 | 3,430 | 2,613 | 3.1 | 0.0 |
| Wisconsin (e)...................... | 20,812 | 23,332 | 20,336 | 1.0 | -6.8 |
| Regional total..................... | 230,718 | 231,113 | 208,939 | N.A. | -1.7 |
| **Southern Region** | | | | | |
| Alabama.............................. | 30,739 | 30,723 | 26,034 | 1.9 | 0.1 |
| Arkansas ............................ | 16,147 | 15,144 | 11,851 | 2.8 | 6.6 |
| Florida................................ | 104,306 | 103,915 | 71,318 | 4.3 | 0.4 |
| Georgia (f).......................... | 47,634 | 52,012 | 44,141 | 1.8 | -8.4 |
| Kentucky............................ | 19,937 | 20,672 | 14,919 | 3.7 | -3.6 |
| Louisiana............................ | 39,444 | 39,780 | 35,207 | 1.4 | -0.8 |
| Mississippi.......................... | 22,275 | 20,768 | 19,239 | 0.9 | -1.9 |
| Missouri.............................. | 30,614 | 30,554 | 27,519 | 1.2 | 0.2 |
| North Carolina.................... | 35,436 | 34,989 | 27,043 | 2.9 | 1.3 |
| Oklahoma........................... | 24,514 | 24,396 | 23,181 | 0.6 | 0.5 |
| South Carolina.................... | 22,822 | 23,486 | 21,017 | 1.2 | -2.8 |
| Tennessee........................... | 27,451 | 26,965 | 22,166 | 2.2 | 1.8 |
| Texas (g)............................. | 164,652 | 162,186 | 158,008 | 0.3 | 1.5 |
| Virginia.............................. | 37,410 | 38,059 | 29,643 | 2.8 | -1.7 |
| West Virginia...................... | 6,642 | 6,313 | 3,795 | 5.8 | 5.2 |
| Regional total..................... | 630,023 | 629,962 | 535,081 | N.A. | 1.0 |
| **Western Region** | | | | | |
| Alaska (a)............................ | 2,429 | 2,508 | 2,128 | 1.8 | -3.1 |
| Arizona (e).......................... | 38,423 | 38,529 | 25,412 | 4.7 | -0.3 |
| California............................ | 164,213 | 170,131 | 160,412 | 0.7 | -3.5 |
| Colorado (d) ....................... | 22,815 | 22,795 | 16,833 | 3.4 | 0.1 |
| Hawaii (a)........................... | 3,939 | 4,119 | 3,553 | 1.7 | -4.4 |
| Idaho................................... | 7,431 | 7,400 | 5,535 | 3.3 | 0.4 |
| Montana............................. | 3,716 | 3,605 | 3,105 | 1.7 | 3.1 |
| Nevada............................... | 12,556 | 12,482 | 10,063 | 2.4 | 0.6 |
| New Mexico........................ | 6,614 | 6,320 | 4,666 | 3.4 | 4.7 |
| Oregon (d).......................... | 13,971 | 14,365 | 10,533 | 3.5 | -2.7 |
| Utah ................................... | 6,795 | 6,524 | 5,541 | 1.8 | 4.2 |
| Washington........................ | 18,212 | 18,199 | 14,666 | 2.4 | 0.1 |
| Wyoming............................ | 2,112 | 2,075 | 1,680 | 2.4 | 1.8 |
| Regional total..................... | 303,226 | 309,052 | 264,127 | N.A. | -1.8 |
| Regional total without California ......... | 139,013 | 138,921 | 103,715 | N.A. | 0.6 |
| Dist. of Columbia.............. | 0 | 0 | 5,008 | 0 | 0 |

Source: U.S. Department of Justice, Bureau of Justice Statistics, *Prisoners in 2010*—NCJ 236096 (December 2011).

Note: Sentenced prisoner is defined as a prisoner sentenced to more than one year.

Key:

N.A. — Not available

(a) Prisons and jails form one integrated system. Data include total jail and prison populations.

(b) Jurisdiction count excludes approximately 3,271 inmates in local jails and houses of corrections serving a sentence of more than 1 year. By law, offenders in Massachusetts may be sentenced to terms of up to 30 months in locally operated jails and correctional institutions. Noncitizen data are self-reported.

(c) Includes some prisoners sentenced to one year.

(d) Includes some prisoners sentenced to one year or less.

(e) Counts include 698 temporary probation and parole placements.

(f) Prison population based on custody counts.

(g) Jurisdiction count includes offenders in custody as well as those held in privately operated prisons, substance abuse felony punishment facilities, halfway houses, offenders temporarily released to a county jail for less than 30 days, and offenders awaiting paperwork for transfer to state-funded custody.

## Table 9.18
## NUMBER OF SENTENCED PRISONERS ADMITTED AND RELEASED FROM STATE AND FEDERAL JURISDICTION, BY REGION: 2000, 2009 and 2010

| State or other jurisdiction | Admissions | | | | | Releases | | | | |
|---|---|---|---|---|---|---|---|---|---|---|
| | 2009 | 2010 | 2000 | Average annual change 2000–2009 | Percent change 2009–2010 | 2009 | 2010 | 2000 | Average annual change 2000–2009 | Percent change 2009–2010 |
| United States.............. | 731,576 | 703,798 | 625,219 | 1.8% | -3.8% | 729,749 | 708,677 | 604,858 | 2.1% | -2.9% |
| Federal....................... | 56,153 | 54,121 | 43,732 | 2.8 | -3.6 | 50,720 | 52,487 | 35,259 | 4.1 | 3.5 |
| State ......................... | 675,423 | 649,677 | 581,487 | 1.7 | -3.8 | 674,707 | 656,190 | 569,599 | 2 | -3.4 |
| **Eastern Region** | | | | | | | | | | |
| Connecticut ................. | 6,293 | 6,182 | 6,185 | 0.2 | -1.8 | 6,850 | 6,095 | 5,918 | 1.6 | -11.0 |
| Delaware ..................... | 1,550 | 1,583 | 2,709 | -6.0 | 2.1 | 1,697 | 1,681 | 2,260 | -3.1 | -0.9 |
| Maine.......................... | 856 | 1,007 | 751 | 1.5 | 17.6 | 1,141 | 1,176 | 677 | 6.0 | 3.1 |
| Maryland...................... | 9,959 | 9,828 | 10,327 | -0.4 | -1.3 | 10,807 | 9,387 | 10,004 | 0.9 | -13.1 |
| Massachusetts.............. | 2,789 | 2,806 | 2,062 | 3.4 | 0.6 | 2,850 | 2,908 | 2,889 | -0.2 | 2.0 |
| New Hampshire ........... | 1,416 | 1,384 | 1,051 | 4.4 | -10.4 | 1,460 | 1,584 | 1,044 | 3.8 | 8.5 |
| New Jersey ................... | 12,251 | 12,409 | 13,653 | -1.2 | 1.3 | 12,860 | 12,821 | 15,362 | -2.0 | -0.3 |
| New York...................... | 24,058 | 23,377 | 27,601 | -1.5 | -2.8 | 25,481 | 25,365 | 28,828 | -1.4 | -0.5 |
| Pennsylvania................. | 16,914 | 16,662 | 11,777 | 4.1 | -1.5 | 14,630 | 16,781 | 11,759 | 2.5 | 14.7 |
| Rhode Island ............... | 959 | 938 | 3,701 | : | -2.2 | 1,246 | 1,113 | 3,223 | : | -10.7 |
| Vermont....................... | 2,106 | 2,079 | 984 | : | -1.3 | 1,973 | 2,130 | 946 | : | 8.0 |
| Regional total.............. | 79,151 | 78,255 | 80,801 | : | -1.1 | 80,995 | 81,041 | 82,910 | : | 0.5 |
| **Midwestern Region** | | | | | | | | | | |
| Illinois........................... | 37,718 | 34,316 | 29,344 | 2.8 | -9.0 | 38,034 | 31,055 | 28,876 | 3.1 | -18.3 |
| Indiana.......................... | 19,689 | 18,501 | 11,876 | 5.8 | -6.0 | 19,699 | 19,911 | 11,053 | 6.6 | 1.1 |
| Iowa.............................. | 4,376 | 4,939 | 4,656 | -0.7 | 12.9 | 4,648 | 4,367 | 4,379 | 0.7 | -6.0 |
| Kansas........................... | 4,816 | 4,962 | 5,002 | -0.4 | 3.0 | 4,721 | 4,553 | 5,231 | -1.1 | -3.6 |
| Michigan........................ | 14,955 | 15,668 | 12,169 | 2.3 | 4.8 | 18,197 | 17,033 | 10,874 | 5.9 | -6.4 |
| Minnesota ..................... | 7,361 | 6,989 | 4,406 | 5.9 | -5.1 | 7,777 | 7,882 | 4,244 | 7.0 | 1.4 |
| Nebraska ....................... | 2,101 | 2,232 | 1,688 | 2.5 | 6.2 | 2,107 | 2,123 | 1,503 | 3.8 | 0.8 |
| North Dakota ............... | 1,042 | 1,008 | 605 | 6.2 | -3.3 | 1,003 | 1,006 | 598 | 5.9 | 0.3 |
| Ohio.............................. | 26,864 | 24,559 | 23,780 | 1.4 | -8.4 | 26,949 | 24,495 | 24,793 | 0.9 | -9.1 |
| South Dakota................ | 3,170 | 2,843 | 1,400 | 9.5 | -10.3 | 3,079 | 2,857 | 1,327 | 9.8 | -7.2 |
| Wisconsin...................... | 7,245 | 7,107 | 8,396 | -1.6 | -1.9 | 8,771 | 8,640 | 8,158 | 0.8 | -1.5 |
| Regional total.............. | 129,337 | 123,124 | 103,322 | : | -4.8 | 134,985 | 123,922 | 101,036 | : | -8.2 |
| **Southern Region** | | | | | | | | | | |
| Alabama........................ | 13,093 | 11,881 | 6,296 | 8.5 | -9.3 | 12,231 | 12,070 | 7,136 | 6.2 | -1.3 |
| Arkansas....................... | 7,383 | 7,603 | 6,941 | 0.7 | 3.0 | 6,990 | 6,664 | 6,308 | 1.1 | -4.7 |
| Florida .......................... | 38,050 | 32,786 | 35,683 | 0.7 | -13.8 | 37,167 | 32,649 | 33,994 | 1.0 | -12.2 |
| Georgia......................... | 17,600 | 16,718 | 17,373 | 0.1 | -5.0 | 16,161 | 16,745 | 14,797 | 1.0 | 3.6 |
| Kentucky....................... | 14,033 | 14,674 | 8,116 | 6.3 | 4.6 | 14,138 | 15,962 | 7,733 | 6.9 | 12.9 |
| Louisiana....................... | 14,940 | 17,191 | 15,735 | -0.6 | 15.1 | 14,924 | 17,262 | 14,536 | 0.3 | 15.7 |
| Mississippi..................... | 8,348 | 8,381 | 5,796 | 4.1 | 0.4 | 9,285 | 8,694 | 4,940 | 7.3 | -6.4 |
| Missouri......................... | 18,216 | 17,740 | 14,454 | 2.6 | -2.6 | 18,097 | 17,799 | 13,346 | 3.4 | -1.6 |
| North Carolina.............. | 12,171 | 11,964 | 9,848 | 2.4 | -1.7 | 11,495 | 11,539 | 9,687 | 1.9 | 0.4 |
| Oklahoma...................... | 8,120 | 8,021 | 7,426 | 1.0 | -1.2 | 8,004 | 7,903 | 6,628 | 2.1 | -1.3 |
| South Carolina ............. | 9,352 | 8,049 | 8,460 | 1.1 | -13.9 | 9,321 | 8,716 | 8,676 | 0.8 | -6.5 |
| Tennessee..................... | 13,783 | 13,806 | 13,675 | 0.1 | 0.2 | 15,762 | 14,735 | 13,593 | 1.4 | -6.5 |
| Texas ............................ | 71,965 | 73,965 | 58,197 | 2.3 | 3.5 | 72,320 | 71,497 | 59,776 | 2.1 | -1.1 |
| Virginia ......................... | 12,631 | 12,221 | 9,791 | 2.9 | -3.2 | 13,168 | 12,989 | 9,148 | 4.1 | -1.4 |
| West Virginia................. | 3,204 | 3,288 | 1,577 | 8.2 | 2.6 | 2,943 | 3,009 | 1,261 | 9.9 | 2.2 |
| Regional total.............. | 262,889 | 258,288 | 219,368 | : | -1.7 | 262,006 | 258,233 | 211,859 | : | -1.4 |
| **Western Region** | | | | | | | | | | |
| Alaska (a)...................... | 2,427 | 2,650 | 2,427 | 1.4 | -4.0 | 3,196 | 3,068 | 2,599 | 2.3 | -4.0 |
| Arizona......................... | 14,526 | 13,249 | 9,560 | 4.8 | -8.8 | 13,854 | 13,500 | 9,100 | 4.8 | -2.6 |
| California...................... | 129,640 | 118,943 | 129,640 | 0.0 | -8.3 | 128,869 | 121,918 | 129,621 | -0.1 | -5.4 |
| Colorado....................... | 7,036 | 10,553 | 7,036 | 5.1 | -4.5 | 10,558 | 10,558 | 5,881 | 7.1 | -2.8 |
| Hawaii.......................... | 1,714 | 1,577 | 1,594 | 0.8 | -8.0 | 1,915 | 1,764 | 1,379 | 3.7 | -7.9 |
| Idaho............................ | 3,857 | 4,301 | 3,386 | 1.5 | 11.5 | 3,743 | 4,264 | 2,697 | 3.7 | 13.9 |
| Montana ....................... | 2,295 | 2,263 | 1,202 | 7.5 | -1.4 | 2,212 | 2,152 | 1,031 | 8.9 | -2.7 |
| Nevada.......................... | 5,409 | 5,554 | 4,929 | 1.0 | 2.7 | 5,967 | 6,036 | 4,374 | 3.5 | 1.2 |
| New Mexico .................. | 5,650 | 4,135 | 3,161 | 6.7 | -26.8 | 3,650 | 3,487 | 3,383 | 0.8 | -4.5 |
| Oregon.......................... | 5,950 | 5,455 | 4,059 | 4.3 | -8.3 | 5,422 | 5,290 | 3,371 | 5.4 | -2.4 |
| Utah............................. | 3,583 | 3,377 | 3,270 | 1.0 | -5.7 | 3,498 | 3,109 | 2,897 | 2.1 | -11.1 |
| Washington................... | 17,084 | 17,084 | 7,094 | 10.3 | 0.1 | 17,035 | 17,060 | 6,764 | 10.8 | 0.1 |
| Wyoming....................... | 815 | 829 | 638 | 2.8 | 1.7 | 824 | 788 | 697 | 1.9 | -4.4 |
| Regional total.............. | 199,986 | 189,970 | 177,996 | : | -5.0 | 200,743 | 192,994 | 173,794 | : | -3.8 |
| Regional total without California.... | 70,346 | 71,027 | 48,356 | : | 1.0 | 71,874 | 71,076 | 44,173 | : | -1.1 |

*Source:* U.S. Department of Justice, Bureau of Justice Statistics, *Prisoners in 2010*—NCJ 236096 (December 2011).

*Note:* Totals based on prisoners with a sentence of more than 1 year. Totals exclude escapees, AWOLS, and transfers to and from other jurisdictions.

*Key:*
: — Not calculated.
(a) The Alaska Department of Corrections was unable to provide admissions and releases by type. These counts were imputed using a ratio adjustment based on the 2009 admission and release data reported by the state.

# Table 9.19
## STATE PRISON CAPACITIES, BY REGION: 2010

| State | Rated capacity | Operational capacity | Design capacity | Highest capacity (a) | Lowest capacity (a) |
|---|---|---|---|---|---|
| | | Type of capacity measure | | Population as a percent of capacity | |
| Federal.................................. | 126,863 | ... | ... | 136% | 136% |
| **Eastern Region** | | | | | |
| Connecticut (b)................. | ... | ... | ... | ... | ... |
| Delaware............................ | 6,378 | 5,210 | 4,161 | 100 | 153 |
| Maine.................................. | 2,339 | 2,133 | 2,339 | 89 | 97 |
| Maryland............................ | ... | 23,016 | ... | 99 | 99 |
| Massachusetts.................... | ... | ... | 8,029 | 139 | 139 |
| New Hampshire................. | ... | 2,281 | 1,945 | 115 | 134 |
| New Jersey ......................... | ... | 22,503 | 16,152 | 96 | 134 |
| New York............................ | 57,505 | 58,546 | 56,590 | 96 | 100 |
| Pennsylvania ..................... | 43,837 | 43,837 | 43,837 | 107 | 107 |
| Rhode Island (c)............... | 4,283 | 4,273 | 4,028 | 74 | 78 |
| Vermont............................. | 1,613 | 1,613 | 1,322 | 94 | 115 |
| **Midwestern Region** | | | | | |
| Illinois............................... | 33,700 | 33,700 | 29,791 | 144 | 163 |
| Indiana.............................. | ... | 29,574 | ... | 83 | 83 |
| Iowa .................................. | ... | ... | 7,209 | 131 | 131 |
| Kansas ............................... | 9,054 | ... | ... | 100 | 100 |
| Michigan............................ | 45,281 | 44,420 | ... | 102 | 104 |
| Minnesota.......................... | ... | 9,099 | ... | 103 | 103 |
| Nebraska ........................... | ... | 3,969 | 3,175 | 116 | 145 |
| North Dakota.................... | 1,044 | 991 | 1,044 | 136 | 143 |
| Ohio................................... | 38,389 | ... | ... | 127 | 127 |
| South Dakota.................... | ... | 3,523 | ... | 96 | 96 |
| Wisconsin (d).................... | ... | ... | 17,596 | 125 | 125 |
| **Southern Region** | | | | | |
| Alabama (f)........................ | ... | ... | 13,403 | 196 | 196 |
| Arkansas............................ | 14,025 | 14,025 | 13,461 | 101 | 105 |
| Florida (f).......................... | ... | 105,814 | ... | 96 | 96 |
| Georgia (g)......................... | 58,763 | 54,137 | ... | 93 | 100 |
| Kentucky ........................... | 13,902 | 13,902 | 14,237 | 87 | 89 |
| Louisiana (g)...................... | 19,008 | 20,333 | ... | 108 | 115 |
| Mississippi (g) ................... | ... | 23,016 | ... | 99 | 99 |
| Missouri............................. | ... | 31,423 | ... | 97 | 97 |
| North Carolina (f) ............ | ... | 41,705 | 35,756 | 97 | 113 |
| Oklahoma (g)..................... | 25,352 | 25,352 | 25,352 | 95 | 95 |
| South Carolina.................. | ... | 24,319 | ... | 95 | 95 |
| Tennessee .........:............... | 20,946 | 20,498 | ... | 71 | 73 |
| Texas (e)............................ | 163,381 | 159,396 | 163,381 | 86 | 89 |
| Virginia.............................. | 32,921 | ... | ... | 92 | 92 |
| West Virginia..................... | 4,304 | 5,114 | 4,304 | 99 | 118 |
| **Western Region** | | | | | |
| Alaska................................ | 3,058 | 3,206 | ... | 122 | 128 |
| Arizona.............................. | 37,089 | 43,011 | 37,089 | 81 | 94 |
| California .......................... | ... | 149,624 | 84,181 | 110 | 196 |
| Colorado............................ | ... | 15,032 | 13,065 | 121 | 140 |
| Hawaii ............................... | ... | 3,327 | 2,291 | 101 | 147 |
| Idaho (g)............................ | 7,028 | 6,677 | 7,028 | 103 | 108 |
| Montana ............................ | ... | 1,679 | ... | 97 | 97 |
| Nevada............................... | / | / | / | / | / |
| New Mexico (g) ................ | 6,139 | 7,123 | 6,128 | 53 | 61 |
| Oregon............................... | / | / | / | / | / |
| Utah ................................... | ... | 6,661 | 6,901 | 79 | 82 |
| Washington........................ | 16,420 | 17,801 | 17,801 | 96 | 104 |
| Wyoming ........................... | 2,381 | 2,281 | 2,221 | 79 | 84 |

*Source:* U.S. Department of Justice, Bureau of Justice Statistics, Prisoners in 2010—NCJ 236096 (December 2011).

*Key:*

... — Not available.

(a) Population counts are based on the number of inmates held in facilities operated by the jurisdiction. Excludes inmates held in local jails, in other states, or in private facilities.

(b) Connecticut no longer reports capacity because of a law passed in 1995.

(c) Prisons and jails form on integrated system. Data include jail and prison populations unless otherwise specified.

(d) Counts include 698 temporary probation and parole placements.

(e) Jurisdiction count includes offenders in custody as well as those held in privately operated prisons, substance abuse felony punishment facilities, halfway houses, offenders temporarily released to a county jail for less than 30 days, and offenders awaiting paperwork for transfer to state-funded custody.

(f) Excludes capacity of county facilities and inmates housed in them.

(g) Includes capacity of private and contract facilities and inmates housed in them.

## Table 9.20
## ADULTS ON PROBATION BY REGION: 2010

| State or other jurisdiction | 1/1/10 | Probation population | | | Percent change during 2010 | Number on probation on 12/31/10 per 100,000 adult residents |
| | | 2010 | | 12/31/10 | | |
| | | Entries (a) | Exits (a) | | | |
|---|---|---|---|---|---|---|
| **United States** ...................... | 4,125,033 | 2,190,200 | 2,261,300 | 4,055,514 | -1.7% | 1,721 |
| Federal........................... | 22,587 | 11,287 | 11,171 | 22,703 | 0.5 | 10 |
| State ............................... | 4,102,446 | 2,178,900 | 2,250,100 | 4,032,811 | -1.7 | 1,711 |
| **Eastern Region** | | | | | | |
| Connecticut (c) .................. | 55,553 | 26,040 | 28,686 | 52,907 | -4.8 | 1,931 |
| Delaware ........................... | 16,831 | 12,992 | 13,510 | 16,313 | -3.1 | 2,365 |
| Maine................................. | 7,316 | 3,517 | 3,555 | 7,278 | -0.5 | 693 |
| Maryland (c) ...................... | 95,017 | 48,438 | 55,274 | 88,181 | -7.2 | 1,999 |
| Massachusetts (b)(c) ........ | 76,249 | 81,800 | 86,000 | 72,049 | -5.5 | 1,378 |
| New Hampshire ................. | 4,600 | 3,082 | 3,335 | 4,347 | -5.5 | 416 |
| New Jersey ........................ | 124,176 | 42,139 | 46,160 | 120,155 | -3.2 | 1,788 |
| New York........................... | 121,182 | 34,126 | 38,277 | 117,031 | -3.4 | 769 |
| Pennsylvania (d) ............... | 171,329 | 91,858 | 83,890 | 179,297 | 4.7 | 1,808 |
| Rhode Island..................... | 25,924 | 5,100 | 5,800 | 25,164 | -2.9 | 3,010 |
| Vermont (b)(c).................. | 6,833 | 3,891 | 4,420 | 6,304 | -7.7 | 1,257 |
| Regional total .................. | 705,010 | 352,983 | 352,983 | 689,026 | -2.6 | : |
| **Midwestern Region** | | | | | | |
| Illinois (c).......................... | 130,910 | 58,600 | 57,600 | 131,910 | 0.8 | 1,344 |
| Indiana (b) ........................ | 131,635 | 92,378 | 95,266 | 128,747 | -2.2 | 2,638 |
| Iowa (b)............................. | 23,163 | 17,461 | 18,245 | 22,379 | -3.4 | 963 |
| Kansas ............................... | 17,236 | 21,537 | 21,371 | 17,402 | 1.0 | 812 |
| Michigan (c)(d).................. | 185,416 | 124,500 | 128,500 | 182,333 | -1.7 | 2,388 |
| Minnesota.......................... | 121,313 | 64,461 | 73,888 | 111,886 | -7.8 | 2,760 |
| Nebraska............................ | 18,910 | 14,719 | 14,023 | 19,606 | 3.7 | 1,460 |
| North Dakota..................... | 4,206 | 2,756 | 2,672 | 4,290 | 2.0 | 834 |
| Ohio (b)(c)(d)..................... | 256,084 | 147,108 | 155,300 | 160,100 | -1.7 | 2,841 |
| South Dakota..................... | 6,602 | 3,202 | 3,264 | 6,540 | -0.9 | 1,046 |
| Wisconsin .......................... | 46,950 | 22,275 | 23,079 | 46,163 | -1.7 | 1,052 |
| Regional total ................... | 942,425 | 568,997 | 593,208 | 831,356 | -11.7 | : |
| **Southern Region** | | | | | | |
| Alabama ............................ | 49,953 | 24,423 | 21,111 | 53,265 | 6.6 | 1,474 |
| Arkansas............................ | 30,642 | 8,520 | 10,340 | 28,822 | -5.9 | 1,307 |
| Florida (c)(d) .................... | 267,448 | 210,600 | 220,400 | 256,220 | -4.2 | 1,743 |
| Georgia (c)(e)..................... | 453,887 | 222,208 | 218,935 | 457,160 | 0.7 | 6,208 |
| Kentucky (c) ...................... | 54,947 | 28,061 | 25,813 | 57,195 | 4.1 | 1,714 |
| Louisiana ........................... | 42,259 | 17,050 | 15,396 | 43,913 | 3.9 | 1,285 |
| Mississippi ........................ | 24,276 | 10,170 | 7,653 | 26,793 | 10.4 | 1,216 |
| Missouri............................. | 57,805 | 23,755 | 24,131 | 57,429 | -0.7 | 1,246 |
| North Carolina (c)............. | 106,581 | 63,113 | 65,466 | 104,228 | -2.2 | 1,442 |
| Oklahoma (c)..................... | 27,067 | 9,635 | 11,045 | 25,657 | -5.2 | 912 |
| South Carolina.................. | 33,876 | 13,431 | 14,122 | 33,185 | -2.0 | 939 |
| Tennessee .......................... | 58,493 | 24,311 | 23,801 | 59,946 | 2.5 | 1,232 |
| Texas ................................. | 426,208 | 165,551 | 173,081 | 418,678 | -1.8 | 2,280 |
| Virginia (c) ........................ | 57,876 | 25,626 | 26,848 | 56,654 | -2.1 | 923 |
| West Virginia (c)(d).......... | 8,409 | 1,800 | 1,600 | 8,623 | 2.5 | 597 |
| Regional total .................. | 1,699,727 | 848,254 | 859,742 | 1,687,768 | -0.7 | : |
| **Western Region** | | | | | | |
| Alaska (b) ......................... | 6,739 | 1,209 | 989 | 6,959 | 3.3 | 1,308 |
| Arizona (c)........................ | 78,243 | 27,500 | 24,800 | 80,910 | 3.4 | 1,626 |
| California (c)...................... | 311,728 | 149,029 | 167,883 | 292,874 | -6.0 | 1,047 |
| Colorado (b)(c)(d) ........... | 78,432 | 53,500 | 55,600 | 76,289 | -2.7 | 1,959 |
| Hawaii (c).......................... | 19,469 | 6,484 | 5,079 | 20,874 | 7.2 | 2,066 |
| Idaho (c)(f)........................ | 56,975 | 43,365 | 47,447 | 52,893 | -7.2 | 4,602 |
| Montana (c)(d) ................. | 10,091 | 4,021 | 4,019 | 10,093 | 0.0 | 1,316 |
| Nevada.............................. | 12,300 | 6,467 | 6,933 | 11,834 | -3.8 | 597 |
| New Mexico (d) ................ | 20,086 | 6,000 | 6,200 | 19,839 | -1.2 | 1,301 |
| Oregon.............................. | 39,607 | 15,103 | 14,864 | 39,846 | 0.6 | 1,328 |
| Utah.................................. | 11,481 | 5,637 | 5,511 | 11,607 | 1.1 | 590 |
| Washington (b)(c)(d) ....... | 98,053 | 73,900 | 74,900 | 97,864 | -0.2 | 1,882 |
| Wyoming (c)...................... | 5,352 | 3,146 | 3,179 | 5,319 | -0.6 | 1,270 |
| Regional total .................. | 748,556 | 395,361 | 417,404 | 727,201 | -2.8 | : |
| Regional total without California......... | 436,828 | 246,332 | 249,521 | 434,327 | -0.5 | : |
| Dist. of Columbia.............. | 8,055 | 6,989 | 5,977 | 9,067 | 12.6 | 1,815 |

See footnotes at end of table.

# ADULTS ON PROBATION BY REGION: 2010 — Continued

*Source:* U.S. Department of Justice, Bureau of Justice Statistics, *Probation and Parole in the United States*, 2010, Statistical Tables NCJ 236019 (November 2011).

*Note:* Because of nonresponse or incomplete data, the probation population for some jurisdictions on December 31, 2010, does not equal the population on January 1, 2010 plus entries, minus exits. Rates were computed using the estimated adult resident population in each state on January 1, 2010. See Methodology for more detail.

: — Not calculated.

(a) Reflects reported data except for jurisdictions in which data were not available. Details may not sum to totals because of rounding.

(b) Population excludes probationers in one of the following categories: inactive, warrant, supervised out of jurisdiction, or probationers who had their location tracked by GPS.

(c) Some or all detailed data are estimated.

(d) Data for entries and exits were estimated for nonreporting agencies.

(e) Counts include private agency cases and may overstate the number of persons under supervision.

(f) Counts include estimates for misdemeanors based on entries during the year.

## Table 9.21
## ADULTS ON PAROLE BY REGION: 2010

| State or other jurisdiction | Parole population | | | | Percent change during 2010 | Number on parole on 12/31/10 per 100,000 adult residents |
|---|---|---|---|---|---|---|
| | 1/1/10 | 2010 | | 12/31/10 | | |
| | | Entries (a) | Exits (a) | | | |
| **United States** .................... | 837,818 | 565,264 | 562,478 | 840,676 | 0.3 | 357 |
| Federal............................. | 100,598 | 47,873 | 42,919 | 105,552 | 4.9 | 45 |
| State .................................. | 737,220 | 517,391 | 519,559 | 735,124 | -0.3 | 312 |
| **Eastern Region** | | | | | | |
| Connecticut (b)................. | 2,873 | 3,413 | 3,392 | 2,894 | 0.7 | 106 |
| Delaware (c) ..................... | 519 | 516 | 475 | 560 | 7.9 | 81 |
| Maine................................. | 32 | 1 | 1 | 32 | 0 | 3 |
| Maryland ........................... | 13,195 | 6,378 | 6,378 | 13,195 | 0 | 299 |
| Massachusetts (d) ............. | 3,253 | 4,507 | 4,500 | 3,260 | 0.2 | 62 |
| New Hampshire (e).......... | 1,883 | 1,284 | 1,194 | 1,973 | 4.8 | 189 |
| New Jersey ........................ | 15,356 | 8,183 | 7,976 | 15,563 | 1.3 | 232 |
| New York........................... | 49,950 | 23,461 | 24,869 | 48,542 | -2.8 | 319 |
| Pennsylvania (v) ............... | 96,014 | 53,156 | 53,300 | 95,870 | -0.1 | 967 |
| Rhode Island (v)............... | 537 | 488 | 469 | 556 | 3.5 | 67 |
| Vermont (f)(u) ................. | 1,087 | 513 | 568 | 1,032 | -5.1 | 206 |
| Regional total ................... | 184,699 | 101,900 | 103,122 | 183,477 | -6.6 | : |
| **Midwestern Region (a)** | | | | | | |
| Illinois............................... | 33,162 | 26,578 | 33,731 | 26,009 | -21.6 | 265 |
| Indiana (v)......................... | 10,989 | 10,607 | 10,724 | 10,872 | -1.1 | 223 |
| Iowa (v) ............................. | 3,259 | 2,312 | 2,374 | 3,197 | -1.9 | 138 |
| Kansas (v) ......................... | 5,010 | 4,793 | 4,740 | 5,063 | 1.1 | 236 |
| Michigan (g)...................... | 24,374 | 12,137 | 12,025 | 24,486 | 0.5 | 321 |
| Minnesota.......................... | 5,435 | 5,706 | 5,334 | 5,807 | 6.8 | 143 |
| Nebraska ........................... | 823 | 1,147 | 1,029 | 941 | 14.3 | 69 |
| North Dakota..................... | 363 | 818 | 754 | 427 | 17.6 | 83 |
| Ohio (h)............................. | 14,575 | 6,655 | 9,154 | 12,076 | -17.1 | 136 |
| South Dakota..................... | 2,748 | 1,706 | 1,611 | 2,843 | 3.5 | 455 |
| Wisconsin (u) .................... | 19,499 | 6,995 | 6,930 | 19,572 | 0.4 | 446 |
| Regional total ................... | 120,237 | 79,454 | 88,406 | 111,293 | -7.4 | : |
| **Southern Region** | | | | | | |
| Alabama (i)........................ | 8,429 | 3,024 | 2,447 | 9,006 | 6.8 | 249 |
| Arkansas............................ | 21,077 | 9,395 | 9,366 | 21,106 | 0.1 | 957 |
| Florida (j)(u)..................... | 4,323 | 6,528 | 6,758 | 4,093 | -5.3 | 28 |
| Georgia.............................. | 23,709 | 13,622 | 12,240 | 25,091 | 5.8 | 341 |
| Kentucky (k) ..................... | 12,601 | 9,154 | 7,127 | 14,628 | 16.1 | 438 |
| Louisiana........................... | 23,607 | 15,755 | 13,160 | 26,202 | 11 | 767 |
| Mississippi (l)................... | 5,426 | 3,423 | 2,415 | 6,434 | 18.6 | 292 |
| Missouri............................ | 18,857 | 11,570 | 11,006 | 19,421 | 3 | 421 |
| North Carolina (m)(u) ...... | 3,544 | 3,833 | 3,756 | 3,621 | 2.2 | 50 |
| Oklahoma (u)..................... | 2,970 | 596 | 939 | 2,627 | -11.5 | 93 |
| South Carolina.................. | 6,419 | 3,053 | 3,060 | 6,412 | -0.1 | 182 |
| Tennessee (n) .................... | 11,556 | 4,595 | 3,854 | 12,157 | 5.2 | 250 |
| Texas (w).......................... | 104,943 | 33,050 | 33,230 | 104,763 | -0.2 | 570 |
| Virginia (o)(u) ................. | 2,565 | 1,060 | 1,001 | 2,624 | 2.3 | 43 |
| West Virginia..................... | 1,889 | 1,302 | 1,395 | 1,796 | -4.9 | 124 |
| Regional total ................... | 251,915 | 119,960 | 111,754 | 259,981 | 3.2 | : |
| **Western Region** | | | | | | |
| Alaska (p) ......................... | 1,923 | 593 | 427 | 2,089 | 8.6 | 393 |
| Arizona (u)........................ | 8,186 | 12,880 | 13,073 | 7,993 | -2.4 | 161 |
| California (v) .................... | 106,371 | 166,340 | 167,782 | 105,133 | -1.2 | 376 |
| Colorado (q) ..................... | 11,655 | 8,978 | 9,619 | 11,014 | -5.5 | 283 |
| Hawaii (r).......................... | 1,831 | 814 | 795 | 1,850 | 1 | 183 |
| Idaho................................. | 3,447 | 1,863 | 1,353 | 3,957 | 14.8 | 344 |
| Montana (s)....................... | 1,007 | 580 | 601 | 986 | -2.1 | 129 |
| Nevada............................... | 4,186 | 4,625 | 3,847 | 4,964 | 18.6 | 250 |
| New Mexico ...................... | 3,157 | 510 | 521 | 3,146 | -0.3 | 206 |
| Oregon............................... | 22,117 | 8,799 | 8,425 | 22,491 | 1.7 | 750 |
| Utah................................... | 3,185 | 1,780 | 2,024 | 2,941 | -7.7 | 150 |
| Washington (t) .................. | 6,563 | 5,733 | 5,340 | 6,956 | 6 | 134 |
| Wyoming ........................... | 749 | 360 | 427 | 682 | -8.9 | 163 |
| Regional total .................. | 174,377 | 213,855 | 214,234 | 174,202 | -0.1 | : |
| Regional total without California......... | 68,006 | 47,515 | 46,452 | 69,069 | 1.5 | : |
| Dist. of Columbia.............. | 5,992 | 2,222 | 2,043 | 6,171 | 3 | 1,235 |

See footnotes at end of table.

## ADULTS ON PAROLE BY REGION: 2010 — Continued

*Source:* U.S. Department of Justice, Bureau of Justice Statistics, *Probation and Parole in the United States,* 2010, Statistical Tables NCJ 236019 (November 2011).

*Note:* Because of nonresponse or incomplete data, the parole population for some jurisdictions on December 31, 2010, does not equal the population on January 1, 2010, plus entries, minus exits. Rates were computed using the estimated adult resident population in each state on January 1, 2011.

*Key:*

: — Not calculated.

(a) Reflects reported data except for jurisdictions in which data were not available. Details may not sum to totals because of rounding.

(b) More than one year includes parolees with a maximum sentence to incarceration of more than two years because Connecticut statute stipulates that parole eligible sentences are sentences of more than two years.

(c) Total parole population on December 31, 2010, includes an additional 167 parolees supervised for another state through an interstate compact agreement.

(d) Total parole population on December 31, 2010, includes an additional 286 parolees supervised for another state through an interstate compact agreement.

(e) Total parole population on December 31, 2010, includes an additional 73 parolees supervised for another state through an interstate compact agreement.

(f) Total parole population on December 31, 2010, excludes an estimated 11 parolees supervised by another state through an interstate compact agreement. The total parole population on December 31, 2010, includes an additional estimated 34 parolees supervised by another state through an interstate compact agreement. Vermont's information system does not include a racial category for Hispanic or Latino and does not collect any ethnicity data; therefore, the number of Hispanic or Latino parolees could not be reported and whether or not other racial categories include Hispanic or Latino parolees could not be determined. Vermont's information system also does not include a racial category for Native Hawaiian/Other Pacific Islander or two or more races.

(g) Number of parolees reported as Hispanic or Latino is an underestimate because Michigan's information system does not include a category which directly tracks and measures parolees who are Hispanic or Latino.

(h) The decrease (down 17.1% or 2,499 parolees) in Ohio's parole population during 2010 was related to an Ohio Supreme Court case from October 2009. The result was a mandate to discharge certain post-prison persons from parole, which was first implemented in November 2009 and continued through February 2010. The decrease was also partially the result of database cleaning that took place during 2010.

(i) Has two reporting agencies—one state agency, representing about 99% of Alabama's total parole population, and one local agency. Alabama's total parole population on December 31, 2010, includes an additional 990 parolees supervised for another state through an interstate compact agreement.

(j) Total parole population on December 31, 2010, includes an additional 167 parolees supervised for another state through an interstate compact agreement.

(k) Total parole population on December 31, 2010, includes an additional 590 parolees supervised for another state through an interstate compact agreement.

(l) The 18.6% increase (1,008 parolees) in Mississippi's parole population during 2010 resulted from modifications in both parole and house arrest laws and state statutes that made more offenders eligible for conditional release.

(m) Total parole population on December 31, 2010, includes offenders under post-release supervision. Post-release supervision is defined under North Carolina's Structured Sentencing Act of 1993 as a reintegration program for serious offenders who served extensive prison terms. Weapon offense is the illegal possession of a weapon, not an offense in which a weapon was used (i.e., does not include armed robbery offenses). Post-release offenders were reported in term of supervised release.

(n) Total parole population on December 31, 2010, includes an additional 987 parolees supervised for another state through an interstate compact agreement.

(o) Reporting changes between 2000 and 2009—for reporting changes in Virginia that occurred in 2007 and 2008, see Methodology and *Probation and Parole in the United States,* 2009, BJS Web, NCJ 231674.

(p) Total parole population on December 31, 2010, includes an additional unknown number of parolees supervised for another state through an interstate compact agreement.

(q) Total parole population on December 31, 2010, includes an additional 304 parolees supervised for another state through an interstate compact agreement. These methods are not comparable to those used between 2005 and 2008. Entries to parole by reinstatement were previously classified as mandatory entries to parole (appendix table 13). Mandatory releases have increased since 2009 as the result of legislative revision that went into effect July 1, 2009, that allows certain offenders to earn additional reductions in time. The 1,980 parolees reported as supervised out of state includes an unspecified number of parolees released to a detainer for other charges and some who were detained by the U.S. Immigration and Customs Enforcement (ICE) agency for deportation.

(r) Total parole population on December 31, 2010, includes an additional 48 parolees supervised for another state through an interstate compact agreement. Hawaii reported absconder, supervised out of state, and other supervision statuses separately from active status to meet BJS definitions; however, Hawaii considers these statuses to be active.

(s) Reporting changes between 2000 and 2009—for changes in reporting methods that occurred in Montana in 2009, see Methodology and *Probation and Parole in the United States,* 2009, BJS Web, NCJ 231674.

(t) Reporting changes between 2000 and 2009—for reporting changes that occurred in Washington in 2004, see *Probation and Parole in the United States,* 2009, BJS Web, NCJ 231674.

(u) Some or all data were estimated.

(v) Population excludes parolees in one of the following categories: absconder or supervised out of state.

# Table 9.22
## ADULTS LEAVING PAROLE BY TYPE OF EXIT, BY REGION: 2010

*Number of adults exiting parole, 2010*

| State or other jurisdiction | Total reported exits | Completion | Returned to prison or jail | | | | Absconder | Other unsatisfactory (a) | Death | Other (b) | Unknown or not reported |
| | | | With new sentence | With revocation | To receive treatment | Other Unknown | | | | | |
|---|---|---|---|---|---|---|---|---|---|---|---|
| **United States** | 562,478 | 288,717 | 49,334 | 127,918 | 1,657 | 5,417 | 47,860 | 9,508 | 5,714 | 14,912 | 11,441 |
| Federal | 42,919 | 23,188 | 2,181 | 9,939 | 0 | 80 | 1,367 | 1,267 | 530 | 442 | 3,925 |
| State | 519,559 | 265,529 | 47,153 | 117,979 | 1,657 | 5,337 | 46,493 | 8,241 | 5,184 | 14,470 | 7,516 |
| **Eastern Region** | | | | | | | | | | | |
| Connecticut | 3,392 | 1,975 | 0 | 0 | 0 | 1,259 | 158 | 0 | ** | 0 | 0 |
| Delaware | 475 | 293 | ** | ** | ** | ** | ** | 77 | 7 | 98 | 0 |
| Maine | 1 | 0 | 0 | 0 | 0 | 0 | 0 | 0 | 1 | 0 | 0 |
| Maryland | 6,378 | 3,597 | 773 | 980 | ** | ** | ** | 932 | 92 | 4 | 0 |
| Massachusetts | 4,500 | 3,454 | 256 | 768 | ** | 3 | 0 | 0 | 19 | 0 | 0 |
| New Hampshire | 1,194 | 560 | ** | ** | ** | 623 | 0 | 0 | 11 | ** | 0 |
| New Jersey | 7,976 | 6,042 | 196 | 1,632 | 1,539 | ~ | ~ | 0 | 106 | ** | 0 |
| New York (c) | 24,869 | 13,934 | 1,539 | 7,549 | 0 | 141 | ~ | 0 | 167 | ** | 0 |
| Pennsylvania | 53,300 | 31,250 | 6,614 | 5,488 | 0 | 0 | 1,379 | 116 | 789 | 2,572 | 5,092 |
| Rhode Island | 469 | 321 | 32 | 113 | ** | 0 | 0 | 0 | 3 | ** | 0 |
| Vermont (d) | 568 | 347 | 80 | 75 | ~ | 16 | 0 | ~ | 6 | 44 | 0 |
| Regional total | 103,122 | 61,773 | 9,490 | 16,605 | 1,539 | 2,042 | 1,537 | 1,125 | 1,201 | 2,718 | 5,092 |
| **Midwestern Region** | | | | | | | | | | | |
| Illinois | 33,731 | 16,716 | 2,483 | 11,448 | ~ | ~ | 1,252 | 0 | 46 | 954 | 832 |
| Indiana | 10,724 | 6,375 | 794 | 1,184 | 0 | ~ | 592 | 0 | 51 | 1,728 | 0 |
| Iowa (e) | 2,374 | 1,431 | ** | ** | ** | 651 | 1 | 1 | 14 | 63 | 214 |
| Kansas | 4,740 | 2,227 | 158 | 1,065 | ~ | 3 | 1,146 | ** | 34 | 107 | 0 |
| Michigan | 12,025 | 7,635 | 1,793 | 2,390 | ~ | ~ | ~ | ~ | 207 | 0 | 0 |
| Minnesota | 5,334 | 2,913 | 222 | 1,762 | 0 | 0 | 422 | 0 | 15 | 0 | 0 |
| Nebraska | 1,029 | 808 | 30 | 188 | ** | ** | 0 | ** | 3 | 0 | 0 |
| North Dakota | 754 | 579 | 17 | 142 | ** | ** | 15 | ** | 1 | ** | 0 |
| Ohio | 9,154 | 7,665 | 687 | 129 | 0 | 0 | 241 | 0 | 120 | 312 | 0 |
| South Dakota | 1,611 | 788 | 140 | 559 | ~ | 114 | ~ | ** | 10 | ** | 0 |
| Wisconsin (f) | 6,930 | 3,873 | 919 | 2,019 | ~ | 0 | ~ | 32 | 87 | ** | 0 |
| Regional total | 88,406 | 51,010 | 7,243 | 20,886 | ~ | 768 | 3,668 | 34 | 588 | 3,164 | 1,046 |
| **Southern Region** | | | | | | | | | | | |
| Alabama | 2,447 | 1,587 | 276 | 223 | ** | 23 | 0 | 0 | 100 | 228 | 10 |
| Arkansas | 9,366 | 5,707 | 1,200 | 1,474 | ** | 0 | 183 | 0 | 145 | 657 | 0 |
| Florida | 6,758 | 4,670 | 365 | 840 | ** | 0 | ~ | 0 | 60 | 666 | 157 |
| Georgia | 12,240 | 8,583 | 5 | 2,491 | 9 | 926 | 90 | 0 | 68 | 0 | 68 |
| Kentucky | 7,127 | 3,306 | 442 | 2,502 | ~ | ~ | 464 | ~ | 95 | 318 | 0 |
| Louisiana | 13,160 | 7,510 | 1,242 | 1,090 | ~ | 65 | ~ | 3,020 | 115 | 118 | 0 |
| Mississippi | 2,415 | 1,509 | ** | ** | ** | 821 | 47 | 0 | 22 | 16 | 0 |
| Missouri | 11,006 | 8,539 | 319 | 2,039 | 109 | ~ | ** | ** | ** | 0 | 0 |
| North Carolina | 3,756 | 3,018 | 118 | 216 | ~ | ~ | 207 | 22 | 34 | 0 | 141 |
| Oklahoma (h) | 939 | 811 | 54 | 44 | 0 | 0 | ** | ** | 30 | ** | 0 |
| South Carolina | 3,060 | 2,183 | 74 | 676 | 0 | 0 | 0 | 0 | 37 | 90 | 0 |
| Tennessee | 3,854 | 2,482 | 729 | 542 | 0 | 0 | ~ | 0 | 101 | 0 | 0 |
| Texas | 33,230 | 25,252 | 5,423 | 1,205 | ~ | ~ | ~ | ~ | 1,350 | ~ | 0 |
| Virginia (g) | 1,001 | 728 | 191 | 34 | 0 | 14 | 0 | 0 | 29 | ~ | 0 |
| West Virginia | 1,395 | 847 | 9 | 493 | 0 | 0 | 37 | 0 | 9 | 5 | 0 |
| Regional total | 111,754 | 76,732 | 10,447 | 13,869 | 118 | 1,849 | 1,028 | 3,042 | 2,195 | 2,098 | 376 |

See footnotes at end of table.

# ADULTS LEAVING PAROLE BY TYPE OF EXIT, BY REGION: 2010—Continued

| State or other jurisdiction | Total reported exits | Completion | Returned to prison or jail — With new sentence | With revocation | To receive treatment | Other Unknown | Absconder | Other unsatisfactory (a) | Death | Other (b) | Unknown or not reported |
|---|---|---|---|---|---|---|---|---|---|---|---|
| **Western Region -----** | | | | | | | | | | | |
| Alaska | 427 | 164 | 37 | 66 | ** | 128 | 1 | ** | 11 | 4 | 16 |
| Arizona (h) | 13,073 | 7,492 | 263 | 3,106 | 0 | 0 | 0 | 2,212 | 0 | ** | 0 |
| California | 167,782 | 48,385 | 17,008 | 55,640 | 0 | 0 | 40,191 | 0 | 660 | 5,898 | 0 |
| Colorado | 9,619 | 4,448 | 1,018 | 4,028 | 0 | 0 | 0 | 0 | 69 | 56 | 0 |
| Hawaii | 795 | 307 | 2 | 231 | 0 | 0 | ~ | 0 | 20 | ~ | 235 |
| Idaho | 1,353 | 466 | 191 | 438 | ~ | 0 | ~ | 249 | 9 | ~ | 0 |
| Montana | 601 | 364 | 9 | 206 | ~ | 0 | 0 | 0 | 11 | 11 | 0 |
| Nevada (c) | 3,847 | 3,283 | 266 | 156 | ** | 47 | 58 | ** | 37 | 0 | 0 |
| New Mexico (c) | 521 | ** | ** | ** | ** | ** | ** | ** | ** | ** | 521 |
| Oregon | 8,425 | 4,831 | 853 | 1,664 | 0 | 0 | 10 | 770 | 142 | 12 | 143 |
| Utah | 2,024 | 453 | 277 | 1,034 | 0 | 3 | 0 | 169 | 25 | 63 | 0 |
| Washington | 5,340 | 4,638 | ** | ** | ** | 0 | ** | 559 | 143 | 0 | 0 |
| Wyoming | 427 | 241 | 49 | 50 | 0 | 0 | 0 | 0 | 0 | ** | 87 |
| Regional total | 214,234 | 75,072 | 19,973 | 66,619 | ** | 178 | 40,260 | 3,959 | 1,127 | 6,044 | 1,002 |
| Regional total w/o California | 46,452 | 26,687 | 2,965 | 10,979 | ** | 178 | 69 | 3,959 | 467 | 146 | 1,002 |
| Dist. of Columbia | 2,043 | 942 | ** | ** | ** | 500 | 0 | 82 | 74 | 445 | 0 |

*Source:* U.S. Department of Justice, Bureau of Justice Statistics, *Probation and Parole in the United States, 2010,* Statistical Tables NCJ 236019 (November 2011).

*Key:*

** – Not known.

~ – Not applicable.

(a) Includes parolees discharged from supervision who failed to meet all conditions of supervision, had their parole sentence rescinded, or had their parole sentence revoked but were not returned to incarceration because their sentence was immediately reinstated, and other types of unsatisfactory exits; includes some early terminations and expirations of sentence.

(b) Includes 7,030 parolees who were transferred to another state and 7,881 parolees who exited for other reasons. Other reasons include parolees who were deported or transferred to the jurisdiction of Immigration and Customs Enforcement (ICE), had their sentence terminated by the court through an appeal, were transferred to another state through an interstate compact agreement or discharged to probation supervision, and other types of exits.

(c) Some or all detailed data are estimated type of exit.

(d) Total parole population on December 31, 2010, excludes an estimated 11 parolees supervised by another state through an interstate compact agreement (appendix tables 12 and 18). The total parole population on December 31, 2010, includes an additional estimated 34 parolees supervised by another state through an interstate compact agreement (appendix tables 12). Vermont's information system does not include a racial category for Hispanic or Latino and does not collect any ethnicity data; therefore, the number of Hispanic or Latino parolees could not be reported and whether or not other racial categories include Hispanic or Latino parolees could not be determined. Vermont's information system also does not include a racial category for Native Hawaiian/Other Pacific Islander or two or more races.

(e) Total parole population on December 31, 2010, excludes 202 parolees supervised by another state through an interstate compact agreement (appendix tables 12 and 18).

(f) Asian includes an unspecified number of parolees who were Native Hawaiian/Other Pacific Islander because Native Hawaiian/Other Pacific Islander could not be reported separately (appendix table 17).

(g) Reporting changes between 2000 and 2009 — for reporting changes in Virginia that occurred in 2007 and 2008, see Methodology and *Probation and Parole in the United States,* 2009 BJS Web, NCJ 231674. Reporting changes between 2009 and 2010, population as the result of the implementation of the Virginia Corrections Information System (VACORIS) and the rebuilding of the offender population data used for analysis. The total change in Virginia's parole population was a decrease of 2,040 parolees on January 1, 2010 (2,565), compared to the population reported for December 31, 2009 (4,605) (appendix table 12).

(h) Total parole population on December 31, 2010, includes an additional 515 parolees supervised for another state through an interstate compact agreement (appendix table 12).

## Table 9.23
## CAPITAL PUNISHMENT

| State or other jurisdiction | Capital offenses by state | Prisoners under sentence of death | Method of execution |
|---|---|---|---|
| Alabama | Intentional murder with 18 aggravating factors (Ala. Stat. Ann. 13A-5-40(a)(1)-(18)). | 206 | Electrocution or lethal injection |
| Alaska | ... | ... | ... |
| Arizona | First-degree murder, including pre-meditated murder and felony murder, accompanied by at least 1 of 14 aggravating factors (A.R.S. § 13-703(F)). | 138 | Lethal gas or lethal injection (a) |
| Arkansas | Capital murder (Ark. Code Ann. 5-10-101) with a finding of at least 1 of 10 aggravating circumstances; treason. | 43 | Lethal injection or electrocution (b) |
| California | First-degree murder with special circumstances; sabotage; train wrecking causing death; treason; perjury causing execution of an innocent person; fatal assault by a prisoner serving a life sentence. | 721 | Lethal injection |
| Colorado | First-degree murder with at least 1 of 17 aggravating factors; first-degree kidnapping resulting in death; treason. | 4 | Lethal injection |
| Connecticut | Capital felony with 8 forms of aggravated homicide (C.G.S. § 53a–54b). | 10 | Lethal injection |
| Delaware | First-degree murder (11Del. C. § 636) with at least 1 statutory aggravating circumstance (11Del. C. § 4209). | 20 | Lethal injection (c) |
| Florida (d) | First-degree murder; felony murder; capital drug trafficking; capital sexual battery. | 398 | Electrocution or lethal injection |
| Georgia | Murder; kidnapping with bodily injury or ransom when the victim dies; aircraft hijacking; treason. | 103 | Lethal injection |
| Hawaii | ... | ... | ... |
| Idaho | First-degree murder with aggravating factors; first-degree kidnapping; perjury resulting in death. | 16 | Lethal injection |
| Illinois | ... (e) | 0 | ... |
| Indiana | Murder with 16 aggravating circumstances (IC 35-50-2-9). | 14 | Lethal injection |
| Iowa | ... | ... | ... |
| Kansas | Capital murder with 8 aggravating circumstances (KSA 21-3439, KSA 21-4625, KSA 21-4636). | 9 | Lethal injection |
| Kentucky | Murder with aggravating factors; kidnapping with aggravating factors (KRS 32.025). | 36 | Electrocution or lethal injection (f) |
| Louisiana (d) | First-degree murder; treason (La. R.S. 14:30 and 14:113). | 86 | Lethal injection |
| Maine | ... | ... | ... |
| Maryland | First-degree murder, either premeditated or during the commission of a felony, provided that certain death eligibility requirements are satisfied. | 5 | Lethal injection |
| Massachusetts | ... | ... | ... |
| Michigan | ... | ... | ... |
| Minnesota | ... | ... | ... |
| Mississippi | Capital murder (Miss Code Ann. § 97-3-19(2)); aircraft piracy (Miss Code Ann. § 97-25-55(1)). | 60 | Lethal injection |
| Missouri | First-degree murder (565.020 RSMO 2000). | 50 | Lethal injection or lethal gas |
| Montana (d) | Capital murder with 1 of 9 aggravating circumstances (Mont. Code Ann. § 46-18-303); aggravated sexual intercourse without consent (Mont. Code Ann. § 45-5-503). | 2 | Lethal injection |
| Nebraska | First-degree murder with a finding of at least 1 statutorily-defined aggravating circumstance. | 12 | Lethal injection |
| Nevada | First-degree murder with at least 1 of 15 aggravating circumstances (NRS 200.030, 200.033, 200.035). | 81 | Lethal injection |
| New Hampshire | Murder committed in the course of rape, kidnapping, or drug crimes; killing of a police officer, judge, or prosecutor; murder for hire; murder by an inmate while serving a sentence of life without parole (RSA 630:1, RSA 630:5). | 1 | Lethal injection or hanging (g) |
| New Jersey | ... (h) | ... | ... |
| New Mexico (i) | ... (i) | 2 | (i) |

See footnotes at end of table.

## CAPITAL PUNISHMENT — Continued

| State or other jurisdiction | Capital offenses by state (a) | Prisoners under sentence of death (b) | Method of execution (a) |
|---|---|---|---|
| New York (j) | First-degree murder with 1 of 13 aggravating factors (NY Penal Law § 125.27). | 0 | Lethal injection |
| North Carolina | First-degree murder (NCGS § 14-17). | 165 | Lethal injection |
| North Dakota | ... | ... | ... |
| Ohio | Aggravated murder with at least 1 of 10 aggravating circumstances (O.R.C. secs. 2903.01, 2929.02, and 2929.04). | 159 | Lethal injection |
| Oklahoma (d) | First-degree murder in conjunction with a finding of at least 1 of 8 statutorily-defined aggravating circumstances. | 77 | Electrocution, lethal injection or firing squad (k) |
| Oregon (l) | Aggravated murder (ORS 163.095-150). | 34 | Lethal injection |
| Pennsylvania | First-degree murder with 18 aggravating circumstances. | 219 | Lethal injection |
| Rhode Island | ... | ... | ... |
| South Carolina (d) | Murder with 1 of 12 aggravating circumstances (§ 16-3-20(C)(a)). | 63 | Electrocution or lethal injection |
| South Dakota | First-degree murder with 1 of 10 aggravating circumstances. | 3 | Lethal injection |
| Tennessee | First-degree murder with 1 of 16 aggravating circumstances (Tenn. Code Ann. § 39-13-204). | 87 | Lethal injection or electrocution (m) |
| Texas (d) | Criminal homicide with 1 of 9 aggravating circumstances (TX Penal Code § 19.03). | 321 | Lethal injection |
| Utah | Aggravated murder (76-5-202, Utah Code Annotated). | 9 | Lethal injection or firing squad (n) |
| Vermont | ... | ... | ... |
| Virginia | First-degree murder with 1 of 15 aggravating circumstances (VA Code § 18.2-31). | 11 | Electrocution or lethal injection |
| Washington | Aggravated first-degree murder. | 9 | Lethal injection or hanging |
| West Virginia | ... | ... | ... |
| Wisconsin | ... | ... | ... |
| Wyoming | First-degree murder; murder during the commission of sexual assault, sexual abuse of a minor, arson, robbery, burglary, escape, resisting arrest, kidnapping, or abuse of a minor under 16 (W.S.A. § 6-2-101 (a)). | 1 | Lethal injection or lethal gas (o) |
| Dist. of Columbia | ... | ... | ... |
| American Samoa | First-degree murder (ASC § 46.3513). (p) | 0 | Hanging (p) |
| Guam | ... | ... | ... |
| No. Mariana Islands | ... | ... | ... |
| Puerto Rico | ... | ... | ... |
| U.S. Virgin Islands | ... | ... | ... |

*Sources:* U.S. Department of Justice, Office of Justice programs, Bureau of Justice Statistics, *Capital Punishment, 2010 — Statistical Tables*, December 2011; The Council of State Governments, February 2012; NAACP Legal Defense Fund, Death Row U.S.A.: As of January 1, 2011 (Spring 2011).

*Note:* At press time, a severe shortage of barbiturate sodium thiopental—one of the three drugs used in most lethal injections—caused many states to switch to pentobarbital. The sole U.S. manufacturer of pentobarbital condemns its use in executions and seeks to prevent its sale for that purpose. If the current supply is exhausted, states will face shortages of tested chemicals once again. February 2012.

The United States Supreme Court ruling in *Roper v. Simmons*, 543 U.S. 551 (2005) declared unconstitutional the imposition of the death penalty on persons under the age of 18.

The United States Supreme Court ruling in *Atkins v. Virginia*, 536 U.S. 304 (2002) declared unconstitutional the imposition of the death penalty on mentally handicapped persons.

The method of execution of Federal prisoners is lethal injection, pursuant to 28 CFR, Part 26. For offenses under the Violent Crime Control and Law Enforcement Act of 1994, the execution method is that of the State in which the conviction took place (18 U.S.C. 3596).

*Key:*

... — No capital punishment statute.

(a) Arizona authorizes lethal injection for persons sentenced after November 15, 1992; inmates sentenced before that date may select lethal injection or gas.

(b) Arkansas authorizes lethal injection for those whose offense occurred on or after July 4, 1983; inmates whose offense occurred before that date may select lethal injection or electrocution.

(c) Delaware authorizes hanging if lethal injection is held to be unconstitutional by a court of competent jurisdiction.

(d) The United States Supreme Court struck a portion of the Louisiana capital statute on June 25, 2008 (*Kennedy v. Louisiana*, U.S. 128 S.Ct. 2641). The statute (La. Rev. Stat. Ann. § 14:42(D)(2)) allowing execution as a punishment for the rape of a minor when no murder had been committed had been ruled constitutionally permissible by the Louisiana Supreme Court. The U.S. Supreme Court found that since no national consensus existed for application of the death penalty in cases of rape where no murder had been committed, such laws constitute cruel and unusual punishment under the Eighth and Fourteenth Amendments. The ruling affects laws passed in Florida, Oklahoma, South Carolina, Texas, and Montana.

(e) Governor Pat Quinn signed a bill (SB 3539) on March 9, 2011 that abolishes the death penalty effective July 1, 2011. He commuted all death sentences to life without parole and said he would commute any other death sentences prior to the effective date.

(f) Kentucky authorizes lethal injection for persons sentenced on or after March 31, 1998; inmates sentenced before that date may select lethal injection or electrocution.

(g) New Hampshire authorizes hanging only if lethal injection cannot be given.

## CAPITAL PUNISHMENT — Continued

(h) New Jersey repealed its death penalty statute in 2007.

(i) Governor Bill Richardson signed a bill in March of 2009 abolishing the death penalty. The law is not retroactive and leaves two inmates on death row.

(j) The New York Court of Appeals has held that a portion of New York's death penalty sentencing statute (CPL 400.27) was unconstitutional (*People v. Taylor*, 9 N.Y.3d 129 (2007)). As a result, no defendants can be sentenced to death until the legislature corrects the errors in this statute.

(k) Oklahoma authorizes electrocution if lethal injection is held to be unconstitutional, and firing squad if both lethal injection and electrocution are held to be unconstitutional.

(l) In November 2011, Governor Kitzhaber placed a moratorium on all executions in Oregon.

(m) Tennessee authorizes lethal injection for those whose capital offense occurred after December 31, 1998; those who committed the offense before that date may select electrocution by written waiver.

(n) Authorizes firing squad if lethal injection is held unconstitutional. Inmates who selected execution by firing squad prior to May 3, 2004, may still be entitled to execution by that method.

(o) Wyoming authorizes lethal gas if lethal injection is ever held to be unconstitutional.

(p) The last execution was in the 1920s.

# Hydraulic Fracturing – An Introduction and Policy Considerations for States

### By Brydon Ross

*Hydraulic fracturing and horizontal drilling have created new domestic energy frontiers and made the United States a net energy exporter for the first time in more than 60 years. Although the process has been used for decades to stimulate production from declining wells, new technological advancements have rapidly accelerated the development of unconventional reserves of fossil fuels that were either unknown or considered uneconomic just a few years ago. Despite the excitement over the potential economic benefits are underlying public safety and environmental concerns.*

Hydraulic fracturing and horizontal drilling have created new domestic energy frontiers and made the United States a net energy exporter for the first time in more than 60 years. Although the process has been used for decades to stimulate production from declining wells, new technological advancements have rapidly accelerated the development of unconventional reserves of fossil fuels that were either unknown or considered uneconomic just a few years ago. According to a study commissioned by the American Natural Gas Association, shale gas supported more than 600,000 jobs in 2010 and projected a growth to 870,000 supported jobs by 2015.[1] The rapid growth of production and well completion alone will add $145 billion to the U.S. economy, an 11-fold increase over the past decade, and has spurred nearly $25 billion in private equity investment in 2011.[2]

The scale and size of the ramp-up in production, as well as the resource estimates that have been unlocked by hydraulic fracturing, are staggering. Federal estimates of perhaps the best-known formation, the Marcellus Shale, are 141 trillion cubic feet of technically recoverable reserves. Ten years ago, the U.S. Geological Survey estimated that the Marcellus region only contained 2 trillion cubic feet of recoverable reserves.[3] That figure itself is hardly an insignificant sum considering that 1 *billion* cubic feet of natural gas can power 10,000 homes a year, but federal energy experts were off by a factor of 70 when it came to predicting the technological breakthrough that would happen only a few years later. The substantial increase in domestic natural gas supplies have led to the lowest prices for natural

gas in a decade. U.S. consumers could save $16.5 billion on home energy bills this year with a typical household saving roughly $145 at current prices, according to an economist with the Federal Reserve Bank of Dallas.[4]

Despite the excitement over the potential economic benefits are underlying public safety and environmental concerns. Many communities and advocacy groups believe that hydraulic fracturing may cause or contribute to groundwater pollution, increase harmful air emissions, increase strains on local water supplies, and could even contribute to seismic events during deep-well injection of wastewater disposal. Some states are pursuing more regulatory oversight of the drilling process to assuage these concerns, including providing more public information on the chemicals used when a well is fracked. States also face significant long-term economic considerations when setting up royalty and tax policy to capture the financial rewards of increased production. In addition, some critics worry that the substantial growth caused by hydraulic fracturing can stress the infrastructure of small communities unprepared for increased traffic, worker housing demands, and the cyclical nature of the industry.

## What is Hydraulic Fracturing?

Hydraulic fracturing is performed after a well is drilled and involves injecting large volumes of water, sand or propping agents and specialized chemicals under high pressure to fracture the formations holding the oil or natural gas. The sand or other propping agents hold the fractures open to allow the oil or natural gas to flow freely out of the formation and into a production well. According to the U.S. Department of Energy and the Ground Water Protection Council, approximately 99.5 percent of the fracking solutions used to develop shale formations are comprised of freshwater and sand.[5] The remaining chemicals in fracking solutions have specifically designed and engineered purposes that vary depending on the formation. For example, some are used to prevent bacteria from corroding well structures or can contain friction-reducing additives for proppants to more effectively target a particular deposit. The use of these chemicals, however, worry public safety advocates and environmental groups because many fracking solutions contain substances like hydrochloric acid, which can be harmful to human health if consumed.

Wells used in the hydraulic fracturing process can be drilled vertically, horizontally or a combination of the two through directional drilling. Vertical segments of the well can extend beyond depths of 8,000 feet, and horizontal drilling can often occur several thousand feet away from a production pad where the well is located. Sound well construction processes are critical to protecting groundwater resources. The primary method used to prevent the migration of drilling fluids into groundwater supplies is called casing. Casing is the cementing of a steel pipe into the shale formation after a wellbore has drilled through different geologic sublevels to access the natural gas or oil. The casing must be able to withstand the pressure of the formation and prevent the drilled borehole from collapsing on itself. The specialized cement must ensure the integrity of the well's operations, as well as prevent corrosion or other factors unique to the formation.[6]

Fracking operations require tremendous amounts of water, depending on the size and type of formation being produced. The Environmental Protection Agency estimates that 50,000 to 350,000 gallons of water may be used to fracture one coalbed methane formation, while 2 million to 5 million gallons may be needed for one horizontal shale well.[7] Local surface water and groundwater supply the vast majority of fracking fluids, although some operators are beginning to develop water recycling efforts. When a formation is cracked, wastewater or flowback that contains heavy metals, salts and elements of the chemicals used in the fracking solution is produced. Typically, flowback is disposed of in permitted, deep underground injection wells or it may be discharged after treatment into surface waters to remove contaminants.[8]

## Environmental Concerns

Environmental advocacy groups and local communities near production areas have raised concerns that hydraulic fracturing has contaminated local drinking water with migration of flammable methane gas into wells and spills of chemical fluids into water tables. The most memorable scenes in the film *Gasland*, which is highly critical of hydraulic fracturing, were shots of homeowners igniting their faucet with a lighter because of methane concentrations in their water. The oil and natural gas industries have sharply objected to allegations of water contamination directly caused by hydraulic fracturing, and have said there is no single documented case proving causality of water contamination from the process itself. They note biogenic, or biologically generated, methane can occur naturally in the environment and can be found in local drinking water supplies when organic materials decompose over time.[9] Further, the industry contends any incidents related to methane well migration are from either naturally occurring methane or operator errors during well-bore casing or the cementing process itself.

Increased production of unconventional fuels also can increase ozone and smog-forming emissions. According to a September 2011 article in *The New York Times*, nearly 30 percent of all the natural gas produced in North Dakota from the Bakken Shale formation is flared, which is a deliberate burning of excess gas that is produced along with oil from wells due to a lack of pipeline infrastructure or other economic incentives to store it. Nationwide, up to 100 million cubic feet of natural gas, which could heat 500,000 homes, is flared.[10]

State regulators are dealing with another challenge—competing interests for water usage, especially in the drought-stricken Southwest and West. For example, the Eagle Ford shale has been a significant financial boon for what is historically a more economically depressed part of south Texas. Because of the formation's unique geology, however, water usage for fracking a single well can take up to 13 million gallons of water or three to four times as much water as is needed to develop a well in the Fort Worth area.[11] Industry supporters have noted a recent study by the Texas Water Development Board to assuage concerns. The study found that oil and gas drilling comprised only 1 percent of the state's overall water usage, compared to 56 percent for commercial agriculture, and that wells are rarely refracked. Critics and opponents of fracking in Texas have disputed those results because the demand for well construction is expected to expand significantly from 2,000 wells to 25,000 wells over the coming decades. Further, concentrated pressure on the usage of freshwater aquifers during drought conditions places added stress on agriculture operations that have property rights, but not mineral rights, which allow drilling operations to tap water resources without the consent of the landowner.[12] To address these resource concerns, Texas law now requires hydraulic fracturing operators, beginning in February 2012, to publicly disclose the total amount of water used to develop a formation.[13]

## The States' Oversight Role

States historically have primary jurisdiction and oversight of hydraulic fracturing production. Regulatory action covering the practice of hydraulic fracturing began soon after the technology was developed in the late 1940s, many years before Congress passed the Clean Water Act or Safe Drinking Water Act.[14] The Safe Drinking Water Act requires the EPA to delegate primary enforcement to states for the underground injection and disposal of fluids or brines regarding oil and natural gas production as long as they have adopted basic federal requirements to prevent injected fluids from contaminating groundwater sources. States may choose to forego their oversight authority and instead have the EPA administer their underground injection control programs.[15] In addition, states may enact more stringent requirements than those found in federal law. The 2005 Energy Policy Act, made the role of state regulation more explicit. It excluded the "underground injection of fluids or propping agents (other than diesel fuels)" of hydraulic fracturing operations from requiring a federal permit under the Safe Drinking Water Act.[16]

## Chemical Disclosure

Several states—including Arkansas, Colorado, Texas and Wyoming—have addressed public concerns regarding the disclosure of fracking solutions used by companies when developing shale formations. Many states and private companies require operators to publicly disclose the chemical makeup of fracturing solutions on the website, *www.FracFocus.org*. Those opposed to hydraulic fracturing contend that disclosure is often a term of art in some states, and that accessing information is too burdensome or that the information does not fully explain to the public the potential health hazards of chemicals in fracking solutions. For example, well operators disclose chemical information to the Pennsylvania Department of Environmental Protection, but the only way concerned citizens can access the entirety of those records is by scheduling an appointment and physically viewing them in person because many small producers do not also disclose information to FracFocus.[17]

Variances in state laws have limited the full description and amount of chemicals used in the fracking process because of industry concerns that trade secrets and proprietary information would be revealed, causing economic harm. Large oilfield services companies like Halliburton have noted that complete disclosure of all its proprietary information would cost the company $375 million, as it has spent tens of millions of dollars in developing new fracking fluids.[18]

In addition, the Obama administration's advisory panel on hydraulic fracturing and other environmental groups have been critical of the format used by FracFocus because the information on the website is not available in spreadsheet format, thus limiting broad analysis, and that some chemicals that are not covered by worker safety laws are often omitted from public disclosure.[19] Despite these criticisms, Wyoming's disclosure law is often described as an effective example of strong state oversight, and it even served as the framework for the Bureau of Land Management's recent proposal to require chemical disclosure of fracking operations on federal land. Under the state law, companies must disclose the chemical compounds used in fracking solutions before operations begin, as well as provide the actual names of chemical additives, compound type and their concentration rates both before and after a well is stimulated. In order to protect a trade secret used in solutions, an operator must obtain approval from the state that the compound is indeed proprietary in nature.

## Moratoriums, Bans and New Regulations

Some states, like New York, have reacted strongly to slow down the development of shale deposits and have been a high-profile battleground for policy related to fracking. Former Gov. David Paterson vetoed the legislature's ban on the practice in 2009, but he issued an executive order directing further environmental review, which has essentially created a de facto moratorium until the state Department of Environmental Conservation issues a final decision. Although a 2011 draft report from the department recommended allowing fracking on private lands, Gov. Andrew Cuomo's 2012 budget did not include any additional funds for new regulatory staff signaling that the state's review will continue for some time.[20] The Vermont House of Representatives in February passed a three-year moratorium on any hydraulic fracturing activities even though no producer has applied for a permit to use the technique. "I don't think we should be fracking for natural gas in Vermont," Gov. Peter Shumlin said in expressing his concerns about chemicals used in the process, according the *Burlington Free Press*.[21]

In addition to outright prohibitions, state legislation relating to wastewater treatment, disposal and transportation has markedly increased. According to an *Associated Press* analysis, hydraulic fracturing generated roughly 10 million barrels of flowback or wastewater in the last half of 2011, with 97 percent of it either being recycled, or sent to deep underground injection wells or waste treatment plants.[22] Sending flowback to municipal sewage treatment plants has become increasingly worrisome for regulators in states like Pennsylvania. The Pennsylvania Department of Environmental Protection has found high concentrations of dissolved salts like bromide in treated water; the dissolved salts have proved harmful to water quality and public health. In April 2011, Gov. Tom Corbett directed that all drilling operations in the state voluntarily comply with a ban on sending flowback to wastewater treatment plants. To date, all drillers in the Marcellus Shale have complied, but the state's unique geology is not suitably porous enough for permanent storage in deep underground injection wells.[23] Large and sophisticated operators are recycling large amounts of their flowback. Range Resources, for example, recycled approximately 90 percent of its wastewater in 2010 and set a goal of 100 percent for 2011.

But the economics and the sheer volumes of flowback have caused producers to look for disposal options out of state. During the last half of 2011, the amount of Marcellus Shale flowback injected into deep reservoirs tripled, with much of it being sent to wells in Ohio. A series of high-profile earthquakes in northeastern Ohio from Christmas 2011 to New Year's Day near well sites have raised the specter of potentially increasing seismic activity when injecting thousands of gallons of water in reservoirs at high pressure. In response to public concerns, Ohio Gov. John Kasich shut down wastewater injection within five miles of the well where the earthquakes were taking place. Ohio state officials have pointed out that 176 wells have been operating since the mid-1980s without any significant incidents, but that well activity near a fault line likely caused pressure to build, which triggered the seismic activity.[24] Legislation introduced in both Maryland and New Jersey would ban the shipment and treating of wastewater from fracking operations in the nearby Marcellus region, further pressuring industry to invest in recycling efforts.

## New Economic Considerations

Expanded drilling has given state policymakers more than just environmental questions to ponder. Newfound revenue from the growth has filled state coffers and rejuvenated economic activity despite the nationally weak recovery. In February 2012, the Pennsylvania legislature approved legislation that would direct more than $200 million a year in shale impact fees to local communities and counties from drilling in the Marcellus region.[25] Some critics of the deal claim that money was left on the table and that more favorable terms could have been negotiated for the state and local communities. They warn against the cyclical boom-bust potential the industry could have on small communities when prices drop or when local services and roads become overwhelmed by increased traffic and growth. Many fracking critics argue that the industry's growth highlights the deficiencies between severance tax and royalty policies of states with mature extraction industries and those beginning to experience the shale wave. Several states outside traditional production areas have property tax laws dating back to the 1930s. For instance, some states may have an income tax on wages, but no laws to tax the royalties a landowner receives from allowing oil and gas operations on their property.[26] Instituting new fees or new taxes requires a careful balancing act by policymakers to harness the economic benefits of shale production without creating voter backlash or negatively impacting jobs dependent on natural gas prices.

## Notes

[1] The Economic and Employment Contributions of Shale Gas in the United States. IHS Global (USA) Inc. December 2011, p.5.

[2] "Oil and Gas Boom Lifts U.S. Economy." Russell Gold, *Wall Street Journal*. February 8, 2012.

[3] 2012 Annual Energy Outlook, Early Release Overview. Energy Information Administration, p. 9.

[4] "Shale Gas $100 Billion Savings to U.S. Exceed Tax Cuts: Energy." Mark Chediak, *Bloomberg*. January 26, 2012.

[5] Modern Shale Gas Development in the United States: A Primer. U.S. Department of Energy Office of Fossil Energy, April 2009, p. 61.

[6] "Hydraulic Fracturing Operations—Well Construction

and Integrity Guidelines." API Guidance Document HF1, First Edition, October 2009, pp. 2–5.

[7] Environmental Protection Agency, Office of Research and Development Hydraulic Fracturing Study Fact Sheet. June 2010. *http://www.epa.gov/owindian/tribal/pdf/hydraulic-fracturing-fact-sheet.pdf*.

[8] "Hydraulic Fracturing and Safe Drinking Water Act Issues." Mary Tiemann, Adam Vann. Congressional Research Service, April 15, 2011, p. 1

[9] Colorado Oil and Gas Conservation Commission Fact Sheet *http://cogcc.state.co.us/library/GASLAND%20DOC.pdf*.

[10] "In North Dakota, Flames of Wasted Natural Gas Light the Prairie." Clifford Krauss, *New York Times*. September 26, 2011.

[11] "Worst Drought in More Than a Century Strikes Texas Oil Boom." Joe Carroll, *Bloomberg*, June 13, 2011.

[12] "Oil's Growing Thirst for Water." Russell Gold and Ana Campoy, *Wall Street Journal*. December 5, 2011.

[13] Texas Administrative Code, Title 16, Chapter 3, Rule §3.29.

[14] Testimony of Gerry Baker, Associate Executive Director of the Interstate Oil and Gas Compact Commission. Before the House Committee on Natural Resources, June 18, 2009, p. 2.

[15] Tiemann, Vann, p.7.

[16] The Energy Policy Act of 2005 (PL 109-58), Section 322.

[17] "More States Ordering Disclosure of Fracking Chemicals." Andrew Maykuth, *Philadelphia Enquirer*. January 22, 2012.

[18] "Wyoming Natural Gas Rules Point the Way for Public Disclosure of Chemicals Used." Mike Soraghan, *Greenwire*. December 20, 2010.

[19] "BLM Proposes More Disclosure than Most States." Mike Soraghan, *Greenwire*. February 6, 2012.

[20] "Cuomo: No Hydrofracking Funds in State Budget." Jon Campbell, *Ithaca Journal*. January 16, 2012.

[21] "Vermont Legislature Considers Ban on Hydrofracking." Terri Hallenbeck, *Burlington Free Press*. January 26, 2012.

[22] "Marcellus Shale Gas Drillers Recycling More Waste." Kevin Begos, *Associated Press*. February 17, 2012.

[23] "PA Drillers Told to Stop Sending Wastewater to Treatment Plants." Andrew Maykuth, *Philadelphia Inquirer*. April 20, 2011.

[24] "Company Cautions Linking Well, Ohio Quakes." Julie Carr Smith, *Columbus Dispatch*. January 12, 2012.

[25] "Pennsylvania Senate Approves Plan to Let Counties Tax Natural Gas Wells." Romy Varghese, *Bloomberg*. February 7, 2012.

[26] "Some States Unprepared for Shale Energy Boom." Dennis Cauchon, *USA Today*. February 23, 2012.

## About the Author

**Brydon Ross** joined CSG in January 2012 as the director of energy and environmental policy after nearly 11 years in Washington, D.C. He worked for the Senate Committee on Environment and Public Works as well as several U.S. senators across the Southeast on energy, natural resource development, environment, wetlands and agricultural policy issues. Most recently, he served as the director of government relations for the Association of Oil Pipe Lines (AOPL) before joining the staff of CSG.

Brydon is a graduate of the U.S. Naval War College with an M.A. in National Security and Strategic Studies and is a graduate of Centre College in Danville, Ky., with a B.A. in History.

# Chapter Ten

# STATE PAGES

# Table 10.1
## OFFICIAL NAMES OF STATES AND JURISDICTIONS, CAPITALS, ZIP CODES AND CENTRAL SWITCHBOARDS

| State or other jurisdiction | Name of state capitol (a) | Capital | Zip code | Area code | Central switchboard |
|---|---|---|---|---|---|
| Alabama, State of............................ | State House | Montgomery | 36130 | 334 | 242-7100 |
| Alaska, State of................................ | State Capitol | Juneau | 99801 | 907 | 465-2111 |
| Arizona, State of.............................. | State Capitol | Phoenix | 85007 | 602 | 542-1500 |
| Arkansas, State of............................ | State Capitol | Little Rock | 72201 | 501 | 682-3000 |
| California, State of .......................... | State Capitol | Sacramento | 95814 | 916 | 322-9900 |
| Colorado, State of............................ | State Capitol | Denver | 80203 | 303 | 866-5000 |
| Connecticut, State of........................ | State Capitol | Hartford | 06106 | 860 | 622-2200 |
| Delaware, State of............................ | Legislative Hall | Dover | 19903 | 800 | 464-4357 |
| Florida, State of............................... | The Capitol | Tallahassee | 32399 | 850 | 488-1234 |
| Georgia, State of.............................. | State Capitol | Atlanta | 30334 | 404 | 656-2000 |
| Hawaii, State of................................ | State Capitol | Honolulu | 96813 | 808 | 586-2211 |
| Idaho, State of.................................. | State Capitol | Boise | 83720 | 208 | 334-2411 |
| Illinois, State of............................... | State House | Springfield | 62706 | 217 | 782-2000 |
| Indiana, State of............................... | State House | Indianapolis | 46204 | 317 | 232-1000 |
| Iowa, State of................................... | State Capitol | Des Moines | 50319 | 515 | 281-5011 |
| Kansas, State of................................ | Statehouse | Topeka | 66612 | 785 | 296-0111 |
| Kentucky, Commonwealth of.............. | State Capitol | Frankfort | 40601 | 502 | 564-7680 |
| Louisiana, State of............................ | State Capitol | Baton Rouge | 70804 | 225 | 342-6600 |
| Maine, State of................................. | State House Station | Augusta | 04333 | 207 | 624-9494 |
| Maryland, State of............................ | State House | Annapolis | 21401 | 410 | 841-3000 |
| Massachusetts, Commonwealth of ...... | State House | Boston | 02133 | 617 | 727-2800 |
| Michigan, State of............................ | State Capitol | Lansing | 48909 | 517 | 373-1837 |
| Minnesota, State of........................... | State Capitol | St. Paul | 55155 | 651 | 296-8338 |
| Mississippi, State of.......................... | State Capitol | Jackson | 39215 | 601 | 359-1000 |
| Missouri, State of............................. | State Capitol | Jefferson City | 65101 | 573 | 751-2000 |
| Montana, State of ............................. | State Capitol | Helena | 59620 | 406 | 444-2511 |
| Nebraska, State of ............................ | State Capitol | Lincoln | 68509 | 402 | 471-2311 |
| Nevada, State of ............................... | State Capitol | Carson City | 89701 | 775 | 684-5670 |
| New Hampshire, State of ................... | State House | Concord | 03301 | 603 | 271-1110 |
| New Jersey, State of.......................... | State House | Trenton | 08625 | 609 | 292-6000 |
| New Mexico, State of........................ | State Capitol | Santa Fe | 87501 | 800 | 825-6639 |
| New York, State of............................ | State Capitol | Albany | 12224 | 518 | 474-2121 |
| North Carolina, State of.................... | State Capitol | Raleigh | 27601 | 919 | 733-1110 |
| North Dakota, State of ...................... | State Capitol | Bismarck | 58505 | 701 | 328-2000 |
| Ohio, State of................................... | Statehouse | Columbus | 43215 | 614 | 466-2000 |
| Oklahoma, State of............................ | State Capitol | Oklahoma City | 73105 | 405 | 521-2011 |
| Oregon, State of............................... | State Capitol | Salem | 97301 | 503 | 986-1000 |
| Pennsylvania, Commonwealth of ........ | Main Capitol Building | Harrisburg | 17120 | 717 | 787-2121 |
| Rhode Island and Providence Plantations, State of .............. | State House | Providence | 02903 | 401 | 222-2000 |
| South Carolina, State of.................... | State House | Columbia | 29211 | 803 | 896-0000 |
| South Dakota, State of ...................... | State Capitol | Pierre | 57501 | 605 | 773-3011 |
| Tennessee, State of........................... | State Capitol | Nashville | 37243 | 615 | 741-2001 |
| Texas, State of.................................. | State Capitol | Austin | 78701 | 512 | 463-4630 |
| Utah, State of................................... | State Capitol | Salt Lake City | 84114 | 801 | 538-3000 |
| Vermont, State of.............................. | State House | Montpelier | 05633 | 802 | 828-1110 |
| Virginia, Commonwealth of................ | State Capitol | Richmond | 23219 | 804 | 698-1470 |
| Washington, State of......................... | Legislative Building | Olympia | 98504 | 360 | 753-5000 |
| West Virginia, State of...................... | State Capitol | Charleston | 25305 | 304 | 558-3456 |
| Wisconsin, State of........................... | State Capitol | Madison | 53702 | 608 | 266-2211 |
| Wyoming, State of ............................ | State Capitol | Cheyenne | 82002 | 307 | 777-7011 |
| District of Columbia.......................... | District Building | . . . | 20004 | 202 | 727-1000 |
| American Samoa, Territory of............. | Maota Fono | Pago Pago | 96799 | 684 | 633-4116 |
| Guam, Territory of............................ | Congress Building | Hagatna | 96932 | 671 | 472-8931 |
| No. Mariana Islands, Commonwealth of ...... | Civic Center Building | Saipan | 96950 | 670 | 664-2282 |
| Puerto Rico, Commonwealth of.......... | The Capitol | San Juan | 00902 | 787 | 721-7000 |
| U.S. Virgin Islands, Territory of......... | Government House | Charlotte Amalie, St. Thomas | 00802 | 340 | 774-0001 |

(a) In some instances the name is not official.

## Table 10.2
## HISTORICAL DATA ON THE STATES

| State or other jurisdiction | Source of state lands | Date organized as territory | Date admitted to Union | Chronological order of admission to Union |
|---|---|---|---|---|
| Alabama | Mississippi Territory, 1798 (a) | March 3, 1817 | Dec. 14, 1819 | 22 |
| Alaska | Purchased from Russia, 1867 | Aug. 24, 1912 | Jan. 3, 1959 | 49 |
| Arizona | Ceded by Mexico, 1848 (b) | Feb. 24, 1863 | Feb. 14, 1912 | 48 |
| Arkansas | Louisiana Purchase, 1803 | March 2, 1819 | June 15, 1836 | 25 |
| California | Ceded by Mexico, 1848 | (c) | Sept. 9, 1850 | 31 |
| Colorado | Louisiana Purchase, 1803 (d) | Feb. 28, 1861 | Aug. 1, 1876 | 38 |
| Connecticut | Fundamental Orders, Jan. 14, 1638; Royal charter, April 23, 1662 | (e) | Jan. 9, 1788 (f) | 5 |
| Delaware | Swedish charter, 1638; English charter, 1638 | (e) | Dec. 7, 1787 (f) | 1 |
| Florida | Ceded by Spain, 1819 | March 30, 1822 | March 3, 1845 | 27 |
| Georgia | Charter, 1732, from George II to Trustees for Establishing the Colony of Georgia | (e) | Jan. 2, 1788 (f) | 4 |
| Hawaii | Annexed, 1898 | June 14, 1900 | Aug. 21, 1959 | 50 |
| Idaho | Treaty with Britain, 1846 | March 4, 1863 | July 3, 1890 | 43 |
| Illinois | Northwest Territory, 1787 | Feb. 3, 1809 | Dec. 3, 1818 | 21 |
| Indiana | Northwest Territory, 1787 | May 7, 1800 | Dec. 11, 1816 | 19 |
| Iowa | Louisiana Purchase, 1803 | June 12, 1838 | Dec. 28, 1846 | 29 |
| Kansas | Louisiana Purchase, 1803 (d) | May 30, 1854 | Jan. 29, 1861 | 34 |
| Kentucky | Part of Virginia until admitted as state | (c) | June 1, 1792 | 15 |
| Louisiana | Louisiana Purchase, 1803 (g) | March 26, 1804 | April 30, 1812 | 18 |
| Maine | Part of Massachusetts until admitted as state | (c) | March 15, 1820 | 23 |
| Maryland | Charter, 1632, from Charles I to Calvert | (e) | April 28, 1788 (f) | 7 |
| Massachusetts | Charter to Massachusetts Bay Company, 1629 | (e) | Feb. 6, 1788 (f) | 6 |
| Michigan | Northwest Territory, 1787 | Jan. 11, 1805 | Jan. 26, 1837 | 26 |
| Minnesota | Northwest Territory, 1787 (h) | March 3, 1849 | May 11, 1858 | 32 |
| Mississippi | Mississippi Territory (i) | April 7, 1798 | Dec. 10, 1817 | 20 |
| Missouri | Louisiana Purchase, 1803 | June 4, 1812 | Aug. 10, 1821 | 24 |
| Montana | Louisiana Purchase, 1803 (j) | May 26, 1864 | Nov. 8, 1889 | 41 |
| Nebraska | Louisiana Purchase, 1803 | May 30, 1854 | March 1, 1867 | 37 |
| Nevada | Ceded by Mexico, 1848 | March 2, 1861 | Oct. 31, 1864 | 36 |
| New Hampshire | Grants from Council for New England, 1622 and 1629; made Royal province, 1679 | (e) | June 21, 1788 (f) | 9 |
| New Jersey | Dutch settlement, 1618; English charter, 1664 | (e) | Dec. 18, 1787 (f) | 3 |
| New Mexico | Ceded by Mexico, 1848 (b) | Sept. 9, 1850 | Jan. 6, 1912 | 47 |
| New York | Dutch settlement, 1623; English control, 1664 | (e) | July 26, 1788 (f) | 11 |
| North Carolina | Charter, 1663, from Charles II | (e) | Nov. 21, 1789 (f) | 12 |
| North Dakota | Louisiana Purchase, 1803 (k) | March 2, 1861 | Nov. 2, 1889 | 39 |
| Ohio | Northwest Territory, 1787 | May 7, 1800 | March 1, 1803 | 17 |
| Oklahoma | Louisiana Purchase, 1803 | May 2, 1890 | Nov. 16, 1907 | 46 |
| Oregon | Settlement and treaty with Britain, 1846 | Aug. 14, 1848 | Feb. 14, 1859 | 33 |
| Pennsylvania | Grant from Charles II to William Penn, 1681 | (e) | Dec. 12, 1787 (f) | 2 |
| Rhode Island | Charter, 1663, from Charles II | (e) | May 29, 1790 (f) | 13 |
| South Carolina | Charter, 1663, from Charles II | (e) | May 23, 1788 (f) | 8 |
| South Dakota | Louisiana Purchase, 1803 | March 2, 1861 | Nov. 2, 1889 | 40 |
| Tennessee | Part of North Carolina until land ceded to U.S. in 1789 | June 8, 1790 (l) | June 1, 1796 | 16 |
| Texas | Republic of Texas, 1845 | (c) | Dec. 29, 1845 | 28 |
| Utah | Ceded by Mexico, 1848 | Sept. 9, 1850 | Jan. 4, 1896 | 45 |
| Vermont | From lands of New Hampshire and New York | (c) | March 4, 1791 | 14 |
| Virginia | Charter, 1609, from James I to London Company | (e) | June 25, 1788 (f) | 10 |
| Washington | Oregon Territory, 1848 | March 2, 1853 | Nov. 11, 1889 | 42 |
| West Virginia | Part of Virginia until admitted as state | (c) | June 20, 1863 | 35 |
| Wisconsin | Northwest Territory, 1787 | April 20, 1836 | May 29, 1848 | 30 |
| Wyoming | Louisiana Purchase, 1803 (d)(j) | July 25, 1868 | July 10, 1890 | 44 |
| Dist. of Columbia | Maryland (m) | ... | ... | ... |
| American Samoa | ......................Became a territory, 1900...................... | | | |
| Guam | Ceded by Spain, 1898 | Aug. 1, 1950 | ... | ... |
| No. Mariana Islands | ... | March 24, 1976 | ... | ... |
| Puerto Rico | Ceded by Spain, 1898 | ... | July 25, 1952 (n) | ... |
| U.S. Virgin Islands | ......................Purchased from Denmark, March 31, 1917...................... | | | |

See footnotes at end of table.

# HISTORICAL DATA ON THE STATES — Continued

*Key*:

(a) By the Treaty of Paris, 1783, England gave up claim to the 13 original Colonies, and to all land within an area extending along the present Canadian to the Lake of the Woods, down the Mississippi River to the 31st parallel, east to the Chattahoochee, down that river to the mouth of the Flint, border east to the source of the St. Mary's down that river to the ocean. The major part of Alabama was acquired by the Treaty of Paris, and the lower portion from Spain in 1813.

(b) Portion of land obtained by Gadsden Purchase, 1853.

(c) No territorial status before admission to Union.

(d) Portion of land ceded by Mexico, 1848.

(e) One of the original 13 Colonies.

(f) Date of ratification of U.S. Constitution.

(g) West Feliciana District (Baton Rouge) acquired from Spain, 1810; added to Louisiana, 1812.

(h) Portion of land obtained by Louisiana Purchase, 1803.

(i) See footnote (a). The lower portion of Mississippi also was acquired from Spain in 1813.

(j) Portion of land obtained from Oregon Territory, 1848.

(k) The northern portion of the Red River Valley was acquired by treaty with Great Britain in 1818.

(l) Date Southwest Territory (identical boundary as Tennessee's) was created.

(m) Area was originally 100 square miles, taken from Virginia and Maryland. Virginia's portion south of the Potomac was given back to that state in 1846. Site chosen in 1790, city incorporated 1802.

(n) On this date, Puerto Rico became a self-governing commonwealth by compact approved by the U.S. Congress and the voters of Puerto Rico as provided in U.S. Public Law 600 of 1950.

# Table 10.3
## STATE STATISTICS

| State or other jurisdiction | Land area — In square miles | Land area — Rank in nation | Population (a) — Size | Population (a) — Rank in nation | Percentage change 2001 to 2011 | Density per square mile | Rank in nation | Number of Representatives in Congress | Capital | Population (b) | Largest city | Rank in state | Population (b) |
|---|---|---|---|---|---|---|---|---|---|---|---|---|---|
| Alabama | 50,645 | 28 | 4,802,740 | 23 | 7.6 | 94.8 | 27 | 7 | Montgomery | 205,764 | Birmingham | 2 | 212,237 |
| Alaska | 570,641 | 1 | 722,718 | 47 | 13.8 | 1.3 | 50 | 1 | Juneau | 31,275 | Anchorage (d) | 3 | 291,826 |
| Arizona | 113,594 | 6 | 6,482,505 | 16 | 22.1 | 57.1 | 33 | 9 | Phoenix | 1,445,632 | Phoenix | 1 | 1,445,632 |
| Arkansas | 52,035 | 27 | 2,937,979 | 32 | 9.1 | 56.5 | 34 | 4 | Little Rock | 193,524 | Little Rock | 1 | 193,524 |
| California | 155,779 | 3 | 37,691,912 | 1 | 9.2 | 242.0 | 11 | 53 | Sacramento | 466,488 | Los Angeles | 6 | 3,792,621 |
| Colorado | 103,642 | 8 | 5,116,796 | 22 | 15.8 | 49.4 | 37 | 7 | Denver | 600,158 | Denver | 1 | 600,158 |
| Connecticut | 4,842 | 48 | 3,580,709 | 29 | 4.5 | 739.5 | 4 | 5 | Hartford | 124,775 | Bridgeport | 3 | 144,229 |
| Delaware | 1,949 | 49 | 907,135 | 45 | 13.9 | 465.5 | 6 | 1 | Dover | 36,047 | Wilmington | 2 | 70,851 |
| Florida | 53,625 | 26 | 19,057,542 | 4 | 16.2 | 355.4 | 8 | 27 | Tallahassee | 181,376 | Jacksonville | 7 | 821,784 |
| Georgia | 57,513 | 21 | 9,815,210 | 9 | 17.1 | 170.7 | 18 | 14 | Atlanta | 420,003 | Atlanta | 1 | 420,003 |
| Hawaii | 6,423 | 47 | 1,374,810 | 40 | 12.3 | 214.1 | 13 | 2 | Honolulu | 337,256 | Honolulu | 1 | 337,256 |
| Idaho | 82,643 | 11 | 1,584,985 | 39 | 20.0 | 19.2 | 44 | 2 | Boise | 205,671 | Boise | 1 | 205,671 |
| Illinois | 55,519 | 24 | 12,869,257 | 5 | 3.1 | 231.8 | 12 | 18 | Springfield | 116,250 | Chicago | 6 | 2,695,598 |
| Indiana | 35,826 | 38 | 6,516,922 | 15 | 6.6 | 181.9 | 16 | 9 | Indianapolis | 829,718 | Indianapolis | 1 | 829,718 |
| Iowa | 55,857 | 23 | 3,062,309 | 30 | 4.8 | 54.8 | 36 | 4 | Des Moines | 203,433 | Des Moines | 1 | 203,433 |
| Kansas | 81,759 | 13 | 2,871,238 | 33 | 6.6 | 35.1 | 40 | 4 | Topeka | 127,473 | Wichita | 4 | 382,368 |
| Kentucky | 39,486 | 37 | 4,369,356 | 26 | 7.5 | 110.7 | 22 | 6 | Frankfort | 25,527 | Louisville (e) | 14 | 741,096 |
| Louisiana | 43,204 | 33 | 4,574,836 | 25 | 2.5 | 105.9 | 23 | 6 | Baton Rouge | 229,493 | New Orleans | 2 | 343,829 |
| Maine | 30,843 | 39 | 1,328,188 | 41 | 3.2 | 43.1 | 38 | 2 | Augusta | 19,136 | Portland | 9 | 66,194 |
| Maryland | 9,707 | 42 | 5,828,289 | 19 | 8.4 | 600.4 | 5 | 8 | Annapolis | 38,394 | Baltimore | 7 | 620,961 |
| Massachusetts | 7,800 | 45 | 6,587,536 | 14 | 3.3 | 844.5 | 3 | 9 | Boston | 617,594 | Boston | 1 | 617,594 |
| Michigan | 56,539 | 22 | 9,876,187 | 8 | -1.1 | 174.7 | 17 | 14 | Lansing | 114,297 | Detroit | 5 | 713,777 |
| Minnesota | 79,627 | 14 | 5,344,861 | 21 | 7.5 | 67.1 | 31 | 8 | St. Paul | 285,068 | Minneapolis | 2 | 382,578 |
| Mississippi | 46,923 | 31 | 2,978,512 | 31 | 4.2 | 63.5 | 32 | 4 | Jackson | 173,514 | Jackson | 1 | 173,514 |
| Missouri | 68,742 | 18 | 6,010,688 | 18 | 6.8 | 87.4 | 28 | 8 | Jefferson City | 43,079 | Kansas City | 15 | 459,787 |
| Montana | 145,546 | 4 | 998,199 | 44 | 10.4 | 6.9 | 48 | 1 | Helena | 28,190 | Billings | 6 | 104,170 |
| Nebraska | 76,824 | 15 | 1,842,641 | 38 | 7.6 | 24.0 | 43 | 3 | Lincoln | 258,379 | Omaha | 2 | 408,958 |
| Nevada | 109,781 | 7 | 2,723,322 | 35 | 29.3 | 24.8 | 42 | 4 | Carson City | 55,274 | Las Vegas | 6 | 583,756 |
| New Hampshire | 8,953 | 44 | 1,318,194 | 42 | 4.7 | 147.2 | 21 | 2 | Concord | 42,695 | Manchester | 3 | 109,565 |
| New Jersey | 7,354 | 46 | 8,821,155 | 11 | 4.0 | 1,199.5 | 1 | 12 | Trenton | 84,913 | Newark | 10 | 277,140 |
| New Mexico | 121,298 | 5 | 2,082,224 | 36 | 13.8 | 17.2 | 45 | 3 | Santa Fe | 67,947 | Albuquerque | 4 | 545,852 |
| New York | 47,126 | 30 | 19,465,197 | 3 | 2.4 | 413.0 | 7 | 27 | Albany | 97,856 | New York City | 6 | 8,175,133 |
| North Carolina | 48,618 | 29 | 9,656,401 | 10 | 18.0 | 198.6 | 15 | 13 | Raleigh | 403,892 | Charlotte | 2 | 731,424 |
| North Dakota | 69,001 | 17 | 683,932 | 48 | 7.8 | 9.9 | 47 | 1 | Bismarck | 61,272 | Fargo | 2 | 105,549 |
| Ohio | 40,861 | 35 | 11,544,951 | 7 | 1.5 | 282.5 | 10 | 16 | Columbus | 787,033 | Columbus | 1 | 787,033 |
| Oklahoma | 68,595 | 19 | 3,791,508 | 28 | 9.6 | 55.3 | 35 | 5 | Oklahoma City | 579,999 | Oklahoma City | 1 | 579,999 |
| Oregon | 95,988 | 10 | 3,871,859 | 27 | 11.5 | 40.3 | 39 | 5 | Salem | 154,637 | Portland | 3 | 583,776 |
| Pennsylvania | 44,743 | 32 | 12,742,886 | 6 | 3.7 | 284.8 | 9 | 18 | Harrisburg | 49,528 | Philadelphia (f) | 15 | 1,526,006 |
| Rhode Island | 1,034 | 50 | 1,051,302 | 43 | -0.7 | 1,016.9 | 2 | 2 | Providence | 178,042 | Providence | 1 | 178,042 |
| South Carolina | 30,061 | 40 | 4,679,230 | 24 | 15.2 | 155.7 | 19 | 7 | Columbia | 129,272 | Columbia | 1 | 129,272 |

See footnotes at end of table.

# STATE STATISTICS — Continued

| State or other jurisdiction | Land area | | Population (a) | | Percentage change 2001 to 2011 | Density per square mile | Rank in nation | Number of Representatives in Congress | Capital | Population (b) | Rank in state | Largest city | Population (b) |
|---|---|---|---|---|---|---|---|---|---|---|---|---|---|
| | In square miles | Rank in nation | Size | Rank in nation | | | | | | | | | |
| South Dakota........ | 75,811 | 16 | 824,082 | 46 | 8.9 | 10.9 | 46 | 1 | Pierre | 13,646 | 8 | Sioux Falls | 153,888 |
| Tennessee............ | 41,235 | 34 | 6,403,353 | 17 | 11.6 | 155.3 | 20 | 9 | Nashville (g) | 626,681 | 2 | Memphis | 646,889 |
| Texas.................. | 261,232 | 2 | 25,674,681 | 2 | 20.4 | 98.3 | 26 | 36 | Austin | 790,390 | 4 | Houston | 2,099,451 |
| Utah................... | 82,170 | 12 | 2,817,222 | 34 | 24.1 | 34.3 | 41 | 4 | Salt Lake City | 186,440 | 1 | Salt Lake City | 186,440 |
| Vermont............... | 9,217 | 43 | 626,431 | 49 | 2.2 | 68.0 | 30 | 1 | Montpelier | 7,855 | 15 | Burlington | 42,417 |
| Virginia............... | 39,490 | 36 | 8,096,604 | 12 | 12.6 | 205.0 | 14 | 11 | Richmond | 204,214 | 4 | Virginia Beach | 437,994 |
| Washington........... | 66,456 | 20 | 6,830,038 | 13 | 14.1 | 102.8 | 25 | 10 | Olympia | 46,478 | 18 | Seattle | 608,660 |
| West Virginia........ | 24,038 | 41 | 1,855,364 | 37 | 3.0 | 77.2 | 29 | 3 | Charleston | 51,400 | 1 | Charleston | 51,400 |
| Wisconsin............ | 54,158 | 25 | 5,711,767 | 20 | 5.7 | 105.5 | 24 | 8 | Madison | 233,209 | 2 | Milwaukee | 594,833 |
| Wyoming.............. | 97,093 | 9 | 568,158 | 50 | 14.9 | 5.9 | 49 | 1 | Cheyenne | 59,466 | 1 | Cheyenne | 59,466 |
| Dist. of Columbia ...... | 61 | ... | 617,996 | ... | 8.1 | 10,131.1 | ... | 1 (h) | ... | | | ... | |
| American Samoa ........ | 77 | ... | 55,519 (b) | ... | -3.1 (c) | 721.0 | ... | 1 (h) | Pago Pago | 3,656 | 3 | Tafuna | 7,945 |
| Guam ................ | 210 | ... | 159,358 (b) | ... | -2.9 (c) | 758.8 | ... | 1 (h) | Hagatna (d) | 1,051 | 13 | Dededo (d) | 44,943 |
| No. Mariana Islands .... | 179 | ... | 53,883 (b) | ... | -22.2 (c) | 301.0 | ... | 1 (h) | Saipan (d) | 48,220 | 1 | Saipan (d) | 48,220 |
| Puerto Rico............ | 3,424 | ... | 3,706,690 | ... | -3.5 | 1,082.6 | ... | 1 (i) | San Juan | 381,931 | 1 | San Juan | 381,931 |
| U.S. Virgin Islands........ | 134 | ... | 106,405 (b) | ... | -2.0 (c) | 794.1 | ... | 1 (h) | Charlotte Amalie, St. Thomas | 18,481 | 1 | Charlotte Amalie, St. Thomas | 18,481 |

*Source:* U.S. Census Bureau.

*Key:*
... — Not applicable.
(a) July 1, 2011 Census Bureau estimates.
(b) 2010 Census Bureau counts.
(c) Population change calculations are from 2000–2010.

(d) Municipality.
(e) This city is part of a consolidated city-county government and is coextensive with Jefferson County.
(f) Philadelphia County and Philadelphia city are coextensive.
(g) This city is part of a consolidated city-county government and is coextensive with Davidson County.
(h) Represented by one non-voting House Delegate.
(i) Represented by one non-voting House Resident Commissioner.

**Table 10.4**
**PER CAPITA PERSONAL INCOME, PERSONAL INCOME, AND POPULATION, BY STATE AND REGION, 2010–2011**

| State or other jurisdiction | Per capita personal income (dollars) | | | | | | | | Personal income (millions of dollars) | | | | Population (thousands of persons) | | | |
|---|---|---|---|---|---|---|---|---|---|---|---|---|---|---|---|---|
| | 2010r | 2011p | Rank in the U.S. 2010r | Rank in the U.S. 2011p | Percent of the U.S. 2010r | Percent of the U.S. 2011p | Percent change 2010–11 | Rank of percent change 2010–11 | 2010r | 2011p | Percent change 2010–11 | Rank of percent change 2010–11 | 2010r | 2011p | Percent change 2010–11 | Rank of percent change 2010–11 |
| United States | $39,937 | $41,663 | -- | -- | 100 | 100 | 4.3 | -- | $12,353,577 | $12,981,741 | 5.1 | -- | 309,330.00 | 311,592.00 | 0.7 | -- |
| Alabama | 33,504 | 34,650 | 42 | 42 | 84 | 83 | 3.4 | 46 | 160,332 | 166,414 | 3.8 | 49 | 4,785 | 4,803 | 0.4 | 35 |
| Alaska | 44,233 | 45,529 | 8 | 10 | 111 | 109 | 2.9 | 50 | 31,589 | 32,905 | 4.2 | 46 | 714 | 723 | 1.2 | 6 |
| Arizona | 34,539 | 35,875 | 40 | 40 | 86 | 86 | 3.9 | 36 | 221,503 | 232,560 | 5.0 | 24 | 6,413 | 6,483 | 1.1 | 8 |
| Arkansas | 32,805 | 34,014 | 44 | 44 | 82 | 82 | 3.7 | 42 | 95,844 | 99,933 | 4.3 | 43 | 2,922 | 2,938 | 0.6 | 29 |
| California | 42,514 | 44,481 | 13 | 12 | 106 | 107 | 4.6 | 14 | 1,587,404 | 1,676,565 | 5.6 | 9 | 37,338 | 37,692 | 0.9 | 11 |
| Colorado | 42,295 | 44,088 | 14 | 15 | 106 | 106 | 4.2 | 25 | 213,494 | 225,591 | 5.7 | 8 | 5,048 | 5,117 | 1.4 | 4 |
| Connecticut | 54,239 | 56,889 | 1 | 1 | 136 | 137 | 4.9 | 10 | 193,932 | 203,703 | 5.0 | 21 | 3,575 | 3,581 | 0.1 | 43 |
| Delaware | 40,097 | 41,635 | 20 | 20 | 100 | 100 | 3.8 | 38 | 36,079 | 37,769 | 4.7 | 31 | 900 | 907 | 0.8 | 19 |
| Florida | 38,210 | 39,563 | 25 | 27 | 96 | 95 | 3.5 | 45 | 719,828 | 753,983 | 4.7 | 29 | 18,839 | 19,058 | 1.2 | 7 |
| Georgia | 34,747 | 36,104 | 38 | 39 | 87 | 87 | 3.9 | 35 | 337,468 | 354,372 | 5.0 | 23 | 9,712 | 9,815 | 1.1 | 9 |
| Hawaii | 41,550 | 43,053 | 17 | 17 | 104 | 103 | 3.6 | 43 | 56,647 | 59,190 | 4.5 | 38 | 1,363 | 1,375 | 0.8 | 17 |
| Idaho | 31,897 | 33,326 | 49 | 49 | 80 | 80 | 4.5 | 21 | 50,114 | 52,821 | 5.4 | 11 | 1,571 | 1,585 | 0.9 | 15 |
| Illinois | 42,040 | 44,140 | 15 | 14 | 105 | 106 | 5.0 | 8 | 539,880 | 568,049 | 5.2 | 16 | 12,842 | 12,869 | 0.2 | 41 |
| Indiana | 33,981 | 35,550 | 41 | 41 | 85 | 85 | 4.6 | 15 | 220,555 | 231,674 | 5.0 | 20 | 6,491 | 6,517 | 0.4 | 33 |
| Iowa | 38,039 | 40,470 | 26 | 24 | 95 | 97 | 6.4 | 2 | 116,027 | 123,933 | 6.8 | 2 | 3,050 | 3,062 | 0.4 | 34 |
| Kansas | 38,977 | 40,481 | 23 | 23 | 98 | 97 | 3.9 | 37 | 111,441 | 116,230 | 4.3 | 42 | 2,859 | 2,871 | 0.4 | 32 |
| Kentucky | 32,316 | 33,667 | 47 | 47 | 81 | 81 | 4.2 | 27 | 140,483 | 147,103 | 4.7 | 30 | 4,347 | 4,369 | 0.5 | 30 |
| Louisiana | 37,039 | 38,578 | 28 | 28 | 93 | 93 | 4.2 | 28 | 168,356 | 176,489 | 4.8 | 27 | 4,545 | 4,575 | 0.6 | 26 |
| Maine | 36,763 | 37,973 | 31 | 31 | 92 | 91 | 3.3 | 49 | 48,799 | 50,435 | 3.4 | 50 | 1,327 | 1,328 | 0.1 | 46 |
| Maryland | 49,023 | 51,038 | 4 | 4 | 123 | 123 | 4.1 | 29 | 283,634 | 297,465 | 4.9 | 26 | 5,786 | 5,828 | 0.7 | 21 |
| Massachusetts | 51,304 | 53,621 | 2 | 2 | 128 | 129 | 4.5 | 19 | 336,320 | 353,228 | 5.0 | 22 | 6,555 | 6,588 | 0.5 | 31 |
| Michigan | 34,714 | 36,533 | 39 | 36 | 87 | 88 | 5.2 | 5 | 342,874 | 360,806 | 5.2 | 15 | 9,877 | 9,876 | -- | 49 |
| Minnesota | 42,798 | 44,672 | 11 | 11 | 107 | 107 | 4.4 | 23 | 227,288 | 238,768 | 5.1 | 19 | 5,311 | 5,345 | 0.6 | 27 |
| Mississippi | 31,071 | 32,176 | 50 | 50 | 78 | 77 | 3.6 | 44 | 92,284 | 95,835 | 3.8 | 48 | 2,970 | 2,979 | 0.3 | 38 |
| Missouri | 36,799 | 38,248 | 30 | 29 | 92 | 92 | 3.9 | 33 | 220,635 | 229,898 | 4.2 | 45 | 5,996 | 6,011 | 0.2 | 39 |
| Montana | 35,053 | 36,573 | 35 | 35 | 88 | 88 | 4.3 | 24 | 34,736 | 36,507 | 5.1 | 18 | 991 | 998 | 0.7 | 22 |
| Nebraska | 39,534 | 41,584 | 21 | 22 | 99 | 100 | 5.2 | 7 | 72,353 | 76,624 | 5.9 | 6 | 1,830 | 1,843 | 0.7 | 25 |
| Nevada | 36,938 | 38,173 | 29 | 30 | 92 | 92 | 3.3 | 47 | 99,892 | 103,957 | 4.1 | 47 | 2,704 | 2,723 | 0.7 | 24 |
| New Hampshire | 43,698 | 45,787 | 9 | 8 | 109 | 110 | 4.8 | 12 | 57,542 | 60,356 | 4.9 | 25 | 1,317 | 1,318 | 0.1 | 44 |
| New Jersey | 51,139 | 53,181 | 3 | 3 | 128 | 128 | 4.0 | 32 | 450,004 | 469,115 | 4.2 | 44 | 8,800 | 8,821 | 0.2 | 40 |
| New Mexico | 33,342 | 34,575 | 43 | 43 | 83 | 83 | 3.7 | 41 | 68,882 | 71,993 | 4.5 | 37 | 2,066 | 2,082 | 0.8 | 20 |
| New York | 48,596 | 50,545 | 5 | 5 | 122 | 121 | 4.0 | 30 | 942,523 | 983,868 | 4.4 | 39 | 19,395 | 19,465 | 0.4 | 36 |
| North Carolina | 35,007 | 36,164 | 36 | 38 | 88 | 87 | 3.3 | 48 | 334,677 | 349,212 | 4.3 | 40 | 9,560 | 9,656 | 1.0 | 10 |
| North Dakota | 42,890 | 45,747 | 10 | 9 | 107 | 110 | 6.7 | 1 | 28,935 | 31,288 | 8.1 | 1 | 675 | 684 | 1.4 | 3 |
| Ohio | 36,162 | 37,791 | 33 | 33 | 91 | 91 | 4.5 | 20 | 417,235 | 436,297 | 4.6 | 36 | 11,538 | 11,545 | 0.1 | 47 |
| Oklahoma | 35,389 | 37,277 | 34 | 34 | 89 | 89 | 5.3 | 3 | 133,070 | 141,335 | 6.2 | 4 | 3,760 | 3,792 | 0.8 | 18 |
| Oregon | 36,317 | 37,909 | 32 | 32 | 91 | 91 | 4.4 | 22 | 139,395 | 146,778 | 5.3 | 14 | 3,838 | 3,872 | 0.9 | 16 |
| Pennsylvania | 40,604 | 42,478 | 18 | 18 | 102 | 102 | 4.6 | 17 | 516,390 | 541,297 | 4.8 | 28 | 12,718 | 12,743 | 0.2 | 42 |
| Rhode Island | 41,995 | 43,992 | 16 | 16 | 105 | 106 | 4.8 | 13 | 44,200 | 46,248 | 4.6 | 35 | 1,053 | 1,051 | (0.1) | 50 |
| South Carolina | 32,462 | 33,673 | 46 | 46 | 81 | 81 | 3.7 | 40 | 150,528 | 157,565 | 4.7 | 32 | 4,637 | 4,679 | 0.9 | 13 |

See footnotes at end of table.

# PER CAPITA PERSONAL INCOME, PERSONAL INCOME, AND POPULATION, BY STATE AND REGION, 2010–2011—Continued

| State or other jurisdiction | Per capita personal income (dollars) | | | | | | | | Personal income (millions of dollars) | | | | Population (thousands of persons) | | | |
| --- | --- | --- | --- | --- | --- | --- | --- | --- | --- | --- | --- | --- | --- | --- | --- | --- |
| | | | Rank in the U.S. | | Percent of the U.S. | | Percent change 2010–11 | Rank of percent change 2010–11 | | | Percent change 2010–11 | Rank of percent change 2010–11 | | | Percent change 2010–11 | Rank of percent change 2010–11 |
| | 2010r | 2011p | 2010r | 2011p | 2010r | 2011p | | | 2010r | 2011p | | | 2010r | 2011p | | |
| South Dakota......... | 39,519 | 41,590 | 22 | 21 | 99 | 100 | 5.2 | 4 | 32,271 | 34,274 | 6.2 | 5 | 817 | 824 | 0.9 | 12 |
| Tennessee ............. | 34,921 | 36,533 | 37 | 36 | 87 | 88 | 4.6 | 16 | 222,007 | 233,933 | 5.4 | 12 | 6,357 | 6,403 | 0.7 | 23 |
| Texas..................... | 37,747 | 39,593 | 27 | 26 | 95 | 95 | 4.9 | 9 | 953,254 | 1,016,529 | 6.6 | 3 | 25,253 | 25,675 | 1.7 | 1 |
| Utah...................... | 32,517 | 33,790 | 45 | 45 | 81 | 81 | 3.9 | 34 | 90,250 | 95,194 | 5.5 | 10 | 2,775 | 2,817 | 1.5 | 2 |
| Vermont................ | 40,134 | 41,832 | 19 | 19 | 100 | 100 | 4.2 | 26 | 25,120 | 26,205 | 4.3 | 41 | 626 | 626 | 0.1 | 45 |
| Virginia................. | 44,267 | 45,920 | 7 | 7 | 111 | 110 | 3.7 | 39 | 355,193 | 371,796 | 4.7 | 33 | 8,024 | 8,097 | 0.9 | 14 |
| Washington........... | 42,589 | 44,294 | 12 | 13 | 107 | 106 | 4.0 | 31 | 287,175 | 302,529 | 5.3 | 13 | 6,743 | 6,830 | 1.3 | 5 |
| West Virginia......... | 32,042 | 33,513 | 48 | 48 | 80 | 80 | 4.6 | 18 | 59,417 | 62,178 | 4.6 | 34 | 1,854 | 1,855 | 0.1 | 48 |
| Wisconsin............. | 38,225 | 40,073 | 24 | 25 | 96 | 96 | 4.8 | 11 | 217,562 | 228,888 | 5.2 | 17 | 5,692 | 5,712 | 0.4 | 37 |
| Wyoming .............. | 44,961 | 47,301 | 6 | 6 | 113 | 114 | 5.2 | 6 | 25,383 | 26,875 | 5.9 | 7 | 565 | 568 | 0.6 | 28 |
| Dist. of Columbia ... | 70,710 | 73,105 | -- | -- | 177 | 175 | 3.4 | -- | 42,773 | 45,178 | 5.6 | -- | 605 | 618 | 2.2 | -- |

*Source:* U.S. Bureau of Economic Analysis and Bureau of the Census, released March 23 and March 25, 2011.
*Key:*
r — revised
p — preliminary

# Alabama

| | |
|---|---|
| Nickname | The Heart of Dixie |
| Motto | *Aldemus Jura Nostra Defendere* |
| | (We Dare Defend Our Rights) |
| Flower | Camellia |
| Bird | Yellowhammer |
| Tree | Southern (Longleaf) Pine |
| Song | *Alabama* |
| Entered the Union | December 14, 1819 |
| Capital | Montgomery |

## STATISTICS

| | |
|---|---|
| Land Area (square miles) | 50,645 |
| Rank in Nation | 28th |
| Population | 4,802,740 |
| Rank in Nation | 23rd |
| Density per square mile | 94.8 |
| Capital City | Montgomery |
| Population | 205,764 |
| Rank in State | 2nd |
| Largest City | Birmingham |
| Population | 212,237 |
| Number of Representatives in Congress | 7 |
| Number of 2012 Electoral Votes | 9 |
| Number of County Governments | 67 |
| Number of Municipal Governments | 458 |
| Number of School Districts | 131 |
| Number of Special Districts | 529 |

## LEGISLATIVE BRANCH

| | |
|---|---|
| Legislative Body | Legislature |
| President of the Senate | Lt. Gov. Kay Ivey |
| President Pro Tem of the Senate | Del Marsh |
| Secretary of the Senate | D. Patrick Harris |
| Speaker of the House | Mike Hubbard |
| Speaker Pro Tem of the House | Victor Gaston |
| Clerk of the House | Greg Pappas |
| 2012 Regular Session | Feb. 7 – mid-May, 2012 |
| Number of Senatorial Districts | 35 |
| Number of Representative Districts | 105 |

## EXECUTIVE BRANCH

| | |
|---|---|
| Governor | Robert J. Bentley |
| Lieutenant Governor | Kay Ivey |
| Secretary of State | Beth Chapman |
| Attorney General | Luther Strange |
| Treasurer | Young Boozer |
| Auditor | Samantha Shaw |
| State Comptroller | Tom White |
| Governor's Present Term | 1/2011 – 1/2015 |
| Number of Elected Officials in the Executive Branch | 7 |
| Number of Members in the Cabinet | 25 |

## JUDICIAL BRANCH

| | |
|---|---|
| Highest Court | Supreme Court |
| Supreme Court Chief Justice | Charles R. Malone |
| Number of Supreme Court Judges | 9 |
| Number of Intermediate Appellate Court Judges | 10 |
| Number of U.S. Court Districts | 3 |
| U.S. Circuit Court | 11th Circuit |

## STATE INTERNET ADDRESSES

| | |
|---|---|
| Official State Website | http://www.alabama.gov |
| Governor's Website | http://www.governor.alabama.gov |
| State Legislative Website | http://www.legislature.state.al.us |
| State Judicial Website | http://www.judicial.alabama.gov |

# Alaska

| | |
|---|---|
| Nickname | The Last Frontier |
| Motto | *North to the Future* |
| Flower | Forget-Me-Not |
| Bird | Willow Ptarmigan |
| Tree | Sitka Spruce |
| Song | *Alaska's Flag* |
| Entered the Union | January 3, 1959 |
| Capital | Juneau |

## STATISTICS

| | |
|---|---|
| Land Area (square miles) | 570,641 |
| Rank in Nation | 1st |
| Population | 722,718 |
| Rank in Nation | 47th |
| Density per square mile | 1.3 |
| Capital City | Juneau |
| Population | 31,275 |
| Rank in State | 3rd |
| Largest City | Anchorage |
| Population | 291,826 |
| Number of Representatives in Congress | 1 |
| Number of 2012 Electoral Votes | 3 |
| Number of Geographic Boroughs | 16 |
| Number of County Governments | 11 |
| Number of Consolidated Governments | 5 |
| Number of Municipal Governments | 148 |
| Number of School Districts | 0 |
| Number of Special Districts | 15 |

## LEGISLATIVE BRANCH

| | |
|---|---|
| Legislative Body | Legislature |
| President of the Senate | Gary Stevens |
| Secretary of the Senate | Kirsten Waid |
| Speaker of the House | Mike Chenault |
| Chief Clerk of the House | Suzanne Lowell |
| 2012 Regular Session | Jan. 17 – April 15, 2012 |
| Number of Senatorial Districts | 20 |
| Number of Representative Districts | 40 |

## EXECUTIVE BRANCH

| | |
|---|---|
| Governor | Sean Parnell |
| Lieutenant Governor | Mead Treadwell |
| Attorney General | Michael C. Geraghty |
| Treasurer | Angela Rodell |
| Auditor | Kris Curtis |
| Comptroller | Scot Arehart |
| Governor's Present Term | 7/2009 – 12/2014 |
| Number of Elected Officials in the Executive Branch | 2 |
| Number of Members in the Cabinet | 19 |

## JUDICIAL BRANCH

| | |
|---|---|
| Highest Court | Supreme Court |
| Supreme Court Chief Justice | Walter Carpeneti |
| Number of Supreme Court Judges | 5 |
| Number of Intermediate Appellate Court Judges | 3 |
| Number of U.S. Court Districts | 1 |
| U.S. Circuit Court | 9th Circuit |

## STATE INTERNET ADDRESSES

| | |
|---|---|
| Official State Website | http://www.alaska.gov |
| Governor's Website | http://www.gov.state.ak.us |
| State Legislative Website | http://www.legis.state.ak.us |
| State Judicial Website | http://www.courts.ak.gov |

# Arizona

| | |
|---|---|
| Nickname | The Grand Canyon State |
| Motto | *Ditat Deus* (God Enriches) |
| Flower | Blossom of the Saguaro Cactus |
| Bird | Cactus Wren |
| Tree | Palo Verde |
| Songs | *Arizona March Song* and *Arizona* |
| Entered the Union | February 14, 1912 |
| Capital | Phoenix |

## STATISTICS

| | |
|---|---|
| Land Area (square miles) | 113,594 |
| Rank in Nation | 6th |
| Population | 6,482,505 |
| Rank in Nation | 16th |
| Density per square mile | 57.1 |
| Capital City | Phoenix |
| Population | 1,445,632 |
| Rank in State | 1st |
| Largest City | Phoenix |
| Number Representatives in Congress | 9 |
| Number of 2012 Electoral Votes | 11 |
| Number of County Governments | 15 |
| Number of Municipal Governments | 90 |
| Number of School Districts | 239 |
| Number of Special Districts | 301 |

## LEGISLATIVE BRANCH

| | |
|---|---|
| Legislative Body | Legislature |
| President of the Senate | Steve Pierce |
| President Pro Tem of the Senate | Sylvia Allen |
| Secretary of the Senate | Charmion Billington |
| Speaker of the House | Andy Tobin |
| Speaker Pro Tem of the House | Steve Montenegro |
| Chief Clerk of the House | Cheryl Laube |
| 2012 Regular Session | Jan. 10 – mid-April 2012 |
| Number of Senatorial Districts | 30 |
| Number of Representative Districts | 30 |

## EXECUTIVE BRANCH

| | |
|---|---|
| Governor | Jan Brewer |
| Secretary of State | Ken Bennett |
| Attorney General | Tom Horne |
| Treasurer | Doug Ducey |
| Auditor | Debra K. Davenport |
| Comptroller | D. Clark Partridge |
| Governor's Present Term | 1/2009 – 1/2015 |
| Number of Elected Officials in the Executive Branch | 11 |
| Number of Members in the Cabinet | 38 |

## JUDICIAL BRANCH

| | |
|---|---|
| Highest Court | Supreme Court |
| Supreme Court Chief Justice | Rebecca White Berch |
| Number of Supreme Court Judges | 5 |
| Number of Intermediate Appellate Court Judges | 22 |
| Number of U.S. Court Districts | 1 |
| U.S. Circuit Court | 9th Circuit |

## STATE INTERNET ADDRESSES

| | |
|---|---|
| Official State Website | http://www.az.gov |
| Governor's Website | http://www.azgovernor.gov |
| State Legislative Website | http://www.azleg.gov |
| State Judicial Website | http://www.azcourts.gov |

# Arkansas

| | |
|---|---|
| Nickname | The Natural State |
| Motto | *Regnat Populus* (The People Rule) |
| Flower | Apple Blossom |
| Bird | Mockingbird |
| Tree | Pine |
| Song | *Arkansas* |
| Entered the Union | June 15, 1836 |
| Capital | Little Rock |

## STATISTICS

| | |
|---|---|
| Land Area (square miles) | 52,035 |
| Rank in Nation | 27th |
| Population | 2,937,979 |
| Rank in Nation | 32nd |
| Density per square mile | 56.5 |
| Capital City | Little Rock |
| Population | 193,524 |
| Rank in State | 1st |
| Largest City | Little Rock |
| Number of Representatives in Congress | 4 |
| Number of 2012 Electoral Votes | 6 |
| Number of County Governments | 75 |
| Number of Municipal Governments | 502 |
| Number of School Districts | 247 |
| Number of Special Districts | 724 |

## LEGISLATIVE BRANCH

| | |
|---|---|
| Legislative Body | General Assembly |
| President of the Senate | Lt. Gov. Mark Darr |
| President Pro Tem of the Senate | Paul Bookout |
| Secretary of the Senate | Ann Cornwell |
| Speaker of the House | Robert Moore |
| Speaker Pro Tem of the House | Bobby Pierce |
| Chief Clerk of the House | Sherri Stacks |
| 2012 Regular Session | Feb. 13 – March 9, 2012 |
| Number of Senatorial Districts | 35 |
| Number of Representative Districts | 100 |

## EXECUTIVE BRANCH

| | |
|---|---|
| Governor | Mike Beebe |
| Lieutenant Governor | Mark Darr |
| Secretary of State | Mark Martin |
| Attorney General | Dustin McDaniel |
| Treasurer | Martha A. Shoffner |
| Auditor | Charlie Daniels |
| Comptroller | Richard Weiss |
| Governor's Present Term | 1/2007 – 1/2015 |
| Number of Elected Officials in the Executive Branch | 7 |
| Number of Members in the Cabinet | 47 |

## JUDICIAL BRANCH

| | |
|---|---|
| Highest Court | Supreme Court |
| Supreme Court Chief Justice | Jim Hannah |
| Number of Supreme Court Judges | 7 |
| Number of Intermediate Appellate Court Judges | 12 |
| Number of U.S. Court Districts | 2 |
| U.S. Circuit Court | 8th Circuit |

## STATE INTERNET ADDRESSES

| | |
|---|---|
| Official State Website | http://arkansas.gov |
| Governor's Website | http://www.governor.arkansas.gov |
| State Legislative Website | http://www.arkleg.state.ar.us |
| State Judicial Website | http://courts.arkansas.gov |

# California

Nickname..................................................................The Golden State
Motto........................................................*Eureka* (I Have Found It)
Flower ...........................................................California Poppy
Bird.........................................................California Valley Quail
Tree..........................................................California Redwood
Song...............................................*I Love You, California*
Entered the Union..................................September 9, 1850
Capital......................................................................Sacramento

## STATISTICS

Land Area (square miles)...............................................155,779
Rank in Nation.........................................................................3rd
Population.........................................................................37,691,912
Rank in Nation........................................................................1st
Density per Square Mile ..........................................................242
Capital City.....................................................................Sacramento
Population.............................................................................466,488
Rank in State...........................................................................7th
Largest City ................................................................ Los Angeles
Population.........................................................................3,792,621
Number of Representatives in Congress .............................53
Number of 2012 Electoral Votes.........................................55
Number of Geographic Counties........................................58
Number of County Governments........................................57
Number of Consolidated Governments..................................1
Number of Municipal Governments ...................................478
Number of School Districts .............................................1,044
Number of Special Districts .............................................2,765

## LEGISLATIVE BRANCH

Legislative Body .......................................................Legislature

President of the Senate ..................Lt. Gov. Gavin Newsom
President Pro Tem of the Senate...............Darrell Steinberg
Secretary of the Senate................................Gregory Schmidt

Speaker of the Assembly ...................................John A. Perez
Speaker Pro Tem of the Assembly...........................Fiona Ma
Chief Clerk of the Assembly ...................E. Dotson Wilson

2012 Regular Session...........................Jan. 4 – Aug. 31, 2012
Number of Senatorial Districts .............................................40
Number of Representative Districts ....................................80

## EXECUTIVE BRANCH

Governor ...........................................Edmund G. Brown Jr.
Lieutenant Governor .....................................Gavin Newsom
Secretary of State............................................. Debra Bowen
Attorney General ...........................................Kamala Harris
Treasurer................................................................Bill Lockyer
Auditor............................................................. Elaine M. Howle
Controller ....................................................................John Chiang

Governor's Present Term........................... 1/2011 – 1/2015
Number of Elected Officials in the Executive Branch.........................8
Number of Members in the Cabinet ....................................11

## JUDICIAL BRANCH

Highest Court..................................................Supreme Court
Supreme Court Chief Justice................. Tani Cantil-Sakauye
Number of Supreme Court Judges .........................................7
Number of Intermediate Appellate Court Judges............................88
Number of U.S. Court Districts.............................................4
U.S. Circuit Court................................................. 9th Circuit

## STATE INTERNET ADDRESSES

Official State Website ......................................http://www.ca.gov
Governor's Website ....................................... http://gov.ca.gov/
State Legislative Website .............................. http://www.leginfo.ca.gov
State Judicial Website.............................. http://www.courtinfo.ca.gov

# Colorado

Nickname...........................................................The Centennial State
Motto.....................................................*Nil Sine Numine*
(Nothing Without Providence)
Flower ......................................Rocky Mountain Columbine
Bird..................................................................... Lark Bunting
Tree..................................................................... Blue Spruce
Song..............................................*Where the Columbines Grow*
Entered the Union.................................... August 1, 1876
Capital............................................................................. Denver

## STATISTICS

Land Area (square miles)...............................................103,642
Rank in Nation.........................................................................8th
Population.........................................................................5,116,796
Rank in Nation........................................................................22nd
Density per square mile ...........................................................49.4
Capital City..................................................................... Denver
Population.............................................................................600,158
Rank in State...........................................................................1st
Largest City ................................................................. Denver
Number of Representatives in Congress ...............................7
Number of 2012 Electoral Votes...........................................9
Number of Geographic Counties........................................64
Number of County Governments........................................62
Number of Consolidated Governments..................................2
Number of Municipal Governments ...................................270
Number of School Districts .............................................180
Number of Special Districts .............................................1,904

## LEGISLATIVE BRANCH

Legislative Body ...................................... General Assembly

President of the Senate ...............................Brandon Shaffer
President Pro Tem of the Senate.............................Betty Boyd
Secretary of the Senate................................ Cindy Markwell

Speaker of the House.......................................Frank McNulty
Speaker Pro Tem of the House ..........................Kevin Priola
Chief Clerk of the House.................................Marilyn Eddins

2012 Regular Session...........................Jan. 11 – May 9, 2012
Number of Senatorial Districts .............................................35
Number of Representative Districts ....................................65

## EXECUTIVE BRANCH

Governor ...................................................... John Hickenlooper
Lieutenant Governor ...........................................Joe Garcia
Secretary of State...............................................Scott Gessler
Attorney General ...........................................John W. Suthers
Treasurer....................................................... Walker Stapleton
Auditor..................................................................Diane Ray
Controller ................................................... David McDermott

Governor's Present Term........................... 1/2011 – 1/2015
Number of Elected Officials in the Executive Branch.........................5
Number of Members in the Cabinet ....................................21

## JUDICIAL BRANCH

Highest Court..................................................Supreme Court
Supreme Court Chief Justice................... Michael L. Bender
Number of Supreme Court Judges .........................................7
Number of Intermediate Appellate Court Judges............................16
Number of U.S. Court Districts.............................................1
U.S. Circuit Court................................................. 10th Circuit

## STATE INTERNET ADDRESSES

Official State Website ...................................... http://www.colorado.gov
Governor's Website .......................http://www.colorado.gov/governor
State Legislative Website .............................. http://www.leg.state.co.us
State Judicial Website.............................http://www.courts.state.co.us

# Connecticut

Nickname............................................................. The Constitution State
Motto.............................................................. *Qui Transtulit Sustinet*
(He Who Transplanted Still Sustains)
Flower ...................................................................Mountain Laurel
Bird .................................................................... American Robin
Tree ........................................................................... White Oak
Song........................................................................ *Yankee Doodle*
Entered the Union.................................................. January 9, 1788
Capital ........................................................................Hartford

## STATISTICS

Land Area (square miles).............................................5,842
Rank in Nation.............................................................48th
Population...........................................................3,580,709
Rank in Nation.............................................................29th
Density per square mile ............................................739.5
Capital City..............................................................Hartford
Population..............................................................124,775
Rank in State.................................................................3rd
Largest City ......................................................... Bridgeport
Population..............................................................144,229
Number of Representatives in Congress .............................5
Number of 2012 Electoral Votes.........................................7
Number of Geographic Counties.........................................8
Number of County Governments.........................................0
Number of Municipal Governments...................................30
Number of School Districts...............................................17
Number of Special Districts .............................................453

## LEGISLATIVE BRANCH

Legislative Body ......................................... General Assembly

President of the Senate .....................Lt. Gov. Nancy Wyman
President Pro Tem of the Senate............................Donald E. Williams
Clerk of the Senate.................................. Garey E. Coleman

Speaker of the House.....................................Christopher G. Donovan
Deputy Speakers of the House ..............Emil Altobello, Bob Godfrey,
Marie Kirkley-Bey, Joe Aresimowicz,
Linda Orange, Kevin Ryan
Clerk of the House ..................................Nicholas A. Varunes

2012 Regular Session.............................Feb. 8 – May 9, 2012
Number of Senatorial Districts.............................................36
Number of Representative Districts ..................................151

## EXECUTIVE BRANCH

Governor .................................................................Dan Malloy
Lieutenant Governor ...................................... Nancy Wyman
Secretary of State........................................Denise W. Merrill
Attorney General .................................... George C. Jepsen
Treasurer........................................................Denise L. Nappier
Auditors ..............................John C. Geragosian and Robert M. Ward
Comptroller ...........................................................Kevin P. Lembo

Governor's Present Term.............................. 1/2011 – 1/2015
Number of Elected Officials in the Executive Branch.........................6
Number of Members in the Cabinet ...................................27

## JUDICIAL BRANCH

Highest Court............................................................Supreme Court
Supreme Court Chief Justice............................Chase T. Rogers
Number of Supreme Court Judges .......................................7
Number of Intermediate Appellate Court Judges............................10
Number of U.S. Court Districts...........................................1
U.S. Circuit Court................................................. 2nd Circuit

## STATE INTERNET ADDRESSES

Official State Website .................................http://www.ct.gov
Governor's Website .....................................http://www.governor.ct.gov
State Legislative Website ......................................http://www.cga.ct.gov
State Judicial Website...........................................http://www.jud.ct.gov

# Delaware

Nickname............................................................... The First State
Motto.............................................................*Liberty and Independence*
Flower ................................................................... Peach Blossom
Bird................................................................. Blue Hen Chicken
Tree ................................................................ American Holly
Song.......................................................................... *Our Delaware*
Entered the Union...........................................December 7, 1787
Capital ........................................................................ Dover

## STATISTICS

Land Area (square miles)...................................................1,949
Rank in Nation...........................................................49th
Population...............................................................907,135
Rank in Nation...........................................................45th
Density per square mile...............................................465.5
Capital City................................................................. Dover
Population...............................................................36,047
Rank in State.................................................................2nd
Largest City ....................................................... Wilmington
Population...............................................................70,851
Number of Representatives in Congress ...............................1
Number of 2012 Electoral Votes.........................................3
Number of County Governments.........................................3
Number of Municipal Governments...................................57
Number of School Districts.............................................19
Number of Special Districts .............................................259

## LEGISLATIVE BRANCH

Legislative Body ........................................ General Assembly

President of the Senate ......................Lt. Gov. Matthew Denn
President Pro Tem of the Senate...........................Anthony J. DeLuca
Secretary of the Senate ........................... Bernard J. Brady

Speaker of the House............................... Robert F. Gilligan
Clerk of the House ...............................................Richard Puffer

2012 Regular Session............................ Jan. 10 – June 30, 2012
Number of Senatorial Districts...........................................21
Number of Representative Districts ..................................41

## EXECUTIVE BRANCH

Governor ................................................................ Jack Markell
Lieutenant Governor ....................................... Matthew Denn
Secretary of State............................................Jeffrey Bullock
Attorney General ......................................Joseph R. Biden III
Treasurer................................................... Chip Flowers Jr.
Auditor....................................................R. Thomas Wagner
Controller ............................................... Thomas J. Cooke

Governor's Present Term.............................. 1/2009 – 1/2013
Number of Elected Officials in the Executive Branch.........................5
Number of Members in the Cabinet ...................................16

## JUDICIAL BRANCH

Highest Court..............................................................Supreme Court
Supreme Court Chief Justice.......................... Myron T. Steele
Number of Supreme Court Judges .......................................5
Number of Intermediate Appellate Court Judges..............................0
Number of U.S. Court Districts...........................................1
U.S. Circuit Court................................................3rd Circuit

## STATE INTERNET ADDRESSES

Official State Website ............................... http://delaware.gov
Governor's Website ................http://governor.delaware.gov
State Legislative Website ................http://legis.delaware.gov
State Judicial Website....................http://courts.delaware.gov

# Florida

Nickname.................................................The Sunshine State
Motto.......................................................*In God We Trust*
Flower..........................................................Orange Blossom
Bird..................................................................Mockingbird
Tree....................................................Sabal Palmetto Palm
Song......................*The Swannee River (Old Folks at Home)*
Entered the Union............................................March 3, 1845
Capital..........................................................Tallahassee

## STATISTICS

Land Area (square miles).......................................53,625
Rank in Nation.......................................................26th
Population.....................................................19,057,542
Rank in Nation..........................................................4th
Density per square mile..........................................355.4
Capital City...................................................Tallahassee
Population...........................................................181,376
Rank in State...........................................................7th
Largest City...................................................Jacksonville
Population...........................................................821,784
Number of Representatives in Congress...........................27
Number of 2012 Electoral Votes..................................29
Number of Geographic Counties.................................67
Number of County Governments.................................66
Number of Consolidated Governments..........................1
Number of Municipal Governments............................411
Number of School Districts.........................................95
Number of Special Districts....................................1,051

## LEGISLATIVE BRANCH

Legislative Body.................................................Legislature

President of the Senate............................Mike Haridopolos
President Pro Tem of the Senate..............Michael S. Bennett
Secretary of the Senate.............................Debbie Brown

Speaker of the House................................Dean Cannon
Speaker Pro Tem of the House........................John Legg
Clerk of the House........................................Bob Ward

2012 Regular Session....................Jan. 10 – March 9, 2012
Number of Senatorial Districts....................................40
Number of Representative Districts............................120

## EXECUTIVE BRANCH

Governor...................................................... Rick Scott
Lieutenant Governor............................Jennifer Carroll
Secretary of State....................................Ken Detzner
Attorney General......................................Pam Bondi
Chief Financial Officer..................Jeffrey H. Atwater
Auditor...................................................David Martin

Governor's Present Term.......................1/2011 – 1/2015
Number of Elected Officials in the Executive Branch...........5
Number of Members in the Cabinet.............................4

## JUDICIAL BRANCH

Highest Court.......................................Supreme Court
Supreme Court Chief Justice............Charles T. Canady
Number of Supreme Court Judges..............................7
Number of Intermediate Appellate Court Judges...........62
Number of U.S. Court Districts...................................3
U.S. Circuit Court....................................11th Circuit

## STATE INTERNET ADDRESSES

Official State Website....................http://www.myflorida.com
Governor's Website..............................http://www.flgov.com
State Legislative Website.................http://www.leg.state.fl.us
State Judicial Website.........................http://www.flcourts.org

# Georgia

Nickname.................................The Empire State of the South
Motto.............................*Wisdom, Justice and Moderation*
Flower...........................................................Cherokee Rose
Bird............................................................. Brown Thrasher
Tree....................................................................Live Oak
Song................................................*Georgia on My Mind*
Entered the Union.......................................January 2, 1788
Capital..................................................................Atlanta

## STATISTICS

Land Area (square miles)........................................57,513
Rank in Nation.........................................................21st
Population.......................................................9,815,210
Rank in Nation...........................................................9th
Density per square mile...........................................170.7
Capital City..............................................................Atlanta
Population...........................................................420,003
Rank in State.............................................................1st
Largest City............................................................Atlanta
Number of Representatives in Congress...........................14
Number of 2012 Electoral Votes..................................16
Number of Geographic Counties...............................159
Number of County Governments...............................154
Number of Consolidated Governments..........................5
Number of Municipal Governments............................535
Number of School Districts.......................................180
Number of Special Districts.......................................570

## LEGISLATIVE BRANCH

Legislative Body.......................................General Assembly

President of the Senate........................Lt. Gov. Casey Cagle
President Pro Tem of the Senate...............Tommie Williams
Secretary of the Senate..............................Bob Ewing

Speaker of the House.............................David Ralston
Speaker Pro Tem of the House......................Jan Jones
Clerk of the House.........................Robert E. Rivers Jr.

2012 Regular Session......................Jan. 9 – March 29, 2012
Number of Senatorial Districts....................................56
Number of Representative Districts............................180

## EXECUTIVE BRANCH

Governor..................................................Nathan Deal
Lieutenant Governor...............................Casey Cagle
Secretary of State......................................Brian Kemp
Attorney General......................................Sam Olens
Treasurer...............................................Steve McCoy
Auditor.......................................Russell W. Hinton

Governor's Present Term.......................1/2011 – 1/2015
Number of Elected Officials in the Executive Branch.........13
Number of Members in the Cabinet...........No formal cabinet system

## JUDICIAL BRANCH

Highest Court.......................................Supreme Court
Supreme Court Chief Justice................,Carol W. Hunstein
Number of Supreme Court Judges..............................7
Number of Intermediate Appellate Court Judges...........12
Number of U.S. Court Districts...................................3
U.S. Circuit Court....................................11th Circuit

## STATE INTERNET ADDRESSES

Official State Website......................................www.georgia.gov
Governor's Website...............................http://gov.georgia.gov
State Legislative Website.......................http://www.legis.ga.gov
State Judicial Website......................http://www.georgiacourts.org

# Hawaii

| | |
|---|---|
| Nickname | The Aloha State |
| Motto | *Ua Mau Ke Ea O Ka Aina I Ka Pono* |
| | (The Life of the Land Is Perpetuated in Righteousness) |
| Flower | Native Yellow Hibiscus |
| Bird | Hawaiian Goose (Nene) |
| Tree | Kukue Tree (Candlenut) |
| Song | *Hawaii Ponoi* |
| Entered the Union | August 21, 1959 |
| Capital | Honolulu |

## STATISTICS

| | |
|---|---|
| Land Area (square miles) | 6,423 |
| Rank in Nation | 47th |
| Population | 1,374,810 |
| Rank in Nation | 40th |
| Density per square mile | 214.1 |
| Capital City | Honolulu |
| Population | 337,256 |
| Rank in State | 1st |
| Largest City | Honolulu |
| Number of Representatives in Congress | 2 |
| Number of 2012 Electoral Votes | 4 |
| Number of Geographic Counties | 4 |
| Number of County Governments | 3 |
| Number of Consolidated Governments | 1 |
| Number of Municipal Governments | 1 |
| Number of School Districts | 0 |
| Number of Special Districts | 15 |

## LEGISLATIVE BRANCH

| | |
|---|---|
| Legislative Body | Legislature |
| | |
| President of the Senate | Shan S. Tsutsui |
| Vice President of the Senate | Donna Mercado Kim |
| Chief Clerk of the Senate | Carol Taniguchi |
| | |
| Speaker of the House | Calvin K.Y. Say |
| Vice Speaker of the House | Joey Manahan |
| Chief Clerk of the House | CJ Leong |
| | |
| 2012 Regular Session | Jan. 18 – late-April 2012 |
| Number of Senatorial Districts | 25 |
| Number of Representative Districts | 51 |

## EXECUTIVE BRANCH

| | |
|---|---|
| Governor | Neil Abercrombie |
| Lieutenant Governor | Brian Schatz |
| Attorney General | David Louie |
| Treasurer | Kalbert Young |
| Auditor | Marion M. Higa |
| Comptroller | Dean Seki |
| | |
| Governor's Present Term | 12/2010 – 12/2014 |
| Number of Elected Officials in the Executive Branch | 2 |
| Number of Members in the Cabinet | 22 |

## JUDICIAL BRANCH

| | |
|---|---|
| Highest Court | Supreme Court |
| Supreme Court Chief Justice | Mark E. Recktenwald |
| Number of Supreme Court Judges | 5 |
| Number of Intermediate Appellate Court Judges | 6 |
| Number of U.S. Court Districts | 1 |
| U.S. Circuit Court | 9th Circuit |

## STATE INTERNET ADDRESSES

| | |
|---|---|
| Official State Website | http://hawaii.gov |
| Governor's Website | http://hawaii.gov/gov |
| State Legislative Website | http://www.capitol.hawaii.gov |
| State Judicial Website | http://www.courts.state.hi.us |

# Idaho

| | |
|---|---|
| Nickname | The Gem State |
| Motto | *Esto Perpetua* (Let It Be Perpetual) |
| Flower | Syringa |
| Bird | Mountain Bluebird |
| Tree | Western White Pine |
| Song | *Here We Have Idaho* |
| Entered the Union | July 3, 1890 |
| Capital | Boise |

## STATISTICS

| | |
|---|---|
| Land Area (square miles) | 82,643 |
| Rank in Nation | 11th |
| Population | 1,584,985 |
| Rank in Nation | 39th |
| Density per square mile | 19.2 |
| Capital City | Boise |
| Population | 205,671 |
| Rank in State | 1st |
| Largest City | Boise |
| Number of Representatives in Congress | 2 |
| Number of 2012 Electoral Votes | 4 |
| Number of County Governments | 44 |
| Number of Municipal Governments | 200 |
| Number of School Districts | 116 |
| Number of Special Districts | 880 |

## LEGISLATIVE BRANCH

| | |
|---|---|
| Legislative Body | Legislature |
| | |
| President of the Senate | Lt. Gov. Brad Little |
| President Pro Tem of the Senate | Brent Hill |
| Secretary of the Senate | Jennifer Novak |
| | |
| Speaker of the House | Lawrence Denney |
| Chief Clerk of the House | Bonnie Alexander |
| | |
| 2012 Regular Session | Jan. 9 – March 29, 2012 |
| Number of Senatorial Districts | 35 |
| Number of Representative Districts | 35 |

## EXECUTIVE BRANCH

| | |
|---|---|
| Governor | C.L. "Butch" Otter |
| Lieutenant Governor | Brad Little |
| Secretary of State | Ben Ysursa |
| Attorney General | Lawrence Wasden |
| Treasurer | Ron Crane |
| Controller | Donna Jones |
| | |
| Governor's Present Term | 1/2007 – 1/2015 |
| Number of Elected Officials in the Executive Branch | 7 |
| Number of Members in the Cabinet | 43 |

## JUDICIAL BRANCH

| | |
|---|---|
| Highest Court | Supreme Court |
| Supreme Court Chief Justice | Roger S. Burdick |
| Number of Supreme Court Judges | 5 |
| Number of Intermediate Appellate Court Judges | 3 |
| Number of U.S. Court Districts | 1 |
| U.S. Circuit Court | 9th Circuit |

## STATE INTERNET ADDRESSES

| | |
|---|---|
| Official State Website | http://www.idaho.gov |
| Governor's Website | http://gov.idaho.gov |
| State Legislative Website | http://www.legislature.idaho.gov |
| State Judicial Website | http://www.isc.idaho.gov |

# Illinois

| | |
|---|---|
| Nickname | The Prairie State |
| Motto | *State Sovereignty—National Union* |
| Flower | Native Violet |
| Bird | Cardinal |
| Tree | White Oak |
| Song | Illinois |
| Entered the Union | December 3, 1818 |
| Capital | Springfield |

## STATISTICS

| | |
|---|---|
| Land Area (square miles) | 55,519 |
| Rank in Nation | 24th |
| Population | 12,869,257 |
| Rank in Nation | 5th |
| Density per square mile | 231.8 |
| Capital City | Springfield |
| Population | 116,250 |
| Rank in State | 6th |
| Largest City | Chicago |
| Population | 2,695,598 |
| Number of Representatives in Congress | 18 |
| Number of 2012 Electoral Votes | 20 |
| Number of County Governments | 102 |
| Number of Municipal Governments | 1,299 |
| Number of School Districts | 912 |
| Number of Special Districts | 3,249 |

## LEGISLATIVE BRANCH

| | |
|---|---|
| Legislative Body | General Assembly |
| | |
| President of the Senate | John J. Cullerton |
| President Pro Tem of the Senate | Don Harmon |
| Secretary of the Senate | Tim Anderson |
| | |
| Speaker of the House | Michael J. Madigan |
| House Chief Clerk | Timothy Mapes |
| | |
| 2012 Regular Session | Jan. 11 – Dec. 31, 2012 |
| Number of Senatorial Districts | 59 |
| Number of Representative Districts | 118 |

## EXECUTIVE BRANCH

| | |
|---|---|
| Governor | Patrick Quinn |
| Lieutenant Governor | Sheila Simon |
| Secretary of State | Jesse White |
| Attorney General | Lisa Madigan |
| Treasurer | Don Rutherford |
| Auditor | William G. Holland |
| Comptroller | Judy Baar Topinka |
| | |
| Governor's Present Term | 1/2009 – 1/2015 |
| Number of Elected Officials in the Executive Branch | 6 |
| Number of Members in the Cabinet | 18 |

## JUDICIAL BRANCH

| | |
|---|---|
| Highest Court | Supreme Court |
| Supreme Court Chief Justice | Thomas L. Kilbride |
| Number of Supreme Court Judges | 7 |
| Number of Intermediate Appellate Court Judges | 53 |
| Number of U.S. Court Districts | 3 |
| U.S. Circuit Court | 7th Circuit |

## STATE INTERNET ADDRESSES

| | |
|---|---|
| Official State Website | http://www.illinois.gov |
| Governor's Website | http://www.illinois.gov/gov |
| State Legislative Website | http://www.ilga.gov |
| State Judicial Website | http://www.state.il.us/courts |

# Indiana

| | |
|---|---|
| Nickname | The Hoosier State |
| Motto | *Crossroads of America* |
| Flower | Peony |
| Bird | Cardinal |
| Tree | Tulip Poplar |
| Song | *On the Banks of the Wabash, Far Away* |
| Entered the Union | December 11, 1816 |
| Capital | Indianapolis |

## STATISTICS

| | |
|---|---|
| Land Area (square miles) | 35,826 |
| Rank in Nation | 38th |
| Population | 6,516,922 |
| Rank in Nation | 15th |
| Density per square mile | 181.9 |
| Capital City | Indianapolis |
| Population | 829,718 |
| Rank in State | 1st |
| Largest City | Indianapolis |
| Number of Representatives in Congress | 9 |
| Number of 2012 Electoral Votes | 11 |
| Number of Geographic Counties | 92 |
| Number of County Governments | 91 |
| Number of Consolidated Governments | 1 |
| Number of Municipal Governments | 567 |
| Number of School Districts | 293 |
| Number of Special Districts | 1,272 |

## LEGISLATIVE BRANCH

| | |
|---|---|
| Legislative Body | General Assembly |
| | |
| President of the Senate | Lt. Gov. Becky Skillman |
| President Pro Tem of the Senate | David C. Long |
| Secretary of the Senate | Jennifer Mertz |
| | |
| Speaker of the House | Brian C. Bosma |
| Clerk of the House | M. Carolyn Spotts |
| | |
| 2012 Regular Session | Jan. 14 – March 10, 2012 |
| Number of Senatorial Districts | 50 |
| Number of Representative Districts | 100 |

## EXECUTIVE BRANCH

| | |
|---|---|
| Governor | Mitch Daniels |
| Lieutenant Governor | Becky Skillman |
| Secretary of State | Connie Lawson |
| Attorney General | Greg Zoeller |
| Treasurer | Richard E. Mourdock |
| Auditor | Tim Berry |
| | |
| Governor's Present Term | 1/2005 – 1/2013 |
| Number of Elected Officials in the Executive Branch | 7 |
| Number of Members in the Cabinet | 16 |

## JUDICIAL BRANCH

| | |
|---|---|
| Highest Court | Supreme Court |
| Acting Supreme Court Chief Justice | Brent E. Dickson |
| Number of Supreme Court Judges | 5 |
| Number of Intermediate Appellate Court Judges | 15 |
| Number of U.S. Court Districts | 2 |
| U.S. Circuit Court | 7th Circuit |

## STATE INTERNET ADDRESSES

| | |
|---|---|
| Official State Website | http://www.in.gov |
| Governor's Website | http://www.in.gov/gov |
| State Legislative Website | http://www.in.gov/legislative |
| State Judicial Website | http://www.in.gov/judiciary |

# Iowa

| | |
|---|---|
| Nickname | The Hawkeye State |
| Motto | *Our Liberties We Prize and Our Rights We Will Maintain* |
| Flower | Wild Rose |
| Bird | Eastern Goldfinch |
| Tree | Oak |
| Song | *The Song of Iowa* |
| Entered the Union | December 28, 1846 |
| Capital | Des Moines |

### STATISTICS

| | |
|---|---|
| Land Area (square miles) | 55,857 |
| Rank in Nation | 23rd |
| Population | 3,062,309 |
| Rank in Nation | 30th |
| Density per square mile | 54.8 |
| Capital City | Des Moines |
| Population | 203,433 |
| Rank in State | 1st |
| Largest City | Des Moines |
| Number of Representatives in Congress | 4 |
| Number of 2012 Electoral Votes | 6 |
| Number of County Governments | 99 |
| Number of Municipal Governments | 947 |
| Number of School Districts | 380 |
| Number of Special Districts | 528 |

### LEGISLATIVE BRANCH

| | |
|---|---|
| Legislative Body | General Assembly |
| | |
| President of the Senate | John P. Kibbie |
| President Pro Tem of the Senate | Jeff Danielson |
| Secretary of the Senate | Michael E. Marshall |
| | |
| Speaker of the House | Kraig Paulsen |
| Speaker Pro Tem of the House | Jeff Kaufmann |
| Chief Clerk of the House | Charlie Smithson |
| | |
| 2012 Regular Session | Jan. 9 – April 17, 2012 |
| Number of Senatorial Districts | 50 |
| Number of Representative Districts | 100 |

### EXECUTIVE BRANCH

| | |
|---|---|
| Governor | Terry Branstad |
| Lieutenant Governor | Kim Reynolds |
| Secretary of State | Matt Schultz |
| Attorney General | Thomas Miller |
| Treasurer | Michael Fitzgerald |
| Auditor | David A. Vaudt |
| Chief Operating Officer | Calvin McKelvogue |
| | |
| Governor's Present Term | 1/2011 – 1/2015 |
| Number of Elected Officials in the Executive Branch | 7 |
| Number of Members in the Cabinet | 30 |

### JUDICIAL BRANCH

| | |
|---|---|
| Highest Court | Supreme Court |
| Supreme Court Chief Justice | Mark S. Cady |
| Number of Supreme Court Judges | 7 |
| Number of Intermediate Appellate Court Judges | 9 |
| Number of U.S. Court Districts | 2 |
| U.S. Circuit Court | 8th Circuit |

### STATE INTERNET ADDRESSES

| | |
|---|---|
| Official State Website | http://www.iowa.gov |
| Governor's Website | http://governor.iowa.gov |
| State Legislative Website | http://www.legis.iowa.gov |
| State Judicial Website | http://www.iowacourts.gov |

# Kansas

| | |
|---|---|
| Nickname | The Sunflower State |
| Motto | *Ad Astra per Aspera* (To the Stars through Difficulties) |
| Flower | Wild Native Sunflower |
| Bird | Western Meadowlark |
| Tree | Cottonwood |
| Song | *Home on the Range* |
| Entered the Union | January 29, 1861 |
| Capital | Topeka |

### STATISTICS

| | |
|---|---|
| Land Area (square miles) | 81,759 |
| Rank in Nation | 13th |
| Population | 2,871,238 |
| Rank in Nation | 33rd |
| Density per square mile | 35.1 |
| Capital City | Topeka |
| Population | 127,473 |
| Rank in State | 4th |
| Largest City | Wichita |
| Population | 382,368 |
| Number of Representatives in Congress | 4 |
| Number of 2012 Electoral Votes | 6 |
| Number of Geographic Counties | 105 |
| Number of County Governments | 103 |
| Number of Consolidated Governments | 2 |
| Number of Municipal Governments | 627 |
| Number of School Districts | 316 |
| Number of Special Districts | 1,531 |

### LEGISLATIVE BRANCH

| | |
|---|---|
| Legislative Body | Legislature |
| | |
| President of the Senate | Stephen Morris |
| President Pro Tem of the Senate | John Vratil |
| Secretary of the Senate | Pat Saville |
| | |
| Speaker of the House | Michael O'Neal |
| Speaker Pro Tem of the House | Jene Vickrey |
| Chief Clerk of the House | Susan W. Kannarr |
| | |
| 2012 Regular Session | Jan. 9 – March 31, 2012 |
| Number of Senatorial Districts | 40 |
| Number of Representative Districts | 125 |

### EXECUTIVE BRANCH

| | |
|---|---|
| Governor | Sam Brownback |
| Lieutenant Governor | Jeff Colyer |
| Secretary of State | Kris Kobach |
| Attorney General | Derek Schmidt |
| Treasurer | Ron Estes |
| Auditor | Scott Frank |
| Director, Division of Accounts & Reports | Kent Olson |
| | |
| Governor's Present Term | 1/2011 – 1/2015 |
| Number of Elected Officials in the Executive Branch | 6 |
| Number of Members in the Cabinet | 14 |

### JUDICIAL BRANCH

| | |
|---|---|
| Highest Court | Supreme Court |
| Supreme Court Chief Justice | Lawton R. Nuss |
| Number of Supreme Court Judges | 7 |
| Number of Intermediate Appellate Court Judges | 12 |
| Number of U.S. Court Districts | 1 |
| U.S. Circuit Court | 10th Circuit |

### STATE INTERNET ADDRESSES

| | |
|---|---|
| Official State Website | http://www.kansas.gov |
| Governor's Website | http://governor.ks.gov |
| State Legislative Website | http://www.kslegislature.org |
| State Judicial Website | http://www.kscourts.org |

# Kentucky

| | |
|---|---|
| Nickname | The Bluegrass State |
| Motto | *United We Stand, Divided We Fall* |
| Flower | Goldenrod |
| Bird | Cardinal |
| Tree | Tulip Poplar |
| Song | *My Old Kentucky Home* |
| Entered the Union | June 1, 1792 |
| Capital | Frankfort |

## STATISTICS

| | |
|---|---|
| Land Area (square miles) | 39,486 |
| Rank in Nation | 37th |
| Population | 4,369,356 |
| Rank in Nation | 26th |
| Density per square mile | 110.7 |
| Capital City | Frankfort |
| Population | 25,527 |
| Rank in State | 7th |
| Largest City | Louisville |
| Population | 741,096 |
| Number of Representatives in Congress | 6 |
| Number of 2012 Electoral Votes | 8 |
| Number of Geographic Counties | 120 |
| Number of County Governments | 118 |
| Number of Consolidated Governments | 2 |
| Number of Municipal Governments | 419 |
| Number of School Districts | 175 |
| Number of Special Districts | 634 |

## LEGISLATIVE BRANCH

| | |
|---|---|
| Legislative Body | General Assembly |
| President of the Senate | David L. Williams |
| President Pro Tem of the Senate | Katie Stine |
| Secretary of the Senate | Donna Holiday |
| Speaker of the House | Gregory Stumbo |
| Speaker Pro Tem of the House | Larry Clark |
| Chief Clerk of the House | Jean Burgin |
| 2012 Regular Session | Jan. 3 – April 9, 2012 |
| Number of Senatorial Districts | 38 |
| Number of Representative Districts | 100 |

## EXECUTIVE BRANCH

| | |
|---|---|
| Governor | Steve Beshear |
| Lieutenant Governor | Jerry Abramson |
| Secretary of State | Alison Lundergan Grimes |
| Attorney General | Jack Conway |
| Treasurer | Todd Hollenbach |
| Auditor | Adam Edelen |
| Controller | Edgar C. Ross |
| Governor's Present Term | 12/2007 – 12/2015 |
| Number of Elected Officials in the Executive Branch | 7 |
| Number of Members in the Cabinet | 15 |

## JUDICIAL BRANCH

| | |
|---|---|
| Highest Court | Supreme Court |
| Supreme Court Chief Justice | John D. Minton |
| Number of Supreme Court Judges | 7 |
| Number of Intermediate Appellate Court Judges | 14 |
| Number of U.S. Court Districts | 2 |
| U.S. Circuit Court | 6th Circuit |

## STATE INTERNET ADDRESSES

| | |
|---|---|
| Official State Website | http://kentucky.gov |
| Governor's Website | http://governor.ky.gov |
| Legislative Website | http://www.lrc.ky.gov |
| Judicial Website | http://courts.ky.gov |

# Louisiana

| | |
|---|---|
| Nickname | The Pelican State |
| Motto | *Union, Justice and Confidence* |
| Flower | Magnolia |
| Bird | Eastern Brown Pelican |
| Tree | Bald Cypress |
| Songs | *Give Me Louisiana* and *You Are My Sunshine* |
| Entered the Union | April 30, 1812 |
| Capital | Baton Rouge |

## STATISTICS

| | |
|---|---|
| Land Area (square miles) | 43,204 |
| Rank in Nation | 33rd |
| Population | 4,574,836 |
| Rank in Nation | 25th |
| Density per square mile | 105.9 |
| Capital City | Baton Rouge |
| Population | 229,493 |
| Rank in State | 2nd |
| Largest City | New Orleans |
| Population | 343,829 |
| Number of Representatives in Congress | 6 |
| Number of 2012 Electoral Votes | 8 |
| Number of Geographic Parishes | 64 |
| Number of Parish Governments | 60 |
| Number of Consolidated Governments | 1 |
| Number of Municipal Governments | 303 |
| Number of School Districts | 68 |
| Number of Special Districts | 95 |

## LEGISLATIVE BRANCH

| | |
|---|---|
| Legislative Body | Legislature |
| President of the Senate | John Alario |
| President Pro Tem of the Senate | Sharon Weston Broome |
| Secretary of Senate | Glenn Koepp |
| Speaker of the House | Chuck Kleckley |
| Speaker Pro Tem of the House | Walt Leger |
| Clerk of the House and Chief of Staff | Alfred W. Speer |
| 2012 Regular Session | March 12 – June 4, 2012 |
| Number of Senatorial Districts | 39 |
| Number of Representative Districts | 105 |

## EXECUTIVE BRANCH

| | |
|---|---|
| Governor | Bobby Jindal |
| Lieutenant Governor | Jay Dardenne |
| Secretary of State | Tom Schedler |
| Attorney General | James D. Caldwell |
| Treasurer | John Neely Kennedy |
| Governor's Present Term | 1/2008 – 1/2016 |
| Number of Elected Officials in the Executive Branch | 8 |
| Number of Members in the Cabinet | 16 |

## JUDICIAL BRANCH

| | |
|---|---|
| Highest Court | Supreme Court |
| Supreme Court Chief Justice | Catherine D. Kimball |
| Number of Supreme Court Judges | 7 |
| Number of Intermediate Appellate Court Judges | 53 |
| Number of U.S. Court Districts | 3 |
| U.S. Circuit Court | 5th Circuit |

## STATE INTERNET ADDRESSES

| | |
|---|---|
| Official State Website | http://louisiana.gov |
| Governor's Website | http://gov.louisiana.gov |
| Legislative Website | http://legis.louisiana.gov |
| Judicial Website | http://louisiana.gov/Government/Judicial_Branch/ |

# Maine

| | |
|---|---|
| Nickname | The Pine Tree State |
| Motto | *Dirigo* (I Direct or I Lead) |
| Flower | White Pine Cone and Tassel |
| Bird | Chickadee |
| Tree | White Pine |
| Song | *State of Maine Song* |
| Entered the Union | March 15, 1820 |
| Capital | Augusta |

## STATISTICS

| | |
|---|---|
| Land Area (square miles) | 30,843 |
| Rank in Nation | 39th |
| Population | 1,328,188 |
| Rank in Nation | 41st |
| Density per square mile | 43.1 |
| Capital City | Augusta |
| Population | 19,136 |
| Rank in State | 9th |
| Largest City | Portland |
| Population | 66,194 |
| Number of Representatives in Congress | 2 |
| Number of 2012 Electoral Votes | 4 |
| Number of County Governments | 16 |
| Number of Municipal Governments | 22 |
| Number of School Districts | 98 |
| Number of Special Districts | 248 |

## LEGISLATIVE BRANCH

| | |
|---|---|
| Legislative Body | Legislature |
| President of the Senate | Kevin L. Raye |
| Secretary of the Senate | Joseph Carleton, Jr. |
| Speaker of the House | Robert W. Nutting |
| Clerk of the House | Heather J.R. Priest |
| 2012 Regular Session | Jan. 4 – April 18, 2012 |
| Number of Senatorial Districts | 35 |
| Number of Representative Districts | 151 |

## EXECUTIVE BRANCH

| | |
|---|---|
| Governor | Paul LePage |
| Secretary of State | Charlie Summers |
| Attorney General | William Schneider |
| Treasurer | Bruce Poliquin |
| Auditor | Neria R. Douglass |
| Controller | Terry Brann |
| Governor's Present Term | 1//2011 – 1/2015 |
| Number of Elected Officials in the Executive Branch | 1 |
| Number of Members in the Cabinet | 16 |

## JUDICIAL BRANCH

| | |
|---|---|
| Highest Court | Supreme Judicial Court |
| Supreme Court Chief Justice | Leigh Ingalls Saufley |
| Number of Supreme Court Judges | 7 |
| Number of Intermediate Appellate Court Judges | 0 |
| Number of U.S. Court Districts | 1 |
| U.S. Circuit Court | 1st Circuit |

## STATE INTERNET ADDRESSES

| | |
|---|---|
| Official State Website | http://www.maine.gov |
| Governor's Website | http://www.maine.gov/governor |
| Legislative Website | http://www.maine.gov/legis |
| Judicial Website | http://www.courts.state.me.us |

# Maryland

| | |
|---|---|
| Nicknames | The Old Line State and Free State |
| Motto | *Fatti Maschii, Parole Femine* |
| | (Manly Deeds, Womanly Words) |
| Flower | Black-eyed Susan |
| Bird | Baltimore Oriole |
| Tree | White Oak |
| Song | *Maryland, My Maryland* |
| Entered the Union | April 28, 1788 |
| Capital | Annapolis |

## STATISTICS

| | |
|---|---|
| Land Area (square miles) | 9,707 |
| Rank in Nation | 42nd |
| Population | 5,828,289 |
| Rank in Nation | 19th |
| Density per square mile | 600.4 |
| Capital City | Annapolis |
| Population | 38,394 |
| Rank in State | 7th |
| Largest City | Baltimore |
| Population | 620,961 |
| Number of Representatives in Congress | 8 |
| Number of 2012 Electoral Votes | 10 |
| Number of Geographic Counties | 24 |
| Number of County Governments | 23 |
| Number of County Equivalents | 1* |
| Number of Municipal Governments | 157 |
| Number of School Districts | 0 |
| Number of Special Districts | 76 |

## LEGISLATIVE BRANCH

| | |
|---|---|
| Legislative Body | General Assembly |
| President of the Senate | Thomas V. Mike Miller Jr. |
| President Pro Tem of the Senate | Nathaniel J. McFadden |
| Secretary of the Senate | William B.C. Addison Jr. |
| Speaker of the House | Michael Erin Busch |
| Speaker Pro Tem of the House | Adrienne A. Jones |
| Clerk of the House | Mary Monahan |
| 2012 Regular Session | Jan. 11 – April 19, 2012 |
| Number of Senatorial Districts | 47 |
| Number of Representative Districts | 47 |

## EXECUTIVE BRANCH

| | |
|---|---|
| Governor | Martin O'Malley |
| Lieutenant Governor | Anthony Brown |
| Secretary of State | John McDonough |
| Attorney General | Douglas Gansler |
| Treasurer | Nancy K. Kopp |
| Auditor | Bruce A. Myers |
| Comptroller | Peter Franchot |
| Governor's Present Term | 1/2011 – 1/2015 |
| Number of Elected Officials in the Executive Branch | 4 |
| Number of Members in the Cabinet | 25 |

## JUDICIAL BRANCH

| | |
|---|---|
| Highest Court | Court of Appeals |
| Court of Appeals Chief Judge | Robert M. Bell |
| Number of Court of Appeals Judges | 7 |
| Number of Intermediate Appellate Court Judges | 13 |
| Number of U.S. Court Districts | 1 |
| U.S. Circuit Court | 4th Circuit |

## STATE INTERNET ADDRESSES

| | |
|---|---|
| Official State Website | http://www.maryland.gov |
| Governor's Website | http://www.gov.state.md.us |
| Legislative Website | http://www.mlis.state.md.us |
| Judicial Website | http://www.courts.state.md.us |

*The city of Baltimore is an Independent City and considered a county equivalent.

# Massachusetts

Nickname......................................................................The Bay State
Motto............................... *Ense Petit Placidam Sub Libertate Quietem*
    (By the Sword We Seek Peace, but Peace Only under Liberty)
Flower .............................................................................Mayflower
Bird...................................................................................Chickadee
Tree...........................................................................American Elm
Song.................................................... *All Hail to Massachusetts*
Entered the Union.............................................February 6, 1788
Capital...................................................................................Boston

## STATISTICS

Land Area (square miles)...................................................7,800
Rank in Nation...................................................................45th
Population.................................................................6,587,536
Rank in Nation...................................................................14th
Density per square mile ....................................................844.5
Capital City......................................................................Boston
Population..................................................................617,594
Rank in State......................................................................1st
Largest City......................................................................Boston
Number of Representatives in Congress ..................................9
Number of 2012 Electoral Votes.............................................11
Number of Geographic Counties.........................................14*
Number of County Governments............................................5
Number of Consolidated Governments....................................2
Number of Municipal Governments ......................................45
Number of School Districts..................................................82
Number of Special Districts ................................................423

## LEGISLATIVE BRANCH

Legislative Body .................................................. General Court

President of the Senate ...............................Therese Murray
President Pro Tem of the Senate...................Stanley C. Rosenberg
Clerk of the Senate.....................................William F. Welch

Speaker of the House.................................Robert A. DeLeo
Speaker Pro Tempore.................................Patricia A. Haddad
Clerk of the House ...................................Steven T. James

2012 Regular Session...............................Jan. 4 – Dec. 31, 2012
Number of Senatorial Districts .............................................40
Number of Representative Districts .....................................160

## EXECUTIVE BRANCH

Governor ..................................................Deval Patrick
Lieutenant Governor ....................................Tim Murray
Secretary of the Commonwealth ..............William F. Galvin
Attorney General......................................Martha Coakley
Treasurer & Receiver General....................Steven Grossman
Auditor...................................................Suzanne Bump
Comptroller..........................................Martin J. Benison

Governor's Present Term.......................... 1/2007 – 1/2015
Number of Elected Officials in the Executive Branch........................6
Number of Members in the Cabinet ......................................10

## JUDICIAL BRANCH

Highest Court..................................Supreme Judicial Court
Supreme Judicial Court Chief Justice.............Roderick L. Ireland
Number of Supreme Judicial Court Judges.............................7
Number of Intermediate Appellate Court Judges....................28
Number of U.S. Court Districts...............................................1
U.S. Circuit Court.........................................................1st Circuit

## STATE INTERNET ADDRESSES

Official State Website ....................... http://www.mass.gov
Governor's Website .............................http://www.mass.gov/governor
Legislative Website ...................... http://www.malegislature.gov
Judicial Website..............................http://www.mass.gov/courts

*Seven counties have been abolished and are only geographic in
nature.

# Michigan

Nickname......................................................The Wolverine State
Motto..........................*Si Quaeris Peninsulam Amoenam Circumspice*
    (If You Seek a Pleasant Peninsula, Look About You)
Flower ....................................................................Apple Blossom
Bird...............................................................................Robin
Tree......................................................................White Pine
Song..................................................*Michigan, My Michigan*
Entered the Union............................................ January 26, 1837
Capital.................................................................................Lansing

## STATISTICS

Land Area (square miles)...............................................56,539
Rank in Nation..................................................................22nd
Population.................................................................9,876,187
Rank in Nation.....................................................................8th
Density per square mile ....................................................174.7
Capital City.....................................................................Lansing
Population.................................................................114,297
Rank in State.....................................................................5th
Largest City.....................................................................Detroit
Population..................................................................713,777
Number of Representatives in Congress ................................14
Number of 2012 Electoral Votes.............................................16
Number of County Governments...........................................83
Number of Municipal Governments ....................................533
Number of School Districts................................................579
Number of Special Districts ..............................................456

## LEGISLATIVE BRANCH

Legislative Body .................................................Legislature

President of the Senate .................................Brian Calley
President Pro Tem of the Senate.................Tonya Schuitmaker
Secretary of the Senate .........................Carol Morey Viventi

Speaker of the House.................................Jase Bolger
Speaker Pro Tem of the House.....................John J. Walsh
Clerk of the House ...................................Gary Randall

2012 Regular Session................................. Jan. 11 – Dec. 31, 2012
Number of Senatorial Districts .............................................38
Number of Representative Districts .....................................110

## EXECUTIVE BRANCH

Governor................................................. Rick Snyder
Lieutenant Governor ................................Brian Calley
Secretary of State....................................... Ruth Johnson
Attorney General........................................ Bill Schuette
Treasurer......................................................Andy Dillon
Auditor................................................Thomas McTavish
Director, Office of Financial Management...............Michael J. Moody

Governor's Present Term............................ 1/2011 – 1/2015
Number of Elected Officials in the Executive Branch..................4
Number of Members in the Cabinet .....................................18

## JUDICIAL BRANCH

Highest Court..................................................Supreme Court
Supreme Court Chief Justice..................Robert P. Young, Jr.
Number of Supreme Court Judges ..........................................7
Number of Intermediate Appellate Court Judges....................28
Number of U.S. Court Districts...............................................2
U.S. Circuit Court.................................................... 6th Circuit

## STATE INTERNET ADDRESSES

Official State Website ........................http://www.michigan.gov
Governor's Website ....................................http://www.michigan.gov/gov
Legislative Website ....................... http://www.michiganlegislature.org
Judicial Website...................................... http://www.courts.michigan.gov

# Minnesota

Nickname......................................................... The North Star State
Motto.................................................*L'Etoile du Nord* (The North Star)
Flower ...................................................... Pink and White Lady-Slipper
Bird...................................................................Common Loon
Tree.......................................................................... Red Pine
Song..................................................................*Hail! Minnesota*
Entered the Union.......................................................May 11, 1858
Capital.......................................................................... St. Paul

## STATISTICS

Land Area (square miles)................................................79,627
Rank in Nation...............................................................14th
Population.............................................................5,344,861
Rank in Nation...............................................................21st
Density per square mile ....................................................67.1
Capital City..............................................................St. Paul
Population.............................................................285,068
Rank in State.................................................................2nd
Largest City ....................................................... Minneapolis
Population.............................................................382,578
Number of Representatives in Congress ...............................8
Number of 2012 Electoral Votes.......................................10
Number of County Governments.......................................87
Number of Municipal Governments.................................854
Number of School Districts ...........................................341
Number of Special Districts ...........................................456

## LEGISLATIVE BRANCH

Legislative Body .....................................................Legislature

President of the Senate ........................... Michelle Fischbach
President Pro Tem of the Senate.............................Gen Olson
Secretary of the Senate .............................Cal Ludeman

Speaker of the House................................ Kurt Zellers
Speakers Pro Tempore of the House....... Greg Davids, Mary Holberg,
                                        Morrie Lanning, Torrey Westrom,
Chief Clerk of the House................................ Al Mathiowetz

2012 Regular Session.............................Jan. 24 – May 21, 2012
Number of Senatorial Districts.........................................67
Number of Representative Districts ..................................67

## EXECUTIVE BRANCH

Governor ....................................................Mark Dayton
Lieutenant Governor .......................Yvonne Prettner Solon
Secretary of State..............................Mark Ritchie
Attorney General ...................................Lori Swanson
Commissioner of Finance ....................Jim Schowalter
Auditor.......................................... Rebecca Otto

Governor's Present Term.............................1/2011 – 1/2015
Number of Elected Officials in the Executive Branch.........5
Number of Members in the Cabinet ................................24

## JUDICIAL BRANCH

Highest Court...............................................Supreme Court
Supreme Court Chief Justice.............Lorie Skjerven Gildea
Number of Supreme Court Judges ..................................7
Number of Intermediate Appellate Court Judges...........16
Number of U.S. Court Districts.........................................1
U.S. Circuit Court...........................................8th Circuit

## STATE INTERNET ADDRESSES

Official State Website ..............................http://www.mn.gov
Governor's Website ...........................http://mn.gov/governor
Legislative Website .......................... http://www.leg.state.mn.us
Judicial Website..............................http://www.mncourts.gov

# Mississippi

Nickname......................................................... The Magnolia State
Motto........................................ *Virtute et Armis* (By Valor and Arms)
Flower .........................................................................Magnolia
Bird........................................................................Mockingbird
Tree..........................................................................Magnolia
Song..................................................................*Go, Mississippi*
Entered the Union................................December 10, 1817
Capital.......................................................................Jackson

## STATISTICS

Land Area (square miles)................................................46,923
Rank in Nation...............................................................31st
Population.............................................................2,978,512
Rank in Nation...............................................................31st
Density per square mile ....................................................63.5
Capital City..............................................................Jackson
Population.............................................................173,514
Rank in State.................................................................1st
Largest City ................................................................Jackson
Number of Representatives in Congress ...............................4
Number of 2012 Electoral Votes.........................................6
Number of County Governments.......................................82
Number of Municipal Governments.................................296
Number of School Districts ...........................................164
Number of Special Districts ...........................................458

## LEGISLATIVE BRANCH

Legislative Body .....................................................Legislature

President of the Senate ...................Lt. Gov. Tate Reeves
President Pro Tem of the Senate........................ Terry Brown
Secretary of the Senate .............................Tressa W. Guynes

Speaker of the House................................ Philip Gunn
Speaker Pro Tem of the House .......................Greg Snowden
Clerk of the House ...................................Andrew Ketchings

2012 Regular Session....................Jan. 3 – May 5, 2012
Number of Senatorial Districts.........................................52
Number of Representative Districts ..................................122

## EXECUTIVE BRANCH

Governor ....................................................Phil Bryant
Lieutenant Governor .......................................Tate Reeves
Secretary of State..............................Delbert Hosemann Jr.
Attorney General ...................................Jim Hood
Treasurer.......................................................Lynn Fitch
Auditor....................................................Stacey Pickering

Governor's Present Term.............................1/2012 – 1/2016
Number of Elected Officials in the Executive Branch.........8
Number of Members in the Cabinet ........... No formal cabinet system

## JUDICIAL BRANCH

Highest Court...............................................Supreme Court
Supreme Court Chief Justice................. William L. Waller Jr.
Number of Supreme Court Judges ..................................9
Number of Intermediate Appellate Court Judges...........10
Number of U.S. Court Districts.........................................2
U.S. Circuit Court...........................................5th Circuit

## STATE INTERNET ADDRESSES

Official State Website ..............................http://www.ms.gov
Governor's Website ...........................http://www.governorbryant.com
Legislative Website ...................... http://billstatus.ls.state.ms.us
Judicial Website..............................http://courts.ms.gov

# Missouri

Nickname................................................................The Show Me State
Motto....................................................*Salus Populi Suprema Lex Esto*
(The Welfare of the People Shall Be the Supreme Law)
Flower ..................................................... White Hawthorn Blossom
Bird ............................................................................... Bluebird
Tree.................................................................Flowering Dogwood
Song.............................................................*Missouri Waltz*
Entered the Union...................................................... August 10, 1821
Capital.............................................................................. Jefferson City

### STATISTICS

Land Area (square miles).........................................68,742
Rank in Nation...........................................................18th
Population..................................................6,010,688
Rank in Nation...........................................................18th
Density per square mile ...............................................87.4
Capital City..................................................... Jefferson City
Population..................................................43,079
Rank in State..............................................................15th
Largest City ..................................................... Kansas City
Population..................................................459,787
Number of Representatives in Congress .............................8
Number of 2012 Electoral Votes.......................................10
Number of Geographic Counties.....................................115
Number of County Governments.....................................114
Number of County Equivalents.......................................1*
Number of Municipal Governments ...............................952
Number of School Districts ...........................................536
Number of Special Districts ...........................................1,809

### LEGISLATIVE BRANCH

Legislative Body ...................................... General Assembly

President of the Senate ....................... Lt. Gov. Peter Kinder
President Pro Tem of the Senate.................. Robert N. Mayer
Secretary of the Senate .................................Terry L. Spieler

Speaker of the House ...................................... Steven Tilley
Speaker Pro Tem of the House ...................Shane Schoeller
Clerk of the House ................................D. Adam Crumbliss

2012 Regular Session...............................Jan. 4 – May 30, 2012
Number of Senatorial Districts .........................................34
Number of Representative Districts ................................163

### EXECUTIVE BRANCH

Governor ...................................................... Jay Nixon
Lieutenant Governor ............................................Peter Kinder
Secretary of State................................Robin Carnahan
Attorney General .........................................Chris Koster
Treasurer.......................................................Clint Zweifel
Auditor.......................................................Tom Schweich
Director, Division of Accounting..........................Stacy Neal

Governor's Present Term.......................... 1/2009 – 1/2013
Number of Elected Officials in the Executive Branch.........6
Number of Members in the Cabinet ...............................17

### JUDICIAL BRANCH

Highest Court.............................................Supreme Court
Supreme Court Chief Justice.......................... Richard B. Teitelman
Number of Supreme Court Judges .....................................7
Number of Intermediate Appellate Court Judges.............32
Number of U.S. Court Districts...........................................2
U.S. Circuit Court.............................................8th Circuit

### STATE INTERNET ADDRESSES

Official State Website ...............................http://www.mo.gov
Governor's Website ........................http://governor.mo.gov
Legislative Website.............................http://www.moga.mo.gov
Judicial Website.......................................http://www.courts.mo.gov

*The city of St. Louis is an Independent City and considered a
county equivalent.

# Montana

Nickname.................................................. The Treasure State
Motto.................................................*Oro y Plata* (Gold and Silver)
Flower .......................................................................Bitterroot
Bird.............................................. Western Meadowlark
Tree..........................................................Ponderosa Pine
Song.............................................................*Montana*
Entered the Union................................... November 8, 1889
Capital.............................................................................Helena

### STATISTICS

Land Area (square miles).........................................145,546
Rank in Nation............................................................4th
Population..................................................998,199
Rank in Nation...........................................................44th
Density per square mile .................................................6.9
Capital City................................................................Helena
Population..................................................28,190
Rank in State..............................................................6th
Largest City ................................................................. Billings
Population..................................................104,170
Number of Representatives in Congress ............................1
Number of 2012 Electoral Votes.......................................3
Number of Geographic Counties.......................................56
Number of County Governments.......................................54
Number of Consolidated Governments...............................2
Number of Municipal Governments ...............................129
Number of School Districts ...........................................332
Number of Special Districts ...........................................758

### LEGISLATIVE BRANCH

Legislative Body ..................................................Legislature

President of the Senate ......................................Jim Peterson
President Pro Tem of the Senate......................Bruce Tutvedt
Secretary of the Senate ............................... Marilyn Miller

Speaker of the House................................ Mike Milburn
Speaker Pro Tem of the House .....................Janna Taylor
Chief Clerk of the House............................... Beth Cargo

2012 Regular Session................................... No regular session in 2012
Number of Senatorial Districts .........................................50
Number of Representative Districts ................................100

### EXECUTIVE BRANCH

Governor ...........................................Brian Schweitzer
Lieutenant Governor .............................John Bohlinger
Secretary of State....................................Linda McCulloch
Attorney General ....................................... Steve Bullock
Treasurer........................................................Janet Kelly
Auditor....................................................Monica Lindeen
Administrator, State Accounting...........Paul Christofferson

Governor's Present Term.......................... 1/2005 – 1/2013
Number of Elected Officials in the Executive Branch.........6
Number of Members in the Cabinet ...............................21

### JUDICIAL BRANCH

Highest Court.............................................Supreme Court
Supreme Court Chief Justice......................... Mike McGrath
Number of Supreme Court Judges .....................................7
Number of Intermediate Appellate Court Judges...............0
Number of U.S. Court Districts...........................................1
U.S. Circuit Court.............................................9th Circuit

### STATE INTERNET ADDRESSES

Official State Website ...............................http://mt.gov
Governor's Website ........................http://governor.mt.gov
Legislative Website.............................http://leg.mt.gov/css/default.asp
Judicial Website.......................................http://courts.mt.gov

# Nebraska

Nickname........................................................... The Cornhusker State
Motto.................................................. *Equality Before the Law*
Flower .................................................................. Goldenrod
Bird.......................................................... Western Meadowlark
Tree........................................................... Western Cottonwood
Song....................................................... *Beautiful Nebraska*
Entered the Union................................................ March 1, 1867
Capital .................................................................. Lincoln

## STATISTICS

Land Area (square miles)...................................................76,824
Rank in Nation................................................................15th
Population.............................................................1,842,641
Rank in Nation................................................................38th
Density per square mile ....................................................22.0
Capital City...............................................................Lincoln
Population................................................................258,379
Rank in State.................................................................2nd
Largest City...............................................................Omaha
Population................................................................408,958
Number of Representatives in Congress .....................................3
Number of 2012 Electoral Votes.............................................5
Number of County Governments............................................93
Number of Municipal Governments.......................................530
Number of School Districts................................................288
Number of Special Districts.............................................1,294

## LEGISLATIVE BRANCH

Legislative Body ..............................Unicameral Legislature

President of the Legislature .................Lt. Gov. Rick Sheehy
Speaker of the Legislature................................. Mike Flood
Chairperson of the Executive Board........................... John Wightman
Clerk of the Legislature ....................... Patrick J. O'Donnell

2012 Regular Session....................Jan. 4 – mid-April, 2012
Number of Legislative Districts................................................49

## EXECUTIVE BRANCH

Governor ........................................................David Heineman
Lieutenant Governor ....................................................Rick Sheehy
Secretary of State..........................................................John Gale
Attorney General ..................................................... Jon Bruning
Treasurer .................................................... Don B. Stenberg
Auditor ...................................................................... Mike Foley
Acting State Accounting Administrator ..........................Wes Mohling

Governor's Present Term.......................... 1/2005 – 1/2015
Number of Elected Officials in the Executive Branch.........................6
Number of Members in the Cabinet ........................................30

## JUDICIAL BRANCH

Highest Court.......................................................Supreme Court
Supreme Court Chief Justice........................... Michael G. Heavican
Number of Supreme Court Judges.............................................7
Number of Intermediate Appellate Court Judges................................6
Number of U.S. Court Districts................................................1
U.S. Circuit Court...........................................................8th Circuit

## STATE INTERNET ADDRESSES

Official State Website ....................................http://www.nebraska.gov
Governor's Website ....................http://www.governor.nebraska.gov
Legislative Website ............................... http://nebraskalegislature.gov
Judicial Website.............................http://www.supremecourt.ne.gov

# Nevada

Nickname..........................................................The Silver State
Motto..........................................................*All for Our Country*
Flower ..................................................................Sagebrush
Bird.............................................................. Mountain Bluebird
Tree.......................Bristlecone Pine and Single-leaf Piñon
Song................................................ *Home Means Nevada*
Entered the Union.................................................. October 31, 1864
Capital ...............................................................Carson City

## STATISTICS

Land Area (square miles)...............................................109,781
Rank in Nation.................................................................7th
Population.............................................................2,723,322
Rank in Nation................................................................35th
Density per square mile ....................................................24.8
Capital City...........................................................Carson City
Population..................................................................55,274
Rank in State.................................................................6th
Largest City ...........................................................Las Vegas
Population................................................................583,756
Number of Representatives in Congress .....................................4
Number of 2012 Electoral Votes.............................................6
Number of Geographic Counties............................................17
Number of County Governments............................................16
Number of County Equivalents.............................................1*
Number of Municipal Governments.........................................19
Number of School Districts................................................17
Number of Special Districts.............................................146

## LEGISLATIVE BRANCH

Legislative Body ..............................................Legislature

President of the Senate ..................Lt. Gov. Brian K. Krolicki
President Pro Tem of the Senate....................... Michael A. Schneider
Secretary of the Senate ......................................David A. Byerman

Speaker of the Assembly .............................. John Oceguera
Speaker Pro Tem of the Assembly......................Deborah June Smith
Chief Clerk of the Assembly ................................Susan Furlong

2012 Regular Session................................ No regular session in 2012
Number of Senatorial Districts .............................................21
Number of Representative Districts .........................................42

## EXECUTIVE BRANCH

Governor ............................................................Brian Sandoval
Lieutenant Governor ...................................................Brian Krolicki
Secretary of State.......................................................... Ross Miller
Attorney General ................................Catherine Cortez Masto
Treasurer.............................................................Kate Marshall
Auditor .................................................... Paul V. Townsend
Controller ............................................................. Kim Wallin

Governor's Present Term............................... 1/2011 – 1/2015
Number of Elected Officials in the Executive Branch.........................6
Number of Members in the Cabinet ........................................23

## JUDICIAL BRANCH

Highest Court..........................................................Supreme Court
Supreme Court Chief Justice.................................Nancy M. Saitta
Number of Supreme Court Judges.............................................7
Number of Intermediate Appellate Court Judges..............................0
Number of U.S. Court Districts................................................1
U.S. Circuit Court...........................................................9th Circuit

## STATE INTERNET ADDRESSES

Official State Website .....................................http://www.nv.gov
Governor's Website ....................................... http://gov.nv.gov
Legislative Website .............................http://www.leg.state.nv.us
Judicial Website.....................................http://www.nevadajudiciary.us

*Carson City is an Independent City and considered a county equivalent.

# New Hampshire

Nickname........................................................The Granite State
Motto..................................................... *Live Free or Die*
Flower .............................................................. Purple Lilac
Bird..................................................................... Purple Finch
Tree........................................................................ White Birch
Song............................................... *Old New Hampshire*
Entered the Union..................................June 21, 1788
Capital............................................................... Concord

## STATISTICS

Land Area (square miles)...................................8,953
Rank in Nation.......................................................44th
Population......................................................1,318,194
Rank in Nation......................................................42nd
Density per square mile ..................................147.2
Capital City.................................................... Concord
Population...........................................................42,695
Rank in State............................................................3rd
Largest City ............................................. Manchester
Population.........................................................109,565
Number of Representatives in Congress ............................2
Number of 2012 Electoral Votes.............................4
Number of County Governments...........................10
Number of Municipal Governments .......................13
Number of School Districts..................................164
Number of Special Districts .................................137

## LEGISLATIVE BRANCH

Legislative Body .............................. General Court

President of the Senate ........................... Peter E. Bragdon
President Pro Tem of the Senate.............................John S. Barnes Jr.
Clerk of the Senate.................................... Tammy L. Wright

Speaker of the House........................... William L. O'Brien
Deputy Speaker of the House.................Pamela Tucker
Clerk of the House ............................... Karen O. Wadsworth

2012 Regular Session...................... Jan. 4 – July 1, 2012
Number of Senatorial Districts...........................24
Number of Representative Districts ...................103

## EXECUTIVE BRANCH

Governor ......................................................John Lynch
Secretary of State.................................... William M. Gardner
Attorney General .....................................Michael A. Delaney
Treasurer........................................ Catherine Provencher
Auditor...................................................Jeffrey A. Pattison
Comptroller.................................................Edgar R. Carter

Governor's Present Term...................... 1/2005 – 1/2013
Number of Elected Officials in the Executive Branch.........................1
Number of Members in the Cabinet ........... No formal cabinet system

## JUDICIAL BRANCH

Highest Court.................................................Supreme Court
Supreme Court Chief Justice......................... Linda S. Dalianis
Number of Supreme Court Judges.............................5
Number of Intermediate Appellate Court Judges.............................0
Number of U.S. Court Districts.............................1
U.S. Circuit Court..........................................1st Circuit

## STATE INTERNET ADDRESSES

Official State Website ................................. http://www.nh.gov
Governor's Website ................... http://www.nh.gov/governor
Legislative Website .............. http://www.gencourt.state.nh.us
Judicial Website..................... http://www.courts.state.nh.us

# New Jersey

Nickname..................................................The Garden State
Motto.........................................*Liberty and Prosperity*
Flower ...............................................................Violet
Bird.........................................................Eastern Goldfinch
Tree.......................................................................Red Oak
Song.......................................... *I'm From New Jersey*
Entered the Union...............................December 18, 1787
Capital .................................................................Trenton

## STATISTICS

Land Area (square miles)...................................7,354
Rank in Nation.......................................................46th
Population......................................................8,821,155
Rank in Nation......................................................11th
Density per square mile ..................................1,199.5
Capital City.......................................................Trenton
Population...........................................................84,913
Rank in State............................................................10th
Largest City ......................................................Newark
Population.........................................................277,140
Number of Representatives in Congress ............................12
Number of 2012 Electoral Votes.............................14
Number of County Governments...........................21
Number of Municipal Governments .......................324
Number of School Districts..................................549
Number of Special Districts .................................247

## LEGISLATIVE BRANCH

Legislative Body ...................................Legislature

President of the Senate ...........................Stephen Sweeney
President Pro Tem of the Senate.............................Nia H. Gill
Secretary of the Senate.................................... Kent Hicks

Speaker of the Assembly ...........................Sheila Y. Oliver
Speaker Pro Tem of the Assembly.......................Jerry Green
Clerk of the General Assembly........................Dana M. Burley

2012 Regular Session................... Jan. 10 – Dec. 31, 2012
Number of Senatorial Districts...........................40
Number of Representative Districts ...................40

## EXECUTIVE BRANCH

Governor ......................................................Chris Christie
Lieutenant Governor .....................................Kim Guadagno
Attorney General .....................................Jeffrey Chiesa
Treasurer........................................Andrew P. Sidamon-Eristoff
Auditor...................................................Stephen Eells
Controller ................................................. Matthew Boxer

Governor's Present Term...................... 1/2010 – 1/2014
Number of Elected Officials in the Executive Branch.........................2
Number of Members in the Cabinet .......................24

## JUDICIAL BRANCH

Highest Court.................................................Supreme Court
Supreme Court Chief Justice.........................Stuart Rabner
Number of Supreme Court Judges.............................7
Number of Intermediate Appellate Court Judges.............................35
Number of U.S. Court Districts.............................1
U.S. Circuit Court..........................................3rd Circuit

## STATE INTERNET ADDRESSES

Official State Website ................................. http://www.nj.gov
Governor's Website ................... http://www.state.nj.us/governor
Legislative Website .............. http://www.njleg.state.nj.us
Judicial Website..................... http://www.judiciary.state.nj.us

# New Mexico

Nickname..............................................The Land of Enchantment
Motto.........................................*Crescit Eundo* (It Grows As It Goes)
Flower ............................................ Yucca (Our Lord's Candles)
Bird..................................................................... Chaparral Bird
Tree.......................................................................................... Piñon
Songs ...................................................*Asi es Nuevo Mexico* and
*O, Fair New Mexico*
Entered the Union.................................................. January 6, 1912
Capital............................................................................. Santa Fe

## STATISTICS

Land Area (square miles)................................................121,298
Rank in Nation...........................................................................5th
Population..................................................................2,082,224
Rank in Nation........................................................................36th
Density per square mile ..........................................................17.2
Capital City......................................................................... Santa Fe
Population..................................................................................67,947
Rank in State.............................................................................4th
Largest City ............................................................ Albuquerque
Population..................................................................................545,852
Number of Representatives in Congress ..................................3
Number of 2012 Electoral Votes.............................................5
Number of County Governments..........................................33
Number of Municipal Governments ...................................101
Number of School Districts .....................................................96
Number of Special Districts ...................................................633

## LEGISLATIVE BRANCH

Legislative Body ..................................................Legislature

President of the Senate ................................ Lt. Gov. John A. Sanchez
President Pro Tem of the Senate............................ Timothy Z. Jennings
Chief Clerk of the Senate ..........................................Lenore Naranjo

Speaker of the House..........................................................Ben Lujan
Chief Clerk of the House.............................................Stephen R. Arias

2012 Regular Session.............................Jan. 17 – Feb. 16, 2012
Number of Senatorial Districts .................................................42
Number of Representative Districts .........................................70

## EXECUTIVE BRANCH

Governor ..........................................................Susana Martinez
Lieutenant Governor ......................................... John A. Sanchez
Secretary of State................................................ Dianna J. Duran
Attorney General ..................................................... Gary King
Treasurer.................................................................... James Lewis
Auditor...............................................................Hector Balderas
Controller .................................................... Ricky Bejarano

Governor's Present Term................................ 1/2011 – 1/2015
Number of Elected Officials in the Executive Branch..........................5
Number of Members in the Cabinet ........................................25

## JUDICIAL BRANCH

Highest Court.........................................................Supreme Court
Supreme Court Chief Justice..............................Petra Jimenez Maes
Number of Supreme Court Judges ..........................................5
Number of Intermediate Appellate Court Judges.............................10
Number of U.S. Court Districts.................................................1
U.S. Circuit Court.................................................10th Circuit

## STATE INTERNET ADDRESSES

Official State Website .........................http://www.newmexico.gov
Governor's Website ...........................http://www.governor.state.nm.us
Legislative Website ..................................http://www.nmlegis.gov
Judicial Website................................http://www.nmcourts.gov

# New York

Nickname......................................................The Empire State
Motto..................................................*Excelsior* (Ever Upward)
Flower ...................................................................................Rose
Bird............................................................................... Bluebird
Tree.............................................................. Sugar Maple
Song ............................................................ *I Love New York*
Entered the Union...............................................July 26, 1788
Capital..............................................................................Albany

## STATISTICS

Land Area (square miles)...............................................47,126
Rank in Nation........................................................................30th
Population.............................................................19,465,197
Rank in Nation..........................................................................3rd
Density per square mile .........................................................413
Capital City..............................................................................Albany
Population..................................................................................97,856
Rank in State........................................................................... 6th
Largest City ......................................................New York City
Population..................................................................8,175,133
Number of Representatives in Congress .............................27
Number of 2012 Electoral Votes............................................29
Number of Geographic Counties...........................................62*
Number of County Governments.........................................57
Number of Consolidated Governments..................................1*
Number of Municipal Governments ...................................618
Number of School Districts ...................................................680
Number of Special Districts ...................................................1,119

## LEGISLATIVE BRANCH

Legislative Body ..................................................Legislature

President of the Senate ..................................... Lt. Gov. Robert Duffy
Majority Leader of the Senate.. ....................................Dean G. Skelos
Secretary of the Senate .................................. Frank Patience

Speaker of the Assembly ............................... Sheldon Silver
Speaker Pro Tempore of the Assembly............................ Peter Rivera
Clerk of the Assembly....................................Laurene R. Kretzler

2012 Regular Session..............................Jan. 4 – Dec. 31, 2012
Number of Senatorial Districts .................................................62
Number of Representative Districts .........................................150

## EXECUTIVE BRANCH

Governor ..........................................................Andrew M. Cuomo
Lieutenant Governor .............................................Robert Duffy
Secretary of State................................................Cesar Perales
Attorney General ...................................... Eric T. Schneiderman
Treasurer................................................................ Aida Brewer
Comptroller....................................................Thomas P. DiNapoli

Governor's Present Term................................ 1/2011 – 1/2015
Number of Elected Officials in the Executive Branch..........................4
Number of Members in the Cabinet ........................................75

## JUDICIAL BRANCH

Highest Court............................................................Court of Appeals
Court of Appeals Chief Justice ................................Jonathan Lippman
Number of Court of Appeals Judges.........................................7
Number of Intermediate Appellate Court Judges.............................57
Number of U.S. Court Districts.................................................4
U.S. Circuit Court.................................................. 2nd Circuit

## STATE INTERNET ADDRESSES

Official State Website .................................... http://www.state.ny.us
Governor's Website ..................................http://www.governor.ny.gov
Senate Website ......................................... http://www.nysenate.gov
Assembly Website.........................................http://assembly.state.ny.us
Judicial Website...................................http://www.courts.state.ny.us

*New York City is coextensive with the five boroughs (counties).

# North Carolina

| | |
|---|---|
| Nickname | The Tar Heel State and Old North State |
| Motto | *Esse Quam Videri* |
| | (To Be Rather Than to Seem) |
| Flower | Dogwood |
| Bird | Cardinal |
| Tree | Long Leaf Pine |
| Song | *The Old North State* |
| Entered the United States | November 21, 1789 |
| Capital | Raleigh |

## STATISTICS

| | |
|---|---|
| Land Area (square miles) | 48,618 |
| Rank in Nation | 29th |
| Population | 9,656,401 |
| Rank in Nation | 10th |
| Density per square mile | 198.6 |
| Capital City | Raleigh |
| Population | 403,892 |
| Rank in State | 2nd |
| Largest City | Charlotte |
| Population | 731,424 |
| Number of Representatives in Congress | 13 |
| Number of 2012 Electoral Votes | 15 |
| Number of County Governments | 100 |
| Number of Municipal Governments | 548 |
| Number of School Districts | 0 |
| Number of Special Districts | 315 |

## LEGISLATIVE BRANCH

| | |
|---|---|
| Legislative Body | General Assembly |
| | |
| President of the Senate | Lt. Gov. Walter Dalton |
| President Pro Tem of the Senate | Phil Berger |
| Principal Clerk of the Senate | Sarah Clapp |
| | |
| Speaker of the House | Thom Tillis |
| Speaker Pro Tempore of the House | Dale Folwell |
| Principal Clerk of the House | Denise Weeks |
| | |
| 2012 Regular Session | Jan. 4 – mid-July 2012 |
| Number of Senatorial Districts | 50 |
| Number of Representative Districts | 120 |

## EXECUTIVE BRANCH

| | |
|---|---|
| Governor | Beverly Perdue |
| Lieutenant Governor | Walter Dalton |
| Secretary of State | Elaine Marshall |
| Attorney General | Roy A. Cooper III |
| Treasurer | Jane Cowell |
| Auditor | Beth Wood |
| Controller | David McCoy |
| | |
| Governor's Present Term | 1/2009 – 1/2013 |
| Number of Elected Officials in the Executive Branch | 10 |
| Number of Members in the Cabinet | 10 |

## JUDICIAL BRANCH

| | |
|---|---|
| Highest Court | Supreme Court |
| Supreme Court Chief Justice | Sarah Parker |
| Number of Supreme Court Judges | 7 |
| Number of Intermediate Appellate Court Judges | 15 |
| Number of U.S. Court Districts | 3 |
| U.S. Circuit Court | 4th Circuit |

## STATE INTERNET ADDRESSES

| | |
|---|---|
| Official State Website | http://www.ncgov.com |
| Governor's Website | http://www.governor.state.nc.us |
| Legislative Website | http://www.ncga.state.nc.us |
| Judicial Website | http://www.nccourts.org |

# North Dakota

| | |
|---|---|
| Nickname | Peace Garden State |
| Motto | *Liberty and Union, Now and Forever,* |
| | *One and Inseparable* |
| Flower | Wild Prairie Rose |
| Bird | Western Meadowlark |
| Tree | American Elm |
| Song | *North Dakota Hymn* |
| Entered the Union | November 2, 1889 |
| Capital | Bismarck |

## STATISTICS

| | |
|---|---|
| Land Area (square miles) | 69,001 |
| Rank in Nation | 17th |
| Population | 683,932 |
| Rank in Nation | 48th |
| Density per square mile | 9.9 |
| Capital City | Bismarck |
| Population | 61,272 |
| Rank in State | 2nd |
| Largest City | Fargo |
| Population | 105,549 |
| Number of Representatives in Congress | 1 |
| Number of 2012 Electoral Votes | 3 |
| Number of County Governments | 53 |
| Number of Municipal Governments | 357 |
| Number of School Districts | 198 |
| Number of Special Districts | 771 |

## LEGISLATIVE BRANCH

| | |
|---|---|
| Legislative Body | Legislative Assembly |
| | |
| President of the Senate | Lt. Gov. Drew Wrigley |
| President Pro Tem of the Senate | Richard Wardner |
| Secretary of the Senate | William Horton |
| | |
| Speaker of the House | David Drovdal |
| Clerk of the House | Buell Reich |
| | |
| 2012 Regular Session | No regular session in 2012 |
| Number of Senatorial Districts | 47 |
| Number of Representative Districts | 47 |

## EXECUTIVE BRANCH

| | |
|---|---|
| Governor | Jack Dalrymple |
| Lieutenant Governor | Drew Wrigley |
| Secretary of State | Alvin Jaeger |
| Attorney General | Wayne Stenehjem |
| Treasurer | Kelly Schmidt |
| Auditor | Robert R. Peterson |
| | |
| Governor's Present Term | 12/2000 – 12/2012 |
| Number of Elected Officials in the Executive Branch | 10 |
| Number of Members in the Cabinet | 18 |

## JUDICIAL BRANCH

| | |
|---|---|
| Highest Court | Supreme Court |
| Supreme Court Chief Justice | Jerry W. VandeWalle |
| Number of Supreme Court Judges | 5 |
| Number of Intermediate Appellate Court Judges | 0 |
| Number of U.S. Court Districts | 1 |
| U.S. Circuit Court | 8th Circuit |

## STATE INTERNET ADDRESSES

| | |
|---|---|
| Official State Website | http://www.nd.gov |
| Governor's Website | http://governor.nd.gov |
| Legislative Website | http://www.legis.nd.gov |
| Judicial Website | http://www.ndcourts.gov |

# Ohio

Nickname................................................................The Buckeye State
Motto...............................................*With God, All Things Are Possible*
Flower .............................................................Scarlet Carnation
Bird.............................................................................. Cardinal
Tree................................................................................. Buckeye
Song..........................................................................*Beautiful Ohio*
Entered the Union................................................... March 1, 1803
Capital...................................................................Columbus

## STATISTICS

Land Area (square miles)........................................40,861
Rank in Nation...............................................................35th
Population..............................................................11,544,951
Rank in Nation.................................................................7th
Density per square mile.........................................282.5
Capital City...................................................Columbus
Population.................................................................787,033
Rank in State....................................................................1st
Largest City...................................................Columbus
Number of Representatives in Congress ...........................16
Number of 2012 Electoral Votes..................................18
Number of County Governments.....................................88
Number of Municipal Governments ...........................938
Number of School Districts ...........................................668
Number of Special Districts ........................................700

## LEGISLATIVE BRANCH

Legislative Body ......................................... General Assembly

President of the Senate ...................................Thomas E. Niehaus
President Pro Tem of the Senate.........................................Keith Faber
Clerk of the Senate ........................................ Vincent Keeran

Speaker of the House............................William G. Batchelder
Speaker Pro Tem of the House ........................ Louis W. Blessing Jr.
Legislative Clerk of the House ................................ Laura P. Clemens

2012 Regular Session.......................................... Jan. 3 – Dec. 31, 2012
Number of Senatorial Districts ...........................................33
Number of Representative Districts ......................................99

## EXECUTIVE BRANCH

Governor .....................................................................John Kasich
Lieutenant Governor ........................................ Mary Taylor
Secretary of State...............................................Jon Husted
Attorney General ........................................Mike DeWine
Treasurer..............................................................Josh Mandel
Auditor..................................................................... David A. Yost

Governor's Present Term........................................ 1/2011 – 1/2015
Number of Elected Officials in the Executive Branch.......................6
Number of Members in the Cabinet ....................................24

## JUDICIAL BRANCH

Highest Court..........................................................Supreme Court
Supreme Court Chief Justice.................................. Maureen O'Connor
Number of Supreme Court Judges ........................................7
Number of Intermediate Appellate Court Judges............................68
Number of U.S. Court Districts...............................................2
U.S. Circuit Court..........................................................6th Circuit

## STATE INTERNET ADDRESSES

Official State Website ............................... http://ohio.gov
Governor's Website .............................http://governor.ohio.gov
Legislative Website ...........................http://www.legislature.state.oh.us
Judicial Website.......................http://www.supremecourt.ohio.gov

# Oklahoma

Nickname............................................................ The Sooner State
Motto...................... *Labor Omnia Vincit* (Labor Conquers All Things)
Flower .....................................................................Mistletoe
Bird..................................................... Scissor-tailed Flycatcher
Tree.............................................................................Redbud
Song.........................................................................*Oklahoma*
Entered the Union................................................ November 16, 1907
Capital............................................................Oklahoma City

## STATISTICS

Land Area (square miles)...........................................68,595
Rank in Nation................................................................19th
Population.............................................................3,791,508
Rank in Nation................................................................28th
Density per square mile .............................................55.3
Capital City....................................................Oklahoma City
Population.............................................................579,999
Rank in State.....................................................................1st
Largest City....................................................Oklahoma City
Number of Representatives in Congress ............................5
Number of 2012 Electoral Votes..................................7
Number of County Governments....................................77
Number of Municipal Governments ...........................594
Number of School Districts .......................................567
Number of Special Districts ........................................642

## LEGISLATIVE BRANCH

Legislative Body ......................................................Legislature

President of the Senate .........................................Lt. Gov. Todd Lamb
President Pro Tem of the Senate..........................Brian Bingman
Secretary of the Senate ...................................... Paul Ziriax

Speaker of the House.............................................Kris Steele
Speaker Pro Tem of the House .............................Jeffrey W. Hickman
Chief Clerk of the House........................................ Jan Harrison

2012 Regular Session......................................Feb. 6 – May 25, 2012
Number of Senatorial Districts ...........................................50
Number of Representative Districts ..................................101

## EXECUTIVE BRANCH

Governor .................................................................Mary Fallin
Lieutenant Governor ........................................... Todd Lamb
Secretary of State...............................................Glenn Coffee
Attorney General ............................................Scott Pruitt
Treasurer..............................................................Ken Miller
Auditor..................................................................... Gary Jones
Comptroller..................................................... Lynne Bajema

Governor's Present Term........................................ 1/2011 – 1/2015
Number of Elected Officials in the Executive Branch.......................8
Number of Members in the Cabinet ....................................16

## JUDICIAL BRANCH

Highest Court..........................................................Supreme Court
Supreme Court Chief Justice..................................Steven W. Taylor
Number of Supreme Court Judges ........................................9
Number of Intermediate Appellate Court Judges............................10
Number of U.S. Court Districts...............................................3
U.S. Circuit Court..........................................................10th Circuit

## STATE INTERNET ADDRESSES

Official State Website ............................... http://www.ok.gov
Governor's Website .............................http://www.ok.gov/governor
Legislative Website ...........................http://www.oklegislature.gov
Judicial Website.......................http://www.oscn.net

# Oregon

| | |
|---|---|
| Nickname | The Beaver State |
| Motto | *She Flies with Her Own Wings* |
| Flower | Oregon Grape |
| Bird | Western Meadowlark |
| Tree | Douglas Fir |
| Song | *Oregon, My Oregon* |
| Entered the Union | February 14, 1859 |
| Capital | Salem |

## STATISTICS

| | |
|---|---|
| Land Area (square miles) | 95,988 |
| Rank in Nation | 10th |
| Population | 3,871,859 |
| Rank in Nation | 27th |
| Density per square mile | 40.3 |
| Capital City | Salem |
| Population | 153,637 |
| Rank in State | 3rd |
| Largest City | Portland |
| Population | 583,776 |
| Number of Representatives in Congress | 5 |
| Number of 2012 Electoral Votes | 7 |
| Number of County Governments | 36 |
| Number of Municipal Governments | 242 |
| Number of School Districts | 234 |
| Number of Special Districts | 1,034 |

## LEGISLATIVE BRANCH

| | |
|---|---|
| Legislative Body | Legislative Assembly |
| | |
| President of the Senate | Peter Courtney |
| President Pro Tem of the Senate | Ginny Burdick |
| Secretary of the Senate | Robert Taylor |
| | |
| Speaker of the House | Bruce Hanna; Arnie Roblan |
| Speaker Pro Tempore of the House | Tina Kotek; Andy Olson |
| Chief Clerk of the House | Ramona Kenady |
| | |
| 2012 Regular Session | Feb. 1 – March 5, 2012 |
| Number of Senatorial Districts | 30 |
| Number of Representative Districts | 60 |

## EXECUTIVE BRANCH

| | |
|---|---|
| Governor | John A. Kitzhaber |
| Secretary of State | Kate Brown |
| Attorney General | John Kroger |
| Treasurer | Ted Wheeler |
| Auditor | Gary Blackmer |
| Acting Controller | Joy Sebastian |
| | |
| Governor's Present Term | 1/2011 – 1/2015 |
| Number of Elected Officials in the Executive Branch | 6 |
| Number of Members in the Cabinet | No formal cabinet system |

## JUDICIAL BRANCH

| | |
|---|---|
| Highest Court | Supreme Court |
| Supreme Court Chief Justice | Paul J. De Muniz |
| Number of Supreme Court Judges | 7 |
| Number of Intermediate Appellate Court Judges | 10 |
| Number of U.S. Court Districts | 1 |
| U.S. Circuit Court | 9th Circuit |

## STATE INTERNET ADDRESSES

| | |
|---|---|
| Official State Website | http://www.oregon.gov |
| Governor's Website | http://governor.oregon.gov |
| Legislative Website | http://www.leg.state.or.us |
| Judicial Website | https://courts.oregon.gov |

# Pennsylvania

| | |
|---|---|
| Nickname | The Keystone State |
| Motto | *Virtue, Liberty and Independence* |
| Bird | Ruffed Grouse |
| Flower | Mountain Laurel |
| Tree | Hemlock |
| Song | *Pennsylvania* |
| Entered the Union | December 12, 1787 |
| Capital | Harrisburg |

## STATISTICS

| | |
|---|---|
| Land Area (square miles) | 44,743 |
| Rank in Nation | 32nd |
| Population | 12,742,886 |
| Rank in Nation | 6th |
| Density per square mile | 284.8 |
| Capital City | Harrisburg |
| Population | 49,528 |
| Rank in State | 15th |
| Largest City | Philadelphia |
| Population | 1,526,006 |
| Number of Representatives in Congress | 18 |
| Number of 2012 Electoral Votes | 20 |
| Number of Geographic Counties | 67 |
| Number of County Governments | 66 |
| Number of Consolidated Governments | 1 |
| Number of Municipal Governments | 1,016 |
| Number of School Districts | 515 |
| Number of Special Districts | 1,728 |

## LEGISLATIVE BRANCH

| | |
|---|---|
| Legislative Body | General Assembly |
| | |
| President of the Senate | Lt. Gov. Jim Cawley |
| President Pro Tem of the Senate | Joseph B. Scarnati |
| Secretary-Parliamentarian of the Senate | Mark R. Corrigan |
| | |
| Speaker of the House | Samuel H. Smith |
| Chief Clerk of the House | Anthony Frank Barbush |
| | |
| 2012 Regular Session | Jan. 3 – Dec. 31, 2012 |
| Number of Senatorial Districts | 50 |
| Number of Representative Districts | 203 |

## EXECUTIVE BRANCH

| | |
|---|---|
| Governor | Tom Corbett |
| Lieutenant Governor | Jim Cawley |
| Secretary of State | Carol Aichele |
| Attorney General | Linda Kelly |
| Treasurer | Robert McCord |
| Comptroller | Anna Marie Kiehl |
| | |
| Governor's Present Term | 1/2011 – 1/2015 |
| Number of Elected Officials in the Executive Branch | 5 |
| Number of Members in the Cabinet | 28 |

## JUDICIAL BRANCH

| | |
|---|---|
| Highest Court | Supreme Court |
| Supreme Court Chief Justice | Ronald D. Castille |
| Number of Supreme Court Judges | 7 |
| Number of Intermediate Appellate Court Judges | 23 |
| Number of U.S. Court Districts | 3 |
| U.S. Circuit Court | 3rd Circuit |

## STATE INTERNET ADDRESSES

| | |
|---|---|
| Official State Website | http://pa.gov |
| Governor's Website | http://www.governor.state.pa.us |
| Legislative Website | http://www.legis.state.pa.us |
| Judicial Website | http://www.apoc.org |

# Rhode Island

Nicknames .................................. Little Rhody and Ocean State
Motto .......................................................................... *Hope*
Flower ......................................................................... Violet
Bird ..................................................... Rhode Island Red
Tree ............................................................. Red Maple
Song ................................................................... *Rhode Island*
Entered the Union ........................................ May 29, 1790
Capital ................................................................. Providence

## STATISTICS

Land Area (square miles) ........................................... 1,034
Rank in Nation ........................................................... 50th
Population ........................................................... 1,051,302
Rank in Nation ........................................................... 43rd
Density per square mile ........................................ 1,016.9
Capital City ....................................................... Providence
Population ............................................................. 178,042
Rank in State ................................................................ 1st
Largest City ...................................................... Providence
Number of Representatives in Congress ........................ 2
Number of 2012 Electoral Votes ................................... 4
Number of Geographic Counties ................................... 5
Number of County Governments ................................... 0
Number of Municipal Governments ............................... 8
Number of School Districts ........................................... 4
Number of Special Districts ........................................ 91

## LEGISLATIVE BRANCH

Legislative Body ....................................... General Assembly

President of the Senate ....................... M. Teresa Paiva-Weed
President Pro Tem of the Senate ............... Juan M. Pichardo
Secretary of the Senate ............................... Joseph Brady

Speaker of the House ..................................... Gordon Fox
Speaker Pro Tem of the House ............... Elaine A. Coderre
Clerk of the House ................................. Frank McCabe

2012 Regular Session ...................... Jan. 3 – mid-June 2012
Number of Senatorial Districts .................................... 38
Number of Representative Districts ............................. 75

## EXECUTIVE BRANCH

Governor ........................................... Lincoln D. Chafee
Lieutenant Governor ..................... Elizabeth H. Roberts
Secretary of State ......................................... Ralph Mollis
Attorney General .............................. Peter F. Kilmartin
Treasurer ........................................... Gina M. Raimondo
Auditor ................................................. Dennis Hoyle
Controller ......................................... Marc Leonetti

Governor's Present Term ..................... 1/2011 – 1/2015
Number of Elected Officials in the Executive Branch ......... 5
Number of Members in the Cabinet ......................... 20

## JUDICIAL BRANCH

Highest Court .................................... Supreme Court
Supreme Court Chief Justice ................... Paul A. Suttell
Number of Supreme Court Judges ............................. 5
Number of Intermediate Appellate Court Judges ............ 0
Number of U.S. Court Districts ................................... 1
U.S. Circuit Court ........................................... 1st Circuit

## STATE INTERNET ADDRESSES

Official State Website ........................... http://www.ri.gov
Governor's Website ................... http://www.governor.ri.gov
Legislative Website ..................... http://www.rilin.state.ri.us
Judicial Website ........................... http://www.courts.ri.gov

# South Carolina

Nickname .......................................... The Palmetto State
Motto ................................................ *Animis Opibusque Parati*
(Prepared in Mind and Resources) and
*Dum Spiro Spero* (While I breathe, I Hope)
Flower ......................................... Yellow Jessamine
Bird ................................................. Carolina Wren
Tree ...................................................... Palmetto
Songs ................... *Carolina* and *South Carolina on My Mind*
Entered the Union .................................. May 23, 1788
Capital .................................................... Columbia

## STATISTICS

Land Area (square miles) ....................................... 30,061
Rank in Nation ........................................................... 40th
Population ........................................................... 4,679,230
Rank in Nation ........................................................... 24th
Density per square mile ........................................... 155.7
Capital City ............................................................ Columbia
Population ............................................................. 129,272
Rank in State ................................................................ 1st
Largest City ............................................................ Columbia
Number of Representatives in Congress ........................ 7
Number of 2012 Electoral Votes ................................... 9
Number of County Governments ................................. 46
Number of Municipal Governments ........................... 268
Number of School Districts ....................................... 85
Number of Special Districts .................................... 299

## LEGISLATIVE BRANCH

Legislative Body ....................................... General Assembly

President of the Senate ................ Lt. Gov. Glenn F. McConnell
President Pro Tem of the Senate .................. John Courson
Clerk of the Senate ............................... Jeffrey S. Gossett

Speaker of the House ......................... Robert W. Harrell Jr.
Speaker Pro Tem of the House ................... James H. Lucas
Clerk of the House ................................. Charles F. Reid

2012 Regular Session ...................... Jan. 11 – June 7, 2012
Number of Senatorial Districts .................................... 46
Number of Representative Districts ........................... 124

## EXECUTIVE BRANCH

Governor ............................................... Nikki Haley
Lieutenant Governor ....................... Glenn McConnell
Secretary of State ............................. Mark Hammond
Attorney General ................................... Alan Wilson
Treasurer ............................................. Curtis Loftis
Auditor ................................... Richard H. Gilbert Jr.
Comptroller .................................... Richard Eckstrom

Governor's Present Term ..................... 1/2011 – 1/2015
Number of Elected Officials in the Executive Branch ......... 9
Number of Members in the Cabinet ......................... 16

## JUDICIAL BRANCH

Highest Court .................................... Supreme Court
Supreme Court Chief Justice ................. Jean Hoefer Toal
Number of Supreme Court Judges ............................. 5
Number of Intermediate Appellate Court Judges .......... 10
Number of U.S. Court Districts ................................... 1
U.S. Circuit Court ........................................... 4th Circuit

## STATE INTERNET ADDRESSES

Official State Website ........................... http://www.sc.gov
Governor's Website ....................... http://governor.sc.gov
Legislative Website ................... http://www.scstatehouse.gov
Judicial Website ..................... http://www.judicial.state.sc.us

# South Dakota

| | |
|---|---|
| Nickname | The Mt. Rushmore State |
| Motto | *Under God the People Rule* |
| Flower | American Pasque |
| Bird | Ring-necked Pheasant |
| Tree | Black Hills Spruce |
| Song | *Hail, South Dakota* |
| Entered the Union | November 2, 1889 |
| Capital | Pierre |

## STATISTICS

| | |
|---|---|
| Land Area (square miles) | 75,811 |
| Rank in Nation | 16th |
| Population | 824,082 |
| Rank in Nation | 46th |
| Density per square mile | 10.9 |
| Capital City | Pierre |
| Population | 13,646 |
| Rank in State | 8th |
| Largest City | Sioux Falls |
| Population | 153,888 |
| Number of Representatives in Congress | 1 |
| Number of 2012 Electoral Votes | 3 |
| Number of County Governments | 66 |
| Number of Municipal Governments | 309 |
| Number of School Districts | 166 |
| Number of Special Districts | 526 |

## LEGISLATIVE BRANCH

| | |
|---|---|
| Legislative Body | Legislature |
| | |
| President of the Senate | Lt. Gov. Matthew Michels |
| President Pro Tem of the Senate | Bob Gray |
| Secretary of the Senate | Trudy Evenstad |
| | |
| Speaker of the House | Val Rausch |
| Speaker Pro Tem of the House | Brian G. Gosch |
| Chief Clerk of the House | Karen Gerdes |
| | |
| 2012 Regular Session | Jan. 10 – March 19, 2012 |
| Number of Senatorial Districts | 35 |
| Number of Representative Districts | 35 |

## EXECUTIVE BRANCH

| | |
|---|---|
| Governor | Dennis Daugaard |
| Lieutenant Governor | Matthew Michels |
| Secretary of State | Jason M. Gant |
| Attorney General | Martin Jackley |
| Treasurer | Rich Sattgast |
| Auditor | Steve Barnett |
| | |
| Governor's Present Term | 1/2011 – 1/2015 |
| Number of Elected Officials in the Executive Branch | 7 |
| Number of Members in the Cabinet | 19 |

## JUDICIAL BRANCH

| | |
|---|---|
| Highest Court | Supreme Court |
| Supreme Court Chief Justice | David E. Gilbertson |
| Number of Supreme Court Judges | 5 |
| Number of Intermediate Appellate Court Judges | 0 |
| Number of U.S. Court Districts | 1 |
| U.S. Circuit Court | 8th Circuit |

## STATE INTERNET ADDRESSES

| | |
|---|---|
| Official State Website | http://sd.gov |
| Governor's Website | http://sd.gov/governor |
| Legislative Website | http://legis.state.sd.us |
| Judicial Website | http://www.sdjudicial.com |

# Tennessee

| | |
|---|---|
| Nickname | The Volunteer State |
| Motto | *Agriculture and Commerce* |
| Flower | Iris |
| Bird | Mockingbird |
| Tree | Tulip Poplar |
| Songs | *When It's Iris Time in Tennessee*; *The Tennessee Waltz*; *My Homeland, Tennessee*; *My Tennessee*; and *Rocky Top* |
| Entered the Union | June 1, 1796 |
| Capital | Nashville |

## STATISTICS

| | |
|---|---|
| Land Area (square miles) | 41,235 |
| Rank in Nation | 34th |
| Population | 6,403,353 |
| Rank in Nation | 17th |
| Density per square mile | 155.3 |
| Capital City | Nashville |
| Population | 626,681 |
| Rank in State | 2nd |
| Largest City | Memphis |
| Population | 646,889 |
| Number of Representatives in Congress | 9 |
| Number of 2012 Electoral Votes | 11 |
| Number of Geographic Counties | 95 |
| Number of County Governments | 92 |
| Number of Consolidated Governments | 3 |
| Number of Municipal Governments | 347 |
| Number of School Districts | 14 |
| Number of Special Districts | 475 |

## LEGISLATIVE BRANCH

| | |
|---|---|
| Legislative Body | General Assembly |
| | |
| Senate President | Lt. Gov. Ron Ramsey |
| Speaker Pro Tem of the Senate | Bo Watson |
| Chief Clerk of the Senate | Russell Humphrey |
| | |
| Speaker of the House | Beth Harwell |
| Speaker Pro Tem of the House | Judd Matheny |
| Chief Clerk of the House | Joe McCord |
| | |
| 2012 Regular Session | Jan. 10 – mid-May 2012 |
| Number of Senatorial Districts | 33 |
| Number of Representative Districts | 99 |

## EXECUTIVE BRANCH

| | |
|---|---|
| Governor | Bill Haslam |
| Lieutenant Governor | Ron Ramsey |
| Secretary of State | Tre Hargett |
| Attorney General | Robert Cooper |
| Treasurer | David H. Lillard Jr. |
| Auditor | Arthur A. Hayes Jr. |
| Comptroller | Jan I. Sylvis |
| | |
| Governor's Present Term | 1/2011 – 1/2015 |
| Number of Elected Officials in the Executive Branch | 1 |
| Number of Members in the Cabinet | 28 |

## JUDICIAL BRANCH

| | |
|---|---|
| Highest Court | Supreme Court |
| Supreme Court Chief Justice | Cornelia Clark |
| Number of Supreme Court Judges | 5 |
| Number of Intermediate Appellate Court Judges | 24 |
| Number of U.S. Court Districts | 3 |
| U.S. Circuit Court | 6th Circuit |

## STATE INTERNET ADDRESSES

| | |
|---|---|
| Official State Website | http://www.tn.gov |
| Governor's Website | http://www.tn.gov/governor |
| Legislative Website | http://www.capitol.tn.gov |
| Judicial Website | http://www.tncourts.gov |

# Texas

Nickname....................................................The Lone Star State
Motto.........................................................................*Friendship*
Flower ......................Bluebonnet (Buffalo Clover, Wolf Flower)
Bird.....................................................................Mockingbird
Tree...............................................................................Pecan
Song.......................................................*Texas, Our Texas*
Entered the Union....................................December 29, 1845
Capital.........................................................................Austin

## STATISTICS

Land Area (square miles)....................................261,232
Rank in Nation.........................................................2nd
Population......................................................25,674,681
Rank in Nation.........................................................2nd
Density per square mile ..........................................98.3
Capital City.............................................................Austin
Population..............................................................790,390
Rank in State.............................................................4th
Largest City ......................................................... Houston
Population.........................................................2,099,451
Number of Representatives in Congress .....................36
Number of 2012 Electoral Votes.................................38
Number of County Governments...............................254
Number of Municipal Governments .......................1,209
Number of School Districts....................................1,081
Number of Special Districts ..................................2,291

## LEGISLATIVE BRANCH

Legislative Body ...........................................Legislature

President of the Senate .................Lt. Gov. David Dewhurst
President Pro Tem of the Senate.......................Mike Jackson
Secretary of the Senate ...................................Patsy Spaw

Speaker of the House.......................................Joe Straus
Speaker Pro Tem of the House ........................ Craig Eiland
Chief Clerk of the House...............................Robert Haney

2012 Regular Session....................No regular session in 2012
Number of Senatorial Districts.....................................31
Number of Representative Districts ...................150

## EXECUTIVE BRANCH

Governor ........................................................Rick Perry
Lieutenant Governor ...............................David Dewhurst
Secretary of State..................................Esperanza Andrade
Attorney General ..........................................Greg Abbott
Comptroller of Public Accounts ........................ Susan Combs
Auditor...........................................................John Keel

Governor's Present Term.................................. 12/2000 – 1/2015
Number of Elected Officials in the Executive Branch.......................9
Number of Members in the Cabinet ........... No formal cabinet system

## JUDICIAL BRANCH

Highest Court.............................................Supreme Court
Supreme Court Chief Justice.................Wallace B. Jefferson
Number of Supreme Court Judges .................................9
Number of Intermediate Appellate Court Judges............................80
Number of U.S. Court Districts......................................4
U.S. Circuit Court........................................ 5th Circuit

## STATE INTERNET ADDRESSES

Official State Website ..............................http://www.texas.gov
Governor's Website ...........................http://www.governor.state.tx.us
Legislative Website ..........................http://www.capitol.state.tx.us
Judicial Website.............................. http://www.courts.state.tx.us

# Utah

Nickname....................................................The Beehive State
Motto.........................................................................*Industry*
Flower ..........................................................Sego Lily
Bird.................................................. California Seagull
Tree..........................................................Blue Spruce
Song....................................................*Utah, We Love Thee*
Entered the Union.................................... January 4, 1896
Capital.........................................................Salt Lake City

## STATISTICS

Land Area (square miles)..........................................82,170
Rank in Nation........................................................12th
Population......................................................2,817,222
Rank in Nation........................................................34th
Density per square mile ..........................................34.3
Capital City......................................................Salt Lake City
Population..............................................................186,440
Rank in State..............................................................1st
Largest City ......................................................Salt Lake City
Number of Representatives in Congress .......................4
Number of 2012 Electoral Votes...................................6
Number of County Governments.................................29
Number of Municipal Governments .........................242
Number of School Districts.........................................40
Number of Special Districts .....................................288

## LEGISLATIVE BRANCH

Legislative Body ...........................................Legislature

President of the Senate .....................Michael G. Waddoups
Secretary of the Senate ...........................Annette B. Moore

Speaker of the House.......................Rebecca D. Lockhart
Chief Clerk of the House............................. Sandy Tenney

2012 Regular Session.............Jan. 23 – March 8, 2012
Number of Senatorial Districts .............................29
Number of Representative Districts .........................75

## EXECUTIVE BRANCH

Governor ........................................................Gary R. Herbert
Lieutenant Governor ............................Gregory Bell
Attorney General ..................................... Mark L. Shurtleff
Treasurer.......................................................Richard Ellis
Auditor...........................................................Auston G. Johnson

Governor's Present Term.............................. 8/2009 – 1/2013
Number of Elected Officials in the Executive Branch.......................5
Number of Members in the Cabinet ..........................21

## JUDICIAL BRANCH

Highest Court.............................................Supreme Court
Supreme Court Chief Justice................Matthew Durrant
Number of Supreme Court Judges .................................5
Number of Intermediate Appellate Court Judges............................7
Number of U.S. Court Districts.......................................1
U.S. Circuit Court................................................. 10th Circuit

## STATE INTERNET ADDRESSES

Official State Website .............................http://www.utah.gov
Governor's Website ....................http://www.utah.gov/governor
Legislative Website ......................... http://www.le.state.ut.us
Judicial Website................................http://www.utcourts.gov

# Vermont

Nickname.........................................................The Green Mountain State
Motto.................................................................*Freedom and Unity*
Flower ...................................................................... Red Clover
Bird................................................................Hermit Thrush
Tree..........................................................................Sugar Maple
Song...................................................................*Hail, Vermont!*
Entered the Union..............................................March 4, 1791
Capital...........................................................................Montpelier

## STATISTICS
Land Area (square miles).............................................9,217
Rank in Nation.............................................................43rd
Population.................................................................626,431
Rank in Nation.............................................................49th
Density per square mile ...............................................68.0
Capital City.............................................................Montpelier
Population.....................................................................7,855
Rank in State..................................................................15th
Largest City .............................................................Burlington
Population...................................................................42,417
Number of Representatives in Congress ...............................1
Number of 2012 Electoral Votes......................................3
Number of County Governments......................................14
Number of Municipal Governments.................................45
Number of School Districts.............................................293
Number of Special Districts ..........................................144

## LEGISLATIVE BRANCH
Legislative Body ....................................... General Assembly

President of the Senate ..............................Lt. Gov. Phil Scott
President Pro Tem of the Senate...................John F. Campbell
Secretary of the Senate ...........................John H. Bloomer Jr.

Speaker of the House................................................Shap Smith
Clerk of the House ............................... Donald G. Milne

2012 Regular Session.........................Jan. 3 – mid-May 2012
Number of Senatorial Districts .........................................13
Number of Representative Districts ...............................106

## EXECUTIVE BRANCH
Governor .........................................................Peter E. Shumlin
Lieutenant Governor ............................................Phil Scott
Secretary of State...............................................Jim Condos
Attorney General ......................................William H. Sorrell
Treasurer........................................................Elizabeth Pearce
Auditor.............................................Thomas M. Salmon

Governor's Present Term.............................. 1/2011 – 1/2013
Number of Elected Officials in the Executive Branch.....................6
Number of Members in the Cabinet ..................................7

## JUDICIAL BRANCH
Highest Court....................................................Supreme Court
Supreme Court Chief Justice............................ Paul L. Reiber
Number of Supreme Court Judges ......................................5
Total Number of Appellant Court Judges ..............................0
Number of U.S. Court Districts...........................................1
U.S. Circuit Court......................................................2nd Circuit

## STATE INTERNET ADDRESSES
Official State Website .................................. http://vermont.gov
Governor's Website ....................................http://governor.vermont.gov
Legislative Website ..........................................http://www.leg.state.vt.us
Judicial Website..............................http://www.vermontjudiciary.org

# Virginia

Nickname................................................. The Old Dominion
Motto...........................*Sic Semper Tyrannis* (Thus Always to Tyrants)
Flower ............................................................ Dogwood
Bird.................................................................... Cardinal
Tree ............................................................... Dogwood
Song, emeritus ..................................*Carry Me Back to Old Virginia*
Entered the Union ......................................June 25, 1788
Capital ........................................................... Richmond

## STATISTICS
Land Area (square miles)...............................................39,490
Rank in Nation.............................................................36th
Population.............................................................8,096,604
Rank in Nation.............................................................12th
Density per square miles...............................................205.0
Capital City.............................................................Richmond
Population.................................................................204,214
Rank in State..................................................................4th
Largest City .......................................................Virginia Beach
Population...................................................................437,994
Number of Representatives in Congress .............................11
Number of 2012 Electoral Votes......................................13
Number of Geographic Counties........................................95
Number of County Governments.................................95*
Number of Consolidated Governments.............................5*
Number of Municipal Governments .................................229
Number of School Districts ................................................1
Number of Special Districts ..........................................186

## LEGISLATIVE BRANCH
Legislative Body ....................................... General Assembly

President of the Senate ..............................Lt. Gov. Bill Bolling
President Pro Tem of the Senate.......................Walter Stosch
Clerk of the Senate ...........................Susan Clarke Schaar

Speaker of the House..............................William J. Howell
Clerk of the House ............................... G. Paul Nardo

2012 Regular Session.....................Jan. 11 – March 10, 2012
Number of Senatorial Districts .........................................40
Number of Representative Districts ...............................100

## EXECUTIVE BRANCH
Governor ..................................................... Bob McDonnell
Lieutenant Governor ............................................Bill Bolling
Secretary of the Commonwealth ....................... Janet Polarek
Attorney General .....................................Ken Cuccinelli
Treasurer.....................................................Manju Ganeriwala
Auditor......................................................Walter J. Kucharski
Comptroller ............................................David Von Moll

Governor's Present Term.............................. 1/2010 – 1/2014
Number of Elected Officials in the Executive Branch.....................3
Number of Members in the Cabinet ..................................14

## JUDICIAL BRANCH
Highest Court....................................................Supreme Court
Supreme Court Chief Justice............................ Cynthia D. Kinser
Number of Supreme Court Judges .......................................7
Total Number of Appellant Court Judges ............................11
Number of U.S. Court Districts............................................2
U.S. Circuit Court...................................................... 4th Circuit

## STATE INTERNET ADDRESSES
Official State Website ..................................http://www.virginia.gov
Governor's Website .........................http://www.governor.virginia.gov
Legislative Website ...........................................http://legis.state.va.us
Judicial Website...............................http://www.courts.state.va.us

*In addition to 95 counties, Virginia has 39 Independent Cities,
considered county equivalents. Five cities in the Hampton Roads
area were formed of entire counties and function at the county level
of government. They are listed with the Independent Cities but
counted as consolidated governments in Virginia.

# Washington

| | |
|---|---|
| Nickname | The Evergreen State |
| Motto | *Alki* (Chinook Indian word meaning By and By) |
| Flower | Coast Rhododendron |
| Bird | Willow Goldfinch |
| Tree | Western Hemlock |
| Song | *Washington, My Home* |
| Entered the Union | November 11, 1889 |
| Capital | Olympia |

## STATISTICS

| | |
|---|---|
| Land Area (square miles) | 66,456 |
| Rank in Nation | 20th |
| Population | 6,830,038 |
| Rank in Nation | 13th |
| Density per square mile | 102.8 |
| Capital City | Olympia |
| Population | 46,478 |
| Rank in State | 18th |
| Largest City | Seattle |
| Population | 608,660 |
| Number of Representatives in Congress | 10 |
| Number of 2012 Electoral Votes | 12 |
| Number of County Governments | 39 |
| Number of Municipal Governments | 281 |
| Number of School Districts | 296 |
| Number of Special Districts | 1,229 |

## LEGISLATIVE BRANCH

| | |
|---|---|
| Legislative Body | Legislature |
| President of the Senate | Lt. Gov. Brad Owen |
| President Pro Tem of the Senate | Margarita Prentice |
| Secretary of the Senate | Tom Hoemann |
| Speaker of the House | Frank Chopp |
| Speaker Pro Tem of the House | Jim Moeller |
| Chief Clerk of the House | Barbara Baker |
| 2012 Regular Session | Jan. 9 – March 8, 2012 |
| Number of Senatorial Districts | 49 |
| Number of Representative Districts | 49 |

## EXECUTIVE BRANCH

| | |
|---|---|
| Governor | Christine O. Gregoire |
| Lieutenant Governor | Brad Owen |
| Secretary of State | Sam Reed |
| Attorney General | Rob McKenna |
| Treasurer | James McIntire |
| Auditor | Brian Sonntag |
| Director of Office of Financial Management | Marty Brown |
| Governor's Present Term | 1/2005 – 1/2013 |
| Number of Elected Officials in the Executive Branch | 9 |
| Number of Members in the Cabinet | 28 |

## JUDICIAL BRANCH

| | |
|---|---|
| Highest Court | Supreme Court |
| Supreme Court Chief Justice | Barbara A. Madsen |
| Number of Supreme Court Judges | 9 |
| Total Number of Appellant Court Judges | 22 |
| Number of U.S. Court Districts | 2 |
| U.S. Circuit Court | 9th Circuit |

## STATE INTERNET ADDRESSES

| | |
|---|---|
| Official State Website | http://access.wa.gov |
| Governor's Website | http://www.governor.wa.gov |
| Legislative Website | http://www.leg.wa.gov |
| Judicial Website | http://www.courts.wa.gov |

# West Virginia

| | |
|---|---|
| Nickname | The Mountain State |
| Motto | *Montani Semper Liberi* (Mountaineers Are Always Free) |
| Flower | Rhododendron |
| Bird | Cardinal |
| Tree | Sugar Maple |
| Songs | *West Virginia, My Home Sweet Home*; *The West Virginia Hills*; and *This is My West Virginia* |
| Entered the Union | June 20, 1863 |
| Capital | Charleston |

## STATISTICS

| | |
|---|---|
| Land Area (square miles) | 24,038 |
| Rank in Nation | 41st |
| Population | 1,855,364 |
| Rank in Nation | 37th |
| Density per square mile | 77.2 |
| Capital City | Charleston |
| Population | 51,400 |
| Rank in State | 1st |
| Largest City | Charleston |
| Number of Representatives in Congress | 3 |
| Number of 2012 Electoral Votes | 5 |
| Number of County Governments | 55 |
| Number of Municipal Governments | 232 |
| Number of School Districts | 55 |
| Number of Special Districts | 321 |

## LEGISLATIVE BRANCH

| | |
|---|---|
| Legislative Body | Legislature |
| Acting President of the Senate | Jeffrey V. Kessler |
| President Pro Tem of the Senate | Joseph Minard |
| Clerk of the Senate | Darrell E. Holmes |
| Speaker of the House of Delegates | Richard Thompson |
| Speaker Pro Tem of the House of Delegates | Ron Fragale |
| Clerk of the House of Delegates | Gregory M. Gray |
| 2012 Regular Session | Jan. 11 – March 16, 2012 |
| Number of Senatorial Districts | 17 |
| Number of Representative Districts | 58 |

## EXECUTIVE BRANCH

| | |
|---|---|
| Governor | Earl Ray Tomblin |
| Lieutenant Governor | Jeffrey V. Kessler |
| Secretary of State | Natalie Tennant |
| Attorney General | Darrell V. McGraw Jr. |
| Treasurer | John D. Perdue |
| Auditor | Glen B. Ganier III |
| Governor's Present Term | 11/2010 – 1/2013 |
| Number of Elected Officials in the Executive Branch | 6 |
| Number of Members in the Cabinet | 9 |

## JUDICIAL BRANCH

| | |
|---|---|
| Highest Court | Supreme Court of Appeals |
| Supreme Court of Appeals Chief Justice | Menis E. Ketchum II |
| Number of Supreme Court of Appeals Judges | 5 |
| Total Number of Appellant Court Judges | 0 |
| Number of U.S. Court Districts | 2 |
| U.S. Circuit Court | 4th Circuit |

## STATE INTERNET ADDRESSES

| | |
|---|---|
| Official State Website | http://www.wv.gov |
| Governor's Website | http://www.governor.wv.gov |
| Legislative Website | http://www.legis.state.wv.us |
| Judicial Website | http://www.courtswv.gov |

# Wisconsin

Nickname*.................................................................... The Badger State
Motto................................................................................*Forward*
Flower ........................................................................Wood Violet
Bird.......................................................................................Robin
Tree.............................................................................. Sugar Maple
Song.....................................................................*On, Wisconsin!*
Entered the Union.....................................................May 29, 1848
Capitol............................................................................. Madison

*unofficial

## STATISTICS
Land Area (square miles)...............................................54,158
Rank in Nation.................................................................25th
Population.............................................................5,711,767
Rank in Nation................................................................20th
Density per square mile .................................................105.5
Capital City................................................................ Madison
Population.............................................................233,209
Rank in State.....................................................................2nd
Largest City ............................................................ Milwaukee
Population.............................................................594,833
Number of Representatives in Congress .................................8
Number of 2012 Electoral Votes.........................................10
Number of County Governments..........................................72
Number of Municipal Governments ...................................592
Number of School Districts ..............................................441
Number of Special Districts ..............................................756

## LEGISLATIVE BRANCH
Legislative Body .......................................................Legislature

President of the Senate .......................................Michael G. Ellis
President Pro Tem of the Senate............................Joseph K. Leibham
Chief Clerk of the Senate .................................... Jeffery Renk

Speaker of the Assembly .......................................Jeff Fitzgerald
Speaker Pro Tem of the Assembly.........................Bill Kramer
Chief Clerk of the Assembly ...........................Patrick Fuller

2012 Regular Session.............................. Jan. 10 – Dec. 31, 2012
Number of Senatorial Districts ...............................................33
Number of Representative Districts .........................................99

## EXECUTIVE BRANCH
Governor ........................................................... Scott K. Walker
Lieutenant Governor ..............................................Rebecca Kleefisch
Secretary of State.................................................Douglas La Follette
Attorney General ..............................................J.B. Van Hollen
Treasurer.......................................................... Kurt W. Schuller
Auditor...................................................................Joe Chrisman
Controller ...........................................................Steve Censky

Governor's Present Term.................................. 1/2011 – 1/2015
Number of Elected Officials in the Executive Branch..........................6
Number of Members in the Cabinet ......................................16

## JUDICIAL BRANCH
Highest Court.....................................................Supreme Court
Supreme Court Chief Justice.......................... Shirley S. Abrahamson
Number of Supreme Court Judges .........................................7
Total Number of Appellant Court Judges .............................16
Number of U.S. Court Districts..............................................2
U.S. Circuit Court................................................... 7th Circuit

## STATE INTERNET ADDRESSES
Official State Website .............................http://www.wisconsin.gov
Governor's Website ...................................http://www.wisgov.state.wi.us
Legislative Website .........................................http://legis.wisconsin.gov
Judicial Website........................................ http://www.wicourts.gov

# Wyoming

Nicknames ..........................The Equality State and The Cowboy State
Motto.................................................................... *Equal Rights*
Flower ................................................................ Indian Paintbrush
Bird......................................................... Western Meadowlark
Tree..................................................................Cottonwood
Song.............................................................................*Wyoming*
Entered the Union.....................................................July 10, 1890
Capital ............................................................................Cheyenne

## STATISTICS
Land Area (square miles)...............................................97,093
Rank in Nation...................................................................9th
Population.............................................................568,158
Rank in Nation................................................................50th
Density per square mile ...................................................14.9
Capital City................................................................Cheyenne
Population.............................................................59,466
Rank in State.......................................................................1st
Largest City ............................................................Cheyenne
Number of Representatives in Congress .................................1
Number of 2012 Electoral Votes...........................................3
Number of County Governments..........................................23
Number of Municipal Governments ......................................99
Number of School Districts ................................................55
Number of Special Districts ..............................................549

## LEGISLATIVE BRANCH
Legislative Body ........................................................Legislature

President of the Senate .......................................Jim Anderson
Vice President of the Senate ....................................Philip A. Nicholas
Chief Clerk of the Senate .....................................Diane Harvey

Speaker of the House .........................................Edward Buchanan
Speaker Pro Tem of the House .......................................Keith Gingery
Chief Clerk of the House.......................................Patricia Benskin

2012 Regular Session.............................. Feb. 13 – March 8, 2012
Number of Senatorial Districts .................................................30
Number of Representative Districts .........................................60

## EXECUTIVE BRANCH
Governor ..........................................................Matthew Mead
Secretary of State.................................................... Max Maxfield
Attorney General ...................................................Bruce A. Salzburg
Treasurer...........................................................Joseph B. Meyer
Auditor...............................................................Cynthia Cloud

Governor's Present Term.................................... 1/2011 – 1/2015
Number of Elected Officials in the Executive Branch.........................5
Number of Members in the Cabinet ......................................20

## JUDICIAL BRANCH
Highest Court............................................................Supreme Court
Supreme Court Chief Justice.......................... Marilyn S. Kite
Number of Supreme Court Judges .........................................5
Total Number of Appellant Court Judges ..............................0
Number of U.S. Court Districts...............................................1
U.S. Circuit Court................................................... 10th Circuit

## STATE INTERNET ADDRESSES
Official State Website ...............................http://www.wyoming.gov
Governor's Website ...................................http://governor.wy.gov
Legislative Website ......................................http://legisweb.state.wy.us
Judicial Website........................................ http://www.courts.state.wy.us

# District of Columbia

Motto...................................................*Justitia Omnibus* (Justice to All)
Flower ...........................................................American Beauty Rose
Bird................................................................................Wood Thrush
Tree.....................................................................................Scarlet Oak
Became U.S. Capital ...................................................December 1, 1800

## STATISTICS
Land Area (square miles)...................................................................61
Population..............................................................................617,996
Density per square mile ...........................................................10,131.1
Delegate to Congress* ..........................................................................1
Number of 2012 Electoral Votes ..........................................................3
Number of Municipal Governments ...................................................1
Number of School Districts ................................................................1
Number of Special Districts ................................................................0

*Committee voting privileges only.

## LEGISLATIVE BRANCH
Legislative Body ...........................Council of the District of Columbia

Chair.......................................................................Kwame R. Brown
Chair Pro Tem ......................................................... Mary M. Cheh
Secretary to the Council .............................................. Nyasha Smith
2012 Regular Session...............................................Jan. 2 – Dec. 31, 2012

## EXECUTIVE BRANCH
Mayor....................................................................... Vincent C. Gray
Secretary of the District of Columbia ................Cynthia Brock-Smith
Attorney General ...................................................... Irvin Nathan
Chief Financial Officer.....................................................Natwar Gandhi
Auditor ................................................................ Yolanda Branche

Mayor's Present Term .......................................... 1/2011 – 1/2015
Number of Elected Officials in the Executive Branch.......................10
Number of Members in the Cabinet .......................................10

## JUDICIAL BRANCH
Highest Court..............................................D.C. Court of Appeals
Court of Appeals Chief Justice ...................................Eric Washington
Number of Court of Appeals Judges......................................................9
Number of U.S. Court Districts................................................................1

## INTERNET ADDRESSES
Official Website ...............................................http://www.dc.gov
Mayor's Website.........................................................http://mayor.dc.gov
Legislative Website .................http://www.dccouncil.washington.dc.us
Judicial Website...............................................http://www.dccourts.gov

# American Samoa

Motto.......................*Samoa-Maumua le Atua* (In Samoa, God Is First)
Flower ......................................................... Paogo (Ula-fala)
Plant .........................................................................................Ava
Song............................................................................*Amerika Samoa*
Became a Territory of the United States ........................................1900
Capital .............................................................................. Pago Pago

## STATISTICS
Land Area (square miles)..................................................................77
Population..............................................................................55,519
Density per square mile ..........................................................721.0
Capital City...............................................................................Pago Pago
Population...............................................................................3,656
Rank in Territory .....................................................................3rd
Largest City ......................................................................Tafuna
Population...............................................................................7,945
Delegate to Congress* ..........................................................................1
Number of School Districts ...............................................................1

*Committee voting privileges only.

## LEGISLATIVE BRANCH
Legislative Body ..................................................................Legislature

President of the Senate ...................................Gaoteote P.T. Gaoteote
President Pro Tem of the Senate........................Tulifua Tini Lam Yuen
Secretary of the Senate .................................................Leo'o V. Ma'o

Speaker of the House.............................................. Savali Talavou Ale
Chief Clerk of the House........................................... Fialupe Lutu

2012 Regular Session...............................................Jan. 10, 2012 – TBD
Number of Senatorial Districts .........................................................12
Number of Representative Districts ..................................................17

## EXECUTIVE BRANCH
Governor ..................................................... Togiola T.A. Tulafono
Lieutenant Governor ........................................... Ipulasi Aito Sunia
Attorney General ............................................ Fepulea'i Afa Ripley Jr.
Treasurer....................................................... Magalei Logovi'i

Governor's Present Term....................................... 4/2003 – 1/2013
Number of Members in the Cabinet ....................................16

## JUDICIAL BRANCH
Highest Court...........................................................................High Court
High Court Chief Justice............................................ F. Michael Kruse
Number of High Court Judges...............................................................6

## INTERNET ADDRESSES
Official Website ....................................http://americansamoa.gov
Governor's Website ...................................http://americansamoa.gov
Legislative Website ....................................http://americansamoa.gov
Judicial Website...............................................http://www.asbar.org

# Guam

| | |
|---|---|
| Nickname | Hub of the Pacific |
| Flower | Puti Tai Nobio (Bougainvillea) |
| Bird | Totot (Fruit Dove) |
| Tree | Ifit (Intsiabijuga) |
| Song | *Stand Ye Guamanians* |
| Stone | Latte |
| Animal | Iguana |
| Ceded to the United States by Spain | December 10, 1898 |
| Became a Territory | August 1, 1950 |
| Request to become a Commonwealth Plebiscite | November 1987 |
| Capital | Hagatna |

## STATISTICS

| | |
|---|---|
| Land Area (square miles) | 210 |
| Population | 159,358 |
| Density per square mile | 758.8 |
| Capital | Hagatna |
| Population | 1,051 |
| Rank in Territory | 13th |
| Largest City | Dededo |
| Population | 44,943 |
| Delegate to Congress* | 1 |
| Number of School Districts | 1 |

*Committee voting privileges only.

## LEGISLATIVE BRANCH

| | |
|---|---|
| Legislative Body | Legislature |
| Speaker | Judith T. Won Pat |
| Vice Speaker | Benjamin J.F. Cruz |
| Clerk of the Legislature | Patricia C. Santos |
| 2012 Regular Session | Jan. 10 – Dec. 31, 2012 |
| Number of Senatorial Districts | 15 |

## EXECUTIVE BRANCH

| | |
|---|---|
| Governor | Edward J.B. Calvo |
| Lieutenant Governor | Ray Tenorio |
| Attorney General | Leonardo Rapadas |
| Treasurer | Rose T. Fejeran |
| Auditor | Doris Flores Brooks |
| Governor's Present Term | 1/2003 – 1/2015 |
| Number of Elected Officials in the Executive Branch | 10 |
| Number of Members in the Cabinet | 55 |

## JUDICIAL BRANCH

| | |
|---|---|
| Highest Court | Supreme Court |
| Supreme Court Chief Justice | F. Phillip Carbullido |
| Number of Supreme Court Judges | 3 |

## INTERNET ADDRESSES

| | |
|---|---|
| Official Website | http://www.guam.gov |
| Governor's Website | http://governor.guam.gov |
| Legislative Website | http://www.guamlegislature.com |
| Judicial Website | http://www.justice.gov.gu |

# Northern Mariana Islands

| | |
|---|---|
| Flower | Plumeria |
| Bird | Marianas Fruit Dove |
| Tree | Flame Tree |
| Song | *Gi TaloGi Halom Tasi* |
| Administered by the United States a trusteeship for the United Nations | July 18, 1947 |
| Voters approved a proposed constitution | June 1975 |
| U.S. president signed covenant agreeing to commonwealth status for the islands | March 24, 1976 |
| Became a self-governing Commonwealth | January 9, 1978 |
| Capital | Saipan |

## STATISTICS

| | |
|---|---|
| Land Area (square miles) | 179 |
| Population | 53,883 |
| Density per square mile | 301.0 |
| Capital City | Saipan |
| Population | 48,220 |
| Largest City | Saipan |
| Delegate to Congress* | 1 |
| Number of School Districts | 1 |

*Committee voting privileges only.

## LEGISLATIVE BRANCH

| | |
|---|---|
| Legislative Body | Legislature |
| President of the Senate | Paul A. Manglona |
| Vice President of the Senate | Jude Hofschneider |
| Clerk of the Senate | Doris Bermudes |
| Speaker of the House | Eliceo D. Cabrera |
| Vice Speaker of the House | Felicidad T. Ogumoro |
| Clerk of the House | Linda B. Muna |
| 2012 Regular Session | Jan. 10, 2012 – TBD |
| Number of Senatorial Districts | 9 |
| Number of Representative Districts | 18 |

## EXECUTIVE BRANCH

| | |
|---|---|
| Governor | Benigno R. Fitial |
| Lieutenant Governor | Eloy S. Inos |
| Attorney General | Edward T. Buckingham |
| Treasurer | Antoinette S. Calvo |
| Governor's Present Term | 1/2006 – 1/2015 |
| Number of Elected Officials in the Executive Branch | 10 |
| Number of Members in the Cabinet | 16 |

## JUDICIAL BRANCH

| | |
|---|---|
| Highest Court | Commonwealth Supreme Court |
| Commonwealth Supreme Court Chief Justice | Alexandro C. Castro |
| Number of Commonwealth Supreme Court Judges | 3 |

## INTERNET ADDRESSES

| | |
|---|---|
| Official Website | www.gksoft.com/govt/en/mp.html |
| Governor's Website | http://www.gov.mp |
| Legislative Website | http://www.cnmileg.gov.mp |
| Judicial Website | http://www.justice.gov.mp |

# Puerto Rico

Nickname............................................................Island of Enchantment
Motto...............................................................*Joannes Est Nomen Ejus*
(John is His Name)
Flower .................................................................................................Maga
Bird..................................................................................................Reinita
Tree................................................................................................... Ceiba
Song.......................................................................... *La Borinqueña*
Became a Territory of the United States ................December 10, 1898
Became a self-governing Commonwealth .........................July 25, 1952
Capital..................................................................................... San Juan

## STATISTICS
Land Area (square miles)...............................................................3,424
Population..............................................................................3,706,690
Density per square mile .............................................................1,082.6
Capital City............................................................................... San Juan
Population..............................................................................381,931
Largest City............................................................................... San Juan
Resident Commissioner in Congress*....................................................1
Number of School Districts .................................................................1

*Committee voting privileges only.

## LEGISLATIVE BRANCH
Legislative Body ....................................Legislative Assembly

President of the Senate ......................................Thomas Rivera Schatz
Vice President of the Senate ....................Margarita Nolasco Santiago
Secretary of the Senate ....................................Manuel A. Torres Nieves

Speaker of the House....................................Jenniffer González-Colón
Speaker Pro Tem............................................Gabriel Rodriguez Aguilo
Clerk of the House ........................................Brunilda Ortiz-Rodriguez

2012 Regular Session........................................... Jan. 10 – June 30, 2012

## EXECUTIVE BRANCH
Governor .................................................................Luis Fortuño
Secretary of State...................................................Kenneth McClintock
Attorney General ................................ Guillermo Somoza Colombani
Treasurer...........................................................Jesús F. Méndez Rodríguez

Governor's Present Term.............................................. 1/2009 – 1/2013
Number of Elected Officials in the Executive Branch.......................10
Number of Members in the Cabinet .....................................................10

## JUDICIAL BRANCH
Highest Court................................................................Supreme Court
Supreme Court Chief Justice.................Frederico Hernandez-Denton
Number of Supreme Court Judges .......................................................7

## INTERNET ADDRESSES
Official State Website ...................................................http://www.pr.gov
Governor's Website ............................. http://www.fortaleza.gobierno.pr
Senate Website ..................................................... http://www.senadopr.us
House Website.........................http://www.camaraderepresentantes.org
Judicial Website...............................................http://www.tribunalpr.org

# U.S. Virgin Islands

Nickname.........................................................The American Paradise
Motto........................................................... *United in Pride and Hope*
Flower ............................................................... The Yellow Cedar
Bird................................................ Yellow Breast or Banana Quit
Song............................................................. *Virgin Islands March*
Purchased from Denmark ........................................... March 31, 1917
Capital........................................................Charlotte Amalie, St. Thomas

## STATISTICS
Land Area (square miles)*...............................................................134
Population..............................................................................106,405
Density per square mile .............................................................794.1
Capital City............................................Charlotte Amalie, St. Thomas
Population..............................................................................18,481
Largest City ............................................Charlotte Amalie, St. Thomas
Delegate to Congress** ....................................................................1
Number of School Districts .................................................................1

*The U.S. Virgin Islands is comprised of three large islands (St. Croix, St. John, and St. Thomas) and 50 smaller islands and cays.
**Committee voting privileges only.

## LEGISLATIVE BRANCH
Legislative Body ....................................................Legislature

President ................................................................. Ronald E. Russell
Vice President ..............................................................Louis Patrick Hill
Legislative Secretary of the Senate .............................. Sammuel Sanes

2012 Regular Session.......................................... Jan. 10 – Dec. 31, 2012

## EXECUTIVE BRANCH
Governor ...................................................................John De Jongh Jr.
Lieutenant Governor ................................................... Gregory Francis
Attorney General .........................................................Vincent Frazer
Commissioner of Finance ................................................ Laurel Payne

Governor's Present Term............................................. 1/2007 – 1/2015
Number of Elected Officials in the Executive Branch.......................10
Number of Members in the Cabinet .....................................................21

## JUDICIAL BRANCH
Highest Court................................................................Supreme Court
Supreme Court Chief Justice............................................. Rhys S. Hodge
Number of Supreme Court Judges .......................................................3
U.S. Circuit Court.............................................................................3rd

## INTERNET ADDRESSES
Official Website ..................................................http://www.gov.vi
Governor's Website ..........................http://www.governordejongh.com
Legislative Website................................................http://www.legvi.org
Judicial Website....................................http://www.visupremecourt.org

# Index

# —F—

# —H—

## —M—

## —N—

## —O—

## —P—